FORD

FULL SIZE TRUCKS
1987-93 REPAIR MANUAL

CHILTON'S

President, Chilton Enterprises	David S. Loewith
Senior Vice President	Ronald A. Hoxter
Publisher & Editor-In-Chief	Kerry A. Freeman, S.A.E.
Managing Editors	Peter M. Conti, Jr., W. Calvin Settle, Jr., S.A.E.
Assistant Managing Editor	Nick D'Andrea
Senior Editors	Debra Gaffney, Ken Grabowski, A.S.E., S.A.E.
	Michael L. Grady, Richard J. Rivele, S.A.E.
	Richard T. Smith, Jim Taylor
	Ron Webb
Project Managers	Martin J. Gunther, Jeffrey M. Hoffman
Production Manager	Andrea Steiger
Director of Manufacturing	Mike D'Imperio
Editor	Richard J. Rivele

CHILTON BOOK COMPANY

ONE OF THE **DIVERSIFIED PUBLISHING COMPANIES**,
A PART OF **CAPITAL CITIES/ABC,INC.**

Manufactured in USA

© 1994 Chilton Book Company
Chilton Way, Radnor, PA 19089
ISBN 0-8019-8492-0
Library of Congress Catalog Card No. 93-070525
2345678901   3210987654

Contents

Contents

DRIVE TRAIN   **7**

STEERING AND SUSPENSION   **8**

BRAKES   **9**

BODY AND TRIM   **10**

GLOSSARY

MASTER INDEX

SAFETY NOTICE

Proper service and repair procedures are vital to the safe, reliable operation of all motor vehicles, as well as the personal safety of those performing repairs. This manual outlines procedures for servicing and repairing vehicles using safe, effective methods. The procedures contain many NOTES, CAUTIONS, and WARNINGS which should be followed along with standard procedures to eliminate the possibility of personal injury or improper service which could damage the vehicle or compromise its safety.

It is important to note that the repair procedures and techniques, tools and parts for servicing motor vehicles, as well as the skill and experience of the individual performing the work vary widely. It is not possible to anticipate all of the conceivable ways or conditions under which vehicles may be serviced, or to provide cautions as to all of the possible hazards that may result. Standard and accepted safety precautions and equipment should be used when handling toxic or flammable fluids, and safety goggles or other protection should be used during cutting, grinding, chiseling, prying, or any other process that can cause material removal or projectiles.

Some procedures require the use of tools specially designed for a specific purpose. Before substituting another tool or procedure, you must be completely satisfied that neither your personal safety, nor the performance of the vehicle will be endangered.

Although information in this manual is based on industry sources and is complete as possible at the time of publication, the possibility exists that some car manufacturers made later changes which could not be included here. While striving for total accuracy, Chilton Book Company cannot assume responsibility for any errors, changes or omissions that may occur in the compilation of this data.

PART NUMBERS

Part numbers listed in this reference are not recommendation by Chilton for any product by brand name. They are references that can be used with interchange manuals and aftermarket supplier catalogs to locate each brand supplier's discrete part number.

SPECIAL TOOLS

Special tools are recommended by the vehicle manufacturer to perform their specific job. Use has been kept to a minimum, but where absolutely necessary, they are referred to in the text by the part number of the tool manufacturer. These tools can be purchased, under the appropriate part number, from your dealer or regional distributor, or an equivalent tool can be purchased locally from a tool supplier or parts outlet. Before substituting any tool for the one recommended, read the SAFETY NOTICE at the top of this page.

ACKNOWLEDGMENTS

The Chilton Book Company expresses appreciation to the Ford Motor Company for their generous assistance.

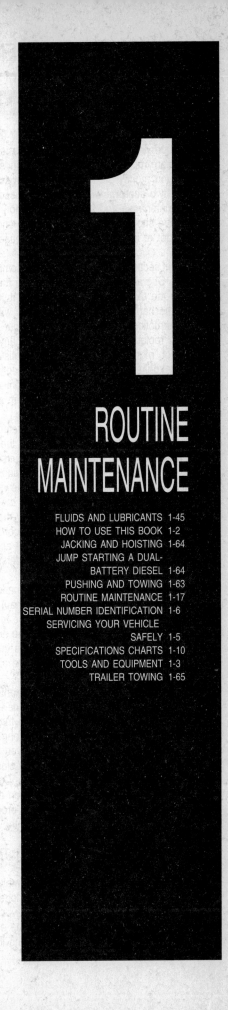

1

ROUTINE
MAINTENANCE

HOW TO USE THIS BOOK

Chilton's Total Car Care Manual for 1987-93 Ford Pickups, Bronco, Super Duty and Motor Home chassis is intended to help you learn more about the inner workings of your vehicle and save you money on its upkeep and operation.

The first two sections will be the most used, since they contain maintenance and tune-up information and procedures. Studies have shown that a properly tuned and maintained truck can get at least 10% better gas mileage than an out-of-tune truck.

The other sections deal with the more complex systems of your truck. Operating systems from engine through brakes are covered to the extent that the average do-it-yourselfer becomes mechanically involved. This book will give you detailed instructions to help you change your own brake pads and shoes, replace spark plugs, and do many more jobs that will save you money, give you personal satisfaction, and help you avoid expensive problems. We will even explain such complicated things as rebuilding the differential even though the expertise required and the investment in special tools may make this task uneconomical.

A secondary purpose of this book is a reference for owners who want to understand their truck and/or their mechanics better. In this case, no tools at all are required.

Before removing any fasteners, read through the entire procedure. This will give you the overall view of what tools and supplies will be required. There is nothing more frustrating than having to walk to the bus stop on Monday morning because you were short one bolt on Sunday afternoon. So read ahead and plan ahead. Each operation should be approached logically and all procedures thoroughly understood before attempting any work.

All sections contain adjustments, maintenance, removal and installation procedures, and repair or overhaul procedures. When repair is not considered practical, we tell you how to remove the part and then how to install the new or rebuilt replacement. In this way, you at least save the labor costs. Backyard repair of such components as the alternator is just not practical.

Two basic mechanic's rules should be mentioned here. One, whenever the left side of the truck or engine is referred to, it is meant to specify the driver's side of the truck. Conversely, the right side of the truck means the passenger's side. Secondly, most screws and bolt are removed by turning counterclockwise, and tightened by turning clockwise.

Safety is always the most important rule. Constantly be aware of the dangers involved in working on an automobile and take the proper precautions. (See the procedure in this section Servicing Your Vehicle Safely and the SAFETY NOTICE on the acknowledgment page.)

Pay attention to the instructions provided. There are 3 common mistakes in mechanical work:

1. Incorrect order of assembly, disassembly or adjustment. When taking something apart or putting it together, doing things in the wrong order usually just cost you extra time; however, it CAN break something. Read the entire procedure before beginning disassembly. Do everything in the order in which the instructions say you should do it, even if you can't immediately see a reason for it. When you're taking apart something that is very intricate (for example, a carburetor), you might want to draw a picture of how it looks when assembled at one point in order to make sure you get everything back in its proper position. (We will supply exploded view whenever possible). When making adjustments, especially tune-up adjustments, do them in order; often, one adjustment affects another, and you cannot expect even satisfactory results unless each adjustment is made only when it cannot be changed by any order.

2. Overtorquing (or undertorquing). While it is more common for over-torquing to cause damage, undertorquing can cause a fastener to vibrate loose causing serious damage. Especially when dealing with aluminum parts, pay attention to torque specifications and utilize a torque wrench in assembly. If a torque figure is not available, remember that if you are using the right tool to do the job, you will probably not have to strain yourself to get a fastener tight enough. The pitch of most threads is so slight that the tension you put on the wrench will be multiplied many, many times in actual force on what you are tightening. A good example of how critical torque is can be seen in the case of spark plug installation, especially where you are putting the plug into an aluminum cylinder head. Too little torque can fail to crush the gasket, causing leakage of combustion gases and consequent overheating of the plug and engine parts. Too much torque can damage the threads, or distort the plug which changes the s park gap.

There are many commercial products available for ensuring that fasteners won't come loose, even if they are not torqued just right (a very common brand is Loctite®). If you're worried about getting something together tight enough to hold, but loose enough to avoid mechanical damage during assembly, one of these products might offer substantial insurance. Read the label on the package and make sure the products is compatible with the materials, fluids, etc. involved before choosing one.

3. Crossthreading. This occurs when a part such as a bolt is screwed into a nut or casting at the wrong angle and forced. Cross threading is more likely to occur if access is difficult. It helps to clean and lubricate fasteners, and to start threading with the part to be installed going straight in. Then, start the bolt, spark plug, etc. with your fingers. If you encounter resistance, unscrew the part and start over again at a different angle until it can be inserted and turned several turns without much effort. Keep in mind that many parts, especially spark plugs, used tapered threads so that gentle turning will automatically bring the part you're threading to the proper angle if you don't force it or resist a change in angle. Don't put a wrench on the part until its's been turned a couple of turns by hand. If you suddenly encounter resistance, and the part has not seated fully, don't force it. Pull it back out and make sure it's clean and threading properly.

Always take your time and be patient; once you have some experience, working on your truck will become an enjoyable hobby.

TOOLS AND EQUIPMENT

▶ **See Figures 1, 2 and 3**

Naturally, without the proper tools and equipment it is impossible to properly service you vehicle. It would be impossible to catalog each tool that you would need to perform each or any operation in this book. It would also be unwise for the amateur to rush out and buy an expensive set of tool on the theory that he may need on or more of them at sometime.

The best approach is to proceed slowly gathering together a good quality set of those tools that are used most frequently. Don't be misled by the low cost of bargain tools. It is far better to spend a little more for better quality. Forged wrenches, 6- or 12-point sockets and fine tooth ratchets are by far preferable to their less expensive counterparts. As any good mechanic

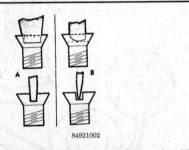

84921002

Fig. 1 Keep screwdrivers in good shape. They should fit the slot as shown in 'A'. If they look like those in 'B', they need grinding or replacing

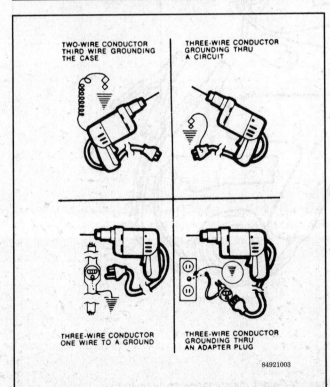

84921003

Fig. 2 When using electric tools, make sure they are properly grounded

can tell you, there are few worse experiences than trying to work on a truck with bad tools. Your monetary savings will be far outweighed by frustration and mangled knuckles.

Begin accumulating those tools that are used most frequently; those associated with routine maintenance and tune-up.

In addition to the normal assortment of screwdrivers and pliers you should have the following tools for routine maintenance jobs:

1. SAE (or Metric) or SAE/Metric wrenches-sockets and combination open end-box end wrenches in sizes from ⅛in. (3mm) to ¾ in. (19mm) and a spark plug socket (11/32 in. or ⅝in. depending on plug type).

➡ **If possible, buy various length socket drive extensions. One break in this department is that the metric sockets available in the U.S. will all fit the ratchet handles and extensions you may already have (¼ in., ⅜in., and ½ in. drive).**

2. Jackstands for support.
3. Oil filter wrench.
4. Oil filler spout for pouring oil.
5. Grease gun for chassis lubrication.
6. Hydrometer for checking the battery.
7. A container for draining oil.
8. Many rags for wiping up the inevitable mess.

In addition to the above items there are several others that are not absolutely necessary, but handy to have around. these include oil dry, a transmission funnel and the usual supply of lubricants, antifreeze and fluids, although these can be purchased as needed. This is a basic list for routine maintenance, but only your personal needs and desire can accurately determine you list of tools.

The second list of tools is for tune-ups. While the tools involved here are slightly more sophisticated, they need not be outrageously expensive. There are several inexpensive tach/dwell meters on the market that are every bit as good for the average mechanic as a $100.00 professional model. Just be sure that it goes to a least 1,200-1,500 rpm on the tach scale and that it works on 4-, 6-, 8-cylinder engines. (A special tach is needed for diesel engines). A basic list of tune-up equipment could include:

9. Tach/dwell meter.
10. Spark plug wrench.
11. Timing light (a DC light that works from the truck's battery is best, although an AC light that plugs into 110V house current will suffice at some sacrifice in brightness).
12. Wire spark plug gauge/adjusting tools.
13. Set of feeler blades.

Here again, be guided by your own needs. A feeler blade will set the points as easily as a dwell meter will read well, but slightly less accurately. And since you will need a tachometer anyway. . . well, make your own decision.

In addition to these basic tools, there are several other tools and gauges you may find useful. These include:

14. A compression gauge. The screw-in type is slower to use, but eliminates the possibility of a faulty reading due to escaping pressure.
15. A manifold vacuum gauge.

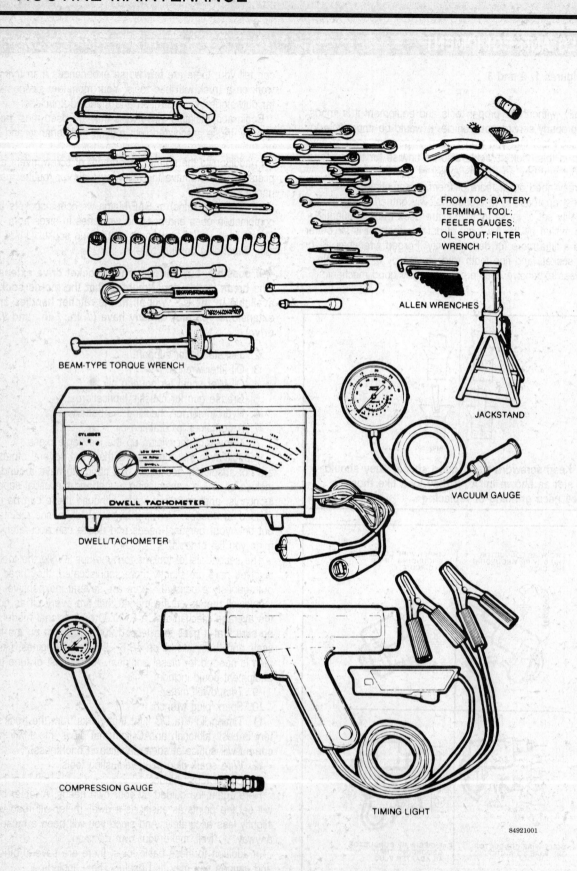

FROM TOP: BATTERY
TERMINAL TOOL;
FEELER GAUGES;
OIL SPOUT; FILTER
WRENCH

ALLEN WRENCHES

JACKSTAND

BEAM-TYPE TORQUE WRENCH

DWELL TACHOMETER

DWELL/TACHOMETER

VACUUM GAUGE

COMPRESSION GAUGE

TIMING LIGHT

84921001

Fig. 3 This basic collection of tools and test instruments is all need for most maintenance on your truck

16. A test light.

17. An induction meter. This is used for determining whether or not there is current in a wire. These are handy for use if a wire is broken somewhere in a wiring harness.

As a final not, you will probably find a torque wrench necessary for all but the most basic work. The beam type models are perfectly adequate, although the newer click type are more precise.

Special Tools

Normally, the use of special factory tools is avoided for repair procedures, since these are not readily available for the do-it-yourself mechanic. When it is possible to preform the job with more commonly available tools, it will be pointed out, but occasionally, a special tool was designed to perform a specific function and should be used. Before substituting another tool, you should be convinced that neither your safety nor the performance of the vehicle will be compromised.

Some special tools are available commercially from major tool manufacturers. Others can be purchased from your Ford Dealer or from the Owatonna Tool Company, Owatonna, Minnesota 55060.

SERVICING YOUR VEHICLE SAFELY

It is virtually impossible to anticipate all of the hazards involved with automotive maintenance and service but care and common sense will prevent most accidents.

The rules of safety for mechanics range from 'don't smoke around gasoline' to 'use the proper tool for the job.' The trick to avoiding injuries is to develop safe work habits and take every possible precaution.

Do's

▸ **See Figure 4**

• Do keep a fire extinguisher and first aid kit within easy reach.

• Do wear safety glasses or goggles when cutting, drilling, grinding, or prying, even if you have 20/20 vision. If you wear glasses for the sake of vision, then they should be made of hardened glass that can serve also as safety glasses, or wear safety glasses over your regular glasses.

• Do shield your eyes whenever you work around the battery. Batteries contain sulfuric acid; in case of contact with the eyes or skin, flush the area with water or a mixture of water and baking soda and get medical attention immediately.

• Do use safety stands for any under-truck service. Jacks are for raising vehicles; safety stands are for making sure the vehicle stays raised until you want it to come down. Whenever the vehicle is raised, block the wheels remaining on the ground and set the parking brake.

• Do use adequate ventilation when working with any chemicals. Like carbon monoxide, the asbestos dust resulting from brake lining wear can be poisonous in sufficient quantities.

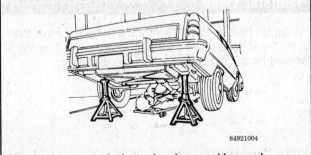

84921004

Fig. 4 Always use jackstands when working under your truck

• Do disconnect the negative battery cable when working on the electrical system. The primary ignition system can contain up to 40,000 volts.

• Do follow manufacturer's directions whenever working with potentially hazardous materials. Both brake fluid and antifreeze are poisonous if taken internally.

• Do properly maintain your tools. Loose hammerheads, mushroomed punches and chisels, frayed or poorly grounded electrical cords, excessively worn screwdrivers, spread wrenches (open end), cracked sockets, slipping ratchets, or faulty drop light sockets can cause accidents.

• Do use the proper size and type of tool for the job being done.

• Do when possible, pull on a wrench handle rather than push on it, and adjust your stance to prevent a fall.

• Do be sure that adjustable wrenches are tightly adjusted on the nut or bolt and pulled so that the face is on the side of the fixed jaw.

• Do select a wrench or socket that fits the nut or bolt. The wrench or socket should sit straight, not cocked.

• Do strike squarely with a hammer. Avoid glancing blows.

• Do set the parking brake and block the drive wheels if the work requires that the engine be running.

Don't's

• Don't run an engine in a garage or anywhere else without proper ventilation — EVER! Carbon monoxide is poisonous; it takes a long time to leave the human body and you can build up a deadly supply of it in your system by simply breathing in a little every day. You may not realize you are slowly poisoning yourself. Always use proper vents, window, fans or open the garage door.

• Don't work around moving parts while wearing a necktie or other loose clothing. Short sleeves are much safer than long, loose sleeves and hard-toed shoes with neoprene soles protect your toes and give a better grip on slippery surfaces. Jewelry such as watches, fancy belt buckles, beads or body adornment of any kind is not safe working around a truck. Long hair should be hidden under a hat or cap.

• Don't use pockets for tool boxes. A fall or bump can drive a screwdriver deep into your body. Even a wiping cloth hanging from the back pocket can wrap around a spinning shaft or fan.

- Don't smoke when working around gasoline, cleaning solvent or other flammable material.
- Don't smoke when working around the battery. When the battery is being charged, it gives off explosive hydrogen gas.
- Don't use gasoline to wash your hands; there are excellent soaps available. Gasoline may contain lead, and lead can enter the body through a cut, accumulating in the body until you are very ill. Gasoline also removes all the natural oils from the skin so that bone dry hands will such up oil and grease.
- Don't service the air conditioning system unless you are equipped with the necessary tools and training. The refrigerant,

R-12, is extremely cold and when exposed to the air, will instantly freeze any surface it comes in contact with, including your eyes. Although the refrigerant is normally non-toxic, R-12 becomes a deadly poisonous gas in the presence of an open flame. One good whiff of the vapors from burning refrigerant can be fatal.
- Don't ever use a bumper jack (the jack that comes with the vehicle) for anything other than changing tires! If you are serious about maintaining your truck yourself, invest in a hydraulic floor jack of at least 1½ ton capacity. It will pay for itself many times over through the years.

SERIAL NUMBER IDENTIFICATION

Vehicle

▶ **See Figures 5, 6 and 7**

The vehicle identification number is located on the left side of the dash panel behind the windshield.

A seventeen digit combination of numbers and letters forms the Vehicle Identification Number (VIN). Refer to the illustration for VIN details.

Vehicle Safety Compliance Certification Label

▶ **See Figure 8**

The label is attached to the driver's door lock pillar. The label contains the name of the manufacturer, the month and year of the vehicle, certification statement and VIN. The label also contains gross vehicle weight and tire data.

Engine

▶ **See Figures 9 and 10**

The engine identification tag identifies the cubic inch displacement of the engine, the model year, the year and month

in which the engine was built, where it was built and the change level number. The change level is usually the number one (1), unless there are parts on the engine that will not be completely interchangeable and will require minor modification.

The engine identification tag is located under the ignition coil attaching bolt on all engines except the 6.9L and 7.3L diesels. The diesel engine I.D. number is stamped on the front of the block, in front of the left cylinder head.

The engine identification code is located in the VIN at the eighth digit. The VIN can be found in the safety certification decal and the VIN plate at the upper left side of the dash panel. Refer to the 'Engine Application' chart for engine VIN codes.

Transmission

▶ **See Figure 11**

The transmission identification letter is located on a metal tag or plate attached to the case or it is stamped directly on the transmission case. Also, the transmission code is located on the Safety Certification Decal. Refer to the 'Transmission Application' chart in this section.

Drive Axle

▶ **See Figure 12**

The drive axle code is found stamped on a flat surface on the axle tube, next to the differential housing, or, on a tag secured by one of the differential housing cover bolts. A separate limited-slip tag is attached to the differential housing cover bolt. The letters L-S signifies a limited-slip differential.

Transfer Case

A tag is affixed to the case mounting bolts. The information on the tag is needed when ordering service parts. If the tag is removed for any reason, make sure it is reinstalled.

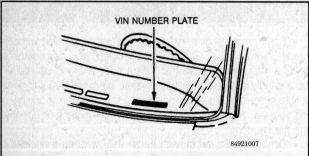

VIN NUMBER PLATE

84921007

Fig. 5 The VIN is located on the driver's side of the dash

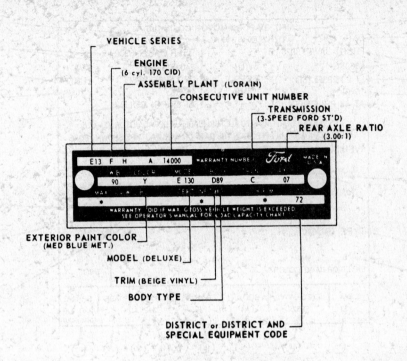

Vehicle Identification Plate

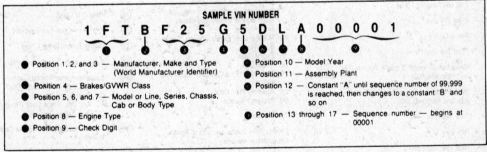

Fig. 6 VIN Code Plates

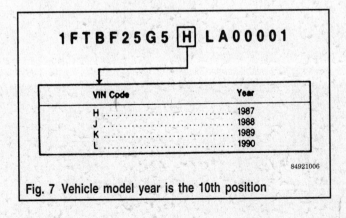

Fig. 7 Vehicle model year is the 10th position

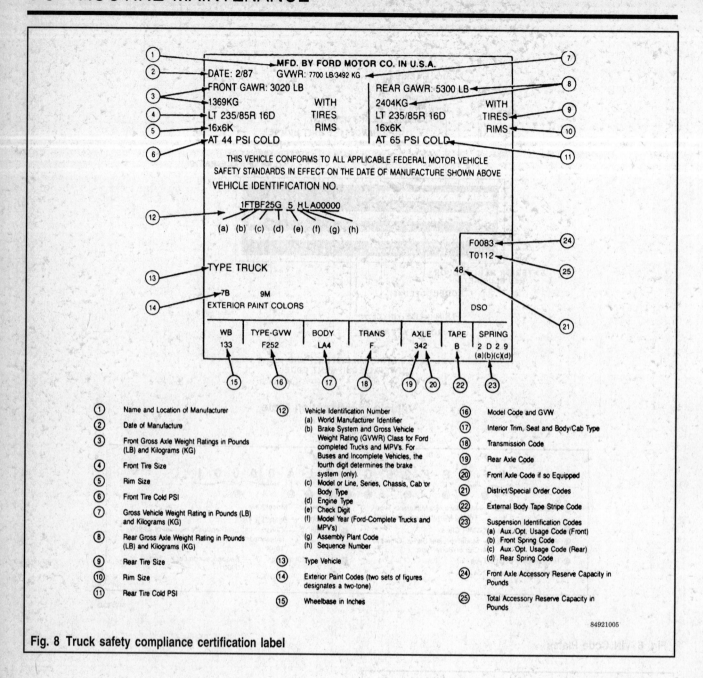

Fig. 8 Truck safety compliance certification label

① Name and Location of Manufacturer

② Date of Manufacture

③ Front Gross Axle Weight Ratings in Pounds (LB) and Kilograms (KG)

④ Front Tire Size

⑤ Rim Size

⑥ Front Tire Cold PSI

⑦ Gross Vehicle Weight Rating in Pounds (LB) and Kilograms (KG)

⑧ Rear Gross Axle Weight Rating in Pounds (LB) and Kilograms (KG)

⑨ Rear Tire Size

⑩ Rim Size

⑪ Rear Tire Cold PSI

⑫ Vehicle Identification Number
(a) World Manufacturer Identifier
(b) Brake System and Gross Vehicle Weight Rating (GVWR) Class for Ford completed Trucks and MPV's. For Buses and Incomplete Vehicles, the fourth digit determines the brake system (only).
(c) Model or Line, Series, Chassis, Cab or Body Type
(d) Engine Type
(e) Check Digit
(f) Model Year (Ford-Complete Trucks and MPV's)
(g) Assembly Plant Code
(h) Sequence Number

⑬ Type Vehicle

⑭ Exterior Paint Codes (two sets of figures designates a two-tone)

⑮ Wheelbase in Inches

⑯ Model Code and GVW

⑰ Interior Trim, Seat and Body/Cab Type

⑱ Transmission Code

⑲ Rear Axle Code

⑳ Front Axle Code if so Equipped

㉑ District/Special Order Codes

㉒ External Body Tape Stripe Code

㉓ Suspension Identification Codes
(a) Aux./Opt. Usage Code (Front)
(b) Front Spring Code
(c) Aux./Opt. Usage Code (Rear)
(d) Rear Spring Code

㉔ Front Axle Accessory Reserve Capacity in Pounds

㉕ Total Accessory Reserve Capacity in Pounds

84921005

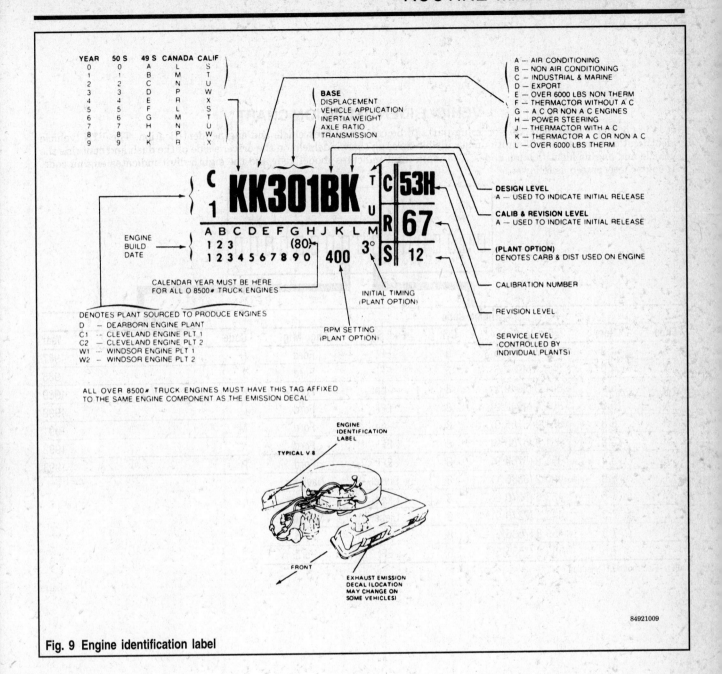

YEAR	50 S	49 S	CANADA	CALIF
0	0		A	L	S
1	1		B	M	T
2	2		C	N	U
3	3		D	P	W
4	4		E	R	X
5	5		F	L	S
6	6		G	M	T
7	7		H	N	U
8	8		J	P	W
9	9		K	R	X

A — AIR CONDITIONING
B — NON AIR CONDITIONING
C — INDUSTRIAL & MARINE
D — EXPORT
E — OVER 6000 LBS NON THERM
F — THERMACTOR WITHOUT A C
G — A C OR NON A C ENGINES
H — POWER STEERING
J — THERMACTOR WITH A C
K — THERMACTOR A C OR NON A C
L — OVER 6000 LBS THERM

BASE
DISPLACEMENT
VEHICLE APPLICATION
INERTIA WEIGHT
AXLE RATIO
TRANSMISSION

KK301BK T C 53H
U R 67
S 12

A B C D E F G H J K L M
1 2 3 (80) 3° 400

ENGINE BUILD DATE

DESIGN LEVEL
A — USED TO INDICATE INITIAL RELEASE

CALIB & REVISION LEVEL
A — USED TO INDICATE INITIAL RELEASE

(PLANT OPTION)
DENOTES CARB & DIST USED ON ENGINE

CALIBRATION NUMBER

REVISION LEVEL

SERVICE LEVEL
(CONTROLLED BY INDIVIDUAL PLANTS)

CALENDAR YEAR MUST BE HERE
FOR ALL O 8500# TRUCK ENGINES

INITIAL TIMING
(PLANT OPTION)

DENOTES PLANT SOURCED TO PRODUCE ENGINES
D — DEARBORN ENGINE PLANT
C1 — CLEVELAND ENGINE PLT 1
C2 — CLEVELAND ENGINE PLT 2
W1 — WINDSOR ENGINE PLT 1
W2 — WINDSOR ENGINE PLT 2

RPM SETTING
(PLANT OPTION)

ALL OVER 8500# TRUCK ENGINES MUST HAVE THIS TAG AFFIXED
TO THE SAME ENGINE COMPONENT AS THE EMISSION DECAL

ENGINE IDENTIFICATION LABEL

TYPICAL V 8

FRONT

EXHAUST EMISSION DECAL (LOCATION MAY CHANGE ON SOME VEHICLES)

84921009

Fig. 9 Engine identification label

VEHICLE IDENTIFICATION CHART

It is important for servicing and ordering parts to be certain of the vehicle and engine identification. The VIN (vehicle identification number) is a 17 digit number visible through the windshield on the driver's side of the dash and contains the vehicle and engine identification codes. The tenth digit indicates model year and the eighth digit indicates engine code. It can be interpreted as follows:

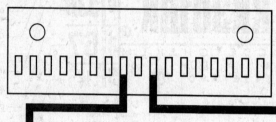

Engine Code							Model Year	
Code	Liters	Cu. In. (cc)	Cyl.	Fuel Sys.	Eng. Mfg.		Code	Year
B	4.9	300.1 (4917.5)	6	EFI	Ford		H	1987
Y	4.9	300.1 (4917.5)	6	EFI	Ford		J	1988
G	5.0	301.5 (4942.2)	8	4-bbl	Ford		K	1989
N	5.0	301.5 (4942.2)	8	EFI	Ford		L	1990
H	5.8	351.9 (5765.9)	8	4-bbl	Ford		M	1991
H	5.8	351.9 (5765.9)	8	EFI	Ford		N	1992
R	5.8	351.9 (5765.9)	8	EFI	Ford		P	1993
1	6.9	420.2 (6886.1)	8	Diesel	Navistar			
M	7.3	433.6 (7270.0)	8	Diesel	Navistar			
C	7.3	443.6 (7270.0)	8	Diesel	Navistar			
L	7.5	459.8 (7535.5)	8	4-bbl	Ford			
G	7.5	459.8 (7535.5)	8	EFI	Ford			

EFI—Electronic Fuel Injection

84921139

ENGINE IDENTIFICATION

Year	Model	Engine Displacement Liters (cc)	Engine Series (ID/VIN)	Fuel System	No. of Cylinders	Engine Type
1987	All	4.9 (4917.5)	B	EFI	6	OHV
	All	5.0 (4942.2)	G	4-bbl	8	OHV
	All	5.0 (4942.2)	N	EFI	8	OHV
	All	5.8 (5765.9)	H	4-bbl	8	OHV
	F-250/350	6.9 (6886.1)	1	Diesel	8	OHV
	F-Series	7.5 (7535.5)	L	4-bbl	8	OHV
1988	All	4.9 (4917.5)	Y	EFI	6	OHV
	All	5.0 (4942.2)	N	EFI	8	OHV
	All	5.8 (5765.9)	H	EFI	8	OHV
	F-Series	7.3 (7270.0)	M	Diesel	8	OHV
	F-Series	7.5 (7535.5)	G	EFI	8	OHV
1989	All	4.9 (4917.5)	Y	EFI	6	OHV
	All	5.0 (4942.2)	N	EFI	8	OHV
	All	5.8 (5765.9)	H	EFI	8	OHV
	F-Series	7.3 (7270.0)	M	Diesel	8	OHV
	F-Series	7.5 (7535.5)	G	EFI	8	OHV
1990	All	4.9 (4917.5)	Y	EFI	6	OHV
	All	5.0 (4942.2)	N	EFI	8	OHV
	All	5.8 (5765.9)	H	EFI	8	OHV
	F-Series	7.3 (7270.0)	M	Diesel	8	OHV
	F-Series	7.5 (7535.5)	G	EFI	8	OHV
1991	All	4.9 (4917.5)	Y	EFI	6	OHV
	All	5.0 (4942.2)	N	EFI	8	OHV
	All	5.8 (5765.9)	H	EFI	8	OHV
	F-Series	7.3 (7270.0)	M	Diesel	8	OHV
	F-Series	7.5 (7535.5)	G	EFI	8	OHV
1992	All	4.9 (4917.5)	Y	EFI	6	OHV
	All	5.0 (4942.2)	N	EFI	8	OHV
	All	5.8 (5765.9)	H	EFI	8	OHV
	F-Series	7.3 (7270.0)	M	Diesel	8	OHV
	F-Series	7.5 (7535.5)	G	EFI	8	OHV
1993	All	4.9 (4917.5)	Y	EFI	6	OHV
	All	5.0 (4942.2)	N	EFI	8	OHV
	All	5.8 (5765.9)	H	EFI	8	OHV
	Lightning	5.8 (5765.9)	R	EFI	8	OHV
	F-Series	7.3 (7270.0)	M	Diesel	8	OHV
	F-Series	7.3 (7270.0)	C	Diesel	8	OHV
	F-Series	7.5 (7535.5)	G	EFI	8	OHV

EFI—Electronic Fuel Injection

TRANSMISSION APPLICATION CHART

Year	Model	Transmission Identification	Transmission Type
1987	Bronco	Borg-Warner T-18	4-sp MT
		New Process 435	4-sp MT
		Ford TOD	4-sp MT
		Ford C6	3-sp AT
		Ford AOD	4-sp AT
	F-150	Borg-Warner T-18	4-sp MT
		New Process 435	4-sp MT
		Ford TOD	4-sp MT
		Ford C6	3-sp AT
		Ford AOD	4-sp AT
	F-250	Borg-Warner T-18	4-sp MT
		New Process 435	4-sp MT
		Ford TOD	4-sp MT
	F-250 HD w/Diesel or 7.5L	Borg-Warner T-19A or C	4-sp MT
	F-250 All	Ford C6	3-sp AT
	F-250 w/4.9L or 5.0L	Ford AOD	4-sp AT
	F-350	Borg-Warner T-18	4-sp MT
		Borg-Warner T-19A or C	4-sp MT
		Ford C6	3-sp AT
	F-350 w/4.9L or 5.0L	Ford AOD	4-sp AT
1988	Bronco	Mazda M50D	5-sp MT
		ZF S5-42	5-sp MT
		Ford C6	3-sp AT
	Bronco w/5.0L	Ford AOD	4-sp AT
	F-150	Mazda M50D	5-sp MT
		ZF S5-42	5-sp MT
		Ford C6	3-sp AT
	F-150 w/4.9L & 5.0L	Ford AOD	4-sp AT
	F-250	ZF S5-42	5-sp MT
		Ford C6	3-sp AT
	F-250 w/4.9L or 5.0L	Ford AOD	4-sp AT
	F-350	ZF S5-42	5-sp MT
		Ford C6	3-sp MT
1989	Bronco	Borg-Warner T-18	4-SP MT
		Mazda M50D	5-sp MT
		ZF S5-42	5-sp MT
		Ford C6	3-sp AT
		Ford AOD	4-sp AT
	F-150	Borg-Warner T-18	4-sp MT
		Mazda M50D	5-sp MT
		ZF S5-42	5-sp MT
		Ford C6	3-sp AT
	F-150 w/4.9L & 5.0L	Ford AOD	4-sp AT

TRANSMISSION APPLICATION CHART

Year	Model	Transmission Identification	Transmission Type
1989	F150 under 8,500 lb. GWV w/V8	Ford E40D	4-sp AT
	F-250	Borg-Warner T-18	4-sp MT
		ZF S5-42	5-sp MT
		Ford C6	3-sp AT
	F-250 w/4.9L or 5.0L	Ford AOD	4-sp AT
	F-250 all w/V8	Ford E40D	4-sp AT
	F-350	ZF S5-42	5-sp MT
		Ford C6	3-sp AT
		Ford E40D	4-sp AT
1990	Bronco	Borg-Warner T-18	4-SP MT
		Mazda M50D	5-sp MT
		ZF S5-42	5-sp MT
		Ford AOD	4-sp AT
		Ford C6	3-sp AT
	F-150	Borg-Warner T-18	4-sp MT
		Mazda M50D	5-sp MT
		ZF S5-42	5-sp MT
		Ford C6	3-sp AT
	F-150 w/4.9L & 5.0L	Ford AOD	4-sp AT
	F150 all w/V8	E40D	4-sp AT
	F-250	Borg-Warner T-18	4-sp MT
		Mazda M50D	5-sp MT
		ZF S5-42	5-sp MT
		Ford C6	3-sp AT
	F-250 w/4.9L or 5.0L	Ford AOD	4-sp AT
	F-250 all w/V8	Ford E40D	4-sp AT
	F-350	ZF S5-42	5-sp MT
		Ford C6	3-sp AT
		Ford E40D	4-sp AT
1991	Bronco	Borg-Warner T-18	4-SP MT
		Mazda M50D	5-sp MT
		Ford C6	3-sp AT
		Ford AOD	4-sp AT
		Ford E40D	4-sp AT
	F-150	Borg-Warner T-18	4-sp MT
		Mazda M50D	5-sp MT
		Ford C6	3-sp AT
	F-150 w/4.9L & 5.0L	Ford AOD	4-sp AT
	F150 all w/V8	Ford E40D	4-sp AT
	F-250	Borg-Warner T-18	4-sp MT
		ZF S5-42	5-sp MT
		Ford C6	3-sp AT
	F-250 w/4.9L or 5.0L	Ford AOD	4-sp AT
	F-250 all w/V8	Ford E40D	4-sp AT

TRANSMISSION APPLICATION CHART

Year	Model	Transmission Identification	Transmission Type
1991	F-350	ZF S5-42	5-sp MT
		Ford C6	3-sp AT
		Ford E40D	4-sp AT
	F-Super Duty	ZF S5-42	5-sp MT
		Ford C6	3-sp AT
		Ford E40D	4-sp AT
1992	Bronco w/4.9L or 5.0L	Borg-Warner T-18	4-SP MT
		Mazda M50D	5-sp MT
	Bronco w/5.0L	Ford AOD	4-sp AT
	Bronco all	Ford E40D	4-sp AT
	F-150 under 8500 lb. GVW w/4.9L or 5.0L	Mazda M50D	5-sp AT
		Borg-Warner T-18	4-sp MT
	F-150 8500 lb. + GVW	ZF S5-42	5-sp MT
	F150 all	Ford C6	3-sp AT
	F150 w/5.0L	Ford AOD	4-sp AT
	F-150 all	Ford E40D	4-sp AT
	F-250 under 8500 lb. GVW w/4.9L or 5.0L	Borg-Warner T-18	4-sp MT
		Mazda M50D	5-sp MT
	F-250 8500 lb. + GVW	ZF S5-42	5-sp MT
	F-250 all	Ford C6	3-sp AT
		Ford E40D	4-sp AT
	F-350	ZF S5-42	5-sp MT
		Ford C6	3-sp AT
		Ford E40D	4-sp AT
	F-Super Duty	ZF S5-42	5-sp MT
		Ford C6	3-sp AT
		Ford E40D	4-sp AT
1993	Bronco all	Borg-Warner T-18	4-SP MT
	Bronco w/4.9L or 5.0L	Mazda M50D	5-sp MT
	Bronco w/5.0L	Ford AOD	4-sp AT
	Bronco all	Ford E40D	4-sp AT
	F-150 under 8500 lb. GVW	Borg-Warner T-18	4-sp MT
	F-150 under 8500 lb. GVW w/4.0L or 5.0L	Mazda M50D	5-sp MT
	F-150 8500 lb. + GVW	ZF S5-42	5-sp MT
	F150 all	Ford C6	3-sp AT
	F150 w/5.0L	Ford AOD	4-sp AT
	F-150 all	Ford E40D	4-sp AT
	F-250 under 8500 lb. GVW	Borg-Warner T-18	4-sp MT
	F-250 under 8500 lb. GVW w/4.9L or 5.0L	Mazda M50D	5-sp MT
	F-250 8500 lb. + GVW	ZF S5-42	5-sp MT
	F-250 all	Ford C6	3-sp AT
		Ford E40D	4-sp AT
	F-350	ZF S5-42	5-sp MT
		Ford C6	3-sp AT
		Ford E40D	4-sp AT
	F-Super Duty	ZF S5-42	5-sp MT
		Ford C6	3-sp AT
		Ford E40D	4-sp AT

84921143

TRANSFER CASE APPLICATION CHART

Year	Model	Transfer Case Identification	Transfer Case Type
1987	Bronco, all	Borg-Warner 13-56	2-sp MS
	Bronco, w/AT	Borg-Warner 13-56	2-sp ES
	F-150	Borg-Warner 13-56	2-sp MS
		Borg-Warner 13-45	2-sp MS
	F-250	Borg-Warner 13-56	2-sp MS
		Borg-Warner 13-45	2-sp MS
	F-350	Borg-Warner 13-56	2-sp MS
1988	Bronco, all	Borg-Warner 13-56	2-sp MS
	Bronco, w/AT	Borg-Warner 13-56	2-sp ES
	F-150	Borg-Warner 13-56	2-sp MS
		Borg-Warner 13-45	2-sp MS
	F-250	Borg-Warner 13-56	2-sp MS
		Borg-Warner 13-45	2-sp MS
	F-350	Borg-Warner 13-56	2-sp MS
1989	Bronco, all	Borg-Warner 13-56	2-sp MS
	Bronco, w/AT	Borg-Warner 13-56	2-sp ES
	F-150	Borg-Warner 13-56	2-sp MS
		Borg-Warner 13-45	2-sp MS
	F-250	Borg-Warner 13-56	2-sp MS
		Borg-Warner 13-45	2-sp MS
	F-350	Borg-Warner 13-56	2-sp MS
1990	Bronco, all	Borg-Warner 13-56	2-sp MS
	Bronco, w/AT	Borg-Warner 13-56	2-sp ES
	F-150	Borg-Warner 13-56	2-sp MS
		Borg-Warner 13-45	2-sp MS
	F-250	Borg-Warner 13-56	2-sp MS
		Borg-Warner 13-45	2-sp MS
	F-350	Borg-Warner 13-56	2-sp MS
1991	Bronco, all	Borg-Warner 13-56	2-sp MS
	Bronco, w/AT	Borg-Warner 13-56	2-sp ES
	F-150	Borg-Warner 13-56	2-sp MS
		Borg-Warner 13-45	2-sp MS
	F-250	Borg-Warner 13-56	2-sp MS
		Borg-Warner 13-45	2-sp MS
	F-350	Borg-Warner 13-56	2-sp MS
1992	Bronco, all	Borg-Warner 13-56	2-sp MS
	Bronco, w/AT	Borg-Warner 13-56	2-sp ES
	F-150, all	Borg-Warner 13-56	2-sp MS
	F-150, w/AT	Borg-Warner 13-56	2-sp ES
	F-250	Borg-Warner 13-56	2-sp MS
	F-350	Borg-Warner 13-56	2-sp MS
1993	Bronco, all	Borg-Warner 13-56	2-sp MS
	Bronco, w/AT	Borg-Warner 13-56	2-sp ES
	F-150, all	Borg-Warner 13-56	2-sp MS
	F-150, w/AT	Borg-Warner 13-56	2-sp ES
	F-250	Borg-Warner 13-56	2-sp MS
	F-350	Borg-Warner 13-56	2-sp MS

AT: Automatic Transmission   ES: Electronic Shift   MS: Manual Shift

84921145

DRIVE AXLE APPLICATION CHART

Year	Model	Axle Identification	Axle Type
1987	Bronco	Dana 44 IFS	Front
		Ford 8.8 inch	Rear
	F-150	Dana 44 IFS	Front
		Ford 8.8 inch	Rear
	F-250	Dana 44 IFS	Front
		Dana 44 IFS-HD	Front
		Dana 50 IFS	Front
		Ford 10.25 inch	Rear
	F-350	Dana 60 Monobeam	Front
		Ford 10.25 inch	Rear
1988	Bronco	Dana 44 IFS	Front
		Ford 8.8 inch	Rear
	F-150	Dana 44 IFS	Front
		Ford 8.8 inch	Rear
	F-250	Dana 44 IFS	Front
		Dana 44 IFS-HD	Front
		Dana 50 IFS	Front
		Ford 10.25 inch	Rear
	F-350	Dana 60 Monobeam	Front
		Ford 10.25 inch	Rear
	F-Super Duty	Dana 80	Rear
1989	Bronco	Dana 44 IFS	Front
		Ford 8.8 inch	Rear
	F-150	Dana 44 IFS	Front
		Ford 8.8 inch	Rear
	F-250	Dana 44 IFS	Front
		Dana 44 IFS-HD	Front
		Dana 50 IFS	Front
		Ford 10.25 inch	Rear
	F-350	Dana 60 Monobeam	Front
		Ford 10.25 inch	Rear
	F-Super Duty	Dana 80	Rear
1990	Bronco	Dana 44 IFS	Front
		Ford 8.8 inch	Rear
	F-150	Dana 44 IFS	Front
		Ford 8.8 inch	Rear
	F-250	Dana 44 IFS	Front
		Dana 44 IFS-HD	Front
		Dana 50 IFS	Front
		Ford 10.25 inch	Rear
	F-350	Dana 60 Monobeam	Front
		Ford 10.25 inch	Rear
	F-Super Duty	Dana 80	Rear

DRIVE AXLE APPLICATION CHART

Year	Model	Axle Identification	Axle Type
1991	Bronco	Dana 44 IFS	Front
		Ford 8.8 inch	Rear
	F-150	Dana 44 IFS	Front
		Ford 8.8 inch	Rear
	F-250	Dana 44 IFS	Front
		Dana 44 IFS-HD	Front
		Dana 50 IFS	Front
		Ford 10.25 inch	Rear
	F-350	Dana 60 Monobeam	Front
		Ford 10.25 inch	Rear
	F-Super Duty	Dana 80	Rear
1992	Bronco	Dana 44 IFS	Front
		Ford 8.8 inch	Rear
	F-150	Dana 44 IFS	Front
		Ford 8.8 inch	Rear
	F-250	Dana 44 IFS	Front
		Dana 44 IFS-HD	Front
		Dana 50 IFS	Front
		Ford 10.25 inch	Rear
	F-350	Dana 60 Monobeam	Front
		Ford 10.25 inch	Rear
	F-Super Duty	Dana 80	Rear
1993	Bronco	Dana 44 IFS	Front
		Ford 8.8 inch	Rear
	F-150	Dana 44 IFS	Front
		Ford 8.8 inch	Rear
	F-250	Dana 44 IFS	Front
		Dana 44 IFS-HD	Front
		Dana 50 IFS	Front
		Ford 10.25 inch	Rear
	F-350	Dana 60 Monobeam	Front
		Ford 10.25 inch	Rear
	F-Super Duty	Dana 80	Rear

84921150

ROUTINE MAINTENANCE

➡ All maintenance procedures included in this Section refer to both gasoline and diesel engines except where noted.

Air Cleaner

▶ See Figures 13, 14, 15, 16, 17, 18, 19, 20, 21 and 22

The air cleaner is a paper element type.

The paper cartridge should be replaced according to the Preventive Maintenance Schedule at the end of this Section.

➡ Check the air filter more often if the vehicle is operated under severe dusty conditions and replace or clean it as necessary.

REPLACEMENT

Carbureted Engines

1. Open the engine compartment hood.
2. Remove the wing nut holding the air cleaner assembly to the top of the carburetor.
3. Disconnect the crankcase ventilation hose at the air cleaner and remove the entire air cleaner assembly from the carburetor.

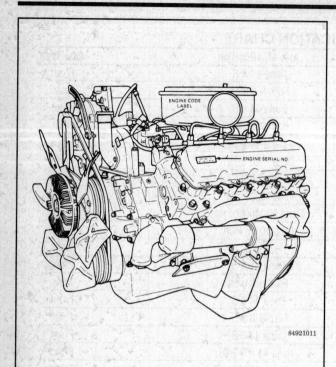

Fig. 10 Diesel engine serial number and identification label locations

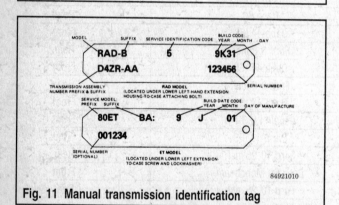

Fig. 11 Manual transmission identification tag

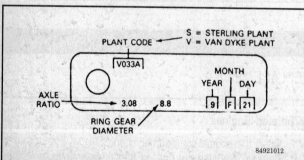

Fig. 12 Differential identification label. Limited slip units have a separate tag secured by a cover bolt

Fig. 13 Removing the carburetor air cleaner element

Fig. 14 Clean out the air cleaner body before installing the new filter

4. Remove and discard the old filter element, and inspect the condition of the air cleaner mounting gasket. Replace the gasket as necessary.

➡ A crankcase ventilation filter is located in the side of the air cleaner body. The filter should be replaced rather than cleaned. Simply pull the old filter out of the body every 20,000 miles (or more frequently if the vehicle has been used in extremely dusty conditions) and push a new filter into place.

5. Install the air cleaner body on the carburetor so that the word **FRONT** faces toward the front of the vehicle.

6. Place the new filter element in the air cleaner body and install the cover and tighten the wing nut. If the word **TOP** appears on the element, make sure that the side that the word appears on is facing up when the element is in place.

7. Connect the crankcase ventilation hose to the air cleaner.

Fuel Injected Gasoline Engines

1. Loosen the two clamps that secure the hose assembly to the air cleaner.

2. Remove the two screws that attach the air cleaner to the bracket.

3. Disconnect the hose and inlet tube from the air cleaner.

4. Remove the screws attaching the air cleaner cover.

5. Remove the air filter and tubes.

To install:

6. Install the air filter and tubes.

7. Install the screws attaching the air cleaner cover. Don't overtighten the hose clamps! A torque of 12-15 inch lbs. is sufficient.

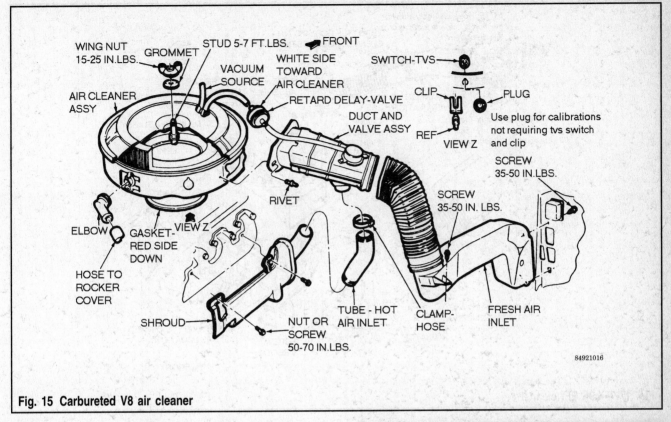

Fig. 15 Carbureted V8 air cleaner

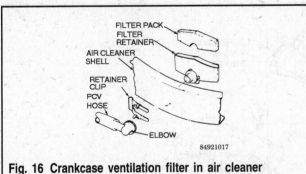

Fig. 16 Crankcase ventilation filter in air cleaner housing

8. Connect the hose and inlet tube to the air cleaner.

9. Install the two screws that attach the air cleaner to the bracket.

10. Tighten the two clamps that secure the hose assembly to the air cleaner.

Diesel Engines

1. Open the engine compartment hood.

2. Remove the wing nut holding the air cleaner assembly.

3. Remove and discard the old filter element, and inspect the condition of the air cleaner mounting gasket. Replace the gasket as necessary.

4. Place the new filter element in the air cleaner body and install the cover and tighten the wing nut.

Fuel Filter

REPLACEMENT

✳✳CAUTION

NEVER SMOKE WHEN WORKING AROUND OR NEAR GASOLINE! MAKE SURE THAT THERE IS NO IGNITION SOURCE NEAR YOUR WORK AREA!

Carbureted Engines

▶ **See Figures 23 and 24**

A carburetor mounted gas filter is used. These filters screw into the float chamber. To replace one of these filters:

1. Wait until the engine is cold.

2. Remove the air cleaner assembly.

3. Place some absorbent rags under the filter.

4. Remove the hose clamp and slide the rubber hose from the filter.

✳✳CAUTION

It is possible for gasoline to spray in all directions when removing the hose! This rarely happens, but it is possible, so protect your eyes!

5. Move the fuel line out of the way and unscrew the filter from the carburetor.

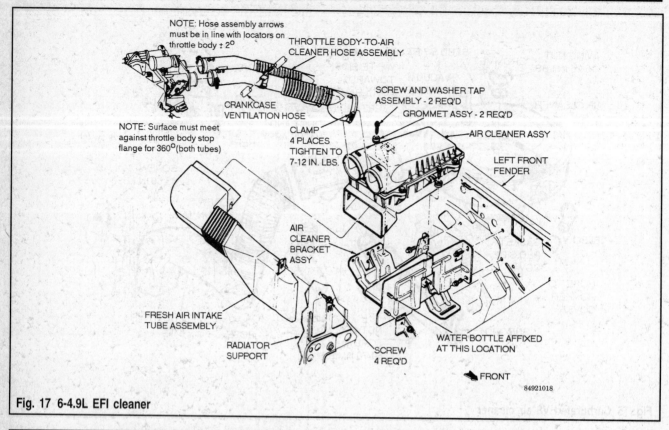

Fig. 17 6-4.9L EFI cleaner

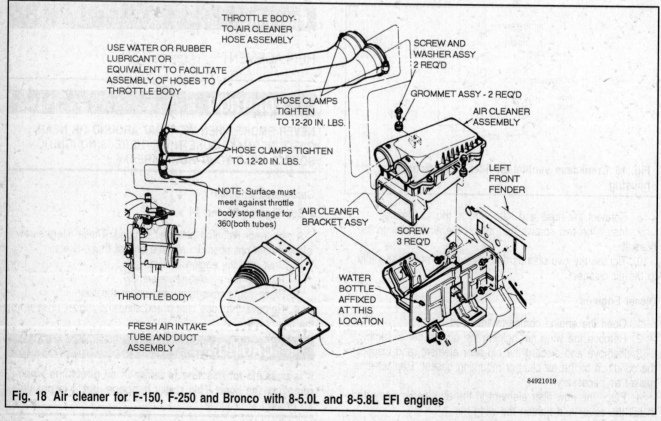

Fig. 18 Air cleaner for F-150, F-250 and Bronco with 8-5.0L and 8-5.8L EFI engines

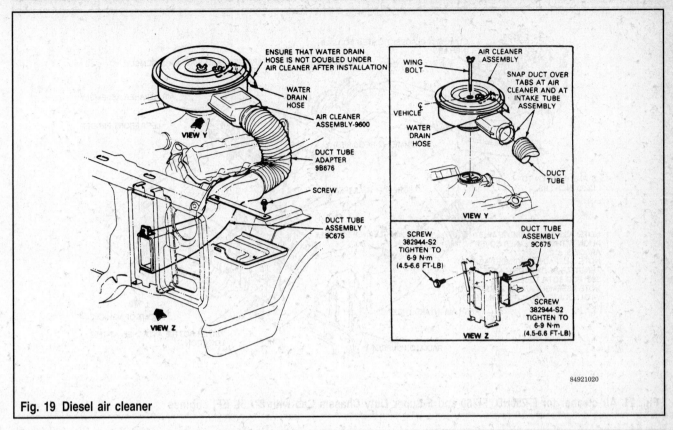

Fig. 19 Diesel air cleaner

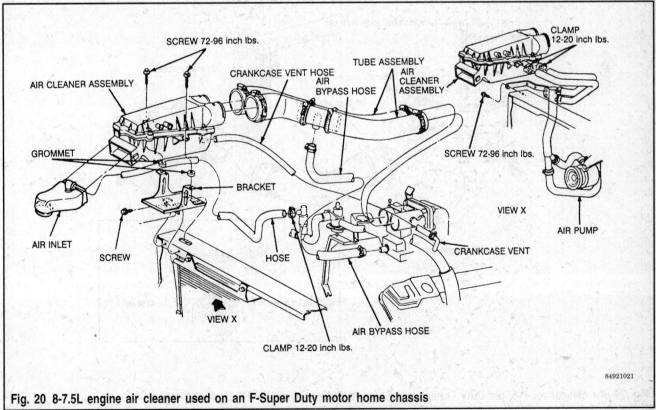

Fig. 20 8-7.5L engine air cleaner used on an F-Super Duty motor home chassis

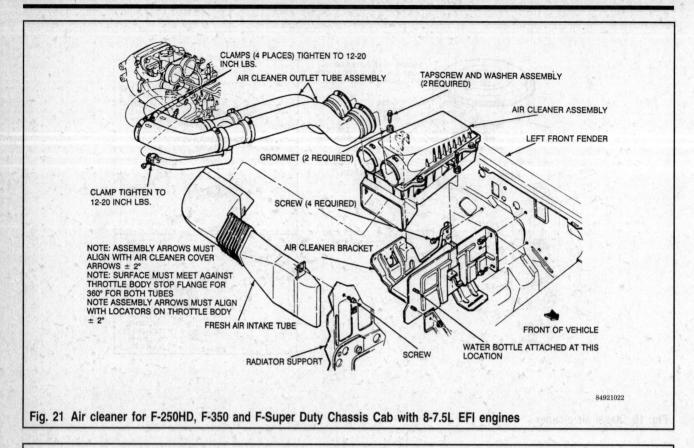

Fig. 21 Air cleaner for F-250HD, F-350 and F-Super Duty Chassis Cab with 8-7.5L EFI engines

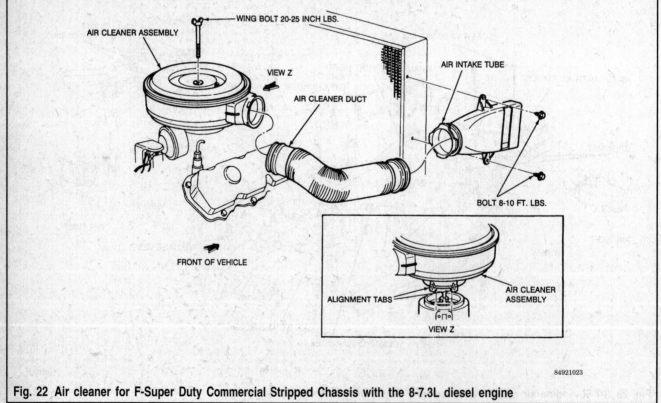

Fig. 22 Air cleaner for F-Super Duty Commercial Stripped Chassis with the 8-7.3L diesel engine

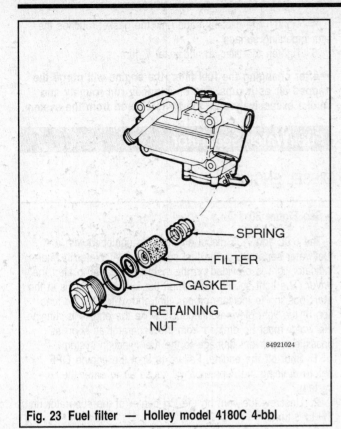

Fig. 23 Fuel filter — Holley model 4180C 4-bbl

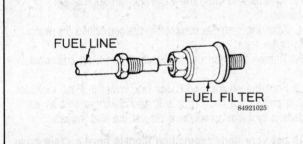

Fig. 24 Some models have the screw-in type fuel filter which threads into the carburetor

To install:

6. Coat the threads of the new filter with non-hardening, gasoline-proof sealer and screw it into place by hand. Tighten it snugly with the wrench.

✳✳WARNING

Do not overtighten the filter! The threads in the carburetor bowl are soft metal and are easily stripped! You don't want to damage these threads!!

7. Connect the hose to the new filter. Most replacement filters come with a new hose and clamps. Use them.

8. Remove the fuel-soaked rags, wipe up any spilled fuel and start the engine. Check the filter connections for leaks.

➥CHILTON TIP: The problem with the screw-in type filter used with the above engines is the possibility of stripping the soft threads in the carburetor float bowl when replac-

ing the filter. Such an occurrence is disastrous! To avoid this possibility, discard the screw-in filter and replace it in the float bowl with a brass fitting having a 5/16 in. OD nipple. To this, attach a length of 5/16 in. ID fuel hose, with a similar length of hose attached to the steel fuel line. Between these 2 hoses you can use an inline type fuel filter such as a Fram G2 or equivalent. Now, filter replacement is simply a matter of removing the inline filter from the hoses. Always use the spring-type hose clamps supplied with the new filter at all hose connection points. Use enough hose to avoid stretching, but not too much, to avoid movement of the filter against nearby components.

Fuel Injected Gasoline Engines

1987-89 ENGINES

▶ **See Figure 25**

The inline filter is mounted on the same bracket as the fuel supply pump on the frame rail under the truck, back by the fuel tank. To replace the filter:

1. Raise and support the rear end on jackstands.

2. With the engine off, depressurize the fuel system. See Section 5.

3. Remove the quick-disconnect fittings at both ends of the filter. See Section 5.

4. Remove the filter and retainer from the bracket.

5. Remove the rubber insulator ring from the filter.

6. Remove the filter from the retainer.

7. Install the new filter into the retainer, noting the direction of the flow arrow.

8. Install a new rubber insulator ring.

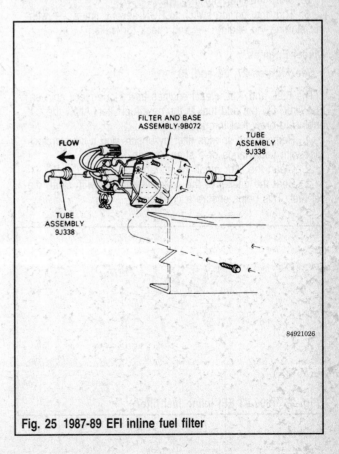

Fig. 25 1987-89 EFI inline fuel filter

9. Install the retainer and filter on the bracket and tighten the screws to 60 inch lbs.
10. Install the fuel lines using new retainer clips.
11. Start the engine and check for leaks.

1990-93 ENGINES
▶ See Figure 26

The filter, with these engines, is located amidships on the left frame rail. Ford states that, under normal use, the filter should last the life of the truck. If, however, you would like to replace the filter:

✳✳CAUTION

To prevent siphoning of fuel from the tank when the filter is removed, raise and support the front end of the truck above the level of the tank.

1. Relieve fuel system pressure. See Section 5. When working in hot weather, work quickly to complete filter replacement before the fuel pressure rebuilds!
2. Unsnap the filter canister from the retaining clips.
3. Disconnect the quick-connect couplings and remove the filter.

✳✳WARNING

Be careful to avoid kinking the fuel lines!

4. Noting the direction-of-flow arrow on the new filter, connect the fuel lines.
5. Snap the filter into the clips.
6. Turn the ignition switch to RUN several times — without starting the engine — and check for leaks.

Diesel Engines
▶ See Figures 27, 28 and 29

The 6.9L and 7.3L diesel engines use a one-piece spin-on fuel filter. Do not add fuel to the new fuel filter. Allow the engine to draw fuel through the filter.
1. Remove the spin-on filter by unscrewing it counterclockwise with your hands or a strap wrench.
2. Clean the filter mounting surface.
3. Coat the gasket or the replacement filter with clean diesel fuel. This helps ensure a good seal.

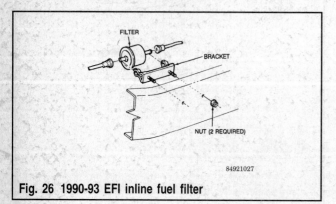

FILTER

BRACKET

NUT (2 REQUIRED)

84921027

Fig. 26 1990-93 EFI inline fuel filter

4. Tighten the filter by hand until the gasket touches the filter mounting surface.
5. Tighten the filter an additional ½ turn.

➡**After changing the fuel filter, the engine will purge the trapped air as it runs. The engine may run roughly and smoke excessively until the air is cleared from the system.**

Fuel/Water Separator

DIESEL ENGINES

▶ See Figure 30

The 6.9L and 7.3L diesel engines are equipped with a fuel/water separator in the fuel supply line. A 'Water in Fuel' indicator light is provided on the instrument panel to alert the driver. The light should glow when the ignition switch is in the **start** position to indicate proper light and water sensor function. If the light glows continuously while the engine is running, the water must be drained from the separator as soon as possible to prevent damage to the fuel injection system.
1. Shut off the engine. Failure to shut the engine **OFF** before draining the separator will cause air to enter the system.
2. Unscrew the vent on the top center of the separator unit 2½ to 3 turns.
3. Unscrew the drain screw on the bottom of the separator 1½ to 2 turns and drain the water into an appropriate container.
4. After the water is completely drained, close the water drain finger tight.
5. Tighten the vent until snug, then turn it an additional ¼ turn.
6. Start the engine and check the 'Water in Fuel' indicator light; it should not be lit. If it is lit and continues to stay so, there is a problem somewhere else in the fuel system.

➡**All but very early production models have a drain hose connected to separator which allows water to drain directly into a container placed underneath the vehicle.**

PCV Valve

GASOLINE ENGINES ONLY

▶ See Figures 31, 32, 33 and 34

Check the PCV valve according to the Preventive Maintenance Schedule at the end of this Section to see if it is free and not gummed up, stuck or blocked. To check the valve, remove it from the engine and work the valve by sticking a screwdriver in the crankcase side of the valve. It should move. It is possible to clean the PCV valve by soaking it in a solvent and blowing it out with compressed air. This can restore the valve to some level of operating order. This should be used only as an emergency measure. Otherwise the valve should be replaced.

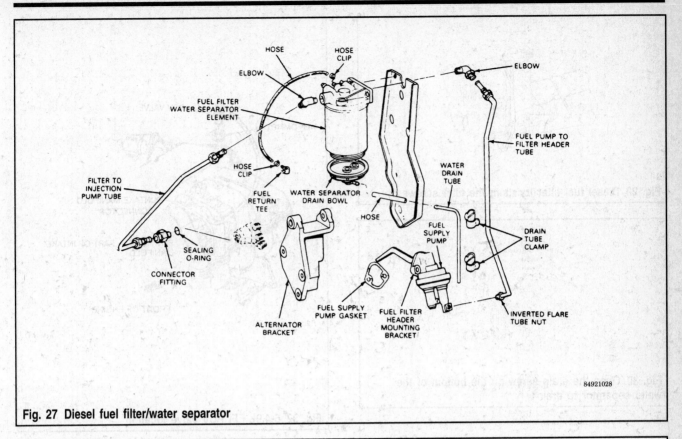

Fig. 27 Diesel fuel filter/water separator

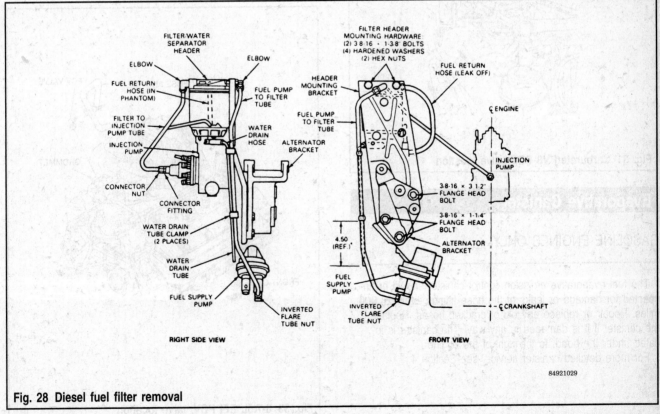

Fig. 28 Diesel fuel filter removal

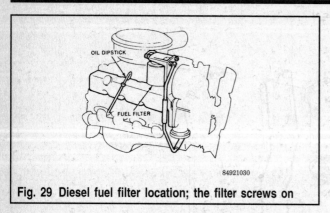

Fig. 29 Diesel fuel filter location; the filter screws on

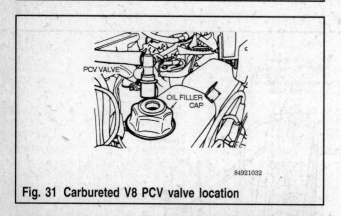

Fig. 30 Open the drain screw on the bottom of the water separator to drain

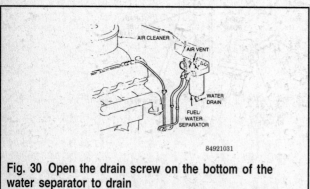

Fig. 31 Carbureted V8 PCV valve location

Evaporative Canister

GASOLINE ENGINES ONLY

The fuel evaporative emission control canister should be inspected for damage or leaks at the hose fittings every 24,000 miles. Repair or replace any old or cracked hoses. Replace the canister if it is damaged in any way. The canister is located under the hood, to the right of the engine.

For more detailed canister service, see Section 4.

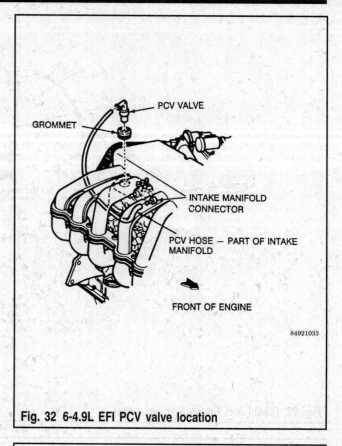

Fig. 32 6-4.9L EFI PCV valve location

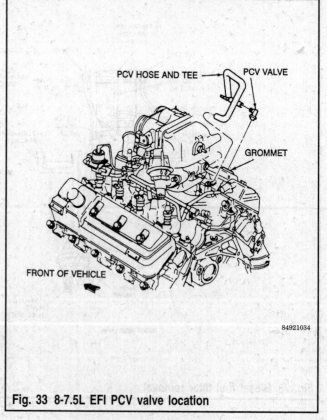

Fig. 33 8-7.5L EFI PCV valve location

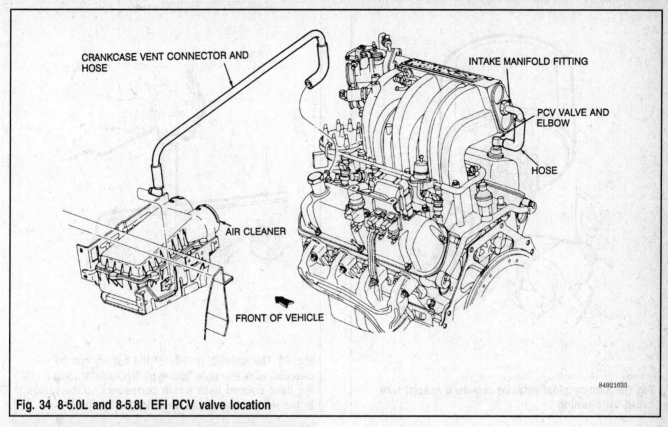

Fig. 34 8-5.0L and 8-5.8L EFI PCV valve location

Battery

▶ See Figures 35, 36, 37, 38, 39, 40 and 41

INSPECTION

Loose, dirty, or corroded battery terminals are a major cause of 'no-start.' Every 3 months or so, remove the battery terminals and clean them, giving them a light coating of petroleum jelly when you are finished. This will help to retard corrosion.

Check the battery cables for signs of wear or chafing and replace any cable or terminal that looks marginal. Battery terminals can be easily cleaned and inexpensive terminal cleaning tools are an excellent investment that will pay for themselves many times over. They can usually be purchased from any well-equipped auto store or parts department. Side terminal batteries require a different tool to clean the threads in the

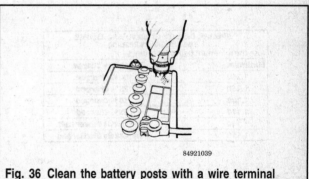

Fig. 36 Clean the battery posts with a wire terminal cleaner

battery case. The accumulated white powder and corrosion can be cleaned from the top of the battery with an old toothbrush and a solution of baking soda and water.

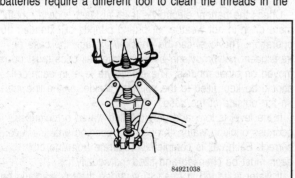

Fig. 35 Top terminal battery cables are easily removed with this inexpensive puller

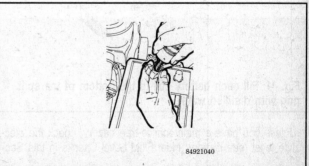

Fig. 37 Clean the cable ends with a stiff cable cleaning tool (male end)

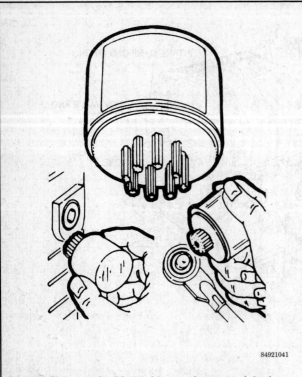

Fig. 38 Side terminal batteries require a special wire brush for cleaning

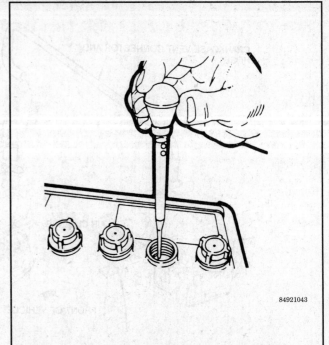

Fig. 40 The specific gravity of the battery can be checked with a simple float-type hydrometer. Some testers have colored balls which correspond to the values in the left column of the specific gravity chart

SPECIFIC GRAVITY (@ 80°F.) AND CHARGE	
Specific Gravity Reading (use the minimum figure for testing)	
Minimum	**Battery Charge**
1.260	100% Charged
1.230	75% Charged
1.200	50% Charged
1.170	25% Charged
1.140	Very Little Power Left
1.110	Completely Discharged

Fig. 39 Battery specific gravity chart

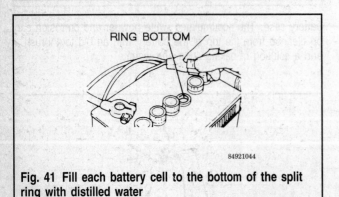

RING BOTTOM

Fig. 41 Fill each battery cell to the bottom of the split ring with distilled water

Unless you have a maintenance-free battery, check the electrolyte level (see Battery under Fluid Level Checks in this Sec-

tion) and check the specific gravity of each cell. Be sure that the vent holes in each cell cap are not blocked by grease or dirt. The vent holes allow hydrogen gas, formed by the chemical reaction in the battery, to escape safely.

REPLACEMENT BATTERIES

The cold power rating of a battery measures battery starting performance and provides an approximate relationship between battery size and engine size. The cold power rating of a replacement battery should match or exceed your engine size in cubic inches.

FLUID LEVEL EXCEPT MAINTENANCE FREE BATTERIES

Check the battery electrolyte level at least once a month, or more often in hot weather or during periods of extended truck operation. The level can be checked through the case on translucent polypropylene batteries; the cell caps must be removed on other models. The electrolyte level in each cell should be kept filled to the split ring inside, or the line marked on the outside of the case.

If the level is low, add only distilled water, or colorless, odorless drinking water, through the opening until the level is correct. Each cell is completely separate from the others, so each must be checked and filled individually.

If water is added in freezing weather, the truck should be driven several miles to allow the water to mix with the electrolyte. Otherwise, the battery could freeze.

SPECIFIC GRAVITY EXCEPT MAINTENANCE FREE BATTERIES

At least once a year, check the specific gravity of the battery. It should be between 1.20 in. Hg and 1.26 in. Hg at room temperature.

The specific gravity can be checked with the use of an hydrometer, an inexpensive instrument available from many sources, including auto parts stores. The hydrometer has a squeeze bulb at one end and a nozzle at the other. Battery electrolyte is sucked into the hydrometer until the float is lifted from its seat. The specific gravity is then read by noting the position of the float. Generally, if after charging, the specific gravity between any two cells varies more than 50 points (0.50), the battery is bad and should be replaced.

It is not possible to check the specific gravity in this manner on sealed (maintenance free) batteries. Instead, the indicator built into the top of the case must be relied on to display any signs of battery deterioration. If the indicator is dark, the battery can be assumed to be OK. If the indicator is light, the specific gravity is low, and the battery should be charged or replaced.

CABLES AND CLAMPS

Once a year, the battery terminals and the cable clamps should be cleaned. Loosen the clamps and remove the cables, negative cable first. On batteries with posts on top, the use of a puller specially made for the purpose is recommended. These are inexpensive, and available in auto parts stores. Side terminal battery cables are secured with a bolt.

Clean the cable lamps and the battery terminal with a wire brush, until all corrosion, grease, etc., is removed and the metal is shiny. It is especially important to clean the inside of the clamp thoroughly, since a small deposit of foreign material or oxidation there will prevent a sound electrical connection and inhibit either starting or charging. Special tools are available for cleaning these parts, one type for conventional batteries and another type for side terminal batteries.

Before installing the cables, loosen the battery holddown clamp or strap, remove the battery and check the battery tray. Clear it of any debris, and check it for soundness. Rust should be wire brushed away, and the metal given a coat of anti-rust paint. Replace the battery and tighten the holddown clamp or strap securely, but be careful not to overtighten, which will crack the battery case.

After the clamps and terminals are clean, reinstall the cables, negative cable last; do not hammer on the clamps to install. Tighten the clamps securely, but do not distort them. Give the clamps and terminals a thin external coat of grease after installation, to retard corrosion.

Check the cables at the same time that the terminals are cleaned. If the cable insulation is cracked or broken, or if the ends are frayed, the cable should be replaced with a new cable of the same length and gauge.

CHARGING

If your truck's battery becomes discharged because of an electrical system failure, or just leaving your lights on, it can be recharged using a battery charger.

A charger rated at 6 amps is more than sufficient for any need. Some battery chargers have a high amperage start feature of 50 amps or more. This will give the battery enough 'boost' to get the truck started when the battery is dead, however, a slow charge is far more beneficial. Follow the charger manufacturer's recommendation when using your charger. A charger with a charging rate gauge will be best, since it shows the rate of charge and can indicate a shorted battery.

✳✳CAUTION

Keep flame or sparks away from the battery; it gives off explosive hydrogen gas. Battery electrolyte contains sulfuric acid. If you should splash any on your skin or in your eyes, flush the affected area with plenty of clear water. If it lands in your eyes, get medical help immediately.

Belts

▶ **See Figures 42, 43, 44, 45, 46, 47, 48, 49, 50, 51, 52, 53, 54 and 55**

Once a year or at 12,000 mile intervals, the tension (and condition) of the alternator, power steering (if so equipped), air conditioning (if so equipped), and Thermactor® air pump drive belts should be checked, and, if necessary, adjusted. Loose accessory drive belts can lead to poor engine cooling and diminish alternator, power steering pump, air conditioning compressor or Thermactor® air pump output. A belt that is too tight places a severe strain on the water pump, alternator, power steering pump, compressor or air pump bearings.

Replace any belt that is so glazed, worn or stretched that it cannot be tightened sufficiently.

➡**The material used in late model drive belts is such that the belts often do not show wear. Replace belts at least every three years.**

On vehicles with matched belts, replace both belts. New ½ in. (13mm), ⅜in. (10mm) and ¹⁵⁄₃₂ in. (12mm) wide belts are to be adjusted to a tension of 140 lbs.; ¼ in. (6mm)wide belts are adjusted to 80 lbs., measured on a belt tension gauge. Any belt that has been operating for a minimum of 10 minutes is considered a used belt. In the first 10 minutes, the belt should stretch to its maximum extent. After 10 minutes, stop the engine and recheck the belt tension. Belt tension for a used belt should be maintained at 110 lbs. (all except ¼ in. wide belts) or 60 lbs. (¼ in. wide belts). If a belt tension gauge is not available, the following procedures may be used.

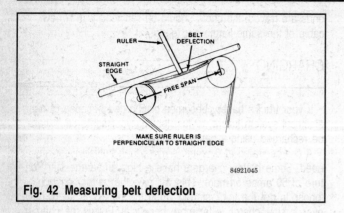

Fig. 42 Measuring belt deflection

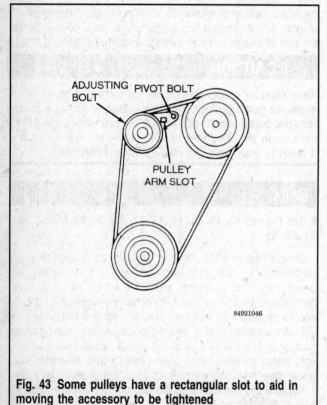

Fig. 43 Some pulleys have a rectangular slot to aid in moving the accessory to be tightened

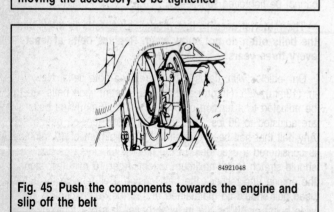

Fig. 45 Push the components towards the engine and slip off the belt

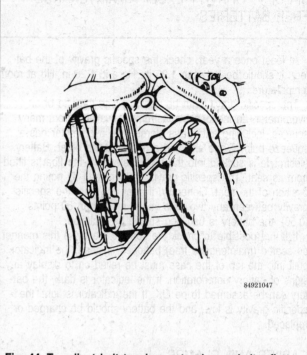

Fig. 44 To adjust belt tension or to change belts, first loosen the component's mounting and adjusting bolts slightly

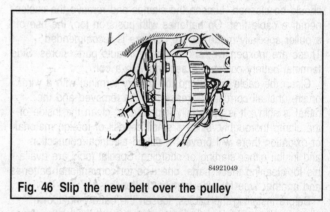

Fig. 46 Slip the new belt over the pulley

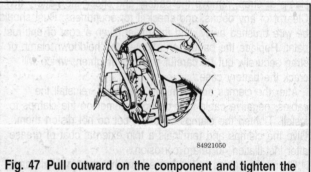

Fig. 47 Pull outward on the component and tighten the mounting bolts

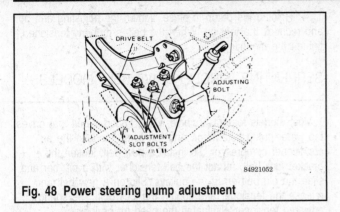

Fig. 48 Power steering pump adjustment

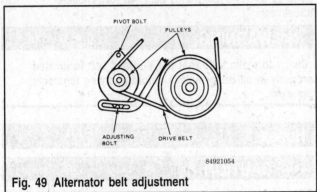

Fig. 49 Alternator belt adjustment

ADJUSTMENTS FOR ALL EXCEPT THE SERPENTINE (SINGLE) BELT

✷✷CAUTION

On models equipped with an electric cooling fan, disconnect the negative battery cable or fan motor wiring harness connector before replacing or adjusting drive belts. The fan may come on, under certain circumstances, even though the ignition is off.

Alternator (Fan Drive) Belt

1. Position the ruler perpendicular to the drive belt at its longest straight run. Test the tightness of the belt by pressing it firmly with your thumb. The deflection should not exceed ¼ in. (6mm).

2. If the deflection exceeds ¼ in. (6mm), loosen the alternator mounting and adjusting arm bolts.

3. Place a 1 in. open-end or adjustable wrench on the adjusting ridge cast on the body, and pull on the wrench until the proper tension is achieved.

4. Holding the alternator in place to maintain tension, tighten the adjusting arm bolt. Recheck the belt tension. When the belt is properly tensioned, tighten the alternator mounting bolt.

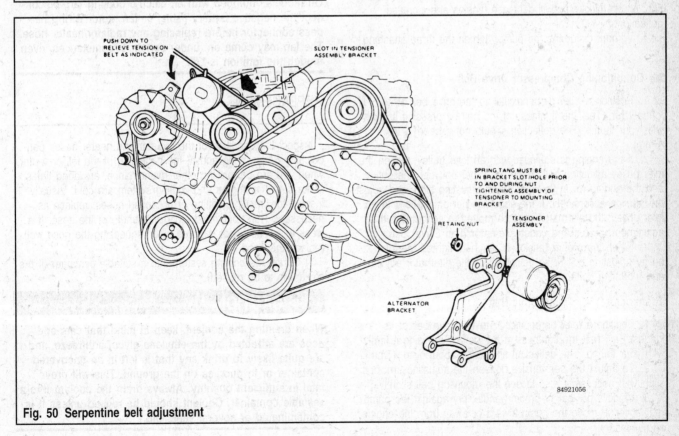

Fig. 50 Serpentine belt adjustment

Power Steering Drive Belt

6-4.9L

1. Hold a ruler perpendicularly to the drive belt at its longest run, test the tightness of the belt by pressing it firmly with your thumb. The deflection should not exceed ¼ in. (6mm).

2. To adjust the belt tension, loosen the adjusting and mounting bolts on the front face of the steering pump cover plate (hub side).

3. Using a pry bar or broom handle on the pump hub, move the power steering pump toward or away from the engine until the proper tension is reached. Do not pry against the reservoir as it is relatively soft and easily deformed.

4. Holding the pump in place, tighten the adjusting arm bolt and then recheck the belt tension. When the belt is properly tensioned tighten the mounting bolts.

V8 MODELS

1. Position a ruler perpendicular to the drive belt at its longest run. Test the tightness of the belt by pressing it firmly with your thumb. The deflection should be about ¼ in. (6mm).

2. To adjust the belt tension, loosen the three bolts in the three elongated adjusting slots at the power steering pump attaching bracket.

3. Turn the steering pump drive belt adjusting nut as required until the proper deflection is obtained. Turning the adjusting nut clockwise will increase tension and decrease deflection; counterclockwise will decrease tension and increase deflection.

4. Without disturbing the pump, tighten the three attaching bolts.

Air Conditioning Compressor Drive Belt

1. Position a ruler perpendicular to the drive belt at its longest run. Test the tightness of the belt by pressing it firmly with your thumb. The deflection should not exceed ¼ in. (6mm).

2. If the engine is equipped with an idler pulley, loosen the idler pulley adjusting bolt, insert a pry bar between the pulley and the engine (or in the idler pulley adjusting slot), and adjust the tension accordingly. If the engine is not equipped with an idler pulley, the alternator must be moved to accomplish this adjustment, as outlined under Alternator (Fan Drive) Belt.

3. When the proper tension is reached, tighten the idler pulley adjusting bolt (if so equipped) or the alternator adjusting and mounting bolts.

Thermactor® Air Pump Drive Belt

1. Position a ruler perpendicular to the drive belt at its longest run. Test the tightness of the belt by pressing it firmly with your thumb. The deflection should be about ¼ in. (6mm).

2. To adjust the belt tension, loosen the adjusting arm bolt slightly. If necessary, also loosen the mounting belt slightly.

3. Using a pry bar or broom handle, pry against the pump rear cover to move the pump toward or away from the engine as necessary.

✳✳CAUTION

Do not pry against the pump housing itself, as damage to the housing may result.

4. Holding the pump in place, tighten the adjusting arm bolt and recheck the tension. When the belt is properly tensioned, tighten the mounting bolt.

SERPENTINE (SINGLE) DRIVE BELT MODELS

Most models feature a single, wide, ribbed V-belt that drives the water pump, alternator, and (on some models) the air conditioner compressor. To install a new belt, loosen the bracket lock bolt, retract the belt tensioner with a pry bar and slide the old belt off of the pulleys. Slip on a new belt and release the tensioner and tighten the lock bolt. The spring powered tensioner eliminates the need for periodic adjustments.

✳✳WARNING

Check to make sure that the V-ribbed belt is located properly in all drive pulleys before applying tensioner pressure.

Hoses

✳✳CAUTION

On models equipped with an electric cooling fan, disconnect the negative battery cable, or fan motor wiring harness connector before replacing any radiator/heater hose. The fan may come on, under certain circumstances, even though the ignition is Off.

REPLACEMENT

Inspect the condition of the radiator and heater hoses periodically. Early spring and at the beginning of the fall or winter, when you are performing other maintenance, are good times. Make sure the engine and cooling system are cold. Visually inspect for cracking, rotting or collapsed hoses, replace as necessary. Run your hand along the length of the hose. If a weak or swollen spot is noted when squeezing the hose wall, replace the hose.

1. Drain the cooling system into a suitable container (if the coolant is to be reused).

✳✳CAUTION

When draining the coolant, keep in mind that cats and dogs are attracted by the ethylene glycol antifreeze, and are quite likely to drink any that is left in an uncovered container or in puddles on the ground. This will prove fatal in sufficient quantity. Always drain the coolant into a sealable container. Coolant should be reused unless it is contaminated or several years old.

2. Loosen the hose clamps at each end of the hose that requires replacement.

3. Twist, pull and slide the hose off the radiator, water pump, thermostat or heater connection.

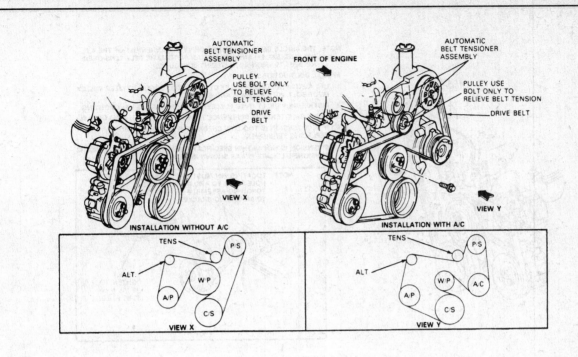

Fig. 51 6-4.9L EFI drive belts

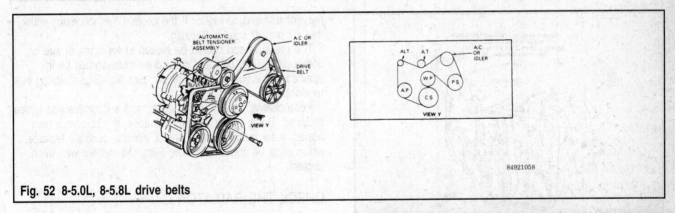

Fig. 52 8-5.0L, 8-5.8L drive belts

4. Clean the hose mounting connections. Position the hose clamps on the new hose.

5. Coat the connection surfaces with a water resistant sealer and slide the hose into position. Make sure the hose clamps are located beyond the raised bead of the connector (if equipped) and centered in the clamping area of the connection.

6. Tighten the clamps to 20-30 inch lbs. Do not overtighten.

7. Fill the cooling system.

8. Start the engine and allow it to reach normal operating temperature. Check for leaks.

Cooling System

✳✳CAUTION

Never remove the radiator cap under any conditions while the engine is running! Failure to follow these instructions could result in damage to the cooling system or engine and/or personal injury. To avoid having scalding hot coolant or steam blow out of the radiator, use extreme care when removing the radiator cap from a hot radiator. Wait until the engine has cooled, then wrap a thick cloth around the radiator cap and turn it slowly to the first stop. Step back while the pressure is released from the cooling system. When you are sure the pressure has been released, press down on the radiator cap (still have the cloth in position) turn and remove the radiator cap.

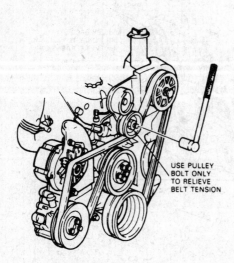

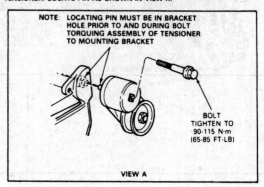

NOTE: THE SINGLE BELT, SERPENTINE DRIVE ARRANGEMENT OF THE 4.9L, 5.0L AND 5.8L EFI ENGINES USE AN AUTOMATIC BELT TENSIONER. NO BELT TENSION ADJUSTMENT IS REQUIRED.

SPECIAL INSTRUCTIONS:

1. LIFT AUTO TENSIONER PULLEY BY APPLYING TORQUE TO IDLER PULLEY PIVOT BOLT WITH WRENCH AND SOCKET.

2. INSTALL DRIVE BELT OVER PULLEYS PER APPROPRIATE BELT ROUTING

3. CHECK BELT TENSION. REFERENCE TENSION CODE (4.9L), (5.0L) OR (5.8L)

4. IF BELT TENSION IS TOO LOW CHECK WITH NEW BELT BEFORE REPLACING TENSIONER.

5. IF TENSION IS NOT WITHIN SPECIFICATION INSTALL A NEW AUTOMATIC TENSIONER. LOCATE PIN AS SHOWN IN VIEW A.

USE PULLEY BOLT ONLY TO RELIEVE BELT TENSION

NOTE: LOCATING PIN MUST BE IN BRACKET HOLE PRIOR TO AND DURING BOLT TORQUING ASSEMBLY OF TENSIONER TO MOUNTING BRACKET

BOLT TIGHTEN TO 90-115 N·m (65-85 FT-LB)

VIEW A

84921059

Fig. 53 Drive belt adjustments on the 6-4.9L, 8-5.0L and 8-5.8L EFI engines

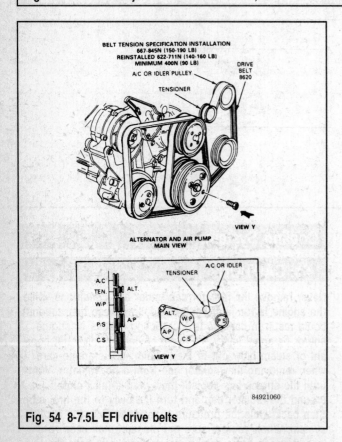

BELT TENSION SPECIFICATION INSTALLATION
667-845N (150-190 LB)
REINSTALLED 622-711N (140-160 LB)
MINIMUM 400N (90 LB)
A/C OR IDLER PULLEY
TENSIONER
DRIVE BELT 8620

VIEW Y

ALTERNATOR AND AIR PUMP MAIN VIEW

A/C OR IDLER
TENSIONER

A.C
TEN.
W/P
P-S
C.S
ALT.
A-P

ALT.
A/P
W/P
C/S
P-S

VIEW Y

84921060

Fig. 54 8-7.5L EFI drive belts

At least once every 2 years, the engine cooling system should be inspected, flushed, and refilled with fresh coolant. If the coolant is left in the system too long, it loses its ability to prevent rust and corrosion. If the coolant has too much water, it won't protect against freezing.

The pressure cap should be looked at for signs of age or deterioration. Fan belt and other drive belts should be inspected and adjusted to the proper tension. (See checking belt tension).

Hose clamps should be tightened, and soft or cracked hoses replaced. Damp spots, or accumulations of rust or dye near hoses, water pump or other areas, indicate possible leakage, which must be corrected before filling the system with fresh coolant.

CHECK THE RADIATOR CAP

▶ **See Figure 56**

While you are checking the coolant level, check the radiator cap for a worn or cracked gasket. It the cap doesn't seal properly, fluid will be lost and the engine will overheat.

Worn caps should be replaced with a new one.

CLEAN RADIATOR OF DEBRIS

▶ **See Figure 57**

Periodically clean any debris — leaves, paper, insects, etc. — from the radiator fins. Pick the large pieces off by hand. The smaller pieces can be washed away with water pressure from a hose.

Carefully straighten any bent radiator fins with a pair of needle nose pliers. Be careful — the fins are very soft. Don't

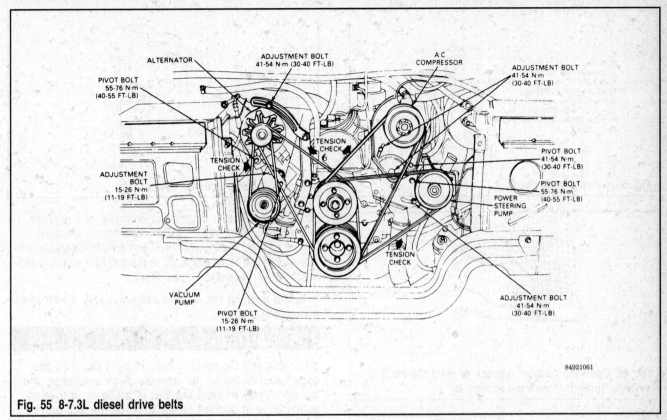

Fig. 55 8-7.3L diesel drive belts

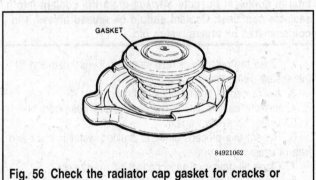

Fig. 56 Check the radiator cap gasket for cracks or wear

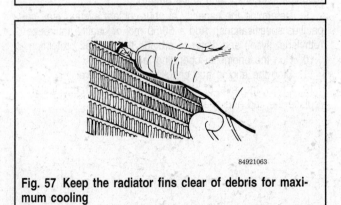

Fig. 57 Keep the radiator fins clear of debris for maximum cooling

wiggle the fins back and forth too much. Straighten them once and try not to move them again.

DRAIN AND REFILL THE COOLING SYSTEM

▶ **See Figures 58, 59, 60, 61 and 62**

Completely draining and refilling the cooling system every two years at least will remove accumulated rust, scale and other deposits. Coolant in late model trucks is a 50/50 mixture of ethylene glycol and water for year round use. Use a good

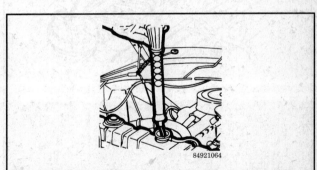

Fig. 58 Check antifreeze protection with an inexpensive tester

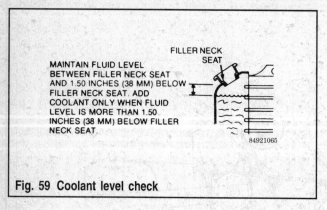

MAINTAIN FLUID LEVEL BETWEEN FILLER NECK SEAT AND 1.50 INCHES (38 MM) BELOW FILLER NECK SEAT. ADD COOLANT ONLY WHEN FLUID LEVEL IS MORE THAN 1.50 INCHES (38 MM) BELOW FILLER NECK SEAT.

FILLER NECK SEAT

84921065

Fig. 59 Coolant level check

84921066

Fig. 60 Open the radiator petcock to drain the cooling system. Spray first with penetrating oil

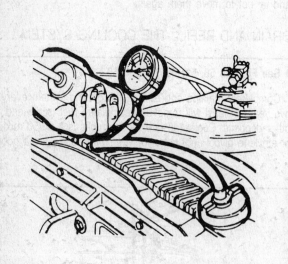

84921067

Fig. 61 The system should be pressure tested once a year

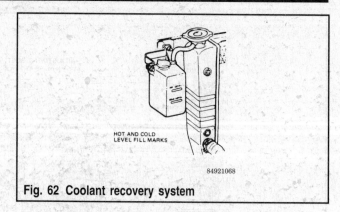

HOT AND COLD LEVEL FILL MARKS

84921068

Fig. 62 Coolant recovery system

quality antifreeze with water pump lubricants, rust inhibitors and other corrosion inhibitors along with acid neutralizers.

1. Drain the existing antifreeze and coolant. Open the radiator and engine drain petcocks, or disconnect the bottom radiator hose, at the radiator outlet.

➡ Before opening the radiator petcock, spray it with some penetrating lubricant.

✳✳CAUTION

When draining the coolant, keep in mind that cats and dogs are attracted by the ethylene glycol antifreeze, and are quite likely to drink any that is left in an uncovered container or in puddles on the ground. This will prove fatal in sufficient quantity. Always drain the coolant into a sealable container. Coolant should be reused unless it is contaminated or several years old.

2. Close the petcock or reconnect the lower hose and fill the system with water.
3. Add a can of quality radiator flush.
4. Idle the engine until the upper radiator hose gets hot.
5. Drain the system again.
6. Repeat this process until the drained water is clear and free of scale.
7. Close all petcocks and connect all the hoses.
8. If equipped with a coolant recovery system, flush the reservoir with water and leave empty.
9. Determine the capacity of your coolant system (see capacities specifications). Add a 50/50 mix of quality antifreeze (ethylene glycol) and water to provide the desired protection.
10. Run the engine to operating temperature.
11. Stop the engine and check the coolant level.
12. Check the level of protection with an antifreeze tester, replace the cap and check for leaks.

Air Conditioning

▸ See Figure 63

GENERAL SERVICING PROCEDURES

✳✳WARNING

R-12 refrigerant is a chlorofluorocarbon which, when released into the atmosphere, contributes to the depletion of the ozone layer in the upper atmosphere. Ozone filters out harmful radiation from the sun. Consult the laws in your area before servicing the air conditioning system. In some states it is illegal to perform repairs involving refrigerant unless the work is done by a certified technician.

The most important aspect of air conditioning service is the maintenance of pure and adequate charge of refrigerant in the system. A refrigeration system cannot function properly if a significant percentage of the charge is lost. Leaks are common because the severe vibration encountered in an automobile can easily cause a sufficient cracking or loosening of the air conditioning fittings. As a result, the extreme operating pressures of the system force refrigerant out.

The problem can be understood by considering what happens to the system as it is operated with a continuous leak. Because the expansion valve regulates the flow of refrigerant to the evaporator, the level of refrigerant there is fairly constant. The receiver/drier stores any excess of refrigerant, and so a loss will first appear there as a reduction in the level of liquid. As this level nears the bottom of the vessel, some refrigerant vapor bubbles will begin to appear in the stream of liquid supplied to the expansion valve. This vapor decreases the capacity of the expansion valve very little as the valve opens to compensate for its presence. As the quantity of liquid in the condenser decreases, the operating pressure will drop there and throughout the high side of the system. As the R-12 continues to be expelled, the pressure available to force the liquid through the expansion valve will continue to decrease, and, eventually, the valve's orifice will prove to be too much of a restriction for adequate flow even with the needle fully withdrawn.

At this point, low side pressure will start to drop, and severe reduction in cooling capacity, marked by freeze-up of the evaporator coil, will result. Eventually, the operating pressure of the evaporator will be lower than the pressure of the atmosphere surrounding it, and air will be drawn into the system wherever there are leaks in the low side.

Because all atmospheric air contains at least some moisture, water will enter the system and mix with the R-12 and the oil. Trace amounts of moisture will cause sludging of the oil, and corrosion of the system. Saturation and clogging of the filter/drier, and freezing of the expansion valve orifice will eventually result. As air fills the system to a greater and greater extend, it will interfere more and more with the normal flows of refrigerant and heat.

A list of general precautions that should be observed while doing this follows:

1. Keep all tools as clean and dry as possible.
2. Thoroughly purge the service gauges and hoses of air and moisture before connecting them to the system. Keep them capped when not in use.

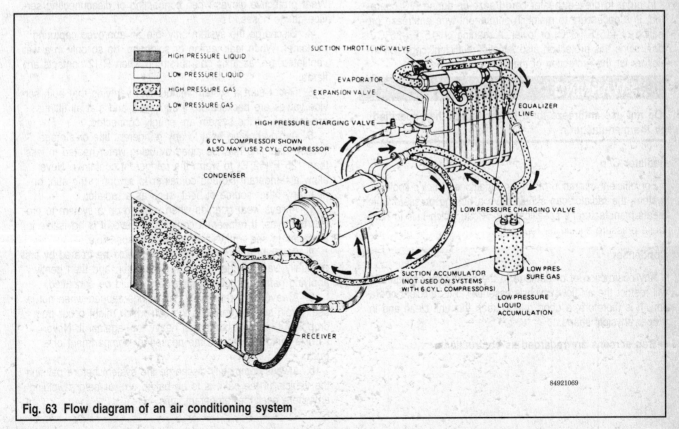

Fig. 63 Flow diagram of an air conditioning system

84921069

3. Thoroughly clean any refrigerant fitting before disconnecting it, in order to minimize the entrance of dirt into the system.

4. Plan any operation that requires opening the system beforehand in order to minimize the length of time it will be exposed to open air. Cap or seal the open ends to minimize the entrance of foreign material.

5. When adding oil, pour it through an extremely clean and dry tube or funnel. Keep the oil capped whenever possible. Do not use oil that has not been kept tightly sealed.

6. Use only refrigerant 12. Purchase refrigerant intended for use in only automotive air conditioning system. Avoid the use of refrigerant 12 that may be packaged for another use, such as cleaning, or powering a horn, as it is impure.

7. Completely evacuate any system that has been opened to replace a component, other than when isolating the compressor, or that has leaked sufficiently to draw in moisture and air. This requires evacuating air and moisture with a good vacuum pump for at least one hour.

If a system has been open for a considerable length of time it may be advisable to evacuate the system for up to 12 hours (overnight).

8. Use a wrench on both halves of a fitting that is to be disconnected, so as to avoid placing torque on any of the refrigerant lines.

ADDITIONAL PREVENTIVE MAINTENANCE CHECKS

Antifreeze

In order to prevent heater core freeze-up during A/C operation, it is necessary to maintain permanent type antifreeze protection of +15°F (-9°C) or lower. A reading of -15°F (-26°C) is ideal since this protection also supplies sufficient corrosion inhibitors for the protection of the engine cooling system.

❋❋WARNING

Do not use antifreeze for a longer period than specified by the manufacturer.

Radiator Cap

For efficient operation of an air conditioned truck's cooling system, the radiator cap should have a holding pressure which meets manufacturer's specifications. A cap which fails to hold these pressure should be replaced.

Condenser

Any obstruction of or damage to the condenser configuration will restrict the air flow which is essential to its efficient operation. It is therefore, a good rule to keep this unit clean and in proper physical shape.

➡**Bug screens are regarded as obstructions.**

Condensation Drain Tube

This single molded drain tube expels the condensation, which accumulates on the bottom of the evaporator housing, into the engine compartment.

If this tube is obstructed, the air conditioning performance can be restricted and condensation buildup can spill over onto the vehicle's floor.

SAFETY PRECAUTIONS

Because of the importance of the necessary safety precautions that must be exercised when working with air conditioning systems and R-12 refrigerant, a recap of the safety precautions are outlined.

1. Avoid contact with a charged refrigeration system, even when working on another part of the air conditioning system or vehicle. If a heavy tool comes into contact with a section of copper tubing or a heat exchanger, it can easily cause the relatively soft material to rupture.

2. When it is necessary to apply force to a fitting which contains refrigerant, as when checking that all system couplings are securely tightened, use a wrench on both parts of the fitting involved, if possible. This will avoid putting torque on the refrigerant tubing. (It is advisable, when possible, to use tube or line wrenches when tightening these flare nut fittings.)

3. Do not attempt to discharge the system by merely loosening a fitting, or removing the service valve caps and cracking these valves. Precise control is possibly only when using the service gauges. Connect the center hose, while discharging the system, to an approved refrigerant capturing container. Wear protective gloves when connecting or disconnecting service gauge hoses.

4. Discharge the system only into an approved capturing container. When leak testing or soldering, do so only in a well ventilated are, as toxic gas is formed when R-12 contacts any flame.

5. Never start a system without first verifying that both service valves are backseated, if equipped, and that all fittings are throughout the system are snugly connected.

6. Avoid applying heat to any refrigerant line or storage vessel. Charging may be aided by using water heated to less than 125°F (52°C) to warm the refrigerant container. Never allow a refrigerant storage container to sit out in the sun, or near any other source of heat, such as a radiator.

7. Always wear goggles when working on a system to protect the eyes. If refrigerant contacts the eye, it is advisable in all cases to see a physician as soon as possible.

8. Frostbite from liquid refrigerant should be treated by first gradually warming the area with cool water, and then gently applying petroleum jelly. A physician should be consulted.

9. Always keep refrigerant can fittings capped when not in use. Avoid sudden shock to the can which might occur from dropping it, or from banging a heavy tool against it. Never carry a refrigerant can in the passenger compartment of a truck.

10. Always completely discharge the system before painting the vehicle (if the paint is to be baked on), or before welding anywhere near the refrigerant lines.

TEST GAUGES

▶ See Figures 64, 65, 66 and 67

Most of the service work performed in air conditioning requires the use of a set of two gauges, one for the high (head) pressure side of the system, the other for the low (suction) side.

The low side gauge records both pressure and vacuum. Vacuum readings are calibrated from 0 to 30 inches Hg and the pressure graduations read from 0 to no less than 60 psi.

The high side gauge measures pressure from 0 to at last 600 psi.

Both gauges are threaded into a manifold that contains two hand shut-off valves. Proper manipulation of these valves and the use of the attached test hoses allow the user to perform the following services:

1. Test high and low side pressures.
2. Remove air, moisture, and contaminated refrigerant.
3. Purge the system (of refrigerant).
4. Charge the system (with refrigerant).

The manifold valves are designed so that they have no direct effect on gauge readings, but serve only to provide for, or cut off, flow of refrigerant through the manifold. During all testing and hook-up operations, the valves are kept in a close position to avoid disturbing the refrigeration system. The valves are opened only to purge the system or refrigerant or to charge it.

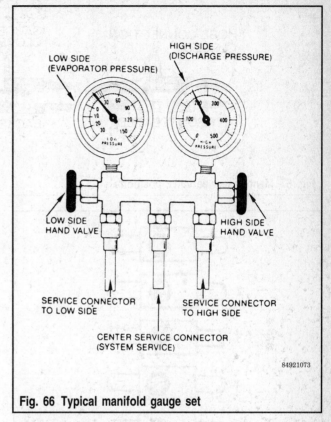

Fig. 66 Typical manifold gauge set

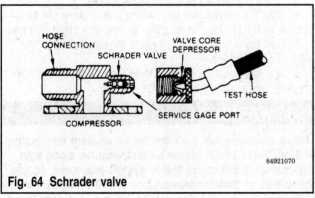

Fig. 64 Schrader valve

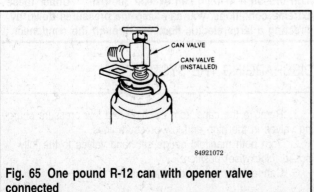

Fig. 65 One pound R-12 can with opener valve connected

INSPECTION

✳✳CAUTION

The compressed refrigerant used in the air conditioning system expands into the atmosphere at a temperature of -21.7°F (-30°C) or lower. This will freeze any surface, including your eyes, that it contacts. In addition, the refrigerant decomposes into a poisonous gas in the presence of a flame. Do not open or disconnect any part of the air conditioning system.

Sight Glass Check
▶ See Figure 68

You can safely make a few simple checks to determine if your air conditioning system needs service. The tests work best if the temperature is warm (about 70°F (21.1°C)).

➡**If your vehicle is equipped with an aftermarket air conditioner, the following system check may not apply. You should contact the manufacturer of the unit for instructions on systems checks.**

1. Place the automatic transmission in Park or the manual transmission in Neutral. Set the parking brake.
2. Run the engine at a fast idle (about 1,500 rpm) either with the help of a friend or by temporarily readjusting the idle speed screw.
3. Set the controls for maximum cold with the blower on High.
4. Locate the sight glass in one of the system lines. Usually it is on the left alongside the top of the radiator.

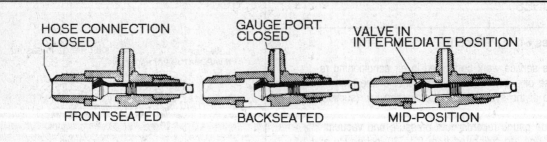

HOSE CONNECTION CLOSED — FRONTSEATED

GAUGE PORT CLOSED — BACKSEATED

VALVE IN INTERMEDIATE POSITION — MID-POSITION

84921074

Fig. 67 Manual service valve positions

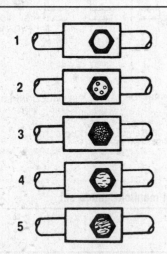

1 Clear sight glass — system correctly charged or over-charged

2 Occasional bubbles — refrigerant charge slightly low

3 Oil streaks on sight glass — total lack of refrigerant

4 Heavy stream of bubbles — serious shortage of refrigerant

5 Dark or clouded sight glass — contaminent present

84921071

Fig. 68 Sight glass inspection

5. If you see bubbles, the system must be recharged. Very likely there is a leak at some point.

6. If there are no bubbles, there is either no refrigerant at all or the system is fully charged. Feel the two hoses going to the belt driven compressor. If they are both at the same temperature, the system is empty and must be recharged.

7. If one hose (high pressure) is warm and the other (low pressure) is cold, the system may be all right. However, you are probably making these tests because you think there is something wrong, so proceed to the next step.

8. Have an assistant in the truck turn the fan control on and off to operate the compressor clutch. Watch the sight glass.

9. If bubbles appear when the clutch is disengaged and disappear when it is engaged, the system is properly charged.

10. If the refrigerant takes more than 45 seconds to bubble when the clutch is disengaged, the system is overcharged. This usually causes poor cooling at low speeds.

❄❄WARNING

If it is determined that the system has a leak, it should be corrected as soon as possible. Leaks may allow moisture to enter and cause a very expensive rust problem. Exercise the air conditioner for a few minutes, every two weeks or so, during the cold months. This avoids the possibility of the compressor seals drying out from lack of lubrication.

TESTING THE SYSTEM

1. Park the truck in the shade, at least 5 feet from any walls.

2. Connect a gauge set.

3. Close (clockwise) both gauge set valves.

4. Start the engine, set the parking brake, place the transmission in NEUTRAL and establish an idle of 1,100-1,300 rpm.

5. Run the air conditioning system for full cooling, in the MAX or COLD mode.

6. The low pressure gauge should read 5-20 psi; the high pressure gauge should indicate 120-180 psi.

❄❄WARNING

These pressures are the norm for an ambient temperature of 70-80°F (21-27°C). Higher air temperatures along with high humidity will cause higher system pressures. At idle speed and an ambient temperature of 110°F (43°C), the high pressure reading can exceed 300 psi. Under these extreme conditions, you can keep the pressures down by directing a large electric floor fan through the condenser.

DISCHARGING THE SYSTEM

1. Remove the caps from the high and low pressure charging valves in the high and low pressure lines.

2. Turn both manifold gauge set hand valves to the fully closed (clockwise) position.

3. Connect the manifold gauge set.

4. If the gauge set hoses do not have the gauge port actuating pins, install fitting adapters T71P-19703-S and R on the manifold gauge set hoses. If the truck does not have a service access gauge port valve, connect the gauge set low pressure hose to the evaporator service access gauge port valve. A special adapter, T77L-19703-A, is required to attach the manifold gauge set to the high pressure service access gauge port valve.

5. Connect the end of the center hose to an approved refrigerant capturing station.

6. Open the low pressure gauge valve slightly and allow the system pressure to bleed off.

7. When the system is just about empty, open the high pressure valve very slowly to avoid losing an excessive amount of refrigerant oil. Allow any remaining refrigerant to escape.

EVACUATING THE SYSTEM

➡**This procedure requires the use of a vacuum pump.**

1. Connect the manifold gauge set.
2. Discharge the system.
3. Make sure that the low pressure gauge set hose is connected to the low pressure service gauge port on the top center of the accumulator/drier assembly and the high pressure hose connected to the high pressure service gauge port on the compressor discharge line.
4. Connect the center service hose to the inlet fitting of the vacuum pump.
5. Turn both gauge set valves to the wide open position.
6. Start the pump and note the low side gauge reading.
7. Operate the pump until the low pressure gauge reads 25-30 in. Hg. Continue running the vacuum pump for 10 minutes more. If you've replaced some component in the system, run the pump for an additional 20-30 minutes.
8. Leak test the system. Close both gauge set valves. Turn off the pump. The needle should remain stationary at the point at which the pump was turned off. If the needle drops to zero rapidly, there is a leak in the system which must be repaired.

LEAK TESTING

Some leak tests can be performed with a soapy water solution. There must be at least a ½ lb. charge in the system for a leak to be detected. The most extensive leak tests are performed with either a Halide flame type leak tester or the more preferable electronic leak tester.

In either case, the equipment is expensive, and, the use of a Halide detector can be **extremely** hazardous!

CHARGING THE SYSTEM

❋❋CAUTION

NEVER OPEN THE HIGH PRESSURE SIDE WITH A CAN OF REFRIGERANT CONNECTED TO THE SYSTEM! OPENING THE HIGH PRESSURE SIDE WILL OVER-PRESSURIZE THE CAN, CAUSING IT TO EXPLODE!

1. Connect the gauge set.
2. Close (clockwise) both gauge set valves.
3. Connect the center hose to the refrigerant can opener valve.
4. Make sure the can opener valve is closed, that is, the needle is raised, and connect the valve to the can. Open the valve, puncturing the can with the needle.
5. Loosen the center hose fitting at the pressure gauge, allowing refrigerant to purge the hose of air. When the air is bled, tighten the fitting.

❋❋CAUTION

IF THE LOW PRESSURE GAUGE SET HOSE IS NOT CONNECTED TO THE ACCUMULATOR/DRIER, KEEP THE CAN IN AN UPRIGHT POSITION!

6. Disconnect the wire harness snap-lock connector from the clutch cycling pressure switch and install a jumper wire across the two terminals of the connector.
7. Open the low side gauge set valve and the can valve.
8. Allow refrigerant to be drawn into the system.
9. When no more refrigerant is drawn into the system, start the engine and run it at about 1,500 rpm. Turn on the system and operate it at the full high position. The compressor will operate and pull refrigerant gas into the system.

➡**To help speed the process, the can may be placed, upright, in a pan of warm water, not exceeding 125°F (52°C).**

10. If more than one can of refrigerant is needed, close the can valve and gauge set low side valve when the can is empty and connect a new can to the opener. Repeat the charging process until the sight glass indicates a full charge. The frost line on the outside of the can will indicate what portion of the can has been used.

❋❋CAUTION

NEVER ALLOW THE HIGH PRESSURE SIDE READING TO EXCEED 240 psi.

11. When the charging process has been completed, close the gauge set valve and can valve. Remove the jumper wire and reconnect the cycling clutch wire. Run the system for at least five minutes to allow it to normalize. Low pressure side reading should be 4-25 psi; high pressure reading should be 120-210 psi at an ambient temperature of 70-90°F (21-32°C).

12. Loosen both service hoses at the gauges to allow any refrigerant to escape. Remove the gauge set and install the dust caps on the service valves.

➡Multi-can dispensers are available which allow a simultaneous hook-up of up to four 1 lb. cans of R-12.

✳✳CAUTION

Never exceed the recommended maximum charge for the system. The maximum charge for systems is 3 lb.

▶ See Figure 69

Intense heat from the sun, snow, and ice, road oils and the chemicals used in windshield washer solvent combine to deteriorate the rubber wiper refills. The refills should be replaced about twice a year or whenever the blades begin to streak or chatter.

WIPER REFILL REPLACEMENT

Normally, if the wipers are not cleaning the windshield properly, only the refill has to be replaced. The blade and arm usually require replacement only in the event of damage. It is not necessary (except on new Tridon® refills) to remove the arm or the blade to replace the refill (rubber part), though you may have to position the arm higher on the glass. You can do this by turning the ignition switch on and operating the wipers. When they are positioned where they are accessible, turn the ignition switch off.

There are several types of refills and your vehicle could have any kind, since aftermarket blades and arms may not use exactly the same type refill as the original equipment.

Most Anco® styles use a release button that is pushed down to allow the refill to slide out of the yoke jaws. The new refill slides in and locks in place.

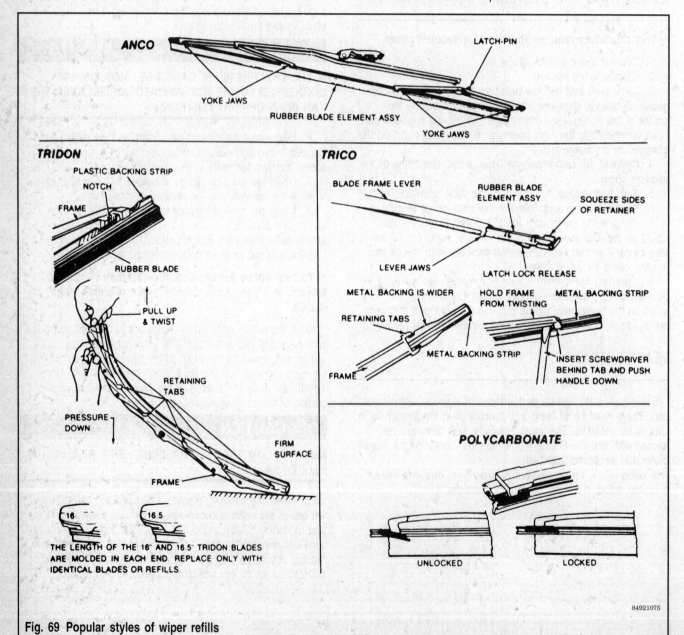

Fig. 69 Popular styles of wiper refills

Some Trico® refills are removed by locating where the metal backing strip or the refill is wider. Insert a small screwdriver blade between the frame and metal backing strip. Press down to release the refill from the retaining tab.

Other Trico® blades are unlocked at one end by squeezing 2 metal tabs, and the refill is slid out of the frame jaws. When the new refill is installed, the tabs will click into place, locking the refill.

The polycarbonate type is held in place by a locking lever that is pushed downward out of the groove in the arm to free the refill. When the new refill is installed, it will lock in place automatically.

The Tridon® refill has a plastic backing strip with a notch about 1 in. (25mm) from the end. Hold the blade (frame) on a hard surface so that the frame is tightly bowed. Grip the tip of the backing strip and pull up while twisting counterclockwise. The backing strip will snap out of the retaining tab. Do this for the remaining tabs until the refill is free of the arm. The length of these refills is molded into the end and they should be replaced with identical types.

No matter which type of refill you use, be sure that all of the frame claws engage the refill. Before operating the wipers, be sure that no part of the metal frame is contacting the windshield.

Tires and Wheels

▶ **See Figures 70, 71, 72, 73, 74 and 75**

The tires should be rotated as specified in the Maintenance Intervals Chart. Refer to the accompanying illustrations for the recommended rotation patterns.

The tires on your truck should have built-in tread wear indicators, which appear as $\frac{1}{2}$ in. (13mm) bands when the tread depth gets as low as 1/16 in. (1.5mm). When the indicators appear in 2 or more adjacent grooves, it's time for new tires.

For optimum tire life, you should keep the tires properly inflated, rotate them often and have the wheel alignment checked periodically.

Some late models have the maximum load pressures listed in the V.I.N. plate on the left door frame. In general, pressure of 28-32 psi would be suitable for highway use with moderate loads and passenger truck type tires (load range B, non-flotation) of original equipment size. Pressures should be checked before driving, since pressure can increase as much as 6 psi due to heat. It is a good idea to have an accurate gauge and to check pressures weekly. Not all gauges on service station

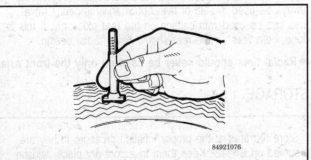

Fig. 70 Checking tread with an inexpensive depth gauge

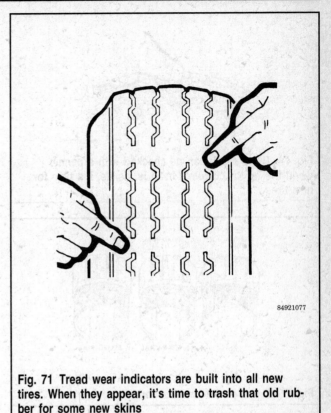

Fig. 71 Tread wear indicators are built into all new tires. When they appear, it's time to trash that old rubber for some new skins

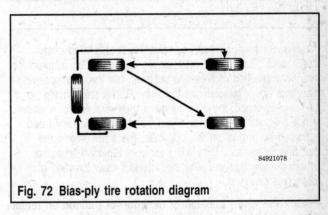

Fig. 72 Bias-ply tire rotation diagram

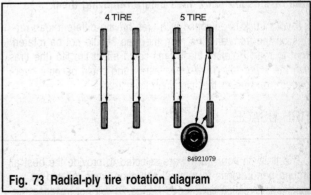

4 TIRE   5 TIRE

Fig. 73 Radial-ply tire rotation diagram

air pumps are to be trusted. In general, truck type tires require higher pressures and flotation type tires, lower pressures.

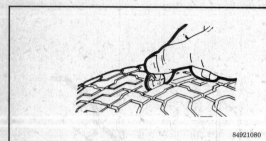

Fig. 74 Tread depth can be checked with a penny; when the top of Lincoln's head is visible, it's time for new tires

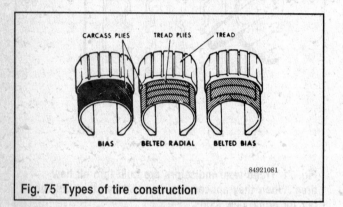

Fig. 75 Types of tire construction

TIRE ROTATION

It is recommended that you have the tires rotated every 6,000 miles. There is no way to give a tire rotation diagram for every combination of tires and vehicles, but the accompanying diagrams are a general rule to follow. Radial tires should not be cross-switched; they last longer if their direction of rotation is not changed. Truck tires sometimes have directional tread, indicated by arrows on the sidewalls; the arrow shows the direction of rotation. They will wear very rapidly if reversed. Studded snow tires will lose their studs if their direction of rotation is reversed.

➡**Mark the wheel position or direction of rotation on radial tires or studded snow tires before removing them.**

If your truck is equipped with tires having different load ratings on the front and the rear, the tires should not be rotated front to rear. Rotating these tires could affect tire life (the tires with the lower rating will wear faster, and could become overloaded), and upset the handling of the truck.

TIRE USAGE

The tires on your truck were selected to provide the best all around performance for normal operation when inflated as specified. Oversize tires (Load Range D) will not increase the maximum carrying capacity of the vehicle, although they will provide an extra margin of tread life. Be sure to check overall height before using larger size tires which may cause interference with suspension components or wheel wells. When re-

placing conventional tire sizes with other tire size designations, be sure to check the manufacturer's recommendations. Interchangeability is not always possible because of differences in load ratings, tire dimensions, wheel well clearances, and rim size. Also due to differences in handling characteristics, 70 Series and 60 Series tires should be used only in pairs on the same axle; radial tires should be used only in sets of four.

The wheels must be the correct width for the tire. Tire dealers have charts of tire and rim compatibility. A mismatch can cause sloppy handling and rapid tread wear. The old rule of thumb is that the tread width should match the rim width (inside bead to inside bead) within an inch. For radial tires, the rim width should be 80% or less of the tire (not tread) width.

The height (mounted diameter) of the new tires can greatly change speedometer accuracy, engine speed at a given road speed, fuel mileage, acceleration, and ground clearance. Tire manufacturers furnish full measurement specifications. Speedometer drive gears are available for correction.

➡**Dimensions of tires marked the same size may vary significantly, even among tires from the same manufacturer.**

The spare tire should be usable, at least for low speed operation, with the new tires.

TIRE DESIGN

For maximum satisfaction, tires should be used in sets of five. Mixing or different types (radial, bias-belted, fiberglass belted) should be avoided. Conventional bias tires are constructed so that the cords run bead-to-bead at an angle. Alternate plies run at an opposite angle. This type of construction gives rigidity to both tread and sidewall. Bias-belted tires are similar in construction to conventional bias ply tires. Belts run at an angle and also at a 90° angle to the bead, as in the radial tire. Tread life is improved considerably over the conventional bias tire. The radial tire differs in construction, but instead of the carcass plies running at an angle of 90° to each other, they run at an angle of 90° to the bead. This gives the tread a great deal of rigidity and the sidewall a great deal of flexibility and accounts for the characteristic bulge associated with radial tires.

Radial tire are recommended for use on all Ford trucks. If they are used, tire sizes and wheel diameters should be selected to maintain ground clearance and tire load capacity equivalent to the minimum specified tire. Radial tires should always be used in sets of five, but in an emergency radial tires can be used with caution on the rear axle only. If this is done, both tires on the rear should be of radial design.

➡**Radial tires should never be used on only the front axle.**

STORAGE

Store the tires at the proper inflation pressure if they are mounted on wheels. Keep them in a cool dry place, laid on their sides. If the tires are stored in the garage or basement, do not let them stand on a concrete floor; set them on strips of wood.

INFLATION PRESSURE

Tire inflation is the most ignored item of auto maintenance. Gasoline mileage can drop as much as 0.8% for every 1 pound per square inch (psi of under inflation).

Two items should be a permanent fixture in every glove compartment; a tire pressure gauge and a tread depth gauge. Check the tire air pressure (including the spare) regularly with a pocket type gauge. Kicking the tires won't tell you a thing, and the gauge on the service station air hose is notoriously inaccurate.

The tire pressures recommended for your care are usually found on the glove box door, on the door jam, or in the owners manual. Ideally, inflation pressure should be checked when the tires are cool. When the air becomes heated it expands and the pressure increases. Every 10 degree rise (or drop) in temperature means a difference of 1 psi, which also explains why the tire appears to lose air on a very cold night. When it is impossible to check the tires cold, allow for pressure build-up due to heat. If the hot pressure exceeds the cold pressure by more than 15 psi, reduce your speed, load or both. Otherwise internal heat is created in the tire. When the heat approaches the temperature at which the tire was cured, during manufacture, the tread can separate from the body.

✳✳CAUTION

Never counteract excessive pressure build-up by bleeding off air pressure (letting some air out). This will only further raise the tire operating temperature.

Before starting a long trip with lots of luggage, you can add about 2-4 psi to the tires to make them run cooler, but never exceed the maximum inflation pressure on the side of the tire.

CARE OF SPECIAL WHEELS

An aluminum wheel may be porous and leak air. Locate the leak by inflating the tire to 40 psi and submerging the tire/wheel assembly in water. Mark the leak areas. Remove the tire from the wheel and scuff the inside rim surface with 80 grit sandpaper. Apply a thick layer of adhesive sealant or equivalent to the leak area and allow to dry for approximately 6 hours.

Clean wheels with a special mag wheel cleaner or mild soap and water. Do not use harsh detergents or solvents or else the protective coating may be damaged.

FLUIDS AND LUBRICANTS

Fluid Disposal

Used fluids such as engine oil, transmission fluid, antifreeze and brake fluid are hazardous wastes and must be disposed of properly. Before draining any fluids, consult with the local authorities; in many areas, waste oil, etc. is being accepted as part of recycling programs. A number of service stations and auto parts stores are also accepting waste fluids for recycling.

Be sure of the recycling center's policies before draining any fluids, as many will not accept different fluids that have been mixed together, such as oil and antifreeze.

Oil and Fuel Recommendations

▶ See Figures 76 and 77

GASOLINE ENGINES

All 1987-93 Ford pickups and Broncos must use lead-free gasoline. It is recommended that 1992-93 trucks avoid the use of premium grade gasoline. This is due to the engine control system being calibrated towards the use of regular grade gasoline. The use of premium grades may actually cause driveability problems.

The recommended oil viscosities for sustained temperatures ranging from below 0°F (-18°C) to above 32°F (0°C) are listed in this Section. They are broken down into multi-viscosity and single viscosities. Multi-viscosity oils are recommended because of their wider range of acceptable temperatures and driving conditions.

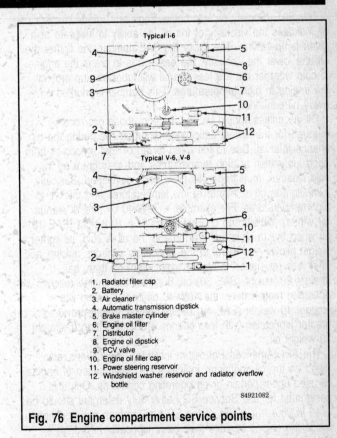

1. Radiator filler cap
2. Battery
3. Air cleaner
4. Automatic transmission dipstick
5. Brake master cylinder
6. Engine oil filter
7. Distributor
8. Engine oil dipstick
9. PCV valve
10. Engine oil filler cap
11. Power steering reservoir
12. Windshield washer reservoir and radiator overflow bottle

84921082

Fig. 76 Engine compartment service points

When adding oil to the crankcase or changing the oil or filter, it is important that oil of an equal quality to original equipment be used in your truck. The use of inferior oils may void the warranty, damage your engine, or both.

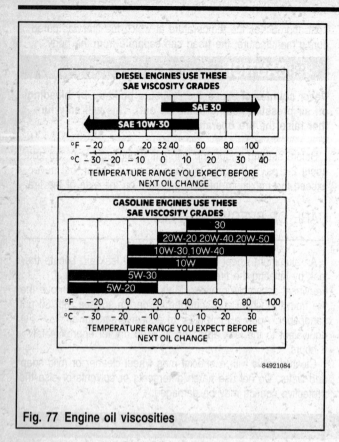

Fig. 77 Engine oil viscosities

The SAE (Society of Automotive Engineers) grade number of oil indicates the viscosity of the oil (its ability to lubricate at a given temperature). The lower the SAE number, the lighter the oil; the lower the viscosity, the easier it is to crank the engine in cold weather but the less the oil will lubricate and protect the engine in high temperatures. This number is marked on every oil container.

Oil viscosities should be chosen from those oils recommended for the lowest anticipated temperatures during the oil change interval. Due to the need for an oil that embodies both good lubrication at high temperatures and easy cranking in cold weather, multigrade oils have been developed. Basically, a multigrade oil is thinner at low temperatures and thicker at high temperatures. For example, a 10W-40 oil (the W stands for winter) exhibits the characteristics of a 10 weight (SAE 10) oil when the truck is first started and the oil is cold. Its lighter weight allows it to travel to the lubricating surfaces quicker and offer less resistance to starter motor cranking than, say, a straight 30 weight (SAE 30) oil. But after the engine reaches operating temperature, the 10W-40 oil begins acting like straight 40 weight (SAE 40) oil, its heavier weight providing greater lubrication with less chance of foaming than a straight 30 weight oil.

The API (American Petroleum Institute) designations, also found on the oil container, indicates the classification of engine oil used under certain given operating conditions. Only oils designated for use Service SG heavy duty detergent should be used in your truck. Oils of the SG type perform may functions inside the engine besides their basic lubrication. Through a balanced system of metallic detergents and polymeric dispersants, the oil prevents high and low temperature deposits and also keeps sludge and dirt particles in suspension. Acids, particularly sulfuric acid, as well as other by-products of engine combustion are neutralized by the oil. If these acids are allowed to concentrate, they can cause corrosion and rapid wear of the internal engine parts.

✳✳CAUTION

Non-detergent motor oils or straight mineral oils should not be used in your Ford gasoline engine.

Synthetic Oil

There are many excellent synthetic and fuel-efficient oils currently available that can provide better gas mileage, longer service life, and in some cases better engine protection. These benefits do not come without a few hitches, however; the main one being the price of synthetic oils, which is three or four times the price per quart of conventional oil.

Synthetic oil is not for every truck and every type of driving, so you should consider your engine's condition and your type of driving. Also, check your truck's warranty conditions regarding the use of synthetic oils.

Both brand new engines and older, high mileage engines are the wrong candidates for synthetic oil. The synthetic oils are so slippery that they can prevent the proper break-in of new engines; most manufacturers recommend that you wait until the engine is properly broken in (3000 miles) before using synthetic oil. Older engines with wear have a different problem with synthetics: they 'use' (consume during operation) more oil as they age. Slippery synthetic oils get past these worn parts easily. If your engine is 'using' conventional oil, it will use synthetics much faster. Also, if your truck is leaking oil past old seals you'll have a much greater leak problem with synthetics.

Consider your type of driving. If most of your accumulated mileage is high speed, highway type driving, the more expensive synthetic oils may be a benefit. Extended highway driving gives the engine a chance to warm up, accumulating less acids in the oil and putting less stress on the engine over the long run. Under these conditions, the oil change interval can be extended (as long as your oil filter can last the extended life of the oil) up to the advertised mileage claims of the synthetics. Trucks with synthetic oils may show increased fuel economy in highway driving, due to less internal friction. However, many automotive experts agree that 50,000 miles (80,000 km) is too long to keep any oil in your engine.

Trucks used under harder circumstances, such as stop-and-go, city type driving, short trips, or extended idling, should be serviced more frequently. For the engines in these trucks, the much greater cost of synthetic or fuel-efficient oils may not be worth the investment. Internal wear increase much quicker on these trucks, causing greater oil consumption and leakage.

➡**The mixing of conventional and synthetic oils is not recommended. If you are using synthetic oil, it might be wise to carry two or three quarts with you no matter where you drive, as not all service stations carry this type of lubricant. Non-detergent or straight mineral oils must never be used.**

Diesel Engines

Diesel engines require different engine oil from those used in gasoline engines. Besides doing the things gasoline engine oil does, diesel oil must also deal with increased engine heat and the diesel blow-by gases, which create sulfuric acid, a high corrosive.

Under the American Petroleum Institute (API) classifications, gasoline engine oil codes begin with an **S**, and diesel engine oil codes begin with a **C**. This first letter designation is followed by a second letter code which explains what type of service (heavy, moderate, light) the oil is meant for. For example, the top of a typical oil can will include: API SERVICES SG, CD. This means the oil in the can is a superior, heavy duty engine oil when used in a diesel engine.

Many diesel manufacturers recommend an oil with both gasoline and diesel engine API classifications.

➡**Ford specifies the use of an engine oil conforming to API service categories of both SG and CD. DO NOT use oils labeled as only SG or only CD as they could cause engine damage.**

FUEL

Fuel makers produce two grades of diesel fuel, No. 1 and No. 2, for use in automotive diesel engines. Generally speaking, No. 2 fuel is recommended over No. 1 for driving in temperatures above 20°F (-7°C). In fact, in many areas, No. 2 diesel is the only fuel available. By comparison, No. 2 diesel fuel is less volatile than No. 1 fuel, and gives better fuel economy. No. 2 fuel is also a better injection pump lubricant.

Two important characteristics of diesel fuel are its cetane number and its viscosity.

The cetane number of a diesel fuel refers to the ease with which a diesel fuel ignites. High cetane numbers mean that the fuel will ignite with relative ease or that it ignites well at low temperatures. Naturally, the lower the cetane number, the higher the temperature must be to ignite the fuel. Most commercial fuels have cetane numbers that range from 35 to 65. No. 1 diesel fuel generally has a higher cetane rating than No. 2 fuel.

Viscosity is the ability of a liquid, in this case diesel fuel, to flow. Using straight No. 2 diesel fuel below 20°F (-7°C) can cause problems, because this fuel tends to become cloudy, meaning wax crystals begin forming in the fuel. 20°F (-7°C) is often call the cloud point for No. 2 fuel. In extremely cold weather, No. 2 fuel can stop flowing altogether. In either case, fuel flow is restricted, which can result in no start condition or poor engine performance. Fuel manufacturers often winterize No. 2 diesel fuel by using various fuel additives and blends (no. 1 diesel fuel, kerosene, etc.) to lower its winter time viscosity. Generally speaking, though, No. 1 diesel fuel is more satisfactory in extremely cold weather.

➡**No. 1 and No. 2 diesel fuels will mix and burn with no ill effects, although the engine manufacturer recommends one or the other. Consult the owner's manual for information.**

Depending on local climate, most fuel manufacturers make winterized No. 2 fuel available seasonally.

Many automobile manufacturers publish pamphlets giving the locations of diesel fuel stations nationwide. Contact the local dealer for information.

Do not substitute home heating oil for automotive diesel fuel. While in some cases, home heating oil refinement levels equal those of diesel fuel, many times they are far below diesel engine requirements. The result of using dirty home heating oil will be a clogged fuel system, in which case the entire system may have to be dismantled and cleaned.

One more word on diesel fuels. Don't thin diesel fuel with gasoline in cold weather. The lighter gasoline, which is more explosive, will cause rough running at the very least, and may cause extensive damage to the fuel system if enough is used.

OPERATION IN FOREIGN COUNTRIES

If you plan to drive your truck outside the United States or Canada, there is a possibility that fuels will be too low in anti-knock quality and could produce engine damage. It is wise to consult with local authorities upon arrival in a foreign country to determine the best fuels available.

ENGINE OIL LEVEL CHECK

▶ **See Figure 78**

Check the engine oil level every time you fill the gas tank. The oil level should be above the ADD mark and not above the FULL mark on the dipstick. Make sure that the dipstick is inserted into the crankcase as far as possible and that the vehicle is resting on level ground. Also, allow a few minutes after turning off the engine for the oil to drain into the pan or an inaccurate reading will result.

1. Open the hood and remove the engine oil dipstick.
2. Wipe the dipstick with a clean, lint-free rag and reinsert it. Be sure to insert it all the way.
3. Pull out the dipstick and note the oil level. It should be between the **SAFE** (MAX) mark and the **ADD** (MIN) mark.
4. If the level is below the lower mark, replace the dipstick and add fresh oil to bring the level within the proper range. Do not overfill.
5. Recheck the oil level and close the hood.

➡**Use a multi-grade oil with API classification SG.**

OIL AND FILTER CHANGE

▶ **See Figures 79, 80, 81, 82, 83 and 84**

➡**The engine oil and oil filter should be changed at the same time, at the recommended intervals on the maintenance schedule chart.**

The oil should be changed more frequently if the vehicle is being operated in very dusty areas. Before draining the oil, make sure that the engine is at operating temperature. Hot oil will hold more impurities in suspension and will flow better, allowing the removal of more oil and dirt.

Loosen the drain plug with a wrench, then, unscrew the plug with your fingers, using a rag or rubber gloves, to shield your fingers from the heat. Push in on the plug as you unscrew it so you can feel when all of the screw threads are out of the hole. You can then remove the plug quickly with the minimum amount of oil running down your arm and you will also have the plug in your hand and not in the bottom of a pan of hot oil. Drain the oil into a suitable receptacle. Be careful of the

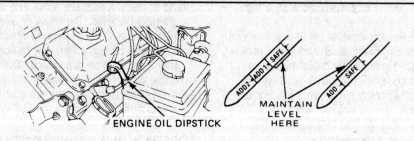

Fig. 78 Checking engine oil level

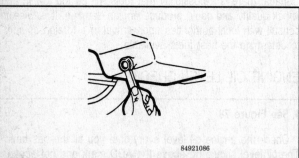

Fig. 79 Loosen, but do not remove, the drain plug at the bottom of the oil pan. Get your drain pan ready

Fig. 82 Wipe clean engine oil around the rubber gasket on the new filter. This helps ensure a good seal

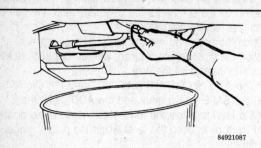

Fig. 80 Unscrew the plug by hand. Keep an inward pressure on the plug as you unscrew it, so the oil won't escape until you pull the plug away

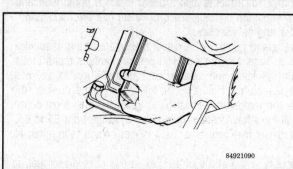

Fig. 83 Install the new filter by hand only; DO NOT use a strap wrench to install

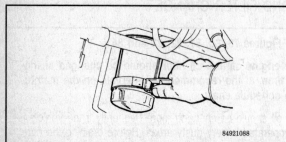

Fig. 81 Move the drain pan underneath the oil filter. Use a strap wrench to remove the filter — remember it is still filled with about a quart of hot, dirty oil

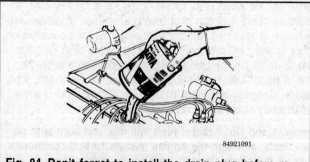

Fig. 84 Don't forget to install the drain plug before re-filling the engine with fresh oil

oil. If it is at operating temperatures it is hot enough to burn you.

The oil filter is located on the left side of all the engines installed in Ford trucks. For longest engine life, it should be changed every time the oil is changed. To remove the filter, you may need an oil filter wrench since the filter may have been fitted too tightly and the heat from the engine may have made it even tighter. A filter wrench can be obtained at an auto parts store and is well worth the investment, since it will save you a lot of grief. Loosen the filter with the filter wrench. With a rag wrapped around the filter, unscrew the filter from the boss on the side of the engine. Be careful of hot oil that will run down the side of the filter. Make sure that you have a pan under the filter before you start to remove it from the engine; should some of the hot oil happen to get on you, you will have a place to dump the filter in a hurry. Wipe the base of the mounting boss with a clean, dry cloth. When you install the new filter, smear a small amount of oil on the gasket with your finger, just enough to coat the entire surface, where it comes in contact with the mounting plate. When you tighten the filter, rotate if only a half turn after it comes in contact with the mounting boss.

Transmission

FLUID RECOMMENDATIONS

Manual Transmissions:
- All 1987 models — SAE 85W/90 gear oil
- All 1988 models — MERCON® (Dexron®II) ATF
- 1989-91 4-speed models — SAE 85W/90 gear oil
- 1992-93 4-speed models — MERCON® (Dexron®II) ATF
- 1989-93 5-speed models — MERCON® (Dexron®II) ATF

Automatic Transmissions:
- All models — MERCON® (Dexron®II) ATF

LEVEL CHECK

Automatic Transmissions
▶ **See Figures 85, 86 and 87**

It is very important to maintain the proper fluid level in an automatic transmission. If the level is either too high or too low, poor shifting operation and internal damage are likely to

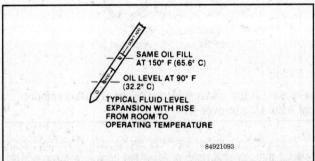

84921093

Fig. 85 Checking the automatic transmission fluid level when it is warmed to operating temperature

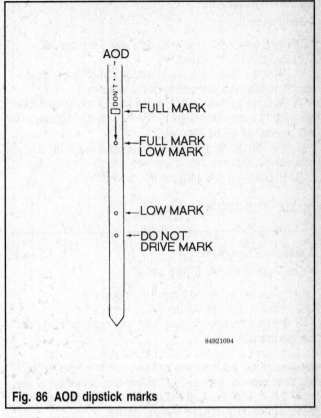

84921094

Fig. 86 AOD dipstick marks

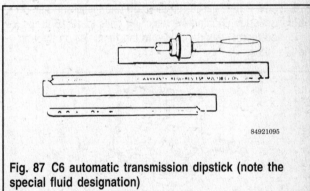

84921095

Fig. 87 C6 automatic transmission dipstick (note the special fluid designation)

occur. For this reason a regular check of the fluid level is essential.

1. Drive the vehicle for 15-20 minutes to allow the transmission to reach operating temperature.

2. Park the truck on a level surface, apply the parking brake and leave the engine idling. Shift the transmission and engage each gear, then place the gear selector in **P** (PARK).

3. Wipe away any dirt in the areas of the transmission dipstick to prevent it from falling into the filler tube. Withdraw the dipstick, wipe it with a clean, lint-free rag and reinsert it until it seats.

4. Withdraw the dipstick and note the fluid level. It should be between the upper (FULL) mark and the lower (ADD) mark.

5. If the level is below the lower mark, use a funnel and add fluid in small quantities through the dipstick filler neck. Keep the engine running while adding fluid and check the level after each small amount. Do not overfill.

Manual Transmission

▶ **See Figure 88**

The fluid level should be checked every 6 months/6,000 miles, whichever comes first.

1. Park the truck on a level surface, turn off the engine, apply the parking brake and block the wheels.
2. Remove the filler plug from the side of the transmission case with a proper size wrench. The fluid level should be even with the bottom of the filler hole.
3. If additional fluid is necessary, add it through the filler hole using a siphon pump or squeeze bottle.
4. Replace the filler plug; do not overtighten.

DRAIN AND REFILL

Automatic Transmission

▶ **See Figures 89, 90, 91, 92 and 93**

1. Raise the truck and support on jackstands.
2. Place a drain pan under the transmission.
3. Loosen the pan attaching bolts and drain the fluid from the transmission.
4. When the fluid has drained to the level of the pan flange, remove the remaining pan bolts working from the rear and both sides of the pan to allow it to drop and drain slowly.
5. When all of the fluid has drained, remove the pan and clean it thoroughly. Discard the pan gasket.
6. Place a new gasket on the pan, and install the pan on the transmission. Tighten the attaching bolts to 12-16 ft. lbs.
7. Add three 3 quarts of fluid to the transmission through the filler tube.

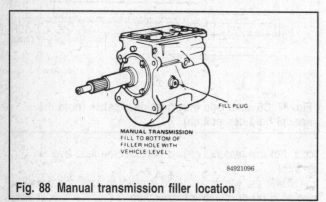

Fig. 88 Manual transmission filler location

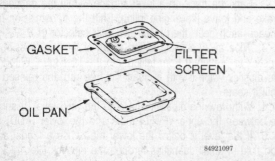

Fig. 89 Automatic transmission filters are found above the transmission oil pan

Fig. 90 Many late model vehicles have no drain plug. Loosen the pan bolts and allow one corner of the pan to hang, so that the fluid will drain out

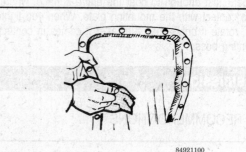

Fig. 91 Clean the pan thoroughly with a safe solvent and allow it to air dry

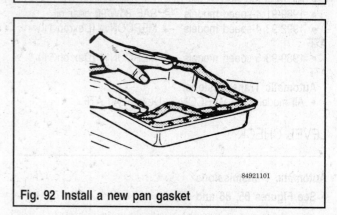

Fig. 92 Install a new pan gasket

Fig. 93 Fill the transmission with the required amount of fluid. Do not over fill

8. Lower the vehicle. Start the engine and move the gear selector through shift pattern. Allow the engine to reach normal operating temperature.

9. Check the transmission fluid. Add fluid, if necessary, to maintain correct level.

Manual Transmission

1. Place a suitable drain pan under the transmission.
2. Remove the drain plug and allow the gear lube to drain out.
3. Replace the drain plug, remove the filler plug and fill the transmission to the proper level with the required fluid.
4. Reinstall the filler plug.

Front (4WD) and Rear Axles

FLUID LEVEL CHECK

▶ **See Figure 94**

Clean the area around the fill plug, which is located in the housing cover, before removing the plug. The lubricant level should be maintained to the bottom of the fill hole with the axle in its normal running position. If lubricant does not appear at the hole when the plug is removed, additional lubricant should be added. Use hypoid gear lubricant SAE 80 or 90.

➡**If the differential is of the limited slip type, be sure and use special limited slip differential additive.**

DRAIN AND REFILL

Drain and refill the front and rear axle housing every 24,000 miles, or every day if the vehicle is operated in deep water. Remove the oil with a suction gun. Refill the axle housings with the proper oil. Be sure and clean the area around the drain plug before removing the plug. See the section on level checks.

Brake Master Cylinder

The master cylinder reservoir is located under the hood, on the left side firewall. Before removing the master cylinder reservoir cap, make sure the vehicle is resting on level ground and clean all dirt away from the top of the master cylinder. On early models, pry off the retaining clip or unscrew the hold-down bolt and remove the cap. On later models, simply unscrew the cap. The brake fluid level should be within ¼ in.

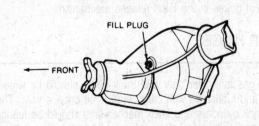

FILL PLUG

← FRONT

84921103

Fig. 94 Differential fill plug location, 2-wheel drive shown. The 4·4 front axle is similar

(6mm) of the top of the reservoir, on cast iron cylinders, or, at the level mark on plastic reservoirs.

If the level of the brake fluid is less than half the volume of the reservoir, it is advised that you check the brake system for leaks. Leaks in the hydraulic brake system most commonly occur at the wheel cylinder.

There is a rubber diaphragm in the top of the master cylinder cap. As the fluid level lowers in the reservoir due to normal brake shoe wear or leakage, the diaphragm takes up the space. This is to prevent the loss of brake fluid out the vented cap and contamination by dirt. After filling the master cylinder to the proper level with heavy duty brake fluid, but before replacing the cap, fold the rubber diaphragm up into the cap, then replace the cap in the reservoir and tighten the retaining bolt or snap the retaining clip into place.

Hydraulic Clutch Reservoir

The hydraulic fluid reservoirs on these systems are mounted on the firewall. Fluid level checks are performed like those on the brake hydraulic system. The proper fluid level is indicated by a step on the reservoir. Keep the reservoir topped up with Ford Heavy-Duty Brake fluid or equivalent; do not overfill.

❋❋CAUTION

Carefully clean the top and sides of the reservoir before opening, to prevent contamination of the system with dirt, etc. Remove the reservoir diaphragm before adding fluid, and replace after filling.

See the illustration of the hydraulic clutch assembly in Section 7.

Manual Steering Gear

2-WHEEL DRIVE

1. Center the steering wheel.
2. Remove the steering gear housing filler plug.
3. Remove the lower cover-to-housing attaching bolt.
4. With a clean punch or similar object, clean out or push the loose lubricant in the filler plug hole and cover-to-housing attaching bolt hole inward.
5. Slowly turn the steering wheel to the left until the linkage reaches its stop. Lubricant should rise within the cover lower bolt hole.
6. Slowly turn the steering wheel to the right until the linkage reaches its stop. Lubricant should rise within the filler plug hole.
7. If lubricant does not rise in both of the holes, add steering gear lubricant until it comes out both the holes during the check.
8. Install the lower cover-to-housing attaching bolt and the filler plug.

4-WHEEL DRIVE

1. Remove the filler plug from the sector shaft cover.

2. Check to see if the lubricant level is visible in the filler plug tower. If the lubricant is visible, install the filler plug. If the lubricant is not visible, add steering gear lubricant until the lubricant is visible about 1 in. (25mm) from the top of the hole in the filler plug tower.

3. Replace the filler plug.

Power Steering Reservoir

▶ **See Figure 95**

Position the vehicle on level ground. Run the engine until the fluid is at normal operating temperature. Turn the steering wheel all the way to the left and right several times. Position the wheels in the straight ahead position, then shut off the engine. Check the fluid level on the dipstick which is attached to the reservoir cap. The level should be between the ADD and FULL marks on the dipstick. Add fluid accordingly. Do not overfill. Use power steering fluid.

Transfer Case

FLUID LEVEL CHECK

Position the vehicle on level ground. Remove the transfer case fill plug located on the left side of the transfer case. The fluid level should be up to the fill hole. If lubricant doesn't run out when the plug is removed, add lubricant until it does run out and then replace the fill plug. Use Ford MERCON® or Dexron®II ATF.

DRAIN AND REFILL

The transfer case is serviced at the same time and in the same manner as the transmission. Clean the area around the filler and drain plugs and remove the filler plug on the side of the transfer case. Remove the drain plug on the bottom of the transfer case and allow the lubricant to drain completely.

Clean and install the drain plug. Add the proper lubricant. See the section on level checks.

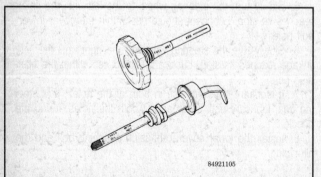

84921105

Fig. 95 Typical power steering pump reservoir dipsticks

Chassis Greasing

KNUCKLES AND STEERING LINKAGE

The lubrication chart indicates where the grease fittings are located. The vehicle should be greased according to the intervals in the Preventive Maintenance Schedule at the end of this Section. Fittings are usually located on the ball joints, steering linkage and driveshaft(s). In some cases, a threaded plug will be found which will have to be removed to allow the installation of a fitting. Fittings are available at most auto parts stores.

Using a grease gun loaded with multi-purpose chassis lube, pump grease through the fitting until some grease is forced from the ball stud or joint being serviced.

Wipe the fitting clean before applying the grease gun and wipe off the excess grease after servicing.

➡**The grease fitting inside the double cardan joint on the driveshaft, will require a special needle adapter for the grease gun**

PARKING BRAKE LINKAGE

Use chassis grease on the parking brake cable where it contacts the cable guides, levers and linkage.

Automatic Transmission Linkage

Apply a small amount of clean engine oil to the kickdown and shift linkage points at 7,500 mile intervals.

Body Lubrication And Maintenance

LOCK CYLINDERS

Apply graphite lubricant sparingly through the key slot. Insert the key and operate the lock several times to be sure that the lubricant is worked into the lock cylinder.

HOOD LATCH AND HINGES

Clean the latch surfaces and apply clean engine oil to the latch pilot bolts and the spring anchor. Also lubricate the hood hinges with engine oil. Use a chassis grease to lubricate all the pivot points in the latch release mechanism.

DOOR HINGES

The gas tank filler door and truck doors should be wiped clean and lubricated with clean engine oil once a year. The door lock cylinders and latch mechanisms should be lubricated periodically with a few drops of graphite lock lubricant or a few shots of silicone spray.

BODY DRAIN HOLES

Be sure that the drain holes in the doors and rocker panels are cleared of obstruction. A small punch, screwdriver or unbent wire coat hanger can be used to clear them of any debris.

2-Wheel Drive Front Wheel Bearings

ADJUSTMENT

▶ **See Figures 96, 97, 98 and 99**

The front wheels each rotate on a set of opposed, tapered roller bearings as shown in the accompanying illustration. The grease retainer at the inside of the hub prevents lubricant from leaking into the brake drum.

1987-89 F-150, F-250, F-350

1. Raise and support the front end on jackstands.
2. Remove the grease cap and remove excess grease from the end of the spindle.
3. Remove the cotter pin and nut lock shown in the illustration.
4. Back off the adjusting nut 2-3 turns.
5. Rotate the wheel, hub and rotor assembly while tightening the adjusting nut to 22-25 ft. lbs. in order to seat the bearings.
6. Back off the adjusting nut ⅛ turn.

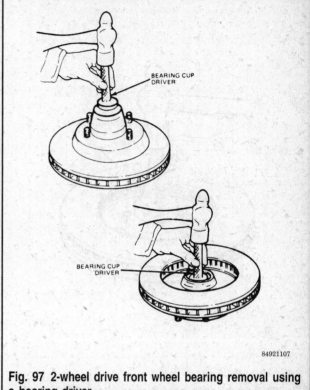

Fig. 97 2-wheel drive front wheel bearing removal using a bearing driver

7. Locate the nut lock on the adjusting nut so that the castellations on the lock are lined up with the cotter pin hole in the spindle. Try to avoid turning the adjusting nut.

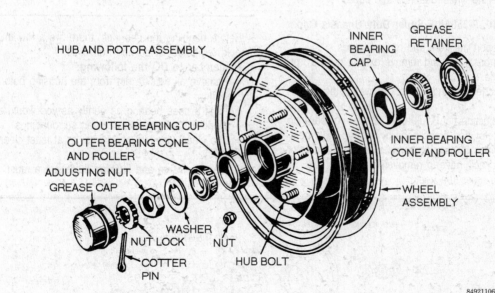

Fig. 96 Front hub, bearing, and grease seal with disc brakes — 2-wheel drive

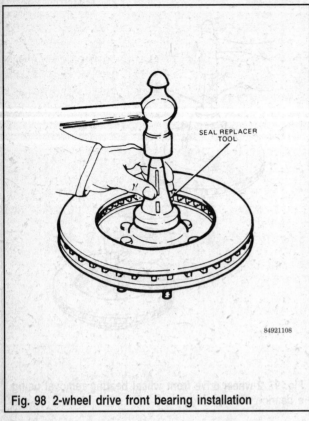

Fig. 98 2-wheel drive front bearing installation

8. Install the new cotter pin, bending the ends of the cotter pin around the castellated flange of the nut lock. If possible, check the bearing end-play. Proper end-play should be 0.001-0.010 in. (O.025-0.254mm).

9. Check the wheel for proper rotation, then install the grease cap. If the wheel still does not rotate properly, inspect and clean or replace the wheel bearings and cups.

1990-93 F-150, F-250, F-350All F-Super Duty Chassis Cab

1. Raise and support the front end on jackstands.
2. Remove the grease cap and remove excess grease from the end of the spindle.
3. Remove the cotter pin and nut lock shown in the illustration.
4. Loosen the adjusting nut 3 full turns. Obtain a clearance between the brake rotor and brake pads by rocking the wheel in and out several times to push the pads away from the rotor. If that doesn't work, you'll have to remove the caliper (see Section 9). The rotor must turn freely.

5. Tighten the adjusting nut to 17-25 ft. lbs. while rotating the rotor in opposite directions.
6. Back off the adjusting nut 120-180° (⅓-½ turn).
7. Install the retainer and cotter pin without additional movement of the locknut.
8. If a dial indicator is available, check the end-play at the hub. End-play should be 0.00024-0.0050 in. (0.006-0.127mm).
9. Install the grease cap.
10. If removed, install the caliper.

F-Super Duty Stripped Chassis Motor Home Chassis

1. Raise and support the front end on jackstands.
2. Remove the grease cap and remove excess grease from the end of the spindle.
3. Remove the cotter pin and nut lock shown in the illustration.
4. Loosen the adjusting nut 3 full turns. Obtain a clearance between the brake rotor and brake pads by rocking the wheel in and out several times to push the pads away from the rotor. If that doesn't work, you'll have to remove the caliper (see Section 9). The rotor must turn freely.
5. Tighten the adjusting nut to 17-25 ft. lbs. while rotating the rotor in the opposite direction.
6. Back off the adjusting nut 120-180° (⅓-½ turn).
7. Tighten the adjusting nut to 18-20 inch lbs. while rotating the rotor.
8. If a dial indicator is available, check the end-play at the hub. End-play should be 0.00024-0.0050 in. (0.006-0.127mm). The torque required to turn the hub should be 10-25 inch lbs.
9. Install the locknut, cotter pin and grease cap.
10. If removed, install the caliper.
11. Install the wheel. Torque the lug nuts to 140 ft. lbs. After 500 miles, retorque the lug nuts.

REMOVAL, REPACKING, AND INSTALLATION

Before handling the bearings, there are a few things that you should remember to do and not to do.

Remember to DO the following:
• Remove all outside dirt from the housing before exposing the bearing.
• Treat a used bearing as gently as you would a new one.
• Work with clean tools in clean surroundings.
• Use clean, dry canvas gloves, or at least clean, dry hands.
• Clean solvents and flushing fluids are a must.

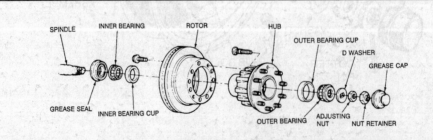

Fig. 99 Front hub, rotor, bearings and related parts for the F-Super Duty

- Use clean paper when laying out the bearings to dry.
- Protect disassembled bearings from rust and dirt. Cover them up.
- Use clean rags to wipe bearings.
- Keep the bearings in oil-proof paper when they are to be stored or are not in use.
- Clean the inside of the housing before replacing the bearing.

Do NOT do the following:

- Don't work in dirty surroundings.
- Don't use dirty, chipped or damaged tools.
- Try not to work on wooden work benches or use wooden mallets.
- Don't handle bearings with dirty or moist hands.
- Do not use gasoline for cleaning; use a safe solvent.
- Do not spin-dry bearings with compressed air. They will be damaged.
- Do not spin dirty bearings.
- Avoid using cotton waste or dirty cloths to wipe bearings.
- Try not to scratch or nick bearing surfaces.
- Do not allow the bearing to come in contact with dirt or rust at any time.

1. Raise and support the front end on jackstands.
2. Remove the wheel cover. Remove the wheel.
3. Remove the caliper from the disc and wire it to the underbody to prevent damage to the brake hose. See Section 9
4. Remove the grease cap from the hub. Then, remove the cotter pin, nut lock, adjusting nut and flat washer from the spindle. Remove the outer bearing assembly from the hub.
5. Pull the hub and disc assembly off the wheel spindle.
6. Remove and discard the old grease retainer. Remove the inner bearing cone and roller assembly from the hub.
7. Clean all grease from the inner and outer bearing cups with solvent. Inspect the cups for pits, scratches, or excessive wear. If the cups are damaged, remove them with a drift.
8. Clean the inner and outer cone and roller assemblies with solvent and shake them dry. If the cone and roller assemblies show excessive wear or damage, replace them with the bearing cups as a unit.
9. Clean the spindle and the inside of the hub with solvent to thoroughly remove all old grease.
10. Covering the spindle with a clean cloth, brush all loose dirt and dust from the brake assembly. Remove the cloth carefully so as to not get dirt on the spindle.
11. If the inner and/or outer bearing cups were removed, install the replacement cups on the hub. Be sure that the cups seat properly in the hub.
12. It is imperative that all old grease be removed from the bearings and surrounding surfaces before repacking. The new lithium-based grease is not compatible with the sodium base grease used in the past.
13. Install the hub and disc on the wheel spindle. To prevent damage to the grease retainer and spindle threads, keep the hub centered on the spindle.
14. Install the outer bearing cone and roller assembly and the flat washer on the spindle. Install the adjusting nut.
15. Adjust the wheel bearings by torquing the adjusting nut to 17-25 ft. lbs. with the wheel rotating to seat the bearing. Then back off the adjusting nut ½ turn. Retighten the adjusting nut to 10-15 inch lbs. Install the locknut so that the castellations are aligned with the cotter pin hole. Install the cotter pin.

Bend the ends of the cotter pin around the castellations of the locknut to prevent interference with the radio static collector in the grease cap. Install the grease cap.

✳✳WARNING

New bolts must be used when servicing floating caliper units. The upper bolt must be tightened first. For caliper service see Section 9.

16. Install the wheels.
17. Install the wheel cover.

Manual Locking Hubs

REMOVAL & INSTALLATION

▶ **See Figures 100 and 101**

1. To remove hub, first separate cap assembly from body assembly by removing the six (6) socket head capscrews from the cap assembly and slip them apart.
2. Remove snapring (retainer ring) from the end of the axle shaft.
3. Remove the lock ring seated in the groove of the wheel hub. The body assembly will now slide out of the wheel hub. If necessary, use an appropriate puller to remove the body assembly.
4. Install hub in reverse order of removal. Torque socket head capscrews to 30-50 inch lbs.

Automatic Locking Hubs

▶ **See Figures 102, 103, 104, 105, 106, 107, 108, 109, 110, 111 and 112**

REMOVAL

1. Remove the 5 capscrews — Torx® bit TX25 — and remove hub cap assembly from the hub.

➡**Take care to avoid dropping the spring, ball bearing, bearing race or retainer!**

2. Remove the rubber seal.
3. Remove the seal bridge — a small metal stamping — from the retainer ring space.
4. Remove lock ring seated in the groove of the wheel hub by compressing the ends with a needle nose pliers, while pulling the hub lock from the hub body. If body assembly does not slide out easily, use an appropriate puller.
5. If the hub and spindle are being removed:
   a. Remove the C-washer from the groove in the stub shaft.
   b. Remove the splined spacer from the shaft.
   c. Remove the outer locknut, locking washer and inner bearing locknut.
   d. Pull the hub and bearings from the spindle.
6. See the Wheel Bearing procedures, below, for cleaning and packing the bearings.

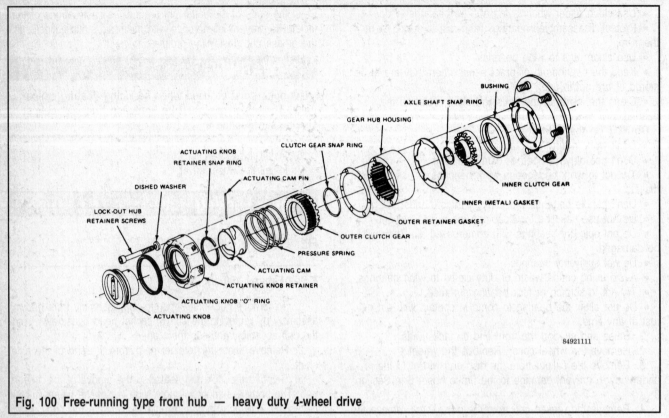

Fig. 100 Free-running type front hub — heavy duty 4-wheel drive

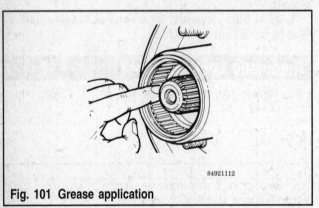

Fig. 101 Grease application

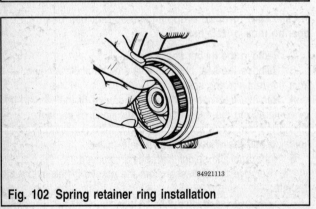

Fig. 102 Spring retainer ring installation

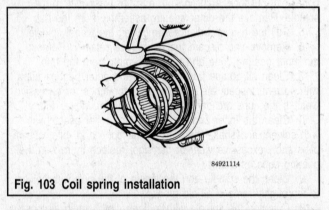

Fig. 103 Coil spring installation

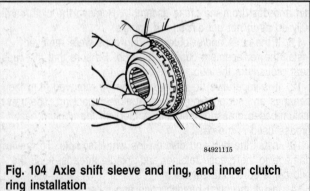

Fig. 104 Axle shift sleeve and ring, and inner clutch ring installation

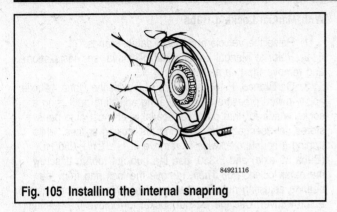

Fig. 105 Installing the internal snapring

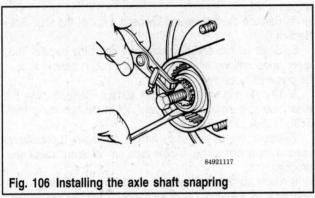

Fig. 106 Installing the axle shaft snapring

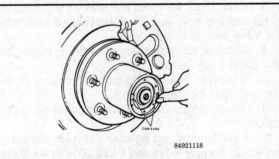

Fig. 107 Applying a small amount of grease on the ears of the cam

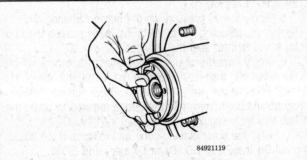

Fig. 108 Installing the cam body ring into the clutch retaining ring

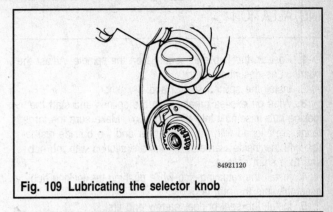

Fig. 109 Lubricating the selector knob

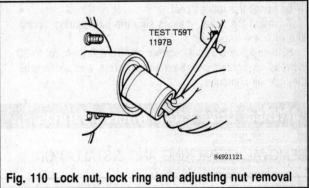

TEST T59T 1197B

Fig. 110 Lock nut, lock ring and adjusting nut removal

DISASSEMBLY

1. Remove the snapring and flat washer from the inner end of the hub lock assembly

2. Pull the hub sleeve and attached parts out of the drag sleeve to unlock the tangs of the brake band. Remove the drag sleeve assembly.

➡Never remove the brake band from the drag sleeve!

ASSEMBLY

1. Wash all parts in a non-flammable solvent and let them air dry.

2. Lubricate the brake band and drag sleeve with 1.5g (0.05 oz.) of Automatic Hublock Grease E1TZ-19590-A (ESL-M1C193A) (Darmex Spec. DX-123-LT), or equivalent. Work the lubricant over and under the spring.

3. Dip the locking hub body (not the cap or brake band/drag sleeve) into Dexron®II ATF and allow it to drip off the excess.

4. Assemble the brake band so that one tang is on each side of the plastic outer cage, located in the window of the steel inner cage. It will probably be necessary to cock these parts to engage the tangs as the drag sleeve is positioned against the face of the cam follower.

5. Install the washer and snapring.

INSTALLATION

1. Position the hub and bearings on the spindle. Adjust the bearings as described below.

2. Install the splined spacer and C-washer.

3. Wipe off excess grease from the splines and start the locking hub assembly into the hub body. Make sure the large tangs are aligned with the lockwasher and the outside diameter, and the inside diameter splines are aligned with the hub and axle shaft splines.

4. Install the retaining ring while pushing the locking hub assembly into the hub body.

5. Install the seal bridge, narrow end first.

6. Install the rubber seal.

7. Install the cover, making sure the ball bearing, spring and race are in position.

8. Install the 5 Torx® screws and tighten them to 40-50 inch lbs. by tighten one, then skipping one, and so on until they are all tightened.

4-Wheel Drive Front Wheel Bearings

REMOVAL, REPACKING AND INSTALLATION

Before handling the bearings, there are a few things that you should remember to do and not to do. **Remember to DO the following:**

• Remove all outside dirt from the housing before exposing the bearing.

• Treat a used bearing as gently as you would a new one.

• Work with clean tools in clean surroundings.

• Use clean, dry canvas gloves, or at least clean, dry hands.

• Clean solvents and flushing fluids are a must.

• Use clean paper when laying out the bearings to dry.

• Protect disassembled bearings from rust and dirt. Cover them up.

• Use clean rags to wipe bearings.

• Keep the bearings in oil-proof paper when they are to be stored or are not in use.

• Clean the inside of the housing before replacing the bearing. **Do NOT do the following:**

• Don't work in dirty surroundings.

• Don't use dirty, chipped or damaged tools.

• Try not to work on wooden work benches or use wooden mallets.

• Don't handle bearings with dirty or moist hands.

• Do not use gasoline for cleaning; use a safe solvent.

• Do not spin-dry bearings with compressed air. They will be damaged.

• Do not spin dirty bearings.

• Avoid using cotton waste or dirty cloths to wipe bearings.

• Try not to scratch or nick bearing surfaces.

• Do not allow the bearing to come in contact with dirt or rust at any time.

With Manual Locking Hubs

1. Raise the vehicle and install safety stands.

2. Refer to Manual Locking Hub Removal and Installation and remove the hub assemblies.

3. On Bronco, F-150 and F-250 LD with the Dana 44 axle: apply inward pressure on the bearing adjusting nut, using a socket made for that purpose, available at most auto parts stores, to disengage the adjusting nut locking splines, while turning it counterclockwise to remove it.   On F-250 HD (Dana 50 axle) and F-350, use the hub nut tool to unscrew the outer locking nut. Then, remove the lock ring from the bearing adjusting nut. This can be done with your finger tips or a screwdriver. Use the locknut socket to remove the bearing adjusting nut.

4. Remove the caliper and suspend it out of the way. See Section 9.

5. Slide the hub and disc assembly off of the spindle. The outer wheel bearing will slide out as the hub is removed, so be prepared to catch it.

6. Lay the hub on a clean work surface. Carefully drive the inner bearing cone and grease seal out of the hub using Tool T69L-1102-A, or equivalent.

7. Inspect the bearing cups for pits or cracks. If necessary, remove them with a drift. If new cups are installed, install new bearings.

8. Lubricate the bearings with Multi-Purpose Lubricant Ford Specification, ESA-MIC7-B or equivalent. Clean all old grease from the hub. Pack the cones and rollers. If a bearing packer is not available, work as much lubricant as possible between the rollers and the cages.

9. Drive new cups into place with a driver, making sure that they are fully seated.

10. Position the inner bearing cone and roller in the inner cup and install the grease retainer.

11. Carefully position the hub and disc assembly on the spindle.

12. Install the outer bearing cone and roller, and the adjusting nut. **On Bronco, F-150 and F-250 LD with the Dana 44 axle:**

a. Make sure the metal stamping on the adjusting nut faces inboard and the inner diameter key on the nut enters the spindle keyway.

b. Apply inward pressure on the hub nut wrench and tighten the adjusting nut to 70 ft. lbs. while rotating the hub back and forth to seat the bearings.

c. Apply inward pressure on the wrench and back off the nut about 90° then, re-tighten the nut to 15-20 ft. lbs.

d. Remove the wrench. End-play of the hub/rotor assembly should be 0 (zero) and the torque required to rotate the hub assembly should not exceed 20 inch lbs.

13. Install the outer bearing cone and roller, and the adjusting nut. **On the F-250 HD (Dana 50 axle) and F-350:**

➤**The adjusting nut has a small dowel on one side. This dowel faces outward to engage the locking ring.**

a. Using the hub nut socket and a torque wrench, tighten the bearing adjusting nut to 50 ft. lbs., while rotating the wheel back and forth to seat the bearings.

b. Back off the adjusting nut approximately 90°.

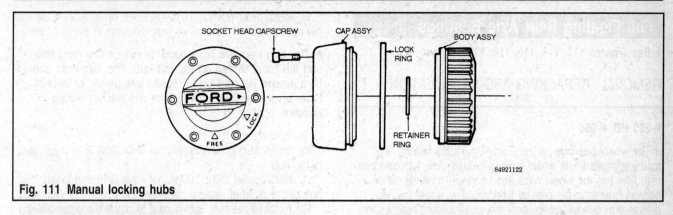

Fig. 111 Manual locking hubs

c. Install the lock ring by turning the nut to the nearest hole and inserting the dowel pin.

✱✱WARNING

The dowel pin must seat in a lock ring hole for proper bearing adjustment and wheel retention!

d. Install the outer lock nut and tighten to 160-205 ft. lbs. Final end-play of the wheel on the spindle should be 0-0.004 in. (0-0.15mm).
14. Assemble the hub parts.
15. Install the caliper.
16. Remove the safety stands and lower the vehicle.

With Automatic Locking Hubs

1. Raise the vehicle and install safety stands.
2. Refer to Automatic Locking Hub Removal and Installation and remove the hub assemblies.
3. Using a socket made for that purpose, available at most auto parts stores, use the hub nut tool to unscrew the outer locking nut.
4. Remove the lock ring from the bearing adjusting nut. This can be done with your finger tips or a screwdriver.
5. Use the locknut socket to remove the bearing adjusting nut.
6. Remove the caliper and suspend it out of the way. See Section 9.
7. Slide the hub and disc assembly off of the spindle. The outer wheel bearing will slide out as the hub is removed, so be prepared to catch it.
8. Lay the hub on a clean work surface. Carefully drive the inner bearing cone and grease seal out of the hub using Tool T69L-1102-A, or equivalent.

9. Inspect the bearing cups for pits or cracks. If necessary, remove them with a drift. If new cups are installed, install new bearings.
10. Lubricate the bearings with Multi-Purpose Lubricant Ford Specification, ESA-MIC7-B or equivalent. Clean all old grease from the hub. Pack the cones and rollers. If a bearing packer is not available, work as much lubricant as possible between the rollers and the cages.
11. Drive new cups into place with a driver, making sure that they are fully seated.
12. Position the inner bearing cone and roller in the inner cup and install the grease retainer.
13. Carefully position the hub and disc assembly on the spindle.
14. Install the outer bearing cone and roller, and the adjusting nut.

➡**The adjusting nut has a small dowel on one side. This dowel faces outward to engage the locking ring.**

15. Using the hub nut socket and a torque wrench, tighten the bearing adjusting nut to 50 ft. lbs., while rotating the wheel back and forth to seat the bearings.
16. Back off the adjusting nut approximately 90°.
17. Install the lock ring by turning the nut to the nearest hole and inserting the dowel pin.

➡**The dowel pin must seat in a lock ring hole for proper bearing adjustment and wheel retention.**

18. Install the outer lock nut and tighten to 160-205 ft. lbs. Final end-play of the wheel on the spindle should be 0-0.004 in. (0-0.15mm).
19. Assemble the hub parts.
20. Install the caliper.
21. Remove the safety stands and lower the vehicle.

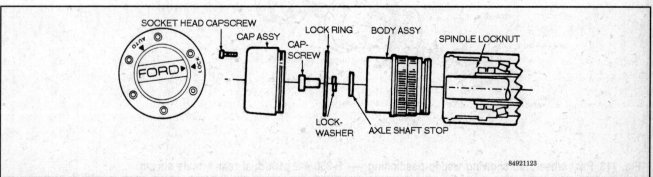

Fig. 112 Automatic locking hubs

Full Floating Rear Axle Bearings

▶ See Figures 113, 114, 115, 116, 117, 118 and 119

REMOVAL, REPACKING AND INSTALLATION

F-250 HD, F-350

The wheel bearings on the Ford 10½ in. full floating rear axle are packed with wheel bearing grease. Axle lubricant can also flow into the wheel hubs and bearings, however, wheel bearing grease is the primary lubricant. The wheel bearing grease provides lubrication until the axle lubricant reaches the bearings during normal operation.

The wheel bearings on the full floating rear axle are packed with wheel bearing grease. Axle lubricant can also flow into the wheel hubs and bearings, however, wheel bearing grease is the primary lubricant. The wheel bearing grease provides lubrication until the axle lubricant reaches the bearings during normal operation.

1. Set the parking brake and loosen the axle shaft bolts.
2. Raise the rear wheels off the floor and place jackstands under the rear axle housing so that the axle is parallel with the floor.
3. Remove the wheels.
4. Remove the brake drums.
5. Remove the axle shaft bolts.
6. Remove the axle shaft and discard the gaskets.
7. With the axle shaft removed, remove the gasket from the axle shaft flange studs.

8. Install Hub Wrench T85T-4252-AH, or equivalent, so that the drive tangs on the tool engage the slots in the hub nut.

➡ The hub nuts are right hand thread on the right hub and left hand thread on the left hub. The hub nuts should be stamped RH and LH. Never use power or impact tools on these nuts! The nuts will ratchet during removal.

9. Remove the hub nut.
10. Install step plate adapter tool D80L-630-7, or equivalent, in the hub.
11. Install puller D80L-1002-L, or equivalent and loosen the hub to the point of removal. Remove the puller and step plate.
12. Remove the hub, taking care to catch the outer bearing as the hub comes off.
13. Install the hub in a soft-jawed vise and pry out the hub seal.
14. Lift out the inner bearing.
15. Drive out the inner and outer bearing races with a drift.
16. Wash all the old grease or axle lubricant out of the wheel hub, using a suitable solvent.
17. Wash the bearing races and rollers and inspect them for pitting, galling, and uneven wear patterns. Inspect the roller for end wear. Replace any bearing and race that appears in any way damaged. Always replace the bearings and races as a set.
18. Coat the race bores with a light coat of clean, water-proof wheel bearing grease and drive the races squarely into the bores until they are fully seated. A good indication that the race is seated is when you notice the grease from the bore squashing out under the race when it contact the shoulder. Another indication is a definite change in the metallic tone

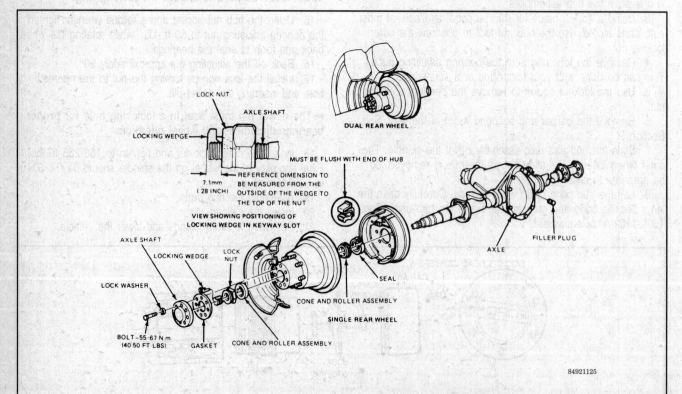

Fig. 113 Rear wheel hub showing wedge positioning — F-350 4·2 with dual rear wheels shown

when you seat the race. Just be very careful to avoid damaging the bearing surface of the race!

19. Pack each bearing cone and roller with a bearing packer or in the manner outlined in Section 1 for the front wheel bearings on 2-Wheel Drive trucks.

20. Place the inner bearing cone and roller assembly in the wheel hub.

➤ **When installing the new seal, the words OIL SIDE must go inwards towards the bearing!**

21. Place the seal squarely in the hub and drive it into place. The best tool for the job is a seal driver such as T85T-1175-AH, which will stop when the seal is at the proper depth.

➤ **If the seal is misaligned or damaged during installation, a new seal must be installed.**

22. Clean the spindle thoroughly. If the spindle is excessively pitted, damaged or has a predominately bluish tint (from overheating), it must be replaced.

23. Coat the spindle with 80W/90 oil.

24. Pack the hub with clean, waterproof wheel bearing grease.

25. Pack the outer bearing with clean, waterproof wheel bearing grease in the same manner as you packed the inner bearing.

26. Place the outer bearing in the hub and install the hub and bearing together on the spindle.

27. Install the hub nut on the spindle. Make sure that the nut tab is located in the keyway prior to thread engagement. Turn the hub nut onto the threads as far as you can by hand, noting the thread direction.

28. Install the hub wrench tool and tighten the nut to 55-65 ft. lbs. Rotate the hub occasionally during nut tightening.

29. Ratchet the nut back 5 teeth. **Make sure that you hear 5 clicks!**

30. Inspect the axle shaft O-ring seal and replace it if it looks at all bad.

31. Install the axle shaft.

32. Coat the axle shaft bolt threads with waterproof seal and install them by hand until they seat. **Do not tighten them with a wrench at this time!**

33. Check the diameter across the center of the brake shoes. Check the diameter of the brake drum. Adjust the brake shoes so that their diameter is 0.030 in. (0.76mm) less than the drum diameter.

34. Install the brake drum.

35. Install the wheel.

36. Loosen the differential filler plug. If lubricant starts to run out, retighten the plug. If not, remove the plug and fill the housing with 80W/90 gear oil.

37. Lower the truck to the floor.

38. Tighten the wheel lugs to 140 ft. lbs.

39. Now tighten the axle shaft bolts. Torque them to 60-80 ft. lbs.

1988-89 F-Super Duty, Stripped Chassis and Motor Home Chassis

The wheel bearings on the Dana 80 full floating rear axles are packed with wheel bearing grease. Axle lubricant can also flow into the wheel hubs and bearings, however, wheel bearing grease is the primary lubricant. The wheel bearing grease provides lubrication until the axle lubricant reaches the bearings during normal operation.

1. Set the parking brake and loosen — do not remove — the axle shaft bolts.

2. Raise the rear wheels off the floor and place jackstands under the rear axle housing so that the axle is parallel with the floor. Release the parking brake.

3. Remove the axle shaft bolts and lockwashers. They should not be re-used.

4. Place a heavy duty wheel dolly under the wheels and raise them so that all weight is off the wheel bearings.

5. Remove the axle shaft and gasket(s).

6. Remove the caliper. See Section 9.

7. Using a special hub nut wrench, remove the hub nut.

➤ **The hub nut on the right spindle is right hand thread; the one on the left spindle is left hand thread. They are marked RH and LH. NEVER use an impact wrench on the hub nut!**

8. Remove the outer bearing cone and pull the wheel straight off the axle.

9. With a piece of hardwood or a brass drift which will just clear the outer bearing cup, drive the inner bearing cone and inner seal out of the wheel hub.

10. Wash all the old grease or axle lubricant out of the wheel hub, using a suitable solvent.

11. Wash the bearing cups and rollers and inspect them for pitting, galling, and uneven wear patterns. Inspect the roller for end wear.

12. If the bearing cups are to be replaced, drive them out with a brass drift. Install the new cups with a block of wood and hammer or press them in.

13. If the bearing cups are properly seated, a 0.0015 in. (0.038mm) feeler gauge will not fit between the cup and the wheel hub. The gauge should not fit beneath the cup. Check several places to make sure the cups are squarely seated.

14. Pack each bearing cone and roller with a bearing packer or in the manner previously outlined for the front wheel bearings on 2WD trucks. Use a multi-purpose wheel bearing grease.

15. Place the inner bearing cone and roller assembly in the wheel hub. Install a new inner seal in the hub with a seal installation tool.

16. Wrap the threads of the spindle with tape and carefully slide the hub straight on the spindle. Take care to avoid damaging the seal! Remove the tape.

17. Install the outer bearing. Start the hub nut, making sure that the hub tab is engaged with the keyway prior to threading.

18. Tighten the nut to 65-75 ft.lbs. while rotating the wheel.

➤ **The hub will ratchet at torque is applied. This ratcheting can be avoided by using Ford tool No. T88T-4252-A. Avoiding ratcheting will give more even bearing preloads.**

19. Back off (loosen) the adjusting nut 90° (¼ turn). Then, tighten it to 15-20 ft. lbs.

20. Using a dial indicator, check end-play of the hub. No end-play is permitted.

21. Clean the hub bolt holes thoroughly. Replace the hub if any cracks are found around the holes or if the threads in the holes are in any way damaged.

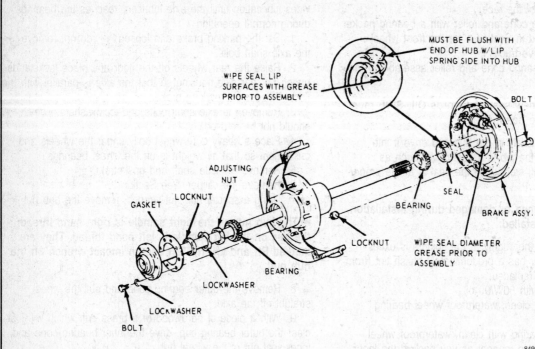

Fig. 114 Single rear hub assembly with full-floating axles, F-250 only

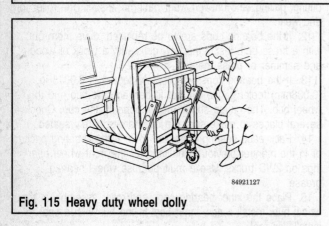

Fig. 115 Heavy duty wheel dolly

22. Install the axle shaft, new flange gasket, lock washers and **new** shaft retaining bolts. Coat the bolt threads with thread adhesive. Tighten them snugly, but not completely.

23. Install the caliper.

24. Install the wheels.

25. Lower the truck to the ground.

26. Tighten the wheel lug nuts.

27. Tighten the axle shaft bolts to 70-85 ft. lbs.

1990-93 F-Super Duty, Stripped Chassis and Motor Home Chassis

The wheel bearings on full floating rear axles are packed with wheel bearing grease. Axle lubricant can also flow into the wheel hubs and bearings, however, wheel bearing grease is the primary lubricant. The wheel bearing grease provides lubrication until the axle lubricant reaches the bearings during normal operation.

1. Set the parking brake and loosen — do not remove — the axle shaft bolts.

2. Raise the rear wheels off the floor and place jackstands under the rear axle housing so that the axle is parallel with the floor. The axle shafts must turn freely, so release the parking brake.

3. Remove the axle shaft bolts and lockwashers. They should not be re-used.

4. Place a heavy duty wheel dolly under the wheels and raise them so that all weight is off the wheel bearings.

5. Remove the axle shaft and gasket(s).

6. Remove the brake caliper. See Section 9.

7. Using a special hub nut wrench, remove the hub nut.

➡The hub nuts for both sides are right hand thread and marked RH.

8. Remove the outer bearing cone and pull the wheel straight off the axle.

9. With a piece of hardwood or a brass drift which will just clear the outer bearing cup, drive the inner bearing cone and inner seal out of the wheel hub.

10. Wash all the old grease or axle lubricant out of the wheel hub, using a suitable solvent.

11. Wash the bearing cups and rollers and inspect them for pitting, galling, and uneven wear patterns. Inspect the roller for end wear.

12. If the bearing cups are to be replaced, drive them out with a brass drift. Install the new cups with a block of wood and hammer or press them in.

13. If the bearing cups are properly seated, a 0.0015 in. (0.038mm) feeler gauge will not fit between the cup and the wheel hub. The gauge should not fit beneath the cup. Check several places to make sure the cups are squarely seated.

14. Pack each bearing cone and roller with a bearing packer or in the manner previously outlined for the front wheel bearings on 2WD trucks. Use a multi-purpose wheel bearing grease.

15. Place the inner bearing cone and roller assembly in the wheel hub. Install a new inner seal in the hub with a seal installation tool.

16. Wrap the threads of the spindle with tape and carefully slide the hub straight on the spindle. Take care to avoid damaging the seal! Remove the tape.

17. Install the outer bearing. Start the hub nut, making sure that the hub tab is engaged with the keyway prior to threading.

18. Tighten the nut to 65-75 ft.lbs. while rotating the wheel.

➡**The hub will ratchet at torque is applied. This ratcheting can be avoided by using Ford tool No. T88T-4252-A. Avoiding ratcheting will give more even bearing preloads.**

19. Back off (loosen) the adjusting nut 90° (¼ turn). Then, tighten it to 15-20 ft. lbs.

20. Using a dial indicator, check end-play of the hub. No end-play is permitted.

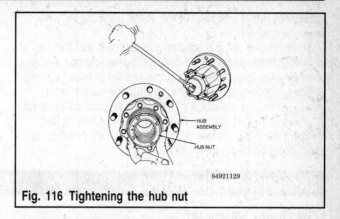

Fig. 116 Tightening the hub nut

21. Clean the hub bolt holes thoroughly. Replace the hub if any cracks are found around the holes or if the threads in the holes are in any way damaged.

22. Install the axle shaft, new flange gasket, lock washers and **new** shaft retaining bolts. Coat the bolt threads with thread adhesive. Tighten them snugly, but not completely.

23. Install the caliper.

24. Install the wheels.

25. Lower the truck to the ground.

26. Tighten the wheel lug nuts.

27. Tighten the axle shaft bolts to 40-55 ft. lbs.

PUSHING AND TOWING

To push-start your vehicle, (manual transmission only), check to make sure that bumpers of both vehicles are aligned so neither will be damaged. Be sure that all electrical system components are turned off (headlight, heater, blower, etc.).

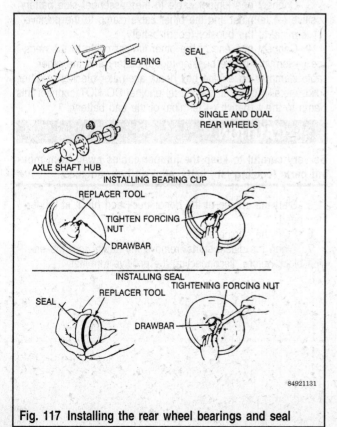

Fig. 117 Installing the rear wheel bearings and seal

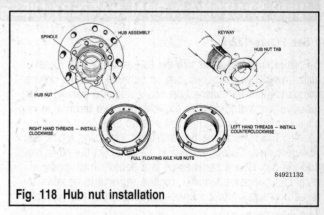

Fig. 118 Hub nut installation

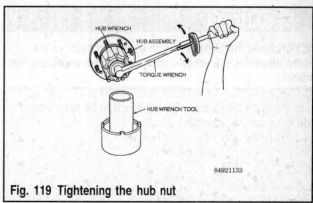

Fig. 119 Tightening the hub nut

Turn on the ignition switch. Place the shift lever in Third or Fourth and push in the clutch pedal. At about 15 mph, signal the driver of the pushing vehicle to fall back, depress the accelerator pedal, and release the clutch pedal slowly. The engine should start.

When you are doing the pushing, make sure that the two bumpers match so you won't damage the vehicle you are to push. Another good idea is to put an old tire between the two vehicles. Try to keep your truck right up against the other vehicle while you are pushing. If the two vehicles do separate, stop and start over again instead of trying to catch up and ramming the other vehicle. Also try, as much as possible, to avoid riding or slipping the clutch.

If your truck has to be towed by a tow truck, it can be towed forward for any distance with the driveshaft connected as long as it is done fairly slowly. Otherwise disconnect the driveshaft at the rear axle and tie it up. On and F-250, the rear axle shafts can be removed and the hub covered to prevent lubricant loss. If your 4-wheel drive truck has to be towed backward, remove the front axle driving hubs, or disengage the lock-out hubs to prevent the front differential from rotating. If the drive hubs are removed, improvise a cover to keep out dust and dirt.

JACKING AND HOISTING

▶ **See Figures 120 and 121**

It is very important to be careful about running the engine on vehicles equipped with limited slip differentials, while the vehicle is up on the jack. This is because when the drive train is engaged, power is transmitted to the wheel with the best traction and the vehicle will drive off the jack if one drive wheel is in contact with the floor, resulting in possible damage or injury.

Jack a Ford truck from under the axles, radius arms, or spring hangers and the frame. Be sure and block the diagonally opposite wheel. Place jackstands under the vehicle at the points mentioned or directly under the frame when you are going to work under the vehicle.

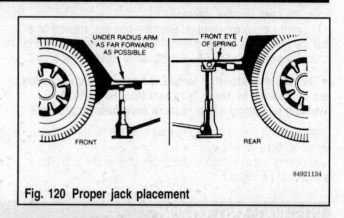

Fig. 120 Proper jack placement

JUMP STARTING A DUAL-BATTERY DIESEL

▶ **See Figure 122**

Ford pickups equipped with the 6.9L and 7.3L V8 diesel utilize two 12 volt batteries, one on either side of the engine compartment. The batteries are connected in a parallel circuit (positive terminal to positive terminal, negative terminal to negative terminal). Hooking the batteries up in parallel circuit increases battery cranking power without increasing total battery voltage output. Output remains at 12 volts. On the other hand, hooking two 12 volt batteries up in a series circuit (positive terminal to negative terminal, positive terminal to negative terminal) increases total battery output to 24 volts (12 volts plus 12 volts).

✳✳CAUTION

NEVER hook the batteries up in a series circuit or the entire electrical system will go up in smoke, especially the starter.

In the event that a diesel pickup needs to be jump started, use the following procedure.
1. Turn all lights off.

2. Turn on the heater blower motor to remove transient voltage.

3. Connect one jumper cable to the passenger side battery positive (+) terminal and the other cable clamp to the positive (+) terminal to the booster (good) battery.

4. Connect one end of the other jumper cable to the negative (-) terminal of the booster (good) battery and the other cable clamp to an engine bolt head, alternator bracket or other solid, metallic point on the diesel engine. DO NOT connect this clamp to the negative (-) terminal of the bad battery.

✳✳CAUTION

Be very careful to keep the jumper cables away from moving parts (cooling fan, belts, etc.) on both engines.

5. Start the engine of the donor truck and run it at moderate speed.
6. Start the engine of the diesel.
7. When the diesel starts, remove the cable from the engine block before disconnecting the positive terminal.

TRAILER TOWING

Factory trailer towing packages are available on most trucks. However, if you are installing a trailer hitch and wiring on your truck, there are a few thing that you ought to know.

Trailer Weight

Trailer weight is the first, and most important, factor in determining whether or not your vehicle is suitable for towing the trailer you have in mind. The horsepower-to-weight ratio should be calculated. The basic standard is a ratio of 35:1. That is, 35 pounds of GVW for every horsepower.

To calculate this ratio, multiply you engine's rated horsepower by 35, then subtract the weight of the vehicle, including passengers and luggage. The resulting figure is the ideal maximum trailer weight that you can tow. One point to consider: a numerically higher axle ratio can offset what appears to be a low trailer weight. If the weight of the trailer that you have in mind is somewhat higher than the weight you just calculated, you might consider changing your rear axle ratio to compensate.

Hitch Weight

There are three kinds of hitches: bumper mounted, frame mounted, and load equalizing.

Bumper mounted hitches are those which attach solely to the vehicle's bumper. Many states prohibit towing with this type of hitch, when it attaches to the vehicle's stock bumper, since it subjects the bumper to stresses for which it was not designed. Aftermarket rear step bumpers, designed for trailer towing, are acceptable for use with bumper mounted hitches.

Frame mounted hitches can be of the type which bolts to two or more points on the frame, plus the bumper, or just to several points on the frame. Frame mounted hitches can also be of the tongue type, for Class I towing, or, of the receiver type, for Classes II and III.

Load equalizing hitches are usually used for large trailers. Most equalizing hitches are welded in place and use equalizing bars and chains to level the vehicle after the trailer is hooked up.

The bolt-on hitches are the most common, since they are relatively easy to install.

Check the gross weight rating of your trailer. Tongue weight is usually figured as 10% of gross trailer weight. Therefore, a trailer with a maximum gross weight of 2,000 lb. will have a

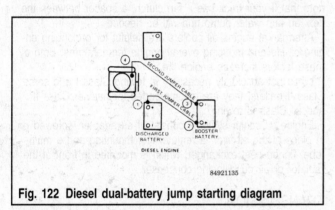

84921135

Fig. 122 Diesel dual-battery jump starting diagram

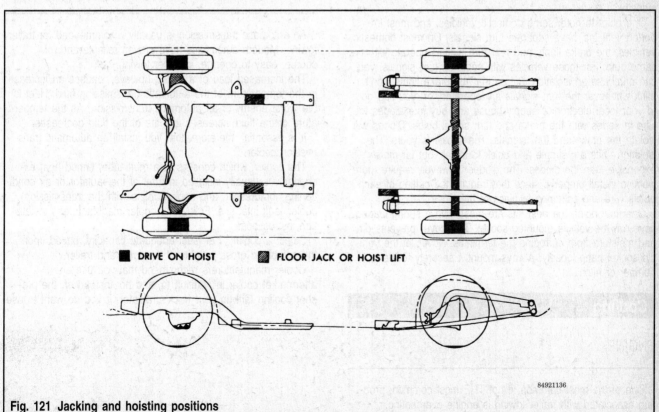

■ DRIVE ON HOIST   ▨ FLOOR JACK OR HOIST LIFT

84921136

Fig. 121 Jacking and hoisting positions

maximum tongue weight of 200 lb. Class I trailers fall into this category. Class II trailers are those with a gross weight rating of 2,000-3,500 lb., while Class III trailers fall into the 3,500-6,000 lb. category. Class IV trailers are those over 6,000 lb. and are for use with fifth wheel trucks, only.

When you've determined the hitch that you'll need, follow the manufacturer's installation instructions, exactly, especially when it comes to fastener torques. The hitch will subjected to a lot of stress and good hitches come with hardened bolts. Never substitute an inferior bolt for a hardened bolt.

Wiring

Wiring the truck for towing is fairly easy. There are a number of good wiring kits available and these should be used, rather than trying to design your own. All trailers will need brake lights and turn signals as well as tail lights and side marker lights. Most states require extra marker lights for overly wide trailers. Also, most states have recently required backup lights for trailers, and most trailer manufacturers have been building trailers with backup lights for several years.

Additionally, some Class I, most Class II and just about all Class III trailers will have electric brakes.

Add to this number an accessories wire, to operate trailer internal equipment or to charge the trailer's battery, and you can have as many as seven wires in the harness.

Determine the equipment on your trailer and buy the wiring kit necessary. The kit will contain all the wires needed, plus a plug adapter set which included the female plug, mounted on the bumper or hitch, and the male plug, wired into, or plugged into the trailer harness.

When installing the kit, follow the manufacturer's instructions. The color coding of the wires is standard throughout the industry.

One point to note, some domestic vehicles, and most imported vehicles, have separate turn signals. On most domestic vehicles, the brake lights and rear turn signals operate with the same bulb. For those vehicles with separate turn signals, you can purchase an isolation unit so that the brake lights won't blink whenever the turn signals are operated, or, you can go to your local electronics supply house and buy four diodes to wire in series with the brake and turn signal bulbs. Diodes will isolate the brake and turn signals. The choice is yours. The isolation units are simple and quick to install, but far more expensive than the diodes. The diodes, however, require more work to install properly, since they require the cutting of each bulb's wire and soldering in place of the diode.

One final point, the best kits are those with a spring loaded cover on the vehicle mounted socket. This cover prevents dirt and moisture from corroding the terminals. Never let the vehicle socket hang loosely. Always mount it securely to the bumper or hitch.

Cooling

ENGINE

One of the most common, if not THE most common, problem associated with trailer towing is engine overheating.

With factory installed trailer towing packages, a heavy duty cooling system is usually included. Heavy duty cooling systems are available as optional equipment on most trucks, with or without a trailer package. If you have one of these extra-capacity systems, you shouldn't have any overheating problems.

If you have a standard cooling system, without an expansion tank, you'll definitely need to get an aftermarket expansion tank kit, preferably one with at least a 2 quart capacity. These kits are easily installed on the radiator's overflow hose, and come with a pressure cap designed for expansion tanks.

Another helpful accessory is a Flex Fan. These fan are large diameter units are designed to provide more airflow at low speeds, with blades that have deeply cupped surfaces. The blades then flex, or flatten out, at high speed, when less cooling air is needed. These fans are far lighter in weight than stock fans, requiring less horsepower to drive them. Also, they are far quieter than stock fans.

If you do decide to replace your stock fan with a flex fan, note that if your truck has a fan clutch, a spacer between the flex fan and water pump hub will be needed.

Aftermarket engine oil coolers are helpful for prolonging engine oil life and reducing overall engine temperatures. Both of these factors increase engine life.

While not absolutely necessary in towing Class I and some Class II trailers, they are recommended for heavier Class II and all Class III towing.

Engine oil cooler systems consist of an adapter, screwed on in place of the oil filter, a remote filter mounting and a multi-tube, finned heat exchanger, which is mounted in front of the radiator or air conditioning condenser.

TRANSMISSION

An automatic transmission is usually recommended for trailer towing. Modern automatics have proven reliable and, of course, easy to operate, in trailer towing.

The increased load of a trailer, however, causes an increase in the temperature of the automatic transmission fluid. Heat is the worst enemy of an automatic transmission. As the temperature of the fluid increases, the life of the fluid decreases.

It is essential, therefore, that you install an automatic transmission cooler.

The cooler, which consists of a multi-tube, finned heat exchanger, is usually installed in front of the radiator or air conditioning compressor, and hooked inline with the transmission cooler tank inlet line. Follow the cooler manufacturer's installation instructions.

Select a cooler of at least adequate capacity, based upon the combined gross weights of the truck and trailer.

Cooler manufacturers recommend that you use an aftermarket cooler in addition to, and not instead of, the present cooling tank in your truck's radiator. If you do want to use it in place of the radiator cooling tank, get a cooler at least two sizes larger than normally necessary.

➡A transmission cooler can, sometimes, cause slow or harsh shifting in the transmission during cold weather, until the fluid has a chance to come up to normal operat-ing temperature. Some coolers can be purchased with or retrofitted with a temperature bypass valve which will allow fluid flow through the cooler only when the fluid has reached operating temperature, or above.

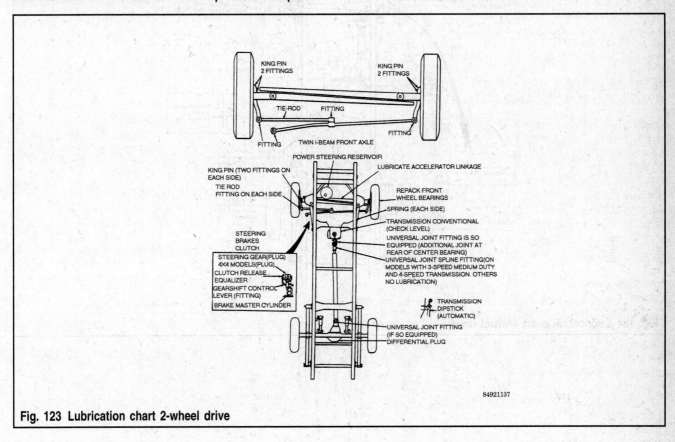

Fig. 123 Lubrication chart 2-wheel drive

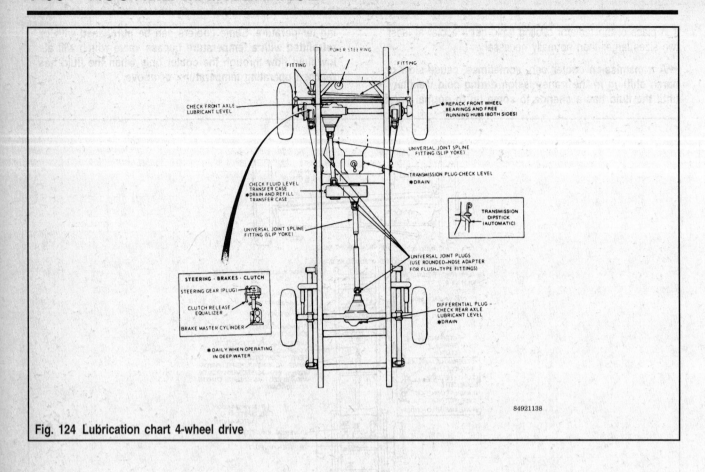

Fig. 124 Lubrication chart 4-wheel drive

PREVENTIVE MAINTENANCE SCHEDULE

Model/Interval	Item	Service
Gasoline Engine Models		
Every 6 months or 6,000 miles	Crankcase	change oil & filter
	Carbureted idle speed and TSP-off speed	adjust
	Chassis fittings	lubricate
	4 x 4 power cylinder	lubricate
	Clutch linkage	inspect and oil
	Exhaust system heat shields	inspect
	Transmission, automatic	check level
Every 15 miles or 15,000 miles	Spark plugs	replace
	Exhaust control valve	check & lubricate
	Drive belts	check and adjust
	Air cleaner temperature control	check
	Choke system	check
	Thermactor system	check
	Crankcase breather cap	clean
	EGR system	clean and inspect
	PCV system	clean and inspect
Every 30 months or 30,000 miles	PCV valve	replace
	Air cleaner element	replace
	Air cleaner crankcase filter	replace
	Fuel vapor system	replace
	Brake master cylinder	check
	Brakes	inspect
	Free-running hubs	clean and repack
	Front wheel bearings	clean and repack
	Rear wheel bearings, Dana axles	clean and repack
Every 6 months or 5,000 miles	Crankcase	change oil and filter
	Idle speed	check and adjust
	Throttle linkage	check operation
	Fuel/water separator	drain water
	U-joints	lubricate
	Front axle spindles	lubricate
Every 6 months or 15,000 miles	Fuel filter	replace
	Drive belts	check/adjust
	Steering linkage	lubricate
Every year	Coolant	check condition/replace
	Cooling hoses, clamps	check condition/replace

84921155

CAPACITIES CHART—PICK-UPS

Year	Engine No. Cyl. Liters	Crankcase Incl. Filter (qt.)	Transmission (pt.) 4-sp	5-sp	Auto.	Transfer Case (pts.)	Drive Axle (pt.)* Front	Rear	Fuel Tank (gal.)	Cooling System (qt.) w/AC	wo/AC
1987	6-4.9	6.0	②	—	③	4.0	④	⑤	⑥	①	①
	8-5.0	6.0	②	—	③	4.0	④	⑤	⑥	18.0	15.0
	8-5.8	6.0	②	—	26.75	4.0	④	⑤	⑥	17.0	17.0
	8-6.9	10.0	②	—	26.75	4.0	④	⑤	⑥	29.0	29.0
	8-7.5	6.0	—	—	26.75	4.0	④	⑤	⑥	18.0	18.0
1988	6-4.9	6.0	3.5	⑦	⑧	4.0	⑩	⑪	⑫	⑬	13.0
	8-5.0	6.0	3.5	7.6	⑨	4.0	⑩	⑪	⑫	⑭	13.0
	8-5.8	6.0	—	6.8	⑨	4.0	⑩	⑪	⑫	⑮	15.0
	8-7.3	10.0	—	6.8	⑨	4.0	⑩	⑪	⑫	31.0	31.0
	8-7.5	6.0	—	6.8	⑨	4.0	⑩	⑪	⑫	18.0	18.0
1989	6-4.9	6.0	3.5	⑦	⑧	4.0	⑩	⑪	⑫	⑬	13.0
	8-5.0	6.0	3.5	7.6	⑨	4.0	⑩	⑪	⑫	⑭	13.0
	8-5.8	6.0	—	6.8	⑨	4.0	⑩	⑪	⑫	⑮	15.0
	8-7.3	10.0	—	6.8	⑨	4.0	⑩	⑪	⑫	31.0	31.0
	8-7.5	6.0	—	6.8	⑨	4.0	⑩	⑪	⑫	18.0	18.0
1990	6-4.9	6.0	3.5	⑦	⑧	4.0	⑩	⑪	⑫	⑬	13.0
	8-5.0	6.0	3.5	7.6	⑨	4.0	⑩	⑪	⑫	⑭	13.0
	8-5.8	6.0	—	6.8	⑨	4.0	⑩	⑪	⑫	⑮	15.0
	8-7.3	10.0	—	6.8	⑨	4.0	⑩	⑪	⑫	31.0	31.0
	8-7.5	6.0	—	6.8	⑨	4.0	⑩	⑪	⑫	18.0	18.0
1991	6-4.9	6.0	3.5	⑦	⑧	4.0	⑩	⑪	⑫	⑬	13.0
	8-5.0	6.0	3.5	7.6	⑨	4.0	⑩	⑪	⑫	⑭	13.0
	8-5.8	6.0	—	6.8	⑨	4.0	⑩	⑪	⑫	⑮	15.0
	8-7.3	10.0	—	6.8	⑨	4.0	⑩	⑪	⑫	34.0	34.0
	8-7.5	6.0	—	6.8	⑨	4.0	⑩	⑪	⑫	18.0	18.0
1992	6-4.9	6.0	3.5	⑦	⑧	4.0	⑩	⑪	⑫	⑬	13.0
	8-5.0	6.0	3.5	7.6	⑨	4.0	⑩	⑪	⑫	⑭	13.0
	8-5.8	6.0	—	6.8	⑨	4.0	⑩	⑪	⑫	⑮	15.0
	8-7.3	10.0	—	6.8	⑨	4.0	⑩	⑪	⑫	34.0	34.0
	8-7.5	6.0	—	6.8	⑨	4.0	⑩	⑪	⑫	18.0	18.0

84921146

CAPACITIES CHART—PICK-UPS

Year	Engine No. Cyl. Liters	Crankcase Incl. Filter (qt.)	Transmission (pt.)			Transfer Case (pts.)	Drive Axle (pt.)*		Fuel Tank (gal.)	Cooling System (qt.)	
			4-sp	5-sp	Auto.		Front	Rear		w/AC	wo/AC
1993	6-4.9	6.0	3.5	⑦	⑧	4.0	⑩	⑪	⑫	⑬	13.0
	8-5.0	6.0	3.5	7.6	⑨	4.0	⑩	⑪	⑫	⑭	13.0
	8-5.8	6.0	—	6.8	⑨	4.0	⑩	⑪	⑫	⑮	15.0
	8-7.3	10.0	—	6.8	⑨	4.0	⑩	⑪	⑫	34.0	34.0
	8-7.5	6.0	—	6.8	⑨	4.0	⑩	⑪	⑫	18.0	18.0

*For limited slip differentials, add the following amounts of Friction Modifier Additive
 Dana front axle: 2 oz.
 Dana rear axle: 8 oz.
 Ford 8.8 in. rear axle: 4 oz.
 Ford 10.25 in. axle: 8 oz.

① Standard cooling with manual transmission: 13.0
 Standard cooling with automatic transmission: 14.0
 With air conditioning: 17.0
 With extra cooling and without air conditioning: 14.0

② Warner T-18 and T-19B; 7.0
 NP-435 with extension housing: 7.0
 NP-435 without extension housing: 6.5
 4-Speed overdrive: 5.0

③ C-6: 23.5
 AOD: 24.0

④ Dana 60-7F: 6.0
 Dana 50-IFS: 4.1
 Dana 44-IFS: 3.8

⑤ Dana 61-1: 6.0
 Dana 61-2: 6.0
 Dana 70: 7.0
 Dana 70HD: 7.4

⑥ F-100 2-wheel drive regular cab: 16.5 standard
 F-100 2-wheel drive regular cab: 19.0 optional behind axle
 F-150 2-wheel drive Crew Cab: 16.5 standard
 F-150 2-wheel drive Crew Cab: 19.0 optional behind axle
 F-150 4x4 regular cab: 16.5 standard
 F-150 4x4 regular cab: 19.0 optional behind axle
 F-250 4x4 regular cab: 16.5 standard
 F-250 4x4 regular cab: 19.0 optional behind axle
 F-150 2-wheel drive regular cab: 16.5 standard
 F-150 2-wheel drive regular cab: 19.0 optional behind axle
 F-250 2-wheel drive regular cab: 16.5 standard
 F-250 2-wheel drive regular cab: 19.0 optional behind axle
 F-150 all 4x4: 19.0 standard
 F-250 all 4x4: 19.0 optional behind axle
 F-350 all models: 19.0 standard
 F-350 all models: 19.0 optional behind axle

⑦ Mazda 5-sp OD: 7.6
 ZF 5-sp Heavy Duty OD: 6.8

⑧ C6 3-sp: 24.5 w/2-wheel drive
  27.5 w/4-wheel drive
 AOD 4-sp: 24.0

⑨ 1988 2-wheel drive: 24.5
  4-wheel drive: 27.5
 1989–93 C6 2-wheel drive: 24.0
  4-wheel drive: 27.0
 AOD: 24.6
 E40D 2-wheel drive: 31.0
  4-wheel drive: 32.0

⑩ F-150 and F-250: 3.6
 F-350 w/Dana 50-IFS: 3.8
 F-350 w/Dana 60 Monobeam: 5.4

⑪ F-150: 5.5
 F-250, F-350: 7.5
 F-Super Duty: 8.25

⑫ F-150 Standard Cab:
  116.8 in. wb—Standard 18.2; optional 16.5
  133.0 in. wb—Standard 19.0; optional 18.2
 F-250, F-350 Standard Cab:
  Standard—19.0 w/gasoline engine;
  20.9 w/diesel engine
  Option—F-250 4x2 and 4x4 and
  F-250 HD 4x4, 17.5
  Optional—F-250 HD 4x2 and F-350 4x2,
  18.2
 F-150, F-250 SuperCab:
  138.8 in. wb—Standard dual tanks 34.7
  155.0 in. wb—Standard dual tanks 37.2
 F-350 Crew Cab: 27.2
 F-350 Chassis Cab and F-Super Duty:
  133.0 in. wb—Standard 19.0 w/gasoline
  engine; 20.0 w/diesel engine
  136.8 & 160.8 in. wb—Optional 19.0

⑬ With air conditioning or Super Cooling: 14.0
 With air conditioning and Super Cooling,
 (MT) 15.0
 With Super Cooling, (AT) 14.0

⑭ With air conditioning: 15.0
 With Super Cooling: 14.0

⑮ With air conditioning and/or Super Cooling: 16.0

CAPACITIES CHART—BRONCO

Year	Engine No. Cyl. Liters	Crankcase Incl. Filter (qt.)	Transmission (pt.)			Transfer Case (pts.)	Drive Axle (pt.)*		Fuel Tank (gal.)	Cooling System (qt.)	
			4-sp	5-sp	Auto.		Front	Rear		w/AC	wo/AC
1987	6-4.9	6.0	⑥	—	27.0	4.0	3.6	5.5	32.0	③	③
	8-5.0	6.0	⑥	—	②	4.0	3.6	5.5	32.0	④	④
	8-5.8	6.0	—	—	27.0	4.0	3.6	5.5	32.0	⑤	⑤
1988	6-4.9	6.0	—	①	27.0	4.0	3.6	5.5	32.0	③	③
	8-5.0	6.0	—	7.6	②	4.0	3.5	5.5	32.0	④	④
	8-5.8	6.0	—	—	27.0	4.0	3.6	5.5	32.0	⑤	⑤
1989	6-4.9	6.0	7.0	①	27.0	4.0	3.6	5.5	32.0	③	③
	8-5.0	6.0	7.0	7.6	②	4.0	3.5	5.5	32.0	④	④
	8-5.8	6.0	—	—	27.0	4.0	3.6	5.5	32.0	⑤	⑤
1990	6-4.9	6.0	7.0	①	27.0	4.0	3.6	5.5	32.0	③	③
	8-5.0	6.0	7.0	7.6	②	4.0	3.5	5.5	32.0	④	④
	8-5.8	6.0	—	—	27.0	4.0	3.6	5.5	32.0	⑤	⑤
1991	6-4.9	6.0	7.0	①	27.0	4.0	3.6	5.5	32.0	③	③
	8-5.0	6.0	7.0	7.6	②	4.0	3.5	5.5	32.0	④	④
	8-5.8	6.0	—	—	27.0	4.0	3.6	5.5	32.0	⑤	⑤
1992	6-4.9	6.0	7.0	7.6	27.0	4.0	3.6	5.5	32.0	③	③
	8-5.0	6.0	7.0	7.6	②	4.0	3.6	5.5	32.0	④	④
	8-5.8	6.0	—	—	27.0	4.0	3.6	5.5	32.0	⑤	⑤
1993	6-4.9	6.0	7.0	7.6	27.0	4.0	3.6	5.5	32.0	③	③
	8-5.0	6.0	7.0	7.6	②	4.0	3.6	5.5	32.0	④	④
	8-5.8	6.0	—	—	27.0	4.0	3.6	5.5	32.0	⑤	⑤

*For limited slip differentials, add the following
amounts of friction modifier additive:
  Front axle: 2 oz.
  Rear axle: 4 oz.
① Mazda M50D: 7.6
  ZF S5-42: 6.8
② C6 and E40D: 27.0
  AOD: 24.6
③ Standard cooling: 13.0
  Manual Transmission w/AC or Super Cooling: 14.0
  Automatic Transmission w/Super Cooling: 14.0
  Man. Tran. or Auto. Tran. w/AC and Super Cooling: 15.0
  Auto. Trans. w/AC: 15.0
④ Man. Tran. w/Standard Cooling: 13.0
  Auto. Tran. w/Standard Cooling: 14.0
  Man. Tran. or Auto. Tran. w/AC: 14.0
  Man. Tran. or Auto. Tran. w/AC or w/AC and Super Cooling: 15.0
⑤ With Standard Cooling or AC: 16.0
  With Super Cooling or Super Cooling and Air Conditioning: 17.0
⑥ Warner T-18: 7.0
  NP-435 with extension housing: 7.0
  Ford 4-Speed overdrive: 5.0

84921148

2

ENGINE PERFORMANCE AND TUNE-UP

TUNE-UP PROCEDURES

In order to extract the full measure of performance and economy from your engine it is essential that it be properly tuned at regular intervals. A regular tune-up will keep your vehicle's engine running smoothly and will prevent the annoying minor breakdowns and poor performance associated with an untuned engine.

Tune-ups should be performed more frequently if the vehicle is operated under severe conditions, such as trailer towing, prolonged idling, continual stop and start driving, or if starting or running problems are noticed. It is assumed that the routine maintenance described in Section 1 has been kept up, as this will have a decided effect on the results of a tune-up. All of the applicable steps of a tune-up should be followed in order, as the result is a cumulative one.

If the specifications on the tune-up sticker in the engine compartment disagree with the Tune-Up Specifications chart in this Section, the figures on the sticker must be used. The sticker often reflects changes made during the production run.

Spark Plugs

▶ **See Figures 1, 2, 3, 4, 5 and 6**

A typical spark plug consists of a metal shell surrounding a ceramic insulator. A metal electrode extends downward through the center of the insulator and protrudes a small distance. Located at the end of the plug and attached to the side of the outer metal shell is the side electrode. The side electrode bends in at a 90° angle so that its tip is even with, and

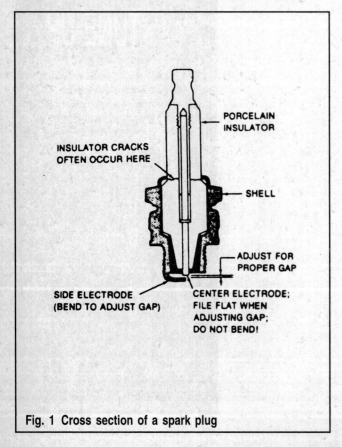

Fig. 1 Cross section of a spark plug

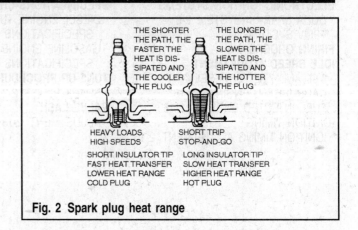

Fig. 2 Spark plug heat range

1 — **R--INDICATES RESISTOR-TYPE PLUG.**
2 — **"4" INDICATES 14 mm THREADS.**
3 — **HEAT RANGE**
4 — **TS--TAPERED SEAT**
    S--EXTENDED TIP
5 — **SPECIAL GAP**

Fig. 3 Spark plug type number chart, using the R45TSX as an example

parallel to, the tip of the center electrode. The distance between these two electrodes (measured in thousandths of an inch) is called the spark plug gap. The spark plug in no way produces a spark but merely provides a gap across which the current can arc. The coil produces anywhere from 20,000 to 40,000 volts which travels to the distributor where it is distributed through the spark plug wires to the spark plugs. The current passes along the center electrode and jumps the gap to the side electrode, and, in do doing, ignites the air/fuel mixture in the combustion chamber.

SPARK PLUG HEAT RANGE

Spark plug heat range is the ability of the plug to dissipate heat. The longer the insulator (or the farther it extends into the engine), the hotter the plug will operate; the shorter the insulator the cooler it will operate. A plug that absorbs little heat and remains too cool will quickly accumulate deposits of oil and carbon since it is not hot enough to burn them off. This leads to plug fouling and consequently to misfiring. A plug that absorbs too much heat will have no deposits, but, due to the excessive heat, the electrodes will burn away quickly and in some instances, preignition may result. Preignition takes place when plug tips get so hot that they glow sufficiently to ignite the fuel/air mixture before the actual spark occurs. This early ignition will usually cause a pinging during low speeds and heavy loads.

The general rule of thumb for choosing the correct heat range when picking a spark plug is: if most of your driving is long distance, high speed travel, use a colder plug; if most of your driving is stop and go, use a hotter plug. Original equipment plugs are compromise plugs, but most people never have occasion to change their plugs from the factory-recommended heat range.

REPLACING SPARK PLUGS

A set of spark plugs usually requires replacement after about 20,000 to 30,000 miles, depending on your style of driving. In normal operation, plug gap increases about 0.001 in. (0.025mm) for every 1,000-2,500 miles. As the gap increases, the plug's voltage requirement also increases. It requires a greater voltage to jump the wider gap and about two to three times as much voltage to fire a plug at high speeds than at idle.

When you're removing spark plugs, you should work on one at a time. Don't start by removing the plug wires all at once, because unless you number them, they may become mixed up. Take a minute before you begin and number the wires with tape. The best location for numbering is near where the wires come out of the cap.

➡ **Apply a small amount of silicone dielectric compound (D7AZ-19A331-A or the equivalent) to the inside of the terminal boots whenever an ignition wire is disconnected from the plug, or coil/distributor cap connection.**

1. Twist the spark plug boot and remove the boot and wire from the plug. Do not pull on the wire itself as this will ruin the wire.

2. If possible, use a brush or gag to clean the area around the spark plug. Make sure that all the dirt is removed so that none will enter the cylinder after the plug is removed.

3. Remove the spark plug using the proper size socket. Truck models use either a $\frac{5}{8}$ in. or $\frac{13}{16}$ in. size socket depending on the engine. Turn the socket counterclockwise to remove the plug. Be sure to hold the socket straight on the plug to avoid breaking the plug, or rounding off the hex on the plug.

4. Once the plug is out, check the center electrode for squareness. If the electrode is rounded, it is worn and should be replaced.

5. Use a round wire feeler gauge to check the plug gap. The correct size gauge should pass through the electrode gap with a slight drag. If you're in doubt, try one size smaller and one larger. The smaller gauge should go through easily while the larger one shouldn't go through at all. If the gap is incorrect, use the electrode bending tool on the end of the gauge to adjust the gap. When adjusting the gap, always bend the side electrode. The center electrode is non-adjustable.

6. Squirt a drop of penetrating oil on the threads of the new plug and install it. Don't oil the threads too heavily. Turn the plug in clockwise by hand until it is snug.

7. When the plug is finger tight, tighten it with a wrench. If you don't have a torque wrench, tighten the plug as shown.

8. Install the plug boot firmly over the plug. Proceed to the next plug.

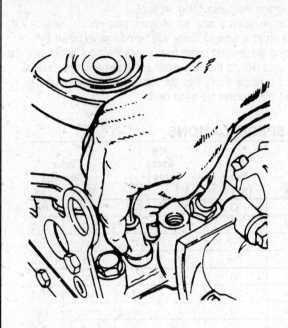

Fig. 4 Twist and pull on the rubber boot to remove the spark wires; never pull on the wire itself

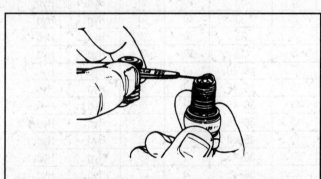

Fig. 5 Always use a wire gauge to check the electrode gap; a flat feeler gauge may not give the proper reading

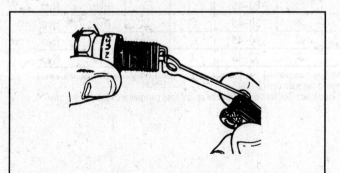

Fig. 6 Adjust the electrode gap by bending the side electrode

CHECKING AND REPLACING SPARK PLUG CABLES

Visually inspect the spark plug cables for burns, cuts, or breaks in the insulation. Check the spark plug boots and the nipples on the distributor cap and coil. Replace any damaged wiring. If no physical damage is obvious, the wires can be checked with an ohmmeter for excessive resistance. (See the tune-up and troubleshooting section).

When installing a new set of spark plug cables, replace the cables on at a time so there will be no mix-up. Start by replacing the longest cable first. Install the boot firmly over the spark plug. Route the wire exactly the same as the original. Insert the nipple firmly into the tower on the distributor cap. Repeat the process for each cable.

GASOLINE ENGINE TUNE-UP SPECIFICATIONS

Year	Engine ID/VIN	Engine Displacement Liters	Spark Plugs Gap (in.)	Ignition Timing (deg.) MT	AT	Fuel Pump (psi) ②	Idle Speed (rpm) MT	AT	Valve Clearance In.	Ex.
1987	B	4.9	0.044	①	①	33	①	①	Hyd.	Hyd.
	G	5.0	0.044	①	①	7–9	①	①	Hyd.	Hyd.
	H	5.8	0.044	①	①	7–9	①	①	Hyd.	Hyd.
	L	7.5	0.044	①	①	7–9	①	①	Hyd.	Hyd.
1988	Y	4.9	0.044	①	①	33	①	①	Hyd.	Hyd.
	N	5.0	0.044	①	①	33	①	①	Hyd.	Hyd.
	H	5.8	0.044	①	①	33	①	①	Hyd.	Hyd.
	G	7.5	0.044	①	①	33	①	①	Hyd.	Hyd.
1989	Y	4.9	0.044	①	①	33	①	①	Hyd.	Hyd.
	N	5.0	0.044	①	①	33	①	①	Hyd.	Hyd.
	H	5.8	0.044	①	①	33	①	①	Hyd.	Hyd.
	G	7.5	0.044	①	①	33	①	①	Hyd.	Hyd.
1990	Y	4.9	0.044	①	①	33	①	①	Hyd.	Hyd.
	N	5.0	0.044	①	①	33	①	①	Hyd.	Hyd.
	H	5.8	0.044	①	①	33	①	①	Hyd.	Hyd.
	G	7.5	0.044	①	①	33	①	①	Hyd.	Hyd.
1991	Y	4.9	0.044	①	①	45–60	①	①	Hyd.	Hyd.
	N	5.0	0.044	①	①	30–45	①	①	Hyd.	Hyd.
	H	5.8	0.044	①	①	30–45	①	①	Hyd.	Hyd.
	G	7.5	0.044	①	①	30–45	①	①	Hyd.	Hyd.
1992	Y	4.9	0.044	①	①	45–60	①	①	Hyd.	Hyd.
	N	5.0	0.044	①	①	30–45	①	①	Hyd.	Hyd.
	H	5.8	0.044	①	①	30–45	①	①	Hyd.	Hyd.
	G	7.5	0.044	①	①	30–45	①	①	Hyd.	Hyd.
1993	Y	4.9	0.044	①	①	45–60	①	①	Hyd.	Hyd.
	N	5.0	0.044	①	①	30–45	①	①	Hyd.	Hyd.
	H	5.8	0.044	①	①	30–45	①	①	Hyd.	Hyd.
	R	5.8	0.044	①	①	30–45	①	①	Hyd.	Hyd.
	G	7.5	0.044	①	①	30–45	①	①	Hyd.	Hyd.

NOTE: The lowest cylinder pressure should be within 75% of the highest cylinder pressure reading. For example, if the highest cylinder is 134 psi, the lowest should be 101. Engine should be at normal operating temperature with throttle valve in the wide open position.
The underhood specifications sticker often reflects tune-up specification changes in production. Sticker figures must be used if they disagree with those in this chart.
① See underhood sticker
② Engine running

TUNE-UP SPECIFICATIONS
Diesel Engines

Year	Engine No. Cyl. Liters	Static Timing	Dynamic Timing	Nozzle Opening Pressure (psi)	Curb Idle Speed (rpm)	Fast Idle Speed (rpm)	Maximum Compression Pressure (psi)
1987	8-6.9	Index	①	1,850	650–700	850–900	440
1988	8-7.3	Index	①	1,850	650–700	850–900	440
1989	8-7.3	Index	①	1,850	650–700	850–900	440
1990	8-7.3	Index	①	1,850	650–700	850–900	440
1991	8-7.3	Index	①	1,850	650–700	850–900	440
1992	8-7.3	Index	①	1,850	650–700	850–900	440
1993	8-7.3	Index	①	1,850	650–700	850–900	440

Static timing is set by aligning the index mark on the pump mounting flange with the index mark on the pump mounting adapter.

① Cetane rating of 38–42: Up to 3,000 ft.—6°
ATDC ± 1°
Over 3,000 ft.—7°
ATDC ± 1°
Cetane rating of 43–46: Up to 3,000 ft.—5°
ATDC ± 1°
Over 3,000 ft.—6°
ATDC ± 1°
Cetane rating of 47–50: Up to 3,000 ft.—4°
ATDC ± 1°
Over 3,000 ft.—5°
ATDC ± 1°

FIRING ORDERS

▶ See Figures 7, 8, 9 and 10

➡ To avoid confusion, replace spark plug wires one at a time.

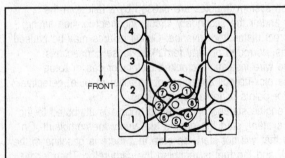

Fig. 7 8-5.8L engine
Firing order: 1-3-7-2-6-5-4-8
Distributor rotation: Counterclockwise

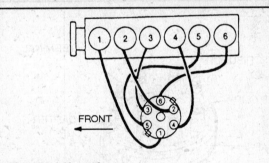

Fig. 8 6-4.9L engine
Firing order: 1-5-3-6-2-4
Distributor rotation: Clockwise

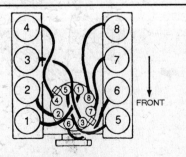

Fig. 9 8-5.0L and 8-7.5L engines
Firing order: 1-5-4-2-6-3-7-8
Distributor rotation: Counterclockwise

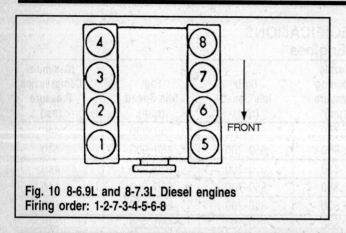

Fig. 10 8-6.9L and 8-7.3L Diesel engines
Firing order: 1-2-7-3-4-5-6-8

ELECTRONIC IGNITION SYSTEMS

➡ **All fuel injected engines use the TFI-IV system. All carbureted engines use the Dura Spark II system.**

Dura Spark II System

SYSTEM OPERATION

◆ **See Figures 11 and 12**

With the ignition switch **ON**, the primary circuit is on and the ignition coil is energized. When the armature spokes approach the magnetic pickup coil assembly, they induce the voltage

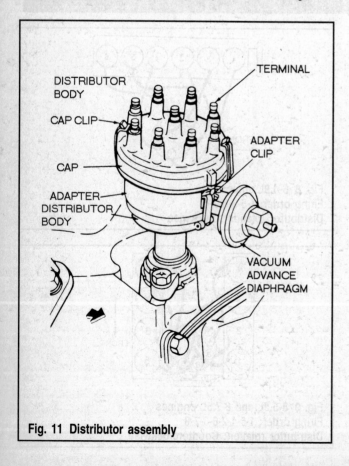

Fig. 11 Distributor assembly

which tells the amplifier to turn the coil primary current off. A timing circuit in the amplifier module will turn the current on again after the coil field has collapsed. When the current is on, it flows from the battery through the ignition switch, the primary windings of the ignition coil, and through the amplifier module circuits to ground. When the current is off, the magnetic field built up in the ignition coil is allowed to collapse, inducing a high voltage into the secondary windings of the coil. High voltage is produced each time the field is thus built up and collapsed. When DuraSpark is used in conjunction with the EEC, the EEC computer tells the DuraSpark module when to turn the coil primary current off or on. In this case, the armature position is only a reference signal of engine timing, used by the EEC computer in combination with other reference signals to determine optimum ignition spark timing.

The high voltage flows through the coil high tension lead to the distributor cap where the rotor distributes it to one of the spark plug terminals in the distributor cap. This process is repeated for every power stroke of the engine.

Ignition system troubles are caused by a failure in the primary and/or the secondary circuit; incorrect ignition timing; or incorrect distributor advance. Circuit failures may be caused by shorts, corroded or dirty terminals, loose connections, defective wire insulation, cracked distributor cap or rotor, defective pick-up coil assembly or amplifier module, defective distributor points or fouled spark plugs.

If an engine starting or operating trouble is attributed to the ignition system, start the engine and verify the complaint. On engines that will not start, be sure that there is gasoline in the fuel tank and the fuel is reaching the carburetor. Then locate the ignition system problem using the following procedures.

TROUBLESHOOTING DURASPARK II

◆ **See Figures 13, 14, 15, 16, 17 and 18**

The following procedures can be used to determine whether the ignition system is working or not. If these procedures fail to correct the problem, a full troubleshooting procedure should be performed.

Preliminary Checks

1. Check the battery's state of charge and connections.

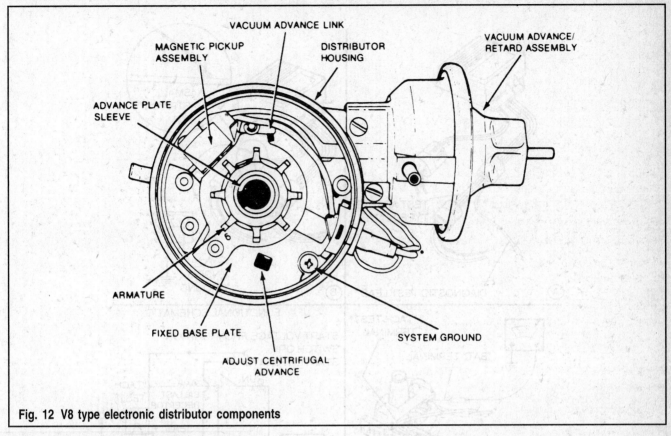

VACUUM ADVANCE LINK

MAGNETIC PICKUP ASSEMBLY

DISTRIBUTOR HOUSING

VACUUM ADVANCE/ RETARD ASSEMBLY

ADVANCE PLATE SLEEVE

ARMATURE

FIXED BASE PLATE

ADJUST CENTRIFUGAL ADVANCE

SYSTEM GROUND

Fig. 12 V8 type electronic distributor components

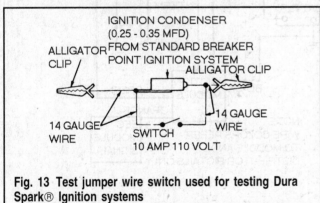

IGNITION CONDENSER
(0.25 - 0.35 MFD)

ALLIGATOR CLIP

FROM STANDARD BREAKER POINT IGNITION SYSTEM

ALLIGATOR CLIP

14 GAUGE WIRE

14 GAUGE WIRE

SWITCH
10 AMP 110 VOLT

Fig. 13 Test jumper wire switch used for testing Dura Spark® Ignition systems

2. Inspect all wires and connections for breaks, cuts, abrasions, or burned spots. Repair as necessary.

3. Unplug all connectors one at a time and inspect for corroded or burned contacts. Repair and plug connectors back together. DO NOT remove the dielectric compound in the connectors.

4. Check for loose or damaged spark plug or coil wires. A wire resistance check is given at the end of this section. If the boots or nipples are removed on 8mm ignition wires, reline the inside of each with new silicone dielectric compound (Motorcraft WA-10).

Special Tools

To perform the following tests, two special tools are needed; the ignition test jumper shown in the illustration and a modified

spark plug. Use the illustration to assembly the ignition test jumper. The test jumper must be used when performing the following tests. The modified spark plug is basically a spark plug with the side electrode removed. Ford makes a special tool called a Spark Tester for this purpose, which besides not having a side electrode is equipped with a spring clip so that it can be grounded to engine metal. It is recommended that the Spark Tester be used as there is less change of being shocked.

Run Mode Spark Test

➡️ **The wire colors given here are the main colors of the wires, not the dots or hashmarks.**

STEP 1

1. Remove the distributor cap and rotor from the distributor.

2. With the ignition off, turn the engine over by hand until one of the teeth on the distributor armature aligns with the magnet in the pickup coil.

3. Remove the coil wire from the distributor cap. Install the modified spark plug (see Special Tools, above) in the coil wire terminal and using heavy gloves and insulated pliers, hold the spark plug shell against the engine block.

4. Turn the ignition to RUN (not START) and tap the distributor body with a screwdriver handle. There should be a spark at the modified spark plug or at the coil wire terminal.

5. If a good spark is evident, the primary circuit is OK: perform the Start Mode Spark Test. If there is no spark, proceed to STEP 2.

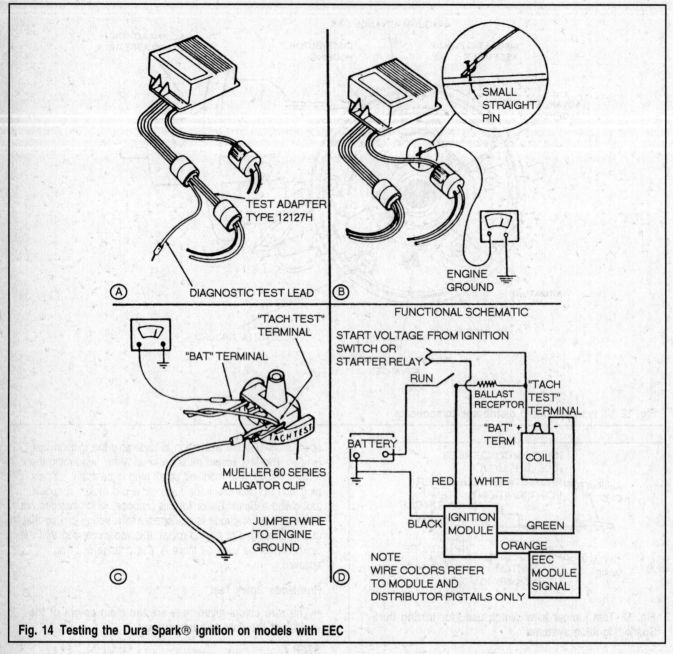

Fig. 14 Testing the Dura Spark® ignition on models with EEC

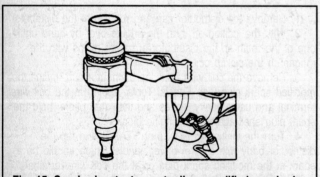

Fig. 15 Spark plug tester; actually a modified spark plug (side electrode removed) with a spring for ground

STEP 2

1. Unplug the module connector(s) which contain(s) the green and black module leads.

2. In the harness side of the connector(s), connect the special test jumper (see Special Tools, above) between the leads which connect to the green and black leads of the module pig tails. Use paper clips on connector socket holes to make contact. Do not allow clips to ground.

3. Turn the ignition switch to RUN (not START) and close the test jumper switch. Leave closed for about 1 second, then open. Repeat several times. There should be a spark each time the switch is opened.

4. If there is no spark, the problem is probably in the primary circuit through the ignition switch, the coil, the green lead or the black lead, or the ground connection in the distributor; Perform STEP 3. If there is a spark, the primary

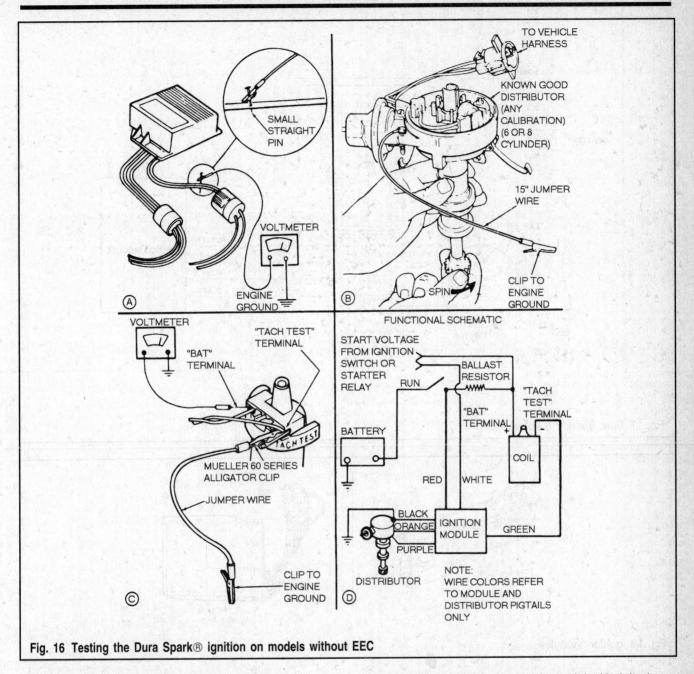

Fig. 16 Testing the Dura Spark® ignition on models without EEC

circuit wiring and coil are probably OK. The problem is probably in the distributor pick-up, the module red wire, or the module: perform STEP 6.

STEP 3

1. Disconnect the test jumper lead from the black lead and connect it to a good ground. Turn the test jumper switch on and off several times as in STEP 2.

2. If there is no spark, the problem is probably in the green lead, the coil, or the coil feed circuit: perform STEP 5.

3. If there is spark, the problem is probably in the black lead or the distributor ground connection: perform STEP 4.

STEP 4

1. Connect an ohmmeter between the black lead and ground. With the meter on its lowest scale, there should be no measurable resistance in the circuit. If there is resistance,

check the distributor ground connection and the black lead from the module. Repair as necessary, remove the ohmmeter, plug in all connections and repeat STEP 1.

2. If there is no resistance, the primary ground wiring is OK: perform STEP 6.

STEP 5

1. Disconnect the test jumper from the green lead and ground and connect it between the TACH-TEST terminal of the coil and a good ground to the engine.

2. With the ignition switch in the RUN position, turn the jumper switch on. Hold it on for about 1 second then turn it off as in Step 2. Repeat several times. There should be a spark each time the switch in turned off. If there is no spark, the problem is probably in the primary circuit running through the ignition switch to the coil BAT terminal, or in the coil itself. Check coil resistance (test given later in this section), and

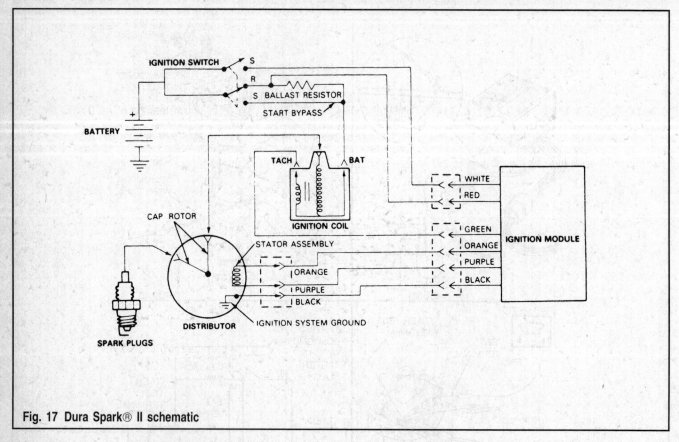

Fig. 17 Dura Spark® II schematic

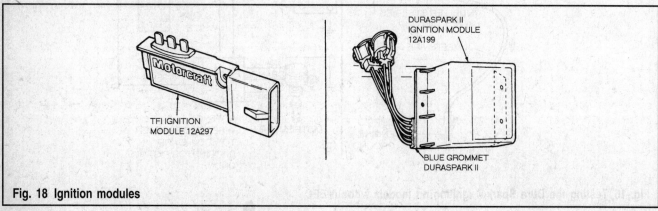

Fig. 18 Ignition modules

check the coil for internal shorts or opens. Check the coil feed circuit for opens, shorts, or high resistance. Repair as necessary, reconnect all connectors and repeat STEP 1. If there is spark, the coil and its feed circuit are OK. The problem could be in the green lead between the coil and the module. Check for an open or short, repair as necessary, reconnect all connectors and repeat STEP 1.

STEP 6

To perform this step, a voltmeter which is not combined with a dwell meter is needed. The slight needle oscillations ($\frac{1}{2}$v)

you'll be looking for may not be detectable on the combined voltmeter/dwell meter unit.

1. Connect a voltmeter between the orange and purple leads on the harness side of the module connectors.

✳✳CAUTION

On catalytic converter equipped trucks, disconnect the air supply line between the Thermactor by-pass valve and the manifold before cranking the engine with the ignition off. This will prevent damage to the catalytic converter. After testing, run the engine for at least 3 minutes before reconnecting the by-pass valve, to clear excess fuel from the exhaust system.

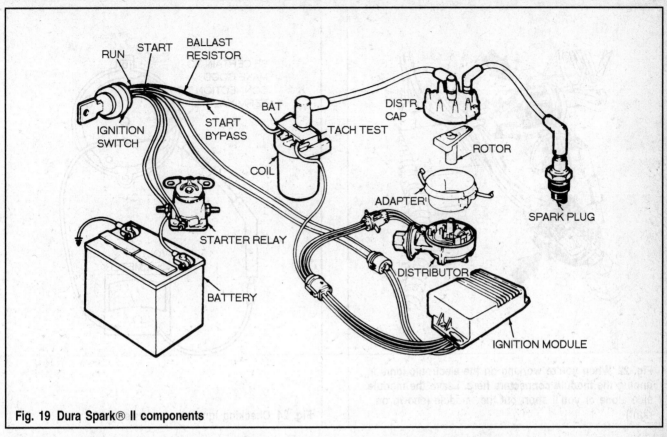

Fig. 19 Dura Spark® II components

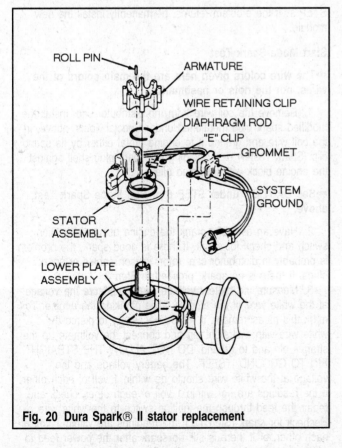

Fig. 20 Dura Spark® II stator replacement

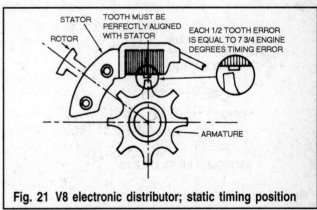

Fig. 21 V8 electronic distributor; static timing position

2. Set the voltmeter on its lowest scale and crank the engine. The meter needle should oscillate slightly (about ½v). If the meter does not oscillate, check the circuit through the magnetic pick-up in the distributor for open, shorts, shorts to ground and resistance. Resistance between the orange and purple leads should be 400-1,000Ω, and between each lead and ground should be more than 70,000Ω. Repair as necessary, reconnect all connectors and repeat STEP 1.

If the meter oscillates, the problem is probably in the power feed to the module (red wire) or in the module itself: proceed to STEP 7.

STEP 7

1. Remove all meters and jumpers and plug in all connectors.

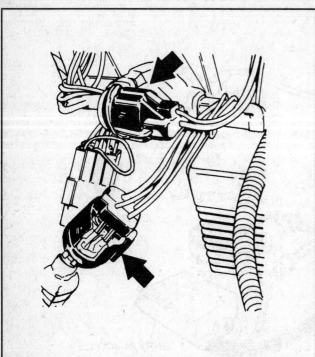

Fig. 22 When you're working on the electronic ignition, unplug the module connectors here. Leave the module side alone or you'll short out the module (shown on right)

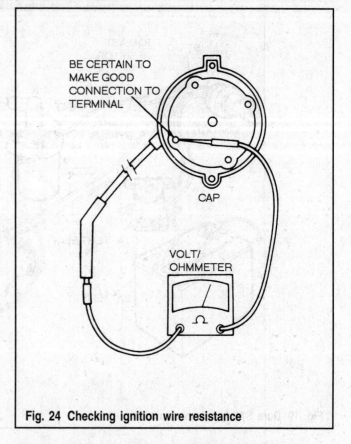

Fig. 24 Checking ignition wire resistance

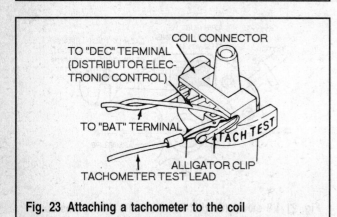

Fig. 23 Attaching a tachometer to the coil

2. Turn the ignition switch to the RUN position and measure voltage between the battery positive terminal and engine ground. It should be 12 volts.

3. Next, measure voltage between the red lead of the module and engine ground. To mark this measurement, it will be necessary to pierce the red wire with a straight pin and connect the voltmeter to the straight pin and to ground. DO NOT ALLOW THE STRAIGHT PIN TO GROUND ITSELF!

4. The two readings should be within one volt of each other. If not within one volt, the problem is in the power feed to the red lead. Check for shorts, open, or high resistance and correct as necessary. After repairs, repeat Step 1. If the readings are within one volt, the problem is probably in the module. Replace it with a good module and repeat STEP 1. If this corrects the problem, reconnect the old module and repeat

STEP 1. If the problem returns, permanently install the new module.

Start Mode Spark Test

➡ The wire colors given here are the main colors of the wires, not the dots or hashmarks.

1. Remove the coil wire from the distributor cap. Install the modified spark plug mentioned under Special Tools, above, in the coil wire and ground it to engine metal either by its spring clip (Spark Tester) or by holding the spark plug shell against the engine block with insulated pliers.

➡ See CAUTION under STEP 6 of Run Mode Spark Test, above.

2. Have an assistant crank the engine using the ignition switch and check for spark. If there is good spark, the problem is probably in distributor cap, rotor, ignition cables or spark plugs. If there is no spark, proceed to Step 3.

3. Measure the battery voltage. Next, measure the voltage at the white wire of the module while cranking the engine. To mark this measurement, it will be necessary to pierce the white wire with a straight pin and connect the voltmeter to the straight pin and to ground. DO NOT ALLOW THE STRAIGHT PIN TO GROUND ITSELF! The battery voltage and the voltage at the white wire should be within 1 volt of each other. If the readings are not within 1 volt of each other, check and repair the feed through the ignition switch to the white wire. Recheck for spark (Step 1). If the readings are within 1 volt of each other, or if there is still no spark after the power feed to white wire is repaired, proceed to Step 4.

4. Measure the coil BAT terminal voltage while cranking the engine. The reading should be within 1 volt of battery voltage. If the readings are not within 1 volt of each other, check and repair the feed through the ignition switch to the coil. If the readings are within 1 volt of each other, the problem is probably in the ignition module. Substitute another module and repeat the test for spark (Step 1).

TFI-IV System

SYSTEM OPERATION

▶ **See Figures 25 and 26**

The Thick Film Integrated (TFI-IV) ignition system uses a camshaft driven distributor with no centrifugal or vacuum advance. The distributor has a diecast base, incorporating a Hall effect stator assembly. The TFI-IV system module is mounted on the distributor base, it has 6 pins and uses an E-Core ignition coil, named after the shape of the laminations making up the core.

The TFI-IV module supplies voltage to the Profile Ignition Pick-up (PIP) sensor, which sends the crankshaft position information to the TFI-IV module. The TFI-IV module then sends this information to the EEC-IV module, which determines the spark timing and sends an electronic signal to the TFI-IV ignition module to turn off the coil and produce a spark to fire the spark plug.

The operation of the universal distributor is accomplished through the Hall effect stator assembly, causing the ignition coil to be switched off and on by the EEC-IV computer and TFI-IV modules. The vane switch is an encapsulated package consisting of a Hall sensor on one side and a permanent magnet on the other side.

A rotary vane cup, made of ferrous metal, is used to trigger the Hall effect switch. When the window of the vane cup is between the magnet and the Hall effect device, a magnetic flux field is completed from the magnet through the Hall effect device back to the magnet. As the vane passes through the opening, the flux lines are shunted through the vane and back to the magnet. A voltage is produced while the vane passes through the opening. When the vane clears the opening, the window causes the signal to go to 0 volts. The signal is then used by the EEC-IV system for crankshaft position sensing and the computation of the desired spark advance based on the engine demand and calibration. The voltage distribution is accomplished through a conventional rotor, cap and ignition wires.

GENERAL TESTING

Ignition Coil Test

The ignition coil must be diagnosed separately from the rest of the ignition system.

1. Primary resistance is measured between the two primary (low voltage) coil terminals, with the coil connector disconnected and the ignition switch off. Primary resistance should be 0.3-1.0Ω.

2. On Dura Spark ignitions, the secondary resistance is measured between the BATT and high voltage (secondary) terminals of the ignition coil with the ignition off, and the wiring

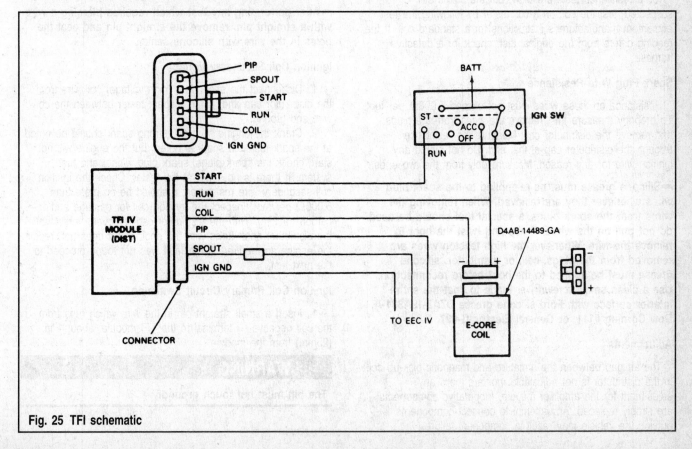

Fig. 25 TFI schematic

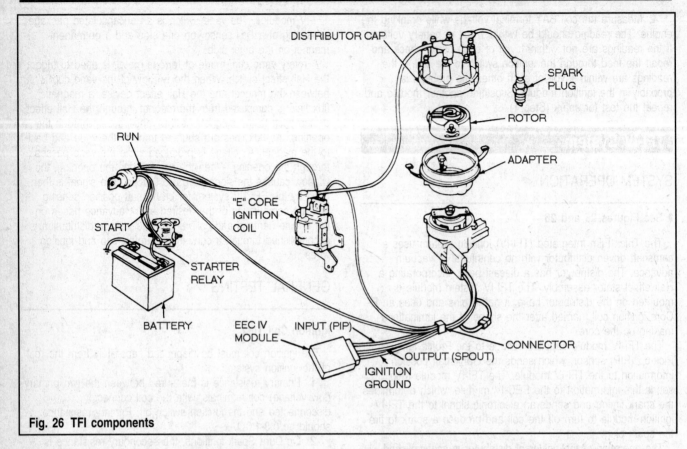

Fig. 26 TFI components

from the coil disconnected. Secondary resistance must be 8,000-11,500Ω.

3. If resistance tests are okay, but the coil is still suspected, test the coil on a coil tester by following the test equipment manufacturer's instructions for a standard coil. If the reading differs from the original test, check for a defective harness.

Spark Plug Wire Resistance

Resistance on these wires must not exceed 5,000Ω per foot. To properly measure this, remove the wires from the plugs, and remove the distributor cap. Measure the resistance through the distributor cap at that end. Do not pierce any ignition wire for any reason. Measure only from the two ends.

➡**Silicone grease must be re-applied to the spark plug wires whenever they are removed. When removing the wires from the spark plugs, a special tool should be used. do not pull on the wires. Grasp and twist the boot to remove the wire. Whenever the high tension wires are removed from the plugs, coil, or distributor, silicone grease must be applied to the boot before reconnection. Use a clean small screwdriver blade to coat the entire interior surface with Ford silicone grease D7AZ-19A331-A, Dow Corning #111, or General Electric G-627.**

Adjustments

The air gap between the armature and magnetic pick-up coil in the distributor is not adjustable, nor are there any adjustment for the amplifier module. Inoperative components are simply replaced. Any attempt to connect components outside the vehicle may result in component failure.

TROUBLESHOOTING THE TFI-IV SYSTEM

➡**After performing any test which requires piercing a wire with a straight pin, remove the straight pin and seal the holes in the wire with silicone sealer.**

Ignition Coil Secondary Voltage

1. Disconnect the secondary (high voltage) coil wire from the distributor cap and install a spark tester between the coil wire and ground.

2. Crank the engine. A good, strong spark should be noted at the spark tester. If spark is noted, but the engine will not start, check the spark plugs, spark plug wiring, and fuel system. If there is no spark at the tester: Check the ignition coil secondary wire resistance; it should be no more than 5,000Ω per foot. Inspect the ignition coil for damage and/or carbon tracking. With the distributor cap removed, verify that the distributor shaft turns with the engine; if it does not, repair the engine as required. If the fault was not found proceed to the next test.

Ignition Coil Primary Circuit Switching

1. Insert a small straight pin in the wire which runs from the coil negative (-) terminal to the TFI module, about 1 in. (25mm) from the module.

✴✴WARNING

The pin must not touch ground!

2. Connect a 12 VDC test lamp between the straight pin and an engine ground.

3. Crank the engine, noting the operation of the test lamp. If the test lamp flashes, proceed to the next test. If the test lamp lights but does not flash, proceed to the Wiring Harness test. If the test lamp does not light at all, proceed to the Primary Circuit Continuity test.

Ignition Coil Resistance

Refer to the General Testing for an explanation of the resistance tests. Replace the ignition coil if the resistance is out of the specification range.

Wiring Harness

1. Disconnect the wiring harness connector from the TFI module; the connector tabs must be PUSHED to disengage the connector. Inspect the connector for damage, dirt, and corrosion.

2. Attach the negative lead of a voltmeter to the base of the distributor. Attach the other voltmeter lead to a small straight pin. With the ignition switch in the RUN position, insert the straight pin into the No. 1 terminal of the TFI module connector. Note the voltage reading. With the ignition switch in the RUN position, move the straight pin to the No. 2 connector terminal. Again, note the voltage reading. Move the straight pin to the No. 3 connector terminal, then turn the ignition switch to the START position. Note the voltage reading then turn the ignition OFF.

3. The voltage readings should all be at least 90% of the available battery voltage. If the readings are okay, proceed to the Stator Assembly and Module test. If any reading is less than 90% of the battery voltage, inspect the wiring, connectors, and/or ignition switch for defects. if the voltage is low only at the No. 1 terminal, proceed to the ignition coil primary voltage test.

Stator Assembly and Module

1. Remove the distributor from the engine.
2. Remove the TFI module from the distributor.
3. Inspect the distributor terminals, ground screw, and stator wiring for damage. Repair as necessary.
4. Measure the resistance of the stator assembly, using an ohmmeter. If the ohmmeter reading is 800-975Ω, the stator is okay, but the TFI module must be replaced. If the ohmmeter reading is less than 800Ω or more than 975Ω; the TFI module is okay, but the stator module must be replaced.
5. Repair as necessary and install the TFI module and the distributor.

TFI Module

1. Remove the distributor cap from the distributor, and set it aside (spark plug wires intact).

2. Disconnect the TFI harness connector.
3. Remove the distributor.
4. Remove the two TFI module retaining screws.

✳✳WARNING

Step 5 must be followed EXACTLY; failure to do so will result in damage to the distributor module connector pins.

5. To disengage the modules terminals from the distributor base connector, pull the right side of the module down the distributor mounting flange and then back up. Carefully pull the module toward the flange and away from the distributor.
6. Coat the TFI module baseplate with a thin layer of silicone grease (FD7AZ-19A331-A or its equivalent).
7. Place the TFI module on the distributor base mounting flange. Position the module assembly toward the distributor bowl and carefully engage the distributor connector pins. Install and torque the two TFI module retaining screws to 9-16 inch lbs.
8. Install the distributor assembly.
9. Install the distributor cap and check the engine timing.

Primary Circuit Continuity

This test is performed in the same manner as the previous Wiring Harness test, but only the No. 1 terminal conductor is tested (ignition switch in Run position). If the voltage is less than 90% of the available battery voltage, proceed to the coil primary voltage test.

Ignition Coil Primary Voltage

1. Attach the negative lead of a voltmeter to the distributor base.
2. Turn the ignition switch ON and connect the positive voltmeter lead to the negative (-) ignition coil terminal. Note the voltage reading and turn the ignition OFF. If the voltmeter reading is less than 90% of the available battery voltage, inspect the wiring between the ignition module and the negative (-) coil terminal, then proceed to the last test, which follows.

Ignition Coil Supply Voltage

1. Attach the negative lead of a voltmeter to the distributor base.
2. Turn the ignition switch ON and connect the positive voltmeter lead to the positive (+) ignition coil terminal. Note the voltage reading then turn the ignition OFF. If the voltage reading is at least 90% of the battery voltage, yet the engine will still not run; first, check the ignition coil connector and terminals for corrosion, dirt, and/or damage; second, replace the ignition switch if the connectors and terminal are okay.
3. Connect any remaining wiring.

IGNITION TIMING

Ignition timing is the measurement, in degrees of crankshaft rotation, of the point at which the spark plugs fire in each of the cylinders. It is measured in degrees before or after Top Dead Center (TDC) of the compression stroke.

Ideally, the air/fuel mixture in the cylinder will be ignited by the spark plug just as the piston passes TDC of the compression stroke. If this happens, the piston will be beginning the power stroke just as the compressed and ignited air/fuel mixture starts to expand. The expansion of the air/fuel mixture then forces the piston down on the power stroke and turns the crankshaft.

Because it takes a fraction of a second for the spark plug to ignite the mixture in the cylinder, the spark plug must fire a little before the piston reaches TDC. Otherwise, the mixture will not be completely ignited as the piston passes TDC and the full power of the explosion will not be used by the engine.

The timing measurement is given in degrees of crankshaft rotation before the piston reaches TDC (BTDC, or Before Top Dead Center). If the setting for the ignition timing is 5°BTDC, each spark plug must fire 5° before each piston reaches TDC. This only holds true, however, when the engine is at idle speed.

As the engine speed increases, the piston go faster. The spark plugs have to ignite the fuel even sooner if it is to be completely ignited when the piston reaches TDC.

With the Dura Spark II system, the distributor has a means to advance the timing of the spark as the engine speed increases. This is accomplished by centrifugal weights within the distributor and a vacuum diaphragm mounted on the side of the distributor. It is necessary to disconnect the vacuum lines from the diaphragm when the ignition timing is being set.

With the TFI-IV system, ignition timing is calculated at all phases of vehicle operation by the TFI module.

If the ignition is set too far advanced (BTDC), the ignition and expansion of the fuel in the cylinder will occur too soon and tend to force the piston down while it is still traveling up. This causes engine ping. If the ignition spark is set too far retarded after TDC (ATDC), the piston will have already passed TDC and started on its way down when the fuel is ignited. This will cause the piston to be forced down for only a portion of its travel. This will result in poor engine performance and lack of power.

The timing must be checked with a timing light. This device is connected in series with the No. 1 spark plug. The current that fires the spark plug also causes the timing light to flash.

There is a notch on the crankshaft pulley on 6-cylinder engines. A scale of degrees of crankshaft rotation is attached to the engine block in such a position that the notch will pass close by the scale.

On V8 engines, the scale is located on the crankshaft pulley and a pointer is attached to the engine block so that the scale will pass close by. When the engine is running, the timing light is aimed at the mark on the crankshaft pulley and the scale.

IGNITION TIMING ADJUSTMENT

With the Dura Spark II system, only an initial timing adjustment is possible. Ignition timing is not considered to be a part of tune-up or routine maintenance.

With the TFI-IV system no ignition timing adjustment is possible and none should be attempted.

IGNITION TIMING CHECK

Dura Spark II Systems

1. Locate the timing marks on the crankshaft pulley and the front of the engine.
2. Clean the timing marks so that you can see them.
3. Mark the timing marks with a piece of chalk or with paint. Color the mark on the scale that will indicate the correct timing when it is aligned with the mark on the pulley or the pointer. It is also helpful to mark the notch in the pulley or the tip of the pointer with a small dab of color.
4. Attach a tachometer to the engine.
5. Attach a timing light according to the manufacturer's instructions. If the timing light has three wires, one is attached to the No. 1 spark plug with an adapter. The other wires are connected to the battery. The red wire goes to the positive side of the battery and the black wire is connected to the negative terminal of the battery.
6. Disconnect the vacuum line to the distributor at the distributor and plug the vacuum line. A golf tee does a fine job.
7. Check to make sure that all of the wires clear the fan and then start the engine.
8. Adjust the idle to the correct setting.
9. Aim the timing light at the timing marks. if the marks that you put on the flywheel or pulley and the engine are aligned with the light flashes, the timing is correct. Turn off the engine and remove the tachometer and the timing light. If the mark are not in alignment, replace the ignition module.

IDLE SPEED ADJUSTMENT

Carbureted Engines

▶ See Figure 27

1. Block the wheels and firmly apply parking brake.
2. Run engine until normal operating temperature is reached.
3. Place the vehicle in Park or Neutral, A/C in OFF position, and set parking brake.
4. Remove air cleaner.
5. Disconnect and plug decel throttle control kicker diaphragm vacuum hose.
6. Connect a slave vacuum hose from an engine manifold vacuum source to the decel throttle control kicker.
7. Run engine at approximately 2,500 rpm for 15 seconds, then release the throttle.

8. If decel throttle control rpm is not within ± 50 rpm of specification, adjust the kicker.
9. Disconnect the slave vacuum hose and allow engine to return to curb idle.
10. Adjust curb idle, if necessary, using the curb idle adjusting screw.
11. Rev the engine momentarily, recheck curb idle and adjust if necessary.
12. Reconnect the decel throttle control vacuum hose to the diaphragm.
13. Reinstall the air cleaner.

Fuel Injected Engines

These engines have idle speed controlled by the TFI-IV/EEC-IV system and no adjustment is possible.

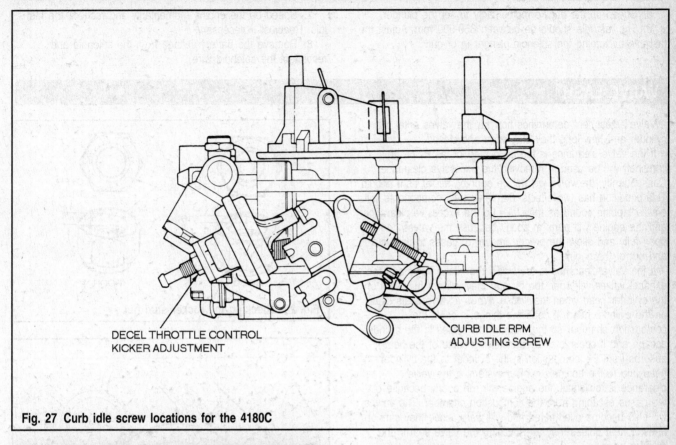

DECEL THROTTLE CONTROL
KICKER ADJUSTMENT

CURB IDLE RPM
ADJUSTING SCREW

Fig. 27 Curb idle screw locations for the 4180C

6.9L and 7.3L V8 Diesel

CURB IDLE ADJUSTMENT

♦ **See Figure 28**

1. Place the transmission in Neutral or Park. Firmly set the parking brake.
2. Bring the engine up to normal operating temperature.
3. Idle speed is measured with manual transmission in Neutral and automatic transmission in Drive, with the wheels blocked and parking brake ON.
4. Check the curb idle speed, using a magnetic pickup tachometer suitable for diesel engines. The part number of the Ford tachometer is Rotunda 99-0001. Adjust the idle speed to 600-700 rpm.

➡**Always check the underhood emissions control information sticker for the latest idle and adjustment specifications.**

5. Place the transmission in Neutral or Park and momentarily speed up the engine. Allow the rpm to drop to idle and recheck the idle speed. Readjust if necessary.

FAST IDLE ADJUSTMENT

1. Place the transmission in Neutral or Park.
2. Start the engine and bring up to normal operating temperatures.

3. Disconnect the wire from the fast idle solenoid.
4. Apply battery voltage to activate the solenoid plunger.

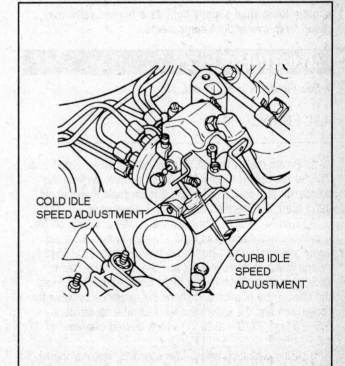

COLD IDLE
SPEED ADJUSTMENT

CURB IDLE
SPEED
ADJUSTMENT

Fig. 28 Diesel injection pump showing idle speed adjustment. Pump is mounted on top (front) of the intake manifold

5. Speed up the engine momentarily to set the plunger.

6. The fast idle should be between 850-900 rpm. Adjust the fast idle by turning the solenoid plunger in or out.

7. Speed up the engine momentarily and recheck the fast idle. Readjust if necessary.

8. Remove the battery voltage from the solenoid and reconnect the solenoid wire.

VALVE LASH

Valve adjustment determines how far the valves enter the cylinder and how long they stay open and closed.

If the valve clearance is too large, part of the lift of the camshaft will be used in removing the excessive clearance. Consequently, the valve will not be opening as far as it should. This condition has two effects: the valve train components will emit a tapping sound as they take up the excessive clearance and the engine will perform poorly because the valves don't open fully and allow the proper amount of gases to flow into and out of the engine.

If the valve clearance is too small, the intake valve and the exhaust valves will open too far and they will not fully seal on the cylinder head when they close. When a valve seats itself on the cylinder head, it does two things: it seals the combustion chamber so that none of the gases in the cylinder escape and it cools itself by transferring some of the heat it absorbs from the combustion in the cylinder to the cylinder head and to the engine's cooling system. If the valve clearance is too small, the engine will run poorly because of the gases escaping from the combustion chamber. The valves will also become overheated and will warp, since they cannot transfer heat unless they are touching the valve seat in the cylinder head.

➡While all valve adjustments must be made as accurately as possible, it is better to have the valve adjustment slightly loose than slightly tight as a burned valve may result from overly tight adjustments.

ADJUSTMENT

▶ **See Figures 29, 30, 31 and 32**

4.9L ENGINE

1. Rotate the crankshaft by hand so that No. 1 piston is at TDC of the compression stroke. Make a chalk mark on the damper at that point, then, make 2 more chalk marks about 120° apart, dividing the damper into 3 equal parts.

2. With No. 1 at TDC, tighten the rocker arm bolts on No. 1 cylinder intake and exhaust to 17 — 23 ft. lbs. Then, slowly apply pressure, using Lifter Bleed-down wrench T70P-6513-A, or equivalent, to completely bottom the lifter. Take care to avoid excessive pressure that might bend the pushrod. Hold the lifter in this position and check the clearance between the rocker arm and the valve stem tip. Allowable clearance is 2.5 — 5.0mm (0.10 — 0.20 in.) with a desired clearance of 3.0 — 4.5mm (0.125 — 0.175 in.).

3. If the clearance is less than specified, install a shorter pushrod. If the clearance is greater than specified, install a longer pushrod.

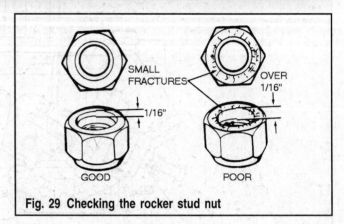

Fig. 29 Checking the rocker stud nut

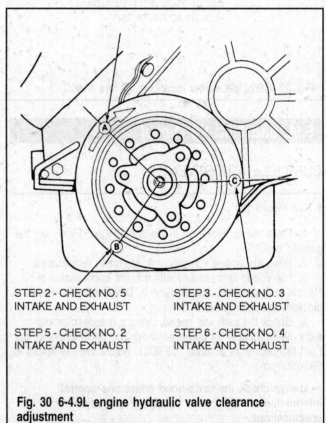

STEP 2 - CHECK NO. 5 INTAKE AND EXHAUST

STEP 3 - CHECK NO. 3 INTAKE AND EXHAUST

STEP 5 - CHECK NO. 2 INTAKE AND EXHAUST

STEP 6 - CHECK NO. 4 INTAKE AND EXHAUST

Fig. 30 6-4.9L engine hydraulic valve clearance adjustment

4. Rotate the crankshaft clockwise — as viewed from the front — until the next chalk mark is aligned with the timing pointer. Repeat the procedure for No. 5 intake and exhaust.

5. Rotate the crankshaft to the next chalk mark and repeat the procedure for No. 3 intake and exhaust.

6. Repeat the rotation/checking procedure for the remaining valves in firing order, that is: 6 — 2 — 4.

5.0L ENGINE

1. Rotate the crankshaft by hand so that No. 1 piston is at TDC of the compression stroke. Make a chalk mark on the damper at that point, then, make 2 more chalk marks about 90° apart in a clockwise direction.

2. With No. 1 at TDC, slowly apply pressure, using Lifter Bleed-down wrench T70P-6513-A, or equivalent, to completely bottom the lifter, on the following valves:

- No. 1 intake and exhaust
- No. 7 intake
- No. 5 exhaust
- No. 8 intake
- No. 4 exhaust

Take care to avoid excessive pressure that might bend the pushrod. Hold the lifter in this position and check the clearance between the rocker arm and the valve stem tip. Allowable clearance is 1.8 — 4.9mm (0.071 — 0.193 in.) with a desired clearance of 2.4 — 4.2mm (0.096 — 0.165 in.).

3. If the clearance is less than specified, install a shorter pushrod. If the clearance is greater than specified, install a longer pushrod.

4. Rotate the crankshaft clockwise — as viewed from the front — 180°, until the next chalk mark is aligned with the timing pointer. Repeat the procedure for:

- No. 5 intake
- No. 2 exhaust
- No. 4 intake
- No. 6 exhaust

5. Rotate the crankshaft to the next chalk mark — 90° — and repeat the procedure for:

- No. 2 intake
- No. 7 exhaust
- No. 3 intake and exhaust
- No. 6 intake
- No. 8 exhaust

5.8L ENGINE

1. Rotate the crankshaft by hand so that No. 1 piston is at TDC of the compression stroke. Make a chalk mark on the damper at that point, then, make 2 more chalk marks about 90° apart in a clockwise direction.

2. With No. 1 at TDC, slowly apply pressure, using Lifter Bleed-down wrench T70P-6513-A, or equivalent, to completely bottom the lifter, on the following valves:

- No. 1 intake and exhaust
- No. 4 intake
- No. 3 exhaust
- No. 8 intake
- No. 7 exhaust

Take care to avoid excessive pressure that might bend the pushrod. Hold the lifter in this position and check the clearance between the rocker arm and the valve stem tip. Allowable clearance is 2.5-5.0mm (0.098-0.198 in.) with a desired clearance of 3.1-4.4mm (0.123-0.173 in.).

3. If the clearance is less than specified, install a shorter pushrod. If the clearance is greater than specified, install a longer pushrod.

4. Rotate the crankshaft clockwise — viewed from the front — 180°, until the next chalk mark is aligned with the timing pointer. Repeat the procedure for:

- No. 3 intake
- No. 2 exhaust
- No. 7 intake
- No. 6 exhaust

5. Rotate the crankshaft to the next chalk mark — 90° — and repeat the procedure for:

- No. 2 intake
- No. 4 exhaust
- No. 5 intake and exhaust
- No. 6 intake
- No. 8 exhaust

7.5L ENGINE

1. Rotate the crankshaft by hand so that No. 1 piston is at TDC of the compression stroke. Make a chalk mark on the damper at that point.

2. With No. 1 at TDC, slowly apply pressure, using Lifter Bleed-down wrench T70P-6513-A, or equivalent, to completely bottom the lifter, on the following valves:

- No. 1 intake and exhaust
- No. 3 intake
- No. 4 exhaust
- No. 7 intake
- No. 5 exhaust
- No. 8 intake and exhaust

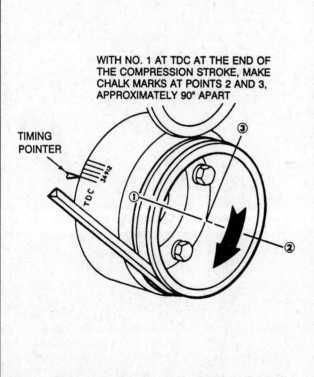

WITH NO. 1 AT TDC AT THE END OF THE COMPRESSION STROKE, MAKE CHALK MARKS AT POINTS 2 AND 3, APPROXIMATELY 90° APART

TIMING POINTER

Fig. 31 Marking the damper on the 8-5.0L and 8-5.8L engines

Take care to avoid excessive pressure that might bend the pushrod. Hold the lifter in this position and check the clearance between the rocker arm and the valve stem tip. Allowable clearance is 1.9-4.4mm (0.075-0.175 in.) with a desired clearance of 2.5-3.8mm (0.100-0.150 in.).

3. If the clearance is less than specified, install a shorter pushrod. If the clearance is greater than specified, install a longer pushrod.

4. Rotate the crankshaft clockwise — viewed from the front — 360°, until the chalk mark is once again aligned with the timing pointer. Repeat the procedure for:

- No. 2 intake and exhaust
- No. 4 intake
- No. 3 exhaust
- No. 5 intake
- No. 7 exhaust
- No. 6 intake and exhaust

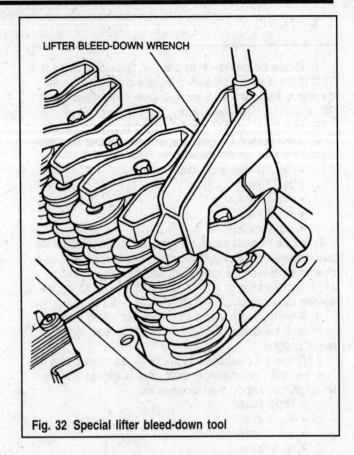

LIFTER BLEED-DOWN WRENCH

Fig. 32 Special lifter bleed-down tool

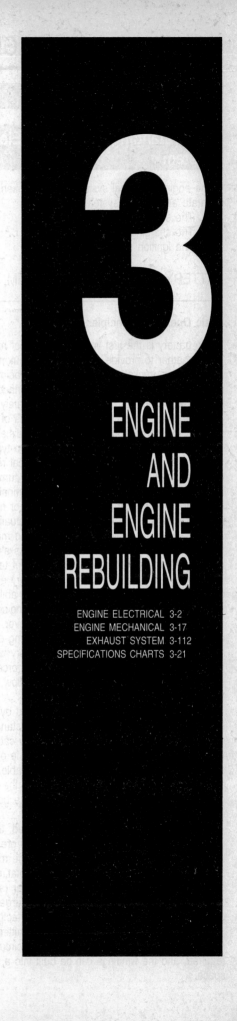

3

ENGINE AND ENGINE REBUILDING

ENGINE ELECTRICAL

Understanding the Engine Electrical System

The engine electrical system can be broken down into three separate and distinct systems:
1. The starting system.
2. The charging system.
3. The ignition system.

BATTERY AND STARTING SYSTEM

Basic Operating Principles

The battery is the first link in the chain of mechanisms which work together to provide cranking of the automobile engine. In most modern trucks, the battery is a lead/acid electrochemical device consisting of six 2v subsections connected in series so the unit is capable of producing approximately 12v of electrical pressure. Each subsection, or cell, consists of a series of positive and negative plates held a short distance apart in a solution of sulfuric acid and water. The two types of plates are of dissimilar metals. This causes a chemical reaction to be set up, and it is this reaction which produces current flow from the battery when its positive and negative terminals are connected to an electrical appliance such as a lamp or motor. The continued transfer of electrons would eventually convert the sulfuric acid in the electrolyte to water, and make the two plates identical in chemical composition. As electrical energy is removed from the battery, its voltage output tends to drop. Thus, measuring battery voltage and battery electrolyte composition are two ways of checking the ability of the unit to supply power. During the starting of the engine, electrical energy is removed from the battery. However, if the charging circuit is in good condition and the operating conditions are normal, the power removed from the battery will be replaced by the generator (or alternator) which will force electrons back through the battery, reversing the normal flow, and restoring the battery to its original chemical state.

The battery and starting motor are linked by very heavy electrical cables designed to minimize resistance to the flow of current. Generally, the major power supply cable that leaves the battery goes directly to the starter, while other electrical system needs are supplied by a smaller cable. During starter operation, power flows from the battery to the starter and is grounded through the truck's frame and the battery's negative ground strap.

The starting motor is a specially designed, direct current electric motor capable of producing a very great amount of power for its size. One thing that allows the motor to produce a great deal of power is its tremendous rotating speed. It drives the engine through a tiny pinion gear (attached to the starter's armature), which drives the very large flywheel ring gear at a greatly reduced speed. Another factor allowing it to produce so much power is that only intermittent operation is required of it. This, little allowance for air circulation is required, and the windings can be built into a very small space.

The starter solenoid is a magnetic device which employs the small current supplied by the starting switch circuit of the ignition switch. This magnetic action moves a plunger which mechanically engages the starter and electrically closes the heavy switch which connects it to the battery. The starting switch circuit consists of the starting switch contained within the ignition switch, a transmission neutral safety switch or clutch pedal switch, and the wiring necessary to connect these in series with the starter solenoid or relay.

A pinion, which is a small gear, is mounted to a one-way drive clutch. This clutch is splined to the starter armature shaft. When the ignition switch is moved to the **start** position, the solenoid plunger slides the pinion toward the flywheel ring gear via a collar and spring. If the teeth on the pinion and flywheel match properly, the pinion will engage the flywheel immediately. If the gear teeth butt one another, the spring will be compressed and will force the gears to mesh as soon as the starter turns far enough to allow them to do so. As the solenoid plunger reaches the end of its travel, it closes the contacts that connect the battery and starter and then the engine is cranked.

As soon as the engine starts, the flywheel ring gear begins turning fast enough to drive the pinion at an extremely high rate of speed. At this point, the one-way clutch begins allowing the pinion to spin faster than the starter shaft so that the starter will not operate at excessive speed. When the ignition switch is released from the starter position, the solenoid is de-energized, and a spring contained within the solenoid assembly pulls the gear out of mesh and interrupts the current flow to the starter.

Some starter employ a separate relay, mounted away from the starter, to switch the motor and solenoid current on and off. The relay thus replaces the solenoid electrical switch, buy does not eliminate the need for a solenoid mounted on the starter used to mechanically engage the starter drive gears. The relay is used to reduce the amount of current the starting switch must carry.

THE CHARGING SYSTEM

Basic Operating Principles

The automobile charging system provides electrical power for operation of the vehicle's ignition and starting systems and all the electrical accessories. The battery services as an electrical surge or storage tank, storing (in chemical form) the energy originally produced by the engine driven generator. The system also provides a means of regulating generator output to protect the battery from being overcharged and to avoid excessive voltage to the accessories.

The storage battery is a chemical device incorporating parallel lead plates in a tank containing a sulfuric acid/water solution. Adjacent plates are slightly dissimilar, and the chemical reaction of the two dissimilar plates produces electrical energy when the battery is connected to a load such as the starter motor. The chemical reaction is reversible, so that when the generator is producing a voltage (electrical pressure) greater than that produced by the battery, electricity is forced into the battery, and the battery is returned to its fully charged state.

The vehicle's generator is driven mechanically, through V-belts, by the engine crankshaft. It consists of two coils of fine wire, one stationary (the stator), and one movable (the rotor). The rotor may also be known as the armature, and consists of fine wire wrapped around an iron core which is mounted on a shaft. The electricity which flows through the two coils of wire (provided initially by the battery in some cases) creates an intense magnetic field around both rotor and stator, and the interaction between the two fields creates voltage, allowing the generator to power the accessories and charge the battery.

There are two types of generators: the earlier is the direct current (DC) type. The current produced by the DC generator is generated in the armature and carried off the spinning armature by stationary brushes contacting the commutator. The commutator is a series of smooth metal contact plates on the end of the armature. The commutator is a series of smooth metal contact plates on the end of the armature. The commutator plates, which are separated from one another by a very short gap, are connected to the armature circuits so that current will flow in one directions only in the wires carrying the generator output. The generator stator consists of two stationary coils of wire which draw some of the output current of the generator to form a powerful magnetic field and create the interaction of fields which generates the voltage. The generator field is wired in series with the regulator.

Newer automobiles use alternating current generators or alternators, because they are more efficient, can be rotated at higher speeds, and have fewer brush problems. In an alternator, the field rotates while all the current produced passes only through the stator winding. The brushes bear against continuous slip rings rather than a commutator. This causes the current produced to periodically reverse the direction of its flow. Diodes (electrical one-way switches) block the flow of current from traveling in the wrong direction. A series of diodes is wired together to permit the alternating flow of the stator to be converted to a pulsating, but unidirectional flow at the alternator output. The alternator's field is wired in series with the voltage regulator.

The regulator consists of several circuits. Each circuit has a core, or magnetic coil of wire, which operates a switch. Each switch is connected to ground through one or more resistors. The coil of wire responds directly to system voltage. When the voltage reaches the required level, the magnetic field created by the winding of wire closes the switch and inserts a resistance into the generator field circuit, thus reducing the output. The contacts of the switch cycle open and close many times each second to precisely control voltage.

While alternators are self-limiting as far as maximum current is concerned, DC generators employ a current regulating circuit which responds directly to the total amount of current flowing through the generator circuit rather than to the output voltage. The current regulator is similar to the voltage regulator except that all system current must flow through the energizing coil on its way to the various accessories.

Ignition Coil

REMOVAL & INSTALLATION

Carbureted Engines

1. Disconnect the battery ground.
2. Disconnect the two small and one large wires from the coil.
3. Disconnect the condenser connector from the coil, if equipped.
4. Unbolt and remove the coil.
5. Installation is the reverse of removal.

Ignition Module

REMOVAL & INSTALLATION

Carbureted Engines

Removing the module, on all models, is a matter of simply removing the fasteners that attach it to the fender or firewall and pulling apart the connectors. When unplugging the connectors, pull them apart with a firm, straight pull. NEVER PRY THEM APART! To pry them will cause damage. When reconnecting them, coat the mating ends with silicone dielectric grease to waterproof the connection. Press the connectors together firmly to overcome any vacuum lock caused by the grease.

➡ If the locking tabs weaken or break, don't replace the unit. Just secure the connection with electrical tape or tie straps.

Fuel Injected Engines

1. Remove the 2 screws securing the TFI heatsink assembly to the left fender apron.
2. Disconnect the harness from the module.
3. Remove the 2 screws securing the TFI module to the heatsink.
4. Coat the baseplate of the module with a uniform covering of silicone dielectric grease, about $1/32$ in. thick.
5. Position the module on the heatsink and tighten the screws to 15-35 inch lbs.
6. Install the heatsink and connect the wiring.

Distributor

REMOVAL

▶ See Figure 1

Carbureted Engines (DuraSpark II)

1. Remove the air cleaner assembly, taking note of the hose locations.
2. Disconnect the distributor wiring connector from the vehicle wiring harness.

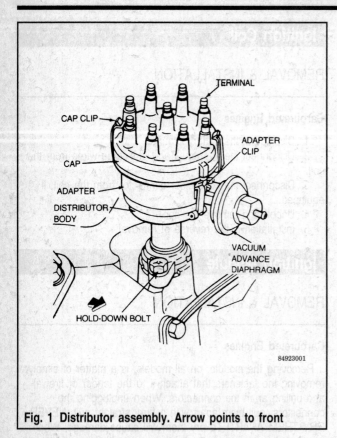

Fig. 1 Distributor assembly. Arrow points to front

3. Noting the position of the vacuum line(s) on the distributor diaphragm, disconnect the lines at the diaphragm. Unsnap the two distributor cap retaining clamps and remove the cap, rotor and adapter.

➡**If it is necessary to disconnect ignition wires from the cap to get enough room to remove the distributor, make sure to label every wire and the cap for easy and accurate reinstallation.**

4. Rotate the engine to align any pole on the armature with the pole on the stator.
5. Install the rotor. Using chalk or paint, carefully mark the position of the distributor rotor in relation to the distributor housing and mark the position of the distributor housing in relation to the engine block. When this is done, you should have a line on the distributor housing directly in line with the tip of the rotor and another line on the engine block directly in line with the mark on the distributor housing. This is very important because the distributor must be installed in the exact same location from which it was removed, if correct ignition timing is to be maintained.
6. Remove the distributor holddown bolt and clamp. Remove the distributor from the engine. Make sure that the oil pump (intermediate) driveshaft does not come out with the distributor. If it does, remove it from the distributor shaft, coat its lower end with heavy grease, and reinsert it, making sure that it fully engages the oil pump drive.

➡**Do not disturb the engine while the distributor is removed. If you turn the engine over with the distributor removed, you will have to retime the engine.**

INSTALLATION ENGINE NOT ROTATED

Carbureted Engines (DuraSpark II)

1. If the engine was not cranked (disturbed) when the distributor was removed, position the distributor in the block with the armature and stator poles aligned, the rotor aligned with the mark previously scribed on the distributor body and the marks on the distributor body and cylinder block in alignment. Install the distributor holddown bolt and clamp finger tight.
2. If the stator and armature poles cannot be aligned by rotating the distributor, pull the distributor out just far enough to disengage the drive gear and rotate the distributor shaft to engage a different gear tooth.
3. Install the distributor cap and wires.
4. Connect the distributor wring connector to the wiring harness. Tighten the holddown bolt.
5. Install the air cleaner, if removed.
6. Check the ignition timing as outlined in Section 2.

INSTALLATION CRANKSHAFT OR CAMSHAFT ROTATED

Carbureted Engines (DuraSpark II)

If the engine is cranked (disturbed) with the distributor removed, it will now be necessary to retime the engine.
1. Rotate the engine so that No. 1 piston is at TDC of the compression stroke.
2. Align the timing marks to the correct initial timing shown on the underhood decal.
3. Install the distributor with the rotor in the No. 1 firing position and any armature pole aligned with the stator pole.

➡**Make sure that the oil pump intermediate shaft properly engages the distributor shaft. It may be necessary to crank the engine after the distributor gear is partially engaged in order to engage the oil pump intermediate shaft and fully seat the distributor in the block.**

4. If it was necessary to rotate the engine to align the oil pump, repeat Steps 1, 2 and 3.
5. Install the holddown bolt finger tight.
6. Install the distributor cap and wires.
7. Connect the distributor wring connector to the wiring harness. Tighten the holddown bolt.
8. Install the air cleaner, if removed.
9. Check the ignition timing as outlined in Section 2.
10. When everything is set, tighten the holddown bolt to 25 ft. lbs.

REMOVAL

Fuel Injected Engines (TFI-IV Systems)

1. Disconnect the primary wiring connector from the distributor.
2. Mark the position of the cap's No. 1 terminal on the distributor base.
3. Unclip and remove the cap. Remove the adapter.

4. Remove the rotor.
5. Remove the TFI connector.
6. Matchmark the distributor base and engine for installation reference.
7. Remove the holddown bolt and lift out the distributor.

INSTALLATION

Fuel Injected Engines (TFI-IV System)

1. Rotate the engine so that the No. 1 piston is at TDC of the compression stroke.
2. Align the timing marks so that the engine is set at the initial timing shown on the underhood sticker.
3. Install the rotor on the shaft and rotate the shaft so that the rotor tip points to the No. 1 mark made on the distributor base.
4. Continue rotating the shaft so that the leading edge of the vane is centered on the vane switch assembly.
5. Position the distributor in the block and rotate the distributor body to align the leading edge of the vane and vane switch. Verify that the rotor tip points to the No. 1 mark on the body.

➡If the vane and vane switch cannot be aligned by rotating the distributor body in the engine, pull the distributor out just far enough to disengage the gears and rotate the shaft to engage a different gear tooth. Repeat Steps 3, 4 and 5.

6. Install and finger tighten the holddown bolt.
7. Connect the TFI and primary wiring.
8. Install the rotor, if not already done.

➡Coat the brass portions of the rotor with a $1/32$ in. (0.8mm) thick coating of silicone dielectric compound.

9. Install the cap and adapter (as necessary). Install the wires and start the engine.
10. Check and set the initial timing.
11. Tighten the holddown bolt to 25 ft. lbs.

STATOR ASSEMBLY REPLACEMENT

Carbureted Engines

1. Disconnect the battery ground cable.
2. Remove the distributor cap.
3. Remove the rotor.
4. Unclip and remove the upper distributor body.
5. Remove the retaining screw and remove the wire harness from the distributor.
6. Using a small gear puller, remove the stator from the distributor shaft. As the stator is pulled up on the shaft, take care to grab the roll pin so that it doesn't fall into the distributor.
   To install:
7. Place the new stator on the shaft, press or dive it down slightly, insert the roll pin and drive it into place inside the stator.

8. Using a deep socket, or similar tool, drive the stator down until it bottoms. Check occasionally to be sure that the roll pin stays in place.
9. Replace the wiring harness, upper body, rotor and cap.

Fuel Injected Engines

EXCEPT THE 6-4.9L

1. Remove the distributor assembly from the engine; refer to the procedure in this Section.
2. Remove the ignition rotor from the distributor shaft.
3. Mark the armature and distributor drive gear with a felt tip pen or equivalent, to note their orientation. While holding the distributor gear, remove the 2 armature retaining screws and remove the armature.

➡Do not hold the armature to loosen the screws.

4. Use a suitable punch to remove the roll pin from the distributor drive gear; discard the roll pin.
5. Position the distributor upside down in a suitable press. Using a press plate and suitable driver, press off the distributor drive gear.
6. Use a file and/or emery paper to remove any burrs or deposits from the distributor shaft, that would keep the shaft from sliding freely from the distributor housing. Remove the shaft assembly.
7. Remove the 2 stator assembly retaining screws.
8. Remove the octane rod and screw.
9. Remove the stator assembly.
10. Inspect the base bushing for wear or signs of excess heat concentration. If damage is evident, the entire distributor assembly must be replaced.
11. Inspect the base O-ring for cuts or damage and replace, as necessary.
12. Inspect the base for cracks and wear. Replace the entire distributor assembly if the base is damaged.
    To install:
13. Position the stator assembly over the bushing and press down to seat.
14. Position the stator connector. The tab should fit in the notch on the base and the fastening eyelets should be aligned with the screw holes. Be sure the wires are positioned out of the way of moving parts.
15. Install the 2 stator retaining screws and tighten to 15-35 inch lbs. (1.7-4.0 Nm). Install the octane rod.
16. Apply a thin coat of clean engine oil to the distributor shaft below the armature. Insert the shaft into the distributor base.
17. Place a $1/2$ in. deep well socket over the distributor shaft, invert the assembly and place on the press plate.
18. Position the distributor drive gear on the end of distributor shaft, aligning the marks on the armature and gear. Make sure the holes in the shaft and drive gear are aligned, so the roll pin can be installed.
19. Place a $5/8$in. deep well socket over the shaft and gear and press the gear until the holes are aligned.

➡If the shaft and gear holes do not align, the gear must be removed and repressed. Do not attempt to use a drift punch to align the holes.

20. Drive a new roll pin through the gear and shaft.

21. Install the armature and tighten the screws to 25-35 inch lbs. (2.8-4.0 Nm).

22. Check that the distributor shaft moves freely over full rotation. If the armature contacts the stator, the entire distributor must be replaced.

23. Make sure the back of the TFI-IV module and and the distributor mounting face are clean. Apply silicone dielectric compound to the back of the module, spreading thinly and evenly.

24. Turn the distributor base upside down, so the stator connector is in full view.

25. Install the ignition rotor onto the distributor shaft. Install the distributor, as described in this Section.

6-4.9L ENGINES

1. Remove the distributor assembly from the engine; refer to the procedure in this Section.

2. Remove the ignition rotor from the distributor shaft.

3. Mark the armature and distributor drive gear with a felt tip pen or equivalent, to note their orientation. While holding the distributor gear, remove the 2 armature retaining screws and remove the armature.

➡**Do not hold the armature to loosen the screws.**

4. Use a suitable punch to remove the roll pin from the distributor drive gear; discard the roll pin.

5. Position the distributor upside down in a suitable press. Using a press plate and suitable driver, press off the distributor drive gear.

6. Remove the thrust washer and save it.

7. Use a file and/or emery paper to remove any burrs or deposits from the distributor shaft, that would keep the shaft from sliding freely from the distributor housing.

8. Remove the shaft assembly.

9. Remove the 2 stator assembly retaining screws.

10. Remove the octane rod and screw.

11. Remove the stator assembly.

12. Inspect the base bushing for wear or signs of excess heat concentration. If damage is evident, the entire distributor assembly must be replaced.

13. Inspect the base O-ring for cuts or damage and replace, as necessary.

14. Inspect the base for cracks and wear. Replace the entire distributor assembly if the base is damaged.

To install:

15. Position the stator assembly over the bushing and press down to seat.

16. Position the stator connector. The tab should fit in the notch on the base and the fastening eyelets should be aligned with the screw holes. Be sure the wires are positioned out of the way of moving parts.

17. Install the 2 stator retaining screws and tighten to 15-35 inch lbs. (1.7-4.0 Nm). Install the octane rod.

18. Apply a thin coat of clean engine oil to the distributor shaft below the armature. Insert the shaft into the distributor base. Install the thrust washer.

19. Place a 1/2 in. deep well socket over the distributor shaft, invert the assembly and place on the press plate.

20. Position the distributor drive gear on the end of the distributor shaft, aligning the marks on the armature and gear. Make sure the holes in the shaft and drive gear are aligned, so the roll pin can be installed.

21. Place a 5/8 in. deep well socket over the shaft and gear and press the gear until the holes are aligned.

➡**If the shaft and gear holes do not align, the gear must be removed and repressed. Do not attempt to use a drift punch to align the holes.**

22. Drive a new roll pin through the gear and shaft.

23. Install the armature and tighten the screws to 25-35 inch lbs. (2.8-4.0 Nm).

24. Check that the distributor shaft moves freely over full rotation. If the armature contacts the stator, the entire distributor must be replaced.

25. Make sure the back of the TFI-IV module and and the distributor mounting face are clean. Apply silicone dielectric compound to the back of the module, spreading thinly and evenly.

26. Turn the distributor base upside down, so the stator connector is in full view.

27. Install the ignition rotor onto the distributor shaft. Install the distributor, as described in this Section.

VACUUM DIAPHRAGM ASSEMBLY REPLACEMENT

1. Disconnect the diaphragm assembly vacuum hose(s).

2. Remove the C-clip securing the diaphragm rod to the base plate pin. Lift the diaphragm rod off the base plate pin.

3. Remove the 2 diaphragm assembly attaching screws and identification tag.

4. Remove the diaphragm assembly from the distributor base.

To install:

5. Adjust the new diaphragm assembly per manufacturer's instructions included with the new diaphragm.

6. Install the diaphragm on the distributor base. Attach the diaphragm assembly and identification tag to the distributor base with the 2 attaching screws and tighten to 15 inch lbs. (1.7 Nm).

7. Place diaphragm rod on the pin and install the C-clip.

8. Reconnect the vacuum hose(s).

Alternator

IDENTIFICATION

There are 4 different types of alternators found on the years and model ranges covered in this manual. They are:

1. Rear Terminal, External Regulator, External Fan Alternator

2. Side Terminal, Internal Regulator, External Fan Alternator

3. Leece-Neville 165 Ampere Alternator

4. Integral Rear Mount Regulator, Internal Fan Alternator

Rear Terminal, External Regulator, External Fan Alternator

This unit utilizes a separate, external electronic regulator. The regulator is non-adjustable. The rear terminal alternator was standard equipment on 1987 trucks, and can be found on some 1992 motor home chassis models equipped with the 7.3L diesel or 7.5L gasoline engine.

Side Terminal, Internal Regulator, External Fan Alternator

This unit was optional on 1987, standard on all 1988-92 models and standard on 1993 models equipped with the 6-4.9L and 8-7.5L engines. The regulator in integrated within the alternator body and is not adjustable.

Integral Rear Mount Regulator, Internal Fan Alternator

This alternator is standard equipment on all 1993 models equipped with 8-5.0L, 8-5.8L gasoline engines and 8-7.3L diesel engines.

Leece-Neville 165 Ampere Alternator

This unit is optional equipment on some 1989-93 trucks and ambulance packages. A separate, electronic, fully adjustable regulator is employed in this system.

OPERATION

The alternator charging system is a negative (-) ground system which consists of an alternator, a regulator, a charge indicator, a storage battery and wiring connecting the components, and fuse link wire.

The alternator is belt-driven from the engine. Energy is supplied from the alternator/regulator system to the rotating field through two brushes to two slip-rings. The slip-rings are mounted on the rotor shaft and are connected to the field coil. This energy supplied to the rotating field from the battery is called excitation current and is used to initially energize the field to begin the generation of electricity. Once the alternator starts to generate electricity, the excitation current comes from its own output rather than the battery.

The alternator produces power in the form of alternating current. The alternating current is rectified by 6 diodes into direct current. The direct current is used to charge the battery and power the rest of the electrical system.

When the ignition key is turned on, current flows from the battery, through the charging system indicator light on the instrument panel, to the voltage regulator, and to the alternator. Since the alternator is not producing any current, the alternator warning light comes on. When the engine is started, the alternator begins to produce current and turns the alternator light off. As the alternator turns and produces current, the current is divided in two ways: part to the battery to charge the battery and power the electrical components of the vehicle, and part is returned to the alternator to enable it to increase its output. In this situation, the alternator is receiving current from the battery and from itself. A voltage regulator is wired into the current supply to the alternator to prevent it from receiving too much current which would cause it to put out too much current. Conversely, if the voltage regulator does not allow the alternator to receive enough current, the battery will not be fully charged and will eventually go dead.

The battery is connected to the alternator at all times, whether the ignition key is turned on or not. If the battery were shorted to ground, the alternator would also be shorted. This would damage the alternator. To prevent this, a fuse link is installed in the wiring between the battery and the alternator. If the battery is shorted, the fuse link is melted, protecting the alternator.

ALTERNATOR PRECAUTIONS

To prevent damage to the alternator and regulator, the following precautions should be taken when working with the electrical system.

1. Never reverse the battery connections.
2. Booster batteries for starting must be connected properly: positive-to-positive and negative-to-ground.
3. Disconnect the battery cables before using a fast charger; the charger has a tendency to force current through the diodes in the opposite direction for which they were designed. This burns out the diodes.
4. Never use a fast charger as a booster for starting the vehicle.
5. Never disconnect the voltage regulator while the engine is running.
6. Avoid long soldering times when replacing diodes or transistors. Prolonged heat is damaging to AC generators.
7. Do not use test lamps of more than 12 volts (V) for checking diode continuity.
8. Do not short across or ground any of the terminals on the AC generator.
9. The polarity of the battery, generator, and regulator must be matched and considered before making any electrical connections within the system.
10. Never operate the alternator on an open circuit. Make sure that all connections within the circuit are clean and tight.
11. Disconnect the battery terminals when performing any service on the electrical system. This will eliminate the possibility of accidental reversal of polarity.
12. Disconnect the battery ground cable if arc welding is to be done on any part of the car.

CHARGING SYSTEM TROUBLESHOOTING

When performing charging system tests, turn off all lights and electrical components. Place the transmission in **P** and apply the parking brake.

To ensure accurate meter indications, the battery terminal posts and battery cable clamps must be clean and tight.

❊❊WARNING

Do not make jumper wire connections except as instructed. Incorrect jumper wire connections can damage the regulator or fuse links.

Preliminary Inspection

1. Make sure the battery cable connections are clean and tight.
2. Check all alternator and regulator wiring connections. Make sure all connections are clean and secure.
3. Check the alternator belt tension. Adjust, if necessary.
4. Check the fuse link between the starter relay and alternator. Replace if burned out.

5. Make sure the fuses/fuse links to the alternator are not burned or damaged. This could cause an open circuit or high resistance, resulting in erratic or intermittent charging problems.

6. If equipped with heated windshield, make sure the wiring connections to the alternator output control relay are correct and tight.

7. If equipped with heated windshield, make sure the connector to the heated windshield module is properly seated and there are no broken wires.

External Regulator Alternator

CHARGING SYSTEM INDICATOR LIGHT TEST

1. If the charging system indicator light does not come on with the ignition key in the **RUN** position and the engine not running, check the ignition switch-to-regulator I terminal wiring for an open circuit or burned out charging system indicator light. Replace the light, if necessary.

2. If the charging system indicator light does not come on, disconnect the electrical connector at the regulator and connect a jumper wire between the I terminal of the connector and the negative battery cable clamp.

3. The charging system indicator light should go on with the ignition switch in the **RUN** position.

4. If the light does not go on, check the light for continuity and replace, if necessary.

5. If the light is not burned out, there is an open circuit between the ignition switch and the regulator.

6. Check the 500 ohm resistor across the indicator light.

BASE VOLTAGE TEST

1. Connect the negative and positive leads of a voltmeter to the negative and positive battery cable clamps.

2. Make sure the ignition switch is in the **OFF** position and all electrical loads (lights, radio, etc.) are OFF.

3. Record the battery voltage shown on the voltmeter; this is the base voltage.

NO-LOAD TEST

1. Connect a suitable tachometer to the engine.

2. Start the engine and bring the engine speed to 1500 rpm. With no other electrical loads (doors closed, foot off the brake pedal), the reading on the voltmeter should increase, but no more than 2.5 volts above the base voltage.

➡The voltage reading should be taken when the voltage stops rising. This may take a few minutes.

3. If the voltage increases as in Step 2, perform the Load Test.

4. If the voltage continues to rise, perform the Over Voltage Tests.

5. If the voltage does not rise to the proper level, perform the Under Voltage Tests.

LOAD TEST

1. With the engine running, turn the blower speed switch to the high speed position and turn the headlights on to high beam.

2. Raise the engine speed to approximately 2000 rpm. The voltmeter reading should be a minimum of 0.5 volts above the base voltage. If not, perform the Under Voltage Tests.

➡If the voltmeter readings in the No-Load Test and Load Test are as specified, the charging system is operating properly. Go to the following tests if one or more of the voltage readings differs, and also check for battery drain.

OVER VOLTAGE TESTS

1. If the voltmeter reading was more than 2.5 volts above the base voltage in the No-Load Test, connect a jumper wire between the voltage regulator base and the alternator frame or housing. Repeat the No-Load Test.

2. If the over voltage condition disappears, check the ground connections on the alternator, regulator and from the engine to the dash panel and to the battery. Clean and securely tighten the connections.

3. If the over voltage condition still exists, disconnect the voltage regulator wiring connector from the voltage regulator. Repeat the No-Load Test.

4. If the over voltage condition disappears (voltmeter reads base voltage), replace the voltage regulator.

5. If the over voltage condition still exists with the voltage regulator wiring connector disconnected, check for a short between circuits A and F in the wiring harness and service, as necessary. Then reconnect the voltage regulator wiring connector.

UNDER VOLTAGE TESTS

1. If the voltage reading was not more than 0.5 volts above the base voltage, disconnect the wiring connector from the voltage regulator and connect an ohmmeter from the F terminal of the connector to ground. The ohmmeter should indicate more than 2.4 ohms.

2. If the ohmmeter reading is less than 2.4 ohms, service the grounded field circuit in the wiring harness or alternator and repeat the Load Test.

✳✳WARNING

Do not replace the voltage regulator before a shorted rotor coil or field circuit has been serviced. Damage to the regulator could result.

3. If the ohmmeter reading is more than 2.4 ohms, connect a jumper wire from the A to F terminals of the wiring connector and repeat the Load Test. If the voltmeter now indicates more than 0.5 volts above the base voltage, the regulator or wiring is damaged or worn. Perform the S and I Circuit Tests and service the wiring or regulator, as required.

4. If the voltmeter still indicates an under voltage problem, remove the jumper wire from the voltage regulator connector and leave the connector disconnected from the regulator.

5. Disconnect the FLD terminal on the alternator and pull back the protective cover from the BAT terminal. Connect a jumper wire between the FLD and BAT terminals and repeat the Load Test.

6. If the voltmeter indicates a 0.5 volts or more, increase above base voltage, perform the S and I Circuit Tests and service the wiring or regulator, as indicated.

7. If the voltmeter still indicates under voltage, shut the engine OFF and move the positive voltmeter lead to the BAT terminal of the alternator. If the voltmeter now indicates the base voltage, service the alternator. If the voltmeter indicates 0 volts, service the alternator-to-starter relay wire.

REGULATOR S AND I CIRCUIT TESTS

1. Disconnect the voltage regulator wiring connector and install a jumper wire between the A and F terminals.

2. With the engine idling and the negative voltmeter lead connected to the negative battery terminal, connect the positive voltmeter lead to the S terminal and then to the I terminal of the regulator wiring connector.

3. The S circuit voltage reading should be approximately ½ the I circuit reading. If the voltage readings are correct, remove the jumper wire. Replace the voltage regulator and repeat the Load Test.

4. If there is no voltage present, service the faulty wiring circuit. Connect the positive voltmeter lead to the positive battery terminal.

5. Remove the jumper wire from the regulator wiring connector and connect the connector to the regulator. Repeat the Load Test

FUSE LINK CONTINUITY

1. Make sure the battery is okay. (See Section 1)

2. Turn on the headlights or any accessory. If the headlights or accessory do not operate, the fuse link is probably burned out.

3. On some vehicles there are several fuse links. Proceed as in Step 2 to test other fuse links.

4. To test the fuse link that protects the alternator, check for voltage at the BAT terminal of the alternator, using a voltmeter. If there is no voltage, the fuse link is probably burned out.

Integral Regulator/External Fan Alternator

CHARGING SYSTEM INDICATOR LIGHT TEST

Two conditions can cause the charging system indicator light to come on when your truck is running: no alternator output, caused by a damaged alternator, regulator or wiring, or an over voltage condition, caused by a shorted alternator rotor, regulator or wiring.

In a normally functioning system, the charging system indicator light will be OFF when the ignition switch is in the OFF position, ON when the ignition switch is in the RUN position and the engine not running, and OFF when the ignition switch is in the RUN position and the engine is running.

1. If the charging system indicator light does not come on, disconnect the wiring connector from the regulator.

2. Connect a jumper wire between the connector I terminal and the negative battery cable clamp.

3. Turn the ignition switch to the RUN position, but leave the engine OFF. If the charging system indicator light does not come on, check for a light socket resistor. If there is a resistor, check the contact of the light socket leads to the flexible printed circuit. If they are good, check the indicator light for continuity and replace if burned out. If the light checks out good, perform the Regulator I Circuit Test.

4. If the indicator light comes on, remove the jumper wire and reconnect the wiring connector to the regulator. Connect

the negative voltmeter lead to the negative battery cable clamp and connect the positive voltmeter lead to the regulator A terminal screw. Battery voltage should be indicated. If battery voltage is not indicated, service the A circuit wiring.

5. If battery voltage is indicated, clean and tighten the ground connections to the engine, alternator and regulator. Tighten loose regulator mounting screws to 15-26 inch lbs. (1.7-2.8 Nm).

6. Turn the ignition switch to the RUN position with the engine OFF. If the charging system indicator light still does not come on, replace the regulator.

BASE VOLTAGE TEST

1. Connect the negative and positive leads of a voltmeter to the negative and positive battery cable clamps.

2. Make sure the ignition switch is in the OFF position and all electrical loads (lights, radio, etc.) are OFF.

3. Record the battery voltage shown on the voltmeter; this is the base voltage.

NO-LOAD TEST

1. Connect a suitable tachometer to the engine.

2. Start the engine and bring the engine speed to 1500 rpm. With no other electrical loads (doors closed, foot off the brake pedal), the reading on the voltmeter should increase, but no more than 2.5 volts above the base voltage.

➡**The voltage reading should be taken when the voltage stops rising. This may take a few minutes.**

3. If the voltage increases as in Step 2, perform the Load Test.

4. If the voltage continues to rise, perform the Over Voltage Tests.

5. If the voltage does not rise to the proper level, perform the Under Voltage Tests.

LOAD TEST

1. With the engine running, turn the blower speed switch to the high speed position and turn the headlights on to high beam.

2. Raise the engine speed to approximately 2000 rpm. The voltmeter reading should be a minimum of 0.5 volts above the base voltage. If not, perform the Under Voltage Tests.

➡**If the voltmeter readings in the No-Load Test and Load Test are as specified, the charging system is operating properly. Go to the following tests if one or more of the voltage readings differs, and also check for battery drain.**

OVER VOLTAGE TESTS

If the voltmeter reading was more than 2.5 volts above base voltage in the No-Load Test, proceed as follows:

1. Turn the ignition switch to the RUN position, but do not start the engine.

2. Connect the negative voltmeter lead to the alternator rear housing. Connect the positive voltmeter lead first to the alternator output connection at the starter solenoid and then to the regulator A screw head.

3. If there is greater than 0.5 volts difference between the 2 locations, service the A wiring circuit to eliminate the high resistance condition indicated by excessive voltage drop.

4. If the over voltage condition still exists, check for loose regulator and alternator grounding screws. Tighten loose regulator grounding screws to 15-26 inch lbs. (1.7-2.8 Nm).

5. If the over voltage condition still exists, connect the negative voltmeter lead to the alternator rear housing. With the ignition switch in the **OFF** position, connect the positive voltmeter lead first to the regulator A screw head and then to the regulator F screw head. If there are different voltage readings at the 2 screw heads, a malfunctioning grounded brush lead or a grounded rotor coil is indicated; service or replace the entire alternator/regulator unit.

6. If the same voltage is obtained at both screw heads in Step 5 and there is no high resistance in the ground of the A+ circuit, replace the regulator.

UNDER VOLTAGE TESTS

If the voltmeter reading was not more than 0.5 volts above base voltage, proceed as follows:

1. Disconnect the electrical connector from the regulator. Connect an ohmmeter between the regulator A and F terminal screws. The ohmmeter reading should be more than 2.4 ohms. If it is less than 2.4 ohms, the regulator has failed. also check the alternator for a shorted rotor or field circuit. Perform the Load Test after servicing.

❋❋WARNING

Do not replace the voltage regulator before a shorted rotor coil or field circuit has been serviced. Damage to the regulator could result.

2. If the ohmmeter reading is greater than 2.4 ohms, connect the regulator wiring connector and connect the negative voltmeter lead to the alternator rear housing. Connect the positive voltmeter lead to the regulator A terminal screw. The voltmeter should indicate battery voltage. If there is no voltage, service the A wiring circuit and then perform the Load Test.

3. If the voltmeter indicates battery voltage, connect the negative voltmeter lead to the alternator rear housing. With the ignition switch in the **OFF** position, connect the positive voltmeter lead to the regulator F terminal screw. The voltmeter should indicate battery voltage. If there is no voltage, there is an open field circuit in the alternator. Service or replace the alternator, then perform the Load Test after servicing.

4. If the voltmeter indicates battery voltage, connect the negative voltmeter lead to the alternator rear housing. Turn the ignition switch to the **RUN** position, leaving the engine off, and connect the positive voltmeter lead to the regulator F terminal screw. The voltmeter should read 1.5 volts or less. If more than 1.5 volts is indicated, perform the I circuit tests and service the I circuit if needed. If the I circuit is normal, replace the regulator, if needed, and perform the Load Test after servicing.

5. If 1.5 volts or less is indicated, disconnect the alternator wiring connector. Connect a set of 12 gauge jumper wires between the alternator B+ terminal blades and the mating wiring connector terminals. Perform the Load Test, but connect the positive voltmeter lead to one of the B+ jumper wire terminals. If the voltage increases more than 0.5 volts above base voltage, service the alternator-to-starter relay wiring. Repeat the Load Test, measuring voltage at the battery cable clamps after servicing.

6. If the voltage does not increase more than 0.5 volts above base voltage, connect a jumper wire from the alternator rear housing to the regulator F terminal. Repeat the Load Test with the positive voltmeter lead connected to one of the B+ jumper wire terminals. If the voltage increases more than 0.5 volts, replace the regulator. If the voltage does not increase more than 0.5 volts, service or replace the alternator.

REGULATOR S AND I CIRCUIT TEST

1. Disconnect the wiring connector from the regulator. Connect a jumper wire between the regulator A terminal and the wiring connector A lead and connect a jumper wire between the regulator F screw and the alternator rear housing.

2. With the engine idling and the negative voltmeter lead connected to the negative battery terminal, connect the positive voltmeter lead first to the S terminal and then to the I terminal of the regulator wiring connector.

3. The S circuit voltage should be approximately ½ that of the I circuit. If the voltage readings are correct, remove the jumper wire. Replace the regulator and connect the regulator wiring connector. Perform the Load Test.

4. If there is no voltage present, remove the jumper wire and service the faulty wiring circuit or alternator.

5. Connect the positive voltmeter lead to the positive battery terminal and connect the wiring connector to the regulator. Repeat the Load Test.

FUSE LINK CONTINUITY

1. Make sure the battery is okay (See Section 1).

2. Turn on the headlights or any accessory. If the headlights or accessory do not operate, the fuse link is probably burned out.

3. On some vehicles there are several fuse links. Proceed as in Step 2 to test other fuse links.

4. To test the fuse link that protects the alternator, check for voltage at the BAT terminal of the alternator and A terminal of the regulator, using a voltmeter. If there is no voltage, the fuse link is probably burned out.

FIELD CIRCUIT DRAIN

In all of the Field Circuit Drain test steps, connect the negative voltmeter lead to the alternator rear housing.

1. With the ignition switch in the **OFF** position, connect the positive voltmeter lead to the regulator F terminal screw. The voltmeter should read battery voltage if the system is operating normally. If less than battery voltage is indicated, go to Step 2.

2. Disconnect the wiring connector from the regulator and connect the positive voltmeter lead to the wiring connector I terminal. There should be no voltage indicated. If voltage is indicated, service the I lead from the ignition switch to identify and eliminate the voltage source.

3. If there was no voltage indicated in Step 2, connect the positive voltmeter lead to the wiring connector S terminal. No voltage should be indicated. If no voltage is indicated, replace the regulator.

4. If there was voltage indicated in Step 3, disconnect the wiring connector from the alternator rectifier connector. Connect the positive voltmeter lead to the regulator wiring connector S terminal. If voltage is indicated, service the S lead to the alternator connector to eliminate the voltage source. If no voltage is indicated, the alternator rectifier assembly is faulty.

Integral Regulator/Internal Fan Alternator

BASE VOLTAGE TEST

1. Connect the negative and positive leads of a voltmeter to the negative and positive battery cable clamps.
2. Make sure the ignition switch is in the **OFF** position and all electrical loads (lights, radio, etc.) are OFF.
3. Record the battery voltage shown on the voltmeter; this is the base voltage.

➡️**Turn the headlights ON for 10-15 seconds to remove any surface charge from the battery, then wait until the voltage stabilizes, before performing the base voltage test.**

NO-LOAD TEST

1. Connect a suitable tachometer to the engine.
2. Start the engine and bring the engine speed to 1500 rpm. With no other electrical loads (doors closed, foot off the brake pedal), the reading on the voltmeter should increase, but no more than 3 volts above the base voltage.

➡️**The voltage reading should be taken when the voltage stops rising. This may take a few minutes.**

3. If the voltage increases as in Step 2, perform the Load Test.
4. If the voltage continues to rise, perform the Over Voltage Tests.
5. If the voltage does not rise to the proper level, perform the Under Voltage Tests.

LOAD TEST

1. With the engine running, turn the blower speed switch to the high speed position and turn the headlights on to high beam.
2. Raise the engine speed to approximately 2000 rpm. The voltmeter reading should be a minimum of 0.5 volts above base voltage. If not, perform the Under Voltage Tests.

➡️**If the voltmeter readings in the No-Load Test and Load Test are as specified, the charging system is operating properly. Go to the following tests if one or more of the voltage readings differs, and also check for battery drain.**

OVER VOLTAGE TESTS

If the voltmeter reading was more than 3 volts above base voltage in the No-Load Test, proceed as follows:
1. Turn the ignition switch to the **RUN** position, but do not start the engine.
2. Connect the negative voltmeter lead to ground. Connect the positive voltmeter lead first to the alternator output connection at the starter solenoid (1992) or load distribution point (1993) and then to the regulator A screw head.
3. If there is greater than 0.5 volts difference between the 2 locations, service the A wiring circuit to eliminate the high resistance condition indicated by excessive voltage drop.
4. If the over voltage condition still exists, check for loose regulator and alternator grounding screws. Tighten loose regulator grounding screws to 16-24 inch lbs. (1.7-2.8 Nm).
5. If the over voltage condition still exists, connect the negative voltmeter lead to ground. Turn the ignition switch to the **OFF** position and connect the positive voltmeter lead first to the regulator A screw head and then to the regulator F screw

head. If there are different voltage readings at the 2 screw heads, a malfunctioning regulator grounded brush lead or a grounded rotor coil is indicated; replace the regulator/brush set or the entire alternator.
6. If the same voltage reading, battery voltage, is obtained at both screw heads in Step 5, then there is no short to ground through the alternator field/brushes. Replace the regulator.

UNDER VOLTAGE TESTS

If the voltmeter reading was not more than 0.5 volts above base voltage, proceed as follows:
1. Disconnect the wiring connector from the regulator and connect an ohmmeter between the regulator A and F terminal screws. The ohmmeter should read more than 2.4 ohms. If the ohmmeter reads less than 2.4 ohms, check the alternator for shorted rotor to field coil or for shorted brushes. Replace the brush holder or the entire alternator assembly. Perform the Load Test after replacement.

✳✳WARNING

Do not replace the regulator if a shorted rotor coil or field circuit has been diagnosed, or regulator damage could result. Replace the alternator assembly.

2. If the ohmmeter reading is greater than 2.4 ohms, connect the regulator wiring connector and connect the negative voltmeter lead to ground. Connect the positive voltmeter lead to the regulator A terminal screw; battery voltage should be indicated. If there is no voltage, service the A wiring circuit and then perform the Load Test.
3. If battery voltage is indicated in Step 2, connect the negative voltmeter lead to ground. Turn the ignition switch to the **OFF** position, then connect the positive voltmeter lead to the regulator F terminal screw. Battery voltage should be indicated on the voltmeter. If there is no voltage, replace the alternator and then perform the Load Test.
4. If battery voltage is indicated in Step 3, connect the negative voltmeter lead to ground. Turn the ignition switch to the **RUN** position, but leave the engine OFF. Connect the positive voltmeter lead to the regulator F terminal screw; the voltmeter reading should be 2 volts or less. If more than 2 volts is indicated, perform the I circuit tests and service the I circuit, if needed. If the I circuit tests normal, replace the regulator, if needed, then perform the Load Test.
5. If 2 volts or less is indicated in Step 4, perform the Load Test, but connect the positive voltmeter lead to the alternator output stud. If the voltage increases more than 0.5 volts above base voltage, service the alternator-to-starter relay (1992) or alternator-to-load distribution point (1993) wiring. Repeat the Load Test, measuring the voltage at the battery cable clamps after servicing.
6. If the voltage does not increase more than 0.5 volts above base voltage in Step 5, perform the Load Test and measure the voltage drop from the battery to the A terminal of the regulator (regulator connected). If the voltage drop exceeds 0.5 volts, service the wiring from the A terminal to the starter relay (1992) or load distribution point (1993).
7. If the voltage drop does not exceed 0.5 volts, connect a jumper wire from the alternator rear housing to the regulator F terminal. Repeat the Load Test with the positive voltmeter lead

connected to the alternator output stud. If the voltage increases more than 0.5 volts, replace the regulator. If voltage does not increase more than 0.5 volts, replace the alternator.

ALTERNATOR S CIRCUIT TEST

1. Disconnect the wiring connector from the regulator. Connect a jumper wire from the regulator A terminal to the wiring connector A lead. Connect a jumper wire from the regulator F screw to the alternator rear housing.
2. With the engine idling and the negative voltmeter lead connected to ground, connect the positive voltmeter lead first to the S terminal and then to the A terminal of the regulator wiring connector. The S circuit voltage should be approximately ½ the A circuit voltage. If the voltage readings are normal, remove the jumper wire, replace the regulator and connect the wiring connector. Repeat the Load Test.
3. If there is no voltage present, remove the jumper wire and service the damaged or worn wiring circuit or alternator.
4. Connect the positive voltmeter lead to the positive battery terminal. Connect the wiring connector to the regulator and repeat the Load Test.

FUSE LINK CONTINUITY

1. Make sure the battery is okay (See Section 1).
2. Turn on the headlights or any accessory. If the headlights or accessory do not operate, the fuse link is probably burned out.
3. On some vehicles there are several fuse links. Proceed as in Step 2 to test other fuse links.
4. To test the fuse link that protects the alternator, check for voltage at the BAT terminal of the alternator and A terminal of the regulator, using a voltmeter. If there is no voltage, the fuse link is probably burned out.

FIELD CIRCUIT DRAIN

In all of the Field Circuit Drain test steps, connect the negative voltmeter lead to the alternator rear housing.
1. With the ignition switch in the **OFF** position, connect the positive voltmeter lead to the regulator F terminal screw. The voltmeter should read battery voltage if the system is operating normally. If less than battery voltage is indicated, go to Step 2.
2. Disconnect the wiring connector from the regulator and connect the positive voltmeter lead to the wiring connector I terminal. There should be no voltage indicated. If voltage is indicated, service the I lead from the ignition switch to identify and eliminate the voltage source.
3. If there was no voltage indicated in Step 2, connect the positive voltmeter lead to the wiring connector S terminal. No voltage should be indicated. If no voltage is indicated, replace the regulator.
4. If there was voltage indicated in Step 3, disconnect the 1-pin S terminal connector. Again, connect the positive voltmeter lead to the regulator wiring connector S terminal. If voltage is indicated, service the S lead wiring to eliminate the voltage source. If no short is found, replace the alternator.

REMOVAL & INSTALLATION

▶ **See Figures 2 and 3**

1. Open the hood and disconnect the battery ground cable.

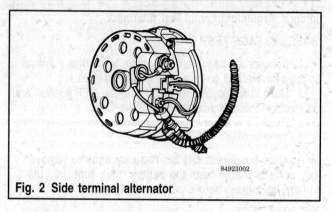

Fig. 2 Side terminal alternator

2. Remove the adjusting arm bolt.
3. Remove the alternator through-bolt. Remove the drive belt from the alternator pulley and lower the alternator.

➡**Some engines are equipped with a ribbed, K-section belt and automatic tensioner. A special tool must be made to remove the tension from the tensioner arm. Loosen the idler pulley pivot and adjuster bolts before using the tool. See the accompanying illustration for tool details.**

4. Label all of the leads to the alternator so that you can install them correctly and disconnect the leads from the alternator.
5. Remove the alternator from the vehicle.
6. To install, reverse the above procedure. Observe the following torques:
- Pivot bolt: 58 ft. lbs.
- Adjusting bolt: 25 ft. lbs.
- Wire terminal nuts: 60-90 inch lbs.

BELT TENSION ADJUSTMENT

The fan belt drives the alternator and water pump. If the belt is too loose, it will slip and the alternator will not be able to produce it rated current. Also, the water pump will not operate efficiently and the engine could overheat.

Check the tension of the belt by pushing your thumb down on the longest span of the belt, midway between the pulleys. Belt deflection should be approximately ½ in. (13mm). To adjust the belt tension, proceed as follows:
1. Loosen the alternator mounting bolt and the adjusting arm bolts.
2. Apply pressure on the alternator front housing only, moving the alternator away from the engine to tighten the belt. Do

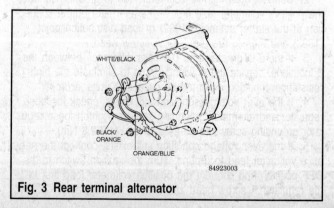

Fig. 3 Rear terminal alternator

not apply pressure to the rear of the cast aluminum housing of an alternator; damage to the housing could result.

3. Tighten the alternator mounting bolt and the adjusting arm bolts when the correct tension is reached.

Regulator

REMOVAL & INSTALLATION

Leece-Neville Alternator

The regulator is mounted on the back of the alternator.

1. Disconnect the diode trio lead from the regulator terminal.
2. Remove the 2 nuts retaining the regulator and the jumper leads.
3. Carefully pull the regulator from its holder.

➡ **The brushes will snap together when the regulator is removed. They can now be checked for length. Brush length minimum is 4.76mm (0.188 in.).**

To install:
4. Push the brushes back into their holders and insert a 1/32 inch pin through the hole provided in the housing. This will hold the brushes in place.
5. Carefully push the regulator into place and **just start** the retaining nuts. Remove the brush holding pin and **then** tighten the retaining nuts.
6. Connect the diode trio leads.

Rear Terminal Alternators

This unit is located on the fender liner, adjacent to the alternator.

1. Disconnect the battery ground.
2. Remove the regulator mounting screws.
3. Disconnect the wiring harness from the regulator.
4. Installation is the reverse of removal.

Starter Motor

TESTING

Place the transmission in **N** or **P**. Disconnect the vacuum line to the Thermactor® bypass valve, if equipped, before performing any cranking tests. After tests, run the engine for 3 minutes before connecting the vacuum line.

Starter Cranks Slowly

1. Connect jumper cables as shown in the Jump Starting procedure in Section 1. If, with the aid of the booster battery, the starter now cranks normally, check the condition of the battery. Recharge or replace the battery, as necessary. Clean the cables and battery posts and make sure connections are tight.
2. If Step 1 does not correct the problem, clean and tighten the connections at the starter relay and battery ground on the engine. You should not be able to rotate the eyelet terminals

easily, by hand. Also make sure the positive cable is not shorted to ground.

3. If the starter still cranks slowly, it must be replaced.

Starter Relay Operates But Starter Doesn't Crank

1. Connect jumper cables as shown in the Jump Starting procedure in Section 1. If, with the aid of the booster battery, the starter now cranks normally, check the condition of the battery. Recharge or replace the battery, as necessary. Clean the cables and battery posts and make sure connections are tight.
2. If Step 1 does not correct the problem, clean and tighten the connections at the starter and relay. Make sure the wire strands are secure in the eyelets.
3. On models with a fender mounted solenoid, if the starter still doesn't crank, it must be replaced.
4. On vehicles with starter mounted solenoid: Connect a jumper cable across terminals B and M of the starter solenoid. If the starter does not operate, replace the starter. If the starter does operate, replace the solenoid.

▓▓CAUTION

Making the jumper connections could cause a spark. Battery jumper cables or equivalent, should be used due to the high current in the starting system.

Starter Doesn't Crank — Relay Chatters or Doesn't Click

1. Connect jumper cables as shown in the Jump Starting procedure in Section 1. If, with the aid of the booster battery, the starter now cranks normally, check the condition of the battery. Recharge or replace the battery, as necessary. Clean the cables and battery posts and make sure connections are tight.
2. If Step 1 does not correct the problem, remove the push-on connector from the relay (red with blue stripe wire). Make sure the connection is clean and secure and the relay bracket is grounded.
3. If the connections are good, check the relay operation with a jumper wire. Remove the push-on connector from the relay and, using a jumper wire, jump from the now exposed terminal on the starter relay to the main terminal (battery side or battery positive post). If this corrects the problem, check the ignition switch, neutral safety switch and the wiring in the starting circuit for open or loose connections.
4. If a jumper wire across the relay does not correct the problem, replace the relay.

Start Spins But Doesn't Crank Engine

1. Remove the starter.
2. Check the armature shaft for corrosion and clean or replace, as necessary.
3. If there is no corrosion, replace the starter drive.

REMOVAL & INSTALLATION

▶ **See Figures 4, 5, 6 and 7**

Except Diesel

1. Disconnect the negative battery cable.

2. Raise the front of the truck and install jackstands beneath the frame. Firmly apply the parking brake and place blocks in back of the rear wheels.

3. Tag and disconnect the wiring at the starter.

4. Turn the front wheels fully to the right. On some later models it will be necessary to remove the frame brace. On many models, it will be necessary to remove the two bolts retaining the steering idler arm to the frame to gain access to the starter.

5. Remove the starter mounting bolts and remove the starter.

6. Reverse the above procedure to install. Observe the following torques:

- Mounting bolts: 12-15 ft. lbs. on starters with 3 mounting bolts and 15-20 ft. lbs. on starters with 2 mounting bolts.
- Idler arm retaining bolts to 28-35 ft. lbs. (if removed).

Make sure that the nut securing the heavy cable to the starter is snugged down tightly.

8-6.9L and 8-7.3L Diesel

1. Disconnect the battery ground cable.

2. Raise the vehicle and disconnect the cables and wires at the starter solenoid.

3. Turn the front wheels to the right and remove the two bolts attaching the steering idler arm to the frame.

4. Remove the starter mounting bolts and remove the starter.

5. Installation is the reverse of removal. Torque the mounting bolts to 20 ft. lbs.

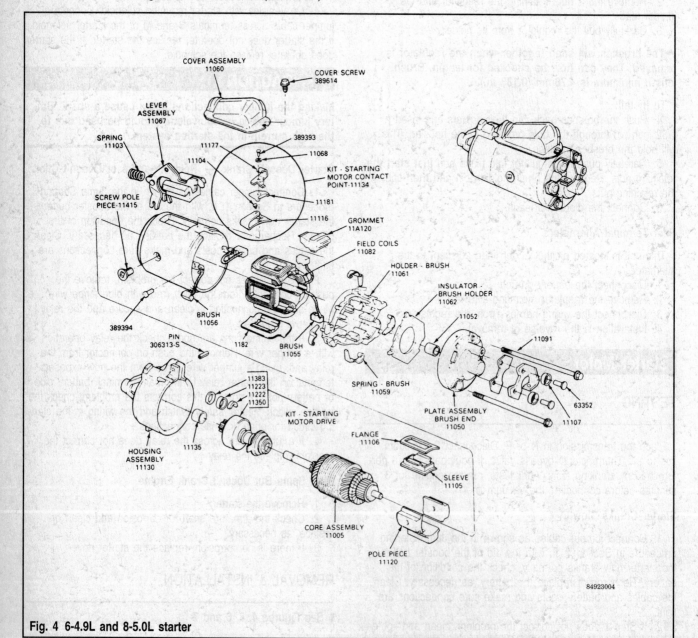

Fig. 4 6-4.9L and 8-5.0L starter

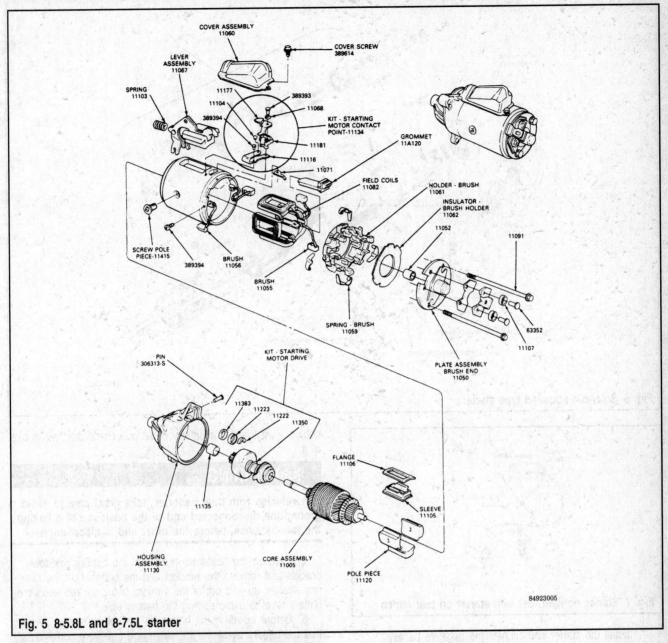

Fig. 5 8-5.8L and 8-7.5L starter

Starter Relay

REMOVAL & INSTALLATION

Fender Mounted Solenoid

1. Disconnect the positive battery cable from the battery terminal. With dual batteries, disconnect the connecting cable at both ends.

2. Remove the nut securing the positive battery cable to the relay.

3. Remove the positive cable and any other wiring under that cable.

4. Tag and remove the push-on wires from the front of the relay.

5. Remove the nut and disconnect the cable from the starter side of the relay.

6. Remove the relay attaching bolts and remove the relay.

7. Installation is the reverse of removal.

Starter Mounted Solenoid

1. Disconnect the negative battery cable.

2. Remove the starter.

3. Remove the positive brush connector from the solenoid M terminal.

4. Remove the solenoid retaining screws and remove the solenoid.

5. Attach the solenoid plunger rod to the slot in the lever and tighten the solenoid retaining screws to 45-54 inch lbs. (5.1-6.1 Nm).

6. Attach the positive brush connector to the solenoid M terminal and tighten the retaining nut to 80-120 inch lbs. (9.0-13.5 Nm).

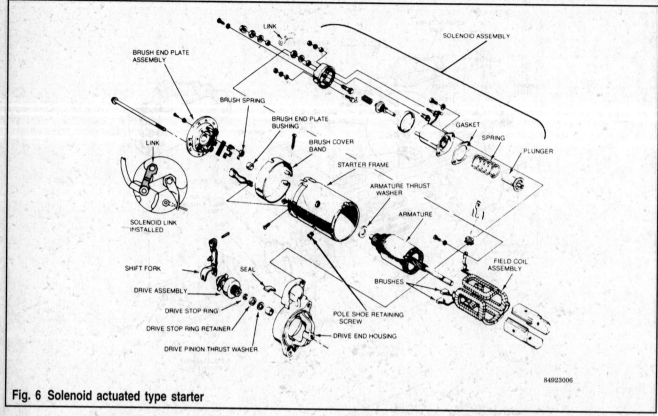

Fig. 6 Solenoid actuated type starter

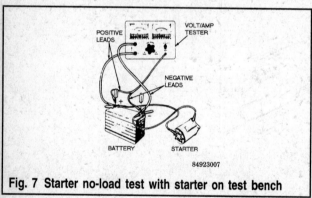

Fig. 7 Starter no-load test with starter on test bench

7. Install the starter and connect the negative battery terminal.

Battery

REMOVAL & INSTALLATION

1. Loosen the nuts which secure the cable ends to the battery terminals. Lift the negative battery cables from the terminals first with a twisting motion, then the positive

cables. If there is a battery cable puller available, make use of it.

✳✳WARNING

On vehicles with dual batteries, take great care to avoid ground the disconnected end of the positive cable linking the two batteries, before the other end is disconnected.

2. Remove the holddown nuts from the battery holddown bracket and remove the bracket and the battery. Lift the battery straight up and out of the vehicle, being sure to keep the battery level to avoid spilling the battery acid.

3. Before installing the battery in the vehicle, make sure that the battery terminals are clean and free from corrosion. Use a battery terminal cleaner on the terminals and on the inside of the battery cable ends. If a cleaner is not available, use coarse grade sandpaper to remove the corrosion. A mixture of baking soda and water poured over the terminals and cable ends will help remove and neutralize any acid buildup.

✳✳WARNING

Take great care to avoid getting any of the baking soda solution inside the battery. If any solution gets inside the battery a violent reaction will take place and/or the battery will be damaged.

4. Before installing the cables onto the terminals, cut a piece of felt cloth, or something similar into a circle about 3 in. (76mm) across. Cut a hole in the middle about the size of the battery terminals at their base. Push the cloth pieces over the terminals so that they lay flat on the top of the battery. Soak

the pieces of cloth with oil. This will keep oxidation to a minimum.

5. Place the battery in the vehicle. Install the cables onto the terminals.

✷✷WARNING

On vehicles with dual batteries, take great care to avoid grounding the disconnected end of the positive cable linking the two batteries, after the other end is connected.

6. Tighten the nuts on the cable ends.

➡See Section 1 for battery maintenance illustrations.

7. Smear a light coating of grease on the cable ends and tops of the terminals. This will further prevent the buildup of oxidation on the terminals and the cable ends.

8. Install and tighten the nuts of the battery holddown bracket.

Sending Units and Sensors

REMOVAL & INSTALLATION

Coolant Temperature Sender/Switch

1. Disconnect the negative battery cable.
2. Drain the cooling system into a suitable container.

✷✷CAUTION

When draining the coolant, keep in mind that cats and dogs are attracted by the ethylene glycol antifreeze, and are quite likely to drink any that is left in an uncovered container or in puddles on the ground. This will prove fatal in sufficient quantity. Always drain the coolant into a sealable container. Coolant should be reused unless it is contaminated or several years old.

3. Disconnect the electrical connector at the temperature sender/switch.
4. Remove the temperature sender/switch.
To install:
5. Apply pipe sealant or Teflon® tape to the threads of the new sender/switch.

ENGINE MECHANICAL

Engine Overhaul Tips

Most engine overhaul procedures are fairly standard. In addition to specific parts replacement procedures and complete specifications for your individual engine, this section also is a guide to accept rebuilding procedures. Examples of standard rebuilding practice are shown and should be used along with specific details concerning your particular engine.

Competent and accurate machine shop services will ensure maximum performance, reliability and engine life.

In most instances it is more profitable for the do-it-yourself mechanic to remove, clean and inspect the component, buy

6. Install the temperature sender/switch and connect the electrical connector.
7. Connect the negative battery cable. Fill the cooling system.
8. Run the engine and check for leaks.

Oil Pressure Sender/Switch

✷✷WARNING

The pressure switch used with the oil pressure warning light is not interchangeable with the sending unit used with the oil pressure gauge. If the incorrect part is installed the oil pressure indicating system will be inoperative and the sending unit or gauge will be damaged.

1. Disconnect the negative battery cable.
2. Disconnect the electrical connector and remove the oil pressure sender/switch.
To install:
3. Apply pipe sealant to the threads of the new sender/switch.
4. Install the oil pressure sender/switch and tighten to 9-11 ft. lbs. (12-16 Nm).
5. Connect the electrical connector to the sender/switch and connect the negative battery cable.
6. Run the engine and check for leaks and proper operation.

Low Oil Level Sensor

1. Disconnect the negative battery cable.
2. Raise and safely support the vehicle.
3. Drain at least 2 quarts of oil from the engine into a suitable container.
4. Disconnect the electrical connector from the sensor.
5. Remove the sensor using a 1 in. socket or wrench.
To install:
6. Install the sensor and tighten to 15-25 ft. lbs. (20-34 Nm).
7. Connect the electrical connector.
8. Tighten the oil pan drain plug. See the specifications chart at the end of this Section.
9. Lower the vehicle.
10. Add oil to the proper level.
11. Connect the negative battery cable, start the engine and check for leaks.

the necessary parts and deliver these to a shop for actual machine work.

On the other hand, much of the rebuilding work (crankshaft, block, bearings, piston rods, and other components) is well within the scope of the do-it-yourself mechanic.

TOOLS

The tools required for an engine overhaul or parts replacement will depend on the depth of your involvement. With a few exceptions, they will be the tools found in a mechanic's tool kit. More in-depth work will require any or all of the following:

• A dial indicator (reading in thousandths) mounted on a universal base
• Micrometers and telescope gauges
• Jaw and screw-type pullers
• Scraper
• Valve spring compressor
• Ring groove cleaner
• Piston ring expander and compressor
• Ridge reamer
• Cylinder hone or glaze breaker
• Plastigage®
• Engine stand

The use of most of these tools is illustrated in this section. Many can be rented for a one-time use from a local parts jobber or tool supply house specializing in automotive work.

Occasionally, the use of special tools is called for. See the information on Special Tools and Safety Notice in the front of this book before substituting another tool.

INSPECTION TECHNIQUES

Procedures and specifications are given in this section for inspecting, cleaning and assessing the wear limits of most major components. Other procedures such as Magnaflux® and Zyglo® can be used to locate material flaws and stress cracks. Magnaflux® is a magnetic process applicable only to ferrous materials. The Zyglo® process coats the material with a fluorescent dye penetrant and can be used on any material. Check for suspected surface cracks can be more readily made using spot check dye. The dye is sprayed onto the suspected area, wiped off and the area sprayed with a developer. Cracks will show up brightly.

OVERHAUL TIPS

Aluminum has become extremely popular for use in engines, due to its low weight. Observe the following precautions when handling aluminum parts:

• Never hot tank aluminum parts (the caustic hot tank solution will eat the aluminum.
• Remove all aluminum parts (identification tag, etc.) from engine parts prior to the tanking.
• Always coat threads lightly with engine oil or anti-seize compounds before installation, to prevent seizure.
• Never overtorque bolts or spark plugs especially in aluminum threads.

Stripped threads in any component can be repaired using any of several commercial repair kits (Heli-Coil® , Microdot® , Keenserts® , etc.).

When assembling the engine, any parts that will be frictional contact must be prelubed to provide lubrication at initial start-up. Any product specifically formulated for this purpose can be used, but engine oil is not recommended as a prelube.

When semi-permanent (locked, but removable) installation of bolts or nuts is desired, threads should be cleaned and coated with Loctite® or other similar, commercial non-hardening sealant.

REPAIRING DAMAGED THREADS

▶ **See Figures 8, 9, 10, 11 and 12**

Several methods of repairing damaged threads are available. Heli-Coil® (shown here), Keenserts® and Microdot® are among the most widely used. All involve basically the same principle — drilling out stripped threads, tapping the hole and installing a prewound insert — making welding, plugging and oversize fasteners unnecessary.

Two types of thread repair inserts are usually supplied: a standard type for most Inch Coarse, Inch Fine, Metric Course and Metric Fine thread sizes and a spark lug type to fit most spark plug port sizes. Consult the individual manufacturer's catalog to determine exact applications. Typical thread repair kits will contain a selection of prewound threaded inserts, a tap (corresponding to the outside diameter threads of the insert) and an installation tool. Spark plug inserts usually differ be-

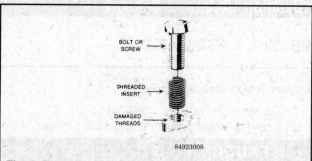
Fig. 8 Damaged bolt holes can be repaired with thread repair inserts

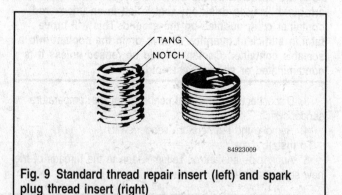
Fig. 9 Standard thread repair insert (left) and spark plug thread insert (right)

Fig. 10 Drill out the damaged threads with specified drill. Drill completely through the hole or to the bottom of a blind hole

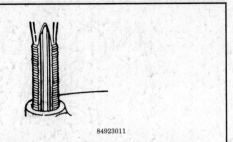

84923011

Fig. 11 With the tap supplied, tap the hole to receive the thread insert. Keep the tap well oiled and back it out frequently to avoid clogging the threads

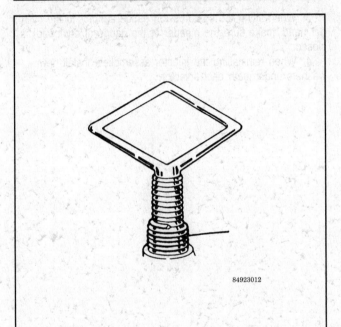

84923012

Fig. 12 Screw the threaded insert onto the installation tool until the tang engages the slot. Screw the insert into the tapped hole until it is ¼-½ turn below the top surface, after installation break off the tang with a hammer and punch

cause they require a tap equipped with pilot threads and a combined reamer/tap section. Most manufacturers also supply blister-packed thread repair inserts separately in addition to a master kit containing a variety of taps and inserts plus installation tools.

Before effecting a repair to a threaded hole, remove any snapped, broken or damaged bolts or studs. Penetrating oil can be used to free frozen threads. The offending item can be removed with locking pliers or with a screw or stud extractor. After the hole is clear, the thread can be repaired, as shown in the series of accompanying illustrations.

Checking Engine Compression

▶ **See Figures 13 and 14**

A noticeable lack of engine power, excessive oil consumption and/or poor fuel mileage measured over an extended pe-

riod are all indicators of internal engine war. Worn piston rings, scored or worn cylinder bores, blown head gaskets, sticking or burnt valves and worn valve seats are all possible culprits here. A check of each cylinder's compression will help you locate the problems.

As mentioned earlier, a screw-in type compression gauge is more accurate that the type you simply hold against the spark plug hole, although it takes slightly longer to use. It's worth it to obtain a more accurate reading. Follow the procedures below.

GASOLINE ENGINES

1. Warm up the engine to normal operating temperature.
2. Remove all the spark plugs.
3. Disconnect the high tension lead from the ignition coil.
4. On fully open the throttle either by operating the carburetor throttle linkage by hand or by having an assistant floor the accelerator pedal.
5. Screw the compression gauge into the No. 1 spark plug hole until the fitting is snug.

✳✳WARNING

Be careful not to crossthread the plug hole. On aluminum cylinder heads use extra care, as the threads in these heads are easily ruined.

6. Ask an assistant to depress the accelerator pedal fully on both carbureted and fuel injected vehicles. Then, while you read the compression gauge, ask the assistant to crank the engine two or three times in short bursts using the ignition switch.
7. Read the compression gauge at the end of each series of cranks, and record the highest of these readings. Repeat this procedure for each of the engine's cylinders. Compare the highest reading to the reading in each cylinder.

A cylinder's compression pressure is usually acceptable if it is not less than 80% of of the highest reading. For example, if the highest reading is 150 psi, the lowest should be no lower than 120 psi.

No cylinder should have a reading below 100 psi.

8. If a cylinder is unusually low, pour a tablespoon of clean engine oil into the cylinder through the spark plug hole and repeat the compression test. If the compression comes up after adding the oil, it appears that the cylinder's piston rings or bore are damaged or worn. If the pressure remains low, the

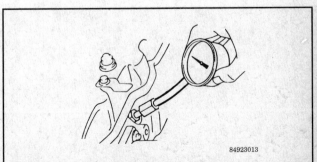

84923013

Fig. 13 The screw-in type compression gauge is more accurate

valves may not be seating properly (a valve job is needed), or the head gasket may be blown near that cylinder. If compression in any two adjacent cylinders is low, and if the addition of oil doesn't help the compression, there is leakage past the head gasket. Oil and coolant water in the combustion chamber can result from this problem. There may be evidence of water droplets on the engine dipstick when a head gasket has blown.

DIESEL ENGINES

Checking cylinder compression on diesel engines is basically the same procedure as on gasoline engines except for the following:

1. A special compression gauge adaptor suitable for diesel engines (because these engines have much greater compression pressures) must be used.

2. Remove the injector tubes and remove the injectors from each cylinder.

✳✳WARNING

Don't forget to remove the washer underneath each injector. Otherwise, it may get lost when the engine is cranked.

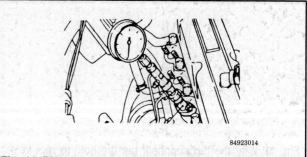

84923014

Fig. 14 Diesel engines require a special compression gauge adaptor

3. When fitting the compression gauge adaptor to the cylinder head, make sure the bleeder of the gauge (if equipped) is closed.

4. When reinstalling the injector assemblies, install new washers underneath each injector.

GENERAL ENGINE SPECIFICATIONS

Year	Engine ID/VIN	Engine Displacement Liters	Fuel System Type	Net Horsepower @ rpm	Net Torque @ rpm (ft. lbs.)	Bore × Stroke (in.)	Compression Ratio	Oil Pressure @ rpm
1987	B	4.9	EFI	120 @ 3200	245 @ 1600	4.00 × 3.98	8.4:1	40–60
	G	5.0	4-bbl	225 @ 3600	280 @ 2800	4.00 × 3.00	9.0:1	40–60
	N	5.0	EFI	170 @ 3800	275 @ 2800	4.00 × 3.00	8.9:1	40–60
	H	5.8	4-bbl	210 @ 4000	305 @ 2800	4.00 × 4.50	8.3:1	40–60
	1	6.9	Diesel	170 @ 3300	315 @ 1400	4.00 × 4.18	21.5:1	40–60
	L	7.5	4-bbl	225 @ 4000	365 @ 2800	4.36 × 3.85	8.0:1	40–65
1988	Y	4.9	EFI	150 @ 3400	265 @ 2000	4.00 × 3.98	8.8:1	40–60
	N	5.0	EFI	170 @ 3800	275 @ 2800	4.00 × 3.00	8.9:1	40–60
	H	5.8	EFI	210 @ 3800	315 @ 2800	4.00 × 3.50	8.8:1	40–60
	M	7.3	Diesel	180 @ 3300	345 @ 1400	4.11 × 4.18	21.5:1	40–70
	G	7.5	EFI	245 @ 4000	380 @ 2800	4.36 × 3.85	8.5:1	40–65
1989	Y	4.9	EFI	150 @ 3400	265 @ 2000	4.00 × 3.98	8.8:1	40–60
	N	5.0	EFI	170 @ 3800	275 @ 2800	4.00 × 3.00	8.9:1	40–60
	H	5.8	EFI	210 @ 3800	315 @ 2800	4.00 × 3.50	8.8:1	40–60
	M	7.3	Diesel	180 @ 3300	345 @ 1400	4.11 × 4.18	21.5:1	40–70
	G	7.5	EFI	245 @ 4000	380 @ 2800	4.36 × 3.85	8.5:1	40–65
1990	Y	4.9	EFI	150 @ 3400	265 @ 2000	4.00 × 3.98	8.8:1	40–60
	N	5.0	EFI	170 @ 3800	275 @ 2800	4.00 × 3.00	8.9:1	40–60
	H	5.8	EFI	210 @ 3800	315 @ 2800	4.00 × 3.50	8.8:1	40–60
	M	7.3	Diesel	180 @ 3300	345 @ 1400	4.11 × 4.18	21.5:1	40–70
	G	7.5	EFI	245 @ 4000	380 @ 2800	4.36 × 3.85	8.5:1	40–65
1991	Y	4.9	EFI	150 @ 3400	265 @ 2000	4.00 × 3.98	8.8:1	40–60
	N	5.0	EFI	170 @ 3800	275 @ 2800	4.00 × 3.00	8.9:1	40–60
	H	5.8	EFI	210 @ 3800	315 @ 2800	4.00 × 3.50	8.8:1	40–60
	M	7.3	Diesel	180 @ 3300	345 @ 1400	4.11 × 4.18	21.5:1	40–70
	G	7.5	EFI	245 @ 4000	380 @ 2800	4.36 × 3.85	8.5:1	40–65
1992	Y	4.9	EFI	150 @ 3400	265 @ 2000	4.00 × 3.98	8.8:1	40–60
	N	5.0	EFI	170 @ 3800	275 @ 2800	4.00 × 3.00	8.9:1	40–60
	H	5.8	EFI	210 @ 3800	315 @ 2800	4.00 × 3.50	8.8:1	40–60
	M	7.3	Diesel	180 @ 3300	345 @ 1400	4.11 × 4.18	21.5:1	40–70
	G	7.5	EFI	245 @ 4000	380 @ 2800	4.36 × 3.85	8.5:1	40–65
1993	Y	4.9	EFI	150 @ 3400	265 @ 2000	4.00 × 3.98	8.8:1	40–60
	N	5.0	EFI	170 @ 3800	275 @ 2800	4.00 × 3.00	8.9:1	40–60
	H	5.8	EFI	210 @ 3800	315 @ 2800	4.00 × 3.50	8.8:1	40–60
	R	5.8	EFI	250 @ 4000	340 @ 2800	4.00 × 3.50	9.0:1	40–60
	M	7.3	Diesel	180 @ 3300	345 @ 1400	4.11 × 4.18	21.5:1	40–70
	C	7.3	Diesel	180 @ 3000	360 @ 1600	4.11 × 4.18	21.5:1	40–70
	G	7.5	EFI	245 @ 4000	380 @ 2800	4.36 × 3.85	8.5:1	40–65

84923611

CAMSHAFT SPECIFICATIONS

All measurements given in inches.

Year	Engine ID/VIN	Engine Displacement Liters	Journal Diameter					Lobe Lift		Bearing Clearance	Camshaft End Play
			1	2	3	4	5	In.	Ex.		
1987	B	4.9	2.0175	2.0175	2.0175	2.0175	—	0.2490	0.2490	0.0020	0.004
	G	5.0	2.0810	2.0660	2.0510	2.0360	2.0210	0.2375	0.2474	0.0020	0.004
	N	5.0	2.0810	2.0660	2.0510	2.0360	2.0210	0.2375	0.2474	0.0020	0.004
	H	5.8	2.0810	2.0660	2.0510	2.0360	2.0210	0.2600	0.2600	0.0020	0.004
	1	6.9	2.0995	2.0995	2.0995	2.0995	2.0995	0.2535	0.2535	0.0030	0.005
	L	7.5	2.1243	2.1243	2.1243	2.1243	2.1243	0.2520	0.2780	0.0020	0.004
1988	Y	4.9	2.0175	2.0175	2.0175	2.0175	—	0.2490	0.2490	0.0020	0.004
	N	5.0	2.0810	2.0660	2.0510	2.0360	2.0210	0.2375	0.2474	0.0020	0.004
	H	5.8	2.0810	2.0660	2.0510	2.0360	2.0210	0.2600	0.2600	0.0020	0.004
	M	7.3	2.0995	2.0995	2.0995	2.0995	2.0995	0.2535	0.2530	0.0025	0.005
	G	7.5	2.1243	2.1243	2.1243	2.1243	2.1243	0.2520	0.2780	0.0020	0.004
1989	Y	4.9	2.0175	2.0175	2.0175	2.0175	—	0.2490①	0.2490①	0.0020	0.004
	N	5.0	2.0810	2.0660	2.0510	2.0360	2.0210	0.2375	0.2474	0.0020	0.004
	H	5.8	2.0810	2.0660	2.0510	2.0360	2.0210	0.2780	0.2830	0.0020	0.004
	M	7.3	2.0995	2.0995	2.0995	2.0995	2.0995	0.2535	0.2530	0.0025	0.005
	G	7.5	2.1243	2.1243	2.1243	2.1243	2.1243	0.2520	0.2780	0.0020	0.004
1990	Y	4.9	2.0175	2.0175	2.0175	2.0175	—	0.2490①	0.2490①	0.0020	0.004
	N	5.0	2.0810	2.0660	2.0510	2.0360	2.0210	0.2375	0.2474	0.0020	0.004
	H	5.8	2.0810	2.0660	2.0510	2.0360	2.0210	0.2780	0.2830	0.0020	0.004
	M	7.3	2.0995	2.0995	2.0995	2.0995	2.0995	0.2535	0.2530	0.0025	0.005
	G	7.5	2.1243	2.1243	2.1243	2.1243	2.1243	0.2520	0.2780	0.0020	0.004
1991	Y	4.9	2.0175	2.0175	2.0175	2.0175	—	0.2490①	0.2490①	0.0020	0.004
	N	5.0	2.0810	2.0660	2.0510	2.0360	2.0210	0.2375	0.2474	0.0020	0.004
	H	5.8	2.0810	2.0660	2.0510	2.0360	2.0210	0.2780	0.2830	0.0020	0.004
	M	7.3	2.0995	2.0995	2.0995	2.0995	2.0995	0.2535	0.2530	0.0025	0.005
	G	7.5	2.1243	2.1243	2.1243	2.1243	2.1243	0.2520	0.2780	0.0020	0.004
1992	Y	4.9	2.0175	2.0175	2.0175	2.0175	—	0.2490①	0.2490①	0.0020	0.004
	N	5.0	2.0810	2.0660	2.0510	2.0360	2.0210	0.2375	0.2474	0.0020	0.004
	H	5.8	2.0810	2.0660	2.0510	2.0360	2.0210	0.2780	0.2830	0.0020	0.004
	M	7.3	2.1020	2.1020	2.1020	2.1020	2.1020	0.2535	0.2530	0.0020	0.006
	G	7.5	2.1243	2.1243	2.1243	2.1243	2.1243	0.2520	0.2780	0.0020	0.004
1993	Y	4.9	2.0175	2.0175	2.0175	2.0175	—	0.2490①	0.2490①	0.0020	0.004
	N	5.0	2.0805	2.0655	2.0505	2.0355	2.0205	0.2375	0.2474	0.0020	0.004
	H	5.8	2.0815	2.0665	2.0515	2.0365	2.0215	0.2780	0.2830	0.0020	0.004
	R	5.8	2.0815	2.0665	2.0515	2.0365	2.0215	0.2600	0.2780	0.0020	0.004
	M	7.3	2.1020	2.1020	2.1020	2.1020	2.1020	0.2535	0.2530	0.0020	0.006
	C	7.3	2.1020	2.1020	2.1020	2.1020	2.1020	0.2535	0.2530	0.0020	0.006
	G	7.5	2.1243	2.1243	2.1243	2.1243	2.1243	0.2520	0.2780	0.0020	0.004

① F-150 4x2 w/2.47:1 or 2.75:1 axle & manual
transmission, 49 states: 0.2470

84923612

CRANKSHAFT AND CONNECTING ROD SPECIFICATIONS

All measurements are given in inches.

| Year | Engine ID/VIN | Engine Displacement Liters | Crankshaft | | | | Connecting Rod | | |
			Main Brg. Journal Dia.	Main Brg. Oil Clearance	Shaft End-play	Thrust on No.	Journal Diameter	Oil Clearance	Side Clearance
1987	B	4.9	2.3982–2.3990	0.0008–0.0015	0.004–0.008	5	2.1228–2.1236	0.0008–0.0015	0.0060–0.0130
	G	5.0	2.2482–2.2490	①	0.004–0.008	3	2.1228–2.1236	0.0008–0.0015	0.0100–0.0200
	N	5.0	2.2482–2.2490	①	0.004–0.008	3	2.1228–2.1236	0.0008–0.0015	0.0100–0.0200
	H	5.8	2.9994–3.0002	①	0.004–0.008	3	2.3103–2.3111	0.0008–0.0015	0.0100–0.0200
	1	6.9	3.1228–3.1236	0.0018–0.0036	0.002–0.009	3	2.4980–2.4990	0.0011–0.0026	0.0120–0.0240
	L	7.5	2.9994–3.0002	0.0008–0.0015	0.004–0.008	3	2.4992–2.5000	0.0008–0.0015	0.0100–0.0200
1988	Y	4.9	2.3982–2.3990	0.0008–0.0015	0.004–0.008	5	2.1228–2.1236	0.0008–0.0015	0.0060–0.0130
	N	5.0	2.2482–2.2490	①	0.004–0.008	3	2.1228–2.1236	0.0008–0.0015	0.0100–0.0200
	H	5.8	2.9994–3.0002	①	0.004–0.008	3	2.3103–2.3111	0.0008–0.0015	0.0100–0.0200
	M	7.3	3.1228–3.1236	0.0018–0.0036	0.002–0.009	3	2.4980–2.4990	0.0011–0.0036	0.0120–0.0240
	G	7.5	2.9994–3.0002	0.0008–0.0015	0.004–0.008	3	2.4992–2.5000	0.0008–0.0015	0.0100–0.0200
1989	Y	4.9	2.3982–2.3990	0.0008–0.0015	0.004–0.008	5	2.1228–2.1236	0.0008–0.0015	0.0060–0.0130
	N	5.0	2.2482–2.2490	①	0.004–0.008	3	2.1228–2.1236	0.0008–0.0015	0.0100–0.0200
	H	5.8	2.9994–3.0002	①	0.004–0.008	3	2.3103–2.3111	0.0008–0.0015	0.0100–0.0200
	M	7.3	3.1228–3.1236	0.0018–0.0036	0.002–0.009	3	2.4980–2.4990	0.0011–0.0036	0.0120–0.0240
	G	7.5	2.9994–3.0002	0.0008–0.0015	0.004–0.008	3	2.4992–2.5000	0.0008–0.0015	0.0100–0.0200
1990	Y	4.9	2.3982–2.3990	0.0008–0.0015	0.004–0.008	5	2.1228–2.1236	0.0008–0.0015	0.0060–0.0130
	N	5.0	2.2482–2.2490	①	0.004–0.008	3	2.1228–2.1236	0.0008–0.0015	0.0100–0.0200
	H	5.8	2.9994–3.0002	①	0.004–0.008	3	2.3103–2.3111	0.0008–0.0015	0.0100–0.0200
	M	7.3	3.1228–3.1236	0.0018–0.0036	0.002–0.009	3	2.4980–2.4990	0.0011–0.0036	0.0120–0.0240
	G	7.5	2.9994–3.0002	0.0008–0.0015	0.004–0.008	3	2.4992–2.5000	0.0008–0.0015	0.0100–0.0200
1991	Y	4.9	2.3982–2.3990	0.0008–0.0015	0.004–0.008	5	2.1228–2.1236	0.0008–0.0015	0.0060–0.0130
	N	5.0	2.2482–2.2490	①	0.004–0.008	3	2.1228–2.1236	0.0008–0.0015	0.0100–0.0200

84923613

CRANKSHAFT AND CONNECTING ROD SPECIFICATIONS

All measurements are given in inches.

Year	Engine ID/VIN	Engine Displacement Liters	Crankshaft				Connecting Rod		
			Main Brg. Journal Dia.	Main Brg. Oil Clearance	Shaft End-play	Thrust on No.	Journal Diameter	Oil Clearance	Side Clearance
1991	H	5.8	2.9994–3.0002	①	0.004–0.008	3	2.3103–2.3111	0.0008–0.0015	0.0100–0.0200
	M	7.3	3.1228–3.1236	0.0018–0.0036	0.003–0.009	3	2.4980–2.4990	0.0011–0.0036	0.0120–0.0240
	G	7.5	2.9994–3.0002	0.0008–0.0015	0.004–0.008	3	2.4992–2.5000	0.0008–0.0015	0.0100–0.0200
1992	Y	4.9	2.3982–2.3990	0.0008–0.0015	0.004–0.008	5	2.1228–2.1236	0.0008–0.0015	0.0060–0.0130
	N	5.0	2.2482–2.2490	②	0.004–0.008	3	2.1228–2.1236	0.0008–0.0015	0.0100–0.0200
	H	5.8	2.9994–3.0002	②	0.004–0.008	3	2.3103–2.3111	0.0008–0.0015	0.0100–0.0200
	M	7.3	3.1228–3.1236	0.0018–0.0036	0.003–0.009	3	2.4980–2.4990	0.0011–0.0036	0.0120–0.0240
	G	7.5	2.9994–3.0002	0.0008–0.0015	0.004–0.008	3	2.4992–2.5000	0.0008–0.0015	0.0100–0.0200
1993	Y	4.9	2.3982–2.3990	0.0008–0.0015	0.004–0.008	5	2.1228–2.1236	0.0008–0.0015	0.0060–0.0130
	N	5.0	2.2482–2.2490	②	0.004–0.008	3	2.1228–2.1236	0.0008–0.0015	0.0100–0.0200
	H	5.8	2.9994–3.0002	②	0.004–0.008	3	2.3103–2.3111	0.0008–0.0015	0.0100–0.0200
	R	5.8	2.9994–3.0002	②	0.004–0.008	3	2.3103–2.3111	0.0008–0.0015	0.0100–0.0200
	M	7.3	3.1228–3.1236	0.0018–0.0036	0.003–0.009	3	2.4980–2.4990	0.0011–0.0036	0.0120–0.0240
	C	7.3	3.1228–3.1236	0.0018–0.0036	0.003–0.009	3	2.4980–2.4990	0.0011–0.0036	0.0120–0.0240
	G	7.5	2.9994–3.0002	0.0008–0.0015	0.004–0.008	3	2.4992–2.5000	0.0008–0.0015	0.0100–0.0200

① No. 1: 0.0001–0.0015
 All others: 0.0005–0.0015
② No. 1: 0.0001–0.0015
 All others: 0.0008–0.0015

84923614

VALVE SPECIFICATIONS

Year	Engine ID/VIN	Engine Displacement Liters	Seat Angle (deg.)	Face Angle (deg.)	Spring Test Pressure (lbs. @ in.)	Spring Installed Height (in.)	Stem-to-Guide Clearance (in.)		Stem Diameter (in.)	
							Intake	Exhaust	Intake	Exhaust
1987	B	4.9	45	44	①	②	0.0010–0.0027	0.0010–0.0027	0.3416–0.3423	0.3416–0.3423
	G	5.0	45	44	③	⑤	0.0010–0.0027	0.0015–0.0032	0.3416–0.3423	0.3411–0.3418
	N	5.0	45	44	③	⑤	0.0010–0.0027	0.0015–0.0032	0.3416–0.3423	0.3411–0.3418
	H	5.8	45	44	200 @ 1.20	⑥	0.0010–0.0027	0.0015–0.0032	0.3416–0.3423	0.3411–0.3418
	1	6.9	⑦	⑦	80 @ 1.833	⑧	0.0012–0.0029	0.0012–0.0029	0.3717–0.3724	0.3717–0.3724
	L	7.5	45	44	229 @ 1.330	1.813	0.0010–0.0027	0.0010–0.0027	0.3415–0.3423	0.3415–0.3423
1988	Y	4.9	45	44	①	②	0.0010–0.0027	0.0010–0.0027	0.3416–0.3423	0.3416–0.3423
	N	5.0	45	44	③	④	0.0010–0.0027	0.0015–0.0032	0.3416–0.3423	0.3411–0.3418
	H	5.8	45	44	200 @ 1.20	⑥	0.0010–0.0027	0.0015–0.0032	0.3416–0.3423	0.3411–0.3418
	M	7.3	⑦	⑦	80 @ 1.833	⑧	0.0055	0.0055	0.3717–0.3724	0.3717–0.3724
	G	7.5	45	44	229 @ 1.330	1.813	0.0010–0.0027	0.0010–0.0027	0.3415–0.3423	0.3415–0.3423
1989	Y	4.9	45	44	①	②	0.0010–0.0027	0.0010–0.0027	0.3416–0.3423	0.3416–0.3423
	N	5.0	45	44	③	④	0.0010–0.0027	0.0015–0.0032	0.3416–0.3423	0.3411–0.3418
	H	5.8	45	44	200 @ 1.20	⑥	0.0010–0.0027	0.0015–0.0032	0.3416–0.3423	0.3411–0.3418
	M	7.3	⑦	⑦	80 @ 1.833	⑧	0.0055	0.0055	0.3717–0.3724	0.3717–0.3724
	G	7.5	45	44	229 @ 1.330	1.813	0.0010–0.0027	0.0010–0.0027	0.3415–0.3423	0.3415–0.3423
1990	Y	4.9	45	44	①	②	0.0010–0.0027	0.0010–0.0027	0.3416–0.3423	0.3416–0.3423
	N	5.0	45	44	③	④	0.0010–0.0027	0.0015–0.0032	0.3416–0.3423	0.3411–0.3418
	H	5.8	45	44	200 @ 1.20	⑥	0.0010–0.0027	0.0015–0.0032	0.3416–0.3423	0.3411–0.3418
	M	7.3	⑦	⑦	80 @ 1.833	⑧	0.0055	0.0055	0.3717–0.3724	0.3717–0.3724
	G	7.5	45	44	229 @ 1.330	1.813	0.0010–0.0027	0.0010–0.0027	0.3415–0.3423	0.3415–0.3423
1991	Y	4.9	45	44	①	②	0.0010–0.0027	0.0010–0.0027	0.3416–0.3423	0.3416–0.3423
	N	5.0	45	44	③	④	0.0010–0.0027	0.0015–0.0032	0.3416–0.3423	0.3411–0.3418

84923615

VALVE SPECIFICATIONS

Year	Engine ID/VIN	Engine Displacement Liters	Seat Angle (deg.)	Face Angle (deg.)	Spring Test Pressure (lbs. @ in.)	Spring Installed Height (in.)	Stem-to-Guide Clearance (in.)		Stem Diameter (in.)	
							Intake	Exhaust	Intake	Exhaust
1991	H	5.8	45	44	200 @ 1.20	⑥	0.0010–0.0027	0.0015–0.0032	0.3416–0.3423	0.3411–0.3418
	M	7.3	⑦	⑦	80 @ 1.833	⑧	0.0055	0.0055	0.3717–0.3724	0.3717–0.3724
	G	7.5	45	44	229 @ 1.330	1.813	0.0010–0.0027	0.0010–0.0027	0.3415–0.3423	0.3415–0.3423
1992	Y	4.9	45	44	①	②	0.0010–0.0027	0.0010–0.0027	0.3416–0.3423	0.3416–0.3423
	N	5.0	45	44	③	④	0.0010–0.0027	0.0015–0.0032	0.3416–0.3423	0.3411–0.3418
	H	5.8	45	44	200 @ 1.20	⑥	0.0010–0.0027	0.0015–0.0032	0.3416–0.3423	0.3411–0.3418
	M	7.3	⑦	⑦	80 @ 1.833	⑧	0.0055	0.0055	0.3717–0.3724	0.3717–0.3724
	G	7.5	45	44	229 @ 1.330	1.813	0.0010–0.0027	0.0010–0.0027	0.3415–0.3423	0.3415–0.3423
1993	Y	4.9	45	44	①	②	0.0010–0.0027	0.0010–0.0027	0.3416–0.3423	0.3416–0.3423
	N	5.0	45	44	③	⑨	0.0010–0.0027	0.0015–0.0032	0.3416–0.3423	0.3410–0.3418
	H	5.8	45	44	200 @ 1.20	⑨	0.0010–0.0027	0.0015–0.0032	0.3416–0.3423	0.3410–0.3418
	R	5.8	45	44	200 @ 1.20	⑨	0.0010–0.0027	0.0015–0.0032	0.3416–0.3423	0.3410–0.3418
	M	7.3	⑦	⑦	80 @ 1.833	⑧	0.0055	0.0055	0.3717–0.3724	0.3717–0.3724
	C	7.3	⑦	⑦	80 @ 1.833	⑧	0.0055	0.0055	0.3717–0.3724	0.3717–0.3724
	G	7.5	45	44	229 @ 1.330	1.813	0.0010–0.0027	0.0010–0.0027	0.3415–0.3423	0.3415–0.3423

① Intake: 166–184 @ 1.240
  Exhaust: 166–184 @ 1.070
② Intake: 1.640
  Exhaust: 1.470
③ Intake: 196–212 @ 1.360
  Exhaust: 190–210 @ 1.200
④ Intake: 1.78
  Exhaust: 1.60
⑤ Intake: 1.6885
  Exhaust: 1.594
⑥ Intake: 1.782
  Exhaust: 1.594
⑦ Intake: 30
  Exhaust: 37.5
⑧ Intake: 1.767
  Exhaust: 1.833
⑨ Intake: 1.780
  Exhaust: 1.610

84923616

PISTON AND RING SPECIFICATIONS

All measurements are given in inches.

Year	Engine ID/VIN	Engine Displacement Liters	Piston Clearance	Ring Gap			Ring Side Clearance		
				Top Compression	Bottom Compression	Oil Control	Top Compression	Bottom Compression	Oil Control
1987	B	4.9	0.0010–0.0018	0.0100–0.0200	0.0100–0.0200	0.015–0.055	0.0019–0.0036	0.0020–0.0040	Snug
	G	5.0	0.0013–0.0030	0.0100–0.0200	0.0100–0.0200	0.015–0.055	0.0013–0.0033	0.0020–0.0040	Snug
	N	5.0	0.0013–0.0030	0.0100–0.0200	0.0100–0.0200	0.015–0.055	0.0013–0.0033	0.0020–0.0040	Snug
	H	5.8	0.0013–0.0030	0.0100–0.0200	0.0100–0.0200	0.015–0.055	0.0013–0.0033	0.0020–0.0040	Snug
	1	6.9	0.0055–0.0065	0.0140–0.0240	0.0600–0.0700	0.0100–0.0240	0.0020–0.0040	0.0020–0.0040	0.0010–0.0030
	L	7.5	0.0022–0.0030	0.0100–0.0200	0.0100–0.0200	0.0100–0.0350	0.0025–0.0045	0.0025–0.0045	Snug
1988	Y	4.9	0.0010–0.0018	0.0100–0.0200	0.0100–0.0200	0.015–0.055	0.0019–0.0036	0.0020–0.0040	Snug
	N	5.0	0.0013–0.0030	0.0100–0.0200	0.0100–0.0200	0.015–0.055	0.0013–0.0033	0.0020–0.0040	Snug
	H	5.8	0.0013–0.0030	0.0100–0.0200	0.0100–0.0200	0.015–0.055	0.0013–0.0033	0.0020–0.0040	Snug
	M	7.3	0.0055–0.0065	0.0140–0.0240	0.0600–0.0700	0.0100–0.0240	0.0020–0.0040	0.0020–0.0040	0.0010–0.0030
	G	7.5	0.0022–0.0030	0.0100–0.0200	0.0100–0.0200	0.0100–0.0350	0.0025–0.0045	0.0025–0.0045	Snug
1989	Y	4.9	0.0010–0.0018	0.0100–0.0200	0.0100–0.0200	0.015–0.055	0.0019–0.0036	0.0020–0.0040	Snug
	N	5.0	0.0013–0.0030	0.0100–0.0200	0.0100–0.0200	0.015–0.055	0.0013–0.0033	0.0020–0.0040	Snug
	H	5.8	0.0013–0.0030	0.0100–0.0200	0.0100–0.0200	0.015–0.055	0.0013–0.0033	0.0020–0.0040	Snug
	M	7.3	①	0.0130–0.0450	0.0600–0.0850	0.0100–0.0240	0.0020–0.0040	0.0020–0.0040	0.0010–0.0030
	G	7.5	0.0022–0.0030	0.0100–0.0200	0.0100–0.0200	0.0100–0.0350	0.0025–0.0045	0.0025–0.0045	Snug
1990	Y	4.9	0.0010–0.0018	0.0100–0.0200	0.0100–0.0200	0.015–0.055	0.0019–0.0036	0.0020–0.0040	Snug
	N	5.0	0.0013–0.0030	0.0100–0.0200	0.0100–0.0200	0.015–0.055	0.0013–0.0033	0.0020–0.0040	Snug
	H	5.8	0.0013–0.0030	0.0100–0.0200	0.0100–0.0200	0.015–0.055	0.0013–0.0033	0.0020–0.0040	Snug
	M	7.3	①	0.0130–0.0450	0.0600–0.0850	0.0100–0.0240	0.0020–0.0040	0.0020–0.0040	0.0010–0.0030
	G	7.5	0.0022–0.0030	0.0100–0.0200	0.0100–0.0200	0.0100–0.0350	0.0025–0.0045	0.0025–0.0045	Snug
1991	Y	4.9	0.0010–0.0018	0.0100–0.0200	0.0100–0.0200	0.015–0.055	0.0019–0.0036	0.0020–0.0040	Snug
	N	5.0	0.0014–0.0022	0.0100–0.0200	0.0100–0.0200	0.015–0.055	0.0013–0.0033	0.0020–0.0040	Snug
	H	5.8	0.0014–0.0022	0.0100–0.0200	0.0100–0.0200	0.015–0.055	0.0020–0.0040	0.0020–0.0040	Snug

84923617

PISTON AND RING SPECIFICATIONS

All measurements are given in inches.

| Year | Engine ID/VIN | Engine Displacement Liters | Piston Clearance | Ring Gap | | | Ring Side Clearance | | |
				Top Compression	Bottom Compression	Oil Control	Top Compression	Bottom Compression	Oil Control
1991	M	7.3	①	0.0130–0.0450	0.0600–0.0850	0.0100–0.0240	0.0020–0.0040	0.0020–0.0040	0.0010–0.0030
	G	7.5	0.0022–0.0030	0.0100–0.0200	0.0100–0.0200	0.0100–0.0350	0.0025–0.0045	0.0025–0.0045	Snug
1992	Y	4.9	0.0010–0.0018	0.0100–0.0200	0.0100–0.0200	0.015–0.055	0.0019–0.0036	0.0020–0.0040	Snug
	N	5.0	0.0014–0.0022	0.0100–0.0200	0.0100–0.0200	0.015–0.055	0.0013–0.0033	0.0020–0.0040	Snug
	H	5.8	0.0018–0.0026	0.0100–0.0200	0.0100–0.0200	0.015–0.055	0.0020–0.0040	0.0020–0.0040	Snug
	M	7.3	①	0.0130–0.0450	0.0600–0.0850	0.0100–0.0240	0.0020–0.0040	0.0020–0.0040	0.0010–0.0030
	G	7.5	0.0022–0.0030	0.0100–0.0200	0.0100–0.0200	0.0100–0.0350	0.0025–0.0045	0.0025–0.0045	Snug
1993	Y	4.9	0.0010–0.0018	0.0100–0.0200	0.0100–0.0200	0.015–0.055	0.0019–0.0036	0.0020–0.0040	Snug
	N	5.0	0.0014–0.0022	0.0100–0.0200	0.0180–0.0280	0.010–0.040	0.0013–0.0033	0.0013–0.0033	Snug
	H	5.8	0.0018–0.0026	0.0100–0.0200	0.0100–0.0200	0.015–0.055	0.0020–0.0040	0.0020–0.0040	Snug
	R	5.8	0.0015–0.0023	0.0100–0.0200	0.0180–0.0280	0.010–0.040	0.0013–0.0033	0.0013–0.0033	Snug
	M	7.3	①	0.0130–0.0450	0.0600–0.0850	0.010–0.035	0.0020–0.0040	0.0020–0.0040	0.0010–0.0030
	C	7.3	①	0.0130–0.0450	0.0600–0.0850	0.010–0.035	0.0020–0.0040	0.0020–0.0040	0.0010–0.0030
	G	7.5	0.0022–0.0030	0.0100–0.0200	0.0100–0.0200	0.010–0.035	0.0025–0.0045	0.0025–0.0045	Snug

① Nos. 1–6: 0.0055–0.0085
No. 7 & 8: 0.0060–0.0085

84923618

TORQUE SPECIFICATIONS
All readings in ft. lbs.

Year	Engine ID/VIN	Engine Displacement Liters (cc)	Cylinder Head Bolts	Main Bearing Bolts	Rod Bearing Bolts	Crankshaft Damper Bolts	Flywheel Bolts	Manifold ⑫ Intake	Manifold ⑫ Exhaust	Spark Plugs
1987	B	4.9	①	60–70	40–45	130–150	75–85	22–32	22–32	15
	G	5.0	②	60–70	19–24	70–90	75–85	23–25	18–24	15
	N	5.0	②	60–70	40–45	70–90	75–85	23–25	18–24	15
	H	5.8	③	95–105	40–45	70–90	75–85	23–25	18–24	15
	1	6.9	④	⑥	⑤	90	44–50	⑦	⑧	—
	L	7.5	⑪	95–105	45–50	70–90	75–85	⑩	28–33	10
1988	Y	4.9	①	60–70	40–45	130–150	75–85	22–32	22–32	15
	N	5.0	②	60–70	19–24	70–90	75–85	23–25	18–24	15
	H	5.8	③	95–105	40–45	70–90	75–85	23–25	18–24	15
	M	7.3	⑨	⑥	⑤	90	44–50	⑦	⑧	—
	G	7.5	⑪	95–105	45–50	70–90	75–85	⑩	22–30	10
1989	Y	4.9	①	60–70	40–45	130–150	75–85	22–32	22–32	15
	N	5.0	②	60–70	19–24	70–90	75–85	23–25	18–24	15
	H	5.8	③	95–105	40–45	70–90	75–85	23–25	18–24	15
	M	7.3	⑨	⑥	⑤	90	44–50	⑦	⑧	—
	G	7.5	⑪	95–105	45–50	70–90	75–85	⑩	22–30	10
1990	Y	4.9	①	60–70	40–45	130–150	75–85	22–32	22–32	15
	N	5.0	②	60–70	19–24	70–90	75–85	23–25	18–24	15
	H	5.8	③	95–105	40–45	70–90	75–85	23–25	18–24	15
	M	7.3	⑨	⑥	⑤	90	44–50	⑦	⑧	—
	G	7.5	⑪	95–105	45–50	70–90	75–85	⑩	22–30	10
1991	Y	4.9	①	60–70	40–45	130–150	75–85	22–32	22–32	15
	N	5.0	②	60–70	19–24	70–90	75–85	23–25	18–24	15
	H	5.8	③	95–105	40–45	70–90	75–85	23–25	18–24	15
	M	7.3	⑨	⑥	⑤	90	44–50	⑦	⑧	—
	G	7.5	⑪	95–105	45–50	70–90	75–85	⑩	22–30	10
1992	Y	4.9	①	60–70	40–45	130–150	75–85	22–32	22–32	15
	N	5.0	②	60–70	19–24	70–90	75–85	23–25	18–24	15
	H	5.8	③	95–105	40–45	70–90	75–85	23–25	18–24	15
	M	7.3	⑬	⑥	⑤	90	44–50	⑦	⑧	—
	G	7.5	⑪	95–105	41–45	70–90	75–85	⑩	22–45	10

84923619

TORQUE SPECIFICATIONS

All readings in ft. lbs.

Year	Engine ID/VIN	Engine Displacement Liters (cc)	Cylinder Head Bolts	Main Bearing Bolts	Rod Bearing Bolts	Crankshaft Damper Bolts	Flywheel Bolts	Manifold ⑫ Intake	Manifold ⑫ Exhaust	Spark Plugs
1993	Y	4.9	①	60–70	40–45	130–150	75–85	22–32	22–32	15
	N	5.0	②	60–70	19–24	70–90	75–85	23–25	18–24	15
	H	5.8	③	95–105	40–45	70–90	75–85	23–25	18–24	15
	R	5.8	③	95–105	40–45	70–90	75–85	23–25	18–24	15
	M	7.3	⑨	⑥	⑤	90	44–50	⑦	⑧	—
	C	7.3	⑨	⑥	⑤	90	44–50	⑦	⑧	—
	G	7.5	⑪	95–105	41–45	70–90	75–85	⑩	22–45	10

① Step 1: 50–55
   Step 2: 60–65
   Step 3: 70–85
② Step 1: 55–65
   Step 2: 65–72
③ Step 1: 85
   Step 2: 95
   Step 3: 105–112
④ Step 1: 40
   Step 2: 70
   Step 3: 80
   Step 4: Run engine to normal operating temperature
   Step 5: Retorque to 80 ft. lbs. while hot
⑤ Step 1: 38
   Step 2: 48–53
⑥ Step 1: 75
   Step 2: 95

⑦ Step 1: 24
   Step 2: Run engine to normal operating temperature
   Step 3: Retorque to 24 ft. lbs. while hot
⑧ Step 1: 35
   Step 2: Run engine to normal operating temperature
   Step 3: Retorque to 35 ft. lbs. while hot
⑨ Step 1: 65
   Step 2: 90
   Step 3: 100
⑩ Step 1: 8–12
   Step 2: 12–22
   Step 3: 22–35
⑪ Step 1: 70–80
   Step 2: 100–110
   Step 3: 130–140
⑫ Manifold to cylinder head
⑬ Step 1: 65
   Step 2: 90
   Step 3: 110

84923620

Engine

REMOVAL & INSTALLATION

▶ See Figures 15, 16, 17, 18, 19, 20, 21, 22 and 23

✳✳WARNING

Disconnect the negative battery cable(s) before beginning any work. Always label all disconnected hoses, vacuum lines and wires, to prevent incorrect reassembly. Do not disconnect any air conditioning lines unless you are thoroughly familiar with air conditioning systems and the hazards involved; escaping refrigerant (Freon®) will freeze any surface it contacts, including skin and eyes. Have the system discharged professionally before required repairs are started.

6-4.9L

1. Drain the cooling system and the crankcase.

❋❋CAUTION

When draining the coolant, keep in mind that cats and dogs are attracted by the ethylene glycol antifreeze, and are quite likely to drink any that is left in an uncovered container or in puddles on the ground. This will prove fatal in sufficient quantity. Always drain the coolant into a sealable container. Coolant should be reused unless it is contaminated or several years old.   The EPA warns that prolonged contact with used engine oil may cause a number of skin disorders, including cancer! You should make every effort to minimize your exposure to used engine oil. Protective gloves should be worn when changing the oil. Wash your hands and any other exposed skin areas as soon as possible after exposure to used engine oil. Soap and water, or waterless hand cleaner should be used.

2. Remove the hood.
3. Remove the throttle body inlet tubes.
4. Disconnect the positive battery cable.
5. Discharge the air conditioning system. (See Section 1).
6. Disconnect the refrigerant lines at the compressor. Cap all openings at once.
7. Remove the compressor.
8. Disconnect the refrigerant lines at the condenser. Cap all openings at once.
9. Remove the condenser.
10. Disconnect the heater hose from the water pump and coolant outlet housing.
11. Disconnect the flexible fuel line from the fuel pump.
12. Remove the radiator.
13. Remove the fan, water pump pulley, and fan belt.
14. Disconnect the accelerator cable.
15. Disconnect the brake booster vacuum hose at the intake manifold.
16. On trucks with automatic transmission, disconnect the transmission kickdown rod at the bellcrank assembly.
17. Disconnect the exhaust pipe from the exhaust manifold.
18. Disconnect the Electronic Engine Control (EEC) harness from all the sensors.
19. Disconnect the body ground strap and the battery ground cable from the engine.
20. Disconnect the engine wiring harness at the ignition coil, the coolant temperature sending unit, and the oil pressure sensing unit. Position the wiring harness out of the way.
21. Remove the alternator mounting bolts and position the alternator out of the way.
22. Remove the power steering pump from the mounting brackets and move it to one side, leaving the lines attached.
23. Raise and support the truck on jackstands.
24. Remove the starter.
25. Remove the automatic transmission filler tube bracket, if so equipped.
26. Remove the rear engine plate upper right bolt.
27. On manual transmission equipped trucks:
    a. Remove the flywheel housing lower attaching bolts.
    b. Disconnect the clutch return spring.

28. On automatic transmission equipped trucks:
    a. Remove the converter housing access cover assembly.
    b. Remove the flywheel-to-converter attaching nuts.
    c. Secure the converter in the housing.
    d. Remove the transmission oil cooler lines from the retaining clip at the engine.
    e. Remove the lower converter housing-to-engine attaching bolts.
29. Remove the nut from each of the two front engine mounts.
30. Lower the vehicle and position a jack under the transmission and support it.
31. Remove the remaining bellhousing-to-engine attaching bolts.
32. Attach an engine lifting device and raise the engine slightly and carefully pull it from the transmission. Lift the engine out of the vehicle.

To install the engine:

33. Remove the engine mount brackets from the frame. Attach them to the engine mounts, making the nuts just tight enough to hold the brackets securely to the mounts.
34. Place a new gasket on the muffler inlet pipe.
35. Carefully lower the engine into the truck. Make sure that the dowels in the engine block engage the holes in the bellhousing and the mount bracket holes align with the frame holes.
36. On manual transmission equipped trucks, start the transmission input shaft into the clutch disc. It may be necessary to adjust the position of the engine or transmission in order for the input shaft to enter the clutch disc. If necessary, turn the crankshaft until the input shaft splines mesh with the clutch disc splines.
37. On automatic transmission equipped trucks, start the converter pilot into the crankshaft. Secure the converter in the housing.
38. Install the bolts securing the mount brackets to the frame.
39. Install the bellhousing upper attaching bolts. Torque the bolts to 50 ft. lbs.
40. Remove the jack supporting the transmission.
41. Remove the lifting device.
42. Install the engine mount nuts and tighten them to 70 ft. lbs. Tighten the bracket-to-frame bolts to 70 ft. lbs.
43. Install the automatic transmission coil cooler lines bracket, if equipped.
44. Install the remaining bellhousing attaching bolts. Torque them to 50 ft. lbs.
45. Connect the clutch return spring, if so equipped.
46. Install the starter and connect the starter cable.
47. Attach the automatic transmission fluid filler tube bracket, if so equipped.
48. On trucks with automatic transmissions, install the transmission oil cooler lines in the bracket at the cylinder block.
49. Connect the exhaust pipe to the exhaust manifold. Tighten the nuts to 25-35 ft. lbs.
50. Connect the engine ground strap and negative battery cable.
51. On a truck with an automatic transmission, connect the kickdown rod to the bellcrank assembly on the intake manifold.
52. Connect the accelerator linkage.
53. Connect the brake booster vacuum line to the intake manifold.

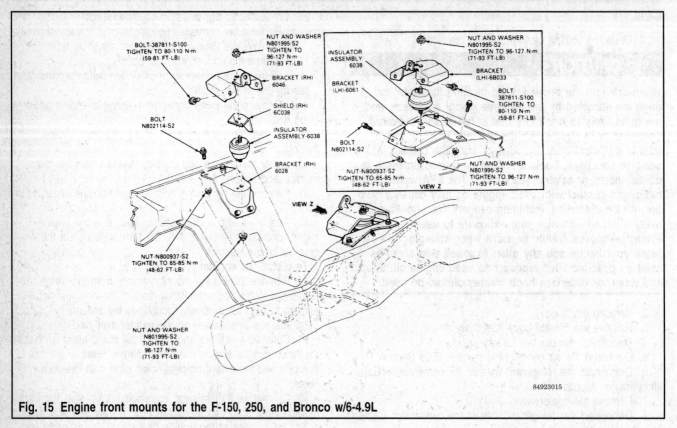

Fig. 15 Engine front mounts for the F-150, 250, and Bronco w/6-4.9L

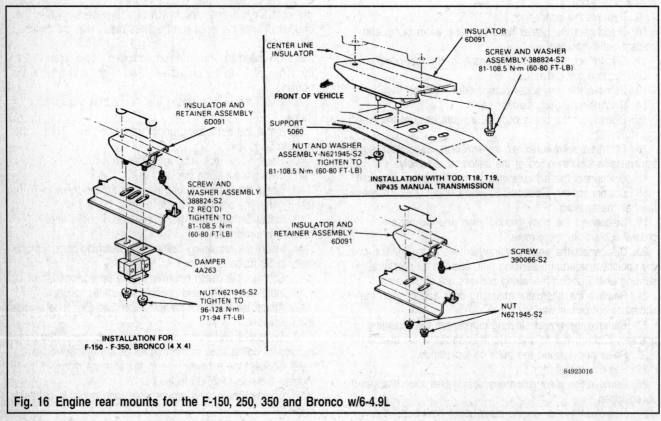

Fig. 16 Engine rear mounts for the F-150, 250, 350 and Bronco w/6-4.9L

54. Connect the coil primary wire, oil pressure and coolant temperature sending unit wires, fuel line, heater hoses, and the battery positive cable.

55. Connect the EEC sensors.
56. Install the alternator on its mounting bracket.
57. Install the power steering pump on its bracket.

58. Install the water pump pulley, spacer, fan, and fan belt. Adjust the belt tension.

59. Install the air conditioning compressor. Connect the refrigerant lines.

60. Install the radiator.

61. Install the condenser and connect the refrigerant lines.

62. Charge the refrigerant system. (See Section 1).

63. Connect the upper and lower radiator hoses to the radiator and engine.

64. Connect the automatic transmission oil cooler lines, if so equipped.

65. Install and adjust the hood.

66. Fill the cooling system.

67. Fill the crankcase.

68. Start the engine and check for leaks.

69. Bleed the cooling system.

70. Adjust the clutch pedal free-play or the automatic transmission control linkage.

71. Install the air cleaner.

8-5.0L or 8-5.7L Engine

1. Remove the hood.
2. Drain the cooling system and crankcase.

✳✳CAUTION

When draining the coolant, keep in mind that cats and dogs are attracted by the ethylene glycol antifreeze, and are quite likely to drink any that is left in an uncovered container or in puddles on the ground. This will prove fatal in sufficient quantity. Always drain the coolant into a sealable container. Coolant should be reused unless it is contaminated or several years old. The EPA warns that prolonged contact with used engine oil may cause a number of skin disorders, including cancer! You should make every effort to minimize your exposure to used engine oil. Protective gloves should be worn when changing the oil. Wash your hands and any other exposed skin areas as soon as possible after exposure to used engine oil. Soap and water, or waterless hand cleaner should be used.

3. Disconnect the battery and alternator cables.

4. On carbureted engines, remove the air cleaner and intake duct assembly, plus the crankcase ventilation hose. On fuel injected engines, remove the air intake hoses, PCV tube and carbon canister hose.

5. Disconnect the upper and lower radiator hoses.

6. Discharge the air conditioning system. (See Section 1).

7. Disconnect the refrigerant lines at the compressor. Cap all openings immediately.

8. If so equipped, disconnect the automatic transmission oil cooler lines.

9. Remove the fan shroud and lay it over the fan.

10. Remove the radiator and fan, shroud, fan, spacer, pulley and belt.

11. Remove the alternator pivot and adjusting bolts. Remove the alternator.

12. Disconnect the oil pressure sending unit lead from the sending unit.

13. Disconnect the fuel tank-to-pump fuel line at the fuel pump and plug the line.

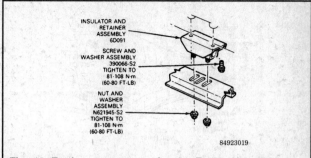

Fig. 19 Engine rear mounts for the F-150, 250, 350 w/8-5.0L

14. On trucks with EFI, disconnect the chassis fuel line at the fuel rails.

15. Disconnect the accelerator linkage and speed control linkage at the carburetor or throttle body.

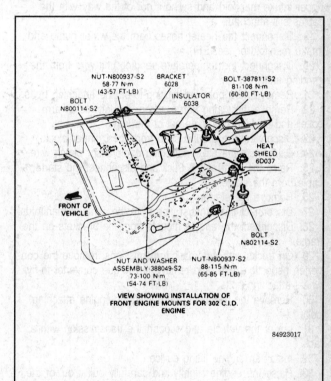

Fig. 17 Engine front mounts for the F-150, 250, 350 and Bronco w/8-5.0L, 5.8L

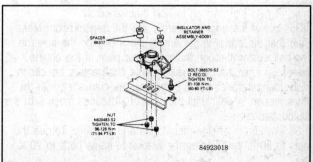

Fig. 18 Engine rear mounts for the Bronco w/8-5.0L, 5.8L

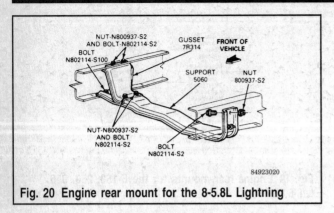

Fig. 20 Engine rear mount for the 8-5.8L Lightning

16. Disconnect the automatic transmission kick-down rod and remove the return spring, if so equipped.

17. Disconnect the power brake booster vacuum hose.

18. On EFI models, disconnect the throttle bracket from the upper intake manifold and swing it out of the way with the cables still attached.

19. Disconnect the heater hoses from the water pump and intake manifold or tee (EFI).

20. Disconnect the temperature sending unit wire from the sending unit.

21. Remove the upper bellhousing-to-engine attaching bolts.

22. Remove the wiring harness from the left rocker arm cover and position the wires out of the way.

23. Disconnect the ground strap from the cylinder block.

24. Disconnect the air conditioning compressor clutch wire.

25. Raise the front of the truck and disconnect the starter cable from the starter.

26. Remove the starter.

27. Disconnect the exhaust pipe from the exhaust manifolds.

28. Disconnect the engine mounts from the brackets on the frame.

29. On trucks with automatic transmissions, remove the converter inspection plate and remove the torque converter-to-flywheel attaching bolts.

30. Remove the remaining bellhousing-to-engine attaching bolts.

31. Lower the vehicle and support the transmission with a jack.

32. Install an engine lifting device.

33. Raise the engine slightly and carefully pull it out of the transmission. Lift the engine out of the engine compartment.

To install:

34. Remove the engine mount brackets from the frame and attach them to the engine mounts. Tighten the mount-to-bracket nuts just enough to hold them securely.

35. Lower the engine carefully into the transmission. Make sure that the dowel in the engine block engage the holes in the bellhousing through the rear cover plate. If the engine hangs up after the transmission input shaft enters the clutch disc (manual transmission only), turn the crankshaft with the transmission in gear until the input shaft splines mesh with the clutch disc splines.

36. Install the engine mount nuts and washers. Torque the nuts to 80 ft. lbs. Tighten the bracket-to-frame bolts to 70 ft. lbs.

37. Remove the engine lifting device.

38. Install the lower bellhousing-to-engine attaching bolts. Torque the bolts to 50 ft. lbs.

39. Remove the transmission support jack.

40. On trucks with automatic transmissions, install the torque converter-to-flywheel attaching bolts. Torque the bolts to 30 ft. lbs.

41. Install the converter inspection plate. Torque the bolts to 60 inch lbs.

42. Connect the exhaust pipe to the exhaust manifolds. Tighten the exhaust pipe-to-exhaust manifold nuts to 25-35 ft. lbs.

43. Install the starter. Torque the mounting bolts to 20 ft. lbs.

44. Connect the starter cable to the starter.

45. Lower the truck.

46. Install the upper bellhousing-to-engine attaching bolts. Torque the bolts to 50 ft. lbs.

47. Connect the wiring harness at the left rocker arm cover.

48. Connect the ground strap to the cylinder block.

49. Connect the air conditioning compressor clutch wire.

50. Connect the heater hoses at the water pump and intake manifold or tee (EFI).

51. Connect the temperature sending unit wire at the sending unit.

52. Connect the accelerator linkage and speed control linkage at the carburetor or throttle body.

53. Connect the automatic transmission kick-down rod and install the return spring, if so equipped.

54. Connect the power brake booster vacuum hose.

55. On EFI models, connect the throttle bracket to the upper intake manifold.

56. Connect the fuel tank-to-pump fuel line at the fuel pump. On trucks with EFI, disconnect the chassis fuel line at the fuel rails.

57. Connect the oil pressure sending unit lead to the sending unit.

58. Install the alternator.

59. Connect the refrigerant lines to the compressor.

60. Install the radiator and fan, shroud, fan, spacer, pulley and belt.

61. Connect the upper and lower radiator hoses, and, if so equipped, the automatic transmission oil cooler lines.

62. On carbureted engines, install the air cleaner and intake duct assembly, plus the crankcase ventilation hose.   On fuel injected engines, install the air intake hoses, PCV tube and carbon canister hose.

63. Connect the battery and alternator cables.

64. Fill the cooling system and crankcase.

65. Charge the air conditioning system. (See Section 1.)

66. Install the hood.

If the torque for a particular fastener was not mentioned above, use the following torque values as a guide:

- $\frac{1}{4}$ in.-20: 6-9 ft. lbs.
- $\frac{5}{16}$ in.-18: 12-18 ft. lbs.
- $\frac{3}{8}$ in.-16: 22-32 ft. lbs.
- $\frac{7}{16}$ in.-14: 45-57 ft. lbs.
- $\frac{1}{2}$ in.-13: 55-80 ft. lbs.
- $\frac{9}{16}$ in.: 85-120 ft. lbs.

8-7.5L Engine

1. Remove the hood.

2. Drain the cooling system.

✳✳CAUTION

When draining the coolant, keep in mind that cats and dogs are attracted by the ethylene glycol antifreeze, and are quite likely to drink any that is left in an uncovered container or in puddles on the ground. This will prove fatal in sufficient quantity. Always drain the coolant into a sealable container. Coolant should be reused unless it is contaminated or several years old.

3. Disconnect the negative battery cable from the block.
4. Remove the air cleaner assembly.
5. Remove the crankcase ventilation hose.
6. Remove the canister hose.
7. Disconnect the upper and lower radiator hoses.
8. Disconnect the transmission oil cooler lines from the radiator.
9. Disconnect the engine oil cooler lines at the oil filter adapter.

✳✳WARNING

Don't disconnect the lines at the quick-connect fittings behind or at the oil cooler. Disconnecting them may permanently damage them.

10. Discharge the air conditioning system. (See Section 1.)
11. Disconnect the refrigerant lines at the compressor. Cap the openings at once!
12. Disconnect the refrigerant lines at the condenser. Cap the openings at once!
13. Remove the condenser.
14. Remove the fan shroud from the radiator and position it up, over the fan.
15. Remove the radiator.
16. Remove the fan shroud.
17. Remove the fan, belts and pulley from the water pump.
18. Remove the compressor.
19. Remove the power steering pump from the engine, if so equipped, and position it to one side. Do not disconnect the fluid lines.
20. Disconnect the fuel pump inlet line from the pump and plug the line.
21. Disconnect the oil pressure sending unit wire at the sending unit.
22. Remove the alternator drive belts and disconnect the alternator from the engine, positioning it aside.
23. Disconnect the ground cable from the right front corner of the engine.
24. Disconnect the heater hoses.
25. Remove the transmission fluid filler tube attaching bolt from the right side valve cover and position the tube out of the way.
26. Disconnect all vacuum lines at the rear of the intake manifold.
27. Disconnect the speed control cable at the carburetor, if so equipped.
28. Disconnect the accelerator rod and the transmission kickdown rod and secure them out of the way.

29. Disconnect the engine wiring harness at the connector on the fire wall. Disconnect the primary wire at the coil.
30. Remove the upper flywheel housing-to-engine bolts.
31. Raise the vehicle and disconnect the exhaust pipes at the exhaust manifolds.
32. Disconnect the starter cable and remove the starter. Bring the starter forward and rotate the solenoid outward to remove the assembly.
33. Remove the access cover from the converter housing and remove the flywheel-to-converter attaching nuts.
34. Remove the lower the converter housing-to-engine attaching bolts.
35. Remove the engine mount through bolts attaching the rubber insulator to the frame brackets.
36. Lower the vehicle and place a jack under the transmission to support it.
37. Remove the converter housing-to-engine block attaching bolts (left side).
38. Remove the coil and bracket assembly from the intake manifold.
39. Attach an engine lifting device and carefully take up the weight of the engine.
40. Move the engine forward to disengage it from the transmission and slowly lift it from the truck.

To install:
41. Remove the engine mount brackets from the frame and attach them to the mounts. Tighten the nuts just enough to hold them securely.
42. Lower the engine slowly into the truck.
43. Slide the engine rearward to engage it with the transmission and slowly lower it onto the supports.
44. Tighten the engine support nuts to 74 ft. lbs. Tighten the bracket bolts to 70 ft. lbs.

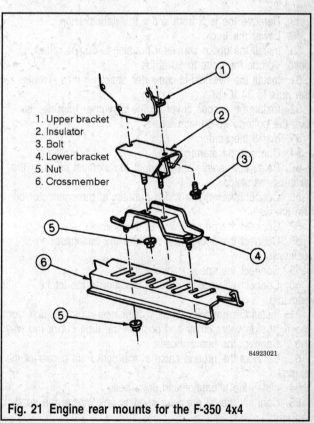

1. Upper bracket
2. Insulator
3. Bolt
4. Lower bracket
5. Nut
6. Crossmember

84923021

Fig. 21 Engine rear mounts for the F-350 4x4

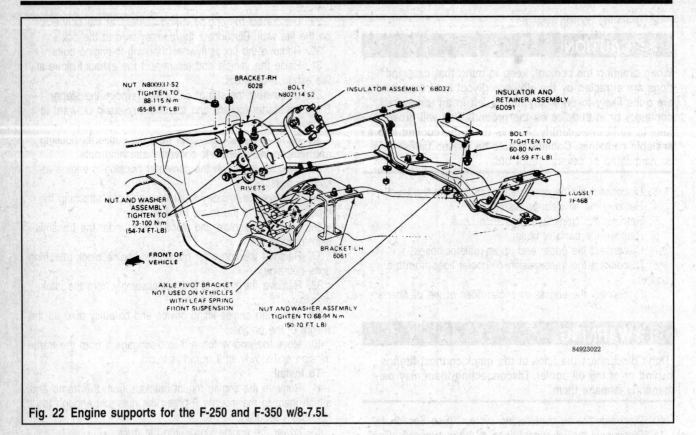

NUT N800937-S2 TIGHTEN TO 88-115 N·m (65-85 FT·LB)

BRACKET-RH 6028

BOLT N802114 S2

INSULATOR ASSEMBLY 6B032

INSULATOR AND RETAINER ASSEMBLY 6D091

BOLT TIGHTEN TO 60-80 N·m (44-59 FT·LB)

GUSSET 7F468

RIVETS

NUT AND WASHER ASSEMBLY TIGHTEN TO 73-100 N·m (54-74 FT·LB)

FRONT OF VEHICLE

AXLE PIVOT BRACKET NOT USED ON VEHICLES WITH LEAF SPRING FRONT SUSPENSION

BRACKET-LH 6061

NUT AND WASHER ASSEMBLY TIGHTEN TO 68-94 N·m (50-70 FT·LB)

84923022

Fig. 22 Engine supports for the F-250 and F-350 w/8-7.5L

45. Remove the engine lifting device.

46. Install the converter housing-to-engine block upper and left side attaching bolts. Torque the bolts to 50 ft. lbs.

47. Install the coil and bracket assembly on the intake manifold.

48. Remove the jack from under the transmission.

49. Lower the truck.

50. Install the upper converter housing-to-engine attaching bolts. Torque the bolts to 50 ft. lbs.

51. Install the flywheel-to-converter attaching nuts. Torque the nuts to 34 ft. lbs.

52. Install the access cover on the converter housing. Torque the bolts to 60-90 inch lbs.

53. Install the starter.

54. Connect the starter cable.

55. Raise the vehicle and connect the exhaust pipes at the exhaust manifolds.

56. Connect the engine wiring harness at the connector on the fire wall.

57. Connect the primary wire at the coil.

58. Connect the accelerator rod and the transmission kickdown rod.

59. Connect the speed control cable.

60. Connect all vacuum lines at the rear of the intake manifold.

61. Install the transmission fluid filler tube attaching bolt from the right side valve cover and position the tube out of the way.

62. Connect the heater hoses.

63. Connect the ground cable at the right front corner of the engine.

64. Install the alternator and drive belts.

65. Connect the oil pressure sending unit wire at the sending unit.

66. Connect the fuel pump inlet line at the pump and plug the line.

67. Install the power steering pump and belt.

68. Install air conditioning compressor. Connect the refrigerant lines.

69. Install the fan, belts and pulley on the water pump.

70. Position the fan shroud over the fan.

71. Install the radiator.

72. Attach the fan shroud.

73. Install the condenser.

74. Connect the refrigerant lines at the condenser.

75. Charge the air conditioning system. (See Section 1.)

76. Connect the engine oil cooler lines at the oil filter adapter.

77. Connect the transmission oil cooler lines at the radiator.

78. Connect the upper and lower radiator hoses.

79. Connect the canister hose.

80. Connect the crankcase ventilation hose.

81. Connect the negative battery cable from the block.

82. Fill the cooling system.

83. Install the air cleaner assembly.

84. Install the hood.

If the torque for a particular fastener was not mentioned above, use the following torque values as a guide:

- ¼ in.-20: 6-9 ft. lbs.
- 5/16 in.-18: 12-18 ft. lbs.
- 3/8 in.-16: 22-32 ft. lbs.
- 7/16 in.-14: 45-57 ft. lbs.
- ½ in.-13: 55-80 ft. lbs.

6.9L and 7.3L Diesel Engines

1. Remove the hood.

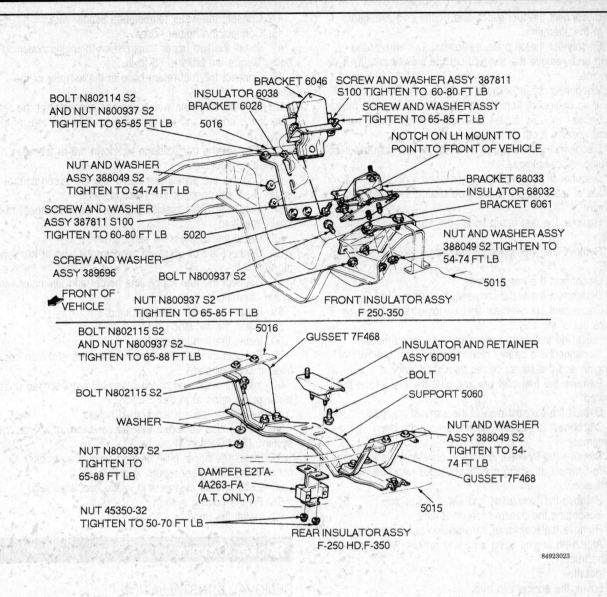

BOLT N802114 S2
AND NUT N800937 S2
TIGHTEN TO 65-85 FT LB

BRACKET 6046
INSULATOR 6038
BRACKET 6028
5016

SCREW AND WASHER ASSY 387811
S100 TIGHTEN TO 60-80 FT LB
SCREW AND WASHER ASSY
TIGHTEN TO 65-85 FT LB

NOTCH ON LH MOUNT TO
POINT TO FRONT OF VEHICLE

NUT AND WASHER
ASSY 388049 S2
TIGHTEN TO 54-74 FT LB

BRACKET 68033
INSULATOR 68032
BRACKET 6061

SCREW AND WASHER
ASSY 387811 S100
TIGHTEN TO 60-80 FT LB   5020

SCREW AND WASHER
ASSY 389696

FRONT OF
VEHICLE

BOLT N800937 S2

NUT N800937 S2
TIGHTEN TO 65-85 FT LB

NUT AND WASHER ASSY
388049 S2 TIGHTEN TO
54-74 FT LB
5015

FRONT INSULATOR ASSY
F 250-350

BOLT N802115 S2
AND NUT N800937 S2
TIGHTEN TO 65-88 FT LB   5016

GUSSET 7F468

INSULATOR AND RETAINER
ASSY 6D091

BOLT

SUPPORT 5060

NUT AND WASHER
ASSY 388049 S2
TIGHTEN TO 54-
74 FT LB

GUSSET 7F468

BOLT N802115 S2

WASHER

NUT N800937 S2
TIGHTEN TO
65-88 FT LB

DAMPER E2TA-
4A263-FA
(A.T. ONLY)

NUT 45350-32
TIGHTEN TO 50-70 FT LB

REAR INSULATOR ASSY
F-250 HD, F-350

5015

84923023

Fig. 23 Engine supports for the F-250, 350 w/diesel

2. Drain the coolant.

❊❊CAUTION

When draining the coolant, keep in mind that cats and dogs are attracted by the ethylene glycol antifreeze, and are quite likely to drink any that is left in an uncovered container or in puddles on the ground. This will prove fatal in sufficient quantity. Always drain the coolant into a sealable container. Coolant should be reused unless it is contaminated or several years old.

3. Remove the air cleaner and intake duct assembly and cover the air intake opening with a clean rag to keep out the dirt.

4. Remove the upper grille support bracket and upper air conditioning condenser mounting bracket.

5. On vehicles equipped with air conditioning, the system MUST be discharged to remove the condenser.

❊❊WARNING

DO NOT attempt to do this yourself, unless you are familiar with air conditioning repair and have the appropriate equipment. (See Section 1).

6. Remove the radiator fan shroud halves.

7. Remove the fan and clutch assembly as described under water pump removal in this Section.

8. Detach the radiator hoses and the transmission cooler lines, if so equipped.

9. Remove the condenser. Cap all openings at once!

10. Remove the radiator.

11. Remove the power steering pump and position it out of the way.

12. Disconnect the fuel supply line heater and alternator wires at the alternator.

13. Disconnect the oil pressure sending unit wire at the sending unit, remove the sender from the firewall and lay it on the engine.

14. Disconnect the accelerator cable and the speed control cable, if so equipped, from the injection pump. Remove the cable bracket with the cables attached, from the intake manifold and position it out of the way.

15. Disconnect the transmission kickdown rod from the injection pump, if so equipped.

16. Disconnect the main wiring harness connector from the right side of the engine and the ground strap from the rear of the engine.

17. Remove the fuel return hose from the left rear of the engine.

18. Remove the two upper transmission-to-engine attaching bolts.

19. Disconnect the heater hoses.

20. Disconnect the water temperature sender wire.

21. Disconnect the overheat light switch wire and position the wire out of the way.

22. Raise the truck and support on it on jackstands.

23. Disconnect the battery ground cables from the front of the engine and the starter cables from the starter.

24. Remove the fuel inlet line and plug the fuel line at the fuel pump.

25. Detach the exhaust pipe at the exhaust manifold.

26. Disconnect the engine insulators from the no. 1 crossmember.

27. Remove the flywheel inspection plate and the four converter-to-flywheel attaching nuts, if equipped with automatic transmission.

28. Remove the jackstands and lower the truck.

29. Supporting the transmission on a jack.

30. Remove the four lower transmission attaching bolts.

31. Attach an engine lifting sling and remove the engine from the truck.

To install:

32. Lower the engine into truck.

33. Align the converter to the flex plate and the engine dowels to the transmission.

34. Install the engine mount bolts and torque them to 80 ft. lbs.

35. Remove the engine lifting sling.

36. Install the four lower transmission attaching bolts. Torque the bolts to 65 ft. lbs.

37. Remove transmission jack.

38. Raise and support the front end on jackstands.

39. If equipped with automatic transmission, install the four converter-to-flywheel attaching nuts. Torque the nuts to 34 ft. lbs.

40. Install the flywheel inspection plate. Torque the bolts to 60-90 inch lbs.

41. Attach the exhaust pipe at the exhaust manifold.

42. Connect the fuel inlet line.

43. Connect the battery ground cables to the front of the engine.

44. Connect the starter cables at the starter.

45. Lower the truck.

46. Connect the overheat light switch wire.

47. Connect the water temperature sender wire.

48. Connect the heater hoses.

49. Install the two upper transmission-to-engine attaching bolts. Torque the bolts to 65 ft. lbs.

50. Connect the fuel return hose at the left rear of the engine.

51. Connect the main wiring harness connector at the right side of the engine and the ground strap from the rear of the engine.

52. Connect the transmission kickdown rod at the injection pump, if so equipped.

53. Connect the accelerator cable and the speed control cable, if so equipped, at the injection pump.

54. Install the cable bracket with the cables attached, to the intake manifold.

55. Install the oil pressure sending unit.

56. Connect the oil pressure sending unit wire at the sending unit.

57. Connect the fuel supply line heater and alternator wires at the alternator.

58. Install the power steering pump.

59. Install the radiator.

60. Install the condenser.

61. Connect the radiator hoses and the transmission cooler lines, if so equipped.

62. Install the fan and clutch assembly as described under water pump removal in this Section.

63. Install the radiator fan shroud halves.

64. On vehicles equipped with air conditioning, charge the system. (See Section 1).

65. Install the upper grille support bracket and upper air conditioning condenser mounting bracket.

66. Install the air cleaner and intake duct assembly.

67. Fill the cooling system.

68. Install the hood.

Rocker Covers

REMOVAL & INSTALLATION

6-4.9L Engine

1. Disconnect the inlet hose at the crankcase filler cap.

2. Remove the throttle body inlet tubes.

3. Disconnect the accelerator cable at the throttle body. Remove the cable retracting spring. Remove the accelerator cable bracket from the upper intake manifold and position the cable and bracket out of the way.

4. Remove the fuel line from the fuel rail. Be careful not to kink the line.

5. Remove the upper intake manifold and throttle body assembly. See Section 5.

6. Remove the ignition coil and wires.

7. Remove the rocker arm cover.

8. Remove and discard the gasket.

To install:

9. Clean the mating surfaces for the cover and head thoroughly.

10. Coat both mating surfaces with gasket sealer and place the new gasket on the head with the locating tabs downward.

11. Place the cover on the head making sure the gasket is evenly seated. Torque the bolts to 48-84 inch lbs.

12. Install the ignition coil and wires.

13. Install the upper intake manifold and throttle body assembly. See Section 5.

14. Install the fuel line at the fuel rail.

15. Install the accelerator cable bracket at the upper intake manifold. Install the cable retracting spring. Connect the accelerator cable at the throttle body.

16. Install the throttle body inlet tubes.

17. Connect the inlet hose at the crankcase filler cap.

8-5.0L or 8-5.8L Engines

1. Disconnect the battery ground cable.

2. Remove the air cleaner and inlet duct.

3. Remove the coil.

4. For the right cover, remove the lifting eye (except Lightning) and Thermactor® tube; for the left cover, remove the oil filler pipe attaching bolt, and, on Lightning, the lifting eye.

5. Mark and remove the spark plug wires. On the Lightning, remove the upper intake manifold.

6. Remove any vacuum lines, wires or pipes in the way. Make sure that you tag them for identification.

7. Remove the cover bolts and lift off the cover. It may be necessary to break the cover loose by rapping on it with a rubber mallet. NEVER pry the cover off!

To install:

8. Thoroughly clean the mating surfaces of both the cover and head.

9. Coat both mating surfaces with gasket sealer and place the new gasket(s) in the cover(s) with the locating tabs engaging the slots.

10. Place the cover on the head making sure the gasket is evenly seated. Torque the bolts to 10-13 ft. lbs. After 2 minutes, retighten the bolts.

11. Install the vacuum lines, wires and pipes.

12. Install the spark plug wires. On the Lightning, install the upper intake manifold.

13. For the right cover, install the lifting eye (except Lightning) and Thermactor® tube; for the left cover, install the oil filler pipe attaching bolt, and, on Lightning, the lifting eye.

14. Install the coil.

15. Install the air cleaner and inlet duct.

16. Connect the battery ground cable.

8-7.5L Engine

1. Disconnect the battery ground cable(s).

2. Remove the air cleaner and inlet duct.

3. Remove the Thermactor® air supply control valve and bracket.

4. Remove the coil.

5. Disconnect the MTA hose at the Thermactor® valve. Disconnect the Thermactor® air control valve-to-air pump hose and tube.

6. Mark and remove the spark plug wires.

7. Remove any vacuum lines, wires or pipes in the way. Make sure that you tag them for identification.

8. Remove the cover bolts and lift off the cover. It may be necessary to break the cover loose by rapping on it with a rubber mallet. NEVER pry the cover off!

To install:

9. Thoroughly clean the mating surfaces of both the cover and head.

10. Place the new cover seal(s) in the cover(s) with the locating tab engaging the slot.

11. Place the cover on the head. Torque the bolts to 6-9 ft. lbs. from right to left.

12. Install the vacuum lines, wires and pipes.

13. Install the spark plug wires.

14. Connect the MTA hose at the Thermactor® valve. Connect the Thermactor® air control valve-to-air pump hose and tube.

15. Install the coil.

16. Install the Thermactor® air supply control valve and bracket.

17. Install the air cleaner and inlet duct.

18. Connect the battery ground cable(s).

-6.9L -7.3L

1. Disconnect the battery ground cables.

2. Remove the cover bolts and lift off the covers. It may be necessary to break the covers loose by rapping on them with a rubber mallet. NEVER pry a cover off!

3. Clean the mating surfaces of the covers and heads thoroughly, coat the mating surfaces with gasket sealer, place new gaskets in the covers, position the covers on the heads and torque the bolts to 72 inch lbs.

Rocker Arms

REMOVAL & INSTALLATION

▶ **See Figures 24 and 25**

6-4.9L Engine

1. Disconnect the inlet hose at the crankcase filler cap.

2. Remove the throttle body inlet tubes.

3. Disconnect the accelerator cable at the throttle body. Remove the cable retracting spring. Remove the accelerator cable bracket from the upper intake manifold and position the cable and bracket out of the way.

4. Remove the fuel line from the fuel rail. Be careful not to kink the line.

5. Remove the upper intake manifold and throttle body assembly. See Section 5.

6. Remove the ignition coil and wires.

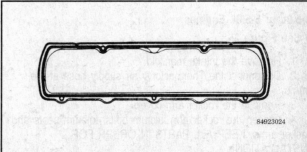

84923024

Fig. 24 Use a silicone sealant when reinstalling the valve covers

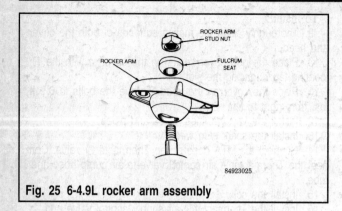

Fig. 25 6-4.9L rocker arm assembly

7. Remove the rocker arm cover.
8. Remove the spark plug wires.
9. Remove the distributor cap.
10. Remove the pushrod cover (engine side cover).
11. Loosen the rocker arm bolts until the pushrods can be removed. KEEP THE PUSHRODS IN ORDER, FOR INSTALLATION!
12. Using a magnetic lifter removal tool, remove the lifters. Wipe clean the exterior of each lifter as it's removed and mark it with an indelible marker, so that it can be installed in its original bore.

To install:

13. Coat the bottom surface of each lifter with multi-purpose grease, and coat the rest of the lifter with clean engine oil.
14. Install each lifter in it original bore using the magnetic tool.
15. Coat each end of each pushrod with multi-purpose grease and install each in its original position. Make sure that each pushrod is properly seated in the lifter socket.
16. Engage the rocker arms with the pushrods and tighten the rocker arm bolts enough to hold the pushrods in place.
17. Adjust the valve clearance as described below.
18. Install the pushrod cover (engine side cover).
19. Install the distributor cap.
20. Install the spark plug wires.
21. Install the rocker arm cover.
22. Install the ignition coil and wires.
23. Install the upper intake manifold and throttle body assembly. See Section 5.
24. Install the fuel line at the fuel rail.
25. Install the accelerator cable bracket on the upper intake manifold. Install the cable retracting spring. Connect the accelerator cable at the throttle body.
26. Install the throttle body inlet tubes.
27. Connect the inlet hose at the crankcase filler cap.

8-5.0L or 8-5.8L Engines

▶ See Figure 26

1. Remove the intake manifold.
2. Disconnect the Thermactor® air supply hose at the pump.
3. Remove the rocker arm covers.
4. Loosen the rocker arm fulcrum bolts, fulcrum seats and rocker arms. KEEP ALL PARTS IN ORDER FOR INSTALLATION!

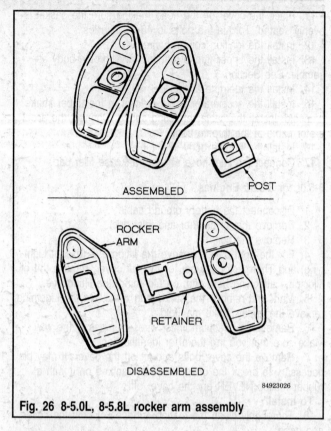

Fig. 26 8-5.0L, 8-5.8L rocker arm assembly

To install:

5. Apply multi-purpose grease to the valve stem tips, the fulcrum seats and sockets.
6. Install the fulcrum guides, rocker arms, seats and bolts. Torque the bolts to 18-25 ft. lbs.
7. Install the rocker arm covers.
8. Connect the Thermactor® air supply hose at the pump.
9. Install the intake manifold.

8-7.5L Engine

▶ See Figure 27

1. Remove the intake manifold.
2. Remove the rocker arm covers.
3. Loosen the rocker arm fulcrum bolts, fulcrum, oil deflector, seat and rocker arms. KEEP EVERYTHING IN ORDER FOR INSTALLATION!

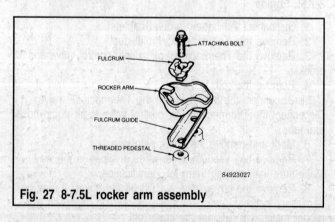

Fig. 27 8-7.5L rocker arm assembly

To install:

4. Coat each end of each pushrod with multi-purpose grease.

5. Coat the top of the valve stems, the rocker arms and the fulcrum seats with multi-purpose grease.

6. Rotate the crankshaft by hand until No. 1 piston is at TDC of compression. The firing order marks on the damper will be aligned at TDC with the timing pointer.

7. Install the rocker arms, seats, deflectors and bolts on the following valves:
   - No. 1 intake and exhaust
   - No. 3 intake
   - No. 8 exhaust
   - No. 7 intake
   - No. 5 exhaust
   - No. 8 intake
   - No. 4 exhaust

Engage the rocker arms with the pushrods and tighten the rocker arm fulcrum bolts to 18-25 ft. lbs.

8. Rotate the crankshaft on full turn — 360° — and re-align the TDC mark and pointer. Install the parts and tighten the bolts on the following valves:
   - No. 2 intake and exhaust
   - No. 4 intake
   - No. 3 exhaust
   - No. 5 intake
   - No. 6 exhaust
   - No. 6 intake
   - No. 7 exhaust

9. Install the rocker arm covers.

10. Install the intake manifold.

11. Check the valve clearance as described under Hydraulic Valve Clearance, below.

Diesel Engines

▶ **See Figures 28 and 29**

1. Disconnect the ground cables from both batteries.

2. Remove the valve cover attaching screws and remove both valve cover.

3. Remove the valve rocker arm post mounting bolts. Remove the rocker arms and posts in order and mark them with tape so they can be installed in their original positions.

4. If the cylinder heads are to be removed, then the pushrods can now be removed. Make a holder for the pushrods out of a piece of wood or cardboard, and remove the pushrods in order. It is very important that the pushrods be re-installed in their original order. The pushrods can remain in position if no further disassembly is required.

5. If the pushrods were removed, install them in their original locations. make sure they are fully seated in the tappet seats.

➡**The copper colored end of the pushrod goes toward the rocker arm.**

6. Apply a polyethylene grease to the valve stem tips. Install the rocker arms and posts in their original positions.

7. Turn the engine over by hand until the valve timing mark is at the 11:00 o'clock position, as viewed from the front of the engine. Install all of the rocker arm post attaching bolts and torque to 20 ft. lbs.

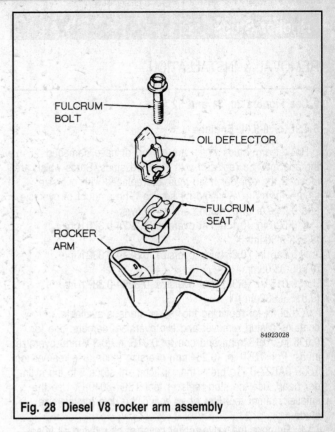

Fig. 28 Diesel V8 rocker arm assembly

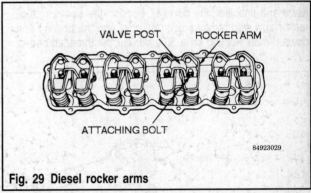

Fig. 29 Diesel rocker arms

8. Install new valve cover gaskets and install the valve cover. Install the battery cables, start the engine and check for leaks.

Hydraulic Lash Adjuster

REMOVAL & INSTALLATION

8-7.5L Engine

1. Remove the lower intake manifold.
2. Remove the rocker arm assemblies.
3. Remove the pushrods.
4. Lift out the hydraulic lash adjuster.
5. Installation is the reverse of removal.

Rocker Studs

REMOVAL & INSTALLATION

▶ See Figures 30, 31 and 32

6-4.9L or 8-5.0L Engines

Rocker arm studs which are broken or have damaged threads may be replaced with standard studs. Studs which are loose in the cylinder head must be replaced with oversize studs which are available for service. The amount of oversize and diameter of the studs are as follows:

- 0.006 in. (0.152mm) oversize: 0.3774-0.3781 in. (9.586-9.604mm)
- 0.010 in. (0.254mm) oversize: 0.3814-0.3821 in. (9.688-9.705mm)
- 0.015 in. (0.381mm) oversize: 0.3864-0.3871 in. (9.815-9.832mm)

A tool kit for replacing the rocker studs is available and contains a stud remover and two oversize reamers: one for 0.006 in. (0.152mm) and one for 0.015 in. (0.381mm) oversize studs. For 0.010 in. (0.254mm) oversize studs, use reamer tool T66P-6A527-B. To press the replacement studs into the cylinder head, use the stud replacer tool T69P-6049-D. Use the smaller reamer tool first when boring the hole for oversize studs.

1. Remove the valve rocker cover(s) by moving all hoses aside and unbolting the cover(s). Position the sleeve of the rocker arm stud remover over the stud with the bearing end down. When working on a 5.0L V8, cut the threaded part of

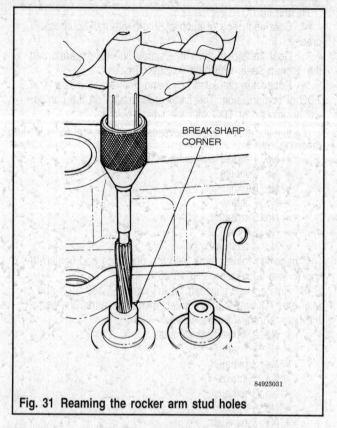

Fig. 31 Reaming the rocker arm stud holes

the stud off with a hacksaw. Thread the puller into the sleeve and over the stud until it is fully bottomed. Hold the sleeve with a wrench and rotate the puller clockwise to remove the stud.

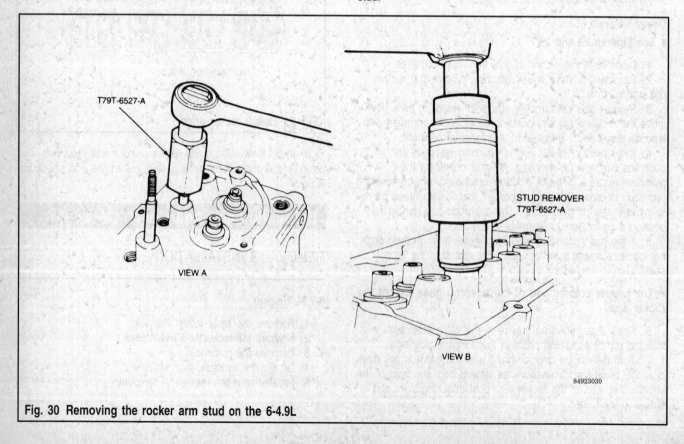

Fig. 30 Removing the rocker arm stud on the 6-4.9L

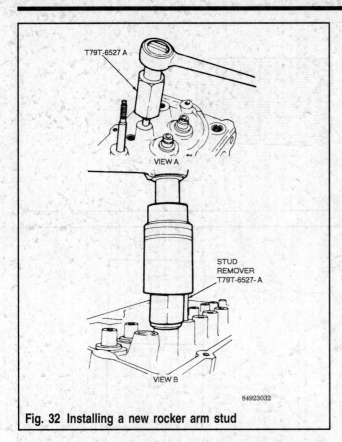

VIEW A

STUD
REMOVER
T79T-6527- A

T79T-6527 A

VIEW B

84923032

Fig. 32 Installing a new rocker arm stud

An alternate method of removing the rocker studs without the special tool is to put spacers over the stud until just enough threads are left showing at the top so a nut can be screwed onto the top of the rocker arm stud and get a full bite. Turn the nut clockwise until the stud is removed, adding spacers under the nut as necessary.

➡**If the rocker stud was broken off flush with the stud boss, use an easy-out tool to remove the broken off part of the stud from the cylinder head.**

2. If a loose rocker arm stud is being replaced, ream the stud bore for the selected oversize stud.

➡**Keep all metal particles away from the valves.**

3. Coat the end of the stud with Lubriplate® . Align the stud and installer with the stud bore and top the sliding driver until it bottoms. When the installer contacts the stud boss, the stud is installed to its correct height.

Radiator

REMOVAL & INSTALLATION

▶ **See Figures 33, 34, 35, 36, 37, 38 and 39**

1. Drain the cooling system.

✳✳CAUTION

When draining the coolant, keep in mind that cats and dogs are attracted by the ethylene glycol antifreeze, and are quite likely to drink any that is left in an uncovered

container or in puddles on the ground. This will prove fatal in sufficient quantity. Always drain the coolant into a sealable container. Coolant should be reused unless it is contaminated or several years old.

2. Disconnect the transmission cooling lines from the bottom of the radiator, if so equipped.

3. Remove the retaining bolts at each of the 4 corners of the shroud, if so equipped, and position the shroud over the fan, clear of the radiator.

4. Disconnect the upper and lower hoses from the radiator.

5. Remove the radiator retaining bolts or the upper supports and lift the radiator from the vehicle.

To install:

6. Lower the radiator into the vehicle. Install the radiator retaining bolts or the upper supports.

7. Connect the upper and lower hoses at the radiator.

8. Install the shroud, if so equipped.

9. Connect the transmission cooling lines at the bottom of the radiator.

10. Fill the cooling system.

Engine Fan and Fan Clutch

REMOVAL & INSTALLATION

▶ **See Figures 40, 41 and 42**

6-4.9L Engine

1. Remove the fan shroud.

2. Remove one of the fan-to-clutch bolts, to access the clutch-to-hub nut.

3. Turn the large fan clutch-to-hub nut counterclockwise to remove the fan and clutch from the hub. There are 2 tools made for this purpose, holding tool T84T-6312-C and nut wrench T84T-6312-D.

4. If the fan and clutch have to be separated, remove the remaining fan-to-clutch bolts.

To install:

5. Attach the fan to the clutch using all but one of the bolts. The bolts are tightened to 18 ft. lbs.

6. Install the assembly on the hub and tighten the hub nut to a maximum of 100 ft. lbs., or a minimum of 30 ft. lbs.

7. Install and torque the last fan-to-clutch bolt.

8. Install the shroud.

8-5.0L, 8-5.8L or 8-7.5L Engines

1. Remove the fan shroud, and, if you need the clearance, the radiator.

2. Remove the 4 fan clutch-to-water pump hub bolts and lift off the fan/clutch assembly.

3. Remove the 4 fan-to-clutch bolts and separate the fan from the clutch.

4. Installation is the reverse of removal. Torque the all the bolts to 18 ft. lbs.

Diesel Engine

1. Remove the fan shroud.

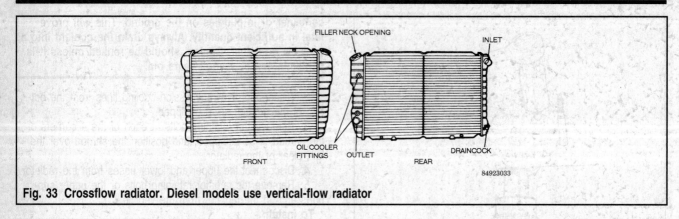

Fig. 33 Crossflow radiator. Diesel models use vertical-flow radiator

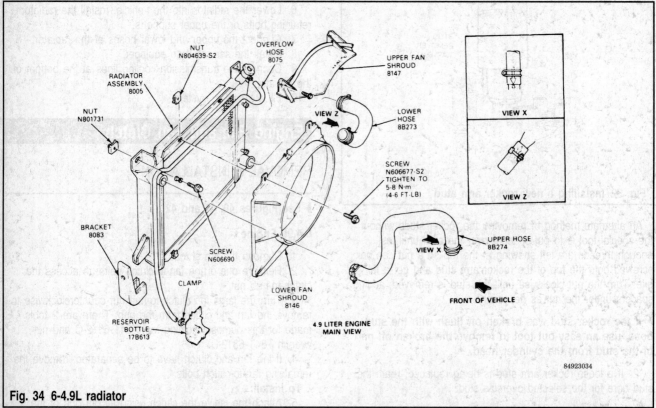

Fig. 34 6-4.9L radiator

2. Turn the large fan clutch-to-hub nut CLOCKWISE (left-handed threads) to remove the fan and clutch from the hub. There are 2 tools made for this purpose, holding tool T84T-6312-A and nut wrench T84T-6312-B.

3. If the fan and clutch have to be separated, remove the fan-to-clutch bolts.

To install:

4. Attach the fan to the clutch. The bolts are tightened to 18 ft. lbs.

5. Install the assembly on the hub and tighten the hub nut to a maximum of 120 ft. lbs., or a minimum of 40 ft. lbs. Remember, the nut is left-handed. Tighten it by turning it COUNTERCLOCKWISE.

6. Install the shroud.

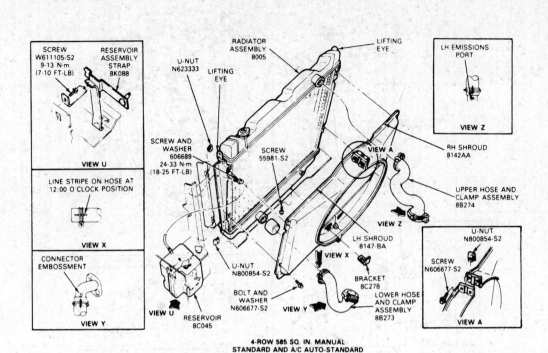

**4-ROW 585 SQ. IN. MANUAL
STANDARD AND A/C AUTO-STANDARD**

**3-AND 4-ROW 735 SQ. IN. AUTO-A/C
AUTO MANUAL SUPER COOL WITH/WITHOUT A/C**

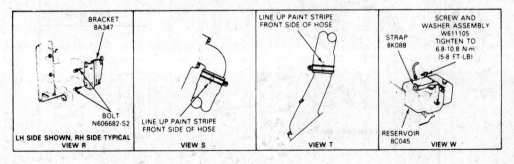

84923035

Fig. 35 Diesel radiators

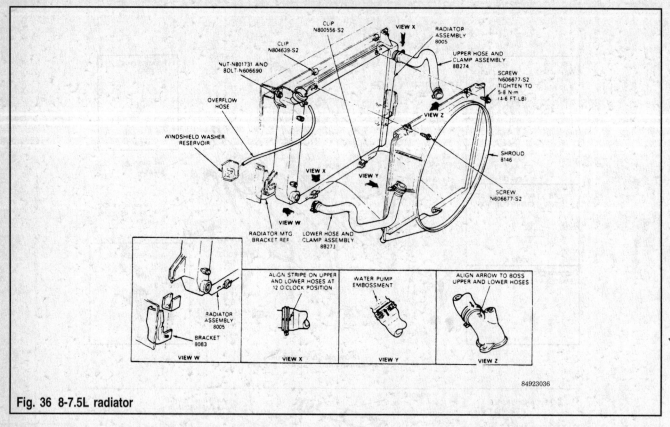

Fig. 36 8-7.5L radiator

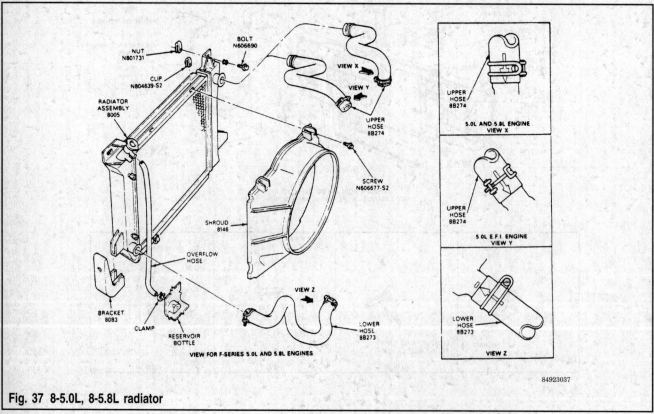

Fig. 37 8-5.0L, 8-5.8L radiator

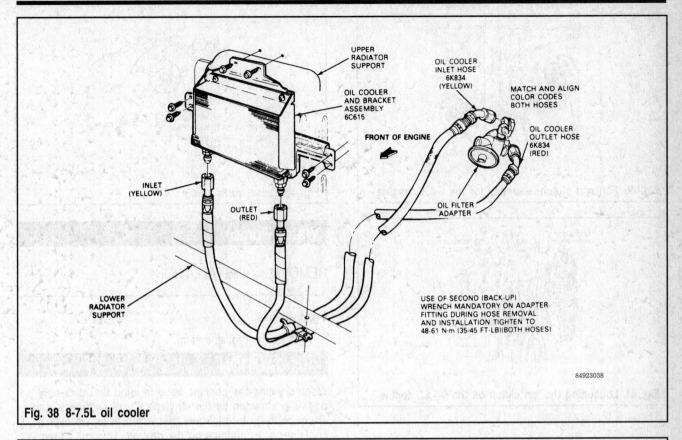

Fig. 38 8-7.5L oil cooler

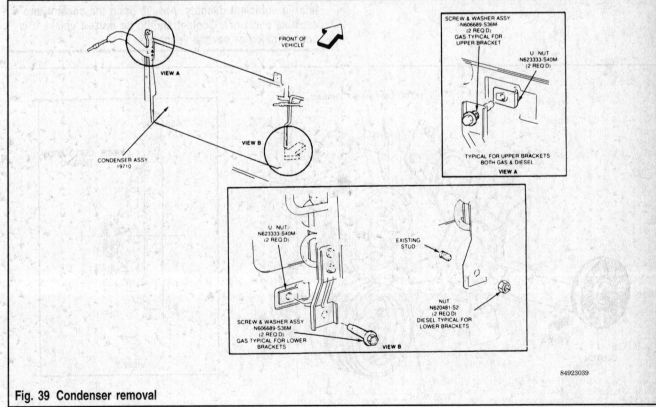

Fig. 39 Condenser removal

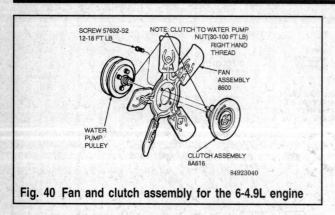

Fig. 40 Fan and clutch assembly for the 6-4.9L engine

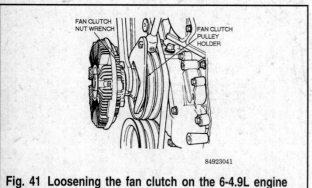

Fig. 41 Loosening the fan clutch on the 6-4.9L engine

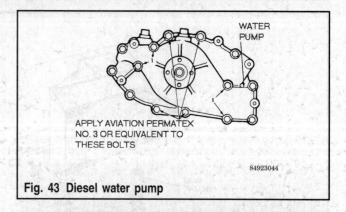

Fig. 43 Diesel water pump

Water Pump

REMOVAL & INSTALLATION

6-4.9L Engine

1. Drain the cooling system.

✳✳CAUTION

When draining the coolant, keep in mind that cats and dogs are attracted by the ethylene glycol antifreeze, and are quite likely to drink any that is left in an uncovered container or in puddles on the ground. This will prove fatal in sufficient quantity. Always drain the coolant into a sealable container. Coolant should be reused unless it is contaminated or several years old.

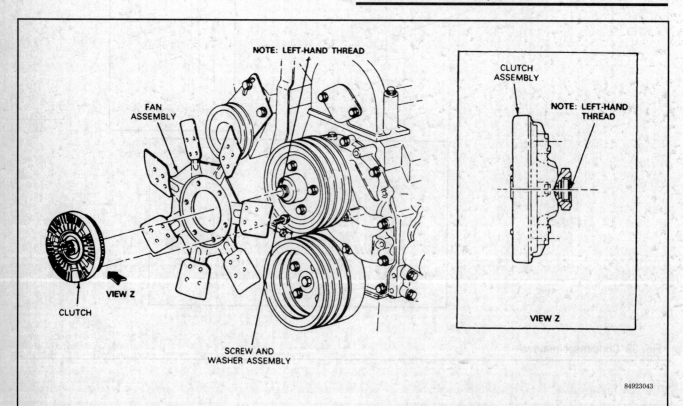

Fig. 42 Diesel fan and clutch assembly

2. Disconnect the lower radiator hose from the water pump.

3. Remove the drive belt, fan, fan spacer, fan shroud, if so equipped, and water pump pulley.

4. Remove the alternator pivot arm from the pump.

5. Disconnect the heater hose at the water pump.

6. Remove the water pump.

To install:

7. Before installing the old water pump, clean the gasket mounting surfaces on the pump and on the cylinder block. If a new water pump is being installed, remove the heater hose fitting from the old pump and install it on the new one.

8. Coat the new gaskets with sealer on both sides and install the water pump. Torque the mounting bolts to 18 ft. lbs.

9. Connect the heater hose at the water pump.

10. Install the alternator pivot arm on the pump.

11. Install the water pump pulley fan shroud, fan spacer, fan, and drive belt.

12. Connect the lower radiator hose at the water pump.

13. Fill the cooling system.

8-5.0L, 8-5.8L or 8-7.5L Engines

1. Drain the cooling system.

✳✳CAUTION

When draining the coolant, keep in mind that cats and dogs are attracted by the ethylene glycol antifreeze, and are quite likely to drink any that is left in an uncovered container or in puddles on the ground. This will prove fatal in sufficient quantity. Always drain the coolant into a sealable container. Coolant should be reused unless it is contaminated or several years old.

2. Remove the bolts securing the fan shroud to the radiator, if so equipped, and position the shroud over the fan.

3. Disconnect the lower radiator hose, heater hose and by-pass hose at the water pump. Remove the drive belts, fan, fan spacer and pulley. Remove the fan shroud, if so equipped.

4. Loosen the alternator pivot bolt and the bolt attaching the alternator adjusting arm to the water pump. Remove the power steering pump bracket from the water pump and position it out of the way.

5. Remove the bolts securing the water pump to the timing chain cover and remove the water pump.

To install:

6. Coat a new gasket with sealer and install the water pump. Torque the bolts to 18 ft. lbs.

7. Install the power steering pump bracket.

8. Connect the lower radiator hose, heater hose and by-pass hose at the water pump.

9. Install the fan shroud, if so equipped.

10. Install the pulley, fan spacer, fan, and drive belts.

11. Fill the cooling system.

6.9L or 7.3L Diesel Engines
▶ See Figure 43

1. Disconnect both battery ground cables.

2. Drain the cooling system.

✳✳CAUTION

When draining the coolant, keep in mind that cats and dogs are attracted by the ethylene glycol antifreeze, and are quite likely to drink any that is left in an uncovered container or in puddles on the ground. This will prove fatal in sufficient quantity. Always drain the coolant into a sealable container. Coolant should be reused unless it is contaminated or several years old.

3. Remove the radiator shroud halves.

4. Remove the fan clutch and fan.

➡**The fan clutch bolts are left hand thread. Remove them by turning them clockwise.**

5. Remove the power steering pump belt.

6. Remove the air conditioning compressor belt.

7. Remove the vacuum pump drive belt.

8. Remove the alternator drive belt.

9. Remove the water pump pulley.

10. Disconnect the heater hose at the water pump.

11. If you're installing a new pump, remove the heater hose fitting from the old pump at this time.

12. Remove the alternator adjusting arm and bracket.

13. Unbolt the air conditioning compressor and position it out of the way. DO NOT DISCONNECT THE REFRIGERANT LINES!

14. Remove the air conditioning compressor brackets.

15. Unbolt the power steering pump and bracket and position it out of the way. DO NOT DISCONNECT THE POWER STEERING FLUID LINES!

16. Remove the bolts attaching the water pump to the front cover and lift off the pump.

17. Thoroughly clean the mating surfaces of the pump and front cover.

18. Get a hold of two dowel pins - anything that will fit into 2 mounting bolt holes in the front cover. You'll need these to ensure proper bolt hole alignment when you're installing the water pump.

19. Using a new gasket, position the water pump over the dowel pins and into place on the front cover.

20. Install the attaching bolts. The 2 top center and 2 bottom center bolts must be coated with RTV silicone sealant prior to installation. See the illustration. Also, the 4 bolts marked No. 1 in the illustration are a different length than the other bolts. Torque the bolts to 14 ft. lbs.

21. Install the water pump pulley.

22. Wrap the heater hose fitting threads with Teflon® tape and screw it into the water pump. Torque it to 18 ft. lbs.

23. Connect the heater hose to the pump.

24. Install the power steering pump and bracket. Install the belt.

25. Install the air conditioning compressor bracket.

26. Install the air conditioning compressor. Install the belt.

27. Install the alternator adjusting arm and install the belt.

28. Install the vacuum pump drive belt.

29. Adjust all the drive belts.

30. Install the fan and clutch. Remember that the bolts are left hand thread. Turn them counterclockwise to tighten them. Torque them to 45 ft. lbs.

31. Install the fan shroud halves.
32. Fill and bleed the cooling system.
33. Connect the battery ground cables.
34. Start the engine and check for leaks.

Thermostat

➡It is a good practice to check the operation of a new thermostat before it is installed in an engine. Place the thermostat in a pan of boiling water. If it does not open more than ¼ in. (6mm), do not install it in the engine.

REMOVAL & INSTALLATION

▶ See Figures 44, 45, 46, 47 and 48

6-4.9L Engine

1. Drain the cooling system below the level of the coolant outlet housing. Use the petcock valve at the bottom of the radiator to drain the system. It is not necessary to remove any of the hoses.

❄❄CAUTION

When draining the coolant, keep in mind that cats and dogs are attracted by the ethylene glycol antifreeze, and are quite likely to drink any that is left in an uncovered container or in puddles on the ground. This will prove fatal in sufficient quantity. Always drain the coolant into a sealable container. Coolant should be reused unless it is contaminated or several years old.

Fig. 44 6-4.9L thermostat installation. V8 thermostat mounted vertically on front of engine, diesel is on side of front of intake manifold

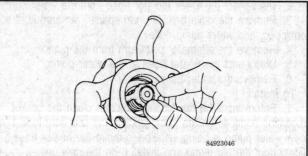

Fig. 45 Thermostat spring always faces down in all engines

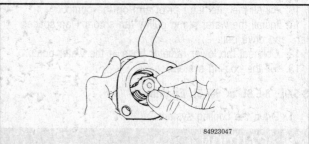

Fig. 46 On gasoline engines, turn the thermostat clockwise to lock it into position on the flats in the outlet elbow

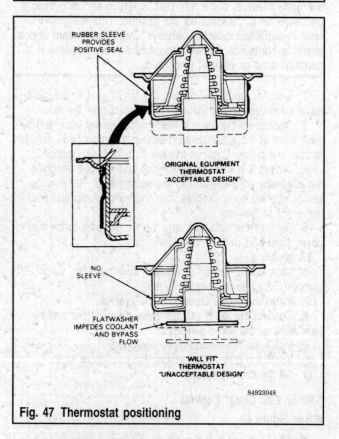

Fig. 47 Thermostat positioning

2. Remove the coolant outlet housing retaining bolts and slide the housing with the hose attached to one side.

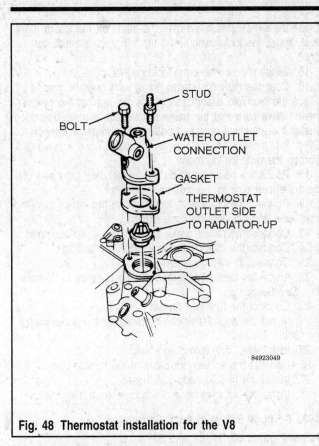

BOLT

STUD

WATER OUTLET
CONNECTION

GASKET

THERMOSTAT
OUTLET SIDE
TO RADIATOR-UP

84923049

Fig. 48 Thermostat installation for the V8

3. Remove the thermostat and gasket from the cylinder head and clean both mating surfaces.

4. To install the thermostat, coat a new gasket with water resistant sealer and position it on the outlet of the engine. The gasket must be in place before the thermostat is installed.

5. Install the thermostat with the bridge (opposite end of the spring) inside the elbow connection.

6. Position the elbow connection onto the mounting surface of the outlet, so that the thermostat flange is resting on the gasket and install the retaining bolts. Torque the bolts to 15 ft. lbs.

7. Fill the radiator and operate the engine until it reaches operating temperature. Check the coolant level and adjust if necessary.

8-5.0L, 8-5.8L or 8-7.5L Engine

1. Drain the cooling system below the level of the coolant outlet housing. Use the petcock valve at the bottom of the radiator to drain the system. It is not necessary to remove any of the hoses.

✳✳CAUTION

When draining the coolant, keep in mind that cats and dogs are attracted by the ethylene glycol antifreeze, and are quite likely to drink any that is left in an uncovered container or in puddles on the ground. This will prove fatal in sufficient quantity. Always drain the coolant into a sealable container. Coolant should be reused unless it is contaminated or several years old.

2. Disconnect the bypass hoses at the water pump and intake manifold.

3. Remove the bypass tube.

4. Remove the coolant outlet housing retaining bolts, bend the hose and lift the housing with the hose attached to one side.

5. Remove the thermostat and gasket from the intake manifold and clean both mating surfaces.

To install:

6. To install the thermostat, coat a new gasket with water resistant sealer and position it on the outlet of the engine. The gasket must be in place before the thermostat is installed.

7. Install the thermostat with the bridge (opposite end of the spring) inside the elbow connection and the thermostat flange positioned in the recess in the manifold.

8. Position the elbow connection onto the mounting surface of the outlet. Torque the bolts to 18 ft. lbs. on the 8-5.0L and 5.8L; 28 ft. lbs. on the 8-7.5L.

9. Install the bypass tube and hoses.

10. Fill the radiator and operate the engine until it reaches operating temperature. Check the coolant level and adjust if necessary.

6.9L and 7.3L Diesel

✳✳WARNING

The factory specified thermostat does not contain an internal bypass. On these engines, an internal bypass is located in the block. The use of any replacement thermostat other than that meeting the manufacturer's specifications will result in engine overheating! Use only thermostats meeting the specifications of Ford part number E5TZ-8575-C or Navistar International part number 1807945-C1.

1. Disconnect both battery ground cables.

2. Drain the coolant to a point below the thermostat housing.

✳✳CAUTION

When draining the coolant, keep in mind that cats and dogs are attracted by the ethylene glycol antifreeze, and are quite likely to drink any that is left in an uncovered container or in puddles on the ground. This will prove fatal in sufficient quantity. Always drain the coolant into a sealable container. Coolant should be reused unless it is contaminated or several years old.

3. Remove the alternator and vacuum pump belts

4. Remove the alternator.

5. Remove the vacuum pump and bracket.

6. Remove all but the lowest vacuum pump/alternator mounting casting bolt.

7. Loosen that lowest bolt and pivot the casting outboard of the engine.

8. Remove the thermostat housing attaching bolts, bend the hose and lift the housing up and to one side.

9. Remove the thermostat and gasket.

10. Clean the thermostat housing and block surfaces thoroughly.

11. Coat a new gasket with waterproof sealer and position the gasket on the manifold outlet opening.

12. Install the thermostat in the manifold opening with the spring element end downward and the flange positioned in the recess in the manifold.

13. Place the outlet housing into position and install the bolts. Torque the bolts to 20 ft. lbs.

14. Reposition the casting.

15. Install the vacuum pump and bracket.

16. Install the alternator.

17. Adjust the drive belts.

18. Fill and bleed the cooling system.

19. Connect both battery cables.

20. Run the engine and check for leaks.

Intake Manifolds

REMOVAL & INSTALLATION

6-4.9L

▶ See Figure 49

The intake and exhaust manifolds on these engines are known as combination manifolds and are serviced as a unit.

1. Remove the air inlet hose at the crankcase filter cap.

2. Remove the throttle body inlet hoses.

3. Disconnect the accelerator cable at the throttle body.

4. Remove the cable retracting spring.

5. Remove the cable bracket from the upper intake manifold.

6. Disconnect the fuel inlet line at the fuel rail. Don't kink the line!

7. Remove the upper intake and throttle body as an assembly. See Section 5.

8. Tag and disconnect all vacuum lines attached to the parts in question.

9. Disconnect the inlet pipe from the exhaust manifold.

10. Disconnect the power brake vacuum line, if so equipped.

11. Remove the bolts and nuts attaching the manifolds to the cylinder head. Lift the manifold assemblies from the engine. Remove and discard the gaskets.

12. To separate the manifold, remove the nuts joining the intake and exhaust manifolds.

To install:

13. Clean the mating surfaces of the cylinder head and the manifolds.

14. If the intake and exhaust manifolds have been separated, coat the mating surfaces lightly with graphite grease and

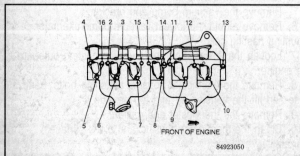

Fig. 49 6-4.9L EFI intake and exhaust manifold bolt torque sequence

place the exhaust manifold over the studs on the intake manifold. Install the lockwashers and nuts. Tighten them finger tight.

15. Install a new intake manifold gasket.

16. Coat the mating surfaces lightly with graphite grease. Place the manifold assemblies in position against the cylinder head. Make sure that the gaskets have not become dislodged. Install the attaching nuts and bolts in the proper sequence to 26 ft. lbs. If the intake and exhaust manifolds were separated, tighten the nuts joining them.

17. Position a new gasket on the muffler inlet pipe and connect the inlet pipe to the exhaust manifold.

18. Connect the crankcase vent hose to the intake manifold inlet tube and position the hose clamp.

19. Connect the power brake vacuum line, if so equipped.

20. Connect the inlet pipe at the exhaust manifold.

21. Connect all vacuum lines.

22. Install the upper intake and throttle body as an assembly. See Section 5.

23. Connect the fuel inlet line at the fuel rail.

24. Install the accelerator cable bracket at the upper intake manifold.

25. Install the cable retracting spring.

26. Connect the accelerator cable at the throttle body.

27. Install the throttle body inlet hoses.

28. Install the air inlet hose at the crankcase filter cap.

1987 8-5.0L & 5.8L with 4-bbl Carburetor

▶ See Figures 50, 51, 52 and 53

1. Drain the cooling system, remove the air cleaner and the intake duct assembly.

✳✳CAUTION

When draining the coolant, keep in mind that cats and dogs are attracted by the ethylene glycol antifreeze, and are quite likely to drink any that is left in an uncovered container or in puddles on the ground. This will prove fatal in sufficient quantity. Always drain the coolant into a sealable container. Coolant should be reused unless it is contaminated or several years old.

2. Disconnect the accelerator rod from the carburetor and remove the accelerator retracting spring. Disconnect the automatic transmission kickdown rod at the carburetor, if so equipped.

3. Disconnect the high tension lead and all other wires from the ignition coil.

4. Disconnect the spark plug wires from the spark plugs by grasping the rubber boots and twisting and pulling at the same time. Remove the wires from the brackets on the rocker covers. Remove the distributor cap and spark plug wire assembly.

5. Remove the carburetor fuel inlet line and the distributor vacuum line from the carburetor.

6. Remove the distributor lockbolt and remove the distributor and vacuum line. See Distributor Removal and Installation.

7. Disconnect the upper radiator hose from the coolant outlet housing and the temperature sending unit wire at the sending unit. Remove the heater hose from the intake manifold.

8. Loosen the clamp on the water pump bypass hose at the coolant outlet housing and slide the hose off the outlet housing.

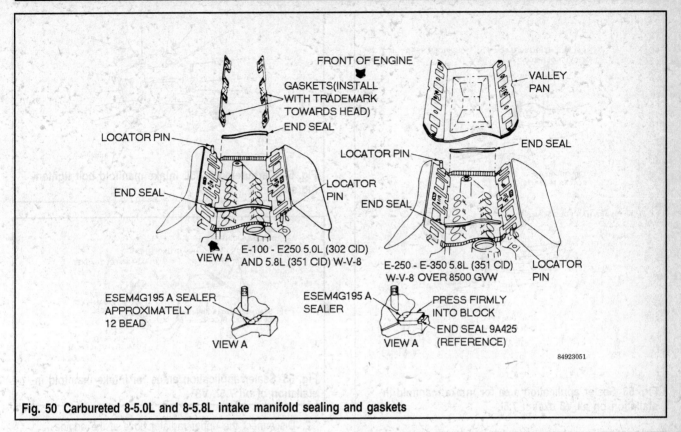

Fig. 50 Carbureted 8-5.0L and 8-5.8L intake manifold sealing and gaskets

9. Disconnect the PCV hose at the rocker cover.

10. If the engine is equipped with the Thermactor® exhaust emission control system, remove the air pump to cylinder head air hose at the air pump and position it out of the way. Also

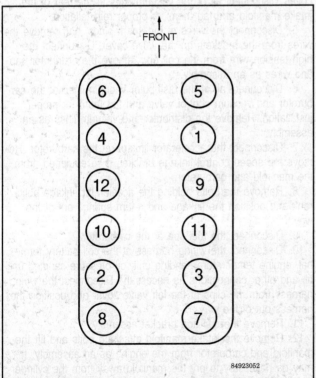

Fig. 51 Carbureted 8-5.0L intake manifold bolt tightening sequence

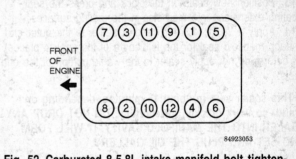

Fig. 52 Carbureted 8-5.8L intake manifold bolt tightening sequence

remove the air hose at the backfire suppressor valve. Remove the air hose bracket from the valve rocker arm cover and position the air hose out of the way.

11. Remove the intake manifold and carburetor as an assembly. It may be necessary to pry the intake manifold from the cylinder head. Remove all traces of the intake manifold-to-cylinder head gaskets and the two end seals from both the manifold and the other mating surfaces of the engine.

Installation is as follows:

12. Clean the mating surfaces of the intake manifold, cylinder heads, and block with lacquer thinner or similar solvent. Apply a ⅛in. (3mm) bead of silicone-rubber RTV sealant at the points shown in the accompanying diagram.

⋇⋇WARNING

Do not apply sealer to the waffle portions of the seals as the sealer will rupture the end seal material.

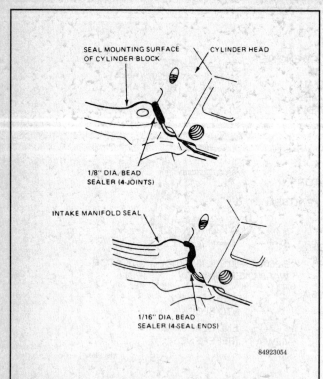

Fig. 53 Sealer application area for intake manifold installation on all V8 except 7.5L

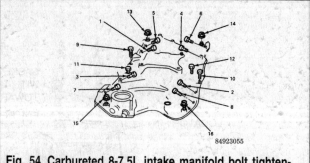

Fig. 54 Carbureted 8-7.5L intake manifold bolt tightening sequence

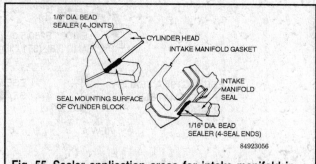

Fig. 55 Sealer application areas for intake manifold installation of on 7.5L V8

13. Position new seals on the block and press the seal locating extensions into the holes in the mating surfaces.

14. Apply a $\frac{1}{16}$ in. (1.5mm) bead of sealer to the outer end of each manifold seal for the full length of the seal (4 places). As before, do not apply sealer to the waffle portion of the end seals.

➡This sealer sets in about 15 minutes, depending on brand, so work quickly but carefully. **DO NOT DROP ANY SEALER INTO THE MANIFOLD CAVITY. IT WILL FORM AND SET AND PLUG THE OIL GALLERY.**

15. Position the manifold gasket onto the block and heads with the alignment notches under the dowels in the heads. Be sure gasket holes align with head holes.

16. Install the manifold and related equipment in reverse order of removal.

1987 8-7.5L with 4-bbl Carburetor

▶ **See Figures 54 and 55**

1. Drain the cooling system and remove the air cleaner assembly.

✳✳CAUTION

When draining the coolant, keep in mind that cats and dogs are attracted by the ethylene glycol antifreeze, and are quite likely to drink any that is left in an uncovered container or in puddles on the ground. This will prove fatal in sufficient quantity. Always drain the coolant into a sealable container. Coolant should be reused unless it is contaminated or several years old.

2. Disconnect the upper radiator hose at the engine.

3. Disconnect the heater hoses at the intake manifold and the water pump. Position them out of the way. Loosen the water pump by-pass hose clamp at the intake manifold.

4. Disconnect the PCV valve and hose at the right valve cover. Disconnect all of the vacuum lines at the rear of the intake manifold and tag them for proper reinstallation.

5. Disconnect the wires at the spark plugs, and remove the wires from the brackets on the valve cover. Disconnect the high tension wire from the coil and remove the distributor cap and wires as an assembly.

6. Disconnect all of the distributor vacuum lines at the carburetor and vacuum control valve and tag them for proper installation. Remove the distributor and vacuum lines as an assembly.

7. Disconnect the accelerator linkage at the carburetor. Remove the speed control linkage bracket, if so equipped, from the manifold and carburetor.

8. Remove the bolts holding the accelerator linkage bellcrank and position the linkage and return springs out of the way.

9. Disconnect the fuel line at the carburetor.

10. Disconnect the wiring harness at the coil battery terminal, engine temperature sending unit, oil pressure sending until, and other connections as necessary. Disconnect the wiring harness from the clips at the left valve cover and position the harness out of the way.

11. Remove the coil and bracket assembly.

12. Remove the intake manifold attaching bolts and lift the manifold and carburetor from the engine as an assembly. It may be necessary to pry the manifold away from the cylinder heads. Do not damage the gasket sealing surfaces.

Installation is as follows:

13. Clean the mating surfaces of the intake manifold, cylinder heads and block with lacquer thinner or similar solvent. Apply a 1/8in. (3mm) bead of silicone-rubber RTV sealant at the points shown in the accompanying diagram.

❋❋WARNING

Do not apply sealer to the waffle portions of the seals as the sealer will rupture the end seal material.

14. Position the new seals on the block and press the seal locating extensions into the holes in the mating surfaces.

15. Apply a 1/16 in. (1.5mm) bead of sealer to the outer end of each manifold seal for the full length of the seal (4 places). As before, do not apply sealer to the waffle portion of the end seals.

➡This sealer sets in about 15 minutes, depending on brand, so work quickly but carefully. DO NOT DROP ANY SEALER INTO THE MANIFOLD CAVITY. IT WILL FORM AND SET AND PLUG THE OIL GALLERY.

16. Position the manifold gasket onto the block and heads with the alignment notches under the dowels in the heads. Be sure gasket holes align with head holes.

17. Install the manifold and related equipment in reverse order of removal.

Fuel Injected V8 Engines Except 5.8L Lightning

▶ See Figures 56, 57, 58 and 59

➡Discharge fuel system pressure before starting any work that involves disconnecting fuel system lines. See Fuel Supply Manifold removal and installation procedures in Section 5 (Gasoline Fuel System section).

UPPER INTAKE MANIFOLD

1. Remove the air cleaner. Disconnect the electrical connectors at the air bypass valve, throttle position sensor and EGR position sensor.

2. Disconnect the throttle linkage at the throttle ball and the AOD transmission linkage from the throttle body. Remove the bolts that secure the bracket to the intake and position the bracket and cables out of the way.

3. Disconnect the upper manifold vacuum fitting connections by removing all the vacuum lines at the vacuum tree (label lines for position identification). Remove the vacuum lines to the EGR valve and fuel pressure regulator.

4. Disconnect the PCV system by disconnecting the hose from the fitting at the rear of the upper manifold.

5. Remove the two canister purge lines from the fittings at the throttle body.

6. Disconnect the EGR tube from the EGR valve by loosening the flange nut.

7. Remove the bolt from the upper intake support bracket to upper manifold. Remove the upper manifold retaining bolts and remove the upper intake manifold and throttle body as an assembly.

8. Clean and inspect all mounting surfaces of the upper and lower intake manifolds.

To install:

9. Position a new mounting gasket on the lower intake manifold.

10. Install the upper intake manifold and throttle body as an assembly. Install the upper manifold retaining bolts and install the bolt at the upper intake support bracket. Mounting bolts are torqued to 12-18 ft. lbs.

11. Connect the EGR tube at the EGR valve.

12. Install the two canister purge lines at the fittings at the throttle body.

13. Connect the PCV system hose at the fitting at the rear of the upper manifold.

14. Connect the upper manifold vacuum lines at the vacuum tree. Install the vacuum lines at the EGR valve and fuel pressure regulator.

15. Install the throttle bracket on the intake manifold. Connect the throttle linkage at the throttle ball and the AOD transmission linkage at the throttle body.

16. Connect the electrical connectors at the air bypass valve, throttle position sensor and EGR position sensor.

17. Install the air cleaner.

UPPER INTAKE MANIFOLD

1. Upper manifold and throttle body must be removed first.
2. Drain the cooling system.

❋❋CAUTION

When draining the coolant, keep in mind that cats and dogs are attracted by the ethylene glycol antifreeze, and are quite likely to drink any that is left in an uncovered container or in puddles on the ground. This will prove fatal in sufficient quantity. Always drain the coolant into a sealable container. Coolant should be reused unless it is contaminated or several years old.

3. Remove the distributor assembly, cap and wires.

4. Disconnect the electrical connectors at the engine, coolant temperature sensor and sending unit, at the air charge temperature sensor and at the knock sensor.

5. Disconnect the injector wiring harness from the main harness assembly. Remove the ground wire from the intake manifold stud. The ground wire must be installed at the same position it was removed from.

6. Disconnect the fuel supply and return lines from the fuel rails.

7. Remove the upper radiator hose from the thermostat housing. Remove the bypass hose. Remove the heater outlet hose at the intake manifold.

8. Remove the air cleaner mounting bracket. Remove the intake manifold mounting bolts and studs. Pay attention to the location of the bolts and studs for reinstallation. Remove the lower intake manifold assembly.

To install:

9. Clean and inspect the mounting surfaces of the heads and manifold.

10. Apply a 1/16 in. (1.5mm) bead of RTV sealer to the ends of the manifold seal (the junction point of the seals and gaskets). Install the end seals and intake gaskets on the cylinder heads. The gaskets must interlock with the seal tabs.

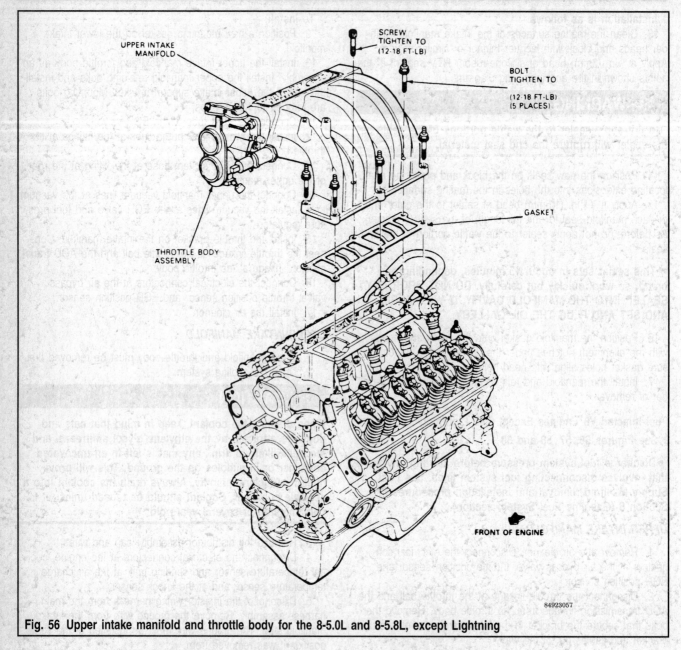

UPPER INTAKE MANIFOLD

SCREW
TIGHTEN TO
(12-18 FT-LB)

BOLT
TIGHTEN TO
(12-18 FT-LB)
(5 PLACES)

THROTTLE BODY
ASSEMBLY

GASKET

FRONT OF ENGINE

84923057

Fig. 56 Upper intake manifold and throttle body for the 8-5.0L and 8-5.8L, except Lightning

11. Install locator bolts at opposite ends of each head and carefully lower the intake manifold into position. Install and tighten the mounting bolts and studs to 23-25 ft. lbs.

12. Install the lower intake manifold assembly. Install the intake manifold mounting bolts and studs. Pay attention to the location of the bolts. Install the air cleaner mounting bracket.

13. Install the heater outlet hose at the intake manifold.

14. Install the bypass hose.

15. Install the upper radiator hose.

16. Connect the fuel supply and return lines at the fuel rails.

17. Connect the injector wiring harness from the main harness assembly. Install the ground wire from the intake manifold stud.

18. Connect the electrical connectors at the engine, coolant temperature sensor and sending unit, at the air charge temperature sensor and at the knock sensor.

19. Install the distributor assembly, cap and wires.

20. Fill the cooling system.

5.8L Lightning

UPPER INTAKE MANIFOLD

▶ **See Figures 60, 61 and 62**

1. Disconnect the battery ground.

2. Remove the air intake tube.

3. Remove the snow/ice shield from the throttle body.

4. Disconnect the electrical connectors at:
   - Throttle position sensor
   - Idle air control valve
   - EVP sensor
   - Emission vacuum control secondary regulator
   - Secondary air injection bypass/secondary air injection diverter solenoids

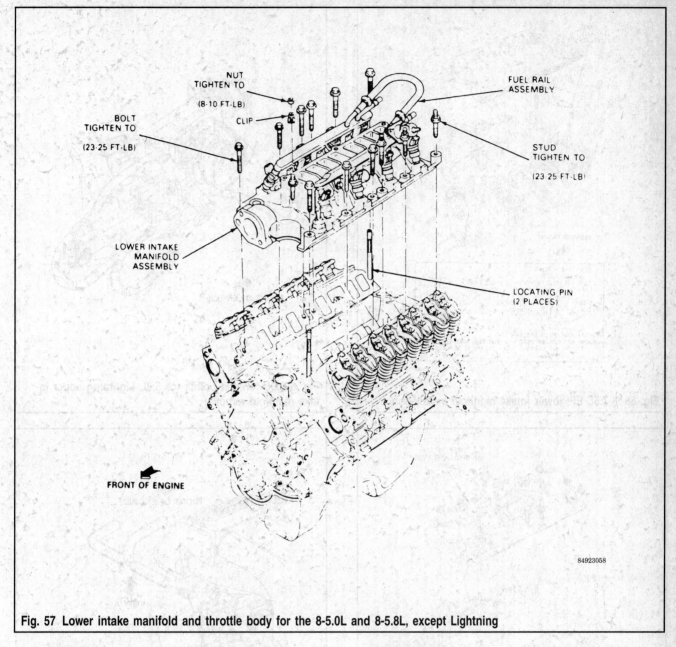

NUT
TIGHTEN TO

(8-10 FT-LB)

CLIP

BOLT
TIGHTEN TO

(23-25 FT-LB)

FUEL RAIL
ASSEMBLY

STUD
TIGHTEN TO

(23-25 FT-LB)

LOWER INTAKE
MANIFOLD
ASSEMBLY

LOCATING PIN
(2 PLACES)

FRONT OF ENGINE

84923058

Fig. 57 Lower intake manifold and throttle body for the 8-5.0L and 8-5.8L, except Lightning

5. Disconnect the vacuum lines from:
- EGR external pressure valve
- EVP sensor
- AIRB/AIRD solenoids
- Vacuum tree

6. Disconnect the PCV fresh air tube from the throttle body and oil fill tube.

7. Loosen the radiator cap.

8. Disconnect and plug the coolant hoses at the EGR spacer.

9. Using a screwdriver, carefully pry the throttle cable from the ball stud. DO NOT PULL IT OFF BY HAND!

10. Reach up behind the upper intake manifold and pull the PCV valve from the lower intake manifold.

11. Disconnect the vacuum line from the brake booster.

12. Remove the mounting bolts, lift the upper manifold up and pull it forward to gain access to the vacuum hoses located below it. Disconnect the hoses and remove the upper manifold.

To install:

13. Clean all gasket surfaces thoroughly and carefully. Don't allow any gasket material to fall into the lower manifold.

14. Position a new gasket on the lower manifold.

15. Place the upper manifold onto the lower and connect all the vacuum hoses.

16. Install the bolts and tighten them, in the sequence shown, to 12-18 ft. lbs.

17. Connect the throttle cable at the ball stud.

18. Connect the coolant hoses at the EGR spacer.

19. Connect the PCV fresh air tube at the throttle body and oil fill tube.

20. Connect the vacuum lines to:
- EGR external pressure valve
- EVP sensor
- AIRB/AIRD solenoids
- Vacuum tree

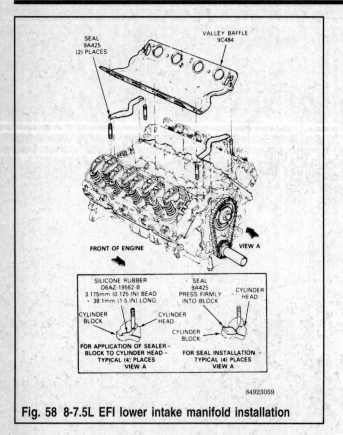

Fig. 58 8-7.5L EFI lower intake manifold installation

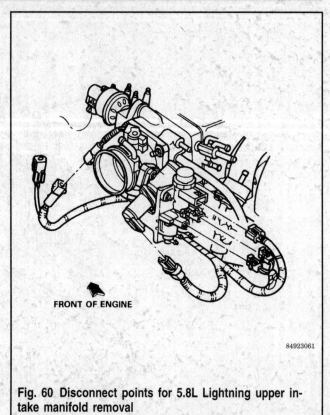

Fig. 60 Disconnect points for 5.8L Lightning upper intake manifold removal

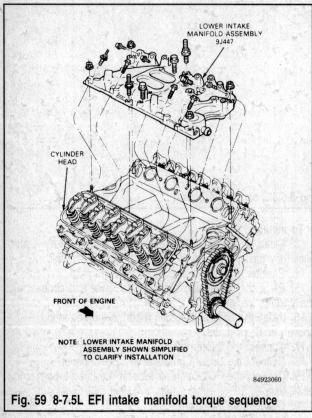

Fig. 59 8-7.5L EFI intake manifold torque sequence

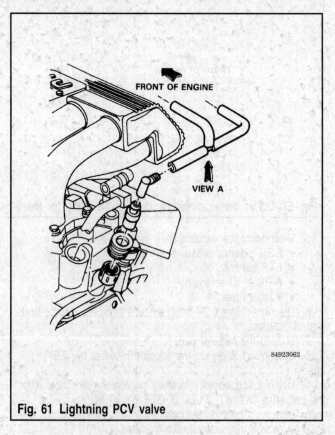

Fig. 61 Lightning PCV valve

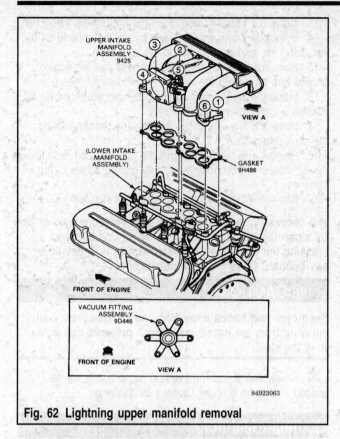

Fig. 62 Lightning upper manifold removal

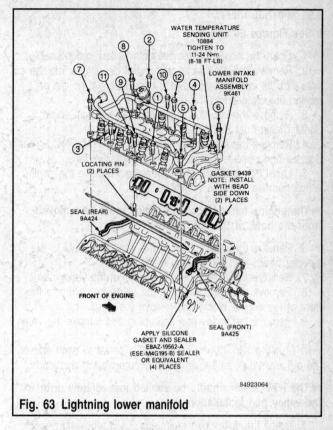

Fig. 63 Lightning lower manifold

21. Connect the electrical connectors at:
- Throttle position sensor
- Idle air control valve
- EVP sensor
- Emission vacuum control secondary regulator
- Secondary air injection bypass/secondary air injection diverter solenoids

22. Install the snow/ice shield on the throttle body.
23. Install the air intake tube.
24. Connect the battery ground.

LOWER MANIFOLD

▶ See Figure 63

1. The upper manifold and throttle body must be removed first.
2. Drain the cooling system.

✳✳CAUTION

When draining the coolant, keep in mind that cats and dogs are attracted by the ethylene glycol antifreeze, and are quite likely to drink any that is left in an uncovered container or in puddles on the ground. This will prove fatal in sufficient quantity. Always drain the coolant into a sealable container. Coolant should be reused unless it is contaminated or several years old.

3. Remove the distributor assembly, cap and wires.
4. Disconnect the electrical connectors at the engine, coolant temperature sensor and sending unit, at the air charge temperature sensor and at the knock sensor.
5. Disconnect the injector wiring harness from the main harness assembly. Remove the ground wire from the intake

manifold stud. The ground wire must be installed at the same position it was removed from.
6. Disconnect the fuel supply and return lines from the fuel rails.
7. Remove the upper radiator hose from the thermostat housing. Remove the bypass hose. Remove the heater outlet hose at the intake manifold.
8. Remove the air cleaner mounting bracket. Remove the intake manifold mounting bolts and studs. Pay attention to the location of the bolts and studs for reinstallation. Remove the lower intake manifold assembly.

To install:
9. Clean and inspect the mounting surfaces of the heads and manifold.
10. Apply a 1/16 in. (1.5mm) bead of RTV sealer to the ends of the manifold seal (the junction point of the seals and gaskets). Install the end seals and intake gaskets on the cylinder heads. The gaskets must interlock with the seal tabs.
11. Install locator bolts at opposite ends of each head and carefully lower the intake manifold into position. Install and tighten the mounting bolts and studs to 23-25 ft. lbs.
12. Install the air cleaner mounting bracket.
13. Install the upper radiator hose at the thermostat housing. Install the bypass hose. Install the heater outlet hose at the intake manifold.
14. Connect the fuel supply and return lines at the fuel rails.
15. Connect the injector wiring harness at the main harness assembly. Install the ground wire at the intake manifold stud.
16. Connect the electrical connectors at the engine, coolant temperature sensor and sending unit, at the air charge temperature sensor and at the knock sensor.
17. Install the distributor assembly, cap and wires.
18. Fill the cooling system.

6.9L and 7.3L Diesel

▶ **See Figures 64 and 65**

1. Open the hood and remove both battery ground cables.
2. Remove the air cleaner and install clean rags into the air intake of the intake manifold. It is important that no dirt or foreign objects get into the diesel intake.
3. Remove the injection pump as described in Section 5 under Diesel Fuel Systems.
4. Remove the fuel return hose from No. 7 and No. 8 rear nozzles and remove the return hose to the fuel tank.
5. Label the positions of the wires and remove the engine wiring harness from the engine.

➡**The engine harness ground cables must be removed from the back of the left cylinder head.**

6. Remove the bolts attaching the intake manifold to the cylinder heads and remove the manifold.
7. Remove the CDR tube grommet from the valley pan.
8. Remove the bolts attaching the valley pan strap to the front of the engine block, and remove the strap.
9. Remove the valley pan drain plug and remove the valley pan.
10. Apply a ⅛in. (3mm) bead of RTV sealer to each end of the cylinder block as shown in the accompanying illustration.

➡**The RTV sealer should be applied immediately prior to the valley pan installation.**

11. Install the valley pan drain plug, CDR tube and new grommet into the valley pan.
12. Install a new O-ring and new back-up ring on the CDR valve.

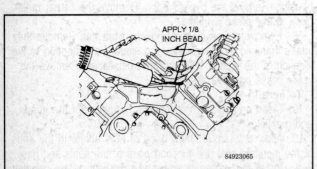

Fig. 64 Apply sealer to the diesel cylinder block-to-intake manifold mating surfaces on each end

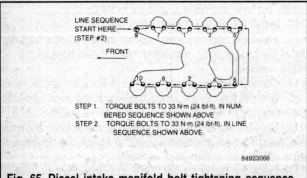

LINE SEQUENCE
START HERE
(STEP #2)

FRONT

STEP 1. TORQUE BOLTS TO 33 N·m (24 lbf-ft), IN NUMBERED SEQUENCE SHOWN ABOVE
STEP 2. TORQUE BOLTS TO 33 N·m (24 lbf-ft), IN LINE SEQUENCE SHOWN ABOVE.

Fig. 65 Diesel intake manifold bolt tightening sequence

13. Install the valley pan strap on the front of the valley pan.
14. Install the intake manifold and torque the bolts to 24 ft. lbs. using the sequence shown in the illustration.
15. Reconnect the engine wiring harness and the engine ground wire located to the rear of the left cylinder head.
16. Install the injection pump using the procedure shown in Section 5 under Diesel fuel Systems.
17. Install the No. 7 and No. 8 fuel return hoses and the fuel tank return hose.
18. Remove the rag from the intake manifold and replace the air cleaner. Reconnect the battery ground cables to both batteries.
19. Run the engine and check for oil and fuel leaks.

➡**If necessary, purge the nozzle high pressure lines of air by loosening the connector one half to one turn and cranking the engine until solid stream of fuel, devoid of any bubbles, flows from the connection.**

✳✳CAUTION

Keep eyes and hands away from the nozzle spray. Fuel spraying from the nozzle under high pressure can penetrate the skin.

20. Check and adjust the injection pump timing, as described in Section 5 under Diesel Fuel Systems.

Exhaust Manifold

REMOVAL & INSTALLATION

6-4.9L

The intake and exhaust manifolds on these engines are known as combination manifolds and are serviced as a unit. See Intake Manifold Removal and Installation.

Gasoline V8

▶ **See Figure 66**

1. Remove the air cleaner if the manifold being removed has the carburetor heat stove attached to it.
2. On the 8-5.0L, remove the dipstick bracket.
3. Disconnect the exhaust pipe or catalytic converter from the exhaust manifold. Remove and discard the doughnut gasket.
4. Remove the exhaust manifold attaching screws and remove the manifold from the cylinder head.
5. Install the exhaust manifold in the reverse order of removal. Apply a light coat of graphite grease to the mating surface of the manifold. Install and tighten the attaching bolts, starting from the center and working to both ends alternately. Tighten to the proper specifications.

6.9L and 7.3L Diesel

▶ **See Figure 67**

1. Disconnect the ground cables from both batteries.
2. Jack up the truck and safely support it with jackstands.
3. Disconnect the muffler inlet pipe from the exhaust manifolds.

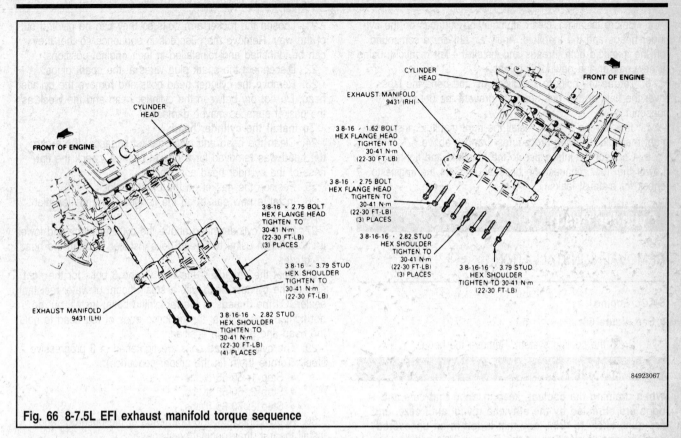

CYLINDER
HEAD

FRONT OF ENGINE

CYLINDER
HEAD

FRONT OF ENGINE

EXHAUST MANIFOLD
9431 (RH)

3 8-16 - 1.62 BOLT
HEX FLANGE HEAD
TIGHTEN TO
30-41 N·m
(22-30 FT-LB)

3 8-16 × 2.75 BOLT
HEX FLANGE HEAD
TIGHTEN TO
30-41 N·m
(22-30 FT-LB)
(3) PLACES

3 8-16 - 2.75 BOLT
HEX FLANGE HEAD
TIGHTEN TO
30-41 N·m
(22-30 FT-LB)
(3) PLACES

3 8-16 - 3.79 STUD
HEX SHOULDER
TIGHTEN TO
30-41 N·m
(22-30 FT-LB)

3 8-16-16 - 2.82 STUD
HEX SHOULDER
TIGHTEN TO
30-41 N·m
(22-30 FT-LB)
(3) PLACES

3 8-16-16 - 3.79 STUD
HEX SHOULDER
TIGHTEN TO 30-41 N·m
(22-30 FT-LB)

EXHAUST MANIFOLD
9431 (LH)

3 8-16-16 × 2.82 STUD
HEX SHOULDER
TIGHTEN TO
30-41 N·m
(22-30 FT-LB)
(4) PLACES

84923067

Fig. 66 8-7.5L EFI exhaust manifold torque sequence

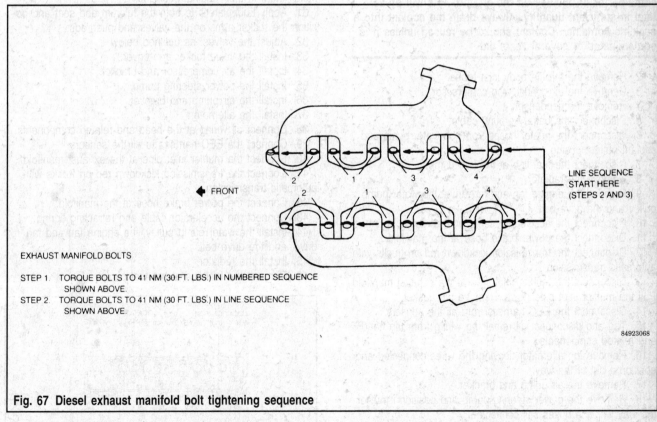

FRONT

LINE SEQUENCE
START HERE
(STEPS 2 AND 3)

EXHAUST MANIFOLD BOLTS

STEP 1. TORQUE BOLTS TO 41 NM (30 FT. LBS.) IN NUMBERED SEQUENCE
SHOWN ABOVE.
STEP 2. TORQUE BOLTS TO 41 NM (30 FT. LBS.) IN LINE SEQUENCE
SHOWN ABOVE.

84923068

Fig. 67 Diesel exhaust manifold bolt tightening sequence

4. Lower the truck to remove the right manifold. When removing the left manifold, jack the tuck up. Bend the tabs on the manifold attaching bolts, then remove the bolts and manifold.

5. Before installing, clean all mounting surfaces on the cylinder heads and the manifold. Apply an anti-seize compound on the manifold both threads and install the left manifold, using a new gasket and new locking tabs.

6. Torque the bolts to specifications and bend the tabs over the flats on the bolt heads to prevent the bolts from loosening.

7. Jack up the truck to install the right manifold. Install the right manifold following procedures 5 and 6 above.

8. Connect the inlet pipes to the manifold and tighten. Lower the truck, connect the batteries and run the engine to check for exhaust leaks.

Cylinder Head

REMOVAL & INSTALLATION

6-4.9L Engine
▶ **See Figure 68**

1. Drain the cooling system. Remove the hood.

✳✳CAUTION

When draining the coolant, keep in mind that cats and dogs are attracted by the ethylene glycol antifreeze, and are quite likely to drink any that is left in an uncovered container or in puddles on the ground. This will prove fatal in sufficient quantity. Always drain the coolant into a sealable container. Coolant should be reused unless it is contaminated or several years old.

2. Remove the throttle body inlet tubes.
3. Remove the air conditioning compressor.
4. Remove the condenser.
5. Disconnect the battery ground cable.
6. Disconnect the heater hoses from the water pump and coolant outlet housing.
7. Disconnect the fuel line at the fuel pump.
8. Remove the radiator.
9. Remove the engine fan and fan drive, the water pump pulley and the drive belt.
10. Disconnect the accelerator cable and retracting spring.
11. Disconnect the power brake hose at the manifold.
12. Disconnect the transmission kickdown rod on trucks with automatic transmission.
13. Disconnect the muffler inlet pipe at the exhaust manifold. Pull the muffler inlet pipe down. Remove the gasket.
14. Disconnect the EEC harness from all the sensors.
15. Tag and disconnect all remaining wiring from the head and related components.
16. Remove the alternator, leaving the wires connected and position it out of the way.
17. Remove the air pump and bracket.
18. Remove the power steering pump and position it out of the way with the hoses still connected.
19. If the truck is equipped with an air compressor, bleed the 2 pressure lines and remove the compressor and bracket.
20. Remove the valve rocker arm cover.

21. Loosen the rocker arm bolts so they can be pivoted out of the way. Remove the pushrods in sequence so that they can be identified and reinstalled in their original positions.
22. Disconnect the spark plug wires at the spark plugs.
23. Remove the cylinder head bolts and remove the cylinder head. Do not pry between the cylinder head and the block as the gasket surfaces maybe damaged.

To install the cylinder head:
24. Clean the head and block gasket surfaces. If the cylinder head was removed for a gasket change, check the flatness of the cylinder head and block.
25. Position the gasket on the cylinder block.
26. Install a new gasket on the flange of the muffler inlet pipe.
27. Lift the cylinder head above the cylinder block and lower it into position using two head bolts installed through the head as guides.
28. Coat the threads of the Nos. 1 and 6 bolts for the right side of the cylinder head with a small mount of water-resistant sealer. Oil the threads of the remaining bolts. Install, but do not tighten, two bolts at the opposite ends of the head to hold the head and gasket in position.
29. The cylinder head bolts are tightened in 3 progressive steps. Torque them (in the proper sequence):
   • Step 1: 50-55 ft. lbs.
   • Step 2: 60-65 ft. lbs.
   • Step 3: 70-85 ft. lbs.
30. Apply Lubriplate® to both ends of the pushrods and install them in their original positions.
31. Apply Lubriplate® to both the fulcrum and seat and position the rocker arms on the valves and pushrods.
32. Adjust the valves, as outlined below.
33. Install the valve rocker arm cover.
34. Install the air compressor and bracket.
35. Install the power steering pump.
36. Install the air pump and bracket.
37. Install the alternator.
38. Connect all wiring at the head and related components.
39. Connect the EEC harness to all the sensors.
40. Connect the muffler inlet pipe at the exhaust manifold.
41. Connect the transmission kickdown rod on trucks with automatic transmission.
42. Connect the power brake hose at the manifold.
43. Connect the accelerator cable and retracting spring.
44. Install the water pump pulley, the engine fan and fan drive, and the drive belt.
45. Install the radiator.
46. Connect the fuel line at the fuel pump.

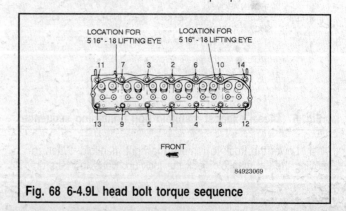

LOCATION FOR
5 16" - 18 LIFTING EYE   LOCATION FOR
5 16" - 18 LIFTING EYE

11 7   3   2   6   10 14

13 9   5   1   4   8   12

FRONT

84923069

Fig. 68 6-4.9L head bolt torque sequence

47. Connect the heater hoses at the water pump and coolant outlet housing.
48. Connect the battery ground cable.
49. Install the condenser.
50. Install the air conditioning compressor.
51. Install the throttle body inlet tubes.
52. Fill and bleed the cooling system.
53. Install the hood.

1987 8-5.8L with 4-bbl. Carburetor

1. Drain the cooling system.

❋❋CAUTION

When draining the coolant, keep in mind that cats and dogs are attracted by the ethylene glycol antifreeze, and are quite likely to drink any that is left in an uncovered container or in puddles on the ground. This will prove fatal in sufficient quantity. Always drain the coolant into a sealable container. Coolant should be reused unless it is contaminated or several years old.

2. Remove the intake manifold and carburetor.
3. Remove the rocker arm cover(s).
4. If the right cylinder head is to be removed, loosen the alternator adjusting arm bolt and remove the alternator mounting bracket bolt and spacer. Swing the alternator down and out of the way. Remove the air cleaner inlet duct from the right cylinder head assembly.

If the left cylinder head is being removed, remove the bolts fastening the accelerator shaft assembly at the front of the cylinder head. On vehicles equipped with air conditioning, the system must be discharged and the compressor removed. The procedure is best left to an air conditioning specialist. Persons not familiar with air conditioning systems can be easily injured when working on the systems.

5. Disconnect the exhaust manifold(s) from the muffler inlet pipe(s).
6. Loosen the rocker arm stud nuts so that the rocker arms can be rotated to the side. Remove the pushrods and identify them so that they can be reinstalled in their original positions.
7. Remove the cylinder head bolts and lift the cylinder head from the block.

To install the cylinder head(s):

8. Clean the cylinder head, intake manifold, the valve cover and the head gasket surfaces.
9. A specially treated composition head gasket is used. Do not apply sealer to a composition gasket. Position the new gasket over the locating dowels on the cylinder block. Then, position the cylinder head on the block and install the attaching bolts.
10. The cylinder head bolts are tightened in progressive steps. Tighten all the bolts in the proper sequence to:
    - Step 1: 85 ft. lbs.
    - Step 2: 95 ft. lbs.
    - Step 3: 105-112 ft. lbs.
11. Clean the pushrods. Blow out the oil passage in the rods with compressed air. Check the pushrods for straightness by rolling them on a piece of glass. Never try to straighten a pushrod; always replace it.
12. Apply Lubriplate® to the ends of the pushrods and install them in their original positions.

13. Apply Lubriplate® to the rocker arms and their fulcrum seats and install the rocker arms. Adjust the valves.
14. Position a new gasket(s) on the muffler inlet pipe(s) as necessary. Connect the exhaust manifold(s) at the muffler inlet pipe(s).
15. If the right cylinder head was removed, install the alternator, ignition coil and air cleaner duct on the right cylinder head. Adjust the drive belt.   If the left cylinder head was removed, install the accelerator shaft assembly at the front of the cylinder head.
16. Clean the valve rocker arm cover and the cylinder head gasket surfaces. Place the new gaskets in the covers, making sure that the tabs of the gasket engage the notches provided in the cover. Install the compressor, evaluate, charge and leak test the system. Let an air conditioning specialist do this.
17. Install the intake manifold and related parts.
18. Fill and bleed the cooling system.

8-5.0L and 8-5.8L Engines with EFI

▶ See Figure 69

1. Drain the cooling system.

❋❋CAUTION

When draining the coolant, keep in mind that cats and dogs are attracted by the ethylene glycol antifreeze, and are quite likely to drink any that is left in an uncovered container or in puddles on the ground. This will prove fatal in sufficient quantity. Always drain the coolant into a sealable container. Coolant should be reused unless it is contaminated or several years old.

2. Remove the intake manifold and EFI throttle body.
3. Remove the rocker arm cover(s).
4. If the right cylinder head is to be removed, lift the tensioner and remove the drive belt. Loosen the alternator adjusting arm bolt and remove the alternator mounting bracket bolt and spacer. Swing the alternator down and out of the way. Remove the air cleaner inlet duct.

If the left cylinder head is being removed, remove the air conditioning compressor. (See Section 1). Persons not familiar with air conditioning systems should exercise extreme caution, perhaps leaving this job to a professional. Remove the oil dipstick and tube. Remove the cruise control bracket.

5. Disconnect the exhaust manifold(s) from the muffler inlet pipe(s).
6. Loosen the rocker arm stud nuts so that the rocker arms can be rotated to the side. Remove the pushrods and identify them so that they can be reinstalled in their original positions.
7. Disconnect the Thermactor® air supply hoses at the check valves. Cover the check valve openings.
8. Remove the cylinder head bolts and lift the cylinder head from the block. Remove the discard the gasket.

To install the cylinder head(s):

9. Clean the cylinder head, intake manifold, the valve cover and the head gasket surfaces.
10. A specially treated composition head gasket is used. Do not apply sealer to a composition gasket. Position the new gasket over the locating dowels on the cylinder block. Then, position the cylinder head on the block and install the attaching bolts.

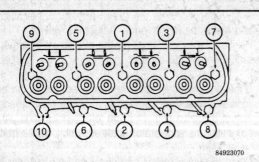

84923070

Fig. 69 Cylinder head bolt torque sequence, all gasoline V8

11. The cylinder head bolts are tightened in progressive steps. Tighten all the bolts in the proper sequence to:

8-5.0L
- Step 1: 55-65 ft. lbs.
- Step 2: 66-72 ft. lbs.

8-5.8L
- Step 1: 85 ft. lbs.
- Step 2: 95 ft. lbs.
- Step 3: 105-112 ft. lbs.

12. Clean the pushrods. Blow out the oil passage in the rods with compressed air. Check the pushrods for straightness by rolling them on a piece of glass. Never try to straighten a pushrod; always replace it.

13. Apply Lubriplate® to the ends of the pushrods and install them in their original positions.

14. Apply Lubriplate® to the rocker arms and their fulcrum seats and install the rocker arms. Adjust the valves.

15. Position a new gasket(s) on the muffler inlet pipe(s) as necessary. Connect the exhaust manifold(s) at the muffler inlet pipe(s).

16. If the right cylinder head was removed, install the alternator, and air cleaner duct. Install the drive belt.   If the left cylinder head was removed, install the compressor. (See Section 1). Install the dipstick and cruise control bracket.

17. Clean the valve rocker arm cover and the cylinder head gasket surfaces. Place the new gaskets in the covers, making sure that the tabs of the gasket engage the notches provided in the cover. Evacuate, charge and leak test the air conditioning system. (See Section 1).

18. Install the intake manifold and related parts. Install the Thermactor® hoses.

19. Fill and bleed the cooling system.

8-7.5L with 4-bbl Carburetor

1. Drain the cooling system.

✳✳CAUTION

When draining the coolant, keep in mind that cats and dogs are attracted by the ethylene glycol antifreeze, and are quite likely to drink any that is left in an uncovered container or in puddles on the ground. This will prove fatal in sufficient quantity. Always drain the coolant into a sealable container. Coolant should be reused unless it is contaminated or several years old.

2. Remove the intake manifold and carburetor as an assembly.

3. Disconnect the exhaust pipe from the exhaust manifold.

4. Loosen the air conditioning compressor drive belt, if so equipped.

5. Loosen the alternator attaching bolts and remove the bolt attaching the alternator bracket to the right cylinder head.

6. Disconnect the air conditioning compressor from the engine and move it aside, out of the way. Do not discharge the air conditioning system.

7. Remove the bolts securing the power steering reservoir bracket to the left cylinder head. Position the reservoir and bracket out of the way.

8. Remove the valve rocker arm covers. Remove the rocker arm bolts, rocker arms, oil deflectors, fulcrums and pushrods in sequence so that they can be reinstalled in their original positions.

9. Remove the cylinder head bolts and lift the head and exhaust manifold off the engine. If necessary, pry at the forward corners of the cylinder head against the casting bosses provided on the cylinder block. Do not damage the gasket mating surfaces of the cylinder head and block by prying against them.

10. Remove all gasket material from the cylinder head and block. Clean all gasket material from the mating surfaces of the intake manifold. If the exhaust manifold was removed, clean the mating surfaces of the cylinder head and exhaust manifold. Apply a thin coat of graphite grease to the cylinder head exhaust port areas and install the exhaust manifold.

11. Position two long cylinder head bolts in the two rear lower bolt holes of the left cylinder head. Place a long cylinder head bolt in the rear lower bolt hole of the right cylinder head. Use rubber bands to keep the bolts in position until the cylinder heads are installed on the cylinder block.

12. Position new cylinder head gaskets on the cylinder block dowels. Do not apply sealer to the gaskets, heads, or block.

13. Place the cylinder heads on the block, guiding the exhaust manifold studs into the exhaust pipe connections. Install the remaining cylinder head bolts. The longer bolts go in the lower row of holes.

14. Tighten all the cylinder head attaching bolts in the proper sequence in three stages: 75 ft. lbs., 105 ft.lbs., and finally to 135 ft. lbs. When this procedure is used, it is not necessary to retorque the heads after extended use.

15. Make sure that the oil holes in the pushrods are open and install the pushrods in their original positions. Place a dab of Lubriplate® to the ends of the pushrods before installing them.

16. Lubricate and install the valve rockers. Make sure that the pushrods remain seated in their lifters.

17. Connect the exhaust pipes to the exhaust manifolds.

18. Install the intake manifold and carburetor assembly. Tighten the intake manifold attaching bolts in the proper sequence to 25-30 ft. lbs.

19. Install the air conditioning compressor to the engine.

20. Install the power steering reservoir to the engine.

21. Apply oil-resistant sealer to one side of the new valve cover gaskets and lay the cemented side in place in the valve cover. Install the covers.

22. Install the alternator to the right cylinder head and adjust the alternator drive belt tension.

23. Adjust the air conditioning compressor drive belt tension.

24. Fill the radiator with coolant.

25. Start the engine and check for leaks.

8-7.5L with EFI

1. Drain the cooling system.

❊❊CAUTION

When draining the coolant, keep in mind that cats and dogs are attracted by the ethylene glycol antifreeze, and are quite likely to drink any that is left in an uncovered container or in puddles on the ground. This will prove fatal in sufficient quantity. Always drain the coolant into a sealable container. Coolant should be reused unless it is contaminated or several years old.

2. Remove the upper and lower intake manifolds. See above and Section 5.

3. Disconnect the exhaust pipe from the exhaust manifold.

4. Loosen the air conditioning compressor drive belt, if so equipped.

5. Loosen the alternator attaching bolts and remove the bolt attaching the alternator bracket to the right cylinder head.

6. Disconnect the air conditioning compressor from the engine and move it aside, out of the way. Do not discharge the air conditioning system.

7. Remove the bolts securing the power steering reservoir bracket to the left cylinder head. Position the reservoir and bracket out of the way. On motor home chassis, remove the oil filler tube.

8. Remove the valve rocker arm covers. Remove the rocker arm bolts, rocker arms, oil deflectors, fulcrums and pushrods in sequence so that they can be reinstalled in their original positions.

9. Remove the cylinder head bolts and lift the head and exhaust manifold off the engine. If necessary, pry at the forward corners of the cylinder head against the casting bosses provided on the cylinder block. Do not damage the gasket mating surfaces of the cylinder head and block by prying against them.

10. Remove all gasket material from the cylinder head and block. Clean all gasket material from the mating surfaces of the intake manifold. If the exhaust manifold was removed, clean the mating surfaces of the cylinder head and exhaust manifold. Apply a thin coat of graphite grease to the cylinder head exhaust port areas and install the exhaust manifold.

11. Position two long cylinder head bolts in the two rear lower bolt holes of the left cylinder head. Place a long cylinder head bolt in the rear lower bolt hole of the right cylinder head. Use rubber bands to keep the bolts in position until the cylinder heads are installed on the cylinder block.

12. Position new cylinder head gaskets on the cylinder block dowels. Do not apply sealer to the gaskets, heads, or block.

13. Place the cylinder heads on the block, guiding the exhaust manifold studs into the exhaust pipe connections. Install the remaining cylinder head bolts. The longer bolts go in the lower row of holes.

14. Tighten all the cylinder head attaching bolts in the proper sequence in three stages: 80-90 ft. lbs., 100-110 ft.lbs., and finally to 130-140 ft. lbs. When this procedure is used, it is not necessary to retorque the heads after extended use.

15. Make sure that the oil holes in the pushrods are open and install the pushrods in their original positions. Place a dab of Lubriplate® to the ends of the pushrods before installing them.

16. Lubricate and install the valve rockers. Make sure that the pushrods remain seated in their lifters.

17. Connect the exhaust pipes to the exhaust manifolds.

18. Install the upper and lower intake manifolds.

19. Install the air conditioning compressor.

20. Install the power steering reservoir.

21. Apply oil-resistant sealer to one side of the new valve cover gaskets and lay the cemented side in place in the valve cover. Install the covers.

22. Install the alternator and adjust the drive belt.

23. Adjust the air conditioning compressor drive belt tension.

24. On motor home chassis, install the oil filler tube.

25. Fill and bleed the cooling system.

26. Start the engine and check for leaks.

6.9L and 7.3L Diesel Engines

◆ See Figures 70, 71 and 72

1. Open the hood and disconnect the negative cables from both batteries.

2. Drain the cooling system and remove the radiator fan shroud halves.

❊❊CAUTION

When draining the coolant, keep in mind that cats and dogs are attracted by the ethylene glycol antifreeze, and are quite likely to drink any that is left in an uncovered container or in puddles on the ground. This will prove fatal in sufficient quantity. Always drain the coolant into a sealable container. Coolant should be reused unless it is contaminated or several years old.

3. Remove the radiator fan and clutch assembly using special tool T83T-6312-A and B. This tool is available through the Owatonna Tool Co. whose address is listed in the front of this boot, or through Ford Dealers. It is also available through many tool rental shops.

➥ The fan clutch uses a left hand thread and must be removed by turning the nut clockwise.

4. Label and disconnect the wiring from the alternator.

5. Remove the adjusting bolts and pivot bolts from the alternator and the vacuum pump and remove both units.

6. Remove the fuel filter lines and cap to prevent fuel leakage.

7. Remove the alternator, vacuum pump, and fuel filter brackets with the fuel filter attached.

8. Remove the heater hose from the cylinder head.

9. Remove the fuel injection pump as described in Section 5 under Diesel Fuel Systems.

10. Remove the intake manifold and valley cover.

11. Jack up the truck and safely support it with jackstands.

12. Disconnect the exhaust pipes from the exhaust manifolds.

13. Remove the clamp holding the engine oil dipstick tube in place and the bolt attaching the transmission oil dipstick to the cylinder head.

14. Lower the truck.

15. Remove the engine oil dipstick tube.

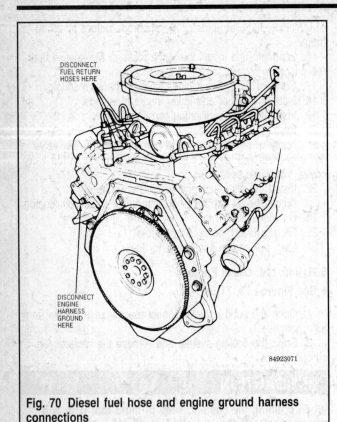

Fig. 70 Diesel fuel hose and engine ground harness connections

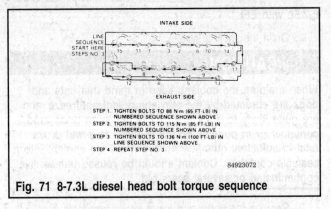

Fig. 71 8-7.3L diesel head bolt torque sequence

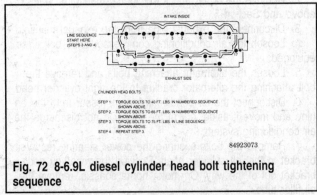

Fig. 72 8-6.9L diesel cylinder head bolt tightening sequence

16. Remove the valve covers, rocker arms and pushrods. Keep the pushrods in order so they can be returned to their original positions.

17. Remove the nozzles and glow plugs as described in Section 5 under Diesel Fuel Systems.

18. Remove the cylinder head bolts and attach lifting eyes, using special tool T70P-6000 or equivalent, to each end of the cylinder heads.

19. Carefully lift the cylinder heads out of the engine compartment and remove the head gaskets.

➡**The cylinder head prechambers may fall out of the heads upon removal.**

To install:

20. Position the cylinder head gasket on the engine block and carefully lower the cylinder head in place.

➡**Use care in installing the cylinder heads to prevent the prechambers from falling out into the cylinder bores.**

21. Install the cylinder head bolt and torque in 4 steps using the sequence shown in the illustration.

➡**Lubricate the threads and the mating surfaces of the bolt heads and washers with engine oil.**

22. Dip the pushrod ends in clean engine oil and install the pushrods with the copper colored ends toward the rocker arms, making sure the pushrods are fully seated in the tappet pushrod seats.

23. Install the rocker arms and posts in their original positions. Apply Lubriplate® grease to the valve stem tips. Turn the engine over by hand until the timing mark is at the 11 o'clock position as viewed from the front. Install the rocker arm posts, bolts, and torque to 27 ft. lbs. Install the valve covers.

24. Install the valley pan and the intake manifold.

25. Install the fuel injection pump as described in Section 5 under Diesel Fuel Systems.

26. Connect the heater hose to the cylinder head.

27. Install the fuel filter, alternator, vacuum pump, and their drive belts.

28. Install the engine oil and transmission dip stick.

29. Connect the exhaust pipe to the exhaust manifolds.

30. Reconnect the alternator wiring harness and replace the air cleaner. Connect both battery ground cables.

31. Refill and bleed the cooling system.

32. Run the engine and check for fuel, coolant and exhaust leaks.

➡**If necessary, purge the high pressure fuel lines of air by loosening the connector one half to one turn and cranking the engine until a solid stream of fuel, free from any bubbles, flows from the connections.**

33. Check the injection pump timing. Refer to Section 5 for these procedures.

34. Install the radiator fan and clutch assembly using special tools T83T-6312A and B or equivalent.

➡**The fan clutch uses a left hand thread. Tighten by turning the nut counterclockwise. Install the radiator fan shroud halves.**

CLEANING AND INSPECTION

▶ **See Figures 73 and 74**

1. With the valves installed to protect the valve seats, remove deposits from the combustion chambers and valve heads

with a scraper and a wire brush. Be careful not to damage the cylinder head gasket surface. After the valves are removed, clean the valve guide bores with a valve guide cleaning tool. Using cleaning solvent to remove dirt, grease and other deposits, clean all bolts holes; be sure the oil passage is clean (V8 engines).

2. Remove all deposits from the valves with a fine wire brush or buffing wheel.

3. Inspect the cylinder heads for cracks or excessively burned areas in the exhaust outlet ports.

4. Check the cylinder head for cracks and inspect the gasket surface for burrs and nicks. Replace the head if it is cracked.

5. On cylinder heads that incorporate valve seat inserts, check the inserts for excessive wear, cracks, or looseness.

RESURFACING

Cylinder Head Flatness

When the cylinder head is removed, check the flatness of the cylinder head gasket surfaces.

1. Place a straightedge across the gasket surface of the cylinder head. Using feeler gauges, determine the clearance at the center of the straightedge.

2. If warpage exceeds 0.003 in. (0.076mm) in a 6 in. (152mm) span, or 0.006 in. (0.152mm) over the total length, the cylinder head must be resurfaced.

3. If necessary to refinish the cylinder head gasket surface, do not plane or grind off more than 0.254mm (0.010 in.) from the original gasket surface.

➡ When milling the cylinder heads of V8 engines, the intake manifold mounting position is altered, and must be corrected by milling the manifold flange a proportionate amount. Consult an experienced machinist about this.

Valves and Springs

REMOVAL & INSTALLATION

▶ **See Figures 75, 76 and 77**

1. Block the head on its side, or install a pair of head-holding brackets made especially for valve removal.

2. Use a socket slightly larger than the valve stem and keepers, place the socket over the valve stem and gently hit the socket with a plastic hammer to break loose any varnish buildup.

3. Remove the valve keepers, retainer, spring shield and valve spring using a valve spring compressor (the locking C-clamp type is the easiest kind to use).

4. Put the parts in a separate container numbered for the cylinder being worked on; do not mix them with other parts removed.

5. Remove and discard the valve stem oil seals. A new seal will be used at assembly time.

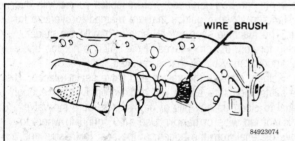

Fig. 73 Remove combustion chamber carbon from the cylinder head with a wire brush and electric drill. Make sure all carbon is removed and not just burnished

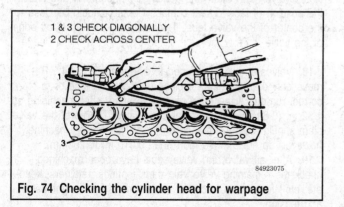

Fig. 74 Checking the cylinder head for warpage

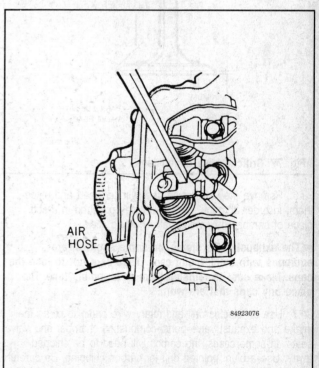

Fig. 75 Compressing gasoline engine valve spring. Note spring compressor position and air hose. Cylinder at TDC

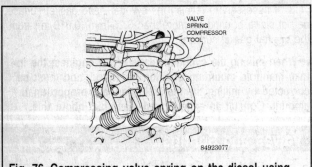

Fig. 76 Compressing valve spring on the diesel using the special tool

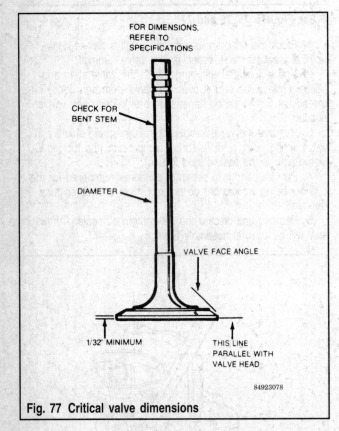

Fig. 77 Critical valve dimensions

6. Remove the valves from the cylinder head and place them, in order, through numbered holes punched in a stiff piece of cardboard or wood valve holding stick.

➡**The exhaust valve stems, on some engines, are equipped with small metal caps. Take care not to lose the caps. Make sure to reinstall them at assembly time. Replace any caps that are worn.**

7. Use an electric drill and rotary wire brush to clean the intake and exhaust valve ports, combustion chamber and valve seats. In some cases, the carbon will need to be chipped away. Use a blunt pointed drift for carbon chipping. Be careful around the valve seat areas.

8. Use a wire valve guide cleaning brush and safe solvent to clean the valve guides.

9. Clean the valves with a revolving wire brush. Heavy carbon deposits may be removed with the blunt drift.

➡**When using a wire brush to clean carbon on the valve ports, valves etc., be sure that the deposits are actually removed, rather than burnished.**

10. Wash and clean all valve springs, keepers, retaining caps etc., in safe solvent.

11. Clean the head with a brush and some safe solvent and wipe dry.

12. Check the head for cracks. Cracks in the cylinder head usually start around an exhaust valve seat because it is the hottest part of the combustion chamber. If a crack is suspected but cannot be detected visually have the area checked with dye penetrant or other method by the machine shop.

13. After all cylinder head parts are reasonably clean, check the valve stem-to-guide clearance. If a dial indicator is not on hand, a visual inspection can give you a fairly good idea if the guide, valve stem or both are worn.

14. Insert the valve into the guide until slight away from the valve seat. Wiggle the valve sideways. A small amount of wobble is normal, excessive wobble means a worn guide or valve stem. If a dial indicator is on hand, mount the indicator so that the stem of the valve is at 90° to the valve stem, as close to the valve guide as possible. Move the valve off the seat, and measure the valve guide-to-stem clearance by rocking the stem back and forth to actuate the dial indicator. Measure the valve stem using a micrometer and compare to specifications to determine whether stem or guide wear is causing excessive clearance.

15. The valve guide, if worn, must be repaired before the valve seats can be resurfaced. Ford supplies valves with oversize stems to fit valve guides that are reamed to oversize for repair. The machine shop will be able to handle the guide reaming for you. In some cases, if the guide is not too badly worn, knurling may be all that is required.

16. Reface, or have the valves and valve seats refaced. The valve seats should be a true 45° angle. Remove only enough material to clean up any pits or grooves. Be sure the valve seat is not too wide or narrow. Use a 60° grinding wheel to remove material from the bottom of the seat for raising and a 30° grinding wheel to remove material from the top of the seat to narrow.

17. After the valves are refaced by machine, hand lap them to the valve seat. Clean the grinding compound off and check the position of face-to-seat contact. Contact should be close to the center of the valve face. If contact is close to the top edge of the valve, narrow the seat; if too close to the bottom edge, raise the seat.

18. Valves should be refaced to a true angle of 44°. Remove only enough metal to clean up the valve face or to correct run-out. If the edge of a valve head, after machining, is 1/32 in. (0.8mm) or less replace the valve. The tip of the valve stem should also be dressed on the valve grinding machine, however, do not remove more than 0.010 in. (0.254mm).

19. After all valve and valve seats have been machined, check the remaining valve train parts (springs, retainers, keepers, etc.) for wear. Check the valve springs for straightness and tension.

20. Install the valves in the cylinder head and metal caps.

21. Install new valve stem oil seals.

22. Install the valve keepers, retainer, spring shield and valve spring using a valve spring compressor (the locking C-clamp type is the easiest kind to use).

23. Check the valve spring installed height, shim or replace as necessary.

CHECKING VALVE SPRINGS

▶ **See Figures 78 and 79**

Place the valve spring on a flat surface next to a carpenter's square. Measure the height of the spring, and rotate the spring against the edge of the square to measure distortion. If the spring height varies (by comparison) by more than $\frac{1}{16}$ in. (1.5mm) or if the distortion exceeds $\frac{1}{16}$ in. (1.5mm), replace the spring.

Have the valve springs tested for spring pressure at the installed and compressed (installed height minus valve lift) height using a valve spring tester. Springs should be within one pound, plus or minus each other. Replace springs as necessary.

VALVE SPRING INSTALLED HEIGHT

After installing the valve spring, measure the distance between the spring mounting pad and the lower edge of the spring retainer. Compare the measurement to specifications. If the installed height is incorrect, add shim washers between the spring mounting pad and the spring. Use only washers designed for valve springs, available at most parts houses.

VALVE SEATS

▶ **See Figures 80, 81, 82, 83 and 84**

If the valve seat is damaged or burnt and cannot be serviced by refacing, it may be possible to have the seat machined and an insert installed. Consult an automotive machine shop for their advice.

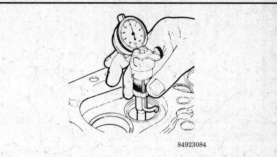

Fig. 79 Have the spring test pressure checked at a machine shop. Make sure the readings are within specifications

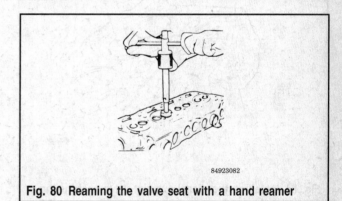

Fig. 82 Checking the valve seat concentricity with a dial gauge

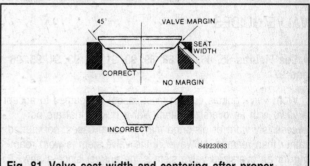

Fig. 80 Reaming the valve seat with a hand reamer

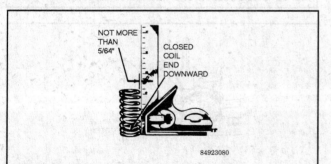

Fig. 78 Check the valve spring free length and squareness

Fig. 81 Valve seat width and centering after proper reaming

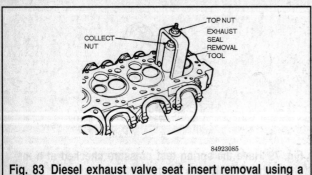

Fig. 83 Diesel exhaust valve seat insert removal using a special tool

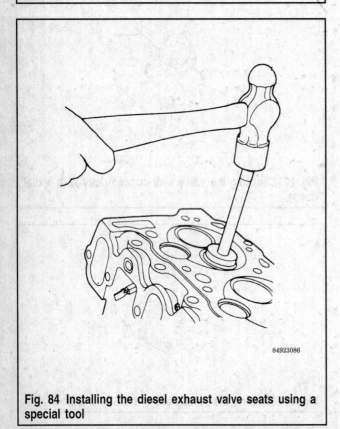

Fig. 84 Installing the diesel exhaust valve seats using a special tool

VALVE GUIDES

▶ **See Figures 85, 86, 87, 88, 89, 90, 91, 92, 93, 94, 95, 96 and 97**

Worn valve guides can, in most cases, be reamed to accept a valve with an oversized stem. Valve guides that are not excessively worn or distorted may, in some cases, be knurled rather than reamed. However, if the valve stem is worn reaming for an oversized valve stem is the answer since a new valve would be required.

Knurling is a process in which metal is displaced and raised, thereby reducing clearance. Knurling also produces excellent oil control. The possibility of knurling instead of reaming the valve guides should be discussed with a machinist.

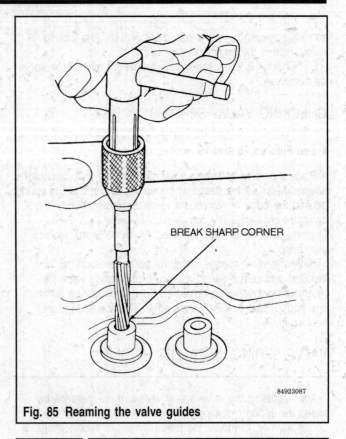

Fig. 85 Reaming the valve guides

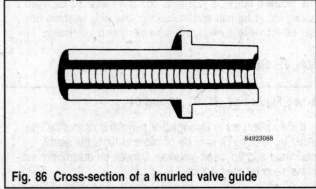

Fig. 86 Cross-section of a knurled valve guide

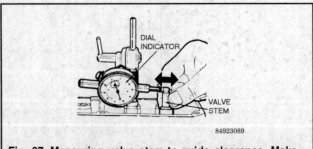

Fig. 87 Measuring valve stem-to-guide clearance. Make sure the indicator is mounted at 90° to the valve stem and as close to the guide as possible

Fig. 88 Lapping the valves by hand. When done, the finish on both the valve faces and the seats should be smooth and evenly shiny

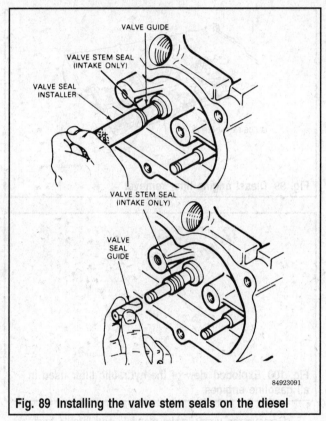

Fig. 89 Installing the valve stem seals on the diesel

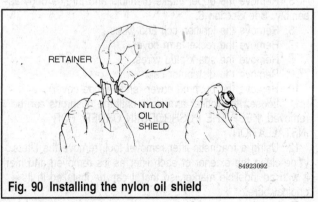

Fig. 90 Installing the nylon oil shield

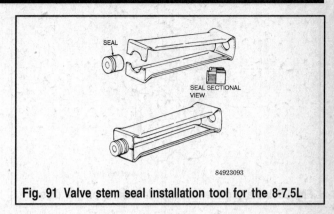

Fig. 91 Valve stem seal installation tool for the 8-7.5L

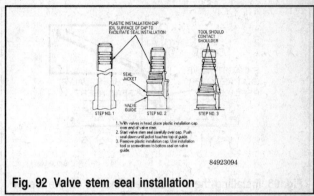

Fig. 92 Valve stem seal installation

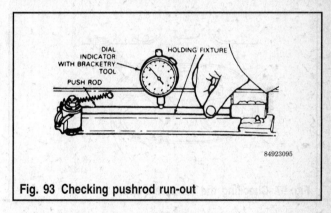

Fig. 93 Checking pushrod run-out

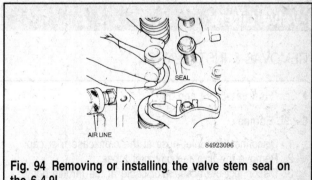

Fig. 94 Removing or installing the valve stem seal on the 6-4.9L

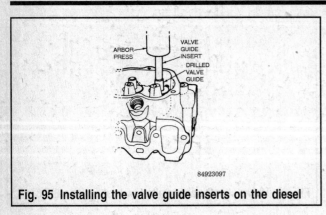

Fig. 95 Installing the valve guide inserts on the diesel

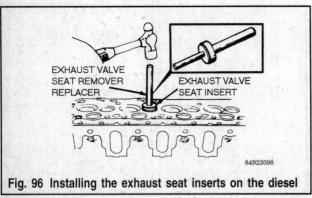

Fig. 96 Installing the exhaust seat inserts on the diesel

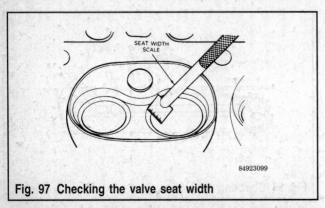

Fig. 97 Checking the valve seat width

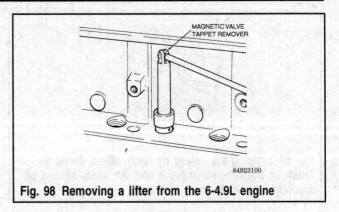

Fig. 98 Removing a lifter from the 6-4.9L engine

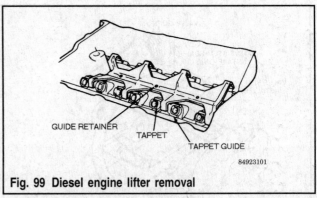

Fig. 99 Diesel engine lifter removal

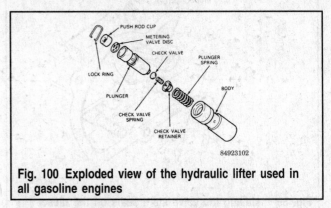

Fig. 100 Exploded view of the hydraulic lifter used in all gasoline engines

Valve Lifters

REMOVAL & INSTALLATION

▶ **See Figures 98, 99 and 100**

6-4.9L Engine

1. Disconnect the inlet hose at the crankcase filler cap.
2. Remove the throttle body inlet tubes.
3. Disconnect the accelerator cable at the throttle body. Remove the cable retracting spring. Remove the accelerator cable bracket from the upper intake manifold and position the cable and bracket out of the way.
4. Remove the fuel line from the fuel rail. Be careful not to kink the line.

5. Remove the upper intake manifold and throttle body assembly. See Section 5.
6. Remove the ignition coil and wires.
7. Remove the rocker arm cover.
8. Remove the spark plug wires.
9. Remove the distributor cap.
10. Remove the pushrod cover (engine side cover).
11. Loosen the rocker arm bolts until the pushrods can be removed. KEEP THE PUSHRODS IN ORDER, FOR INSTALLATION!
12. Using a magnetic lifter removal tool, remove the lifters. Wipe clean the exterior of each lifter as it's removed and mark it with an indelible marker, so that it can be installed in its original bore.
    To install:
13. Coat the bottom surface of each lifter with multi-purpose grease, and coat the rest of the lifter with clean engine oil.

14. Install each lifter in it original bore using the magnetic tool.

15. Coat each end of each pushrod with multi-purpose grease and install each in its original position. Make sure that each pushrod is properly seated in the lifter socket.

16. Engage the rocker arms with the pushrods and tighten the rocker arm bolts enough to hold the pushrods in place.

17. Adjust the valve clearance.

18. Install the pushrod cover (engine side cover).

19. Install the distributor cap.

20. Install the spark plug wires.

21. Install the rocker arm cover.

22. Install the ignition coil and wires.

23. Install the upper intake manifold and throttle body assembly. See Section 5.

24. Install the fuel line at the fuel rail.

25. Install the accelerator cable bracket at the upper intake manifold. Install the cable retracting spring. Connect the accelerator cable at the throttle body.

26. Install the throttle body inlet tubes.

27. Connect the inlet hose at the crankcase filler cap.

8-5.0L and 8-5.8L Engines

➡ **The 1993 5.0L engine uses roller lifters.**

1. Remove the intake manifold.

2. Disconnect the Thermactor® air supply hose at the pump.

3. Remove the rocker arm covers.

4. Loosen the rocker arm fulcrum bolts until the rocker arms can be rotated off the pushrods.

5. Remove the pushrods. KEEP THE PUSHRODS IN ORDER, FOR INSTALLATION!

6. Using a magnetic lifter removal tool, remove the lifters. Wipe clean the exterior of each lifter as it's removed and mark it with an indelible marker, so that it can be installed in its original bore.

To install:

7. Coat the bottom surface of each lifter with multi-purpose grease, and coat the rest of the lifter with clean engine oil.

8. Install each lifter in it original bore using the magnetic tool.

9. Coat each end of each pushrod with multi-purpose grease and install each in its original position. Make sure that each pushrod is properly seated in the lifter socket.

10. Engage the rocker arms with the pushrods and tighten the rocker arm fulcrum bolts to 18-25 ft. lbs. No valve adjustment should be necessary, however, if there is any question as to post-assembly collapsed lifter clearance, see the Hydraulic Lifter Clearance procedure below.

11. Install the rocker arm covers.

12. Connect the Thermactor® air supply hose at the pump.

13. Install the intake manifold.

8-7.5L Engine

1. Remove the intake manifold.

2. Remove the rocker arm covers.

3. Loosen the rocker arm fulcrum bolts until the rocker arms can be rotated off the pushrods.

4. Remove the pushrods. KEEP THE PUSHRODS IN ORDER, FOR INSTALLATION!

5. Using a magnetic lifter removal tool, remove the lifters. Wipe clean the exterior of each lifter as it's removed and mark it with an indelible marker, so that it can be installed in its original bore.

To install:

6. Coat the bottom surface of each lifter with multi-purpose grease, and coat the rest of the lifter with clean engine oil.

7. Install each lifter in it original bore using the magnetic tool.

8. Coat each end of each pushrod with multi-purpose grease and install each in its original position. Make sure that each pushrod is properly seated in the lifter socket.

9. Rotate the crankshaft by hand until No. 1 piston is at TDC of compression. The firing order marks on the damper will be aligned at TDC with the timing pointer.

10. Engage the rocker arms with the pushrods and tighten the rocker arm fulcrum bolts to 18-25 ft. lbs. in the following sequence:
- No. 1 intake and exhaust
- No. 3 intake
- No. 8 exhaust
- No. 7 intake
- No. 5 exhaust
- No. 8 intake
- No. 4 exhaust

11. Rotate the crankshaft on full turn — 360° — and realign the TDC mark and pointer. Tighten the fulcrum bolt on the following valves:
- No. 2 intake and exhaust
- No. 4 intake
- No. 3 exhaust
- No. 5 intake
- No. 6 exhaust
- No. 6 intake
- No. 7 exhaust

12. Check the valve clearance as described under Hydraulic Valve Clearance, below.

13. Install the intake manifold.

14. Install the rocker arm covers.

Diesel Engine

1. Remove the intake manifold.

2. Remove the CDR tube and grommet from the valley pan.

3. Remove the valley pan strap from the front of the block.

4. Remove the valley pan drain plug and lift out the valley pan.

5. Remove the rocker arm covers.

6. Remove the rocker arms. KEEP THEM IN ORDER FOR INSTALLATION!

7. Remove the pushrods. KEEP THEM IN ORDER FOR INSTALLATION!

8. Remove the lifter guide retainer.

9. Using a magnetic lifter removal tool, remove the lifters. Wipe clean the exterior of each lifter as it's removed and mark it with an indelible marker, so that it can be installed in its original bore.

To install:

10. Coat the bottom surface of each lifter with multi-purpose grease, and coat the rest of the lifter with clean engine oil.

11. Install each lifter in it original bore using the magnetic tool.

12. Install the lifter guide retainer.

13. Install the pushrods, copper colored end up, into their original locations, making sure that they are firmly seated in the lifters.

14. Coat the valve stem tips with multi-purpose grease and install the rocker arms and posts in their original positions.

15. Turn the crankshaft by hand, until the timing mark is at the 11 o'clock position — viewed from the front.

16. Install all the rocker arm post bolts and torque them to 20 ft. lbs.

17. Install the rocker arm covers.

18. Clean all old RTV gasket material from the block and run a 1/8in. (3mm) bead of new RTV gasket material at each end of the block. Within 15 minutes, install the valley pan. Install the pan drain plug.

19. Install the CDR tube, new grommet and new O-ring.

20. Install the intake manifold and related parts.

DISASSEMBLY AND ASSEMBLY

➡**Each lifter is an assembly of matched parts. When disassembling more than one lifter, keep the parts segregated. Mixing of parts between or among different lifters will result in improper operation of the lifter(s). Always mark the lifters so that you won't forget which bore from which they originally came. Lifters must be returned to their original bore. Always work on a clean work surface.**

1. Using needle-nosed pliers, remove the plunger lockring from the lifter. It may be necessary to depress the plunger.

2. Remove the pushrod cup, metering valve, plunger and spring from the lifter body.

3. Invert the plunger and remove the check valve retainer by prying up on it carefully. Remove the check valve (either a disc or ball) and the spring.

4. Clean all parts thoroughly and replace any damaged or worn parts.

To install:

5. Place the plunger upside down on the clean work surface.

6. Place the check valve in position over the oil hole on the bottom of the plunger. Place the check valve spring on top of the check valve.

7. Place the check valve retainer over the check valve and spring. Push the retainer down, into place on the plunger.

8. Place the plunger spring and plunger, with the open end up, into the lifter body.

9. Place the metering valve in the plunger, followed by the pushrod cup.

10. Depress the plunger and install the lockring. Release the plunger and make sure the lockring stays in place with the spring pressure against it.

DIESEL HYDRAULIC VALVE LIFTER INSPECTION

➡**The lifters used on diesel engines require a special test fluid, kerosene is not satisfactory.**

Remove the lifters from their bores and remove any gum and varnish with safe solvent. Check the lifters for concave wear. If the bottom of the lifter is worn concave or flat, replace the lifter. Lifters are built with a convex bottom, flatness indicates wear. If a worn lifter is detected, carefully check the camshaft for wear.

To test lifter leak down, submerge the lifter in a container of kerosene. Chuck a used pushrod or its equivalent into a drill press. Position the container of kerosene so the pushrod acts on the lifter plunger. Pump the lifter with the drill press until resistance increases. Pump several more times to bleed any air from the lifter. Apply very firm, constant pressure to the lifter and observe the rate which fluid bleeds out of the lifter. If the lifter bleeds down very quickly (less than 15 seconds), the lifter should be replaced. If the time exceeds 60 seconds, the lifter is sticking and should be cleaned or replaced. If the lifter is operating properly (leak down time 15-60 seconds) and not worn, lubricate and reinstall in engine.

➡**Always inspect the valve pushrods for wear, straightness and oil blockage. Damaged pushrods will cause erratic valve operation.**

GASOLINE ENGINE HYDRAULIC VALVE CLEARANCE ADJUSTMENT

▶ **See Figures 101, 102, 103, 104 and 105**

When a valve in the engine is in the closed position, the valve lifter is resting on the base circle of the camshaft lobe and the pushrod is in its lowest position. To remove this additional clearance from the valve train, the valve lifter expands to maintain zero clearance in the valve system. When a rocker arm is loosened or removed from the engine, the lifter expands to it fullest travel. When the rocker arm is reinstalled on the engine, the proper valve setting is obtained by tightening the rocker arm to a specified limit. But with the lifter fully expanded, if the camshaft lobe is on a high point it will require excessive torque to compress the lifter and obtain the proper setting. Because of this, when any component of the valve system has been removed, a preliminary valve adjustment procedure must be followed to ensure that when the rocker arm is reinstalled on the engine and tightened, the camshaft lobe for that cylinder is in the low position.

To determine whether a shorter or longer pushrod is necessary, make the following check:

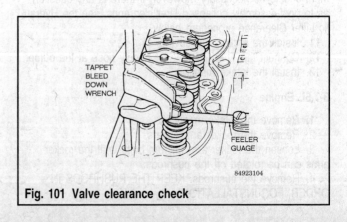

Fig. 101 Valve clearance check

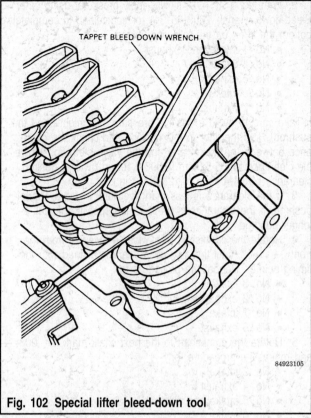

Fig. 102 Special lifter bleed-down tool

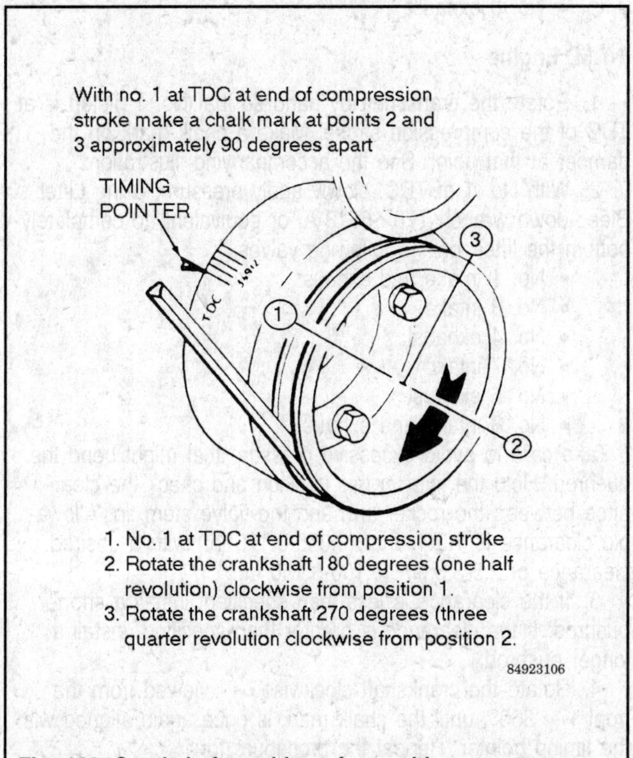

Step 1. Set no. 1 piston on TDC at end of
compression stroke adjust no. 1 intake
and exhaust
Step 4. Check no. 6 intake and exhaust

Step 2. Check no. 5
intake and exhaust
Step 5. Check no. 2
intake and exhaust

Step 3. Check no. 3
intake and exhaust
Step 6. Check no. 4
intake and exhaust

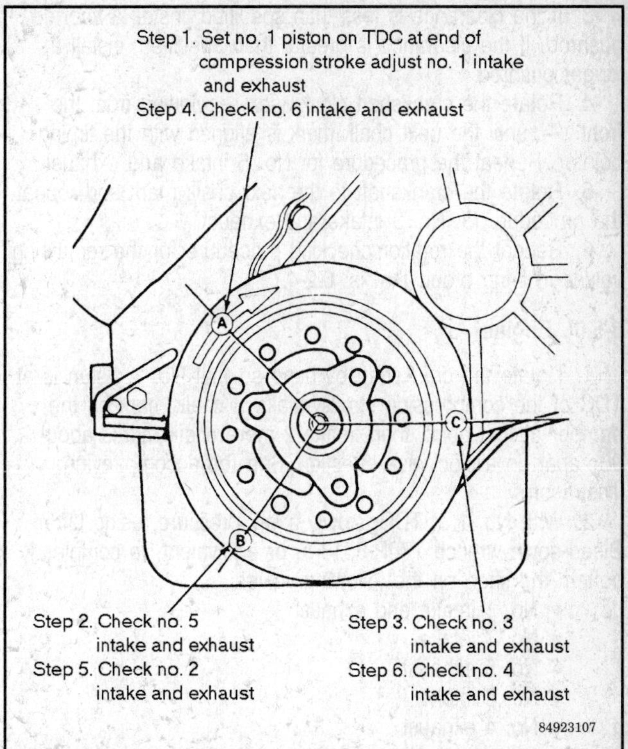

**Fig. 104 6-4.9L engine hydraulic valve clearance
adjustment**

With no. 1 at TDC at end of compression
stroke make a chalk mark at points 2 and
3 approximately 90 degrees apart

TIMING
POINTER

1. No. 1 at TDC at end of compression stroke
2. Rotate the crankshaft 180 degrees (one half
   revolution) clockwise from position 1.
3. Rotate the crankshaft 270 degrees (three
   quarter revolution clockwise from position 2.

**Fig. 103 Crankshaft positions for positive stop-type
valve adjustment — 8-5.0L**

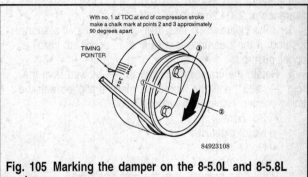

With no. 1 at TDC at end of compression stroke
make a chalk mark at points 2 and 3 approximately
90 degrees apart.

TIMING
POINTER

**Fig. 105 Marking the damper on the 8-5.0L and 8-5.8L
engines**

6-4.9L Engine

1. Rotate the crankshaft by hand so that No. 1 piston is at
TDC of the compression stroke. Make a chalk mark on the
damper at that point, then, make 2 more chalk marks about
120° apart, dividing the damper into 3 equal parts. See the
accompanying illustration.

2. With No. 1 at TDC, tighten the rocker arm bolts on No.
1 cylinder intake and exhaust to 17-23 ft. lbs. Then, slowly
apply pressure, using Lifter Bleed-down wrench T70P-6513-A,
or equivalent, to completely bottom the lifter. Take care to
avoid excessive pressure that might bend the pushrod. Hold
the lifter in this position and check the clearance between the
rocker arm and the valve stem tip. Allowable clearance is
2.5-5.0mm (0.10-0.20 in.) with a desired clearance of
3.0-4.5mm (0.125-0.175 in.).

3. If the clearance is less than specified, install a shorter pushrod. If the clearance is greater than specified, install a longer pushrod.

4. Rotate the crankshaft clockwise — viewed from the front — until the next chalk mark is aligned with the timing pointer. Repeat the procedure for No. 5 intake and exhaust.

5. Rotate the crankshaft to the next chalk mark and repeat the procedure for No. 3 intake and exhaust.

6. Repeat the rotation/checking procedure for the remaining valves in firing order, that is: 6-2-4.

8-5.0L Engine

1. Rotate the crankshaft by hand so that No. 1 piston is at TDC of the compression stroke. Make a chalk mark on the damper at that point, then, make 2 more chalk marks about 90° apart in a clockwise direction. See the accompanying illustration.

2. With No. 1 at TDC, slowly apply pressure, using Lifter Bleed-down wrench T70P-6513-A, or equivalent, to completely bottom the lifter, on the following valves:
- No. 1 intake and exhaust
- No. 7 intake
- No. 5 exhaust
- No. 8 intake
- No. 4 exhaust

Take care to avoid excessive pressure that might bend the pushrod. Hold the lifter in this position and check the clearance between the rocker arm and the valve stem tip. Allowable clearance is 1.8-4.9mm (0.071-0.193 in.) with a desired clearance of 2.4-4.2mm (0.096-0.165 in.).

3. If the clearance is less than specified, install a shorter pushrod. If the clearance is greater than specified, install a longer pushrod.

4. Rotate the crankshaft clockwise — viewed from the front — 180°, until the next chalk mark is aligned with the timing pointer. Repeat the procedure for:
- No. 5 intake
- No. 2 exhaust
- No. 4 intake
- No. 6 exhaust

5. Rotate the crankshaft to the next chalk mark — 90° — and repeat the procedure for:
- No. 2 intake
- No. 7 exhaust
- No. 3 intake and exhaust
- No. 6 intake
- No. 8 exhaust

8-5.8L Engine

1. Rotate the crankshaft by hand so that No. 1 piston is at TDC of the compression stroke. Make a chalk mark on the damper at that point, then, make 2 more chalk marks about 90° apart in a clockwise direction. See the accompanying illustration.

2. With No. 1 at TDC, slowly apply pressure, using Lifter Bleed-down wrench T70P-6513-A, or equivalent, to completely bottom the lifter, on the following valves:
- No. 1 intake and exhaust
- No. 4 intake
- No. 3 exhaust
- No. 8 intake
- No. 7 exhaust

Take care to avoid excessive pressure that might bend the pushrod. Hold the lifter in this position and check the clearance between the rocker arm and the valve stem tip. Allowable clearance is 2.5-5.0mm (0.098-0.198 in.) with a desired clearance of 3.1-4.4mm (0.123-0.173 in.).

3. If the clearance is less than specified, install a shorter pushrod. If the clearance is greater than specified, install a longer pushrod.

4. Rotate the crankshaft clockwise — viewed from the front — 180°, until the next chalk mark is aligned with the timing pointer. Repeat the procedure for:
- No. 3 intake
- No. 2 exhaust
- No. 7 intake
- No. 6 exhaust

5. Rotate the crankshaft to the next chalk mark — 90° — and repeat the procedure for:
- No. 2 intake
- No. 4 exhaust
- No. 5 intake and exhaust
- No. 6 intake
- No. 8 exhaust

8-7.5L Engine

1. Rotate the crankshaft by hand so that No. 1 piston is at TDC of the compression stroke. Make a chalk mark on the damper at that point. See the accompanying illustration.

2. With No. 1 at TDC, slowly apply pressure, using Lifter Bleed-down wrench T70P-6513-A, or equivalent, to completely bottom the lifter, on the following valves:
- No. 1 intake and exhaust
- No. 3 intake
- No. 4 exhaust
- No. 7 intake
- No. 5 exhaust
- No. 8 intake and exhaust

Take care to avoid excessive pressure that might bend the pushrod. Hold the lifter in this position and check the clearance between the rocker arm and the valve stem tip. Allowable clearance is 1.9-4.4mm (0.075-0.175 in.) with a desired clearance of 2.5-3.8mm (0.100-0.150 in.).

3. If the clearance is less than specified, install a shorter pushrod. If the clearance is greater than specified, install a longer pushrod.

4. Rotate the crankshaft clockwise — viewed from the front — 360°, until the chalk mark is once again aligned with the timing pointer. Repeat the procedure for:
- No. 2 intake and exhaust
- No. 4 intake
- No. 3 exhaust
- No. 5 intake
- No. 7 exhaust
- No. 6 intake and exhaust

Valve Stem Oil Seals

REPLACEMENT

Cylinder Head Removed

1. Remove the cylinder head.
2. Block the head on its side, or install a pair of head-holding brackets made especially for valve removal.
3. Using a socket slightly larger than the valve stem and keepers, place the socket over the valve spring retainer and gently hit the socket with a plastic hammer to break loose any varnish buildup.
4. Remove the valve keepers, retainer, (sleeve on 5.0L and 5.8L engine intake valve) and valve spring using a valve spring compressor (the locking C-clamp type is the easiest to use).
5. Place the parts from each valve in a separate container, numbered and identified for the valve and cylinder.
6. Remove and discard the valve stem oil seal.
7. On the 5.0L and 5.8L engines, install new valve seals, using a ⅝in. deep-well socket and a light mallet to seat the seal on the cylinder head and valve stem.
8. Install any required shims, the valve spring and the retainer over the valve stem. Compress the spring with the valve spring compressor and install the keepers.
9. After all the valves and springs have been assembled, take a mallet and lightly strike each valve stem tip squarely to seat the keepers.

Cylinder Head Installed

1. Disconnect the negative battery cable.
2. Remove the rocker arm cover.
3. Remove the spark plug from the cylinder where the seals are to be replaced.
4. Rotate the crankshaft until the piston is at Top Dead Center (TDC) with both valves closed.
5. Install a suitable adapter in the spark plug hole and connect an air supply line to the adapter. Turn on the air supply.

➡**If the air pressure does not hold the valves closed during the following steps, there is probably valve and/or valve seat damage; remove the cylinder head.**

6. Remove the rocker arm fulcrum bolts, fulcrum, rocker arm, fulcrum guide and pushrod. Note their positions so they can be reinstalled in their original locations.
7. Install the fulcrum bolt and position valve spring compressor tool T70P-6049-A or equivalent. Compress the valve spring and remove the keepers, sleeve (intake valve only), retainer and spring.
8. Remove and discard the valve stem seal.

➡**If air pressure has forced the piston to the bottom of the cylinder, any loss of air pressure will let the valve(s) fall into the cylinder. Wrap a rubber band, tape or string around the end of the valve stem to prevent this.**

9. Make sure the piston is at TDC. Remove the air pressure from the spark plug adapter and inspect the valve stem for damage. Rotate the valve and check the valve stem tip for eccentric movement. Move the valve up and down in the guide through its normal travel and check for binding. If the valve is damaged, the cylinder head must be removed.
10. If the valve is okay, apply clean engine oil to the valve stem and hold the valve closed. Apply the air pressure to the cylinder.
11. Install a new valve seal using a ⅝in. deep well socket and light hammer or mallet to seat the seal on the valve stem or use valve seal installer kit (guide mounted) T87L-6571-BH or equivalent.
12. Position the spring and retainer (and sleeve, if equipped) over the valve stem and compress the valve spring. Install the keepers and release the compressor. Remove the compressor and fulcrum bolt.
13. Turn off the air pressure and remove the air line and adaptor.
14. Apply multi-purpose grease or equivalent lubricant to the pushrod ends and install the pushrods. Apply multi-purpose grease or equivalent lubricant to the valve stem tips.
15. Apply multi-purpose grease or equivalent lubricant to the rocker arm pushrod socket, fulcrum seat and valve stem pad.
16. Install the rocker arms, fulcrum seats and fulcrum bolts. Rotate the crankshaft until the lifter is on the base circle of the camshaft, then tighten the fulcrum bolt to 18-25 ft. lbs. (24-34 Nm).
17. Install the spark plug and the rocker arm cover.
18. Connect the negative battery cable, start the engine and check for leaks.

Valve Seats

REMOVAL & INSTALLATION

6.9L and 7.3L Diesel

➡**The diesel is the only engine covered in this guide which has removable valve seats.**

1. Using Ford Rotunda tool 14-0309 the exhaust valve seats may be removed. Position the remover collet into the insert and rotate the collet nut clockwise to expand the collet jaws under the lip of the seat insert.
2. Rotate the top nut clockwise to remove the insert.

➡**If an oversize seat insert is required, the cylinder head should be sent out to a qualified machine shop.**

3. To install a new exhaust valve seat, drive the seat in place using Rotunda tool 14-0309 and a hammer.
Valve seat inserts are supplied for service in standard size, 0.015 in. (0.381mm) oversize and 0.030 in. (0.762mm) oversize.

Valve Guides

REAMING VALVE GUIDES

If it becomes necessary to ream a valve guide to install with an oversize stem, a reaming kit is available which contains a oversize reamers and pilot tools.

When replacing a standard size valve with an oversize valve always use the reamer in sequence (smallest oversize first, then next smallest, etc.) so as not to overload the reamers. Always reface the valve seat after the valve guide has been reamed, and use a suitable scraper to brake the sharp corner at the top of the valve guide.

KNURLING

Valve guides which are not excessively worn or distorted may, in some cases, be knurled rather than reamed. Knurling is a process in which metal inside the valve guide bore is displaced and raised (forming a very fine cross-hatch pattern), thereby reducing clearance. Knurling also provides for excellent oil control. The possibility of knurling rather than reaming the guides should be discussed with a machinist.

STEM-TO-GUIDE CLEARANCE

Valve stem-to-guide clearance should be checked upon assembling the cylinder head, and is especially necessary if the valve guides have been reamed or knurled, or if oversize valve have been installed. Excessive oil consumption often is a result of too much clearance between the valve guide and valve stem.

1. Clean the valve stem with lacquer thinner or a similar solvent to remove all gum and varnish. Clean the valve guides using solvent and an expanding wire-type valve guide cleaner (a rifle cleaning brush works well here).

2. Mount a dial indicator so that the stem is 90° to the valve stem and as close to the valve guide as possible.

3. Move the valve off its seat, and measure the valve guide-to-stem clearance by rocking the stem back and forth to actuate the dial indicator. Measure the valve stems using a micrometer and compare to specifications, to determine whether stem or guide wear is responsible for excessive clearance.

VALVE LAPPING

The valve must be lapped into their seats after resurfacing, to ensure proper sealing. Even if the valve have not been refaced, they should be lapped into the head before reassembly.

Set the cylinder head on the workbench, combustion chamber side up. Rest the head on wooden blocks on either end,

so there are 2-3 in. (51-76mm) between the tops of the valve guides and the bench.

1. Lightly lube the valve stem with clean engine oil. Coat the valve seat completely with valve grinding compound. Use just enough compound so that the full width and circumference of the seat are covered.

2. Install the valve in its proper location in the head. Attach the suction cup end of the valve lapping tool to the valve head. It usually helps to put a small amount of saliva into the suction cup to aid it sticking to the valve.

3. Rotate the tool between the palms, changing position and lifting the tool often to prevent grooving. Lap the valve in until a smooth, evenly polished seat and valve face are evident.

4. Remove the valve from the head. Wipe away all traces of grinding compound from the valve face and seat. Wipe out the port with a solvent soaked rag, and swab out the valve guide with a piece of solvent soaked rag to make sure there are no traces of compound grit inside the guide. This cleaning is very important, as the engine will ingest any grit remaining when started.

5. Proceed through the remaining valves, one at a time. Make sure the valve faces, sets, cylinder ports and valve guides are clean before reassembling the valve train.

Crankshaft Pulley (Vibration Damper)

REMOVAL & INSTALLATION

◗ See Figures 106, 107, 108 and 109

1. Remove the fan shroud, as required. If necessary, drain the cooling system and remove the radiator. Remove drive belts from pulley.

✳✳CAUTION

When draining the coolant, keep in mind that cats and dogs are attracted by the ethylene glycol antifreeze, and are quite likely to drink any that is left in an uncovered container or in puddles on the ground. This will prove fatal in sufficient quantity. Always drain the coolant into a sealable container. Coolant should be reused unless it is contaminated or several years old.

2. On those engines with a separate pulley, remove the retaining bolts and separate the pulley from the vibration damper.

3. Remove the vibration damper/pulley retaining bolt from the crankshaft end.

4. Using a puller, remove the damper/pulley from the crankshaft.

5. Upon installation, align the key slot of the pulley hub to the crankshaft key. Complete the assembly in the reverse order of removal. Torque the retaining bolts to the specifications found in the Torque Specifications Chart.

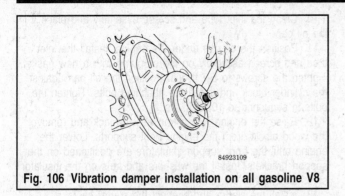

Fig. 106 Vibration damper installation on all gasoline V8

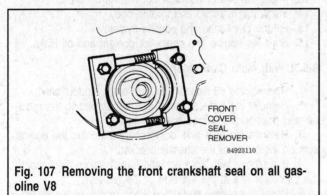

FRONT
COVER
SEAL
REMOVER

84923110

Fig. 107 Removing the front crankshaft seal on all gasoline V8

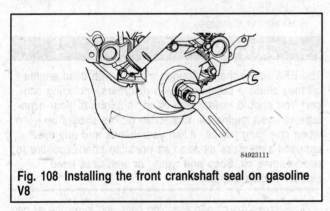

84923111

Fig. 108 Installing the front crankshaft seal on gasoline V8

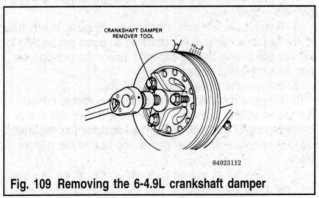

CRANKSHAFT DAMPER
REMOVER TOOL

84923112

Fig. 109 Removing the 6-4.9L crankshaft damper

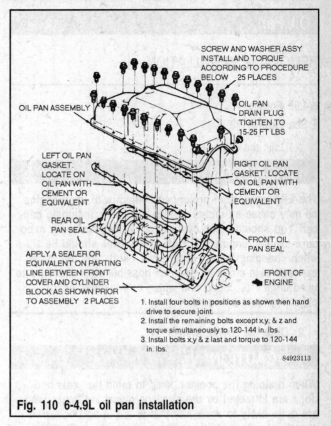

SCREW AND WASHER ASSY
INSTALL AND TORQUE
ACCORDING TO PROCEDURE
BELOW 25 PLACES

OIL PAN ASSEMBLY

OIL PAN
DRAIN PLUG
TIGHTEN TO
15-25 FT LBS

LEFT OIL PAN
GASKET.
LOCATE ON
OIL PAN WITH
CEMENT OR
EQUIVALENT

RIGHT OIL PAN
GASKET. LOCATE
ON OIL PAN WITH
CEMENT OR
EQUIVALENT

REAR OIL
PAN SEAL

FRONT OIL
PAN SEAL

APPLY A SEALER OR
EQUIVALENT ON PARTING
LINE BETWEEN FRONT
COVER AND CYLINDER
BLOCK AS SHOWN PRIOR
TO ASSEMBLY 2 PLACES

FRONT OF
ENGINE

1. Install four bolts in positions as shown then hand drive to secure joint.
2. Install the remaining bolts except x,y, & z and torque simultaneously to 120-144 in. lbs.
3. Install bolts x,y & z last and torque to 120-144 in. lbs.

84923113

Fig. 110 6-4.9L oil pan installation

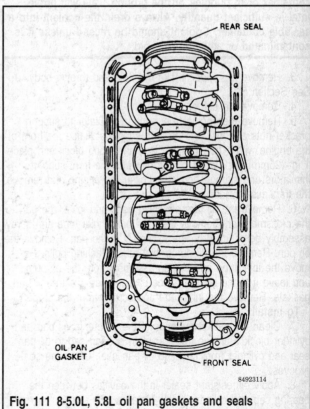

REAR SEAL

OIL PAN
GASKET

FRONT SEAL

84923114

Fig. 111 8-5.0L, 5.8L oil pan gaskets and seals

Oil Pan

REMOVAL & INSTALLATION

6-4.9L Engine

▶ See Figure 110

1. Drain the crankcase.

※※CAUTION

The EPA warns that prolonged contact with used engine oil may cause a number of skin disorders, including cancer! You should make every effort to minimize your exposure to used engine oil. Protective gloves should be worn when changing the oil. Wash your hands and any other exposed skin areas as soon as possible after exposure to used engine oil. Soap and water, or waterless hand cleaner should be used.

2. Drain the cooling system.

※※CAUTION

When draining the coolant, keep in mind that cats and dogs are attracted by the ethylene glycol antifreeze, and are quite likely to drink any that is left in an uncovered container or in puddles on the ground. This will prove fatal in sufficient quantity. Always drain the coolant into a sealable container. Coolant should be reused unless it is contaminated or several years old.

3. Remove the upper intake manifold and throttle body. See Section 5.
4. Remove the starter.
5. Remove the engine front support insulator to support bracket nuts and washers on both supports. Raise the front of the engine with a transmission jack and wood block and place 1 in. (25mm) thick wood blocks between the front support insulators and support brackets. Lower the engine and remove the transmission jack.
6. Remove the oil pan attaching bolts and lower the pan to the crossmember. Remove the 2 oil pump inlet tube and screw assembly bolts and drop the assembly in the pan. Remove the oil pan. Remove the oil pump inlet tube attaching bolts. Remove the inlet tube and screen assembly from the oil pump and leave it in the bottom of the oil pan. Remove the oil pan gaskets. Remove the inlet tube and screen from the oil pan.

To install:

7. Clean the gasket surfaces of the oil pump, oil pan and cylinder block. Remove the rear main bearing cap to oil pan seal and cylinder front cover to oil pan seal. Clean the seal grooves.
8. Apply oil-resistant sealer in the cavities between the bearing cap and cylinder block. Install a new seal in the rear main bearing cap and apply a bead of oil-resistant sealer to the tapered ends of the seal.
9. Install new side gaskets on the oil pan with oil-resistant sealer. Position a new oil pan to cylinder front cover seal on the oil pan.

10. Clean the inlet tube and screen assembly and place it in the oil pan.
11. Position the oil pan under the engine. Install the inlet tube and screen assembly on the oil pump with a new gasket. Tighten the screws to 5-7 ft. lbs. Position the oil pan against the cylinder block and install the attaching bolts. Tighten the bolts in sequence to 10-12 ft. lbs.
12. Raise the engine with a transmission jack and remove the wood blocks from the engine front supports. Lower the engine until the front support insulators are positioned on the support brackets. Install the washers and nuts on the insulator studs and tighten the nuts.
13. Install the starter and connect the starter cable.
14. Install the manifold and throttle body.
15. Fill the crankcase and cooling system.
16. Start the engine and check for coolant and oil leaks.

8-5.8L with 4-bbl Carburetor

1. Remove the oil dipstick (on pan entry models only).
2. Remove the bolts attaching the fan shroud to the radiator and position the shroud over the fan.
3. Remove the nuts and lockwashers attaching the engine support insulators to the chassis bracket.
4. If equipped with an automatic transmission, disconnect the oil cooler line at the left side of the radiator.
5. Raise the engine and place wood blocks under the engine supports.
6. Drain the crankcase.

※※CAUTION

The EPA warns that prolonged contact with used engine oil may cause a number of skin disorders, including cancer! You should make every effort to minimize your exposure to used engine oil. Protective gloves should be worn when changing the oil. Wash your hands and any other exposed skin areas as soon as possible after exposure to used engine oil. Soap and water, or waterless hand cleaner should be used.

7. Remove the oil pan attaching bolts and lower the oil pan onto the crossmember.
8. Remove the two bolts attaching the oil pump pickup tube to the oil pump. Remove nut attaching oil pump pickup tube to the number 3 main bearing cap stud. Lower the pick-up tube and screen into the oil pan.
9. Remove the oil pan from the vehicle.
10. Clean oil pan, inlet tube and gasket surfaces. Inspect the gasket sealing surface for damages and distortion due to overtightening of the bolts. Repair and straighten as required.
11. Position a new oil pan gasket and seal to the cylinder block.
12. Position the oil pick-up tube and screen to the oil pump, and install the lower attaching bolt and gasket loosely. Install nut attaching to number 3 main bearing cap stud.
13. Place the oil pan on the crossmember. Install the upper pick-up tube bolt. Tighten the pick-up tube bolts.
14. Position the oil pan to the cylinder block and install the attaching bolts. Tighten to 10-12 ft. lbs.

8-5.0L, 8-5.8L with EFI Engines

▶ **See Figure 111**

1. Drain the cooling system.

❋❋CAUTION

When draining the coolant, keep in mind that cats and dogs are attracted by the ethylene glycol antifreeze, and are quite likely to drink any that is left in an uncovered container or in puddles on the ground. This will prove fatal in sufficient quantity. Always drain the coolant into a sealable container. Coolant should be reused unless it is contaminated or several years old.

2. Remove the bolts attaching the fan shroud to the radiator and position the shroud over the fan.
3. Remove the upper intake manifold and throttle body. See Section 5.
4. Remove the nuts and lockwashers attaching the engine support insulators to the chassis bracket.
5. If equipped with an automatic transmission, disconnect the oil cooler line at the left side of the radiator.
6. Remove the exhaust system.
7. Raise the engine and place wood blocks under the engine supports.
8. Drain the crankcase.

❋❋CAUTION

The EPA warns that prolonged contact with used engine oil may cause a number of skin disorders, including cancer! You should make every effort to minimize your exposure to used engine oil. Protective gloves should be worn when changing the oil. Wash your hands and any other exposed skin areas as soon as possible after exposure to used engine oil. Soap and water, or waterless hand cleaner should be used.

9. Support the transmission with a floor jack and remove the transmission crossmember.
10. Remove the oil pan attaching bolts and lower the oil pan onto the crossmember.
11. Remove the two bolts attaching the oil pump pickup tube to the oil pump. Remove nut attaching oil pump pickup tube to the number 3 main bearing cap stud. Lower the pickup tube and screen into the oil pan.
12. Remove the oil pan from the vehicle.
To install:
13. Clean the oil pan, inlet tube and gasket surfaces. Inspect the gasket sealing surface for damages and distortion due to overtightening of the bolts. Repair and straighten as required.
14. Position a new oil pan gasket and seal to the cylinder block.
15. Position the oil pick-up tube and screen to the oil pump, and install the lower attaching bolt and gasket loosely. Install nut attaching to number 3 main bearing cap stud.
16. Place the oil pan on the crossmember. Install the upper pick-up tube bolt. Tighten the pick-up tube bolts.
17. Position the oil pan to the cylinder block and install the attaching bolts. Tighten to 10-12 ft. lbs.

18. Install the transmission crossmember.
19. Raise the engine and remove the blocks under the engine supports. Bolt the engine to the supports.
20. Install the exhaust system.
21. If equipped with an automatic transmission, connect the oil cooler line at the left side of the radiator.
22. Install the nuts and lockwashers attaching the engine support insulators to the chassis bracket.
23. Install the upper intake manifold and throttle body. See Section 5.
24. Install the fan shroud.
25. Fill the crankcase.
26. Fill and bleed the cooling system.

8-7.5L with 4-bbl. Carburetor

1. Raise and support the truck on jackstands. Remove the oil dipstick.
2. Remove the bolts attaching the fan shroud and position it over the fan.
3. Remove the engine support insulators-to-chassis bracket attaching nuts and washers. Disconnect the exhaust pipe at the manifolds.
4. If the vehicle is equipped with an automatic transmission, disconnect the oil cooler line at the left side of the radiator.
5. Raise the engine with a jack placed under the crankshaft damper and a block of wood to act as a cushion. Place wood blocks under the engine supports.
6. Drain the crankcase. Remove the oil filter.

❋❋CAUTION

The EPA warns that prolonged contact with used engine oil may cause a number of skin disorders, including cancer! You should make every effort to minimize your exposure to used engine oil. Protective gloves should be worn when changing the oil. Wash your hands and any other exposed skin areas as soon as possible after exposure to used engine oil. Soap and water, or waterless hand cleaner should be used.

7. Remove the oil pan attaching screws and lower the oil pan onto the crossmember. Remove the two bolts attaching the oil pump pick-up tube to the oil pump. Lower the assembly from the oil pump. Leave it on the bottom of the oil pan. Remove the oil pan and gaskets. Remove the inlet tube and screen from the oil pan.
To install:
8. In preparation for installation, clean the gasket surfaces of the oil pump, oil pan and cylinder block. Remove the rear main bearing cap-to-oil pan seal and engine front cover-to-oil pan seal. Clean the seal grooves.
9. Position the oil pan front and rear seal on the engine front cover and the rear main bearing cap, respectively. Be sure that the tabs on the seals are over the oil pan gasket.
10. Clean the inlet tube and screen assembly and place it in the oil pan.
11. Position the oil pan under the engine and install the inlet tube and screen assembly on the oil pump with a new gasket. Using new gaskets, position the oil pan against the cylinder block and install the retaining bolts.
12. Install the oil filter.
13. Remove the wood blocks and lower the engine.

14. If the vehicle is equipped with an automatic transmission, connect the oil cooler line at the left side of the radiator.

15. Install the engine support insulators-to-chassis bracket attaching nuts and washers. Connect the exhaust pipe at the manifolds.

16. Install the fan shroud.

17. Install the oil dipstick.

18. Fill the crankcase with oil.

8-7.5L with EFI

1. Remove the hood.
2. Disconnect the battery ground cable.
3. Drain the cooling system.

❊❊CAUTION

When draining the coolant, keep in mind that cats and dogs are attracted by the ethylene glycol antifreeze, and are quite likely to drink any that is left in an uncovered container or in puddles on the ground. This will prove fatal in sufficient quantity. Always drain the coolant into a sealable container. Coolant should be reused unless it is contaminated or several years old.

4. Remove the air intake tube and air cleaner assembly.
5. Disconnect the throttle linkage at the throttle body.
6. Disconnect the power brake vacuum line at the manifold.
7. Disconnect the fuel lines at the fuel rail.
8. Disconnect the air tubes at the throttle body.
9. Remove the radiator.
10. Remove the power steering pump and position it out of the way without disconnecting the lines.
11. Remove the oil dipstick tube. On motor home chassis, remove the oil filler tube.
12. Remove the front engine mount through-bolts.
13. Position the air conditioner refrigerant hoses so that they are clear of the firewall. If necessary, discharge the system and remove the compressor. (See Section 1).
14. Remove the upper intake manifold and throttle body. See Section 5.
15. Drain the crankcase. Remove the oil filter.

❊❊CAUTION

The EPA warns that prolonged contact with used engine oil may cause a number of skin disorders, including cancer! You should make every effort to minimize your exposure to used engine oil. Protective gloves should be worn when changing the oil. Wash your hands and any other exposed skin areas as soon as possible after exposure to used engine oil. Soap and water, or waterless hand cleaner should be used.

16. Disconnect the exhaust pipe at the manifolds.
17. Disconnect the transmission linkage at the transmission.
18. Remove the driveshaft(s).
19. Remove the transmission fill tube.
20. Raise the engine with a jack placed under the crankshaft damper and a block of wood to act as a cushion. Raise the engine until the transmission contacts the underside of the floor. Place wood blocks under the engine supports. The en-

gine **must** remain centralized at a point at least 4 in. (102mm) above the mounts, to remove the oil pan!

21. Remove the oil pan attaching screws and lower the oil pan onto the crossmember. Remove the two bolts attaching the oil pump pick-up tube to the oil pump. Lower the assembly from the oil pump. Leave it on the bottom of the oil pan. Remove the oil pan and gaskets. Remove the inlet tube and screen from the oil pan.

To install:

22. Clean the gasket surfaces of the oil pan and cylinder block.
23. Apply a coating of gasket adhesive on the block mating surface and stick the 1-piece silicone gasket on the block.
24. Clean the inlet tube and screen assembly and place on the pump.
25. Position the oil pan against the cylinder block and install the retaining bolts. Torque all bolts to 10 ft. lbs.
26. Lower the engine and bolt it in place.
27. Install the transmission fill tube.
28. Install the driveshaft(s).
29. Connect the transmission linkage at the transmission.
30. Connect the exhaust pipe at the manifolds.
31. Install the oil filter.
32. Install the upper intake manifold and throttle body. See Section 5.
33. Install the compressor or reposition the hoses.
34. Install the oil dipstick tube. On motor home chassis, install the oil filler tube.
35. Install the power steering pump.
36. Install the radiator.
37. Connect the air tubes at the throttle body.
38. Connect the fuel lines at the fuel rail.
39. Connect the power brake vacuum line at the manifold.
40. Connect the throttle linkage at the throttle body.
41. Install the air intake tube and air cleaner assembly.
42. Fill and bleed the cooling system.
43. Fill the crankcase.
44. Connect the battery ground cable.
45. Install the hood.

8-6.9L, 8-7.3L Diesel Engines

1. Disconnect both battery ground cables.
2. Remove the engine oil dipstick.
3. Remove the transmission oil dipstick.
4. Remove the air cleaner and cover the intake opening.
5. Remove the fan and fan clutch.

➡The fan uses left hand threads. Remove them by turning them clockwise.

6. Drain the cooling system.

❊❊CAUTION

When draining the coolant, keep in mind that cats and dogs are attracted by the ethylene glycol antifreeze, and are quite likely to drink any that is left in an uncovered container or in puddles on the ground. This will prove fatal in sufficient quantity. Always drain the coolant into a sealable container. Coolant should be reused unless it is contaminated or several years old.

7. Disconnect the lower radiator hose.

8. Disconnect the power steering return hose and plug the line and pump.

9. Disconnect the alternator wiring harness.

10. Disconnect the fuel line heater connector from the alternator.

11. Raise and support the front end on jackstands.

12. On trucks with automatic transmission, disconnect the transmission cooler lines at the radiator and plug them.

13. Disconnect and plug the fuel pump inlet line.

14. Drain the crankcase and remove the oil filter.

❋❋CAUTION

The EPA warns that prolonged contact with used engine oil may cause a number of skin disorders, including cancer! You should make every effort to minimize your exposure to used engine oil. Protective gloves should be worn when changing the oil. Wash your hands and any other exposed skin areas as soon as possible after exposure to used engine oil. Soap and water, or waterless hand cleaner should be used.

15. Remove the engine oil filler tube.

16. Disconnect the exhaust pipes at the manifolds.

17. Disconnect the muffler inlet pipe from the muffler and remove the pipe.

18. Remove the upper inlet mounting stud from the right exhaust manifold.

19. Unbolt the engine from the No. 1 crossmember.

20. Lower the vehicle.

21. Install lifting brackets on the front of the engine.

22. Raise the engine until the transmission contact the body.

23. Install wood blocks — 2¾ in. (70mm) on the left side; 2 in. (50mm) on the right side — between the engine insulators and crossmember.

24. Lower the engine onto the blocks.

25. Raise and support the front end on jackstands.

26. Remove the flywheel inspection plate.

27. Position fuel pump inlet line No. 1 rearward of the crossmember and position the oil cooler lines out of the way.

28. Remove the oil pan bolts.

29. Lower the oil pan.

➡The oil pan is sealed to the crankcase with RTV silicone sealant in place of a gasket. It may be necessary to separate the pan from the crankcase with a utility knife.

➡CHILTON TIP: The crankshaft may have to be turned to allow the pan to clear the crankshaft throws.

30. Clean the pan and crankcase mating surfaces thoroughly.

To install:

31. Apply a ⅛in. (3mm) bead of RTV silicone sealant to the pan mating surfaces, and a ¼ in. (6mm) bead on the front and rear covers and in the corners. You have 15 minutes within which to install the pan!

32. Install locating dowels (which you supply) into position as shown.

33. Position the pan on the engine and install the pan bolts loosely.

34. Remove the dowels.

35. Torque the pan bolts to 7 ft. lbs. for ¼ in.-20 bolts; 14 ft. lbs. for 5/16 in.-18 bolts; 24 ft.lb for ⅜in.-16 bolts.

36. Install the flywheel inspection cover.

37. Lower the truss.

38. Raise the engine and remove the wood blocks.

39. Lower the engine onto the crossmember and remove the lifting brackets.

40. Raise and support the front end on jackstands.

41. Torque the engine-to-crossmember nuts to 70 ft. lbs.

42. Install the upper inlet pipe mounting stud.

43. Install the inlet pipe, using a new gasket.

44. Install the transmission oil filler tube, using a new gasket.

45. Install the oil pan drain plug.

46. Install a new oil filter.

47. Connect the fuel pump inlet line. Make sure that the clip is installed on the crossmember.

48. Connect the transmission cooler lines.

49. Lower the truck.

50. Connect all wiring.

51. Connect the power steering return line.

52. Connect the lower radiator hose.

53. Install the fan and fan clutch.

➡The fan uses left hand threads. Install them by turning them counterclockwise.

54. Remove the cover and install the air cleaner.

55. Install the dipsticks.

56. Fill the crankcase.

57. Fill and bleed the cooling system.

58. Fill the power steering reservoir.

59. Connect the batteries.

60. Run the engine and check for leaks.

➡The fan uses left hand threads. Install them by turning them counterclockwise.

61. Remove the cover and install the air cleaner.

62. Install the dipsticks.

63. Fill the crankcase.

64. Fill and bleed the cooling system.

65. Fill the power steering reservoir.

66. Connect the batteries.

67. Run the engine and check for leaks.

Oil Pump

REMOVAL & INSTALLATION

Gasoline Engines
◆ See Figures 112, 113 and 114

1. Remove the oil pan.

2. Remove the oil pump inlet tube and screen assembly.

3. Remove the oil pump attaching bolts and remove the oil pump gasket and intermediate driveshaft.

4. Before installing the oil pump, prime it by filling the inlet and outlet port with engine oil and rotating the shaft of the pump to distribute it.

5. Position the intermediate driveshaft into the distributor socket.

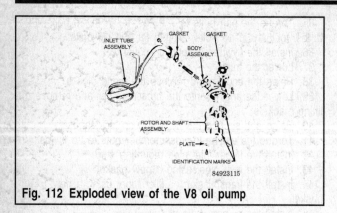

Fig. 112 Exploded view of the V8 oil pump

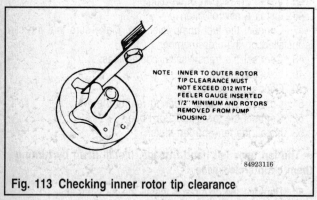

NOTE: INNER TO OUTER ROTOR TIP CLEARANCE MUST NOT EXCEED .012 WITH FEELER GAUGE INSERTED 1/2" MINIMUM AND ROTORS REMOVED FROM PUMP HOUSING

Fig. 113 Checking inner rotor tip clearance

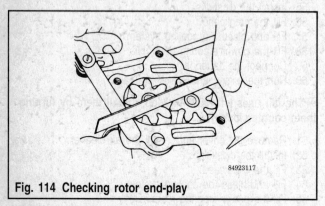

Fig. 114 Checking rotor end-play

6. Position the new gasket on the pump body and insert the intermediate driveshaft into the pump body.

7. Install the pump and intermediate driveshaft as an assembly. Do not force the pump if it does not seal readily. The driveshaft may be misaligned with the distributor shaft. To align it, rotate the intermediate driveshaft into a new position.

8. Install the oil pump attaching bolts and torque them to 12-15 ft. lbs. on the inline sixes and to 20-25 ft. lbs. on the V8s.

Diesel Engines
▶ **See Figures 115 and 116**

1. Remove the oil pan.
2. Remove the oil pick-up tube from the pump.
3. Unbolt and remove the oil pump.
4. Assemble the pick-up tube and pump. Use a new gasket.

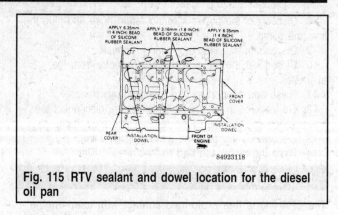

Fig. 115 RTV sealant and dowel location for the diesel oil pan

5. Install the oil pump and torque the bolts to 14 ft. lbs.

OVERHAUL

1. Wash all parts in solvent and dry them thoroughly with compressed air. Use a brush to clean the inside of the pump housing and the pressure relief valve chamber. Be sure all dirt and metal particles are removed.

2. Check the inside of the pump housing and the outer race and rotor for damage or excessive wear or scoring.

3. Check the mating surface of the pump cover for wear. If the cover mating surface is worn, scored, or grooved, replace the pump.

4. Measure the inner rotor tip clearance.

5. With the rotor assembly installed in the housing, place a straight edge over the rotor assembly and the housing. Measure the clearance (rotor end-play) between the straight edge and the rotor and the outer race.

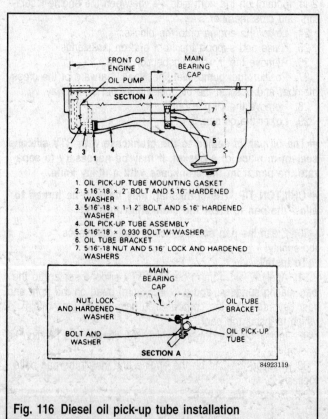

1. OIL PICK-UP TUBE MOUNTING GASKET
2. 5.16"-18 × 2" BOLT AND 5.16" HARDENED WASHER
3. 5.16"-18 × 1-1.2" BOLT AND 5.16" HARDENED WASHER
4. OIL PICK-UP TUBE ASSEMBLY
5. 5.16"-18 × 0.930 BOLT W WASHER
6. OIL TUBE BRACKET
7. 5.16"-18 NUT AND 5.16" LOCK AND HARDENED WASHERS

Fig. 116 Diesel oil pick-up tube installation

6. Check the drive shaft to housing bearing clearance by measuring the OD of the shaft and the ID of the housing bearing.

7. Components of the oil pump are not serviced. If any part of the pump requires replacement, replace the complete pump assembly.

8. Inspect the relief valve spring to see if it is collapsed or worn.

9. Check the relief valve piston for scores and free operation in the bore.

Oil Cooler

REMOVAL & INSTALLATION

8-5.8L Lightning
▶ See Figure 117

1. Drain the cooling system.

✻✻CAUTION

When draining the coolant, keep in mind that cats and dogs are attracted by the ethylene glycol antifreeze, and are quite likely to drink any that is left in an uncovered container or in puddles on the ground. This will prove fatal in sufficient quantity. Always drain the coolant into a sealable container. Coolant should be reused unless it is contaminated or several years old.

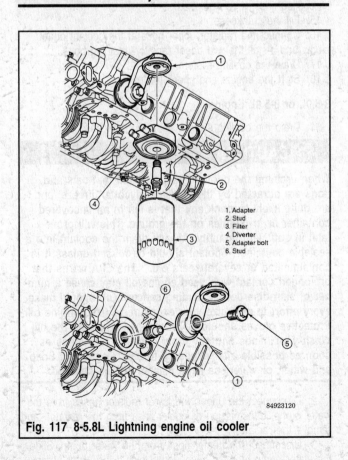

1. Adapter
2. Stud
3. Filter
4. Diverter
5. Adapter bolt
6. Stud

Fig. 117 8-5.8L Lightning engine oil cooler

2. Raise and support the front end on jackstands.
3. Loosen the clamps and remove the hoses from the cooler.
4. Remove the oil filter.
5. Remove the adapter from the engine and separate the cooler from it.
6. Installation is the reverse of removal.

6.9L and 7.3L Diesel
▶ See Figure 118

The diesel oil cooler should be disassembled if the cooler O-rings begin to leak.

1. Gently rap the front and oil cooler headers to loosen the O-rings. Carefully twist the oil cooler apart.
2. Using a suitable solvent, thoroughly clean the oil cooler and the front and filter headers.
3. Always use new O-rings when reassembling. Lubricate the new rings and all O-ring mating surfaces with clean engine oil. Install the two narrow O-rings into their respective grooves inside the front and filter headers.
4. Place the large O-ring over the oil cooler shell.
5. Press the assembly together, making sure the locating clips align with the slots.

Front Cover and Oil Seal

REMOVAL & INSTALLATION

6-4.9L Engine
▶ See Figures 119 and 120

1. Drain the cooling system and disconnect the radiator upper hose at the coolant outlet elbow and remove the two upper radiator retaining bolts.

✻✻CAUTION

When draining the coolant, keep in mind that cats and dogs are attracted by the ethylene glycol antifreeze, and are quite likely to drink any that is left in an uncovered container or in puddles on the ground. This will prove fatal in sufficient quantity. Always drain the coolant into a sealable container. Coolant should be reused unless it is contaminated or several years old.

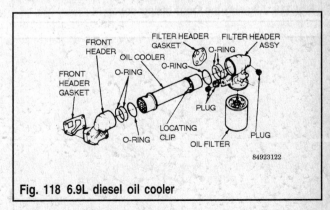

Fig. 118 6.9L diesel oil cooler

2. Raise the vehicle and drain the crankcase.

❊❊CAUTION

The EPA warns that prolonged contact with used engine oil may cause a number of skin disorders, including cancer! You should make every effort to minimize your exposure to used engine oil. Protective gloves should be worn when changing the oil. Wash your hands and any other exposed skin areas as soon as possible after exposure to used engine oil. Soap and water, or waterless hand cleaner should be used.

3. Remove the splash shield and the automatic transmission oil cooling lines, if so equipped, then remove the radiator.
4. Loosen and remove the fan belt, fan and pulley.
5. Use a gear puller to remove the crankshaft pulley damper.

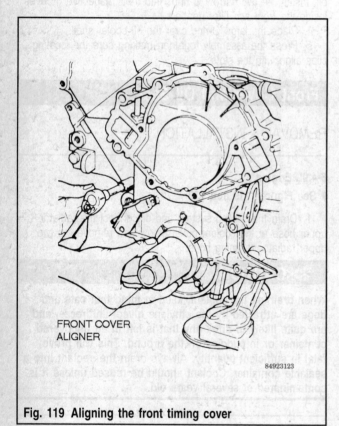

FRONT COVER
ALIGNER

84923123

Fig. 119 Aligning the front timing cover

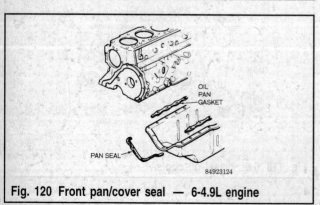

OIL
PAN
GASKET

PAN SEAL

84923124

Fig. 120 Front pan/cover seal — 6-4.9L engine

6. Remove the cylinder front cover retaining bolts and gently pry the cover away from the block. Remove the gasket.
7. Drive out the old seal with a pin punch from the rear of the cover. Clean out the recess in the cover.

To install:

8. Coat the new seal with grease and drive it into the cover until it is fully seated. Check the seal to make sure that the spring around the seal is in the proper position.
9. Clean the cylinder front cover and the gasket surface of the cylinder block. Apply an oil-resistant sealer to the new front cover gasket and install the gasket onto the cover.
10. Position the front cover assembly over the end of the crankshaft and against the cylinder block. Start, but do not tighten, the cover and pan attaching screws. Slide a front cover alignment tool (Ford part no. T68P-6019-A or equivalent) over the crank stub and into the seal bore of the cover. Tighten all front cover and oil pan attaching screws to 12-18 ft. lbs. front cover; 10-15 ft. lbs. oil pan, tightening the oil pan screws first.

➡Trim away the exposed portion of the old oil pan gasket flush with the front of the engine block. Cut and position the required portion of a new gasket to the oil pan and apply sealer to both sides.

11. Lubricate the hub of the crankshaft damper pulley with Lubriplate® to prevent damage to the seal during installation or on initial starting of the engine.
12. Install the fan belt, fan and pulley.
13. Install the radiator.
14. Install the splash shield and the automatic transmission oil cooling lines, if so equipped.
15. Fill the crankcase.
16. Connect the radiator upper hose at the coolant outlet elbow and install the two upper radiator retaining bolts.
17. Drain the cooling system.
18. Start the engine and check for leaks.

8-5.0L or 8-5.8L Engine

1. Drain the cooling system and the crankcase.

❊❊CAUTION

When draining the coolant, keep in mind that cats and dogs are attracted by the ethylene glycol antifreeze, and are quite likely to drink any that is left in an uncovered container or in puddles on the ground. This will prove fatal in sufficient quantity. Always drain the coolant into a sealable container. Coolant should be reused unless it is contaminated or several years old. The EPA warns that prolonged contact with used engine oil may cause a number of skin disorders, including cancer! You should make every effort to minimize your exposure to used engine oil. Protective gloves should be worn when changing the oil. Wash your hands and any other exposed skin areas as soon as possible after exposure to used engine oil. Soap and water, or waterless hand cleaner should be used.

2. Disconnect the upper and lower radiator hoses from the water pump, transmission oil cooler lines from the radiator, and remove the radiator.
3. Disconnect the heater hose from the water pump. Slide the water pump by-pass hose clamp toward the water pump.

4. Loosen the alternator pivot bolt and the bolt which secures the alternator adjusting arm to the water pump. Position the alternator out of the way.

5. Remove the power steering pump and air conditioning compressor from their mounting brackets, if so equipped.

6. Remove the bolts holding the fan shroud to the radiator, if so equipped. Remove the fan, spacer, pulley and drive belts.

7. Remove the crankshaft pulley from the crankshaft damper. Remove the damper attaching bolt and washer and remove the damper with a puller.

8. Disconnect the fuel pump outlet line at the fuel pump. Disconnect the vacuum inlet and outlet lines from the fuel pump. Remove the fuel pump attaching bolts and lay the pump to one side with the fuel inlet line still attached.

9. Remove the oil level dipstick and the bolt holding the dipstick tube to the exhaust manifold on the 8-5.0L.

10. Remove the oil pan-to-cylinder front cover attaching bolts. Use a sharp, thin cutting blade to cut the oil pan gasket flush with the cylinder block. Remove the front cover and water pump as an assembly.

11. Discard the front cover gasket.

To install:

12. Place the front seal removing tool (Ford part no. T70P-6B070-A or equivalent) into the front cover plate and over the front of the seal as shown in the illustration. Tighten the two through bolts to force the seal puller under the seal flange, then alternately tighten the four puller bolts a half turn at a time to pull the oil seal from the cover.

13. Coat a new front cover oil seal with Lubriplate® or equivalent and place it onto the front oil seal alignment and installation tool (Ford part no. T70P-6B070-A or equivalent) as shown in the illustration. Place the tool and the seal onto the end of the crankshaft and push it toward the engine until the seal starts into the front cover.

14. Place the installation screw, washer, and nut onto the end of the crankshaft, then thread the screw into the crankshaft. Tighten the nut against the washer and tool to force the seal into the front cover plate. Remove the tool.

15. Apply Lubriplate® or equivalent to the oil seal rubbing surface of the vibration damper inner hub to prevent damage to the seal. Coat the front of the crankshaft with engine oil for damper installation.

16. To install the damper, line up the damper keyway with the key on the crankshaft, then install the damper onto the crankshaft. Install the cap screw and washer, and tighten the screw to 80 ft. lbs. Install the crankshaft pulley.

17. Install the fan, spacer, pulley and drive belts.

18. Install the bolts holding the fan shroud to the radiator, if so equipped.

19. Install the power steering pump and air conditioning compressor.

20. Position and tighten the alternator.

21. Connect the heater hose at the water pump.

22. Install the radiator.

23. Connect the upper and lower radiator hoses, and transmission oil cooler lines.

24. Fill the cooling system and the crankcase.

8-7.5L Engine

▶ See Figures 121 and 122

1. Drain the cooling system and crankcase.

✳✳CAUTION

When draining the coolant, keep in mind that cats and dogs are attracted by the ethylene glycol antifreeze, and are quite likely to drink any that is left in an uncovered container or in puddles on the ground. This will prove fatal in sufficient quantity. Always drain the coolant into a sealable container. Coolant should be reused unless it is contaminated or several years old. The EPA warns that prolonged contact with used engine oil may cause a number of skin disorders, including cancer! You should make every effort to minimize your exposure to used engine oil. Protective gloves should be worn when changing the oil. Wash your hands and any other exposed skin areas as soon as possible after exposure to used engine oil. Soap and water, or waterless hand cleaner should be used.

2. Remove the radiator shroud and fan.

3. Disconnect the upper and lower radiator hoses, and the automatic transmission oil cooler lines from the radiator.

4. Remove the radiator upper support and remove the radiator.

5. Loosen the alternator attaching bolts and air conditioning compressor idler pulley and remove the drive belts with the water pump pulley. Remove the bolts attaching the compressor support to the water pump and remove the bracket (support), if so equipped.

6. Remove the crankshaft pulley from the vibration damper. Remove the bolt and washer attaching the crankshaft damper and remove the damper with a puller. Remove the woodruff key from the crankshaft.

7. Loosen the by-pass hose at the water pump, and disconnect the heater return tube at the water pump.

8. Disconnect and plug the fuel inlet and outlet lines at the fuel pump, and remove the fuel pump.

9. Remove the bolts attaching the front cover to the cylinder block. Cut the oil pan seal flush with the cylinder block face with a thin knife blade prior to separating the cover from the cylinder block. Remove the cover and water pump as an assembly. Discard the front cover gasket and oil pan seal.

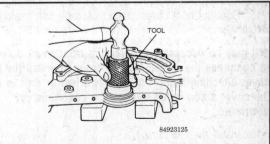

84923125

Fig. 121 Installing the oil seal into the 8-7.5L front cover. The tool makes it easier to drive in the seal evenly

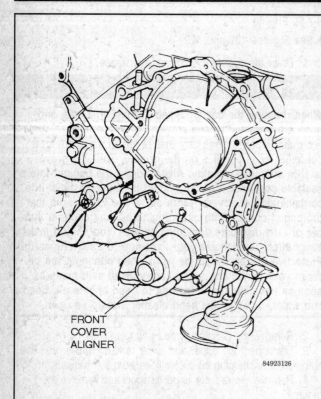

FRONT
COVER
ALIGNER

84923126

Fig. 122 Aligning the front cover on the 8-7.5L

To install:

10. Transfer the water pump if a new cover is going to be installed. Clean all of the gasket sealing surfaces on both the front cover and the cylinder block.

11. Coat the gasket surface of the oil pan with sealer. Cut and position the required sections of a new seal on the oil pan. Apply sealer to the corners.

12. Drive out the old front cover oil seal with a pin punch. Clean out the seal recess in the cover. coat a new seal with Lubriplate® or equivalent grease. Install the seal, making sure the seal spring remains in the proper position. A front cover seal tool, Ford part no. T72J-117 or equivalent, makes installation easier.

13. Coat the gasket surfaces of the cylinder block and cover with sealer and position the new gasket on the block.

14. Position the front cover on the cylinder block. Use care not to damage the seal and gasket or misplace them.

15. Coat the front cover attaching screws with sealer and install them.

➡**It may be necessary to force the front cover downward to compress the oil pan seal in order to install the front cover attaching bolts. Use a screwdriver or drift to engage the cover screw holes through the cover and pry downward.**

16. Install the fuel pump.
17. Connect the fuel inlet and outlet lines at the fuel pump.
18. Tighten the by-pass hose at the water pump.
19. Connect the heater return tube at the water pump.
20. Install the woodruff key from the crankshaft.
21. Install the damper.

22. Install the crankshaft pulley on the vibration damper.
23. Install the compressor support on the water pump and install the bracket (support), if so equipped.
24. Install the drive belts with the water pump pulley.
25. Install the radiator and upper support.
26. Connect the upper and lower radiator hoses, and the automatic transmission oil cooler lines.
27. Install the radiator shroud and fan.
28. Fill the cooling system and crankcase.
   Observe the following torques:
   • Front cover bolts — 15-20 ft. lbs.
   • Water pump attaching screws — 12-15 ft. lbs.
   • Crankshaft damper — 70-90 ft. lbs.
   • Crankshaft pulley — 35-50 ft. lbs.
   • Fuel pump — 19-27 ft. lbs.
   • Oil pan bolts — 9-11 ft. lbs. for the $\frac{5}{16}$ in. screws and to 7-9 ft. lbs. for the $\frac{1}{4}$ in. screws
   • Alternator pivot bolt — 45-57 ft. lbs.

6.9L and 7.3L Diesel Engines

▶ **See Figures 123, 124, 125, 126, 127, 128, 129, 130 and 131**

1. Disconnect both battery ground cables. Drain the cooling system.

✳✳CAUTION

When draining the coolant, keep in mind that cats and dogs are attracted by the ethylene glycol antifreeze, and are quite likely to drink any that is left in an uncovered container or in puddles on the ground. This will prove fatal in sufficient quantity. Always drain the coolant into a sealable container. Coolant should be reused unless it is contaminated or several years old.

2. Remove the air cleaner and cover the air intake on the manifold with clean rags. Do not allow any foreign material to enter the intake.

3. Remove the radiator fan shroud halves.

4. Remove the fan and fan clutch assembly. You will need a puller or ford tool No. T83T-6312-A for this.

➡**The nut is a left hand thread; remove by turning the nut clockwise.**

5. Remove the injection pump as described in Section 5 under Diesel Fuel Systems.

6. Remove the water pump.

7. Jack up the truck and safely support it with jackstands.

8. Remove the crankshaft pulley and vibration damper as described in this Section.

9. Remove the engine ground cables at the front of the engine.

10. Remove the five bolts attaching the engine front cover to the engine block and oil pan.

11. Lower the truck.

12. Remove the front cover.

➡**The front cover oil seal on the diesel must be driven out with an arbor press and a 3¼ in. (82.5mm) spacer. Take the cover to a qualified machinist or engine specialist for this procedure. See also steps 14 and 15.**

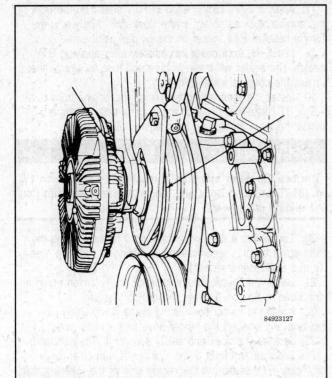

Fig. 123 Removing the diesel fan clutch using a puller (arrows)

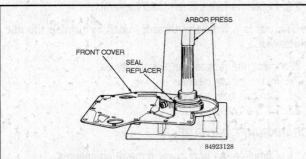

Fig. 124 Diesel front oil seal removal and installation using an arbor press

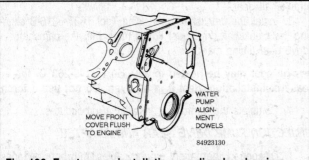

Fig. 126 Front cover installation on diesels, showing the alignment dowels

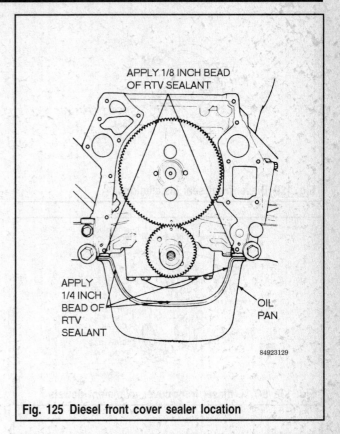

Fig. 125 Diesel front cover sealer location

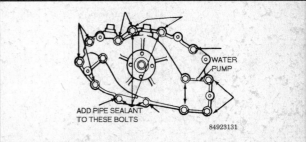

Fig. 127 Water pump-to-front cover installation on the diesel. The two top pump bolts must be no more than 31.75mm (1¼ in.) long

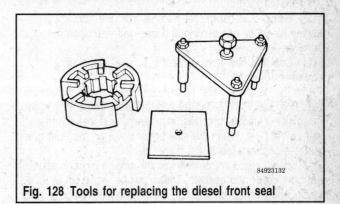

Fig. 128 Tools for replacing the diesel front seal

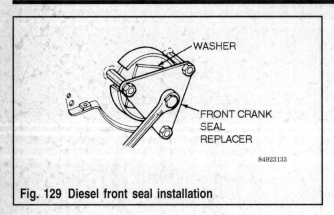

Fig. 129 Diesel front seal installation

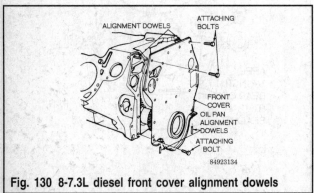

Fig. 130 8-7.3L diesel front cover alignment dowels

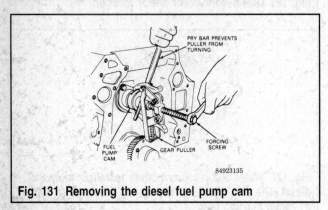

Fig. 131 Removing the diesel fuel pump cam

To install:

13. Remove all old gasket material from the front cover, engine block, oil pan sealing surfaces and water pump surfaces.

14. Coat the new front oil seal with Lubriplate® or equivalent grease.

15. The new seal must be installed using a seal installation tool, Ford part no. T83T-6700-A or an arbor press. A qualified machinist or engine specialist can handle seal installation as well as removal. When the seal bottoms out on the front cover surface, it is installed at the proper depth.

16. Install alignment dowels into the engine block to align the front cover and gaskets. These can be made out of round stock. Apply a gasket sealer to the engine block sealing surfaces, then install the gaskets on the block.

17. Apply a ⅛ in. (3mm) bead of RTV sealer on the front of the engine block as shown in the illustration. Apply a ¼ in. (6mm) bead of RTV sealer on the oil pan as shown.

18. Install the front cover immediately after applying RTV sealer. The sealer will begin to cure and lose its effectiveness unless the cover is installed quickly.

19. Install the water pump gasket on the engine front cover. Apply RTV sealer to the four water pump bolts illustrated. Install the water pump and hand tighten all bolts.

❈❈WARNING

The two top water pump bolts must be no more than 1¼ in. (31.75mm) long bolts any longer will interfere with (hit) the engine drive gears.

20. Torque the water pump bolts to 19 ft. lbs. Torque the front cover bolts to specifications according to bolt size (see Torque Specifications chart).

21. Install the injection pump adaptor and injection pump as described in Section 5 under Diesel Fuel System.

22. Install the heater hose fitting in the pump using pipe sealant, and connect the heater hose to the water pump.

23. Jack up the truck and safely support it with jackstands.

24. Lubricate the front of the crankshaft with clean engine oil. Apply RTV sealant to the engine side of the retaining bolt washer to prevent oil seepage past the keyway. Install the crankshaft vibration damper using Ford Special tools T83T-6316B. Torque the damper-to-crankshaft bolt to 90 ft. lbs.

25. Install the fan and fan clutch assembly.

➡ **The nut is a left hand thread; Install by turning the nut clockwise.**

26. Install the radiator fan shroud halves.

27. Install the air cleaner.

28. Connect both battery ground cables.

29. Fill the cooling system.

CRANKSHAFT DRIVE GEAR

1. Complete the front cover removal procedures.

2. Install the crankshaft drive gear remover Tool T83T-6316-A, and using a breaker bar to prevent crankshaft rotation, or flywheel holding Tool T74R-6375-A, remove the crankshaft gear.

3. Install the crankshaft gear using Tool T83T-6316-B aligning the crankshaft drive gear timing mark with the camshaft drive gear timing mark.

➡ **The gear may be heated to 300-350°F (149-260°C) for ease of installation. Heat it in an oven. Do not use a torch.**

4. Complete the front cover installation procedures.

INJECTION PUMP DRIVE GEAR AND ADAPTER

1. Disconnect the battery ground cables from both batteries. Remove the air cleaner and install an intake opening cover.

2. Remove the injection pump. Remove the bolts attaching the injection pump adapter to the engine block, and remove the adapter.

3. Remove the engine front cover. Remove the drive gear.

4. Clean all gasket and sealant surfaces of the components removed with a suitable solvent and dry them thoroughly.

To install:

5. Install the drive gear in position, aligning all the drive gear timing marks.

➡️To determine that the No. 1 piston is at TDC of the compression stroke, position the injection pump drive gear dowel at the 4 o'clock position. The scribe line on the vibration damper should be at TDC.   Use extreme care to avoid disturbing the injection pump drive gear, once it is in position.

6. Install the engine front cover. Apply a ⅛in. (3mm) bead of RTV Sealant along the bottom surface of the injection pump adapter.

➡️RTV should be applied immediately prior to adapter installation.

7. Install the injection pump adaptor. Apply sealer to the bolt threads before assembly.

➡️With the injection pump adapter installed, the injection pump drive gear cannot jump timing.

8. Install all removed components. Run the engine and check for leaks.

➡️If necessary, purge the high pressure fuel lines of air by loosening the connector one half to one turn and crank the engine until a solid flow of fuel, free of air bubbles, flows from the connection.

CAMSHAFT DRIVE GEAR, FUEL PUMP CAM, SPACER AND THRUST PLATE

▶ See Figures 132, 133, 134, 135, 136, 137 and 138

1. Complete the front cover removal procedures.
2. Remove the camshaft allen screw.
3. Install a gear puller, Tool T83T-6316-A and remove the gear. Remove the fuel supply pump, if necessary.
4. Install a gear puller, Tool T77E-4220-B and shaft protector T83T-6316-A and remove the fuel pump cam and spacer, if necessary.
5. Remove the bolts attaching the thrust plate, and remove the thrust plate, if necessary.
6. Install a new thrust plate, if removed.
7. Install the spacer and fuel pump cam against the camshaft thrust flange, using installation sleeve and replacer Tool T83T-6316-B, if removed.
8. Install the camshaft drive gear against the fuel pump cam, aligning the timing mark with the timing mark on the

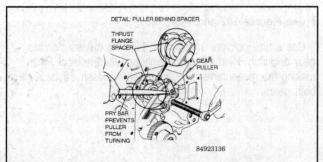

Fig. 132 Removing the thrust flange spacer on the diesel

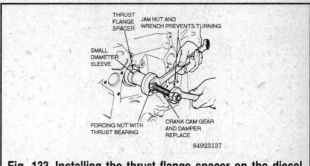

Fig. 133 Installing the thrust flange spacer on the diesel

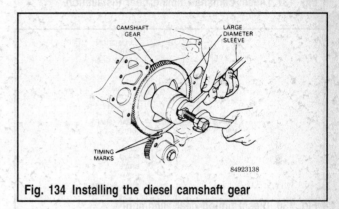

Fig. 134 Installing the diesel camshaft gear

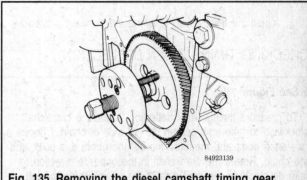

Fig. 135 Removing the diesel camshaft timing gear

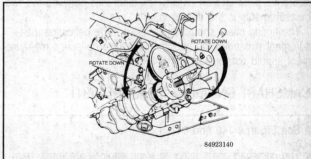

Fig. 136 Diesel crankshaft drive gear removal — engine out of truck

crankshaft drive gear, using installation sleeve and replacer Tool T83T-6316-B.

9. Install the camshaft allen screw and tighten to 18 ft. lbs.
10. Install the fuel pump, if removed.

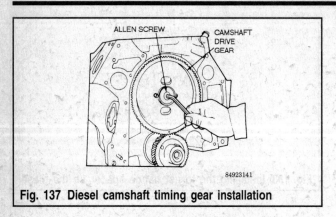

Fig. 137 Diesel camshaft timing gear installation

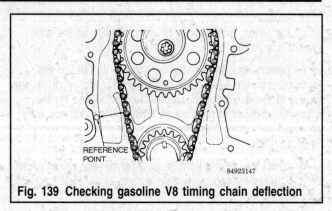

Fig. 139 Checking gasoline V8 timing chain deflection

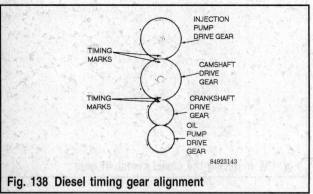

Fig. 138 Diesel timing gear alignment

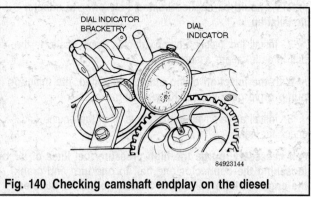

Fig. 140 Checking camshaft endplay on the diesel

11. Install the front cover, following the previous procedure.

CHECKING TIMING CHAIN DEFLECTION

▶ **See Figure 139**

To measure timing chain deflection, rotate the crankshaft clockwise to take up slack on the left side of chain. Choose a reference point and measure the distance from this point and the chain. Rotate the crankshaft in the opposite direction to take up slack on the right side of the chain. Force the left (slack) side of the chain out and measure the distance to the reference point chosen earlier. The difference between the two measurements is the deflection.

The timing chain should be replaced if the deflection measurement exceeded the specified limit. The deflection measurement should not exceed $1/2$ in. (13mm).

CAMSHAFT END-PLAY MEASUREMENT

▶ **See Figures 140 and 141**

The camshaft gears used on some engines are easily damaged if pried upon while the valve train load is on the camshaft. Loosen the rocker arm nuts or rocker arm shaft support bolts before checking the camshaft end-play.

Push the camshaft toward the rear of engine, install and zero a dial indicator, then pry between the camshaft gear and

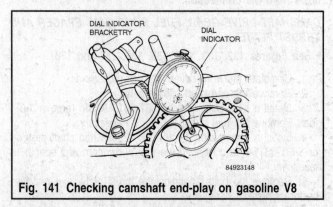

Fig. 141 Checking camshaft end-play on gasoline V8

the block to pull the camshaft forward. If the end-play is excessive, check for correct installation of the spacer. If the spacer is installed correctly, replace the thrust plate.

MEASURING TIMING GEAR BACKLASH

▶ **See Figures 142 and 143**

Use a dial indicator installed on block to measure timing gear backlash. Hold the gear firmly against the block while making the measurement. If excessive backlash exists, replace both gears.

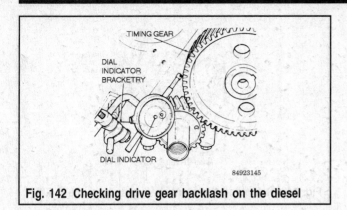

Fig. 142 Checking drive gear backlash on the diesel

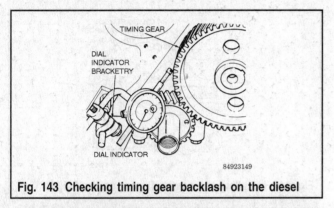

Fig. 143 Checking timing gear backlash on the diesel

Timing Chain

REMOVAL & INSTALLATION

8-5.0L, 8-5.8L and 8-7.5L Engines
▶ See Figures 144 and 145

1. Remove the front cover.
2. Rotate the crankshaft counterclockwise to take up the slack on the left side of the chain.
3. Establish a reference point on the cylinder block and measure from this point to the chain.
4. Rotate the crankshaft in the opposite direction to take up the slack on the right side of the chain.
5. Force the left side of the chain out with your fingers and measure the distance between the reference point and the chain. The timing chain deflection is the difference between the two measurements. If the deflection exceeds ½ in. (13mm), replace the timing chain and sprockets.
   To replace the timing chain and sprockets:
6. Turn the crankshaft until the timing marks on the sprockets are aligned vertically.

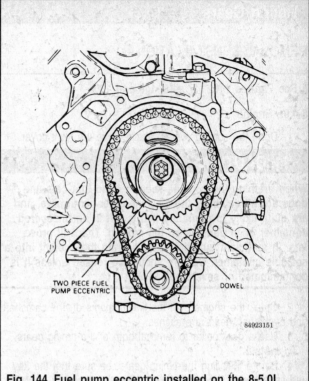

Fig. 144 Fuel pump eccentric installed on the 8-5.0L and 8-5.8L

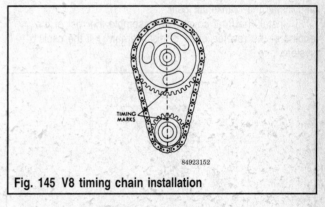

Fig. 145 V8 timing chain installation

7. Remove the camshaft sprocket retaining screw and remove the fuel pump eccentric and washers.
8. Alternately slide both of the sprockets and timing chain off the crankshaft and camshaft until free of the engine.
9. Position the timing chain on the sprockets so that the timing marks on the sprockets are aligned vertically. Alternately slide the sprockets and chain onto the crankshaft and camshaft sprockets.
10. Install the fuel pump eccentric washers and attaching bolt on the camshaft sprocket. Tighten to 40-45 ft. lbs.
11. Install the front cover.

Timing Gears

REMOVAL & INSTALLATION

▶ See Figures 146, 147, 148, 149 and 150

6-4.9L Engine

1. Drain the cooling system and remove the front cover.

✳✳CAUTION

When draining the coolant, keep in mind that cats and dogs are attracted by the ethylene glycol antifreeze, and are quite likely to drink any that is left in an uncovered container or in puddles on the ground. This will prove fatal in sufficient quantity. Always drain the coolant into a sealable container. Coolant should be reused unless it is contaminated or several years old.

2. Crank the engine until the timing marks on the camshaft and crankshaft gears are aligned.

3. Use a gear puller to removal both of the timing gears.

To install:

4. Before installing the timing gears, be sure that the key and spacer are properly installed. Align the gear key way with the key and install the gear on the camshaft. Be sure that the timing marks line up on the camshaft and the crankshaft gears and install the crankshaft gear.

5. Install the front cover, and assemble the rest of the engine in the reverse order of disassembly. Fill the cooling system.

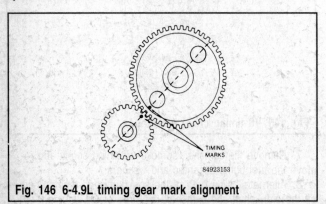

Fig. 146 6-4.9L timing gear mark alignment

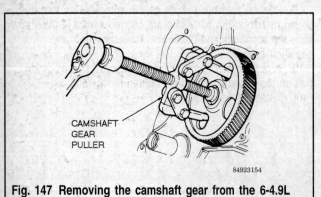

Fig. 147 Removing the camshaft gear from the 6-4.9L

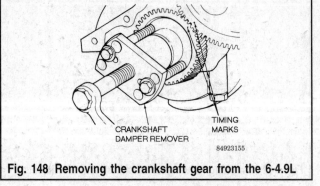

Fig. 148 Removing the crankshaft gear from the 6-4.9L

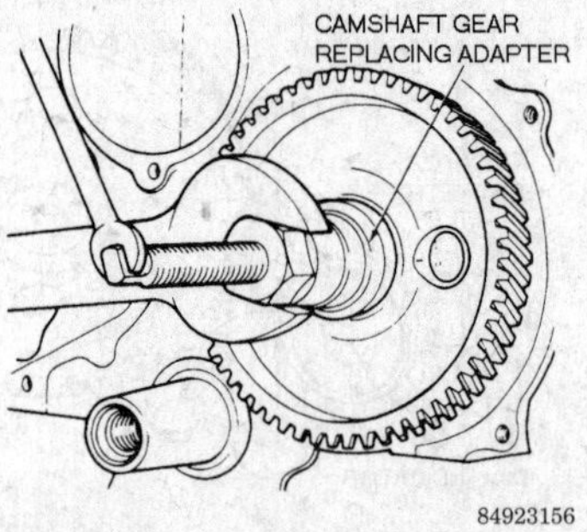

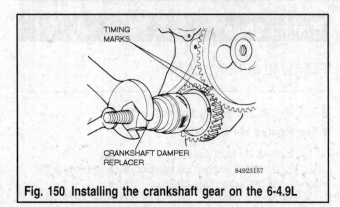

Fig. 149 Installing the camshaft gear on the 6-4.9L

Fig. 150 Installing the crankshaft gear on the 6-4.9L

6.9L and 7.3L Diesel Engines

1. Follow the procedures for timing gear cover removal and installation, and remove the front cover.

2. To remove the crankshaft gear, install gear puller (Ford part) no. T83T-6316-A or equivalent, and using a breaker bar to prevent the crankshaft from rotating, remove the crankshaft gear. To install the crankshaft gear use tool (Ford part) no. T83T-6316-B or equivalent while aligning the timing marks as shown in the illustration, and press the gear into place.

3. The camshaft gear may be removed by taking out the Allen screw and installing a gear puller, Ford part no. T83T-6316-A or equivalent and removing the gear. The gear may be replaced by using tool (Ford part) no. T83T-6316-B or equivalent. Torque the Allen screw to 12-18 ft. lbs.

Camshaft

REMOVAL & INSTALLATION

▶ See Figures 151 and 152

6-4.9L Engine

1. Remove the grille, radiator, air conditioner condenser, and timing cover.

2. Remove the distributor, fuel pump, oil pan and oil pump.

3. Align the timing marks. Unbolt the camshaft thrust plate, working through the holes in the camshaft gear.

4. Loosen the rocker arms, remove the pushrods, take off the side cover and remove the valve lifter with a magnet.

5. Remove the camshaft very carefully to prevent nicking the bearings.

6. Oil the camshaft bearing journals and use Lubriplate® or something similar on the lobes. Install the camshaft, gear, and thrust plate, aligning the gear marks. Tighten down the thrust plate. Make sure that the camshaft end-play is not excessive.

7. The last item to be replaced is the distributor. The rotor should be at the firing position for no. 1 cylinder, with the timing gear marks aligned.

8-5.0L, 8-5.8L, 8-6.9L, 8-7.3L and 8-7.5L Engines

▶ See Figure 153

➡Ford recommends removing the diesel engine for camshaft removal.

1. Remove the intake manifold and valley pan, if so equipped.

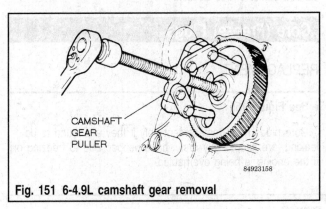

Fig. 151 6-4.9L camshaft gear removal

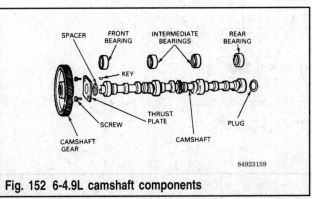

Fig. 152 6-4.9L camshaft components

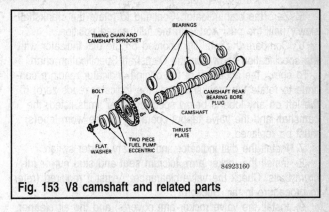

Fig. 153 V8 camshaft and related parts

2. Remove the rocker covers, and either remove the rocker arm shafts or loosen the rockers on their pivots and remove the pushrods. The pushrods must be reinstalled in their original positions.

3. Remove the valve lifters in sequence with a magnet. They must be replaced in their original positions.

4. Remove the timing gear cover and timing chain (timing gear on V8 diesel) and sprockets.

5. In addition to the radiator and air conditioning condenser, if so equipped, it may be necessary to remove the front grille assembly and the hook lock assembly to gain the necessary clearance to code the camshaft out of the front of the engine.

➡A camshaft removal tool, Ford part no. T65L-6250-A and adaptor 14-0314 are needed to remove the diesel camshaft.

6. Coat the camshaft with engine oil liberally before installing it. Slide the camshaft into the engine very carefully so as not to scratch the bearing bores with the camshaft lobes. Install the camshaft thrust plate and tighten the attaching screws to 9-12 ft. lbs. Measure the camshaft end-play. If the end-play is more than 0.009 in. (0.228mm), replace the thrust plate. Assemble the remaining components in the reverse order of removal.

CHECKING CAMSHAFT

Camshaft Lobe Lift

Check the lift of each lobe in consecutive order and make a note of the reading.

1. Remove the fresh air inlet tube and the air cleaner. Remove the heater hose and crankcase ventilation hoses. Remove valve rocker arm cover(s).

2. Remove the rocker arm stud nut or fulcrum bolts, fulcrum seat and rocker arm.

3. Make sure the pushrod is in the valve tappet socket. Install a dial indicator D78P-4201-B or equivalent, so that the actuating point of the indicator is in the push rod socket (or the indicator ball socket adaptor tool 6565-AB is on the end of the push rod) and in the same plane as the push rod movement.

4. Disconnect the I terminal and the S terminal at the starter relay. Install an auxiliary starter switch between the battery and S terminals of the start relay. Crank the engine with the ignition switch off. Turn the crankshaft over until the tappet is on the base circle of the camshaft lobe. At this position, the push rod will be in its lowest position.

5. Zero the dial indicator. Continue to rotate the crankshaft slowly until the push rod is in the fully raised position.

6. Compare the total lift recorded on the dial indicator with the specification shown on the Camshaft Specification chart.

To check the accuracy of the original indicator reading, continue to rotate the crankshaft until the indicator reads zero. If the left on any lobe is below specified wear limits listed, the camshaft and the valve tappet operating on the worn lobe(s) must be replaced.

7. Install the dial indicator and auxiliary starter switch.

8. Install the rocker arm, fulcrum seat and stud nut or fulcrum bolts. Check the valve clearance. Adjust if required (refer to procedure in this Section).

9. Install the valve rocker arm cover(s) and the air cleaner.

Camshaft End-Play

➡On all gasoline V8 engines, prying against the aluminum-nylon camshaft sprocket, with the valve train load on the camshaft, can break or damage the sprocket. Therefore, the rocker arm adjusting nuts must be backed off, or the rocker arm and shaft assembly must be loosened sufficiently to free the camshaft. After checking the camshaft end-play, check the valve clearance. Adjust if required (refer to procedure in this Section).

1. Push the camshaft toward the rear of the engine. Install a dial indicator (Tool D78P-4201-F, -G or equivalent so that the indicator point is on the camshaft sprocket attaching screw.

2. Zero the dial indicator. Position a prybar between the camshaft gear and the block. Pull the camshaft forward and release it. Compare the dial indicator reading with the specifications.

3. If the end-play is excessive, check the spacer for correct installation before it is removed. If the spacer is correctly installed, replace the thrust plate.

4. Remove the dial indicator.

CAMSHAFT BEARING REPLACEMENT

▶ **See Figure 154**

1. Remove the engine following the procedures in this Section and install it on a work stand.

2. Remove the camshaft, flywheel and crankshaft, following the appropriate procedures. Push the pistons to the top of the cylinder.

3. Remove the camshaft rear bearing bore plug. Remove the camshaft bearings with Tool T65L-6250-A or equivalent.

4. Select the proper size expanding collet and back-up nut and assemble on the mandrel. With the expanding collet collapsed, install the collet assembly in the camshaft bearing and tighten the back-up nut on the expanding mandrel until the collet fits the camshaft bearing.

5. Assemble the puller screw and extension (if necessary) and install on the expanding mandrel. Wrap a cloth around the threads of the puller screw to protect the front bearing or journal. Tighten the pulling nut against the thrust bearing and pulling plate to remove the camshaft bearing. Be sure to hold a wrench on the end of the puller screw to prevent it from turning.

6. To remove the front bearing, install the puller from the rear of the cylinder block.

7. Position the new bearings at the bearing bores, and press them in place with tool T65L-6250-A or equivalent. Be sure to center the pulling plate and puller screw to avoid damage to the bearing. Failure to use the correct expanding collet can cause severe bearing damage. Align the oil holes in the bearings with the oil holes in the cylinder block before pressing bearings into place.

➡Be sure the front bearing is installed 0.020-0.035 in. (0.508-0.889mm) for the inline six cylinder engines, 0.005-0.020 in. (0.127-0.508mm) for the gasoline V8, 0.040-0.060 in. (1.016-1.524mm) for the diesel V8, below the front face of the cylinder block.

8. Install the camshaft rear bearing bore plug.

9. Install the camshaft, crankshaft, flywheel and related parts, following the appropriate procedures.

10. Install the engine in the truck, following procedures described earlier in this Section.

Core (Freeze) Plugs

REPLACEMENT

▶ **See Figure 155**

Core plugs need replacement only if they are found to be leaking, are excessively rusty, have popped due to freezing or, if the engine is being overhauled.

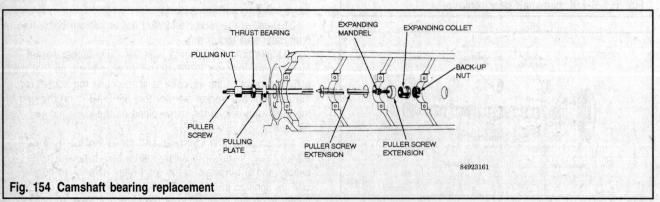

Fig. 154 Camshaft bearing replacement

If the plugs are accessible with the engine in the truck, they can be removed as-is. If not, the engine will have to be removed.

1. If necessary, remove the engine and mount it on a work stand. If the engine is being left in the truck, drain the engine coolant and engine oil

✳✳CAUTION

When draining the coolant, keep in mind that cats and dogs are attracted by the ethylene glycol antifreeze, and are quite likely to drink any that is left in an uncovered container or in puddles on the ground. This will prove fatal in sufficient quantity. Always drain the coolant into a sealable container. Coolant should be reused unless it is contaminated or several years old.   The EPA warns that prolonged contact with used engine oil may cause a number of skin disorders, including cancer! You should make every effort to minimize your exposure to used engine oil. Protective gloves should be worn when changing the oil. Wash your hands and any other exposed skin areas as soon as possible after exposure to used engine oil. Soap and water, or waterless hand cleaner should be used.

2. Remove anything blocking access to the plug or plugs to be replaced.

3. Drill or center-punch a hole in the plug. For large plugs, drill a ½ in. hole; for small plugs, drill a ¼ in. hole.

4. For large plugs, using a slide-hammer, thread a machine screw adapter or insert 2-jawed puller adapter into the hole in the plug. Pull the plug from the block; for small plugs, pry the plug out with a pin punch.

5. Thoroughly clean the opening in the block, using steel wool or emery paper to polish the hole rim.

6. Coat the outer diameter of the new plug with sealer and place it in the hole.   For cup-type core plugs: These plugs are installed with the flanged end outward. The maximum diameter of this type of plug is located at the outer edge of the flange. Carefully and evenly, drive the new plug into place.   For expansion-type plugs: These plugs are installed with the flanged end inward. The maximum diameter of this type of plug is located at the base of the flange. It is imperative that the correct type of installation tool is used with this type of plug. Under no circumstances is this type of plug to be driven in using a tool that contacts the crowned portion of the plug. Driving in this plug incorrectly will cause the plug to expand prior to installation. When installed, the trailing (maximum) diameter of the plug MUST be below the chamfered

edge of the bore to create an effective seal. If the core plug replacing tool has a depth seating surface, do not seat the tool against a non-machined (casting) surface.

7. Install any removed parts and, if necessary, install the engine in the truck.

8. Refill the cooling system and crankcase.

9. Start the engine and check for leaks.

Pistons and Connecting Rods

REMOVAL & INSTALLATION

▶ See Figures 156, 157, 158, 159, 160, 161 and 162

6-4.9L Engine

1. Drain the cooling system and the crankcase.

✳✳CAUTION

When draining the coolant, keep in mind that cats and dogs are attracted by the ethylene glycol antifreeze, and are quite likely to drink any that is left in an uncovered container or in puddles on the ground. This will prove fatal in sufficient quantity. Always drain the coolant into a sealable container. Coolant should be reused unless it is contaminated or several years old.   The EPA warns that prolonged contact with used engine oil may cause a number of skin disorders, including cancer! You should make every effort to minimize your exposure to used engine oil. Protective gloves should be worn when changing the oil. Wash your hands and any other exposed skin areas as soon as possible after exposure to used engine oil. Soap and water, or waterless hand cleaner should be used.

2. Remove the cylinder head.

3. Remove the oil pan, the oil pump inlet tube and the oil pump.

4. Turn the crankshaft until the piston to be removed is at the bottom of its travel and place a cloth on the piston head to collect filings. Using a ridge reaming tool, remove any ridge of carbon or any other deposit from the upper cylinder walls where piston travel ends. Do not cut into the piston ring travel area more than 1/32 in. (0.8mm) while removing the ridge.

5. Mark all of the connecting rod caps so that they can be reinstalled in the original positions from which they are removed and remove the connecting rod bearing cap. Also iden-

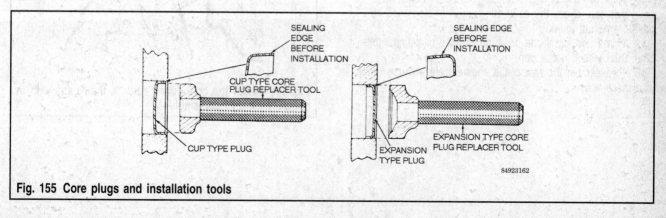

SEALING EDGE BEFORE INSTALLATION

CUP TYPE CORE PLUG REPLACER TOOL

CUP TYPE PLUG

SEALING EDGE BEFORE INSTALLATION

EXPANSION TYPE CORE PLUG REPLACER TOOL

EXPANSION TYPE PLUG

84923162

Fig. 155 Core plugs and installation tools

tify the piston assemblies as they, too, must be reinstalled in the same cylinder from which removed.

6. With the bearing caps removed, the connecting rod bearing bolts are potentially damaging to the cylinder walls during removal. To guard against cylinder wall damage, install 4 in. (101.6mm) or 5 in. (127mm) lengths of ⅜in. (9.5mm) rubber tubing onto the connecting rod bolts. These will also protect the crankshaft journal from scratches when the connecting rod is installed, and will serve as a guide for the rod.

7. Squirt some clean engine oil into each cylinder before removing the pistons. Using a wooden hammer handle, push the connecting rod and piston assembly out of the top of the cylinder (pushing from the bottom of the rod). Be careful to avoid damaging both the crank journal and the cylinder wall when removing the rod and piston assembly.

8. Before installing the piston/connecting rod assembly, be sure to clean all gasket mating surfaces, oil the pistons, piston rings and the cylinder walls with light engine oil.

9. Be sure to install the pistons in the cylinders from which they were removed. The connecting rod and bearing caps are numbered from 1 to 6 beginning at the front of the engine. The numbers on the connecting rod and bearing cap must be on the same side when installed in the cylinder bore. If a connecting rod is ever transposed from one engine or cylinder to another, new bearings should be fitted and the connecting rod should be numbered to correspond with the new cylinder number. The notch on the piston head goes toward the front of the engine.

10. Make sure the ring gaps are properly spaced around the circumference of the piston. Make sure rubber hose lengths are fitted to the rod bolts. Fit a piston ring compressor around the piston and slide the piston and connecting rod assembly down into the cylinder bore, pushing it in with the wooden hammer handle. Push the piston down until it is only slightly below the top of the cylinder bore. Guide the connecting rods onto the crankshaft bearing journals carefully, using the rubber hose lengths, to avoid damaging the crankshaft.

11. Check the bearing clearance of all the rod bearings, fitting them to the crankshaft bearing journals.

12. After the bearings have been fitted, apply a light coating of engine oil to the journals and bearings.

13. Turn the crankshaft until the appropriate bearing journal is at the bottom of its stroke, then push the piston assembly all the way down until the connecting rod bearing seats on the crankshaft journal. Be careful not to allow the bearing cap screws to strike the crankshaft bearing journals and damage them.

14. After the piston and connecting rod assemblies have been installed, check the connecting rod side clearance on each crankshaft journal.

15. Prime and install the oil pump and the oil pump intake tube, then install the oil pan.

16. Reassemble the rest of the engine in the reverse order of disassembly.

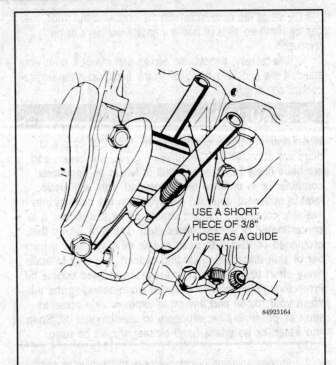

Fig. 156 Make connecting rod bolt guides out of rubber tubing; these also protect the cylinder walls and crankshaft journal from scratches

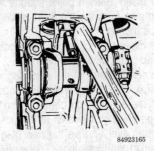

Fig. 157 Push the piston assembly out with a hammer handle

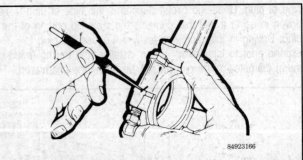

Fig. 158 Match the connecting rods to their caps with a scribe mark for reassembly

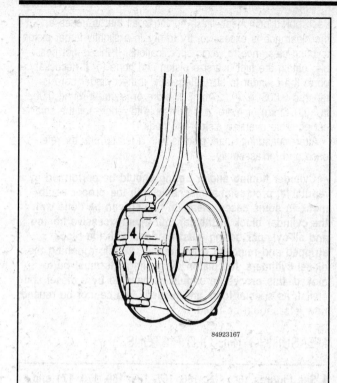

Fig. 159 Number each rod and cap with its cylinder number for correct assembly

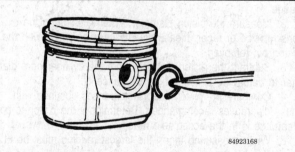

Fig. 160 Use needle-nose or snapring pliers to remove the piston pin clips

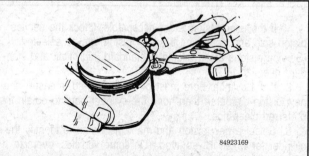

Fig. 161 Remove and install the rings with a ring expander

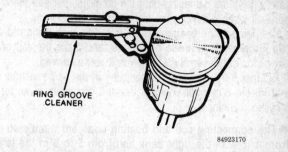

Fig. 162 Clean the ring grooves with this tool or the edge of an old ring

8-5.0L, 8-5.8L, 8-6.9L, 8-7.3L, 8-7.5L

1. Drain the cooling system and the crankcase.

> ### ✳✳CAUTION
>
> When draining the coolant, keep in mind that cats and dogs are attracted by the ethylene glycol antifreeze, and are quite likely to drink any that is left in an uncovered container or in puddles on the ground. This will prove fatal in sufficient quantity. Always drain the coolant into a sealable container. Coolant should be reused unless it is contaminated or several years old.   The EPA warns that prolonged contact with used engine oil may cause a number of skin disorders, including cancer! You should make every effort to minimize your exposure to used engine oil. Protective gloves should be worn when changing the oil. Wash your hands and any other exposed skin areas as soon as possible after exposure to used engine oil. Soap and water, or waterless hand cleaner should be used.

2. Remove the intake manifold.
3. Remove the cylinder heads.
4. Remove the oil pan.
5. Remove the oil pump.
6. Turn the crankshaft until the piston to be removed is at the bottom of its travel, then place a cloth on the piston head to collect filings.
7. Remove any ridge of deposits at the end of the piston travel from the upper cylinder bore, using a ridge reaming tool. Do not cut into the piston ring travel area more than 3/8 in. (0.8mm) when removing the ridge.
8. Make sure that all of the connecting rod bearing caps can be identified, so they will be reinstalled in their original positions.
9. Turn the crankshaft until the connecting rod that is to be removed is at the bottom of its stroke and remove the connecting rod nuts and bearing cap.
10. With the bearing caps removed, the connecting rod bearing bolts are potentially damaging to the cylinder walls during removal. To guard against cylinder wall damage, install four or five inch lengths of ⅜in. (0.8mm) rubber tubing onto the connecting rod bolts. These will also protect the crankshaft journal from scratches when the connecting rod is installed, and will serve as a guide for the rod.
11. Squirt some clean engine oil into each cylinder before removing the piston assemblies. Using a wooden hammer handle, push the connecting rod and piston assembly out of the top of the cylinder (pushing from the bottom of the rod). Be

careful to avoid damaging both the crank journal and the cylinder wall when removing the rod and piston assembly.

12. Remove the bearing inserts from the connecting rod and cap if the bearings are to be replace, and place the cap onto the piston/rod assembly from which it was removed.

13. Install the piston/rod assemblies in the same manner as that for the 6-cylinder engines. See the procedure given for 6-cylinder engines.

➡**The connecting rod and bearing caps are numbered from 1 to 4 in the right bank and from 5 to 8 in the left bank, beginning at the front of the engine. The numbers on the rod and cap must be on the same side when they are installed in the cylinder bore. Also, the largest chamfer at the bearing end of the rod should be positioned toward the crank pin thrust face of the crankshaft and the notch in the head of the piston faces toward the front of the engine.**

14. See the appropriate component procedures to assemble the engine.

Piston Ring and Wrist Pin

REMOVAL

▶ **See Figure 163**

All of the Ford gasoline engines covered in this guide utilize pressed-in wrist pins, which can only be removed by an arbor press. The diesel pistons are removed in the same way, only the pistons are heated before the wrist pins are pressed out. On both gasoline and diesel engines, the piston/connecting rod assemblies should be taken to an engine specialist or qualified machinist for piston removal and installation.

A piston ring expander is necessary for removing the piston rings without damaging them; any other method (screwdriver blades, pliers, etc.) usually results in the rings being bent, scratched or distorted, or the piston itself being damaged. When the rings are removed, clean the ring grooves using an appropriate ring groove cleaning tool, using care not to cut too deeply. Thoroughly clean all carbon and varnish from the piston with solvent.

❋❋WARNING

Do not use a wire brush or caustic solvent (acids, etc.) on pistons.

Inspect the pistons for scuffing, scoring, cracks, pitting, or excessive ring groove wear. If these are evident, the piston must be replaced.

The piston should also be checked in relation to the cylinder diameter. Using a telescoping gauge and micrometer, or a dial gauge, measure the cylinder bore diameter perpendicular (90%) to the piston pin, 2½ in. (64mm) below the cylinder block deck (surface where the block mates with the heads). Then, with the micrometer, measure the piston, perpendicular to its wrist pin on the skirt. the difference between the two measurements is the piston clearance. If the clearance is within specifications or slightly below (after the cylinders have

been bored or hones), finish honing is all that is necessary. If the clearance is excessive, try to obtain a slightly larger piston to bring clearance to within specifications. If this is not possible, obtain the first oversize piston and hone (or if necessary, bore) the cylinder to size. Generally, if the cylinder bore is tapered 0.005 in. (0.127mm) or more or is out-of-round 0.003 in. (0.076mm) or more, it is advisable to rebore for the small est possible oversize piston and rings.

After measuring, mark pistons with a felt tip pen for reference and for assembly.

➡**Cylinder honing and/or boring should be performed by a reputable, professional mechanic with the proper equipment. In some cases, clean-up honing can be done with the cylinder block in the car, but most excessive honing and all cylinder boring must be done with the block stripped and removed from the car. Before honing the diesel cylinders, the piston oil cooling jets must be removed. this procedure should be handled by a diesel specialist, as special tools are needed. Jets cannot be reused; new jets should be fitted.**

MEASURING THE OLD PISTONS

▶ **See Figures 164, 165, 166, 167, 168, 169, 170, 171 and 172**

Check used piston-to-cylinder bore clearance as follows:
1. Measure the cylinder bore diameter with a telescope gauge.
2. Measure the piston diameter. When measuring the pistons for size or taper, measurements must be made with the piston pin removed.
3. Subtract the piston diameter from the cylinder bore diameter to determine piston-to-bore clearance.
4. Compare the piston-to-bore clearances obtained with those clearances recommended. Determine if the piston-to-bore clearance is in the acceptable range.
5. When measuring taper, the largest reading must be at the bottom of the skirt.

SELECTING NEW PISTONS

1. If the used piston is not acceptable, check the service piston size and determine if a new piston can be selected. (Service pistons are available in standard, high limit and standard oversize.
2. If the cylinder bore must be reconditioned, measure the new piston diameter, then hone the cylinder bore to obtain the preferred clearance.
3. Select a new piston and mark the piston to identify the cylinder for which it was fitted. (On some vehicles, oversize pistons may be found. These pistons will be 0.254mm oversize).

CYLINDER HONING

1. When cylinders are being honed, follow the manufacturer's recommendations for the use of the hone.

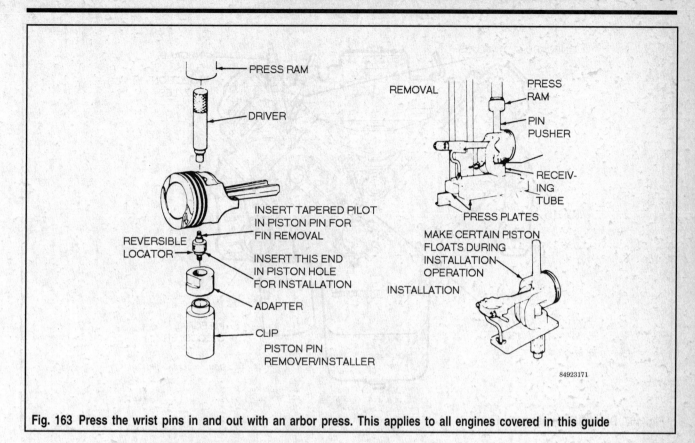

Fig. 163 Press the wrist pins in and out with an arbor press. This applies to all engines covered in this guide

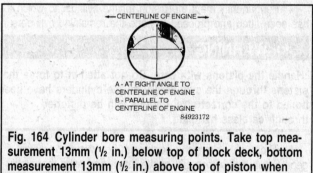

Fig. 164 Cylinder bore measuring points. Take top measurement 13mm (½ in.) below top of block deck, bottom measurement 13mm (½ in.) above top of piston when piston is at BDC

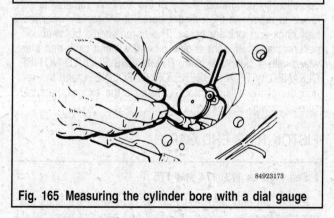

Fig. 165 Measuring the cylinder bore with a dial gauge

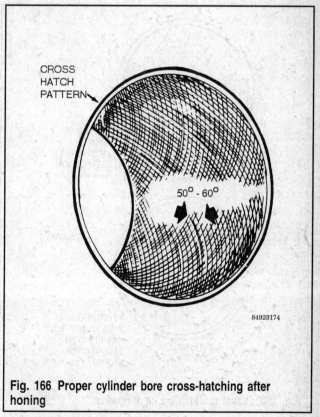

Fig. 166 Proper cylinder bore cross-hatching after honing

2. Occasionally, during the honing operation, the cylinder bore should be thoroughly cleaned and the selected piston checked for correct fit.

3. When finish-honing a cylinder bore, the hone should be moved up and down at a sufficient speed to obtain a very fine uniform surface finish in a cross-hatch pattern of approximately

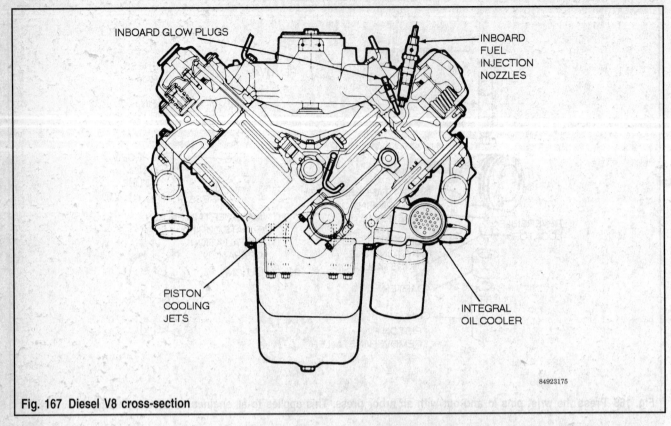

Fig. 167 Diesel V8 cross-section

INBOARD GLOW PLUGS

INBOARD FUEL INJECTION NOZZLES

PISTON COOLING JETS

INTEGRAL OIL COOLER

84923175

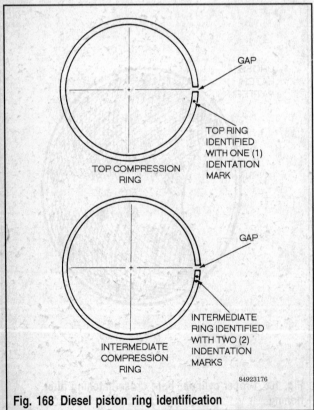

TOP COMPRESSION RING

GAP

TOP RING IDENTIFIED WITH ONE (1) IDENTATION MARK

INTERMEDIATE COMPRESSION RING

GAP

INTERMEDIATE RING IDENTIFIED WITH TWO (2) INDENTATION MARKS

84923176

Fig. 168 Diesel piston ring identification

45-65° included angle. The finish marks should be clean but not sharp, free from embedded particles and torn or folded metal.

4. Permanently mark the piston for the cylinder to which it has been fitted and proceed to hone the remaining cylinders.

❋❋WARNING

Handle the pistons with care. Do not attempt to force the pistons through the cylinders until the cylinders have been honed to the correct size. Pistons can be distorted through careless handling.

5. Thoroughly clean the bores with hot water and detergent. Scrub well with a stiff bristle brush and rinse thoroughly with hot water. It is extremely essential that a good cleaning operation be performed. If any of the abrasive material is allowed to remain in the cylinder bores, it will rapidly wear the new rings and cylinder bores. The bores should be swabbed several times with light engine oil and a clean cloth and then wiped with a clean dry cloth. CYLINDERS SHOULD NOT BE CLEANED WITH KEROSENE OR GASOLINE! Clean the remainder of the cylinder block to remove the excess material spread during the honing operation.

PISTON RING END GAP

▶ **See Figures 173, 174 and 175**

Piston ring end gap should be checked while the rings are removed from the pistons. Incorrect end gap indicates that the wrong size rings are being used; ring breakage could occur.

Compress the piston rings to be used in a cylinder, one at a time, into that cylinder. Squirt clean oil into the cylinder, so that the rings and the top 2 in. (51mm) of cylinder wall are coated. Using an inverted piston, press the rings approximately

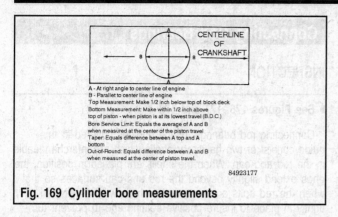

Fig. 169 Cylinder bore measurements

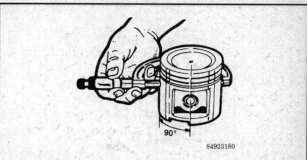

Fig. 172 Check piston diameter at these points with a micrometer

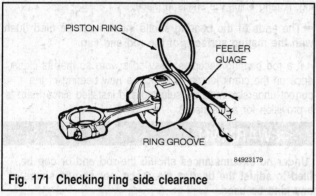

Fig. 171 Checking ring side clearance

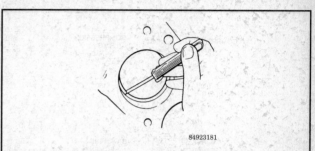

Fig. 173 Check piston ring end gap with a feeler gauge, with the ring positioned in the cylinder, one inch below the deck of the block

1 in. (25mm) below the deck of the block (on diesels, measure ring gap clearance with the ring positioned at the bottom of ring travel in the bore). Measure the ring end gap with the

feeler gauge, and compare to the Ring Gap chart in this Section. Carefully pull the ring out of the cylinder and file the ends squarely with a fine file to obtain the proper clearance.

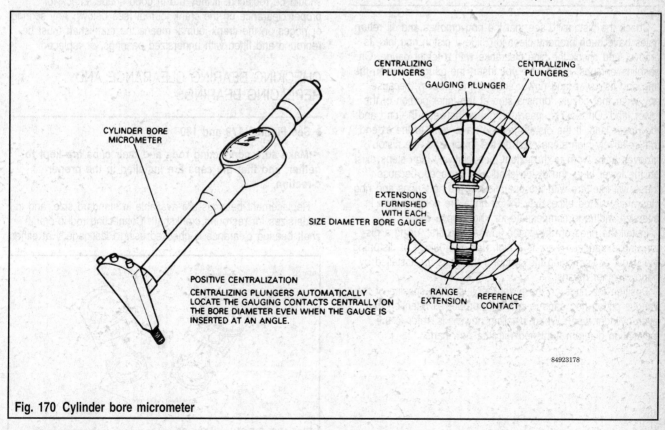

Fig. 170 Cylinder bore micrometer

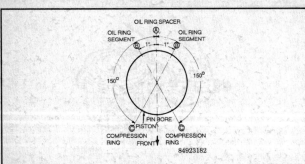

Fig. 174 Proper spacing of the piston ring gaps around the circumference of the piston, for gasoline engines

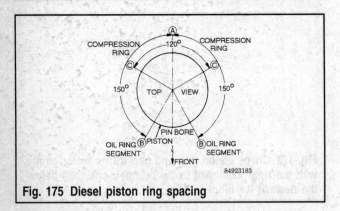

Fig. 175 Diesel piston ring spacing

PISTON RING SIDE CLEARANCE CHECK AND INSTALLATION

Check the pistons to see that the ring grooves and oil return holes have been properly cleaned. Slide a piston ring into its groove, and check the side clearance with a feeler gauge. On gasoline engines, make sure you insert the gauge between the ring and its lower land (lower edge of the groove), because any wear that occurs forms a step at the inner portion of the lower land. On diesels, insert the gauge between the ring and the upper land. If the piston grooves have worn to the extend that relatively high steps exist on the lower land, the piston grooves have worn to the extent that relatively high steps exist on the lower land, the piston should be replaced, because these will interfere with the operation of the new rings and ring clearance will be excessive. Piston rings are not furnished in oversize widths to compensate for ring groove wear.

Install the rings on the piston, lowest ring first, using a piston ring expander. There is a high risk of breaking or distorting the rings, or scratching the piston, if the rings are installed by hand or other means.

Position the rings on the piston as illustrated; spacing of the various piston ring gaps is crucial to proper oil retention and even cylinder wear. When installing new rings, refer to the installation diagram furnished with the new parts.

Connecting Rod Bearings

INSPECTION

▶ **See Figures 176, 177 and 178**

Connecting rod bearings for the engines covered in this guide consist of two halves or shells which are interchangeable in the rod and cap. When the shells are placed in position, the ends extend slightly beyond the rod and cap surfaces so that when the rod bolts are torqued the shells will be clamped tightly in place to insure positive seating and to prevent turning. A tang holds the shells in place.

➡ **The ends of the bearing shells must never be filed flush with the mating surfaces of the rod and cap.**

If a rod bearing becomes noisy or is worn so that its clearance on the crank journal is sloppy, a new bearing of the correct undersize must be selected and installed since there is a provision for adjustment.

✳✳WARNING

Under no circumstances should the rod end or cap be filed to adjust the bearing clearance, nor should shims of any kind be used.

Inspect the rod bearings while the rod assemblies are out of the engine. If the shells are scored or show flaking, they should be replaced. If they are in good shape, check for proper clearance on the crank journal (see below). Any scoring or ridges on the crank journal means the crankshaft must be reground and fitted with undersized bearings, or replaced.

CHECKING BEARING CLEARANCE AND REPLACING BEARINGS

▶ **See Figures 179 and 180**

➡ **Make sure connecting rods and their caps are kept together, and that the caps are installed in the proper direction.**

Replacement bearings are available in standard size, and in undersizes for reground crankshaft. Connecting rod-to-crankshaft bearing clearance is checked using Plastigage® at either

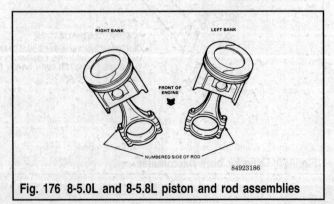

Fig. 176 8-5.0L and 8-5.8L piston and rod assemblies

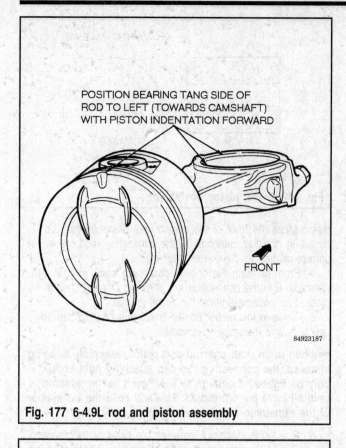

POSITION BEARING TANG SIDE OF
ROD TO LEFT (TOWARDS CAMSHAFT)
WITH PISTON INDENTATION FORWARD

FRONT

84923187

Fig. 177 6-4.9L rod and piston assembly

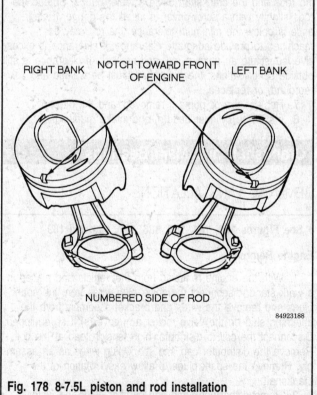

RIGHT BANK   NOTCH TOWARD FRONT   LEFT BANK
OF ENGINE

NUMBERED SIDE OF ROD

84923188

Fig. 178 8-7.5L piston and rod installation

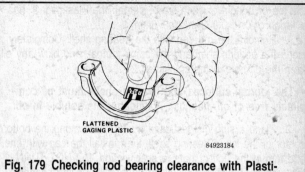

FLATTENED
GAGING PLASTIC

84923184

Fig. 179 Checking rod bearing clearance with Plasti-gage® or equivalent

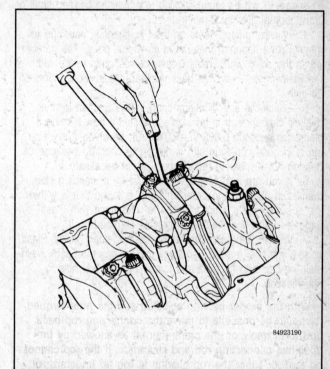

84923190

Fig. 180 Checking connecting rod side clearance with a feeler gauge. Use a small pry bar to spread the connecting rods

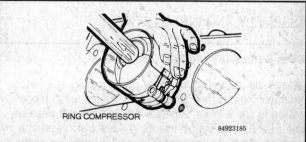

RING COMPRESSOR

84923185

Fig. 181 Tap the piston assembly into the cylinder with a wooden hammer handle. The notches on piston crown face the front of the engine

the top or bottom of each crank journal. the Plastigage® has a range of 0 to 0.003 in. (0.076mm).

1. Remove the rod cap with the bearing shell. Completely clean the bearing shell and the crank journal, and blow any oil from the oil hole in the crankshaft.

➥**The journal surfaces and bearing shells must be completely free of oil, because Plastigage® is soluble in oil.**

2. Place a strip of Plastigage® lengthwise along the bottom center of the lower bearing shell, then install the cap with shell and torque the bolt or nuts to specification. DO NOT TURN the crankshaft with the Plastigage® installed in the bearing.

3. Remove the bearing cap with the shell. The flattened Plastigage® will be found sticking to either the bearing shell or crank journal. Do not remove it yet.

4. Use the printed scale on the Plastigage® envelope to measure the flattened material at its widest point. The number within the scale which most closely corresponds to the width of the Plastigage® indicated bearing clearance in thousandths of an inch.

5. Check the specifications chart in this Section for the desired clearance. It is advisable to install a new bearing if clearance exceeds 0.003 in. (0.076mm); however, if the bearing is in good condition and is not being checked because of bearing noise, bearing replacement is not necessary.

6. If you are installing new bearings, try a standard size, then each undersize in order until one is found that is within the specified limits when checked for clearance with Plastigage® . Each under size has its size stamped on it.

7. When the proper size shell is found, clean off the Plastigage® material from the shell, oil the bearing thoroughly, reinstall the cap with its shell and torque the rod bolt nuts to specification.

➥**With the proper bearing selected and the nuts torqued, it should be possible to move the connecting rod back and forth freely on the crank journal as allowed by the specified connecting rod end clearance. If the rod cannot be moved, either the rod bearing is too far undersize or the rod is misaligned.**

Piston and Connecting Rod

ASSEMBLY AND INSTALLATION

▶ **See Figures 181 and 182**

Install the connecting rod to the piston making sure piston installation notches and any marks on the rod are in proper relation to one another. Lubricate the wrist pin with clean engine oil and install the pin into the rod and piston assembly by using an arbor press as required. Install the wrist pin snaprings if equipped, and rotate them in their grooves to make sure they are seated. To install the piston and rod assemblies:

1. Make sure the connecting rod big bearings (including end cap) are of the correct size and properly installed.

2. Fit rubber hoses over the connecting rod bolt to protect the crankshaft journals, as in the Piston Removal procedure. Coat the rod bearings with clean oil.

3. Using the proper ring compressor, insert the piston assembly into the cylinder so that the notch in the top of the

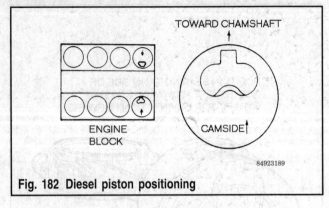

Fig. 182 Diesel piston positioning

piston faces the front of the engine (this assumes that the dimple(s) or other markings on the connecting rods are in correct relation to the piston notch(s)).

4. From beneath the engine, coat each crank journal with clean oil. Pull the connecting rod, with the bearing shell in place, into position against the crank journal.

5. Remove the rubber hoses. Install the bearing cap and cap nuts and torque to specification.

➥**When more than one rod and piston assembly is being installed, the connecting rod cap attaching nuts should only be tightened enough to keep each rod in position until all have been installed. This will ease the installation of the remaining piston assemblies.**

6. Check the clearance between the sides of the connecting rods and the crankshaft using a feeler gauge. Spread the rods slightly with a screwdriver to insert the gauge. If clearance is below the minimum tolerance, the rod may be machined to provide adequate clearance. If clearance is excessive, substitute an unworn rod, and recheck. If clearance is still outside specifications, the crankshaft must be welded and reground, or replaced.

7. Replace the oil pump if removed, and the oil pan.

8. Install the cylinder head(s) and intake manifold.

Crankshaft and Main Bearings

REMOVAL & INSTALLATION

▶ **See Figures 183, 184, 185, 186, 187, 188 and 189**

Engine Removed

1. With the engine removed from the vehicle and placed in a work stand, disconnect the spark plug wires from the spark plugs and remove the wires and bracket assembly from the attaching stud on the valve rocker arm cover(s) if so equipped. Disconnect the coil to distributor high tension lead at the coil. Remove the distributor cap and spark plug wires as an assembly. Remove the spark plugs to allow easy rotation of the crankshaft.

2. Remove the fuel pump and oil filter. Slide the water pump by-pass hose clamp (if so equipped) toward the water pump. Remove the alternator and mounting brackets.

3. Remove the crankshaft pulley from the crankshaft vibration damper. Remove the capscrew and washer from the end of the crankshaft. Install a universal puller, Tool T58P-6316-D

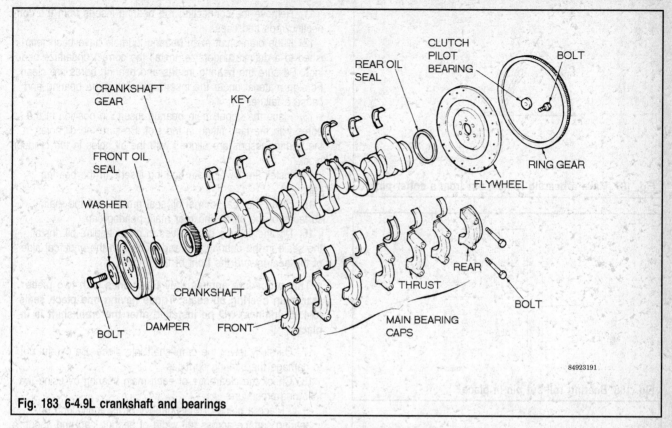

Fig. 183 6-4.9L crankshaft and bearings

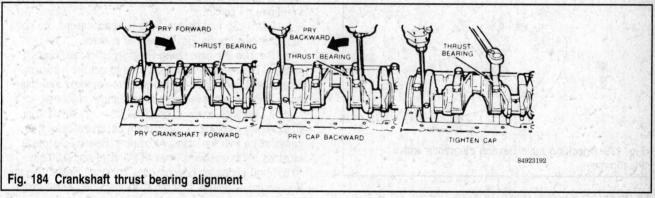

Fig. 184 Crankshaft thrust bearing alignment

or equivalent on the crankshaft vibration damper and remove the damper.

4. Remove the cylinder front cover and crankshaft gear, refer to Cylinder Front Cover and Timing Chain in this Section.

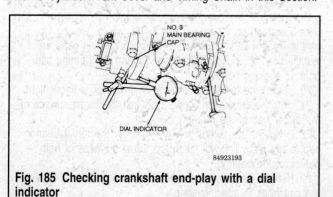

Fig. 185 Checking crankshaft end-play with a dial indicator

Fig. 186 Crankshaft end-play can also be checked with a feeler gauge

5. Invert the engine on the work stand. Remove the clutch pressure plate and disc (manual shift transmission). Remove

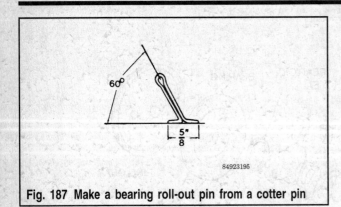

Fig. 187 Make a bearing roll-out pin from a cotter pin

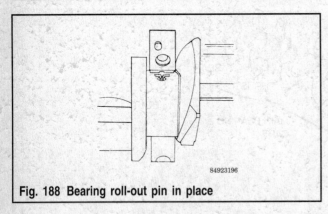

Fig. 188 Bearing roll-out pin in place

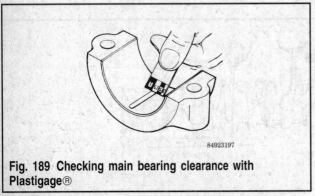

Fig. 189 Checking main bearing clearance with Plastigage®

the flywheel and engine rear cover plate. Remove the oil pan and gasket. Remove the oil pump.

6. Make sure all bearing caps (main and connecting rod) are marked so that they can be installed in their original locations. Turn the crankshaft until the connecting rod from which the cap is being removed is down, and remove the bearing cap. Push the connecting rod and piston assembly up into the cylinder. Repeat this procedure until all the connecting rod bearing caps are removed.

7. Remove the main bearings caps.

8. Carefully lift the crankshaft out of the block so that the thrust bearing surfaces are not damaged. Handle the crankshaft with care to avoid possible fracture to the finished surfaces.

9. Remove the rear journal seal from the block and rear main bearing cap.

10. Remove the main bearing inserts from the block and bearing caps.

11. Remove the connecting rod bearing inserts from the connecting rods and caps.

12. If the crankshaft main bearing journals have been refinished to a definite undersize, install the correct undersize bearings. Be sure the bearing inserts and bearing bores are clean. Foreign material under the inserts will distort the bearing and cause a failure.

13. Place the upper main bearing inserts in position in the bores with the tang fitting in the slot. Be sure the oil holes in the bearing inserts are aligned with the oil holes in the cylinder block.

14. Install the lower main bearing inserts in the bearing caps.

15. Clean the rear journal oil seal groove and the mating surfaces of the block and rear main bearing cap.

16. Dip the lip-type seal halves in clean engine oil. Install the seals in the bearing cap and block with the undercut side of the seal toward the front of the engine.

➡This procedure applies only to engines with two piece rear main bearing oil seals. Those having one piece seals (6-4.9L engines) will be installed after the crankshaft is in place.

17. Carefully lower the crankshaft into place. Be careful not to damage the bearing surfaces.

18. Check the clearance of each main bearing by using the following procedure:

a. Place a piece of Plastigage® or its equivalent, on bearing surface across full width of bearing cap and about ¼ in. (6mm) off center.

b. Install cap and tighten bolts to specifications. Do not turn crankshaft while Plastigage® is in place.

c. Remove the cap. Using Plastigage® scale, check width of Plastigage® at widest point to get the minimum clearance. Check at narrowest point to get maximum clearance. Difference between readings is taper of journal.

d. If clearance exceeds specified limits, try a 0.001 in. (0.0254mm) or 0.002 in. (0.051mm) undersize bearing in combination with the standard bearing. Bearing clearance must be within specified limits. If standard and 0.002 in. (0.051mm) undersize bearing does not bring clearance within desired limits, refinish crankshaft journal, then install undersize bearings.

➡Refer to Rear Main Oil Seal removal and installation, for special instructions in applying RTV sealer to rear main bearing cup.

19. Install all the bearing caps except the thrust bearing cap (No. 3 bearing on all except the 6-4.9L which use the No. 5 as the thrust bearing). Be sure the main bearing caps are installed in their original locations. Tighten the bearing cap bolts to specifications.

20. Install the thrust bearing cap with the bolts finger tight.

21. Pry the crankshaft forward against the thrust surface of the upper half of the bearing.

22. Hold the crankshaft forward and pry the thrust bearing cap to the rear. This will align the thrust surfaces of both halves of the bearing.

23. Retain the forward pressure on the crankshaft. Tighten the cap bolts to specifications.

24. Check the crankshaft end-play using the following procedures:

a. Force the crankshaft toward the rear of the engine.

b. Install a dial indicator (tools D78P-4201-F, -G or equivalent) so that the contact point rests against the crankshaft flange and the indicator axis is parallel to the crankshaft axis.

c. Zero the dial indicator. Push the crankshaft forward and note the reading on the dial.

d. If the end-play exceeds the wear limit listed in the Crankshaft and Connecting Rod Specifications chart, replace the thrust bearing. If the end-play is less than the minimum limit, inspect the thrust bearing faces for scratches, burrs, nicks, or dirt. If the thrust faces are not damaged or dirty, then they probably were not aligned properly. Lubricate and install the new thrust bearing and align the faces following procedures 21 through 24.

25. On 6-4.9L engines with one piece rear main bearing oil seal, coat a new crankshaft rear oil seal with oil and install using Tool T65P-6701-A or equivalent. Inspect the seal to be sure it was not damaged during installation.

26. Install new bearing inserts in the connecting rods and caps. Check the clearance of each bearing, following the procedure (18a through 18d).

27. After the connecting rod bearings have been fitted, apply a light coat of engine oil to the journals and bearings.

28. Turn the crankshaft throw to the bottom of its stroke. Push the piston all the way down until the rod bearing seats on the crankshaft journal.

29. Install the connecting rod cap. Tighten the nuts to specification.

30. After the piston and connecting rod assemblies have been installed, check the side clearance with a feeler gauge between the connecting rods on each connecting rod crankshaft journal. Refer to Crankshaft and Connecting Rod specifications chart in this Section.

31. Install the timing chain and sprockets or gears, cylinder front cover and crankshaft pulley and adapter, following steps under Cylinder Front Cover and Timing Chain Installation in this Section.

Engine in the Truck

1. With the oil pan, oil pump and spark plugs removed, remove the cap from the main bearing needing replacement and remove the bearing from the cap.

2. Make a bearing roll-out pin, using a bent cotter pin as shown in the illustration. Install the end of the pin in the oil hole in the crankshaft journal.

3. Rotate the crankshaft clockwise as viewed from the front of the engine. This will roll the upper bearing out of the block.

4. Lube the new upper bearing with clean engine oil and insert the plain (un-notched) end between the crankshaft and the indented or notched side of the block. Roll the bearing into place, making sure that the oil holes are aligned. Remove the roll pin from the oil hole.

5. Lube the new lower bearing and install it in the main bearing cap. Install the main bearing cap onto the block, making sure it is positioned in proper direction with the matchmarks in alignment.

6. Torque the main bearing cap to specification.

➡See Crankshaft Installation for thrust bearing alignment.

CRANKSHAFT CLEANING AND INSPECTION

➡**Handle the crankshaft carefully to avoid damage to the finish surfaces.**

1. Clean the crankshaft with solvent, and blow out all oil passages with compressed air. On the 6-4.9L engine, clean the oil seal contact surface at the rear of the crankshaft with solvent to remove any corrosion, sludge or varnish deposits.

2. Use crocus cloth to remove any sharp edges, burrs or other imperfections which might damage the oil seal during installation or cause premature seal wear.

➡**Do not use crocus cloth to polish the seal surfaces. A finely polished surface may produce poor sealing or cause premature seal wear.**

3. Inspect the main and connecting rod journals for cracks, scratches, grooves or scores.

4. Measure the diameter of each journal at least four places to determine out-of-round, taper or undersize condition.

5. On an engine with a manual transmission, check the fit of the clutch pilot bearing in the bore of the crankshaft. A needle roller bearing and adapter assembly is used as a clutch pilot bearing. It is inserted directly into the engine crank shaft. The bearing and adapter assembly cannot be serviced separately. A new bearing must be installed whenever a bearing is removed.

6. Inspect the pilot bearing, when used, for roughness, evidence of overheating or loss of lubricant. Replace if any of these conditions are found.

7. On the 6-4.9L engine, inspect the rear oil seal surface of the crankshaft for deep grooves, nicks, burrs, porosity, or scratches which could damage the oil seal lip during installation. Remove all nicks and burrs with crocus cloth.

Main Bearings

1. Clean the bearing inserts and caps thoroughly in solvent, and dry them with compressed air.

➡**Do not scrape varnish or gum deposits from the bearing shells.**

2. Inspect each bearing carefully. Bearings that have a scored, chipped, or worn surface should be replaced.

3. The copper-lead bearing base may be visible through the bearing overlay in small localized areas. This may not mean that the bearing is excessively worn. It is not necessary to replace the bearing if the bearing clearance is within recommended specifications.

4. Check the clearance of bearings that appear to be satisfactory with Plastigage® or its equivalent. Fit the new bearings following the procedure Crankshaft and Main Bearings removal and installation, they should be reground to size for the next undersize bearing.

5. Regrind the journals to give the proper clearance with the next undersize bearing. If the journal will not clean up to maximum undersize bearing available, replace the crankshaft.

6. Always reproduce the same journal shoulder radius that existed originally. Too small a radius will result in fatigue failure of the crankshaft. Too large a radius will result in bearing failure due to radius ride of the bearing.

7. After regrinding the journals, chamfer the oil holes, then polish the journals with a #320 grit polishing cloth and engine oil. Crocus cloth may also be used as a polishing agent.

COMPLETING THE REBUILDING PROCESS

Fill the oil pump with oil, to prevent cavitating (sucking air) on initial engine start up. Install the oil pump and the pickup tube on the engine. Coat the oil pan gasket as necessary, and install the gasket and the oil pan. Mount the flywheel and the crankshaft vibration damper or pulley on the crankshaft.

➡**Always use new bolts when installing the flywheel. Inspect the clutch shaft pilot bushing in the crankshaft. If the bushing is excessively worn, remove it with an expanding puller and a slide hammer, and tap a new bushing into place.**

Position the engine, cylinder head side up. Lubricate the lifters, and install them into their bores. Install the cylinder head, and torque it as specified. Insert the pushrods (where applicable), and install the rocker shaft(s) (if so equipped) or position the rocker.

Install the intake and exhaust manifolds, the carburetor(s), the distributor and spark plugs. Mount all accessories and install the engine in the car. Fill the radiator with coolant, and the crankcase with high quality engine oil.

BREAK-IN PROCEDURE

Start the engine, and allow it to run at low speed for a few minutes, while checking for leaks. Stop the engine, check the oil level, and fill as necessary. Restart the engine, and fill the cooling system to capacity. Check and adjust the ignition timing. Run the engine at low to medium speed (800-2,500 rpm) for approximately ½ hour, and retorque the cylinder head bolts. Road test the car, and check again for leaks.

➡**Some gasket manufacturers recommend not retorquing the cylinder head(s) due to the composition of the head gasket. Follow the directions in the gasket set.**

Flywheel/Flex Plate and Ring Gear

➡**Flex plate is the term for a flywheel mated with an automatic transmission.**

REMOVAL & INSTALLATION

All Engines
◆ See Figure 190

➡**The ring gear is replaceable only on engines mated with a manual transmission. Engines with automatic transmissions have ring gears which are welded to the flex plate.**

1. Remove the transmission and transfer case.
2. Remove the clutch, if equipped, or torque converter from the flywheel. The flywheel bolts should be loosened a little at a time in a cross pattern to avoid warping the flywheel. On

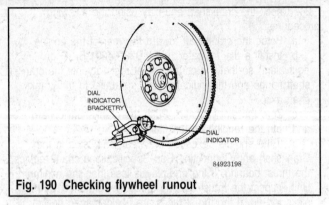

Fig. 190 Checking flywheel runout

trucks with manual transmissions, replace the pilot bearing in the end of the crankshaft if removing the flywheel.

3. The flywheel should be checked for cracks and glazing. It can be resurfaced by a machine shop.
4. If the ring gear is to be replaced, drill a hole in the gear between two teeth, being careful not to contact the flywheel surface. Using a cold chisel at this point, crack the ring gear and remove it.
5. Polish the inner surface of the new ring gear and heat it in an oven to about 600°F (316°C). Quickly place the ring gear on the flywheel and tap it into place, making sure that it is fully seated.

✳✳WARNING

Never heat the ring gear past 800°F (426°C), or the tempering will be destroyed.

6. Position the flywheel on the end of the crankshaft. Torque the bolts a little at a time, in a cross pattern, to the torque figure shown in the Torque Specifications Chart.
7. Install the clutch or torque converter.
8. Install the transmission and transfer case.

Rear Main Oil Seal

REPLACEMENT

Early 1987 8-7.5L Engines with a 2-Piece Seal
◆ See Figures 191, 192 and 193

1. Remove the oil pan and the oil pump (if required).
2. Loosen all the main bearing cap bolts, thereby lowering the crankshaft slightly but not to exceed 1/32 in. (0.8mm).
3. Remove the rear main bearing cap, and remove the oil seal from the bearing cap and cylinder block. On the block half of the seal use a seal removal tool, or install a small metal screw in one end of the seal, and pull on the screw to remove the seal. Exercise caution to prevent scratching or damaging the crankshaft seal surfaces.
4. Remove the oil seal retaining pin from the bearing cap if so equipped. The pin is not used with the split-lip seal.
5. Carefully clean the seal groove in the cap and block with a brush and solvent such as lacquer thinner, spot remover, or equivalent, or trichloroethylene. Also, clean the area thoroughly, so that no solvent touches the seal.

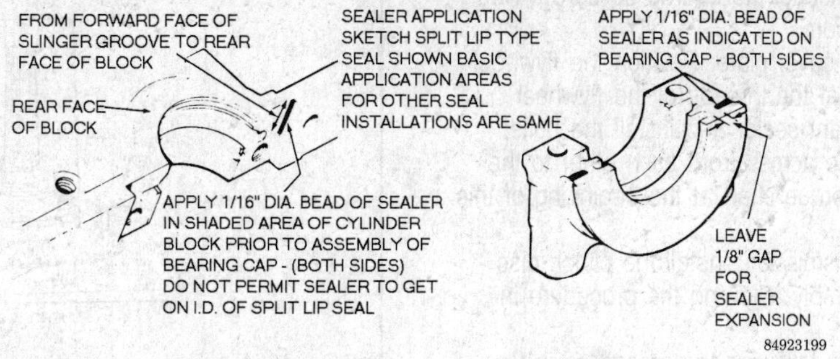

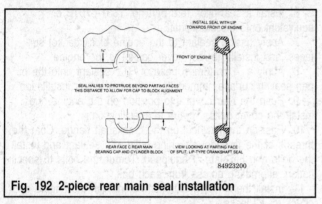

Fig. 191 RTV sealant application on the main bearing cap

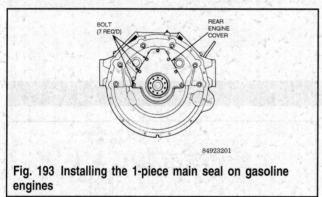

Fig. 192 2-piece rear main seal installation

Fig. 193 Installing the 1-piece main seal on gasoline engines

6. Dip the split lip-type seal halves in clean engine oil.

7. Carefully install the upper seal (cylinder block) into its groove with undercut side of the seal toward the FRONT of the engine, by rotating it on the seal journal of the crankshaft until approximately ⅜in. (9.5mm) protrudes below the parting surface.   Be sure no rubber has been shaved from the outside diameter of the seal by the bottom edge of the groove. Do not allow oil to get on the sealer area.

8. Tighten the remaining bearing cap bolts to the specifications listed in the Torque chart at the beginning of this Section.

9. Install the lower seal in the rear main bearing cap under undercut side of seal toward the FRONT of the engine, allow the seal to protrude approximately ⅜in. (9.5mm) above the parting surface to mate with the upper seal when the cap is installed.

10. Apply an even 1/16 in. (1.6mm) bead of RTV silicone rubber sealer, to the areas shown, following the procedure given in the illustration.

➡This sealer sets up in 15 minutes.

11. Install the rear main bearing cap. Tighten the cap bolts to specifications.

12. Install the oil pump and oil pan. Fill the crankcase with the proper amount and type of oil.

13. Operate the engine and check for oil leaks.

4.9L, 5.0L, 5.8L, most 1987 7.5L, and All 1988 and Later 8-7.5L Engines

▶ See Figure 193

If the crankshaft rear oil seal replacement is the only operation being performed, it can be done in the vehicle as detailed in the following procedure. If the oil seal is being replaced in conjunction with a rear main bearing replacement, the engine must be removed from the vehicle and installed on a work stand.

1. Remove the starter.

2. Remove the transmission from the vehicle, following procedures in Section 6.

3. On manual shift transmission, remove the pressure plate and cover assembly and the clutch disc following the procedure in Section 7.

4. Remove the flywheel attaching bolts and remove the flywheel and engine rear cover plate.

5. Use an awl to punch two holes in the crankshaft rear oil seal. Punch the holes on opposite sides of the crankshaft and just above the bearing cap to cylinder block split line. Install a sheet metal screw in each hole. Use two large screwdrivers or small pry bars and pry against both screws at the same time to remove the crankshaft rear oil seal. It may be necessary to place small blocks of wood against the cylinder block to provide a fulcrum point for the pry bars. Use caution throughout this procedure to avoid scratching or otherwise damaging the crankshaft oil seal surface.

6. Clean the oil seal recess in the cylinder block and main bearing cap.

7. Clean, inspect and polish the rear oil seal rubbing surface on the crankshaft. Coat the new oil seal and the crankshaft with a light film of engine oil. Start the seal in the recess with the seal lip facing forward and install it with a seal driver. Keep the tool straight with the centerline of the crankshaft and install the seal until the tool contacts the cylinder block sur-

face. Remove the tool and inspect the seal to be sure it was not damaged during installation.

8. Install the engine rear cover plate. Position the flywheel on the crankshaft flange. Coat the threads of the flywheel attaching bolts with oil-resistant sealer and install the bolts. Tighten the bolts in sequence across from each other to the specifications listed in the Torque chart at the beginning of this Section.

9. On a manual shift transmission, install the clutch disc and the pressure plate assembly following the procedure in Section 7.

10. Install the transmission, following the procedure in Section 7.

6.9L and 7.3L Diesel Engines

▶ **See Figures 194, 195 and 196**

1. Remove the transmission, clutch and flywheel assemblies.
2. Remove the engine rear cover.
3. Using an arbor press and a 4 1/8 in. (104.775mm) diameter spacer, press out the rear oil seal from the cover.

To install:

4. Clean the rear cover and engine block surfaces. Remove all traces of old RTV sealant from the oil pan and rear cover sealing surface by cleaning with a suitable solvent and drying thoroughly.
5. Coat the new rear oil seal with Lubriplate® or equivalent. Using an arbor press and spacer, install the new seal into the cover.

➡**The seal must be installed from the engine block side of the rear cover, flush with the seal bore inner surface.**

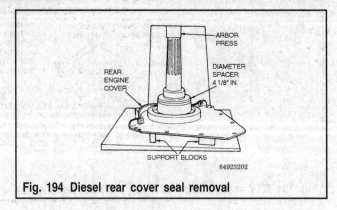

Fig. 194 Diesel rear cover seal removal

6. Install a seal pilot, ford part no. T83T-6701B or equivalent onto the crankshaft.
7. Apply gasket sealant to the engine block gasket surfaces, and install the rear cover gasket to the engine.
8. Apply a 1/4 in. (6mm) bead of RTV sealant onto the oil pan sealing surface, immediately after rear cover installation.
9. Push the rear cover into position on the engine and install the cover bolts. Torque to specification.
10. Position the flywheel on the crankshaft flange. Coat the threads of the flywheel attaching bolts with sealant and install the bolts and flexplate, if equipped. Torque the bolts to specification, alternating across from each bolt.
11. Install the clutch and transmission. Run the engine and check for oil leaks.

EXHAUST SYSTEM

✳✳CAUTION

When working on exhaust systems, ALWAYS wear protective goggles! Avoid working on a hot exhaust system!

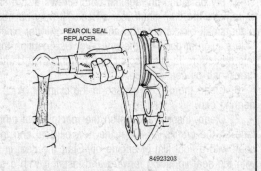

Fig. 195 1-piece diesel rear main seal removal or installation

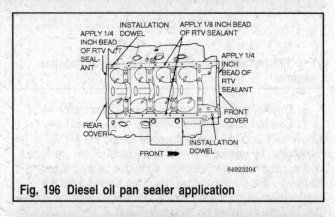

Fig. 196 Diesel oil pan sealer application

Muffler, Catalytic Converter, Inlet and Outlet Pipes

▶ **See Figures 197, 198, 199, 200 and 201**

REMOVAL & INSTALLATION

➡**The following applies to exhaust systems using clamped joints. Some models, use welded joints at the muffler. These joints will, of course, have to be cut.**

1. Raise and support the truck on jackstands.

2. Remove the U-clamps securing the muffler and outlet pipe.

3. Disconnect the muffler and outlet pipe bracket and insulator assemblies.

4. Remove the muffler and outlet pipe assembly. It may be necessary to heat the joints to get the parts to come off. Special tools are available to aid in breaking loose the joints.

5. On Super Cab and Crew Cab models, remove the extension pipe.

6. Disconnect the catalytic converter bracket and insulator assembly.

➡**For rod and insulator type hangers, apply a soap solution to the insulator surface and rod ends to allow easier removal of the insulator from the rod end. Don't use oil-based or silicone-based solutions since they will allow the insulator to slip back off once it's installed.**

7. Remove the catalytic converter.

8. On models with Managed Thermactor® Air, disconnect the MTA tube assembly.

9. Remove the inlet pipe assembly.

10. Install the components making sure that all the components in the system are properly aligned before tightening any fasteners. Make sure all tabs are indexed and all parts are clear of surrounding body panels. See the accompanying illustrations for proper clearances and alignment.   Observe the following torque specifications:

- Inlet pipe-to-manifold: 35 ft. lbs.
- MTA U-bolt: 60-96 inch lbs.
- Inlet pipe or converter-to-muffler or extension: 45 ft. lbs.

- Hanger bracket and insulator-to-frame: 24 ft. lbs.
- Bracket and insulator-to-exhaust: 15 ft. lbs.
- Flat flange bolts (8-7.5L and diesel) 30 ft. lbs.

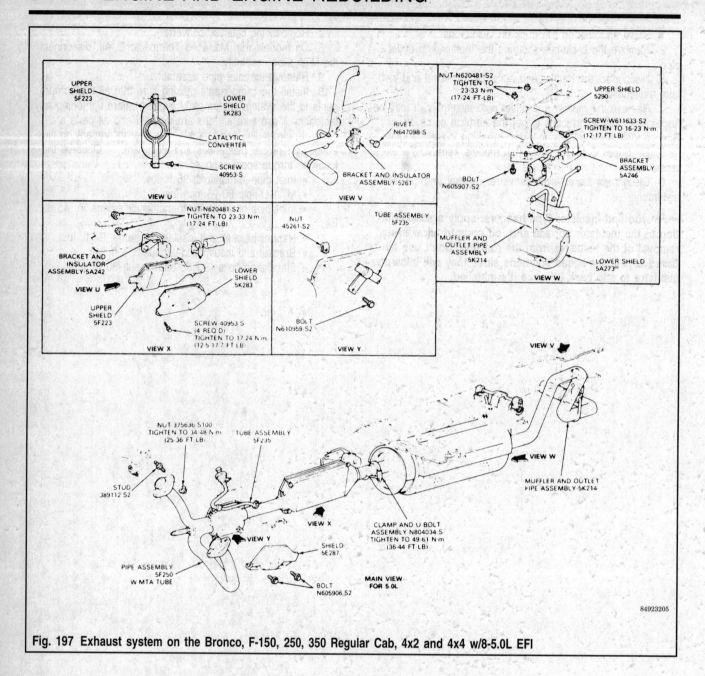

Fig. 197 Exhaust system on the Bronco, F-150, 250, 350 Regular Cab, 4x2 and 4x4 w/8-5.0L EFI

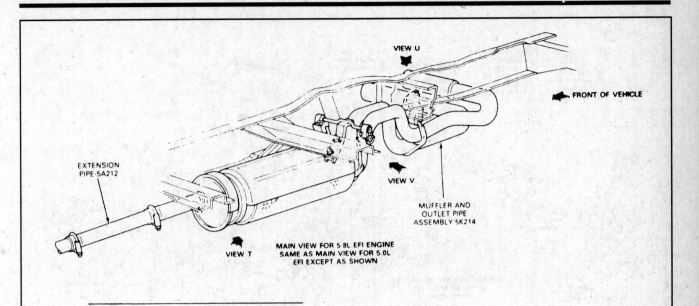

EXTENSION
PIPE-5A212

VIEW U

FRONT OF VEHICLE

VIEW V

MUFFLER AND
OUTLET PIPE
ASSEMBLY 5K214

VIEW T

MAIN VIEW FOR 5.8L EFI ENGINE
SAME AS MAIN VIEW FOR 5.0L
EFI EXCEPT AS SHOWN

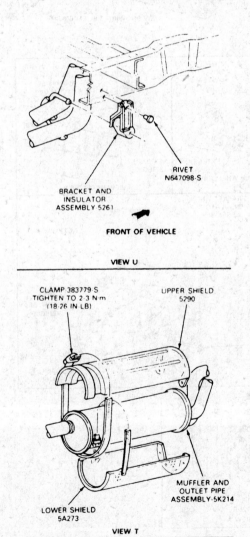

RIVET
N647098-S

BRACKET AND
INSULATOR
ASSEMBLY 5261

FRONT OF VEHICLE

VIEW U

CLAMP 383779-S
TIGHTEN TO 2-3 N·m
(18-26 IN·LB)

UPPER SHIELD
5290

MUFFLER AND
OUTLET PIPE
ASSEMBLY-5K214

LOWER SHIELD
5A273

VIEW T

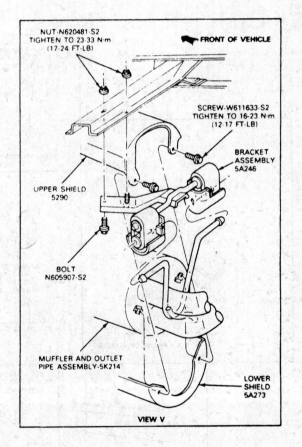

NUT-N620481-S2
TIGHTEN TO 23-33 N·m
(17-24 FT·LB)

FRONT OF VEHICLE

SCREW-W611633-S2
TIGHTEN TO 16-23 N·m
(12-17 FT·LB)

BRACKET
ASSEMBLY
5A246

UPPER SHIELD
5290

BOLT
N605907-S2

MUFFLER AND OUTLET
PIPE ASSEMBLY-5K214

LOWER
SHIELD
5A273

VIEW V

84923207

Fig. 198 Exhaust system on the Bronco, F-150, 250, 350 Regular Cab, Super Cab, 4x2 and 4x4 w/8-5.8L EFI

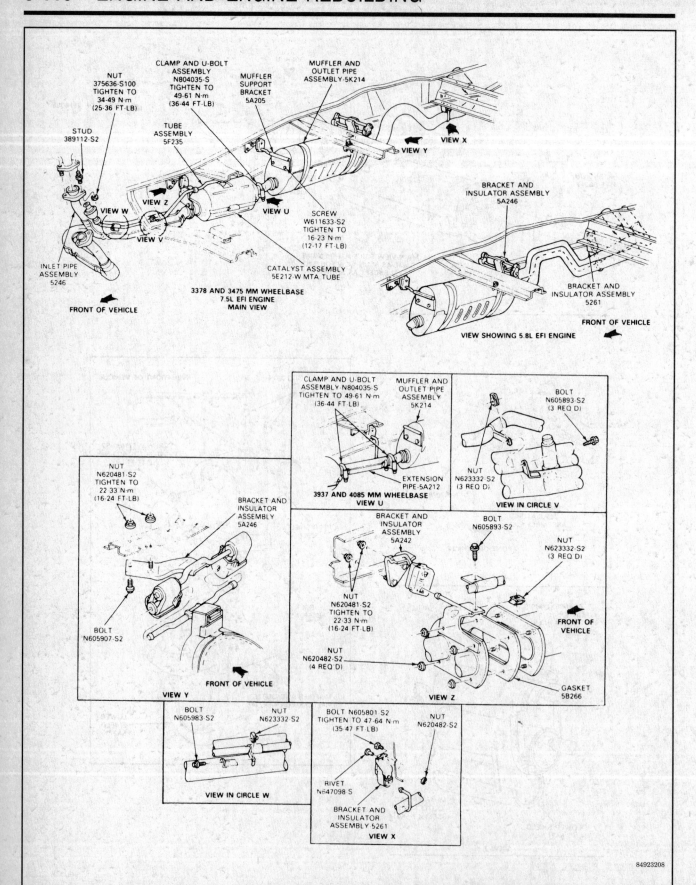

Fig. 199 Exhaust system on the F-250, 350 Regular Cab, Super Cab Chassis 4x2 and 4x4 w/8-5.8L EFI and 8-7.5L EFI

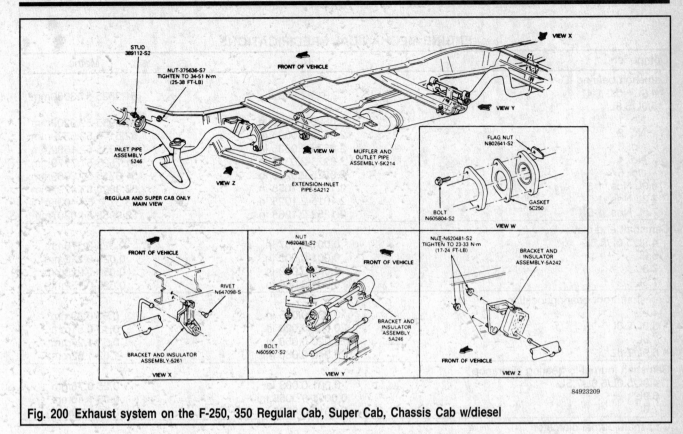

Fig. 200 Exhaust system on the F-250, 350 Regular Cab, Super Cab, Chassis Cab w/diesel

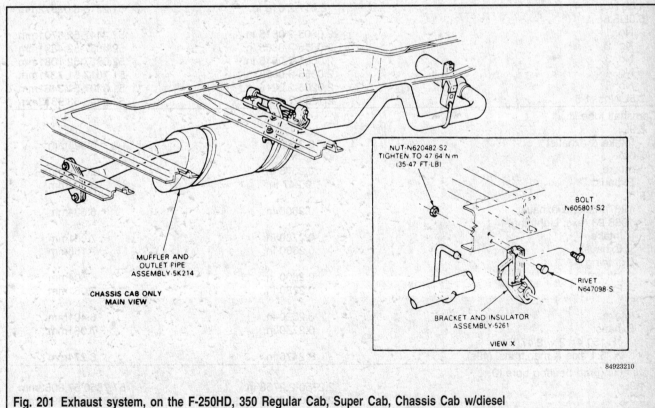

Fig. 201 Exhaust system, on the F-250HD, 350 Regular Cab, Super Cab, Chassis Cab w/diesel

ENGINE MECHANICAL SPECIFICATIONS

Component	U.S.	Metric
Camshaft bearing ID		
4.9L Nos. 1-4	2.019-2.020 in.	51.2826-51.3080mm
5.0L/5.8L		
No. 1	2.0825-2.0835 in.	52.8955-52.9209mm
No. 2	2.0675-2.0685 in.	52.5145-52.5399mm
No. 3	2.0525-2.0535 in.	52.1335-52.1589mm
No. 4	2.0375-2.0385 in.	51.7525-51.7779mm
No. 5	2.0225-2.0235 in.	51.3715-51.3969mm
6.9L Nos. 1-5	2.1020-2.1055 in.	53.3908-53.4797mm
7.3L Nos. 1-5	2.1015-2.1025 in.	53.3781-53.4035mm
7.5L Nos. 1-5	2.1258-2.1268 in.	53.9953-54.0207mm
Camshaft end-play		
4.9L/5.0L/5.8L	0.001-0.007 in.	0.025-0.178mm
6.9L	0.001-0.009 in.	0.025-0.229mm
7.3L	0.002-0.009 in.	0.051-0.229mm
7.5L	0.001-0.006 in.	0.025-0.152mm
Camshaft front bearing location		
4.9L	0.020-0.035 in.	0.51-0.89mm
5.0L/5.8L	0.005-0.020 in.	0.13-0.51mm
7.3L	0.020-0.050 in.	0.51-1.27mm
6.9L/7.5L	0.040-0.060 in.	1.02-1.52mm
Camshaft journal-to-bearing clearance		
4.9L/5.0L/5.8L/7.5L	0.001-0.003 in.	0.25-0.76mm
6.9L	0.0001-0.0055 in.	0.03-1.40mm
7.3L	0.0015-0.0035 in.	0.38-0.89mm
Camshaft journal diameter		
4.9L Nos. 1-4	2.017-2.018 in.	51.2318-51.2572mm
5.0L/5.8L		
No. 1	2.0805-2.0815 in.	52.8447-52.8701mm
No. 2	2.0655-2.0665 in.	52.4637-52.4891mm
No. 3	2.0505-2.0515 in.	52.0827-52.1081mm
No. 4	2.0355-2.0365 in.	51.7017-51.7271mm
No. 5	2.0205-2.0215 in.	51.3207-51.3461mm
7.5L Nos. 1-5	2.1238-2.1248 in.	53.9445-53.9670mm
Camshaft lobe lift		
4.9L		
Intake & exhaust*	0.2490 in.	6.325mm
5.0L		
Intake	0.2375 in.	6.0325mm
Exhaust	0.247 in.	6.274mm
5.8L		
1987 intake & exhaust	0.2600 in.	6.604mm
1988-93 (exc. Lightning)		
Intake	0.2780 in.	7.061mm
Exhaust	0.2830 in.	7.188mm
Lightning		
Intake	0.2600 in.	6.604mm
Exhaust	0.2780 in.	7.061mm
7.5L		
Intake	0.2520 in.	6.401mm
Exhaust	0.2780 in.	7.061mm
*F-150 4×2 w/2.47:1 or		
2.75:1 axle & man.trans. (49s)	0.2470 in.	6.274mm
Connecting rod bearing bore ID		
4.9L	2.2750-2.2758 in.	57.7850-57.8053mm
5.0L	2.2390-2.2398 in.	56.8706-56.8909mm
5.8L	2.4265-2.4273 in.	61.6331-61.6534mm
6.9L/7.3L	2.5001-2.5016 in.	63.5025-63.5406mm
7.5L	2.6522-2.6530 in.	67.3659-67.3862mm

84923221

ENGINE MECHANICAL SPECIFICATIONS

Component	U.S.	Metric
Connecting rod bearing clearance		
4.9L/5.0L/5.8L/7.5L	0.0008-0.0015 in.	0.020-0.038mm
6.9L	0.0011-0.0026 in.	0.0279-0.0660mm
7.3L	0.0011-0.0036 in.	0.0279-0.0914mm
Connecting rod bend (max.)		
4.9L/5.0L/5.8L/7.5L	0.012 in.	0.305mm
6.9L	0.008 in.	0.20mm
7.3L	0.002 in.	0.05mm
Connecting rod-to-crankshaft side clearance		
4.9L	0.006-0.013 in.	0.152-0.330mm
5.0L/5.8L/7.5L	0.010-0.020 in.	0.254-0.500mm
6.9L/7.3L	0.012-0.024 in.	0.305-0.610mm
Connecting rod journal diameter		
4.9L	2.1228-2.1236 in.	53.9191-53.9394mm
5.0L	2.1228-2.1236 in.	53.9191-53.8384mm
5.8L	2.3103-2.3111 in.	58.6816-58.7019mm
6.9L/7.3L	2.4980-2.4990 in.	63.4492-63.4746mm
7.5L	2.4992-2.5000 in.	63.4797-63.5000mm
Connecting rod journal taper		
4.9L/5.0L/5.8L/7.5L	0.0006 in. per 1 in.	0.0152mm per 25.4mm
6.9L/7.3L	0.0005 in. per 1 in.	0.0127mm per 25.4mm
Connecting rod length (center-to-center)		
4.9L	6.2082-6.2112 in.	157.8828-157.7645mm
5.0L	5.0885-5.0915 in.	129.2479-129.3241mm
5.8L	5.9545-5.9575 in.	151.2443-151.3205mm
7.3L	7.1280-7.1320 in.	181.0512-181.1528mm
7.5L	6.6035-6.6065 in.	167.7289-167.8051mm
Connecting rod piston pin bore ID		
4.9L	0.9734-0.9742 in.	24.7244-24.7447mm
5.0L	0.9096-0.9112 in.	23.1038-23.1445mm
5.8L	0.9097-0.9112 in.	23.1064-23.1445mm
6.9L	1.1105-1.1107 in.	28.2067-28.2118mm
7.3L	1.1105-1.1108 in.	28.1105-28.2143mm
7.5L	1.0386-1.0393 in.	26.3804-26.3982mm
Connecting rod twist (max.)		
4.9L/5.8L/7.5L	0.024 in.	0.61mm
5.0L		
1987-92	0.024 in.	0.61mm
1993	0.015 in.	0.38mm
6.9L	0.016 in.	0.41mm
7.3L	0.002 in.	0.05mm
Crankshaft end-play		
4.9L/5.0L/5.8L/7.5L	0.0040-0.0080 in.	0.10-0.20mm
6.9L	0.0020-0.0090 in.	0.05-0.23mm
7.3L	0.0025-0.0085 in.	0.06-0.22mm
Crankshaft thrust bearing journal length		
4.9L	1.1990-1.2010 in.	30.4546-30.5054mm
5.0L/5.8L	1.137-1.139 in.	28.8798-28.9306mm
6.9L/7.3L	1.1325-1.1355 in.	28.7655-28.8417mm
7.5L	1.124-1.126 in.	28.5496-28.6004mm
Cylinder block head gasket surface flatness		
4.9L/5.0L/5.8L/6.9L/7.3L/7.5L	0.003 in. per 6 in.	0.076mm per 152.4mm

ENGINE MECHANICAL SPECIFICATIONS

Component	U.S.	Metric
Cylinder bore diameter		
4.9L	4.0000-4.0048 in.	101.6000-101.7219mm
5.0L	4.0004-4.0052 in.	101.6102-101.7321mm
5.8L	4.0000-4.0048 in.	101.6000-101.7219mm
6.9L	3.9995-4.0015 in.	101.5873-101.6381mm
7.3L	4.1095-4.1115 in.	104.3813-104.4321mm
7.5L	4.3600-4.3636 in.	110.7440-110.8354mm
Cylinder bore max. taper		
4.9L/5.0L/5.8L/7.5L	0.010 in.	0.254mm
6.9L	0.0050 in.	0.127mm
7.3L	0.0020 in.	0.051mm
Cylinder bore out-of-round (max.)		
4.9L/5.0L/5.8L/7.5L	0.0015 in.	0.038mm
6.9L/7.3L	0.0020 in.	0.051mm
Cylinder head gasket surface flatness		
4.9L	0.006 in. per 6 in.	0.152mm per 152.4mm
5.0L/5.8L/6.9L/7.3L/7.5L	0.003 in. per 6 in.	0.076mm per 152.4mm
Flywheel ring gear lateral run-out		
4.9L		
Manual trans.	0.040 in.	1.016mm
Automatic trans.	0.060 in.	1.524mm
6.9L	0.008 in.	0.203mm
7.3L	0.020 in.	0.508mm
Flywheel run-out		
4.9L/5.0L/5.8L	0.010 in.	0.254mm
6.9L	0.008 in.	0.203mm
7.3L	0.030 in.	0.762mm
Lifter-to-bore clearance		
4.9L/5.0L/5.8L/7.5L	0.0007-0.0027 in.	0.0178-0.0686mm
6.9L/7.3L	0.0011-0.0034 in.	0.0279-0.0864mm
Lifter bore diameter		
4.9L/5.0L/5.8L/7.5L	0.8752-0.8767 in.	22.2300-22.2682mm
Lifter collapsed gap		
4.9L	0.100-0.200 in.	2.540-5.080mm
5.0L		
1987-92	0.071-0.193 in.	1.803-4.902mm
1993	0.071-0.171 in.	1.803-4.343mm
5.8L		
1987-92	0.098-0.198 in.	2.489-5.029mm
1993	0.092-0.192 in.	2.337-4.877mm
6.9L/7.3L	0.185 in. max.	4.700mm max.
7.5L	0.075-0.175 in.	1.905-4.445mm
Lifter diameter		
4.9L/5.0L/5.8L/7.5L	0.8740-0.8745 in.	22.2000-22.2123mm
6.9L/7.3L	0.9209-0.9217 in.	23.3908-23.4112mm
Lifter leakdown rate		
4.9L/5.0L/5.8L/7.5L	10-50 sec. per $\frac{1}{16}$ in.	10-50 sec. per 1.6mm
6.9L	12-90 sec. per $\frac{1}{8}$ in.	12-90 sec per 3.2mm
7.3L	20-110 sec. per $\frac{1}{8}$ in.	20-110 sec. per 3.2mm
Main bearing bore diameter		
4.9L	2.5902-2.5910 in.	65.7911-65.8114mm
5.0L	2.4412-2.4420 in.	62.0065-62.0268mm
5.8L	3.1922-3.1930 in.	81.0819-81.1022mm
6.9L	3.1254-3.1274 in.	79.3852-79.4360mm
7.3L	3.3152-3.3162 in.	84.2061-84.2315mm
7.5L	3.1922-3.1934 in.	81.0819-81.1124mm

84923223

ENGINE MECHANICAL SPECIFICATIONS

Component	U.S.	Metric
Main bearing clearance		
4.9L	0.0008-0.0015 in.	0.0203-0.0381mm
5.0L/5.8L		
1987		
No. 1	0.0001-0.0015 in.	0.0025-0.0381mm
Nos. 2-5	0.0005-0.0015 in.	0.0127-0.0381mm
1988-92		
No. 1	0.0001-0.0015 in.	0.0025-0.0381mm
Nos. 2-5	0.0008-0.0015 in.	0.0203-0.0381mm
1993		
No. 1	0.0001-0.0015 in.	0.0025-0.0381mm
Nos. 2-5	0.0005-0.0015 in.	0.0203-0.0381mm
6.9L/7.3L	0.0018-0.0036 in.	0.0457-0.0914mm
7.5L	0.0008-0.0015 in.	0.0203-0.0381mm
Main bearing journal diameter		
4.9L	2.3982-2.3990 in.	60.9143-60.9346mm
5.0L	2.2482-2.2490 in.	57.1043-57.1246mm
5.8L/7.5L	2.9994-3.0002 in.	76.1848-76.2051mm
6.9L/7.3L	3.1228-3.1236 in.	79.3191-79.3394mm
Main bearing journal run-out		
4.9L/5.0L/5.8L/6.9L/7.3L/7.5L	0.002 in.	0.051mm
Main bearing journal taper		
4.9L/5.0L/5.8L/6.9L/7.3L/7.5L	0.0005 in. per 1 in.	0.0127mm per 25.4mm
Main bearing thrust face run-out		
4.9L/5.0L/5.8L/6.9L/7.3L/7.5L	0.001 in.	0.0254mm
Oil pump gear backlash		
6.9L	0.0015-0.0130 in.	0.0381-0.3302mm
7.3L	0.0056-0.0100 in.	0.1422-0.2540mm
Oil pump driveshaft-to-housing clearance		
4.9L/5.0L/5.8L/7.5L	0.0015-0.0030 in.	0.0381-0.0762mm
Oil pump outer race-to-housing clearance		
4.9L/5.0L/5.8L/7.5L	0.001-0.003 in.	0.0254-0.0762mm
Oil pump relief valve-to-housing clearance		
4.9L/5.0L/5.8L/7.5L	0.0015-0.0030 in.	0.0381-0.0762mm
Oil pump relief valve spring pressure		
4.9L/7.5L	21 psi @ 2.49 in.	149kPa @ 63.25mm
5.0L	11 psi @ 1.74 in.	78kPa @ 44mm
5.8L	19 psi @ 2.49 in.	132kPa @ 63.25mm
Oil pump rotor end clearance		
4.9L/5.0L/5.8L/7.5L	0.004 in. max.	0.10mm max.
Oil pump rotor-to-rotor tip clearance		
4.9L/7.5L	0.012 in. max.	0.30mm max.
Piston diameter (centerline)		
4.9L		
Coded red	3.9982-3.9988 in.	101.5543-101.5695mm
Coded blue	3.9994-4.0000 in.	101.5848-101.6000mm
0.003 in. o/s	4.0008-4.0014 in.	101.6203-101.6356mm
5.0L		
1987		
Coded red	3.9991-3.9985 in.	101.5771-101.5619mm
Coded blue	3.9990-4.0000 in.	101.5746-101.6000mm
0.003 o/s	4.0008-4.0014 in.	101.6203-101.6356mm
1988-93		
Coded red	3.9989-3.9995 in.	101.5721-101.5873mm
Coded blue	4.0001-4.0007 in.	101.6025-101.6178mm
0.003 in. o/s	4.0013-4.0019 in.	101.6330-101.6483mm

84923224

ENGINE MECHANICAL SPECIFICATIONS

Component	U.S.	Metric
5.8L (exc. Lightning)		
Coded red	3.9978-3.9984 in.	101.5441-101.5594mm
Coded blue	3.9990-3.9996 in.	101.5746-101.5898mm
0.003 in. o/s	4.0002-4.0008 in.	101.6051-101.6203mm
5.8L Lightning		
Coded red	3.9984-3.9990 in.	101.5594-101.5746mm
Coded blue	3.9996-4.0002 in.	101.5898-101.6051mm
0.003 o/s	4.0008-4.0018 in.	101.6203-101.6457mm
6.9L (skirt)	3.9935-3.9955 in.	101.4349-101.4857mm
7.3L (skirt)	4.1035-4.1040 in.	104.2290-104.2417mm
7.5L		
1987		
Coded red	4.3585-4.3591 in.	110.7059-110.7211mm
Coded blue	4.3597-4.3603 in.	110.7364-110.7516mm
0.003 o/s	4.3609-4.3615 in.	110.7669-110.7821mm
1988-93		
Coded red	4.3577-4.3583 in.	110.6856-110.7002mm
Coded blue	4.3589-4.3595 in.	110.7161-110.7313mm
0.003 in. o/s	4.3601-4.3607 in.	110.7465-110.7618mm
Piston-to-bore clearance		
4.9L	0.0010-0.0018 in.	0.0254-0.0457mm
5.0L		
1987	0.0013-0.0030 in.	0.033-0.076mm
1988-93	0.0014-0.0022 in.	0.0356-0.0559mm
5.8L		
Exc. Lightning	0.0018-0.0026 in.	0.0457-0.0660mm
Lightning	0.0015-0.0023 in.	0.0381-0.0584mm
6.9L	0.0055-0.0075 in.	0.0140-0.0190mm
7.3L		
Nos. 1-6	0.0055-0.0085 in.	0.0140-0.2159mm
Nos. 7 & 8	0.0060-0.0085 in.	0.1524-0.2159mm
7.5L	0.0022-0.0030 in.	0.0559-0.0762mm
Piston height above crankcase		
6.9L/7.3L	0.010-0.031 in.	0.254-0.787mm
Piston pin bore diameter in piston		
4.9L	0.9754-0.9757 in.	24.775-24.783mm
5.0L	0.9123-0.9126 in.	23.172-23.180mm
5.8L	0.9124-0.9127 in.	23.175-23.183mm
6.9L/7.3L	1.1104-1.1106 in.	28.204-28.209mm
7.5L	1.0401-1.0406 in.	26.419-26.431mm
Piston pin diameter (standard)		
4.9L	0.9749-0.9754 in.	24.762-24.775mm
5.0L/5.8L	0.9119-0.9124 in.	23.162-23.175mm
6.9L/7.3L	1.1099-1.1101 in.	28.191-28.197mm
7.5L	1.0398-1.0403 in.	26.411-26.424mm
Piston pin length		
4.9L	3.150-3.170 in.	80.00-80.50mm
5.0L/5.8L	3.010-3.040 in.	76.5-77.2mm
6.9L/7.3L	2.692-2.702 in.	68.4-68.6mm
7.5L	3.290-3.320 in.	83.6-84.3mm
Piston pin-to-piston bore clearance		
4.9L		
Under 8500 lbs. GVW	0.0003-0.0005 in.	0.0076-0.0127mm
8500 lbs. + GVW	0.0002-0.0004 in.	0.0051-0.0102mm
5.0L	0.0002-0.0004 in.	0.0051-0.0102mm
5.8L	0.0003-0.0005 in.	0.0076-0.0127mm
6.9L/7.3L	0.0003-0.0007 in.	0.0076-0.0178mm
7.5L	0.0002-0.0005 in.	0.0051-0.0127mm

84923225

ENGINE MECHANICAL SPECIFICATIONS

Component	U.S.	Metric
Piston pin-to-rod clearance		
4.9L/5.0L/5.8L/7.5L	interference fit	
6.9L/7.3L	0.0004-0.0009 in.	0.0102-0.0228mm
Piston ring diameter		
6.9L	4.00 in.	101.6mm
7.3L	4.11 in.	104.4mm
Piston ring end gap		
4.9L		
Top	0.010-0.020 in.	0.254-0.508mm
Second	0.010-0.020 in.	0.254-0.508mm
Oil	0.015-0.055 in.	0.381-1.397mm
5.0L		
1987-92		
Top	0.010-0.020 in.	0.254-0.508mm
Second	0.010-0.020 in.	0.254-0.508mm
Oil	0.015-0.055 in.	0.381-1.397mm
1993		
Top	0.010-0.020 in.	0.254-0.508mm
Second	0.018-0.028 in.	0.457-0.711mm
Oil	0.010-0.040 in.	0.254-1.016mm
5.8L (exc. Lightning)		
Top	0.010-0.020 in.	0.254-0.508mm
Second	0.010-0.020 in.	0.254-0.508mm
Oil	0.015-0.055 in.	0.381-1.397mm
Lightning		
Top	0.010-0.020 in.	0.254-0.508mm
Second	0.018-0.028 in.	0.457-0.711mm
Oil	0.010-0.040 in.	0.254-1.016mm
Intake	1.769-1.793 in.	44.9326-45.5422mm
Exhaust	1.551-1.569 in.	39.3954-39.8526mm
5.0L		
Intake	1.690-1.694 in.	42.926-43.0276mm
Exhaust	1.439-1.463 in.	36.5506-37.1602mm
5.8L (exc. Lightning)		
Intake	1.770-1.794 in.	44.9580-45.5676mm
Exhaust	1.453-1.468 in.	36.9062-37.2872mm
5.8L Lightning		
Intake	1.837-1.847 in.	46.6598-46.9138mm
Exhaust	1.536-1.546 in.	39.0144-39.2684mm
7.5L		
1987		
Intake	2.075-2.090 in.	52.705-53.086mm
Exhaust	1.646-1.661 in.	41.808-42.189mm
1988-93		
Intake	1.965-1.989 in.	49.911-50.521mm
Exhaust	1.646-1.661 in.	41.808-42.189mm
Valve head recession in deck		
6.9L		
Intake	0.042-0.054 in.	1.067-1.372mm
Exhaust	0.043-0.055 in.	1.092-1.397mm
7.3L		
Intake	0.042-0.054 in.	1.067-1.372mm
Exhaust	0.051-0.063 in.	1.295-1.600mm
Valve seat run-out		
4.9L/5.0L/5.8L/6.9L/7.3L/7.5L	0.002 in.	0.05mm

ENGINE MECHANICAL SPECIFICATIONS

Component	U.S.	Metric
Valve seat width		
4.9L		
Intake		
1987	0.060-0.080 in.	1.524-2.032mm
1988-93	0.060-0.090 in.	1.524-2.286mm
Exhaust	0.070-0.090 in.	1.778-2.286mm
5.0L/5.8L/7.5L		
Intake & exhaust	0.060-0.080 in.	1.524-2.032mm
6.9L/7.3L intake & exhaust	0.065-0.095 in.	1.651-2.413mm
Valve spring compression pressure		
4.9L		
Intake	175 psi @ 1.240 in.	1207kPa @ 31.5mm
Exhaust	175 psi @ 1.070 in.	1207kPa @ 27.2mm
5.0L		
Intake	204 psi @ 1.36 in.	1407kPa @ 34.5mm
Exhaust	200 psi @ 1.20 in.	1379kPa @ 30.5mm
5.8L		
Intake	200 psi @ 1.20 in.	1379kPa @ 30.5mm
Exhaust	200 psi @ 1.20 in.	1379kPa @ 30.5mm
6.9L intake & exhaust	60 psi @ 1.798 in.	414kPa @ 45.7mm
7.3L intake & exhaust	80 psi @ 1.833 in.	552kPa @ 46.5mm
7.5L		
Intake	229 psi @ 1.33 in.	1579kPa @ 33.8mm
Exhaust	229 psi @ 1.33 in.	1579kPa @ 33.8mm
Valve spring free length		
4.9L		
Intake	1.96 in.	49.78mm
Exhaust	1.78 in.	45.21mm
5.0L/5.8L		
1987-92 intake & exhaust	2.04 in.	51.8mm
1993 intake & exhaust	2.06 in.	52.3mm
6.9L intake & exhaust	2.04 in.	51.8mm
7.3L intake & exhaust	2.075 in.	52.7mm
7.5L intake & exhaust	2.06 in.	52.3mm
Valve spring installed height		
4.9L		
Intake	1.61-1.67 in.	40.89-42.42mm
Exhaust	1.44-1.50 in.	36.58-38.10mm
5.0L		
1987-92		
Intake	1.67-1.70 in.	42.42-43.18mm
Exhaust	1.58-1.61 in.	40.13-40.89mm
1993		
Intake	1.75-1.81 in.	44.45-45.97mm
Exhaust	1.58-1.64 in.	40.13-41.66mm
5.8L		
1987-92		
Intake	1.77-1.80 in.	44.96-45.72mm
Exhaust	1.58-1.61 in.	40.13-40.89mm
1993		
Intake	1.75-1.81 in.	44.45-45.97mm
Exhaust	1.58-1.64 in.	40.13-41.66mm
6.9L/7.3L		
Intake	1.767 in.	44.88mm
Exhaust	1.833 in.	46.56mm
7.5L		
Intake & exhaust	1.80-1.83 in.	45.72-46.56mm
Valve spring out-of-square		
4.9L/5.0L/5.8L/6.9L/7.3L/7.5L	0.078 in.	1.981mm

84923227

ENGINE MECHANICAL SPECIFICATIONS

Component	U.S.	Metric
Valve stem diameter (standard)		
4.9L		
Intake	0.3416-0.3423 in.	8.6766-8.6944mm
Exhaust	0.3416-0.3423 in.	8.6766-8.6944mm
5.0L/5.8L		
Intake	0.3416-0.3423 in.	8.6766-8.6944mm
Exhaust	0.3411-0.3418 in.	8.6634-8.6817mm
6.9L/7.3L intake & exhaust	0.37165-0.37235 in.	9.4400-9.4577mm
7.5L		
Intake	0.3415-0.3423 in.	8.6741-8.6944mm
Exhaust	0.3415-0.3423 in.	8.6741-8.6944mm
Valve stem-to-guide clearance		
4.9L/7.5L		
Intake	0.0010-0.0027 in.	0.0254-0.0686mm
Exhaust	0.0010-0.0027 in.	0.0254-0.0686mm
5.0L/5.8L		
Intake	0.0010-0.0027 in.	0.0254-0.0686mm
Exhaust	0.0015-0.0032 in.	0.0381-0.0813mm
6.9L intake & exhaust	0.0012-0.0029 in.	0.0305-0.0737mm
7.3L intake & exhaust	0.0055 in.	0.1397mm
6.9L		
Top	0.014-0.024 in.	0.356-0.610mm
Second	0.060-0.070 in.	1.524-1.778mm
Oil	0.010-0.024 in.	0.254-0.610mm
7.3L		
Top	0.013-0.045 in.	0.330-1.143mm
Second	0.060-0.085 in.	1.524-2.159mm
7.5L		
Top	0.010-0.020 in.	0.254-0.508mm
Second	0.010-0.020 in.	0.254-0.508mm
Oil	0.010-0.035 in.	0.254-0.889mm
Piston ring groove width		
4.9L		
Top	0.080-0.081 in.	2.032-2.057mm
Second	0.080-0.081 in.	2.032-2.057mm
Oil	0.188-0.189 in.	4.775-4.800mm
5.0L		
Top	0.060-0.061 in.	1.524-1.549mm
Second	0.060-0.061 in.	1.524-1.549mm
Oil	0.1587-0.1597 in.	4.031-4.056mm
5.8L		
Top	0.080-0.081 in.	2.032-2.057mm
Second	0.080-0.081 in.	2.032-2.057mm
Oil	0.188-0.189 in.	4.775-4.800mm
7.5L		
Top	0.0805-0.0815 in.	2.045-2.070mm
Second	0.0805-0.0815 in.	2.045-2.070mm
Oil	0.188-0.189 in.	4.775-4.800mm
Piston ring side clearance		
4.9L		
Top	0.0019-0.0036 in.	0.048-0.091mm
Second	0.0020-0.0040 in.	0.051-0.102mm
Oil	snug	
5.0L		
1987-92		
Top	0.0013-0.0033 in.	0.033-0.084mm
Second	0.002-0.004 in.	0.051-0.102mm
Oil	snug	

84923228

ENGINE MECHANICAL SPECIFICATIONS

Component	U.S.	Metric
1993		
Top	0.0013-0.0033 in.	0.033-0.084mm
Second	0.0013-0.0033 in.	0.033-0.084mm
Oil	snug	
5.8L		
1987-92		
Top	0.0013-0.0033 in.	0.033-0.084mm
Second	0.002-0.004 in.	0.051-0.102mm
Oil	snug	
1993 (exc. Lightning)		
Top	0.0020-0.0040 in.	0.051-0.102mm
Second	0.0020-0.0040 in.	0.051-0.102mm
Oil	snug	
Lightning		
Top	0.0013-0.0033 in.	0.033-0.084mm
Second	0.0013-0.0033 in.	0.033-0.084mm
Oil	snug	
6.9L/7.3L		
Top	0.002-0.004 in.	0.051-0.102mm
Second	0.002-0.004 in.	0.051-0.102mm
Oil	0.001-0.003 in.	0.0254-0.0762mm
7.5L		
Top	0.0025-0.0045 in.	0.0635-0.1143mm
Second	0.0025-0.0045 in.	0.0635-0.1143mm
oil	snug	
Piston ring width		
4.9L		
Top	0.0774-0.0781 in.	1.9660-1.9837mm
Second	0.0770-0.0780 in.	1.9558-1.9812mm
5.0L		
Top	0.0577-0.0587 in.	1.4656-1.4910mm
Second	0.0577-0.0587 in.	1.4656-1.4910mm
5.8L		
1987		
Top	0.0577-0.0587 in.	1.4656-1.4910mm
Second	0.0577-0.0587 in.	1.4656-1.4910mm
1988-93 (exc. Lightning)		
Top	0.0770-0.0780 in.	1.9558-1.9812mm
Second	0.0770-0.0780 in.	1.9558-1.9812mm
Lightning		
Top	0.0577-0.0587 in.	1.4656-1.4910mm
Second	0.0577-0.0587 in.	1.4656-1.4910mm
7.5L		
Top	0.0770-0.0780 in.	1.9558-1.9812mm
Second	0.0770-0.0780 in.	1.9558-1.9812mm
Pushrod run-out		
4.9L/5.0L/5.8L/6.9L/7.3L/7.5L	0.015 in.	0.881mm
Rocker arm lift ratio		
4.9L/5.0L/5.8L		
1987-92	1.61:1	
1993	1.59:1	
7.5L	1.73:1	
Timing chain deflection (max.)		
5.0L/5.8L/7.5L	0.50 in.	12.7mm
Timing gears assembled face run-out		
4.9L	0.005 in.	0.127mm
Timing gear backlash		
6.9L/7.3L	0.0015-0.0130 in.	0.0381-0.330mm

ENGINE MECHANICAL SPECIFICATIONS

Component	U.S.	Metric
Valve face minimum margin		
7.3L		
Intake	0.112 in.	2.845mm
Exhaust	0.053 in.	1.346mm
Valve face run-out		
4.9L/5.0L/5.8L/6.9L/7.5L	0.0020 in.	0.05mm
7.3L	0.0015 in.	0.38mm
Valve guide bore		
4.9L/5.0L/5.8L/7.5L		
Intake	0.3433-0.3443 in.	8.7198-8.7452mm
Exhaust	0.3433-0.3443 in.	8.7198-8.7452mm
6.9L/7.3L intake & exhaust	0.3736-0.3746 in.	9.4894-9.5148mm
Valve head diameter		
4.9L		
Intake	1.769-1.793 in.	44.9326-45.5422mm
Exhaust	1.551-1.569 in.	39.3954-39.8526mm
5.0L		
Intake	1.690-1.694 in.	42.926-43.0276mm
Exhaust	1.439-1.463 in.	36.5506-37.1602mm
5.8L (exc. Lightning)		
Intake	1.770-1.794 in.	44.9580-45.5676mm
Exhaust	1.453-1.468 in.	36.9062-37.2872mm
5.8L Lightning		
Intake	1.837-1.847 in.	46.6598-46.9138mm
Exhaust	1.536-1.546 in.	39.0144-39.2684mm
7.5L		
1987		
Intake	2.075-2.090 in.	52.705-53.086mm
Exhaust	1.646-1.661 in.	41.808-42.189mm
1988-93		
Intake	1.965-1.989 in.	49.911-50.521mm
Exhaust	1.646-1.661 in.	41.808-42.189mm
Valve head recession in deck		
6.9L		
Intake	0.042-0.054 in.	1.067-1.372mm
Exhaust	0.043-0.055 in.	1.092-1.397mm
7.3L		
Intake	0.042-0.054 in.	1.067-1.372mm
Exhaust	0.051-0.063 in.	1.295-1.600mm
Valve seat run-out		
4.9L/5.0L/5.8L/6.9L/7.3L/7.5L	0.002 in.	0.05mm
Valve seat width		
4.9L		
Intake		
1987	0.060-0.080 in.	1.524-2.032mm
1988-93	0.060-0.090 in.	1.524-2.286mm
Exhaust	0.070-0.090 in.	1.778-2.286mm
5.0L/5.8L/7.5L		
Intake & exhaust	0.060-0.080 in.	1.524-2.032mm
6.9L/7.3L intake & exhaust	0.065-0.095 in.	1.651-2.413mm
Valve spring compression pressure		
4.9L		
Intake	175 psi @ 1.240 in.	1207kPa @ 31.5mm
Exhaust	175 psi @ 1.070 in.	1207kPa @ 27.2mm

ENGINE MECHANICAL SPECIFICATIONS

Component	U.S.	Metric
5.0L		
Intake	204 psi @ 1.36 in.	1407kPa @ 34.5mm
Exhaust	200 psi @ 1.20 in.	1379kPa @ 30.5mm
5.8L		
Intake	200 psi @ 1.20 in.	1379kPa @ 30.5mm
Exhaust	200 psi @ 1.20 in.	1379kPa @ 30.5mm
6.9L intake & exhaust	60 psi @ 1.798 in.	414kPa @ 45.7mm
7.3L intake & exhaust	80 psi @ 1.833 in.	552kPa @ 46.5mm
7.5L		
Intake	229 psi @ 1.33 in.	1579kPa @ 33.8mm
Exhaust	229 psi @ 1.33 in.	1579kPa @ 33.8mm
Valve spring free length		
4.9L		
Intake	1.96 in.	49.78mm
Exhaust	1.78 in.	45.21mm
5.0L/5.8L		
1987-92 intake & exhaust	2.04 in.	51.8mm
1993 intake & exhaust	2.06 in.	52.3mm
6.9L intake & exhaust	2.04 in.	51.8mm
7.3L intake & exhaust	2.075 in.	52.7mm
7.5L intake & exhaust	2.06 in.	52.3mm
Valve spring installed height		
4.9L		
Intake	1.61-1.67 in.	40.89-42.42mm
Exhaust	1.44-1.50 in.	36.58-38.10mm
5.0L		
1987-92		
Intake	1.67-1.70 in.	42.42-43.18mm
Exhaust	1.58-1.61 in.	40.13-40.89mm
1993		
Intake	1.75-1.81 in.	44.45-45.97mm
Exhaust	1.58-1.64 in.	40.13-41.66mm
5.8L		
1987-92		
Intake	1.77-1.80 in.	44.96-45.72mm
Exhaust	1.58-1.61 in.	40.13-40.89mm
1993		
Intake	1.75-1.81 in.	44.45-45.97mm
Exhaust	1.58-1.64 in.	40.13-41.66mm
6.9L/7.3L		
Intake	1.767 in.	44.88mm
Exhaust	1.833 in.	46.56mm
7.5L		
Intake & exhaust	1.80-1.83 in.	45.72-46.56mm
Valve spring out-of-square		
4.9L/5.0L/5.8L/6.9L/7.3L/7.5L	0.078 in.	1.981mm
Valve stem diameter (standard)		
4.9L		
Intake	0.3416-0.3423 in.	8.6766-8.6944mm
Exhaust	0.3416-0.3423 in.	8.6766-8.6944mm
5.0L/5.8L		
Intake	0.3416-0.3423 in.	8.6766-8.6944mm
Exhaust	0.3411-0.3418 in.	8.6634-8.6817mm
6.9L/7.3L intake & exhaust	0.37165-0.37235 in.	9.4400-9.4577mm
7.5L		
Intake	0.3415-0.3423 in.	8.6741-8.6944mm
Exhaust	0.3415-0.3423 in.	8.6741-8.6944mm

84923231

ENGINE MECHANICAL SPECIFICATIONS

Component	U.S.	Metric
Valve stem-to-guide clearance		
4.9L/7.5L		
Intake	0.0010-0.0027 in.	0.0254-0.0686mm
Exhaust	0.0010-0.0027 in.	0.0254-0.0686mm
5.0L/5.8L		
Intake	0.0010-0.0027 in.	0.0254-0.0686mm
Exhaust	0.0015-0.0032 in.	0.0381-0.0813mm
6.9L intake & exhaust	0.0012-0.0029 in.	0.0305-0.0737mm
7.3L intake & exhaust	0.0055 in.	0.1397mm

TORQUE SPECIFICATIONS

Component	U.S.	Metric
Air Conditioning Compressor		
6-4.9L		
Mounting bolts	50 ft. lbs.	68 Nm
Compressor manifold bolts	13–17 ft. lbs.	18-23 Nm
V8 Gasoline		
Mounting bolts	32 ft. lbs.	44 Nm
Compressor manifold bolts	13–17 ft. lbs.	18-23 Nm
Diesel		
Mounting bolts	32 ft. lbs.	44 Nm
Compressor manifold bolts	13–17 ft. lbs.	18-23 Nm
Alternator		
Adjusting arm-to-support		
Diesel	40-55 ft. lbs.	54-75 Nm
Adjusting arm-to-water pump		
8-7.5L	30-40 ft. lbs.	41-54 Nm
Adjusting bolt		
6-4.9L	25 ft. lbs.	34 Nm
8-5.0L, 8-5.8L, 8-7.5L	30-40 ft. lbs.	41-54 Nm
Diesel	40-55 ft. lbs.	54-75 Nm
Bracket-to-engine		
6-4.9L, except bottom bolt	30-40 ft. lbs.	40-55 Nm
6-4.9L bottom bolt	39-53 ft. lbs.	53-72 Nm
8-5.0L/8-5.8L	40-50 ft. lbs.	54-68 Nm
8-7.5L	30-40 ft. lbs.	41-54 Nm
Diesel	40-55 ft. lbs.	54-75 Nm
Pivot bolt		
6-4.9L	50 ft. lbs.	68 Nm
8-5.0L/8-5.8L		
1987-91	58 ft. lbs.	79 Nm
1992-93	40-50 ft. lbs.	54-68 Nm
8-7.5L	40-53 ft. lbs.	54-71 Nm
Diesel	53-72 ft. lbs.	72-98 Nm
Support bracket-to-water pump		
Diesel	40-55 ft. lbs.	54-75 Nm
Wire terminal nuts	60–90 inch lbs.	7-10 Nm
Bellhousing attaching bolts		
6–4.9L	50 ft. lbs.	68 Nm
8–5.0L/8–5.7L	50 ft. lbs.	68 Nm
8–7.5L	50 ft. lbs.	68 Nm
Diesel	65 ft. lbs.	88 Nm
Camshaft		
Camshaft allen screw		
Diesel	18 ft. lbs.	24 Nm
Gear-to-camshaft		
8-5.0L, 8-5.8L, 8-7.5L	40-45 ft. lbs.	55-61 Nm
Diesel	15 ft. lbs.	20 Nm
Thrust plate attaching screws		
6-4.9L	12-18 ft. lbs.	16-24 Nm
8-5.0L/8-5.8L	9–12 ft. lbs.	12-16 Nm
8-7.5L	70-105 inch lbs.	8-12 Nm
Connecting rod nuts		
6-4.9L	40-45 ft. lbs.	55-61 Nm
8-5.0L	19-24 ft. lbs.	26-32 Nm
8-5.8L	40-45 ft. lbs.	55-61 Nm
8-7.5L	41-45 ft. lbs.	55-61 Nm
Diesel		
Step 1:	38 ft. lbs.	51 Nm
Step 2:	51 ft. lbs.	69 Nm

TORQUE SPECIFICATIONS

Component	U.S.	Metric
Crankshaft damper		
6-4.9L	130-150 ft. lbs.	177-203 Nm
8-5.0L/8-5.8L	70-90 ft. lbs.	95-122 Nm
8-7.5L	70–90 ft. lbs.	95-122 Nm
Diesel	90 ft. lbs.	122 Nm
Crankshaft pulley-to-damper		
6-4.9L	35-50 ft. lbs.	48-68 Nm
8-5.0L/8-5.8L	40-50 ft. lbs.	54-68 Nm
8-7.5L		
1987-91	35-50 ft. lbs.	48-68 Nm
1992-93	40-53 ft. lbs.	54-71 Nm
Cylinder Head		
6-4.9L		
Step 1:	50–55 ft. lbs.	68-75 Nm
Step 2:	60–65 ft. lbs.	82-88 Nm
Step 3:	70–85 ft. lbs.	95-116 Nm
1987 8-5.0L/8-5.8L w/4-bbl. Carburetor		
Step 1:	85 ft. lbs.	116 Nm
Step 2:	95 ft. lbs.	129 Nm
Step 3:	105–112 ft. lbs.	143-152 Nm
8-5.0L with EFI		
Step 1:	55–65 ft. lbs.	75-88 Nm
Step 2:	66–72 ft. lbs.	90-98 Nm
8-5.8L with EFI		
Step 1:	85 ft. lbs.	116 Nm
Step 2:	95 ft. lbs.	129 Nm
Step 3:	105–112 ft. lbs.	143-152 Nm
8-7.5L with 4-bbl Carburetor		
Step 1:	75 ft. lbs.	102 Nm
Step 2:	105 ft.lbs.	143 Nm
Step 3:	135 ft. lbs.	184 Nm
8-7.5L with EFI		
Step 1:	80–90 ft. lbs.	109-122 Nm
Step 2:	100–110 ft.lbs.	136-150 Nm
Step 3:	130–140 ft. lbs.	177-190 Nm
Diesel		
Step 1:	65 ft. lbs.	88 Nm
Step 2:	90 ft. lbs.	122 Nm
Step 3:	110 ft. lbs.	135 Nm
Distributor holddown bolt	25 ft. lbs.	34 Nm
Engine fan and fan clutch		
6-4.9L		
Fan-to-clutch	18 ft. lbs.	24 Nm
Clutch-to-water pump	30-100 ft. lbs.	41-135 Nm
8-5.0L/8-5.8L/8-7.5L	18 ft. lbs.	24 Nm
Diesel		
Fan-to-clutch	18 ft. lbs.	24 Nm
Hub nut	40-120 ft. lbs.	54-163 Nm
Engine mount nuts		
6-4.9L	70 ft. lbs.	95 Nm
8-5.0L/8-5.7L	80 ft. lbs.	109 Nm
8-7.5L	74 ft. lbs.	101 Nm
Diesel	80 ft. lbs.	109 Nm
Engine-to-crossmember nuts		
Diesel	70 ft. lbs.	95 Nm

TORQUE SPECIFICATIONS

Component	U.S.	Metric
Exhaust Manifold		
6-4.9L	22-32 ft. lbs.	30-43 Nm
8-5.0L/8-5.8L	18-24 ft. lbs.	25-32 Nm
8-7.5L	22-45 ft. lbs.	30-60 Nm
Diesel		
Step 1:	35 ft. lbs.	47 Nm
Step 2: retighten to	35 ft. lbs.	47 Nm
Exhaust pipe to the exhaust manifold		
6-4.9L	25-35 ft. lbs.	34 Nm
8-5.0L/8-5.7L	25-35 ft. lbs.	34-48 Nm
Flywheel-to-crankshaft		
6-4.9L	75-85 ft. lbs.	102-115 Nm
8-5.0L/8-5.8L	75-85 ft. lbs.	102-115 Nm
8-7.5L	75-85 ft. lbs.	102-115 Nm
Diesel		
To crankshaft	47 ft. lbs.	64 Nm
Secondary-to-primary	47 ft. lbs.	64 Nm
Front Cover		
6-4.9L	12-18 ft. lbs.	16-24 Nm
8-5.0L/8-5.8L	12-18 ft. lbs.	17-24 Nm
8-7.5L		
1987-91	15-20 ft. lbs.	20-27 Nm
1992-93	12-18 ft. lbs.	17-24 Nm
Diesel		
¼ in.	7 ft. lbs.	10 Nm
⁵⁄₁₆ in.	14 ft. lbs.	19 Nm
⅜ in.	24 ft. lbs.	32 Nm
Fuel pump-to-block		
6-4.9L	12-18 ft. lbs.	17-24 Nm
Fuel pump eccentric bolt		
V8 Gasoline	40-45 ft. lbs.	54-61 Nm
Glow plugs	12 ft. lbs.	16 Nm
Heater hose fitting		
Diesel	18 ft. lbs.	24 Nm
Intake manifold		
Manifold-to-cylinder head		
6-4.9L	26 ft. lbs.	35 Nm
1987 8-5.0L/8-5.8L w/4-bbl Carburetor	23-25 ft. lbs.	31-34 Nm
1987 8-7.5L w/4-bbl Carburetor	23-25 ft. lbs.	31-34 Nm
8-5.0L/8-5.8L w/EFI	23-25 ft. lbs.	31-34 Nm
8-7.5L w/EFI		
Step 1:	8-12 ft. lbs.	11-16 Nm
Step 2:	12-22 ft. lbs.	16-30 Nm
Step 3:	22-35 ft. lbs.	30-47 Nm
Diesel		
Step 1:	24 ft. lbs.	33 Nm
Step 2: Retighten to	24 ft. lbs.	33 Nm
Upper intake manifold-to-lower		
8-5.0L/8-5.8L	12-18 ft. lbs.	17-24 Nm
Main bearing cap bolts		
6-4.9L	60-70 ft. lbs.	82-94 Nm
8-5.0L	60-70 ft. lbs.	82-94 Nm
8-5.8L	95-105 ft. lbs.	129-142 Nm
8-7.5L	95-105 ft. lbs.	129-142 Nm
Diesel		
Step 1:	75 ft. lbs.	101 Nm
Step 2:	95 ft. lbs.	129 Nm

84923235

TORQUE SPECIFICATIONS

Component	U.S.	Metric
Exhaust system		
Inlet pipe-to-manifold	35 ft. lbs.	48 Nm
MTA U-bolt	60–96 inch lbs.	7-11 Nm
Inlet pipe or converter-to-muffler or extension	45 ft. lbs.	61 Nm
Hanger bracket and insulator-to-frame	24 ft. lbs.	33 Nm
Bracket and insulator-to-exhaust	15 ft. lbs.	20 Nm
Flat flange bolts		
8–7.5L	30 ft. lbs.	41 Nm
Diesel	30 ft. lbs.	41 Nm
Oil cooler-to-block		
8-7.5L	40-65 ft. lbs.	54-88 Nm
Oil Pan-to-block		
6–4.9L	10–12 ft. lbs.	14-16 Nm
8-5.0L/8-5.8L		
1987-91	10–12 ft. lbs.	14-16 Nm
1992-93	9-11 ft. lbs.	12-14 Nm
8–7.5L		
1/4 in.	7-9 ft. lbs.	10-12 Nm
5/16 in.	8-11 ft. lbs.	11-15 Nm
Diesel		
1/4 in.-20 bolts	7 ft. lbs.	10 Nm
5/16 in.-18 bolts	14 ft. lbs.	19 Nm
3/8 in.-16 bolts	24 ft. lbs.	33 Nm
Oil pan drain plug		
6-4.9L	15-25 ft. lbs.	21-33 Nm
8-5.0L/8-5.8L	15-25 ft. lbs.	21-33 Nm
8-7.5L	15-25 ft. lbs.	21-33 Nm
Diesel	28 ft. lbs.	37 Nm
Oil Pump-to-block		
6-4.9L	12–15 ft. lbs.	16-20 Nm
8-5.0L/8-5.8L		
1987-91	20–25 ft. lbs.	27-34 Nm
1992-93	22-32 ft. lbs.	30-43 Nm
8-7.5L	22-32 ft. lbs.	30-43 Nm
Diesel	14 ft. lbs.	19 Nm
Rocker arm bolts		
6-4.9L	17-23 ft. lbs.	24-31 Nm
8-5.0L/8-5.8L	18–25 ft. lbs.	24-34 Nm
8-7.5L	18–25 ft. lbs.	24-34 Nm
Diesel	20 ft.lbs.	27 Nm
Rocker arm stud-to-head		
8-5.0L/8-5.8L	18-25 ft. lbs.	25-33 Nm
8-7.5L	18-25 ft. lbs.	25-33 Nm
Rocker Covers		
6-4.9L		
1987-91	48-84 inch lbs.	5-9 Nm
1992-93	70-105 inch lbs.	8-12 Nm
8-5.0L/8-5.8L		
1987-91	10-13 ft. lbs.	14-18 Nm
1992-93	36-60 inch lbs.	4-6 Nm
8-7.5L		
1987-91	6-9 ft. lbs.	8-12 Nm
1992-93	9-11 ft. lbs.	12-15 Nm
Diesel	72 inch lbs.	8 Nm
Side cover		
6-4.9L	25-35 inch lbs.	3-4 Nm

84923236

TORQUE SPECIFICATIONS

Component	U.S.	Metric
Spark plugs		
6-4.9L	10-15 ft. lbs.	14-20 Nm
8-5.0L/8-5.8L	10-15 ft. lbs.	14-20 Nm
8-7.5L	5-10 ft. lbs.	7-13 Nm
Starter Mounting bolts		
Exc. diesel		
Starters w/3 mounting bolts	12–15 ft. lbs.	16-20 Nm
Starters w/2 mounting bolts	15–20 ft. lbs.	20-27 Nm
Diesel	20 ft. lbs.	
Thermostat housing		
6–4.9L	15 ft. lbs.	20 Nm
8-5.0L/8-5.8L		
1987-91	18 ft. lbs.	24 Nm
1992-93	9-12 ft. lbs.	13-16 Nm
8-7.5L		
1987-91	28 ft. lbs.	38 Nm
1992-93	12-18 ft. lbs.	16-24 Nm
Diesel	20 ft. lbs.	27 Nm
Torque converter-to-flywheel		
8–5.0L/8–5.7L	30 ft. lbs.	41 Nm
8–7.5L	34 ft. lbs.	46 Nm
Diesel	34 ft. lbs.	46 Nm
Torque converter inspection plate bolts		
8–5.0L/8–5.7L	60 inch lbs.	7 Nm
8–7.5L	60–90 inch lbs.	7-8 Nm
Diesel	60–90 inch lbs.	7-8 Nm
Vacuum pump		
Bracket and pump		
Diesel	14-19 ft. lbs.	19-26 Nm
Water Pump bolts		
6–4.9L	18 ft. lbs.	24 Nm
8–5.0L/8–5.8L	18 ft. lbs.	24 Nm
8-7.5L	12-18 ft. lbs.	16-24 Nm
Diesel	14 ft. lbs.	19 Nm

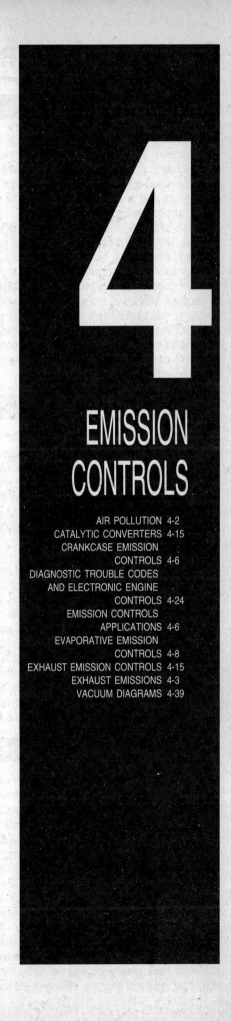

4

EMISSION CONTROLS

AIR POLLUTION

The earth's atmosphere, at or near sea level, consists of 78% nitrogen, 21% oxygen and 1% other gases, approximately. If it were possible to remain in this state, 100% clean air would result. However, many varied causes allow other gases and particulates to mix with the clean air, causing the air to become unclean or polluted.

Certain of these pollutants are visible while others are invisible, with each having the capability of causing distress to the eyes, ears, throat, skin and respiratory system. Should these pollutants be concentrated in a specific area and under the right conditions, death could result due to the displacement or chemical change of the oxygen content in the air. These pollutants can cause much damage to the environment and to the many man made objects that are exposed to the elements.

To better understand the causes of air pollution, the pollutants can be categorized into 3 separate types, natural, industrial and automotive.

Natural Pollutants

Natural pollution has been present on earth before man appeared and is still a factor to be considered when discussing air pollution, although it causes only a small percentage of the present overall pollution problem existing in our country. It is the direct result of decaying organic matter, wind born smoke and particulates from such natural events as plains and forest fires (ignited by heat or lightning), volcanic ash, sand and dust which can spread over a large area of the countryside.

Such a phenomenon of natural pollution has been recent volcanic eruptions, with the resulting plume of smoke, steam and volcanic ash blotting out the sun's rays as it spreads and rises higher into the atmosphere, where the upper air currents catch and carry the smoke and ash, while condensing the steam back into water vapor. As the water vapor, smoke and ash traveled on their journey, the smoke dissipates into the atmosphere while the ash and moisture settle back to earth in a trail hundreds of miles long. In many cases, lives are lost and millions of dollars of property damage result, and ironically, man can only stand by and watch it happen.

Industrial Pollution

Industrial pollution is caused primarily by industrial processes, the burning of coal, oil and natural gas, which in turn produces smoke and fumes. Because the burning fuels contain much sulfur, the principal ingredients of smoke and fumes are sulfur dioxide (SO_2) and particulate matter. This type of pollutant occurs most severely during still, damp and cool weather, such as at night. Even in its less severe form, this pollutant is not confined to just cities. Because of air movements, the pollutants move for miles over the surrounding countryside, leaving in its path a barren and unhealthy environment for all living things.

Working with Federal, State and Local mandated rules, regulations and by carefully monitoring the emissions, industries have greatly reduced the amount of pollutant emitted from their industrial sources, striving to obtain an acceptable level. Because of the mandated industrial emission clean up, many land areas and streams in and around the cities that were formerly barren of vegetation and life, have now begun to move back in the direction of nature's intended balance.

Automotive Pollutants

The third major source of air pollution is the automotive emissions. The emissions from the internal combustion engine were not an appreciable problem years ago because of the small number of registered vehicles and the nation's small highway system. However, during the early 1950's, the trend of the American people was to move from the cities to the surrounding suburbs. This caused an immediate problem in the transportation areas because the majority of the suburbs were not afforded mass transit conveniences. This lack of transportation created an attractive market for the automobile manufacturers, which resulted in a dramatic increase in the number of vehicles produced and sold, along with a marked increase in highway construction between cities and the suburbs. Multi-vehicle families emerged with much emphasis placed on the individual vehicle per family member. As the increase in vehicle ownership and usage occurred, so did the pollutant levels in and around the cities, as the suburbanites drove daily to their businesses and employment in the city and its fringe area returning at the end of the day to their homes in the suburbs.

It was noted that a fog and smoke type haze was being formed and at times, remained in suspension over the cities and did not quickly dissipate. At first this 'smog', derived from the words 'smoke' and 'fog', was thought to result from industrial pollution but it was determined that the automobile emissions were largely to blame. It was discovered that as normal automobile emissions were exposed to sunlight for a period of time, complex chemical reactions would take place.

It was found the smog was a photo chemical layer and was developed when certain oxides of nitrogen (NOx) and unburned hydrocarbons (HC) from the automobile emissions were exposed to sunlight and was more severe when the smog would remain stagnant over an area in which a warm layer of air would settle over the top of a cooler air mass at ground level, trapping and holding the automobile emissions, instead of the emissions being dispersed and diluted through normal air flows. This type of air stagnation was given the name 'Temperature Inversion'.

Temperature Inversion

In normal weather situations, the surface air is warmed by the heat radiating from the earth's surface and the sun's rays and will rise upward, into the atmosphere, to be cooled through a convection type heat expands with the cooler upper air. As the warm air rises, the surface pollutants are carried upward and dissipated into the atmosphere.

When a temperature inversion occurs, we find the higher air is no longer cooler but warmer than the surface air, causing the cooler surface air to become trapped and unable to move. This warm air blanket can extend from above ground level to a few hundred or even a few thousand feet into the air. As the surface air is trapped, so are the pollutants, causing a severe smog condition. Should this stagnant air mass extend to a few thousand feet high, enough air movement with the inversion takes place to allow the smog layer to rise above ground level but the pollutants still cannot dissipate. This inversion can remain for days over an area, with only the smog level rising or lowering from ground level to a few hundred feet high. Meanwhile, the pollutant levels increases, causing eye irritation, respirator problems, reduced visibility, plant damage and in some cases, cancer type diseases.

This inversion phenomenon was first noted in the Los Angeles, California area. The city lies in a basin type of terrain and during certain weather conditions, a cold air mass is held in the basin while a warmer air mass covers it like a lid.

Because this type of condition was first documented as prevalent in the Los Angeles area, this type of smog was named Los Angeles Smog, although it occurs in other areas where a large concentration of automobiles are used and the air remains stagnant for any length of time.

Internal Combustion Engine Pollutants

Consider the internal combustion engine as a machine in which raw materials must be placed so a finished product comes out. As in any machine operation, a certain amount of wasted material is formed. When we relate this to the internal combustion engine, we find that by putting in air and fuel, we obtain power from this mixture during the combustion process to drive the vehicle. The by-product or waste of this power is, in part, heat and exhaust gases with which we must concern ourselves.

EXHAUST EMISSIONS

Composition Of The Exhaust Gases

The exhaust gases emitted into the atmosphere are a combination of burned and unburned fuel. To understand the exhaust emission and its composition review some basic chemistry.

When the air/fuel mixture is introduced into the engine, we are mixing air, composed of nitrogen (78%), oxygen (21%) and other gases (1%) with the fuel, which is 100% hydrocarbons (HC), in a semi-controlled ratio. As the combustion process is accomplished, power is produced to move the vehicle while the heat of combustion is transferred to the cooling system. The exhaust gases are then composed of nitrogen, a diatomic gas (N2), the same as was introduced in the engine, carbon dioxide (CO2), the same gas that is used in beverage carbonation and water vapor (H2O). The nitrogen (N2), for the most part passes through the engine unchanged, while the oxygen (O_2) reacts (burns) with the hydrocarbons (HC) and produces the carbon dioxide (CO_2) and the water vapors (H2O). If this chemical process would be the only process to take place, the exhaust emissions would be harmless. However, during the combustion process, other pollutants are formed and are considered dangerous. These pollutants are carbon monoxide (CO), hydrocarbons (HC), oxides of nitrogen (NOx) oxides of sulfur (SOx) and engine particulates.

HEAT TRANSFER

The heat from the combustion process can rise to over 4000°F (2204°C). The dissipation of this heat is controlled by a ram air effect, the use of cooling fans to cause air flow and having a liquid coolant solution surrounding the combustion area and transferring the heat of combustion through the cylinder walls and into the coolant. The coolant is then directed to a thin-finned, multi-tubed radiator, from which the excess heat is transferred to the outside air by 1 or all of the 3 heat transfer methods, conduction, convection or radiation.

The cooling of the combustion area is an important part in the control of exhaust emissions. To understand the behavior of the combustion and transfer of its heat, consider the air/fuel charge. It is ignited and the flame front burns progressively across the combustion chamber until the burning charge reaches the cylinder walls. Some of the fuel in contact with the walls is not hot enough to burn, thereby snuffing out or Quenching the combustion process. This leaves unburned fuel in the combustion chamber. This unburned fuel is then forced out of the cylinder along with the exhaust gases and into the exhaust system.

Many attempts have been made to minimize the amount of unburned fuel in the combustion chambers due to the snuffing out or 'Quenching', by increasing the coolant temperature and lessening the contact area of the coolant around the combustion area. Design limitations within the combustion chambers prevent the complete burning of the air/fuel charge, so a certain amount of the unburned fuel is still expelled into the exhaust system, regardless of modifications to the engine.

Lead (Pb), is considered 1 of the particulates and is present in the exhaust gases whenever leaded fuels are used. Lead (Pb) does not dissipate easily. Levels can be high along roadways when it is emitted from vehicles and can pose a health threat. Since the increased usage of unleaded gasoline and the phasing out of leaded gasoline for fuel, this pollutant is gradually diminishing. While not considered a major threat lead is still considered a dangerous pollutant.

HYDROCARBONS

Hydrocarbons (HC) are essentially unburned fuel that have not been successfully burned during the combustion process or have escaped into the atmosphere through fuel evaporation. The main sources of incomplete combustion are rich air/fuel mixtures, low engine temperatures and improper spark timing. The main sources of hydrocarbon emission through fuel evaporation come from the vehicle's fuel tank and carburetor bowl.

To reduce combustion hydrocarbon emission, engine modifications were made to minimize dead space and surface area in the combustion chamber. In addition the air/fuel mixture was made more lean through improved carburetion, fuel injection and by the addition of external controls to aid in further combustion of the hydrocarbons outside the engine.

Two such methods were the addition of an air injection system, to inject fresh air into the exhaust manifolds and the installation of a catalytic converter, a unit that is able to burn traces of hydrocarbons without affecting the internal combustion process or fuel economy.

To control hydrocarbon emissions through fuel evaporation, modifications were made to the fuel tank and carburetor bowl to allow storage of the fuel vapors during periods of engine shut-down, and at specific times during engine operation, to purge and burn these same vapors by blending them with the air/fuel mixture.

CARBON MONOXIDE

Carbon monoxide is formed when not enough oxygen is present during the combustion process to convert carbon (C) to carbon dioxide (CO_2). An increase in the carbon monoxide (CO) emission is normally accompanied by an increase in the hydrocarbon (HC) emission because of the lack of oxygen to completely burn all of the fuel mixture.

Carbon monoxide (CO) also increases the rate at which the photo chemical smog is formed by speeding up the conversion of nitric oxide (NO) to nitrogen dioxide (NO_2). To accomplish this, carbon monoxide (CO) combines with oxygen (O_2) and nitrogen dioxide (NO_2) to produce carbon dioxide (CO_2) and nitrogen dioxide (NO_2). ($CO + O_2 + NO = CO_2 + NO_2$).

The dangers of carbon monoxide, which is an odorless, colorless toxic gas are many. When carbon monoxide is inhaled into the lungs and passed into the blood stream, oxygen is replaced by the carbon monoxide in the red blood cells, causing a reduction in the amount of oxygen being supplied to the many parts of the body. This lack of oxygen causes headaches, lack of coordination, reduced mental alertness and should the carbon monoxide concentration be high enough, death could result.

NITROGEN

Normally, nitrogen is an inert gas. When heated to approximately 2500°F (1371°C) through the combustion process, this gas becomes active and causes an increase in the nitric oxide (NOx) emission.

Oxides of nitrogen (NOx) are composed of approximately 97-98% nitric oxide (NO2). Nitric oxide is a colorless gas but when it is passed into the atmosphere, it combines with oxygen and forms nitrogen dioxide (NO2). The nitrogen dioxide then combines with chemically active hydrocarbons (HC) and when in the presence of sunlight, causes the formation of photo chemical smog.

OZONE

To further complicate matters, some of the nitrogen dioxide (NO2) is broken apart by the sunlight to form nitric oxide and oxygen. (NO2 + sunlight = NO + O). This single atom of oxygen then combines with diatomic (meaning 2 atoms) oxygen (O2) to form ozone (O3). Ozone is 1 of the smells associated with smog. It has a pungent and offensive odor,

irritates the eyes and lung tissues, affects the growth of plant life and causes rapid deterioration of rubber products. Ozone can be formed by sunlight as well as electrical discharge into the air.

The most common discharge area on the automobile engine is the secondary ignition electrical system, especially when inferior quality spark plug cables are used. As the surge of high voltage is routed through the secondary cable, the circuit builds up an electrical field around the wire, acting upon the oxygen in the surrounding air to form the ozone. The faint glow along the cable with the engine running that may be visible on a dark night, is called the 'corona discharge.' It is the result of the electrical field passing from a high along the cable, to a low in the surrounding air, which forms the ozone gas. The combination of corona and ozone has been a major cause of cable deterioration. Recently, different types and better quality insulating materials have lengthened the life of the electrical cables.

Although ozone at ground level can be harmful, ozone is beneficial to the earth's inhabitants. By having a concentrated ozone layer called the 'ozonosphere', between 10 and 20 miles (16-32km) up in the atmosphere much of the ultra violet radiation from the sun's rays are absorbed and screened. If this ozone layer were not present, much of the earth's surface would be burned, dried and unfit for human life.

There is much discussion concerning the ozone layer and its density. A feeling exists that this protective layer of ozone is slowly diminishing and corrective action must be directed to this problem. Much experimenting is presently being conducted to determine if a problem exists and if so, the short and long term effects of the problem and how it can be remedied.

OXIDES OF SULFUR

Oxides of sulfur (SOx) were initially ignored in the exhaust system emissions, since the sulfur content of gasoline as a fuel is less than 1/10 of 1%. Because of this small amount, it was felt that it contributed very little to the overall pollution problem. However, because of the difficulty in solving the sulfur emissions in industrial pollutions and the introduction of catalytic converter to the automobile exhaust systems, a change was mandated. The automobile exhaust system, when equipped with a catalytic converter, changes the sulfur dioxide (SO2) into the sulfur trioxide (SO3).

When this combines with water vapors (H2O), a sulfuric acid mist (H2SO4) is formed and is a very difficult pollutant to handle and is extremely corrosive. This sulfuric acid mist that is formed, is the same mist that rises from the vents of an automobile storage battery when an active chemical reaction takes place within the battery cells.

When a large concentration of vehicles equipped with catalytic converters are operating in an area, this acid mist will rise and be distributed over a large ground area causing land, plant, crop, paints and building damage.

PARTICULATE MATTER

A certain amount of particulate matter is present in the burning of any fuel, with carbon constituting the largest percentage of the particulates. In gasoline, the remaining percentage of particulates is the burned remains of the various other compounds used in its manufacture. When a gasoline engine is in good internal condition, the particulate emissions are low but as the engine wears internally, the particulate emissions increase. By visually inspecting the tail pipe emissions, a determination can be made as to where an engine defect may exist. An engine with light gray smoke emitting from the tail pipe normally indicates an increase in the oil consumption through burning due to internal engine wear. Black smoke would indicate a defective fuel delivery system, causing the engine to operate in a rich mode. Regardless of the color of the smoke, the internal part of the engine or the fuel delivery system should be repaired to a 'like new' condition to prevent excess particulate emissions.

Diesel and turbine engines emit a darkened plume of smoke from the exhaust system because of the type of fuel used. Emission control regulations are mandated for this type of emission and more stringent measures are being used to prevent excess emission of the particulate matter. Electronic components are being introduced to control the injection of the fuel at precisely the proper time of piston travel, to achieve the optimum in fuel ignition and fuel usage. Other particulate after-burning components are being tested to achieve a cleaner particular emission.

Good grades of engine lubricating oils should be used, meeting the manufacturers specification. 'Cut-rate' oils can contribute to the particulate emission problem because of their low 'flash' or ignition temperature point. Such oils burn prematurely during the combustion process causing emissions of particulate matter.

The cooling system is an important factor in the reduction of particulate matter. With the cooling system operating at a temperature specified by the manufacturer, the optimum of combustion will occur. The cooling system must be maintained in the same manner as the engine oiling system, as each system is required to perform properly in order for the engine to operate efficiently for a long time.

Other Automobile Emission Sources

Before emission controls were mandated on the internal combustion engines, other sources of engine pollutants were discovered, along with the exhaust emission. It was determined the engine combustion exhaust produced 60% of the total emission pollutants, fuel evaporation from the fuel tank and carburetor vents produced 20%, with the another 20% being produced through the crankcase as a by-product of the combustion process.

CRANKCASE EMISSIONS

Crankcase emissions are made up of water, acids, unburned fuel, oil fumes and particulates. The emissions are classified as hydrocarbons (HC) and are formed by the small amount of unburned, compressed air/fuel mixture entering the crankcase from the combustion area during the compression and power strokes, between the cylinder walls and piston rings. The head of the compression and combustion help to form the remaining crankcase emissions.

Since the first engines, crankcase emissions were allowed to go into the air through a road draft tube, mounted on the lower side of the engine block. Fresh air came in through an open oil filler cap or breather. The air passed through the crankcase mixing with blow-by gases. The motion of the vehicle and the air blowing past the open end of the road draft tube caused a low pressure area at the end of the tube. Crankcase emissions were simply drawn out of the road draft tube into the air.

To control the crankcase emission, the road draft tube was deleted. A hose and/or tubing was routed from the crankcase to the intake manifold so the blow-by emission could be burned with the air/fuel mixture. However, it was found that intake manifold vacuum, used to draw the crankcase emissions into the manifold, would vary in strength at the wrong time and not allow the proper emission flow. A regulating type valve was needed to control the flow of air through the crankcase.

Testing, showed the removal of the blow-by gases from the crankcase as quickly as possible, was most important to the longevity of the engine. Should large accumulations of blow-by gases remain and condense, dilution of the engine oil would occur to form water, soots, resins, acids and lead salts, resulting in the formation of sludge and varnishes. This condensation of the blow-by gases occur more frequently on vehicles used in numerous starting and stopping conditions, excessive idling and when the engine is not allowed to attain normal operating temperature through short runs. The crankcase purge control or PCV system will be described in detail later in this section.

FUEL EVAPORATIVE EMISSIONS

Gasoline fuel is a major source of pollution, before and after it is burned in the automobile engine. From the time the fuel is refined, stored, pumped and transported, again stored until it is pumped into the fuel tank of the vehicle, the gasoline gives off unburned hydrocarbons (HC) into the atmosphere. Through redesigning of the storage areas and venting systems, the pollution factor has been diminished but not eliminated, from the refinery standpoint. However, the automobile still remained the primary source of vaporized, unburned hydrocarbon (HC) emissions.

Fuel pumped form an underground storage tank is cool but when exposed to a warmer ambient temperature, will expand. Before controls were mandated, an owner would fill the fuel tank with fuel from an underground storage tank and park the vehicle for some time in a warm area, such as a parking lot. As the fuel would warm, it would expand and should no provisions or area be provided for the expansion, the fuel would spill out the filler neck and onto the ground, causing hydrocarbon (HC) pollution and creating a severe fire hazard. To correct this condition, the vehicle manufacturers added overflow plumbing and/or gasoline tanks with built in expansion areas or domes.

However, this did not control the fuel vapor emission from the fuel tank and the carburetor bowl. It was determined that most of the fuel evaporation occurred when the vehicle was stationary and the engine not operating. Most vehicles carry 5-25 gallons (19-95 liters) of gasoline. Should a large concentration of vehicles be parked in one area, such as a large parking lot, excessive fuel vapor emissions would take place, increasing as the temperature increases.

To prevent the vapor emission from escaping into the atmosphere, the fuel system is designed to trap the fuel vapors while the vehicle is stationary, by sealing the fuel system from the atmosphere. A storage system is used to collect and hold the fuel vapors from the carburetor and the fuel tank when the engine is not operating. When the engine is started, the storage system is then purged of the fuel vapors, which are drawn into the engine and burned with the air/fuel mixture.

The components of the fuel evaporative system will be described in detail later in this section.

EMISSION CONTROLS APPLICATIONS

6-4.9L:
Positive Crankcase Ventilation system (PCV)
Evaporative Emission system (canister)
Three-way Catalyst (TWC)
Conventional Oxidation Catalyst (COC)
Electronic Fuel Injection Fuel System (EFI)
Electronic Engine Control IV system (EEC-IV)
Electronic (Sonic) Exhaust Gas Recirculation (EEGR)
Managed Thermactor Air system (MTA)
Air Management 1 system (AM1)
Air Management 2 system (AM2)
Thick Film Ignition system (TFI-IV)
Bypass Air idle speed control (BPA)
8-5.0L & 8-5.8L w/4-bbl Carburetor:
Positive Crankcase Ventilation system (PCV)
Evaporative Emission system (canister)
Three-way Catalyst (TWC)
Conventional Oxidation Catalyst (COC)
Holley 4180C 4-bbl carburetor
Integral backpressure EGR valve (IBP)
Managed Thermactor Air System (MTA)
Dura Spark II Ignition System (DS-II)
8-5.0L & 8-5.8L w/Fuel Injection:
Positive Crankcase Ventilation system (PCV)
Evaporative Emission system (canister)
Three-way Catalyst (TWC)
Conventional Oxidation Catalyst (COC)

Electronic Fuel Injection Fuel System (EFI)
Electronic Engine Control IV system (EEC-IV)
Electronic (Sonic) Exhaust Gas Recirculation (EEGR)
Managed Thermactor Air system (MTA)
Air Management 1 system (AM1)
Air Management 2 system (AM2)
Thick Film Ignition system (TFI-IV)
Bypass Air idle speed control (BPA)
8-7.5L w/4-bbl Carburetor:
Positive Crankcase Ventilation system (PCV)
Evaporative Emission system (canister)
Holley 4180C 4-bbl carburetor
Exhaust Gas Recirculation system (EGR)
Managed Thermactor Air System (MTA)
Dura Spark II Ignition System (DS-II)
8-7.5L w/Fuel Injection:
Positive Crankcase Ventilation system (PCV)
Evaporative Emission system (canister)
4 Reduction-Oxidation Catalysts (REDOX)
Electronic Fuel Injection fuel system (EFI)
Electronic Engine Control IV system (EEC-IV)
Electronic (Sonic) Exhaust Gas Recirculation (EEGR)
Managed Thermactor Air System (MTA)
Thick Film Ignition ignition system (TFI-IV)
Bypass Air idle speed control (BPA)

CRANKCASE EMISSION CONTROLS

Positive Crankcase Ventilation System

▶ **See Figures 1, 2 and 3**

The crankcase emission control equipment consists of a positive crankcase ventilation (PCV) valve, a closed oil filler cap and the hoses that connect this equipment.

When the engine is running, a small portion of the gases which are formed in the combustion chamber leak by the piston rings and enter the crankcase. Since these gases are under pressure they tend to escape from the crankcase and enter into the atmosphere. If these gases are allowed to remain in the crankcase for any length of time, they would contaminate the engine oil and cause sludge to build up. If the gases are allowed to escape into the atmosphere, they would pollute the air, as they contain unburned hydrocarbons. The crankcase emission control equipment recycles these gases back into the engine combustion chamber, where they are burned.

Crankcase gases are recycled in the following manner. While the engine is running, clean filtered air is drawn into the crank-

case through the intake air filter and then through a hose leading to the oil filler cap. As the air passes through the crankcase it picks up the combustion gases and carries them out of the crankcase, up through the PCV valve and into the intake manifold. After they enter the intake manifold they are drawn into the combustion chamber and are burned.

The most critical component of the system is the PCV valve. This vacuum-controlled valve regulates the amount of gases which are recycled into the combustion chamber. At low engine speeds the valve is partially closed, limiting the flow of gases into the intake manifold. As engine speed increases, the valve opens to admit greater quantities of the gases into the intake manifold. If the valve should become blocked or plugged, the gases will be prevented from escaping the crankcase by the normal route. Since these gases are under pressure, they will find their own way out of the crankcase. This alternate route is usually a weak oil seal or gasket in the engine. As the gas escapes by the gasket, it also creates an oil leak. Besides causing oil leaks, a clogged PCV valve also allows these gases to remain in the crankcase for an extended

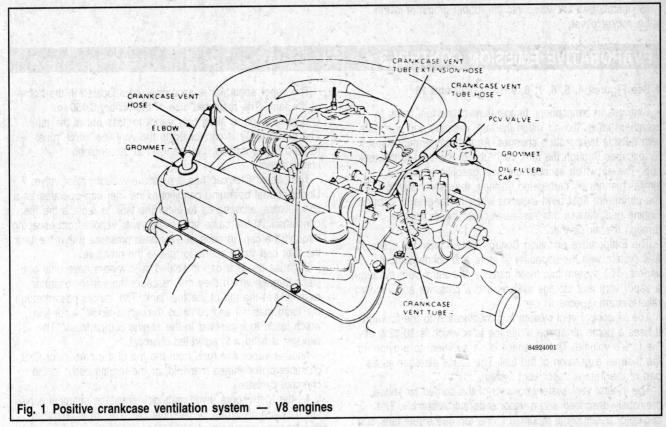

Fig. 1 Positive crankcase ventilation system — V8 engines

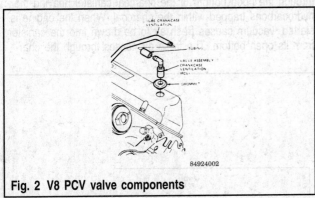

Fig. 2 V8 PCV valve components

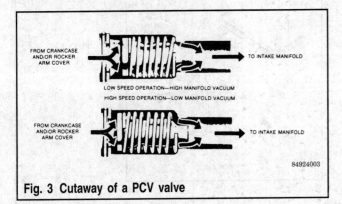

Fig. 3 Cutaway of a PCV valve

period of time, promoting the formation of sludge in the engine.

The above explanation and the troubleshooting procedure which follows applies to all of the gasoline engines installed in Ford trucks, since all are equipped with PCV systems.

TROUBLESHOOTING

With the engine running, pull the PCV valve and hose from the valve rocker cover rubber grommet.

A hissing noise should be heard as air passes through the valve and a strong vacuum should be felt when you place a finger over the valve inlet if the valve is working properly. While you have your finger over the PCV valve inlet, check for vacuum leaks in the hose and at the connections.

When the PCV valve is removed from the engine, a metallic clicking noise should be heard when it is shaken. This indicates that the metal check ball inside the valve is still free and is not gummed up.

REPLACEMENT

1. Pull the PCV valve and hose from the rubber grommet in the rocker cover.
2. Remove the PCV valve from the hose. Inspect the inside of the PCV valve. If it is dirty, disconnect it from the intake manifold and replace it.
To install:
3. If the PCV valve hose was removed, connect it to the intake manifold.
4. Connect the PCV valve to its hose.

5. Install the PCV valve into the rubber grommet in the valve rocker cover.

EVAPORATIVE EMISSION CONTROLS

▶ **See Figures 4, 5, 6, 7, 8, 9, 10, 11, 12 and 13**

Changes in atmospheric temperature cause fuel tanks to breathe; that is, the air within the tank expands and contracts with outside temperature changes. As the temperature rises, air escapes through the tank vent tube or the vent in the tank cap. The air which escapes contains gasoline vapors. In a similar manner on carbureted engines, the gasoline which fills the carburetor float bowl expands when the engine is stopped. Engine heat causes this expansion. The vapors escape through the air cleaner.

The Evaporative Emission Control System provides a sealed fuel system with the capability to store and condense fuel vapors. The system has three parts: a fill control vent system; a vapor vent and storage system; and a pressure and vacuum relief system (special fill cap).

The fill control vent system is a modification to the fuel tank. It uses a dome air space within the tank which is 10-12% of the tank's volume. The air space is is sufficient to provide for the thermal expansion of the fuel. The space also serves as part of the in-tank vapor vent system.

The in-tank vent system consists of the domed air space previously described and a vapor separator assembly. The separator assembly is mounted to the top of the fuel tank and is secured by a cam-lockring, similar to the one which secures the fuel sending unit. Foam material fills the vapor separator assembly. The foam material separates raw fuel and vapors, thus retarding the entrance of fuel into the vapor line.

The vapor separator is an orifice valve located in the dome of the tank. The restricted size of the orifice, 0.050 in. (1.27mm) tends to allow only vapor to pass out of the tank. The orifice valve is connected to the vent line which runs forward to the carbon filled canister in the engine compartment.

The sealed filler cap has a pressure-vacuum relief valve. Under normal operating conditions, the filler cap operates as a check valve, allowing air to enter the tank to replace the fuel consumed. At the same time, it prevents vapors from escaping through the cap. In case of excessive pressure within the tank, the filler cap valve opens to relieve the pressure.

Because the filler cap is sealed, fuel vapors have only one place through which they may escape: the vapor separator assembly at the top of the fuel tank. The vapors pass through the foam material and continue through a single vapor line which leads to a canister in the engine compartment. The canister is filled with activated charcoal.

Another vapor line runs from the top of the carburetor float chamber or the intake manifold, or the throttle body, to the charcoal canister.

As the fuel vapors (hydrocarbons), enter the charcoal canister, they are absorbed by the charcoal. The air is dispelled through the open bottom of the charcoal canister, leaving the hydrocarbons trapped within the charcoal. When the engine is started, vacuum causes fresh air to be drawn into the canister from its open bottom. The fresh air passes through the char-

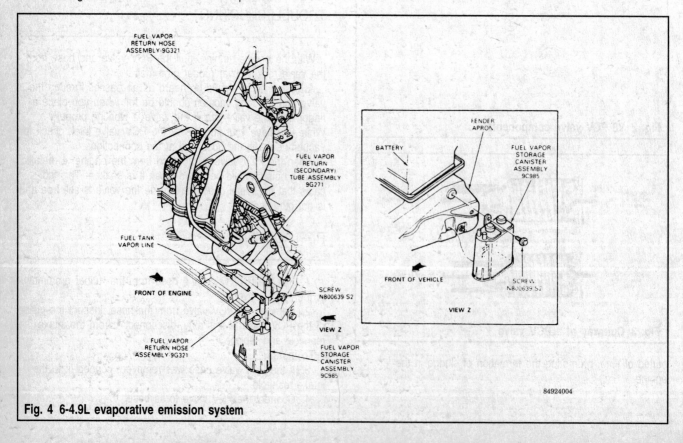

Fig. 4 6-4.9L evaporative emission system

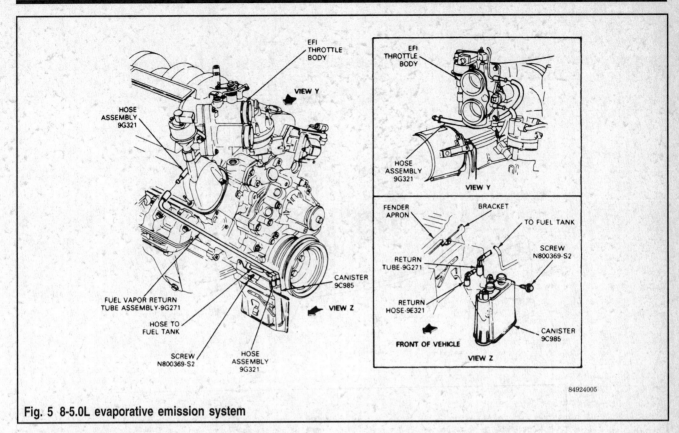

Fig. 5 8-5.0L evaporative emission system

coal picking up the hydrocarbons which are trapped there and feeding them into the engine for burning with the fuel mixture.

Diagnosis and Testing

CANISTER PURGE REGULATOR VALVE

1. Disconnect the hoses at the purge regulator valve. Disconnect the electrical lead.
2. Connect a vacuum pump to the vacuum source port.
3. Apply 5 in. Hg to the port. The valve should hold the vacuum. If not, replace it.

CANISTER PURGE VALVE

1. Apply vacuum to port **A**. The valve should hold vacuum. If not, replace it.
2. Apply vacuum to port **B**. Valves E5VE-AA, E4VE-AA and E77E-AA should show a slight vacuum leak-down. All other valves should hold vacuum. If the valve doesn't operate properly, replace it.
3. Apply 16 in. Hg to port **A** and apply vacuum to port **B**. Air should pass. On valves E5VE-AA, E4VE-AA and E77E-AA, the flow should be greater than that noted in Step 2.

➡**Never apply vacuum to port C. Doing so will damage the valve.**

4. If the valve fails to perform properly in any of these tests, replace it.

FUEL TANK VAPOR ORIFICE AND ROLLOVER VALVE ASSEMBLY

Fuel vapor in the fuel tank is vented to the carbon canister through the vapor valve assembly. The valve is mounted in a rubber grommet at a central location in the upper surface of the fuel tank. A vapor space between the fuel level and the tank upper surface is combined with a small orifice and float shut-off valve in the vapor valve assembly to prevent liquid fuel from passing to the carbon canister. The vapor space also allows for thermal expansion of the fuel.

FUEL BOWL SOLENOID VENT VALVE

The fuel bowl solenoid vent valve is located in the fuel bowl vent line on carbureted engines. The valve is open when the ignition switch is in the **OFF** position and closes when the engine is running.

➡**If lean fuel mixture is suspected as the cause of improper engine operation, check either the solenoid vent valve or the carburetor's built-in fuel bowl vent valve to make sure they are closed when the engine is running. If the valve is open, purge vacuum will affect the fuel bowl balanced air pressure, and the carburetor will have a leaner air/fuel mixture.**

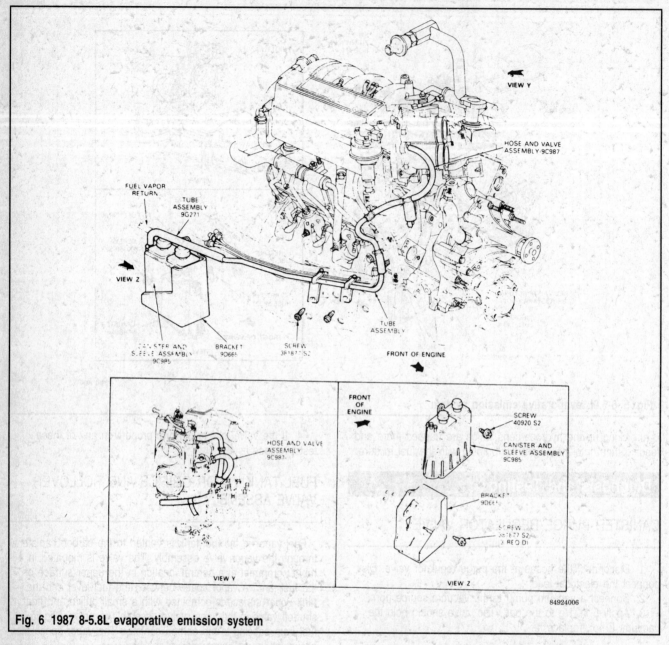

Fig. 6 1987 8-5.8L evaporative emission system

FUEL BOWL THERMAL VENT VALVE

The thermal vent valve is located in the carburetor-to-carbon canister vent line. The valve's function is to prevent fuel tank vapors from being vented through the carburetor fuel bowl when the engine is cold.

The valve is closed when the engine compartment is cold, blocking fuel vapors from entering the now-open carburetor fuel bowl vent, and instead routing them to the carbon canister. When the engine runs and the engine compartment warms up, the thermal vent valve opens. When the engine is turned off, the fuel bowl (or solenoid) vent valve opens, allowing fuel vapor to flow through the open thermal vent valve and into the carbon canister. The thermal vent valve closes as it cools, and the cycle repeats.

AUXILIARY FUEL BOWL VENT TUBE

On some carbureted vehicles, an auxiliary fuel bowl vent tube is connected to the fuel bowl vent tube to vent the fuel bowl when the internal fuel bowl vent or the solenoid vent valve is closed and the thermal vent valve is also closed. An air filter is installed on the air cleaner end of the tube to prevent the entrance of contaminants into the carburetor fuel bowl.

PRESSURE/VACUUM RELIEF FUEL CAP

The fuel cap contains an integral pressure and vacuum relief valve. The vacuum valve acts to allow air into the fuel tank to replace the fuel as it is used, while preventing vapors from escaping the tank through the atmosphere. The vacuum relief

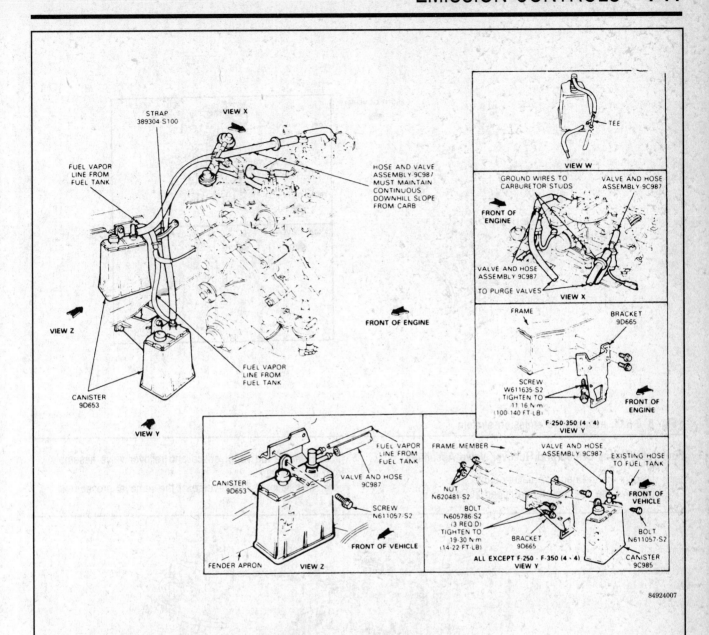

Fig. 7 8-7.5L California evaporative emission system

valve opens after a vacuum of -0.5 psi. The pressure valve acts as a backup pressure relief valve in the event the normal venting system is overcome by excessive generation of internal pressure or restriction of the normal venting system. The pressure relief range is 1.6-2.1 psi. Fill cap damage or contamination that stops the pressure vacuum valve from working may result in deformation of the fuel tank.

SERVICE

System Inspection

1. Visually inspect the vapor and vacuum lines and connections for looseness, pinching, leakage, or other damage. If fuel line, vacuum line, or orifice blockage is suspected as the obvious cause of a malfunction, correct the cause before proceeding further.

2. If applicable, check the wiring and connectors to the purge solenoid for looseness, corrosion, damage or other problems.

3. If all checks are okay, go to the diagnostic charts

REMOVAL & INSTALLATION

Carbon Canister

1. Disconnect the negative battery cable.

2. Label and disconnect the vapor hoses from the carbon canister.

3. Remove the canister attaching screws and remove the canister.

4. Installation is the reverse of the removal procedure.

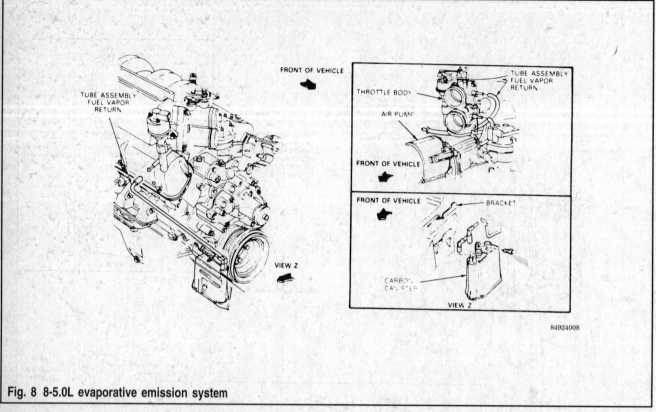

Fig. 8 8-5.0L evaporative emission system

Fuel Tank Vapor Orifice and Rollover Valve Assembly

1. Disconnect the negative battery cable.
2. Remove the fuel tank as described in Section 5.

3. Remove the vapor orifice and rollover valve assembly from the fuel tank.
4. Installation is the reverse of the removal procedure.

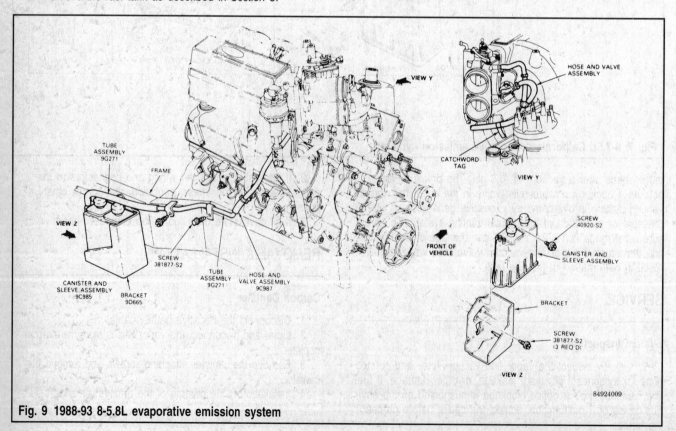

Fig. 9 1988-93 8-5.8L evaporative emission system

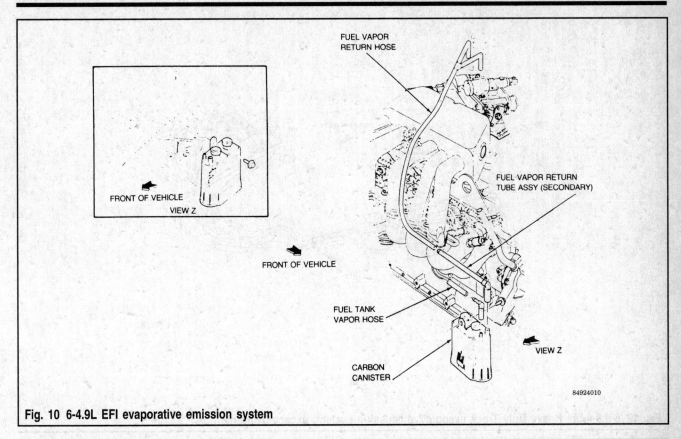

Fig. 10 6-4.9L EFI evaporative emission system

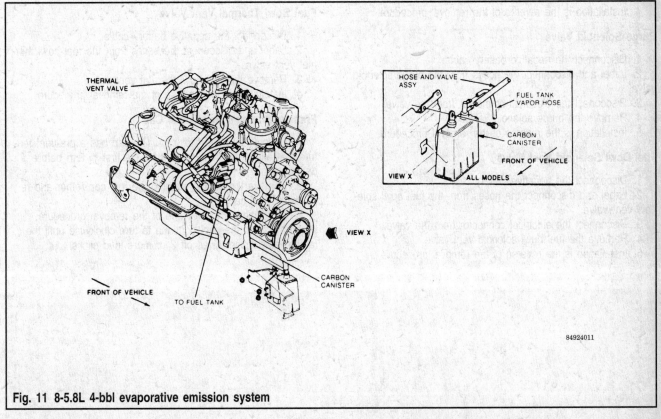

Fig. 11 8-5.8L 4-bbl evaporative emission system

Purge Control Valve

1. Disconnect the negative battery cable.

2. Label and disconnect the hoses from the purge control valve.
3. Remove the purge control valve.

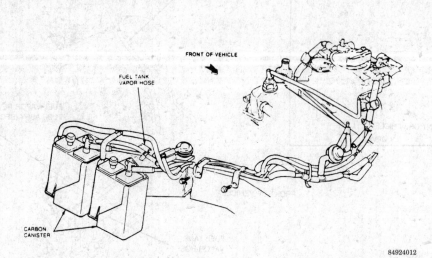

FRONT OF VEHICLE

FUEL TANK
VAPOR HOSE

CARBON
CANISTER

84924012

Fig. 12 8-5.8 4-bbl Heavy Duty Truck evaporative emission system, except California

4. Installation is the reverse of the removal procedure.

Purge Solenoid Valve

1. Disconnect the negative battery cable.
2. Label and disconnect the hoses from the purge solenoid valve.
3. Disconnect the electrical connector from the valve.
4. Remove the purge solenoid valve.
5. Installation is the reverse of the removal procedure.

Fuel Bowl Solenoid Vent Valve

1. Disconnect the negative battery cable.
2. Label and disconnect the hoses from the fuel bowl solenoid vent valve.
3. Disconnect the electrical connector from the valve.
4. Remove the fuel bowl solenoid vent valve.
5. Installation is the reverse of the removal procedure.

Fuel Bowl Thermal Vent Valve

1. Disconnect the negative battery cable.
2. Label and disconnect the hoses from the fuel bowl thermal vent valve.
3. Remove the fuel bowl thermal vent valve.
4. Installation is the reverse of the removal procedure.

Pressure/Vacuum Relief Fuel Cap

1. Unscrew the fuel filler cap. The cap has a pre-vent feature that allows the tank to vent for the first ¾ turn before unthreading.
2. Remove the screw retaining the fuel cap tether and remove the fuel cap.
3. Installation is the reverse of the removal procedure. When installing the cap, continue to turn clockwise until the ratchet mechanism gives off 3 or more loud clicks.

CATALYTIC CONVERTERS

The catalytic converter, mounted in the truck's exhaust system is a muffler-shaped device containing a ceramic honeycomb shaped material coated with alumina and impregnated with catalytically active precious metals such as platinum, palladium and rhodium.

The catalyst's job is to reduce air pollutants by oxidizing hydrocarbons (HC) and carbon monoxide (CO). Catalysts containing palladium and rhodium also oxidize nitrous oxides (NOx).

On some trucks, the catalyst is also fed by the secondary air system, via a small supply tube in the side of the catalyst.

No maintenance is possible on the converter, other than keeping the heat shield clear of flammable debris, such as leaves and twigs.

Other than external damage, the only significant damage possible to a converter is through the use of leaded gasoline, or by way of a too rich fuel/air mixture. Both of these problems will ruin the converter through contamination of the catalyst and will eventually plug the converter causing loss of power and engine performance.

When this occurs, the catalyst must be replaced. For catalyst replacement, see the Exhaust System section in Section 3.

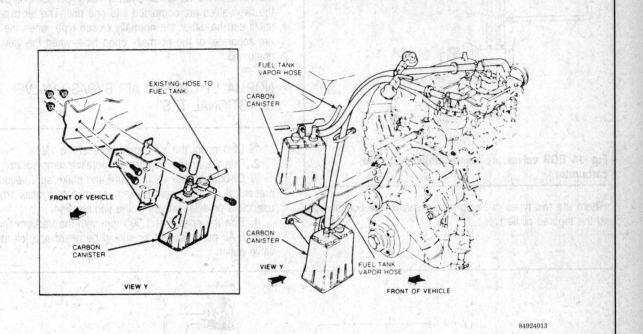

Fig. 13 8-7.5L California Heavy Duty Truck evaporative emission system

EXHAUST EMISSION CONTROLS

Exhaust Gas Recirculation

▶ **See Figures 14, 15, 16, 17, 18, 19, 20, 21, 22 and 23**

ELECTRONIC EGR (EEGR) SYSTEM

The Electronic EGR system (EEGR) is found in all systems in which EGR flow is controlled according to computer commands by means of an EGR valve position sensor (EVP) attached to the valve.

The EEGR valve is operated by a vacuum signal from the dual EGR Solenoid Valves, or the electronic vacuum regulator which actuates the valve diaphragm.

As supply vacuum overcomes the spring load, the diaphragm is actuated lifting the pintle off of its seat allowing the exhaust gas to flow. The amount of flow is directly proportional to the pintle position. The EVP sensor sends an electrical signal to notify the EEC of its position.

The EEGR valve is not serviceable. The EVP sensor must be serviced separately.

INTEGRAL BACKPRESSURE (IBP) EGR SYSTEM

The Integral Backpressure (IBP) EGR system combines inputs of EGR port vacuum and backpressure into one unit. The valve requires both inputs for proper operation. The valve won't operate on vacuum alone.

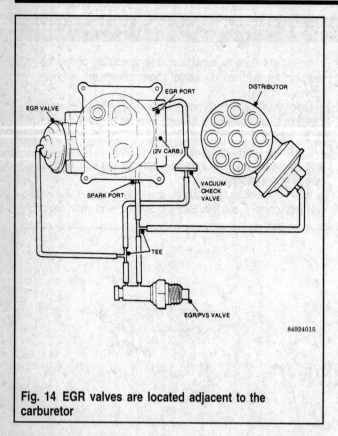

Fig. 14 EGR valves are located adjacent to the carburetor

There are two types of backpressure valves: the poppet type and the tapered pintle type.

PORTED EGR

The ported EGR valve is operated by engine vacuum alone. A vacuum signal from the carburetor activates the EGR valve diaphragm. As the vacuum signal increase it gradually opens the valve pintle allowing exhaust gases to flow. The amount of flow is directly proportional to the pintle position.

Managed Thermactor Air System

The MTA system is used to inject fresh air into the exhaust manifolds or catalytic converters via an air control valve. Under some operating conditions, the air can be dumped back into the atmosphere via an air bypass valve. On some applications the two valves are combined into one unit. The air bypass valve can be either the normally closed type, when the valves are separate, or the normally open type, when the valves are combined.

NORMALLY CLOSED AIR BYPASS VALVE FUNCTIONAL TEST

1. Disconnect the air supply hose at the valve.
2. Run the engine to normal operating temperature.
3. Disconnect the vacuum line and make sure vacuum is present. If no vacuum is present, remove or bypass any restrictors or delay valves in the vacuum line.
4. Run the engine at 1,500 rpm with the vacuum line connected. Air pump supply air should be heard and felt at the valve outlet.

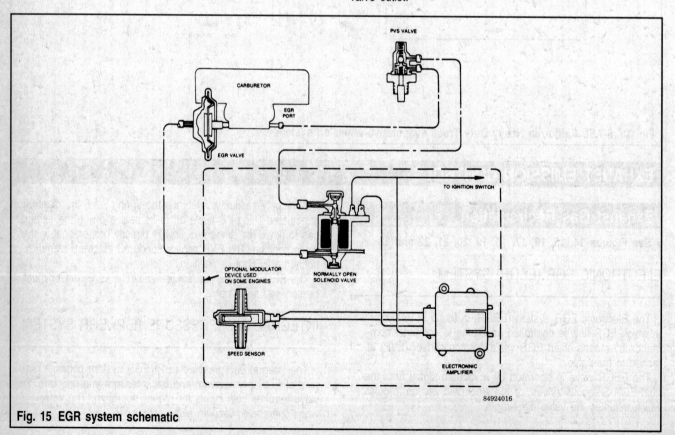

Fig. 15 EGR system schematic

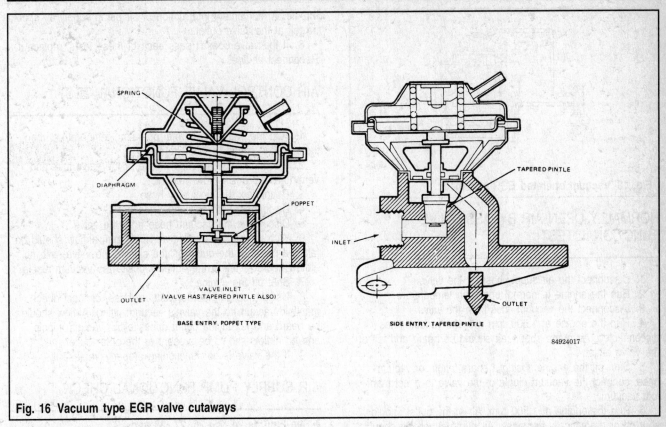

Fig. 16 Vacuum type EGR valve cutaways

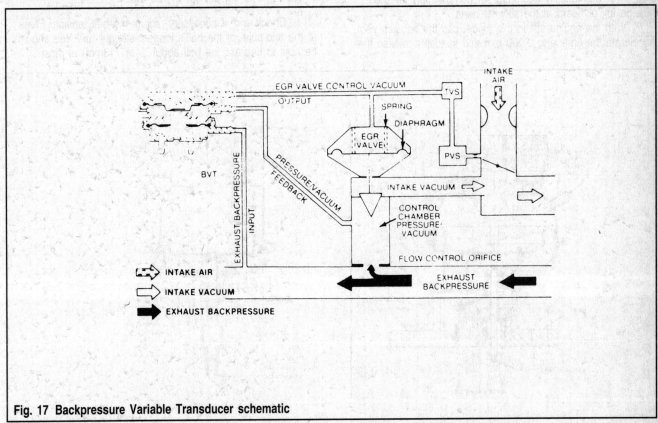

Fig. 17 Backpressure Variable Transducer schematic

5. With the engine still at 1,500 rpm, disconnect the vacuum line. Air at the outlet should shut off or dramatically decrease. Air pump supply air should now be felt or heard at the silencer ports.

6. If the valve doesn't pass each of these tests, replace it.

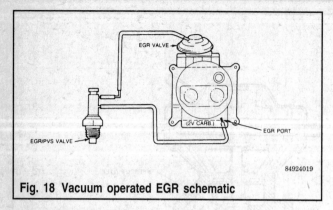

Fig. 18 Vacuum operated EGR schematic

NORMALLY OPEN AIR BYPASS VALVE FUNCTIONAL TEST

1. Disconnect the air supply hose at the valve.
2. Run the engine to normal operating temperature.
3. Disconnect the vacuum lines from the valve.
4. Run the engine at 1,500 rpm with the vacuum lines disconnected. Air pump supply air should be heard and felt at the valve outlet.
5. Shut off the engine. Using a spare length of vacuum hose, connect the vacuum nipple of the valve to direct manifold vacuum.
6. Run the engine at 1,500 rpm. Air at the outlet should shut off or dramatically decrease. Air pump supply air should now be felt or heard at the silencer ports.
7. With the engine still in this mode, cap the vacuum vent. Accelerate the engine to 2,000 rpm and suddenly release the

throttle. A momentary interruption of air pump supply air should be felt at the valve outlet.

8. If the valve doesn't pass each of these tests, replace it. Reconnect all lines.

AIR CONTROL VALVE FUNCTIONAL TEST

1. Run the engine to normal operating temperature, then increase the speed to 1,500 rpm.
2. Disconnect the air supply hose at the valve inlet and verify that there is airflow present.
3. Reconnect the air supply hose.
4. Disconnect both air supply hoses.
5. Disconnect the vacuum hose from the valve.
6. With the engine running at 1,500 rpm, airflow should be felt and heard at the outlet on the side of the valve, with no airflow heard or felt at the outlet opposite the vacuum nipple.
7. Shut off the engine.
8. Using a spare piece of vacuum hose, connect direct manifold vacuum to the valve's vacuum fitting. Airflow should be heard and felt at the outlet opposite the vacuum nipple, and no airflow should be present at the other outlet.
9. If the valve is not functioning properly, replace it.

AIR SUPPLY PUMP FUNCTIONAL CHECK

▶ See Figures 24, 25, 26, 27, 28 and 29

1. Check and, if necessary, adjust the belt tension. Press at the mid-point of the belt's longest straight run. You should be able to depress the belt about ½ in. (13mm) at most.

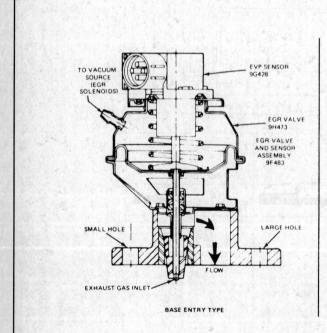

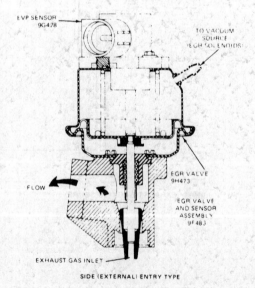

Fig. 19 Electronic EGR valve

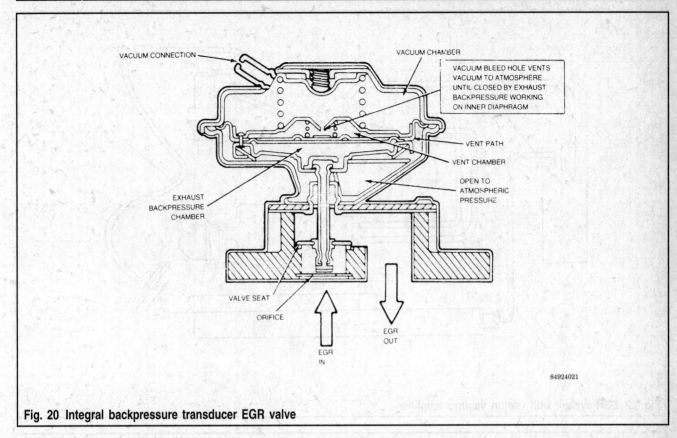

Fig. 20 Integral backpressure transducer EGR valve

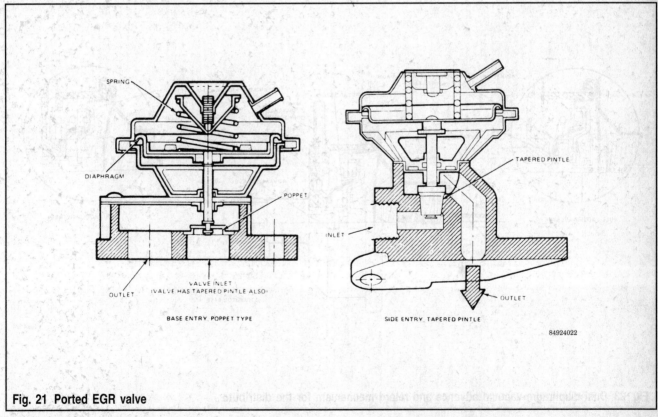

Fig. 21 Ported EGR valve

2. Run the engine to normal operating temperature and let it idle.

3. Disconnect the air supply hose from the bypass control valve. If the pump is operating properly, airflow should be felt at the pump outlet. The flow should increase as you increase

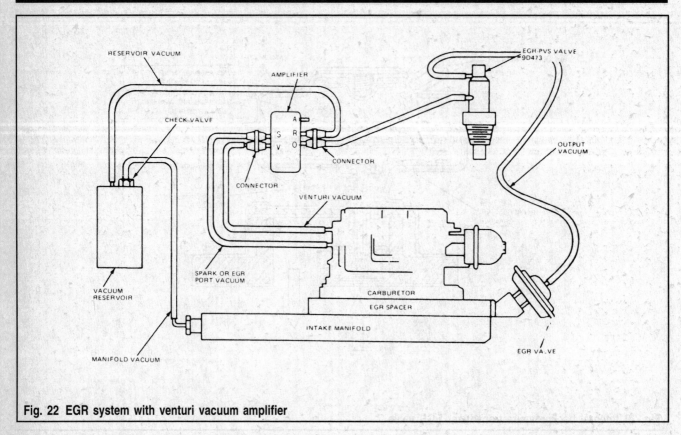

Fig. 22 EGR system with venturi vacuum amplifier

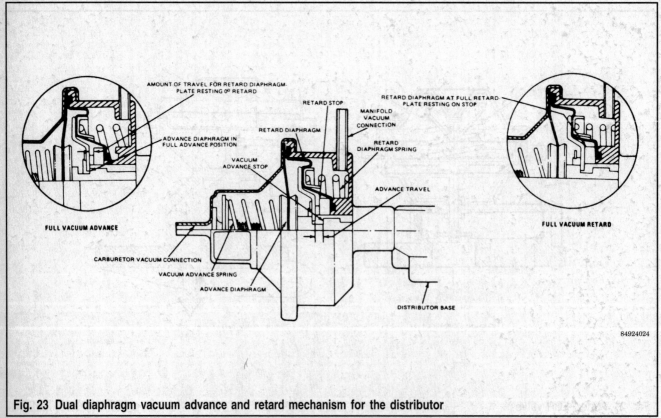

Fig. 23 Dual diaphragm vacuum advance and retard mechanism for the distributor

the engine speed. The pump is not serviceable and should be replaced if it is not functioning properly.

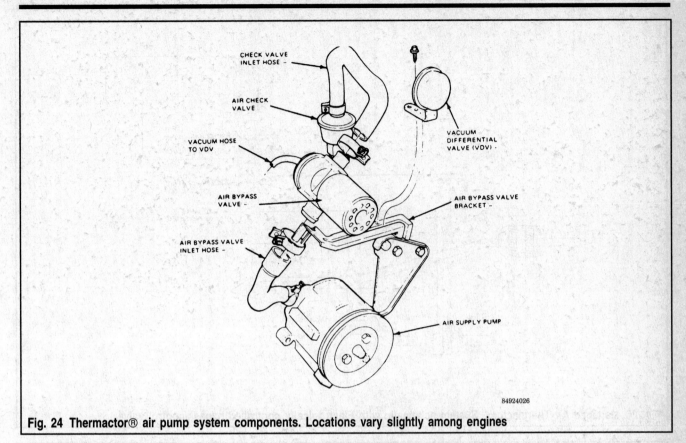

84924026

Fig. 24 Thermactor® air pump system components. Locations vary slightly among engines

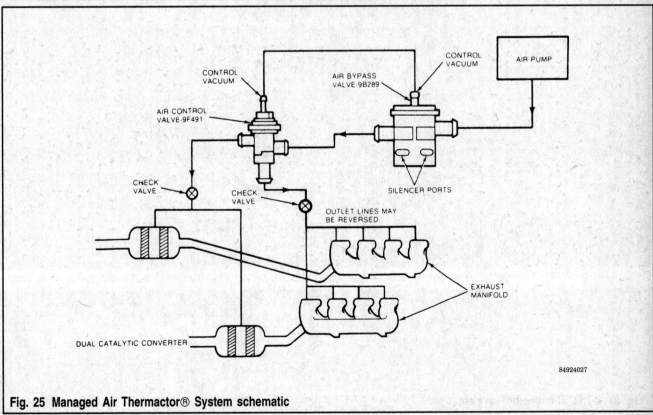

84924027

Fig. 25 Managed Air Thermactor® System schematic

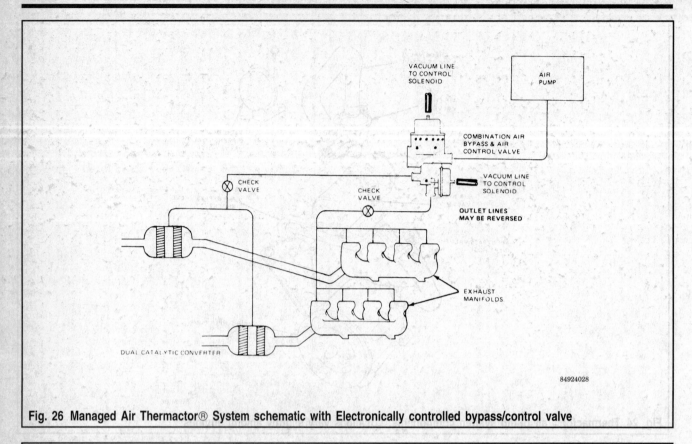

Fig. 26 Managed Air Thermactor® System schematic with Electronically controlled bypass/control valve

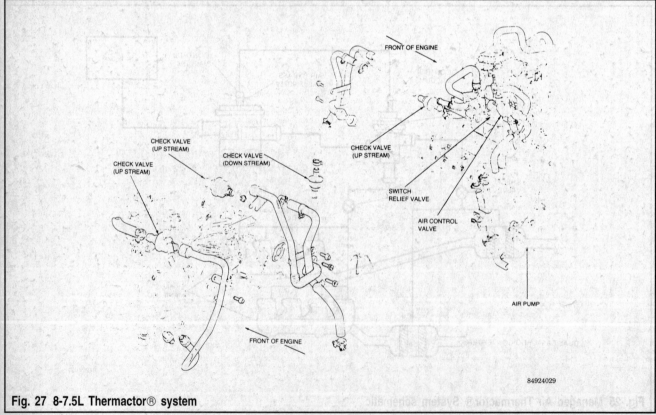

Fig. 27 8-7.5L Thermactor® system

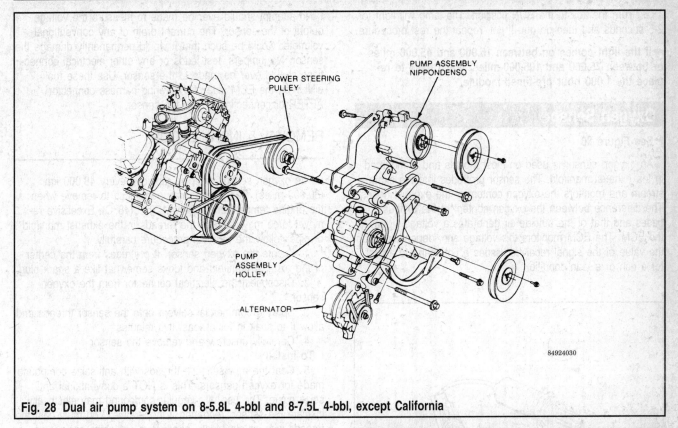

Fig. 28 Dual air pump system on 8-5.8L 4-bbl and 8-7.5L 4-bbl, except California

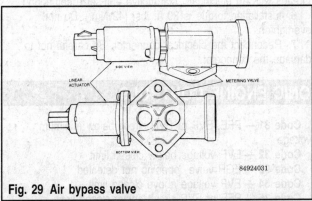

Fig. 29 Air bypass valve

Bypass Air Idle Speed Control

The air bypass solenoid is used to control the engine idle speed and is operated by the EEC module.

The valve allows air to pass around the throttle plates to control:

- Cold engine fast idle
- Cold starting
- Dashpot operation
- Over-temperature idle boost
- Engine load correction

The valve is not serviceable and correction is by replacement only.

Emissions Maintenance Warning Light (EMW)

DESCRIPTION

All gasoline engine equipped light trucks built for sale outside of California employ this device.

The EMW consists of an instrument panel mounted amber light imprinted with the word EGR, EMISS, or EMISSIONS. The light is connected to a sensor module located under the instrument panel. The purpose is the warn the driver that the 60,000 mile emission system maintenance is required on the vehicle. Specific emission system maintenance requirements are listed in the truck's owner's manual maintenance schedule.

RESETTING THE LIGHT

1. Turn the key to the OFF position.
2. Lightly push a Phillips screwdriver through the 0.2 in. (5mm) diameter hole labeled RESET, and lightly press down and hold it.
3. While maintaining pressure with the screwdriver, turn the key to the RUN position. The EMW lamp will light and stay lit as long as you keep pressure on the screwdriver. Hold the screwdriver down for about 5 seconds.
4. Remove the screwdriver. The lamp should go out within 2-5 seconds. If not, repeat Steps 1-3.
5. Turn the key OFF.

6. Turn the key to the RUN position. The lamp will light for 2-5 seconds and then go out. If not, repeat the rest procedure.

➡**If the light comes on between 15,000 and 45,000 miles or between 75,000 and 105,000 miles, you'll have to replace the 1,000 hour pre-timed module.**

Oxygen Sensor

▶ **See Figure 30**

An oxygen sensor is used on most models and is mounted in the exhaust manifold. The sensor protrudes into the exhaust stream and monitors the oxygen content of the exhaust hoses. The difference between the oxygen content of the exhaust gases and that of the outside air generates a voltage signal to the ECM. The ECM monitors this voltage and, depending upon the value of the signal received, issues a command to adjust for a rich or a lean condition.

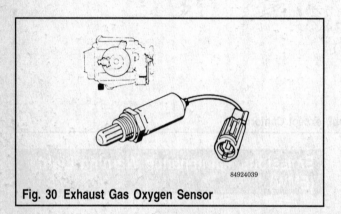

84924039

Fig. 30 Exhaust Gas Oxygen Sensor

No attempt should ever be made to measure the voltage output of the sensor. The current drain of any conventional voltmeter would be such that it would permanently damage the sensor. No jumpers, test leads or any other electrical connections should ever be made to the sensor. Use these tools ONLY on the ECM side of the wiring harness connector AFTER disconnecting it from the sensor.

REMOVAL & INSTALLATION

The oxygen sensor must be replaced every 48,000 km (30,000 miles). The sensor may be difficult to remove when the engine temperature is blow 120°F (48°C). Excessive removal force may damage the threads in the exhaust manifold or pipe; follow the removal procedure carefully.

1. Locate the oxygen sensor. It protrudes from the center of the exhaust manifold and looks somewhat like a spark plug.
2. Disconnect the electrical connector from the oxygen sensor.
3. Spray a commercial solvent onto the sensor threads and allow it to soak in for at least five minutes.
4. Carefully unscrew and remove the sensor.
   To install:
5. Coat the new sensor's threads with anti-seize compound made for oxygen sensors. This is NOT a conventional anti-seize paste. The use of a regular compound may electrically insulate the sensor, rendering it inoperative. You must coat the threads with an electrically conductive anti-seize compound.
6. Installation torque is 30 ft. lbs. (42 Nm.). Do not overtighten.
7. Reconnect the electrical connector. Be careful not to damage the connector.

DIAGNOSTIC TROUBLE CODES AND ELECTRONIC ENGINE CONTROLS

Diagnostic Trouble Codes (DTC)

Code 11 — System pass
Code 12 — RPM unable to reach upper test limit
Code 13 — RPM unable to reach lower test limit
Code 14 — Pip circuit failure
Code 15 — ECA read only memory test failed
Code 15 — ECA keep alive memory test failed
Code 16 — IDM signal not recieved
Code 18 — SPOUT circuit open or spark angle word failure
Code 18 — IDM circuit failure or SPOUT circuit grounded
Code 19 — Failure in ECA internal voltage
Code 21 — ECT out ot self test range
Code 22 — BP sensor out of self test range
Code 22 — BP sensor or MAP out of range
Code 23 — TP sensor out of self test range
Code 24 — ACT sensor out of self test range
Code 25 — Knock not sensed during dynamic test
Code 26 — VAF/MAF out of self test range
Code 26 — TOT out of self test range
Code 26 — TOT sensor out of self test range (E-400)
Code 28 — Loss of IDM, right side
Code 29 — Insufficient input from vehicle speed sensor

Code 31 — PFE, EVP or EVR circuit below minimum voltage
Code 32 — EVP voltage below closed limit
Code 33 — EGR valve opening not detected
Code 34 — EVP voltage above closed limit
Code 35 — PFE or EVP circuit above closed limit
Code 41 — HEGO sensor circuit indicates system lean
Code 41 — No HEGO switching detected
Code 42 — HEGO sensor circuit indicates system rich
Code 44 — Thermactor air system inoperative-right side
Code 45 — Thermactor air upstream during self test
Code 45 — Coil 1,2 or 3 failure
Code 46 — Thermactor air not bypassed during self test
Code 47 — 4WD switch closed (E40D)
Code 48 — Loss of IDM, left side
Code 49 — 1-2 shift error (E40D)
Code 51 — ECT/ACT reads -40°F or circuit open
Code 52 — Power steering pressure switch circuit open
Code 52 — Power steering pressure switch always open or closed
Code 53 — TP circuit above maximum voltage
Code 54 — ACT sensor circuit open
Code 56 — VAF or MAF circuit above maximum voltage
Code 56 — TOT reads -40°F or circuit open (E40D)
Code 59 — 2-3 shift error (E40D)

Code 61 — ECT reads 254°F or circuit grounded

Code 63 — TP circuit below minimum voltage

Code 64 — ACT sensor grounded or input reads 254°F

Code 65 — Overdrive cancel switch open, no change seen (E40D)

Code 66 — MAF sensor input below minimum voltage

Code 66 — TOT grounded or reads 290°F (E40D)

Code 67 — Neutral/drive switch open or A/C on

Code 67 — Clutch switch circuit failure

Code 67 — MLP sensor out of range or A/C on (E40D)

Code 69 — 3-4 shift error

Code 72 — Insufficient MAF/MAP change during dynamic test

Code 73 — Insufficient TP change during dynamic test

Code 74 — Brake on/off switch failure or not actuated

Code 77 — Operator error

Code 79 — A/C on during self test

Code 79 — A/C or defrost on during self test

Code 81 — Air management 2 circuit failure

Code 82 — Air management 1 circuit failure

Code 84 — EGR vacuum solenoid circuit failure

Code 85 — Canister purge solenoid circuit failure

Code 86 — Shift solenoid circuit failure

Code 87 — Fuel pump primary circuit failure

Code 88 — Loss of dual plug input control

Code 89 — Converter clutch solenoid circuit failure

Code 91 — Shift solenoid 1 circuit failure (E40D)

Code 92 — Shift solenoid 2 circuit failure (E40D)

Code 93 — Coast clutch solenoid circuit failure (E40D)

Code 94 — Converter clutch solenoid circuit failure (E40D)

Code 95 — Fuel pump secondary circuit failure — ECA to ground

Code 96 — Fuel pump secondary circuit failure — battery to ECA

Code 97 — Overdrive cancel indicator light — circuit failure(E40D)

Code 98 — Electronic pressure control driver open in ECA (E40D)

Code 98 — Hard fault present

Code 99 — Electronic pressure control circuit failure (E40D)

Code 111 — System pass

Code 112 — ACT sensor circuit grounded or reads 254° F

Code 113 — ACT sensor circuit open or reads -40° F

Code 114 — ACT outside test limits during KOEO or KOER tests

Code 116 — ECT outside test limits during KOEO or KOER tests

Code 117 — ECT sensor circuit grounded

Code 117 — ECT sensor circuit below minimum voltage or reads 254°F

Code 118 — ECT sensor circuit open

Code 118 — ECT sensor circuit below maximum voltage or reads -40°F

Code 121 — Closed throttle voltage higher or lower than expected

Code 122 — TP sensor circuit below minimum voltage

Code 123 — TP sensor circuit below maximum voltage

Code 126 — BP or MAP sensor higher or lower than expected

Code 128 — MAP vacuum circuit failure

Code 129 — Insufficient MAF or MAP change during dynamic responded test

Code 144 — No HEGO switching detected

Code 167 — Insufficient TP change during dynamic response test

Code 171 — Fuel system at adaptive limit, HEGO unable to switch

Code 172 — HEGO shows system always lean

Code 173 — HEGO shows system always rich

Code 174 — HEGO switching time is slow

Code 179 — Fuel at lean adaptive limit at part throttle; system rich

Code 181 — Fuel at rich adaptive limit at part throttle; system lean

Code 182 — Fuel at lean adaptive limit at idle; system rich

Code 183 — Fuel at rich adaptive limit at idle; system lean

Code 211 — PIP circuit fault

Code 212 — Loss of IDM input to ECA or SPOUT circuit grounded

Code 213 — Spout circuit open

Code 224 — Erratic IDM input to processor

Code 225 — Knocked not sensed during dynamic response test

Code 311 — Thermactor air system inoperative

Code 312 — Thermactor air upstream during self test

Code 313 — Thermactor air not bypassed during self test

Code 327 — EVP or DPFE circuit below minimum voltage

Code 328 — EGR closed voltage higher than expected

Code 332 — Insufficient EGR flow detected

Code 334 — EGR closed voltage higher than expected

Code 337 — EVP or DPFE circuit above maximum voltage

Code 411 — Cannot control rpm during KOER low rpm check

Code 412 — Cannot control rpm during KOER high rpm check

Code 452 — Insufficient input from vehicle speed sensor

Code 511 — EEC processor ROM test failed

Code 512 — EEC processor Keep Alive Memory test failed

Code 513 — Failure in EEC processor internal voltage

Code 519 — Power steering pressure switch circuit open

Code 521 — Power steering pressure switch did not change state

Code 525 — Vehicle in gear or A/C on during self test

Code 536 — Brake on/off circuit failure, switch not actuated during KOER test

Code 538 — Insufficient RPM change during KOER dynamic response test

Code 538 — Operator error

Code 542 — Fuel pump secondary circuit failure: ECA to ground

Code 543 — Fuel pump secondary circuit failure: Battery to ECA

Code 552 — Air management 1 circuit failure

Code 553 — Air management 2 circuit failure

Code 556 — Fuel pump primary circuit failure

Code 558 — EGR vacuum regulator circuit failure

Code 565 — Canister purge circuit failure

Code 569 — Canister purge 2 circuit failure

Code 617 — 1-2 shift error (E40D)

Code 618 — 2-3 shift error (E40D)

Code 619 — 3-4 shift error (E40D)

Code 621 — Shift solenoid 1 circuit failure

Code 622 — Shift solenoid 2 circuit failure

Code 624 — EPC solenoid or driver circuit failure

Code 625 — EPC driver open in ECA
Code 626 — Coast clutch solenoid circuit failure (E40D)
Code 627 — Converter clutch solenoid circuit failure (E40D)
Code 628 — Converter clutch error (E40D)
Code 629 — Converter clutch control circuit failure
Code 631 — Overdrive cancel indicator light circuit failure
Code 632 — Overdrive cancel switch not changing states (E40D)
Code 633 — 4WD switch is closed
Code 634 — MLP sensor voltage out ot self test range, A/C on
Code 636 — TOT sensor voltage out of self test range
Code 637 — TOT sensor circuit above maximum voltage
Code 638 — TOT sensor circuit below minimum voltage
Code 654 — MLP sensor not in park position
Code 998 — Hard fault present

General Information

Ford vehicles employ the 4th generation Electronic Engine Control system, commonly designated EEC-IV, to manage fuel, ignition and emissions on vehicle engines.

ENGINE CONTROL SYSTEM

The Engine Control Assembly (ECA) is given responsibility for the operation of the emission control devices, cooling fans, ignition and advance and in some cases, automatic transmission functions. Because the EEC-IV oversees both the ignition timing and the fuel injector operation, a precise air/fuel ratio will be maintained under all operating conditions. The ECA is a microprocessor or small computer which receives electrical inputs from several sensors, switches and relays on and around the engine.

Based on combinations of these inputs, the ECA controls outputs to various devices concerned with engine operation and emissions. The engine control assembly relies on the signals to form a correct picture of current vehicle operation. If any of the input signals is incorrect, the ECA reacts to whatever picture is painted for it. For example, if the coolant temperature sensor is inaccurate and reads too low, the ECA may see a picture of the engine never warming up. Consequently, the engine settings will be maintained as if the engine were cold. Because so many inputs can affect one output, correct diagnostic procedures are essential on these systems.

One part of the ECA is devoted to monitoring both input and output functions within the system. This ability forms the core of the self-diagnostic system. If a problem is detected within a circuit, the controller will recognize the fault, assign it an identification code, and store the code in a memory section. Depending on the year and model, the fault code(s) may be represented by two or three digit numbers. The stored code(s) may be retrieved during diagnosis.

While the EEC-IV system is capable of recognizing many internal faults, certain faults will not be recognized. Because the computer system sees only electrical signals, it cannot sense or react to mechanical or vacuum faults affecting engine operation. Some of these faults may affect another component which will set a code. For example, the ECA monitors the output signal to the fuel injectors, but cannot detect a partially clogged injector. As long as the output driver responds correctly, the computer will read the system as functioning correctly. However, the improper flow of fuel may result in a lean mixture. This would, in turn, be detected by the oxygen sensor and noticed as a constantly lean signal by the ECA. Once the signal falls outside the pre-programmed limits, the engine control assembly would notice the fault and set an identification code.

Additionally, the EEC-IV system employs adaptive fuel logic. This process is used to compensate for normal wear and variability within the fuel system. Once the engine enters steady-state operation, the engine control assembly watches the oxygen sensor signal for a bias or tendency to run slightly rich or lean. If such a bias is detected, the adaptive logic corrects the fuel delivery to bring the air/fuel mixture towards a centered or 14.7:1 ratio. This compensating shift is stored in a non-volatile memory which is retained by battery power even with the ignition switched off. The correction factor is then available the next time the vehicle is operated.

➡ **If the battery cable(s) is disconnected for longer than 5 minutes, the adaptive fuel factor will be lost. After repair it will be necessary to drive the truck at least 10 miles to allow the processor to relearn the correct factors. The driving period should include steady-throttle open road driving if possible. During the drive, the vehicle may exhibit driveability symptoms not noticed before. These symptoms should clear as the ECA computes the correction factor. The ECA will also store Code 19 indicating loss of power to the controller.**

Failure Mode Effects Management (FMEM)

The engine controller assembly contains back-up programs which allow the engine to operate if a sensor signal is lost. If a sensor input is seen to be out of range — either high or low — the FMEM program is used. The processor substitutes a fixed value for the missing sensor signal. The engine will continue to operate, although performance and driveability may be noticeably reduced. This function of the controller is sometimes referred to as the limp-in or fail-safe mode. If the missing sensor signal is restored, the FMEM system immediately returns the system to normal operation. The dashboard warning lamp will be lit when FMEM is in effect.

Hardware Limited Operation Strategy (HLOS)

This mode is only used if the fault is too extreme for the FMEM circuit to handle. In this mode, the processor has ceased all computation and control; the entire system is run on fixed values. The vehicle may be operated but performance and driveability will be greatly reduced. The fixed or default settings provide minimal calibration, allowing the vehicle to be carefully driven in for service. The dashboard warning lamp will be lit when HLOS is engaged. Codes cannot be read while the system is operating in this mode.

DASHBOARD WARNING LAMP (MIL)

◆ **See Figures 31, 32, 33, 34, 35, 36 and 37**

The CHECK ENGINE or SERVICE ENGINE SOON dashboard warning lamp is referred to as the Malfunction Indicator

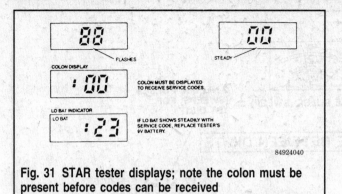

Fig. 31 STAR tester displays; note the colon must be present before codes can be received

Lamp (MIL). The lamp is connected to the engine control assembly and will alert the driver to certain malfunctions within the EEC-IV system. When the lamp is lit, the ECA has detected a fault and stored an identity code in memory. The engine control system will usually enter either FMEM or HLOS mode and driveability will be impaired.

The light will stay on as long as the fault causing it is present. Should the fault self-correct, the MIL will extinguish but the stored code will remain in memory.

Under normal operating conditions, the MIL should light briefly when the ignition key is turned **ON**. As soon as the ECA receives a signal that the engine is cranking, the lamp will be extinguished. The dash warning lamp should remain out during the entire operating cycle.

Tools and Equipment

Although stored codes may be read through the flashing of the CHECK ENGINE or SERVICE ENGINE SOON lamp, the

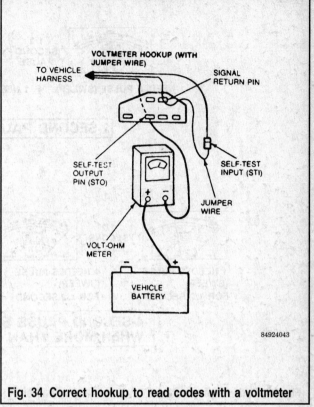

Fig. 34 Correct hookup to read codes with a voltmeter

use of hand-held scan tools such as Ford's Self-Test Automatic Readout (STAR) tester or the second generation SUPER STAR II tester or their equivalent is highly recommended.

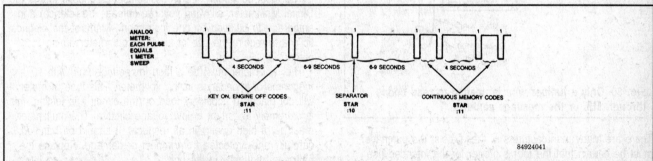

Fig. 32 Code transmission during KOEO test. Note that the continuous memory codes are transmitted after a pause and a separator pulse

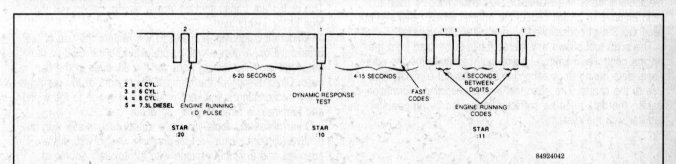

Fig. 33 Code transmission during KOER testing begins with the engine identification pulse and may include a dynamic response prompt

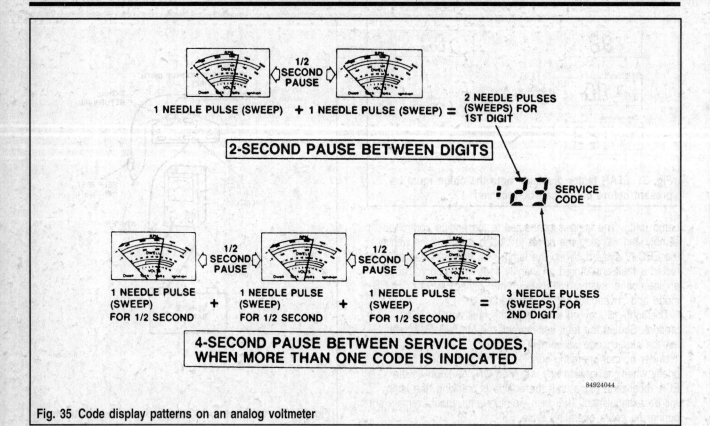

1 NEEDLE PULSE (SWEEP) **+** 1 NEEDLE PULSE (SWEEP) **=** 2 NEEDLE PULSES (SWEEPS) FOR 1ST DIGIT

1/2 SECOND PAUSE

2-SECOND PAUSE BETWEEN DIGITS

:23 SERVICE CODE

1 NEEDLE PULSE (SWEEP) FOR 1/2 SECOND **+** 1 NEEDLE PULSE (SWEEP) FOR 1/2 SECOND **+** 1 NEEDLE PULSE (SWEEP) FOR 1/2 SECOND **=** 3 NEEDLE PULSES (SWEEPS) FOR 2ND DIGIT

1/2 SECOND PAUSE

1/2 SECOND PAUSE

4-SECOND PAUSE BETWEEN SERVICE CODES, WHEN MORE THAN ONE CODE IS INDICATED

84924044

Fig. 35 Code display patterns on an analog voltmeter

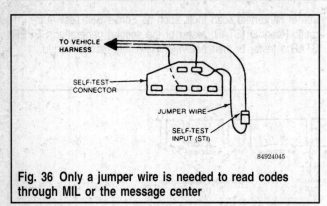

TO VEHICLE HARNESS

SELF-TEST CONNECTOR

JUMPER WIRE

SELF-TEST INPUT (STI)

84924045

Fig. 36 Only a jumper wire is needed to read codes through MIL or the message center

There are many manufacturers of these tools; the purchaser must be certain that the tool is proper for the intended use.

Both the STAR and SUPER STAR testers are designed to communicate directly with the EEC-IV system and interpret the electrical signals. The SUPER STAR tester may be used to read either 2 or 3 digit codes; the original STAR tester will not read the 3 digit codes used on many 1990-93 vehicles.

The scan tool allows any stored faults to be read from the engine controller memory. Use of the scan tool provides additional data during troubleshooting but does not eliminate the use of the charts. The scan tool makes collecting information easier; the data must be correctly interpreted by an operator familiar with the system.

ELECTRICAL TOOLS

▶ See Figures 38, 39, 40, 41 and 42

The most commonly required electrical diagnostic tool is the Digital Multimeter, allowing voltage, ohmage (resistance) and amperage to be read by one instrument. Many of the diagnostic charts require the use of a volt or ohmmeter during diagnosis.

The multimeter must be a high impedance unit, with 10 megohms of impedance in the voltmeter. This type of meter will not place an additional load on the circuit it is testing; this is extremely important in low voltage circuits. The multimeter must be of high quality in all respects. It should be handled carefully and protected from impact or damage. Replace the batteries frequently in the unit.

Additionally, an analog (needle type) voltmeter may be used to read stored fault codes if the STAR tester is not available. The codes are transmitted as visible needle sweeps on the face of the instrument.

Almost all diagnostic procedures will require the use of the Breakout Box, a device which connects into the EEC-IV harness and provides testing ports for the 60 wires in the harness. Direct testing of the harness connectors at the terminals or by backprobing is not recommended; damage to the wiring and terminals is almost certain to occur.

Other necessary tools include a quality tachometer with inductive (clip-on) pickup, a fuel pressure gauge with system adapters and a vacuum gauge with an auxiliary source of vacuum.

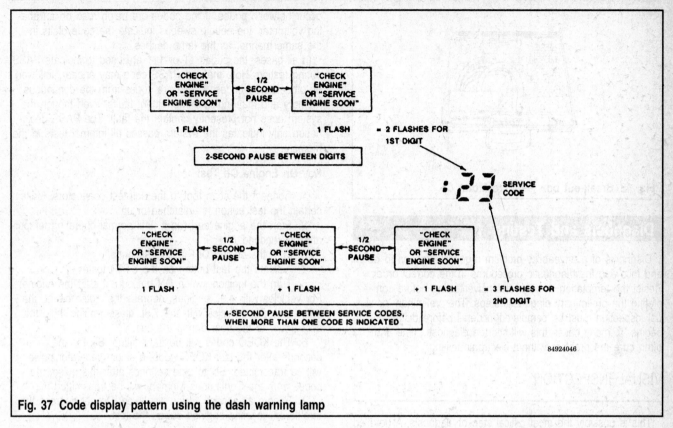

Fig. 37 Code display pattern using the dash warning lamp

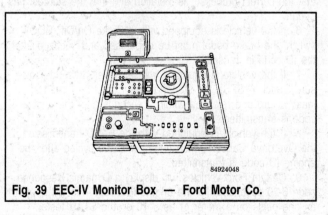

Fig. 38 Super Star II tester — Ford Motor Co.

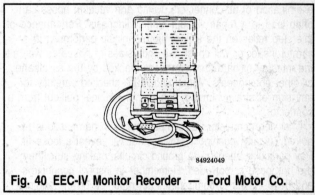

Fig. 40 EEC-IV Monitor Recorder — Ford Motor Co.

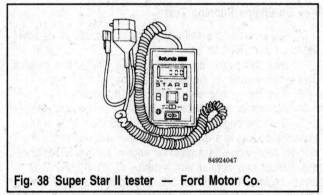

Fig. 39 EEC-IV Monitor Box — Ford Motor Co.

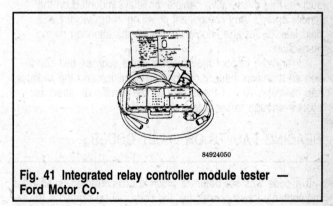

Fig. 41 Integrated relay controller module tester — Ford Motor Co.

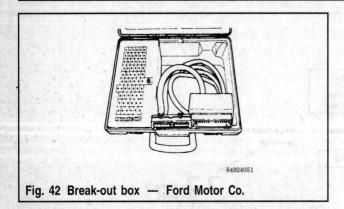

84924051

Fig. 42 Break-out box — Ford Motor Co.

Diagnosis and Testing

Diagnosis of a driveability problem requires attention to detail and following the diagnostic procedures in the correct order. Resist the temptation to begin extensive testing before completing the preliminary diagnostic steps. The preliminary or visual inspection must be completed in detail before diagnosis begins. In many cases this will shorten diagnostic time and often cure the problem without electronic testing.

VISUAL INSPECTION

This is possibly the most critical step of diagnosis. A detailed examination of all connectors, wiring and vacuum hoses can often lead to a repair without further diagnosis. Performance of this step relies on the skill of the technician performing it; a careful inspector will check the undersides of hoses as well as the integrity of hard-to-reach hoses blocked by the air cleaner or other components. Wiring should be checked carefully for any sign of strain, burning, crimping or terminal pull-out from a connector.

Checking connectors at components or in harnesses is required; usually, pushing them together will reveal a loose fit. Pay particular attention to ground circuits, making sure they are not loose or corroded. Remember to inspect connectors and hose fittings at components not mounted on the engine, such as the evaporative canister or relays mounted on the fender aprons. Any component or wiring in the vicinity of a fluid leak or spillage should be given extra attention during inspection.

Additionally, inspect maintenance items such as belt condition and tension, battery charge and condition and the radiator cap carefully. Any of these very simple items may affect the system enough to set a fault.

READING FAULTS OR FAULT CODES

If a code was set before a problem self-corrected (such as a momentarily loose connector), the code will be erased if the problem does not reoccur within 80 warm-up cycles. Codes will be output and displayed as numbers on the hand scan tool, i.e. 23. If the codes are being read through the dashboard warning lamp, the codes will be displayed as groups of flashes separated by pauses. Code 23 would be shown as two flashes, a pause and three more flashes. A longer pause will

occur between codes. If the codes are being read on an analog voltmeter, the needle sweeps indicate the code digits in the same manner as the lamp flashes.

In all cases, the codes 11 or 111 are used to indicate PASS during testing. Note that the PASS code may appear, followed by other stored codes. These are codes from the continuous memory and may indicate intermittent faults, even though the system does not presently contain the fault. The PASS designation only indicates the system passes all internal tests at the moment.

Key On Engine Off Test

1. Connect the scan tool to the self-test connectors. Make certain the test button is unlatched or up.
2. Start the engine and run it until normal operating temperature is reached.
3. Turn the engine **OFF** for 10 seconds.
4. Activate the test button on the STAR tester.
5. Turn the ignition switch **ON** but do not start the engine. For vehicles with 4.9L engines, depress the clutch during the entire test. For vehicles with the 7.3L diesel engine, hold the accelerator to the floor during the test.
6. The KOEO codes will be transmitted. Six to nine seconds after the last KOEO code, a single separator pulse will be transmitted. Six to nine seconds after this pulse, the codes from the Continuous Memory will be transmitted.
7. Record all service codes displayed. Do not depress the throttle on gasoline engines during the test.

Key On Engine Running Test

1. Make certain the self-test button is released or de-activated on the STAR tester.
2. Start the engine and run it at 2000 rpm for two minutes. This action warms up the oxygen sensor.
3. Turn the ignition switch **OFF** for 10 seconds.
4. Activate or latch the self-test button on the scan tool.
5. Start the engine. The engine identification code will be transmitted. This is a single digit number representing ½ the number of cylinders in a gasoline engine. On the STAR tester, this number may appear with a zero, i.e., 20 = 2. For 7.3L diesel engines, the ID code is 5. The code is used to confirm that the correct processor is installed and that the self-test has begun.
6. If the vehicle is equipped with a Brake On/Off (BOO) switch, the brake pedal must be depressed and released after the ID code is transmitted.
7. If the vehicle is equipped with a Power Steering Pressure Switch (PSPS), the steering wheel must be turned at least ½ turn and released within 2 seconds after the engine ID code is transmitted.
8. If the vehicle is equipped with the E4OD transmission, the Overdrive Cancel Switch (OCS) must be cycled after the engine ID code is transmitted.
9. Certain Ford vehicles will display a Dynamic Response code 6-20 seconds after the engine ID code. This will appear as one pulse on a meter or as a 10 on the STAR tester. When this code appears, briefly take the engine to wide open throttle. This allows the system to test the throttle position, MAF and MAP sensors.
10. All relevant codes will be displayed and should be recorded. Remember that the codes refer only to faults present

during this test cycle. Codes stored in Continuous Memory are not displayed in this test mode.

11. Do not depress the throttle during testing unless a dynamic response code is displayed.

Reading Codes With Analog Voltmeter

In the absence of a scan tool, an analog voltmeter may be used to retrieve stored fault codes. Set the meter range to read DC 0-15 volts. Connect the + lead of the meter to the battery positive terminal and connect the - lead of the meter to the self-test output pin of the diagnostic connector.

Follow the directions given previously for performing the KOEO and KOER tests. To activate the tests, use a jumper wire to connect the signal return pin on the diagnostic connector to the self-test input connector. The self-test input line is the separate wire and connector with or near the diagnostic connector.

The codes will be transmitted as groups of needle sweeps. This method may be used to read either 2 or 3 digit codes. The Continuous Memory codes are separated from the KOEO codes by 6 seconds, a single sweep and another 6 second delay.

Reading Codes With MIL

The Malfunction Indicator Lamp on the dashboard may also be used to retrieve the stored codes. This method displays only the stored codes and does not allow for any system investigation.

Follow the directions given previously for performing the KOEO and KOER tests. To activate the tests, use a jumper wire to connect the signal return pin on the diagnostic connector to the self-test input connector. The self-test input line is the separate wire and connector with or near the diagnostic connector.

Codes are transmitted by place value with a pause between the digits; Code 32 would be sent as 3 flashes, a pause and 2 flashes. A slightly longer pause divides codes from each other. Be ready to count and record codes; the only way to repeat a code is to re-cycle the system. This method may be used to read either 2 or 3 digit codes. The Continuous Memory codes are separated from the KOEO codes by 6 seconds, a single flash and another 6 second delay.

To perform the KOER test:

1. Hold in all 3 buttons, start the engine and release the buttons.
2. Press the SELECT or GAUGE SELECT button 3 times. The message **dealer 4** should appear at the bottom of the message panel.
3. Initiate the test by using a jumper wire to connect the signal return pin on the diagnostic connector to the self-test input connector. The self-test input line is the separate wire and connector with or near the diagnostic connector.
4. The stored codes will be output to the vehicle display.
5. To exit the test, turn the ignition switch **OFF** and disconnect the jumper wire.

Other Test Modes

CONTINUOUS MONITOR OR WIGGLE TEST MODE

Once entered, this mode allows the technician to attempt to recreate intermittent faults by wiggling or tapping components, wiring or connectors. The test may be performed during either KOEO or KOER procedures. The test requires the use of either an analog voltmeter or a hand scan tool.

To enter the continuous monitor mode during KOEO testing, turn the ignition switch **ON**. Activate the test, wait 10 seconds, then deactivate and reactivate the test; the system will enter the continuous monitor mode. Tap, move or wiggle the harness, component or connector suspected of causing the problem; if a fault is detected, the code will store in the memory. When the fault occurs, the dash warning lamp will illuminate, the STAR tester will light a red indicator (and possibly beep) and the analog meter needle will sweep once.

To enter this mode in the KOER test:

1. Start the engine and run it at 2000 rpm for two minutes. This action warms up the oxygen sensor.
2. Turn the ignition switch **OFF** for 10 seconds.
3. Start the engine.
4. Activate the test, wait 10 seconds, then deactivate and reactivate the test; the system will enter the continuous monitor mode.
5. Tap, move or wiggle the harness, component or connector suspected of causing the problem; if a fault is detected, the code will store in the memory.
6. When the fault occurs, the dash warning lamp will illuminate, the STAR tester will light a red indicator (and possibly beep) and the analog meter needle will sweep once.

OUTPUT STATE CHECK

This testing mode allows the operator to energize and de-energize most of the outputs controlled by the EEC-IV system. Many of the outputs may be checked at the component by listening for a click or feeling the item move or engage by a hand placed on the case. To enter this check:

1. Enter the KOEO test mode.
2. When all codes have been transmitted, depress the accelerator all the way to the floor and release it.
3. The output actuators are now all ON. Depressing the throttle pedal to the floor again switches the all the actuator outputs OFF.
4. This test may be performed as often as necessary, switching between ON and OFF by depressing the throttle.
5. Exit the test by turning the ignition switch **OFF**, disconnecting the jumper at the diagnostic connector or releasing the test button on the scan tool.

CLEARING CODES

Continuous Memory Codes

These codes are retained in memory for 80 warm-up cycles. To clear the codes for the purposes of testing or confirming repair, perform the KOEO test. When the fault codes begin to be displayed, de-activate the test by either disconnecting the jumper wire (meter, MIL or message center) or releasing the test button on the hand scanner. Stopping the test during code transmission will erase the Continuous Memory. Do not disconnect the negative battery cable to clear these codes; the Keep Alive memory will be cleared and a new code, 19, will be stored for loss of ECA power.

Keep Alive Memory

The Keep Alive Memory (KAM) contains the adaptive factors used by the processor to compensate for component tolerances and wear. It should not be routinely cleared during diagnosis. If an emissions related part is replaced during repair, the KAM must be cleared. Failure to clear the KAM may cause severe driveability problems since the correction factor for the old component will be applied to the new component.

To clear the Keep Alive Memory, disconnect the negative battery cable for at least 5 minutes. After the memory is cleared and the battery reconnected, the vehicle must be driven at least 10 miles so that the processor may relearn the needed correction factors. The distance to be driven depends on the engine and vehicle, but all drives should include steady-throttle cruise on open roads. Certain driveability problems may be noted during the drive because the adaptive factors are not yet functioning.

EEC-IV Operation

The EEC-IV engine control system is divided into 3 major systems:

FUEL DELIVERY SYSTEM

This includes the fuel tank and lines, fuel pump and fuel injection components. On fuel injected models, this includes the fuel supply manifold, fuel pressure regulator, injectors and fuel filter.

AIR INDUCTION SYSTEM

This includes the air cleaner and ducts, intake manifold, fuel injection throttle body, throttle air bypass valve, vane airflow meter, and related vacuum hoses and air ducts.

ELECTRONIC CONTROL SYSTEM

Which consists of the ECA and its various engine sensors (such as the oxygen sensor and coolant temperature sensor, etc.), along with the wiring harness, relays, fuses, battery and self-diagnostic system. It includes the throttle position switch and the wire harness to the fuel injectors, but not the fuel injectors themselves.

EEC-IV SYSTEM OPERATION

Crank Mode

The crank mode is entered after initial engine starting, or after engine stall when restarting. A special operation program is used in the crank mode to aid engine starting. After engine starts, a run mode is entered and normal engine operation is performed. If the engine stumbles during a run mode, the underspeed mode is entered to help it recover from the stumble and prevent stalling. When cranking the engine, the fuel control is in the open loop mode (no feedback to the ECA) of

operation and the ECA sets engine timing at 10-15 degrees BTDC.

On fuel injected models, the injectors fire either in a simultaneous, double-fire manner, to provide the base crank air/fuel control. The throttle air bypass valve solenoid is set to open the bypass valve to provide the fast idle/no-touch start.

Underspeed Mode

Operation in the underspeed mode (under 500 rpm) is similar to that previously described for the crank mode. The system switches from the underspeed mode to the normal run mode when the required rpm is reached. The underspeed mode is used to provide a good pulse width to the injectors and ignores any signal from the vane meter. During this mode, the vane meter flutters and the signal generated would vary with the flutter. Therefore, the vane meter signal is ignored by the ECA in the underspeed mode.

Closed Throttle Mode (Idle or Deceleration)

In the closed throttle mode, the air/fuel ratio is trimmed by either varying the pulse width of the output from the ECA to the injectors to obtain the desired mixture. To calculate what this output signal should be, the ECA evaluates inputs from the ECT sensor, the vane meter, the TP sensor, the EGO sensor, the PIP sensor and the air conditioning clutch. These sensors inform the ECA of the various conditions that must be evaluated in order for the ECA to detect the EGO sensor has cooled off, and the system goes to open-loop fuel control. Under a deceleration condition, the TP sensor signal indicates closed throttle and the ECA shut-off fuel for improved fuel economy and emissions. The injectors are turned off to determine the correct air/fuel ratio for the closed-throttle condition present. Therefore, with the input from the EGO sensor, the system is maintained in closed-loop operation at idle. If the EGO sensor fails to switch rich/lean, the ECA programming assumes the EGO sensor has cooled off, and the system goes to open-loop fuel control. Under a deceleration condition, the TP signal indicates closed throttle and the ECA shut-off fuel for improved fuel economy and emissions. The injectors are turned back on, as required, to prevent engine stalling.

➡**The point at which the injectors are turned back on will occur at different rpm's, depending on calibration factors and engine temperature, although the injectors are turned back on if the throttle is opened.**

Ignition timing is also determined by ECA using these same inputs. The ECA has a series of tables programmed into the assembly at the factory. These tables provide the ECA with a reference of desired ignition timing for the various operating conditions reflected by the sensor inputs. The throttle air bypass valve position is determined by the ECA as a function of RPM, ECT, air conditioning on or off, throttle mode and time since start-up inputs. The signal from the TP sensor to the ECA indicates that the throttle plate is closed, and the ECA de-energizes the EGR shut-off solenoid to close the EGR valve.

Part Throttle Mode (Cruise)

The air/fuel mixture ratio and ignition timing are calculated in the same manner as previously described for the closed throttle mode. The fuel control system remains in closed-loop during part throttle operation, as long as the EGO sensor is operational. In part throttle operation, the throttle air bypass valve is positioned to provide an electronic dashpot function in the event the throttle is closed. Again, as in the closed throttle mode, the ECA makes this determination based on the inputs from the applicable sensors. The TP sensor provides the throttle plate position signal to the ECA. With the throttle plate being in a partial open position, the ECA energizes the EGR shut-off solenoid to open the EGR valve.

Wide Open Throttle (WOT) Mode

Control of the air/fuel ratio in WOT mode is the same as in part, or closed throttle situations, except that fuel control switches to open-loop, and the fuel injector pulse width is increased to provide additional fuel enrichment. This pulse width increase is applied as a result of the WOT signal from the TP sensor to the ECA. This signal from the TP sensor also causes the ECA to remove the energizing signal from the EGR shut-off solenoid. More spark advance is added in WOT for improved performance.

Cold or Hot Engine Operation

This modified operation changes the normal engine operation output signals, as required, to adjust for uncommon engine operating conditions. These include cold or excessively hot engine.

Limited Operation Strategy (LOS)

In this operation, the ECA provides the necessary output signals to allow the vehicle to 'limp home' when an electronic malfunction occurs, sometimes referred to as limp-in mode. The EGR valve is shut-off, the air bypass valve goes to a fixed voltage, timing is locked at the fixed timing (depends on calibration), and the injector pulse width is constant.

Fuel Charging Assembly

The fuel charging assembly controls air/fuel ratio. It consists of a butterfly valve throttle body. It has bore(s) without venturis. The throttle shaft and valves control engine air flow based on driver demand. The throttle body attaches to the intake manifold mounting pad.

A throttle position sensor is attached to the throttle shaft. It includes a potentiometer that electrically senses throttle opening. Some vehicles incorporate a throttle kicker solenoid fastens opposite the throttle position sensor. During air conditioning operation, the solenoid extends to slightly increase engine idle speed.

Fuel Pressure Regulator

The fuel pressure regulator controls critical injector fuel pressure. The regulator receives fuel from the electric fuel pump and then adjusts the fuel pressure for uniform pressure differential between the intake plenum and the fuel injector pressure. The regulator sets fuel pressure at 13-17 psi (90-120 kPa).

Fuel Manifold

The fuel manifold (or fuel rail) distributes fuel to each injector. The end of the fuel rail contains a relief valve for testing

fuel pressure during engine operation and relieving fuel system pressure before work is performed on the system.

Fuel Injectors

The fuel injectors are electromechanical devices. The electrical solenoid operates a pintle or ball metering valve which always travels the same distance from closed to open to closed. Injection is controlled by varying the length of time the valve is open.

The computer, based on voltage inputs from the crank position sensor, operates each injector solenoid 2 times per engine revolution. When the injector metering valve unseats, fuel is sprayed in a fine mist into the intake manifold. The computer varies fuel enrichment based on voltage inputs from the exhaust gas oxygen sensor, barometric pressure sensor, manifold absolute pressure sensor, etc., by calculating how long to hold the injectors open. The longer the injectors remain open, the richer the mixture. This injector 'ON' time is called pulse duration.

Fuel Pump

The fuel delivery system uses either a high or low-pressure in-line or in-tank electric fuel pump, with some models equipped with both. It is a recirculating system that delivers fuel to a pressure regulating valve in the throttle body and returns excess fuel from the throttle body regulator back to the fuel tank. The electrical system uses 2 types of control relays, 1 controlled by a vacuum switch and the other controlled by the electronic control assembly (ECA) to provide power to the fuel pump under various operating conditions.

✳✳CAUTION

Fuel supply lines on vehicles equipped with a high pressure fuel system will remain pressurized for long periods of time after engine shutdown. The fuel pressure must be relieved before servicing the fuel system.

An inertia switch is used as a safety device in the fuel system. The inertia switch is located in the trunk, near the left rear wheel well. It is designed to open the fuel pump power circuit in the event of a collision. The switch is reset by pushing each of 2 buttons on the switch simultaneously (some models use switches with only 1 reset button). The inertia switch should not be reset until the fuel system has been inspected for damage or leaks.

When the ignition switch is **ON**, it turns the EEC power relay **ON**. The EEC power relay provides power to the electronic control assembly (ECA) and the control side of the fuel pump relay. Power for the fuel pump(s) is supplied through a fuse link or high current fuse attached to the starter solenoid (battery side). From the fuse link or high current fuse, current flows through the fuel pump relay and inertia switch to the fuel pump(s). The fuel pump relay is controlled by the ECA.

When the ignition switch is turned **ON**, the fuel pump(s) will operate. If the ignition switch is not turned to the **START** position the ECA will shut the fuel pump(s) **OFF** after 1 second. The ECA will operate the fuel pump(s) operate the fuel pump(s) when the ignition switch is turn to **START** position to provide fuel while cranking.

After the engine starts, the ECA will continue to operate the fuel pump(s) unless the engine stops, drops below 120 rpm or the inertia switch is tripped.

Electronic Control Assembly (ECA)

The Electronic Control Assembly (ECA) is usually located under the instrument panel or passenger's seat and is usually covered by a kick panel. A multi-pin connector links the ECA with all system components. The processor provides a continuous reference voltage to the B/MAP, EVP and TP sensors. EEC-IV systems use a 5 volt reference signal. Different calibration information is used in different vehicle applications, such as California or Federal models. For this reason, careful identification of the engine, year, model and type of electronic control system is essential to insure correct component replacement.

Air Charge Temperature (ACT) Sensor

The ACT sensor is threaded into the intake manifold air runner. It is located next to the throttle body on 4 cylinder engines, behind the distributor on V6 engines and directly below the accelerator linkage on V8 engines. The ACT sensor monitors air/fuel charge temperature and sends an appropriate signal to the ECA. This information is used to correct fuel enrichment for variations in intake air density due to temperature changes.

Barometric and Manifold Absolute Pressure (B/MAP) Sensors

▶ See Figure 43

The B/MAP sensor on V8 engines is located on the right fender panel in the engine compartment. The MAP sensor used on V6 engines is separate from the barometric sensor and is located on the left fender panel in the engine compartment. The barometric sensor signals the ECA of changes in atmospheric pressure and density to regulate calculated air flow into the engine. The MAP sensor monitors and signals the ECA of changes in intake manifold pressure which result from engine load, speed and atmospheric pressure changes.

Crankshaft Position (CP) Sensor

The CP sensor is mounted on the right front of some 5.0L V8 engines. Its purpose is to provide the ECA with an accurate ignition timing reference (when the piston reaches 10 degrees BTDC) and injector operation information (twice each crankshaft revolution). The crankshaft vibration damper is fitted with a 4 lobe pulse ring. As the crankshaft rotates, the pulse ring lobes interrupt the magnetic field at the tip of the CP sensor.

EGR Valve Position (EVP) Sensor

This sensor, mounted on EGR valve, signals the computer of EGR opening so that it may subtract EGR flow from total air flow into the manifold. In this way, EGR flow is excluded from air flow information used to determine mixture requirements.

Engine Coolant Temperature (ECT) Sensor

The ECT is threaded into the intake manifold water jacket directly above the water pump bypass hose. The ECT monitors coolant temperature and signals the ECA, which then uses these signals for mixture enrichment (during cool operation), ignition timing and EGR operation. The resistance value of the ECT increases with temperature, causing a voltage signal drop as the engine warms up.

Exhaust Gas Oxygen (EGO) Sensor

▶ See Figure 44

An exhaust gas oxygen sensor or heated exhaust gas oxygen (HEGO) sensor, mounted in the exhaust manifold, is used on all engines. The EGO is mounted in the right side exhaust manifold on some V8 engines, while other V8 engines use a sensor in both right and left manifolds. The EGO monitors oxygen content of exhaust gases and sends a constantly changing voltage signal to the ECA. The ECA analyzes this signal and adjusts the air/fuel mixture to obtain the optimum (stoichiometric) ratio for combustion and 3-way catalyst performance.

Knock Sensor (KS)

This sensor is attached to the intake manifold in front of the ACT sensor. The KS detects engine vibrations caused by pre-ignition (or detonation) and provides signals to the ECA, which then retards the ignition timing to eliminate detonation in the affected cylinder(s).

Thick Film Integrated (TFI) Module Sensor

▶ See Figure 45

The TFI module sensor plugs into the distributor just below the distributor cap and replaces the CP sensor for some engines. Its function is to provide the ECA with ignition timing information, similar to what the CP sensor provides. On man-

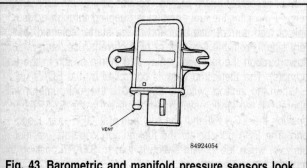

VENT

84924054

Fig. 43 Barometric and manifold pressure sensors look alike

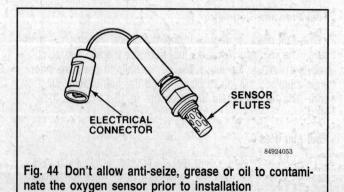

ELECTRICAL CONNECTOR

SENSOR FLUTES

84924053

Fig. 44 Don't allow anti-seize, grease or oil to contaminate the oxygen sensor prior to installation

ual transmission models, the TFI module allows the vehicle to be push-started if necessary.

Throttle Position (TP) Sensor

The TP sensor is mounted on the side of the throttle body, directly connected to the throttle shaft. The TP sensor senses throttle movement and position and transmits an appropriate electrical signal to the ECA. These signals are used by the ECA to adjust the air/fuel mixture, spark timing and EGR operation according to engine load at idle, part throttle, or full throttle. The TP sensor has 2 versions, an adjustable and a non-adjustable; the difference being elongated mounting holes that allow the rotary sensor to be turned slightly to adjust the output voltage. The rotary TP sensor with round mounting holes are not adjustable.

MULTI-POINT FUEL INJECTION SYSTEMS

▶ See Figure 46

The Multi-Point (EFI) and Sequential (SEFI) Fuel Injection sub systems include a high pressure inline electric fuel pump, a low-pressure tank-mounted fuel pump, fuel charging manifold, pressure regulator, fuel filter and both solid and flexible fuel lines. The fuel charging manifold includes 6 or 8 electronically controlled fuel injectors, each mounted directly above an intake port in the lower intake manifold. On the 6 cylinder EFI system, all injectors are energized simultaneously and spray once every crankshaft revolution, delivering a predetermined quantity of fuel into the intake air stream. On the V8 EFI engines, the injectors are energized in 2 banks of 4, once each crankshaft revolution.

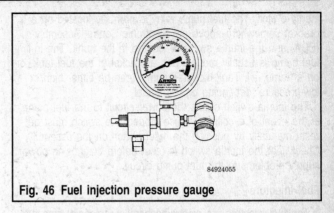

Fig. 46 Fuel injection pressure gauge

The fuel pressure regulator maintains a constant pressure drop across the injector nozzles. The regulator is referenced to intake manifold vacuum and is connected parallel to the fuel injectors and positioned on the far end of the fuel rail. Any excess fuel supplied by the pump passes through the regulator and is returned to the fuel tank via a return line.

➡**The pressure regulator reduces fuel pressure to 39-40 psi under normal operating conditions. At idle or high manifold vacuum condition, fuel pressure is reduced to approximately 30 psi.**

The fuel pressure regulator is a diaphragm operated relief valve in which the inside of the diaphragm senses fuel pressure and the other side senses manifold vacuum. Normal fuel pressure is established by a spring preload applied to the diaphragm. Control of the fuel system is maintained through the EEC power relay and the EEC-IV control unit, although electrical power is routed through the fuel pump relay and an

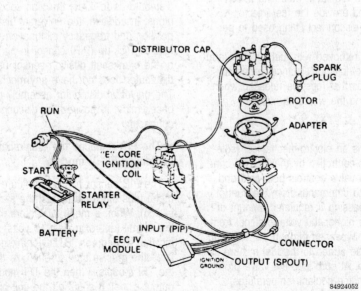

Fig. 45 Thick Film Integrated (TFI) ignition system — 5.0L engine shown

inertia switch. The fuel pump relay is normally located on a bracket somewhere above the Electronic Control Assembly (ECA) and the inertia switch is located in the trunk. The in-line fuel pump is usually mounted on a bracket at the fuel tank, or on a frame rail. Tank-mounted pumps can be either high or low-pressure, depending on the model.

The inertia switch opens the power circuit to the fuel pump in the event of a collision. Once tripped, the switch must be reset manually by pushing the reset button on the assembly. Check that the inertia switch is reset before diagnosing power supply problems to the fuel pump circuit.

Fuel Injectors

The fuel injectors are electromechanical (solenoid) type designed to meter and atomize fuel delivered to the intake ports of the engine. The injectors are mounted in the lower intake manifold and positioned so that their spray nozzles direct the fuel charge in front of the intake valves. The injector body consists of a solenoid actuated pintle and needle valve assembly. The control unit sends an electrical impulse that activates the solenoid, causing the pintle to move inward off the seat and allow the fuel to flow. The amount of fuel delivered is controlled by the length of time the injector is energized (pulse width), since the fuel flow orifice is fixed and the fuel pressure drop across the injector tip is constant. Correct atomization is achieved by contouring the pintle at the point where the fuel enters the pintle chamber.

➡️**Exercise care when handling fuel injectors during service. Be careful not to lose the pintle cap and replace O-rings to assure a tight seal. Never apply direct battery voltage to test a fuel injector.**

The injectors receive high pressure fuel from the fuel manifold (fuel rail) assembly. The complete assembly includes a single, preformed tube with 4, 6, or 8 injector connectors, mounting flange for the pressure regulator, mounting attachments to locate the manifold and provide the fuel injector retainers and a Schrader® quick-disconnect fitting used to perform fuel pressure tests.

The fuel manifold is normally removed with fuel injectors and pressure regulator attached. Fuel injector electrical connectors are plastic and have locking tabs that must be released when disconnecting when disconnecting the wiring harness.

Throttle Air Bypass Valve

The throttle air bypass valve is an electro-mechanical (solenoid) device whose operation is controlled by the EEC-IV control unit. A variable air metering valve controls both cold and warm idle air flow in response to commands from the control unit. The valve operates by bypassing a regulated amount of air around the throttle plate; the higher the voltage signal from the control unit, the more air is bypassed through the valve. In this manner, additional air can be added to the fuel mixture without moving the throttle plate. At curb idle, the valve provides smooth idle for various engine coolant temperatures, compensates for air conditioning load and compensates for transmission load and no-load conditions. The valve also provides fast idle for start-up, replacing the fast idle cam, throttle kicker and anti-dieseling solenoid common to previous models.

There are no curb idle or fast idle adjustments. As in curb idle operation, the fast idle speed is proportional to engine coolant temperature. Fast idle kick-down will occur when the throttle is kicked. A time-out feature in the ECA will also automatically kick-down fast idle to curb idle after a time period of approximately 15-25 seconds; after coolant has reached approximately 71°C (160°F). The signal duty cycle from the ECA to the valve will be at 100% (maximum current) during the crank to provide maximum air flow to allow no touch starting at any time (engine cold or hot).

Electronic Engine Control
➡️ **See Figure 47**

The electronic engine control sub system consists of the ECA and various sensors and actuators. The ECA reads inputs from engine sensors, then outputs a voltage signal to various components (actuators) to control engine functions. The period of time that the injectors are energized ('ON' time or 'pulse width') determines the amount of fuel delivered to each cylinder. The longer the pulse width, the richer the fuel mixture.

➡️**The operating reference voltage (Vref) between the ECA and its sensors and actuators is 5 volts. This allows these components to work during the crank operation even though the battery voltage drops.**

In order for the ECA to properly control engine operation, it must first receive current status reports on various operating conditions. The control unit constantly monitors crankshaft position, throttle plate position, engine coolant temperature, exhaust gas oxygen level, air intake volume and temperature, air conditioning (On/Off), spark knock and barometric pressure.

Universal Distributor

The primary function of the TFI-IV ignition system universal distributor is to direct the high secondary voltage to the spark plugs. In addition, the universal distributor supplies crankshaft position and frequency information to the ECA using a Profile Ignition Pick-up (PIP) sensor in place of the magnetic pick-up or the crankshaft position sensor used on other models. This distributor does not have any mechanical or vacuum advance. The universal distributor assembly is adjustable for resetting base timing, if required, by disconnecting the SPOUT connector.

➡️**The PIP replaces the crankshaft position sensor found on other EEC-IV models.**

The PIP sensor has an armature with 4 windows and 4 metal tabs that rotates past the stator assembly (Hall effect switch). When a metal tab enters the stator assembly, a positive signal (approximately 10 volts) is sent to the ECA, indicating the 10 degrees BTDC crankshaft position. The ECA calculates the precise time to energize the spark output signal to the TFI module. When the TFI module receives the spark output signal, it shuts off the coil primary current and the collapsing field energizes the secondary output.

➡️**Misadjustment of the base timing affects the spark advance in the same manner as a conventional solid-state ignition system.**

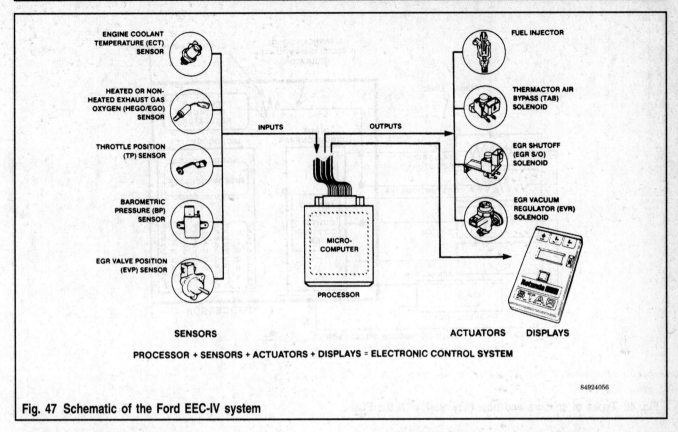

Fig. 47 Schematic of the Ford EEC-IV system

Thick Film Ignition (TFI IV) Module

The TFI IV ignition module has 6 connector pins at the engine wiring harness that supply the following signals:

- Ignition switch in **RUN** position
- Engine cranking
- Tachometer
- PIP (crankshaft position to ECA)
- Spark advance (from ECA)
- Internal ground from the ECA to the distributor

The TFI IV module supplies the spark to the distributor through the ignition coil and calculates the duration. It receives its control signal from the ECA (spark output).

Throttle Position (TP) Sensor

▶ See Figure 48

The TP sensor is mounted on the throttle body. This sensor provides the ECA with a signal that indicates the opening angle of the throttle plate. The sensor output signal uses the 5 volt reference voltage (Vref) previously described. From this input, the ECA controls:

1. Operating modes, which are Wide Open Throttle (WOT), Part Throttle (PT) and Closed Throttle (CT).
2. Fuel enrichment at WOT.
3. Additional spark advance at WOT.
4. EGR cut off during WOT, deceleration and idle.
5. Air conditioning cut off during WOT (30 seconds maximum).
6. Cold start kick-down.
7. Fuel cut off during deceleration.
8. WOT dechoke during crank mode (starting).

On the EEC-IV system, the TP sensor signal to the ECA only changes the spark timing during the WOT mode. As the throttle plate rotates, the TP sensor varies its voltage output. As the throttle plate moves from a closed throttle position to a WOT Position, the voltage output of the TP sensor will change from a low voltage (approximately 1.0 volt) to a high voltage (approximately 4.75 volts). The TP sensor used is not adjustable and must be replaced if it is out of specification. The EEC-IV programming compensates for differences between sensors.

Engine Coolant Temperature (ECT) Sensor

The ECT sensor is located either in the heater supply tube at the rear of the engine, or in the lower intake manifold. The ECT sensor is a thermistor (changes resistance as temperature changes). The sensor detects the temperature of engine coolant and provides a corresponding signal to the ECA. From this signal, the ECA will modify the air/fuel ratio (mixture), idle speed, spark advance, EGR and Canister purge control. When the engine coolant is cold, the ECT sensor signal causes the ECA to provide enrichment to the air/fuel ratio for good cold drive away as engine coolant warms up, the voltage will drop.

Exhaust Gas Oxygen (EGO) Sensor

The EGO or HEGO sensor on the EEC-IV system is a little different from others used and is mounted in its own mounting boss, located between the 2 downstream tubes in the header near the exhaust system. The EGO sensor works between 0-1 volt output, depending on the presence (lean) or absence (rich) of oxygen in the exhaust gas. A voltage reading greater than

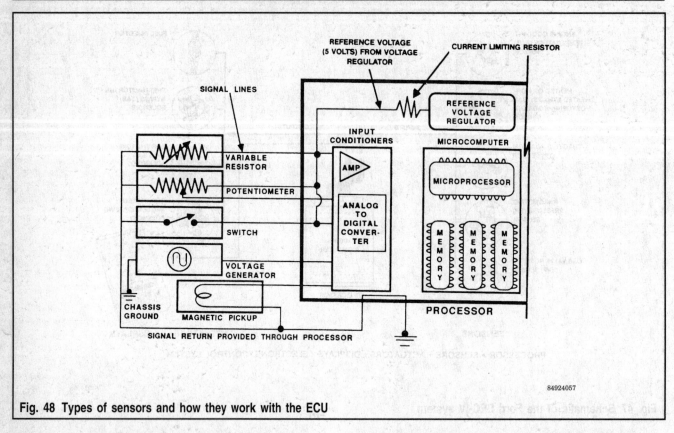

Fig. 48 Types of sensors and how they work with the ECU

0.6 volts indicates a rich air/fuel ratio, while a reading of less than 0.4 volts indicates a lean air/fuel ratio.

➡**Never apply voltage to the EGO sensor because it could destroy the sensor's calibration. This includes the use of an ohmmeter. Before connecting and using a voltmeter, make sure it has a high-input impedance (at least 10 megohms) and is set on the proper resistance range. Any attempt to use a powered voltmeter to measure the EGO voltage output directly will damage or destroy the sensor.**

Operation of the sensor is the same as previous models. A difference that should be noted is that the rubber protective cap used on top of the sensor on the earlier models has been replaced with a metal cap. In addition, later model sensors incorporate a heating element (HEGO), to bring the sensor up to operating temperature more quickly and keep it there during extended idle periods to prevent the sensor from cooling off and placing the system into open loop operation.

Vane Meter

The vane meter is actually 2 sensors in 1 assembly — a Vane Air Flow (VAF) sensor and Vane Air Temperature (VAT) sensor. This meter measures air flow to the engine and the temperature of the air stream. The vane meter is located either behind or under the air cleaner.

Air flow through the body moves a vane mounted on a pivot pin. The more air flowing through the meter, the further the vane rotates about the pivot pin. The air vane pivot pin is connected to a variable resistor (potentiometer) on top of the assembly. The vane meter uses the 5 volt reference voltage. The output of the potentiometer to the ECA varies between 0

and Vref (5 volts), depending on the volume of air flowing through the sensor. A higher volume of air will produce a higher voltage output.

The volume of air measured through the meter has to be converted into an air mass value. The mass (weight) of a specific volume of air varies with pressure and temperature. To compensate for these variables, a temperature sensor in front of the vane measures incoming air temperature. The ECA uses the air temperature and a programmed pressure value to convert the VAF signal into a mass air flow value. This value is used to calculate the fuel flow necessary for the optimum air/fuel ratio. The VAT also affects spark timing as a function of air temperature.

Air Conditioning Clutch Compressor (ACC) Signal

Anytime battery voltage is applied to the A/C clutch, the same signal is also applied to the ECA. The ECA then maintains the engine idle speed with the throttle air bypass valve control solenoid (fuel injection) to compensate for the added load created by the A/C clutch operation. Shutting down the A/C clutch will have a reverse effect. The ECA will maintain the engine idle speed at 850-950 rpm.

Knock Sensor (KS)

The knock sensor is used to detect detonation. In situations of excessive knock the ECA receives a signal from this sensor and retards the spark accordingly. The operation of the knock sensor during boost on turbocharged models improves the engine's durability. It is mounted in the lower intake manifold at the rear of the engine.

Barometric (BAP) Sensor

The barometric sensor is used to compensate for altitude variations. From this signal, the ECA modifies the air/fuel ratio, spark timing, idle speed, and EGR flow. The barometric sensor is a design that produces a frequency based on atmospheric pressure (altitude). The barometric sensor is mounted on the right-hand fender apron.

Manifold Absolute Pressure (MAP) Sensor

The MAP sensor measures manifold vacuum and outputs a variable frequency. This gives the ECA information on engine load. It replaces the BAP sensor by providing the ECA updated barometric pressure readings during key **ON** engine **OFF** and wide open throttle. The MAP sensor output is used by the ECA to control spark advance, EGR flow and air/fuel ratio.

EGR Shut-Off Solenoid

The electrical signal to the EGR shut-off solenoid is controlled by the ECA. The signal is either **ON** or **OFF**. It is **OFF** during cold start, closed throttle or WOT. It is **ON** at all other times.

➡**The canister purge valve is controlled by vacuum from the EGR solenoid. The purge valve is a standard-type valve and operates the same as in previous systems.**

The solenoid is the same as the EGR control solenoid used on previous EEC systems. It is usually mounted on the LH side of the dash panel in the engine compartment, or on the RH shock tower in the engine compartment. The solenoid is normally closed, and the control vacuum from the solenoid is applied to the EGR valve.

ELECTRIC FUEL DELIVERY SYSTEMS

✳✳CAUTION

Fuel pressure must be relieved before attempting to disconnect any fuel lines.

Fuel System Types

Fuel delivery systems using electronic fuel injection differ in their design and arrangement. To simplify diagnostic instructions they will be classified by Type-1 through Type-4. The types shown in the diagnostic charts and schematics are listed as follows:
- Type 1 — Single tank, single pump
- Type 2 — Single tank, dual pump
- Type 3 — Dual tank with electric selector valve
- Type 4 — Dual tank with mechanical selector valve and reservoir

VACUUM DIAGRAMS

▸ **See Figures 49, 50, 51, 52, 53 and 54**

Pressure Tests

The diagnostic pressure valve (Schrader type) is located on the fuel rail on multi-point systems. This valve provides a convenient point for service personnel to monitor fuel pressure, release the system pressure prior to maintenance, and to bleed out air which may become trapped in the system during filter replacement. A pressure gauge with an adapter is required to perform pressure tests.

If the pressure tap is not installed or an adapter is not available, use a T-fitting to install the pressure gauge between the fuel filter line and the throttle body fuel inlet or fuel rail.

Testing fuel pressure requires the use of a special pressure gauge (T80L-9974-A or equivalent) that attaches to the diagnostic pressure tap fitting. Depressurize the fuel system before disconnecting any lines.

EEC-IV SYSTEM TESTING

As in any service procedure, a routine inspection of the EEC-IV system for loose connections, broken wires or obvious damage is the best way to start. Check all vacuum connections and secondary ignition wiring before assuming that the problem lies with the EEC-IV system. A self-diagnosis capability is built into the EEC-IV system to aid in troubleshooting. The primary tool necessary to read the trouble codes stored in the system is an analog voltmeter or special Self Test Automatic Readout (STAR) tester (Motorcraft No. 007-0M004, or equivalent). While the self-test is not conclusive by itself, when activated it checks the EEC-IV system by testing its memory integrity and processing capability. The self-test also verifies that all sensors and actuators are connected and working properly.

FORD EEC MONITOR FOR INTERMITTENTS

The Ford monitor and recorder act as a scan tool into the ECA system. They view the same sensor and actuator values that the ECA uses. The monitor displays these values for both static and dynamic conditions. The purpose of this monitor is to let the technician see the same information that the processor sees and observe how the processor reacts to the information.

Connecting the EEC Monitor requires disconnecting the ECA and connecting special harness adapter to the ECA, monitor and engine control harness. The monitor can then view all circuits going to or from the ECA. The Ford monitor comes with special overlays for each vehicle to be tested, along with instructions.

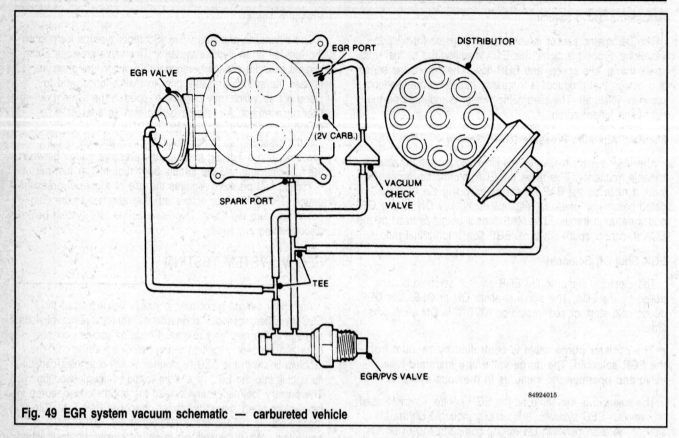

Fig. 49 EGR system vacuum schematic — carbureted vehicle

84924015

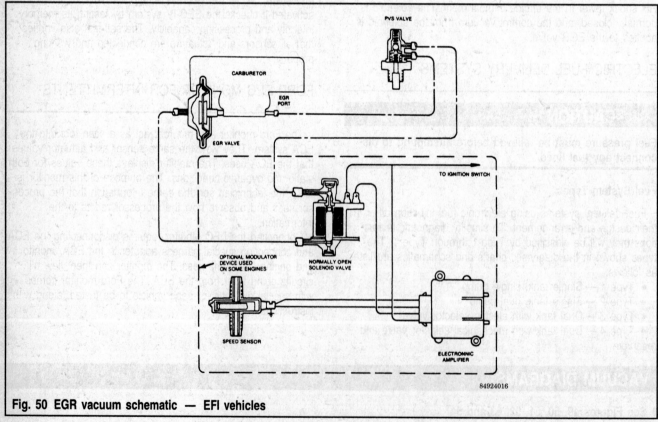

Fig. 50 EGR vacuum schematic — EFI vehicles

84924016

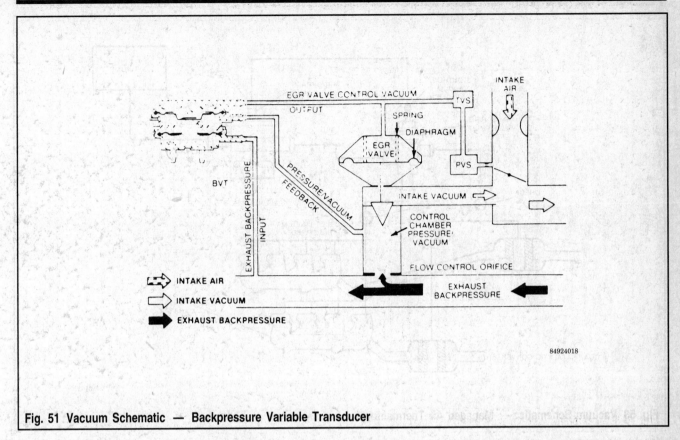

Fig. 51 Vacuum Schematic — Backpressure Variable Transducer

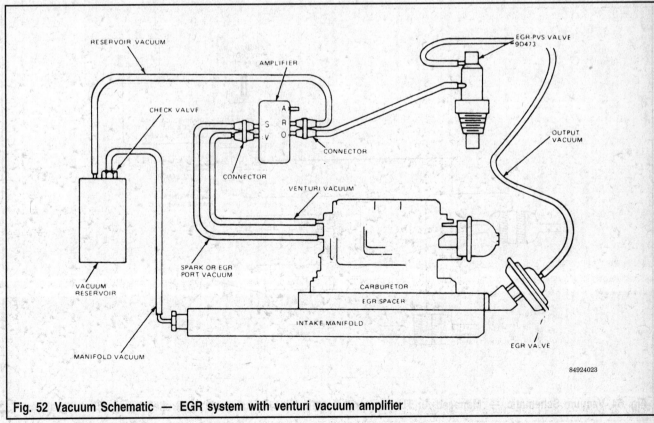

Fig. 52 Vacuum Schematic — EGR system with venturi vacuum amplifier

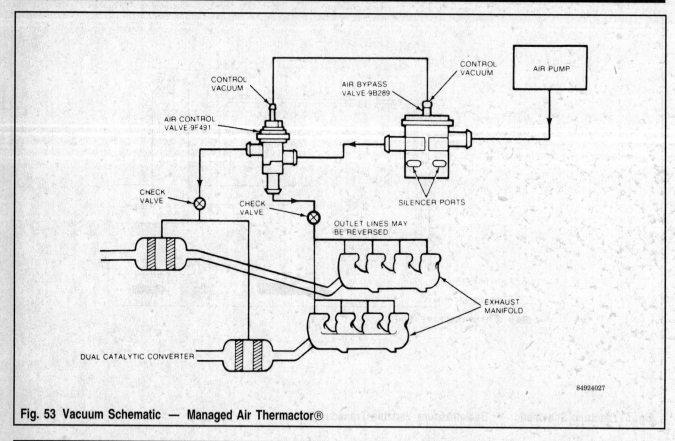

Fig. 53 Vacuum Schematic — Managed Air Thermactor®

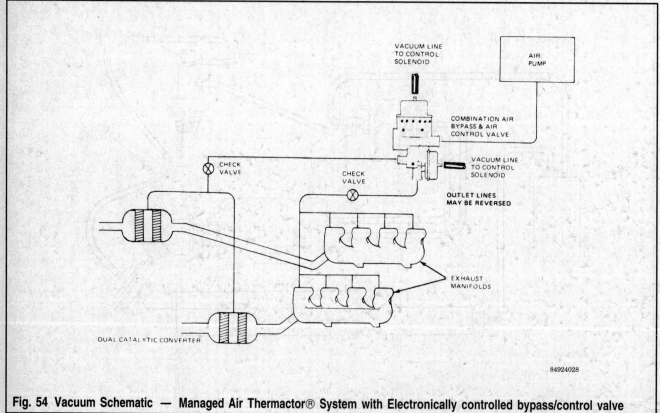

Fig. 54 Vacuum Schematic — Managed Air Thermactor® System with Electronically controlled bypass/control valve

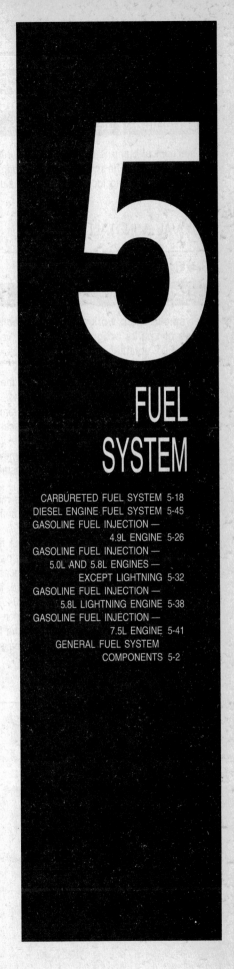

5

FUEL
SYSTEM

GENERAL FUEL SYSTEM COMPONENTS

Mechanical Fuel Pump

A mechanical pump is used on all carbureted engines, except the 8-7.5L. The mechanical fuel pump is camshaft eccentric-actuated and located on the left side of the front cover on V8 engines.

REMOVAL & INSTALLATION

▶ **See Figure 1**

✳✳CAUTION

Never smoke when working around gasoline! Avoid all sources of sparks or ignition. Gasoline vapors are EXTREMELY volatile!

1. Disconnect the fuel inlet and outlet lines at the fuel pump. Discard the fuel inlet retaining clamp.
2. Remove the pump retaining bolts. Remove the pump assembly and gasket from the engine. Discard the gasket.
   To install:
3. If a new pump is to be installed, remove the fuel line connector fitting from the old pump and install it in the new pump.
4. Remove all gasket material from the mounting pad and pump flange. Apply oil resistant sealer to both sides of a new gasket.
5. Position the new gasket on the pump flange and hold the pump in position against the mounting pad. Make sure that the rocker arm is riding on the camshaft eccentric.
6. Press the pump tight against the pad, install the retaining bolts and alternately torque them to 20-24 ft. lbs. on the 8-5.0L; 14-20 on the 8-5.8L; 19-27 ft. lbs. on the 8-7.5L. Connect the fuel lines. Use a new clamp on the fuel inlet lines.
7. Operate the engine and check for leaks.

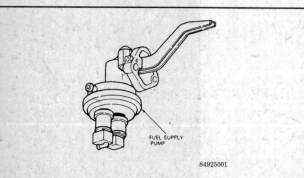

FUEL SUPPLY PUMP

84925001

Fig. 1 Carbureted V8 fuel pump

TESTING

✳✳CAUTION

Never smoke when working around gasoline! Avoid all sources of sparks or ignition. Gasoline vapors are EXTREMELY volatile!

Incorrect fuel pump pressure and low volume (flow rate) are the two most likely fuel pump troubles that will affect engine performance. Low pressure will cause a lean mixture and fuel starvation at high speeds and excessive pressure will cause high fuel consumption and carburetor flooding.

To determine that the fuel pump is in satisfactory operating condition, tests for both fuel pump pressure and volume should be performed.

The test are performed with the fuel pump installed on the engine and the engine at normal operating temperature and at idle speed.

Before the test, make sure that the replaceable fuel filter has been changed at the proper mileage interval. If in doubt, install a new filter.

Pressure Test

1. Remove the air cleaner assembly. Disconnect the fuel inlet line of the fuel filter at the carburetor. Use care to prevent fire, due to fuel spillage. Place an absorbent cloth under the connection before removing the line to catch any fuel that might flow out of the line.
2. Connect a pressure gauge, a restrictor and a flexible hose between the fuel filter and the carburetor.
3. Position the flexible hose and the restrictor so that the fuel can be discharged into a suitable, graduated container.
4. Before taking a pressure reading, operate the engine at the specified idle rpm and vent the system into the container by opening the hose restrictor momentarily.
5. Close the hose restrictor, allow the pressure to stabilize and note the reading. The pressure should be 5 psi.

If the pump pressure is not within 4-6 psi and the fuel lines and filter are in satisfactory condition, the pump is defective and should be replaced.

If the pump pressure is within the proper range, perform the test for fuel volume.

Volume Test

1. Operate the engine at the specified idle rpm.
2. Open the hose restrictor and catch the fuel in the container while observing the time it takes to pump 1 pint. 1 pint should be pumped in 20 seconds. If the pump does not pump to specifications, check for proper fuel tank venting or a restriction in the fuel line leading from the fuel tank to the carburetor before replacing the fuel pump.

Electric Fuel Pump

CARBURETED 7.5L ENGINE

Models equipped with the 7.5L carbureted engine use a single low pressure pump mounted in the fuel tank.

1987-89 FUEL INJECTED ENGINES

Two electric pumps are used on fuel injected models; a low pressure boost pump mounted in the fuel tank and a high pressure pump mounted on the vehicle frame.

On injected models the low pressure pump is used to provide pressurized fuel to the inlet of the high pressure pump and helps prevent noise and heating problems. The externally mounted high pressure pump is capable of supplying 15.9 gallons of fuel an hour. System pressure is controlled by a pressure regulator mounted on the engine.

1990-93 ENGINES

These trucks employ a single, high pressure pump which is part of the modular, in-tank reservoir assembly (ITR). Besides the pump, the ITR consists of a venturi jet pump, a supply check valve and a shuttle selector valve. All this is mounted on the fuel gauge sender flange. The sending unit is separate from the ITR module.

➡On internal fuel tank mounted pumps, tank removal is required. Frame mounted models can be accessed from under the vehicle. Prior to servicing, release the fuel system pressure. Refer to the applicable Fuel Injection System procedures listed in this Section for details. Disconnect the negative battery cable prior to pump removal.

REMOVAL & INSTALLATION

▶ **See Figures 2, 3, 4, 5, 6, 7, 8 and 9**

In-Tank Pump

1. Release the fuel system pressure. Disconnect the negative battery cable.
2. Remove the fuel tank as described below.
3. On steel tanks:
   a. Disconnect the wiring at the connector.
   b. Remove all dirt from the area of the sender.
   c. Disconnect the fuel lines.
   d. Turn the locking ring counterclockwise to remove it. There is a wrench designed for this purpose. If the wrench is not available, you can loosen the locking ring by placing a

WOOD dowel against on the the tabs on the locking ring and hammering it loose. NEVER USE A METAL DRIFT!

✳✳CAUTION

Use of metal will result in sparks which could cause an explosion!

4. Lift out the fuel pump and sending unit. Discard the gasket.
5. On plastic tanks:
   a. Disconnect the wiring at the connector.
   b. Remove all dirt from the area of the sender.
   c. Disconnect the fuel lines.
   d. Turn the locking ring counterclockwise to remove it. A band-type oil filter wrench is ideal for this purpose. Lift out the fuel pump and sending unit. Discard the gasket.

To install:

6. Place a new gasket in position in the groove in the tank.
7. Place the sending unit/fuel pump assembly in the tank, indexing the tabs with the slots in the tank. Make sure the gasket stays in place.
8. Hold the assembly in place and position the locking ring.
   • On steel tanks, turn the locking ring clockwise until the stop is against the retainer ring tab.
   • On plastic tanks, turn the retaining ring clockwise until hand-tight. There is a special too available to set the tightening torque for the locking ring. If you have this tool, torque the ring to 40-55 ft. lbs. If you don't have the tool, just tighten the ring securely with the oil filter wrench.
9. Make sure the gasket is still in place.
10. Connect the fuel lines and wiring.
11. Install the tank.

External Pump

1. Disconnect the negative battery cable.

✳✳CAUTION

Never smoke when working around gasoline! Avoid all sources of sparks or ignition. Gasoline vapors are EXTREMELY volatile!

2. Depressurize the fuel system.
3. Raise and support the rear of the vehicle on jackstands.
4. Disconnect the inlet and outlet fuel lines.
5. Remove the pump from the mounting bracket.
6. Install in reverse order, make sure the pump is indexed correctly in the mounting bracket insulator.
7. Check the pump as follows:
   a. Disconnect the fuel inlet line of the fuel filter at the carburetor. Use care to prevent fire, due to fuel spillage. Place an absorbent cloth under the connection before removing the line to catch any fuel that might flow out of the line.
   b. Connect a pressure gauge, a restrictor and flexible hose between the fuel filter and the carburetor.
   c. Position the flexible hose and the restrictor so that the fuel can be discharged into a suitable, graduated container.
   d. Before taking a pressure reading, operate the engine at the specified idle rpm and vent the system into the container by opening the hose restrictor momentarily.

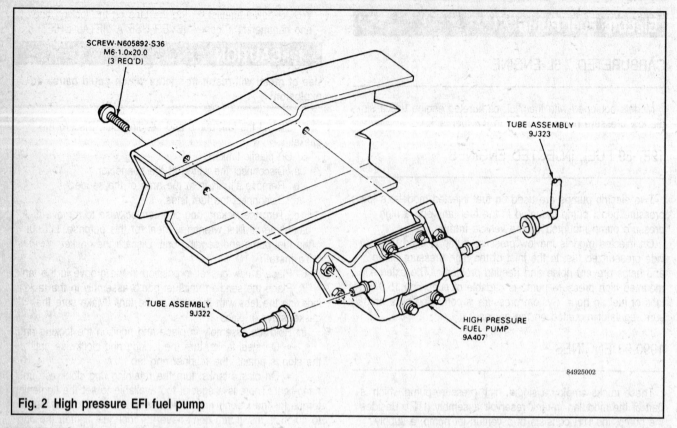

SCREW-N605892-S36
M6-1.0x20.0
(3 REQ'D)

TUBE ASSEMBLY
9J323

TUBE ASSEMBLY
9J322

HIGH PRESSURE
FUEL PUMP
9A407

84925002

Fig. 2 High pressure EFI fuel pump

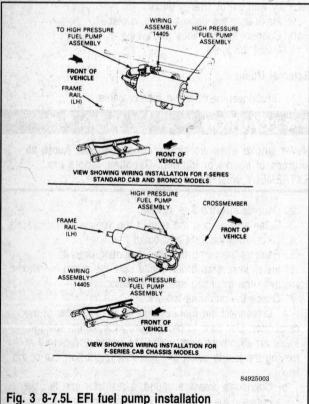

TO HIGH PRESSURE
FUEL PUMP
ASSEMBLY

WIRING
ASSEMBLY
14405

HIGH PRESSURE
FUEL PUMP
ASSEMBLY

FRONT OF
VEHICLE

FRAME
RAIL
(LH)

**VIEW SHOWING WIRING INSTALLATION FOR F-SERIES
STANDARD CAB AND BRONCO MODELS**

HIGH PRESSURE
FUEL PUMP
ASSEMBLY

CROSSMEMBER

FRAME
RAIL
(LH)

FRONT OF
VEHICLE

WIRING
ASSEMBLY
14405

TO HIGH PRESSURE
FUEL PUMP
ASSEMBLY

FRONT OF
VEHICLE

**VIEW SHOWING WIRING INSTALLATION FOR
F-SERIES CAB CHASSIS MODELS**

84925003

Fig. 3 8-7.5L EFI fuel pump installation

e. Close the hose restrictor, allow the pressure to stabilize and note the reading. The pressure should be 5 psi.

If the pump pressure is not within 4-6 psi and the fuel lines and filter are in satisfactory condition, the pump is defective and should be replaced. If the pump pressure is within the proper range, perform the test for fuel volume.

VOLUME TEST

1. Operate the engine at the specified idle rpm.

✳✳CAUTION

Never smoke when working around gasoline! Avoid all sources of sparks or ignition. Gasoline vapors are EXTREMELY volatile!

2. Open the hose restrictor and catch the fuel in the container while observing the time it takes to pump 1 pint. 1 pint should be pumped in 20 seconds. If the pump does not pump to specifications, check for proper fuel tank venting or a restriction in the fuel line leading from the fuel tank to the carburetor before replacing the fuel pump.

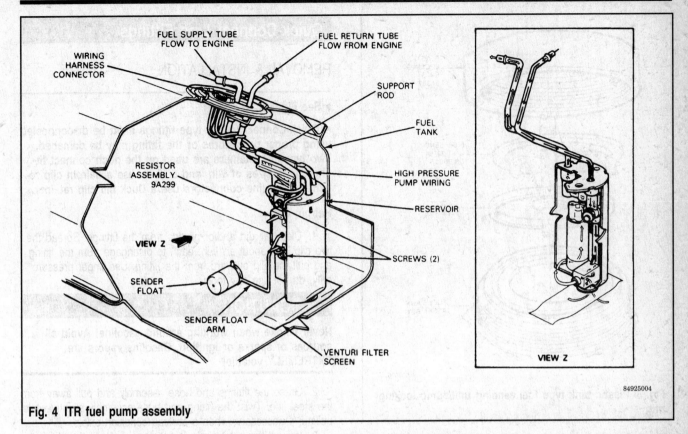

Fig. 4 ITR fuel pump assembly

WIRING HARNESS CONNECTOR

FUEL SUPPLY TUBE FLOW TO ENGINE

FUEL RETURN TUBE FLOW FROM ENGINE

SUPPORT ROD

FUEL TANK

HIGH PRESSURE PUMP WIRING

RESISTOR ASSEMBLY 9A299

RESERVOIR

VIEW Z

SCREWS (2)

SENDER FLOAT

SENDER FLOAT ARM

VENTURI FILTER SCREEN

VIEW Z

84925004

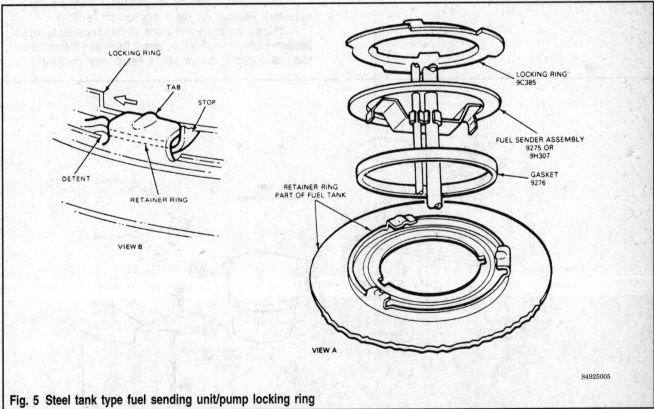

Fig. 5 Steel tank type fuel sending unit/pump locking ring

LOCKING RING

TAB

STOP

DETENT

RETAINER RING

VIEW B

LOCKING RING 9C385

FUEL SENDER ASSEMBLY 9275 OR 9H307

GASKET 9276

RETAINER RING PART OF FUEL TANK

VIEW A

84925005

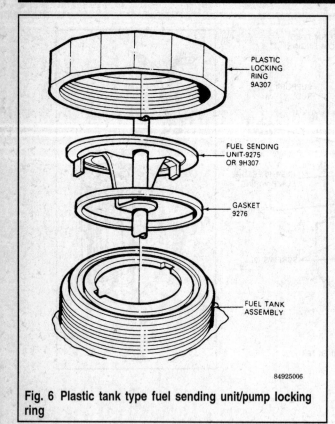

Fig. 6 Plastic tank type fuel sending unit/pump locking ring

Quick-Connect Line Fittings

REMOVAL & INSTALLATION

◆ **See Figures 10 and 11**

➡Quick-Connect (push) type fittings must be disconnected using proper procedures or the fitting may be damaged. Two types of retainers are used on the push connect fittings. Line sizes of ⅜in. and 5/16 in. use a hairpin clip retainer. ¼ in. line connectors use a Duck bill clip retainer.

Hairpin Clip

1. Clean all dirt and/or grease from the fittings. Spread the two clip legs about an ⅛in. each to disengage from the fitting and pull the clip outward from the fitting. Use finger pressure only, do not use any tools.

✳✳CAUTION

Never smoke when working around gasoline! Avoid all sources of sparks or ignition. Gasoline vapors are EXTREMELY volatile!

2. Grasp the fittings and hose assembly and pull away from the steel line. Twist the fitting and hose assembly slightly while pulling, if necessary, when a sticking condition exists.
3. Inspect the hairpin clip for damage, replace the clip if necessary. Reinstall the clip in position on the fitting.
4. Inspect the fitting and inside of the connector to insure freedom of dirt or obstruction. Install fitting into the connector and push together. A click will be heard when the hairpin

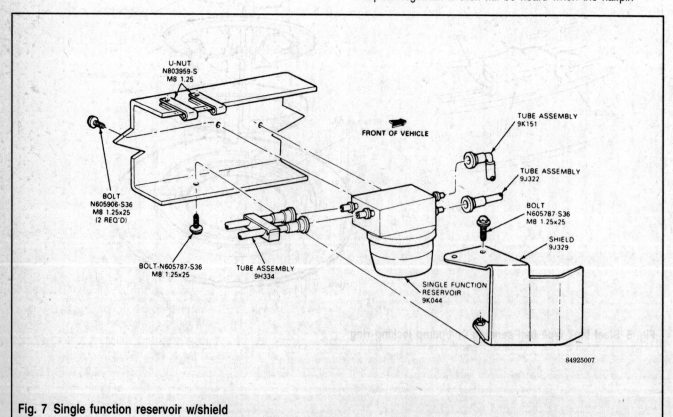

Fig. 7 Single function reservoir w/shield

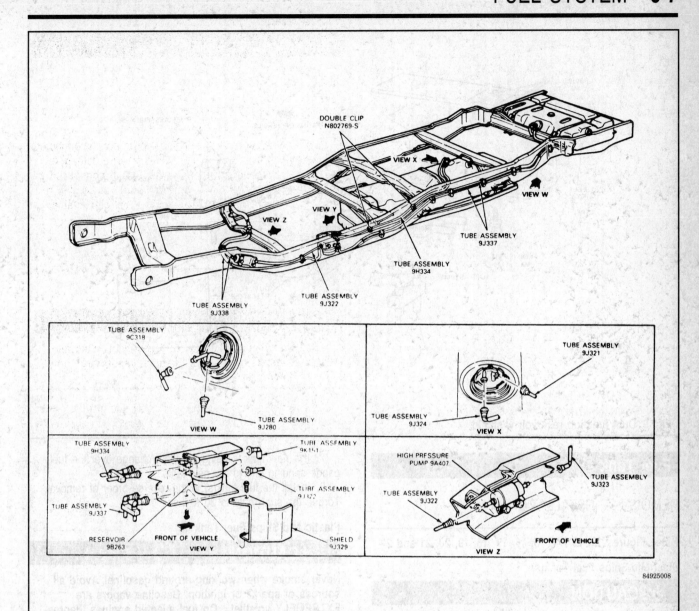

Fig. 8 8-5.0L EFI dual fuel tanks

snaps into proper connection. Pull on the line to insure full engagement.

Duck Bill Clip

1. A special tool is available for Ford for removing the retaining clip (Ford Tool No. T82L-9500-AH). If the tool is not on hand see Step 2. Align the slot on the push connector disconnect tool with either tab on the retaining clip. Pull the line from the connector.

❄❄CAUTION

Never smoke when working around gasoline! Avoid all sources of sparks or ignition. Gasoline vapors are EXTREMELY volatile!

2. If the special clip tool is not available, use a pair of narrow 6 in. (152mm) locking pliers with a jaw width of 0.2 in. (5mm) or less. Align the jaws of the pliers with the openings of the fitting case and compress the part of the retaining clip that engages the case. Compressing the retaining clip will release the fitting which may be pulled from the connector. Both sides of the clip must be compressed at the same time to disengage.

3. Inspect the retaining clip, fitting end and connector. Replace the clip if any damage is apparent.

4. Push the line into the steel connector until a click is heard, indicating the clip is in place. Pull on the line to check engagement.

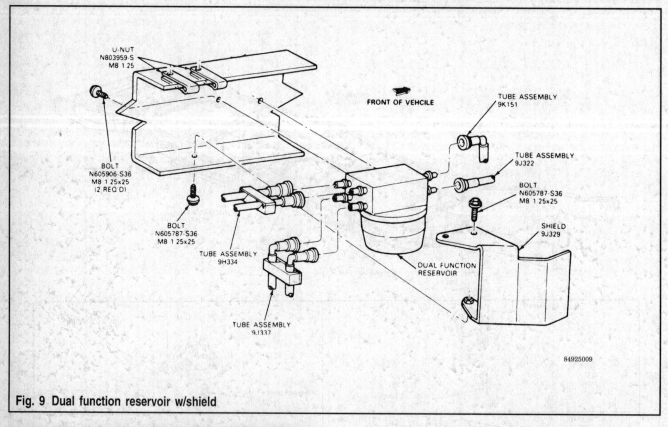

Fig. 9 Dual function reservoir w/shield

Fuel Tank

REMOVAL & INSTALLATION

▶ **See Figures 12, 13, 14, 15, 16, 17, 18, 19, 20, 21 and 22**

Steel Mid-Ships Fuel Tank(s)

❋❋CAUTION

Never smoke when working around gasoline! Avoid all sources of sparks or ignition. Gasoline vapors are EXTREMELY volatile! On fuel injected engines, depressurize the fuel system. Refer to the applicable Fuel Injection System procedures listed in this Section for details.

1. On vehicles with a single fuel tank, disconnect the battery ground cable, then, drain the fuel from the tank into a suitable container by either removing the drain plug, if so equipped, or siphoning through the filler cap opening.
2. On vehicles with dual tanks, drain the fuel tanks by disconnecting the connector hoses, then disconnect the battery ground cable.
3. Disconnect the fuel gauge sending unit wire and fuel outlet line.
4. Disconnect the air relief tube from the filler neck and fuel tank.
5. Loosen the filler neck hose clamp at the fuel tank and pull the filler neck away from the tank.
6. Remove the retaining strap mounting nuts and/or bolts and lower the tank(s) to the floor.

7. If a new tank is being installed, change over the fuel gauge sending unit to the new tank.
8. Install the fuel tank(s) in the reverse order of removal. Torque the strap nuts to 30 ft. lbs.

Plastic Mid-Ships Fuel Tank

❋❋CAUTION

Never smoke when working around gasoline! Avoid all sources of sparks or ignition. Gasoline vapors are EXTREMELY volatile! On fuel injected engines, depressurize the fuel system. Refer to the applicable Fuel Injection System procedures listed in this Section for details.

1. Drain the fuel from the tank into a suitable container by either removing the drain plug, if so equipped, or siphoning through the filler cap opening.
2. Disconnect the battery ground cable(s).
3. Remove the skid plate and heat shields.
4. Disconnect the fuel gauge sending unit wire at the tank.
5. Loosen the filler neck hose clamp at the fuel tank and pull the filler neck away from the tank.
6. Disconnect the fuel line push-connect fittings at the fuel gauge sending unit.
7. Support the tank. Remove the retaining strap mounting bolts and lower the tank to the floor.
8. If a new tank is being installed, change over the fuel gauge sending unit to the new tank.
9. Install the fuel tank(s) in the reverse order of removal. Torque the strap bolts to 12-18 ft. lbs.

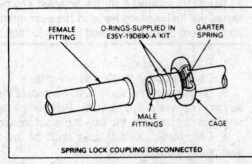

FEMALE FITTING

O-RINGS-SUPPLIED IN E35Y-19D690-A KIT

GARTER SPRING

MALE FITTINGS

CAGE

SPRING LOCK COUPLING DISCONNECTED

TO CONNECT COUPLING

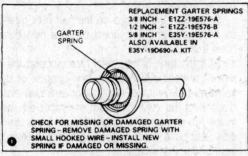

GARTER SPRING

REPLACEMENT GARTER SPRINGS
3/8 INCH – E1ZZ-19E576-A
1/2 INCH – E1ZZ-19E576-B
5/8 INCH – E35Y-19E576-A
ALSO AVAILABLE IN
E35Y-19D690-A KIT

CHECK FOR MISSING OR DAMAGED GARTER SPRING – REMOVE DAMAGED SPRING WITH SMALL HOOKED WIRE – INSTALL NEW SPRING IF DAMAGED OR MISSING.

①

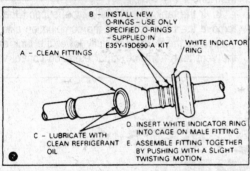

B – INSTALL NEW O-RINGS – USE ONLY SPECIFIED O-RINGS – SUPPLIED IN E35Y-19D690-A KIT

WHITE INDICATOR RING

A – CLEAN FITTINGS

C – LUBRICATE WITH CLEAN REFRIGERANT OIL

D. INSERT WHITE INDICATOR RING INTO CAGE ON MALE FITTING.
E. ASSEMBLE FITTING TOGETHER BY PUSHING WITH A SLIGHT TWISTING MOTION

②

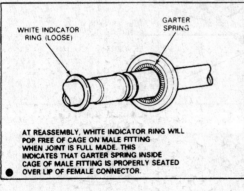

WHITE INDICATOR RING (LOOSE)

GARTER SPRING

AT REASSEMBLY, WHITE INDICATOR RING WILL POP FREE OF CAGE ON MALE FITTING WHEN JOINT IS FULL MADE. THIS INDICATES THAT GARTER SPRING INSIDE CAGE OF MALE FITTING IS PROPERLY SEATED OVER LIP OF FEMALE CONNECTOR.

③

TO DISCONNECT COUPLING
CAUTION – DISCHARGE SYSTEM BEFORE DISCONNECTING COUPLING

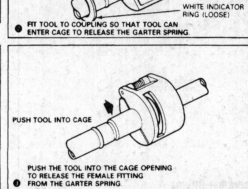

TOOL
D87L-9280-A – 3/8 INCH
D87L-9280-B – 1/2 INCH
T83P-19623-C – 5/8 INCH

CAGE

WHITE INDICATOR RING (LOOSE)

❶ BEFORE DISASSEMBLY, LOCATE WHITE INDICATOR RING WHICH MAY HAVE SLIPPED DOWN LENGTH OF FUEL LINE.

❷ FIT TOOL TO COUPLING SO THAT TOOL CAN ENTER CAGE TO RELEASE THE GARTER SPRING.

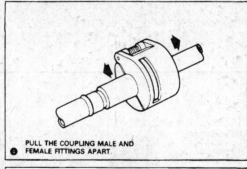

PUSH TOOL INTO CAGE

❸ PUSH THE TOOL INTO THE CAGE OPENING TO RELEASE THE FEMALE FITTING FROM THE GARTER SPRING.

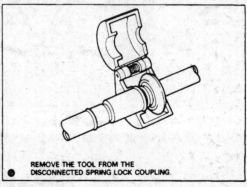

PULL THE COUPLING MALE AND FEMALE FITTINGS APART.

❹

REMOVE THE TOOL FROM THE DISCONNECTED SPRING LOCK COUPLING.

❺

84925010

Fig. 10 EFI Fuel line connectors

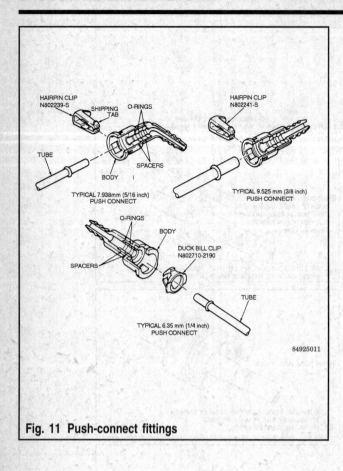

Fig. 11 Push-connect fittings

Plastic or Steel Behind-The-Axle Fuel Tank

✳✳CAUTION

Never smoke when working around gasoline! Avoid all sources of sparks or ignition. Gasoline vapors are EXTREMELY volatile! On fuel injected engines, depressurize the fuel system. Refer to the appropriate Fuel Injection System procedures listed in this Section for details.

1. Raise the rear of the truck.
2. Disconnect the negative battery cable.
3. On trucks with a single tank, disconnect the fuel gauge sending unit wire at the fuel tank. Remove the fuel drain plug or siphon the fuel from the tank into a suitable container.
4. On vehicles with dual tanks, drain the fuel tanks by disconnecting the connector hoses.
5. Disconnect the fuel line push-connect fittings at the fuel gauge sending unit.
6. Loosen the clamps on the fuel filler pipe and vent hose as necessary and disconnect the filler pipe hose and vent hose from the tank.
7. If the tank is the metal type, support the tank and remove the bolts attaching the tank support or skid plate to the frame. Carefully lower the tank or tank/skid plate assembly and disconnect the vent tube from the vapor emission control valve in the top of the tank. Finish removing the filler pipe and filler pipe vent hose if not possible previously. Remove the tank from under the vehicle.
8. If the tank is the plastic type, support the tank and remove the bolts attaching the combination skid plate and tank support to the frame. Carefully lower the tank and disconnect the vent tube from the vapor emission control valve in the top

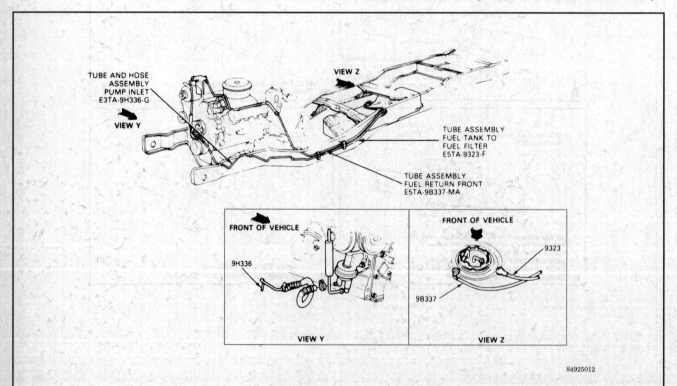

Fig. 12 Diesel fuel lines w/midship tank

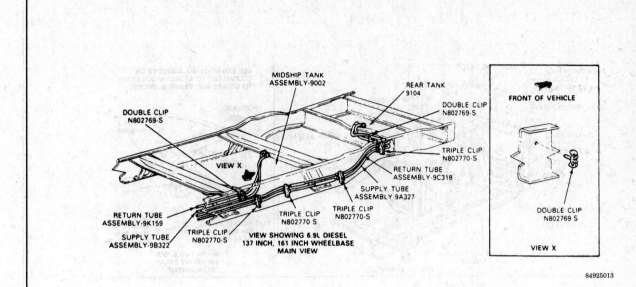

Fig. 13 Diesel fuel lines w/dual tanks

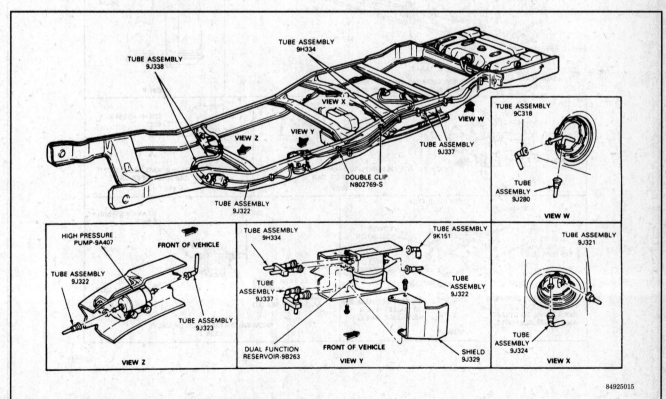

Fig. 14 8-5.0L EFI dual tanks w/139 in. (353cm) wheel base

of the tank. Finish removing the filler pipe and filler pipe vent hose if it was not possible previously. Remove the skid plate and tank from under the vehicle. Remove the skid plate from the tank.

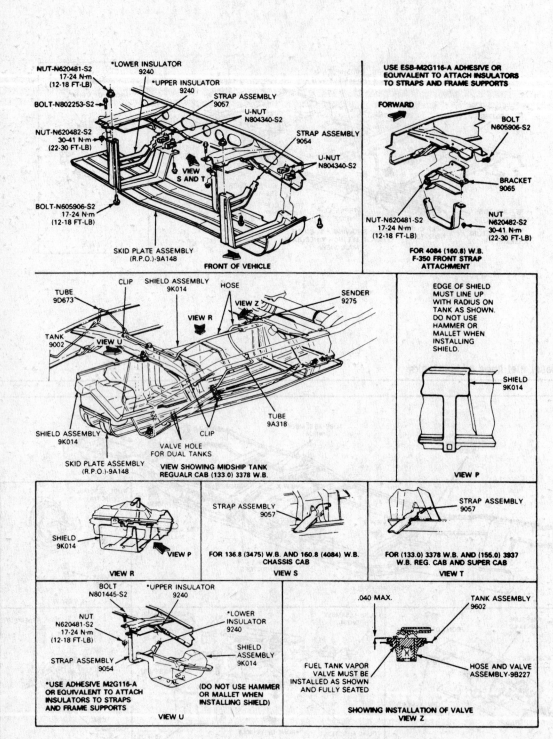

Fig. 15 19 gallon (72L) midships fuel tank

84925020

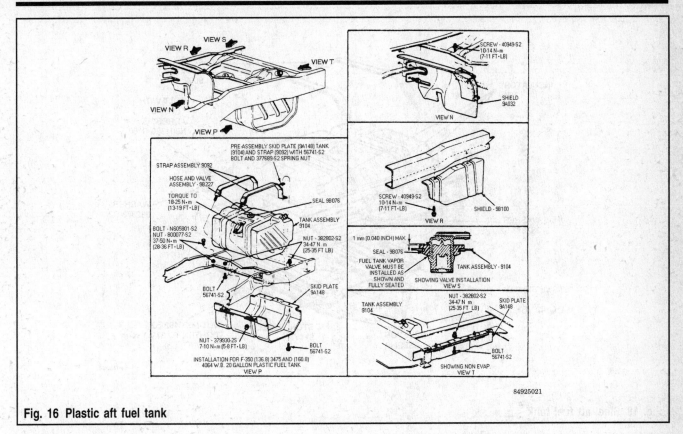

Fig. 16 Plastic aft fuel tank

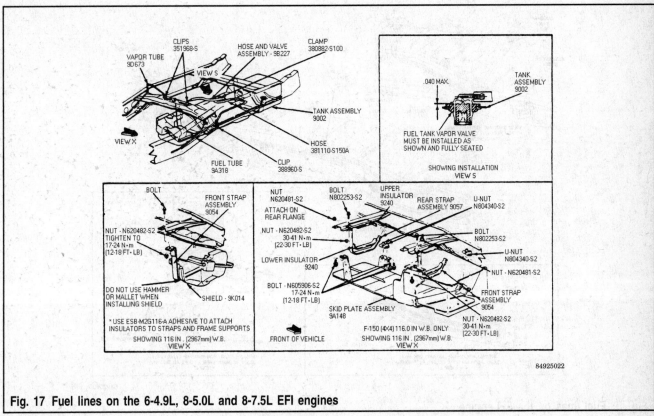

Fig. 17 Fuel lines on the 6-4.9L, 8-5.0L and 8-7.5L EFI engines

9. If the sending unit is to be removed, turn the unit retaining ring counterclockwise and remove the sending unit, retaining ring and gasket. Discard the gasket.

10. Install the tank in the reverse order of removal. With metal tanks, use thread adhesive such as Loctite® on the bolt threads, and torque these bolts to 27-37 ft. lbs. With plastic

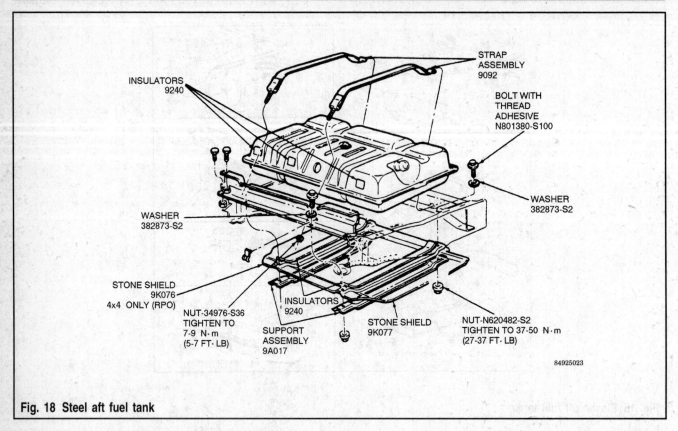

STRAP ASSEMBLY 9092

INSULATORS 9240

BOLT WITH THREAD ADHESIVE N801380-S100

WASHER 382873-S2

WASHER 382873-S2

STONE SHIELD 9K076 4x4 ONLY (RPO)

NUT-34976-S36 TIGHTEN TO 7-9 N·m (5-7 FT·LB)

INSULATORS 9240

SUPPORT ASSEMBLY 9A017

STONE SHIELD 9K077

NUT-N620482-S2 TIGHTEN TO 37-50 N·m (27-37 FT·LB)

84925023

Fig. 18 Steel aft fuel tank

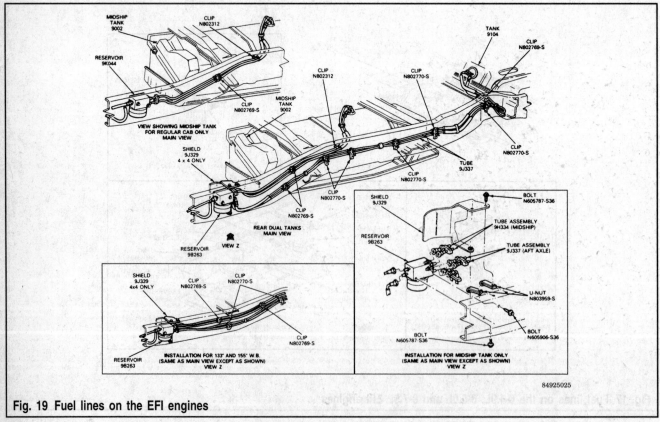

MIDSHIP TANK 9002

CLIP N802312

RESERVOIR 9K044

CLIP N802769-S

MIDSHIP TANK 9002

CLIP N802312

CLIP N802770-S

TANK 9104

CLIP N802769-S

CLIP N802770-S

VIEW SHOWING MIDSHIP TANK FOR REGULAR CAB ONLY MAIN VIEW

SHIELD 9J329 4 x 4 ONLY

CLIP N802770-S

CLIP N802770-S

TUBE 9J337

SHIELD 9J329

BOLT N605787-S36

TUBE ASSEMBLY 9H334 (MIDSHIP)

CLIP N802769-S

RESERVOIR 9B263

TUBE ASSEMBLY 9J337 (AFT AXLE)

U-NUT N803959-S

REAR DUAL TANKS MAIN VIEW

CLIP N802770-S

RESERVOIR 9B263

VIEW Z

SHIELD 9J339 4x4 ONLY

CLIP N802769-S

CLIP N802770-S

CLIP N802769-S

BOLT N605787-S36

BOLT N605906-S36

RESERVOIR 9B263

INSTALLATION FOR 133" AND 155" W.B. (SAME AS MAIN VIEW EXCEPT AS SHOWN) VIEW Z

INSTALLATION FOR MIDSHIP TANK ONLY (SAME AS MAIN VIEW EXCEPT AS SHOWN) VIEW Z

84925025

Fig. 19 Fuel lines on the EFI engines

tanks, DO NOT use thread adhesive. Torque the bolts to 25-35 ft. lbs.

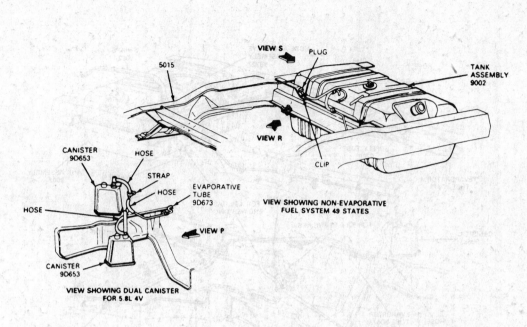

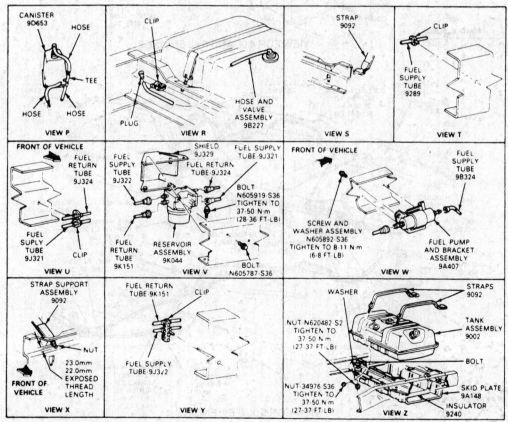

Fig. 20 Bronco fuel tank

84925027

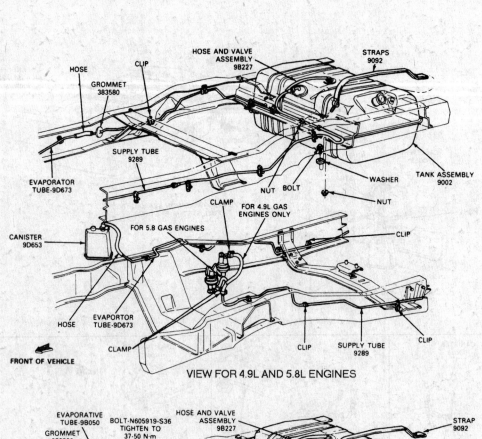

VIEW FOR 4.9L AND 5.8L ENGINES

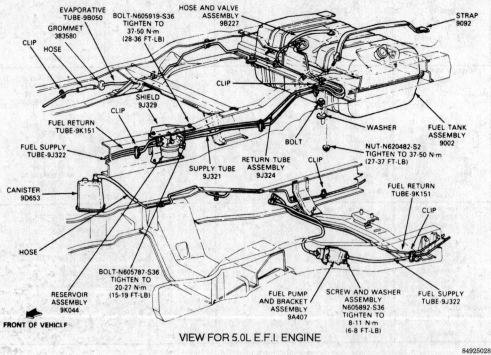

VIEW FOR 5.0L E.F.I. ENGINE

84925028

Fig. 21 Bronco fuel tank, cont.

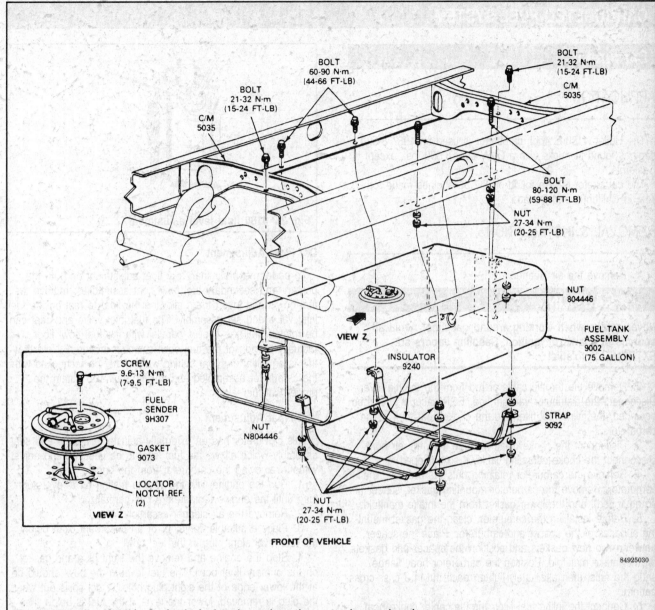

BOLT
60-90 N·m
(44-66 FT-LB)

BOLT
21-32 N·m
(15-24 FT-LB)

C/M
5035

BOLT
21-32 N·m
(15-24 FT-LB)

C/M
5035

BOLT
80-120 N·m
(59-88 FT-LB)

NUT
27-34 N·m
(20-25 FT-LB)

NUT
804446

FUEL TANK
ASSEMBLY
9002
(75 GALLON)

VIEW Z

INSULATOR
9240

STRAP
9092

NUT
N804446

NUT
27-34 N·m
(20-25 FT-LB)

FRONT OF VEHICLE

SCREW
9.6-13 N·m
(7-9.5 FT-LB)

FUEL
SENDER
9H307

GASKET
9073

LOCATOR
NOTCH REF.
(2)

VIEW Z

84925030

Fig. 22 75 gallon (284L) aft-of-axle fuel tank used on the motor home chassis

Bronco Fuel Tank

✷✷CAUTION

Never smoke when working around gasoline! Avoid all sources of sparks or ignition. Gasoline vapors are EXTREMELY volatile!

1. Raise and support the rear end on jackstands.
2. Disconnect the negative battery cable.
3. Disconnect the fuel gauge sending unit wire at the fuel tank.
4. Remove the fuel drain plug or siphon the fuel from the tank into a suitable container.
5. Loosen the fuel line hose clamps, slide the clamps forward and disconnect the fuel one at the fuel gauge sending unit.

6. Loosen the clamps on the fuel filler pipe and vent hose as necessary and disconnect the filler pipe hose and vent hose from the tank.
7. Support the tank and remove the lower attaching bolts or skid plate bolts supporting the tank to the frame. Carefully lower the tank or tank/skid plate assembly and disconnect the vent tube from the vapor emission control valve in the top of the tank. Finish removing the filler pipe and filler pipe vent hose if not possible previously. Remove the tank from under the vehicle.
8. If the sending unit is being removed, turn the unit's retaining ring counterclockwise and remove the sending unit, retaining ring and gasket. Discard the gasket.
9. Install the tank in the reverse order of removal. Use thread locking compound on the bolt threads and torque the bolts to 27-37 ft. lbs.

CARBURETED FUEL SYSTEM

Carburetor

APPLICATION

The Holley 4180-C 4bbl. carburetor is used on 1987 8-5.8L engines found in trucks with a GVW over 8,500 lbs., except in California.

The carburetor is also found on 8-7.5L engines made for sale in California and Canada.

REMOVAL & INSTALLATION

1. Remove the air cleaner.

❋❋CAUTION

Never smoke when working around gasoline! Avoid all sources of sparks or ignition. Gasoline vapors are EXTREMELY volatile!

2. Remove the throttle cable or rod from the throttle lever. Disconnect the distributor vacuum line, EGR vacuum line, if so equipped, the inline fuel filter and the choke heat tube at the carburetor.

3. Disconnect the choke clean air tube from the air horn. Disconnect the choke actuating cable, if so equipped.

4. Remove the carburetor retaining nuts then remove the carburetor. Remove the carburetor mounting gasket, spacer (if so equipped), and the lower gasket from the intake manifold.

5. Before installing the carburetor, clean the gasket mounting surfaces of the spacer and carburetor. Place the spacer between two new gaskets and position the spacer and gaskets on the intake manifold. Position the carburetor body flange, snug the nuts, then alternately tighten each nut in a criss-cross pattern.

6. Connect the inline fuel filter, throttle cable, choke heat tube, distributor vacuum line, EGR vacuum line, and choke cable.

7. Connect the choke clean air line to the air horn.

8. Adjust the engine idle speed, the idle fuel mixture and anti-stall dashpot (if so equipped). Install the air cleaner.

FLOAT AND FUEL LEVEL ADJUSTMENT

▶ See Figure 23

❋❋CAUTION

Never smoke when working around gasoline! Avoid all sources of sparks or ignition. Gasoline vapors are EXTREMELY volatile!

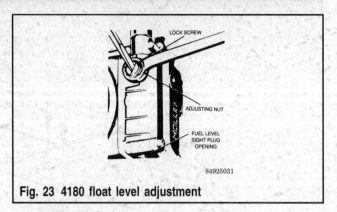

Fig. 23 4180 float level adjustment

Dry Float Adjustment

To perform a preliminary dry float adjustment on both the primary and secondary fuel bowl float assemblies, remove the fuel bowls and invert them allowing the float to rest on the fuel inlet valve and set assembly. The fuel inlet valve and seat can be rotated until the float is parallel with the fuel bowl floor (actually the top of the fuel bowl chamber inverted). Note that this is an initial dry float setting which must be rechecked with the carburetor assembled and on the engine to obtain the proper wet fuel level.

Wet Float Adjustment

This carburetor has an externally adjustable needle and seat assembly which allows the fuel level to be checked and adjust without removing the carburetor from the engine.

1. Run the engine with the vehicle resting on a level surface until the engine temperature has normalized.

2. Remove the air cleaner assembly.

3. Place a suitable container or an absorbent cloth below the fuel level sight plug in the fuel bowl.

4. Stop the engine and remove the sight plug and gasket on the primary float bowl. The fuel level in the bowl should be at the lower edge of the sight plug hole. If fuel spills out when the plug is removed, lower the level; if the fuel is below the hole, raise the level.

❋❋CAUTION

Never loosen the lockscrew or nut, or attempt to adjust the fuel level with the sight plug removed or the engine running, since fuel will spray out creating a fire hazard!

5. To adjust the fuel level, install the sight plug and gasket. Loosen the lockscrew on top of the fuel bowl just enough to allow the adjusting nut to be turned. Turn the adjusting nut about ½ of a turn in to lower the fuel level and out to raise the fuel level. By turning the adjusting nut 5/32 of a turn, the fuel level will change 1/32 in. (0.8mm) at the sight plug.

6. Start the engine and allow the fuel level to stabilize. Check the fuel level as outlined in Step 4.

7. Repeat the procedure for the secondary float bowl adjustment.

8. Install the air cleaner assembly if no further adjustments are necessary.

SECONDARY THROTTLE PLATE ADJUSTMENT

1. Remove the carburetor.

❋❋CAUTION

Never smoke when working around gasoline! Avoid all sources of sparks or ignition. Gasoline vapors are EXTREMELY volatile!

2. Hold the secondary throttle plates closed.
3. Turn the secondary throttle shaft lever stop screw out until the secondary throttle plates seat in the throttle bores.
4. Turn the screw back in until the screw just touches the lever, then ⅜ turn more.

FAST IDLE ADJUSTMENT

▶ See Figure 24

1. Remove the spark delay valve, if so equipped, from the distributor vacuum advance line, and route the vacuum line directly to the advance side of the distributor.

❋❋CAUTION

Never smoke when working around gasoline! Avoid all sources of sparks or ignition. Gasoline vapors are EXTREMELY volatile!

2. Trace the EGR signal vacuum line from the EGR valve to the carburetor and if there is EGR/PVS valve or temperature vacuum switch located in the vacuum line routing, disconnect the EGR vacuum line at the EGR valve and plug the line.
3. If not equipped with an EGR/PVS valve or temperature vacuum switch do not detach the EGR vacuum line.
4. Trace the purge valve vacuum line from the purge valve located on the canister, to the first point where the vacuum line can be detached from the underhood hose routing. Disconnect the vacuum line at that point, cap the open port, and plug the vacuum line.

❋❋WARNING

To prevent damage to the purge valve do not disconnect the vacuum line at the purge valve.

5. With the engine running at normal operating temperature, the choke plate fully opened and the manual transmission in Neutral and the automatic transmission in Park, place the fast idle level on the 2nd or kickdown step of the fast idle cam.
6. Adjust the fast idle screw to within 100 rpm of the specified speed given on the Vehicle Emission Control Decal.
7. Reconnect all vacuum lines.

VACUUM OPERATED THROTTLE MODULATOR ADJUSTMENT

▶ See Figure 25

1. Set the parking brake, put the transmission in Park or Neutral and run the engine up to operating temperature.

❋❋CAUTION

Never smoke when working around gasoline! Avoid all sources of sparks or ignition. Gasoline vapors are EXTREMELY volatile!

2. Turn off the air conditioning and heater controls.
3. Disconnect and plug the vacuum hoses at the air control valve and EGR valve and purge control valve.
4. Place the transmission in the position specified on the underhood decal.
5. If necessary, check and adjust the curb idle rpm.
6. Place the transmission in Neutral or Park and rev the engine. Place the transmission in the specified position according to the underhood decal and recheck the curb idle rpm. Readjust if necessary.
7. Connect an external vacuum source which provides a minimum of 10 in. Hg of vacuum to the VOTM (Vacuum Operated Throttle Modulator) kicker.
8. Place the transmission in the specified position.
9. Adjust the VOTM (throttle kicker) locknut if necessary to obtain the proper idle rpm.
10. Reconnect all vacuum hoses.

CHOKE PLATE PULL-DOWN CLEARANCE ADJUSTMENT

▶ See Figure 26

1. Remove the choke thermostat housing, gasket and retainer.

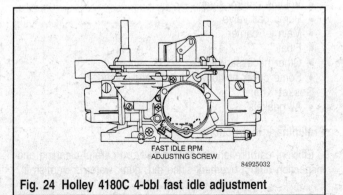

FAST IDLE RPM
ADJUSTING SCREW

84925032

Fig. 24 Holley 4180C 4-bbl fast idle adjustment

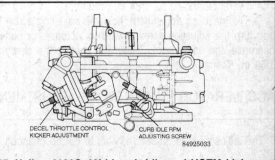

DECEL THROTTLE CONTROL
KICKER ADJUSTMENT

CURB IDLE RPM
ADJUSTING SCREW

84925033

Fig. 25 Holley 4180C 40bbl curb idle and VOTM kicker adjustments location

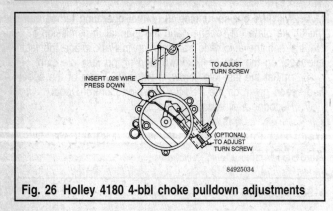

INSERT .026 WIRE PRESS DOWN

TO ADJUST TURN SCREW

(OPTIONAL) TO ADJUST TURN SCREW

84925034

Fig. 26 Holley 4180 4-bbl choke pulldown adjustments

2. Insert a piece of wire into the choke piston bore to move the piston down against the stop screw.

✳✳CAUTION

Never smoke when working around gasoline! Avoid all sources of sparks or ignition. Gasoline vapors are EXTREMELY volatile!

3. Measure the gap between the lower edge of the choke plate and the air horn wall.
4. Turn the adjustment screw to specifications.
5. Reinstall the choke thermostat housing, gasket and retainer.

AUTOMATIC CHOKE HOUSING ADJUSTMENT

This adjustment is present and should not be changed.

ACCELERATOR PUMP LEVER ADJUSTMENT

1. Hold the primary throttle plates in the wide open position.

✳✳CAUTION

Never smoke when working around gasoline! Avoid all sources of sparks or ignition. Gasoline vapors are EXTREMELY volatile!

2. Using a feeler gauge, check the clearance at the accelerator pump operating lever adjustment screw head and the pump arm while depressing the pump arm with your finger. The clearance should be 1/64 in. (0.38mm).
3. To make an adjustment, hold the adjusting screw locknut and turn the adjusting screw inward to increase, or outward to decrease, the adjustment. ½ turn will change the clearance by 1/64 in. (0.4mm).

ACCELERATOR PUMP STROKE ADJUSTMENT

This adjustment is preset and should not be changed.

CARBURETOR TROUBLESHOOTING

The best way to diagnose a bad carburetor is to eliminate all other possible sources of the problem. If the carburetor is suspected to be the problem, first perform all of the adjustments given in this Section. If this doesn't correct the difficulty, then check the following. Check the ignition system to make sure that the spark plugs are in good condition and adjusted to the proper specifications. Examine the emission control equipment to make sure that all the vacuum lines are connected and none are blocked or clogged. See the first half of this Section. Check the ignition timing adjustment. Check all of the vacuum lines on the engine for loose connections, slips or breaks. Torque the carburetor and intake manifold attaching bolts to the proper specifications. If, after performing all of these checks and adjustments, the problem is still not solved, then you can safely assume that the carburetor is the source of the problem.

OVERHAUL

✳✳CAUTION

Never smoke when working around gasoline! Avoid all sources of sparks or ignition. Gasoline vapors are EXTREMELY volatile!

Overhaul Kits

Carburetor overhaul kits are recommended for each overhaul. These kits contain all gaskets and new parts to replace those which deteriorate most rapidly. Failure to replace all of the parts supplied with the kit (especially gaskets) can result in poor performance later.

Most carburetor manufacturers supply overhaul kits of three basic types:

Minor Repair Kits:
- All gaskets
- Float needle valve
- Volume control screw
- All diaphragms
- Spring for the pump diaphragm

Major Repair Kits:
- All jets and gaskets
- All diaphragms
- Float needle valve
- Volume control screw
- Pump ball valve
- Main jet carrier
- Float
- Other necessary items
- Some cover holddown screws and washers

Gasket Kits:
- All gaskets

Preliminary Instructions

Efficient carburetion depends greatly on careful cleaning and inspection during overhaul since dirt, gum, water or varnish in or on the carburetor parts are often responsible for poor performance.

Overhaul the carburetor in a clean, dust free area. Carefully disassemble the carburetor, referring often to the exploded views. Keep all similar and look-alike parts segregated during disassembly and cleaning to avoid accidental interchange during assembly. Make a note of all jet sizes.

When the carburetor is disassembled, wash all parts (except diaphragms, electric choke units, pump plunger and any other plastic, leather, fiber, or rubber parts) in clean carburetor solvent. Do not leave the parts in the solvent any longer than is necessary to sufficiently loosen the dirt and deposits. Excessive cleaning may remove the special finish from the float bowl and choke valve bodies, leaving these parts unfit for service. Rinse all parts in clean solvent and blow them dry with compressed air or allow them to air dry, while resting on clean, lintless paper. Wipe clean all cork, plastic, leather and fiber parts with clean, lint free cloth.

Blow out all passages and jets with compressed air and be sure that there are no restrictions or blockages. Never use wire or similar tools to clean jets, fuel passages or air bleeds. Clean all jets and valves separately to avoid accidental interchange.

Examine all parts for wear or damage. If wear or damage is found, replace the defective parts. Especially, inspect the following:

1. Check the float needle and seat for wear. If wear is found, replace the complete assembly.

2. Check the float hinge pin for wear and the float(s) for dents or distortion. Replace the float if fuel has leaked into it.

3. Check the throttle and choke shaft bores for wear or an out-of-round condition. Damage or wear to the throttle arm, shaft or shaft bore will often require replacement of the throttle body. These parts require a close tolerance of fit; wear may allow air leakage, which could affect starting and idling.

➡**Throttle shaft and bushings are not normally included in overhaul kits. They can be purchased separately.**

4. Inspect the idle mixture adjusting needles for burrs and grooves. Any such condition requires replacement of the needle, since you will not be able to obtain a satisfactory idle.

5. Test the accelerator pump check valves. They should pass air one way, but not the other. Test for proper seating by blowing and sucking on the valve. Replace the valve as necessary. If the valve is satisfactory, wash the valve again to remove moisture.

6. Check the bowl cover for warped surfaces with a straightedge.

7. Closely inspect the valves and seats for wear and damage, replacing as necessary.

8. After the carburetor is assembled, check the choke valve for freedom of operation.

After cleaning and checking all components, reassemble the carburetor, using new parts and referring to the exploded view. When reassembling, make sure that all screws and jets are right in their seat, but do not overtighten, as the tip will be distorted. Tighten all screws gradually, in rotation. Do not tighten needle valves into their seats; uneven jetting will result. Always use new gaskets. Be sure to adjust the float level.

DISASSEMBLY

▶ **See Figures 27, 28, 29 and 30**

Primary Fuel Bowl and Metering Block

1. Remove the fuel bowl and gasket and metering block and gasket. Discard the gaskets.

2. Remove the pump transfer tube from the main housing or metering block and discard the O-rings.

3. Remove the fuel line tube and discard the O-ring.

4. Remove the main jets.

5. Remove the power valve and gasket.

6. Remove the fuel level adjustment lockscrew and gasket. Remove the adjusting screw and the inlet needle and seat assembly. The needle and seat assembly is a matched set and must be replaced by a matched set. Discard the inlet gasket.

7. Remove the float shaft retainer clip and slide the float off the shaft. Remove the spring from the float.

8. Remove the baffle plate from the float bowl.

9. Remove the fuel level sight plug and gasket.

10. Remove the fuel inlet fitting, gasket and filter screen.

11. Invert the float bowl and remove the accelerator pump cover, diaphragm and spring. The pump inlet check ball should not be removed.

Secondary Fuel Bowl and Metering Plate
▶ **See Figure 31**

1. Remove the fuel bowl.

2. Using a clutch-type screwdriver, remove the metering body, plate and gaskets. Discard the gaskets.

3. Remove the fuel level adjustment lockscrew and gasket. Remove the adjusting screw and the inlet needle and seat assembly. The needle and seat assembly is a matched set and must be replaced by a matched set. Discard the inlet gasket.

4. Remove the float shaft retainer clip and slide the float off the shaft. Remove the spring from the float.

5. Remove the baffle plate from the float bowl.

6. Remove the fuel level sight plug and gasket.

Main Body
▶ **See Figures 32 and 33**

1. Remove the air cleaner anchor stud.

2. Remove the secondary diaphragm link C-clip.

3. Invert the carburetor and remove the throttle body attaching screws and lockwashers. Lift off the throttle body and discard the gasket.

4. Remove the choke housing cap and gasket.

5. Remove the 3 choke housing retaining screws and pull the housing from the main body while pushing the choke rod out of the retainer on the choke housing shaft lever.

6. Remove the choke housing shaft nut, star washer, spacer, lever, fast idle cam spring, spring perch and fast idle cam.

7. Remove the over-center spring and choke housing shaft.

8. Remove the choke diaphragm cover screws and separate the diaphragm cover from the diaphragm.

9. Remove the diaphragm spring.

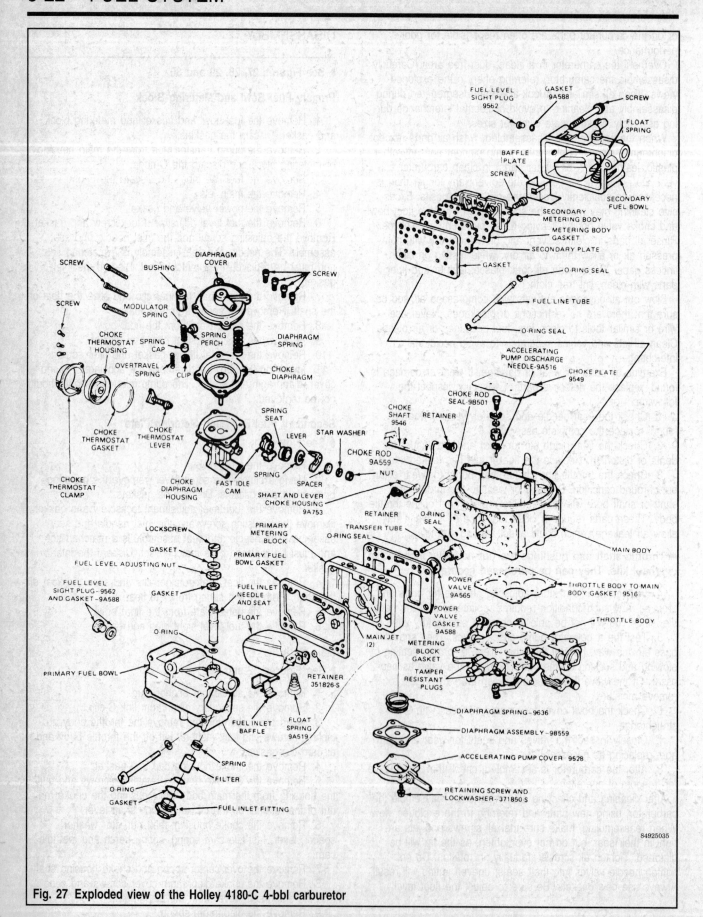

Fig. 27 Exploded view of the Holley 4180-C 4-bbl carburetor

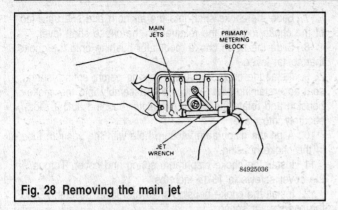

Fig. 28 Removing the main jet

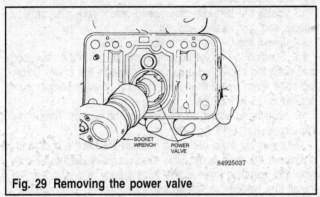

Fig. 29 Removing the power valve

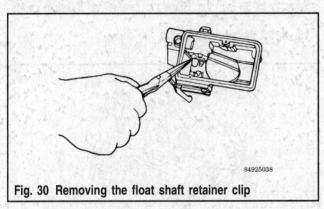

Fig. 30 Removing the float shaft retainer clip

10. Slide the diaphragm and shaft assembly out as far as it will go and remove the choke modulator spring retaining clip. Remove the modulator spring, spring seat and spring perch.

11. Slide the diaphragm assembly out of the choke housing. Remove the nylon choke modulator bushing from the housing.

12. Snap the choke rod from the choke shaft lever retainer.

13. Pull the choke rod up and remove it from the dust seal.

14. Remove the choke plate from the choke shaft and slide the shaft and lever from the air horn.

➡The retaining screws are staked. If the staking is excessive, it will have to be filed off. Be careful to avoid damage to surrounding parts when filing.

15. Remove the 3 screws and remove the secondary diaphragm and O-ring from the main body.

➡The housing must be removed before the cover can be removed.

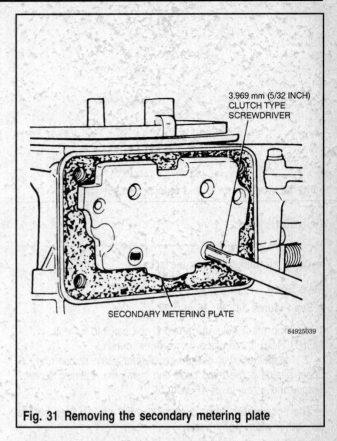

Fig. 31 Removing the secondary metering plate

16. Remove the diaphragm housing cover, then remove the spring and diaphragm, and the check ball from the housing.

17. Remove the accelerator pump discharge nozzle screw. Lift the pump discharge nozzle and gaskets out of the main body.

18. Invert the main body and let the accelerator pump discharge check ball fall into your hand.

➡Your carburetor may use a needle instead of a ball.

Throttle Body

The throttle body should not be disassembled. These parts are a matched assembly designed to maintain emission control standards and the only service to the throttle body should be replacement of the unit.

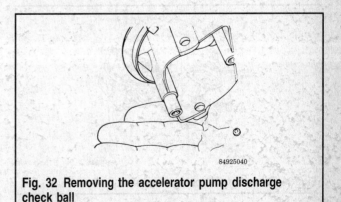

Fig. 32 Removing the accelerator pump discharge check ball

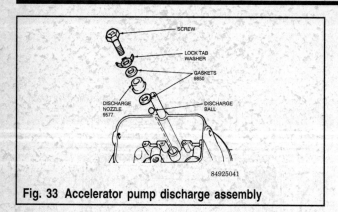

Fig. 33 Accelerator pump discharge assembly

ASSEMBLY

➡ **Clean all gasket mating surfaces.**

Main Body

▶ **See Figures 34, 35, 36 and 37**

1. Drop the accelerator pump check ball into its well. LIGHTLY tap it into place with a brass punch.

2. Install the lower gasket, accelerator pump nozzle and upper gasket in the main body and install the retaining screw. Torque the screw to 27-43 inch lbs.

➡ **The accelerator pump assembly must be installed before any other main body parts.**

3. Install the spring in the secondary diaphragm housing cover. Drop the check ball into the vacuum port and position the secondary diaphragm in the housing. Make sure that the diaphragm is seated evenly and the vacuum opening is aligned. Install the cover and tighten the attaching screws. Torque the screws to 13-17 inch lbs.

➡ **The diaphragm housing must be removed from the main body to install the cover.**

4. Place the O-ring on the secondary vacuum tube in the secondary housing. Place the diaphragm in position on the main body and install the lockwashers and screws.

5. Install the choke rod seal in the main body. Slide the bottom of the choke rod through the seal.

6. Install the choke rod retainer onto the choke shaft lever.

7. Slide the choke shaft into the air horn and snap the top of the choke rod into the retainer on the choke shaft lever.

8. Slide the nylon choke modulator bushing onto the choke thermostat lever.

9. Install the choke modulator, spring perch, spring, spring seat and retaining clip. Position this assembly into the choke housing and rotate the choke modulator bushing until it slide securely into place.

10. Align the diaphragm vacuum hole with the vacuum tube in the choke housing.

11. Install the choke diaphragm spring and cover. Torque the cover screws to 13-17 inch lbs.

12. Install the choke housing shaft and lever assembly, and the over-center spring.

13. Install the fast idle cam, spring perch, spring, lever, spacer and star washer and nut.

14. Install the O-ring on the vacuum tube.

15. Position the choke housing assembly onto the main body and push the choke rod onto the retainer on the choke housing shaft lever. Install the choke housing screws. Torque the screws to 20-30 inch lbs.

16. Install and adjust the choke cap and gasket. Torque the cap screws to 16-18 inch lbs.

17. Invert the main body and position the throttle body and gasket on the main body. Slide the secondary diaphragm rod onto the operating lever as the throttle body is positioned. Install and tighten the screws and lockwashers. Torque the screws to 39-52 inch lbs. Place the retainer on the diaphragm rod.

18. Install the air cleaner stud.

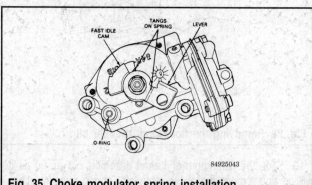

Fig. 35 Choke modulator spring installation

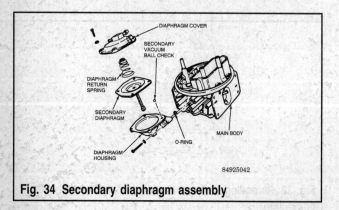

Fig. 34 Secondary diaphragm assembly

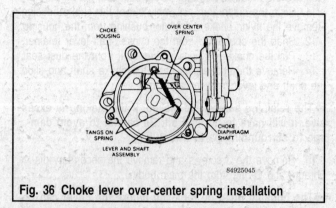

Fig. 36 Choke lever over-center spring installation

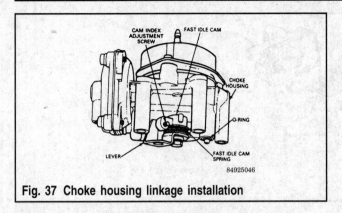

Fig. 37 Choke housing linkage installation

Primary Fuel Bowl and Metering Block

▶ See Figure 38

1. Place the accelerator pump diaphragm spring and diaphragm into the accelerator pump chamber. The diaphragm must be positioned so that the large end of the rivet will be against the pump cover arm.

2. Install the cover and tighten the screws finger-tight. Make sure that the diaphragm is center, depress the diaphragm with the arm and tighten the screws.

3. Install the filter spring, filter, gasket and inlet fitting. Torque the fitting to 22-26 ft. lbs.

4. Install the fuel level sight plug and gasket.

5. Slide the baffle plate onto the ridges in the fuel bowl.

6. Install the float spring on the float and slide the float onto the shaft. Make sure that the float spring is centered between the ridges on the boss. Install the E-clip.

7. Coat a new O-ring with petroleum jelly and slide it onto the needle and seat assembly.

8. Position the needle and seat assembly into the float bowl.

9. Position the adjusting nut gasket and nut on the needle and seat assembly. Align the flat on the inside diameter of the nut with the flat on the outside diameter of the needle and seat. Install the lockscrew and gasket.

10. Perform a preliminary (dry) float adjustment, described above.

11. Install the power valve and gasket in the metering block. Torque the power valve to 9-12 ft. lbs.

12. Install the pump transfer tube and new O-rings in the metering block.

13. Install the jets in the metering block. Torque the jets to 18-20 inch lbs.

14. Place the metering block gaskets on the dowels on the back of the block. Place the block and gasket on the main body. Place the fuel bowl gasket on the metering block. Place the retaining screws and new compression gaskets in the fuel bowl. Place the bowl on the metering block and tighten the retaining screws to 50-60 inch lbs.

15. Coat the fuel line tube O-ring with petroleum jelly. Place the O-ring against the flange on the end of the fuel line tube. Install this end into the recess the the primary bowl. make sure the O-ring isn't pinched.

Secondary Fuel Bowl and Metering Body

▶ See Figure 39

1. Install the fuel level sight plug and gasket.

2. Install the baffle plate in the float bowl.

3. Install the float spring on the float and slide the float onto the shaft. Make sure that the float spring is centered between the ridges on the boss. Install the E-clip.

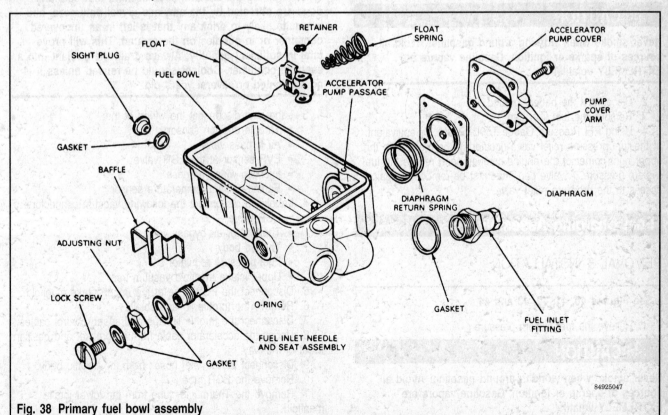

Fig. 38 Primary fuel bowl assembly

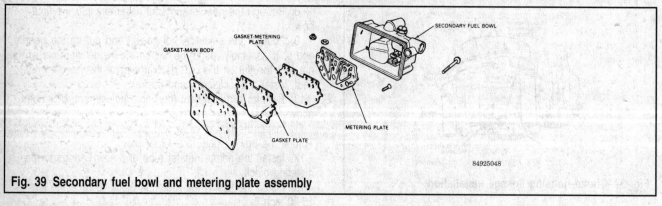

Fig. 39 Secondary fuel bowl and metering plate assembly

4. Coat a new O-ring with petroleum jelly and slide it onto the needle and seat assembly.

5. Position the needle and seat assembly into the float bowl.

6. Position the adjusting nut gasket and nut on the needle and seat assembly. Align the flat on the inside diameter of the nut with the flat on the outside diameter of the needle and seat. Install the lockscrew and gasket.

7. Perform a preliminary (dry) float adjustment, described above.

8. Using a clutch-type screwdriver, install the metering body, plate and gaskets.

9. Coat the fuel line tube O-ring with petroleum jelly and position it against the flange on the fuel line tube.

10. Install the fuel bowl on the main body, guiding the tube into the recess in the bowl. Install the retaining screws and new compression gaskets. Torque the screws to 50-60 inch lbs.

11. Perform all necessary adjustments described above.

GASOLINE FUEL INJECTION — 4.9L ENGINE

Relieving Fuel System Pressure

➡A special tool is necessary for this procedure.

1. Make sure the ignition switch is in the OFF position.

✳✳CAUTION

Never smoke when working around gasoline! Avoid all sources of sparks or ignition. Gasoline vapors are EXTREMELY volatile!

2. Disconnect the battery ground.
3. Remove the fuel filler cap.
4. Using EFI Pressure Gauge T80L-9974-A, or equivalent, at the fuel pressure relief valve (located in the fuel line in the upper right corner of the engine compartment) relieve the fuel system pressure. A valve cap must first be removed to gain access to the pressure relief valve.

Fuel Charging Assembly

REMOVAL & INSTALLATION

◆ **See Figures 40, 41, 42, 43 and 44**

1. Relieve the fuel system pressure.

✳✳CAUTION

Never smoke when working around gasoline! Avoid all sources of sparks or ignition. Gasoline vapors are EXTREMELY volatile!

2. Disconnect the battery ground cable and drain the cooling system.

✳✳CAUTION

When draining the coolant, keep in mind that cats and dogs are attracted by the ethylene glycol antifreeze, and are quite likely to drink any that is left in an uncovered container or in puddles on the ground. This will prove fatal in sufficient quantity. Always drain the coolant into a sealable container. Coolant should be reused unless it is contaminated or several years old.

3. Label and disconnect the wiring at the:
 • Throttle position sensor
 • Air bypass valve
 • EVP sensor at the EGR valve
 • Injection wiring harness
 • Engine coolant temperature sensor
4. Label and disconnect the following vacuum connectors:
 • EGR valve
 • Thermactor air bypass valve
 • Throttle body
 • Fuel pressure regulator
 • Upper intake manifold vacuum tree
5. Disconnect the PCV hose at the upper intake manifold.
6. Remove the throttle linkage shield.
7. Disconnect the throttle linkage and speed control cables.
8. Unbolt the accelerator cable from its bracket and position it out of the way.
9. Disconnect the air inlet hoses from the throttle body.
10. Remove the EGR tube.
11. Remove the Thermactor tube from the lower intake manifold.

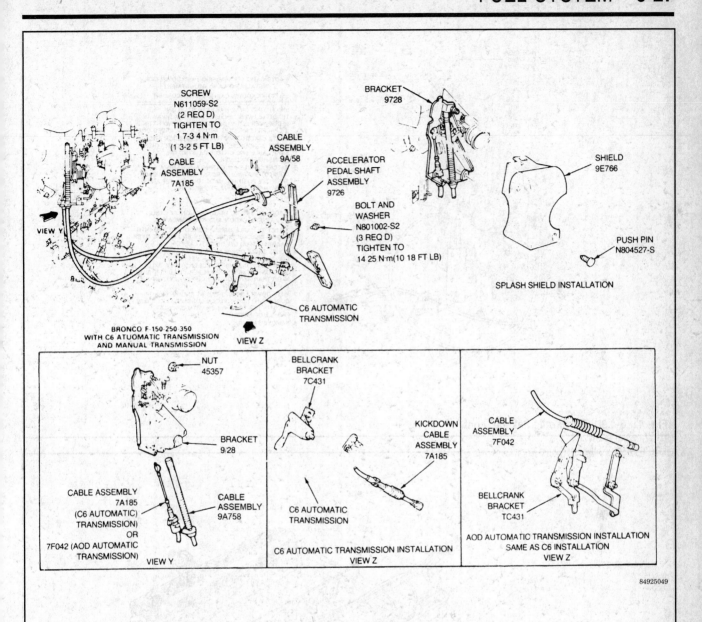

SCREW
N611059-S2
(2 REQ D)
TIGHTEN TO
1 7-3 4 N·m
(1 3-2 5 FT LB)

CABLE
ASSEMBLY
7A185

CABLE
ASSEMBLY
9A/58

ACCELERATOR
PEDAL SHAFT
ASSEMBLY
9726

BOLT AND
WASHER
N801002-S2
(3 REQ D)
TIGHTEN TO
14 25 N·m(10 18 FT LB)

BRACKET
9728

SHIELD
9E766

PUSH PIN
N804527-S

SPLASH SHIELD INSTALLATION

VIEW Y

C6 AUTOMATIC
TRANSMISSION

BRONCO F-150-250-350
WITH C6 ATUOMATIC TRANSMISSION
AND MANUAL TRANSMISSION

VIEW Z

NUT
45357

BRACKET
9/28

CABLE ASSEMBLY
7A185
(C6 AUTOMATIC)
TRANSMISSION)
OR
7F042 (AOD AUTOMATIC
TRANSMISSION)   VIEW Y

CABLE
ASSEMBLY
9A758

BELLCRANK
BRACKET
7C431

KICKDOWN
CABLE
ASSEMBLY
7A185

C6 AUTOMATIC
TRANSMISSION

C6 AUTOMATIC TRANSMISSION INSTALLATION
VIEW Z

CABLE
ASSEMBLY
7F042

BELLCRANK
BRACKET
TC431

AOD AUTOMATIC TRANSMISSION INSTALLATION
SAME AS C6 INSTALLATION
VIEW Z

84925049

Fig. 40 6-4.9L EFI throttle linkage

12. Remove the nut attaching the Thermactor bypass valve bracket to the lower intake manifold.

13. Remove the injector heat shield (2 clips).

14. Remove the 7 studs which retain the upper intake manifold.

15. Remove the screw and washer which retains the upper intake manifold support bracket to the upper intake manifold.

16. Remove the upper intake manifold assembly from the lower intake manifold.

17. Move the vacuum harness away from the lower intake manifold.

18. Remove the injector cooling manifold from the lifting eye attachment.

19. Disconnect the fuel supply and return lines at the quick disconnect couplings using tools T81P-19623-G or T81P-19623-G1.

20. Remove the 16 attaching bolts that the lower intake manifold and exhaust manifolds have in common. DON'T

REMOVE THE BOLTS THAT ATTACH ONLY THE EXHAUST MANIFOLDS!

21. Remove the lower intake manifold from the head.

22. Clean and inspect all mating surfaces. All surfaces MUST be flat and free from debris or damage!

To install:

23. Clean and oil all fastener threads.

24. Position the lower manifold on the head using a new gasket. Tighten the bolts to 30 ft. lbs.

25. Reconnect the vacuum lines at the fuel pressure regulator.

26. Position the upper manifold and new gasket on the lower manifold. Install the fasteners finger tight.

27. Install the upper intake manifold support on the manifold and tighten the retaining screw to 30 ft. lbs.

28. Torque the upper-to-lower manifold fasteners to 18 ft. lbs.

29. Install the injector heat shield.

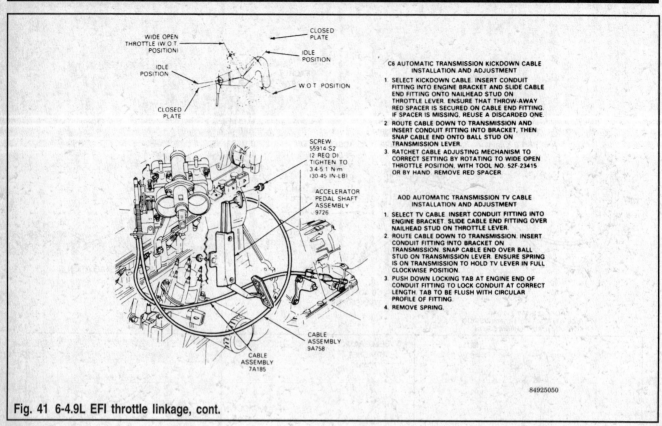

C6 AUTOMATIC TRANSMISSION KICKDOWN CABLE
INSTALLATION AND ADJUSTMENT

1. SELECT KICKDOWN CABLE. INSERT CONDUIT
    FITTING INTO ENGINE BRACKET AND SLIDE CABLE
    END FITTING ONTO NAILHEAD STUD ON
    THROTTLE LEVER. ENSURE THAT THROW-AWAY
    RED SPACER IS SECURED ON CABLE END FITTING.
    IF SPACER IS MISSING, REUSE A DISCARDED ONE.
2. ROUTE CABLE DOWN TO TRANSMISSION AND
    INSERT CONDUIT FITTING INTO BRACKET, THEN
    SNAP CABLE END ONTO BALL STUD ON
    TRANSMISSION LEVER.
3. RATCHET CABLE ADJUSTING MECHANISM TO
    CORRECT SETTING BY ROTATING TO WIDE OPEN
    THROTTLE POSITION, WITH TOOL NO. 52F-23415
    OR BY HAND. REMOVE RED SPACER.

AOD AUTOMATIC TRANSMISSION TV CABLE
INSTALLATION AND ADJUSTMENT

1. SELECT TV CABLE. INSERT CONDUIT FITTING INTO
    ENGINE BRACKET. SLIDE CABLE END FITTING OVER
    NAILHEAD STUD ON THROTTLE LEVER.
2. ROUTE CABLE DOWN TO TRANSMISSION. INSERT
    CONDUIT FITTING INTO BRACKET ON
    TRANSMISSION. SNAP CABLE END OVER BALL
    STUD ON TRANSMISSION LEVER. ENSURE SPRING
    IS ON TRANSMISSION TO HOLD TV LEVER IN FULL
    CLOCKWISE POSITION.
3. PUSH DOWN LOCKING TAB AT ENGINE END OF
    CONDUIT FITTING TO LOCK CONDUIT AT CORRECT
    LENGTH. TAB TO BE FLUSH WITH CIRCULAR
    PROFILE OF FITTING.
4. REMOVE SPRING.

84925050

Fig. 41 6-4.9L EFI throttle linkage, cont.

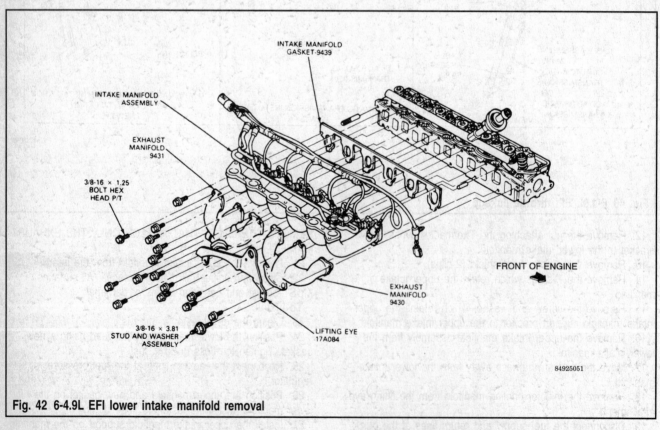

84925051

Fig. 42 6-4.9L EFI lower intake manifold removal

30. Install the EGR tube. The tube should be routed between the no. 4 and 5 lower intake runners. Torque the fittings to 35 ft. lbs.

31. Install the injector cooling manifold and torque the fasteners to 12 ft. lbs.

32. Connect the PCV hose.

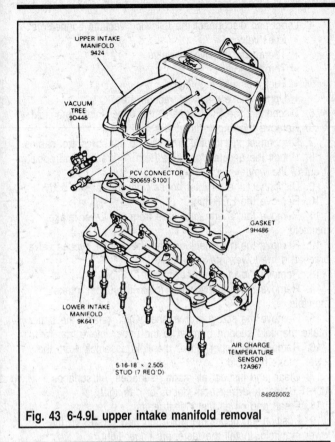

Fig. 43 6-4.9L upper intake manifold removal

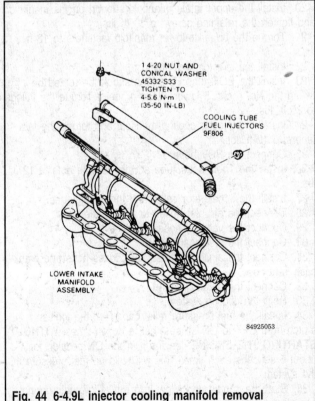

Fig. 44 6-4.9L injector cooling manifold removal

33. Install the Thermactor tube and tighten the nuts to 12 ft. lbs.

34. Install the accelerator cable and throttle linkages.

35. Connect the air inlet hoses to the throttle body.

36. Connect the vacuum hoses.

37. Connect the electrical wiring.

38. Connect the air intake hose, air bypass hose and crankcase vent hose.

39. Connect the battery ground.

40. Refill the cooling system.

41. Install the fuel pressure relief cap. Turn the ignition switch from OFF to ON at least half a dozen times, **WITHOUT STARTING THE ENGINE,** leaving it in the ON position for about 5 seconds each time. This will build up fuel pressure in the system.

42. Start the engine and allow it to run at idle until normal operating temperature is reached. Check for leaks.

Fuel Injector

REMOVAL & INSTALLATION

1. Relieve the fuel system pressure.

❋❋CAUTION

Never smoke when working around gasoline! Avoid all sources of sparks or ignition. Gasoline vapors are EXTREMELY volatile!

2. Remove the upper intake manifold assembly.

3. Remove the fuel supply manifold.

4. Disconnect the wiring at each injector.

5. Pull upward on the injector body while gently rocking it from side-to-side.

6. Inspect the O-rings on the injector for any sign of leakage or damage. Replace any suspected O-rings.

7. Inspect the plastic cap at the top of each injector and replace it if any sign of deterioration is noticed.

To install:

8. Lubricate the O-rings with clean engine oil ONLY!

9. Install the injectors by pushing them in with a gentle rocking motion.

10. Install the fuel supply manifold.

11. Connect the electrical wiring.

12. Install the upper intake manifold.

Fuel Pressure Regulator

REMOVAL & INSTALLATION

1. Relieve the fuel system pressure.

❋❋CAUTION

Never smoke when working around gasoline! Avoid all sources of sparks or ignition. Gasoline vapors are EXTREMELY volatile!

2. Disconnect the vacuum line at the regulator.

3. Remove the 3 Allen screws from the regulator housing.

4. Remove the regulator.

5. Inspect the regulator O-ring for signs of deterioration or damage. Discard the gasket.

To install:

6. Lubricate the O-ring with clean engine oil ONLY!

7. Make sure that the mounting surfaces are clean.

8. Using a new gasket, install the regulator. Tighten the retaining screws to 40 inch lbs.

9. Connect the vacuum line.

Pressure Relief Valve

REMOVAL & INSTALLATION

1. Relieve the fuel system pressure.

❊❊CAUTION

Never smoke when working around gasoline! Avoid all sources of sparks or ignition. Gasoline vapors are EXTREMELY volatile!

2. Unscrew the valve from the fuel line.

3. When installing the valve, tighten it to 80 inch lbs.

4. Tighten the cap to 5 inch lbs.

Upper Intake Manifold

REMOVAL & INSTALLATION

1. Relieve the fuel system pressure.

❊❊CAUTION

Never smoke when working around gasoline! Avoid all sources of sparks or ignition. Gasoline vapors are EXTREMELY volatile!

2. Disconnect the battery ground cable and drain the cooling system.

❊❊CAUTION

When draining the coolant, keep in mind that cats and dogs are attracted by the ethylene glycol antifreeze, and are quite likely to drink any that is left in an uncovered container or in puddles on the ground. This will prove fatal in sufficient quantity. Always drain the coolant into a sealable container. Coolant should be reused unless it is contaminated or several years old.

3. Label and disconnect the wiring at the:
   - Throttle position sensor
   - Air bypass valve
   - EVP sensor at the EGR valve
   - Injection wiring harness
   - Engine coolant temperature sensor

4. Label and disconnect the following vacuum connectors:
   - EGR valve
   - Thermactor air bypass valve
   - Throttle body
   - Fuel pressure regulator
   - Upper intake manifold vacuum tree

5. Disconnect the PCV hose at the upper intake manifold.

6. Remove the throttle linkage shield.

7. Disconnect the throttle linkage and speed control cables.

8. Unbolt the accelerator cable from its bracket and position it out of the way.

9. Disconnect the air inlet hoses from the throttle body.

10. Remove the EGR tube.

11. Remove the Thermactor tube from the lower intake manifold.

12. Remove the nut attaching the Thermactor bypass valve bracket to the lower intake manifold.

13. Remove the injector heat shield (2 clips).

14. Remove the 7 studs which retain the upper intake manifold.

15. Remove the screw and washer which retains the upper intake manifold support bracket to the upper intake manifold.

16. Remove the upper intake manifold assembly from the lower intake manifold.

17. Clean and inspect all mating surfaces. All surfaces MUST be flat and free from debris or damage!

18. Clean and oil all fastener threads.

19. Position the upper manifold and new gasket on the lower manifold. Install the fasteners finger tight.

20. Install the upper intake manifold support on the manifold and tighten the retaining screw to 30 ft. lbs.

21. Torque the upper-to-lower manifold fasteners to 18 ft. lbs.

22. Install the injector heat shield.

23. Install the EGR tube. The tube should be routed between the No. 4 and 5 lower intake runners. Torque the fittings to 35 ft. lbs.

24. Install the injector cooling manifold and torque the fasteners to 12 ft. lbs.

25. Connect the PCV hose.

26. Install the Thermactor tube and tighten the nuts to 12 ft. lbs.

27. Install the accelerator cable and throttle linkages.

28. Connect the air inlet hoses to the throttle body.

29. Connect the vacuum hoses.

30. Connect the electrical wiring.

31. Connect the air intake hose, air bypass hose and crankcase vent hose.

32. Connect the battery ground.

33. Refill the cooling system.

34. Install the fuel pressure relief cap. Turn the ignition switch from OFF to ON at least half a dozen times, **WITHOUT STARTING THE ENGINE**, leaving it in the ON position for about 5 seconds each time. This will build up fuel pressure in the system.

35. Start the engine and allow it to run at idle until normal operating temperature is reached. Check for leaks.

Air Intake Throttle Body

REMOVAL & INSTALLATION

▶ **See Figure 45**

1. Disconnect the air intake hose.

✳✳CAUTION

Never smoke when working around gasoline! Avoid all sources of sparks or ignition. Gasoline vapors are EXTREMELY volatile!

2. Disconnect the throttle position sensor and air by-pass valve connectors.
3. Remove the four throttle body mounting nuts and carefully separate the air throttle body from the upper intake manifold.
4. Remove and discard the mounting gasket. Clean all mounting surfaces using care not to damage the gasket surfaces of the throttle body and manifold. Do not allow any material to drop into the intake manifold.
5. Install the throttle body in the reverse order of removal. The mounting nuts are tightened to 12-15 ft. lbs.

Throttle Position Sensor (TPS)

REMOVAL & INSTALLATION

▶ **See Figure 46**

1. Disconnect the wiring harness from the TPS.
2. Matchmark the sensor and throttle body for installation reference.

✳✳CAUTION

Never smoke when working around gasoline! Avoid all sources of sparks or ignition. Gasoline vapors are EXTREMELY volatile!

3. Remove the 2 retaining screws and remove the TPS.

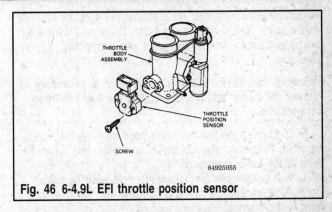

Fig. 46 6-4.9L EFI throttle position sensor

4. Install the TPS so that the wiring harness is parallel with the venturi bores, then, rotate the TPS clockwise to align the scribe marks.

✳✳CAUTION

Slide the rotary tanks into position over the throttle shaft blade, then rotate the TPS CLOCKWISE ONLY to the installed position. FAILURE TO INSTALL THE TPS IN THIS MANNER WILL RESULT IN EXCESSIVE IDLE SPEEDS!

5. Tighten the retaining screws to 16 inch lbs.

➡ **When correctly installed, the TPS wiring harness should be pointing directly at the air bypass valve.**

6. Connect the wiring.

Fuel Supply Manifold

REMOVAL & INSTALLATION

▶ **See Figure 47**

✳✳CAUTION

Never smoke when working around gasoline! Avoid all sources of sparks or ignition. Gasoline vapors are EXTREMELY volatile!

1. Remove the fuel tank fill cap. Relieve fuel system pressure by locating and disconnecting the electrical connection to either the fuel pump relay, the inertia switch or the in line high pressure fuel pump. Crank the engine for about ten seconds. If

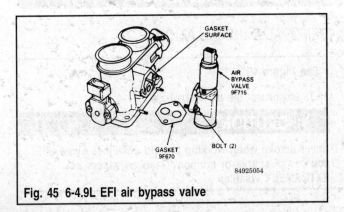

Fig. 45 6-4.9L EFI air bypass valve

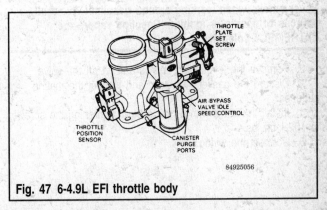

Fig. 47 6-4.9L EFI throttle body

the engine starts, crank for an additional five seconds after the engine stalls. Reconnect the connector. Disconnect the negative battery cable. Remove the upper intake manifold assembly.

➡Special tool T81P-19623-G or equivalent is necessary to release the garter springs that secure the fuel line/hose connections.

2. Disconnect the fuel crossover hose from the fuel supply manifold. Disconnect the fuel supply and return line connections at the fuel supply manifold.

3. Remove the two fuel supply manifold retaining bolts. Carefully disengage the manifold from the fuel injectors and remove the manifold.

4. When installing: make sure the injector caps are clean and free of contamination. Place the fuel supply manifold over each injector and seat the injectors into the manifold. Make sure the caps are seated firmly.

5. Torque the fuel supply manifold retaining bolts to 15-22 ft. lbs. Install the remaining components in the reverse order of removal.

➡Fuel injectors may be serviced after the fuel supply manifold is removed. Grasp the injector and pull up on it while gently rocking injector from side to side. Inspect the mounting O-rings and replace any that show deterioration.

GASOLINE FUEL INJECTION — 5.0L AND 5.8L ENGINES — EXCEPT LIGHTNING

Relieving Fuel System Pressure

➡A special tool is necessary for this procedure.

1. Make sure the ignition switch is in the OFF position.

✳✳CAUTION

Never smoke when working around gasoline! Avoid all sources of sparks or ignition. Gasoline vapors are EXTREMELY volatile!

2. Disconnect the battery ground.
3. Remove the fuel filler cap.
4. Using EFI Pressure Gauge T80L-9974-A, or equivalent, at the fuel pressure relief valve (located in the fuel line in the upper right corner of the engine compartment) relieve the fuel system pressure. A valve cap must first be removed to gain access to the pressure relief valve.

Air Bypass Valve

REMOVAL & INSTALLATION

▶ **See Figure 48**

1. Disconnect the wiring at the valve.

✳✳CAUTION

Never smoke when working around gasoline! Avoid all sources of sparks or ignition. Gasoline vapors are EXTREMELY volatile!

2. Remove the 2 retaining screws and lift off the valve.
3. Discard the gasket and clean and inspect the mating surfaces.
4. Install the valve with a new gasket, tightening the screws to 102 inch lbs.
5. Connect the wiring.

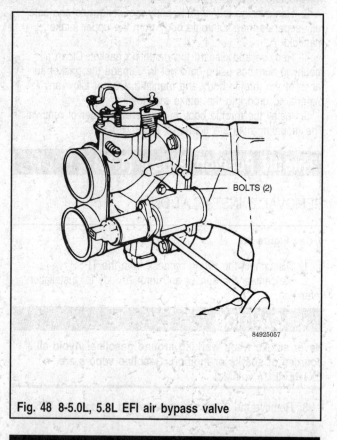

BOLTS (2)

84925057

Fig. 48 8-5.0L, 5.8L EFI air bypass valve

Air Intake Throttle Body

REMOVAL & INSTALLATION

▶ **See Figure 49**

1. Disconnect the air intake hose.

✳✳CAUTION

Never smoke when working around gasoline! Avoid all sources of sparks or ignition. Gasoline vapors are EXTREMELY volatile!

2. Disconnect the throttle position sensor and air by-pass valve connectors.

3. Remove the four throttle body mounting nuts and carefully separate the air throttle body from the upper intake manifold.

4. Remove and discard the mounting gasket. Clean all mounting surfaces using care not to damage the gasket surfaces of the throttle body and manifold. Do not allow any material to drop into the intake manifold.

5. Install the throttle body in the reverse order of removal. The mounting nuts are tightened to 12-18 ft. lbs.

Fuel Charging Assembly

REMOVAL & INSTALLATION

▶ See Figures 50 and 51

1. Relieve the fuel system pressure.

✳✳CAUTION

Never smoke when working around gasoline! Avoid all sources of sparks or ignition. Gasoline vapors are EXTREMELY volatile!

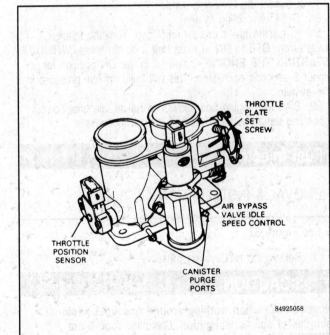

Fig. 49 8-5.0L, 5.8L air throttle body

THROTTLE PLATE SET SCREW

AIR BYPASS VALVE IDLE SPEED CONTROL

THROTTLE POSITION SENSOR

CANISTER PURGE PORTS

84925058

2. Disconnect the battery ground cable and drain the cooling system.

✳✳CAUTION

When draining the coolant, keep in mind that cats and dogs are attracted by the ethylene glycol antifreeze, and are quite likely to drink any that is left in an uncovered container or in puddles on the ground. This will prove fatal in sufficient quantity. Always drain the coolant into a sealable container. Coolant should be reused unless it is contaminated or several years old.

3. Label and disconnect the wiring at the:
- Throttle position sensor
- Air bypass valve
- EGR sensor

4. Label and disconnect the following vacuum connectors:
- EGR valve
- Fuel pressure regulator
- Upper intake manifold vacuum tree

5. Disconnect the PCV hose at the upper intake manifold.

6. Remove the throttle linkage at the throttle ball and AOD transmission linkage at the throttle body.

7. Unbolt the cable bracket from the manifold and position the cables and bracket away from the engine.

8. Disconnect the 2 canister purge lines at the throttle body.

9. Disconnect the water heater lines from the throttle body.

10. Remove the EGR tube.

11. Remove the screw and washer which retains the upper intake manifold support bracket to the upper intake manifold.

12. Remove the 6 bolts which retain the upper intake manifold.

13. Remove the upper intake manifold assembly from the lower intake manifold.

14. Remove the distributor. (See Section 3).

15. Disconnect the wiring at the:
- Engine coolant temperature sensor.
- Engine temperature sending unit.
- Air charge temperature sensor.
- Knock sensor.
- Electrical vacuum regulator.
- Thermactor solenoids.

16. Disconnect the injector wiring harness at the main harness.

17. Remove the EGO ground wire at its intake manifold stud. Note the position of the stud and ground wire for installation.

18. Disconnect the fuel supply and return lines from the fuel rails using tool T81P-19623-G or G1.

19. Remove the upper radiator hose.

20. Remove the coolant bypass hose.

21. Disconnect the heater outlet hose at the manifold.

22. Remove the air cleaner bracket.

23. Remove the coil.

24. Noting the location of each bolt, remove the intake manifold retaining bolts.

25. Remove the lower intake manifold from the head.

26. Clean and inspect all mating surfaces. All surfaces MUST be flat and free from debris or damage!

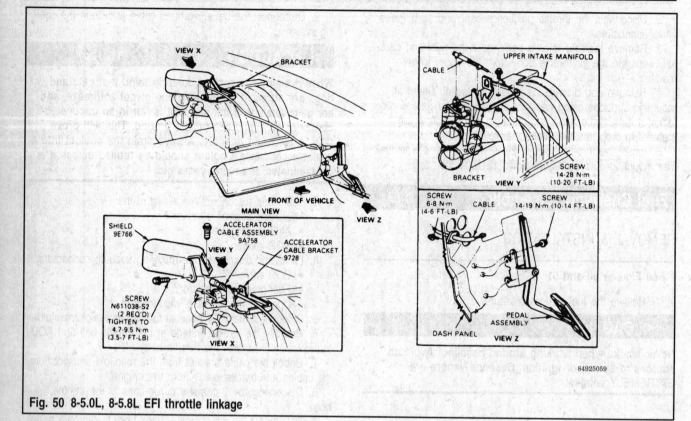

Fig. 50 8-5.0L, 8-5.8L EFI throttle linkage

To install:

27. Clean and oil all fastener threads.
28. Place a 1/16 in. (1.5mm) bead of RTV silicone sealant to both end seal junctions.
29. Position the end seals on the block.
30. Install 2 locator pins at opposite corners of the block.
31. Position the lower manifold on the head using new gaskets. Install the bolts and remove the locating pins.
32. Tighten the bolts to 25 ft. lbs. in sequence. Wait ten minutes and retorque the bolts in sequence.
33. Install the coil.
34. Connect the cooling system hoses.
35. Connect the fuel supply and return lines.
36. Connect the wiring at the:
  • Engine coolant temperature sensor.
  • Engine temperature sending unit.
  • Air charge temperature sensor.
  • Knock sensor.
  • Electrical vacuum regulator.
  • Thermactor solenoids.
37. Install the distributor.
38. Position the upper manifold and new gasket on the lower manifold. Install the fasteners finger tight.
39. Install the upper intake manifold support on the manifold and tighten the retaining screw to 30 ft. lbs.
40. Torque the upper-to-lower manifold fasteners to 18 ft. lbs.
41. Install the EGR tube. Torque the fittings to 35 ft. lbs.
42. Install the canister purge lines at the throttle body.
43. Connect the water heater lines at the throttle body.
44. Connect the PCV hose.
45. Install the accelerator cable and throttle linkages.
46. Connect the vacuum hoses.

47. Connect the electrical wiring.
48. Connect the air intake hose, air bypass hose and crankcase vent hose.
49. Connect the battery ground.
50. Refill the cooling system.
51. Install the fuel pressure relief cap. Turn the ignition switch from OFF to ON at least half a dozen times, **WITHOUT STARTING THE ENGINE**, leaving it in the ON position for about 5 seconds each time. This will build up fuel pressure in the system.
52. Start the engine and allow it to run at idle until normal operating temperature is reached. Check for leaks.

Fuel Injectors

REMOVAL & INSTALLATION

▶ **See Figure 52**

1. Relieve the fuel system pressure.

✳✳CAUTION

Never smoke when working around gasoline! Avoid all sources of sparks or ignition. Gasoline vapors are EXTREMELY volatile!

2. Disconnect the battery ground.
3. Remove the upper intake manifold.
4. Disconnect the wiring at the injectors.
5. Pull upward on the injector body while gently rocking it from side-to-side.

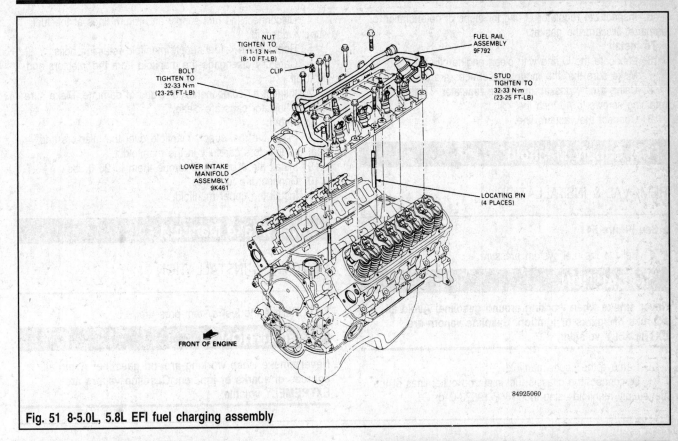

Fig. 51 8-5.0L, 5.8L EFI fuel charging assembly

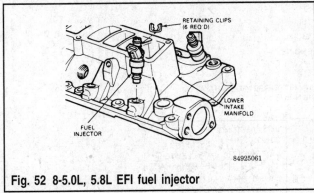

Fig. 52 8-5.0L, 5.8L EFI fuel injector

6. Inspect the O-rings on the injector for any sign of leakage or damage. Replace any suspected O-rings.

7. Inspect the plastic cap at the top of each injector and replace it if any sign of deterioration is noticed.

To install:

8. Lubricate the O-rings with clean engine oil ONLY!

9. Install the injectors by pushing them in with a gentle rocking motion.

10. Install the fuel supply manifold.

11. Connect the electrical wiring.

12. Install the upper intake manifold.

Fuel Pressure Regulator

REMOVAL & INSTALLATION

▶ See Figure 53

1. Relieve the fuel system pressure.

✳✳CAUTION

Never smoke when working around gasoline! Avoid all sources of sparks or ignition. Gasoline vapors are EXTREMELY volatile!

2. Disconnect the vacuum line at the regulator.

3. Remove the 3 allen screws from the regulator housing.

4. Remove the regulator.

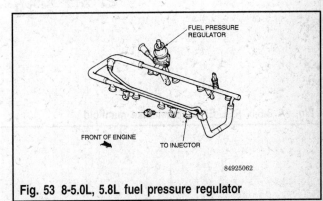

Fig. 53 8-5.0L, 5.8L fuel pressure regulator

5. Inspect the regulator O-ring for signs of deterioration or damage. Discard the gasket.

To install:

6. Lubricate the O-ring with clean engine oil ONLY!

7. Make sure that the mounting surfaces are clean.

8. Using a new gasket, install the regulator. Tighten the retaining screws to 40 inch lbs.

9. Connect the vacuum line.

Fuel Supply Manifold

REMOVAL & INSTALLATION

▶ **See Figure 54**

1. Relieve the fuel system pressure.

❋❋CAUTION

Never smoke when working around gasoline! Avoid all sources of sparks or ignition. Gasoline vapors are EXTREMELY volatile!

2. Remove the upper manifold.

3. Disconnect the chassis fuel inlet and outlet lines at the fuel supply manifold using tool T81P-19623-G or G1.

4. Disconnect the fuel supply and return lines at the fuel supply manifold.

5. Remove the 4 fuel supply manifold retaining bolts.

6. Carefully disengage the manifold from the injectors and lift it off.

7. Inspect all components for signs of damage. Make sure that the injector caps are clean.

To install:

8. Place the fuel supply manifold over the injectors and seat the injectors carefully in the manifold.

9. Install the 4 bolts and torque them to 20 ft. lbs.

10. Connect the fuel lines.

11. Install the upper manifold.

Lower Intake Manifold

REMOVAL & INSTALLATION

1. Relieve the fuel system pressure.

❋❋CAUTION

Never smoke when working around gasoline! Avoid all sources of sparks or ignition. Gasoline vapors are EXTREMELY volatile!

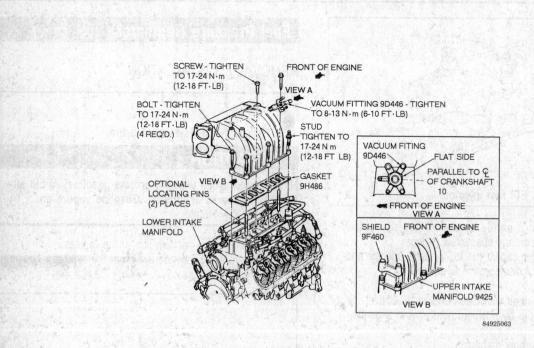

Fig. 54 8-5.0, 5.8L EFI upper intake manifold

2. Disconnect the battery ground cable and drain the cooling system.

3. Label and disconnect the wiring at the:
- Throttle position sensor
- Air bypass valve
- EGR sensor

4. Label and disconnect the following vacuum connectors:
- EGR valve
- Fuel pressure regulator
- Upper intake manifold vacuum tree

5. Disconnect the PCV hose at the upper intake manifold.

6. Remove the throttle linkage at the throttle ball and AOD transmission linkage at the throttle body.

7. Unbolt the cable bracket from the manifold and position the cables and bracket away from the engine.

8. Disconnect the 2 canister purge lines at the throttle body.

9. Disconnect the water heater lines from the throttle body.

10. Remove the EGR tube.

11. Remove the screw and washer which retains the upper intake manifold support bracket to the upper intake manifold.

12. Remove the 6 bolts which retain the upper intake manifold.

13. Remove the upper intake manifold assembly from the lower intake manifold.

14. Remove the distributor. (See Section 3).

15. Disconnect the wiring at the:
- Engine coolant temperature sensor.
- Engine temperature sending unit.
- Air charge temperature sensor.
- Knock sensor.
- Electrical vacuum regulator.
- Thermactor solenoids.

16. Disconnect the injector wiring harness at the main harness.

17. Remove the EGO ground wire at its intake manifold stud. Note the position of the stud and ground wire for installation.

18. Disconnect the fuel supply and return lines from the fuel rails using tool T81P-19623-G or G1.

19. Remove the upper radiator hose.

20. Remove the coolant bypass hose.

21. Disconnect the heater outlet hose at the manifold.

22. Remove the air cleaner bracket.

23. Remove the coil.

24. Noting the location of each bolt, remove the intake manifold retaining bolts.

25. Remove the lower intake manifold from the head.

26. Clean and inspect all mating surfaces. All surfaces MUST be flat and free from debris or damage!

To install:

27. Clean and oil all fastener threads.

28. Place a 1/16 in. (1.5mm) bead of RTV silicone sealant to both of the the the end seal junctions.

29. Position the end seals on the block.

30. Install 2 locator pins at opposite corners of the block.

31. Position the lower manifold on the head using new gaskets. Install the bolts and remove the locating pins.

32. Tighten the bolts to 25 ft. lbs. in sequence. Wait ten minutes and retorque the bolts in sequence.

33. Install the coil.

34. Connect the cooling system hoses.

35. Connect the fuel supply and return lines.

36. Connect the wiring at the:
- Engine coolant temperature sensor.
- Engine temperature sending unit.
- Air charge temperature sensor.
- Knock sensor.
- Electrical vacuum regulator.
- Thermactor solenoids.

37. Install the distributor.

38. Position the upper manifold and new gasket on the lower manifold. Install the fasteners finger tight.

39. Install the upper intake manifold support on the manifold and tighten the retaining screw to 30 ft. lbs.

40. Torque the upper-to-lower manifold fasteners to 18 ft. lbs.

41. Install the EGR tube. Torque the fittings to 35 ft. lbs.

42. Install the canister purge lines at the throttle body.

43. Connect the water heater lines at the throttle body.

44. Connect the PCV hose.

45. Install the accelerator cable and throttle linkages.

46. Connect the vacuum hoses.

47. Connect the electrical wiring.

48. Connect the air intake hose, air bypass hose and crankcase vent hose.

49. Connect the battery ground.

50. Refill the cooling system.

51. Install the fuel pressure relief cap. Turn the ignition switch from OFF to ON at least half a dozen times, **WITHOUT STARTING THE ENGINE**, leaving it in the ON position for about 5 seconds each time. This will build up fuel pressure in the system.

52. Start the engine and allow it to run at idle until normal operating temperature is reached. Check for leaks.

Throttle Position Sensor (TPS)

REMOVAL & INSTALLATION

▶ See Figures 55 and 56

1. Disconnect the wiring harness from the TPS.

2. Matchmark the sensor and throttle body for installation reference.

3. Remove the 2 retaining screws and remove the TPS.

To install:

4. Install the TPS so that the wiring harness is parallel with the venturi bores, then, rotate the TPS clockwise to align the scribe marks.

✳✳CAUTION

Slide the rotary tangs into position over the throttle shaft blade, then rotate the TPS CLOCKWISE ONLY to the installed position. FAILURE TO INSTALL THE TPS IN THIS MANNER WILL RESULT IN EXCESSIVE IDLE SPEEDS!

5. Tighten the retaining screws to 16 inch lbs.

➡When correctly installed, the TPS wiring harness should be pointing directly at the air bypass valve.

6. Connect the wiring.

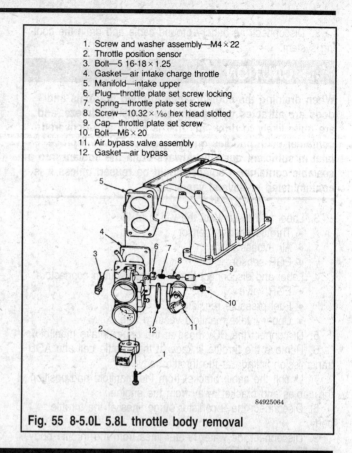

1. Screw and washer assembly—M4 × 22
2. Throttle position sensor
3. Bolt—5 16-18 × 1.25
4. Gasket—air intake charge throttle
5. Manifold—intake upper
6. Plug—throttle plate set screw locking
7. Spring—throttle plate set screw
8. Screw—10.32 × 1/50 hex head slotted
9. Cap—throttle plate set screw
10. Bolt—M6 × 20
11. Air bypass valve assembly
12. Gasket—air bypass

84925064

Fig. 55 8-5.0L 5.8L throttle body removal

GASOLINE FUEL INJECTION — 5.8L LIGHTNING ENGINE

Relieving Fuel System Pressure

➡A special tool is necessary for this procedure.

1. Make sure the ignition switch is in the OFF position.

✳✳CAUTION

Never smoke when working around gasoline! Avoid all sources of sparks or ignition. Gasoline vapors are EXTREMELY volatile!

2. Disconnect the battery ground.
3. Remove the fuel filler cap.

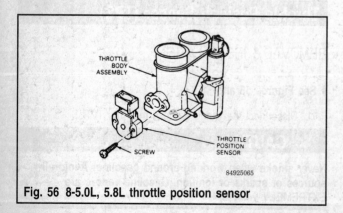

THROTTLE BODY ASSEMBLY

THROTTLE POSITION SENSOR

SCREW

84925065

Fig. 56 8-5.0L, 5.8L throttle position sensor

4. Using EFI Pressure Gauge T80L-9974-A, or equivalent, at the fuel pressure relief valve (located in the fuel line in the upper right corner of the engine compartment) relieve the fuel system pressure. A valve cap must first be removed to gain access to the pressure relief valve.

Air Intake Throttle Body

REMOVAL & INSTALLATION

▶ See Figure 57

1. Disconnect the battery ground cable.

➡On EEC equipped vehicles, disconnecting and reconnecting the battery may cause abnormal drive symptoms as the powertrain control module relearns its codes. The truck may need to be driven 10 miles or more until normal driveability is restored.

2. Remove the snow/ice shield.
3. Disconnect the air intake hose.

✳✳CAUTION

Never smoke when working around gasoline! Avoid all sources of sparks or ignition. Gasoline vapors are EXTREMELY volatile!

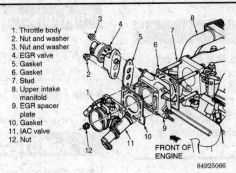

1. Throttle body
2. Nut and washer
3. Nut and washer
4. EGR valve
5. Gasket
6. Gasket
7. Stud
8. Upper intake manifold
9. EGR spacer plate
10. Gasket
11. IAC valve
12. Nut

FRONT OF ENGINE

84925066

Fig. 57 Lightning air throttle body

4. Remove the PCV fresh air tube from the throttle body.

5. Disconnect the throttle position sensor and air by-pass valve connectors.

6. With the engine cool, remove the radiator cap and remove the plug the coolant hoses at the EGR spacer.

7. Remove the AIRB/AIRD bracket nuts and position the bracket out of the way.

8. Remove the throttle body mounting nuts and carefully separate the air throttle body from the EGR spacer.

9. Disconnect the throttle cable from the ball stud by prying it off. DO NOT pull it off!

10. Remove and discard the mounting gasket. Clean all mounting surfaces using care not to damage the gasket surfaces of the throttle body and manifold. Do not allow any material to drop into the intake manifold.

11. Install the throttle body in the reverse order of removal. The mounting nuts are tightened to 12-18 ft. lbs.

Fuel Charging Assembly

REMOVAL & INSTALLATION

Upper Intake Manifold

1. Disconnect the battery ground.
2. Remove the air intake tube.
3. Remove the snow/ice shield from the throttle body.
4. Disconnect the electrical connectors at:
   - Throttle position sensor
   - Idle air control valve
   - EVP sensor
   - Emission vacuum control secondary regulator
   - Secondary air injection bypass/secondary air injection diverter solenoids
5. Disconnect the vacuum lines from:
   - EGR external pressure valve
   - EVP sensor
   - AIRB/AIRD solenoids
   - Vacuum tree
6. Disconnect the PCV fresh air tube from the throttle body and oil fill tube.

7. Loosen the radiator cap.

8. Disconnect and plug the coolant hoses at the EGR spacer.

9. Using a screwdriver, carefully pry the throttle cable from the ball stud. DO NOT PULL IT OFF BY HAND!

10. Reach up behind the upper intake manifold and pull the PCV valve from the lower intake manifold.

11. Disconnect the vacuum line from the brake booster.

12. Remove the mounting bolts, lift the upper manifold up and pull it forward to gain access to the vacuum hoses located below it. Disconnect the hoses and remove the upper manifold.

To install:

13. Clean all gasket surfaces thoroughly and carefully. Don't allow any gasket material to fall into the lower manifold.

14. Position a new gasket on the lower manifold.

15. Place the upper manifold onto the lower and connect all the vacuum hoses.

16. Install the bolts and tighten them, in the sequence shown, to 12-18 ft. lbs.

17. Connect the throttle cable at the ball stud.

18. Connect the coolant hoses at the EGR spacer.

19. Connect the PCV fresh air tube at the throttle body and oil fill tube.

20. Connect the vacuum lines to:
   - EGR external pressure valve
   - EVP sensor
   - AIRB/AIRD solenoids
   - Vacuum tree
21. Connect the electrical connectors at:
   - Throttle position sensor
   - Idle air control valve
   - EVP sensor
   - Emission vacuum control secondary regulator
   - Secondary air injection bypass/secondary air injection diverter solenoids
22. Install the snow/ice shield on the throttle body.
23. Install the air intake tube.
24. Connect the battery ground.

Lower Manifold

1. The upper manifold and throttle body must be removed first.

2. Drain the cooling system.

✳✳CAUTION

When draining the coolant, keep in mind that cats and dogs are attracted by the ethylene glycol antifreeze, and are quite likely to drink any that is left in an uncovered container or in puddles on the ground. This will prove fatal in sufficient quantity. Always drain the coolant into a sealable container. Coolant should be reused unless it is contaminated or several years old.

3. Remove the distributor assembly, cap and wires.
4. Disconnect the electrical connectors at the engine, coolant temperature sensor and sending unit, at the air charge temperature sensor and at the knock sensor.
5. Disconnect the injector wiring harness from the main harness assembly. Remove the ground wire from the intake manifold stud. The ground wire must be installed at the same position it was removed from.
6. Disconnect the fuel supply and return lines from the fuel rails.
7. Remove the upper radiator hose from the thermostat housing. Remove the bypass hose. Remove the heater outlet hose at the intake manifold.
8. Remove the air cleaner mounting bracket. Remove the intake manifold mounting bolts and studs. Pay attention to the location of the bolts and studs for reinstallation. Remove the lower intake manifold assembly.

To install:

9. Clean and inspect the mounting surfaces of the heads and manifold.
10. Apply a 1/16 in. (1.5mm) bead of RTV sealer to the ends of the manifold seal (the junction point of the seals and gaskets). Install the end seals and intake gaskets on the cylinder heads. The gaskets must interlock with the seal tabs.
11. Install locator bolts at opposite ends of each head and carefully lower the intake manifold into position. Install and tighten the mounting bolts and studs to 23-25 ft. lbs.
12. Install the air cleaner mounting bracket.
13. Install the upper radiator hose at the thermostat housing. Install the bypass hose. Install the heater outlet hose at the intake manifold.
14. Connect the fuel supply and return lines at the fuel rails.
15. Connect the injector wiring harness at the main harness assembly. Install the ground wire at the intake manifold stud.
16. Connect the electrical connectors at the engine, coolant temperature sensor and sending unit, at the air charge temperature sensor and at the knock sensor.
17. Install the distributor assembly, cap and wires.
18. Fill the cooling system.

Fuel Injectors

REMOVAL & INSTALLATION

▶ See Figure 58

1. Relieve the fuel system pressure.

✳✳CAUTION

Never smoke when working around gasoline! Avoid all sources of sparks or ignition. Gasoline vapors are EXTREMELY volatile!

2. Disconnect the battery ground.
3. Remove the upper intake manifold.
4. Disconnect the wiring at the injectors.
5. Pull upward on the injector body while gently rocking it from side-to-side.
6. Inspect the O-rings on the injector for any sign of leakage or damage. Replace any suspected O-rings.
7. Inspect the plastic cap at the top of each injector and replace it if any sign of deterioration is noticed.
8. Lubricate the O-rings with clean engine oil ONLY!
9. Install the injectors by pushing them in with a gentle rocking motion.
10. Install the fuel supply manifold.
11. Connect the electrical wiring.
12. Install the upper intake manifold.

Fuel Pressure Regulator

REMOVAL & INSTALLATION

1. Relieve the fuel system pressure.

✳✳CAUTION

Never smoke when working around gasoline! Avoid all sources of sparks or ignition. Gasoline vapors are EXTREMELY volatile!

2. Remove the fuel supply manifold.
3. Remove the 3 Allen screws from the regulator housing.
4. Remove the regulator.

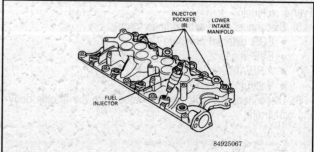

84925067

Fig. 58 Lightning lower intake manifold showing injector positions

5. Inspect the regulator O-ring for signs of deterioration or damage. Discard the gasket.

6. Lubricate the O-ring with clean engine oil ONLY!

7. Make sure that the mounting surfaces are clean.

8. Using a new gasket, install the regulator. Tighten the retaining screws to 40 inch lbs.

9. Install the fuel supply manifold.

Fuel Supply Manifold

REMOVAL & INSTALLATION

1. Relieve the fuel system pressure.

✳✳CAUTION

Never smoke when working around gasoline! Avoid all sources of sparks or ignition. Gasoline vapors are EXTREMELY volatile!

2. Remove the upper manifold.

3. Disconnect the fuel supply and return lines at the fuel supply manifold, using tools D87L-9280-A and D87L-9287-B, or equivalents.

4. Remove the 4 fuel supply manifold retaining bolts.

5. Carefully disengage the manifold from the injectors and lift it off.

To install:

6. Inspect all components for signs of damage. Make sure that the injector caps are clean.

7. Place the fuel supply manifold over the injectors and seat the injectors carefully in the manifold.

8. Install the 4 bolts and torque them to 70-150 inch lbs.

9. Connect the fuel lines.

10. Install the upper manifold.

GASOLINE FUEL INJECTION — 7.5L ENGINE

Relieving Fuel System Pressure

▶ **See Figure 59**

➡ **A special tool is necessary for this procedure.**

1. Make sure the ignition switch is in the OFF position.

✳✳CAUTION

Never smoke when working around gasoline! Avoid all sources of sparks or ignition. Gasoline vapors are EXTREMELY volatile!

2. Disconnect the battery ground.

3. Remove the fuel filler cap.

4. Using EFI Pressure Gauge T80L-9974-A, or equivalent, at the fuel pressure relief valve (located in the fuel line in the upper right corner of the engine compartment) relieve the fuel system pressure. A valve cap must first be removed to gain access to the pressure relief valve.

Throttle Position Sensor (TPS)

REMOVAL & INSTALLATION

1. Disconnect the wiring harness from the TPS.

✳✳CAUTION

Never smoke when working around gasoline! Avoid all sources of sparks or ignition. Gasoline vapors are EXTREMELY volatile!

2. Matchmark the sensor and throttle body for installation reference.

3. Remove the 2 retaining screws and remove the TPS.

To install:

4. Install the TPS aligning the scribe marks.

5. Tighten the retaining screws to 18 inch lbs.

6. Connect the wiring.

7. Start the engine and check for proper operation.

Idle Air Control Valve

REMOVAL & INSTALLATION

1. Disconnect the wiring and vacuum lines from the EVR, AIRB/AIRD solenoids and the idle air control valve

2. Remove the AIRB/AIRD solenoid bracket.

3. Remove the IAC valve retaining screws and remove the valve and gasket.

4. Installation is the reverse of removal. Use new gaskets. Tighten the IAC valve screws to 71-97 inch lbs. and the AIRB/AIRD solenoid bracket nuts to 12-18 ft. lbs.

Upper Intake Manifold

REMOVAL & INSTALLATION

▶ **See Figures 60 and 61**

1. Disconnect the throttle and transmission linkages at the throttle body.

✳✳CAUTION

Never smoke when working around gasoline! Avoid all sources of sparks or ignition. Gasoline vapors are EXTREMELY volatile!

2. Remove the two canister purge lines from the throttle body.

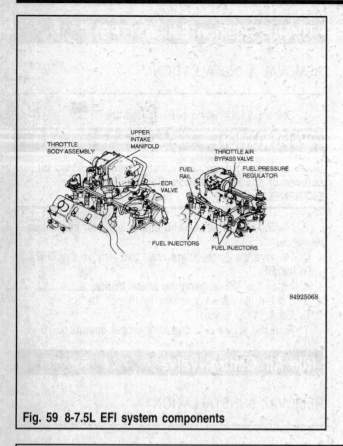

Fig. 59 8-7.5L EFI system components

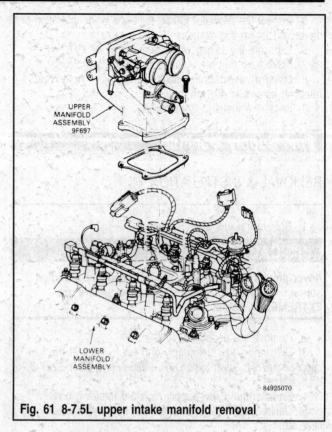

Fig. 61 8-7.5L upper intake manifold removal

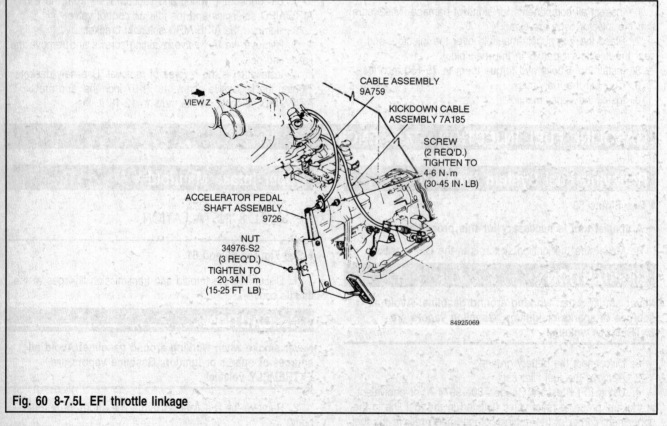

Fig. 60 8-7.5L EFI throttle linkage

3. Tag and disconnect the following:
- Throttle bypass valve wire
- Throttle position sensor wire
- EGR position sensor wire
- MAP sensor vacuum line
- EGR vacuum line
- Fuel pressure regulator vacuum line
- EGR valve flange nut
- PCV hose

4. Disconnect the water lines at the throttle body.

5. Remove the 4 upper intake manifold bolts and lift off the manifold.

6. Installation is the reverse of removal. Always use new gaskets. Torque the manifold bolts to 18 ft. lbs.

Throttle Body

REMOVAL & INSTALLATION

▶ See Figure 62

1. Relieve the fuel system pressure.

✳✳CAUTION

Never smoke when working around gasoline! Avoid all sources of sparks or ignition. Gasoline vapors are EXTREMELY volatile!

2. Disconnect the throttle position sensor wire.

3. Disconnect the water lines at the throttle body.

4. Remove the 4 throttle body bolts and carefully lift off the throttle body. Discard the gasket.

5. Installation is the reverse of removal. Torque the bolts to 18 ft. lbs.

Throttle Position Sensor (TPS)

REMOVAL & INSTALLATION

1. Disconnect the wiring harness from the TPS.

✳✳CAUTION

Never smoke when working around gasoline! Avoid all sources of sparks or ignition. Gasoline vapors are EXTREMELY volatile!

2. Matchmark the sensor and throttle body for installation reference.

3. Remove the 2 retaining screws and remove the TPS.

4. Install the TPS so that the wiring harness is parallel with the venturi bores, then, rotate the TPS clockwise to align the scribe marks.

5. Tighten the retaining screws to 16 inch lbs.

➡When correctly installed, the TPS wiring harness should be pointing directly at the air bypass valve.

6. Connect the wiring.

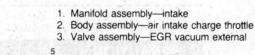

1. Manifold assembly—intake
2. Body assembly—air intake charge throttle
3. Valve assembly—EGR vacuum external
4. Valve assembly—throttle air bypass
5. Gasket—air charge control intake manifold
6. Gasket—EGR valve
7. Gasket—air bypass valve
8. Bolt 5/16 × 1.5 hex head UBS (6 reqd)
9. Bolt M6 × 25mm hex head UBS (2 reqd)
10. Connector 3/8" hose × 3/8" external pipe
11. Connector 3/8" hose × 3/8" external pipe
12. Connector 1/4" hose × 3/8" external pipe

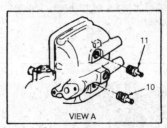

VIEW A

84925071

Fig. 62 8-7.5L throttle body and upper intake manifold

Air Bypass Valve

REMOVAL & INSTALLATION

▶ See Figure 63

1. Disconnect the wiring at the valve.

✳✳CAUTION

Never smoke when working around gasoline! Avoid all sources of sparks or ignition. Gasoline vapors are EXTREMELY volatile!

2. Remove the 2 retaining screws and lift off the valve.
3. Discard the gasket and clean and inspect the mating surfaces.
4. Install the valve with a new gasket, tightening the screws to 102 inch lbs.
5. Connect the wiring.

Fuel Supply Manifold

REMOVAL & INSTALLATION

1. Relieve the fuel system pressure.

✳✳CAUTION

Never smoke when working around gasoline! Avoid all sources of sparks or ignition. Gasoline vapors are EXTREMELY volatile!

2. Remove the upper manifold.
3. Disconnect the chassis fuel inlet and outlet lines at the fuel supply manifold using tool T81P-19623-G or G1.
4. Disconnect the fuel supply and return lines at the fuel supply manifold.
5. Remove the 4 fuel supply manifold retaining bolts.
6. Carefully disengage the manifold from the injectors and lift it off.
7. Inspect all components for signs of damage. Make sure that the injector caps are clean.

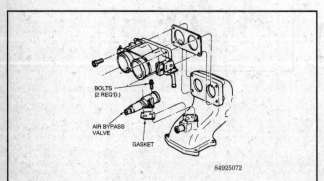

Fig. 63 8-7.5L air bypass valve removal

BOLTS
(2 REQ'D.)

AIR BYPASS
VALVE

GASKET

84925072

8. Place the fuel supply manifold over the injectors and seat the injectors carefully in the manifold.
9. Install the 4 bolts and torque them to 20 ft. lbs.
10. Connect the fuel lines.
11. Install the upper manifold.

Fuel Pressure Regulator

REMOVAL & INSTALLATION

1. Relieve the fuel system pressure.

✳✳CAUTION

Never smoke when working around gasoline! Avoid all sources of sparks or ignition. Gasoline vapors are EXTREMELY volatile!

2. Disconnect the vacuum line at the regulator.
3. Remove the 3 Allen screws from the regulator housing.
4. Remove the regulator.
5. Inspect the regulator O-ring for signs of deterioration or damage. Discard the gasket.
   To install:
6. Lubricate the O-ring with clean engine oil ONLY!
7. Make sure that the mounting surfaces are clean.
8. Using a new gasket, install the regulator. Tighten the retaining screws to 40 inch lbs.
9. Connect the vacuum line.

Fuel Injectors

REMOVAL & INSTALLATION

1. Relieve the fuel system pressure.

✳✳CAUTION

Never smoke when working around gasoline! Avoid all sources of sparks or ignition. Gasoline vapors are EXTREMELY volatile!

2. Disconnect the battery ground.
3. Remove the fuel supply manifold.
4. Disconnect the wiring at the injectors.
5. Pull upward on the injector body while gently rocking it from side-to-side.
6. Inspect the O-rings (2 per injector) on the injector for any sign of leakage or damage. Replace any suspected O-rings.
7. Inspect the plastic cap at the top of each injector and replace it if any sign of deterioration is noticed.
   To install:
8. Lubricate the O-rings with clean engine oil ONLY!
9. Install the injectors by pushing them in with a gentle rocking motion.
10. Install the fuel supply manifold.
11. Connect the electrical wiring.

DIESEL ENGINE FUEL SYSTEM

Fuel Pump

REMOVAL & INSTALLATION

▶ **See Figures 64 and 65**

1. Loosen the threaded connections with the proper size wrench (a flare nut wrench is preferred) and retighten snugly. Do not remove the lines at this time.
2. Loosen the mounting bolts, one to two turns. Apply force with your hand to loosen the fuel pump if the gasket is stuck. Rotate the engine by nudging the starter, until the fuel pump cam lobe is at the low position. At this position, spring tension against the fuel pump bolts will be greatly reduced.
3. Disconnect the fuel supply pump inlet, outlet and fuel return line.

✳✳CAUTION

Use care to prevent combustion of the spilled fuel.

4. Remove the fuel pump attaching bolts and remove the pump and gasket. Discard the old gasket.
5. Remove the remaining fuel pump gasket material from the engine and from the fuel pump if you are reinstalling the old pump. Make sure both mounting surfaces are clean.
   To install:
6. Install the attaching bolts into the fuel supply pump and install a new gasket on the bolts. Position the fuel pump onto the mounting pad. Turn the attaching bolts alternately and evenly and tighten the bolts to the specifications according to the size bolts used on the pump. See the accompanying standard torque chart for reference.

➡**The cam must be at its low position before attempting to install the fuel supply pump. If it is difficult to start the mounting bolts, remove the pump and reinstall with a lever on the bottom side of the cam.**

7. Install the fuel outlet line. Start the fitting by hand to avoid crossthreading.
8. Install the inlet line and the fuel return line.
9. Start the engine and observe all connections for fuel leaks for two minutes.

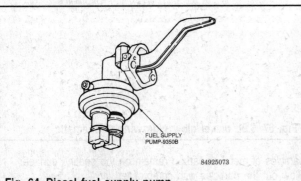

FUEL SUPPLY PUMP-9350B

84925073

Fig. 64 Diesel fuel supply pump

10. Stop the engine and check all fuel supply pump fuel line connections. Check for oil leaks at the pump mounting pad.

Glow Plug System

▶ **See Figures 66, 67 and 68**

The diesel engine utilizes an electric glow plug system to aid in the start of the engine. The function of this stem is to preheat the combustion chamber to aid ignition of the fuel.

The system consists of eight glow plugs (one for each cylinder), control switch, power relay, after glow relay, wait lamp latching relay, wait lamp and the eight fusible links located between the harness and the glow plug terminal.

On initial start with cold engine, the glow plug system operates as follows: The glow plug control switch energizes the power relay (which is a magnetic switch) and the power relay contacts close. Battery current energizes the glow plugs. Current to the glow plugs and a wait lamp will be shut off when the glow plugs are hot enough. This takes from 2 to 10 second after the key is first turned on. When the wait lamp goes off, the engine is ready to start. After the engine is started the glow plugs begin an on-off cycle for about 40 to 90 seconds. This cycle helps to clear start-up smoke. The control switch (the brain of the operation) is threaded into the left cylinder head coolant jacket. the control unit senses engine coolant temperature. Since the control unit senses temperature and glow plug operation the glow plug system will not be activated unless needed. On a restart (warm engine) the glow plug system will not be activated unless the coolant temperature drops before 165°F (91°C).

Since the fast start system utilizes 6 volt glow plugs in a 12 volt system to achieve rapid heating of the glow plug, a cycling device is required in the circuit.

✳✳CAUTION

Never bypass the power relay of the glow plug system. Constant battery current (12 volts) to glow plugs will cause them to overheat and fail.

REMOVAL & INSTALLATION

▶ **See Figure 69**

➡**Before removing the nozzle assemblies, clean the exterior of each nozzle assembly and the surrounding area with clean fuel oil or solvent to prevent entry of dirt into the engine when nozzle assemblies are removed. Also, clean the fuel inlet and fuel leak-off piping connections. Blow dry with compressed air.**

1. Remove the fuel line retaining clamp(s) from the nozzle lines that are to be removed.
2. Disconnect the nozzle fuel inlet (high pressure) and fuel leak-off tees from each nozzle assembly and position out of the way. Cover the open ends of the fuel inlet and outlet or nozzles with protective caps, to prevent dirt from entering.

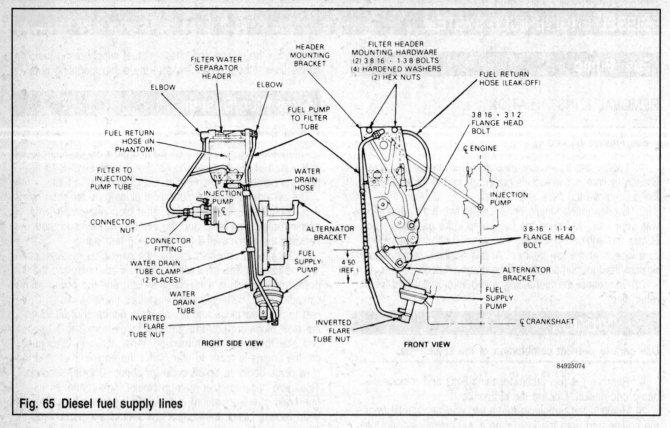

Fig. 65 Diesel fuel supply lines

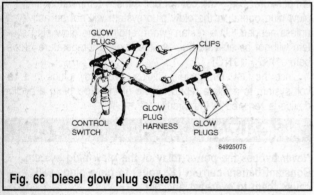

Fig. 66 Diesel glow plug system

3. Remove the injection nozzles by turning them counter-clockwise. Pull the nozzle assembly with the copper washer attached from the engine. Cover the nozzle fuel opening and spray tip, with plastic caps, to prevent the entry of dirt.

➡**Remove the copper injector nozzle gasket from the nozzle bore with special tool, T71P-19703-C, or equivalent, whenever the gasket does not come out with the nozzle.**

4. Place the nozzle assemblies in a fabricated holder as they are removed from the heads. The holder should be marked with numbers corresponding to the cylinder numbering of the engine. This will allow for reinstallation of the nozzle in the same ports from which they were removed.

To install:

5. Thoroughly clean the nozzle bore in cylinder head before reinserting the nozzle assembly with nozzle seat cleaner, special tool T83T-9527-A or equivalent. Make certain that no small

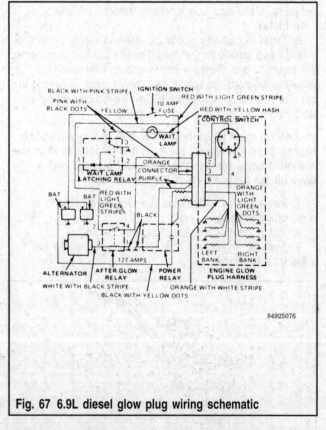

Fig. 67 6.9L diesel glow plug wiring schematic

particles of metal or carbon remain on the seating surface. Blow out the particles with compressed air.

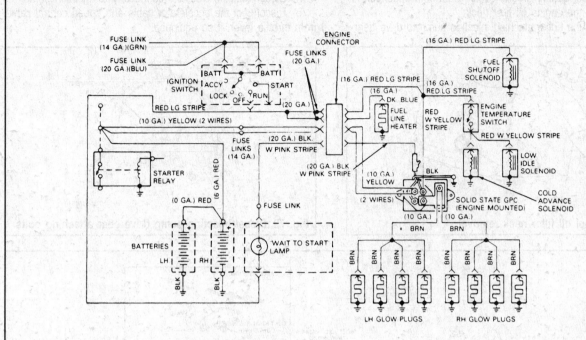

Fig. 68 7.3L diesel glow plug wiring schematic

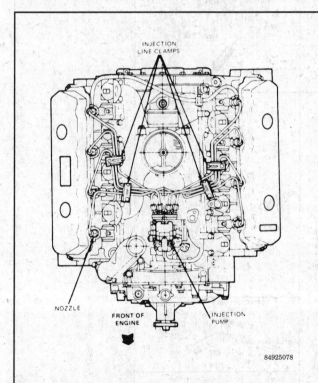

Fig. 69 Injection line clamps, Diesel V8. Injection lines also shown

6. Remove the protective cap and install a new copper gasket on the nozzle assembly, with a small dab of grease.

➡ **Anti-seize compound or equivalent should be used on nozzle threads to aid in installation and future removal.**

7. Install the nozzle assembly into the cylinder head nozzle bore.
8. Tighten the nozzle assembly to 33 ft. lbs.
9. Remove the protective caps from nozzle assemblies and fuel lines.
10. Install the leak-off tees to the nozzle assemblies.

➡ **Install two new O-ring seals for each fuel return tee.**

11. Connect the high pressure fuel line and tighten, using a flare nut wrench.
12. Install the fuel line retainer clamps.
13. Start the engine and check for leaks.

Injection Pump

REMOVAL & INSTALLATION

▶ See Figures 70, 71, 72, 73, 74, 75, 76, 77 and 78

❊❊WARNING

Before removing the fuel lines, clean the exterior with clean fuel oil or solvent to prevent entry of dirt into the engine when the fuel lines are removed. Do not wash or steam clean engine while engine is running. Serious damage to injection pump could occur.

1. Disconnect battery ground cables from both batteries.
2. Remove the engine oil filler neck.
3. Remove the bolts attaching injection pump to drive gear.

4. Disconnect the electrical connectors to injection pump.
5. Disconnect the accelerator cable and speed control cable from throttle lever, if so equipped.

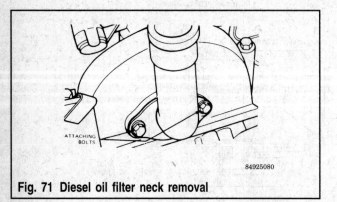

Fig. 71 Diesel oil filter neck removal

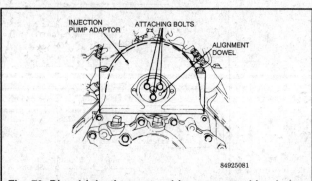

Fig. 72 Diesel injection pump drive gear attaching bolts

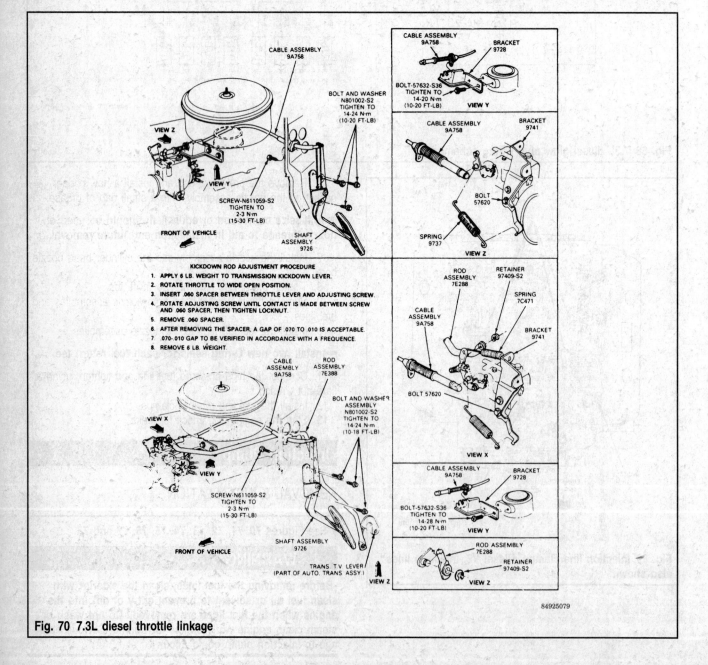

KICKDOWN ROD ADJUSTMENT PROCEDURE

1. APPLY 6 LB. WEIGHT TO TRANSMISSION KICKDOWN LEVER.
2. ROTATE THROTTLE TO WIDE OPEN POSITION.
3. INSERT .060 SPACER BETWEEN THROTTLE LEVER AND ADJUSTING SCREW.
4. ROTATE ADJUSTING SCREW UNTIL CONTACT IS MADE BETWEEN SCREW AND .060 SPACER, THEN TIGHTEN LOCKNUT.
5. REMOVE .060 SPACER.
6. AFTER REMOVING THE SPACER, A GAP OF .070 TO .010 IS ACCEPTABLE.
7. .070-.010 GAP TO BE VERIFIED IN ACCORDANCE WITH A FREQUENCE.
8. REMOVE 6 LB. WEIGHT.

Fig. 70 7.3L diesel throttle linkage

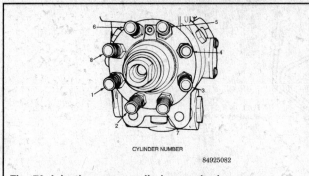

Fig. 73 Injection pump cylinder numbering sequence

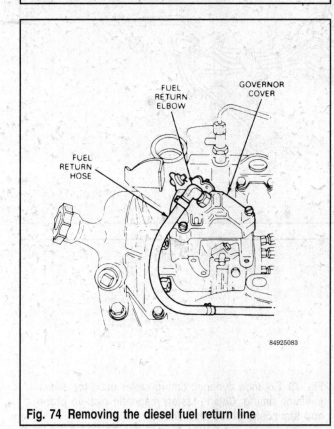

Fig. 74 Removing the diesel fuel return line

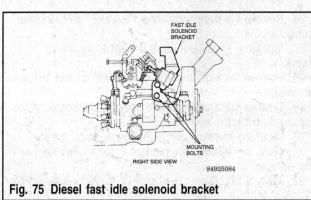

Fig. 75 Diesel fast idle solenoid bracket

6. Remove the air cleaner and install clean rags to prevent dirt from entering the intake manifold.

7. Remove the accelerator cable bracket, with cables attached, from the intake manifold and position out of the way.

➡All fuel lines and fittings must be capped using Fuel System Protective Cap Set T83T-9395-A or equivalent, to prevent fuel contamination.

8. Remove the fuel filter-to-injection pump fuel line and cap fittings.

9. Remove and cap the injection pump inlet elbow and the injection pump fitting adapter.

10. Remove the fuel return line on injection pump, rotate out of the way, And cap all fittings.

➡It is not necessary to remove injection lines from injection pump. If lines are to be removed, loosen injection line fittings at injection pump before removing it from engine.

11. Remove the fuel injection lines from the nozzles and cap lines and nozzles.

12. Remove the three nuts attaching the Injection pump to injection pump adapter using Tool T83T-9000-B.

13. If the injection pump is to be replaced, loosen the injection line retaining clips and the injection nozzle fuel lines with Tool T83T-9396-A and cap all fittings at this time with protective cap set T83T-9395-A or equivalent. Do not install the injection nozzle fuel lines until the new pump is installed in the engine.

14. Lift the Injection pump, with the nozzle lines attached, up and out of the engine compartment.

✳✳WARNING

Do not carry injection pump by injection nozzle fuel lines as this could cause lines to bend or crimp.

To install:

15. Install a new O-ring on the drive gear end of the injection pump.

16. Move the injection pump down and into position.

17. Position the alignment dowel on injection pump into the alignment hole on drive gear.

18. Install the bolts attaching the injection pump to drive gear and tighten.

19. Install the nuts attaching injection pump to adapter. Align scribe lines on the injection pump flange and the injection pump adapter and tighten to 14 ft. lbs.

20. If the injection nozzle fuel lines were removed from the injection pump install at this time, refer to Fuel Lines — Installation, in this Section.

21. Remove the caps from nozzles and the fuel lines and install the fuel line nuts on the nozzles and tighten to 22 ft. lbs.

22. Connect the fuel return line to injection pump and tighten the nuts.

23. Install the injection pump fitting adapter with a new O-ring.

24. Clean the old sealant from the injection pump elbow threads, using clean solvent, and dry thoroughly. Apply a light coating of pipe sealant to the elbow threads.

25. Install the elbow in the injection pump adapter and tighten to a minimum of 6 ft. lbs. Then tighten further, if necessary, to align the elbow with the injection pump fuel inlet line, but do not exceed 360 degrees of rotation or 10 ft. lbs.

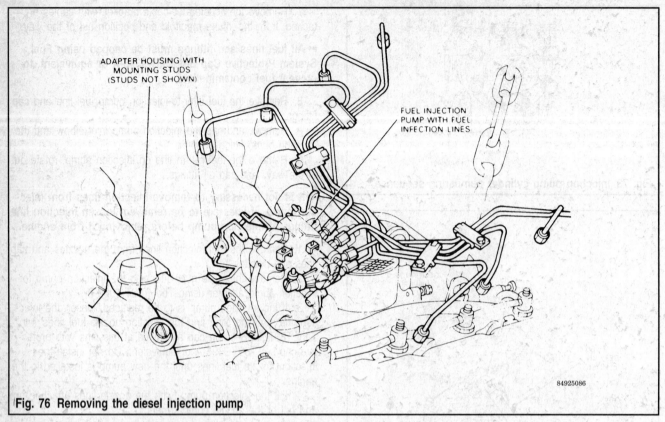

Fig. 76 Removing the diesel injection pump

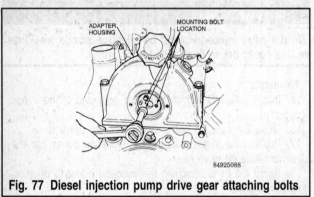

Fig. 77 Diesel injection pump drive gear attaching bolts

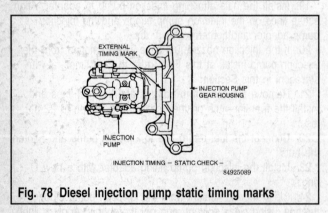

Fig. 78 Diesel injection pump static timing marks

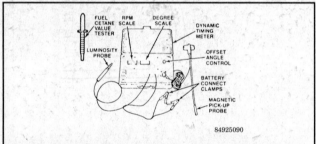

Fig. 79 Rotunda dynamic timing meter used for diesel injection timing. Cetane tester, magnetic pick-up probe and luminosity probe also shown

26. Remove the caps and connect the fuel filter-to-injection pump fuel line.

27. Install the accelerator cable bracket to the intake manifold.

28. Remove the rags from the intake manifold and install the air cleaner.

29. Connect the accelerator and speed control cable, if so equipped, to throttle lever.

30. Install the electrical connectors on injection pump.

31. Clean the injection pump adapter and oil filler neck sealing surfaces.

32. Apply a ⅛in. (3mm) bead of RTV sealant on the adapter housing.

33. Install the oil filler neck and tighten the bolts.

34. Connect the battery ground cables to both batteries.

35. Run the engine and check for fuel leaks.

36. If necessary, purge high pressure fuel lines of air by loosening connector one half to one turn and cranking engine until solid fuel, free from bubbles flows from connection.

✳✳CAUTION

Keep eyes and hands away from nozzle spray. Fuel spraying from the nozzle under high pressure can penetrate the skin.

37. Check and adjust injection pump timing as described in this Section.

Fuel Lines

REMOVAL & INSTALLATION

➡**Before removing any fuel lines, clean the exterior with clean fuel oil, or solvent to prevent entry of dirt into fuel system when the fuel lines are removed. Blow dry with compressed air.**

1. Disconnect the battery ground cables from both batteries.
2. Remove the air cleaner and cap intake manifold opening with clean rags.
3. Disconnect the accelerator cable and speed control cable, if so equipped, from the injection pump.
4. remove the accelerator cable bracket from the intake manifold and position out of the way with cable(s) attached.

✳✳WARNING

To prevent fuel system contamination, cap all fuel lines and fittings.

5. Disconnect the fuel line from the fuel filter to injection pump and cap all fittings.
6. Disconnect and cap the nozzle fuel lines at nozzles.
7. Remove the fuel line clamps from the fuel lines to be removed.
8. Remove and cap the injection pump inlet elbow.
9. Remove and cap the inlet fitting adapter.
10. Remove the injection nozzle lines, one at a time, from injection pump using Tool T83T-9396-A.

➡**Fuel lines must be removed following this sequence: 5-6-4-8-3-1-7-2. Install caps on the end of each fuel line and pump fitting as the line is disconnected and identify each fuel line accordingly.**

To install:
11. Install fuel lines on injection pump, one at a time, and tighten to 22 ft.lbs.

➡**Fuel lines must be installed in the sequence: 2-7-1-3-8-4-6-5.**

12. Clean the old sealant from the injection pump elbow, using clean solvent, and dry thoroughly.
13. Apply a light coating of pipe sealant on the elbow threads.

Diesel Injection Timing

▸ **See Figures 79, 80, 81 and 82**

STATIC TIMING

1. Break the torque of the injection pump mounting nuts (keeping the nuts snug).
2. Rotate the injection pump using Tool T83-9000-C or equivalent to bring the mark on the pump into alignment with the mark on pump mounting adapter.
3. Visually recheck the alignment of the timing marks and tighten injection pump mounting nuts.

DYNAMIC TIMING

1. Bring the engine up to normal operating temperature.
2. Stop the engine and install a dynamic timing meter, Rotunda 78-0100 or equivalent, by placing the magnetic probe pick-up into the probe hole.
3. Remove the no. 1 glow plug wire and remove the glow plug, install the luminosity probe and tighten to 12 ft.lbs. Install the photocell over the probe.
4. Connect the dynamic timing meter to the battery and adjust the offset of the meter.
5. Set the transmission in neutral and raise the rear wheels off the ground. Using Rotunda 14-0302, throttle control, set the

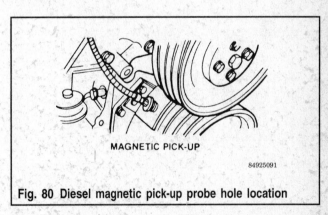

MAGNETIC PICK-UP

84925091

Fig. 80 Diesel magnetic pick-up probe hole location

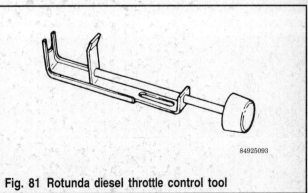

84925093

Fig. 81 Rotunda diesel throttle control tool

Dynamic Timing Specifications

Fuel Cetane Value	Altitude	
	0–3000 Ft ①	Above 3000 Ft ①
38–42	6° ATDC	7° ATDC
43–46	5° ATDC	6° ATDC
47–50	4° ATDC	5° ATDC

① Installation of resetting tolerance for dynamic timing is ± 1°. Service limit is ± 2°.

84925094

Fig. 82 Diesel timing specifications

engine speed to 1,400 rpm with no accessory load. Observe the injection timing on the dynamic timing meter.

➡Obtain the fuel sample from the vehicle and check the cetane value using the tester supplied with the Ford special tools 78-0100 or equivalent. Refer to the dynamic timing chart to find the correct timing in degrees.

6. If the dynamic timing is not within plug or minus 2 degrees of specification, then the injection pump timing will require adjustment.

7. Turn the engine off. Note the timing mark alignment. Loosen the injection pump-to-adapter nuts.

8. Rotate the injection pump clockwise (when viewed from the front of the engine) to retard and counterclockwise to advance timing. Two degrees of dynamic timing is approximately 0.030 in. (0.76mm) of timing mark movement.

9. Start the engine and recheck the timing. If the timing is not within plus or minus 1 degree of specification, repeat steps 7 through 9.

10. Turn off the engine. Remove the dynamic timing equipment. Lightly coat the glow plug thread with anti-seize compound, install the glow plugs and tighten to 12 ft. lbs. Connect the glow plug wires.

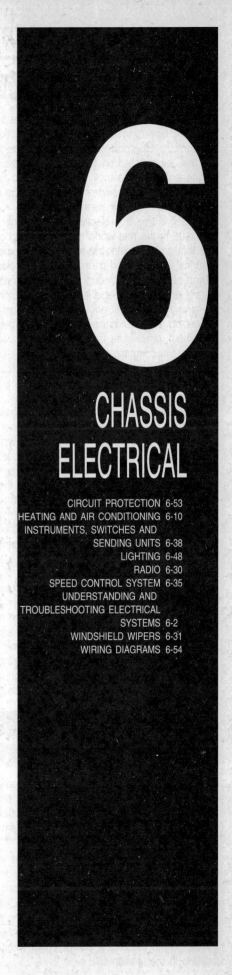

6

CHASSIS
ELECTRICAL

UNDERSTANDING AND TROUBLESHOOTING ELECTRICAL SYSTEMS

Both import and domestic manufacturers are incorporating electronic control systems into their production lines. Most vehicles are equipped with one or more on-board computer, like the unit installed on your vehicle. These electronic components (with no moving parts) should theoretically last the life of the vehicle, provided nothing external happens to damage the circuits or memory chips.

While it is true that electronic components should never wear out, in the real world malfunctions do occur. It is also true that any computer-based system is extremely sensitive to electrical voltages and cannot tolerate careless or haphazard testing or service procedures. An inexperienced individual can literally do major damage looking for a minor problem by using the wrong kind of test equipment or connecting test leads or connectors with the ignition switch ON. When selecting test equipment, make sure the manufacturers instructions state that the tester is compatible with whatever type of electronic control system is being serviced. Read all instructions carefully and double check all test points before installing probes or making any test connections.

The following section outlines basic diagnosis techniques for dealing with computerized automotive control systems. Along with a general explanation of the various types of test equipment available to aid in servicing modern electronic automotive systems, basic repair techniques for wiring harnesses and connectors is given. Read the basic information before attempting any repairs or testing on any computerized system, to provide the background of information necessary to avoid the most common and obvious mistakes that can cost both time and money. Although the replacement and testing procedures are simple in themselves, the systems are not, and unless one has a thorough understanding of all components and their function within a particular computerized control system, the logical test sequence these systems demand cannot be followed. Minor malfunctions can make a big difference, so it is important to know how each component affects the operation of the overall electronic system to find the ultimate cause of a problem without replacing good components unnecessarily. It is not enough to use the correct test equipment; the test equipment must be used correctly.

Safety Precautions

✳✳CAUTION

Whenever working on or around any computer based microprocessor control system, always observe these general precautions to prevent the possibility of personal injury or damage to electronic components.

• Never install or remove battery cables with the key ON or the engine running. Jumper cables should be connected with the key OFF to avoid power surges that can damage electronic control units. Engines equipped with computer controlled systems should avoid both giving and getting jump starts due to the possibility of serious damage to components from arcing in the engine compartment when connections are made with the ignition ON.

• Always remove the battery cables before charging the battery. Never use a high output charger on an installed battery or attempt to use any type of 'hot shot' (24 volt) starting aid.

• Exercise care when inserting test probes into connectors to insure good connections without damaging the connector or spreading the pins. Always probe connectors from the rear (wire) side, NOT the pin side, to avoid accidental shorting of terminals during test procedures.

• Never remove or attach wiring harness connectors with the ignition switch ON, especially to an electronic control unit.

• Do not drop any components during service procedures and never apply 12 volts directly to any component (like a solenoid or relay) unless instructed specifically to do so. Some component electrical windings are designed to safely handle only 4 or 5 volts and can be destroyed in seconds if 12 volts are applied directly to the connector.

• Remove the electronic control unit if the vehicle is to be placed in an environment where temperatures exceed approximately 176°F (80°C), such as a paint spray booth or when arc or gas welding near the control unit location in the car.

ORGANIZED TROUBLESHOOTING

When diagnosing a specific problem, organized troubleshooting is a must. The complexity of a modern automobile demands that you approach any problem in a logical, organized manner. There are certain troubleshooting techniques that are standard:

1. Establish when the problem occurs. Does the problem appear only under certain conditions? Were there any noises, odors, or other unusual symptoms?

2. Isolate the problem area. To do this, make some simple tests and observations; then eliminate the systems that are working properly. Check for obvious problems such as broken wires, dirty connections or split or disconnected vacuum hoses. Always check the obvious before assuming something complicated is the cause.

3. Test for problems systematically to determine the cause once the problem area is isolated. Are all the components functioning properly? Is there power going to electrical switches and motors? Is there vacuum at vacuum switches and/or actuators? Is there a mechanical problem such as bent linkage or loose mounting screws? Doing careful, systematic checks will often turn up most causes on the first inspection without wasting time checking components that have little or no relationship to the problem.

4. Test all repairs after the work is done to make sure that the problem is fixed. Some causes can be traced to more than one component, so a careful verification of repair work is important to pick up additional malfunctions that may cause a problem to reappear or a different problem to arise. A blown fuse, for example, is a simple problem that may require more than another fuse to repair. If you don't look for a problem that caused a fuse to blow, for example, a shorted wire may go undetected.

Experience has shown that most problems tend to be the result of a fairly simple and obvious cause, such as loose or corroded connectors or air leaks in the intake system; making careful inspection of components during testing essential to quick and accurate troubleshooting. Special, hand held computerized testers designed specifically for diagnosing the EEC-IV system are available from a variety of aftermarket sources, as well as from the vehicle manufacturer, but care should be taken that any test equipment being used is designed to diagnose that particular computer controlled system accurately without damaging the control unit (ECU) or components being tested.

➡Pinpointing the exact cause of trouble in an electrical system can sometimes only be accomplished by the use of special test equipment. The following describes commonly used test equipment and explains how to put it to best use in diagnosis. In addition to the information covered below, the manufacturer's instructions booklet provided with the tester should be read and clearly understood before attempting any test procedures.

TEST EQUIPMENT

Jumper Wires

Jumper wires are simple, yet extremely valuable, pieces of test equipment. Jumper wires are merely wires that are used to bypass sections of a circuit. The simplest type of jumper wire is merely a length of multistrand wire with an alligator clip at each end. Jumper wires are usually fabricated from lengths of standard automotive wire and whatever type of connector (alligator clip, spade connector or pin connector) that is required for the particular vehicle being tested. The well equipped tool box will have several different styles of jumper wires in several different lengths. Some jumper wires are made with three or more terminals coming from a common splice for special purpose testing. In cramped, hard-to-reach areas it is advisable to have insulated boots over the jumper wire terminals in order to prevent accidental grounding, sparks, and possible fire, especially when testing fuel system components.

Jumper wires are used primarily to locate open electrical circuits, on either the ground (-) side of the circuit or on the hot (+) side. If an electrical component fails to operate, connect the jumper wire between the component and a good ground. If the component operates only with the jumper installed, the ground circuit is open. If the ground circuit is good, but the component does not operate, the circuit between the power feed and component is open. You can sometimes connect the jumper wire directly from the battery to the hot terminal of the component, but first make sure the component uses 12 volts in operation. Some electrical components, such as fuel injectors, are designed to operate on about 4 volts and running 12 volts directly to the injector terminals can burn out the wiring. By inserting an inline fuse holder between a set of test leads, a fused jumper wire can be used for bypassing open circuits. Use a 5 amp fuse to provide protection against voltage spikes. When in doubt, use a voltmeter to check the voltage input to the component and measure how much voltage is being applied normally. By moving the jumper wire

successively back from the lamp toward the power source, you can isolate the area of the circuit where the open is located. When the component stops functioning, or the power is cut off, the open is in the segment of wire between the jumper and the point previously tested.

✷✷CAUTION

Never use jumpers made from wire that is of lighter gauge than used in the circuit under test. If the jumper wire is of too small gauge, it may overheat and possibly melt. Never use jumpers to bypass high resistance loads (Such as motors) in a circuit. Bypassing resistances, in effect, creates a short circuit which may, in turn, cause damage and fire. Never use a jumper for anything other than temporary bypassing of components in a circuit.

12 Volt Test Light

The 12 volt test light is used to check circuits and components while electrical current is flowing through them. It is used for voltage and ground tests. Twelve volt test lights come in different styles but all have three main parts; a ground clip, a probe, and a light. The most commonly used 12 volt test lights have pick-type probes. To use a 12 volt test light, connect the ground clip to a good ground and probe wherever necessary with the pick. The pick should be sharp so that it can penetrate wire insulation to make contact with the wire, without making a large hole in the insulation. The wrap-around light is handy in hard to reach areas or where it is difficult to support a wire to push a probe pick into it. To use the wrap around light, hook the wire to probed with the hook and pull the trigger. A small pick will be forced through the wire insulation into the wire core.

✷✷CAUTION

Do not use a test light to probe electronic ignition spark plug or coil wires. Never use a pick-type test light to probe wiring on computer controlled systems unless specifically instructed to do so. Any wire insulation that is pierced by the test light probe should be taped and sealed with silicone after testing.

Like the jumper wire, the 12 volt test light is used to isolate opens in circuits. But, whereas the jumper wire is used to bypass the open to operate the load, the 12 volt test light is used to locate the presence of voltage in a circuit. If the test light glows, you know that there is power up to that point; if the 12 volt test light does not glow when its probe is inserted into the wire or connector, you know that there is an open circuit (no power). Move the test light in successive steps back toward the power source until the light in the handle does glow. When it does glow, the open is between the probe and point previously probed.

➡The test light does not detect that 12 volts (or any particular amount of voltage) is present; it only detects that some voltage is present. It is advisable before using the test light to touch its terminals across the battery posts to make sure the light is operating properly.

Self-Powered Test Light

The self-powered test light usually contains a 1.5 volt penlight battery. One type of self-powered test light is similar in design to the 12 volt test light. This type has both the battery and the light in the handle and pick-type probe tip. The second type has the light toward the open tip, so that the light illuminates the contact point. The self-powered test light is dual purpose piece of test equipment. It can be used to test for either open or short circuits when power is isolated from the circuit (continuity test). A powered test light should not be used on any computer controlled system or component unless specifically instructed to do so. Many engine sensors can be destroyed by even this small amount of voltage applied directly to the terminals.

Open Circuit Testing

To use the self-powered test light to check for open circuits, first isolate the circuit from the vehicle's 12 volt power source by disconnecting the battery or wiring harness connector. Connect the test light ground clip to a good ground and probe sections of the circuit sequentially with the test light. (start from either end of the circuit). If the light is out, the open is between the probe and the circuit ground. If the light is on, the open is between the probe and end of the circuit toward the power source.

Short Circuit Testing

By isolating the circuit both from power and from ground, and using a self-powered test light, you can check for shorts to ground in the circuit. Isolate the circuit from power and ground. Connect the test light ground clip to a good ground and probe any easy-to-reach test point in the circuit. If the light comes on, there is a short somewhere in the circuit. To isolate the short, probe a test point at either end of the isolated circuit (the light should be on). Leave the test light probe connected and open connectors, switches, remove parts, etc., sequentially, until the light goes out. When the light goes out, the short is between the last circuit component opened and the previous circuit opened.

➡The 1.5 volt battery in the test light does not provide much current. A weak battery may not provide enough power to illuminate the test light even when a complete circuit is made (especially if there are high resistances in the circuit). Always make sure that the test battery is strong. To check the battery, briefly touch the ground clip to the probe; if the light glows brightly the battery is strong enough for testing. Never use a self-powered test light to perform checks for opens or shorts when power is applied to the electrical system under test. The 12 volt vehicle power will quickly burn out the 1.5 volt light bulb in the test light.

Voltmeter

A voltmeter is used to measure voltage at any point in a circuit, or to measure the voltage drop across any part of a circuit. It can also be used to check continuity in a wire or circuit by indicating current flow from one end to the other. Voltmeters usually have various scales on the meter dial and a selector switch to allow the selection of different voltages. The voltmeter has a positive and a negative lead. To avoid damage to the meter, always connect the negative lead to the negative (-) side of circuit (to ground or nearest the ground side of the circuit) and connect the positive lead to the positive (+) side of the circuit (to the power source or the nearest power source). Note that the negative voltmeter lead will always be black and that the positive voltmeter will always be some color other than black (usually red). Depending on how the voltmeter is connected into the circuit, it has several uses.

A voltmeter can be connected either in parallel or in series with a circuit and it has a very high resistance to current flow. When connected in parallel, only a small amount of current will flow through the voltmeter current path; the rest will flow through the normal circuit current path and the circuit will work normally. When the voltmeter is connected in series with a circuit, only a small amount of current can flow through the circuit. The circuit will not work properly, but the voltmeter reading will show if the circuit is complete or not.

Available Voltage Measurement

Set the voltmeter selector switch to the 20V position and connect the meter negative lead to the negative post of the battery. Connect the positive meter lead to the positive post of the battery and turn the ignition switch ON to provide a load. Read the voltage on the meter or digital display. A well charged battery should register over 12 volts. If the meter reads below 11.5 volts, the battery power may be insufficient to operate the electrical system properly. This test determines voltage available from the battery and should be the first step in any electrical trouble diagnosis procedure. Many electrical problems, especially on computer controlled systems, can be caused by a low state of charge in the battery. Excessive corrosion at the battery cable terminals can cause a poor contact that will prevent proper charging and full battery current flow.

Normal battery voltage is 12 volts when fully charged. When the battery is supplying current to one or more circuits it is said to be 'under load'. When everything is off the electrical system is under a 'no-load' condition. A fully charged battery may show about 12.5 volts at no load; will drop to 12 volts under medium load; and will drop even lower under heavy load. If the battery is partially discharged the voltage decrease under heavy load may be excessive, even though the battery shows 12 volts or more at no load. When allowed to discharge further, the battery's available voltage under load will decrease more severely. For this reason, it is important that the battery be fully charged during all testing procedures to avoid errors in diagnosis and incorrect test results.

Voltage Drop

When current flows through a resistance, the voltage beyond the resistance is reduced (the larger the current, the greater the reduction in voltage). When no current is flowing, there is no voltage drop because there is no current flow. All points in the circuit which are connected to the power source are at the same voltage as the power source. The total voltage drop always equals the total source voltage. In a long circuit with many connectors, a series of small, unwanted voltage drops due to corrosion at the connectors can add up to a total loss of voltage which impairs the operation of the normal loads in the circuit.

INDIRECT COMPUTATION OF VOLTAGE DROPS

1. Set the voltmeter selector switch to the 20 volt position.
2. Connect the meter negative lead to a good ground.
3. Probe all resistances in the circuit with the positive meter lead.
4. Operate the circuit in all modes and observe the voltage readings.

DIRECT MEASUREMENT OF VOLTAGE DROPS

1. Set the voltmeter switch to the 20 volt position.
2. Connect the voltmeter negative lead to the ground side of the resistance load to be measured.
3. Connect the positive lead to the positive side of the resistance or load to be measured.
4. Read the voltage drop directly on the 20 volt scale.

Too high a voltage indicates too high a resistance. If, for example, a blower motor runs too slowly, you can determine if there is too high a resistance in the resistor pack. By taking voltage drop readings in all parts of the circuit, you can isolate the problem. Too low a voltage drop indicates too low a resistance. If, for example, a blower motor runs too fast in the MED and/or LOW position, the problem can be isolated in the resistor pack by taking voltage drop readings in all parts of the circuit to locate a possibly shorted resistor. The maximum allowable voltage drop under load is critical, especially if there is more than one high resistance problem in a circuit because all voltage drops are cumulative. A small drop is normal due to the resistance of the conductors.

HIGH RESISTANCE TESTING

1. Set the voltmeter selector switch to the 4 volt position.
2. Connect the voltmeter positive lead to the positive post of the battery.
3. Turn on the headlights and heater blower to provide a load.
4. Probe various points in the circuit with the negative voltmeter lead.
5. Read the voltage drop on the 4 volt scale. Some average maximum allowable voltage drops are:

> FUSE PANEL — 7 volts
> IGNITION SWITCH — 5volts
> HEADLIGHT SWITCH — 7 volts
> IGNITION COIL (+) — 5 volts
> ANY OTHER LOAD — 1.3 volts

➡**Voltage drops are all measured while a load is operating; without current flow, there will be no voltage drop.**

Ohmmeter

The ohmmeter is designed to read resistance (ohms) in a circuit or component. Although there are several different styles of ohmmeters, all will usually have a selector switch which permits the measurement of different ranges of resistance (usually the selector switch allows the multiplication of the meter reading by 10, 100, 1000, and 10,000). A calibration knob allows the meter to be set at zero for accurate measurement. Since all ohmmeters are powered by an internal battery (usually 9 volts), the ohmmeter can be used as a self-powered test light. When the ohmmeter is connected, current from the ohmmeter flows through the circuit or component

being tested. Since the ohmmeter's internal resistance and voltage are known values, the amount of current flow through the meter depends on the resistance of the circuit or component being tested.

The ohmmeter can be used to perform continuity test for opens or shorts (either by observation of the meter needle or as a self-powered test light), and to read actual resistance in a circuit. It should be noted that the ohmmeter is used to check the resistance of a component or wire while there is no voltage applied to the circuit. Current flow from an outside voltage source (such as the vehicle battery) can damage the ohmmeter, so the circuit or component should be isolated from the vehicle electrical system before any testing is done. Since the ohmmeter uses its own voltage source, either lead can be connected to any test point.

➡**When checking diodes or other solid state components, the ohmmeter leads can only be connected one way in order to measure current flow in a single direction. Make sure the positive (+) and negative (-) terminal connections are as described in the test procedures to verify the one-way diode operation.**

In using the meter for making continuity checks, do not be concerned with the actual resistance readings. Zero resistance, or any resistance readings, indicate continuity in the circuit. Infinite resistance indicates an open in the circuit. A high resistance reading where there should be none indicates a problem in the circuit. Checks for short circuits are made in the same manner as checks for open circuits except that the circuit must be isolated from both power and normal ground. Infinite resistance indicates no continuity to ground, while zero resistance indicates a dead short to ground.

RESISTANCE MEASUREMENT

The batteries in an ohmmeter will weaken with age and temperature, so the ohmmeter must be calibrated or 'zeroed' before taking measurements. To zero the meter, place the selector switch in its lowest range and touch the two ohmmeter leads together. Turn the calibration knob until the meter needle is exactly on zero.

➡**All analog (needle) type ohmmeters must be zeroed before use, but some digital ohmmeter models are automatically calibrated when the switch is turned on. Self-calibrating digital ohmmeters do not have an adjusting knob, but its a good idea to check for a zero readout before use by touching the leads together. All computer controlled systems require the use of a digital ohmmeter with at least 10 megohms impedance for testing. Before any test procedures are attempted, make sure the ohmmeter used is compatible with the electrical system or damage to the on-board computer could result.**

To measure resistance, first isolate the circuit from the vehicle power source by disconnecting the battery cables or the harness connector. Make sure the key is OFF when disconnecting any components or the battery. Where necessary, also isolate at least one side of the circuit to be checked to avoid reading parallel resistances. Parallel circuit resistances will always give a lower reading than the actual resistance of either of the branches. When measuring the resistance of parallel circuits, the total resistance will always be lower than the smallest resistance in the circuit. Connect the meter leads to both sides of the circuit (wire or component) and read the actual measured ohms on the meter scale. Make sure the selector switch is set to the proper ohm scale for the circuit being tested to avoid misreading the ohmmeter test value.

✳✳CAUTION

Never use an ohmmeter with power applied to the circuit. Like the self-powered test light, the ohmmeter is designed to operate on its own power supply. The normal 12 volt automotive electrical system current could damage the meter.

Ammeters

An ammeter measures the amount of current flowing through a circuit in units called amperes or amps. Amperes are units of electron flow which indicate how fast the electrons are flowing through the circuit. Since Ohms Law dictates that current flow in a circuit is equal to the circuit voltage divided by the total circuit resistance, increasing voltage also increases the current level (amps). Likewise, any decrease in resistance will increase the amount of amps in a circuit. At normal operating voltage, most circuits have a characteristic amount of amperes, called 'current draw' which can be measured using an ammeter. By referring to a specified current draw rating, measuring the amperes, and comparing the two values, one can determine what is happening within the circuit to aid in diagnosis. An open circuit, for example, will not allow any current to flow so the ammeter reading will be zero. More current flows through a heavily loaded circuit or when the charging system is operating.

An ammeter is always connected in series with the circuit being tested. All of the current that normally flows through the circuit must also flow through the ammeter; if there is any other path for the current to follow, the ammeter reading will not be accurate. The ammeter itself has very little resistance to current flow and therefore will not affect the circuit, but it will measure current draw only when the circuit is closed and electricity is flowing. Excessive current draw can blow fuses and drain the battery, while a reduced current draw can cause motors to run slowly, lights to dim and other components to not operate properly. The ammeter can help diagnose these conditions by locating the cause of the high or low reading.

Multimeters

Different combinations of test meters can be built into a single unit designed for specific tests. Some of the more common combination test devices are known as Volt/Amp testers, Tach/Dwell meters, or Digital Multimeters. The Volt/Amp tester is used for charging system, starting system or battery tests and consists of a voltmeter, an ammeter and a variable resistance carbon pile. The voltmeter will usually have at least two ranges for use with 6, 12 and 24 volt systems. The ammeter also has more than one range for testing various levels of battery loads and starter current draw and the carbon pile can be adjusted to offer different amounts of resistance. The Volt/Amp tester has heavy leads to carry large amounts of current and many later models have an inductive ammeter pickup that clamps around the wire to simplify test

connections. On some models, the ammeter also has a zero-center scale to allow testing of charging and starting systems without switching leads or polarity. A digital multimeter i s a voltmeter, ammeter and ohmmeter combined in an instrument which gives a digital readout. These are often used when testing solid state circuits because of their high input impedance (usually 10 megohms or more).

The tach/dwell meter combines a tachometer and a dwell (cam angle) meter and is a specialized kind of voltmeter. The tachometer scale is marked to show engine speed in rpm and the dwell scale is marked to show degrees of distributor shaft rotation. In most electronic ignition systems, dwell is determined by the control unit, but the dwell meter can also be used to check the duty cycle (operation) of some electronic engine control systems. Some tach/dwell meters are powered by an internal battery, while others take their power from the truck's battery in use. The battery powered testers usually require calibration much like an ohmmeter before testing.

Special Test Equipment

A variety of diagnostic tools are available to help troubleshoot and repair computerized engine control systems. The most sophisticated of these devices are the console type engine analyzers that usually occupy a garage service bay, but there are several types of aftermarket electronic testers available that will allow quick circuit tests of the engine control system by plugging directly into a special connector located in the engine compartment or under the dashboard. Several tool and equipment manufacturers offer simple, hand held testers that measure various circuit voltage levels on command to check all system components for proper operation. Although these testers usually cost about $300-500, consider that the average computer control unit (or ECM) can cost just as much and the money saved by not replacing perfectly good sensors or components in an attempt to correct a problem could justify the purchase price of a special diagnostic tester the first time it's used.

These computerized testers can allow quick and easy test measurements while the engine is operating or while the truck is being driven. In addition, the on-board computer memory can be read to access any stored trouble codes; in effect allowing the computer to tell you where it hurts and aid trouble diagnosis by pinpointing exactly which circuit or component is malfunctioning. In the same manner, repairs can be tested to make sure the problem has been corrected. The biggest advantage these special testers have is their relatively easy hookups that minimize or eliminate the chances of making the wrong connections and getting false voltage readings or damaging the computer accidentally.

➡**It should be remembered that these testers check voltage levels in circuits; they don't detect mechanical problems or failed components if the circuit voltage falls within the preprogrammed limits stored in the tester PROM unit. Also, most of the hand held testers are designed to work only on one or two systems made by a specific manufacturer.**

A variety of aftermarket testers are available to help diagnose different computerized control systems. Owatonna Tool Company (OTC), for example, markets a device called the OTC Monitor which plugs directly into the assembly line diagnostic link (ALDL). The OTC tester makes diagnosis a simple matter of pressing the correct buttons and, by changing the internal PROM or inserting a different diagnosis cartridge, it will work on any model from full size to subcompact, over a wide range of years. An adapter is supplied with the tester to allow connection to all types of ALDL links, regardless of the number of pin terminals used. By inserting an updated PROM into the OTC tester, it can be easily updated to diagnose any new modifications of computerized control systems.

Wiring Harnesses

The average automobile contains about ½ mile of wiring, with hundreds of individual connections. To protect the many wires from damage and to keep them from becoming a confusing tangle, they are organized into bundles, enclosed in plastic or taped together and called wire harnesses. Different wiring harnesses serve different parts of the vehicle. Individual wires are color coded to help trace them through a harness where sections are hidden from view.

A loose or corroded connection or a replacement wire that is too small for the circuit will add extra resistance and an additional voltage drop to the circuit. A ten percent voltage drop can result in slow or erratic motor operation, for example, even though the circuit is complete. Automotive wiring or circuit conductors can be in any one of three forms:
1. Single strand wire
2. Multistrand wire
3. Printed circuitry

Single strand wire has a solid metal core and is usually used inside such components as alternators, motors, relays and other devices. Multistrand wire has a core made of many small strands of wire twisted together into a single conductor. Most of the wiring in an automotive electrical system is made up of multistrand wire, either as a single conductor or grouped together in a harness. All wiring is color coded on the insulator, either as a solid color or as a colored wire with an identification stripe. A printed circuit is a thin film of copper or other conductor that is printed on an insulator backing. Occasionally, a printed circuit is sandwiched between two sheets of plastic for more protection and flexibility. A complete printed circuit, consisting of conductors, insulating material and connectors for lamps or other components is called a printed circuit board. Printed circuitry is used in place of individual wires or harnesses in places where space is limited, such as behind instrument panel.

WIRE GAUGE

Since computer controlled automotive electrical systems are very sensitive to changes in resistance, the selection of properly sized wires is critical when systems are repaired. The wire gauge number is an expression of the cross section area of the conductor. The most common system for expressing wire size is the American Wire Gauge (AWG) system.

Wire cross section area is measured in circular mils. A mil is 1/1000 in. (0.001 in.); a circular mil is the area of a circle one mil in diameter. For example, a conductor ¼ in. in diameter is 0.250 in. or 250 mils. The circular mil cross section area of the wire is 250 squared (250^2) or 62,500 circular mils. Imported

truck models usually use metric wire gauge designations, which is simply the cross section area of the conductor in square millimeters (mm^2).

Gauge numbers are assigned to conductors of various cross section areas. As gauge number increases, area decreases and the conductor becomes smaller. A 5 gauge conductor is smaller than a 1 gauge conductor and a 10 gauge is smaller than a 5 gauge. As the cross section area of a conductor decreases, resistance increases and so does the gauge number. A conductor with a higher gauge number will carry less current than a conductor with a lower gauge number.

➡**Gauge wire size refers to the size of the conductor, not the size of the complete wire. It is possible to have two wires of the same gauge with different diameters because one may have thicker insulation than the other.**

12 volt automotive electrical systems generally use 10, 12, 14, 16 and 18 gauge wire. Main power distribution circuits and larger accessories usually use 10 and 12 gauge wire. Battery cables are usually 4 or 6 gauge, although 1 and 2 gauge wires are occasionally used. Wire length must also be considered when making repairs to a circuit. As conductor length increases, so does resistance. An 18 gauge wire, for example, can carry a 10 amp load for 10 feet without excessive voltage drop; however if a 15 foot wire is required for the same 10 amp load, it must be a 16 gauge wire.

An electrical schematic shows the electrical current paths when a circuit is operating properly. It is essential to understand how a circuit works before trying to figure out why it doesn't. Schematics break the entire electrical system down into individual circuits and show only one particular circuit. In a schematic, no attempt is made to represent wiring and components as they physically appear on the vehicle; switches and other components are shown as simply as possible. Face views of harness connectors show the cavity or terminal locations in all multi-pin connectors to help locate test points.

If you need to backprobe a connector while it is on the component, the order of the terminals must be mentally reversed. The wire color code can help in this situation, as well as a keyway, lock tab or other reference mark.

WIRING REPAIR

Soldering is a quick, efficient method of joining metals permanently. Everyone who has the occasion to make wiring repairs should know how to solder. Electrical connections that are soldered are far less likely to come apart and will conduct electricity much better than connections that are only 'pig-tailed' together. The most popular (and preferred) method of soldering is with an electrical soldering gun. Soldering irons are available in many sizes and wattage ratings. Irons with higher wattage ratings deliver higher temperatures and recover lost heat faster. A small soldering iron rated for no more than 50 watts is recommended, especially on electrical systems where excess heat can damage the components being soldered.

There are three ingredients necessary for successful soldering; proper flux, good solder and sufficient heat. A soldering flux is necessary to clean the metal of tarnish, prepare it for soldering and to enable the solder to spread into tiny crevices. When soldering, always use a resin flux or resin core solder which is non-corrosive and will not attract moisture once the job is finished. Other types of flux (acid core) will leave a residue that will attract moisture and cause the wires to corrode. Tin is a unique metal with a low melting point. In a molten state, it dissolves and alloys easily with many metals. Solder is made by mixing tin with lead. The most common proportions are 40/60, 50/50 and 60/40, with the percentage of tin listed first. Low priced solders usually contain less tin, making them very difficult for a beginner to use because more heat is required to melt the solder. A common solder is 40/60 which is well suited for all-around general use, but 60/40 melts easier, has more tin f or a better joint and is preferred for electrical work.

Soldering Techniques

Successful soldering requires that the metals to be joined be heated to a temperature that will melt the solder — usually 360-460°F (182-238°C). Contrary to popular belief, the purpose of the soldering iron is not to melt the solder itself, but to heat the parts being soldered to a temperature high enough to melt the solder when it is touched to the work. Melting flux-cored solder on the soldering iron will usually destroy the effectiveness of the flux.

➡**Soldering tips are made of copper for good heat conductivity, but must be 'tinned' regularly for quick transference of heat to the project and to prevent the solder from sticking to the iron. To 'tin' the iron, simply heat it and touch the flux-cored solder to the tip; the solder will flow over the hot tip. Wipe the excess off with a clean rag, but be careful as the iron will be hot.**

After some use, the tip may become pitted. If so, simply dress the tip smooth with a smooth file and 'tin' the tip again. An old saying holds that 'metals well cleaned are half soldered.' Flux-cored solder will remove oxides but rust, bits of insulation and oil or grease must be removed with a wire brush or emery cloth. For maximum strength in soldered parts, the joint must start off clean and tight. Weak joints will result in gaps too wide for the solder to bridge.

If a separate soldering flux is used, it should be brushed or swabbed on only those areas that are to be soldered. Most solders contain a core of flux and separate fluxing is unnecessary. Hold the work to be soldered firmly. It is best to solder on a wooden board, because a metal vise will only rob the piece to be soldered of heat and make it difficult to melt the solder. Hold the soldering tip with the broadest face against the work to be soldered. Apply solder under the tip close to the work, using enough solder to give a heavy film between the iron and the piece being soldered, while moving slowly and making sure the solder melts properly. Keep the work level or the solder will run to the lowest part and favor the thicker parts, because these require more heat to melt the solder. If the soldering tip overheats (the solder coating on the face of the tip burns up), it should be retinned. Once the soldering is completed, let the soldered joint stand until cool. Tape and seal all soldered wire splices after the repair has cooled.

Wire Harness and Connectors

The on-board computer (ECM) wire harness electrically connects the control unit to the various solenoids, switches and sensors used by the control system. Most connectors in the engine compartment or otherwise exposed to the elements are protected against moisture and dirt which could create oxidation and deposits on the terminals. This protection is important because of the very low voltage and current levels used by the computer and sensors. All connectors have a lock which secures the male and female terminals together, with a secondary lock holding the seal and terminal into the connector. Both terminal locks must be released when disconnecting ECM connectors.

These special connectors are weather-proof and all repairs require the use of a special terminal and the tool required to service it. This tool is used to remove the pin and sleeve terminals. If removal is attempted with an ordinary pick, there is a good chance that the terminal will be bent or deformed. Unlike standard blade type terminals, these terminals cannot be straightened once they are bent. Make certain that the connectors are properly seated and all of the sealing rings in place when connecting leads. On some models, a hinge-type flap provides a backup or secondary locking feature for the terminals. Most secondary locks are used to improve the connector reliability by retaining the terminals if the small terminal lock tangs are not positioned properly.

Molded-on connectors require complete replacement of the connection. This means splicing a new connector assembly into the harness. All splices in on-board computer systems should be soldered to insure proper contact. Use care when probing the connections or replacing terminals in them as it is possible to short between opposite terminals. If this happens to the wrong terminal pair, it is possible to damage certain components. Always use jumper wires between connectors for circuit checking and never probe through weatherproof seals.

Open circuits are often difficult to locate by sight because corrosion or terminal misalignment are hidden by the connectors. Merely wiggling a connector on a sensor or in the wiring harness may correct the open circuit condition. This should always be considered when an open circuit or a failed sensor is indicated. Intermittent problems may also be caused by oxidized or loose connections. When using a circuit tester for diagnosis, always probe connections from the wire side. Be careful not to damage sealed connectors with test probes.

All wiring harnesses should be replaced with identical parts, using the same gauge wire and connectors. When signal wires are spliced into a harness, use wire with high temperature insulation only. With the low voltage and current levels found in the system, it is important that the best possible connection at all wire splices be made by soldering the splices together. It is seldom necessary to replace a complete harness. If replacement is necessary, pay close attention to insure proper harness routing. Secure the harness with suitable plastic wire clamps to prevent vibrations from causing the harness to wear in spots or contact any hot components.

➡**Weatherproof connectors cannot be replaced with standard connectors. Instructions are provided with replacement connector and terminal packages. Some wire harnesses have mounting indicators (usually pieces of colored tape) to mark where the harness is to be secured.**

In making wiring repairs, it's important that you always replace damaged wires with wires that are the same gauge as the wire being replaced. The heavier the wire, the smaller the gauge number. Wires are color-coded to aid in identification and whenever possible the same color coded wire should be used for replacement. A wire stripping and crimping tool is necessary to install solderless terminal connectors. Test all crimps by pulling on the wires; it should not be possible to pull the wires out of a good crimp.

Wires which are open, exposed or otherwise damaged are repaired by simple splicing. Where possible, if the wiring harness is accessible and the damaged place in the wire can be located, it is best to open the harness and check for all possible damage. In an inaccessible harness, the wire must be bypassed with a new insert, usually taped to the outside of the old harness.

When replacing fusible links, be sure to use fusible link wire, NOT ordinary automotive wire. Make sure the fusible segment is of the same gauge and construction as the one being replaced and double the stripped end when crimping the terminal connector for a good contact. The melted (open) fusible link segment of the wiring harness should be cut off as close to the harness as possible, then a new segment spliced in as described. In the case of a damaged fusible link that feeds two harness wires, the harness connections should be replaced with two fusible link wires so that each circuit will have its own separate protection.

➡**Most of the problems caused in the wiring harness are due to bad ground connections. Always check all vehicle ground connections for corrosion or looseness before performing any power feed checks to eliminate the chance of a bad ground affecting the circuit.**

Repairing Hard Shell Connectors

Unlike molded connectors, the terminal contacts in hard shell connectors can be replaced. Weatherproof hard-shell connectors with the leads molded into the shell have non-replaceable terminal ends. Replacement usually involves the use of a special terminal removal tool that depress the locking tangs (barbs) on the connector terminal and allow the connector to be removed from the rear of the shell. The connector shell should be replaced if it shows any evidence of burning, melting, cracks, or breaks. Replace individual terminals that are burnt, corroded, distorted or loose.

➡**The insulation crimp must be tight to prevent the insulation from sliding back on the wire when the wire is pulled. The insulation must be visibly compressed under the crimp tabs, and the ends of the crimp should be turned in for a firm grip on the insulation.**

The wire crimp must be made with all wire strands inside the crimp. The terminal must be fully compressed on the wire strands with the ends of the crimp tabs turned in to make a firm grip on the wire. Check all connections with an ohmmeter to insure a good contact. There should be no measurable resistance between the wire and the terminal when connected.

Mechanical Test Equipment

VACUUM GAUGE

Most gauges are graduated in inches of mercury (in. Hg), although a device called a manometer reads vacuum in inches of water (in. H2O). The normal vacuum reading usually varies between 18 and 22 in. Hg at sea level. To test engine vacuum, the vacuum gauge must be connected to a source of manifold vacuum. Many engines have a plug in the intake manifold which can be removed and replaced with an adapter fitting. Connect the vacuum gauge to the fitting with a suitable rubber hose or, if no manifold plug is available, connect the vacuum gauge to any device using manifold vacuum, such as EGR valves, etc. The vacuum gauge can be used to determine if enough vacuum is reaching a component to allow its actuation.

HAND VACUUM PUMP

Small, hand-held vacuum pumps come in a variety of designs. Most have a built-in vacuum gauge and allow the component to be tested without removing it from the vehicle. Operate the pump lever or plunger to apply the correct amount of vacuum required for the test specified in the diagnosis routines. The level of vacuum in inches of Mercury (in. Hg) is indicated on the pump gauge. For some testing, an additional vacuum gauge may be necessary.

Intake manifold vacuum is used to operate various systems and devices on late model vehicles. To correctly diagnose and solve problems in vacuum control systems, a vacuum source is necessary for testing. In some cases, vacuum can be taken from the intake manifold when the engine is running, but vacuum is normally provided by a hand vacuum pump. These hand vacuum pumps have a built-in vacuum gauge that allow testing while the device is still attached to the component. For some tests, an additional vacuum gauge may be necessary.

HEATING AND AIR CONDITIONING

Blower

REMOVAL & INSTALLATION

▶ **See Figures 1, 2, 3, 4 and 5**

Without Air Conditioning

1. Disconnect the battery ground.
2. On trucks built for sale in California, remove the emission module located in front of the blower.
3. Disconnect the wiring harness at the blower.
4. Disconnect the blower motor cooling tube at the blower.
5. Remove the 3 blower motor mounting screws.
6. Hold the cooling tube to one side and pull the blower motor from the housing.
7. Installation is the reverse of removal.

With Air Conditioning

1. Disconnect the blower motor wiring at the blower.
2. Disconnect the cooling tube at the blower.
3. Remove the 4 mounting screws and pull the motor from the housing.
4. Installation is the reverse of removal. Cement the cooling tube on the nipple at the housing using Liquid Butyl Sealer D9AZ-19554-A, or equivalent.

Heater Core

REMOVAL & INSTALLATION

▶ **See Figures 6, 7, 8, 9, 10, 11, 12 and 13**

Without Air Conditioning

1. Drain the cooling system to a level below the heater core.

✳✳CAUTION

When draining the coolant, keep in mind that cats and dogs are attracted by the ethylene glycol antifreeze, and are quite likely to drink any that is left in an uncovered container or in puddles on the ground. This will prove fatal in sufficient quantity. Always drain the coolant into a sealable container. Coolant should be reused unless it is contaminated or several years old.

2. Disconnect the coolant hoses at the heater core tubes.
3. From inside the passenger compartment, remove the 7 screws that secure the heater core access cover to the plenum chamber. Remove the cover. On some models, it might be easier to first remove the glove compartment.
4. Remove the heater core.
5. Installation is the reverse of removal. Replace any damaged sealer.

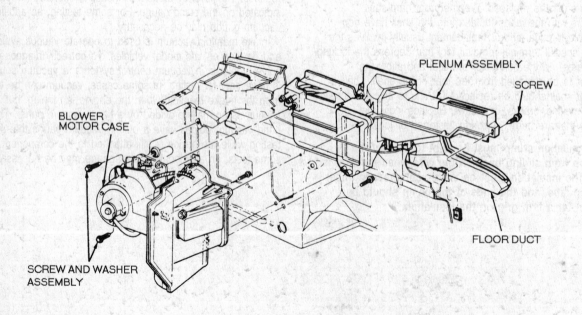

PLENUM ASSEMBLY

SCREW

BLOWER MOTOR CASE

FLOOR DUCT

SCREW AND WASHER ASSEMBLY

84926001

Fig. 1 Heater assembly and plenum removal — without air conditioning

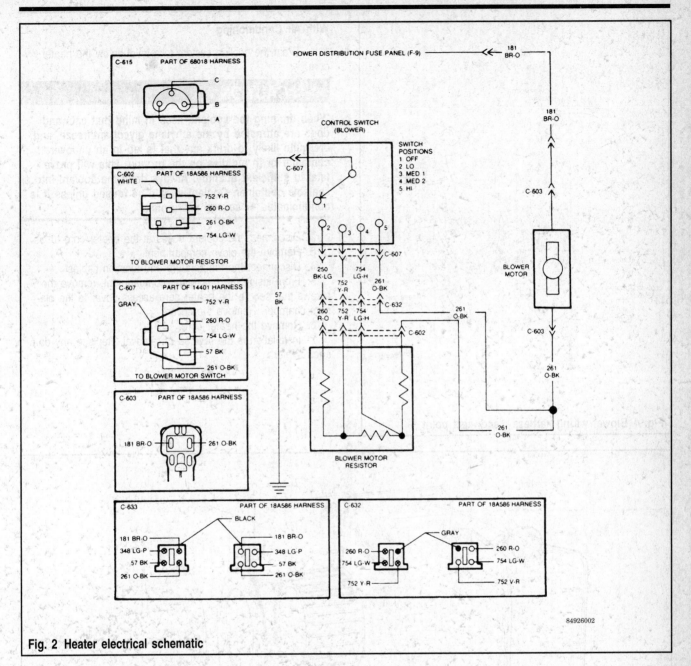

Fig. 2 Heater electrical schematic

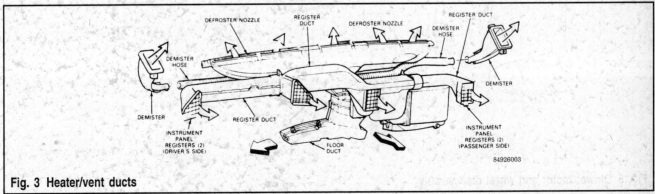

Fig. 3 Heater/vent ducts

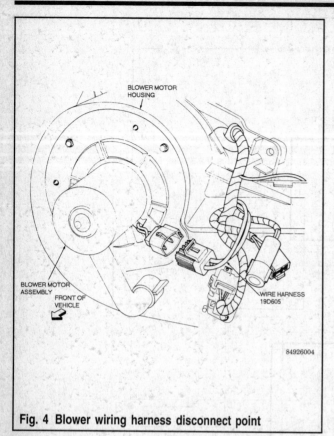

Fig. 4 Blower wiring harness disconnect point

With Air Conditioning

1. Drain the cooling system to a level below the heater core.

❄❄CAUTION

When draining the coolant, keep in mind that cats and dogs are attracted by the ethylene glycol antifreeze, and are quite likely to drink any that is left in an uncovered container or in puddles on the ground. This will prove fatal in sufficient quantity. Always drain the coolant into a sealable container. Coolant should be reused unless it is contaminated or several years old.

2. Disconnect the coolant hoses at the heater core tubes.
3. Remove the glove compartment.
4. Disconnect the temperature and function cables.
5. From inside the passenger compartment, remove the 7 screws that secure the heater core access cover to the plenum chamber. Remove the cover.
6. Remove the heater core.
7. Installation is the reverse of removal. Replace any damaged sealer.

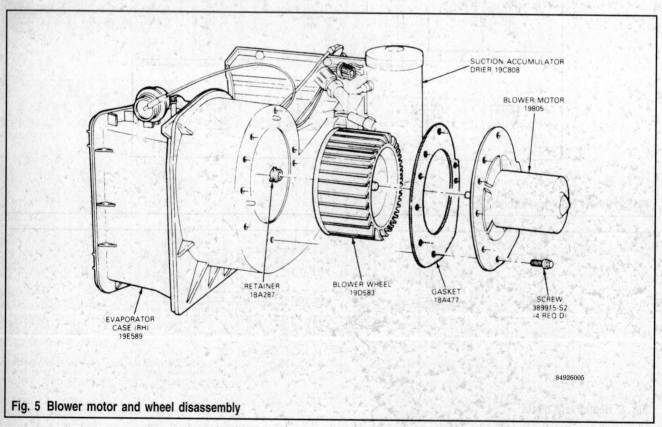

Fig. 5 Blower motor and wheel disassembly

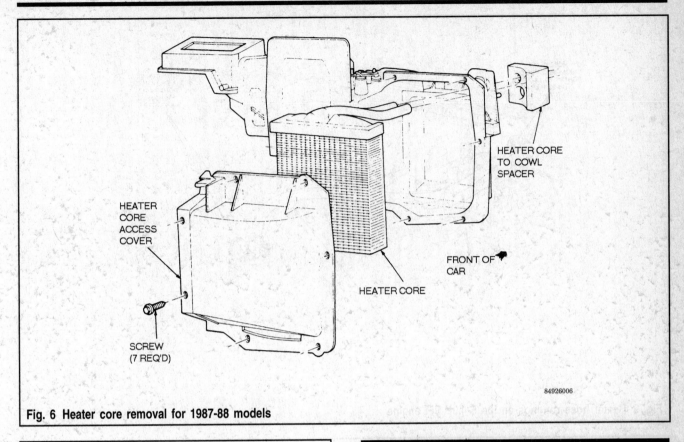

HEATER CORE TO COWL SPACER

HEATER CORE ACCESS COVER

SCREW (7 REQ'D)

HEATER CORE

FRONT OF CAR

84926006

Fig. 6 Heater core removal for 1987-88 models

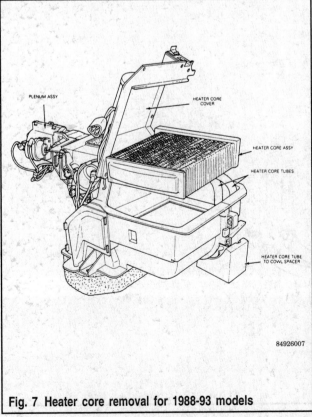

PLENUM ASSY

HEATER CORE COVER

HEATER CORE ASSY

HEATER CORE TUBES

HEATER CORE TUBE TO COWL SPACER

84926007

Fig. 7 Heater core removal for 1988-93 models

Control Unit

REMOVAL & INSTALLATION

▶ See Figures 14 and 15

Without Air Conditioning

1. Disconnect the battery ground.
2. Pull the center finish panel away from the instrument panel, exposing the control attaching screws.
3. Remove the 4 attaching screws.
4. Pull the control towards you just enough to allow disconnection of the wiring and vacuum hoses.
5. Carefully release the function control cable snap-in flag from the underside of the control unit, using a screwdriver.
6. Pull enough cable through the instrument panel to allow the cable to be held vertical to the control unit.
7. Carefully release the temperature control cable snap-in flag from the topside of the control unit, using a screwdriver.
8. Rotate the control unit 90° and disconnect the temperature control cable from the temperature control lever.
9. Pull out the control unit.
10. Installation is the reverse of removal. Check the operation of the unit.

With Air Conditioning

1. Remove the instrument panel center finish panel.
2. Remove the control unit knobs by prying on the spring retainer while pulling out on the knob.
3. Remove the 4 control unit attaching screws.

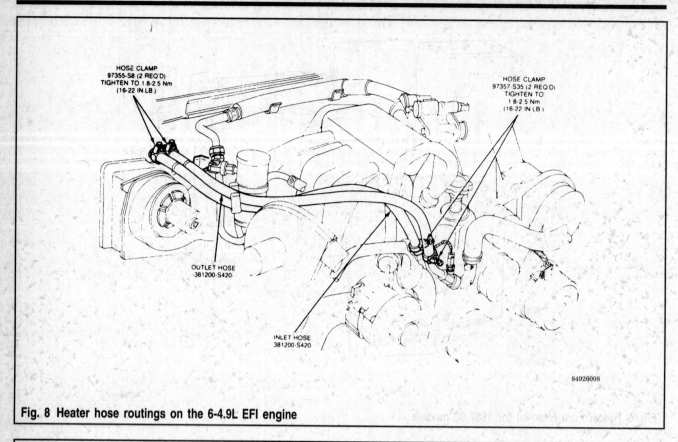

Fig. 8 Heater hose routings on the 6-4.9L EFI engine

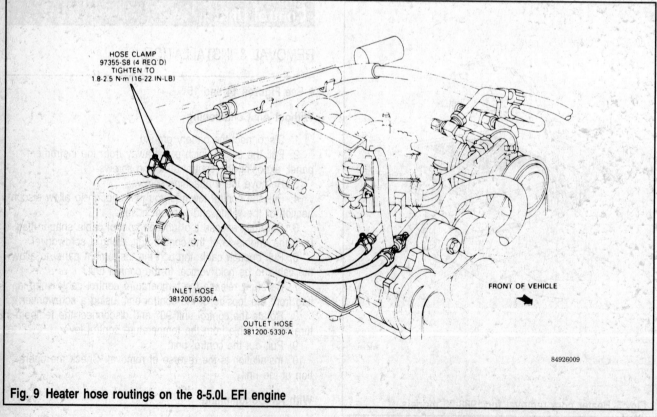

Fig. 9 Heater hose routings on the 8-5.0L EFI engine

4. Disconnect the wiring and vacuum lines from the control unit.

5. Disengage the temperature cable by depressing the locking tabs on the connector.

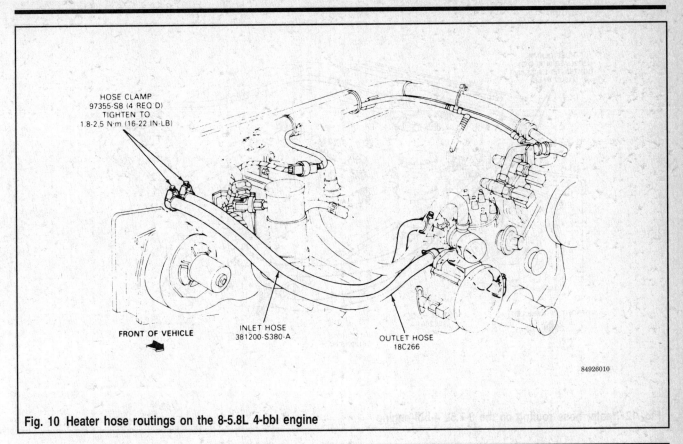

Fig. 10 Heater hose routings on the 8-5.8L 4-bbl engine

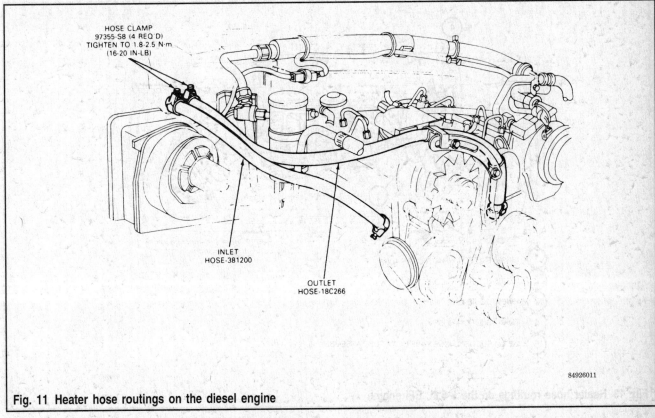

Fig. 11 Heater hose routings on the diesel engine

6. Rotate the control unit 180° and disconnect the function cable from the control assembly. Remove the control assembly by compressing the locking tabs on the connector.

7. Installation is the reverse of removal. Check the operation of the unit.

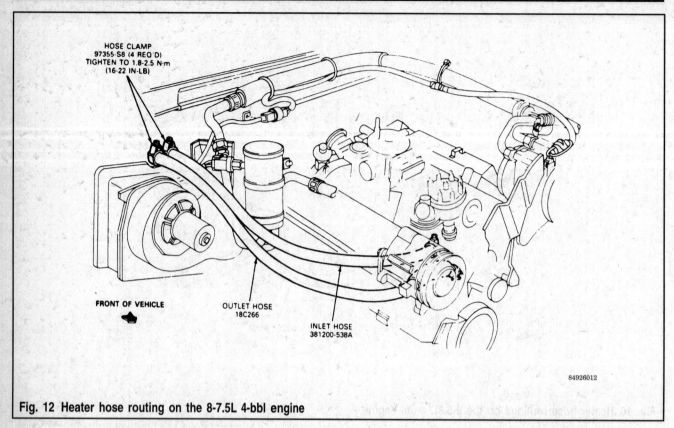

HOSE CLAMP
97355-S8 (4 REQ'D)
TIGHTEN TO 1.8-2.5 N·m
(16-22 IN-LB)

FRONT OF VEHICLE

OUTLET HOSE
18C266

INLET HOSE
381200-538A

84926012

Fig. 12 Heater hose routing on the 8-7.5L 4-bbl engine

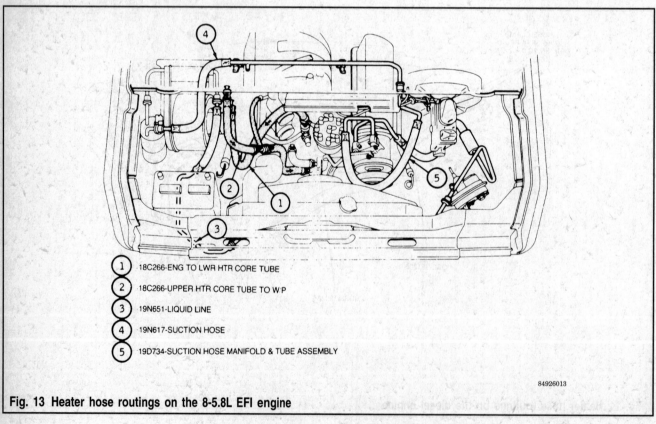

① 18C266-ENG TO LWR HTR CORE TUBE

② 18C266-UPPER HTR CORE TUBE TO W·P

③ 19N651-LIQUID LINE

④ 19N617-SUCTION HOSE

⑤ 19D734-SUCTION HOSE MANIFOLD & TUBE ASSEMBLY

84926013

Fig. 13 Heater hose routings on the 8-5.8L EFI engine

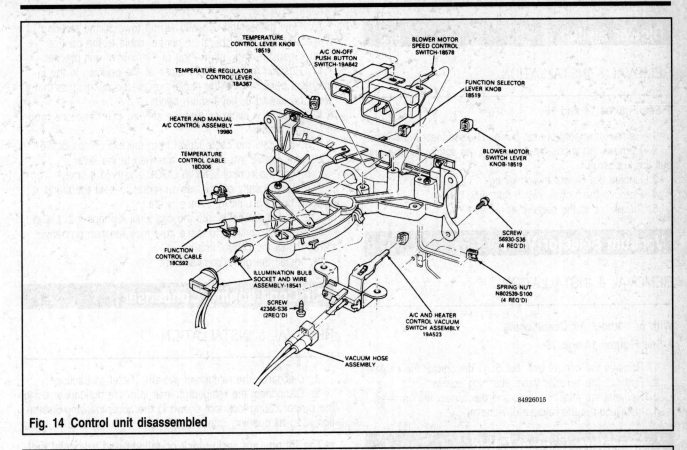

Fig. 14 Control unit disassembled

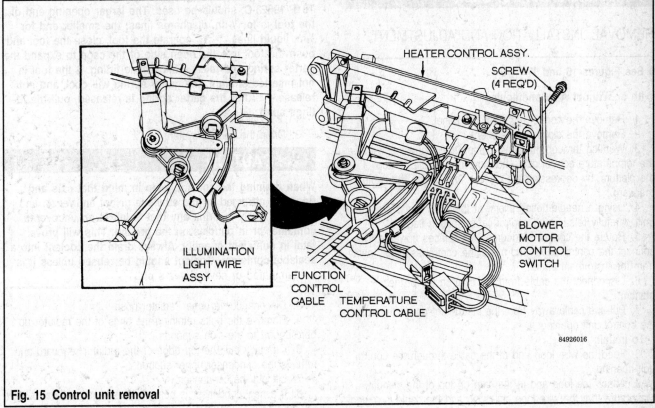

Fig. 15 Control unit removal

Blower Switch

REMOVAL & INSTALLATION

▶ See Figures 14 and 15

1. Remove the control unit, but don't disconnect the cables.
2. Remove the knobs by depressing the spring retainer and pull the knobs off.
3. Unplug the blower switch wiring.
4. Remove the blower switch attaching screw.
5. Installation is the reverse of removal.

Vacuum Selector Valve

REMOVAL & INSTALLATION

With or Without Air Conditioning
▶ See Figures 14 and 15

1. Remove the control unit, but don't disconnect the cables.
2. Remove the selector valve attaching screws.
3. Remove the attaching nuts and disconnect the harness.
4. Installation is the reverse of removal.

Temperature Control Cable

REMOVAL, INSTALLATION AND ADJUSTMENT

▶ See Figures 16 and 17

With or Without Air Conditioning

1. Remove the control unit from the panel.
2. Remove the glove compartment.
3. Working through the glove compartment opening, remove the temperature control cable housing from its clip on top of the plenum, by depressing the clip tab and pulling the cable rearward.
4. Using a needle-nosed pliers, at the bottom of the control unit, carefully release the control cable snap-in flag.
5. Rotate the control 90 degrees, so it faces upwards. Disconnect the control cable and move the control assembly away from the instrument panel.
6. Disconnect the cable from the cam on top of the plenum.
7. Pull the cable away from the instrument panel, through the control unit opening.
To install:
8. Feed the wire loop end of the cable through the control unit opening.
9. Attach the loop end to the cam on top of the plenum. Make sure that the wire loop coil is up and the cable is routed under its hold-down on the cam.

10. Hold the control unit with its top towards the steering wheel. Attach the temperature control cable to the control lever. Snap the flag into the top of the control unit bracket.
11. Position the control unit close to the opening in the instrument panel. Route the cable through the opening so that it won't be kinked or have sharp bends.
12. Adjust the cable so that the plenum door functions properly in all modes:
   a. Remove the cable jacket from the clip on top of the plenum. Leave the cable end attached to the lever.
   b. Set the control lever to **COOL** and hold it firmly.
   c. Push gently on the cable bracket to seat the blend door, pushing until resistance is felt.
   d. Install the cable into the clip, until it snaps into place. Operate the controls to make sure they function properly.
13. Install the control unit.
14. Install the glove compartment.

Air Conditioning Condenser

REMOVAL & INSTALLATION

1. Discharge the refrigerant system. (Refer to Section 1)
2. Disconnect the refrigerant lines from the condenser using the proper spring lock tool shown in the accompanying illustration. Cap all opening immediately!

➡ **The fittings are spring-lock couplings and a special tool, T81P-19623-G, should be used. The larger opening end of the tool is for ½ in. discharge lines; the smaller end for ⅜ in. liquid lines. To operate the tool, close the tool and push the tool into the open side of the cage to expand the garter spring and release the female fitting. If the tool is not inserted straight, the garter spring will cock and not release. After the garter spring is released, pull the fittings apart.**

3. Drain the cooling system.

✳✳CAUTION

When draining the coolant, keep in mind that cats and dogs are attracted by the ethylene glycol antifreeze, and are quite likely to drink any that is left in an uncovered container or in puddles on the ground. This will prove fatal in sufficient quantity. Always drain the coolant into a sealable container. Coolant should be reused unless it is contaminated or several years old.

4. Disconnect the upper radiator hose.
5. Remove the bolts retaining the ends of the radiator upper support to the side supports.
6. Carefully pull the top edge of the radiator rearward and remove the condenser upper support.
7. Lift out the condenser.
8. If a new condenser is being installed, add 1 fl.oz. of new refrigerant oil to the new condenser. Installation is the reverse of removal. Always use new O-rings coated with clean refrigerant oil on the line fittings. Evacuate, charge and leak test the system.

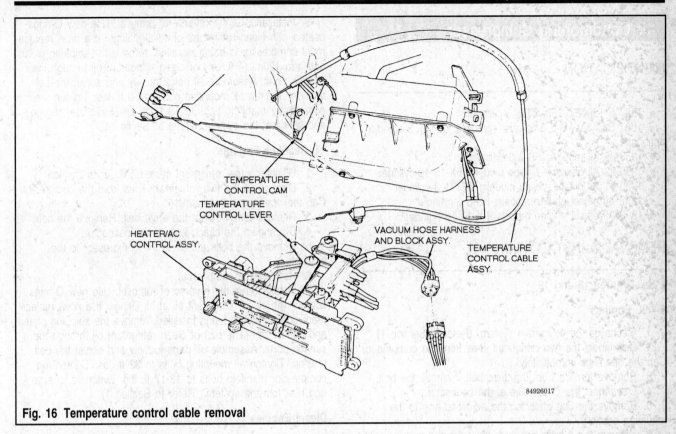

Fig. 16 Temperature control cable removal

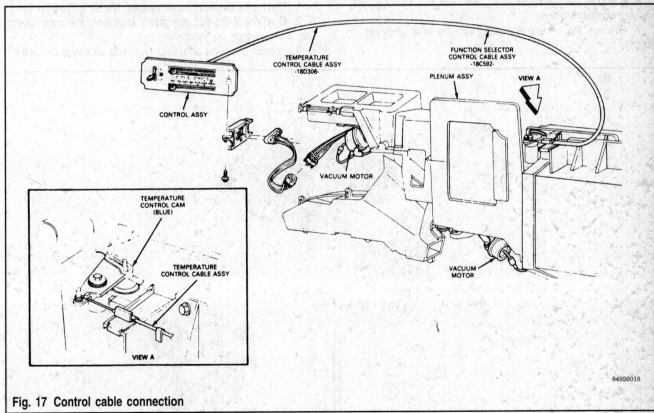

Fig. 17 Control cable connection

Air Conditioning Compressor

IDENTIFICATION

- 1987 F-150/250/350: FS-6 3-cylinder
- 1987 Bronco: FS-6 3-cylinder standard; 6E171 3-cylinder optional
- 1988-89 All models: FS-6 3-cylinder
- 1990-93 All gasoline engine models: FX-15 10-cylinder
- 1990-91 All diesel engine models: 6E171 3-cylinder
- 1992 All diesel engine models: FS-6 3-cylinder
- 1993 All diesel engine models: FX-15 10-cylinder

REMOVAL & INSTALLATION

▶ **See Figures 18 and 19**

6-4.9L Engines

1. Discharge the refrigerant system. (Refer to Section 1)
2. Disconnect the two refrigerant lines from the compressor. Cap the openings immediately!
3. Remove tension from the drive belt. Remove the belt.
4. Disconnect the clutch wire at the connector.
5. Remove the bolt attaching the adjusting arm to the mounting bracket.
6. Remove the 4 bolts attaching the front and rear support to the mounting bracket.
7. Remove the compressor along with the front and rear braces.

8. Installation is the reverse of removal. Use new O-rings coated with clean refrigerant oil at all fittings. If a new, replacement compressor is being installed, remove the shipping plates and add 120ml (4 fl. oz.) of clean refrigerant oil through the service ports. Assemble all parts loosely and adjust the belt tension. Tighten all mounting bolts to 50 ft. lbs. Tighten the compressor manifold bolts to 13-17 ft. lbs. Evacuate, charge and leak test the system. (Refer to Section 1)

V8 Gasoline Engines

1. Discharge the refrigerant system. (Refer to Section 1)
2. Disconnect the two refrigerant lines from the compressor. Cap the openings immediately!
3. Remove tension from the drive belt. Remove the belt.
4. Disconnect the clutch wire at the connector.
5. Remove the bolts attaching the compressor to the brackets.
6. Remove the compressor.
7. Installation is the reverse of removal. Use new O-rings coated with clean refrigerant oil at all fittings. If a new, replacement compressor is being installed, remove the shipping plates and add 120ml (4 fl. oz.) of clean refrigerant oil through the service ports. Assemble all parts loosely and adjust the belt tension. Tighten all mounting bolts to 32 ft. lbs. Tighten the compressor manifold bolts to 13-17 ft. lbs. Evacuate, charge and leak test the system. (Refer to Section 1)

Diesel Engines

1. Discharge the refrigerant system. (Refer to Section 1)
2. Disconnect the two refrigerant lines from the compressor. Cap the openings immediately!
3. Loosen the pivot and adjusting bolts. Remove the belt.

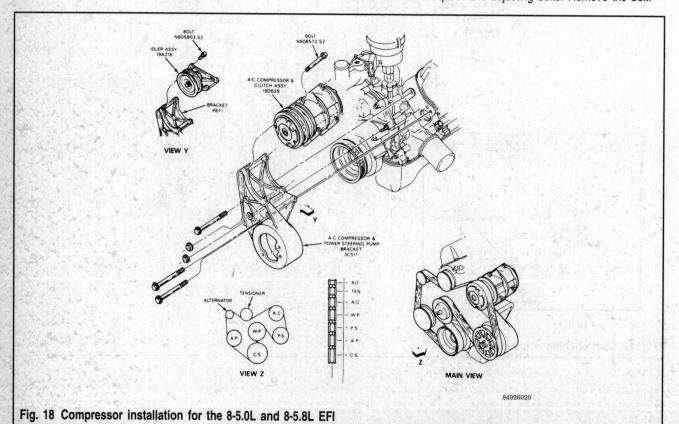

Fig. 18 Compressor installation for the 8-5.0L and 8-5.8L EFI

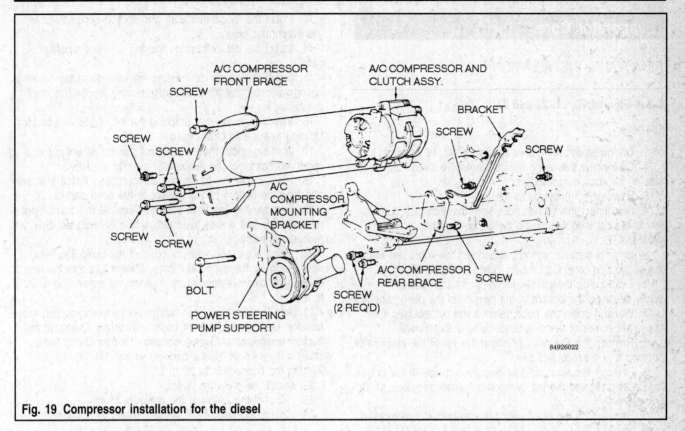

Fig. 19 Compressor installation for the diesel

4. Disconnect the clutch wire at the connector.

5. Remove the 5 bolts attaching the compressor to the mounting bracket.

6. Remove the compressor.

7. Installation is the reverse of removal. Use new O-rings coated with clean refrigerant oil at all fittings. If a new, replacement compressor is being installed, remove the shipping plates and add 120ml (4 fl. oz.) of clean refrigerant oil through the service ports. Assemble all parts loosely and adjust the belt tension. Tighten all mounting bolts to 32 ft. lbs. Tighten the compressor manifold bolts to 13-17 ft. lbs. Evacuate, charge and leak test the system. (Refer to Section 1)

Evaporator Case

REMOVAL & INSTALLATION

1. Discharge the system. (Refer to Section 1)

2. Disconnect the vacuum supply hose at the dash panel. Position the check valve away from the case.

3. Using a quick-disconnect coupling tool, disconnect the liquid line at the evaporator core. Cap all openings at once!

4. Using a back-up wrench, disconnect the suction line at the accumulator. Cap all openings at once!

5. Drain the cooling system.

❈❈CAUTION

When draining the coolant, keep in mind that cats and dogs are attracted by the ethylene glycol antifreeze, and are quite likely to drink any that is left in an uncovered container or in puddles on the ground. This will prove fatal in sufficient quantity. Always drain the coolant into a sealable container. Coolant should be reused unless it is contaminated or several years old.

6. Disconnect the heater hoses at the core.

7. Working in the passenger compartment, remove the 2 screws or nuts attaching the bottom of the case to the dash panel. One screw also secures the lower edge of the plenum.

8. Disconnect the vacuum and wiring harnesses located at the right end of the plenum.

9. Remove the 2 screws attaching the right side of the recirc duct to the dash panel.

10. Remove the 2 nuts attaching the evaporator case and recirc duct to the dash panel.

11. Pull the evaporator case and recirc duct forward and out of the truck.

To install:

12. Position the case assembly in the truck and install the screws and nuts attaching it to the dash panel.

13. Connect the vacuum and wiring harnesses.

14. Using new O-rings coated with clean refrigerant oil, connect the refrigerant lines. Torque the suction line, using a back-up wrench, to 28-33 ft. lbs.

15. Connect the heater hoses.

16. Fill the cooling system.

17. Evacuate, charge and leak test the refrigerant system. (Refer to Section 1)

Evaporator Core

REMOVAL & INSTALLATION

▶ **See Figures 20, 21, 22 and 23**

1987-88

1. Discharge the refrigerant system. (Refer to Section 1)
2. Disconnect the wiring from the pressure switch on the side of the suction accumulator.
3. Remove the pressure switch.
4. Disconnect the suction hose from the suction accumulator. Use a back-up wrench on the fitting. Cap the suction line IMMEDIATELY!
5. Using a back-up wrench, disconnect the liquid line from the evaporator core. Cap the liquid line IMMEDIATELY!
6. From inside the passenger compartment, remove 1 screw attaching the bottom of the plenum to the dash panel.
7. Working under the hood, remove the nut retaining the upper left corner of the evaporator case to the firewall.
8. Remove the 6 screws attaching the left of the evaporator housing to the evaporator case.
9. Remove the spring clip holding the left side of the housing cover plate and the left evaporator housing together, at the firewall.
10. Remove the left evaporator housing from the evaporator case.
11. Remove the evaporator core and suction accumulator from the evaporator case.
12. Transfer the suction accumulator support straps and spring nuts to the core.

13. Install the evaporator core and suction accumulator in the evaporator case.
14. Install the left evaporator housing on the evaporator case.
15. Install the spring clip holding the left side of the housing cover plate and the left evaporator housing together, at the firewall.
16. Install the 6 screws attaching the left of the evaporator housing to the evaporator case.
17. Working under the hood, install the nut retaining the upper left corner of the evaporator case to the firewall.
18. From inside the passenger compartment, install 1 screw attaching the bottom of the plenum to the dash panel.
19. Remove the cap from the liquid line. At this point, Ford recommends that a new fixed orifice tube be installed. See the procedures below.
20. Using a back-up wrench, connect the liquid line, with new O-ring, to the evaporator core. Always lubricate the new O-ring with clean refrigerant oil. Tighten the connection to 20 ft. lbs.
21. Add 3 ounces of clean refrigerant oil to the suction accumulator. Connect the suction hose, with a new O-ring, at the suction accumulator. Always lubricate the new O-ring with clean refrigerant oil. Use a back-up wrench on the fitting. Tighten the connection to 20 ft. lbs.
22. Install the pressure switch.
23. Connect the wiring at the pressure switch.
24. Charge the refrigerant system. (Refer to Section 1)

1989-93

1. Discharge the refrigerant system. (Refer to Section 1)
2. Disconnect the wiring from the pressure switch on the side of the suction accumulator.

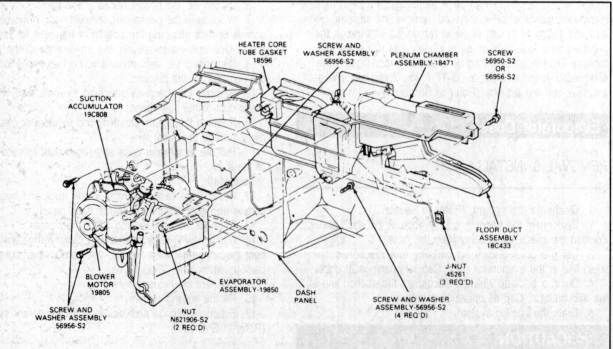

Fig. 20 1987-88 evaporator case components

HEATER CORE TUBE GASKET 18596

SCREW AND WASHER ASSEMBLY 56956-S2

PLENUM CHAMBER ASSEMBLY-18471

SCREW 56950-S2 OR 56956-S2

SUCTION ACCUMULATOR 19C808

FLOOR DUCT ASSEMBLY 18C433

BLOWER MOTOR 19805

J-NUT 45261 (3 REQ'D)

SCREW AND WASHER ASSEMBLY 56956-S2

NUT N621906-S2 (2 REQ'D)

EVAPORATOR ASSEMBLY-19850

DASH PANEL

SCREW AND WASHER ASSEMBLY-56956-S2 (4 REQ'D)

84926024

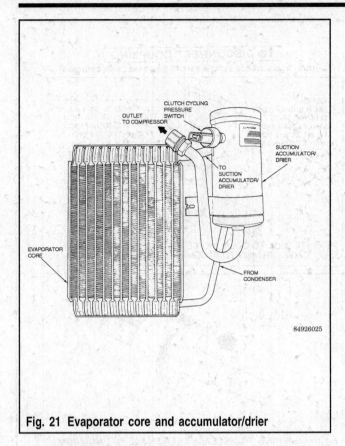

Fig. 21 Evaporator core and accumulator/drier

3. Remove the pressure switch.

4. Disconnect the suction hose from the suction accumulator. Use a back-up wrench on the fitting. Cap the suction line IMMEDIATELY!

5. Using a quick-disconnect coupling tool, disconnect the liquid line from the evaporator core. Cap the liquid line IMMEDIATELY!

6. Remove the nut holding the MAP sensor to the left corner of the evaporator case. Remove the spring clip and left the sensor away from the case.

7. Working under the hood, remove the nut retaining the upper left corner of the evaporator case to the firewall.

8. Remove the 6 screws attaching the left of the evaporator housing to the evaporator case.

9. Remove the left evaporator cover from the evaporator case.

10. Remove the evaporator core and suction accumulator from the evaporator case.

To install:

11. Transfer the suction accumulator support straps and spring nuts to the core.

12. Install the evaporator core and suction accumulator in the evaporator case.

13. Install the left evaporator cover on the evaporator case.

14. Install the 6 screws attaching the left evaporator cover to the evaporator case.

15. Working under the hood, install the nut retaining the upper left corner of the evaporator case to the firewall.

16. Install the MAP sensor.

17. Remove the cap from the liquid line. At this point, Ford recommends that a new fixed orifice tube be installed. See the procedures below.

18. Connect the liquid line, with new O-ring, to the evaporator core. Always lubricate the new O-ring with clean refrigerant oil. Push the coupling together until it snaps securely. Pull back on the coupling to make sure it is correctly connected.

19. Add 3 ounces of clean refrigerant oil to the suction accumulator.

20. Connect the suction hose, with a new O-ring, at the suction accumulator. Always lubricate the new O-ring with clean refrigerant oil. Use a back-up wrench on the fitting. Tighten the connection to 20 ft. lbs.

21. Install the pressure switch using a new O-ring coated with clean refrigerant oil.

22. Connect the wiring at the pressure switch.

23. Charge the refrigerant system. (Refer to Section 1)

Fixed Orifice Tube

REPLACEMENT

▶ **See Figure 24**

➡ **Do not attempt to remove the tube with pliers or to twist or rotate the tube in the evaporator. To do so will break the tube in the evaporator core. Use only the tools recommended in the procedure.**

1. Discharge the system. (Refer to Section 1)

2. Using back-up wrenches (1987-88) or a quick-disconnect coupling tool (1989-91), disconnect the liquid line. Cap all openings at once!

3. Pour a small amount of clean refrigerant oil into the core inlet tube to ease removal.

4. Using remover tool T83L-19990-A, engage the 2 tangs on the orifice tube. DON NOT TWIST OR ROTATE THE TUBE!

5. Tighten the nut on the tool until the orifice tube is withdrawn from the core.

6. If the orifice tube breaks in the core, it must be extracted using tool T-83L-1990-B. Thread the end of the tool into the brass tube end of the orifice tube. Pull the orifice tube from the core. If only the brass tube comes out, thread the tool back into the orifice body and pull that out.

To install:

7. Coat the new O-rings with clean refrigerant oil. Place the O-rings on the new orifice tube.

8. Place the new orifice tube onto tool T83L-1990-A and insert it into the core until it is seated at its stop. Remove the tool.

9. Using a new O-ring coated with clean refrigerant oil, connect the liquid line.

   a. On 1987-88 models, use a back-up wrench and tighten the connection to 20 ft. lbs.

   b. On 1989-91 models, push the coupling firmly together until is snaps securely. Test the coupling by trying to pull it apart.

10. Evacuate, charge and leak test the system. (Refer to Section 1)

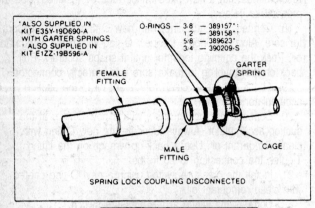

*ALSO SUPPLIED IN
KIT E35Y-19D690-A
WITH GARTER SPRINGS
* ALSO SUPPLIED IN
KIT E1ZZ-19B596-A

O-RINGS — 3.8 — 389157*
1.2 — 389158*
5/8 — 389623*
3/4 — 390209-S

FEMALE
FITTING

GARTER
SPRING

MALE
FITTING

CAGE

SPRING LOCK COUPLING DISCONNECTED

TO DISCONNECT COUPLING

CAUTION — DISCHARGE SYSTEM BEFORE DISCONNECTING COUPLING

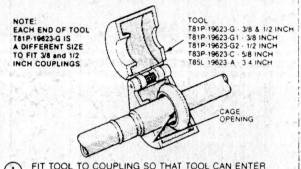

NOTE:
EACH END OF TOOL
T81P-19623-G IS
A DIFFERENT SIZE
TO FIT 3/8 and 1/2
INCH COUPLINGS

TOOL
T81P-19623-G · 3/8 & 1/2 INCH
T81P-19623-G1 · 3/8 INCH
T81P-19623-G2 · 1/2 INCH
T83P-19623-C · 5/8 INCH
T85L-19623-A · 3/4 INCH

CAGE
OPENING

① FIT TOOL TO COUPLING SO THAT TOOL CAN ENTER
CAGE OPENING TO RELEASE THE GARTER SPRING.

TO CONNECT COUPLING

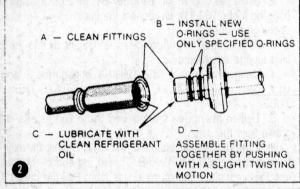

GARTER
SPRING

① CHECK FOR MISSING OR DAMAGED GARTER
SPRING — REMOVE DAMAGED SPRING WITH
SMALL HOOKED WIRE — INSTALL NEW SPRING
IF DAMAGED OR MISSING.

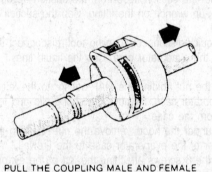

PUSH TOOL INTO
CAGE OPENING

② PUSH THE TOOL INTO THE CAGE
OPENING TO RELEASE THE FEMALE FITTING FROM
THE GARTER SPRING.

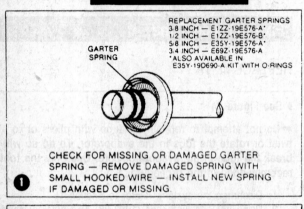

A — CLEAN FITTINGS

B — INSTALL NEW
O-RINGS — USE
ONLY SPECIFIED O-RINGS

C — LUBRICATE WITH
CLEAN REFRIGERANT
OIL

D —
ASSEMBLE FITTING
TOGETHER BY PUSHING
WITH A SLIGHT TWISTING
MOTION

② REPLACEMENT GARTER SPRINGS
3.8 INCH — E1ZZ-19E576-A*
1/2 INCH — E1ZZ-19E576-B*
5/8 INCH — E35Y-19E576-A*
3/4 INCH — E69Z-19E576-A
*ALSO AVAILABLE IN
E35Y-19D690-A KIT WITH O-RINGS

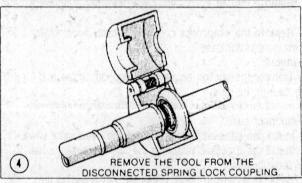

③ PULL THE COUPLING MALE AND FEMALE
FITTINGS APART.

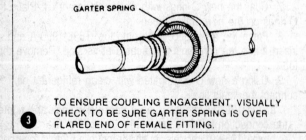

GARTER SPRING

③ TO ENSURE COUPLING ENGAGEMENT, VISUALLY
CHECK TO BE SURE GARTER SPRING IS OVER
FLARED END OF FEMALE FITTING.

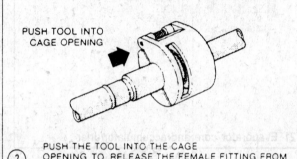

④ REMOVE THE TOOL FROM THE
DISCONNECTED SPRING LOCK COUPLING.

84926026

Fig. 22 Quick-disconnect couplings and tools

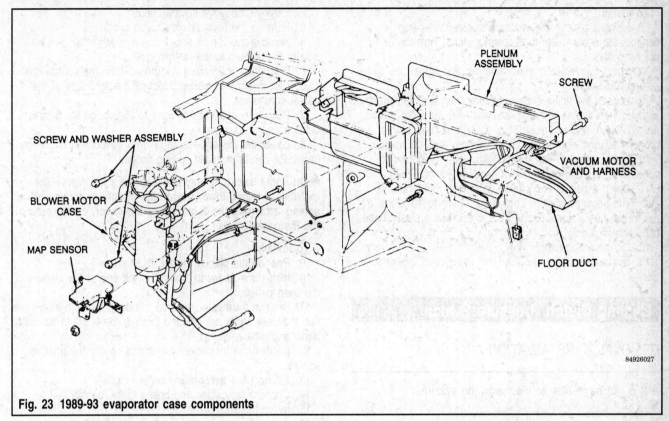

Fig. 23 1989-93 evaporator case components

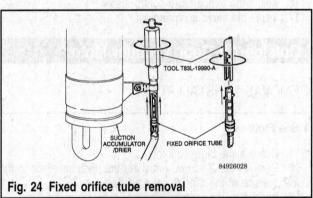

Fig. 24 Fixed orifice tube removal

Accumulator/Drier

REMOVAL & INSTALLATION

▶ See Figure 25

1. Discharge the refrigerant system. (Refer to Section 1)
2. Disconnect the wiring from the pressure switch.
3. Unscrew the pressure switch from the accumulator.
4. Using a back-up wrench, disconnect the suction hose from the accumulator. Cap all openings at once!
5. Using a back-up wrench, loosen the accumulator-to-evaporator fitting.
6. Remove the 2 accumulator attaching strap screws, remove the inlet tube clip and remove the accumulator. Cap all openings at once!

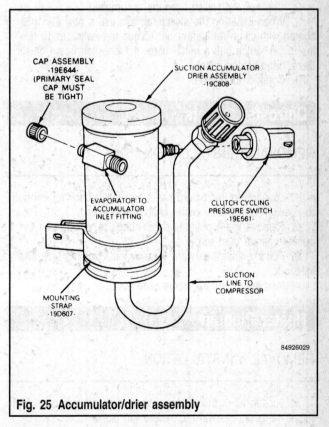

Fig. 25 Accumulator/drier assembly

To install:

7. Using a new O-ring coated with clean refrigerant oil, connect the accumulator-to-evaporator fitting. Turn the fitting nut hand tight.

8. Install the retaining strap tube clip and tighten the strap screws hand tight.

9. Loosen the fitting and make sure everything is correctly aligned, then tighten the strap screws. After the strap screws are tightened, and you're satisfied that the accumulator is properly aligned, tighten the fitting, using a back-up wrench.

10. Using a new O-ring coated with clean refrigerant oil, connect the suction hose. Use a back-up wrench.

11. Using a new O-ring coated with clean refrigerant oil, install the pressure switch. Torque the switch to 10 ft. lbs. if the switch has a metal base. If the switch has a plastic base, hand-tighten it only!

12. Connect the wiring.

13. Evacuate, charge and lean test the system. (Refer to Section 1)

Cycling Clutch Pressure Switch

REMOVAL & INSTALLATION

➡**It is not necessary to discharge the system.**

1. Disconnect the wiring at the switch.
2. Unscrew the switch from the accumulator.
3. When installing the switch, always use a new O-ring coated with clean refrigerant oil. Torque the switch to 10 ft. lbs. if the switch has a metal base. If the switch has a plastic base, hand-tighten it only!
4. Connect the wiring.

Defroster Outlets

REMOVAL & INSTALLATION

1. Loosen the instrument panel and pull it back far enough to access the defroster outlet attaching screws.
2. Remove the 4 outlet-to-panel attaching screws and the 1 outlet-to-center duct screw.
3. Pull the outlet rearward to clear the mounting tabs and lift it out.
4. Installation is the reverse of removal.

Heater Plenum

REMOVAL & INSTALLATION

1. Loosen all of the instrument panel attaching screws and move the panel rearward to access the plenum.

2. Remove the glove compartment.
3. Remove the floor air distribution duct.
4. Remove the 2 nuts and 1 screw which retain the left side of the plenum to the dash panel.
5. Disconnect the cables and hoses from the control unit.
6. Disconnect the vacuum block at the right side of the heater core cover.
7. Pull the heater case forward to disengage the 3 case studs from the dash panel.
8. Lower the plenum assembly from its location under the panel. Be careful to avoid spilling coolant.

➡**On some trucks, it may be necessary to remove the instrument panel, lower, right side attaching screw and the screws attaching the 2 braces to the lower, center area of the instrument panel.**

To install:

9. Position the plenum on the dash panel.
10. Install one screw to attach the left end of the plenum to the dash panel.
11. Position the heater case on the dash panel, making sure that the case studs are inserted through the holes in the dash panel and plenum flange.
12. Position the instrument panel and tighten the attaching screws.
13. Connect the temperature control cable.
14. Connect the cables and hoses to the control unit.
15. Install the floor duct.
16. Adjust the temperature control cable.
17. Install the glove compartment.

Outside Air Door Vacuum Motor

REMOVAL & INSTALLATION

▶ **See Figure 26**

1. Remove the blower motor.
2. Remove the 2 screws attaching the vacuum motor to the upper surface of the outside door air duct.
3. Pry the motor and arm assembly upward at the arm end, to free it from the peg. The arm retaining flange may break during prying. If it does, use a 3/16 in. spring nut to retain the motor arm during installation.
4. Installation is the reverse of removal.

Panel/Defrost Door Motor

REMOVAL & INSTALLATION

▶ **See Figure 27**

1. Disconnect the vacuum hose at the motor.

2. Remove the 2 motor attaching screws.

3. Rotate the assembly so that the slot in the bracket is parallel to the tee-shaped end of the door crank arm, and pull the motor and bracket off the crank arm.

4. Installation is the reverse of removal.

Floor/Defrost Motor

REMOVAL & INSTALLATION

1. Remove the floor duct.
2. Disconnect the vacuum hoses from the motor.
3. Remove the 2 motor attaching screws.
4. Using a small screwdriver, depress the tang on the side of the door operating lever and pull the motor arm out of the lever.
5. Installation is the reverse of removal.

Refrigerant Hoses

REPLACEMENT

▶ See Figures 28, 29, 30 and 31

To replace a refrigerant line, the A/C system must be first evacuated. (Refer to Section 1) Following, is a series of

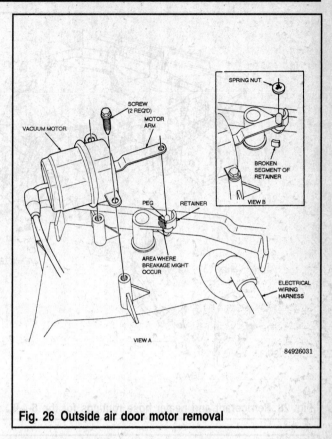

Fig. 26 Outside air door motor removal

schematics showing the refrigerant line routings and installation details.

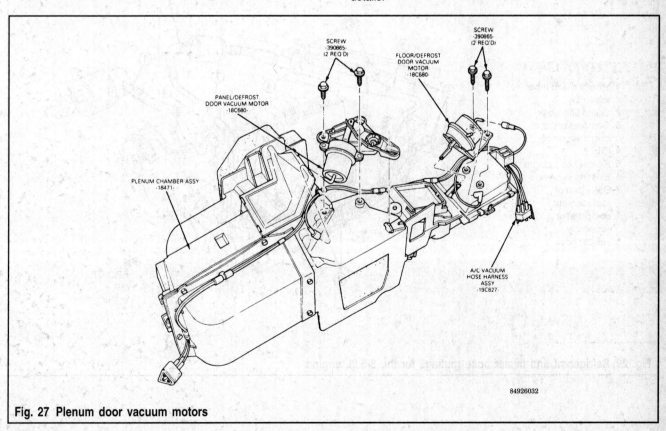

Fig. 27 Plenum door vacuum motors

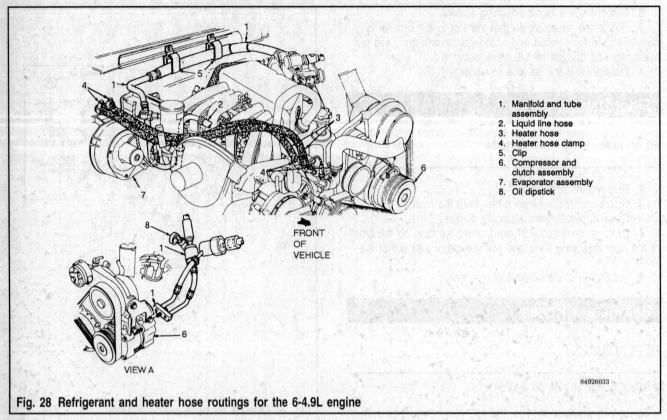

1. Manifold and tube assembly
2. Liquid line hose
3. Heater hose
4. Heater hose clamp
5. Clip
6. Compressor and clutch assembly
7. Evaporator assembly
8. Oil dipstick

VIEW A

FRONT OF VEHICLE

84926033

Fig. 28 Refrigerant and heater hose routings for the 6-4.9L engine

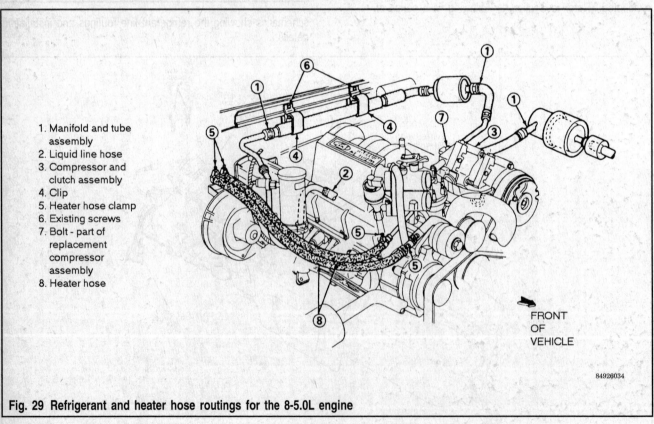

1. Manifold and tube assembly
2. Liquid line hose
3. Compressor and clutch assembly
4. Clip
5. Heater hose clamp
6. Existing screws
7. Bolt - part of replacement compressor assembly
8. Heater hose

FRONT OF VEHICLE

84926034

Fig. 29 Refrigerant and heater hose routings for the 8-5.0L engine

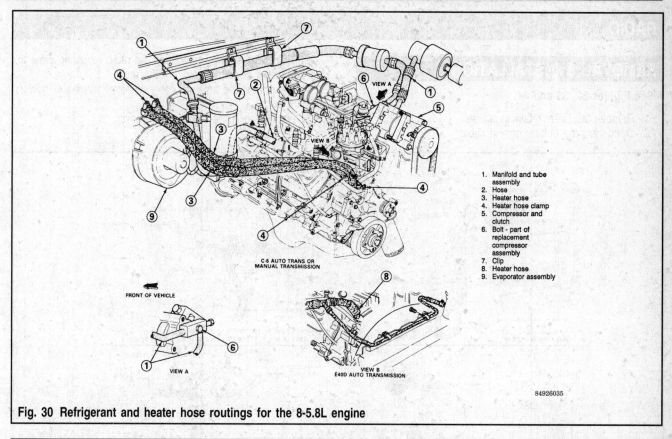

1. Manifold and tube assembly
2. Hose
3. Heater hose
4. Heater hose clamp
5. Compressor and clutch
6. Bolt - part of replacement compressor assembly
7. Clip
8. Heater hose
9. Evaporator assembly

Fig. 30 Refrigerant and heater hose routings for the 8-5.8L engine

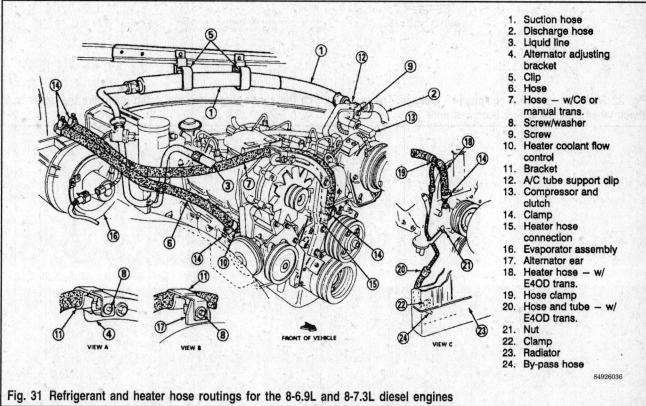

1. Suction hose
2. Discharge hose
3. Liquid line
4. Alternator adjusting bracket
5. Clip
6. Hose
7. Hose — w/C6 or manual trans.
8. Screw/washer
9. Screw
10. Heater coolant flow control
11. Bracket
12. A/C tube support clip
13. Compressor and clutch
14. Clamp
15. Heater hose connection
16. Evaporator assembly
17. Alternator ear
18. Heater hose — w/ E4OD trans.
19. Hose clamp
20. Hose and tube — w/ E4OD trans.
21. Nut
22. Clamp
23. Radiator
24. By-pass hose

Fig. 31 Refrigerant and heater hose routings for the 8-6.9L and 8-7.3L diesel engines

RADIO

REMOVAL & INSTALLATION

▶ **See Figures 32, 33 and 34**

1. Remove the bezel retaining screws.
2. Disconnect the battery ground cable.

3. Remove the screws securing the radio mounting plate to the instrument panel and pull out the radio.
4. Disconnect the antenna cable, speaker wires and power wire.
5. Installation is the reverse of removal.

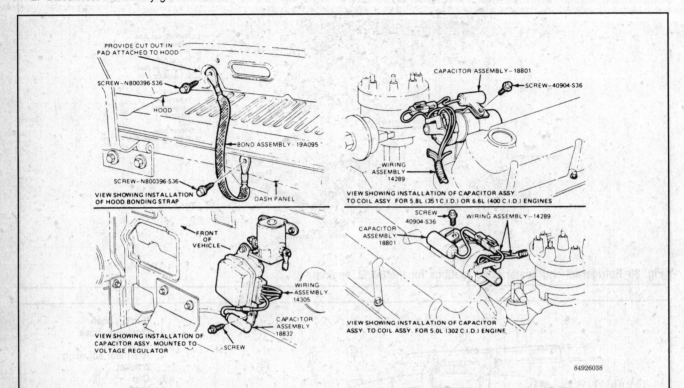

PROVIDE CUT OUT IN PAD ATTACHED TO HOOD
SCREW–N800396·S36
HOOD
BOND ASSEMBLY–19A095
SCREW–N800396·S36
VIEW SHOWING INSTALLATION OF HOOD BONDING STRAP
DASH PANEL

CAPACITOR ASSEMBLY–18801
SCREW–40904·S36
WIRING ASSEMBLY 14289
VIEW SHOWING INSTALLATION OF CAPACITOR ASSY. TO COIL ASSY. FOR 5.8L (351 C.I.D.) OR 6.6L (400 C.I.D.) ENGINES

FRONT OF VEHICLE
WIRING ASSEMBLY 14305
CAPACITOR ASSEMBLY 18832
SCREW
VIEW SHOWING INSTALLATION OF CAPACITOR ASSY. MOUNTED TO VOLTAGE REGULATOR

SCREW 40904·S36
WIRING ASSEMBLY–14289
CAPACITOR ASSEMBLY 18801
VIEW SHOWING INSTALLATION OF CAPACITOR ASSY. TO COIL ASSY. FOR 5.0L (302 C.I.D.) ENGINE

84926038

Fig. 32 Radio suppression equipment - pickups. These, along with the spark plug wires and radio itself, are the areas to check when radio reception becomes poor

WINDSHIELD WIPERS

Motor

REMOVAL & INSTALLATION

▶ **See Figures 35, 36, 37, 38, 39 and 40**

1. Disconnect the battery ground cable.
2. Remove both wiper arm and blade assemblies.
3. Remove the cowl grille attaching screws and lift the cowl grille slightly.
4. Disconnect the washer nozzle hose and remove the cowl grille assembly.

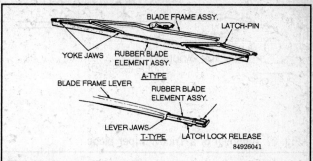

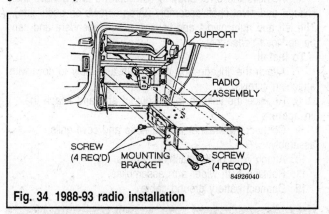

Fig. 34 1988-93 radio installation

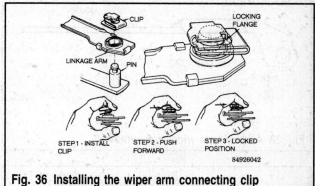

Fig. 35 Anco® (A) and Trico® (T) type wiper blade installation

Fig. 36 Installing the wiper arm connecting clip

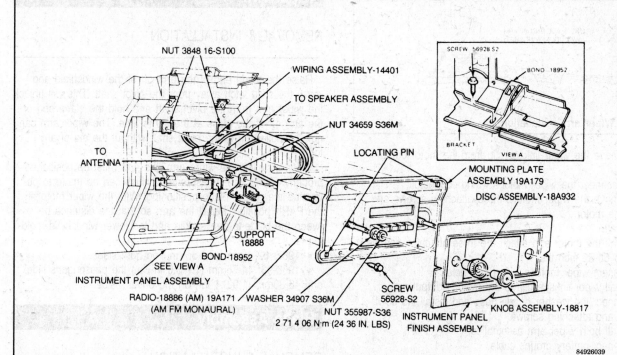

Fig. 33 1987 radio installation

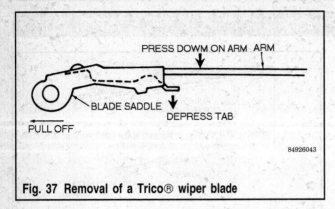

Fig. 37 Removal of a Trico® wiper blade

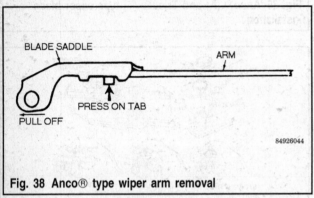

Fig. 38 Anco® type wiper arm removal

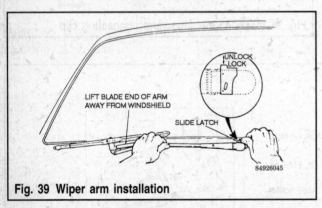

Fig. 39 Wiper arm installation

5. Remove the wiper linkage clip from the motor output arm.

6. Disconnect the wiper motor's wiring connector.

7. Remove the wiper motor's three attaching screws and remove the motor.

To install:

8. Install the motor and attach the three attaching screws. Tighten to 60-85 inch lbs.

9. Connect wiper motor's wiring connector.

10. Install wiper linkage clip to the motor's output arm.

11. Connect the washer nozzle hose and install the cowl assembly and attaching screws.

12. Install both wiper arm assemblies.

13. Connect battery ground cable.

Wiper Linkage

REMOVAL & INSTALLATION

▶ **See Figure 41**

1. Disconnect the battery ground cable.

2. Remove both wiper arm assemblies.

3. Remove the cowl grille attaching screws and lift the cowl grille slightly.

4. Disconnect the washer nozzle hose and remove the cowl grille assembly.

5. Remove the wiper linkage clip from the motor output arm and pull the linkage from the output arm.

6. Remove the pivot body to cowl screws and remove the linkage and pivot shaft assembly (three screws on each side). The left and right pivots and linkage are independent and can be serviced separately.

To install:

7. Attach the linkage and pivot shaft assembly to cowl with attaching screws.

8. Replace the linkage to the output arm and attach the linkage clip.

9. Connect the washer nozzle hose and cowl grills assembly.

10. Attach cowl grille attaching screws.

11. Replace both wiper arm assemblies.

12. Connect battery ground cable.

Wiper Arm

REMOVAL & INSTALLATION

Raise the blade end of the arm off of the windshield and move the slide latch away from the pivot shaft. This will unlock the wiper arm from the pivot shaft and hold the blade end of the arm off of the glass at the same time. The wiper arm can now be pulled off of the pivot shaft without the aid of any tools.

When installing the wiper arm, the arm must be positioned properly. There is a measurement which can be made to determine the proper blade positioning. With the wiper motor in the PARK position, install the arm so that the distance between the blade-to-arm saddle and the lower windshield molding is:

• 1987: 62-93mm (2.4-3.7 in.) on both sides

• 1988-93: 44-76mm (1.7-3.0 in.) on the passenger's side, and 48-80mm (1.9-3.1 in.) on the driver's side.

Blade Assembly

REMOVAL & INSTALLATION

1. Cycle arm and blade assembly to a position on the windshield where removal of blade assembly can be performed without difficulty. Turn ignition key off at desired position.

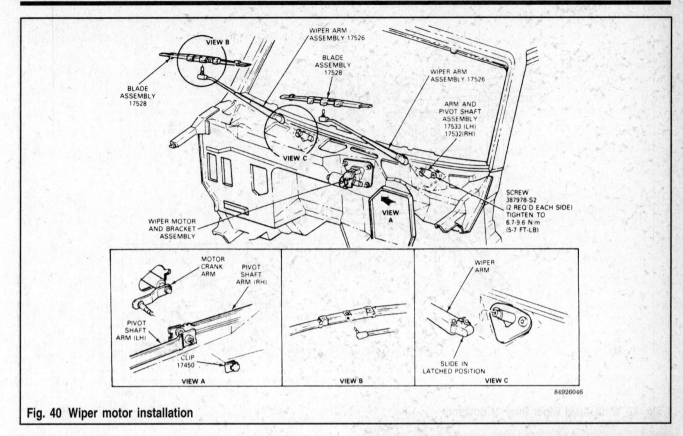

Fig. 40 Wiper motor installation

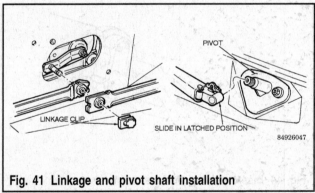

Fig. 41 Linkage and pivot shaft installation

2. With the blade assembly resting on windshield, grasp either end of the wiper blade frame and pull away from windshield, then pull blade assembly from pin.

➡**Rubber element extends past frame. To prevent damage to the blade element, be sure to grasp blade frame and not the end of the blade element.**

3. To install, push blade assembly onto pin until fully seated. Be sure blade is securely attached to the wiper arm.

Interval Governor

REMOVAL & INSTALLATION

▶ **See Figure 42**

1. Reach up under the instrument panel, behind the wiper switch, and locate the governor. Unplug the wiring connector and remove the wiring clip from the panel reinforcement.
2. Remove the governor attaching screw and remove the governor.
3. Installation is the reverse of removal.

Washer Reservoir and Pump Motor

REMOVAL & INSTALLATION

Reservoir

1. Disconnect the wiring at the pump motor. Use a small screwdriver to unlock the connector tabs.
2. Remove the washer hose.
3. Remove the reservoir attaching screws or nuts and lift the assembly from the truck. Depending on the year, model and optional equipment, the reservoir could be on the fender apron, radiator support, or air cleaner bracket.

➡**The cover is not removable from the reservoir.**

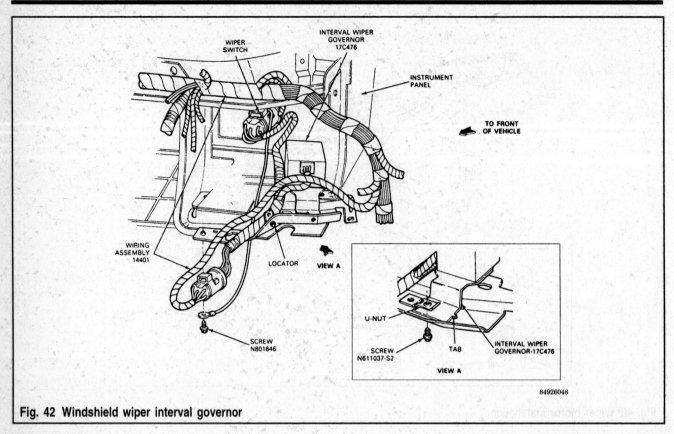

Fig. 42 Windshield wiper interval governor

Motor/Impeller

▶ **See Figures 43 and 44**

1. Remove the reservoir.
2. Using a small screwdriver, pry out the motor retaining ring.
3. Using pliers, grip one edge of the electrical connector ring and pull the motor, seal and impeller from the reservoir.

➡**If the seal and impeller come apart from the motor, it can all be re-assembled.**

To install:

4. Take the time to clean out the reservoir before installing the motor.

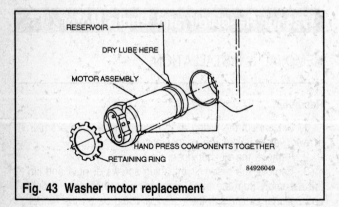

Fig. 43 Washer motor replacement

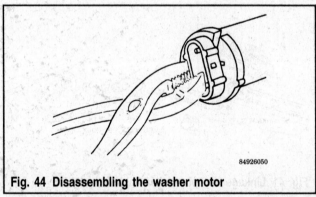

Fig. 44 Disassembling the washer motor

5. Coat the seal with a dry lubricant, such as powdered graphite or spray Teflon®. This will aid assembly.
6. Align the small projection on the motor end cap with the slot in the reservoir and install the motor so that the seal seats against the bottom of the motor cavity.
7. Press the retaining ring into position. A 1 in., 12-point socket or length of 1 in. tubing, will do nicely as an installation tool.
8. Install the reservoir and connect the wiring.

➡**It's not a good idea to run a new motor without filling the reservoir first. Dry-running will damage a new motor.**

SPEED CONTROL SYSTEM

Speed Sensor

REMOVAL & INSTALLATION

1. Unplug the wiring at the sensor on the transmission.
2. Disconnect the speedometer cable from the speed sensor.
3. Remove the retaining bolt and remove the sensor. Remove the drive gear.
4. Installation is the reverse of removal.

Control Switches

Please refer to Section 8, under Steering Wheel Removal and Installation.

Amplifier

▶ **See Figure 45**

REMOVAL & INSTALLATION

1. Disconnect the wiring at the amplifier, located behind the instrument panel.
2. Remove the amplifier mounting bracket attaching screws or nuts and remove the amplifier and bracket.
3. Remove the amplifier from the bracket.
4. Installation is the reverse of removal.

Servo Assembly

The servo is the throttle actuator and is located under the hood.

REMOVAL & INSTALLATION

▶ **See Figures 46 and 47**

1. Disconnect the wiring at the servo.

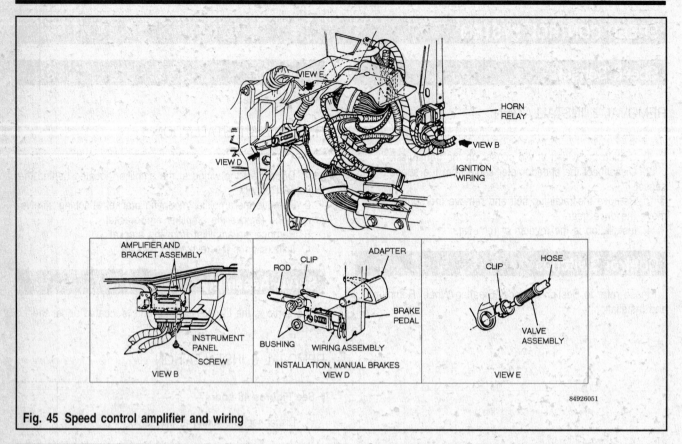

Fig. 45 Speed control amplifier and wiring

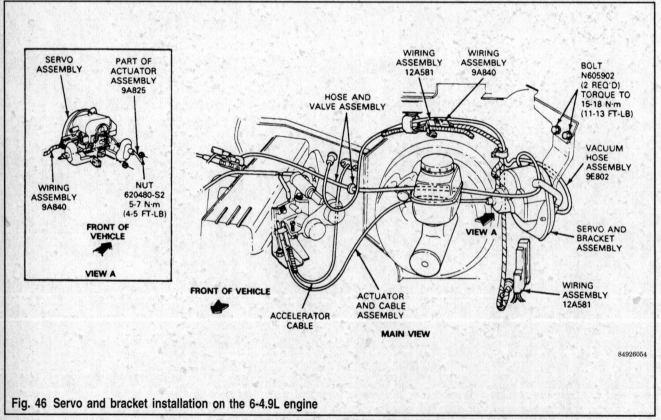

Fig. 46 Servo and bracket installation on the 6-4.9L engine

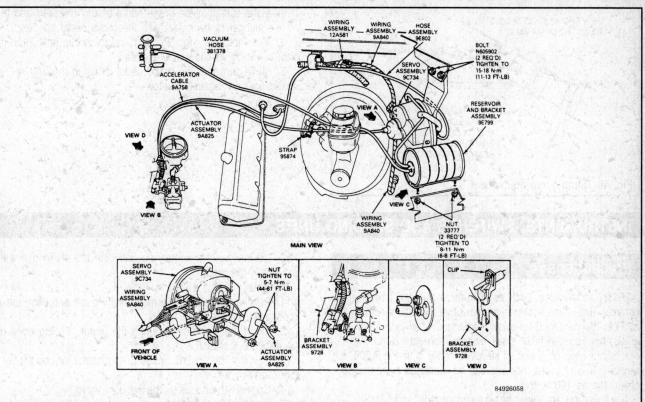

Fig. 47 Servo and bracket installation on the diesel engines

2. Disconnect the adjuster from the accelerator cable.

3. Disconnect the vacuum line at the servo.

4. Remove the actuator cable-to-bracket screw.

5. Remove the pins and nuts retaining the servo to its mounting bracket and lift it out.

6. Installation is the reverse of removal.

LINKAGE ADJUSTMENT

1. Snap the molded cable retainer over the accelerator cable end fitting attached, to the throttle ball stud.

2. Remove the adjuster retainer clip, if installed, from the adjuster mounting tab.

3. Insert the speed control actuator cable adjuster mounting tab in the slot provided in the accelerator cable support bracket.

4. Pull the cable through the adjuster until a slight tension is felt **without** opening the throttle plate.

5. Insert the adjuster cable retainer clip slowly, until engagement is felt, then, push it downwards until it locks in position.

Vacuum Dump Valve

REMOVAL & INSTALLATION

1. Remove the vacuum hose at the valve.

2. Remove the valve and bracket. Separate the valve from the bracket.

3. Installation is the reverse of removal.

ADJUSTMENT

▶ **See Figure 48**

The dump valve disconnects the speed control whenever the brake pedal is depressed.

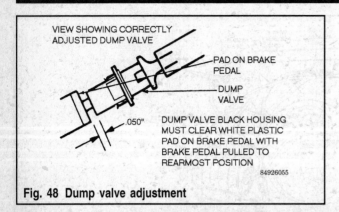

VIEW SHOWING CORRECTLY ADJUSTED DUMP VALVE

PAD ON BRAKE PEDAL

DUMP VALVE

.050"

DUMP VALVE BLACK HOUSING MUST CLEAR WHITE PLASTIC PAD ON BRAKE PEDAL WITH BRAKE PEDAL PULLED TO REARMOST POSITION

84926055

Fig. 48 Dump valve adjustment

1. Make sure that the brake pedal is fully released and the valve's plunger is in contact with the brake pedal adapter.
2. Move the valve forward in its retaining clip until 3mm (⅛ inch) of the valve plunger is exposed.
3. Make sure that the brake pedal is still in the fully released position, against its stop.

INSTRUMENTS, SWITCHES AND SENDING UNITS

Precautions

Electronic modules, such as instrument clusters, powertrain controls and sound systems are sensitive to static electricity and can be damaged by static discharges which are below the levels that you can hear 'snap' or detect on your skin. A detectable snap or shock of static electricity is in the 3,000 volt range. Some of these modules can be damaged by a charge of as little as 100 volts.

The following are some basic safeguards to avoid static electrical damage:

• Leave the replacement module in its original packing until you are ready to install it.
• Avoid touching the module connector pins
• Avoid placing the module on a non-conductive surface
• Use a commercially available static protection kit. These kits contain such things as grounding cords and conductive mats.

Instrument Panel

REMOVAL & INSTALLATION

▶ See Figures 49 and 50

1. Disconnect the battery(ies).
2. Remove the nut attaching the panel to the brake pedal, or, brake and clutch pedal, support.
3. Remove the bolt attaching the panel to the firewall brace.
4. Remove the 4 quarter-turn pins which attach the steering column opening cover and remove the cover.
5. Remove the 2 panel-to-side cowl attaching screws.
6. Unplug the wiring connectors at:
• blower switch
• air conditioner control switch
• heater/air conditioner control bulb
7. Disconnect the hoses at the vacuum valve.
8. Disconnect the control cables at the heater/air conditioner control assembly.
9. Remove the 4 screws securing the upper, leading edge of the panel to the dash.

10. Lift the panel assembly up and over the steering wheel and out of the truck.
To install:
11. Position the panel assembly in the truck and align the 4 upper edge screw holes.
12. Install the 4 screws securing the upper, leading edge of the panel to the dash.
13. Connect the control cables at the heater/air conditioner control assembly.
14. Connect the hoses at the vacuum valve.
15. Connect the wiring at:
• blower switch
• air conditioner control switch
• heater/air conditioner control bulb
16. Install the 2 panel-to-side cowl attaching screws.
17. Install the steering column opening cover.
18. Install the bolt attaching the panel to the firewall brace.
19. Install the nut attaching the panel to the brake pedal, or, brake and clutch pedal, support.
20. Connect the battery(ies).

Instrument Cluster

REMOVAL & INSTALLATION

▶ See Figures 51, 52, 53, 54 and 55

1. Disconnect the battery ground cable.
2. Remove the wiper-washer knob. Use a hook tool to release each knob lock tab.
3. Remove the knob from the head lamp switch. Remove the fog lamp switch knob, if so equipped.
4. Remove the steering column shroud. Care must be taken not to damage the transmission control selector indicator (PRNDL) cable on vehicles equipped with an automatic transmission.
5. On vehicles equipped with an automatic transmission, remove the loop on the indicator cable assembly from the retainer pin. Remove the bracket screw from the cable bracket and slide the bracket out of the slot in the tube.
6. Remove the cluster trim cover. Remove the four cluster attaching screws, disconnect the speedometer cable, wire con-

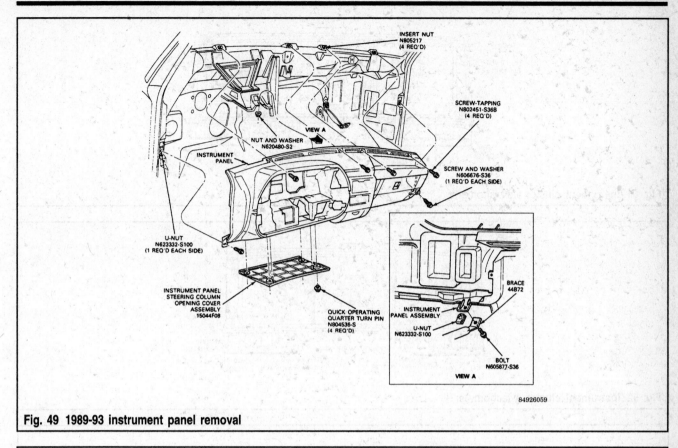

Fig. 49 1989-93 instrument panel removal

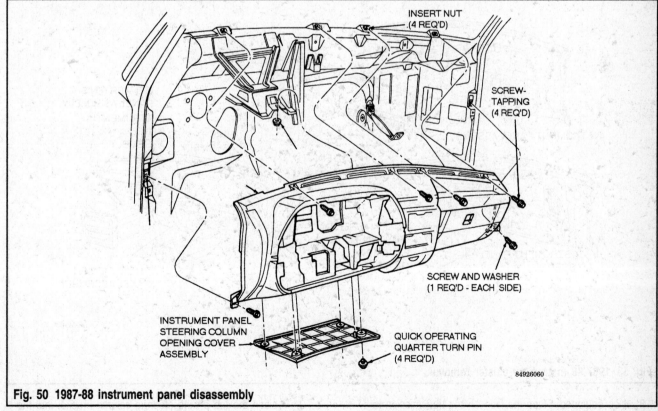

Fig. 50 1987-88 instrument panel disassembly

nector from the printed circuit, 4x4 indicator light and remove the cluster.

7. Position cluster at the opening and connect the multiple connector, the speedometer cable and 4x4 indicator light. Install the four cluster retaining screws.

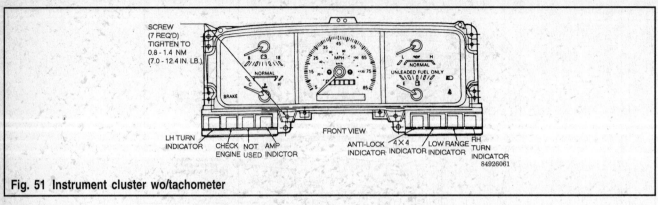

Fig. 51 Instrument cluster wo/tachometer

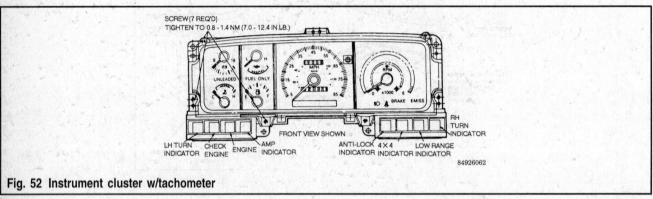

Fig. 52 Instrument cluster w/tachometer

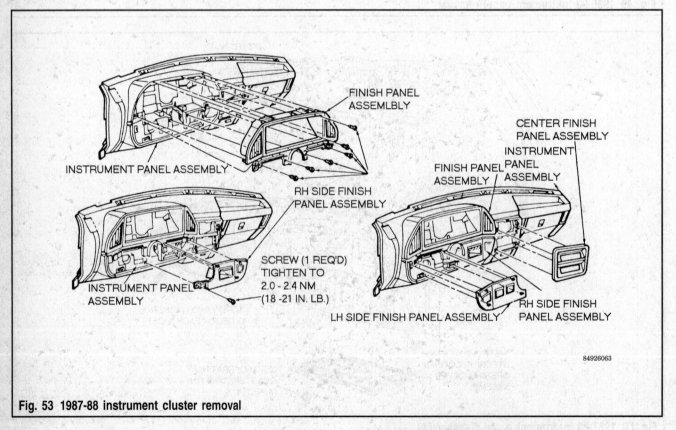

Fig. 53 1987-88 instrument cluster removal

8. If so equipped, place the loop on the transmission indicator cable assembly over the retainer on the column.

9. Position the tab on the steering column bracket into the slot on the column. Align and attach the screw.

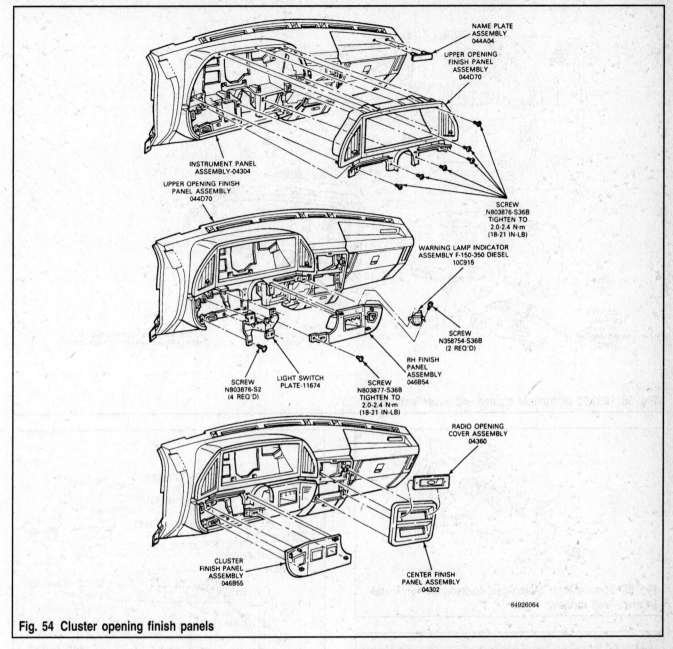

NAME PLATE
ASSEMBLY
044A04

UPPER OPENING
FINISH PANEL
ASSEMBLY
044D70

INSTRUMENT PANEL
ASSEMBLY-04304

UPPER OPENING FINISH
PANEL ASSEMBLY
044D70

SCREW
N803876-S36B
TIGHTEN TO
2.0-2.4 N·m
(18-21 IN-LB)

WARNING LAMP INDICATOR
ASSEMBLY F-150-350 DIESEL
10C915

SCREW
N358754-S36B
(2 REQ'D)

RH FINISH
PANEL
ASSEMBLY
046B54

SCREW
N803876-S2
(4 REQ'D)

LIGHT SWITCH
PLATE-11674

SCREW
N803877-S36B
TIGHTEN TO
2.0-2.4 N·m
(18-21 IN-LB)

RADIO OPENING
COVER ASSEMBLY
04360

CLUSTER
FINISH PANEL
ASSEMBLY
046B55

CENTER FINISH
PANEL ASSEMBLY
04302

84926064

Fig. 54 Cluster opening finish panels

10. Place the transmission selector lever on the steering column into **D** position.

11. Adjust the slotted bracket so the pin is within the letter band.

12. Install the trim cover.

13. Install the head lamp switch knob. If so equipped, install the fog lamp switch.

14. Install the wiper washer control knobs.

15. Connect the battery cable, and check the operation of all gauges, lights and signals.

Speedometer Cable Core

REMOVAL & INSTALLATION

▶ **See Figures 56, 57, 58 and 59**

➡ **1988-91 models equipped with the 6-4.9L EFI, 8-5.0L EFI and 8-5.8L EFI engines have a speed sensor attached to the transmission. This device sends information on vehicle speed to the Engine Management System and Speed Control System. For replacement of this unit, see the Speed Control procedures, above.**

1. Reach up behind the cluster and disconnect the cable by depressing the quick disconnect tab and pulling the cable away.

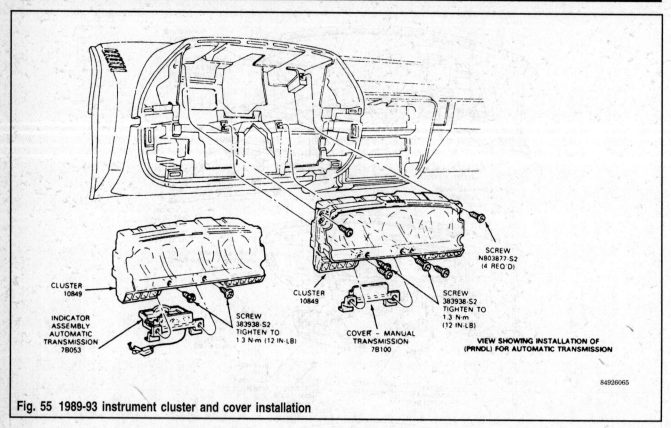

Fig. 55 1989-93 instrument cluster and cover installation

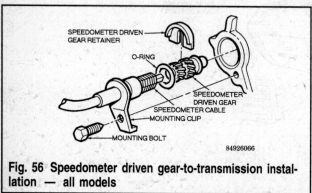

Fig. 56 Speedometer driven gear-to-transmission installation — all models

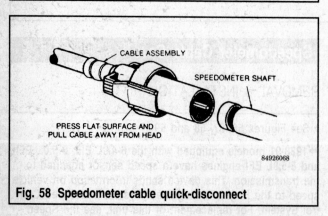

Fig. 58 Speedometer cable quick-disconnect

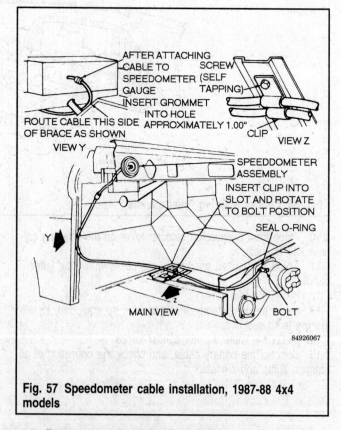

Fig. 57 Speedometer cable installation, 1987-88 4x4 models

2. Remove the cable from the casing. If the cable is broken, raise the vehicle on a hoist and disconnect the cable from the transmission.

3. Remove the cable from the casing.

4. To remove the casing from the vehicle pull it through the floor pan.

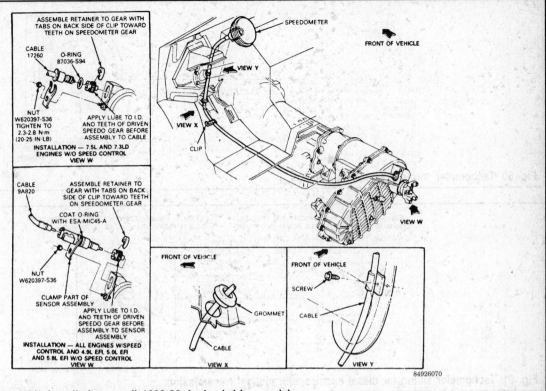

Fig. 59 Speedometer cable installation on all 1989-93 4-wheel drive models

To install:

5. To replace the cable, slide the new cable into the casing and connect it at the transmission.

6. Route the cable through the floor pan and position the grommet in its groove in the floor.

7. Push the cable onto the speedometer head.

Speedometer Head

REMOVAL & INSTALLATION

1. Remove the instrument cluster.
2. Disconnect the cable from the head.
3. Remove the lens and any surrounding trim.
4. Remove the 2 attaching screws.
5. Installation is the reverse of removal. Place a glob of silicone grease on the end of the cable core prior to connection.

Tachometer

REMOVAL & INSTALLATION

▶ **See Figures 60, 61 and 62**

1. Disconnect the battery ground.
2. Remove the instrument cluster.

3. Remove the cluster mask and lens.
4. Remove the tachometer by prying the dial away from the cluster backplate. The tachometer is retained by clips.
5. Installation is the reverse of removal. Make sure the clips are properly seated.

Fuel Gauge

REMOVAL & INSTALLATION

1. Disconnect the battery ground.
2. Remove the instrument cluster.
3. Remove the cluster mask and lens.
4. Remove the 2 nuts attaching the gauge to the cluster backplate.
5. Installation is the reverse of removal.

Clock

REMOVAL & INSTALLATION

1. Disconnect the battery ground.
2. Remove the 3 clock retaining screws.
3. Pull the clock from the dash slowly and disconnect the wiring.
4. Installation is the reverse of removal.

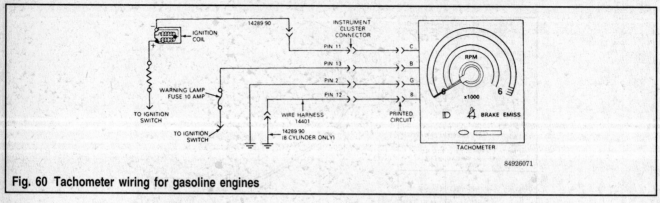

Fig. 60 Tachometer wiring for gasoline engines

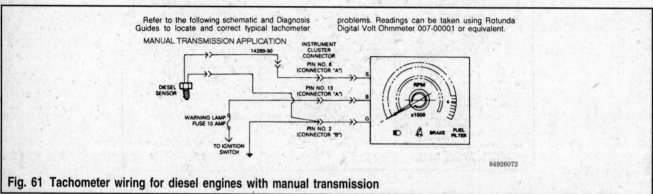

Fig. 61 Tachometer wiring for diesel engines with manual transmission

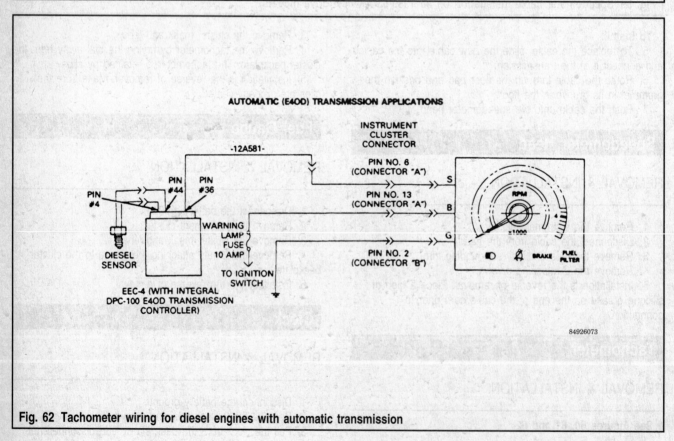

Fig. 62 Tachometer wiring for diesel engines with automatic transmission

Windshield Wiper Switch

REMOVAL & INSTALLATION

1. Disconnect the battery ground.
2. Remove the switch knob, bezel nut and bezel.
3. Pull the switch out from under the panel and unplug the wiring.
4. Installation is the reverse of removal.

Headlight Switch

REMOVAL & INSTALLATION

▶ See Figure 63

1. Disconnect the battery ground cable.
2. Depending on the year and model remove the wiper-washer and fog lamp switch knob if they will interfere with the headlight switch knob removal. Check the switch body (behind dash, see Step 3) for a release button. Press in on the button and remove the knob and shaft assembly. If not equipped with a release button, a hook tool may be necessary for knob removal.
3. Remove the steering column shrouds and cluster panel finish panel if they interfere with the required clearance for working behind the dash.
4. Unscrew the switch mounting nut from the front of the dash. Remove the switch from the back of the dash and disconnect the wiring harness.
5. Install in reverse order.

Sending Units

REMOVAL & INSTALLATION

Oil Pressure
▶ See Figures 64, 65 and 66

For the location of your unit, see the accompanying illustrations.
1. Disconnect the wiring at the unit.
2. Unscrew the unit.
3. Coat the threads with electrically conductive sealer and screw the unit into place. The torque should be 10-18 ft. lbs.

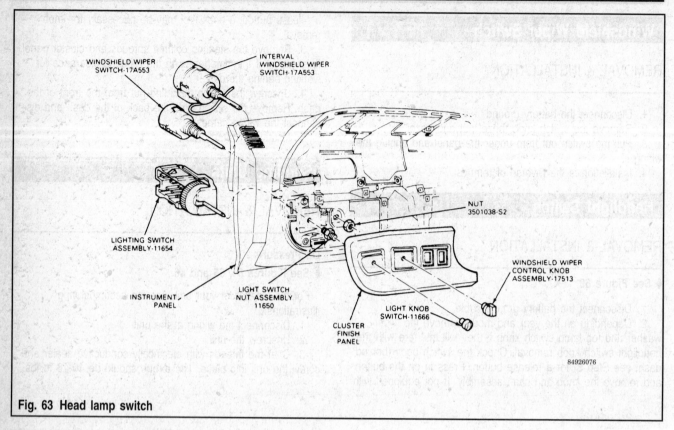

Fig. 63 Head lamp switch

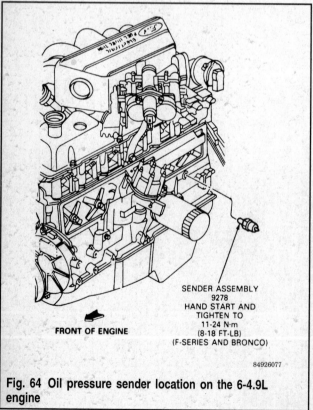

SENDER ASSEMBLY
9278
HAND START AND
TIGHTEN TO
11-24 N·m
(8-18 FT-LB)
(F-SERIES AND BRONCO)

FRONT OF ENGINE

84926077

Fig. 64 Oil pressure sender location on the 6-4.9L engine

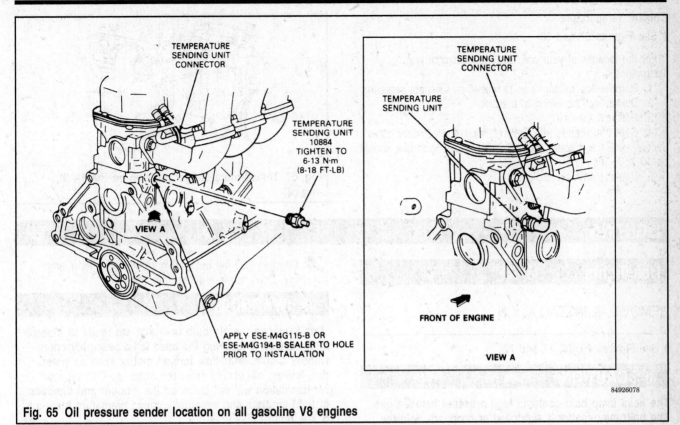

Fig. 65 Oil pressure sender location on all gasoline V8 engines

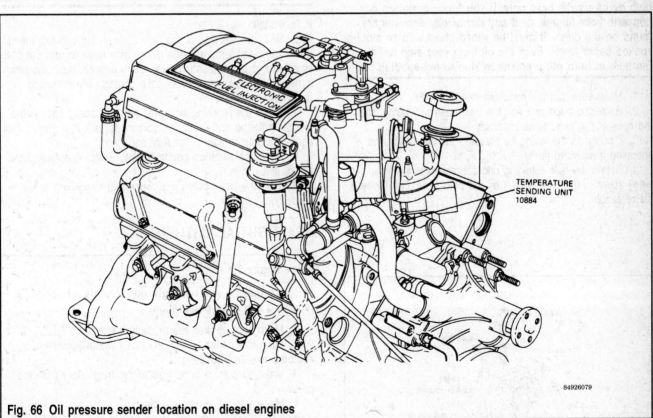

Fig. 66 Oil pressure sender location on diesel engines

Coolant Temperature

▶ **See Figures 67 and 68**

For the location of your unit, see the accompanying illustrations.

1. Remove the radiator cap to relieve any system pressure.
2. Disconnect the wiring at the unit.
3. Unscrew the unit.
4. Coat the threads with Teflon® tape or electrically conductive sealer and screw the unit into place. The torque should be 10-18 ft. lbs.
5. Replace any lost coolant.

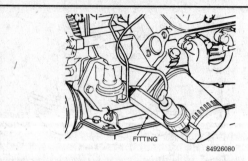

Fig. 67 Temperature sender location on the 6-4.9L engine

LIGHTING

Headlights

REMOVAL & INSTALLATION

▶ **See Figures 69, 70, 71 and 72**

✳✳CAUTION

The head lamp bulb contains high pressure halogen gas. The bulb may shatter if scratched or dropped! Hold the bulb by its plastic base only. If you touch the glass portion with your fingers, or if any dirt or oily deposits are found on the glass, it must be wiped clean with an alcohol soaked paper towel. Even the oil from your skin will cause the bulb to burn out prematurely due to hot-spotting.

1. Make sure that the headlight switch is **OFF**.
2. Raise the hood and find the bulb base protruding from the back of the head lamp assembly
3. Disconnect the wiring by grasping the connector and snapping it rearward firmly.
4. Rotate the bulb retaining ring counterclockwise (rear view) about ⅛ turn and slide it off the bulb base. Don't lose it; it's re-usable.

5. Carefully pull the bulb straight out of the head lamp assembly. Don't rotate it during removal.

✳✳WARNING

Don't remove the old bulb until you are ready to immediately replace it! Leaving the head lamp assembly open, without a bulb, will allow foreign matter such as water, dirt, leaves, oil, etc. to enter the housing. This type of contamination will cut down on the amount and direction of light emitted, and eventually cause premature blow-out of the bulb.

To install:

6. With the flat side of the bulb base facing upward, insert it into the head lamp assembly. You may have to turn the bulb slightly to align the locating tabs. Once aligned, push the bulb firmly into place until the bulb base contacts the mounting flange in the socket.
7. Place the retaining ring over the bulb base, against the mounting flange and rotate it clockwise to lock it. It should lock against a definite stop when fully engaged.
8. Snap the electrical connector into place. A definite snap will be felt.
9. Turn the headlights on a check that everything works properly.

HEADLIGHT ADJUSTMENT

▶ **See Figure 73**

➡**Before making any headlight adjustments, preform the following steps for preparation:**

1. Make sure all tires are properly inflated.
2. Take into consideration any faulty wheel alignment or improper rear axle tracking.
3. Make sure there is no load in the truck other than the driver.
4. Make sure all lenses are clean.

Each headlight is adjusted by means of two screws located at the 10 o'clock and 3 o'clock positions on the headlight underneath the trim ring. Always bring each beam into final position by turning the adjusting screws clockwise so that the

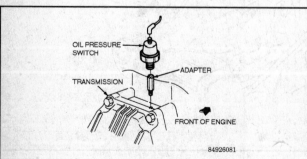

Fig. 68 Temperature sender location on all gasoline V8 engines

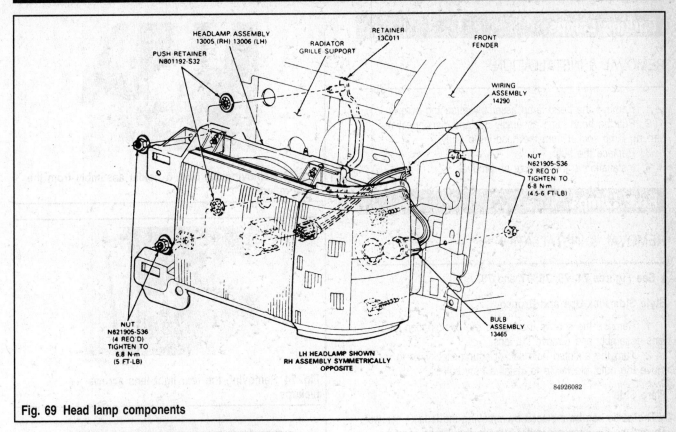

Fig. 69 Head lamp components

Fig. 70 Grasp the bulb socket base

Fig. 72 Pull the bulb socket assembly from the head lamp housing

Fig. 71 Twist it counterclockwise

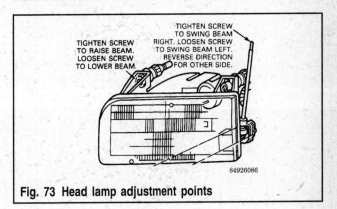

Fig. 73 Head lamp adjustment points

headlight will be held against the tension springs when the operation is completed.

Parking Lamps

REMOVAL & INSTALLATION

1. Remove the head lamp assembly attaching screws.
2. Pull the head lamp assembly out and disconnect the parking lamp socket from the head lamp body.
3. Replace the bulb.
4. Installation is the reverse of removal.

Rear Lamps

REMOVAL & INSTALLATION

▶ **See Figures 74, 75, 76, 77 and 78**

Style Side Pick-Ups and Bronco

1. Remove the screws that attach the combination lamp lens assembly and remove the lens.
2. Turn the affected bulb socket counterclockwise to remove the bulb; clockwise to install a new bulb.

Flare Side

The bulbs can be replaced by removing the lens (4 screws). To replace the lamp assembly, remove the 3 nuts from the mounting studs, disconnect the wiring inside the frame rail, unhook the wiring from the retaining clip, pull out the wires and remove the lamp assembly.

Installation is the reverse of removal.

84926091
Fig. 76 Removing the bulb & holder assembly from the lamp reflector

84926089
Fig. 74 Removing the rear light lens screws — pickups

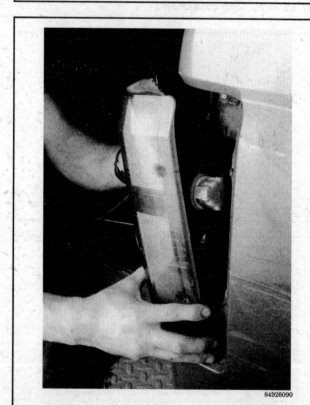
84926090
Fig. 75 Removing the rear light lens — pickups

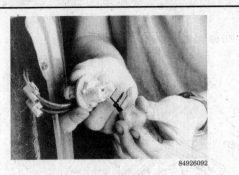

Fig. 77 Removing the bulb from the holder

Interior Lamps

REMOVAL & INSTALLATION

Dome/Map Lamp

BRONCO

1. Carefully pry the dome lamp lens, at the corners, from the housing.

2. Remove the 2 screws attaching the map lamp lens housing to the lamp base and remove the bulbs. The lamp base is retained to the roof by 4 screws.

3. Installation is the reverse of removal.

F-150/250/350 and SUPER DUTY

▶ See Figures 79 and 80

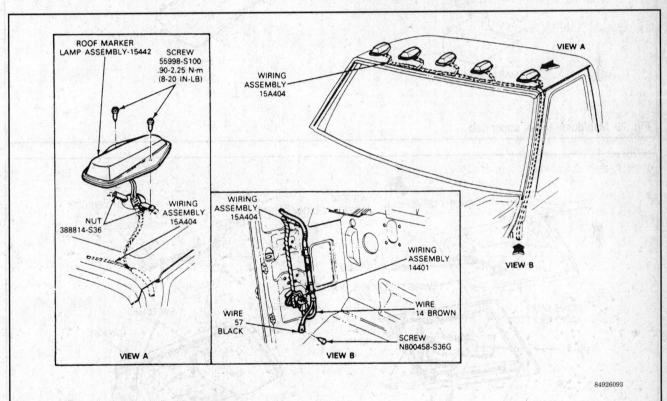

Fig. 78 Roof marker lamps for all models

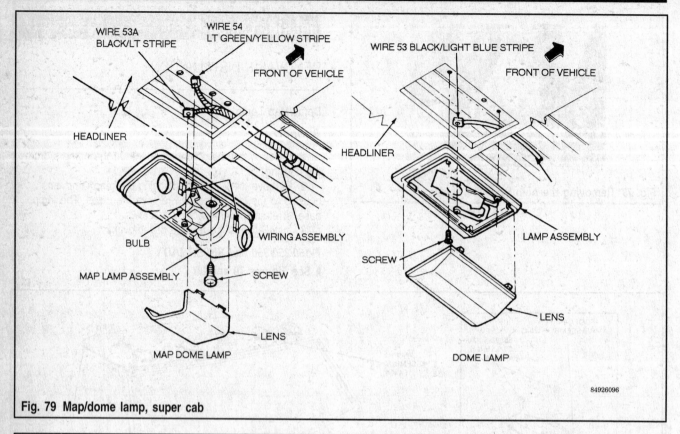

Fig. 79 Map/dome lamp, super cab

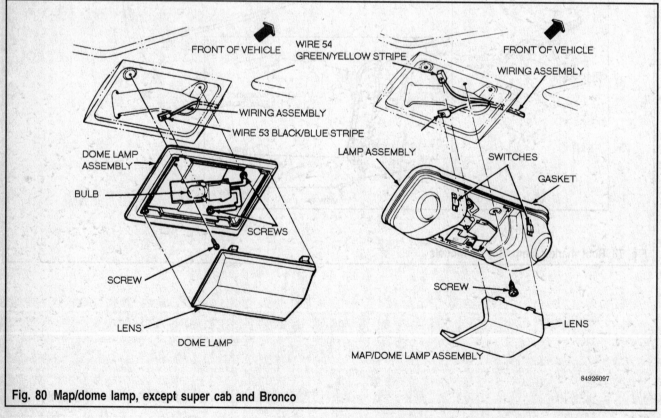

Fig. 80 Map/dome lamp, except super cab and Bronco

1. To replace the bulb, snap the lens out of the lamp body and remove the bulb.

2. To remove the lamp body, remove the 4 retaining screws.

3. Installation is the reverse of removal.

Cargo Lamp

REMOVAL & INSTALLATION

F-150/250/350 and Super Duty

Remove the 2 lamp retaining screws and remove the lamp. Remove the bulb from the lamp. Installation is the reverse of removal.

Bronco

Carefully unsnap the lamp from the side of the truck, disconnect the wiring and remove the bulb. Installation is the reverse of removal.

CIRCUIT PROTECTION

▶ See Figures 81 and 82

Fuses

On earlier models, the fuse panel is located on the firewall above the driver's left foot.

On later models, the fuse panel is located on the underside of the instrument panel, covered with an access door.

Circuit Breakers

▶ See Figures 81 and 82

Two circuits are protected by circuit breakers located in the fuse panel: the power windows (20 amp) or power windows and Shift-On-The-Fly (30 amp) and the power door locks (30 amp). The breakers are self-resetting.

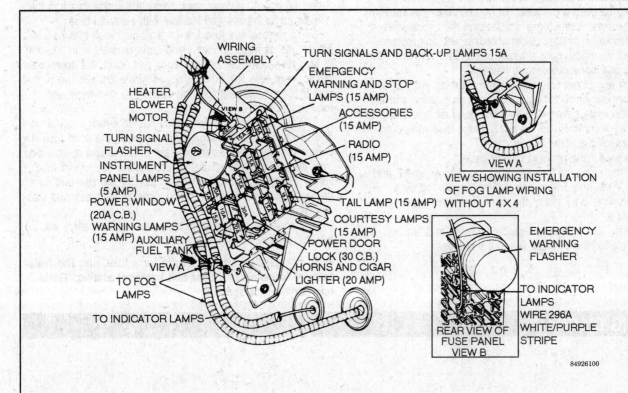

Fig. 81 Firewall-mounted fuse box, turn signal and hazard flashers

84926101

Fig. 82 Instrument panel-mounted fuse box

Turn Signal and Hazard Flasher Locations

▶ See Figures 81 and 82

Both the turn signal flasher and the hazard warning flasher are mounted on the fuse panel. The turn signal flasher is mounted on the front of the fuse panel, and the hazard warning flasher is mounted on the rear of the fuse panel.

Fuse Link

The fuse link is a short length of special, Hypalon (high temperature) insulated wire, integral with the engine compartment wiring harness and should not be confused with standard wire. It is several wire gauges smaller than the circuit which it protects. Under no circumstances should a fuse link replacement repair be made using a length of standard wire cut from bulk stock or from another wiring harness.

To repair any blown fuse link use the following procedure:

1. Determine which circuit is damaged, its location and the cause of the open fuse link. If the damaged fuse link is one of three fed by a common No. 10 or 12 gauge feed wire, determine the specific affected circuit.

2. Disconnect the negative battery cable.

3. Cut the damaged fuse link from the wiring harness and discard it. If the fuse link is one of three circuits fed by a single feed wire, cut it out of the harness at each splice end and discard it.

4. Identify and procure the proper fuse link and butt connectors for attaching the fuse link to the harness.

5. To repair any fuse link in a 3-link group with one feed:

a. After cutting the open link out of the harness, cut each of the remaining undamaged fuse links close to the feed wire weld.

b. Strip approximately ½ in. (13mm) of insulation from the detached ends of the two good fuse links. Then insert two wire ends into one end of a butt connector and carefully push one stripped end of the replacement fuse link into the same end of the butt connector and crimp all three firmly together.

➡Care must be taken when fitting the three fuse links into the butt connector as the internal diameter is a snug it for three wires. Make sure to use a proper crimping tool. Pliers, side cutters, etc. will not apply the proper crimp to retain the wires and withstand a pull test.

c. After crimping the butt connector to the three fuse links, cut the weld portion from the feed wire and strip approximately ½ in. (13mm) of insulation from the cut end. Insert the stripped end into the open end of the butt connector and crimp very firmly.

d. To attach the remaining end of the replacement fuse link, strip approximately ½ in. (13mm) of insulation from the wire end of the circuit from which the blown fuse link was removed, and firmly crimp a butt connector or equivalent to the stripped wire. Then, insert the end of the replacement link into the other end of the butt connector and crimp firmly.

e. Using rosin core solder with a consistency of 60 percent tin and 40 percent lead, solder the connectors and the wires at the repairs and insulate with electrical tape.

6. To replace any fuse link on a single circuit in a harness, cut out the damaged portion, strip approximately ½ in. (13mm) of insulation from the two wire ends and attach the appropriate replacement fuse link to the stripped wire ends with two proper size butt connectors. Solder the connectors and wires and insulate the tape.

7. To repair any fuse link which has an eyelet terminal on one end such as the charging circuit, cut off the open fuse link behind the weld, strip approximately ½ in. (13mm) of insulation from the cut end and attach the appropriate new eyelet fuse link to the cut stripped wire with an appropriate size butt connector. Solder the connectors and wires at the repair and insulate with tape.

8. Connect the negative battery cable to the battery and test the system for proper operation.

➡Do not mistake a resistor wire for a fuse link. The resistor wire is generally longer and has print stating, 'Resistor: don't cut or splice.'

WIRING DIAGRAMS

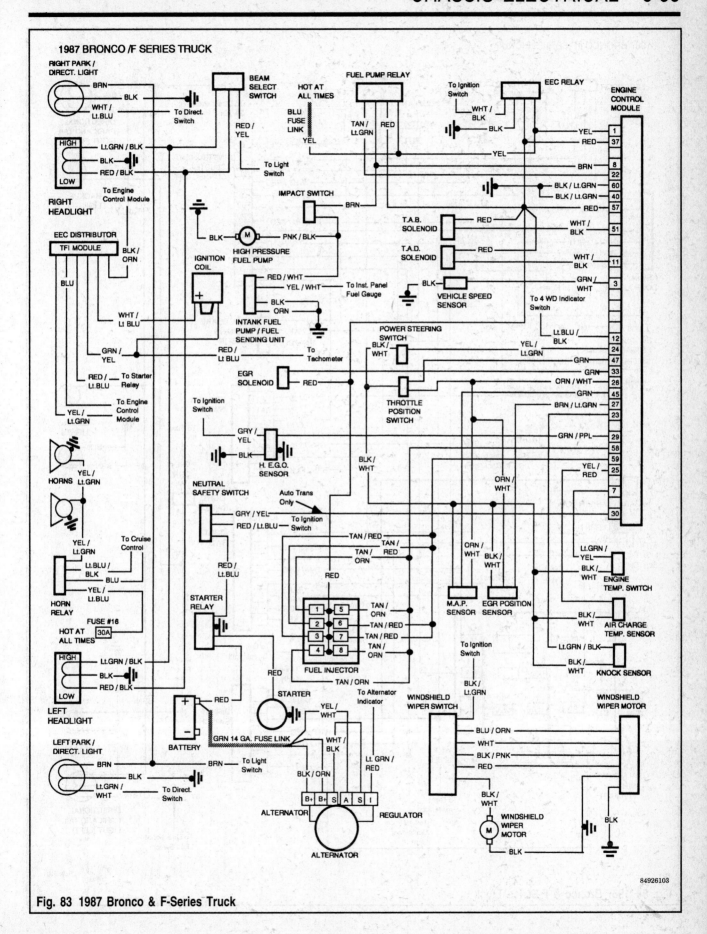

Fig. 83 1987 Bronco & F-Series Truck

84926103

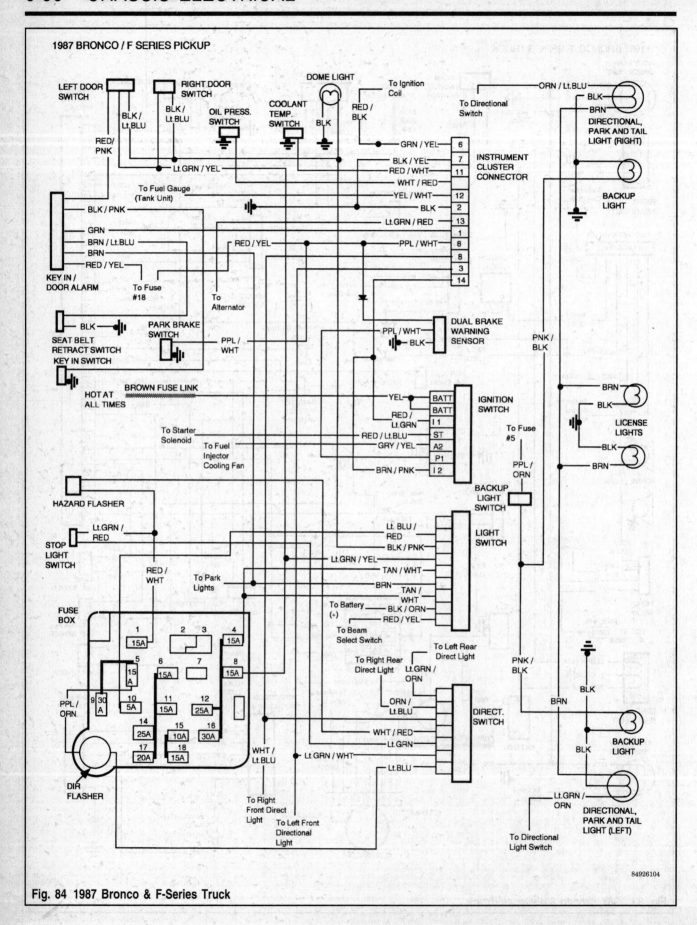

Fig. 84 1987 Bronco & F-Series Truck

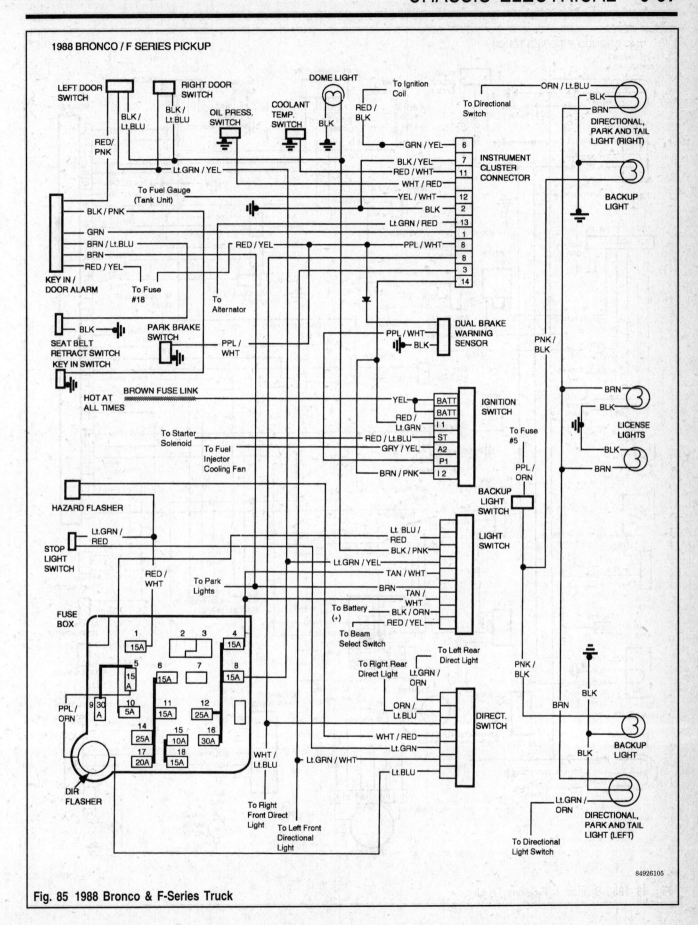

1988 Bronco / F Series Pickup

Fig. 85 1988 Bronco & F-Series Truck

84926105

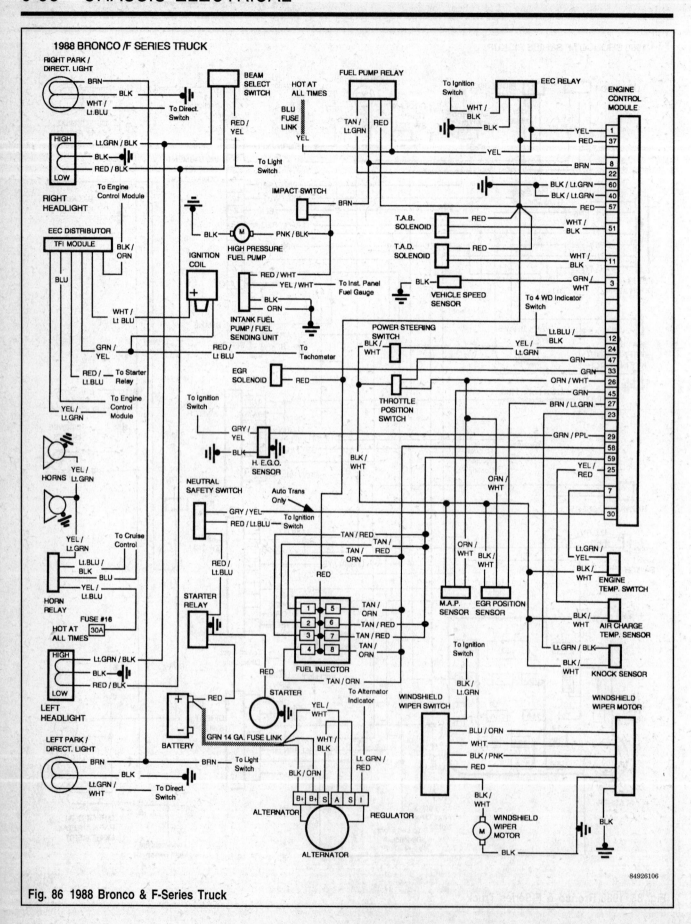

Fig. 86 1988 Bronco & F-Series Truck

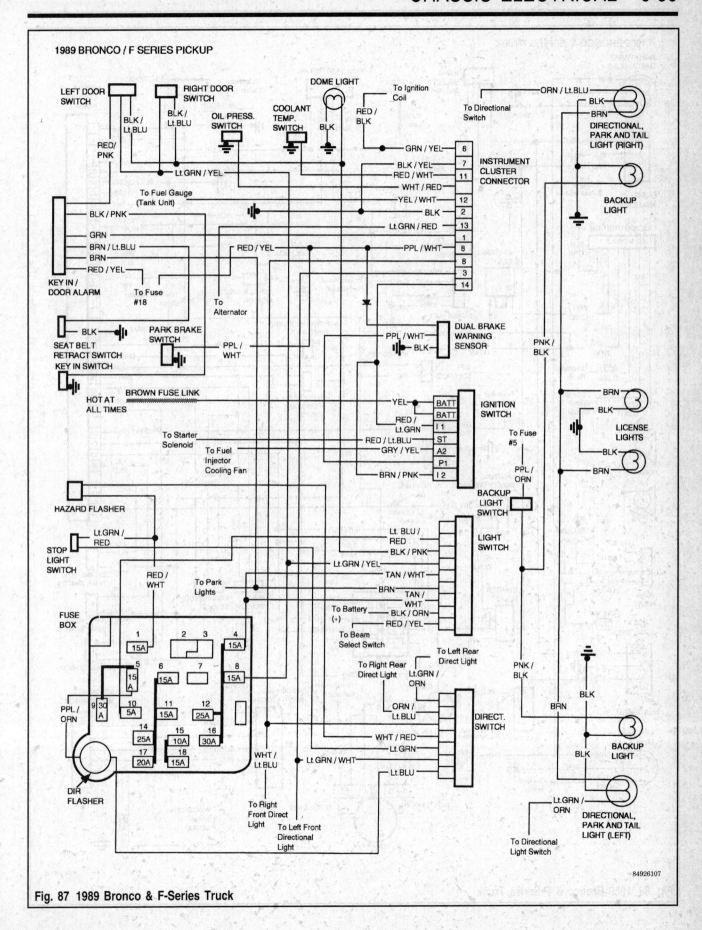

1989 Bronco / F Series Pickup

LEFT DOOR SWITCH
RIGHT DOOR SWITCH
DOME LIGHT
To Ignition Coil
To Directional Switch
ORN / Lt.BLU
BLK
BRN
DIRECTIONAL, PARK AND TAIL LIGHT (RIGHT)

BLK / Lt.BLU
BLK / Lt.BLU
OIL PRESS. SWITCH
COOLANT TEMP. SWITCH
BLK
RED / BLK

RED / PNK
GRN / YEL — 6
BLK / YEL — 7
RED / WHT — 11
WHT / RED —
YEL / WHT — 12
BLK — 2
Lt.GRN / RED — 13
INSTRUMENT CLUSTER CONNECTOR

BACKUP LIGHT

Lt.GRN / YEL
To Fuel Gauge (Tank Unit)
BLK / PNK
GRN
BRN / Lt.BLU
BRN
RED / YEL
RED / YEL
1
PPL / WHT — 8
8
3
14

KEY IN / DOOR ALARM
To Fuse #18
To Alternator

PPL / WHT
DUAL BRAKE WARNING SENSOR
PNK / BLK

BLK
BLK
SEAT BELT RETRACT SWITCH
KEY IN SWITCH
PARK BRAKE SWITCH
PPL / WHT

BRN
BLK
LICENSE LIGHTS

HOT AT ALL TIMES
BROWN FUSE LINK
YEL
RED / Lt.GRN
RED / Lt.BLU
GRY / YEL
BRN / PNK
BATT
BATT
I 1
ST
A2
P1
I 2
IGNITION SWITCH

To Starter Solenoid
To Fuel Injector Cooling Fan

BLK
BRN

To Fuse #5
PPL / ORN

BACKUP LIGHT SWITCH

HAZARD FLASHER

Lt.GRN / RED
STOP LIGHT SWITCH

Lt. BLU / RED
BLK / PNK
Lt.GRN / YEL
TAN / WHT
BRN
TAN / WHT
BLK / ORN
RED / YEL
LIGHT SWITCH

To Park Lights
To Battery (+)
To Beam Select Switch

RED / WHT

FUSE BOX

1   15A
2   3
4   15A
5   15 A
6   15A
7
8   15A
9 30 A
PPL / ORN
10 5A
11 15A
12 25A
14 25A
15 10A
16 30A
17 20A
18 15A

DIR FLASHER

To Right Rear Direct Light
To Left Rear Direct Light
Lt.GRN / ORN
ORN / Lt.BLU
WHT / RED
Lt.GRN
Lt.GRN / WHT
Lt.BLU
DIRECT. SWITCH

PNK / BLK
BRN
BLK

BACKUP LIGHT

WHT / Lt.BLU
To Right Front Direct Light
To Left Front Directional Light
Lt.GRN / ORN
DIRECTIONAL, PARK AND TAIL LIGHT (LEFT)
To Directional Light Switch

84926107

Fig. 87 1989 Bronco & F-Series Truck

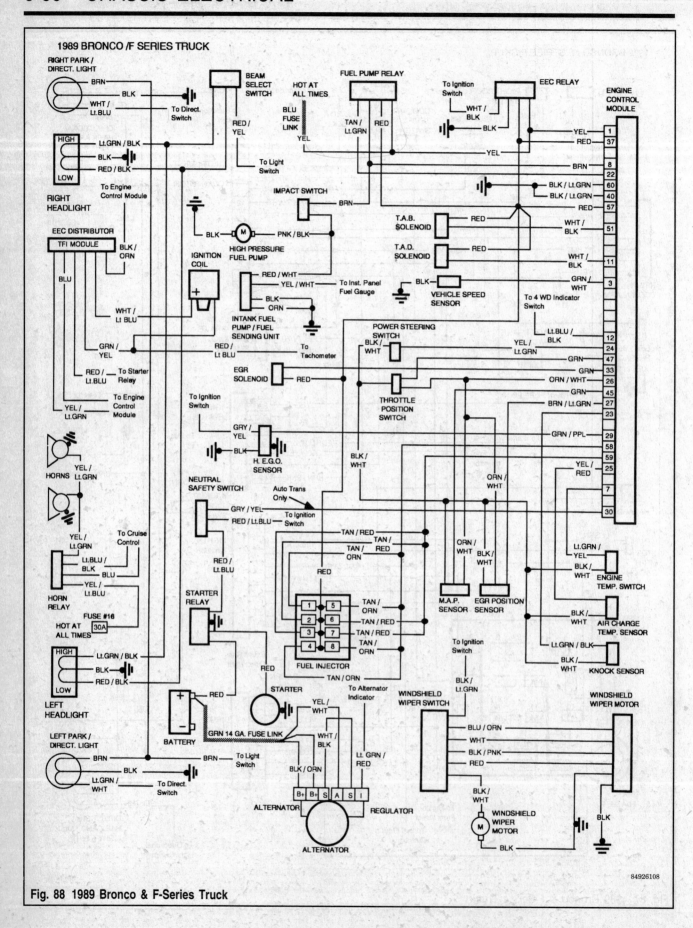

Fig. 88 1989 Bronco & F-Series Truck

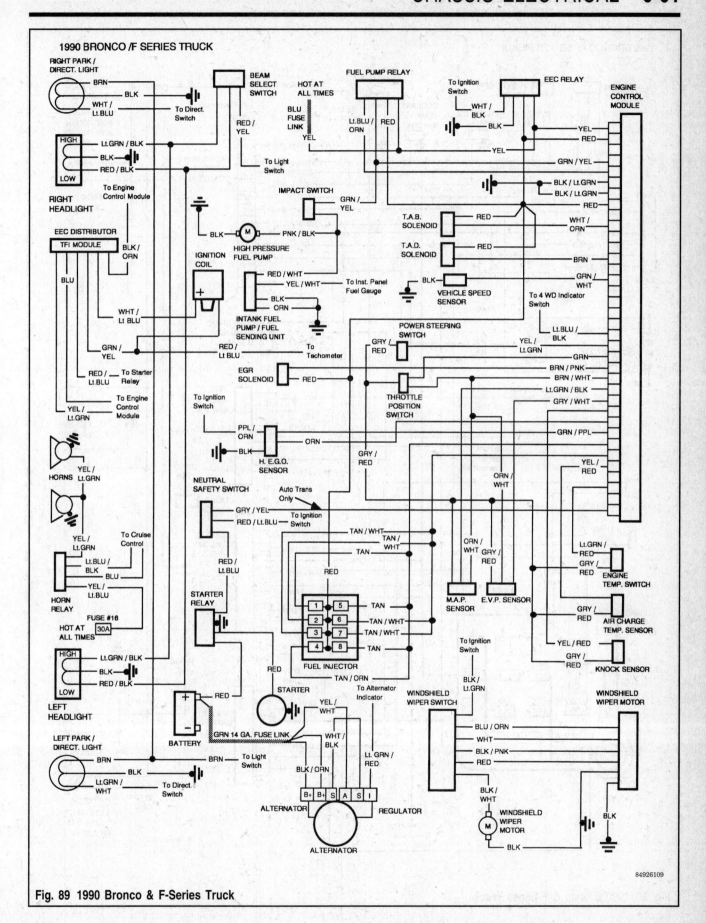

Fig. 89 1990 Bronco & F-Series Truck

84926109

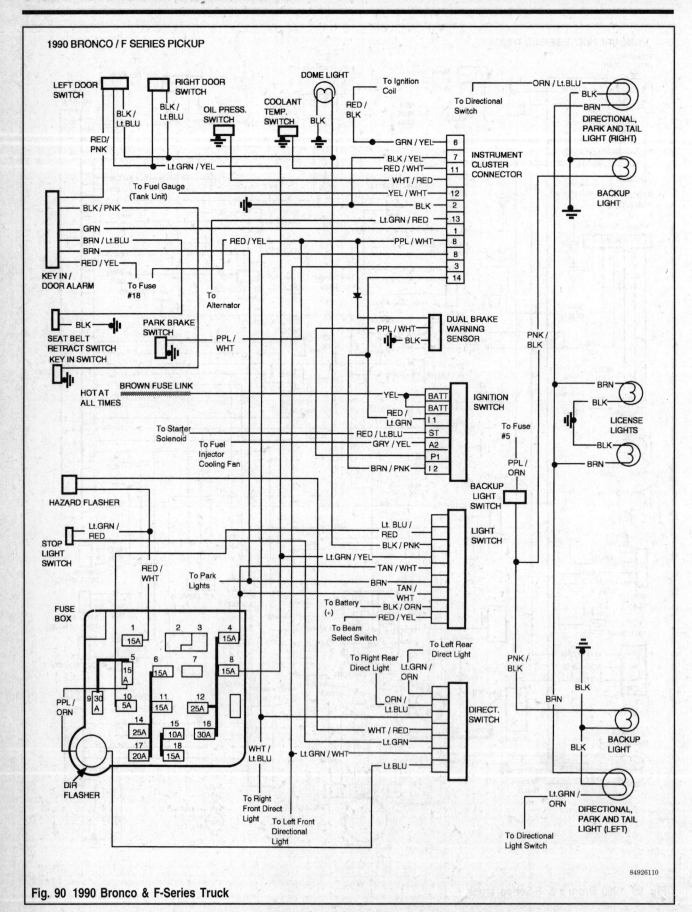

Fig. 90 1990 Bronco & F-Series Truck

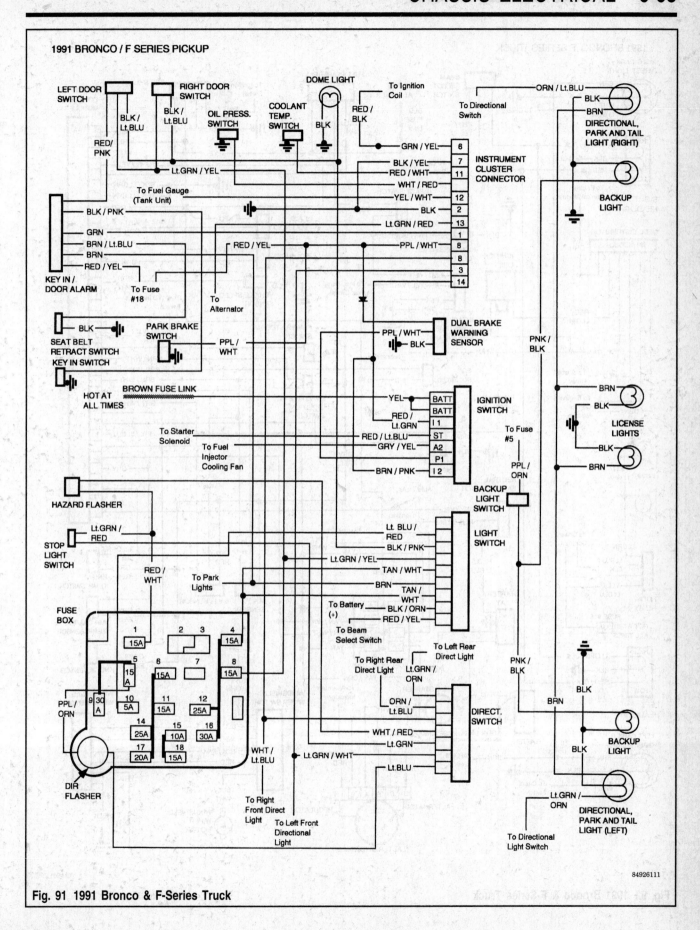

Fig. 91 1991 Bronco & F-Series Truck

84926111

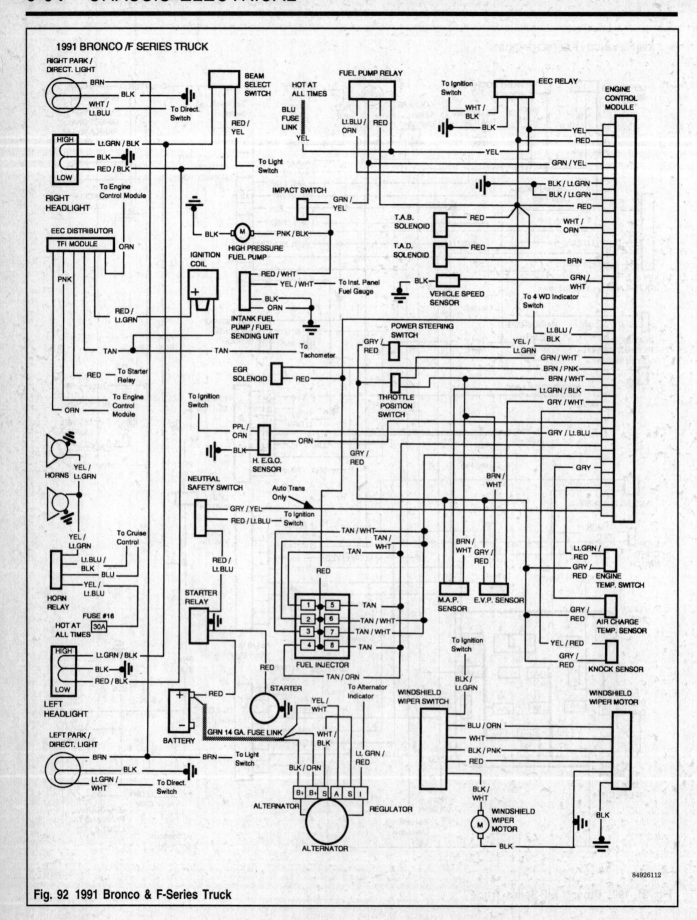

Fig. 92 1991 Bronco & F-Series Truck

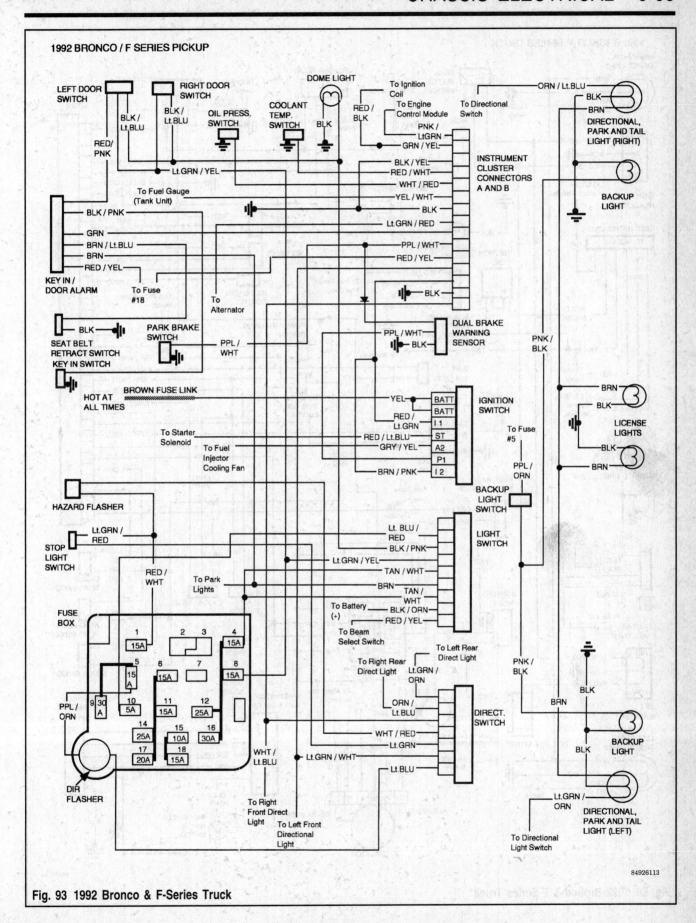

Fig. 93 1992 Bronco & F-Series Truck

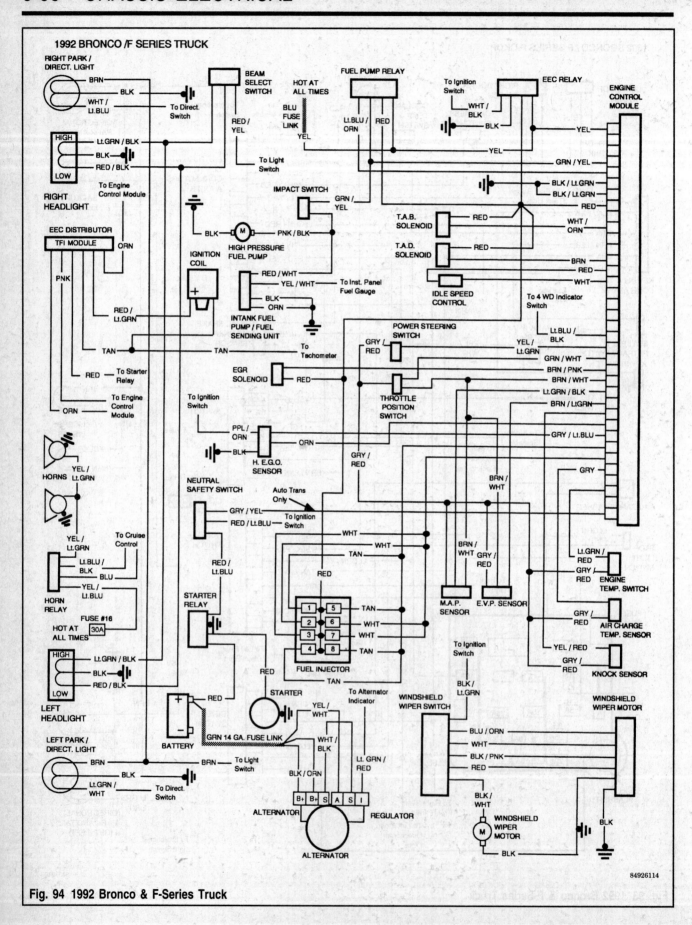

Fig. 94 1992 Bronco & F-Series Truck

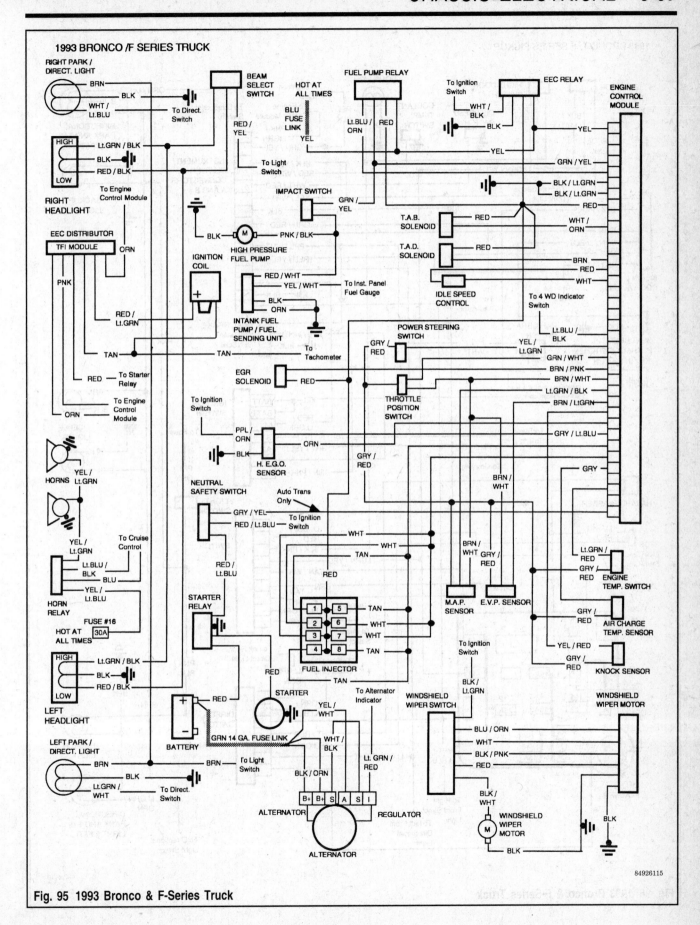

Fig. 95 1993 Bronco & F-Series Truck

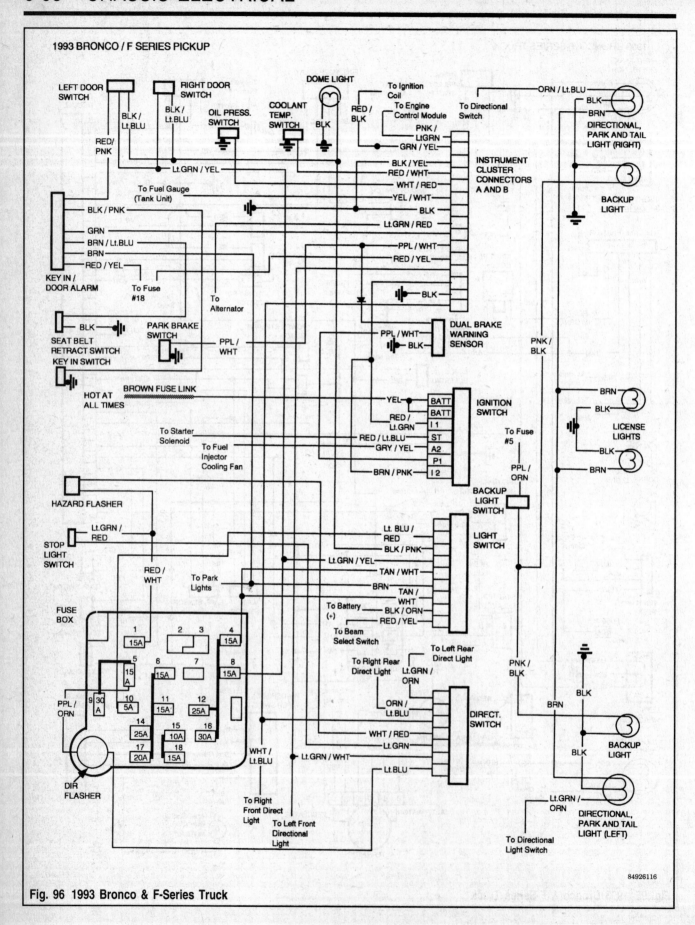

Fig. 96 1993 Bronco & F-Series Truck

7

DRIVE
TRAIN

UNDERSTANDING THE MANUAL TRANSMISSION

Because of the way an internal combustion engine breathes, it can produce torque, or twisting force, only within a narrow speed range. Most modern, overhead valve engines must turn at about 2,500 rpm to produce their peak torque. By 4,500 rpm they are producing so little torque that continued increases in engine speed produce no power increases.

The torque peak on overhead camshaft engines is, generally, much higher, but much narrower.

The manual transmission and clutch are employed to vary the relationship between engine speed and the speed of the wheels so that adequate engine power can be produced under all circumstances. The clutch allows engine torque to be applied to the transmission input shaft gradually, due to mechanical slippage. The truck can, consequently, be started smoothly from a full stop.

The transmission changes the ratio between the rotating speeds of the engine and the wheels by the use of gears. 4-speed or 5-speed transmissions are most common. The

lower gears allow full engine power to be applied to the rear wheels during acceleration at low speeds.

The transmission contains a mainshaft which passes all the way through the transmission, from the clutch to the driveshaft. This shaft is separated at one point, so that front and rear portions can turn at different speeds.

Power is transmitted by a countershaft in the lower gears and reverse. The gears of the countershaft mesh with gears on the mainshaft, allowing power to be carried from one to the other. All the countershaft gears are integral with that shaft, while several of the mainshaft gears can either rotate independently of the shaft or be locked to it. Shifting from one gear to the next causes one of the gears to be freed from rotating with the shaft and locks another to it. Gears are locked and unlocked by internal dog clutches which slide between the center of the gear and the shaft. The forward gears usually employ synchronizers; friction members which smoothly bring gear and shaft to the same speed before the toothed dog clutches are engaged.

MANUAL TRANSMISSION

Back-Up Light Switch

▶ See Figures 1 and 2

REMOVAL & INSTALLATION

The back-up light switch is mounted on the transmission extension housing. this switch is not adjustable. To remove, place the transmission shift lever in any gear but neutral, and disconnect the electrical connector from the switch. Remove the switch assembly from the transmission and install a new switch in the reverse order of removal.

Shift Linkage

LINKAGE ADJUSTMENT

Ford TOD 4-Speed Overdrive

1. Attach the shift rods in the levers.
2. Rotate the output shaft to determine that the transmission is in neutral.
3. Insert a alignment pin into the shift control assembly alignment hole.
4. Attach the slotted end of the shift rods over the flats of the studs in the shift control assembly.
5. Install the lock nuts and remove the alignment pin.

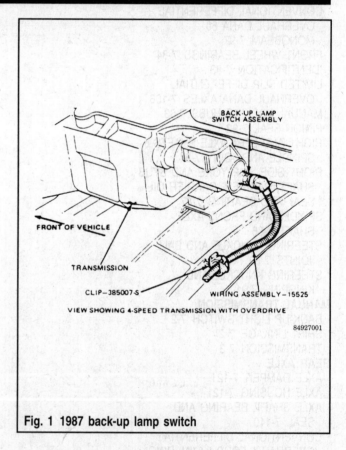

BACK-UP LAMP SWITCH ASSEMBLY

FRONT OF VEHICLE

TRANSMISSION

CLIP—385007-S

WIRING ASSEMBLY—15525

VIEW SHOWING 4-SPEED TRANSMISSION WITH OVERDRIVE

84927001

Fig. 1 1987 back-up lamp switch

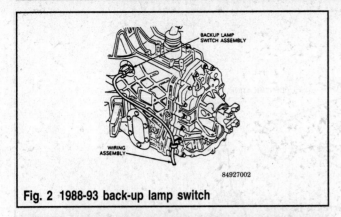

Fig. 2 1988-93 back-up lamp switch

Transmission

REMOVAL & INSTALLATION

❋❋CAUTION

The clutch driven disc contains asbestos, which has been determined to be a cancer causing agent. Never clean clutch surfaces with compressed air! Avoid inhaling any dust from any clutch surface! When cleaning clutch surfaces, use a commercially available brake cleaning fluid.

Warner T-18, T-19A, T-19C 4-Speed

▶ See Figures 3 and 4

2-WHEEL DRIVE

1. Remove the rubber boot, floor mat, and the body floor pan cover.
2. Remove the gearshift lever, shift ball and boot as an assembly.
3. Raise the vehicle and support it with jackstands.
4. Drain the transmission.
5. Remove the driveshaft.
6. Disconnect the speedometer cable.
7. Remove the crossmember-to-transmission bolts.
8. Secure the transmission to a transmission jack.
9. Remove the crossmember.
10. Remove the 4 transmission-to-bell housing bolts, roll the transmission rearward and remove it.

To install:

➡You can make installation a lot easier if you fabricate 2 guide pins, made by cutting the heads off of 2 long bolts. These guide pins are inserted into the upper bolt holes in the back of the bell housing and serve to align the bolt holes.

11. Raise the transmission and roll it forward using the guide pins to align the bolt holes. Turn the output shaft by hand to align the input shaft splines with the clutch.
12. Install the 2 lower bolts and snug them down.
13. Remove the guide pins and install the 2 remaining bolts. Torque all 4 bolts to 50 ft. lbs.

14. Install the crossmember. Crossmember-to-frame bolt torque is 55 ft. lbs.
15. Remove the transmission jack.
16. Install the Crossmember-to-transmission bolts. Torque the bolts to 50 ft. lbs.
17. Connect the speedometer cable.
18. Install the driveshaft.
19. Install the drain plug and fill the transmission. Drain plug torque is 50 ft. lbs.
20. Lower the vehicle.
21. Install the gearshift lever, shift ball and boot as an assembly.
22. Install the body floor pan cover, floor mat, and the rubber boot.

4-WHEEL DRIVE

1. Remove the rubber boot, floor mat, and the body floor pan cover. Remove the gearshift lever. Remove the weather pad.
2. Remove the transfer case shift lever, shift ball and boot as an assembly.
3. Disconnect the back-up light switch at the rear of the gearshift housing cover.
4. Raise the vehicle and support it with jackstands. Remove the drain and fill plugs and drain the lubricant.
5. Position a transmission jack under the transfer case and disconnect the speedometer cable.
6. Matchmark the flanges and disconnect the rear driveshaft from the transfer case. Wire it up and out of the way.
7. Matchmark and disconnect the front driveshaft at the transfer case. Wire it up and out of the way.
8. Remove the shift link from the transfer case.
9. Unbolt the transfer case from the transmission (6 bolts) and lower the transfer case from the vehicle.
10. Position the transmission jack under the transmission.
11. Remove the 8 rear transmission support-to-transmission bolts.
12. Remove the rear transmission support.
13. Remove the 4 transmission-to-clutch housing attaching bolts.
14. Move the transmission to the rear until the input shaft clears the flywheel housing and lower the transmission.

To install:

➡You can make installation a lot easier if you fabricate 2 guide pins, made by cutting the heads off of 2 long bolts. These guide pins are inserted into the upper bolt holes in the back of the bell housing and serve to align the bolt holes.

15. Before installing the transmission, apply a light film of grease to the inner hub surface of the clutch release bearing, the release lever fulcrum and the front bearing retainer of the transmission. Do not apply excessive grease because it will fly off onto the clutch disc.
16. Install the transmission in the reverse order of removal. It may be necessary to turn the output shaft with the transmission in gear to align the input shaft splines with the splines in the clutch disc. Fill the transmission with SAE 80W/90 lubricant

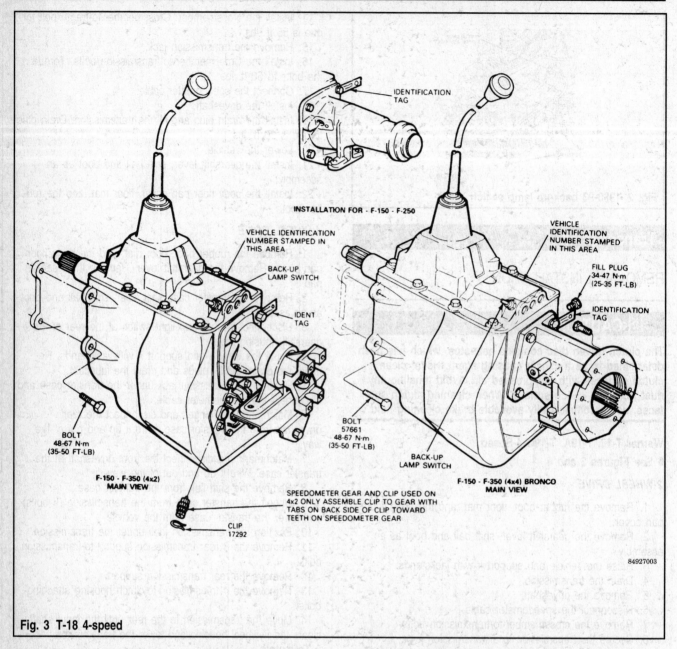

INSTALLATION FOR - F-150 - F-250

IDENTIFICATION TAG

VEHICLE IDENTIFICATION NUMBER STAMPED IN THIS AREA

BACK-UP LAMP SWITCH

IDENT TAG

BOLT 48-67 N·m (35-50 FT-LB)

F-150 - F-350 (4x2) MAIN VIEW

SPEEDOMETER GEAR AND CLIP USED ON 4x2 ONLY ASSEMBLE CLIP TO GEAR WITH TABS ON BACK SIDE OF CLIP TOWARD TEETH ON SPEEDOMETER GEAR

CLIP 17292

VEHICLE IDENTIFICATION NUMBER STAMPED IN THIS AREA

FILL PLUG 34-47 N·m (25-35 FT-LB)

IDENTIFICATION TAG

BOLT 57661 48-67 N·m (35-50 FT-LB)

BACK-UP LAMP SWITCH

F-150 - F-350 (4x4) BRONCO MAIN VIEW

84927003

Fig. 3 T-18 4-speed

if it was drained. The transfer case is filled with Dexron®II ATF. Observe the following torque specifications:

- Back-up light switch: 25 ft. lbs.
- Transmission-to-clutch housing bolts: 65 ft. lbs.
- Transfer case-to-transmission: 40 ft. lbs.
- Drain plug: 50 ft. lbs.
- Fill plug: 50 ft. lbs.
- Transmission to rear support: 80 ft. lbs.
- Rear support-to-frame: 55 ft. lbs.

New Process 435 4-Speed
▶ See Figure 5

2-WHEEL DRIVE

1. Remove the floor mat.
2. Remove the shift lever boot.

3. Remove the floor pan, transmission cover plate, and weather pad. It may be necessary to remove the seat assembly.

4. Remove the shift lever and knob by first removing the inner cap using tool T73T-7220-A, or equivalent. Then, remove the spring seat and spring. Remove the shift lever from the housing.

5. Disconnect the back-up light switch located in the left side of the gearshift housing cover.

6. Raise the vehicle and place jackstands under the frame to support it. Place a transmission jack under the transmission and disconnect the speedometer cable.

7. Matchmark and disconnect the driveshaft.

8. Remove the transmission rear support.

9. Remove the transmission-to-flywheel housing attaching bolts, slide the transmission rearward until the input shaft clears the flywheel housing and lower it out from under the truck.

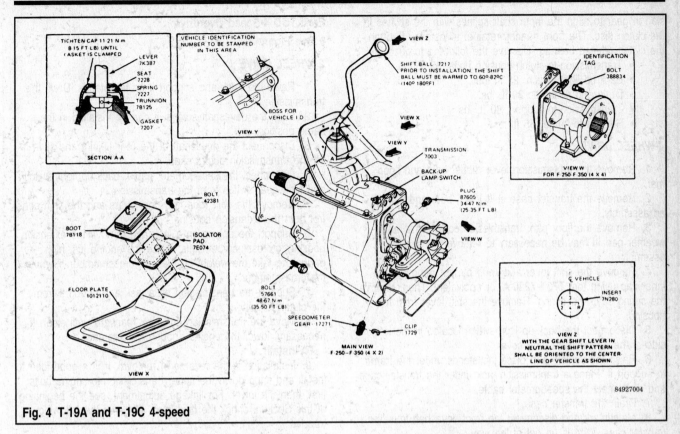

Fig. 4 T-19A and T-19C 4-speed

10. Before installing the transmission, apply a light film of grease of the inner hub surface of the clutch release bearing, release lever fulcrum and fork, and the front bearing retainer of the transmission. Do not apply excessive grease because if will fly off and contaminate the clutch disc.

11. Install the transmission in the reverse order of removal. It may be necessary to turn the output shaft with the transmis-

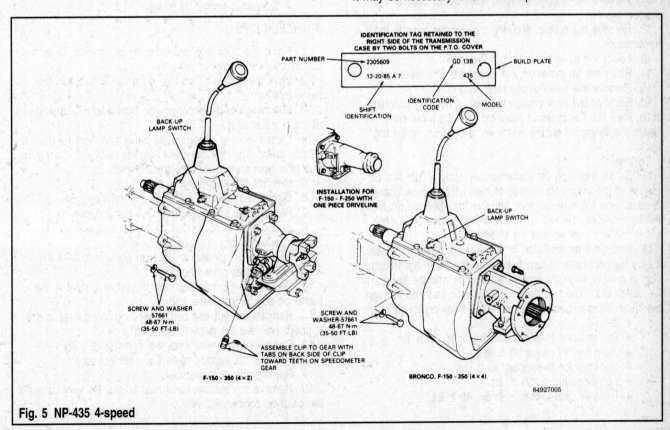

Fig. 5 NP-435 4-speed

sion in gear to align the input shaft splines with the splines in the clutch disc. The front bearing retainer is installed through the clutch release bearing. Observe the following torques:

- Transmission-to-clutch housing bolts: 65 ft. lbs.
- Back-up light switch: 25 ft. lbs.
- Drain and fill plugs: 30 ft. lbs.
- Transmission-to-support: 80 ft. lbs.
- Support-to-frame: 55 ft. lbs.

4-WHEEL DRIVE

1. Remove the transmission lever rubber boot and floor mat.
2. Remove the transfer case shift lever, boot and ball as an assembly.
3. Remove the floor pan, transmission cover plate, and weather pad. It may be necessary to remove the seat assembly.
4. Remove the shift lever and knob by first removing the inner cap using tool T73T-7220-A, or equivalent. Then, remove the spring seat and spring. Remove the shift lever from the housing.
5. Disconnect the back-up light switch located in the left side of the gearshift housing cover.
6. Raise the vehicle and place jackstands under the frame to support it. Place a transmission jack under the transfer case and disconnect the speedometer cable.
7. Drain the transfer case.
8. Matchmark and disconnect the front driveshaft from the transfer case. Wire is up out of the way.
9. Matchmark and disconnect the rear driveshaft from the transfer case. Wire it up out of the way.
10. Disconnect the shift link from the transfer case.
11. Remove the 3 bolts securing the transfer case to the support bracket.
12. Remove the 6 bolts securing the transfer case to the transmission.
13. Lower the transfer case from the truck.
14. Place the transmission jack under the transmission.
15. Remove the transmission rear support.
16. Remove the transmission-to-flywheel housing attaching bolts, slide the transmission rearward until the input shaft clears the flywheel housing and lower it out from under the truck.

To install:

17. Before installing the transmission, apply a light film of grease of the inner hub surface of the clutch release bearing, release lever fulcrum and fork, and the front bearing retainer of the transmission. Do not apply excessive grease because if will fly off and contaminate the clutch disc.
18. Install the transmission in the reverse order of removal. It may be necessary to turn the output shaft with the transmission in gear to align the input shaft splines with the splines in the clutch disc. The front bearing retainer is installed through the clutch release bearing. Observe the following torques:

- Back-up light switch: 25 ft. lbs.
- Transmission-to-clutch housing bolts: 65 ft. lbs.
- Drain and fill plugs: 30 ft. lbs.
- Transmission-to-support: 80 ft. lbs.
- Support-to-frame: 55 ft. lbs.
- Transfer case-to-transmission: 40 ft. lbs.

Ford TOD 4-Speed Overdrive
▶ See Figure 6

2-WHEEL DRIVE

1. Raise the truck and support it on jackstands. Drain the transmission.
2. Mark the driveshaft so that it can be installed in the same position.
3. Disconnect the driveshaft at the rear U-joint and slide it off the transmission output shaft.
4. Disconnect the speedometer cable, back-up light switch and high gear switch from the transmission.
5. Remove the shift rods from the levers and the shift control from the extension housing.
6. Support the engine on a jack and remove the extension housing-to-crossmember bolts. Raise the engine just high enough to take the weight off the rear crossmember. Remove the crossmember.
7. Support the transmission on a jack and unbolt it from the clutch housing.
8. Move the transmission and jack rearward until clear. If necessary, lower the engine enough for clearance.

To install:

9. Installation is the reverse of removal. It is a good idea to install and snug down the upper transmission-to-engine bolts first, then the lower. For linkage adjustment, see the beginning of this Section. check the fluid level. Observe the following torques:

- Back-up light switch: 25 ft. lbs.
- Transmission-to-clutch housing bolts: 65 ft. lbs.
- Drain and fill plugs: 30 ft. lbs.
- Transmission-to-support: 80 ft. lbs.
- Support-to-frame: 55 ft. lbs.

4-WHEEL DRIVE

1. Raise the truck and support it on jackstands. Drain the transmission and transfer case.
2. Mark the driveshaft so that it can be installed in the same position.
3. Matchmark and disconnect the front and rear driveshafts at the transfer case.
4. Disconnect the speedometer cable and 4-wheel drive indicator switch from the transfer case; the back-up light switch and high gear switch from the transmission.
5. Remove the skid plate.
6. Disconnect the shift link from the transfer case.
7. Remove the shift lever from the transmission.
8. Support the transmission on a jack and remove the transmission housing rear support bracket.
9. Raise the transmission just high enough to take the weight off the rear crossmember.
10. Remove the 2 nuts securing the upper gusset to the frame on both sides of the frame.
11. Remove the nut and bolt connecting the gusset to the support. Remove the gusset on the left side.
12. Remove the transmission-to-support plate bolts.
13. Remove the support plate and right gusset.
14. Remove the crossmember.
15. Remove the transfer case heat shield. Be very careful if the catalytic converter is hot!

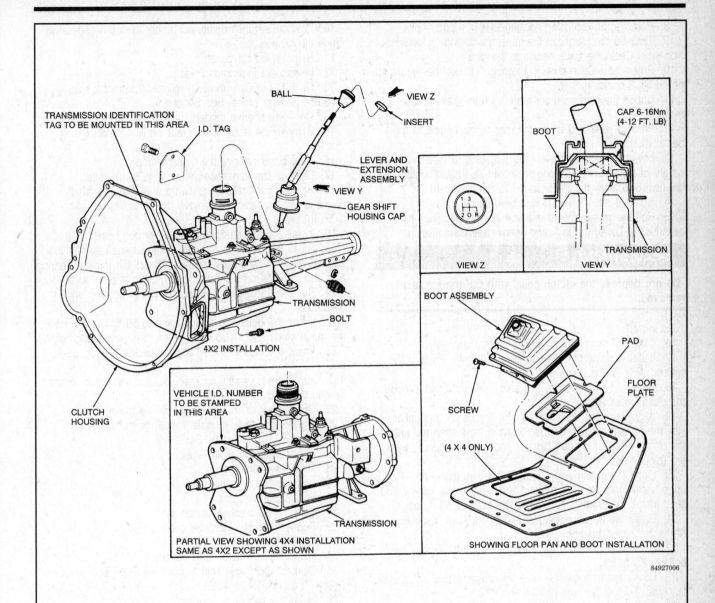

BALL

VIEW Z

INSERT

TRANSMISSION IDENTIFICATION
TAG TO BE MOUNTED IN THIS AREA

I.D. TAG

LEVER AND
EXTENSION
ASSEMBLY

VIEW Y

GEAR SHIFT
HOUSING CAP

CAP 6-16Nm
(4-12 FT. LB)

BOOT

TRANSMISSION

VIEW Z

VIEW Y

BOOT ASSEMBLY

PAD

FLOOR
PLATE

SCREW

(4 X 4 ONLY)

TRANSMISSION

BOLT

4X2 INSTALLATION

CLUTCH
HOUSING

VEHICLE I.D. NUMBER
TO BE STAMPED
IN THIS AREA

TRANSMISSION

PARTIAL VIEW SHOWING 4X4 INSTALLATION
SAME AS 4X2 EXCEPT AS SHOWN

SHOWING FLOOR PAN AND BOOT INSTALLATION

84927006

Fig. 6 TOD 4-speed

16. Support the transfer case on a jack and unbolt it from the transmission.

17. Move the transfer case and jack rearward until clear and lower it. Discard the adapter gasket.

18. Support the transmission on a jack and unbolt it from the clutch housing.

19. Move the transmission and jack rearward until clear. If necessary, lower the engine for clearance.

To install:

20. Installation is the reverse of removal. It is a good idea to install and snug down the upper transmission-to-clutch housing bolts first, then the lower. For linkage adjustment, see the beginning of this Section. Check the fluid level. Observe the following torques:

- Back-up light switch: 25 ft. lbs.
- Transmission-to-clutch housing bolts: 65 ft. lbs.
- Transfer case-to-transmission: 40 ft. lbs.
- Rear driveshaft-to-yoke: 25 ft. lbs.

- Front driveshaft-to-yoke: 15 ft. lbs.
- Drain and fill plugs: 30 ft. lbs.
- Transmission-to-support: 80 ft. lbs.
- Support-to-frame: 55 ft. lbs.

Mazda M5OD 5-Speed

1. Raise and support the truck on jackstands. Prop the clutch pedal in the full up position with a block of wood.

2. Matchmark the driveshaft-to-flange relation.

3. Disconnect the driveshaft at the rear axle and slide it off of the transmission output shaft. Lubricant will leak out of the transmission so be prepared to catch it, or plug the opening with rags or a seal installation tool.

4. Disconnect the speedometer cable at the transmission.

5. Disconnect the shift rods from the shift levers.

6. Remove the shift control from the extension housing and transmission case.

7. On 4-wheel drive models, remove the transfer case.

8. Remove the extension housing-to-rear support bolts.

9. Take up the weight of the transmission with a transmission jack. Chain the transmission to the jack.

10. Raise the transmission just enough to take the weight off of the No.3 crossmember.

11. Unbolt the crossmember from the frame rails and remove it.

12. Place a jackstand under the rear of the engine at the bellhousing.

13. Lower the jack and allow the jackstand to take the weight of the engine. The engine should be angled slightly downward to allow the transmission to roll backward.

14. Remove the transmission-to bellhousing bolts.

15. Roll the jack rearward until the input shaft clears the bellhousing. Lower the jack and remove the transmission.

❉❉WARNING

Do not depress the clutch pedal with the transmission removed.

To install:

16. Clean all machined mating surfaces thoroughly.

17. Install a guide pin in each lower bolt hole. Position the spacer plate on the guide pins.

18. Raise the transmission and start the input shaft through the clutch release bearing.

19. Align the input shaft splines with the clutch disc splines. Roll the transmission forward so that the input shaft will enter the clutch disc. If the shaft binds in the release bearing, work the release arm back and forth.

20. Once the transmission is all the way in, install the 2 upper retaining bolts and washers and remove the lower guide pins. Install the lower bolts. Torque the bolts to 50 ft. lbs.

21. Raise the transmission just enough to allow installation of the No.3 crossmember.

22. Install the crossmember on the frame rails. Torque the bolts to 80 ft. lbs.

23. Lower the transmission onto the crossmember and install the nuts. Torque the nuts to 70 ft. lbs.

24. Remove the transmission jack.

25. Install the transfer case.

26. Install the shift control on the extension housing and transmission case.

27. Connect the shift rods at the shift levers.

28. Connect the speedometer cable at the transmission.

29. Slide the driveshaft onto the output shaft and connect the driveshaft at the rear axle, aligning the matchmarks.

ZF S5-42 5-Speed

1. Place the transmission in neutral.

2. Remove the carpet or floor mat.

3. Remove the ball from the shift lever.

4. Remove the boot and bezel assembly from the floor.

5. Remove the 2 bolts and disengage the upper shift lever from the lower shift lever.

6. Raise and support the tuck on jackstands.

7. Disconnect the speedometer cable.

8. Disconnect the back-up switch wire.

9. Place a drain pan under the case and drain the case through the drain plug.

10. Position a transmission jack under the case and safety-chain the case to the jack.

11. Remove the driveshaft.

12. Disconnect the clutch linkage.

13. On F-Super Duty models, remove the transmission-mounted parking brake. See Section 9.

14. On 4-wheel drive models, remove the transfer case.

15. Remove the transmission rear insulator and lower retainer.

16. Unbolt and remove the crossmember.

17. Remove the transmission-to-engine block bolts.

18. Roll the transmission rearward until the input shaft clears, lower the jack and remove the transmission.

To install:

19. Install 2 guide studs into the lower bolt holes.

20. Raise the transmission until the input shaft splines are aligned with the clutch disc splines. The clutch release bearing and hub must be properly positioned in the release lever fork.

21. Roll the transmission forward and into position on the front case.

22. Install the bolts and torque them to 50 ft. lbs. Remove the guide studs and install and tighten the 2 remaining bolts.

23. Install the crossmember and torque the bolts to 55 ft. lbs.

24. Install the transmission rear insulator and lower retainer. Torque the bolts to 60 ft. lbs.

25. On 4-wheel drive models, install the transfer case.

26. On F-Super Duty models, install the transmission-mounted parking brake. See Section 9.

27. Connect the clutch linkage.

28. Install the driveshaft.

29. Remove the transmission jack.

30. Fill the transmission.

31. Connect the back-up switch wire.

32. Connect the speedometer cable.

33. Lower the van.

34. Install the boot and bezel assembly.

35. Connect the upper shift to from the lower shift lever. Tighten the bolts to 20 ft. lbs.

36. Install the carpet or floor mat.

37. Install the ball from the shift lever.

OVERHAUL

Ford TOD 4-Speed Overdrive

▶ **See Figures 7, 8, 9, 10, 11, 12, 13, 14, 15, 16, 17, 18 and 19**

The Ford TOD 4-speed overdrive transmission is fully synchronized in all forward gears. The 4-speed shift control is serviced as a unit and should not be disassembled. The lubricant capacity is 4.5 pints.

DISASSEMBLY

1. Remove retaining clips and flat washers from the shift rods at the levers.

2. Remove shift linkage control bracket attaching screws and remove shift linkage and control brackets.

3. Remove cover attaching screws. Then lift cover and gasket from the case. Remove the long spring that holds the detent plug in the case. Remove the plug with a magnet.

1. Transmission case assy.
2. Transmission case
3. Chip magnet
4. Spring push-on nut
5. Expansion cup plug
6. Gearshift housing assy.
7. Gearshift housing
8. Gearshift lever pin
9. Dowel
10. Third overdrive shift bias spring
11. Spring retainer plate
12. Rivet
13. Reverse idler gear
14. Idler shaft roller bearings (44)
15. Reverse idler sliding gear
16. Pin
17. Reverse idler gear shaft
18. Countershaft gear
19. Countershaft gear roller bearings (42)
20. ⅞ Flatwasher
21. Front input shaft ball bearing
22. ¾ Flatwasher
23. Retainer ring
24. Snap ring
25. Output shaft
26. First speed gear
27. First and second gear synchronizer assy.
28. First and second clutch hub
29. Reverse sliding gear
30. Synchronizer hub insert
31. Retaining spring
32. Blocking ring
33. Snap ring
34. Second speed gear
35. Low gear thrust washer
36. Retaining ring
37. Overdrive gear
38. Third and fourth gear synchronizer assy.
39. Blocking ring
40. Hub insert
41. Clutch sleeve
42. Retaining spring
44. Third and fourth gear clutch hub
47. Snap ring
48. Reverse rocker arm assy.
49. Pin and housing arm
50. Rocker arm pivot pin
51. Reverse plunger housing
52. Reverse rocker arm
53. O-ring seal
54. ⅜ Retaining ext. ring
55. Reverse plunger spring
56. Reverse rocker plunger
57. Input shaft
58. Input shaft roller bearings (15)
59. Output shaft rear ball bearing
60. Snap ring
61. Snap ring
62. First-second shifter rail
63. Third/overdrive shifter rail
64. Reverse gear shifter rail
65. Speedometer drive gear
66. Extension housing assy.
67. Extension housing
68. Extension housing bushing
69. Extension housing oil seal
70. Third-fourth shift rail
71. Bolt ⁷⁄₁₆-14 × 1.25
72. ⁷⁄₁₆ Ext. tooth washer
73. Input shaft bearing retainer
74. Input shaft oil seal
75. Expansion plug
76. Bolt ⁵⁄₁₆-18 × 0.94
77. Shifter interlock spring
78. Meshlock plunger
79. Countershaft thrust washer
80. Drive screw
81. Filler plug
82. Bolt ⁵⁄₁₆-18 × 1.0
83. Ext. tooth washer
84. Countershaft
85. Reverse idler gear thrust washer
86. Third/overdrive shift pawl
87. Third/overdrive shift gate
88. Service identification tag

89. Back-up lamp switch
90. Back-up lamp switch gasket
91. Electrical wiring clip
92. First-second gearshift fork
93. Third-fourth gearshift fork
94. Reverse gearshift fork
95. Ball 0.25 inch
96. Interlock pin
97. Interlock plunger
98. Plug
99. Overdrive shift control link and pin
100. Retaining ext. ring
101. Finger pin
102. Overdrive shift control link pin assy.
103. Overdrive shift control link shaft
104. Overdrive shift control link
105. Shift control finger pin
106. Cup plug

107. Output shaft thrust washer
108. Screw and washer
109. Pin
110. Housing cap
111. Fourth gear sensing switch
112. Synchro blocking ring
113. Output shaft seal

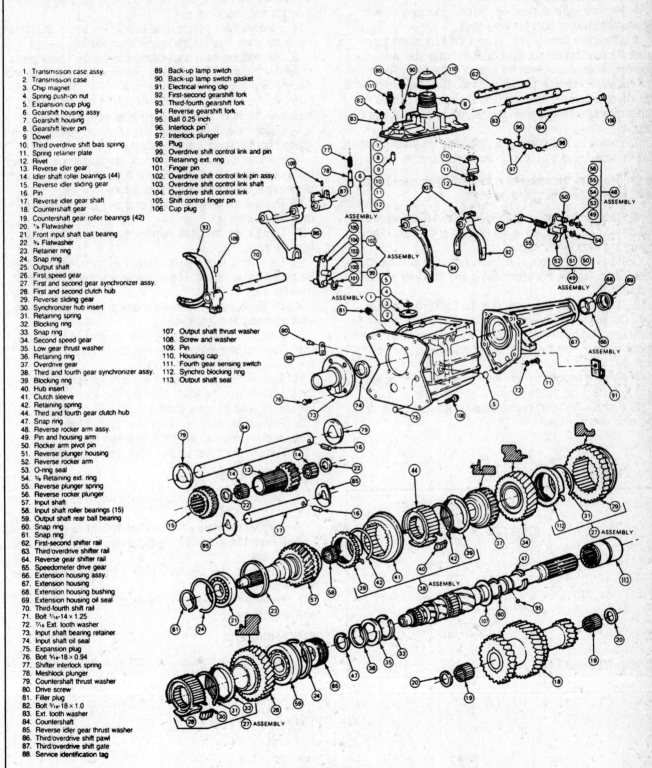

Fig. 7 TOD 4-speed exploded view

84927007

4. Remove extension housing attaching screws. Then, remove extension housing and gasket.

5. Remove input shaft bearing retainer attaching screws. Then, slide retainer from the input shaft.

6. Working a dummy shaft in from the front of the case, drive the countershaft out the rear of the case. Let the countergear assembly lie in the bottom of the case. Remove the set screw from the 1st/2nd shift fork. Slide the 1st/2nd shift rail out of the rear of the case. Use a magnet to remove the interlock detent from between the 1st/2nd and 3rd/4th shift rails.

7. Locate 1st/2nd speed gear shift lever in neutral. Locate 3rd/4th speed gear shift lever in 3rd speed position.

➡**On overdrive transmissions, locate 3rd/4th speed gear shift lever in the 4th speed position.**

8. Remove the lockbolt that holds the 3rd/4th speed shift rail detent spring and plug in the left side of the case. Remove spring and plug with a magnet.

9. Remove the detent mechanism set screw from top of case. Then, remove the detent spring and plug with a small magnet.

10. Remove attaching screw from the 3rd/4th speed shift fork. Tap lightly on the inner end of the shift rail to remove the expansion plug from front of case. Then, withdraw the 3rd/4th speed shift rail from the front. Do not lose the interlock pin from rail.

11. Remove attaching screw from the 1st and 2nd speed shift fork. Slide the 1st/2nd shift rail from the rear of case.

12. Remove the interlock and detent plugs from the top of the case with a magnet.

13. Remove the snapring or disengage retainer that holds the speedometer drive gear to the output shaft, then remove speedometer gear drive ball.

14. Remove the snapring used to hold the output shaft bearing to the shaft. Pull out the output shaft bearing.

15. Remove the input shaft bearing snaprings. Use a press to remove the input shaft bearing. Remove the input shaft and blocking ring from the front of the case.

16. Move output shaft to the right side of the case. Then, maneuver the forks to permit lifting them from the case.

17. Support the thrust washer and 1st speed gear to prevent sliding from the shaft, then lift output shaft from the case.

18. Remove reverse gear shift fork attaching screw. Rotate the reverse shift rail 90°, then, slide the shift rail out the rear of the case. Lift out the reverse shift fork.

19. Remove the reverse detent plug and spring from the case with a magnet.

20. Using a dummy shaft, remove the reverse idler shaft from the case.

21. Lift reverse idler gear and thrust washers from the case. Be careful not to drop the bearing rollers or the dummy shaft from the gear.

22. Lift the countergear, thrust washers, rollers and dummy shaft assembly from the case.

23. Remove the next snapring from the front of the output shaft. Then, slide the 3rd/4th synchronizer blocking ring and the 3rd speed gear from the shaft.

24. Remove the next snapring and the 2nd speed gear thrust washer from the shaft. Slide the 2nd speed gear and the blocking ring from the shaft.

25. Remove the snapring, then slide the 1st/2nd synchronizer, blocking ring and the 1st speed gear from the shaft.

26. Remove the thrust washer from rear of the shaft.

CAM & SHAFT SEALS

1. Remove attaching nut and washers from each shift lever, then remove the three levers.

2. Remove the three cams and shafts from inside the case.

3. Replace the old O-rings with new ones that have been well lubricated.

4. Slide each cam and shaft into its respective bore in the transmission.

5. Install the levers and secure them with their respective washers and nuts.

SYNCHRONIZERS

1. Push the synchronizer hub from each synchronizer sleeve.

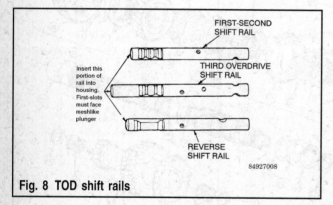

Insert this portion of rail into housing. First-slots must face meshlike plunger

FIRST-SECOND SHIFT RAIL

THIRD OVERDRIVE SHIFT RAIL

REVERSE SHIFT RAIL

84927008

Fig. 8 TOD shift rails

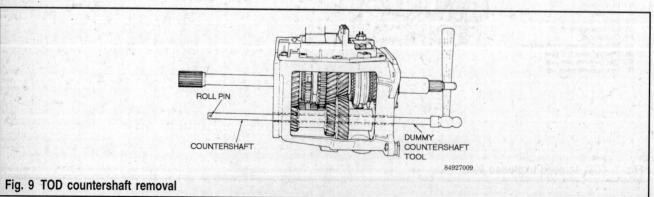

ROLL PIN

COUNTERSHAFT

DUMMY COUNTERSHAFT TOOL

84927009

Fig. 9 TOD countershaft removal

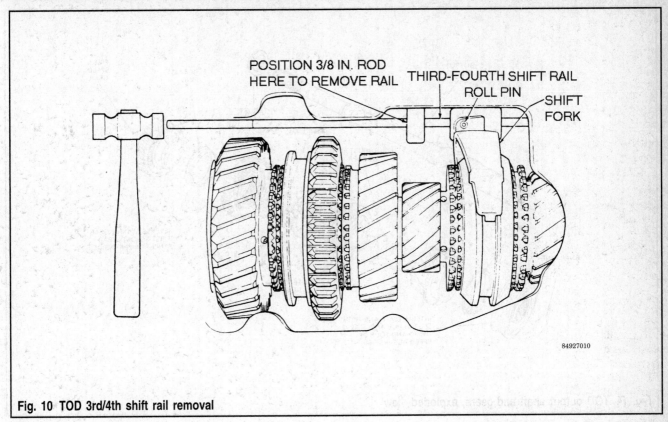

Fig. 10 TOD 3rd/4th shift rail removal

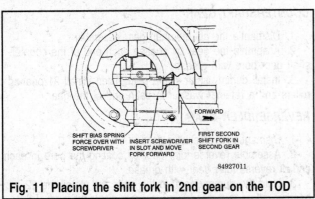

Fig. 11 Placing the shift fork in 2nd gear on the TOD

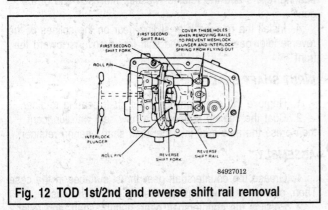

Fig. 12 TOD 1st/2nd and reverse shift rail removal

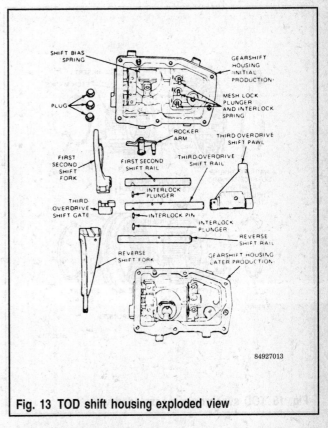

Fig. 13 TOD shift housing exploded view

2. Separate the inserts and springs from the hubs. Do not mix parts of the 1st/2nd with parts of 3rd/4th synchronizers.

3. To assemble, position the hub in the sleeve. Be sure the alignment marks are properly indexed.

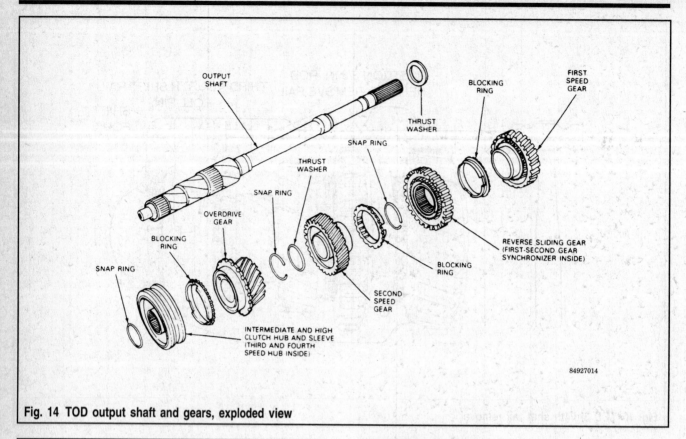

Fig. 14 TOD output shaft and gears, exploded view

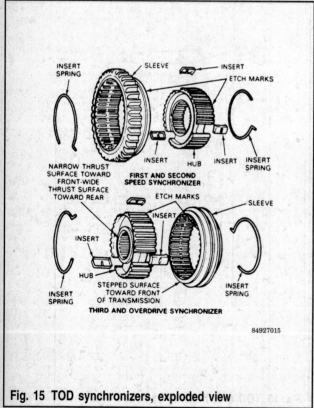

Fig. 15 TOD synchronizers, exploded view

4. Place the three inserts into place on the hub. Install the insert springs so that the irregular surface (hump) is seated in one of the inserts. Do not stagger the springs.

COUNTERSHAFT GEAR

1. Dismantle the countershaft gear assembly.
2. Assemble the gear by coating each end of the countershaft gear bore with grease.
3. Install dummy shaft in the gear. Then install 21 bearing rollers and a retainer washer in each end of the gear.

REVERSE IDLER GEAR

1. Dismantle reverse idler gear.
2. Assemble reverse idler gear by coating the bore in each end of reverse idler gear with grease.
3. Hold the dummy shaft in the gear and install the 22 bearing rollers and the retainer washer into each end of the gear.
4. Install the reverse idler sliding gear on the splines of the reverse idler gear. Be sure the shift fork groove is toward the front.

INPUT SHAFT SEAL

1. Remove the seal from the input shaft bearing retainer.
2. Coat the sealing surface of a new seal with lubricant, then press the new seal into the input shaft bearing retainer.

ASSEMBLY

1. Grease the countershaft gear thrust surfaces in the case. Then, position a thrust washer at each end of the case.
2. Position the countershaft gear, dummy shaft, and roller bearings in the case.
3. Align the gear bore and thrust washers with the bores in the case. Install the countershaft.

4. With the case in a horizontal position, countershaft gear end-play should be from 0.004-0.018 in. (0.10-0.25mm). Use thrust washers to obtain play within these limits.

5. After establishing correct endplay, place the dummy shaft in the countershaft gear and allow the gear assembly to remain on the bottom of the case.

6. Grease the reverse idler gear thrust surfaces in the case, and position the two thrust washers.

7. Position the reverse idler gear, sliding gear, dummy, etc., in place. Make sure that the shift fork groove in the sliding gear is toward the front.

8. Align the gear bore and thrust washers with the case bores and install the reverse idler shaft.

9. Reverse idler gear end-play should be 0.004-0.018 in. (0.10-0.25mm). Use selective thrust washers to obtain play within these limits.

10. Position reverse gear shift rail detent spring and detent plug in the case. Hold the reverse shift fork in place on the reverse idler sliding gear and install the shift rail from the rear of the case. Lock the fork to the rail with the Allen head set screws.

11. Install the 1st/2nd synchronizer onto the output shaft. The 1st and reverse synchronizer hub are a press fit and should be installed with gear teeth facing the rear of the shaft.

➡**On overdrive transmissions, 1st and reverse synchronizer hub is a slip fit.**

12. Place the blocking ring on 2nd gear. Slide 2nd speed gear onto the front of the shaft with the synchronizer coned surface toward the rear.

13. Install the 2nd speed gear thrust washer and snapring.

14. Slide the 4th gear onto the shaft with the synchronizer coned surface front.

15. Place a blocking ring on the 4th gear.

16. Slide the 3rd/4th speed gear synchronizer onto the shaft. Be sure that the inserts in the synchronizer engage the notches in the blocking ring. Install the snapring onto the front of the output shaft.

17. Put the blocking ring on the 1st gear.

18. Slide the 1st gear onto the rear of the output shaft. Be sure that the inserts engage the notches in the blocking ring and that the shift fork groove is toward the rear.

19. Install heavy thrust washer onto the rear of the output shaft.

20. Lower the output shaft assembly into the case.

21. Position the 1st/2nd speed shift fork and the 3rd/4th speed shift fork in place on their respective gears. Rotate them into place.

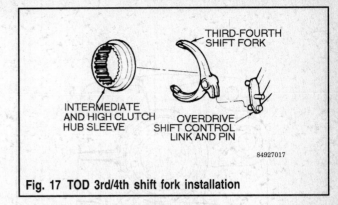

Fig. 17 TOD 3rd/4th shift fork installation

22. Place a spring and detent plug in the detent bore. Place the reverse shift rail into neutral position.

23. Coat the 3rd/4th speed shift rail interlock pin (tapered ends) with grease, then position it in the shift rail.

24. Align the 3rd/4th speed shift fork with the shift rail bores and slide the shift rail into place. Be sure that the three detents are facing the outside of the case. Place the front synchronizer into 4th speed position and install the set screw into the 3rd/4th speed shift fork. Move the synchronizer to neutral position. Install the 3rd/4th speed shift rail detent plug, spring and bolt into the left side of the transmission case. Place the detent plug (tapered ends) in the detent bore.

25. Align 1st/2nd speed shift fork with the case bores and slide the shift rail into place. Lock the fork with the set screw.

26. Coat the input gear bore with a small amount of grease. Then install the 15 bearing rollers.

27. Put the blocking ring in the 3rd/4th synchronizer. Place the input shaft gear in the case. Be sure that the output shaft pilot enters the roller bearing of the input shaft gear.

28. With a new gasket on the input bearing retainer, dip attaching bolts in sealer, install bolts and torque to 30-36 ft. lbs.

29. Press on the output shaft bearing, then install the snapring to hold the bearing.

30. Position the speedometer gear drive ball in the output shaft and slide the speedometer drive gear into place. Secure gear with snapring.

31. Align the countershaft gear bore and thrust washers with the bore in the case. Install the countershaft.

32. With a new gasket in place, install and secure the extension housing. Dip the extension housing screws in sealer, then torque screws to 42-50 ft. lbs.

33. Install the filler plug and the drain plug.

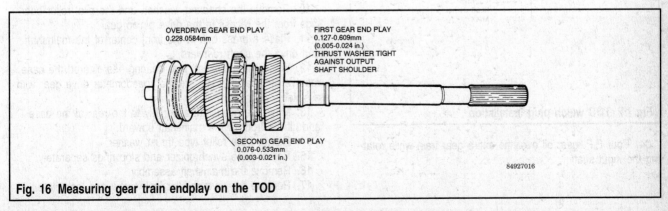

Fig. 16 Measuring gear train endplay on the TOD

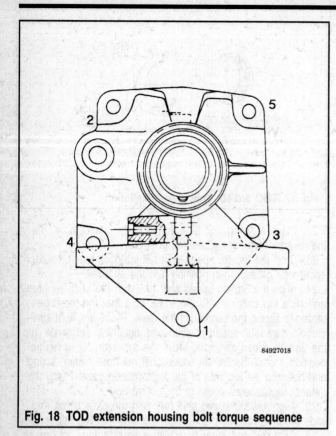

84927018

Fig. 18 TOD extension housing bolt torque sequence

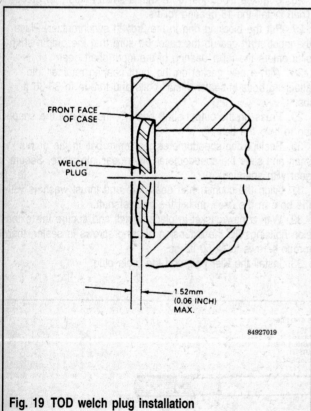

FRONT FACE
OF CASE

WELCH
PLUG

1.52mm
(0.06 INCH)
MAX.

84927019

Fig. 19 TOD welch plug installation

34. Pour E.P. gear oil over the entire gear train while rotating the input shaft.

35. Place each shift fork in all positions to make sure they function properly. Install the remaining detent plug in the case, followed by the spring.

36. With a new cover gasket in place, install the cover. Dip attaching screws in sealer, then torque screws to 14-19 ft. lbs.

37. Coat the 3rd/4th speed shift rail plug bore with sealer. Install a new plug.

38. Secure each shift rod to its respective lever with a spring washer, flat washer and retaining pin.

39. Position the shift linkage control bracket to the extension housing. Install and torque the attaching screws to 12-15 ft. lbs.

NP-435 4-Speed

▶ **See Figures 20 and 21**

DISASSEMBLY

1. Mount the transmission in a holding fixture. Remove the parking brake assembly, if one is installed.

2. Shift the gears into neutral by replacing the gear shift lever temporarily, or by using a bar or screw driver.

3. Remove the cover screws, the 2nd screw from the front on each side is shouldered with a split washer for installation alignment.

4. While lifting the cover, rotate slightly counterclockwise to provide clearance for the shift levers. Remove the cover.

5. Lock the transmission in two gears and remove the output flange nut, the yoke, and the parking brake drum as a unit assembly.

➡ **The drum and yoke are balanced and unless replacement of parts are required, it is recommended that the drum and yoke be removed as a assembly.**

6. Remove the speedometer drive gear pinion and the mainshaft rear bearing retainer.

7. Before removal and disassembly of the drive pinion and mainshaft, measure the end play between the synchronizer stop ring and the 3rd gear. Clearance should be within 0.050-0.070 in. (1.27-1.78mm). If necessary, add corrective shims during assembly.

➡ **Record this reading for reference during assembly.**

8. Remove the drive pinion bearing retainer.

9. Rotate the drive pinion gear to align the space in the pinion gear clutch teeth with the countershaft drive gear teeth. Remove the drive pinion gear and the tapered roller bearing from the transmission by pulling on the pinion shaft, and rapping the face of the case lightly with a brass hammer.

10. Remove the snapring, washer, and the pilot roller bearings from the recess in the drive pinion gear.

11. Place a brass drift in the front center of the mainshaft and drive the shaft rearward.

12. When the mainshaft rear bearing has cleared the case, remove the rear bearing and the speedometer drive gear with a suitable gear puller.

13. Move the mainshaft assembly to the rear of the case and tilt the front of the mainshaft upward.

14. Remove the roller type thrust washer.

15. Remove the synchronizer and stop rings separately.

16. Remove the mainshaft assembly.

17. Remove the reverse idler lock screw and lock plate.

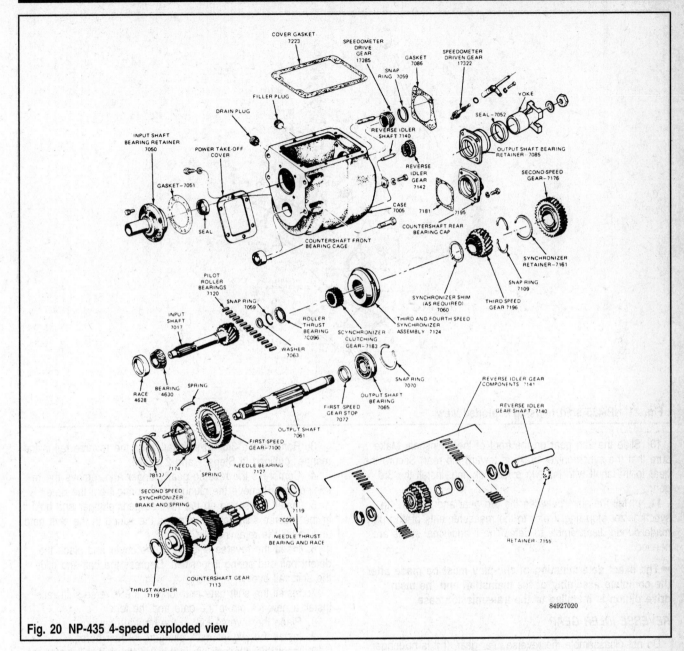

Fig. 20 NP-435 4-speed exploded view

18. Using a brass drift held at an angle, drive the idler shaft to the rear while pulling.

19. Lift the reverse idler gear out of the case.

➡️**If the countershaft gear does not show signs of excessive side play or end play and the teeth are not badly worn or chipped, it may not be necessary to replace the countershaft gear.**

20. Remove the bearing retainer at the rear end of the countershaft. The bearing assembly will remain with the retainer.

21. Tilt the cluster gear assembly and work it out of the transmission case.

22. Remove the front bearings from the case with a suitable driver.

MAINSHAFT

1. Remove the clutch gear snapring.

2. Remove the clutch gear, the synchronizer outer stop ring to 3rd gear shim, and the 3rd gear.

3. Remove the special split lock ring with two screw drivers. Remove the 2nd gear and synchronizer.

4. Remove the 1st/reverse sliding gear.

5. Drive the old seal out of the bearing retainer.

6. Place the mainshaft in a soft-jawed vise with the rear end up.

7. Install the 1st/reverse gear. Be sure the two spline springs, if used, are in place inside the gear as the gear is installed on the shaft.

8. Place the mainshaft in a soft-jawed vise with the front end up.

9. Assemble the 2nd speed synchronizer spring and synchronizer brake on the 2nd gear. Secure the brake with a snapring making sure that the snapring tangs are away from the gear.

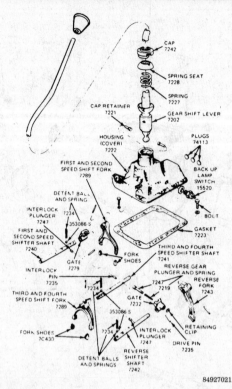

Fig. 21 NP-435 shift housing exploded view

10. Slide the 2nd gear on the front of the mainshaft. Make sure that the synchronizer brake is toward the rear. Secure the gear to the shaft with the two piece lock ring. Install the 3rd gear.

11. Install the shim between the 3rd gear and the 3rd/4th synchronizer stop ring. Refer to the measurements of end play made during disassembly to determine if additional shims are needed.

➡The exact determination of end-play must be made after the complete assembly of the mainshaft and the main drive pinion is installed in the transmission case.

REVERSE IDLER GEAR

Do not disassemble the reverse idler gear. If it is no longer serviceable, replace the assembly complete with the integral bearings.

COVER & SHIFT FORK UNIT

➡The cover and shift fork assembly should be disassembled only if inspection shows worn or damaged parts, or if the assembly is not working properly.

1. Remove the roll pin from the 1st/2nd shift fork and the shift gate with a screw extractor.

➡A square type or a closely wound spiral screw extractor mounted in a tap is preferable for this operation.

2. Move the 1st/2nd shift rail forward and force the expansion plug out of the cover. Cover the detent ball access hole in the cover with a cloth to prevent it from flying out. Remove the rail, fork, and gate from the cover.

3. Remove the 3rd/4th shift rail, then the reverse rail in the manner outlined in Steps 1 and 2 above.

4. Compress the reverse gear plunger and remove the retaining clip. Remove the plunger and spring from the gate.

5. Install the spring on the reverse gear plunger and hold it in the reverse shift gate. Compress the spring in the shift gate and install the retaining clip.

6. Insert the reverse shift rail in the cover and place the detent ball and spring in position. Depress the ball and slide the shift rail over it.

7. Install the shift gate and fork on the reverse shift rail. Install a new roll pin in the gate and the fork.

8. Place the reverse fork in the neutral position.

9. Install the two interlock plungers in their bores.

10. Insert the interlock pin in the 3rd/4th shift rail. Install the shift rail in the same manner as the reverse shift rail.

11. Install the 1st/2nd shift rail in the same manner as outlined above. Make sure the interlock plunger is in place.

12. Check the interlocks by shifting the reverse shift rail into the Reverse position. It should be impossible to shift the other rails with the reverse rail in this position.

13. If the shift lever is to be installed at this point, lubricate the spherical ball seat and place the cap in place.

14. Install the back-up light switch.

15. Install new expansion plugs in the bores of the shift rail holes in the cover. Install the rail interlock hole plug.

DRIVE PINION & BEARING RETAINER
▶ See Figures 22 and 23

1. Remove the tapered roller bearing from the pinion shaft with a suitable tool.

2. Remove the snapring, washer, and the pilot rollers from the gear bore, if they have not been previously removed.

3. Pull the bearing race from the front bearing retainer with a suitable puller.

4. Remove the pinion shaft seal with a suitable tool.

5. Position the drive pinion in an arbor press.

6. Place a wood block on the pinion gear and press it into the bearing until it contacts the bearing inner race.

7. Coat the roller bearings with a light film of grease to hold the bearings in place, and insert them in the pocket of the drive pinion gear.

8. Install the washer and snapring.

9. Press a new seal into the bearing retainer. Make sure that the lip of the seal is toward the mounting surface.

10. Press the bearing race into the retainer.

ASSEMBLY

▶ **See Figures 24 and 25**

1. Press the front countershaft roller bearings into the case until the cage is flush with the front of the transmission case. Coat the bearings with a light film of grease.

2. Place the transmission with the front of the case facing down. If uncaged bearings are used, hold the loose rollers in place in the cap with a light film of grease.

3. Lower the countershaft assembly into the case placing the thrust washer tangs in the slots in the case, and inserting the front end of the shaft into the bearing.

4. Place the roller thrust bearing and race on the rear end of the countershaft. Hold the bearing in place with a light film of grease.

5. While holding the gear assembly in alignment, install the rear bearing retainer gasket, retainer, and bearing assembly. Install and tighten the cap screws.

6. Position the reverse idler gear and bearing assembly in the case.

7. Align the idler shaft so that the lock plate groove in the shaft is in position to install the lock plate.

8. Install the lock plate, washer, and cap screw.

9. Make sure the reverse idler gear turns freely.

10. Lower the rear end of the mainshaft assembly into the case, holding the 1st gear on the shaft. Maneuver the shaft through the rear bearing opening.

➡**With the mainshaft assembly moved to the rear of the case, be sure the 3rd/4th synchronizer and shims remain in position.**

11. Install the roller type thrust bearing.

12. Place a wood block between the front of the case and the front of the mainshaft.

13. Install the rear bearing on the mainshaft by carefully driving the bearing onto the shaft and into the case, snapring flush against the case.

14. Install the drive pinion shaft and bearing assembly. Make sure that the pilot rollers remain in place.

15. Install the spacer and speedometer drive gear.

16. Install the rear bearing retainer and gasket.

17. Place the drive pinion bearing retainer over the pinion shaft, without the gasket.

18. Hold the retainer tight against the bearing and measure the clearance between the retainer and the case with a feeler gauge.

➡**End play in Steps 19 and 20 below allows for normal expansion of parts during operation, preventing seizure and damage to bearings, gears, synchronizers, and shafts.**

19. Install a gasket shim pack 0.010-0.015 in. (0.25-0.38mm) thicker than measured clearance between the retainer and case to obtain the required 0.007-0.017 in. (0.43mm) pinion shaft end play. Tighten the front retainer bolts and recheck the end play.

20. Check the synchronizer end play clearance. It should be 0.050-0.070 in. (1.27-1.78mm) after all mainshaft components are in position and properly tightened. Two sets of feeler gauges are used to measure the clearance. Care should be used to keep both gauges as close as possible to both sides of the mainshaft for best results.

➡**In some cases, it may be necessary to disassemble the mainshaft and change the thickness of the shims to keep the end play clearance within the specified limits, 0.050-0.070 in. (1.27-1.78mm). Shims are available in two thicknesses.**

21. Install the speedometer drive pinion.

22. Install the yoke flange, drum, and drum assembly.

23. Place the transmission in two gears at once, and tighten the yoke flange nut.

24. Shift the gears and/or synchronizers into all gear positions and check for free rotation.

25. Cover all transmissions components with a film of transmission oil to prevent damage during start up after initial lubricant fill-up.

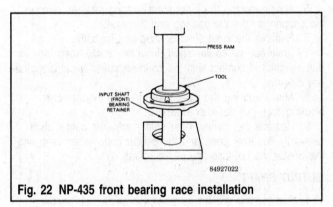

Fig. 22 NP-435 front bearing race installation

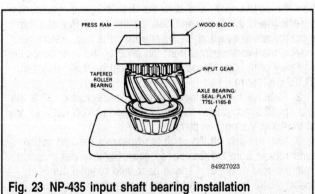

Fig. 23 NP-435 input shaft bearing installation

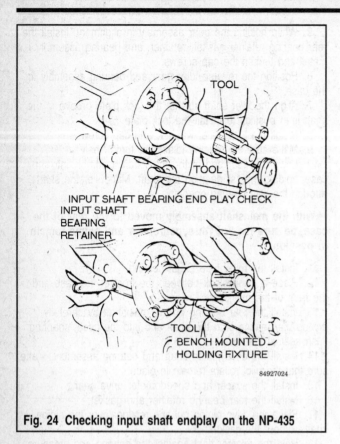

Fig. 24 Checking input shaft endplay on the NP-435

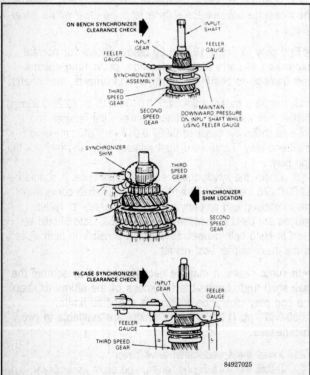

Fig. 25 Measuring input shaft-to-synchronizer clearance on the NP-435

26. Move the gears to the neutral position.
27. Place a new cover gasket on the transmission case, and lower the cover over the transmission.

28. Carefully engage the shift forks into their proper gears. Align the cover.
29. Install a shouldered alignment screw with split washer in the screw hole 2nd from the front of the cover. Try out gear operation by shifting through all ranges. Make sure everything moves freely.
30. Install the remaining cover screws.

T-18, T-19A & T-19C 4-Speed

▶ **See Figures 26, 27, 28, 29, 30, 31, 32, 33, 34, 35, 36, 37, 38, 39, 40 and 41**

The Warner T-18, T-19A and T-19C transmissions have four forward speeds and one reverse. A power take-off opening is provided on certain transmissions, depending upon the models and applications and can be located on either the right or left sides of the case. The T-18 transmissions are synchronized in 2nd, 3rd and 4th speeds only, while the T-19 transmission is synchronized in all forward gears. The disassembly and assembly remains basically the same for the transmission models.

DISASSEMBLY

1. After draining the transmission and removing the parking brake drum (or shoe assembly), lock the transmission in two gears and remove the U-joint flange, oil seal, speedometer driven gear and bearing assembly. Lubricant capacity is 6½ pints.
2. Remove the output shaft bearing retainer and the speedometer drive gear and spacer.
3. Remove the output shaft bearing snapring, and remove the bearing.
4. Remove the countershaft and idler shaft retainer and the power take-off cover.
5. After removing the input shaft bearing retainer, remove the snaprings from the bearing and the shaft.
6. Remove the input shaft bearing and oil baffle.
7. Drive out the countershaft (from the front). Keep the dummy shaft in contact with the countershaft to avoid dropping any rollers.
8. After removing the input shaft and the synchronizer blocking ring, pull the idler shaft.
9. Remove the reverse gear shifter arm, the output shaft assembly, the idler gear, and the cluster gear. When removing the cluster, do not lose any of the rollers.

OUTPUT SHAFT

1. Remove the 3rd/4th speed synchronizer hub snapring from the output shaft, and slide the 3rd/4th speed synchronizer assembly and the 3rd speed gear off the shaft. Remove the synchronizer sleeve and the inserts from the hub. Before removing the two snaprings from the ends of the hub, check the end play of the 2nd speed gear. It should be 0.005-0.024 in. (0.127-0.610mm).
2. Remove the 2nd speed synchronizer snapring. Slide the 2nd speed synchronizer hub gear off the hub. Do not lose any of the balls, springs, or plates.
3. Pull the hub off the shaft, and remove the 2nd speed synchronizer from the 2nd speed gear. Remove the snapring from the rear of the 2nd speed gear, and remove the gear, spacer, roller bearings, and thrust washer from the output shaft. Remove the remaining snapring from the shaft.

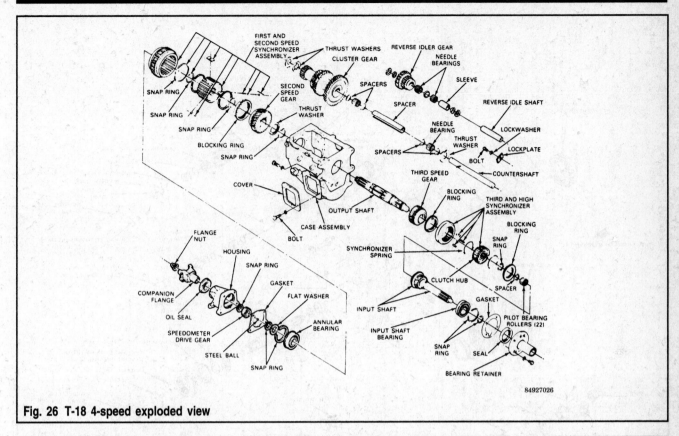

Fig. 26 T-18 4-speed exploded view

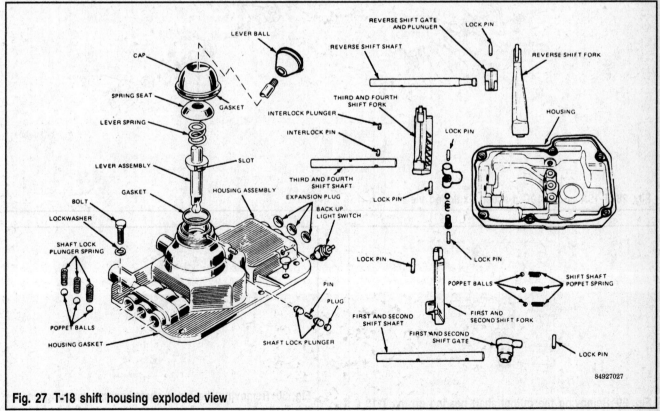

Fig. 27 T-18 shift housing exploded view

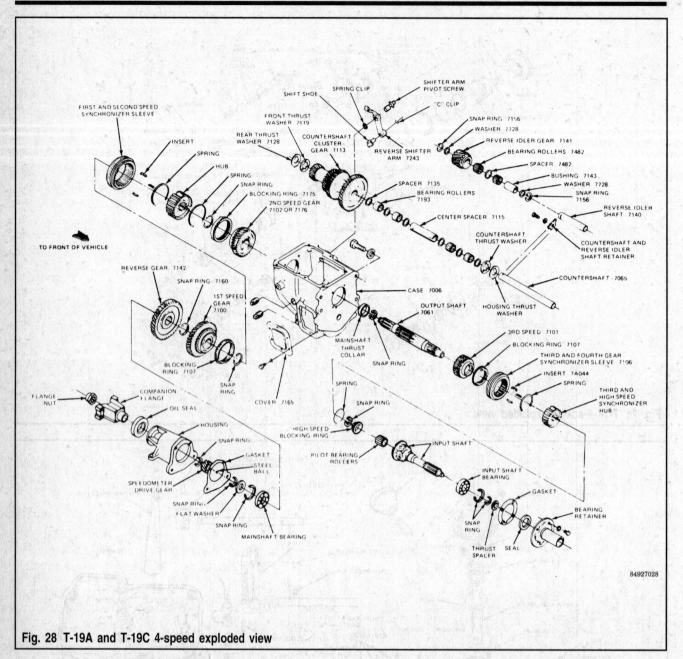

Fig. 28 T-19A and T-19C 4-speed exploded view

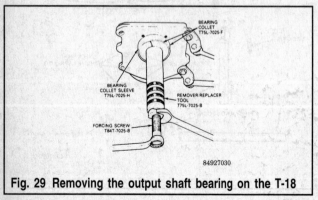

Fig. 29 Removing the output shaft bearing on the T-18

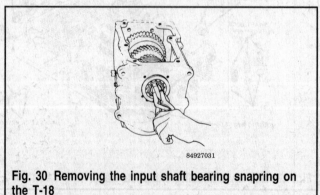

Fig. 30 Removing the input shaft bearing snapring on the T-18

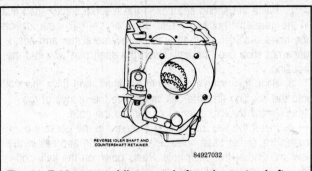

Fig. 31 T-18 reverse idle gear shaft and countershaft retainer

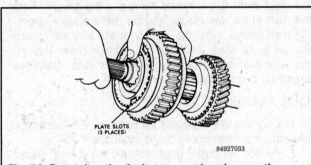

Fig. 32 Removing the 2nd gear synchronizer on the T-18

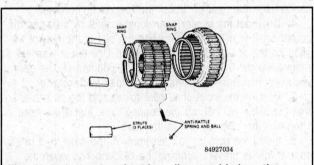

Fig. 33 2nd gear synchronizer disassembled on the T-18

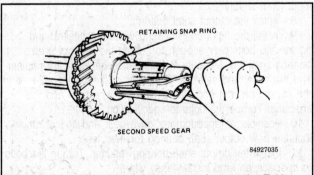

Fig. 34 Removing the 2nd gear snapring on the T-18

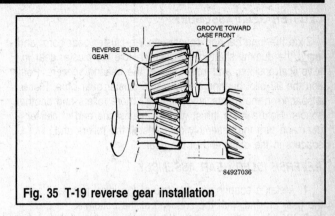

Fig. 35 T-19 reverse gear installation

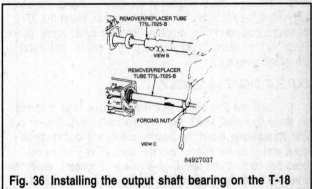

Fig. 36 Installing the output shaft bearing on the T-18

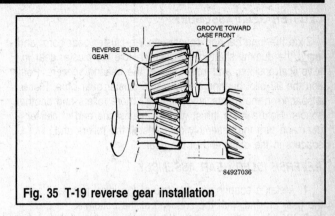

Fig. 37 T-19 reverse shift arm installation

CLUSTER GEAR

Remove the dummy shaft, pilot bearing rollers, bearing spacers, and center spacer from the cluster gear.

REVERSE IDLER GEAR

Rotate the reverse idler gear on the shaft, and if it turns freely and smoothly, disassembly of the unit is not necessary. If any roughness is noticed, disassemble the unit.

GEAR SHIFT HOUSING

1. Remove the housing cap and lever. Be sure all shafts are in neutral before disassembly.
2. Tap the shifter shafts out of the housing while holding one hand over the holes in the housing to prevent loss of the springs and balls. Remove the two shaft lock plungers from the housing.

CLUSTER GEAR ASSEMBLY

Slide the long bearing spacer into the cluster gear bore, and insert the dummy shaft in the spacer. Hold the cluster gear in a vertical position, and install one of the bearing spacers. Position the 22 pilot bearing rollers in the cluster gear bore. Place a spacer on the rollers, and install 22 more rollers and another spacer. Hold a large thrust washer against the end of cluster gear and turn the assembly over. Install the rollers and spacers in the other end of the gear.

REVERSE IDLER GEAR ASSEMBLY

1. Install a snapring in one end of the idler gear, and set the gear on end, with the snapring at the bottom.
2. Position a thrust washer in the gear on top of the snapring. Install the bushing on top of the washer, insert the 37 bearing rollers, and then a spacer followed by 37 more rollers. Place the remaining thrust washer on the rollers, and install the other snapring.

OUTPUT SHAFT ASSEMBLY

1. Install the 2nd speed gear thrust washer and snapring on the output shaft. Hold the shaft vertically, and slide on the 2nd speed gear. Insert the bearing rollers in the 2nd speed gear, and slide the spacer into the gear. (The T-18 model does not contain 2nd speed gear rollers or spacer). Install the snapring on the output shaft at the rear of the 2nd speed gear. Position the blocking ring on the 2nd speed gear. Do not invert the shaft because the bearing rollers will slide out of the gear.
2. Press the 2nd speed synchronizer hub onto the shaft, and install the snapring. Position the shaft vertically in a soft-jawed vise. Position the springs and plates in the 2nd speed synchronizer hub, and place the hub gear on the hub.
3. With the T-19 model, press the 1st and 2nd speed synchronizer onto the shaft and install the snapring. Install the 1st speed gear and snapring on the shaft and press on the reverse gear. For the T-19, ignore Steps 2 and 4.
4. Hold the gear above the hub spring and ball holes, and position one ball at a time in the hub, and slide the hub gear downward to hold the ball in place. Push the plate upward, and insert a small block to hold the plate in position, thereby holding the ball in the hub. Follow these procedures for the remaining balls.
5. Install the 3rd speed gear and synchronizer blocking ring on the shaft.
6. Install the snaprings at both ends of the 3rd and 4th speed synchronizer hub. Stagger the openings of the snaprings so that they are not aligned. Place the inserts in the synchronizer sleeve, and position the sleeve on the hub.
7. Slide the synchronizer assembly onto the output shaft. The slots in the blocking ring must be in line with the synchronizer inserts. Install the snapring at the front of the synchronizer assembly.

GEAR SHIFT HOUSING

1. Place the spring on the reverse gear shifter shaft gate plunger, and install the spring and plunger in the reverse gate. Press the plunger through the gate, and fasten it with the clip. Place the spring and ball in the reverse gate poppet hole. Compress the spring and install the cotter pin.
2. Place the spring and ball in the reverse shifter shaft hole in the gear shift housing. Press down on the ball, and position the reverse shifter shaft so that the reverse shifter arm notch does not slide over the ball. Insert the shaft part way into the housing.
3. Slide the reverse gate onto the shaft, and drive the shaft into the housing until the ball snaps into the groove of the shaft. Install the lock screw lock wire to the gate.
4. Insert the two interlocking plungers in the pockets between the shifter shaft holes. Place the spring and ball in the low and 2nd shifter shaft hole. Press down on the ball, and insert the shifter shaft part way into the housing.
5. Slide the low and 2nd shifter shaft gate onto the shaft, and install the corresponding shifter fork on the shaft so that the offset of the fork is toward the rear of the housing. Push the shaft all the way into the housing until the ball engages the shaft groove. Install the lock screw and wire that fastens the fork to the shaft. Install the 3rd and high shifter shaft in the same manner. Check the interlocking system. Install new expansion plugs in the shaft bores.

CASE ASSEMBLY

1. Coat all parts, especially the bearings, with transmission lubricant to prevent scoring during initial operation.
2. Position the cluster gear assembly in the case. Do not lose any rollers.
3. Place the idler gear assembly in the case, and install the idler shaft. Position the slot in the rear of the shaft so that it can engage the retainer. Install the reverse shifter arm.
4. Drive out the cluster gear dummy shaft by installing the countershaft from the rear. Position the slot in the rear of the shaft so that it can engage the retainer. Use thrust washers as required to get 0.006-0.020 in. (0.152-0.508mm) cluster gear end play. Install the countershaft and idler shaft retainer.
5. Position the input shaft pilot rollers and the oil baffle, so that the baffle will not rub the bearing race. Install the input shaft and the blocking ring in the case.
6. Install the output shaft assembly in the case, and use a special tool to prevent jamming the blocking ring when the input shaft bearing is installed.
7. Drive the input shaft bearing onto the shaft. Install the thickest select-fit snapring that will fit on the bearing. Install the input shaft snapring.
8. Install the output shaft bearing.
9. Install the input shaft bearing without a gasket, and tighten the bolts only enough to bottom the retainer on the bearing snapring. Measure the clearance between the retainer and the case, and select a gasket (or gaskets) that will seal in the oil and prevent end play between the retainer and the snapring. Torque the bolts to specification.
10. Position the speedometer drive gear and spacer, and install a new output shaft bearing retainer seal.
11. Install the output shaft bearing retainer. Torque the bolts to specification, and install safety wire.
12. Install the brake shoe (or drum), and torque the bolts to specification. Install the U-joint flange. Lock the transmission in two gears and torque the nut to specification.
13. Install the power take-off cover plates with new gaskets. Fill the transmission according to specifications.

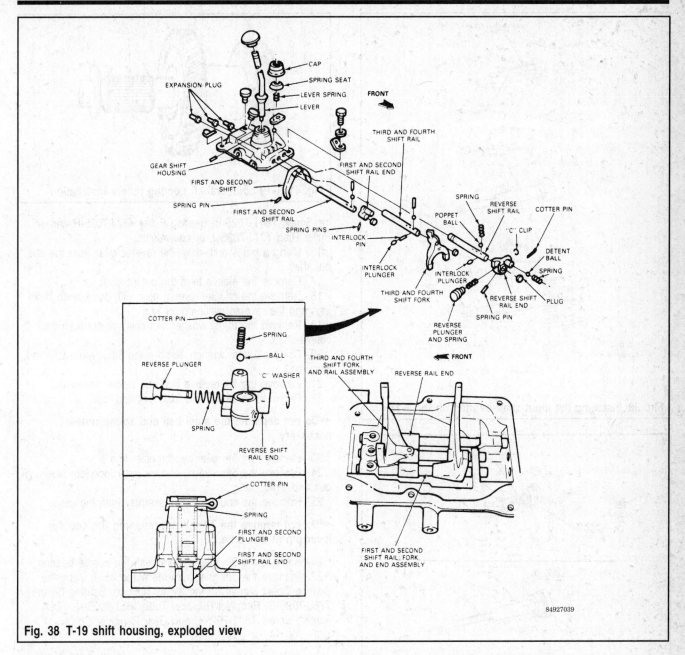

Fig. 38 T-19 shift housing, exploded view

Mazda M5OD 5-Speed

▶ See Figures 42, 43, 44, 45, 46, 47, 48, 49, 50, 51, 52, 53, 54, 55 and 56

CASE DISASSEMBLY

1. Remove the drain plug.
2. Remove the shift lever from the top cover.
3. Remove the 10 top cover bolts and lift off the cover. Discard the gasket.
4. Remove the 9 extension housing bolts. Pry gently at the indentations provided and separate the extension housing from the case.

➡**If you would like to remove the extension housing seal, remove it with a puller BEFORE separating the extension housing from the case.**

5. Remove the rear oil passage from the extension housing using a 10mm socket.

6. Remove and discard the anti-spill seal from the output shaft.
7. Remove the speedometer drive gear and ball. If you're going to replace the gear, replace it with one of the same color.
8. Lock the transmission into 1st and 3rd gears.
9. Using a hammer and chisel, release the staked areas securing the output shaft and countershaft locknuts.
10. Using a 32mm socket, remove and discard the countershaft rear bearing locknut.
11. Remove the countershaft bearing and thrust washer.
12. Using Mainshaft Locknut Wrench T88T-7025-A and Remover Tube T75L-7025-B, or equivalents, remove and discard the output shaft locknut.
13. Using a 17mm wrench, remove the reverse idler shaft bolt.
14. Remove the reverse idler gear assembly by pulling it rearward.

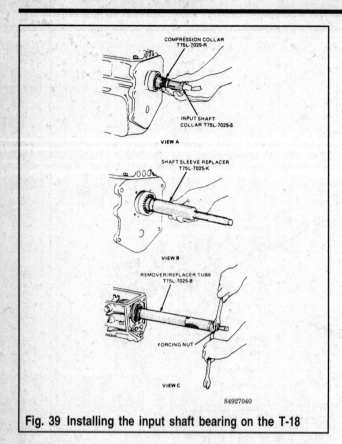

Fig. 39 Installing the input shaft bearing on the T-18

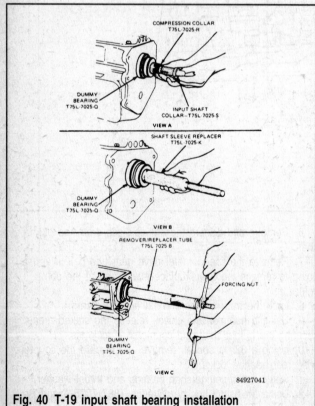

Fig. 40 T-19 input shaft bearing installation

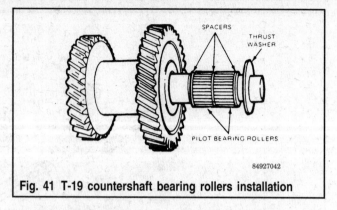

Fig. 41 T-19 countershaft bearing rollers installation

ing Screw T84T-7025-B, Bearing Puller T77J-7025-H and Puller Ring T77J-7025-J, or equivalents.

16. Using a brass drift, drive the reverse gear from the output shaft.

17. Remove the sleeve from the output shaft.

18. Remove the counter/reverse gear with two needle bearings and the reverse synchronizer ring.

19. Remove the thrust washer and split washer from the countershaft.

20. Using a 12mm wrench, remove the 5th/reverse shift rod fixing bolt.

21. Remove the 5th/reverse hub and sleeve assembly.

22. Remove the 5th/reverse shift fork and rod.

➡**Do not separate the steel ball and spring unless necessary.**

23. Remove the 5th gear synchronizer ring.

24. Remove the 5th/reverse counter lever lockplate retaining bolt and inner circlip.

25. Remove the counter lever assembly from the case.

➡**Do not remove the Torx® nut retaining the counter lever pin at this time.**

26. Remove the 5th gear counter with the needle bearing.

27. Remove the 5th gear from the output shaft using the Bearing Collet Sleeve for the 3½ in. (89mm). Bearing Collets T75L-7025-G, Remover/Replacer Tube T85T-7025-A, TOD Forcing Screw T84T-7025-B and Gear Remover Collet T88T-7061-A, or equivalents.

➡**For reference during assembly, observe that the longer of the 2 collars on the 5th gear faces forward.**

28. Remove the 5th gear sleeve and Woodruff key using TOD Forcing Screw T84T-7025-B, Countershaft 5th Gear Sleeve Puller T88T-7025-J, Gear Removal Collets T88T-7025-J1 and Remover/Replacer Tube T77J-7025-B, or equivalents.

29. Remove the 6 center bearing cover retaining bolts and lift off the cover.

➡**There is a reference arrow on the cover which points upward.**

30. Remove the 6 front bearing cover bolts.

31. Remove the front bearing cover by threading 2 of the retaining bolts back into the cover at the service bolt locations

15. Remove the output shaft rear bearing from the output shaft using Remover/Replacer Tube T75L-7025-B, TOD Forc-

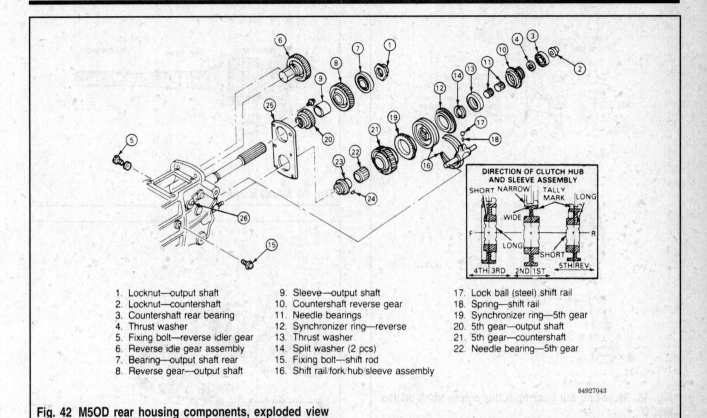

1. Locknut—output shaft
2. Locknut—countershaft
3. Countershaft rear bearing
4. Thrust washer
5. Fixing bolt—reverse idler gear
6. Reverse idle gear assembly
7. Bearing—output shaft rear
8. Reverse gear—output shaft
9. Sleeve—output shaft
10. Countershaft reverse gear
11. Needle bearings
12. Synchronizer ring—reverse
13. Thrust washer
14. Split washer (2 pcs)
15. Fixing bolt—shift rod
16. Shift rail/fork/hub/sleeve assembly
17. Lock ball (steel) shift rail
18. Spring—shift rail
19. Synchronizer ring—5th gear
20. 5th gear—output shaft
21. 5th gear—countershaft
22. Needle bearing—5th gear

84927043

Fig. 42 M5OD rear housing components, exploded view

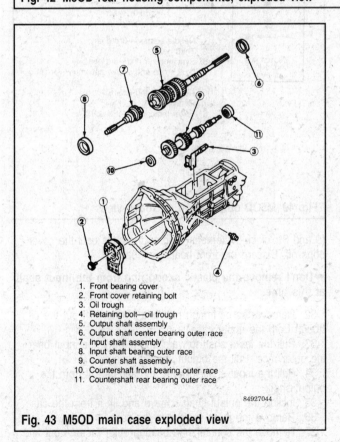

1. Front bearing cover
2. Front cover retaining bolt
3. Oil trough
4. Retaining bolt—oil trough
5. Output shaft assembly
6. Output shaft center bearing outer race
7. Input shaft assembly
8. Input shaft bearing outer race
9. Counter shaft assembly
10. Countershaft front bearing outer race
11. Countershaft rear bearing outer race

84927044

Fig. 43 M5OD main case exploded view

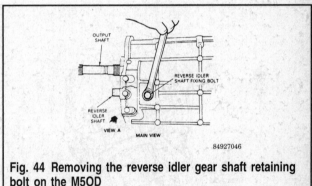

84927046

Fig. 44 Removing the reverse idler gear shaft retaining bolt on the M5OD

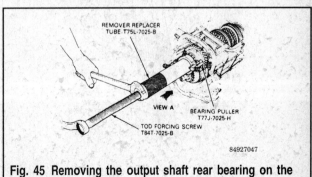

84927047

Fig. 45 Removing the output shaft rear bearing on the M5OD

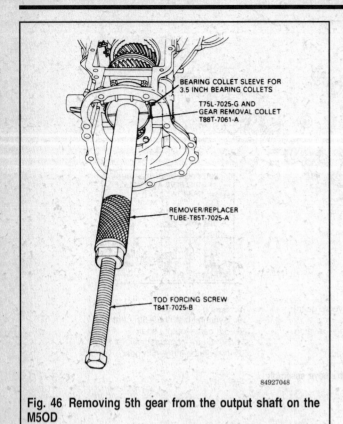

BEARING COLLET SLEEVE FOR
3.5 INCH BEARING COLLETS

T75L-7025-G AND
GEAR REMOVAL COLLET
T88T-7061-A

REMOVER/REPLACER
TUBE-T85T-7025-A

TOD FORCING SCREW
T84T-7025-B

84927048

Fig. 46 Removing 5th gear from the output shaft on the M5OD

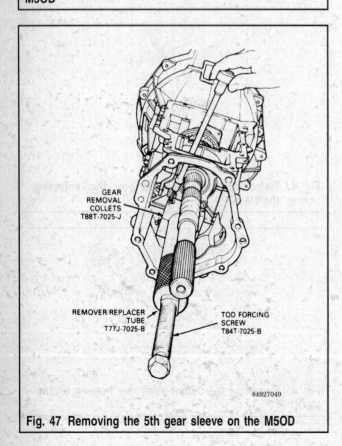

GEAR
REMOVAL
COLLETS
T88T-7025-J

REMOVER/REPLACER
TUBE
T77J-7025-B

TOD FORCING
SCREW
T84T-7025-B

84927049

Fig. 47 Removing the 5th gear sleeve on the M5OD

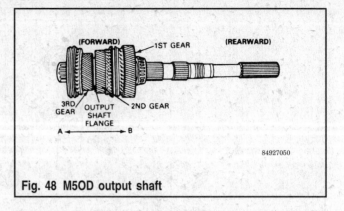

(FORWARD)   1ST GEAR   (REARWARD)

3RD
GEAR   OUTPUT   2ND GEAR
SHAFT
FLANGE

A ← → B

84927050

Fig. 48 M5OD output shaft

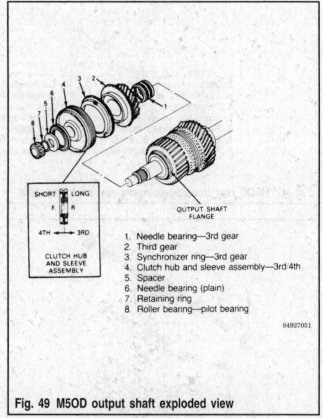

SHORT   LONG
F   R
4TH ← → 3RD

CLUTCH HUB
AND SLEEVE
ASSEMBLY

OUTPUT SHAFT
FLANGE

1. Needle bearing—3rd gear
2. Third gear
3. Synchronizer ring—3rd gear
4. Clutch hub and sleeve assembly—3rd/4th
5. Spacer
6. Needle bearing (plain)
7. Retaining ring
8. Roller bearing—pilot bearing

84927051

Fig. 49 M5OD output shaft exploded view

(9 and 3 o'clock). Alternately tighten the bolts until the cover pops off. Discard the front bearing oil baffle.

➡**Don't remove the plastic scoop ring from the input shaft at this time.**

32. Remove the oil trough retaining bolt and lift out the oil trough from the upper case.

33. Pull the input shaft forward and remove the input bearing outer race. Pull the output shaft rearward.

34. Pull the input shaft forward and separate it from the output shaft.

35. Incline the output shaft upward and lift it from the case.

36. Remove the input shaft from the case.

37. Remove the countershaft bearing outer races (front and center) by moving the countershaft forward and rearward.

38. Pull the countershaft rearward far enough to permit tool clearance behind the front countershaft bearing. Using Bearing

Race Puller T88T-7120-A and Slide Hammer T50T-100-A, or equivalents, remove the front countershaft bearing.

✳✳WARNING

Tap gently during bearing removal. A forceful blow can cause damage to the bearing and/or case.

39. Remove the countershaft through the upper opening of the case.

40. Input Shaft Disassembly and Assembly:

a. Remove and discard the plastic scoop ring.

b. Press the tapered roller bearing from the input shaft using Bearing Cone Remover T71P-4621 — b, or equivalent, and an arbor press.

c. Install the input shaft tapered roller bearing onto the input shaft using a press and Bearing Cone Replacer T88T-7025-B, or equivalent.

d. Install the plastic scoop ring onto the input shaft. Manually rotate the ring clockwise to ensure that the input shaft oil holes properly engage the scoop ring. A click should be heard as the scoop ring notches align with the input shaft holes.

41. Output Shaft Disassembly and Assembly:

a. Remove the pilot bearing needle roller, snapring, needle bearing and spacer from the front (short side) of the output shaft.

b. Position the front (short side) of the shaft upward and lift off the 3rd/4th clutch hub and sleeve assembly, 3rd gear synchronizing ring, 3rd gear, and needle bearing.

c. Turn the shaft so that the long end faces upward.

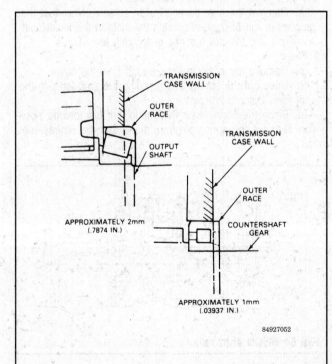

Fig. 50 Installing the output shaft center bearing on the M5OD

d. Place the output shaft into a press with the press cradle contacting the lower part of the 2nd gear.

➡**Make sure that the output shaft flange doesn't contact or ride up on the press cradle.**

42. Press off the following as a unit:
- center bearing,
- 1st gear sleeve,
- 1st gear,
- needle bearing,
- 1st/2nd clutch hub and sleeve,
- 1st/2nd synchronizer rings,
- 2nd gear, and
- needle bearing using Bearing Replacer T53T-4621-B and Bearing Cone Replacer T88T-7025-B, or equivalents. Use T53T-4621-B as a press plate, and Bearing Cone Replacer T88T-7025-B to protect the inner race rollers.

43. Position the output shaft so the rear (long end) faces upward and press on the following parts, in the order listed, using T53T-4621-B and T75L-1165-B, or equivalents:
- 2nd gear needle bearing
- 2nd gear
- 2nd gear synchronizer ring
- 1st/2nd clutch hub and sleeve
- 1st gear synchronizer ring
- 1st gear needle bearing
- 1st gear
- 1st gear sleeve
- center bearing

➡**Make sure that the center bearing race ins installed in the case. When installing the 1st/2nd clutch hub and sleeve make sure that the smaller width sleeve faces the 2nd gear side. Make sure that the reference marks face the rear of the transmission.**

44. Install the center bearing on the output shaft.

45. Position the output shaft so that the front of the shaft flange faces upward. Install the 3rd gear needle bearing, 3rd gear and 3rd gear synchronizer ring.

46. Install the 3rd/4th clutch hub and sleeve:

• Mate the clutch hub synchronizer key groove with the reference mark on the clutch hub sleeve. The mark should face rearward.

• Install the longer flange on the clutch hub sleeve towards the 3rd gear side.

➡**The front and rear sides of the clutch hub are identical, except for the reference mark.**

47. Install the spacer, needle bearing (with rollers upward), retaining ring, and pilot bearing roller.

48. Install the original retaining ring. Using a feeler gauge, check the clutch hub endplay. Endplay should be 0-0.05mm (0-0.0019 in.). If necessary, adjust the endplay by using a new retaining ring. Retaining ring are available in 0.05mm increments in sizes ranging from 1.5mm to 1.95mm.

49. Countershaft Disassembly and Assembly:

a. Place the countershaft in a press with Bearing Cone Remover T71P-4621-B, or equivalent, and remove the countershaft bearing inner race.

b. Using a press and bearing splitter D84L-1123-A, or equivalent, remove the countershaft front bearing inner race.

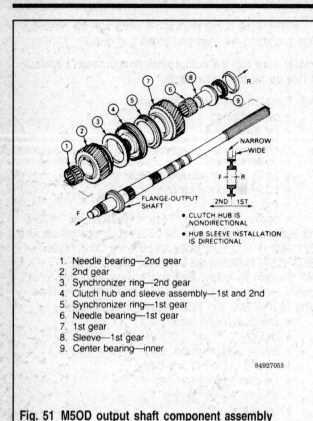

1. Needle bearing—2nd gear
2. 2nd gear
3. Synchronizer ring—2nd gear
4. Clutch hub and sleeve assembly—1st and 2nd
5. Synchronizer ring—1st gear
6. Needle bearing—1st gear
7. 1st gear
8. Sleeve—1st gear
9. Center bearing—inner

84927053

Fig. 51 M5OD output shaft component assembly

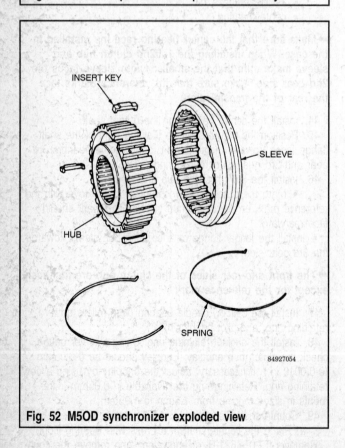

84927054

Fig. 52 M5OD synchronizer exploded view

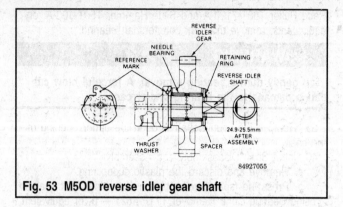

84927055

Fig. 53 M5OD reverse idler gear shaft

c. Assemble the shaft in the press in the reverse order of disassembly.

50. Reverse Idler Gear Shaft Disassembly and Assembly:

51. Remove the following parts:
- Retaining ring
- Spacer
- Idler gear
- Needle bearings
- Thrust washer

52. Install the thrust washer making sure that the tab mates with the groove in the shaft.

53. Install the needle bearings, idler gear and spacer.

54. Install the original retaining ring onto the shaft.

55. Insert a flat feeler gauge between the retaining ring and the reverse idler gear to measure the reverse idler gear endplay. Endplay should be 0.1-0.2mm. If not, use a new retaining ring. Retaining rings are available in 0.5mm increments in thicknesses ranging from 1.5 to 1.9mm.

56. Top Cover Disassembly and Assembly:

a. Remove the dust cover (3 allen screws). Note that the grooves in the bushing align with the slots in the lower shift lever ball and the notch in the lower shift lever faces forward.

b. Remove the back-up lamp switch from the cover.

c. Drive out the spring pins retaining the shift forks to the shift rails. Discard the pins.

d. Place the 5th/reverse shift rail in the fully forward position. Remove the spring pin from the end of the 5th/reverse rail.

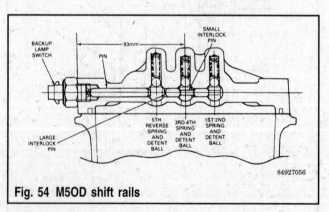

84927056

Fig. 54 M5OD shift rails

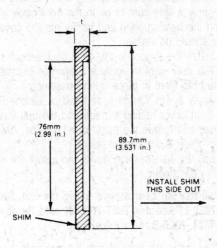

SHIM SELECT CHART — M50D R2

Part Number	Thickness (t)
E8TZ-7029-FA	1.4mm (0.0551 in.)
E8TZ-7029-GA	1.5mm (0.0590 in.)
E8TZ-7029-Ha	1.6mm (0.0629 in.)
E8TZ-7029-Ja	1.7mm (0.0669 in.)
E8TZ-7029-S	1.8mm (0.0708 in.)
E8TZ-7029-T	1.9mm (0.0748 in.)
E8TZ-7029-U	2.0mm (0.0787 in.)
E8TZ-7029-V	2.1mm (0.0826 in.)
E8TZ-7029-W	2.2mm (0.0866 in.)
E8TZ-7029-X	2.3mm (0.0905 in.)
E8TZ-7029-Y	2.4mm (0.0944 in.)
E8TZ-7029-Z	2.5mm (0.0984 in.)
E8TZ-7029-AA	2.6mm (0.1023 in.)
E8TZ-7029-BA	2.7mm (0.1062 in.)
E8TZ-7029-CA	2.8mm (0.1102 in.)
E8TZ-7029-DA	2.9mm (0.1141 in.)
E8TZ-7029-EA	3.0mm (0.1181 in.)

84927057

Fig. 55 M5OD shift selection chart

e. Remove the 3 rubber plugs from the shift rod service bores.

✳✳CAUTION

Wear safety goggles when performing the shift rail removal procedure! Cover the lock ball bores and friction device and spring seats with a heavy cloth held firmly in place. The ball/friction device and spring can fly out during removal, causing possible personal injury!

f. Remove the 5th/reverse shift rail from the top cover through the service bore. It may be necessary to rock the shift rail from side-to-side with a $5/16$ in. (8mm) punch while maintaining rearward pressure.

g. Remove the 1st/2nd shift rail from the cover through the service bore. It may be necessary to rock the shift rail from side-to-side with a $5/16$ in. (8mm) punch while maintaining rearward pressure.

h. Remove the 3rd/4th shift rail from the cover through the service bore. It may be necessary to rock the shift rail from side-to-side with a $5/16$ in. (8mm) punch while maintaining rearward pressure.

i. Remove the 5th/reverse cam lockout plate retaining bolts using a 10mm socket. Remove the plate.

j. Install the 5th/reverse cam lockout plate. Torque the bolts to 72-84 inch lbs.

k. Position the 3rd/4th shift rail into the cover through the service bore. It may be necessary to rock the shift rail from side-to-side with a $5/16$ in. (8mm) punch, while maintaining forward pressure.

l. Engage the 3rd/4th shift fork with the shift rail.

m. Position the detent ball and spring into the cover spring seats. Compress the detent ball and spring and push the shift rail into position over the detent ball.

n. Position the friction device and spring into the cover spring seats. Compress the friction device and spring and push the shift rail into position over the friction device.

o. Install the spring pins retaining the shift rail to the cover.

p. Install the spring retaining the 3rd/4th shift fork to the shift rail.

q. Position the 1st/2nd shift rail in the cover through the service bore. It may be necessary to rock the shift rail from side-to-side with a $5/16$ in. (8mm) punch, while maintaining forward pressure.

r. Engage the 1st/2nd shift fork with the shift rail.

s. Position the detent ball and spring into the cover seats.

t. Compress the detent ball and spring and push the shift rail into position over the detent ball.

u. Position the friction device and spring into the cover seats. Compress the friction device and spring and push the shift rail into position over the friction device.

v. Install the spring pins retaining the shift rail to the cover. Install the spring pin retaining the 1st/2nd shift fork to the shift rail.

w. Position the 5th/reverse shift rail in the top cover through the service bore. It may be necessary to rock the shift rail from side-to-side with a $5/16$ in. (8mm) punch, while maintaining forward pressure. Engage the 5th/reverse shift fork with the shift rail. Position the detent ball and spring into the cover seats. Compress the detent ball and spring and push the shift rail into position over the detent ball.

x. Install the spring pins retaining the shift rail to the cover. Install the spring pin retaining the 5th/reverse shift fork to the shift rail.

y. Install the rubber plugs.

z. Install the interlock pins into the 1st/2nd and 3rd/4th shift rails. Note that the pins are different sizes.

❋❋WARNING

Use of the wrong size pins will affect neutral start and/or back-up light switch operation.

Apply non-hardening sealer to the threads of the back-up light switch and install it. Torque the switch to 18-26 ft. lbs. Install the dust cover.

GENERAL INSPECTION

Inspect all parts for wear or damage. Replace any part that seems suspect. Output shaft runout must not exceed 0.05mm. Replace the shaft is it does. Synchronizer-to-gear clearance must not exceed 0.8mm. Replace the synchronizer ring or gear if necessary. Shift fork-to-clutch hub clearance must not exceed 0.8mm.

GENERAL CASE ASSEMBLY

1. Place the countershaft assembly into the case.
2. Place the input shaft in the case. Make sure that the needle roller bearing is on the shaft.
3. Place the output shaft assembly in the case. Mate the input and out shafts. Make sure that the 4th gear synchronizer is installed.
4. Drive the output shaft center bearing into place with a brass drift.
5. Install the countershaft center bearing. Make sure that the center bearing outer races are squarely seated in their bores.
6. Position the center bearing cover on the case with the arrow upwards. Torque the cover bolts to 14-19 ft. lbs. Use only bolts marked with a grade **8** on the bolt head.
7. Position the transmission on end with the input end up. Make sure that the input shaft front bearing outer race is squarely positioned in its bore. Install the front cover oil seal with a seal driver.
8. Install the countershaft front bearing.
9. Check and record the following dimensions:

a. Check and record the height of the input shaft bearing outer race above the transmission front bearing cover mating surface.

b. Check and record the depth of the front cover outer race bore at the input shaft.

c. Check and record the depth of the countershaft front bearing race (case-to-cover mating surface).

d. Check and record the depth of the front cover outer race bore at the output shaft.

10. Select the proper shims using the following formulae:

- Dimension b - (dimension a + the shim thickness) = 0.05-0.15mm
- Dimension c + (dimension d - the shim thickness) = 0.15-0.25mm

Shims are available in 0.1mm increments ranging from 1.4mm to 3.0mm thick.

11. Clean the mating surfaces of the transmission and front cover.

12. Wrap the input shaft splines with masking tape.

13. Apply a light coat of oil to the front cover oil seal lip. Position the bearing shim and baffle into the cover. The shim groove should be visible.

14. Install the spacer in the case countershaft front bearing bore. You may want to apply a coating of chassis grease to parts to hold them in place during assembly.

15. Apply a 1/8in. (3mm) wide bead of silicone RTV sealant to the front cover mating surface and the bolt threads. Install the cover and torque the bolts to 9-12 ft. lbs. Always us bolts marked grade **6** on the bolt head.

16. Lay the transmission down and install the woodruff key and 5th gear sleeve.

➡**Install the 5th gear sleeve using the nut, Shaft Adapter T75L-7025-L, Adapter T88T-7025-J2 and Remover/Replacer Tube T75L-7025-B, or equivalents.**

17. Install the 5th gear needle bearing onto the countershaft 5th gear.

18. Install the 5th gear onto the output shaft using Gear Installation Spacers T88T-7025-F, and -G, Shaft Adapter T75L-7025-P, Shaft Adapter Screw T75L-7025-K, Remover/Replacer Tube T75L-7025-B (2-wheel drive only) or Remover/Replacer Tube T85T-7025-A (4-wheel drive models), nut and washer, or equivalents. Make sure that the long flange on the 5th gear faces forward.

19. On 2-wheel drive models: install T88T-7025-F. When the tool bottoms, add T88T-7025-G and press the 5th gear assembly all the way into position.   On 4-wheel drive models: follow the procedure for 2-wheel drive, except use T85T-7025-A and T84T-7025-A.

20. Position counterlever assembly in the transmission and install the thrust washer and retaining ring. Apply sealant on the counterlever fixing bolt threads. Install the counterlever fixing bolt and torque it to 72-84 inch lbs.

21. Position the 5th/reverse shift fork and shift rail in the top cover. Insert the 5th/reverse shift rail through the top cover bore and the 5th/reverse shift fork. Install the spring and detent ball on the lower part of the rod.

22. Assemble the 5th/reverse synchronizer hub, sleeve and 5th gear synchronizer ring on the 5th/reverse shift fork and rod. The longer flange faces front. The reference mark on the synchronizer sleeve faces the reverse gear side.

23. Install the 5th/reverse shift fork and rail assembly on the countershaft. Mate the shift fork gate to the 5th/reverse counterlever end. Install the 5th/reverse fork and shift rail with the threaded fixing bolt bores aligned.

➡**It's easier if you place the 5th/reverse shift fork into the rearmost of the three detent positions. Return the shift fork to the neutral position after assembly.**

24. Apply sealant to the 5th/reverse shift rail fixing bolt threads. Install the 5th/reverse shift rail fixing bolt in the case. Torque the 5th/reverse shift rail bolt to 16-22 ft. lbs.

25. Apply sealant to the oil passage retaining bolt. Position the oil passage in the case and torque the bolt to 72-84 inch lbs.

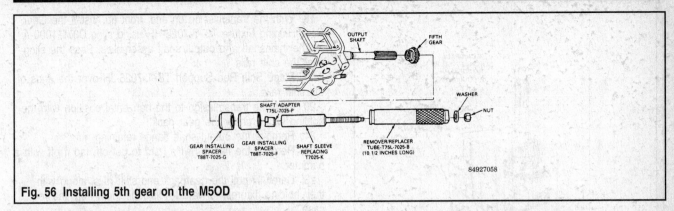

Fig. 56 Installing 5th gear on the M5OD

26. Install the split washer and thrust washer onto the countershaft. If the clutch hub and/or counter reverse gear have been replaced, new split washers must be selected to maintain endplay within specifications. Check the endplay with a flat feeler gauge. Endplay should be 0.2-0.3mm. Split washers are provided in 0.1mm increments ranging from 3.0-3.5mm.

27. Install the reverse synchronizer ring and needle bearings into the counter reverse gear. Install the counter reverse gear and needle bearings onto the countershaft. Install the thrust washer.

28. Push the thrust washer forward by hand against the shoulder on the countershaft. Maintain forward pressure and insert a flat feeler gauge between the thrust washer and the counter reverse gear. Counter reverse endplay should be 0.2-0.3mm. Thrust washers are available in 0.2mm increments ranging from 7.4-7.8mm thicknesses.

29. Temporarily install a spacer, with an inner bore larger than 21mm and an outer diameter smaller than 36mm, 15-20mm overall length, in place of the countershaft bearing. Loosely install the locknut.

30. Install the reverse idler gear assembly. Apply sealant to the threads of the reverse idler gear fixing bolt. Torque the bolt to 58-86 ft. lbs.

31. Drive the sleeve and reverse gear assembly into place on the output shaft using Gear Installation Spacer T88T-7025-G, Shaft Adapter T75L-7025-P, Shaft Adapter Screw T75L-7025-P, Shaft Adapter Screw T75L-7025-K, Remover/Replacer Tube T75L-7025-B (2-wheel drive), Remover/Replacer Tube T85T-7025-A (4-wheel drive), nut and washer, or equivalents. Install the reverse gear with the longer flange facing forward.

32. Install the output shaft rear bearing using Gear Installation Spacer T88T-7025-G, Shaft Adapter T75L-7025-P, Shaft Adapter Screw T75L-7025-K, Remover/Replacer Tube T75L-7025-B (2-wheel drive) or T85T-7025-A (4-wheel drive), nut and washer, or equivalents.

33. Remove the temporary spacer.

34. Install the countershaft rear bearing.

35. Lock the transmission in 1st and 3rd. Install new output shaft and countershaft locknuts. Torque the output shaft locknut to 160-200 ft. lbs.; torque the countershaft locknut to 94-144 ft. lbs.

✳✳WARNING

Always use new locknuts. Make sure that the bearings are fully seated before torquing the locknuts.

36. Using a centerpunch, stake the locknuts.

37. Install the speedometer drive gear and steel ball on the output shaft. The ball can be installed in any of the three detents. Make sure, if you are installing a new speedometer gear, make sure that it is the same color code as the old one.

38. Clean the mating surfaces of the extension housing and case. Apply a ⅛in. (3mm) wide bead of silicone RTV sealant to the case.

➡**If the extension housing bushing is defective, the entire extension housing must be replaced.**

39. Position the extension housing on the case and torque the bolts to 24-34 ft. lbs.

40. Place the synchronizers in the neutral position. Make sure that the shift forks in the cover are also in neutral.

41. Using a new gasket, without sealant, place the cover on the case and carefully engage the shift forks in the synchronizers. Apply sealant to the two rearmost cover bolts and install them. Install the remaining bolts without sealant. Torque the bolts to 12-16 ft. lbs.

42. Install the drain plug. Torque it to 40 ft. lbs.

43. Install the rear oil seal into the extension housing. Make sure that the drain hole faces downward.

44. Fill the case with Dexron®II fluid.

ZF S5-42 5-Speed Overdrive

▶ **See Figures 57, 58, 59, 60, 61, 62, 63, 64, 65, 66, 67, 68, 69, 70, 71, 72, 73, 74, 75, 76, 77 and 78**

MAIN COMPONENT DISASSEMBLY

1. Place the transmission face downward on a clean work surface.

2. Using a hammer and chisel, bend back the tab on the output shaft flange locknut.

3. Install a holding tool on the flange and loosen, but don't remove, the output shaft locknut.

4. Remove 15 of the 17 bolts holding the rear case cover to the case. Leave 2 bolts at opposite corners.

5. Remove any power take-off (pto) equipment.

6. Remove the shift tower assembly from the case.

7. Remove the interlock plate and compression spring which serves as a reverse gear interlock.

➡**Be careful...these parts tend to fall into the case.**

8. Place a punch against the detent bolt cap, at an angle and slightly off center. Drive the cap inward until spring pressure against its underside forces the cap out of its hole. Re-

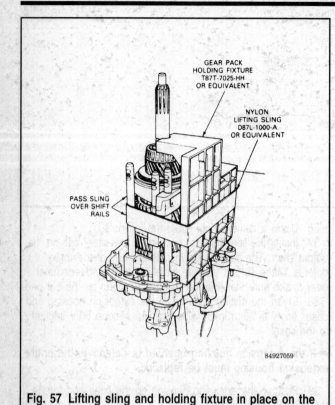

GEAR PACK
HOLDING FIXTURE
T87T-7025-HH
OR EQUIVALENT

NYLON
LIFTING SLING
D87L-1000-A
OR EQUIVALENT

PASS SLING
OVER SHIFT
RAILS

84927059

Fig. 57 Lifting sling and holding fixture in place on the ZF

peat this procedure for the other two detent bolt sealing caps in the front case.

❈❈CAUTION

Always wear goggles! The cap is under spring pressure.

9. Remove the springs from the sealing cap holes.
10. Drive out the sealing caps from the two reverse idler shaft cap screws. Remove the screws.
11. Remove the back-up light switch and switch sealing ring.
12. Using a punch remove the two dowel pins from the two upper corners of the rear case mating surface. Drive them out towards the rear.
13. Remove the two remaining hex bolts from the rear case.
14. Carefully separate the front and rear cases. It may be necessary to push the central shift rail inwards to prevent it from hanging up on the front case. Be careful to ensure that the central shift rail is not lifted off with the front case.

❈❈WARNING

The case mating surfaces are sealed with RTV sealant in place of a gasket. If you experience difficulty in separating the case sections DON'T PRY THEM APART! Tap around the rear case section to break it loose with a rubber or plastic mallet.

15. Remove the central shift rail and shift finger assembly.
16. Lift the shaft out of the reverse idler gear and remove the gear and two caged roller bearings from the rear case.
17. Remove the three capscrews that retain the shift interlock to the rear case.

18. With the transmission on end, front up, install the Gear Pack Holding Fixture T87T-7025-HH using sling D87L-1000-A on the mainshaft and output shaft assemblies. Pass the sling over the shift rails.
19. Place Shift Rod Support T87T-7025-JH over the ends of the shift rails.
20. Turn the transmission to the horizontal position with the holding fixture under the gear pack.
21. Remove the output shaft flange retaining nut.
22. Remove the flange. If it's hard to get off, tap it off with a hammer.
23. Carefully pull the gearpack and shift rails, along with their holding fixtures, forward to dislodge them from the rear case.
24. Remove the speedometer drive gear from the mainshaft.
25. Remove the sling from around the shift rails, gearpack and fixture.
26. Turn the shift rails 45° to release them from the shift hubs.
27. Lift the shift rails, forks and interlock, together with the Support Tool from the mainshaft.
28. Using the shift rod support tool as a base, set the shift rail assembly on a work bench with the shift rails in a vertical position. Remove the interlock.
29. Make identifying marks on each shift fork and shift rail and position them in the holding fixture. Lift the shift rails from the support tool.
30. Lift the countershaft off of the workbench stand. Separate the input shaft from the mainshaft. Lift the mainshaft and output shaft from the stand.
31. Remove the rear cover from the holding fixture.

SUBASSEMBLIES

1. Shift Tower:
   a. Remove the lever cover from the shift housing.
   b. Lift the lever, boot, cover and attached parts off the housing.
   c. Slide the two pieces off the cardan joint.
   d. Slide the boot and cover off the top of the gearshift lever.
   e. Invert the cover and remove the boot snapring.
   f. Assemble the parts in reverse order of disassembly.
2. Shift Rails:
   a. Install each shift rail in a soft-jawed vise and drive the roll pins out of the shift forks with a punch.
   b. Assembly is the reverse of disassembly.
3. Rear Case:
   a. Drive the two dowel pins out of the rear case.
   b. Using a slide hammer and internal puller, remove the mainshaft rear bearing outer race from the rear case.
   c. Using a drift, drive the mainshaft rear seal out of the rear cover. Discard the seal.
   d. Using a slide hammer and bearing cup puller, remove the countershaft rear bearing outer race from the rear case.
   e. Remove the central shift rail bearing from the rear cover using Blind Hole Puller D80L-100-Q and Slide Hammer T50T-100-A.
   f. To install the central shift rail bearing, heat the rear case bore area to 320°F (160°C) with a heat gun. Insert the ball sleeve and drive the bearing in until it seats against its stop using Needle Bearing Replacer T87T-7025-DH.

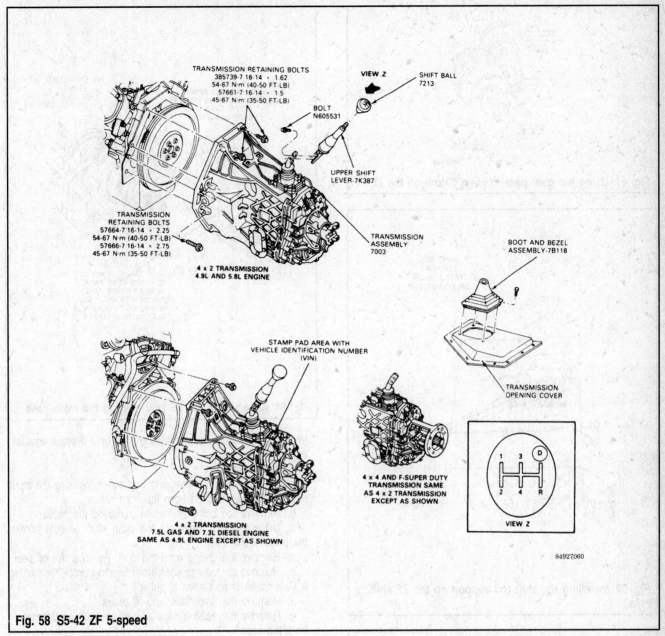

Fig. 58 S5-42 ZF 5-speed

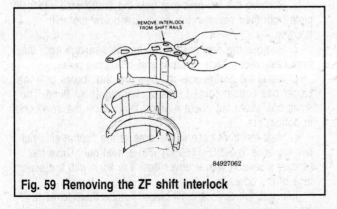

Fig. 59 Removing the ZF shift interlock

Fig. 60 Removing the reverse idler shaft cap screws on the ZF

g. Heat the rear case in the area around the countershaft rear bearing outer race to 320°F (160°C) with a heat gun.

Install the countershaft bearing outer race with a driver until it seats against its stop.

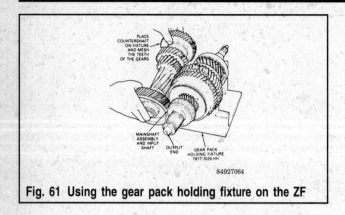

Fig. 61 Using the gear pack holding fixture on the ZF

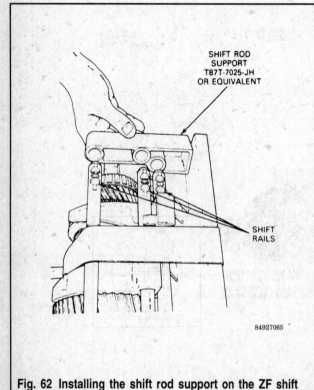

Fig. 62 Installing the shift rod support on the ZF shift rails

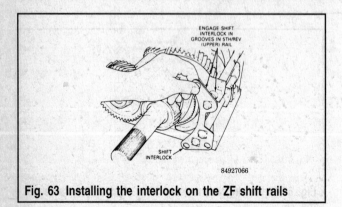

Fig. 63 Installing the interlock on the ZF shift rails

h. Heat the case in the area of the mainshaft outer race to 320°F (160°C) with a heat gun. Drive the bearing cup

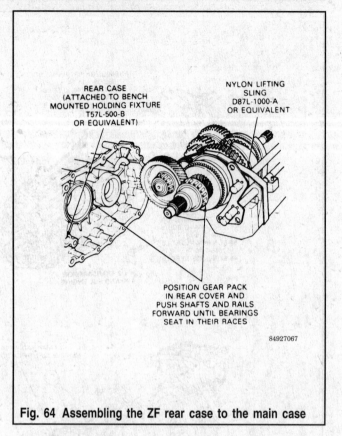

Fig. 64 Assembling the ZF rear case to the main case

into its bore with a driver and cup tool, until it seats against its stop.

4. Front Case:

a. Using a slide hammer and cup puller, remove the input shaft bearing outer race from the front case.

b. Remove the baffle and shims. Discard the baffle.

c. Using a punch, drive out the input shaft oil seal from the base of the quill.

d. Remove the O-ring from the quill. Remove the oil seal.

e. Remove the countershaft front bearing outer race using a slide hammer and internal puller.

f. Remove the fluid drain and fill plugs.

g. Remove the sealing caps and three shift rail detents from the case.

h. Remove the roll pins that hold the 5th/reverse interlock plate from their bores in the case, just below the shift housing.

i. Remove the central shift rail needle bearings from the front case with a slide hammer and blind hole puller.

j. Install the 5th/reverse roll pins into their bores until the bigger one bottoms out. It should stick out about 8mm. The small one sticks out about 4-5mm. Don't allow the small one to bottom out.

k. Heat the front case in the area of the central shift rail bearing bore to 320°F (160°C) with a heat gun. Drive the bearing sleeve in with a driver until it is flush with the surface of the bore.

l. Install the drain and fill plugs. Torque them to 44 ft. lbs.

m. Insert the three shift rail detent bolts into their bores. They must seat in the detents and must move freely when installed.

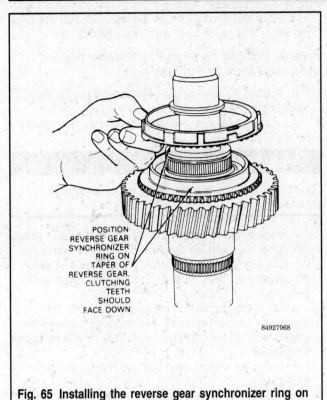

POSITION
REVERSE GEAR
SYNCHRONIZER
RING ON
TAPER OF
REVERSE GEAR.
CLUTCHING
TEETH
SHOULD
FACE DOWN

84927068

Fig. 65 Installing the reverse gear synchronizer ring on the ZF

n. Place a new O-ring on the input shaft quill.

o. Position the seal in the front case. Drive it in with a seal driver until it seats against its stop in the quill.

➡️**If the countershaft, input shaft, mainshaft or any tapered roller bearing is replaced, it will be necessary to adjust the tapered roller bearings to obtain a preload of 0.02-0.11mm. See the ADJUSTMENTS section below.**

p. Heat the mounting bore in the front case for the tapered roller bearing outer race of the countershaft to 320°F (160°C) with a heat gun. Position the proper thickness shim in the bore. Using a bearing driver, drive the race in until it seats against the stop in the case.

q. Heat the front case in the area of the input shaft tapered roller bearing outer race to 320°F (160°C) with a heat gun.

r. Using the ADJUSTMENT procedures below, position the correct shim pack in the bore for the input shaft bearing outer race. Using a driver, drive the bearing cup into place until it seats against its stop in the bore.

5. Mainshaft:

a. Clamp the output end of the mainshaft in a soft-jawed vise.

b. Remove the 4th gear synchronizer ring from the 3rd/4th synchronizer assembly.

c. Place the bearing collets T87T-7025-FH on either side of the mainshaft front bearing. Position Puller Tube T77J-7025-B in the collets. Pass the Collet Retaining Ring T75L-7025-G over the puller and into the collets so they clamp firmly on the bearing. Pull the bearing from the mainshaft.

d. Remove the 3rd/4th gear sliding sleeve from the mainshaft. Place a cloth around the synchronizer to catch the

compression springs, pressure pieces and balls that will be released when the sliding sleeves are removed.

e. Remove the cap ring that retains the 3rd/4th synchronizer body to the mainshaft.

f. Place the Collet Retaining ring T87T-7025-OH over the mainshaft and let it rest on the mainshaft 1st gear.

g. Position the two collet halves T87T-7025-NH on the 3rd/4th synchronizer body and slide the collet retaining ring over the collet halves to hold them in place on the synchronizer body.

h. Place the Shaft Protector D80L-625-4 on the end of the mainshaft. Place a 3-jawed puller on the collet halves and retaining ring, and pull the synchronizer body from the mainshaft.

i. Remove the synchronizer ring from the mainshaft 3rd gear.

j. Remove the 3rd gear from the mainshaft.

k. Remove the 3rd gear caged needle rollers from the mainshaft.

l. Lift the 1st/2nd gear sliding sleeve up as far as it will go. Position Collet Retaining Ring T87T-7025-OH over the mainshaft and let it rest on the 1st gear.

m. Position the two Collet Halves T87T-7025-MH so they seat in the groove in the 1st/2nd sliding sleeve. Pass the retaining ring from below over the two halves and secure them to the sliding sleeve.

n. Position the shaft protector D80L-625-4 on the end of the mainshaft. Position a 3-jawed puller on the collet retaining ring and pull off the 1st/2nd sliding sleeve, 2nd gear, thrust washer, and 3rd gear bearing inner race from the mainshaft.

✳✳CAUTION

Wrap a heavy cloth around the 1st/2nd synchronizer body to catch the springs, pressure pieces and balls.

o. Remove the snapring retaining the 1st/2nd synchronizer to the mainshaft.

p. Reposition the mainshaft in the vise so that the output end is facing upward.

q. On 4-wheel drive and F-Super Duty models, a snapring retaining the tapered roller bearing inner race should be removed.

r. Place a bearing gripper on the mainshaft rear tapered roller bearing. The gripper must be used to back the bearing during removal. Place a 3-jawed puller over the mainshaft and onto the gripper. Pull the bearing from the mainshaft.

s. Remove 5th gear from the mainshaft along with its caged needle rollers.

t. Remove the synchronizer ring from the 5th/reverse synchronizer.

u. Remove the snapring from the 5th/ reverse synchronizer body. Remove the 5th/reverse sliding sleeve.

✳✳CAUTION

Wrap a heavy cloth around the 1st/2nd synchronizer body to catch the springs, pressure pieces and balls.

v. Position Collet Retaining Ring T87T-7025-OH over the mainshaft and let it rest on the 1st gear. Position the two

Collet Halves T87T-7025-NH so the ridge rests between the synchronizer body and the synchronizer ring. Slide the retaining ring upwards around the collets to secure them in position.

w. Position a 3-jawed puller on the collet retaining ring and pull the 5th/reverse synchronizer body from the mainshaft. Remove the synchronizer ring from the reverse gear. Remove the reverse gear from the mainshaft along with the caged needle bearings.

x. Remove the mainshaft from the vise. Position the mainshaft in a press and press off the 1st gear and 1st/2nd synchronizer body.

y. Remove the 1st gear caged needle rollers.

6. To assemble the mainshaft:

a. Clamp the input end of the mainshaft in a soft-jawed vise.

b. Place the reverse gear caged needle roller on the mainshaft.

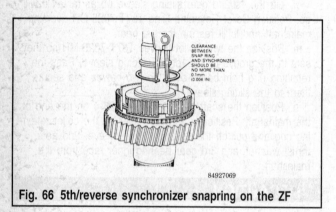

Fig. 66 5th/reverse synchronizer snapring on the ZF

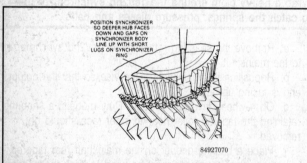

Fig. 67 Installing the synchronizer body on the ZF mainshaft

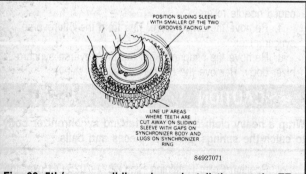

Fig. 68 5th/reverse sliding sleeve installation on the ZF

c. Place the reverse gear on the mainshaft over the needle rollers. The clutch teeth must face upwards.

➡**Before installing the original synchronizer ring and body, check them for excessive wear.**

d. Position the reverse gear synchronizer ring on the taper of the first gear.

e. Using a heat gun, heat the 5th/reverse synchronizer body to 320°F (160°C).

❋❋WARNING

Don't heat the synchronizer body for more than 15 minutes.

f. Position the synchronizer body on the mainshaft splines so that the side with the deeper hub faces downwards and the short lugs on the synchronizer ring engage the gaps in the synchronizer body. Push or lightly tap the synchronizer body down until it stops.

g. Install the snapring on the mainshaft next to the 5th/reverse synchronizer body. The clearance between the snapring and the synchronizer body should be 0-0.1mm, with 0 preferable.

h. Check the reverse gear endplay. Endplay should be 0.15-0.35mm.

i. Position the 5th/reverse sliding sleeve over the synchronizer body with the 2 grooves facing upwards. Align the tooth gaps and lugs. Slide the sleeve down until it rests against the reverse gear clutching teeth.

j. Insert the 3 compression springs and pressure pieces in the recesses of the synchronizer body. If the original springs are being reused, inspect them carefully and replace them if they appear worn or damaged.

k. Push the pressure pieces back with a screwdriver. Push the balls in with a screwdriver and slide the pressure piece against the ball.

l. Place the 5th gear synchronizer ring on the synchronizer body. The short lugs on the synchronizer ring should be located over the gaps in the 5th/reverse synchronizer body.

m. Push the 5th gear synchronizer ring downwards while pulling the sliding sleeve into the center position.

n. Pace the 5th gear caged needle rollers on the mainshaft. Install the 5th gear on the mainshaft over the caged needle rollers.

o. Heat the inner race of the mainshaft rear tapered roller bearing to 320°F (160°C) with a heat gun. Place it on the mainshaft and drive it until it seats against its stop.

❋❋WARNING

Don't heat the bearing for more than 15 minutes.

p. Check the 5th gear endplay. Endplay should be 0.15-0.35mm. On 4-wheel drive and F-Super Duty models, fit an additional retaining ring in the groove next to the tapered roller bearing inner race. It should have an endplay of 0-0.1mm, with 0 preferred.

q. Turn the mainshaft over and clamp it on the input end. Place the 1st gear caged needle rollers on the shaft. Place 1st gear over the rollers with the taper facing upward.

r. Place the 1st gear synchronizer ring on the 1st gear taper. Heat the 1st/2nd synchronizer body with a heat gun to 320°F (160°C). Position the synchronizer body on the mainshaft splines so that the short lugs on the synchronizer ring engage the gaps in the synchronizer body. Push the synchronizer body down until it stops against the ring. If the installation was correct, the word ENGINE will appear on the synchronizer body.

✳✳WARNING

Don't heat the bearing for more than 15 minutes.

s. Install a snapring on the mainshaft next to the 1st/2nd synchronizer body. Clearance between the snapring and synchronizer body should be 0-0.1mm. 1st gear endplay should be 0.15-0.35mm.

t. Position the sliding sleeve over the synchronizer body with its tapered collar facing downward. Align the lugs and tooth gaps, and push the sleeve down until it rests against 1st gear.

u. Insert the three compression springs and pressure pieces in the recesses of the synchronizer body. Push the pressure pieces back with a screwdriver. Push the balls in with a screwdriver and slide the pressure piece against the ball.

v. Place the 2nd gear synchronizer ring on the synchronizer body. The short lugs on the synchronizer ring should be located over the gaps in the 1st/2nd synchronizer body.

w. Push the 2nd gear synchronizer ring downwards while pulling the sliding sleeve into the center position. Pace the 2nd gear caged needle rollers on the mainshaft. Install the 2nd gear on the mainshaft over the caged needle rollers.

x. Heat the thrust washer to 320°F (160°C) with a heat gun. Place it on the mainshaft and drive it until it seats against its stop.

✳✳WARNING

Don't heat the washer for more than 15 minutes.

y. Heat the 3rd gear bearing inner race to 320°F (160°C) with a heat gun. Place the race on the mainshaft and push it down until it seats against its stop. Check the 2nd gear endplay. Endplay should be 0.15-0.45mm. After the 3rd gear has cooled, place the 3rd gear caged needle rollers over it. Place the 3rd gear over the needle rollers with the taper upwards. Place the 3rd gear synchronizer ring on the 3rd gear taper. Heat the 3rd/4th synchronizer body with a heat gun to 320°F (160°C). Position the body on the mainshaft splines so that the short lugs on the synchronizer ring engage the gaps in the body. Push the body down until it stops against the ring. The recess in the body must face upwards.

z. Install a snapring on the mainshaft next to the 1st/2nd synchronizer body. Clearance between the snapring and synchronizer body should be 0-0.1mm. 1st gear endplay should be 0.15-0.35mm. Position the sliding sleeve over the synchronizer body with its tapered collar facing downward. Align the lugs and tooth gaps, and push the sleeve down until it rests against 1st gear. Insert the three compression springs

and pressure pieces in the recesses of the synchronizer body. Push the pressure pieces back with a screwdriver. Push the balls in with a screwdriver and slide the pressure piece against the ball. Place the 2nd gear synchronizer ring on the synchronizer body. The short lugs on the synchronizer ring should be located over the gaps in the 1st/2nd synchronizer body. Push the 2nd gear synchronizer ring downwards while pulling the sliding sleeve into the center position. Pace the 2nd gear caged needle rollers on the mainshaft. Install the 2nd gear on the mainshaft over the caged needle rollers. Heat the thrust washer to 320°F (160°C) with a heat gun. Place it on the mainshaft and drive it until it seats against its stop.

✳✳WARNING

Don't heat the washer for more than 15 minutes.

7. Input Shaft Disassembly and Assembly:

a. Position the two Collet Halves (44803 and 44797) of Universal Bearing Remover Set D81L-4220-A around the input shaft bearing cone. Install the pulling tube and pull the bearing from the shaft.

b. Inspect the bearing and shaft thoroughly. Replace any worn or damaged parts.

c. Place the bearing on the shaft.

d. Place the Bearing Cone Replacer T85T-4621-AH over the bearing.

e. Position the shaft, bearing and tool in Press Plate T75L-1165-B.

f. Press the bearing on until it seats against its stop.

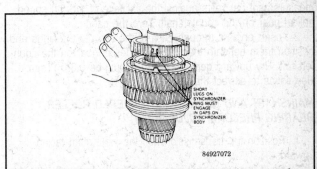

Fig. 69 Synchronizer ring installation showing engaging lugs, on the ZF

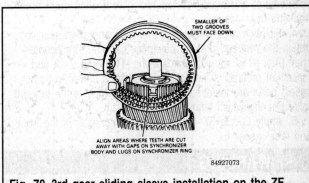

Fig. 70 3rd gear sliding sleeve installation on the ZF

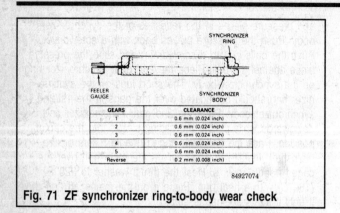

GEARS	CLEARANCE
1	0.6 mm (0.024 inch)
2	0.6 mm (0.024 inch)
3	0.6 mm (0.024 inch)
4	0.6 mm (0.024 inch)
5	0.6 mm (0.024 inch)
Reverse	0.2 mm (0.008 inch)

84927074

Fig. 71 ZF synchronizer ring-to-body wear check

INPUT SHAFT AND MAINSHAFT TAPERED ROLLER BEARING PRELOAD MEASUREMENT

This adjustment is necessary whenever a major, related component is replaced.

1. Place the transmission on a holding fixture with the output shaft facing upward.

2. Attach a dial indicator with a magnetic base so that the measurement bar rests on the output end of the mainshaft.

3. Zero the indicator and pry up on the input shaft and mainshaft with a prybar. Note the indicator reading. The shim and shaft seal must have a combined thickness equal to the indicator reading plus 0.02-0.11mm.

COUNTERSHAFT TAPERED ROLLER BEARING PRELOAD MEASUREMENT

1. Using two 10mm hex screws, attach the magnetic mount dial indicator near the pto opening on the front case. Position the dial indicator gauge on the support in such a way that the measurement bar rests against the flat face of the 5th speed helical gear on the countershaft. Zero the gauge.

2. Insert prybars through each of the two pto openings and position them beneath the 5th speed helical gear on the countershaft. Pry upward gently. Preload should be 0.0-0.11mm. Use shims to correct the preload.

MAINSHAFT AND INPUT SHAFT TAPERED ROLLER BEARING PRELOAD ADJUSTMENT

1. Position the transmission with the input shaft facing upwards.

2. Drive the two dowel pins out of their holes in the front and rear cases, and lift the front case off of the rear case.

3. Using a slide hammer and internal puller, remove the countershaft and mainshaft tapered roller bearing outer races from the front case.

4. Fit each race with a shim, or shim and shaft seal, to obtain the required preload determined above. The countershaft preload is set with shims alone. The input shaft and mainshaft preload is set using shims and a baffle. In both cases, parts are installed under the outer race of the tapered roller bearing which seats in the front case.

5. Apply Loctite 574® to the mating surfaces of the front and rear cases.

✳✳WARNING

Do not use silicone type sealer.

6. Join the case sections and torque the bolts to 16 ft. lbs.

SYNCHRONIZER RING AND SYNCHRONIZER BODY WEAR CHECK

1. Install the ring on the body.

2. Insert a feeler gauge and measure the clearance at two opposite positions. If clearance is less than 0.6mm for the forward speed synchronizers and 0.2mm for the reverse synchronizer, replace the ring and/or synchronizer body as required.

SYNCHRONIZER COMPRESSION SPRING TENSION CHECK

The length of all springs should be 14.8mm; the outer diameter should be 5.96mm and the wire diameter should be 0.95mm. Replace any spring that is not to specifications.

MAIN COMPONENT ASSEMBLY

1. Place the input shaft and synchronizer ring assembly over the tapered roller bearing on the input end of the mainshaft.

2. Place the mainshaft and input shaft on Gear Pack Holding Fixture T87T-7025-HH. Place the countershaft on the fixture and mesh the gears of the two shafts.

3. Place the three shift rails and fork assemblies into Shift Rod Support Tool T87T-7025-JH in the same position from which they were removed during disassembly.

4. Position the three shift rail together with the shift rod support tool and interlock, so that the shift forks engage in the correct mainshaft sliding sleeves.

5. Place the shift interlock on the three gearshift rails and engage it in the interlock grooves in the 5th/reverse upper rail.

6. Slide the speedometer worm gear onto the mainshaft until it seats against its stop.

7. Secure the rear cover on the holding fixture T57L-500-B.

8. Position nylon lifting sling D87L-1000-A around the shift rails, holding fixture and mainshaft and countershaft.

9. Position the gear pack into the rear cover and push the shafts and rails forward until the bearings seat in their races and the gearshift rails slide into their retaining holes.

10. Rotate the gear pack and rear case upwards so that the input shaft faces up.

11. Slide the output shaft flange onto the output end of the mainshaft so that it seats against its stop. Screw the hex nut onto the shaft finger-tightly.

➡**Make sure that the mainshaft bearing is not pushed off its race when the flange is installed.**

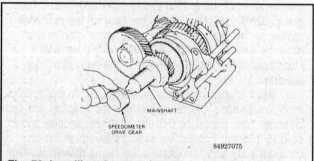

84927075

Fig. 72 Installing the speedometer gear on the ZF mainshaft

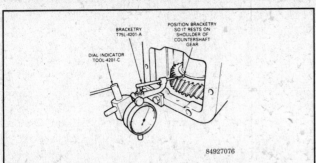

Fig. 73 Measuring the ZF countershaft tapered roller bearing preload

12. Remove the shift rod support tool from the ends of the shift rails.

13. Remove the strap and gear pack holding fixture.

14. Attach the three capscrews that secure the shift interlock to the rear housing. Torque them to 84 inch lbs. Make sure that the interlock still moves freely.

15. Mesh the reverse idler gear and reverse gear. Slide the reverse idler shaft downward through the bearings and into the rear case. Tighten the bolt finger-tightly.

16. Insert the central shift rail and finger assembly into its bore in the rear case.

17. If the tapered roller bearings on the mainshaft or countershaft do not need adjustment, place a thin coating of Loctite 574® on the rear case mating surface. If the bearings need adjustment, do it at this time, then, apply sealer.

➡**Do not use silicone type sealers.**

18. Push the three shift rail detents back into their holes in the front case.

19. Carefully place the front case half over the shafts and gearshift rails until it rests on the mating surface of the rear case. It may be necessary to push the central shift rail inward to clear the inner surfaces of the front case.

20. Drive in the two dowels that align the rear case and front case. Insert the two hex screws and tighten them finger-tightly.

21. Screw to additional hex screws into the rear case and make them finger tight.

22. If shaft preload adjustment is not necessary, install all the hex screws and torque all of them to 18 ft. lbs. If adjustment is necessary, do it at this time, then install and tighten all the hex screws.

23. Insert the reverse idler shaft screws and torque them to 16 ft. lbs. Push the sealing cover into the screw heads.

24. Turn the transmission so that the input shaft is facing down.

25. Install the speedometer drive gear on the mainshaft.

26. On 2-wheel drive vehicles, remove the hex nut that secures the output shaft flange to the mainshaft. Position the output shaft seal on the Output Shaft Seal Replacer Tool T87T-7025-BH. Position the seal and tool in the opening in the rear case. using a plastic or rubber mallet tap the seal in until it seats in the opening.

On 4-wheel drive models, use Output Shaft Seal Replacer T87T-7025-LH and Installer Tube T77J-7025-B to install the output shaft oil seal.

27. On 2-wheel drive models, install the output shaft flange on the shaft. Hold the flange with a holding fixture and torque the shaft nut to 184 ft. lbs.

28. Lock the nut by bending the locktabs.

29. Using new gaskets, install the pto covers and torque the bolts 28 ft. lbs.

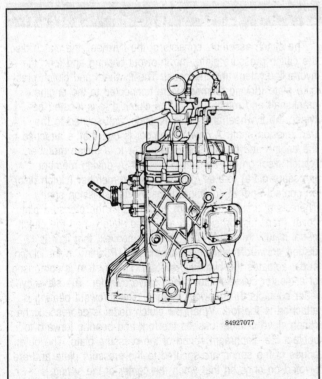

Fig. 74 Measuring the preload on the ZF input shaft and mainshaft roller bearings

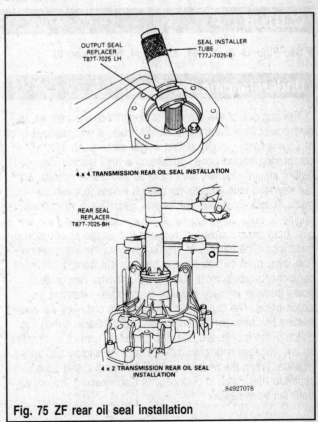

Fig. 75 ZF rear oil seal installation

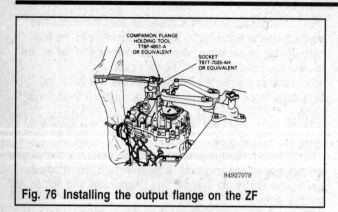

Fig. 76 Installing the output flange on the ZF

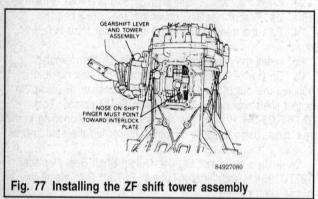

Fig. 77 Installing the ZF shift tower assembly

30. Place the 5th/reverse gear interlock plate into position. Place the gasket over the shift tower mating surface on the front case. Make sure that the stop plate moves freely. Make sure that the plate and spring do not drop into the case.

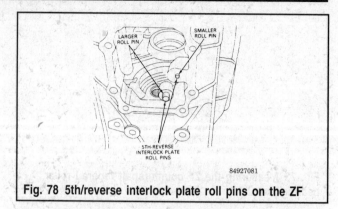

Fig. 78 5th/reverse interlock plate roll pins on the ZF

31. Place the spring above the nose on the interlock plate and move both parts into their proper positions.

✴✴WARNING

Follow this sequence exactly to ensure proper interlock function!

32. Install the shift tower. The nose on the gearshift finger must point towards the interlock plate. Install the spring washers and torque the screws to 18 ft. lbs.
33. Check the interlock operation.
34. Install the compression springs over each detent bolt.
35. Drive the sealing caps over the springs and detent bolts. Each cap should seat $3/64$ in. (1.2mm) below the case surface. If you install them any deeper it will cause increased shift effort.
36. Install the back-up lamp switch and new sealing ring. Torque the switch to 15 ft. lbs.

CLUTCH

▶ **See Figures 79, 80, 81, 82, 83, 84, 85, 86 and 87**

Understanding the Clutch

The purpose of the clutch is to disconnect and connect engine power from the transmission. A truck at rest requires a lot of engine torque to get all that weight moving. An internal combustion engine does not develop a high starting torque (unlike steam engines), so it must be allowed to operate without any load until it builds up enough torque to move the truck. Torque increases with engine rpm. The clutch allows the engine to build up torque by physically disconnecting the engine from the transmission, relieving the engine of any load or resistance. The transfer of engine power to the transmission (the load) must be smooth and gradual; if it weren't, drive line components would wear out or break quickly. This gradual power transfer is made possible by gradually releasing the clutch pedal. The clutch disc and pressure plate are the connecting link between the engine and transmission. When the clutch pedal is released, the disc and plate contact each other (clutch engagement), physically joining t he engine and transmission. When the pedal is pushed in, the disc and plate separate (the clutch is disengaged), disconnecting the engine from the transmission.

The clutch assembly consists of the flywheel, the clutch disc, the clutch pressure plate, the throwout bearing and fork, the hydraulic system and the pedal. The flywheel and clutch pressure plate (driving members) are connected to the engine crankshaft and rotate with it. The clutch disc is located between the flywheel and pressure plate, and splined to the transmission shaft. A driving member is one that is attached to the engine and transfers engine power to a driven member (clutch disc) on the transmission shaft. A driving member (pressure plate) rotates (drives) a driven member (clutch disc) on contact and, in so doing, turns the transmission shaft. There is a circular diaphragm spring within the pressure plate cover (transmission side). In a relaxed state (when the clutch pedal is fully released), this spring is convex; that it, it is dished outward toward the transmission. Pushing in the clutch pedal actuates the hydraulic system. This system is comprised of a master cylinder, tubing and slave cylinder. The slave cylinder contacts the throwout bearing. The throwout bearing is attached to the fork. When the clutch pedal is depressed, the clutch slave cylinder pushes the fork and bearing forward to contact the diaphragm spring of the pressure plate. The outer edges of the spring are secured to the pressure plate and are pivoted on rings so that when the center of the spring is compressed by the throwout bearing, the outer edges bow outward and, by so doing, pull the pressure plate in the same direction — away from the clutch disc. This action separates the disc from the plate, disengaging the clutch and allowing the transmission to be shifted into another gear. A coil type clutch return spring attached to the clutch pedal arm permits full release of the pedal. Releasing the pedal pulls the throwout bearing away from the diaphragm spring resulting in a reversal of spring position. As bearing pressure is gradually released from the spring center, the outer edges of the spring bow outward, pushing the pressure plate into closer contact with the clutch disc. As the disc and plate move closer together, friction between the two increases and slippage is reduced until, when full spring pressure is applied (by fully releasing the pedal), The speed of the disc and plate are the same. This stops all slipping, creating a direct connection between the plate and disc which results in the transfer of power from the engine to the transmission. The clutch disc is now rotating with the pressure plate at engine speed and, because it is splined to the transmission shaft, the shaft now turns at the same engine speed. Understanding clutch operation can be rather difficult at first; if you're still confused after reading this, consider the following analogy. The action of the diaphragm spring can be compared to that of an oil can bottom. The bottom of an oil can is shaped very much like the clutch diaphragm spring and pushing in on the can bottom an d then releasing it produces a similar effect. As mentioned earlier, the clutch pedal return spring permits full release of the pedal.

The diaphragm spring type clutches used are available in two different designs: flat diaphragm springs or bent spring. The bent fingers are bent back to create a centrifugal boost ensuring quick re-engagement at higher engine speeds. This design enables pressure plate load to increase as the clutch disc wears and makes low pedal effort possible even with a heavy-duty clutch. The throwout bearing used with the bent finger design is 1¼ in. (31.75mm) long and is shorter than the bearing used with the flat finger design. These bearings are not interchangeable. If the longer bearing is used with the bent finger clutch, free-pedal travel will not exist. This results in clutch slippage and rapid wear.

The transmission varies the gear ratio between the engine and rear wheels. It can be shifted to change engine speed as driving conditions and loads change. The transmission allows disengaging and reversing power from the engine to the wheels.

Clutch Pedal

REMOVAL & INSTALLATION

▶ **See Figure 88**

All except F-Super Duty Stripped Chassis and Motor Home Chassis

1. Disconnect the clutch pedal pull-back spring.
2. Remove the nut that secures the pedal to the shaft and remove the pedal.
3. Installation is the reverse of removal.

F-Super Duty Stripped Chassis and Motor Home Chassis

1. Disconnect the clutch master cylinder pushrod from the pedal.

2. Remove the through-bolt and nut from the clutch pedal bracket.
3. Remove the pedal, along with the bushings, washer and spacer.
4. Installation is the reverse of removal. Torque the nut to 50-70 ft. lbs.

Hydraulic System

▶ **See Figures 89, 90, 91, 92, 93, 94, 95, 96, 97, 98 and 99**

The hydraulic clutch system operates much like a hydraulic brake system. When you push down (disengage) the clutch pedal, the mechanical clutch pedal movement is converted into hydraulic fluid movement, which is then converted back into mechanical movement by the slave cylinder to actuate the clutch release lever.

The system consists of a combination clutch fluid reservoir/master cylinder assembly, a slave cylinder mounted on the bellhousing, and connecting tubing.

Fluid level is checked at the master cylinder reservoir. The hydraulic clutch system continually remains in adjustment, like a hydraulic disc brake system, so not clutch linkage or pedal adjustment is necessary.

REMOVAL

There are 2 types of slave cylinders used: an internally mounted (in the bell housing) and an externally mounted type.

- 1987 — All models use the externally mounted type
- 1988-89 — Diesel engines and the 8-7.5L gasoline engine use the externally mounted type; all others use the internally mounted type
- 1990-93 — Diesel engines, 8-7.5L gasoline engines, and V8 gasoline engines equipped with the M50DHD transmission use the externally mounted type; all others use the internally mounted type.

✳✳WARNING

Prior to any service on models with the externally mounted slave cylinder, that requires removal of the slave cylinder, such as transmission and/or clutch housing removal, the clutch master cylinder pushrod must be disconnected from the clutch pedal. Failure to do this may damage the slave cylinder if the clutch pedal is depressed while the slave cylinder is disconnected.

1. From inside the truck cab, remove the cotter pin retaining the clutch master cylinder pushrod to the clutch pedal lever. Disconnect the pushrod and remove the bushing.
2. Remove the two nuts retaining the clutch reservoir and master cylinder assembly to the firewall.
3. From the engine compartment, remove the clutch reservoir and master cylinder assembly from the firewall. Note here how the clutch tubing routes to the slave cylinder.
4. Push the release lever forward to compress the slave cylinder.
5. On all models with the internally mounted slave cylinder, remove the plastic clip that retains the slave cylinder to the bracket. Remove the slave cylinder.

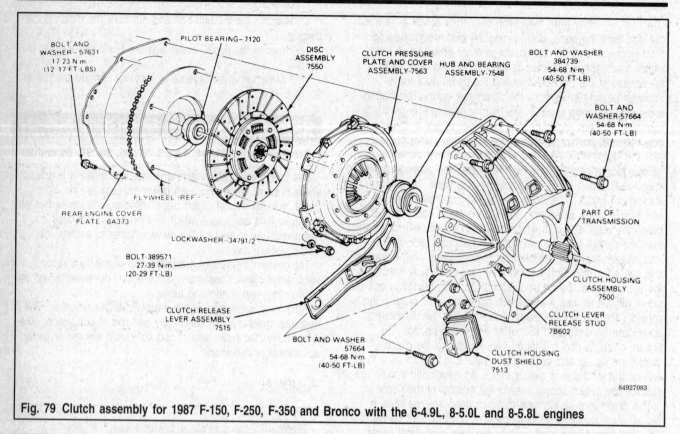

BOLT AND WASHER - 57631
17-23 N·m
(12-17 FT·LBS)

PILOT BEARING-7120

DISC ASSEMBLY 7550

CLUTCH PRESSURE PLATE AND COVER ASSEMBLY-7563

HUB AND BEARING ASSEMBLY-7548

BOLT AND WASHER 384739
54-68 N·m
(40-50 FT-LB)

BOLT AND WASHER-57664
54-68 N·m
(40-50 FT-LB)

FLYWHEEL (REF)

REAR ENGINE COVER PLATE-6A373

LOCKWASHER-34791/2

BOLT-389571
27-39 N·m
(20-29 FT-LB)

CLUTCH RELEASE LEVER ASSEMBLY 7515

BOLT AND WASHER 57664
54-68 N·m
(40-50 FT-LB)

PART OF TRANSMISSION

CLUTCH HOUSING ASSEMBLY 7500

CLUTCH LEVER RELEASE STUD 7B602

CLUTCH HOUSING DUST SHIELD 7513

84927083

Fig. 79 Clutch assembly for 1987 F-150, F-250, F-350 and Bronco with the 6-4.9L, 8-5.0L and 8-5.8L engines

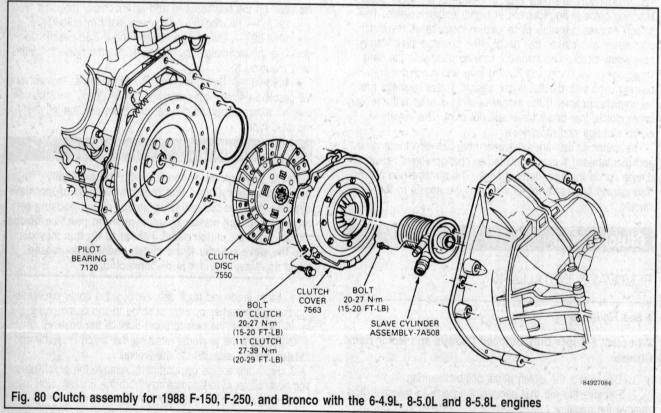

PILOT BEARING 7120

CLUTCH DISC 7550

CLUTCH COVER 7563

BOLT
10" CLUTCH
20-27 N·m
(15-20 FT-LB)
11" CLUTCH
27-39 N·m
(20-29 FT-LB)

BOLT
20-27 N·m
(15-20 FT-LB)

SLAVE CYLINDER ASSEMBLY-7A508

84927084

Fig. 80 Clutch assembly for 1988 F-150, F-250, and Bronco with the 6-4.9L, 8-5.0L and 8-5.8L engines

6. On models with the externally mounted slave cylinder, the steel retaining clip is permanently attached to the slave cylinder. Remove the slave cylinder by prying on the clip to free the tangs while pulling the cylinder clear.

7. Remove the release lever by pulling it outward.

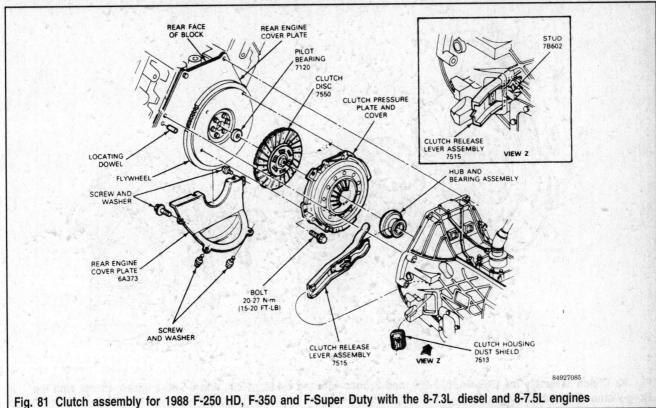

Fig. 81 Clutch assembly for 1988 F-250 HD, F-350 and F-Super Duty with the 8-7.3L diesel and 8-7.5L engines

8. Remove the clutch hydraulic system from the truck.

INSTALLATION

1. Position the clutch pedal reservoir and master cylinder assembly into the firewall from inside the cab, and install the two nuts and tighten.

2. Route the clutch tubing and slave cylinder to the bell housing, taking care that the nylon lines are kept away from any hot exhaust system components.

3. Install the slave cylinder by pushing the slave cylinder pushrod into the cylinder. Engage the pushrod into the release lever and slide the slave cylinder into the bell housing lugs. Seat the cylinder into the recess in the lugs.

➡When installing a new hydraulic system, you'll notice that the slave cylinder contains a shipping strap that pro-positions the pushrod for installation, and also provides a bearing insert. Following installation of the new slave cylinder, the first actuation of the clutch pedal will break the shipping strap and give normal clutch action.

4. Clean the master cylinder pushrod bearing and apply a light film of SAE 30 engine oil.

5. From inside the cab, install the bushing on the clutch pedal lever. Connect the clutch master cylinder pushrod to the clutch pedal lever and install the cotter pin.

6. Check the clutch reservoir and add fluid if required. Depress the clutch pedal at least ten times to verify smooth operation and proper clutch release.

HYDRAULIC SYSTEM BLEEDING

Externally Mounted Slave Cylinder

1. Clean the reservoir cap and the slave cylinder connection.

2. Remove the slave cylinder from the housing.

3. Using a $^{3}/_{32}$ in. punch, drive out the pin that holds the tube in place.

4. Remove the tube from the slave cylinder and place the end of the tube in a container.

5. Hold the slave cylinder so that the connector port is at the highest point, by tipping it about 30° from horizontal. Fill the cylinder with DOT 3 brake fluid through the port. It may be necessary to rock the cylinder or slightly depress the pushrod to expel all the air.

❄❄WARNING

Pushing too hard on the pushrod will spurt fluid from the port!

6. When all air is expelled — no more bubble are seen — install the slave cylinder.

➡Some fluid will be expelled during installation as the pushrod is depressed.

7. Remove the reservoir cap. Some fluid will run out of the tube end into the container. Pour fluid into the reservoir until a steady stream of fluid runs out of the tube and the reservoir is filled. Quickly install the diaphragm and cap. The flow should stop.

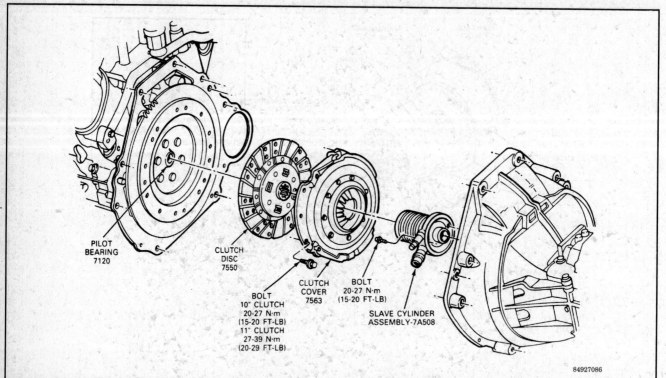

Fig. 82 Clutch assembly for 1989 F-150, F-250, and Bronco with the 6-4.9L, 8-5.0L and 8-5.8L engines, except with the Borg-Warner T-18 transmission

8. Connect the tube and install the pin. Check the fluid level.

9. Check the clutch operation.

Internally Mounted Slave Cylinder

➡With the quick-disconnect coupling, no air should enter the system when the coupling is disconnected. However, if air should somehow enter the system, it must be bled.

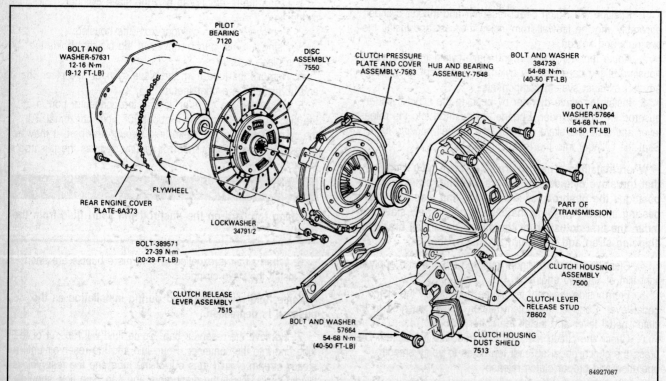

Fig. 83 Clutch assembly for 1989 F-150, F-250, and Bronco with the 6-4.9L, and 8-5.0L engines with the Borg-Warner T-18 transmission

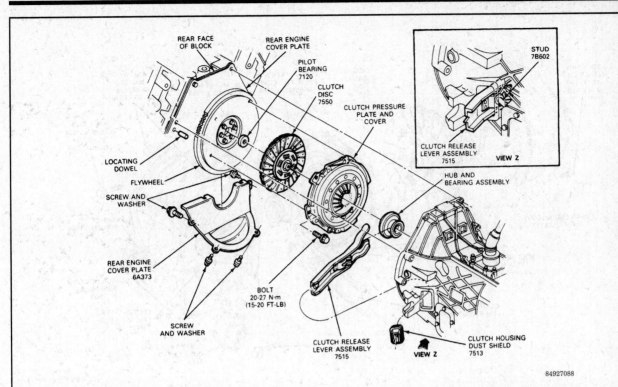

Fig. 84 Clutch assembly for 1989 F-250 HD, F-350, F-Super Duty Chassis Cab and Stripped Chassis with the 8-7.3L diesel and 8-7.5L engines

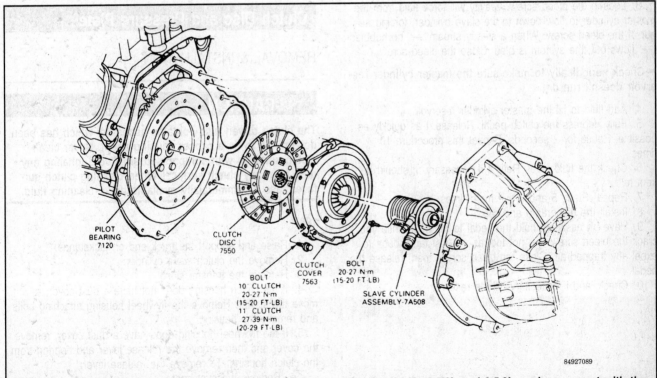

Fig. 85 Clutch assembly for 1990-93 F-150, F-250, and Bronco with the 6-4.9L, 8-5.0L and 8-5.8L engines, except with the Borg-Warner T-18 transmission

1. Remove the reservoir cap and diaphragm. Fill the reservoir with DOT 3 brake fluid.

2. Connect a piece of rubber tubing to the slave cylinder bleed screw. Place the other end in a container.

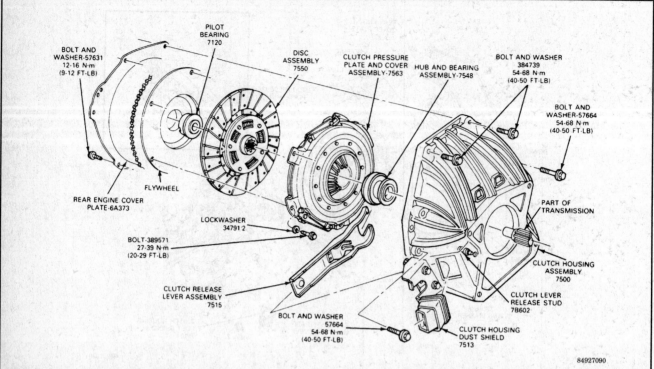

Fig. 86 Clutch assembly for 1990-93 F-150, F-250, and Bronco with 6-4.9L, and 8-5.0L engines, with the Borg-Warner T-18 transmission

3. Loosen the bleed screw. Gravity will force fluid from the master cylinder to flow down to the slave cylinder, forcing air out of the bleed screw. When a steady stream — no bubbles — flows out, the system is bled. Close the bleed screw.

➡**Check periodically to make sure the master cylinder reservoir doesn't run dry.**

4. Add fluid to fill the master cylinder reservoir.
5. Fully depress the clutch pedal. Release it as quickly as possible. Pause for 2 seconds. Repeat this procedure 10 times.
6. Check the fluid level. Refill it if necessary. It should be kept full.
7. Repeat Steps 5 and 6 five more times.
8. Install the diaphragm and cap.
9. Have an assistant hold the pedal to the floor while you crack the bleed screw — not too far — just far enough to expel any trapped air. Close the bleed screw, then, release the pedal.
10. Check, and if necessary, fill the reservoir.

Clutch Disc and Pressure Plate

REMOVAL & INSTALLATION

✳✳CAUTION

The clutch driven disc contains asbestos, which has been determined to be a cancer causing agent. Never clean clutch surfaces with compressed air! Avoid inhaling any dust from any clutch surface! When cleaning clutch surfaces, use a commercially available brake cleaning fluid.

1987

1. Raise and support the truck end on jackstands.
2. Remove the clutch slave cylinder.
3. Remove the transmission.
4. If the clutch housing does not have a dust cover, remove the starter. Remove the flywheel housing attaching bolts and remove the housing.
5. If the flywheel housing does have a dust cover, remove the cover and then remove the release lever and bearing from the clutch housing. To remove the release lever:
   a. Remove the dust boot.
   b. Push the release lever forward to compress the slave cylinder.
   c. On all engines except the diesel and the 7.5L gasoline engines, remove the plastic clip that retains the slave cylinder to the bracket. Remove the slave cylinder.
   d. On the diesel and the 7.5L, the steel retaining clip is permanently attached to the slave cylinder. Remove the

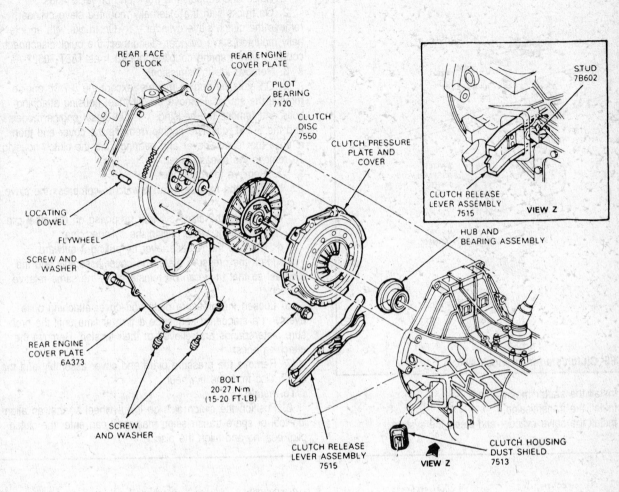

84927091

Fig. 87 Clutch assembly for 1990-93 F-250 HD, F-350, F-Super Duty Chassis Cab and Stripped Chassis with the 8-7.4L diesel and 8-7.5L engines

slave cylinder by prying on the clip to free the tangs while pulling the cylinder clear.

    e. Remove the release lever by pulling it outward.

6. Mark the pressure plate and cover assembly and the flywheel so that they can be reinstalled in the same relative position.

7. Loosen the pressure plate and cover attaching bolts evenly in a staggered sequence a turn at time until the pressure plate springs are relieved of their tension. Remove the attaching bolts.

8. Remove the pressure plate and cover assembly and the clutch disc from the flywheel.

To install:

9. Position the clutch disc on the flywheel so that an aligning tool or spare transmission mainshaft can enter the clutch pilot bearing and align the disc.

10. When reinstalling the original pressure plate and cover assembly, align the assembly and flywheel according to the marks made during removal. Position the pressure plate and cover assembly on the flywheel, align the pressure plate and disc, and install the retaining bolts. Tighten the bolts in an alternating sequence a few turns at a time until the proper torque is reached:

- 10 in. and 12 in. clutch: 15-20 ft. lbs.
- 11 in. clutch: 20-29 ft. lbs.

11. Remove the tool used to align the clutch disc.

12. With the clutch fully released, apply a light coat of grease on the sides of the driving lugs.

13. Position the clutch release bearing and the bearing hub on the release lever. Install the release lever on the fulcrum in the flywheel housing. Apply a light coating of grease to the release lever fingers and the fulcrum. Fill the groove of the release bearing hub with grease.

14. If the flywheel housing has been removed, position it against the rear engine cover plate and install the attaching bolts and tighten them to 40-50 ft. lbs.

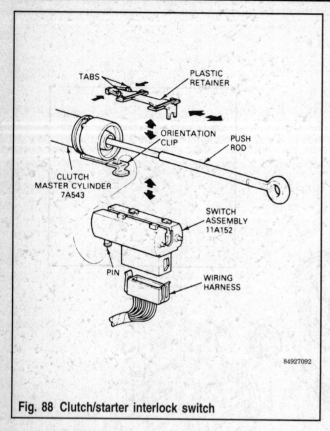

Fig. 88 Clutch/starter interlock switch

15. Install the starter motor.
16. Install the transmission.
17. Install the salve cylinder and bleed the system.

1988-89

1. Raise and support the truck end on jackstands.
2. On trucks with the externally mounted slave cylinder, remove the clutch slave cylinder.   On trucks with an internally mounted slave cylinder, disconnect the quick-disconnect coupling with a spring coupling tool such as T88T-70522-A.
3. Remove the transmission.
4. On gasoline engine models, except the 8-7.5L engine, remove the starter. Remove the flywheel housing attaching bolts and remove the housing.   On diesel engine models and the 8-7.5L gasoline engine, remove the cover and then remove the release lever and bearing from the clutch housing. To remove the release lever:
   a. Remove the dust boot.
   b. Push the release lever forward to compress the slave cylinder.
   c. Remove the slave cylinder by prying on the steel clip to free the tangs while pulling the cylinder clear.
   d. Remove the release lever by pulling it outward.
5. Mark the pressure plate and cover assembly and the flywheel so that they can be reinstalled in the same relative position.
6. Loosen the pressure plate and cover attaching bolts evenly in a staggered sequence a turn at time until the pressure plate springs are relieved of their tension. Remove the attaching bolts.
7. Remove the pressure plate and cover assembly and the clutch disc from the flywheel.
  To install:
8. Position the clutch disc on the flywheel so that an aligning tool or spare transmission mainshaft can enter the clutch pilot bearing and align the disc.

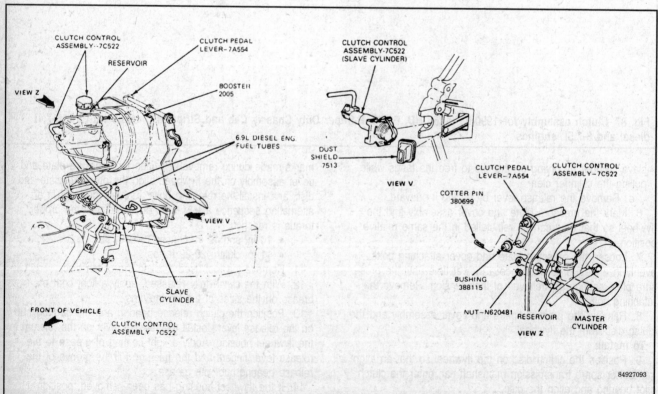

Fig. 89 Clutch hydraulic system used on 1987-89 trucks with the Diesel and 8-7.5L gasoline engines

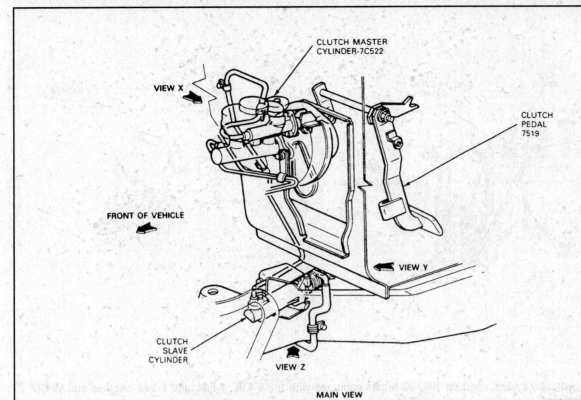

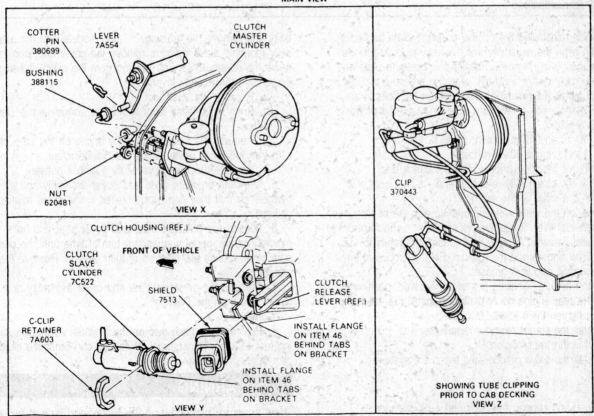

Fig. 90 Clutch hydraulic system used on trucks with the 6-4.9L, 8-5.0L and 8-5.8L engines

84927094

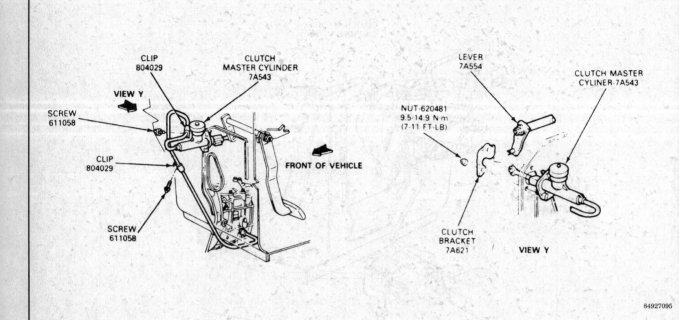

Fig. 91 Clutch hydraulic system used on 1990-93 trucks equipped with the 6-4.9L, 8-5.0L and 8-5.8L engines and M5OD and ZF transmissions

9. When reinstalling the original pressure plate and cover assembly, align the assembly and flywheel according to the marks made during removal. Position the pressure plate and cover assembly on the flywheel, align the pressure plate and disc, and install the retaining bolts. Tighten the bolts in an alternating sequence a few turns at a time until the proper torque is reached:

• 10 in. and 12 in. clutch: 15-20 ft. lbs.
• 11 in. clutch: 20-29 ft. lbs.

10. Remove the tool used to align the clutch disc.

11. With the clutch fully released, apply a light coat of grease on the sides of the driving lugs.

12. Position the clutch release bearing and the bearing hub on the release lever. Install the release lever on the fulcrum in the flywheel housing. Apply a light coating of grease to the release lever fingers and the fulcrum. Fill the groove of the release bearing hub with grease.

13. If the flywheel housing has been removed, position it against the rear engine cover plate and install the attaching bolts and tighten them to 40-50 ft. lbs.

14. Install the starter motor, if removed.

15. Install the transmission.

16. Install the salve cylinder and bleed the system.

1990-93

1. Raise and support the truck end on jackstands.

2. On trucks with the externally mounted slave cylinder, remove the clutch slave cylinder.   On trucks with an internally mounted slave cylinder, disconnect the quick-disconnect coupling with a spring coupling tool such as T88T-70522-A.

3. Remove the transmission.

4. On models with the internally mounted slave cylinder, remove the starter. Remove the flywheel housing attaching

bolts and remove the housing.   On models with the externally mounted slave cylinder, remove the cover and then remove the release lever and bearing from the clutch housing. To remove the release lever:

a. Remove the dust boot.

b. Push the release lever forward to compress the slave cylinder.

c. Remove the slave cylinder by prying on the steel clip to free the tangs while pulling the cylinder clear.

d. Remove the release lever by pulling it outward.

5. Mark the pressure plate and cover assembly and the flywheel so that they can be reinstalled in the same relative position.

6. Loosen the pressure plate and cover attaching bolts evenly in a staggered sequence a turn at time until the pressure plate springs are relieved of their tension. Remove the attaching bolts.

7. Remove the pressure plate and cover assembly and the clutch disc from the flywheel.

To install:

8. Position the clutch disc on the flywheel so that an aligning tool or spare transmission mainshaft can enter the clutch pilot bearing and align the disc.

✳✳WARNING

New pressure plate/cover bolts have been issued for use on the diesel and the 8-7.5L gasoline engine. The bolts for the diesel are 5/16 in. x 18 x 3/4 in. The bolts for the 8-7.5L are 5/16 in. x 18 x 59/64 in. The 59/64 in. bolts cannot be used with the dual mass flywheel used on the diesel, since they would interfere with the operation of the primary flywheel.

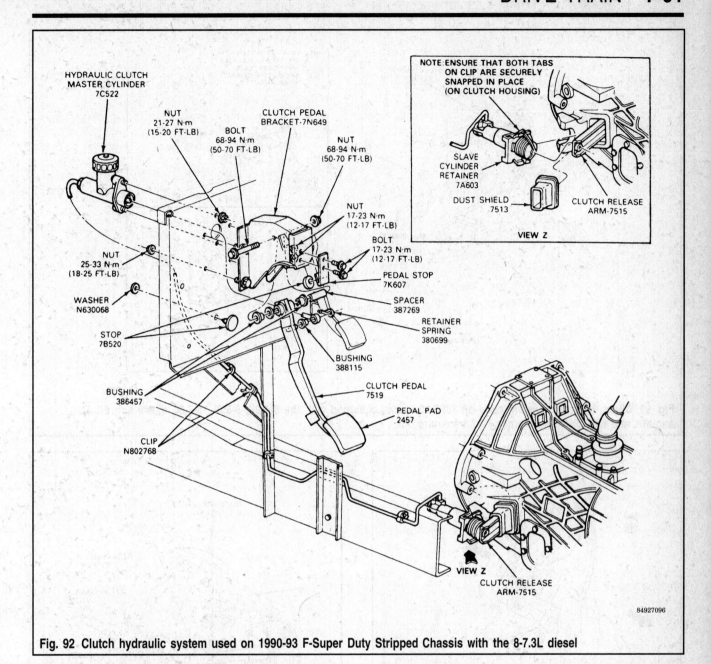

Fig. 92 Clutch hydraulic system used on 1990-93 F-Super Duty Stripped Chassis with the 8-7.3L diesel

9. When reinstalling the original pressure plate and cover assembly, align the assembly and flywheel according to the marks made during removal. Position the pressure plate and cover assembly on the flywheel, align the pressure plate and disc, and install the retaining bolts. Tighten the bolts in an alternating sequence a few turns at a time until the proper torque is reached:

- 10 in. and 12 in. clutch: 15-20 ft. lbs.
- 11 in. clutch: 20-29 ft. lbs.

10. Remove the tool used to align the clutch disc.

11. With the clutch fully released, apply a light coat of grease on the sides of the driving lugs.

12. Position the clutch release bearing and the bearing hub on the release lever. On the diesel and the 8-7.5L engine, clean and lubricate the transmission bearing retainer. Install the release lever on the fulcrum in the flywheel housing. Apply a light coating of grease to the release lever fingers and the fulcrum. Fill the groove of the release bearing hub with grease.

13. If the flywheel housing has been removed, position it against the rear engine cover plate and install the attaching bolts and tighten them to 40-50 ft. lbs.

14. Install the starter motor, if removed.

15. Install the transmission.

16. Install the salve cylinder and bleed the system.

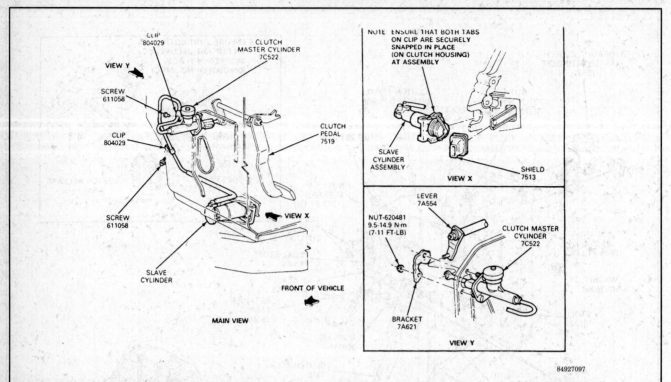

Fig. 93 Clutch hydraulic system used on 1990-93 trucks equipped with the 6-4.9L, 8-5.0L, 8-7.3L diesel and 8-7.5L engines and M5ODHD and Warner T-18 transmissions

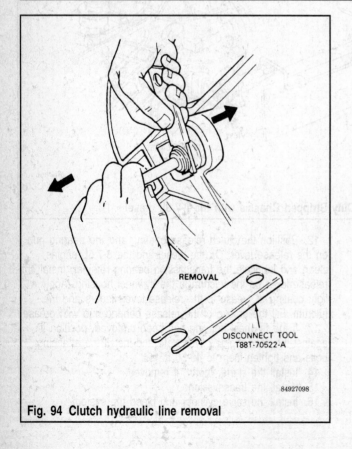

Fig. 94 Clutch hydraulic line removal

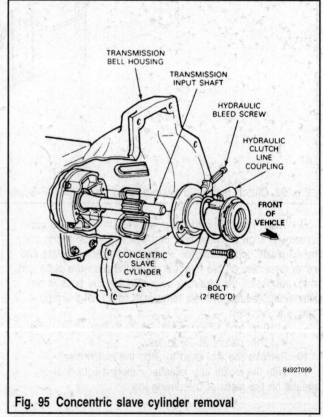

Fig. 95 Concentric slave cylinder removal

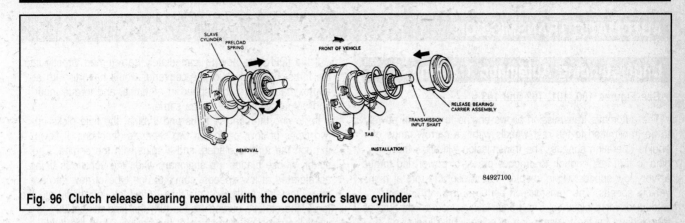

Fig. 96 Clutch release bearing removal with the concentric slave cylinder

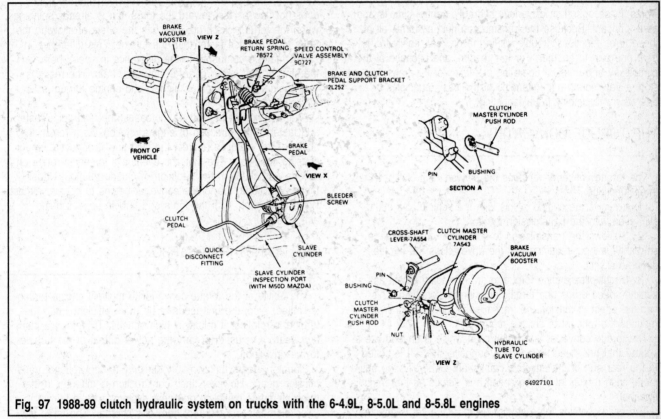

Fig. 97 1988-89 clutch hydraulic system on trucks with the 6-4.9L, 8-5.0L and 8-5.8L engines

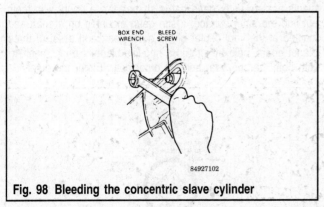

Fig. 98 Bleeding the concentric slave cylinder

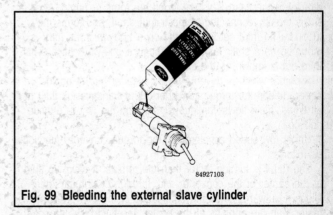

Fig. 99 Bleeding the external slave cylinder

AUTOMATIC TRANSMISSION

Understanding Automatic Transmissions

♦ **See Figures 100, 101, 102 and 103**

The automatic transmission allows engine torque and power to be transmitted to the rear wheels within a narrow range of engine operating speeds. The transmission will allow the engine to turn fast enough to produce plenty of power and torque at very low speeds, while keeping it at a sensible rpm at high vehicle speeds. The transmission performs this job entirely without driver assistance. The transmission uses a light fluid as the medium for the transmission of power. This fluid also works in the operation of various hydraulic control circuits and as a lubricant. Because the transmission fluid performs all of these three functions, trouble within the unit can easily travel from one part to another. For this reason, and because of the complexity and unusual operating principles of the transmission, a very sound understanding of the basic principles of operation will simplify troubleshooting.

THE TORQUE CONVERTER

The torque converter replaces the conventional clutch. It has three functions:

1. It allows the engine to idle with the vehicle at a standstill, even with the transmission in gear.
2. It allows the transmission to shift from range to range smoothly, without requiring that the driver close the throttle during the shift.
3. It multiplies engine torque to an increasing extent as vehicle speed drops and throttle opening is increased. This has the effect of making the transmission more responsive and reduces the amount of shifting required.

The torque converter is a metal case which is shaped like a sphere that has been flattened on opposite sides. It is bolted to the rear end of the engine's crankshaft. Generally, the entire metal case rotates at engine speed and serves as the engine's flywheel.

The case contains three sets of blades. One set is attached directly to the case. This set forms the torus or pump. Another set is directly connected to the output shaft, and forms the turbine. The third set is mounted on a hub which, in turn, is mounted on a stationary shaft through a one-way clutch. This third set is known as the stator.

A pump, which is driven by the converter hub at engine speed, keeps the torque converter full of transmission fluid at all times. Fluid flows continuously through the unit to provide cooling.

Under low speed acceleration, the torque converter functions as follows:

The torus is turning faster than the turbine. It picks up fluid at the center of the converter and, through centrifugal force, slings it outward. Since the outer edge of the converter moves faster than the portions at the center, the fluid picks up speed.

The fluid then enters the outer edge of the turbine blades. It then travels back toward the center of the converter case along the turbine blades. In impinging upon the turbine blades, the fluid loses the energy picked up in the torus.

If the fluid were now to immediately be returned directly into the torus, both halves of the converter would have to turn at approximately the same speed at all times, and torque input and output would both be the same.

In flowing through the torus and turbine, the fluid picks up two types of flow, or flow in two separate directions. It flows through the turbine blades, and it spins with the engine. The stator, whose blades are stationary when the vehicle is being accelerated at low speeds, converts one type of flow into another. Instead of allowing the fluid to flow straight back into the torus, the stator's curved blades turn the fluid almost 90° toward the direction of rotation of the engine. Thus the fluid does not flow as fast toward the torus, but is already spinning when the torus picks it up. This has the effect of allowing the torus to turn much faster than the turbine. This difference in speed may be compared to the difference in speed between the smaller and larger gears in any gear train. The result is that engine power output is higher, and engine torque is multiplied.

As the speed of the turbine increases, the fluid spins faster and faster in the direction of engine rotation. As a result, the ability of the stator to redirect the fluid flow is reduced. Under cruising conditions, the stator is eventually forced to rotate on its one-way clutch in the direction of engine rotation. Under these conditions, the torque converter begins to behave almost like a solid shaft, with the torus and turbine speeds being almost equal.

THE PLANETARY GEARBOX

The ability of the torque converter to multiply engine torque is limited. Also, the unit tends to be more efficient when the turbine is rotating at relatively high speeds. Therefore, a planetary gearbox is used to carry the power output of the turbine to the driveshaft.

Planetary gears function very similarly to conventional transmission gears. However, their construction is different in that three elements make up one gear system, and, in that all three elements are different from one another. The three elements are: an outer gear that is shaped like a hoop, with teeth cut into the inner surface; a sun gear, mounted on a shaft and located at the very center of the outer gear; and a set of three planet gears, held by pins in a ring-like planet carrier, meshing with both the sun gear and the outer gear. Either the outer

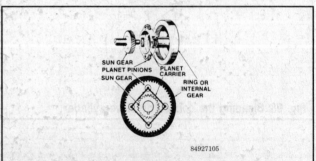

84927105

Fig. 100 Planetary gears are similar to manual transmission gears but are composed of three parts

Fig. 101 Planetary gears in the maximum reduction (low) range. The ring gear is held an a lower gear ration is obtained

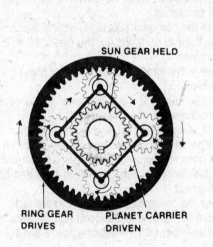

Fig. 102 Planetary gears in the minimum reduction (drive) range. The ring gear is allowed to revolve, providing a higher gear ratio

Fig. 103 Servos, operated by pressure, are used to apply or release the bands, to either hold the ring gear or allow it to rotate

THE SERVOS AND ACCUMULATORS

The servos are hydraulic pistons and cylinders. They resemble the hydraulic actuators used on many familiar machines, such as bulldozers. Hydraulic fluid enters the cylinder, under pressure, and forces the piston to move to engage the band or clutches.

The accumulators are used to cushion the engagement of the servos. The transmission fluid must pass through the accumulator on the way to the servo. The accumulator housing contains a thin piston which is sprung away from the discharge passage of the accumulator. When fluid passes through the accumulator on the way to the servo, it must move the piston against spring pressure, and this action smooths out the action of the servo.

THE HYDRAULIC CONTROL SYSTEM

The hydraulic pressure used to operate the servos comes from the main transmission oil pump. This fluid is channeled to the various servos through the shift valves. There is generally a manual shift valve which is operated by the transmission selector lever and an automatic shift valve for each automatic upshift the transmission provides: i.e., 2-speed automatics have a low/high shift valve, while 3-speeds have a 1-2 valve, and a 2-3 valve.

There are two pressures which effect the operation of these valves. One is the governor pressure which is affected by vehicle speed. The other is the modulator pressure which is affected by intake manifold vacuum or throttle position. Governor pressure rises with an increase in vehicle speed, and modulator pressure rises as the throttle is opened wider. By responding to these two pressures, the shift valves cause the upshift points to be delayed with increased throttle opening to make the best use of the engine's power output.

Most transmissions also make use of an auxiliary circuit for downshifting. This circuit may be actuated by the throttle linkage or the vacuum line which actuates the modulator, or by a cable or solenoid. It applies pressure to a special downshift surface on the shift valve or valves.

The transmission modulator also governs the line pressure, used to actuate the servos. In this way, the clutches and bands will be actuated with a force matching the torque output of the engine.

gear or the sun gear may be held stationary, providing more than one possible torque multiplication factor for each set of gears. Also, if all three gears are forced to rotate at the same speed, the gearset forms, in effect, a solid shaft.

Most modern automatics use the planetary gears to provide either a single reduction ratio of about 1.8:1, or two reduction gears: a low of about 2.5:1, and an intermediate of about 1.5:1. Bands and clutches are used to hold various portions of the gearsets to the transmission case or to the shaft on which they are mounted. Shifting is accomplished, then, by changing the portion of each planetary gearset which is held to the transmission case or to the shaft.

Transmission

REMOVAL & INSTALLATION

C6

▶ **See Figure 104**

1. From in the engine compartment, remove the two upper converter housing-to-engine bolts.

2. Disconnect the neutral switch wire at the inline connector.

3. Remove the bolt securing the fluid filler tube to the engine cylinder head.

4. Raise and support the truck on jackstands.

5. Place the drain pan under the transmission fluid pan. Starting at the rear of the pan and working toward the front, loosen the attaching bolts and allow the fluid to drain. Finally remove all of the pan attaching bolts except two at the front, to allow the fluid to further drain. With fluid drained, install two bolts on the rear side of the pan to temporarily hold it in place.

6. Remove the converter drain plug access cover from the lower end of the converter housing.

7. Remove the converter-to-flywheel attaching nuts. Place a wrench on the crankshaft pulley attaching bolt to turn the converter to gain access to the nuts.

8. With the wrench on the crankshaft pulley attaching bolt, turn the converter to gain access to the converter drain plug. Place a drain pan under the converter to catch the fluid and remove the plug. After the fluid has been drained, reinstall the plug.

9. On 2-wheel drive models, disconnect the driveshaft from the rear axle and slide shaft rearward from the transmission. Install a seal installation tool in the extension housing to prevent fluid leakage.

10. Disconnect the speedometer cable from the extension housing.

11. Disconnect the downshift and manual linkage rods from the levers at the transmission.

12. Disconnect the oil cooler lines from the transmission.

13. Remove the vacuum hose from the vacuum diaphragm unit. Remove the vacuum line retaining clip.

14. Disconnect the cable from the terminal on the starter motor. Remove the three attaching bolts and remove the starter motor.

15. On 4-wheel drive models remove the transfer case.

16. Remove the two engine rear support and insulator assembly-to-attaching bolts.

17. Remove the two engine rear support and insulator assembly-to-extension housing attaching bolts.

18. Remove the six bolts securing the No. 2 crossmember to the frame side rails.

19. Raise the transmission with a transmission jack and remove both crossmembers.

20. Secure the transmission to the jack with the safety chain.

21. Remove the remaining converter housing-to-engine attaching bolts.

22. Move the transmission away from the engine. Lower the jack and remove the converter and transmission assembly from under the vehicle.

To install:

23. Tighten the converter drain plug.

24. Position the converter on the transmission making sure the converter drive flats are fully engaged in the pump gear.

25. With the converter properly installed, place the transmission on the jack. Secure the transmission on the jack with the chain.

26. Rotate the converter until the studs and drain plug are in alignment with their holes in the flywheel.

27. Move the converter and transmission assembly forward into position, using care not to damage the flywheel and the converter pilot. The converter must rest squarely against the flywheel. This indicates that the converter pilot is not binding in the engine crankshaft.

28. Install the converter housing-to-engine attaching bolts and torque them to 65 ft. lbs. for the diesel; 50 ft. lbs. for gasoline engines.

29. Remove the transmission jack safety chain from around the transmission.

30. Position the No. 2 crossmember to the frame side rails. Install and tighten the attaching bolts.

31. Install transfer case on 4-wheel drive models.

32. Position the engine rear support and insulator assembly above the crossmember. Install the rear support and insulator assembly-to-extension housing mounting bolts and tighten the bolts to 45 ft. lbs.

33. Lower the transmission and remove the jack.

34. Secure the engine rear support and insulator assembly to the crossmember with the attaching bolts and tighten them to 80 ft. lbs.

35. Connect the vacuum line to the vacuum diaphragm making sure that the line is in the retaining clip.

36. Connect the oil cooler lines to the transmission.

37. Connect the downshift and manual linkage rods to their respective levers on the transmission.

38. Connect the speedometer cable to the extension housing.

39. Secure the starter motor in place with the attaching bolts. Connect the cable to the terminal on the starter.

40. Install a new O-ring on the lower end of the transmission filler tube and insert the tube in the case.

41. Secure the converter-to-flywheel attaching nuts and tighten them to 30 ft. lbs.

42. Install the converter housing access cover and secure it with the attaching bolts.

43. Connect the driveshaft.

44. Adjust the shift linkage as required.

45. Lower the vehicle. Then install the two upper converter housing-to-engine bolts and tighten them.

46. Position the transmission fluid filler tube to the cylinder head and secure with the attaching bolts.

47. Make sure the drain pan is securely attached, and fill the transmission to the correct level with the Dexron®II fluid.

AOD

▶ **See Figure 105**

1. Raise the vehicle on hoist or stands.

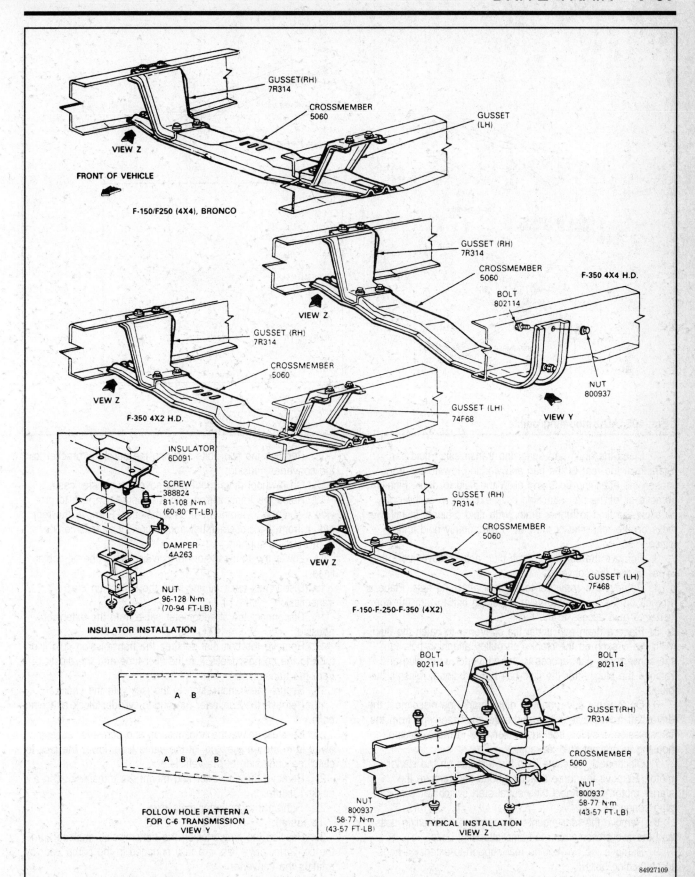

Fig. 104 C6 mounting points

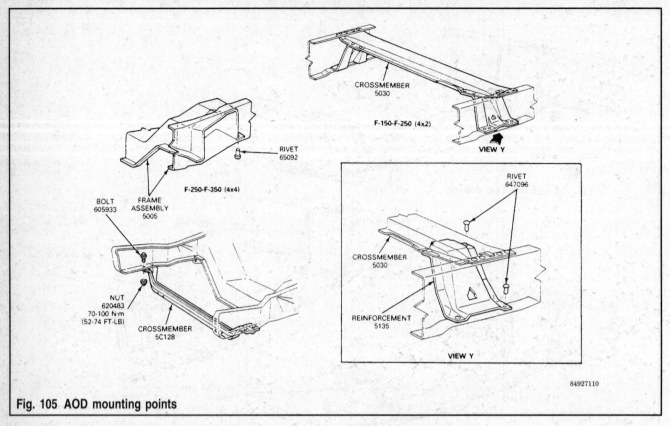

Fig. 105 AOD mounting points

2. Place the drain pan under the transmission fluid pan. Starting at the rear of the pan and working toward the front, loosen the attaching bolts and allow the fluid to drain. Finally remove all of the pan attaching bolts except two at the front, to allow the fluid to further drain. With fluid drained, install two bolts on the rear side of the pan to temporarily hold it in place.

3. Remove the converter drain plug access cover from the lower end of the converter.

4. Remove the converter-to-flywheel attaching nuts. Place a wrench on the crankshaft pulley attaching bolt to turn the converter to gain access to the nuts.

5. Place a drain pan under the converter to catch the fluid. With the wrench on the crankshaft pulley attaching bolt, turn the converter to gain access to the converter drain plug and remove the plug. After the fluid has been drained, reinstall the plug.

6. On 2-wheel drive models, matchmark and disconnect the driveshaft from the rear axle and slide shaft rearward from the transmission. Install a seal installation tool in the extension housing to prevent fluid leakage.

7. Disconnect the cable from the terminal on the starter motor. Remove the three attaching bolts and remove the starter motor. Disconnect the neutral start switch wires at the plug connector.

8. Remove the rear mount-to-crossmember attaching bolts and the two crossmember-to-frame attaching bolts.

9. Remove the two engine rear support-to-extension housing attaching bolts.

10. Disconnect the TV linkage rod from the transmission TV lever. Disconnect the manual rod from the transmission manual lever at the transmission.

11. Remove the two bolts securing the bellcrank bracket to the converter housing.

12. On 4-wheel drive models, remove the transfer case.

13. Raise the transmission with a transmission jack to provide clearance to remove the crossmember. Remove the rear mount from the crossmember and remove the crossmember from the side supports.

14. Lower the transmission to gain access to the oil cooler lines.

15. Disconnect each oil line from the fittings on the transmission.

16. Disconnect the speedometer cable from the extension housing.

17. Remove the bolt that secures the transmission fluid filler tube to the cylinder block. Lift the filler tube and the dipstick from the transmission.

18. Secure the transmission to the jack with the chain.

19. Remove the converter housing-to-cylinder block attaching bolts.

20. Carefully move the transmission and converter assembly away from the engine and, at the same time, lower the jack to clear the underside of the vehicle.

21. Remove the converter and mount the transmission in a holding fixture.

22. Tighten the converter drain plug.

To install:

23. Position the converter on the transmission, making sure the converter drive flats are fully engaged in the pump gear by rotating the converter.

24. With the converter properly installed, place the transmission on the jack. Secure the transmission to the jack with a chain.

25. Rotate the converter until the studs and drain plug are in alignment with the holes in the flywheel.

26. Move the converter and transmission assembly forward into position, using care not to damage the flywheel and the converter pilot. The converter must rest squarely against the flywheel. This indicates that the converter pilot is not binding in the engine crankshaft.

27. Install and tighten the converter housing-to-engine attaching bolts to 40-50 ft. lbs.

28. Remove the safety chain from around the transmission.

29. Install a new O-ring on the lower end of the transmission filler tube. Insert the tube in the transmission case and secure the tube to the engine with the attaching bolt.

30. Connect the speedometer cable to the extension housing.

31. Connect the oil cooler lines to the right side of transmission case.

32. Position the crossmember on the side supports. Torque the bolts to 55 ft. lbs. Position the rear mount on the crossmember and install the attaching nuts to 90 ft. lbs.

33. On 4-wheel drive models, install the transfer case.

34. Secure the rear support to the extension housing and tighten the bolts to 80 ft. lbs.

35. Lower the transmission and remove the jack.

E4OD

▶ **See Figures 106, 107, 108 and 109**

1. Raise and support the truck on jackstands.

2. Place the drain pan under the transmission fluid pan. Starting at the rear of the pan and working toward the front, loosen the attaching bolts and allow the fluid to drain. Finally remove all of the pan attaching bolts except two at the front,

to allow the fluid to further drain. With fluid drained, install two bolts on the rear side of the pan to temporarily hold it in place.

3. Remove the dipstick from the transmission.

4. On 4-wheel drive models, matchmark and remove the front driveshaft.

5. Matchmark and remove the rear driveshaft. Install a seal installation tool in the extension housing to prevent fluid leakage.

6. Disconnect the linkage from the transmission.

7. On 4-wheel drive models, disconnect the transfer case linkage.

8. Remove the heat shield and remove the manual lever position sensor connector by squeezing the tabs and pulling on the connector. NEVER ATTEMPT TO PRY THE CONNECTOR APART!

9. Remove the solenoid body heat shield.

10. Remove the solenoid body connector by pushing on the center tab and pulling on the wiring harness. NEVER ATTEMPT TO PRY APART THE CONNECTOR!

11. On 4-wheel drive models, remove the 4**x**4 switch connector from the transfer case. Be careful not to over-extend the tabs.

12. Pry the harness connector from the extension housing wire bracket.

13. On 4-wheel drive models, remove the wiring harness locators from the left side of the connector.

14. Disconnect the speedometer cable.

15. On 4-wheel drive models, remove the transfer case.

16. Remove the converter cover bolts.

17. Remove the rear engine cover plate bolts.

18. Disconnect the cable from the terminal on the starter motor. Remove the three attaching bolts and remove the

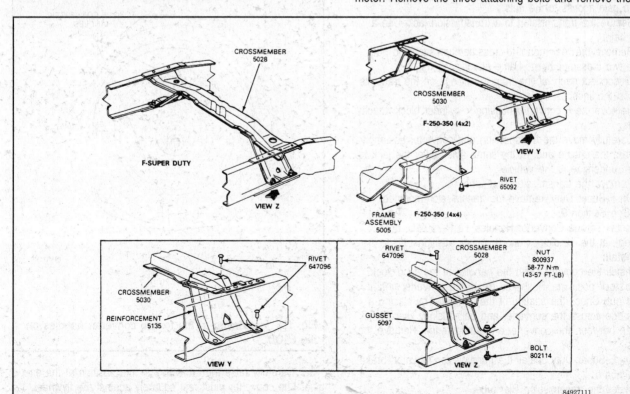

Fig. 106 E4OD mounting points

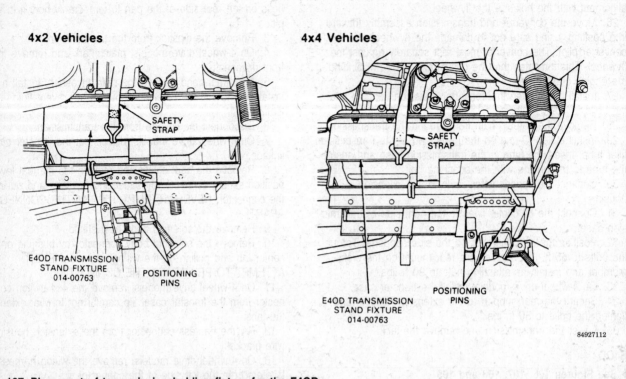

Fig. 107 Placement of transmission holding fixture for the E4OD

starter motor. Disconnect the neutral start switch wires at the plug connector.

19. Remove the converter-to-flywheel attaching nuts. Place a wrench on the crankshaft pulley attaching bolt to turn the converter to gain access to the nuts.

20. Secure the transmission to a transmission jack. Use a safety chain.

21. Remove the rear mount-to-crossmember attaching nuts and the two crossmember-to-frame attaching bolts.

22. Disconnect each oil line from the fittings on the transmission. Cap the lines.

23. Remove the 6 converter housing-to-cylinder block attaching bolts.

24. Carefully move the transmission and converter assembly away from the engine and, at the same time, lower the jack to clear the underside of the vehicle.

25. Remove the transmission filler tube.

26. On F-Super Duty, remove the transmission-mounted brake. See Section 9.

27. Install Torque Converter Handles T81P-7902-C, or equivalent, at the 12 o'clock and 6 o'clock positions.

To install:

28. Install the converter with the handles at the 12 o'clock and 6 o'clock positions. Push and rotate the converter until it bottoms out. Check the seating of the converter by placing a straightedge across the converter and bellhousing. There must be a gap between the converter and straightedge. Remove the handles.

29. On F-Super Duty, install the transmission-mounted brake. See Section 9.

30. Install the transmission filler tube.

31. Rotate the converter to align the studs with the flywheel mounting holes.

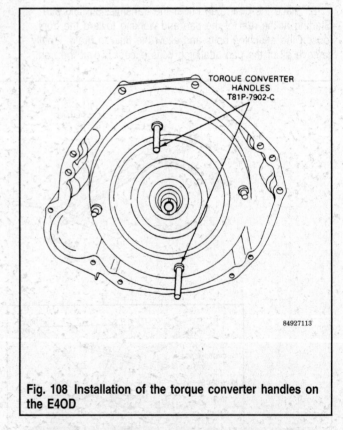

Fig. 108 Installation of the torque converter handles on the E4OD

32. Carefully raise the transmission into position at the engine. The converter must rest squarely against the flywheel.

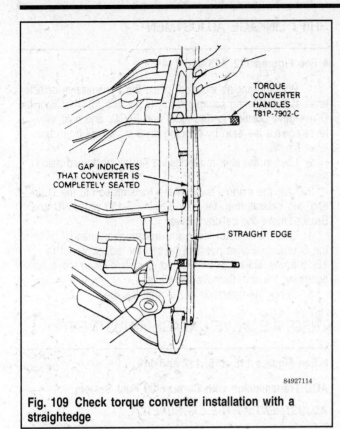

Fig. 109 Check torque converter installation with a straightedge

33. Install the 6 converter housing-to-cylinder block attaching bolts. Snug them alternately and evenly, then, tighten them alternately and evenly to 40-50 ft. lbs.

34. Install the converter drain plug cover.

35. Connect each oil line at the fittings on the transmission.

36. Install the rear mount-to-crossmember attaching nuts and the two crossmember-to-frame attaching bolts. Torque the nuts and bolts to 50 ft. lbs.

37. Remove the transmission jack.

38. Install the converter-to-flywheel attaching nuts. Place a wrench on the crankshaft pulley attaching bolt to turn the converter to gain access to the nuts. Torque the nuts to 20-30 ft. lbs.

39. Install the starter motor. Connect the cable at the terminal on the starter motor. Connect the neutral start switch wires at the plug connector.

40. Install the rear engine cover plate bolts.

41. Install the converter cover bolts.

42. On 4-wheel drive models, install the transfer case.

43. Connect the speedometer cable.

44. On 4-wheel drive models, install the wiring harness locators at the left side of the connector.

45. Connect the harness connector at the extension housing wire bracket.

46. On 4-wheel drive models, install the 4x4 switch connector at the transfer case.

47. Install the solenoid body connector. An audible click indicates connection.

48. Install the solenoid body heat shield.

49. Install the manual lever position sensor connector and the heat shield.

50. On 4-wheel drive models, connect the transfer case linkage.

51. Connect the linkage at the transmission.

52. Install the rear driveshaft.

53. On 4-wheel drive models, install the front driveshaft.

54. Install the dipstick.

55. Install the drain pan using a new gasket and sealer.

56. Lower the truck.

57. Refill the transmission and check for leaks.

Fluid Pan

REMOVAL & INSTALLATION

1. Raise the truck on a hoist or jackstands.

2. Place a drain pan under the transmission.

3. Loosen the pan attaching bolts and drain the fluid from the transmission.

4. When the fluid has drained to the level of the pan flange, remove the remaining pan bolts working from the rear and both sides of the pan to allow it to drop and drain slowly.

5. When all of the fluid has drained, remove the pan and clean it thoroughly, Discard the pan gasket.

To install:

6. Place the new gasket on the pan, and install the pan on the transmission. Tighten the attaching bolts to 12-16 ft. lbs.

7. Add three quarts of fluid to the transmission through the filler tube.

FILTER SERVICE

1. Remove the transmission oil pan and gasket.

2. Remove the screws holding the fine mesh screen to the lower valve body.

3. Install the new filter screen and transmission oil pan gasket in the reverse order of removal.

Vacuum Modulator

REMOVAL & INSTALLATION

▶ **See Figure 110**

C6

1. Disconnect the vacuum hose at the unit.

2. Remove the bracket bolt and bracket.

3. Pull the vacuum unit from the transmission.

4. Installation is the reverse of removal. Torque the bolt to 12-16 ft. lbs. Connect the vacuum hose.

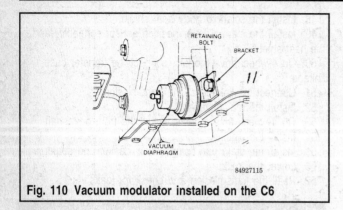

Fig. 110 Vacuum modulator installed on the C6

Adjustments

INTERMEDIATE BAND ADJUSTMENT

C6 Only

▶ See Figure 111

1. Raise the truck on a hoist or jackstands.
2. Clean all dirt away from the band adjusting screw. Remove and discard the locknut.
3. Install a new locknut and tighten the adjusting screw to 10 ft. lbs.
4. Back off the adjusting screw exactly 1½ turns.
5. Hold the adjusting screw from turning and tighten the locknut to 35-40 ft. lbs.
6. Remove the jackstands and lower the vehicle.

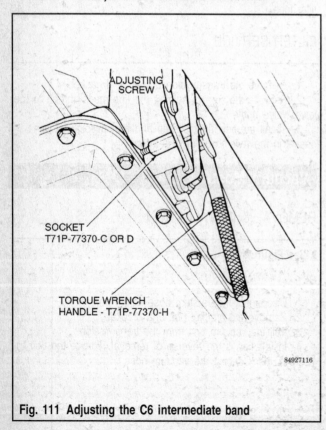

Fig. 111 Adjusting the C6 intermediate band

SHIFT LINKAGE ADJUSTMENT

▶ See Figures 112, 113 and 114

1. With the engine stopped, place the transmission selector lever at the steering column in the D position for the C6 or the D overdrive position for the AOD and E4OD, and hold the lever against the stop by hanging an 8 lb. weight from the lever handle.
2. Loosen the shift rod adjusting nut at the transmission lever.
3. Shift the manual lever at the transmission to the **D** position, two detents from the rear. On the F-150 with 4WD and Bronco, move the bellcrank lever.
4. With the selector lever and transmission manual lever in the D or D overdrive position, tighten the adjusting nut to 12-18 ft. lbs. Do not allow the rod or shift lever to move while tightening the nut. Remove the weight.
5. Check the operation of the shift linkage.

THROTTLE VALVE LINKAGE ADJUSTMENT

▶ See Figures 115, 116, 117 and 118

AOD Transmission with Carbureted Fuel System

ADJUSTMENT AT THE CARBURETOR

The TV control linkage may be adjusted at the carburetor using the following procedure:

1. Check that engine idle speed is set at the specification.
2. De-cam the fast idle cam on the carburetor so that the throttle lever is at its idle stop. Place shift lever in N (neutral), set park brake (engine off).
3. Back out the linkage lever adjusting screw all the way (screw end if flush with lever face).
4. Turn in adjusting screw until a thin shim (0.005 in. max.) or piece of writing paper fits snugly between end of screw and Throttle Lever. To eliminate effect of friction, push linkage lever forward (tending to close gap) and release before checking clearance between end of screw and throttle lever. Do not apply any load on levers with tools or hands while checking gap.
5. Turn in adjusting screw an additional four turns. (Four turns are preferred. Two turns minimum is permissible if screw travel is limited).
6. If it is not possible to turn in adjusting screw at least two addition turns or if there was sufficient screw adjusting capacity to obtain an initial gap in Step 2 above, refer to Linkage Adjustment at Transmission. Whenever it is required to adjust idle speed by more than 50 rpm, the adjustment screw on the linkage lever at the carburetor should also be readjusted as shown.

Idle Speed Change/Turns on Linkage Lever Adjustment Screw

- Less than 50 rpm: No change required
- 50 to 100 rpm increase: 1½ turns out
- 50 to 100 rpm decrease: 1½ turns in
- 100 to 150 rpm increase: 2½ turns out
- 100 to 150 rpm decrease: 2½ turns in

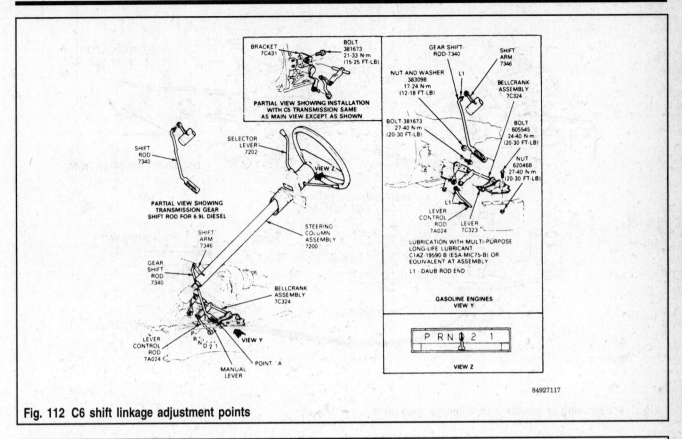

Fig. 112 C6 shift linkage adjustment points

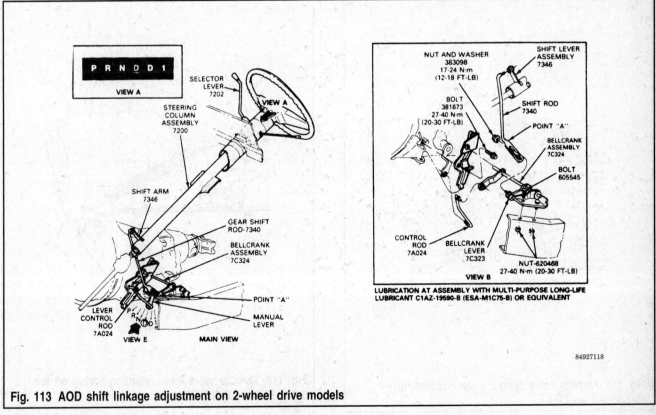

Fig. 113 AOD shift linkage adjustment on 2-wheel drive models

After making any idle speed adjustments, always verify the linkage lever and throttle lever are in contact with the throttle lever at its idle stop and the shift lever is in N (neutral).

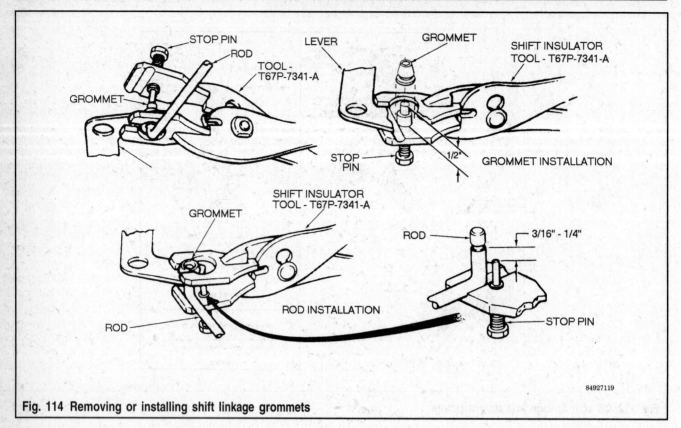

Fig. 114 Removing or installing shift linkage grommets

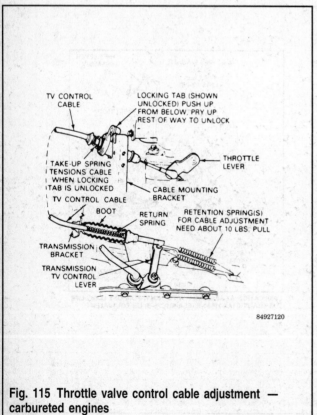

Fig. 115 Throttle valve control cable adjustment — carbureted engines

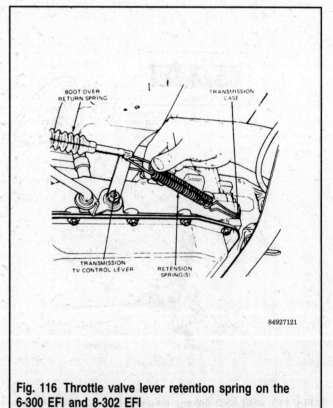

Fig. 116 Throttle valve lever retention spring on the 6-300 EFI and 8-302 EFI

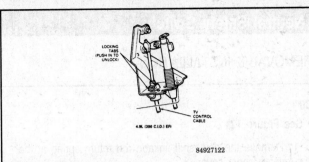

Fig. 117 AOD throttle valve control cable locking tab installation

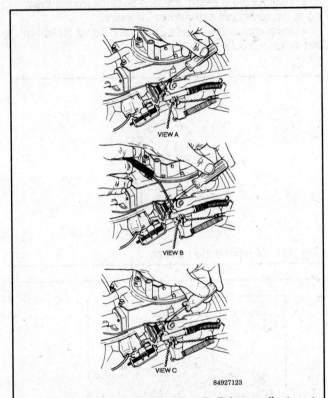

Fig. 118 Automatic overdrive throttle linkage adjustment

ADJUSTMENT AT TRANSMISSION

The linkage lever adjustment screw has limited adjustment capability. It is not possible to adjust the TV linkage using this screw, the length of the TV control rod assembly must be readjusted using the following procedure. This procedure must also be followed whenever a new TV control rod assembly is installed.

This procedure requires placing the vehicle on jackstands to give access to the linkage components at the transmission TV control lever.

1. Set the engine curb idle speed to specification.
2. With engine off, de-cam the fast idle cam on the carburetor so that the throttle lever is against the idle stop. Place shift lever in Neutral and set park brake (engine off).
3. Set the linkage lever adjustment screw at its approximately mid-range.

4. If a new TV control rod assembly is being installed, connect the rod to the linkage lever at the carburetor.

✻✻CAUTION

The following steps involve working in proximity to the exhaust system. Allow the exhaust system to cool before proceeding.

5. Raise the vehicle on the hoist.
6. Using a 13mm box end wrench, loosen the bolt on the sliding trunnion block on the TV control rod assembly. Remove any corrosion from the control rod and free-up the trunnion block so that it slides freely on the control rod. Insert pin into transmission lever grommet.
7. Push up on the lower end of the control rod to insure that the linkage lever at carburetor is firmly against the throttle lever. Release force on rod. Rod must stay up.
8. Push the TV control lever on the transmission up against its internal stop with a firm force (approximately 5 pounds) and tighten the bolt on the trunnion block. do not relax force on lever until nut is tightened.
9. Lower the vehicle and verify that the throttle lever is still against the idle stop. If not, repeat steps 2 through 9.

THROTTLE VALVE CABLE ADJUSTMENT

▶ **See Figures 119 and 120**

AOD Transmission with EFI Fuel System

ADJUSTMENT WITH ENGINE OFF

1. Set the parking brake and put the selector lever in **N**.
2. Remove the protective cover from the cable.
3. Make sure that the throttle lever is at the idle stop. If it isn't, check for binding or interference. NEVER ATTEMPT TO ADJUST THE IDLE STOP!
4. Make sure that the cable is free of sharp bends or is not rubbing on anything throughout its entire length.
5. Lubricate the TV lever ball stud with chassis lube.
6. Unlock the locking tab at the throttle body by prying with a small screwdriver.
7. Install a spring on the TV control lever, to hold it in the rearmost travel position. The spring must exert at least 10 lbs. of force on the lever.
8. Rotate the transmission outer TV lever 10-30° and slowly allow it to return.
9. Push down on the locking tab until flush.
10. Remove the retaining spring from the lever.

THROTTLE KICKDOWN LINKAGE ADJUSTMENT

1. Move the carburetor throttle linkage to the wide open position.
2. Insert a 0.060 in. thick spacer between the throttle lever and the kickdown adjusting screw.
3. Rotate the transmission kickdown lever until the lever engages the transmission internal stop. Do not use the kickdown rod to turn the transmission lever.

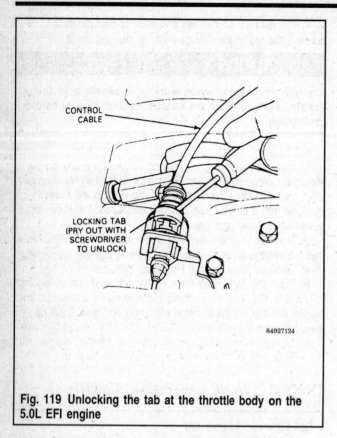

CONTROL CABLE

LOCKING TAB
(PRY OUT WITH
SCREWDRIVER
TO UNLOCK)

84927124

Fig. 119 Unlocking the tab at the throttle body on the 5.0L EFI engine

4. Turn the adjusting screw until it contacts the 0.060 in. spacer.

5. Remove the spacer.

Neutral Safety Switch

REMOVAL & INSTALLATION

C6

♦ **See Figure 121**

1. Remove the downshift linkage rod return spring at the low-reverse servo cover.

2. Coat the outer lever attaching nut with penetrating oil. Remove the nut and lever.

3. Remove the 2 switch attaching bolts, disconnect the wiring at the connectors and remove the switch.

4. Installation is the reverse of removal. Adjust the switch and torque the bolts to 55-75 inch lbs.

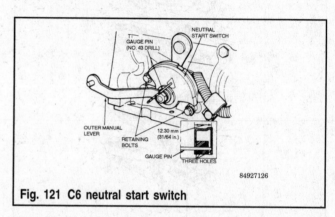

NEUTRAL START SWITCH

TV GAUGE PIN
(NO. 43 DRILL)

OUTER MANUAL LEVER

RETAINING BOLTS

12.30 mm
(31/64 in.)

GAUGE PIN

THREE HOLES

84927126

Fig. 121 C6 neutral start switch

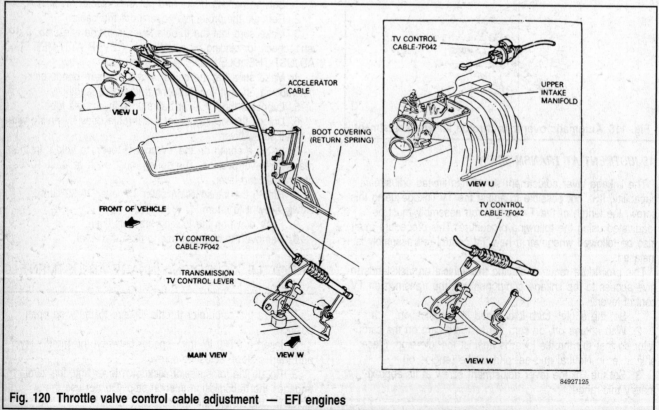

ACCELERATOR CABLE

VIEW U

BOOT COVERING
(RETURN SPRING)

FRONT OF VEHICLE

TV CONTROL
CABLE-7F042

TRANSMISSION
TV CONTROL LEVER

MAIN VIEW

VIEW W

TV CONTROL
CABLE-7F042

UPPER INTAKE MANIFOLD

VIEW U

TV CONTROL
CABLE-7F042

VIEW W

84927125

Fig. 120 Throttle valve control cable adjustment — EFI engines

AOD

▶ See Figure 122

1. Disconnect the wiring from the switch.
2. Using a deep socket, unscrew the switch.
3. Installation is the reverse of removal. Torque the switch to 10 ft. lbs.

ADJUSTMENT

1. Hold the steering column transmission selector lever against the Neutral stop.
2. Move the sliding block assembly on the neutral switch to the neutral position and insert a 0.091 in. (2.3mm) gauge pin in the alignment hole on the terminal side of the switch.

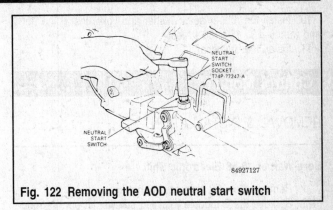

Fig. 122 Removing the AOD neutral start switch

3. Move the switch assembly housing so that the sliding block contacts the actuating pin lever. Secure the switch to the outer tube of the steering column and remove the gauge pin.
4. Check the operation of the switch. The engine should only start in Neutral and Park.

TRANSFER CASE

Front or Rear Output Shaft Seal

REMOVAL & INSTALLATION

Borg-Warner 13-45

1. Raise and support the truck on jackstands.
2. Disconnect the driveshaft at the yoke.
3. Remove the yoke nut and washer.
4. Pull the yoke from the shaft.
5. Center-punch the seal and carefully pry it from its bore. Don't scratch the bore!

To install:

6. Clean the bore thoroughly.
7. Coat the OD of the new seal with sealer and the ID with clean Dexron®II ATF.
8. Position the seal squarely in the bore and drive it into place with a seal driver, or similar tool. Don't hammer directly on the seal.
9. Install the washer and yoke. Coat the threads of the shaft with a thread locking compound. Install the nut and torque it to 120-150 ft. lbs.
10. Install the driveshaft.

Borg-Warner 13-56 Manual Shift

FIXED YOKE TYPE

1. Raise and support the truck on jackstands.
2. Disconnect the driveshaft at the yoke.
3. Remove the 30mm yoke nut, washer and rubber seal.
4. Pull the yoke from the shaft.
5. Center-punch the seal and carefully pry it from its bore. Don't scratch the bore!

To install:

6. Clean the bore thoroughly.
7. Coat the OD and ID of the new seal with clean Dexron®II ATF.

8. Position the seal squarely in the bore and drive it into place with a seal driver, or similar tool. Don't hammer directly on the seal.
9. Install a new seal slinger.
10. Install the rubber seal, washer and yoke. Install the nut and torque it to 150-180 ft. lbs.
11. Install the driveshaft.

SLIP-TYPE REAR SPLINE SEAL

1. Raise and support the truck on jackstands.
2. Disconnect the driveshaft at the rear axle and slide it from the transfer case.
3. Center-punch the seal and carefully pry it from its bore. Don't scratch the bore!
4. Remove and discard the bushing from the retainer.

To install:

5. Drive a new bushing into place with a seal driver or equivalent tool
6. Position the seal in the retainer so the notch on the seal faces upwards and the drain hole in the rubber boot is downwards. Drive it into place with a seal driver, or similar tool. Don't hammer directly on the seal.
7. Install the driveshaft.

Borg-Warner 13-56 Electronic Shift

1. Raise and support the truck on jackstands.
2. Disconnect the driveshaft at the yoke.
3. Remove the 30mm yoke nut, washer and rubber seal.
4. Pull the yoke from the shaft.
5. Center-punch the seal and carefully pry it from its bore. Don't scratch the bore!

To install:

6. Clean the bore thoroughly.
7. Coat the OD and ID of the new seal with clean Dexron®II ATF.
8. Position the seal squarely in the bore and drive it into place with a seal driver, or similar tool. Don't hammer directly on the seal.
9. Install a new seal slinger.

10. Install the rubber seal, washer and yoke. Install the nut and torque it to 150-180 ft. lbs.

11. Install the driveshaft.

Control Module

REMOVAL & INSTALLATION

Borg-Warner 13-56 Electronic Shift

1. Remove the right side cowl panel kick pad.
2. Remove the 2 module retaining screws, lift out the module and unplug the wiring.
3. Installation is the reverse of removal.

Transfer Case

REMOVAL & INSTALLATION

Borg-Warner Model 13-45

▶ See Figure 123

1. Raise and support the truck on jackstands.
2. Drain the fluid from the transfer case.
3. Disconnect the four wheel drive indicator switch wire connector at the transfer case.
4. Remove the skid plate from the frame, if so equipped.
5. Matchmark and disconnect the front driveshaft from the front output yoke.
6. Matchmark and disconnect the rear driveshaft from the rear output shaft yoke.
7. Disconnect the speedometer driven gear from the transfer case rear bearing retainer.
8. Remove the retaining rings and shift rod from the transfer case shift lever.
9. Disconnect the vent hose from the transfer case.
10. Remove the heat shield from the frame.
11. Support the transfer case with a transmission jack.
12. Remove the bolts retaining the transfer case to the transmission adapter.
13. Lower the transfer case from the vehicle.
To install:
14. When installing place a new gasket between the transfer case and the adapter.
15. Raise the transfer case with the transmission jack so that the transmission output shaft aligns with the splined transfer case input shaft. Install the bolts retaining the transfer case to the adapter.
16. Remove the transmission jack from the transfer case.
17. Connect the rear driveshaft to the rear output shaft yoke. Torque the bolts to 15 ft. lbs.
18. Install the shift lever to the transfer case and install the retaining nut.
19. Connect the speedometer driven gear to the transfer case.
20. Connect the four wheel drive indicator switch wire connector at the transfer case.

21. Connect the front driveshaft to the front output yoke. Torque the bolts to 15 ft. lbs.
22. Position the heat shield to the frame crossmember and the mounting lug on the transfer case. Install and tighten the retaining bolts.
23. Install the skid plate to the frame.
24. Install the drain plug. Remove the filler plug and install six pints of Dexron®II type transmission fluid or equivalent.
25. Lower the vehicle.

Borg-Warner 13-56 Manual Shift

▶ See Figure 124

1. Raise and support the truck on jackstands.
2. Drain the fluid from the transfer case.
3. Disconnect the four wheel drive indicator switch wire connector at the transfer case.
4. Remove the skid plate from the frame, if so equipped.
5. Matchmark and disconnect the front driveshaft from the front output yoke.
6. Matchmark and disconnect the rear driveshaft from the rear output shaft yoke.
7. Disconnect the speedometer driven gear from the transfer case rear bearing retainer.
8. Remove the retaining rings and shift rod from the transfer case shift lever.
9. Disconnect the vent hose from the transfer case.
10. Remove the heat shield from the frame.
11. Support the transfer case with a transmission jack.
12. Remove the bolts retaining the transfer case to the transmission adapter.
13. Lower the transfer case from the vehicle.
To install:
14. When installing place a new gasket between the transfer case and the adapter.
15. Raise the transfer case with the transmission jack so that the transmission output shaft aligns with the splined transfer case input shaft. Install the bolts retaining the transfer case to the adapter. Torque the bolts to 40 ft. lbs. in the pattern shown.
16. Remove the transmission jack from the transfer case.
17. Connect the rear driveshaft to the rear output shaft yoke. Torque the bolts to 15 ft. lbs.
18. Install the shift lever to the transfer case and install the retaining nut.
19. Connect the speedometer driven gear to the transfer case.
20. Connect the four wheel drive indicator switch wire connector at the transfer case.
21. Connect the front driveshaft to the front output yoke. Torque the bolts to 15 ft. lbs.
22. Position the heat shield to the frame crossmember and the mounting lug on the transfer case. Install and tighten the retaining bolts.
23. Install the skid plate to the frame.
24. Install the drain plug. Remove the filler plug and install six pints of Dexron®II type transmission fluid or equivalent.
25. Lower the vehicle.

Borg-Warner 13-56 Electronic Shift

▶ See Figures 125 and 126

1. Raise and support the truck on jackstands.

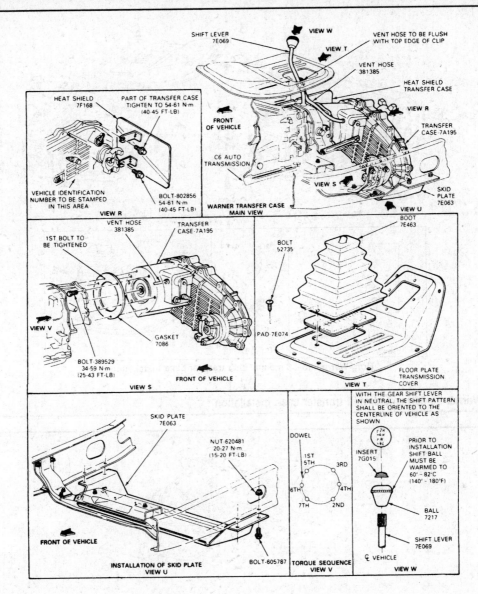

Fig. 123 Borg-Warner 13-45 transfer case installation

2. Drain the fluid from the transfer case.

3. Disconnect the wire connector at the transfer case.

4. Remove the skid plate from the frame, if so equipped.

5. Matchmark and disconnect the front driveshaft from the front output yoke.

6. Matchmark and disconnect the rear driveshaft from the rear output shaft yoke.

7. Disconnect the speedometer driven gear from the transfer case rear bearing retainer.

8. Disconnect the vent hose from the transfer case.

9. Remove the heat shield from the frame.

10. Support the transfer case with a transmission jack.

11. Remove the bolts retaining the transfer case to the transmission adapter.

12. Lower the transfer case from the vehicle.

13. When installing place a new gasket between the transfer case and the adapter.

To install:

14. Raise the transfer case with the transmission jack so that the transmission output shaft aligns with the splined transfer case input shaft. Install the bolts retaining the transfer case to the adapter. Torque the bolts to 40 ft. lbs. in the pattern illustrated.

15. Remove the transmission jack from the transfer case.

16. Connect the rear driveshaft to the rear output shaft yoke. Torque the bolts to 28 ft. lbs.

17. Install the shift lever to the transfer case and install the retaining nut.

18. Connect the speedometer driven gear to the transfer case. Tighten the bolt to 25 inch lbs.

19. Connect the wire connector at the transfer case.

20. Connect the front driveshaft to the front output yoke. Torque the bolts to 15 ft. lbs.

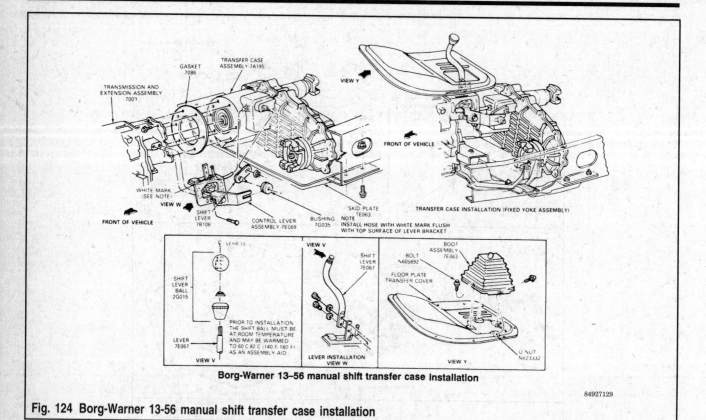

Borg-Warner 13–56 manual shift transfer case installation

Fig. 124 Borg-Warner 13-56 manual shift transfer case installation

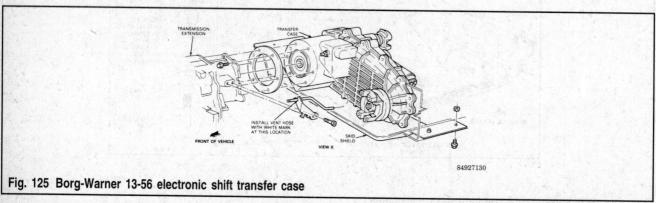

Fig. 125 Borg-Warner 13-56 electronic shift transfer case

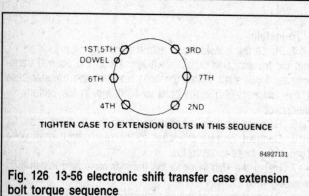

TIGHTEN CASE TO EXTENSION BOLTS IN THIS SEQUENCE

Fig. 126 13-56 electronic shift transfer case extension bolt torque sequence

21. Position the heat shield to the frame crossmember and the mounting lug on the transfer case. Install and tighten the retaining bolts.

22. Install the skid plate to the frame.
23. Install the drain plug. Remove the filler plug and install six pints of Dexron®II type transmission fluid or equivalent.
24. Lower the vehicle.

TRANSFER CASE OVERHAUL

Borg-Warner 13-45

▶ **See Figures 127, 128 and 129**

1. Drain the fluid from the case.
2. Remove both output shaft yokes.
3. Remove the 4WD indicator switch.
4. Unbolt and remove the case cover. The cover may be pried off using a screwdriver in the pry bosses.
5. Remove the magnetic chip collector from the bottom of the case.

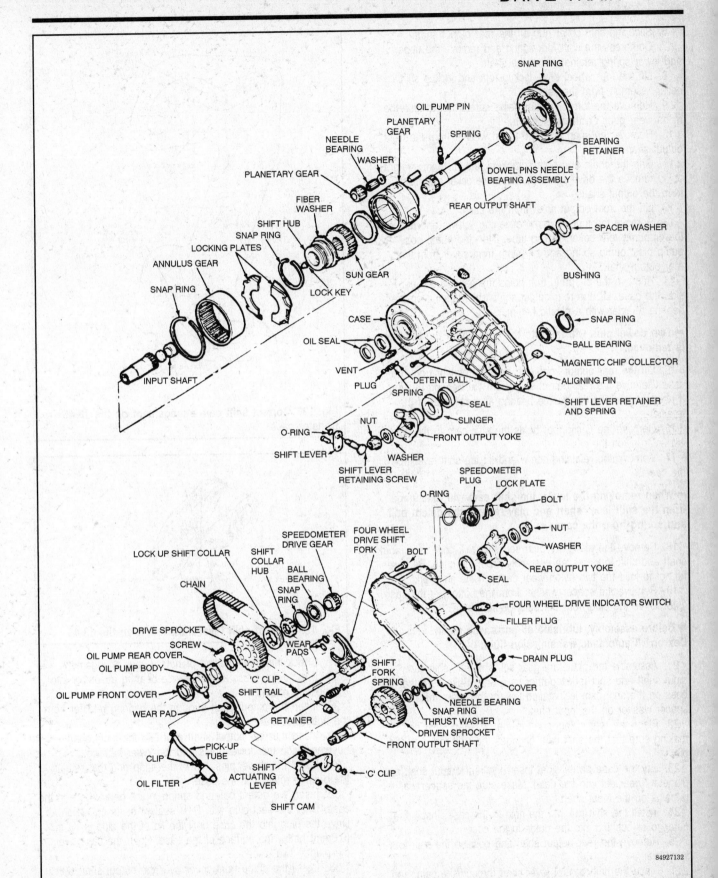

Fig. 127 Borg-Warner 13-45 transfer case explode view

84927132

6. Slide the shift collar hub off the rear output shaft.

7. Compress the shift fork spring and remove the upper and lower spring retainers from the shaft.

8. Lift the four wheel drive lockup fork and lockup shift collar assembly from the case.

9. Remove the thrust washer being careful not to lose the nylon wear pads on the lockup fork.

10. Remove the snap ring and thrust washer from the front output shaft.

11. Grip the chain and both sprockets and lift them straight up to remove the drive sprocket, driven sprocket and chain from the output shafts.

12. Lift the front output shaft from the case.

13. Remove the four oil pump attaching screws and remove the oil pump rear cover, pickup tube, filter and pump body, two pump pins, pump spring and oil pump front cover from the rear output shaft.

14. Remove the snapring that holds the bearing retainer inside the case. Lift the rear output shaft while tapping on the bearing retainer with a plastic hammer.

➡**Two dowel pins will fall into the case when the retainer is removed.**

15. Lift the rear output shaft and bearing retainer from the case. Remove the rear output shaft from the bearing retainer. If necessary, press the needle bearing assembly out of the retainer.

16. Remove the C-clip that holds the shift cam to the actuating lever inside the case.

17. Remove the retaining screw and lift the shift lever from the case.

➡**When removing the lever, the shift cam will disengage from the shift lever shaft and may release the detent ball and spring from the case.**

18. Remove the planetary gear set, shift rail, shift cam, input shaft and shift forks, as an assembly, from the case. Be careful not to lose the two nylon wear pads on the shift fork.

19. Remove the spacer washer from the bottom of the case.

20. Drive the plug from the detent spring bore.

➡**Before assembly, lubricate all parts with clean Dexron®II automatic transmission fluid.**

21. Assemble the planetary gear set, shift rail, shift cam, input shaft and shift fork together as a unit. Make sure that the boss on the shift cam is installed toward the case. Install the spacer washer on the input shaft.

22. Place the rear output shaft in the planetary gear set, making sure that the shift cam engages the shift fork actuating pin.

23. Lay the case on its side. Insert the rear output shaft and planetary gear set into the case. Make sure the spacer washer remains on the input shaft.

24. Install the shift rail into the hole in the case. Install the outer roller bushing into the guide in the case.

25. Remove the rear output shaft and position the shift fork in neutral.

26. Place the shift control lever shaft through the cam, and install the clip ring. Make sure that the shift control lever is pointed downward and is parallel to the front face of the case.

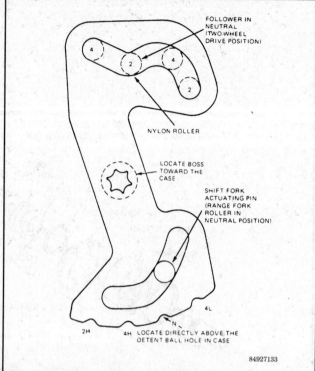

Fig. 128 Correct shift cam engagement on the 13-45 transfer case

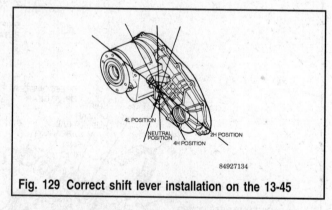

Fig. 129 Correct shift lever installation on the 13-45

27. Check the shift fork and planetary gear engagement.

28. If removed, press a new needle bearing assembly into the bearing retainer.

29. Insert the output shaft through the bearing retainer from the bottom outward.

30. Insert the rear output shaft pilot into the input shaft bushing. Align the dowel holes and the lower bearing.

31. Install the dowel pins. Install the snap ring that retains the bearing retainer in the case.

32. Insert the detent ball and spring in the detent bore in the case. Coat the seal plug with RTV sealant or its equivalent. Drive the plug into the case until the lip of the plug is 5/16 in. (0.8mm) below the surface of the case. Peen the case over the plug in two places.

33. Install the pump front cover over the output shaft with the flanged side down. The word **TOP** must be facing the top of the transfer case.

34. Install the oil pump spring and two pump pins with the flat side outward in the hole in the output shaft. Push both pins in to install the oil pump body, pickup tube and filter.

35. Place the oil pump rear cover on the output shaft with the flanged side outward. The word **TOP** must be positioned toward the top of the case. Apply Loctite® or its equivalent to the oil pump bolts and torque them to 36-40 inch lbs.

36. Install the thrust washer on the rear output shaft nest to the oil pump.

37. Place the drive sprocket on the front output shaft. Install the snap ring and thrust washer.

38. Install the chain on the drive sprocket and driven sprocket. Lower the chain into position in the case. The driven sprocket is installed through the front output shaft bearing and the drive sprocket is installed in the rear output shaft.

39. Engage the 4WD shift fork on the shift collar. Slide the shift fork over the shift shaft and the shift collar over the rear output shaft. Make sure the nylon wear pads are installed on the shift fork tips and the necked-down part of the shift collar is facing downward.

40. Push the 4WD shift spring downward and install the upper spring retainer. Push the spring upward and install the lower retainer.

41. Install the shift collar hub on the rear output shaft.

42. Apply a bead of RTV sealant on the case mounting surface. Lower the cover over the rear output shaft. Align the shift rail with its blind hole in the cover. Make sure the front output shaft is fully seated in its support bearing. Install and tighten the bolts to 40-45 ft. lbs. Allow one hour curing time for the RTV sealant prior to using the case.

43. Install the 4WD indicator switch. Torque to 8-12 ft. lbs.

44. Press the oil slinger on the front yoke. Install the front and rear output shaft yckes. Coat the nuts with Loctite® or equivalent and torque to 100-130 ft. lbs.

45. Fill the unit with 6 pints of Dexron® II. Tighten the fill plug to 18 ft. lbs.

46. Install the unit in the vehicle and start the engine. Remove the level plug. If the fluid is flowing from the hole in a stream, the pump is not operating properly. The fluid should drip slowly from the hole.

Borg-Warner 13-56 Manual Shift

◆ See Figures 130, 131, 132, 133 and 134

✳✳WARNING

The transfer case shell is made of magnesium. It is VERY susceptible to damage, such a scratches, nicks and chipping!

1. Drain the fluid from the case.

2. Remove the speedometer cover.

3. Remove both output shaft yokes.

4. Remove the 4WD indicator switch. DO NOT LOSE THE ALUMINUM WASHER! This washer controls switch operation.

5. Remove the front and rear yoke seals using tools T74P-77248-A and T50L-100-A.

6. Using the same tools, remove the input shaft seal.

7. Unbolt and remove the rear bearing retainer from the case cover. The retainer may be pried off using a ½ in. breaker bar in the pry bosses. Remove all traces of RTV sealer.

8. Lift the rear output shaft and remove the speedometer gear retaining clip.

9. Slide the speedometer gear forward and remove the ball with a small magnet. Pull the gear off the output shaft.

10. Remove the snapring from the rear output shaft that retains the upper rear ball bearing.

11. Unbolt and remove front case cover from the rear case cover. The case halves may be separated using a ½ in. breaker bar in the pry bosses. Remove all traces of RTV sealer.

12. Remove the front output shaft inner needle bearing from the rear cover using a puller-type slidehammer.

13. Drive out the rear output shaft bearing from the inside of the case.

14. Remove the output shaft clutch hub snapring. Slide the 4WD hub off of the shaft.

15. Remove the spring from the shift rail and lift the mode shift fork along with the shift collar, from the upper sprocket spline.

16. Disassemble the 2WD-4WD lockup assembly by removing the internal snapring and pull the lockup hub and spring from the collar.

17. Remove the snapring retaining the lower sprocket to the lower output shaft. Grasp the upper and lower sprocket along with the chain, and lift them, simultaneously, from the upper and lower shafts.

18. Remove the shift rail by sliding it straight out of the shift fork.

19. Remove the high/low shift fork by first rotating it until the roller is free from the cam, then sliding it out of engagement from the shift hub.

20. Remove the magnetic chip collector from the bottom of the case.

21. Lift the pump screen and remove the output shaft assembly with the pump assembled on it. If you are going to disassemble the pump, remove the 4 bolts from the pump body. Note the position of the pump front body, pins, spring, rear cover and pump retainer before disassembly.

22. Remove the high/low shift hub.

23. Remove the front output shaft from the case.

24. Turn the front case over and remove the front oil seal with a puller.

25. Expand the snapring on the input shaft and allow it to drop out of the bearing. If either the bearing or bushing is defective, both must be replaced as a unit. Drive them out together.

26. Remove the ring gear by prying out the internal snapring and lift out the gear.

27. Remove the PTO drive gear from the input shaft carrier assembly.

28. Remove the internal snapring holding the input shaft bearing and drive out the bearing from the outside.

29. Remove the internal snapring holding the front output shaft bearing and drive out the bearing from the front of the case.

30. Remove the shift cam by removing the retaining clip and sliding the shift shaft out of the case.

31. Remove the shift shaft seal by carefully prying it out of the case, being careful to avoid damaging the magnesium surfaces.

32. Remove the shift cam, assist spring and assist spring bushing.

➡**Before assembly, lubricate all parts with clean Dexron®II automatic transmission fluid. Remove any chips from the bolt holes or the case cover.**

33. Install the input shaft and front output shaft bearings in the case using drivers.
34. Install the internal snaprings.
35. Drive the front output shaft seal into the case until it is fully seated.
36. Install the front output shaft through the lower bearing.
37. Install the front yoke assembly onto the shaft, followed by the rubber seal, flat washer and 30mm locknut. Torque the nut to 130-180 ft. lbs.
38. Press the PTO drive gear onto the input shaft.
39. Press the needle bearing and bronze bushing into the input shaft.

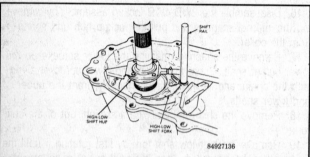

Fig. 131 High/low shift fork and rail on the 13-56 manual shift

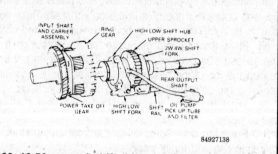

Fig. 132 13-56 manual shift drive train components, exploded view

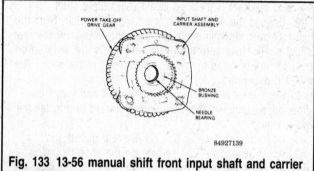

Fig. 133 13-56 manual shift front input shaft and carrier assembly

40. Install the ring gear into the slots in the case and retain it with the large internal snapring, making certain that it is fully seated.

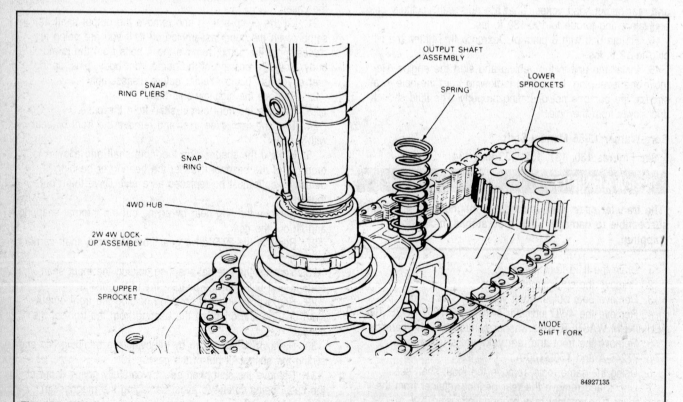

Fig. 130 2W/4W sprockets, 2W/4W lock-up assembly, chain and upper and lower sprockets on the 13-56 manual shift

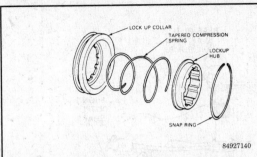

LOCK UP COLLAR
TAPERED COMPRESSION SPRING
LOCKUP HUB
SNAP RING
84927140

Fig. 134 13-56 manual shift 2W/4W lock-up collar assembly

41. Install the input shaft and carrier in the case through the input shaft bearing bore, carefully aligning the gear teeth.

42. Support the carrier assembly and install a new snapring on the front side of the input shaft bearing, making sure that it is fully seated in the groove.

43. Install the upper input shaft oil seal in the case.

44. Install a new shifter shaft seal in the case.

45. Assemble the shift cam assembly in the case by sliding the shift shaft and lever assembly through the case and seal into engagement with the shift cam. Secure the cam with the retaining clip.

46. Install the shift cam assist spring into position in the bushing of the shift cam in the recess of the case.

47. Assemble the pump and output shaft as follows:

    a. Install the oil pump cover with the word FRONT facing the front of the case.

    b. Install the two pins, with the flats facing upward, with the springs between the pins, and place the assembly in the oil pump bore in the output shaft.

    c. Place the oil pump body and pickup tube over the shaft, and make certain that the pins are riding against the inside of the pump body.

    d. Place the oil pump rear cover, with the words TOP REAR facing the rear of the case.

    e. Install the pump retainer with the tabs facing the front of the case.

    f. Install the 4 retaining bolts and rotate the output shaft while tightening the bolts to prevent the pump from binding. Torque the bolts to 40 inch lbs.

    g. Lubricate the whole assembly with clean transmission fluid. The output shaft should turn freely. If not, loosen and retorque the bolts.

48. Install the high/low shift hub.

49. Install the shift rail through the high/low fork bore and into the rail bore in the case.

50. Install the output shaft and oil pump assembly in the input shaft. Make certain that the external splines of the output shaft engage the internal splines of the high/low shift hub. Make sure that the oil pump retainer and oil filter leg are in the groove and notch of the front case.

51. Install the collector magnet.

52. Assemble the upper and lower sprockets with the chain, and place them on the upper and lower shafts. Install the washer and snapring that retain the lower sprocket.

53. Assemble the 2WD/4WD lock-up assembly:

    a. Install the tapered compression spring in the lock-up collar with the small end installed first.

    b. Place the lock-up hub over the spring and compress the spring while installing the internal snapring which holds the assembly together.

54. Install the lock-up assembly and its shift fork over the external splines of the upper sprocket and the shift rail, with the long boss of the shift rail facing forward.

55. Assemble the 4WD return spring over the shift rail and against the shift fork.

56. Place the 4WD hub over the external splines of the output shaft. Install the snapring.

57. Press the lower output needle bearing into its bore in the rear cover.

58. Press the rear output shaft bearing into the cover. Install the snapring.

59. Install the rear output shaft seal in the bearing retainer.

60. Coat the mating surface of the front case with a non-acidic silicone rubber gasket material.

61. Place the cover on the case making sure that the shafts and shift rail are all aligned. Torque the bolts to 36 ft. lbs.

62. Install the rear bearing snapring on the output shaft.

63. Place the speedometer drive gear over the shaft aligning the slot with the drive ball hole. The gear should go completely against the snapring retaining the output shaft. Place the ball in the hole and pull the gear over the ball. Snap the retaining clip between the snapring and speedometer gear.

64. Apply a bead of non-acidic silicone rubber gasket material on the face of the rear bearing retainer.

65. Place the retainer in position and torque the 4 bolts to 36 ft. lbs.

66. If the case has a slip yoke rear bearing retainer housing, remove the extension yoke oil seal and bushing and install a new bushing and seal. Use puller and drivers for this operation.

67. Install the rear output shaft yoke and slinger. Install the rubber seal, flat washer and locking nut. Torque the nut to 150-180 ft. lbs.

68. Install the drain plug.

69. Install the 4WD indicator light switch and aluminum washer.

70. Fill the case with 64 ounces of Dexron®II fluid and install the fill plug.

Borg-Warner 13-56 Electronic Shift

◗ See Figures 135, 136, 137, 138 and 139

✳✳WARNING

The transfer case shell is made of magnesium. It is VERY susceptible to damage, such as scratches, nicks and chipping!

1. Drain the fluid from the case.

2. Remove the speedometer cover and the wire connector assembly from the mounting bracket on the rear cover. If necessary, remove the bracket.

3. Remove both output shaft yokes.

4. Remove the 4WD indicator switch. DO NOT LOSE THE ALUMINUM WASHER! This washer controls switch operation.

5. Bend a paper clip to form a small hook. Remove the locking sleeve from the wire connector by hooking it with the paper clip and pull it up from the bottom. Take care not to damage the locking sleeve.

6. Remove the brown wire from the No.1 center position in the connector. If required, remove the speed sensor green wire from the No.4 connector position and the blue wire from the No.5 position.

7. Remove the front and rear yoke seals using tools T74P-77248-A and T50L-100-A.

8. Using the same tools, remove the input shaft seal.

9. Unbolt and remove the rear bearing retainer from the case cover. The retainer may be pried off using a ½ in. breaker bar in the pry bosses. Remove all traces of RTV sealer.

10. Lift the rear output shaft and remove the speedometer gear retaining clip.

11. Slide the speedometer gear forward and remove the ball with a small magnet. Pull the gear off the output shaft.

12. Remove the speed sensor from the rear cover.

13. Remove the 3 bolts attaching the shift motor to the rear cover and remove the shift motor. Note the position of the

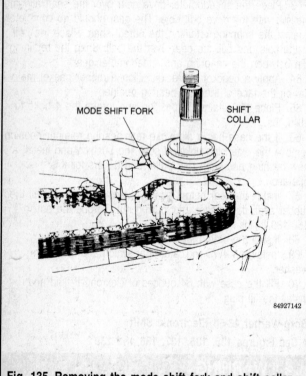

Fig. 135 Removing the mode shift fork and shift collar on the 13-56 electronic shift

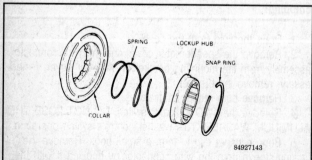

Fig. 136 2W/4W lock-up assembly exploded view for the 13-56 electronic shift

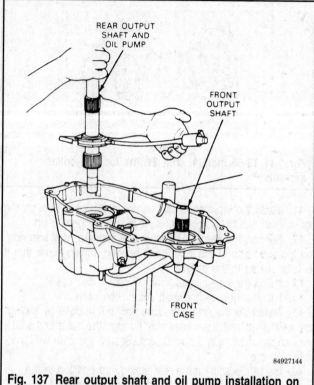

Fig. 137 Rear output shaft and oil pump installation on the 13-56 electronic shift

triangular shaft extending out of the rear cover and the triangular slot in the motor.

➡ **Don't disassemble the motor!**

14. Remove the snapring from the rear output shaft that retains the upper rear ball bearing.

15. Unbolt and remove front case cover from the rear case cover. The case halves may be separated using a ½ in. breaker bar in the pry bosses. Remove all traces of RTV sealer.

16. Remove the front output shaft inner needle bearing from the rear cover using a puller-type slidehammer.

17. Drive out the rear output shaft bearing from the inside of the case.

18. Remove the nuts retaining the clutch coil assembly to the rear cover. Pull the assembly, along with the O-rings and brown wire, from the cover.

19. Remove the shift shaft bushing and seal from the rear cover.

20. Remove the output shaft clutch hub snapring. Slide the 4WD hub off of the shaft.

21. Remove the spring from the shift shaft and lift the mode shift fork along with the shift collar, from the upper rear output shaft sprocket splines.

22. Disassemble the 2WD-4WD lockup assembly by removing the internal snapring and pull the lockup hub and spring from the collar.

23. Remove the snapring retaining the lower sprocket to the lower output shaft. Grasp the upper and lower sprocket along with the chain, and lift them, simultaneously, from the upper and lower shafts.

24. Remove the shift rail by sliding it straight out of the shift fork.

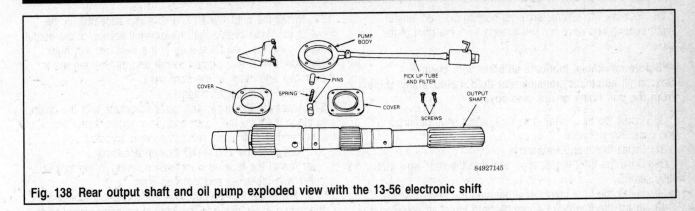

Fig. 138 Rear output shaft and oil pump exploded view with the 13-56 electronic shift

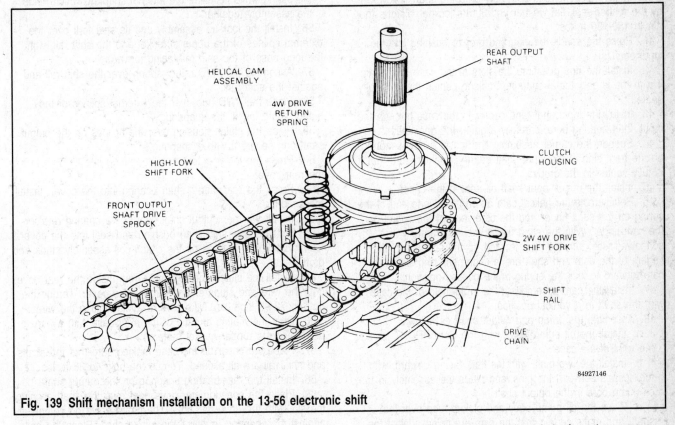

Fig. 139 Shift mechanism installation on the 13-56 electronic shift

25. Remove the high/low shift fork by first rotating it until the roller is free from the cam, then sliding it out of engagement from the shift hub.

26. Remove the helical cam assembly from the front case. If you are going to disassemble the helical cam assembly, be careful when the cam is slid rearward to disengage it from the spring. The spring is energized and can fly out with considerable force. The spring must be removed from the helical cam and the shift finger. Don't get your fingers in the way. It will rotate to the point that the spring ends will be about 180° apart.

27. Remove the magnetic chip collector from the bottom of the case.

28. Lift the pump screen and remove the output shaft assembly with the pump assembled on it. If you are going to

disassemble the pump, remove the 4 bolts from the pump body. Note the position of the pump front body, pins, spring, rear cover and pump retainer before disassembly.

29. Remove the high/low shift hub.

30. Remove the front output shaft from the case.

31. Turn the front case over and remove the front oil seal with a puller.

32. Expand the snapring on the input shaft and allow it to drop out of the bearing. If either the bearing or bushing is defective, both must be replaced as a unit. Drive them out together.

33. Remove the ring gear by prying out the internal snapring and lift out the gear.

34. Remove the internal snapring holding the input shaft bearing and drive out the bearing from the outside.

35. Remove the internal snapring holding the front output shaft bearing and drive out the bearing from the front of the case.

➡**Before assembly, lubricate all parts with clean Dexron®II automatic transmission fluid. Remove any chips from the bolt holes or the case cover.**

36. Install the input shaft and front output shaft bearings in the case using drivers.
37. Install the internal snaprings.
38. Drive the front output shaft seal into the case until it is fully seated.
39. Install the front output shaft through the lower bearing.
40. Install the front yoke assembly onto the shaft, followed by the rubber seal, flat washer and 30mm locknut. Torque the nut to 150-180 ft. lbs.
41. Press the needle bearing and bronze bushing into the input shaft.
42. Install the ring gear into the slots in the case and retain it with the large internal snapring, making certain that it is fully seated.
43. Install the input shaft and carrier in the case through the input shaft bearing bore, carefully aligning the gear teeth.
44. Support the carrier assembly and install a new snapring on the front side of the input shaft bearing, making sure that it is fully seated in the groove.
45. Install the upper input shaft oil seal in the case.
46. Reassemble the helical cam by engaging one end of the spring on the shaft finger and the other end of the spring on the cam finger. With the shaft finger secured carefully in a soft-jawed vise, turn the cam to wind up the spring until the fingers of the cam and shaft are in alignment, and slide the cam forward to lock the spring in the cocked position.
47. Install the cam assembly in the small hole of the case with the shaft in a vertical position.
48. Assemble the pump and output shaft as follows:
   a. Install the oil pump cover with the word FRONT facing the front of the case.
   b. Install the two pins, with the flats facing upward, with the springs between the pins, and place the assembly in the oil pump bore in the output shaft.
   c. Place the oil pump body and pickup tube over the shaft, and make certain that the pins are riding against the inside of the pump body.
   d. Place the oil pump rear cover, with the words TOP REAR facing the rear of the case.
   e. Install the pump retainer with the tabs facing the front of the case.
   f. Install the 4 retaining bolts and rotate the output shaft while tightening the bolts to prevent the pump from binding. Torque the bolts to 40 inch lbs.
   g. Lubricate the whole assembly with clean transmission fluid. The output shaft should turn freely. If not, loosen and retorque the bolts.
49. Install the high/low shift hub.
50. Install the high/low shift fork by engaging it with the shift hub flange and rotating it until the roller is engaged with the lower groove of the helical cam.
51. Install the shift rail through the high/low fork bore and into the rail bore in the case.

52. Install the output shaft and oil pump assembly in the input shaft. Make certain that the external splines of the output shaft engage the internal splines of the high/low shift hub. Make sure that the oil pump retainer and oil filter leg are in the groove and notch of the front case.
53. Install the collector magnet.
54. Assemble the upper and lower sprockets with the chain, and place them on the upper and lower shafts. Install the washer and snapring that retain the lower sprocket.
55. Assemble the 2WD/4WD lock-up assembly:
   a. Install the tapered compression spring in the lock-up collar with the small end installed first.
   b. Place the lock-up hub over the spring and compress the spring while installing the internal snapring which holds the assembly together.
56. Install the lock-up assembly and its shift fork over the external splines of the upper sprocket and the shift rail, with the long boss of the shift rail facing forward.
57. Assemble the 4WD return spring over the shift rail and against the shift fork.
58. Place the 4WD hub over the external splines of the output shaft. Install the snapring.
59. Place the clutch housing over the splines on the output shaft and secure it with a snapring.
60. Press the lower output needle bearing into its bore in the rear cover.
61. Press the rear output shaft bearing into the cover. Install the snapring.
62. Install the rear output shaft seal in the bearing retainer.
63. Install a new shift shaft bushing and seal into the cover.
64. Install new O-rings on the clutch coil assembly studs and grommet.
65. Install the clutch coil assembly from inside the rear cover until the wire and studs extend through the cover. Torque the nuts to 72-96 inch lbs. Take care to avoid kinking the wires.
66. Coat the mating surface of the front case with a non-acidic silicone rubber gasket material.
67. Place the cover on the case making sure that the shafts and shift rail are all aligned. Torque the bolts to 36 ft. lbs.
68. Install the rear bearing snapring on the output shaft.
69. Place the speedometer drive gear over the shaft aligning the slot with the drive ball hole. The gear should go completely against the snapring retaining the output shaft. Place the ball in the hole and pull the gear over the ball. Snap the retaining clip between the snapring and speedometer gear.
70. Install the speed sensor in the cover.
71. Apply a bead of non-acidic silicone rubber gasket material on the face of the rear bearing retainer.
72. Place the retainer in position and torque the 4 bolts to 36 ft. lbs.

✳✳WARNING

Be careful to avoid trapping the brown wire beneath the retainer.

73. Install the rear output shaft yoke and slinger. Install the rubber seal, flat washer and locking nut. Torque the nut to 150-180 ft. lbs.

74. Using soft-jawed pliers, rotate the triangular shift shaft so that it is aligned with the triangular slot in the motor. Install the motor. Torque the retaining screws to 72-96 inch lbs.

➡️**If the shaft will not stay in the 4H position, rotate the shaft to the 2H position. Install the motor and rotate it counterclockwise until the motor is aligned with the mounting holes.**

75. Install the brown clutch coil wire to the No.1 center terminal.

76. Connect the speed sensor green wire to the No.4 connector.
77. Connect the blue wire to the No.5 connector.
78. Install the locking sleeve.
79. Install the wire connector mounting bracket and torque the bolts to 72-96 inch lbs.
80. Install the wire connector on the mounting bracket.
81. Install the drain plug. Torque it to 20 ft. lbs.
82. Fill the case with Dexron®II fluid and install the fill plug. Torque the fill plug to 20 ft. lbs.

DRIVELINE

Driveshaft

◆ **See Figures 140, 141, 142 and 143**

REMOVAL & INSTALLATION

Single Type U-Joint

REAR ONE PIECE DRIVESHAFT

1. Matchmark the driveshaft yoke and axle pinion flange.
2. Remove the U-bolt nuts and U-bolts attaching the yoke to the axle flange.
3. Separate the yoke from the flange. It may be necessary to pry it free with a small prybar. Immediately after separation, wrap tape around the U-joint caps to keep them from falling off.
4. Slip the driveshaft off the transmission splines.

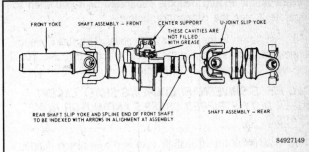
Fig. 142 Two-piece driveshaft with a fixed yoke at the transmission end

5. Installation is the reverse of removal. Align the yoke-to-flange matchmarks. Torque the U-bolt nuts to 15 ft. lbs.

FRONT DRIVESHAFT

1. Matchmark the driveshaft yoke and axle pinion flange.

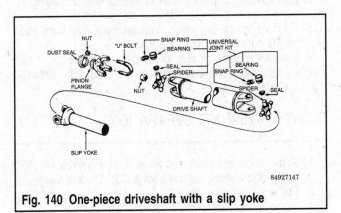
Fig. 140 One-piece driveshaft with a slip yoke

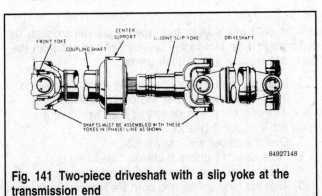
Fig. 141 Two-piece driveshaft with a slip yoke at the transmission end

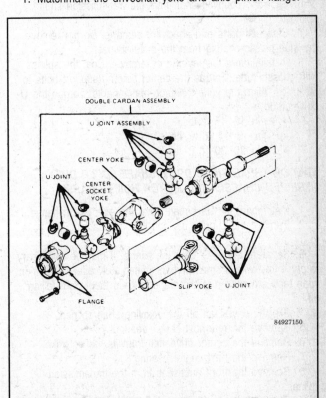
Fig. 143 Rear driveshaft components on the Bronco and F-150 4x4

2. Matchmark the driveshaft yoke and transfer case flange.

3. Remove the U-bolt nuts and U-bolts attaching the yoke to the axle flange.

4. Separate the yoke from the flange. It may be necessary to pry it free with a small prybar. Immediately after separation, wrap tape around the U-joint caps to keep them from falling off.

5. Remove the U-bolts and nuts (bolts for the F-350) and disconnect the driveshaft from the transfer case. It may be necessary to pry it free with a small prybar. Immediately after separation, wrap tape around the U-joint caps to keep them from falling off.

→**Avoid separating the driveshaft parts at the slip joint. If the driveshaft should become separated or if you wish to separate it, see the procedure, below.**

6. Installation is the reverse of removal. Align the yoke-to-flange matchmarks. Torque the U-bolt nuts to 15 ft. lbs. Torque the F-350 bolts to 20-28 ft. lbs.

TWO PIECE DRIVESHAFT/COUPLING SHAFT EXCEPT F-SUPER DUTY STRIPPED CHASSIS AND MOTOR HOME CHASSIS

1. Matchmark the driveshaft yoke and axle pinion flange.

2. Remove the U-bolt nuts and U-bolts attaching the yoke to the axle flange.

3. Separate the yoke from the flange. It may be necessary to pry it free with a small prybar. Immediately after separation, wrap tape around the U-joint caps to keep them from falling off.

4. Slip the driveshaft off the coupling shaft splines.

5. Remove the center bearing.

6. Slide the coupling shaft from the transmission shaft splines.

7. Clean all parts and check for damage. Do not remove the blue plastic coating from the male splines.

8. Installation is the reverse of removal. Coat the splines with chassis lube. Torque the center bearing support bolts to 50 ft. lbs. Align the yoke-to-flange matchmarks. Torque the U-bolt nuts to:

- $5/16$ in.-18: 15 ft. lbs.
- $3/8$ in.-18: 17-26 ft. lbs.
- $7/16$ in.-20: 30-40 ft. lbs.

TWO OR THREE PIECE DRIVE SHAFT-SUPER DUTY STRIPPED CHASSIS AND MOTOR HOME CHASSIS

1. Matchmark the driveshaft yoke and axle pinion flange.

2. Remove the U-bolt nuts and U-bolts attaching the yoke to the axle flange.

3. Separate the yoke from the flange. It may be necessary to pry it free with a small prybar. Immediately after separation, wrap tape around the U-joint caps to keep them from falling off.

4. Slip the driveshaft off the coupling shaft splines.

5. Remove the rearmost center bearing.

6. Remove the center driveshaft from its mating yoke.

7. Remove the next center bearing.

8. Remove the front driveshaft from the transmission splines.

9. Clean all parts and check for damage. Do not remove the blue plastic coating from the male splines.

10. Installation is the reverse of removal. Coat the splines with chassis lube. Torque the center bearing support bolts to 50 ft. lbs. Align the yoke-to-flange matchmarks. Torque the U-bolt nuts to:

- $5/16$ in.-18: 15 ft. lbs.
- $3/8$ in.-18: 17-26 ft. lbs.
- $7/16$ in.-20: 30-40 ft. lbs.

Double Cardan Type U-Joint

BRONCO REAR DRIVESHAFT

1. Matchmark the rear yoke and axle flange.

2. Matchmark the front cardan joint and the transfer case yoke.

3. Remove the U-bolt nuts and U-bolts attaching the yoke to the axle flange.

4. Separate the yoke from the flange. It may be necessary to pry it free with a small prybar. Immediately after separation, wrap tape around the U-joint caps to keep them from falling off.

5. Remove the cardan joint-to transfer case yoke bolts and separate the cardan joint from the yoke.

6. Installation is the reverse of removal. Align the matchmarks. Torque the U-bolt nuts to 15 ft. lbs.; the cardan joint bolts to 25 ft. lbs.

F-350 FRONT DRIVESHAFT

1. Matchmark the front yoke and front axle flange.

2. Matchmark the cardan joint and the transfer case yoke.

3. Remove the U-bolt nuts and U-bolts attaching the yoke to the axle flange.

4. Separate the yoke from the flange. It may be necessary to pry it free with a small prybar. Immediately after separation, wrap tape around the U-joint caps to keep them from falling off.

5. Remove the cardan joint-to transfer case yoke bolts and separate the cardan joint from the yoke.

6. Installation is the reverse of removal. Align the matchmarks. Torque the U-bolt nuts to 15 ft. lbs.; the cardan joint bolts to 25 ft. lbs.

FRONT DRIVESHAFT SEPARATION

1. Remove the driveshaft and place it on a workbench.

2. Using side cutters, cut the boot bands. Discard them.

3. Pull the 2 sections apart.

4. Remove and inspect the boot. If it is in any way damaged, replace it.

→**If the boot was split or torn, the grease will probably be contaminated, so thoroughly clean all old grease from the parts and replace it with fresh grease.**

5. Install the boot on the splined shaft as far as it will go.

6. Install a new small clamp and crimp it with crimping pliers. Use only crimp type clamps as hose type clamps can throw the shaft out of balance.

7. Coat the splines with chassis lube.

8. Place about 10 grams of chassis lube in the boot.

9. Place a new large crimp clamp on the rear yoke.

10. Align the blind splines and push the rear yoke onto the driveshaft splines.

11. Remove the excess grease and position the rear end of the boot in the slip yoke boot groove. On trucks with single type U-joints at each end, move the yoke in or out as required to obtain a total driveshaft length of:

- F-150, 250 and Bronco; C6 and ZF trans.: 892mm
- AOD trans.: 917mm
- M5OD trans.: 978mm

This measurement is made between the centerlines of the U-joints.

- F-350 ;C6 trans.: 819mm
- E4OD trans.: 970mm ;ZF trans. w/8-7.3L or 8-7.5L: 832mm
- ZF trans. w/8-5.8L: 905.8mm

This measurement is made between the centerlines of the U-joints with the shaft fully collapsed.

12. Make sure that the boot has stayed in its groove, dispel any trapped air from the boot and crimp the clamp in place.

DRIVESHAFT BALANCING

▶ **See Figures 144, 145 and 146**

Driveline vibration or shudder, felt mainly on acceleration, coasting or under engine braking, can be caused, among other things, by improper driveshaft installation or imbalance.

If the condition follows driveshaft replacement or installation after disconnection, try disconnecting the driveshaft at the axle and rotating it 180°. Then, reconnect it. If that doesn't work, try the following procedure:

1. Raise and support the truck on jackstands so that all wheels are off the ground and free to rotate. The truck must be as level as possible.

2. Remove the wheels. Install the lug nuts to retain the brake drums or rotors.

3. Start the engine, place the transmission in gear and increase engine speed to the point at which the vibration is most severe. Record this speedometer speed as a reference point.

4. Shift into neutral and shut off the engine.

5. Check all driveshaft attachment fasteners, U-joint bearing caps, U-joint cap retaining rings or cap locating lugs. Tighten any loose fasteners, replace any missing, damaged or shaved retaining rings or lugs. If worn U-joints are suspected, replace them. If everything is normal, or if any corrections made do not solve the problem, continue.

6. Start the engine, place the transmission in gear and increase engine speed to an indicated road speed of 40-50 mph (64-80 kmh). Maintain this speed with some sort of accelerator control, such as a weight on the pedal, or have an assistant hold the pedal.

✳✳CAUTION

The following procedure can be dangerous! Be careful when approaching the spinning driveline parts!

7. Carefully raise a piece of chalk until it *just barely* touches the driveshaft at the front, middle and rear. At either end, try touching the shaft about an inch or so from the yokes. Don't touch any existing driveshaft balancing weights. The

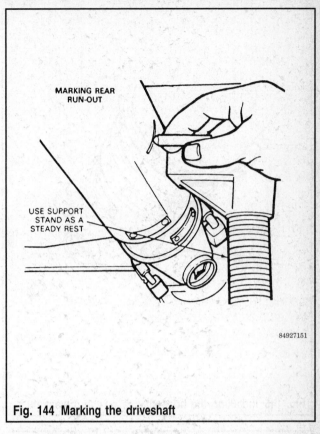

MARKING REAR RUN-OUT

USE SUPPORT STAND AS A STEADY REST

84927151

Fig. 144 Marking the driveshaft

chalk marks will indicate the heavy points of the driveshaft. Shut off the engine.

➡ **It helps greatly to steady your hand on some sort of support.**

8. Check the driveshaft end of the shaft first. If the chalk mark is continuous around the shaft proceed to the opposite end, then the middle.   If the chalk mark is not continuous, install 2 screw-type hose clamps on the shaft so that their heads are 180° from the center of the chalk mark.

9. Start the engine and run it to the speed recorded previously. If the vibration persists, stop the engine and move the screw portions of the clamps 45° from each other. Try the run test again.

✳✳WARNING

Check the engine temperature!

10. If the vibration persists, move the screw portions of the clamps apart in small increments until the vibration disappears. If this doesn't cure the problem, proceed to the other end, then the middle, performing the operation all over again. If the problem persists, investigate other driveline components.

U-JOINT OVERHAUL

▶ **See Figures 147, 148, 149 and 150**

Except Double Cardan Universal

1. Remove the driveshaft from the vehicle and place it in a vise, being careful not to damage it.

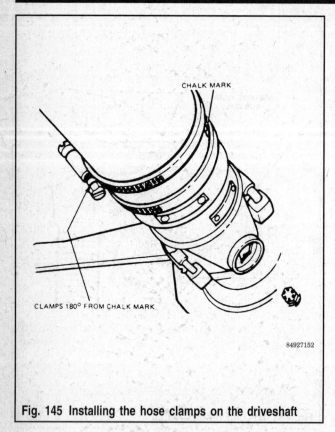

Fig. 145 Installing the hose clamps on the driveshaft

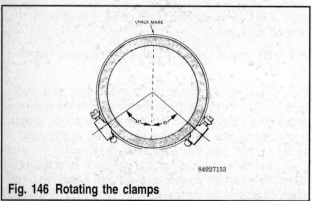

Fig. 146 Rotating the clamps

2. Remove the snaprings which retain the bearings in the flange and in the driveshaft.

3. Remove the driveshaft tube from the vise and position the U-joint in the vise with a socket smaller than the bearing cap on one side and a socket larger than the bearing cap on the other side.

4. Slowly tighten the jaws of the vise so that the smaller socket forces the U-joint spider and the opposite bearing into the larger socket.

5. Remove the other side of the spider in the same manner (if applicable) and remove the spider assembly from the driveshaft. Discard the spider assemblies.

6. Clean all foreign matter from the yoke areas at the end of the driveshaft(s).

7. Start the new spider and one of the bearing cap assemblies into a yoke by positioning the yoke in a vise with the spider positioned in place with one of the bearing cap assem-

blies positioned over one of the holes in the yoke. Slowly close the vise, pressing the bearing cap assembly in the yoke. Press the cap in far enough so that the retaining snapring can be installed. Use the smaller socket to recess the bearing cap.

8. Open the vise and position the opposite bearing cap assembly over the proper hole in the yoke with the socket that is smaller than the diameter of the bearing cap located on the cap. Slowly close the vise, pressing the bearing cap into the hole in the yoke with the socket. Make sure that the spider assembly is in line with the bearing cap as it is pressed in. Press the bearing cap in far enough so that the retaining snapring can be installed.

9. Install all remaining U-joints in the same manner.

10. Install the driveshaft and grease the new U-joints.

Double Cardan Joint

1. Working at the rear axle end of the shaft, mark the position of the spiders, the center yoke, and the centering socket yoke as related to the companion flange. The spiders must be assembled with the bosses in their original position to provide proper clearances.

2. Using a large vise or an arbor press and a socket smaller than the bearing cap on one side and a socket larger than the bearing cap on the other side, drive one of the bearings in toward the center of the universal joint, which will force the opposite bearing out.

3. Remove the driveshaft from the vise.

4. Tighten the bearing in the vise and tap on the yoke to free the bearing from the center yoke. Do not tap on the driveshaft tube.

5. Reposition the sockets on the yoke and force the opposite bearing outward and remove it.

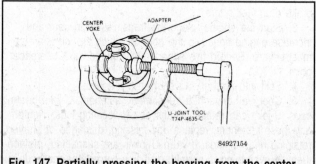

Fig. 147 Partially pressing the bearing from the center yoke

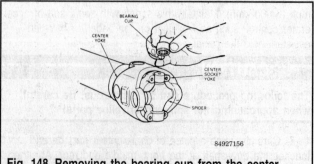

Fig. 148 Removing the bearing cup from the center yoke socket

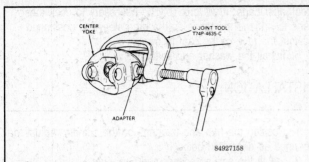

Fig. 149 Removing the bearing from the rear of the center yoke

6. Position the sockets on one of the remaining bearings and force it outward approximately ⅜in. (9.5mm).

7. Grip the bearing in the vise and tap on the weld yoke to free the bearing from the center yoke. Do not tap on the driveshaft tube.

8. Reposition the sockets on the yoke to press out the remaining bearing.

9. Remove the spider from the center yoke.

10. Remove the bearings from the driveshaft yoke as outlined above and remove the spider from the yoke.

11. Insert a suitable tool into the centering ball socket located in the companion flange and pry out the rubber seal. Remove the retainer, three piece ball seat, washer and spring from the ball socket.

12. Inspect the centering ball socket assembly for worn or damaged parts. If any damage is evident replace the entire assembly.

13. Insert the spring, washer, three piece ball seat and retainer into the ball socket.

14. Using a suitable tool, install the centering ball socket seal.

15. Position the spider in the driveshaft yoke. Make sure the spider bosses are in the same position as originally installed. Press in the bearing cups with the sockets and vise. Install the internal snaprings provided in the repair kit.

16. Position the center yoke over the spider ends and press in the bearing cups. Install the snaprings.

17. Install the spider in the companion flange yoke. Make sure the spider bosses are in the position as originally installed. Press on the bearing cups and install the snaprings.

18. Position the center yoke over the spider ends and press on the bearing cups. Install the snaprings.

Center Bearing

REMOVAL & INSTALLATION

1. Remove the driveshafts.

2. Remove the two center support bearing attaching bolts and remove the assembly from the vehicle.

3. Do not immerse the sealed bearing in any type of cleaning fluid. Wipe the bearing and cushion clean with a cloth dampened with cleaning fluid.

4. Check the bearing for wear or rough action by rotating the inner race while holding the outer race. If wear or roughness is evident, replace the bearing. Examine the rubber cushion for evidence of hardening, cracking, or deterioration. Replace it if it is damaged in any way.

5. Place the bearing in the rubber support and the rubber support in the U-shaped support and install the bearing in the reverse order of removal. Torque the bearing to support bracket fasteners to 50 ft. lbs.

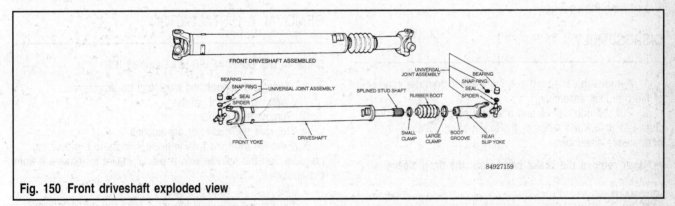

Fig. 150 Front driveshaft exploded view

FRONT DRIVE AXLE

▶ See Figures 151, 152, 153, 154, 155, 156, 157, 158, 159, 160, 161, 162, 163, 164, 165, 166 and 167

Identification

Axle identification and ratio can be determined from the I.D. tag located under one of the bolts on the differential carrier housing. See the drive axle section of the Capacities Chart in Section 1 for complete model application.

Manual Locking Hubs

REMOVAL & INSTALLATION

1. To remove hub, first separate cap assembly from body assembly by removing the six (6) socket head capscrews from the cap assembly and slip apart.

2. Remove snapring (retainer ring) from the end of the axle shaft.

3. Remove the lock ring seated in the groove of the wheel hub. The body assembly will now slide out of the wheel hub. If necessary, use an appropriate puller to remove the body assembly.

4. Install hub in reverse order of removal. Torque socket head capscrews to 30-50 inch lbs.

Automatic Locking Hubs

REMOVAL

1. Remove the 5 capscrews — Torx® bit TX25 — and remove hub cap assembly from the hub.

➡**Take care to avoid dropping the spring, ball bearing, bearing race or retainer!**

2. Remove the rubber seal.

3. Remove the seal bridge — a small metal stamping — from the retainer ring space.

4. Remove lock ring seated in the groove of the wheel hub by compressing the ends with a needle nose pliers, while pulling the hub lock from the hub body. If body assembly does not slide out easily, use an appropriate puller.

5. If the hub and spindle are being removed:

a. Remove the C-washer from the groove in the stub shaft.

b. Remove the splined spacer from the shaft.

c. Remove the outer locknut, locking washer and inner bearing locknut.

d. Pull the hub and bearings from the spindle.

6. See the Wheel Bearing procedures, below, for cleaning and packing the bearings.

DISASSEMBLY

1. Remove the snapring and flat washer from the inner end of the hub lock assembly

2. Pull the hub sleeve and attached parts out of the drag sleeve to unlock the tangs of the brake band, Remove the drag sleeve assembly.

➡**Never remove the brake band from the drag sleeve!**

ASSEMBLY

1. Wash all parts in a non-flammable solvent and let them air dry.

2. Lubricate the brake band and drag sleeve with 1.5g (0.05 oz.) of Automatic Hublock Grease E1TZ-19590-A (ESL-M1C193A) (Darmex Spec. DX-123-LT), or equivalent. Work the lubricant over and under the spring.

3. Dip the locking hub body (not the cap or brake band/drag sleeve) into Dexron®II ATF and allow it to drip off the excess.

4. Assemble the brake band so that one tang is on each side of the plastic outer cage, located in the window of the

steel inner cage. It will probably be necessary to cock these parts to engage the tangs as the drag sleeve is positioned against the face of the cam follower.

5. Install the washer and snapring.

INSTALLATION

1. Position the hub and bearings on the spindle. Adjust the bearings as described below.

2. Install the splined spacer and C-washer.

3. Wipe off excess grease from the splines and start the locking hub assembly into the hub body. Make sure the large tangs are aligned with the lockwasher and the outside diameter, and the inside diameter splines are aligned with the hub and axle shaft splines.

4. Install the retaining ring while pushing the locking hub assembly into the hub body.

5. Install the seal bridge, narrow end first.

6. Install the rubber seal.

7. Install the cover, making sure the ball bearing, spring and race are in position.

8. Install the 5 Torx® screws and tighten them to 40-50 inch lbs. by tighten one, then skipping one, and so on until they are all tightened.

Front Wheel Bearings

For Removal, Repacking and Installation of front wheel bearings, see Section 1.

Right and Left Axle Shafts, Spindle and Joint

REMOVAL & INSTALLATION

Dana 44 IFS Dana 44 IFS-HD Dana 50 IFS

1. Raise and support the front end on jackstands.

2. Remove the front wheels.

3. Remove the calipers.

4. Remove the hub/rotor assemblies.

5. Remove the nuts retaining the spindle to the steering knuckle. Tap the spindle with a plastic mallet to remove it from the knuckle.

6. Remove the splash shield.

7. On the left side, pull the shaft from the carrier, through the knuckle.

8. On the right side, remove and discard the keystone clamp from the shaft and joint assembly and the stub shaft. Slide the rubber boot onto the shaft and pull the shaft and joint assembly from the splines of the stub shaft.

9. Place the spindle in a soft-jawed vise clamped on the second step of the spindle.

10. Using a slidehammer and bearing puller, remove the needle bearing from the spindle.

11. Inspect all parts. If the spindle is excessively corroded or pitted it must be replaced. If the U-joints are excessively loose

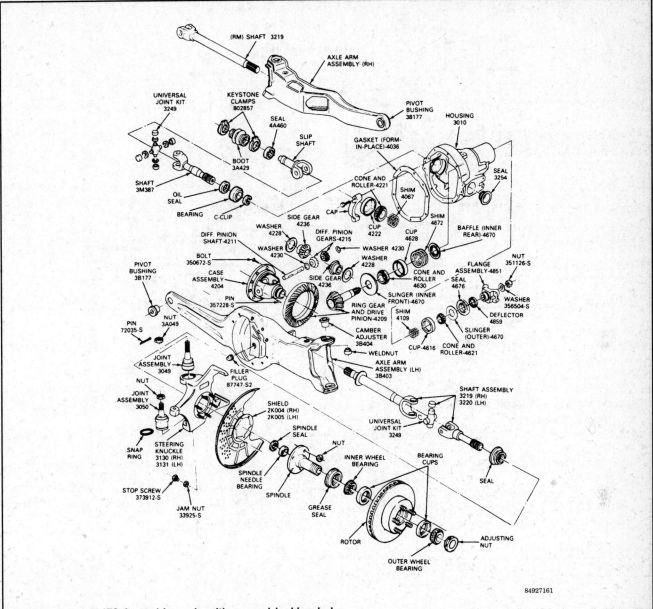

Fig. 151 Dana 44-IFS front drive axle with manual locking hubs

or don't move freely, they must be replaced. If any shaft is bent, it must be replaced.

To install:

12. Clean all dirt and grease from the spindle bearing bore. The bore must be free of nicks and burrs.

13. Insert a new spindle bearing in its bore with the printing facing outward. Drive it into place with drive T80T-4000-S for F-150 and Bronco and F-250, or T80T-4000-R for the F-350, or their equivalents. Install a new bearing seal with the lip facing away from the bearing.

14. Pack the bearing and hub seal with grease. Install the hub seal with a driver.

15. Place the thrust washer on the axle shaft.

16. Place a new slinger on the axle shaft.

17. Install the rubber V-seal on the slinger. The seal lip should face the spindle.

18. Install the plastic spacer on the axle shaft. The chamfered side of the spacer should be inboard against the axle shaft.

19. Pack the thrust face of the seal in the spindle bore and the V-seal on the axle shaft with heavy duty, high temperature, waterproof wheel bearing grease.

20. On the right side, install the rubber boot and new keystone clamps on the stub shaft and slip yoke. The splines permit only one way of meshing so you'll have to properly align the missing spline in the slip yoke with the gapless male spline on the shaft. Slide the right shaft and joint assembly into the slip yoke, making sure that the splines are fully engaged. Slide the boot over the assembly and crimp the keystone clamp.

21. On the left side, slide the shaft and joint assembly through the knuckle and engage the splines in the carrier.

22. Install the splash shield and spindle on the knuckle. Tighten the spindle nuts to 60 ft. lbs.

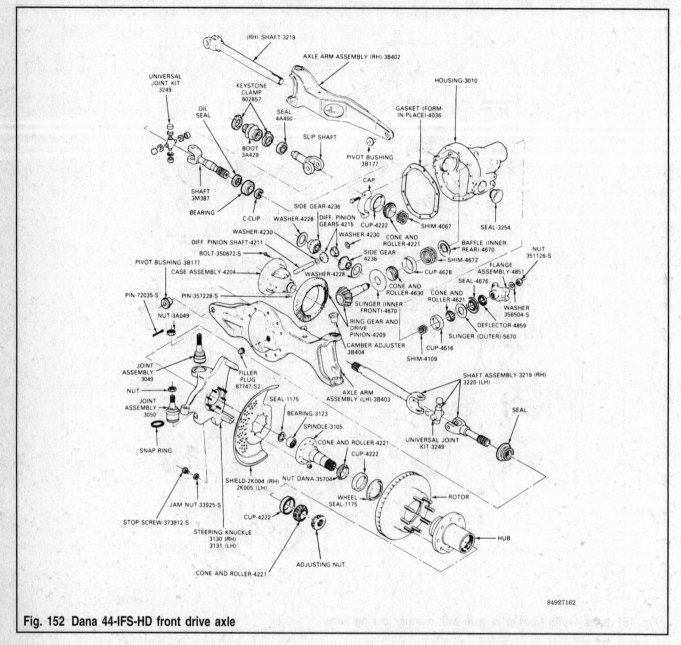

Fig. 152 Dana 44-IFS-HD front drive axle

23. Install the rotor on the spindle. Install the outer wheel bearing into the cup. Make sure that the grease seal lip totally encircles the spindle.

24. Install the wheel bearing, locknut, thrust bearing, snapring and locking hubs. See Section 1.

25. Install the caliper.

Spindle and Front Axle Shaft

REMOVAL & INSTALLATION

Dana 60 Monobeam

1. Raise and support the front end on jackstands.

2. Remove the caliper from the knuckle and wire it out of the way.

3. Remove the free-running hub.

4. Remove the front wheel bearing. See Section 1.

5. Remove the hub and rotor assembly.

6. Remove the spindle-to-knuckle bolts. Tap the spindle from the knuckle using a plastic mallet.

7. Remove the splash shield and caliper support.

8. Pull the axle shaft out through the knuckle.

9. Using a slidehammer and bearing cup puller, remove the needle bearing from the spindle.

10. Clean the spindle bore thoroughly and make sure that it is free of nicks and burrs. If the bore is excessively pitted or scored, the spindle must be replaced.

   To install:

11. Insert a new spindle bearing in its bore with the printing facing outward. Drive it into place with driver T80T-4000-R, or its equivalent. Install a new bearing seal with the lip facing away from the bearing.

12. Pack the bearing with waterproof wheel bearing grease.

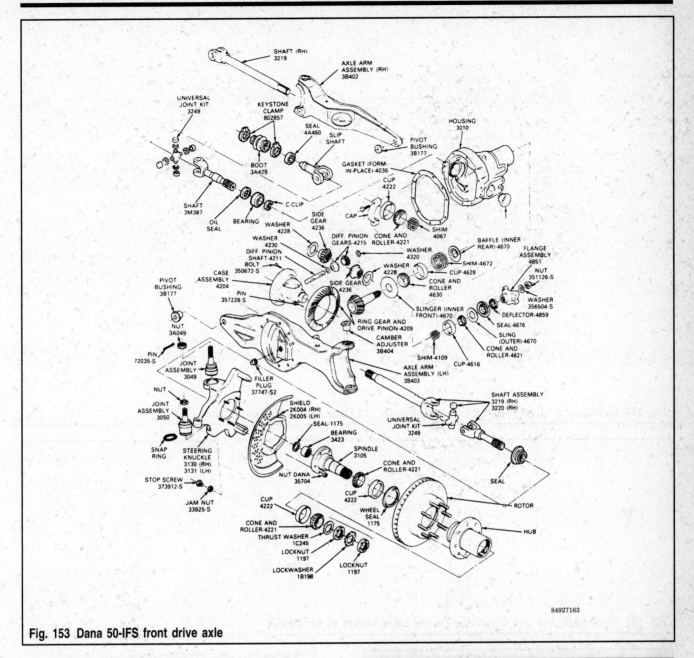

Fig. 153 Dana 50-IFS front drive axle

13. Pack the thrust face of the seal in the spindle bore and the V-seal on the axle shaft with waterproof wheel bearing grease.

14. Carefully guide the axle shaft through the knuckle and into the housing. Align the splines and fully seat the shaft.

15. Place the bronze spacer on the shaft. The chamfered side of the spacer must be inboard.

16. Install the splash shield and caliper support.

17. Place the spindle on the knuckle and install the bolts. Torque the bolts to 50-60 ft. lbs.

18. Install the hub/rotor assembly on the spindle.

19. Assemble the wheel bearings.

20. Assemble the free-running hub.

Right Side Slip Yoke and Stub Shaft, Carrier, Carrier Oil Seal and Bearing

REMOVAL & INSTALLATION

Independent Front Axles

➡This procedure requires the use of special tools.

1. Raise and support the front end on jackstands.

2. Disconnect the front driveshaft from the carrier and wire it up out of the way.

3. Remove the left and right axle shafts and both spindles.

4. Support the carrier with a floor jack and unbolt the carrier from the support arm.

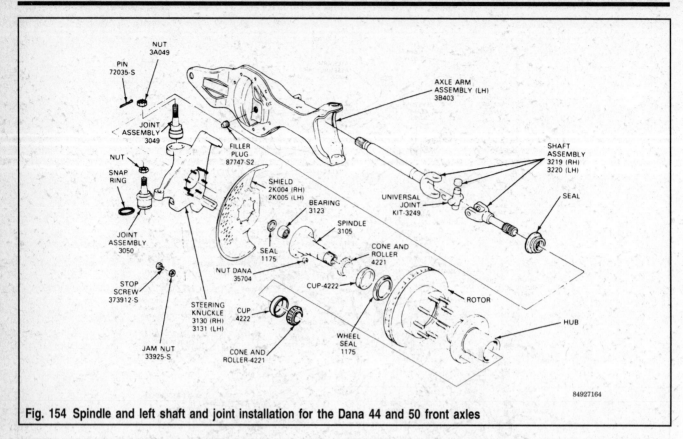

Fig. 154 Spindle and left shaft and joint installation for the Dana 44 and 50 front axles

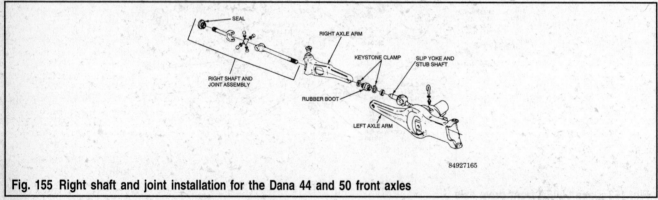

Fig. 155 Right shaft and joint installation for the Dana 44 and 50 front axles

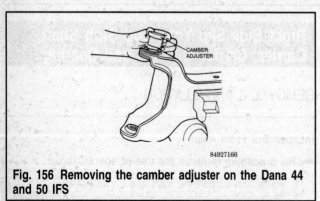

Fig. 156 Removing the camber adjuster on the Dana 44 and 50 IFS

5. Place a drain pan under the carrier, separate the carrier from the support arm and drain the carrier.

6. Remove the carrier from the truck.
7. Place the carrier in holding fixture T57L-500-B with adapters T80T-4000-B.
8. Rotate the slip yoke and shaft assembly from the carrier.

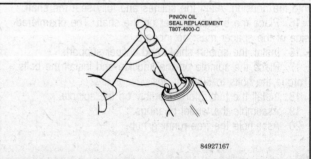

Fig. 157 Pinion oil seal installation on the Dana 44 and 50 IFS

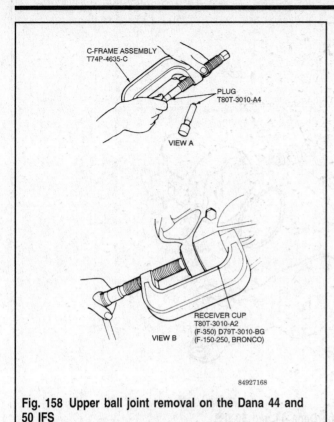

Fig. 158 Upper ball joint removal on the Dana 44 and 50 IFS

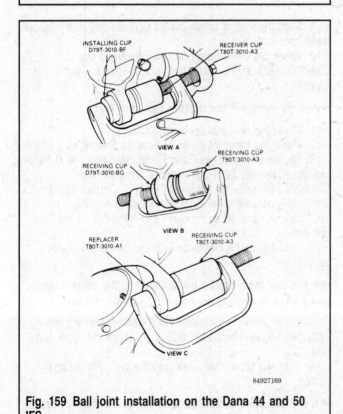

Fig. 159 Ball joint installation on the Dana 44 and 50 IFS

9. Using a slidehammer/puller remove the caged needle bearing and oil seal as a unit. Discard the oil seal and bearing.

To install:

10. Clean the bearing bore thoroughly and make sure that it is free of nicks and burrs.

11. Insert a new bearing in its bore with the printing facing outward. Drive it into place with driver T83T-1244-A, or its equivalent. Install a new bearing seal with the lip facing away from the bearing. Coat the bearing and seal with waterproof wheel bearing grease.

12. Install the slip yoke and shaft assembly into the carrier so that the groove in the shaft is visible in the differential case.

13. Install the snapring in the groove in the shaft. It may be necessary to force the snapring into place with a small prybar. Don't strike the snapring!

14. Remove the carrier from the holding fixture.

15. Clean all traces of sealant from the carrier and support arm. Make sure the mating surfaces are clean. Apply a ¼ in. (6mm) wide bead of RTV sealant to the mating surface of the carrier. The bead must be continuous and should not pass through or outside of the holes. Install the carrier with 5 minutes of applying the sealer.

16. Position the carrier on the jack and raise it into position using guide pins to align it if you'd like. Install and hand-tighten the bolts. Torque the bolts in a circular pattern to 30-40 ft. lbs.

17. Install the support arm tab bolts and torque them to 85-100 ft. lbs.

18. Install all other parts in reverse order of removal.

AXLE SHAFT U-JOINT OVERHAUL

Follow the procedures outlined under Axle Shaft Removal and Installation to gain access to the U-joints. Overhaul them as described under U-joints.

Steering Knuckle and Ball Joints

REMOVAL & INSTALLATION

Independent Front Axles

1. Raise and support the front end on jackstands.
2. Remove the spindles and left and right shafts and joint.
3. Remove the tie rod nut and disconnect the tie rod from the steering arm.
4. Remove the cotter pin from the top ball joint stud. Remove the nut from the top stud and loosen the nut on the lower stud inside the knuckle.
5. Hit the top stud sharply with a plastic mallet to free the knuckle from the axle arm. Remove and discard the bottom nut. New nuts should be used at assembly.
6. Note the positioning of the camber adjuster carefully for reassembly. Remove the camber adjuster. If it's hard to remove, use a puller.
7. Place the knuckle in a vise and remove the snapring from the bottom ball joint. Not all ball joints will have this snapring.
8. Remove the plug from C-frame tool T74P-4635-C and replace it with plug T80T-3010-A. Assemble C-frame tool

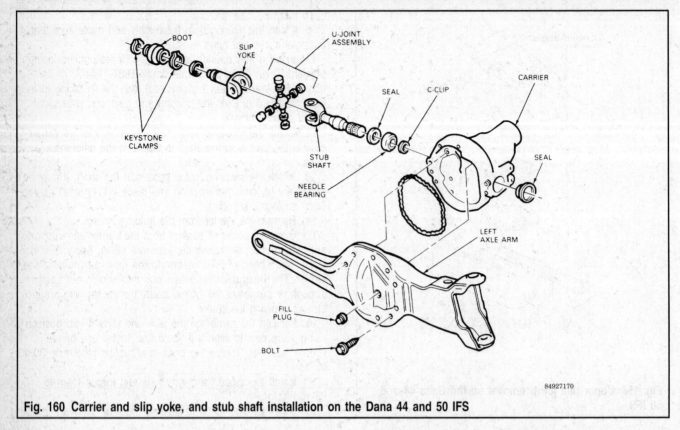

Fig. 160 Carrier and slip yoke, and stub shaft installation on the Dana 44 and 50 IFS

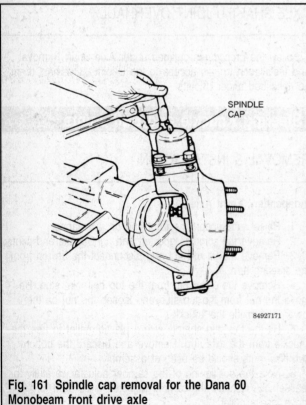

Fig. 161 Spindle cap removal for the Dana 60 Monobeam front drive axle

T74P-4635-C and receiving cup D79T-3010-G (Bronco, F-150 and 250) or T80T-3010-A2 (F-250HD and F-350). on the knuckle.

9. Turn the forcing screw inward until the ball joint is separated from the knuckle.

10. Assemble the C-frame tool with receiving cup D79P-3010-BG on the upper ball joint and force it out of the knuckle.

➡**Always force out the bottom ball joint first.**

11. Clean the ball joint bores thoroughly.

12. Insert the lower joint into its bore as straight as possible.

13. On the Bronco, F-150 and F-250, assemble the C-frame tool, receiving cup T80T-3010-A3 and installing cup D79T-3010-BF onto the lower ball joint.   On the F-250HD and F-350, assemble the C-frame tool, receiving cup T80T-3010-A3 and receiving cup D79T-3010-BG on the lower ball joint.

14. Turn the screw clockwise until the ball joint is firmly seated.

➡**If the ball joint cannot be installed to the correct depth, you'll have to realign the receiving cup on the tool.**

15. On all models, assemble the C-frame, receiving cup T80T-3010-A3 and replacer T80T-3010-A1 on the upper ball joint.

16. Turn the screw clockwise until the ball joint is firmly seated.

➡**If the ball joint cannot be installed to the correct depth, you'll have to realign the receiving cup on the tool.**

17. Place the knuckle into position on the axle arm. Install the camber adjuster on the upper ball joint stud with the arrow point to positive or negative as noted before disassembly.

18. Install a new nut on the bottom stud, finger tight. Install a new nut on the top stud finger tight.

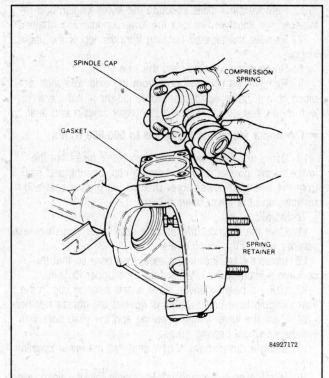

Fig. 162 Compression spring removal for the Dana 60 Monobeam front drive axle

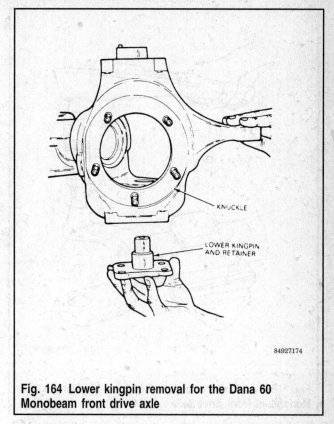

Fig. 164 Lower kingpin removal for the Dana 60 Monobeam front drive axle

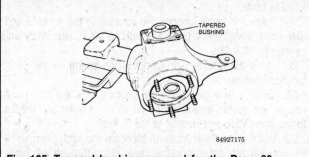

Fig. 165 Tapered bushing removal for the Dana 60 Monobeam, front drive axle

19. Tighten the bottom nut to 80 ft. lbs.
20. Tighten the top nut to 100 ft. lbs., then, (tighten) advance the nut until the cotter pin hole align with the castellations. Install a new cotter pin.

21. Again tighten the bottom nut, this time to 110 ft. lbs.
22. Install all other parts as described elsewhere in this Section.

Steering Knuckle and Kingpins

REMOVAL & INSTALLATION

Monobeam Front Axle

➡For this job you'll need a torque wrench with a capacity of at least 600 ft. lbs.

1. Raise and support the front end on jackstands.
2. Remove the axle shafts.
3. Alternately and evenly remove the 4 bolts that retain the spindle cap to the knuckle. This will relieve spring tension.
4. When spring tension is relieved, remove the bolts.

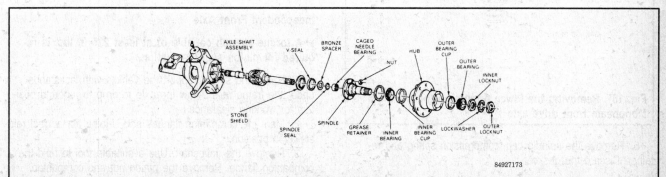

Fig. 163 Axle shift components for the Dana 60 Monobeam front drive axle

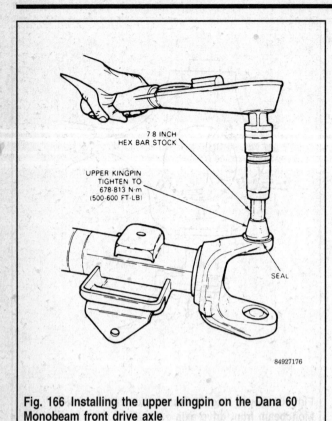

Fig. 166 Installing the upper kingpin on the Dana 60 Monobeam front drive axle

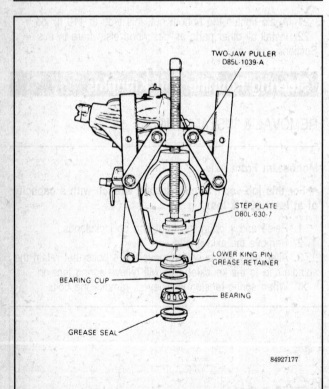

Fig. 167 Removing the lower kingpin on the Dana 60 Monobeam front drive axle

5. Remove the spindle cap, compression spring and retainer. Discard the gasket.

6. Remove the 4 bolts securing the lower kingpin and retainer to the knuckle. Remove the lower kingpin and retainer.

7. Remove the tapered bushing from the top of the upper kingpin.

8. Remove the knuckle from the axle yoke.

9. Remove the upper kingpin from the axle yoke with a piece of 7⁄8in. hex-shaped case hardened metal bar stock, or, with a 7⁄8in. hex socket. Discard the upper kingpin and seal.

➡**The upper kingpin is tightened to 500-600 ft. lbs.**

10. Using a 2-jawed puller and step plate, press out the lower kingpin grease retainer, bearing cup, bearing and seal from the axle yoke lower bore. Discard the grease seal and retainer, and the lower bearing cup.

To install:

11. Coat the mating surfaces of a new lower kingpin grease retainer with RTV silicone sealer.

12. Install the retainer in the axle yoke bore so that the concave portion of the retainer faces the upper kingpin.

13. Using a bearing driver, drive a new bearing cup in the lower kingpin bore until it bottoms against the grease retainer.

14. Pack the lower kingpin bearing and the yoke bore with waterproof wheel bearing grease.

15. Using a driver, drive a new seal into the lower kingpin bore.

16. Install a new seal and upper kingpin into the yoke using tool T86T-3110-AH. Tighten the kingpin to 500-600 ft. lbs.

17. Install the knuckle on the yoke.

18. Place the tapered bushing over the upper kingpin in the knuckle bore.

19. Place the lower kingpin and retainer in the knuckle and axle yoke. Install the 4 bolts and tighten them, alternately and evenly, to 90 ft. lbs.

20. Place the retainer and compression spring on the tapered bushing.

21. Install a new gasket on the knuckle. Position the spindle cap on the gasket and knuckle. Install the 4 bolts and tighten them, alternately and evenly, to 90 ft. lbs.

22. Install the axle shafts and lubricate the upper kingpin through the zerk fitting and the lower fitting through the flush fitting. The lower fitting may be lubricated with Alemite adapter #6783, or equivalent.

Pinion Seal

REMOVAL & INSTALLATION

Independent Front Axle

➡**A torque wrench capable of at least 225 ft. lbs. is required for pinion seal installation.**

1. Raise and safely support the vehicle with jackstands under the frame rails. Allow the axle to drop to rebound position for working clearance.

2. Mark the companion flanges and U-joints for correct reinstallation position.

3. Remove the driveshaft. Use a suitable tool to hold the companion flange. Remove the pinion nut and companion flange.

4. Use a slide hammer and hook or sheet metal screw to remove the oil seal.

To install:

5. Install a new pinion seal after lubricating the sealing surfaces. Use a suitable seal driver. Install the companion flange and pinion nut. Tighten the nut to 200-220 ft. lbs.

Monobeam Front Axle

➡**A torque wrench capable of at least 300 ft. lbs. is required for pinion seal installation.**

1. Raise and support the truck on jackstands.
2. Allow the axle to hang freely.
3. Matchmark and disconnect the driveshaft from the front axle.
4. Using a tool such as T75T-4851-B, or equivalent, hold the pinion flange while removing the pinion nut.
5. Using a puller, remove the pinion flange.
6. Use a puller to remove the seal, or punch the seal out using a pin punch.

To install:

7. Thoroughly clean the seal bore and make sure that it is not damaged in any way. Coat the sealing edge of the new seal with a small amount of 80W/90 oil and drive the seal into the housing using a seal driver.
8. Coat the inside of the pinion flange with clean 80W/90 oil and install the flange onto the pinion shaft.
9. Install the nut on the pinion shaft and tighten it to 250-300 ft. lbs.
10. Connect the driveshaft.

Axle Unit

REMOVAL & INSTALLATION

Independent Front Axles

1. Raise and support the front end on jackstands placed under the radius arms.
2. Remove the wheels.
3. Remove the calipers and wire them out of the way. Don't disconnect the brake lines.
4. Support the axle arm with a jack and remove the upper coil spring retainers.
5. Lower the jack and remove the coil springs, spring cushions and lower spring seats.
6. Disconnect the shock absorbers at the radius arms and upper mounting brackets.
7. Remove the studs and spring seats at the radius arms and axle arms.
8. Remove the bolts securing the upper attachment to the axle arm and the lower attachment to the axle arm.

9. Disconnect the vent tube at the housing. Remove the vent fitting and install a 1/8 in. pipe plug.
10. Remove the pivot bolt securing the right side axle arm to the crossmember. Remove and discard the boot clamps and remove the boot from the shaft. Remove the right drive axle assembly and pull the axle shaft from the slip shaft.
11. Support the housing with a floor jack. Remove the bolt securing the left side axle assembly to the crossmember. Remove the left side drive axle assembly.

To install:

12. Installation is, basically, a reversal of the removal procedure. Always use new boot clamps. Observe the following torques:
    - Left and right drive axles-to-crossmember: 120-150 ft. lbs.
    - Axle arm-to-radius arm: 180-240 ft. lbs.
    - Coil spring insulator: 30-70 ft. lbs.
    - Upper spring retainer: 13-18 ft. lbs.

Monobeam Axle

1. Raise and support the front end on jackstands placed under the frame.
2. Remove the wheels.
3. Remove the calipers and wire them out of the way. Don't disconnect the brake lines.
4. Disconnect the stabilizer links at the stabilizer bar.
5. Remove the U-bolts securing the stabilizer bar and mounting brackets to the axle.
6. Remove the cotter pins and nuts securing the spindle connecting rod to the steering knuckles. Separate the connecting rod to the steering knuckles. Separate the connecting rods from the knuckles with a pitman arm puller. Wire the steering linkage to the spring.
7. Matchmark and disconnect the driveshaft from the front axle.
8. Disconnect the vent tube at the axle and plug the fitting.
9. On the right side, disconnect the track bar from the right spring cap.
10. Raise the front end and position jackstands under front springs at a point about half way between the axle and spring rear hanger. Remove the jackstands from the front of the frame and lower the truck onto the stands under the springs. Make sure that the truck is securely supported.
11. Support the axle with a floor jack.
12. Remove the U-bolts securing the springs to the axle.
13. Lower the axle from the truck.

To install:

14. Installation is the reverse of removal. Observe the following torques:
    - Driveshaft-to-flange: 15-20 ft. lbs.
    - Track bar nut and bolt: 160-200 ft. lbs.
    - Stabilizer link nut: 20-30 ft. lbs.
    - Stabilizer bar U-bolt: 50-65 ft. lbs.
    - Spindle connecting rod-to-knuckle: 70-100 ft. lbs.
    - Front spring U-bolts: 85-100 ft. lbs.

Conventional Differential Overhaul Dana 44 and 50 Units

▶ See Figures 168, 169, 170, 171, 172, 173, 174, 175, 176, 177, 178, 179, 180, 181, 182, 183, 184, 185, 186, 187, 188 and 189

DISASSEMBLY

Differential

1. Remove the left axle arm-to carrier case bolts, the left arm and drain the lubricant.

2. Remove the right axle stub shaft by performing the following procedures:

    a. Rotate the stub shaft so the open end of the snapring is exposed.

    b. Using 2 prybars, force the snapring from the stub shaft.

    c. Remove the stub shaft from the carrier.

3. Using an axle spreader tool, mount it onto the axle housing and spread the housing enough to remove the differential.

4. Using a dial indicator, measure the amount the opening is being spread; do not spread the housing more than 0.010 in. (0.25mm), for damage to the housing may occur.

5. Mark the differential bearing caps for reassembly purposes.

6. Loosen the bearing caps until 2-3 threads are engaged.

7. Using a prybar, pry the differential loose.

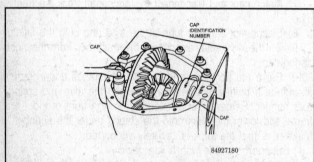

Fig. 169 Removing the bearing caps — Dana 44 and 50 IFS

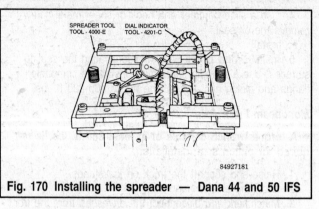

Fig. 170 Installing the spreader — Dana 44 and 50 IFS

8. Remove the bearing caps and the differential.

9. Mount the differential into a vise.

10. Remove and discard the ring gear bolts; they are not reusable.

11. Using a brass drift and a hammer, tap the ring gear from the differential.

12. Using a differential bearing puller, press the differential bearings from the differential.

13. Remove the differential bearing shims.

14. Remove the pinion shaft lockpin and pinion shaft.

15. Rotate the pinions to remove them through the case opening.

16. Remove the side gears and thrust washers.

Pinion Gear

1. Remove the differential case from the axle carrier housing.

2. Using a pinion yoke holding tool, remove the pinion gear nut.

3. Remove the pinion washer. Using a pinion yoke holder tool and a pinion puller tool, press the yoke from the pinion gear.

4. Using a soft hammer, drive the pinion gear assembly from the axle carrier housing.

5. Using a bearing cup puller tool and a slide hammer, remove the pinion gear oil seal and discard it. Remove the outer pinion bearing and the oil slinger from the carrier input bore.

6. Remove the pinion bearing preload shims.

7. Using a shop press, press the inner pinion bearing cup and baffle from the bore.

8. Rotate the carrier housing. Using a shop press, press the outer pinion bearing cup from the bore.

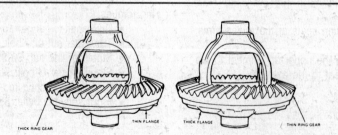

Fig. 168 Differential cases and ring gears used in the Dana 44 and 50 IFS

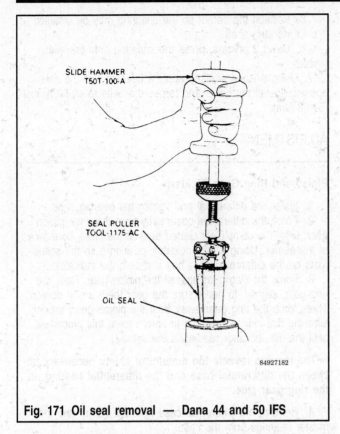

Fig. 171 Oil seal removal — Dana 44 and 50 IFS

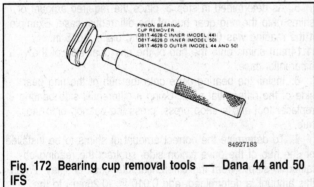

Fig. 172 Bearing cup removal tools — Dana 44 and 50 IFS

9. Using a universal bearing remover tool, press the bearing and the oil slinger from the pinion gear.

INSPECTION

1. Clean the differential components in solvent and use compressed air to dry them; do not use compressed air on the bearings, only shop towels.
2. Check the components for wear or damage; replace them, if necessary.
3. Inspect the bearings and bearing cups for wear, cracks or scoring; replace them, if necessary.
4. Inspect the differential side and pinion gears for wear, cracks or chips; replace them, if necessary.
5. Inspect the ring and pinion gears for wear and/or damage; replace them, if necessary.

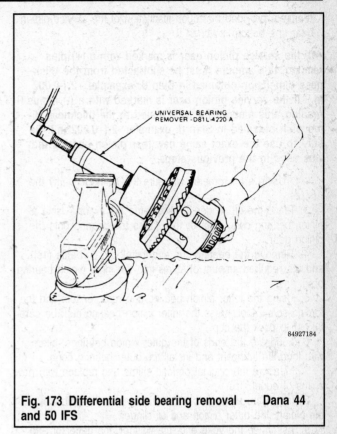

Fig. 173 Differential side bearing removal — Dana 44 and 50 IFS

6. Inspect the differential case for cracks or damage; replace it, if necessary.

ASSEMBLY

Pinion Gear

1. Make sure the ring and pinion are a matched set.
2. Perform the depth gauge check, performing the following procedures:
    a. Using pinion bearing cup replacer tools and the forcing screw from the depth gauge tool set, install the inner and outer pinion cups.
    b. Place a new rear pinion bearing over the aligning adapter and insert it into the pinion bearing retainer assembly. Place the front pinion bearing into the bearing cup in the carrier and assemble the handle onto the screw and hand tighten.

➡️The ⅜in. drive in the handle is to be used for obtaining the proper pinion bearing preload.

    c. Center the gauge tube into the differential bearing bore. Install the bearing caps and tighten the handle until the bearing preload is 20-40 inch lbs. (2.3-4.5 Nm).
    d. Using a feeler gauge or shims, select the thickest feeler shim that will fit between the gauge tube and the gauge block. Insert the feeler gauge or shims directly along the gauge block to insure a correct reading. The feeler gauge, installed between the gauge tube and the gauge block, should have a slight drag feeling.
    e. After the correct shims or feeler gauge thickness is obtained, check the reading, this is the thickness of shim(s)

required, provided that upon inspection of the service pinion gear, the button is etched **0**.

➡️If the service pinion gear is marked with a (+) plus reading, this amount must be subtracted from the thickness dimension obtained in Step d; example: +2 (-0.002 in.). If the service pinion gear is marked with a (-) minus reading, this amount must be added to the thickness dimension obtained in Step d; example: -2 (+0.002 in.). Be sure to use the exact same new rear pinion bearing that was used in the previous steps.

f. Using a micrometer, measure the shims to verify the sizes.

3. Place the oil slinger (if used) onto the pinion. Using a pinion bearing cone installer tool, press the bearing onto the pinion gear.

4. Remove the bearing cup and install the oil baffle (1st) and the required amount of shims into the inner pinion bearing bore.

5. Using the inner pinion bearing cup replacer tool and the forcing screw tool, press the inner pinion bearing cup; be careful not to cock the cup.

6. Lubricate the ends of the outer pinion bearings rollers with long life lubricant and install the outer bearing cone.

7. Measure the original preload shims and replace with new shims of equal size.

8. Install the pinion into the carrier. Install the shims over the pinion, the outer pinion and oil slinger.

9. Assemble the yoke end, the washer, the deflector and slinger onto the pinion shaft and align.

10. Using a companion flange holder tool, seat the yoke, install a new pinion nut and torque to 200-220 ft. lbs. (271-298 Nm).

11. Using an inch lb. torque wrench, rotate the pinion gear and check the preload; it should be 20-40 inch lbs. (2.25-4.52 Nm).

➡️To increase the preload, remove shims; to decrease the preload, install shims.

12. After the preload is adjusted, remove the yoke and washer.

13. Lubricate the pinion oil seal lip. Using an oil seal installation tool, drive a new oil seal into the carrier housing.

14. Using a companion flange holder tool, seat the yoke, install a new pinion nut and torque to 200-220 ft. lbs. (271-298 Nm).

Differential

1. Install the side gears, the thrust washers and the pinion gears into the differential case.

2. Install the pinion shaft and lockpin into the case; peen some differential case metal over the pin to lock it in two places 180° apart.

3. Assemble the ring gear to the differential case and torque the bolts, alternately, to 45-60 ft. lbs. (61-81 Nm).

4. Place the differential assembly into the carrier housing with the master bearings installed.

5. Adjust the pinion and ring gear backlash.

6. Install the right stub shaft by performing the following procedures:

a. Insert the stub shaft into the differential carrier.

b. Position the carrier so the snapring may be installed onto the stub shaft.

c. Using 2 prybars, press the snapring onto the stub shaft.

7. Using silicone sealant, apply a bead of it to the axle housing. Install the cover and torque the bolts to 40-50 ft. lbs. (54-68 Nm).

ADJUSTMENT

Pinion and Ring Gear Backlash

1. Install the differential and tighten the bearing caps.

2. Force the differential case away from the drive pinion gear, until it is completely seated against the cross bore face of the carrier. Using a dial indicator, position it so the stylus rests on the differential case bolt and zero the indicator.

3. Force the ring gear against the pinion gear. Rock the ring gear, slightly, to make sure the gear teeth are in contact. Then, force the ring gear away from the pinion gear, making sure the dial indicator returns to zero; repeat this procedure until the dial indicator reading is the same.

➡️The reading reveals the amount of shims necessary between the differential case and the differential bearing on the ring gear side.

4. Remove the differential case from the carrier and the master bearings from the case.

5. As determined in step 3, place the required amount of shims onto the ring gear hub of the differential case. Example: if the reading was 0.045 in. (1.14mm), place 0.045 in. (1.14mm) shims onto the hub of the ring gear side of the differential case.

6. Install the bearing cone onto the hub of the ring gear side of the differential case. Using a differential side bearing replacer tool and a shop press, press the bearing onto the hub.

7. To determine the correct amount of shims to be installed on the hub of the drive pinion side, subtract the reading obtained in step 3 from the differential total case endplay. When this amount is determined, add 0.010 in. (0.26mm) to the amount; this is the required amount of shims to be placed on the hub of the drive pinion side of the differential.

Example: Total case endplay was 0.091 in. (2.30mm) and the reading in step 3 was 0.045 in. (1.14mm). Subtract the reading from the endplay; the result is 0.046 in. (1.16mm). Then, add 0.010 in. (0.26mm) to the result; 0.056 in. (1.42mm) is the amount of shims to be added on the hub of the drive pinion side of the differential case.

8. Place the required amount of shims onto the hub of the drive pinion side of the differential case.

9. Install the bearing cone onto the hub of the drive pinion side of the differential case. Using a step plate tool, placed on the ring gear side bearing, and a differential side bearing replacer tool, drive the bearing onto the hub of the drive pinion side of the differential case.

10. Using a differential bearing replacer tool, install the bearing cone onto the pinion side of the differential case; be sure to position a pinion bearing cone replacer tool on the ring gear bearing to prevent damage to it.

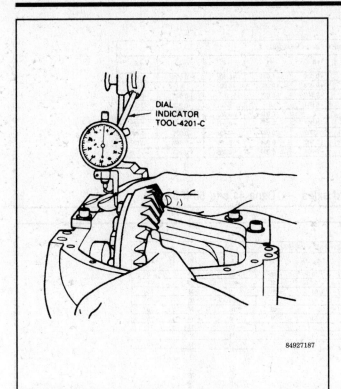

Fig. 174 Checking differential case endplay — Dana 44 and 50 IFS

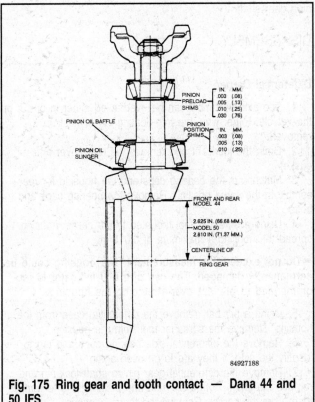

Fig. 175 Ring gear and tooth contact — Dana 44 and 50 IFS

11. Install the differential bearing cups onto the bearing cones.

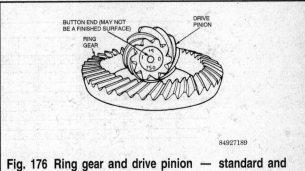

Fig. 176 Ring gear and drive pinion — standard and metric — Dana 44 and 50 IFS

12. Using a case spreader tool and a dial indicator, spread the carrier housing to 0.015 in. (0.25mm) max.

13. Install the differential case into the carrier; it may be necessary to use a soft hammer to seat the differential case into the carrier case cross bore.

14. Install the bearing caps; make sure the letters or numbers stamped on the caps correspond in both direction and position with the numbers stamped in the carrier. Torque the bolts to 80-90 ft. lbs. (108-122 Nm).

15. Install a dial indicator to the case and check the ring gear backlash at 3 equally spaced points; the backlash should be 0.005-0.009 in. (0.13-0.23mm) and should not vary more than 0.003 in. (0.08mm) between the points.

➡ **If the backlash is high, the ring gear must be moved closer to the pinion, by moving the shims to the ring gear side from the opposite side. If the backlash is low, the ring gear must be moved away from the pinion by moving the shims from the ring gear side to the opposite side.**

16. Check and/or adjust the gear tooth pattern.

17. Install the right stub shaft by performing the following procedures:

    a. Insert the stub shaft into the differential carrier.

    b. Position the carrier so the snapring may be installed onto the stub shaft.

    c. Using 2 prybars, press the snapring onto the stub shaft.

18. Using silicone sealant, apply it to the mating surface of the carrier support arm.

➡ **Allow silicone sealant 1 hour to cure.**

19. Using 2 guide pins, assemble the carrier housing to the carrier support arm and torque the new bolts to 30-40 ft. lbs. (41-54 Nm).

20. Install the support arm tab bolt to the side of the carrier and torque the bolts to 85 ft. lbs. (115-136 Nm).

Conventional Differential Overhaul Dana 60 Monobeam

▶ See Figures 190, 191, 192, 193, 194, 195, 196, 197, 198, 199, 200, 201, 202, 203, 204, 205, 206, 207, 208, 209, 210, 211, 212, 213, 214, 215, 216, 217, 218, 219, 220, 221, 222 and 223

The differential side bearing shims are located between the side bearing cup assembly and the differential case. The axle use inner and outer shims on the pinion gear. The inner shims

OLD PINION MARKING	NEW PINION MARKING								
	−4	−3	−2	−1	0	+1	+2	+3	+4
+4	+0.008	+0.007	+0.006	+0.005	+0.004	+0.003	+0.002	+0.001	0
+3	+0.007	+0.006	+0.005	+0.004	+0.003	+0.002	+0.001	0	−0.001
+2	+0.006	+0.005	+0.004	+0.003	+0.002	+0.001	0	−0.001	−0.002
+1	+0.005	+0.004	+0.003	+0.002	+0.001	0	−0.001	−0.002	−0.003
0	+0.004	+0.003	+0.002	+0.001	0	−0.001	−0.002	−0.003	−0.004
−1	+0.003	+0.002	+0.001	0	−0.001	−0.002	−0.003	−0.004	−0.005
−2	+0.002	+0.001	0	−0.001	−0.002	−0.003	−0.004	−0.005	−0.006
−3	+0.001	0	−0.001	−0.002	−0.003	−0.004	−0.005	−0.006	−0.007
−4	0	−0.001	−0.002	−0.003	−0.004	−0.005	−0.006	−0.007	−0.008

Fig. 177 Shim adjustment for pinion replacement — standard axles — Dana 44 and 50 IFS

OLD PINION MARKING	NEW PINION MARKING								
	−10	−8	−5	−3	0	+3	+5	+8	+10
+10	+.20	+.18	+.15	+.13	+.10	+.08	+.05	+.03	0
+8	+.18	+.15	+.13	+.10	+.08	+.05	+.03	0	−.03
+5	+.15	+.13	+.10	+.08	+.05	+.03	0	−.03	−.05
+3	+.13	+.10	+.08	+.05	+.03	0	−.03	−.05	−.08
0	+.10	+.08	+.05	+.03	0	−.03	−.05	−.08	−.10
−3	+.08	+.05	+.03	0	−.03	−.05	−.08	−.10	−.13
−5	+.05	+.03	0	−.03	−.05	−.08	−.10	−.13	−.15
−8	+.03	0	−.03	−.05	−.08	−.10	−.13	−.15	−.18
−10	0	−.03	−.05	−.08	−.10	−.13	−.15	−.18	−.20

Fig. 178 Shim adjustment for pinion replacement — metric axles — Dana 44 and 50 IFS

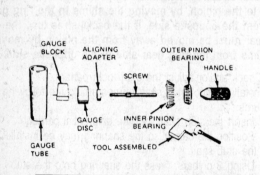

Tool	Tool Number	Axle Model 44	Axle Model 50
Aligning Adapter	T75P-4020-A2	X	X
Gauge Disc	T80T-4020-F40		X
	D80T-4020-F44	X	
Gauge Block	T80T-4020-F42	X	X
Screw	T80T-4020-F43	X	X
Handle	T76P-4020-A11	X	X
Gauge Tube	T80T-4020-F41		X
	D80T-4020-F47	X	

Fig. 179 Depth gauge tool selection — Dana 44 and 50 IFS

are used to control the pinion depth in the housing, while the outer shims are used to preload the pinion bearings. The axle uses a solid differential carrier with a removable side and pinion gear shaft.

DISASSEMBLY

Differential Carrier

1. The axle assembly can be overhauled either in or out of the vehicle. Either way, the free-floating axles must be removed.
2. Drain the lubricant and remove the rear cover and gasket.
3. Matchmark the bearing caps and the housing for reassembly in the same position. Remove the bearing caps and bolts.
4. Using a spreader tool mounted to the carrier housing, spread the housing a maximum of 0.015 in.

➡**Do not exceed this measurement. The housing could be permanently damaged. The use of a dial indicator is recommended to prevent over-stretching the housing.**

5. Using a pry bar, remove the differential case from the housing. Remove the spreader tool from the housing.
6. Remove the differential side bearing cups and tag to identify the side, if they are to be used again.
7. Remove the differential gear pinion shaft lock pin and remove the shaft. Rotate the side and pinion gears to remove them from the carrier. Remove the thrust bearings.
8. Remove the bearing cones and rollers from the carrier, marking and noting the shim locations.
9. Remove the ring gear bolts and tap the ring gear from the carrier housing.

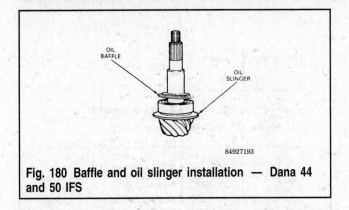

Fig. 180 **Baffle and oil slinger installation — Dana 44 and 50 IFS**

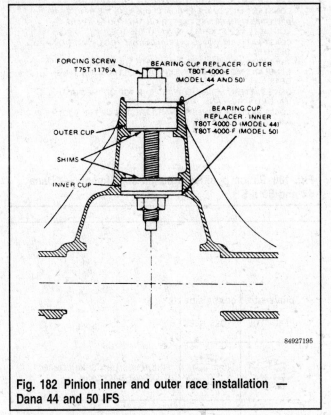

Fig. 182 **Pinion inner and outer race installation — Dana 44 and 50 IFS**

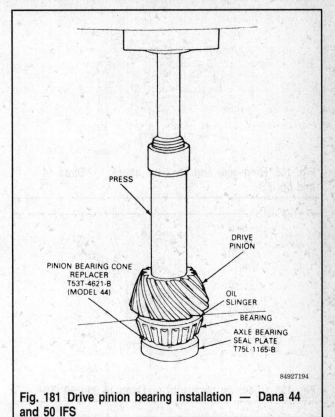

Fig. 181 **Drive pinion bearing installation — Dana 44 and 50 IFS**

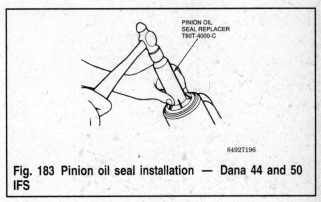

Fig. 183 **Pinion oil seal installation — Dana 44 and 50 IFS**

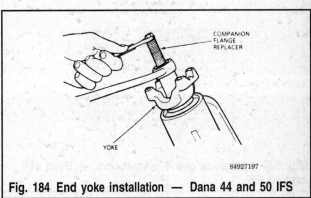

Fig. 184 **End yoke installation — Dana 44 and 50 IFS**

10. Inspect the components.

Drive Pinion

1. Remove the pinion nut and flange from the pinion gear.

2. Remove the pinion gear assembly from the housing. It may be necessary to tap the pinion from the housing with a soft faced hammer. Catch the pinion so as not to allow it to drop on the floor.

3. With a long drift, remove the inner bearing cup, pinion seal, slinger, gasket, outer pinion bearing and the shim pack. Label the shim pack for reassembly.

4. Remove the rear pinion bearing cup and shim pack from the housing. Label the shims for reassembly.

5. Remove the rear pinion bearing from the pinion gear with an arbor press and special plates.

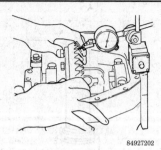

84927202

Fig. 185 Ring gear and backlash check — Dana 44 and 50 IFS

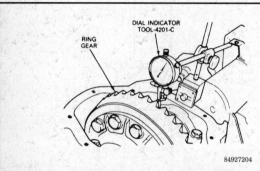

RING GEAR

DIAL INDICATOR TOOL-4201-C

84927204

Fig. 186 Checking backlash — Dana 44 and 50 IFS

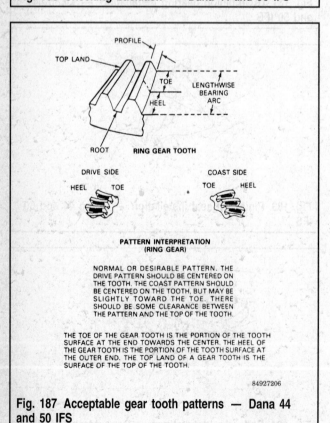

PROFILE

TOP LAND

TOE

LENGTHWISE BEARING ARC

HEEL

ROOT   **RING GEAR TOOTH**

DRIVE SIDE
HEEL   TOE

COAST SIDE
TOE   HEEL

PATTERN INTERPRETATION (RING GEAR)

NORMAL OR DESIRABLE PATTERN. THE DRIVE PATTERN SHOULD BE CENTERED ON THE TOOTH. THE COAST PATTERN SHOULD BE CENTERED ON THE TOOTH, BUT MAY BE SLIGHTLY TOWARD THE TOE. THERE SHOULD BE SOME CLEARANCE BETWEEN THE PATTERN AND THE TOP OF THE TOOTH.

THE TOE OF THE GEAR TOOTH IS THE PORTION OF THE TOOTH SURFACE AT THE END TOWARDS THE CENTER. THE HEEL OF THE GEAR TOOTH IS THE PORTION OF THE TOOTH SURFACE AT THE OUTER END. THE TOP LAND OF A GEAR TOOTH IS THE SURFACE OF THE TOP OF THE TOOTH.

84927206

Fig. 187 Acceptable gear tooth patterns — Dana 44 and 50 IFS

DRIVE SIDE		COAST SIDE	
HEEL	TOE	TOE	HEEL

  BACKLASH CORRECT. THINNER PINION POSITION SHIM SHIM REQUIRED.

BACKLASH CORRECT. THICKER PINION POSITION SHIM REQUIRED.

THICKER PINION POSITION SHIM WITH THE BACKLASH CONSTANT MOVES THE PINION CLOSER TO THE RING GEAR.
DRIVE PATTERN MOVES DEEPER ON THE TOOTH (FLANK CONTACT) AND SLIGHTLY TOWARD THE TOE.
COAST PATTERN MOVES DEEPER ON THE TOOTH AND TOWARD THE HEEL.
THINNER PINION POSITION SHIM WITH THE BACKLASH CONSTANT MOVES THE PINION FURTHER FROM THE RING GEAR.
DRIVE PATTERN MOVES TOWARD THE TOP OF THE TOOTH (FACE CONTACT) AND TOWARD THE HEEL.
COAST PATTERN MOVES TOWARD THE TOP OF THE TOOTH AND SLIGHTLY TOWARD THE TOE.

84927207

Fig. 188 Pinion positioning shim adjustment — Dana 44 and 50 IFS

DRIVE SIDE		COAST SIDE	
HEEL	TOE	TOE	HEEL

PINION POSITION SHIM CORRECT DECREASE BACKLASH.

PINION POSITION SHIM CORRECT. INCREASE BACKLASH.

HIGH BACKLASH IS CORRECTED BY MOVING THE RING GEAR CLOSER TO THE PINION. LOW BACKLASH IS CORRECTED BY MOVING THE RING GEAR AWAY FROM THE PINION. THESE CORRECTIONS ARE MADE BY SWITCHING SHIMS FROM ONE SIDE OF THE DIFFERENTIAL CASE TO THE OTHER.

84927208

Fig. 189 Ring gear positioning shim adjustment — Dana 44 and 50 IFS

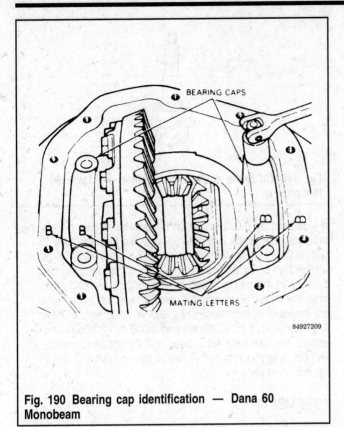

Fig. 190 Bearing cap identification — Dana 60 Monobeam

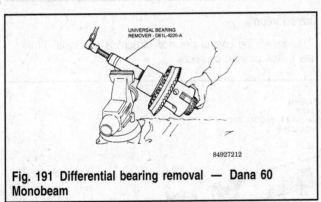

Fig. 191 Differential bearing removal — Dana 60 Monobeam

Fig. 192 Removing the ring gear — Dana 60 Monobeam

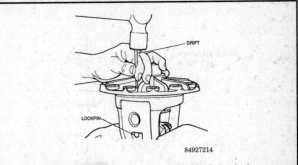

Fig. 193 Driving out the pinion mate shaft lockpin — Dana 60 Monobeam

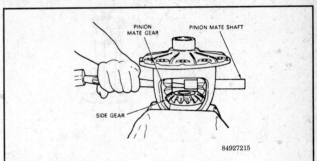

Fig. 194 Driving out the pinion mate shaft — Dana 60 Monobeam

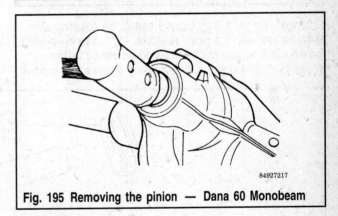

Fig. 195 Removing the pinion — Dana 60 Monobeam

INSPECTION

1. Clean the gears, bearings and component parts with solvent and inspect for scoring, chipping or excessive wear.
2. Inspect the flanges and splines for excessive wear.
3. Replace the necessary parts as required.

PINION SHIM SELECTION

Ring gears and pinions are supplied in matched sets only. The matched numbers are etched on both gears for verification. On the rear face of the pinion, a plus (+) or a minus (-) number will be etched, indicating the best running position for each particular gear set. This dimension is controlled by the shimming behind the inner bearing cup. Whenever baffles or

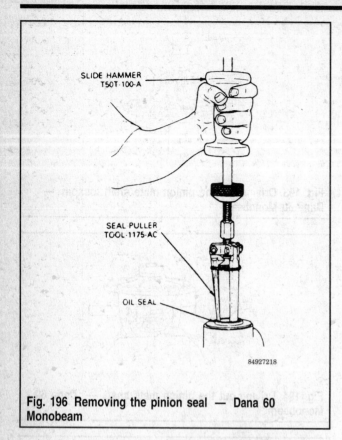

Fig. 196 Removing the pinion seal — Dana 60 Monobeam

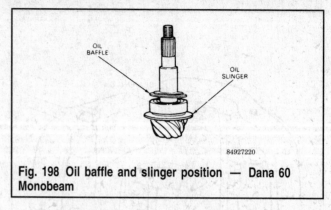

Fig. 198 Oil baffle and slinger position — Dana 60 Monobeam

is increased by 0.003 in., which is just what a plus (+) etching indicates. If a pinion is etched -3, it would be necessary to add 0.003 in. more shims than would be required if the pinion was etched 0. By adding the 0.003 in. shims, the mounting distance of the pinion is decreased 0.003 in., which is just what the minus (-) etching indicates. Pinion adjusting shims are available in thicknesses of 0.003 in. (0.08mm), 0.005 in. (0.13mm), 0.010 in. (0.25mm) and 0.030 in. (0.76mm). An example: If a new gear set is used and the old pinion reads +2 and the new pinion reads -2, add 0.004 in. shims to the original shim pack.

ASSEMBLY

Drive Pinion

1. Select the correct pinion depth shims and install in the rear pinion bearing cup bore.

oil slingers are used, they become part of the adjusting shim pack. An example: If a pinion is etched +3, this pinion would require 0.003 in. less shims than a pinion etched 0. This means by removing shims, the mounting distance of the pinion

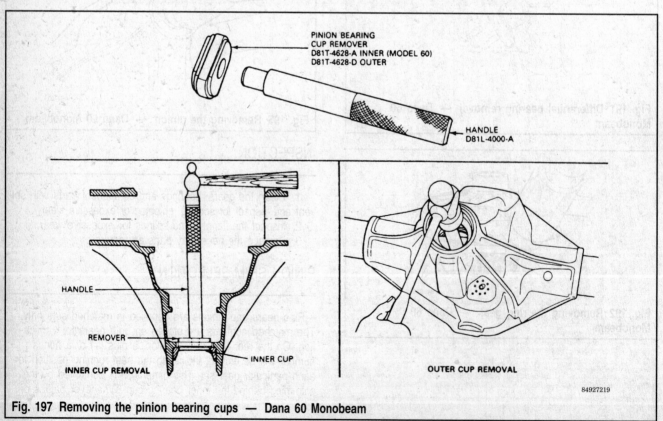

Fig. 197 Removing the pinion bearing cups — Dana 60 Monobeam

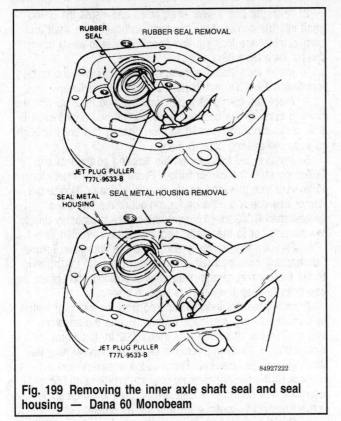

Fig. 199 Removing the inner axle shaft seal and seal housing — Dana 60 Monobeam

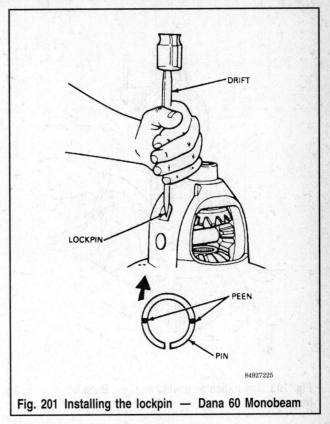

Fig. 201 Installing the lockpin — Dana 60 Monobeam

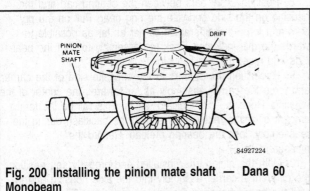

Fig. 200 Installing the pinion mate shaft — Dana 60 Monobeam

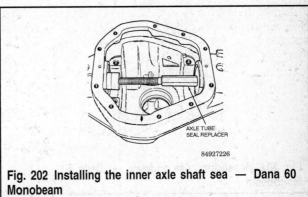

Fig. 202 Installing the inner axle shaft sea — Dana 60 Monobeam

2. Install the rear bearing cup in the axle housing.

3. Add or subtract an equal amount of shim thickness to or from the preload or outer shim pack, as was added or subtracted from the inner shim pack.

4. Install the front pinion bearing cup into its bore in the axle housing.

5. Press the rear pinion bearing onto the pinion gear shaft and install the pinion gear with bearing into the axle housing.

6. Install the preload shims and the front pinion bearing; do not install the oil seal at this time.

7. Install the flange with the holding bar tool attached, the washer and the nut on the pinion shaft end. Torque the nut to 220-280 ft. lbs. (298-379 Nm).

8. Remove the holding bar from the flange and with an inch lb. torque wrench, measure the rotating torque of the pinion gear. The rotating torque should be 10-20 inch lbs. with the original bearings or 15-35 inch lbs. with new bearings.

Disregard the torque reading necessary to start the shaft to turn.

9. If the preload torque is not in specifications, adjust the shim pack as required.

a. To increase preload, decrease the thickness of the preload shim pack.

b. To decrease preload, increase the thickness of the preload shim pack.

10. When the proper preload is obtained, remove the nut, washer and flange from the pinion shaft.

11. Install a new pinion seal into the housing and reinstall the flange, washer and nut. Using the holder tool, torque the nut to 220-280 ft. lbs. (298-379 Nm).

Differential Carrier

1. Install the differential side gears, the differential pinion gears and new thrust washers into the differential carrier.

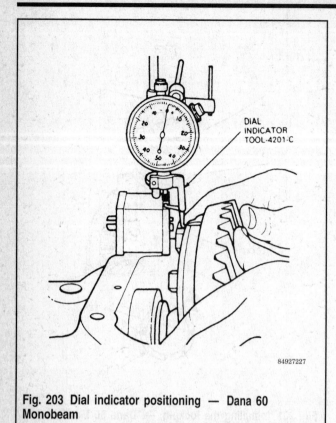

Fig. 203 Dial indicator positioning — Dana 60 Monobeam

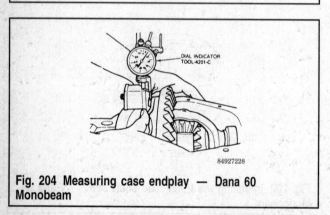

Fig. 204 Measuring case endplay — Dana 60 Monobeam

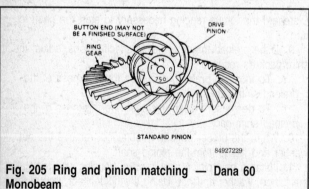

Fig. 205 Ring and pinion matching — Dana 60 Monobeam

2. Align the pinion gear shaft holes and install the pinion shaft into the carrier. Align the lock pin hole in the shaft and carrier. Install the lock pin and peen the hole to avoid having the pin drop from the carrier.

3. Install the differential case side bearings with the proper installation tools. Do not install the shims at this time.

4. Place the carrier assembly into the axle housing with the bearing cups on the bearing cones. Install the bearing caps in their original position and tighten the bearing cap bolts enough to keep the bearing caps in place.

5. Install a dial indicator on the housing so the indicator button contacts the carrier flange. Press the differential carrier to prevent side-play and center the dial indicator. Rotate the carrier and check the flange for run-out. If the run-out is greater than 0.002 in. (0.05mm), the defect is probably due to the bearings or to the carrier and should be corrected.

6. Remove the assembly and install the ring gear. Torque the retaining bolts and reinstall the assembly into the housing. Install the bearing caps in their original position and tighten the cap bolts to keep the bearings caps in place.

7. Install the dial indicator and position the indicator button to contact the ring gear back surface. Rotate the assembly and the run-out should be less than 0.002 in. (0.05mm). If over 0.002 in. (0.05mm), remove the assembly and relocate the ring gear 180 degrees. Reinstall the assembly and recheck. If the run-out remains over the 0.002 in. (0.05mm) tolerance, the ring gear is defective. If the measurement is within tolerances, continue on with the assembly.

8. Position 2 pry bars between the bearing cap and the housing on the side opposite the ring gear. Pull on the pry bars and force the differential carrier as far as possible towards the dial indicator. Rock the assembly to seat the bearings and reset the dial indicator to 0.

9. Reposition the prybars to the opposite side of the carrier and force the carrier assembly as far towards the center of the housing. Read the dial indicator scale. This will be the total amount of shims required for setting the backlash during the reassembly, less the bearing preload. Record the measurement.

10. With the pinion gear installed and properly set, position the differential carrier assembly into the axle housing and install the bearing caps in their proper positions. Tighten the cap bolts just to hold the bearing cups in place.

11. Install a dial indicator on the axle housing with the indicator button contacting the back of the ring gear.

12. Position 2 prybars between the bearing cup and the axle housing on the ring gear side of the case and pry the ring gear into mesh with the pinion gear teeth, as far as possible. Rock the ring gear to allow the teeth to mesh and the bearings to seat. With the pressure still applied by the prybars, set the dial indicator to 0.

13. Reposition the prybars on the opposite side of ring gear and pry the gear as far as it will go. Take the dial indicator reading. Repeat this procedure until the same reading is obtained each time. This reading represents the necessary amount of shims between the differential carrier and the bearing on the ring gear side.

14. Remove the bearing from the differential carrier on the ring gear side and install the proper amount of shims. Reinstall the bearing.

PINION SETTING CHART — ENGLISH

Old Pinion Marking	New Pinion Marking								
	−4	−3	−2	−1	0	+1	+2	+3	+4
+4	+0.008	+0.007	+0.006	+0.005	+0.004	+0.003	+0.002	+0.001	0
+3	+0.007	+0.006	+0.005	+0.004	+0.003	+0.002	+0.001	0	−0.001
+2	+0.006	+0.005	+0.004	+0.003	+0.002	+0.001	0	−0.001	−0.002
+1	+0.005	+0.004	+0.003	+0.002	+0.001	0	−0.001	−0.002	−0.003
0	+0.004	+0.003	+0.002	+0.001	0	−0.001	−0.002	−0.003	−0.004
−1	+0.003	+0.002	+0.001	0	−0.001	−0.002	−0.003	−0.004	−0.005
−2	+0.002	+0.001	0	−0.001	−0.002	−0.003	−0.004	−0.005	−0.006
−3	+0.001	0	−0.001	−0.002	−0.003	−0.004	−0.005	−0.006	−0.007
−4	0	−0.001	−0.002	−0.003	−0.004	−0.005	−0.006	−0.007	−0.008

84927230

Fig. 206 Pinion setting chart — English measure — Dana Monobeam

PINION SETTING CHART — METRIC

Old Pinion Marking	New Pinion Marking								
	−10	−8	−5	−3	0	+3	+5	+8	+10
+10	+.20	+.18	+.15	+.13	+.10	+.08	+.05	+.03	0
+8	+.18	+.15	+.13	+.10	+.08	+.05	+.03	0	−.03
+5	+.15	+.13	+.10	+.08	+.05	+.03	0	−.03	−.05
+3	+.13	+.10	+.08	+.05	+.03	0	−.03	−.05	−.08
0	+.10	+.08	+.05	+.03	0	−.03	−.05	−.08	−.10
−3	+.08	+.05	+.03	0	−.03	−.05	−.08	−.10	−.13
−5	+.05	+.03	0	−.03	−.05	−.08	−.10	−.13	−.15
−8	+.03	0	−.03	−.05	−.08	−.10	−.13	−.15	−.18
−10	0	−.03	−.05	−.08	−.10	−.13	−.15	−.18	−.20

84927231

Fig. 207 Pinion setting chart — Metric measure — Dana 60 Monobeam

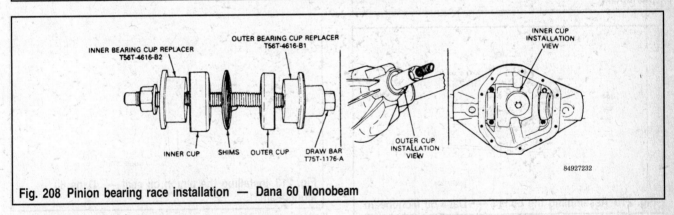

84927232

Fig. 208 Pinion bearing race installation — Dana 60 Monobeam

15. Remove the differential carrier bearing from the opposite side of the ring gear. To determine the amount of shims needed, use the following method.

 a. Subtract the size of the shim pack just installed on the ring gear side of the carrier from the reading obtained and recorded when measurement was taken without the pinion gear in place.

 b. To this figure, add an additional 0.015 in. to compensate for preload and backlash. An example: If the first reading was 0.085 in. and the shims installed on the ring gear side of the carrier were 0.055 in., the correct amount of shims would be 0.085 in. - 0.055 in. + 0.015 in. = 0.045 in.

16. Install the required shims as determined under Step 15 and install the differential side bearing. The installation of the shims should give the proper preload to the bearings and the proper backlash to the ring and pinion gears.

17. Spread the axle housing with the spreader tool no more than 0.015 in. (0.38mm). Install the differential bearing outer cups in their correct locations and install the cups in their respective locations.

18. Install the bolts and tighten finger-tight. Rotate the differential carrier and ring gear and tap with a soft-faced hammer to insure proper seating of the assembly in the axle housing.

19. Remove the spreader tool and torque the cap bolts to 80-90 ft. lbs. (108-122 Nm).

20. Install a dial indicator and check the ring gear backlash at 4 equally spaced points of the ring gear circle. The backlash must be within a range of 0.005-0.009 in. (0.127-0.229mm) and must not vary more than 0.003 in. (0.076mm) between the points checked.

21. If the backlash is not within specifications, the shim packs must be corrected to bring the backlash within limits.

22. Check the tooth contact pattern and verify.

23. Install the cover and torque the bolts to 30-40 ft. lbs. (41-54 Nm). Refill to proper level with lubricant and operate to verify proper assembly.

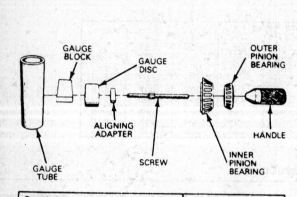

Fig. 209 Depth gauge checking tools — Dana 60 Monobeam

Description	Number
Handle	T76P-4020-A11
Screw	T80T-4020-F43
Gauge Block	T80T-4020-F42
Aligning Adapter	T76P-4020-A3
Gauge Disc	T78P-4020-A15
Gauge Tube	D80T-4020-F48

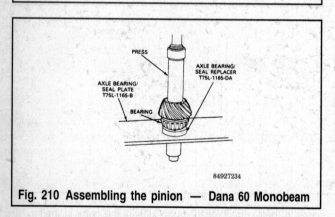

Fig. 210 Assembling the pinion — Dana 60 Monobeam

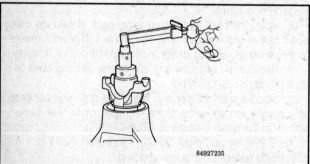

Fig. 211 Checking pinion rotating torque — Dana 60 Monobeam

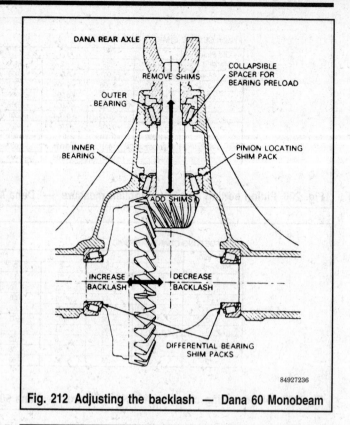

Fig. 212 Adjusting the backlash — Dana 60 Monobeam

Fig. 213 Installing the pinion oil seal — Dana 60 Monobeam

Limited Slip Differential Overhaul Dana Axles

A locking differential is available on the 44 IFS, 44 IFS HD and 60 series. The locking differential construction is the same for all axles. Overhaul of this differential, except for the differential case, is identical to that of the conventional differential.

1. Remove the ring gear.
2. Place the case on a holding fixture mounted in a vise.
3. Use a small punch to drive out the roll pin retaining the cross-shaft and drive out the cross-shaft.
4. Position the Step Plate T83T-4205-A4, or equivalent, into the bottom side gear. Apply a small amount of grease in the centering hole.
5. Insert the forcing nut and screw into the case. Guide the forcing screw onto the step plate.

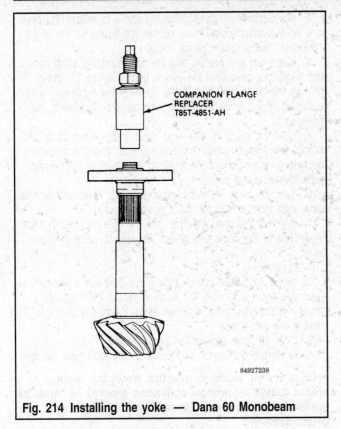

Fig. 214 Installing the yoke — Dana 60 Monobeam

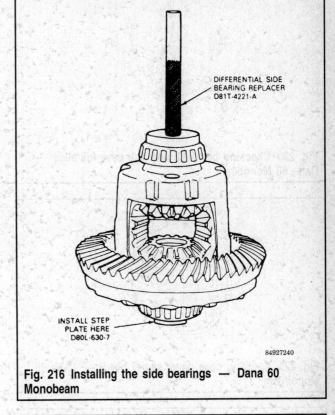

Fig. 216 Installing the side bearings — Dana 60 Monobeam

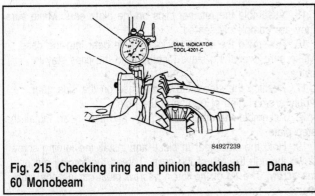

Fig. 215 Checking ring and pinion backlash — Dana 60 Monobeam

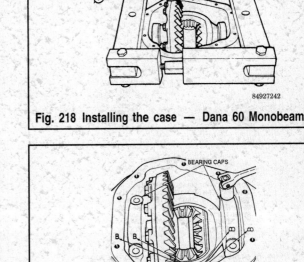

Fig. 218 Installing the case — Dana 60 Monobeam

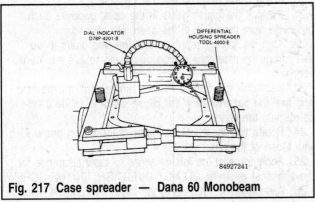

Fig. 217 Case spreader — Dana 60 Monobeam

Fig. 219 Installing the bearing caps — Dana 60 Monobeam

6. Tighten the forcing screw securely. This will move the side gears away from the pinion gears and relieve the nor-

mally loaded condition. Using a piece of 0.03 in. (0.762mm) shim stock, push out the differential spherical washers.

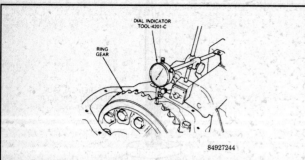

Fig. 220 Checking backlash with the case installed — Dana 60 Monobeam

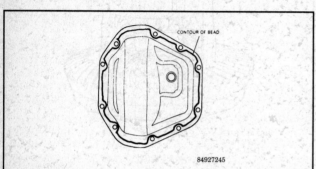

Fig. 221 Applying case cover sealer bead — Dana 60 Monobeam

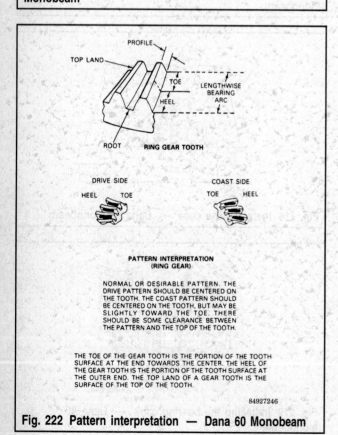

Fig. 222 Pattern interpretation — Dana 60 Monobeam

7. Momentarily loosen the forcing screw to relieve the pressure on the clutch pack, then, tighten the screw until a slight movement of the pinion gears is seen.

8. Insert the tool handle into the pinion mating shaft bore and rotate the case until the pinion gears can be removed through the large openings in the case. Some tightening and loosening of the forcing screw will be required to permit gear movement.

9. Hold the top side gear and clutch pack in the case and remove the forcing screw and rotating tool. Then, remove the top side gear and clutch pack. Keep the stack of plates and discs in their exact order.

10. Turn the case so that the flange is up. Remove the step plate, side gear and clutch pack out of the case.

11. Remove the retainer clips from the clutch packs to allow separation of the discs and plates. Be sure to keep them in order!

To assemble:

12. Install the clutch packs, side gears and thrust washers. Assemble them is exactly the same order as the originals. Never replace just some of these parts. If any are damaged, replace the whole set.

13. Coat all parts with limited slip lubricant.

14. Assemble the plates and discs on the side gear splines.

➡**Discs for the model 60 axle that are of the newer, coated design — without concentric grooves — must be soaked for 20 minutes in limited slip friction additive before assembly.**

15. Assemble the retainer clips on the plate ears. Make sure they are completely seated.

16. Assemble the clutch pack and side gear into the case. Make sure everything stays together and the clips stay in place.

17. Position the step plate in the case on the side gear. Apply a small glob of grease in the hole.

18. Assemble the other clutch pack and side gear. Install the step plate.

19. Hold the side gear in place and install the forcing screw down through the top of the case. Thread the forcing nut on the screw. The tip of the forcing screw must contact the step plate.

20. Position the case on the holding fixture.

21. Position the pinion gears in the case, opposite each other. Be sure the holes in the gears are aligned.

22. Turn the forcing screw so that the side gears move away from the differential pinion gears and relieve the loaded condition.

23. Insert the tool handle into the pinion shaft mating hole and turn the case to allow the pinion gears to rotate themselves into the case.

24. Rotate the case until the holes of the pinion gears align with those of the case.

25. Apply force to the forcing screw to allow clearance for the spherical washers. DO NOT OVERTIGHTEN THE SCREW!

26. Assemble the washers in the case. Be sure the holes in the washers and gears are aligned.

27. Remove all special tools.

28. Install the pinion shaft.

29. Install the cross-shaft locking pin.

30. Install the ring gear.

REAR AXLE

Understanding Drive Axles

The drive axle is a special type of transmission that reduces the speed of the drive from the engine and transmission and divides the power to the wheels. Power enters the axle from the driveshaft via the companion flange. The flange is mounted on the drive pinion shaft. The drive pinion shaft and gear which carry the power into the differential turn at engine speed. The gear on the end of the pinion shaft drives a large ring gear the axis of rotation of which is 90° away from the of the pinion. The pinion and gear reduce the gear ratio of the axle, and change the direction of rotation to turn the axle shafts which drive both wheels. The axle gear ratio is found by dividing the number of pinion gear teeth into the number of ring gear teeth.

The ring gear drives the differential case. The case provides the two mounting points for the ends of a pinion shaft on which are mounted two pinion gears. The pinion gears drive the two side gears, one of which is located on the inner end of each axle shaft.

By driving the axle shafts through the arrangement, the differential allows the outer drive wheel to turn faster than the inner drive wheel in a turn.

The main drive pinion and the side bearings, which bear the weight of the differential case, are shimmed to provide proper bearing preload, and to position the pinion and ring gears properly.

✳✳WARNING

The proper adjustment of the relationship of the ring and pinion gears is critical. It should be attempted only by those with extensive equipment and/or experience.

Limited-slip differentials include clutches which tend to link each axle shaft to the differential case. Clutches may be engaged either by spring action or by pressure produced by the torque on the axles during a turn. During turning on a dry pavement, the effects of the clutches are overcome, and each wheel turns at the required speed. When slippage occurs at either wheel, however, the clutches will transmit some of the power to the wheel which has the greater amount of traction. Because of the presence of clutches, limited-slip units require a special lubricant.

DETERMINING AXLE RATIO

The drive axle is said to have a certain axle ratio. This number (usually a whole number and a decimal fraction) is actually a comparison of the number of gear teeth on the ring gear and the pinion gear. For example, a 4.11 rear means that theoretically, there are 4.11 teeth on the ring gear and one tooth on the pinion gear or, put another way, the driveshaft must turn 4.11 times to turn the wheels once. Actually, on a 4.11 rear, there might be 37 teeth on the ring gear and 9 teeth on the pinion gear. By dividing the number of teeth on the pinion gear into the number of teeth on the ring gear, the numerical axle ratio (4.11) is obtained. This also provides a good method of ascertaining exactly what axle ratio one is dealing with.

Another method of determining gear ratio is to jack up and support the truck so that both rear wheels are off the ground. Make a chalk mark on the rear wheel and the driveshaft. Put the transmission in neutral. Turn the rear wheel one complete turn and count the number of turns that the driveshaft makes. The number of turns that the driveshaft makes in one complete revolution of the rear wheel is an approximation of the rear axle ratio.

DIFFERENTIAL OVERHAUL

A differential overhaul is a complex, highly technical, and time-consuming operation, which requires a great many tools, extensive knowledge of the unit and the way it works, and a high degree of mechanical experience and ability. While complete overhaul procedures are provided here, it is highly advisable that the amateur mechanic not attempt any work on the differential unit.

IMPROVED TRACTION DIFFERENTIALS

In this assembly, a multiple-disc clutch is employed to control differential action.

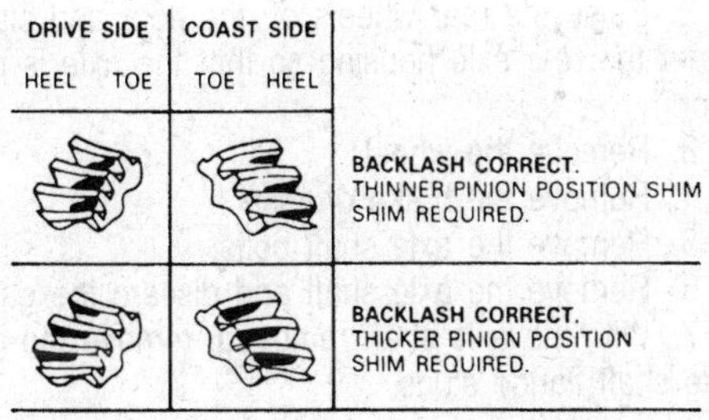

DRIVE SIDE		COAST SIDE		
HEEL	TOE	TOE	HEEL	
				BACKLASH CORRECT. THINNER PINION POSITION SHIM REQUIRED.
				BACKLASH CORRECT. THICKER PINION POSITION SHIM REQUIRED.

THICKER PINION POSITION SHIM WITH THE BACKLASH CONSTANT MOVES THE PINION CLOSER TO THE RING GEAR.
DRIVE PATTERN MOVES DEEPER ON THE TOOTH (FLANK CONTACT) AND SLIGHTLY TOWARD THE TOE.
COAST PATTERN MOVES DEEPER ON THE TOOTH AND TOWARD THE HEEL.
THINNER PINION POSITION SHIM WITH THE BACKLASH CONSTANT MOVES THE PINION FURTHER FROM THE RING GEAR.
DRIVE PATTERN MOVES TOWARD THE TOP OF THE TOOTH (FACE CONTACT) AND TOWARD THE HEEL.
COAST PATTERN MOVES TOWARD THE TOP OF THE TOOTH AND SLIGHTLY TOWARD THE TOE.

84927248

Fig. 223 Tooth pattern adjustment — Dana 60 Monobeam

Identification

Four types of rear axles are used on Ford F-150 and Bronco, F-250 and F-350 pickups:

1. The Ford integral carrier type semi-floating 8.8 in. (223.5mm) ring gear axle used on F-150 and Bronco models.

2. The Ford integral carrier type semi-floating 10.25 in. (260.35mm) ring gear axle used on F-250 Light Duty models.

3. The Ford integral carrier type full-floating 10.25 in. (260.35mm) ring gear axle used on F-250 Heavy Duty models and F-350 models.

4. The Dana 80 integral carrier full-floating 11.25 in. (285.75mm) ring gear rear axle used on F-Super Duty models.

On a full floating rear axle, the weight of the vehicle is supported by the axle housing. The axle shafts can be removed without disturbing the wheel bearings.

On a semi-floating axle, the outboard end of the axle shaft is supported by the bearing which is mounted in a recess in the end of the axle housing.

The axle shaft on a full-floating rear axle is held in place by a flange and bolts attaching it to the hub on the outboard side. The hub is held to the rear spindle by nuts which are also used to adjust the preload of the rear axle bearings.

The axle shaft on the semi-floating rear axle is held in position by C-locks in the differential housing.

Axle Identification and Ratio are found on an I.D. tag located under one of the bolts on the differential housing. Also refer to the Drive Axle Section of the Capacities Chart in Section 1 for complete model application.

Axle Shaft, Bearing and Seal

REMOVAL & INSTALLATION

◆ **See Figures 224, 225, 226, 227 and 228**

Ford 8.8 in. (223.5mm) Ring Gear Integral Carrier Ford 10.25 in. (260.35mm) Ring Gear, Semi-floating Integral Carrier

1. Raise and safely support the vehicle on jackstands.
2. Remove the wheels from the brake drums.
3. Place a drain pan under the housing and drain the lubricant by loosening the housing cover.
4. Remove the locks securing the brake drums to the axle shaft flanges and remove the drums.
5. Remove the housing cover and gasket.
6. Remove the side gear pinion shaft lockbolt and the side gear pinion shaft.
7. Push the axle shafts inward and remove the C-locks from the inner end of the axle shafts. Temporarily replace the shaft and lockbolt to retain the differential gears in position.
8. Remove the axle shafts with a slide hammer. Be sure the seal is not damaged by the splines on the axle shaft.
9. Remove the bearing and oil seal from the housing. Both the seal and bearing can be removed with a slide hammer
10. Two types of bearings are used on some axles, one requiring a press fit and the other a loose fit. A loose fitting bearing does not necessarily indicate excessive wear.

11. Inspect the axle shaft housing and axle shafts for burrs or other irregularities. Replace any work or damaged parts. A light yellow color on the bearing journal of the axle shaft is normal, and does not require replacement of the axle shaft. Slight pitting and wear is also normal.

12. Lightly coat the wheel bearing rollers with axle lubricant. Install the bearings in the axle housing until the bearing seats firmly against the shoulder.

13. Wipe all lubricant from the oil seal bore, before installing the seal.

14. Inspect the original seals for wear. If necessary, these may be replaced with new seals, which are prepacked with lubricant and do not require soaking.

To install:

15. Install the oil seal.

16. Remove the lockbolt and pinion shaft. Carefully slide the axle shafts into place. Be careful that you do not damage the seal with the splined end of the axle shaft. Engage the splined end of the shaft with the differential side gears.

17. Install the axle shaft C-locks on the inner end of the axle shafts and seat the C-locks in the counterbore of the differential side gears.

18. Rotate the differential pinion gears until the differential pinion shaft can be installed. Install the differential pinion shaft lockbolt. Tighten to 15-22 ft. lbs.

19. Install the brake drum on the axle shaft flange.

20. Install the wheel and tire on the brake drum and tighten the attaching nuts.

21. Clean the gasket surface of the rear housing and install a new cover gasket and the housing cover. Some covers do not use a gasket. On these models, apply a bead of silicone sealer on the gasket surface. The bead should run inside of the bolt holes.

22. Raise the rear axle so that it is in the running position. Add the amount of specified lubricant to bring the lubricant level to 1/2 in. (12.7mm) below the filler hole.

Ford 10.25 in. (260.35mm) Ring Gear, Full Floating Integral Carrier

◆ **See Figures 229, 230, 231, 232, 233, 234, 235, 236, 237 and 238**

The wheel bearings on the full floating rear axle are packed with wheel bearing grease. Axle lubricant can also flow into the wheel hubs and bearings, however, wheel bearing grease is the primary lubricant. The wheel bearing grease provides lubrication until the axle lubricant reaches the bearings during normal operation.

1. Set the parking brake and loosen the axle shaft bolts.
2. Raise the rear wheels off the floor and place jackstands under the rear axle housing so that the axle is parallel with the floor.
3. Remove the wheels.
4. Remove the brake drums.
5. Remove the axle shaft bolts.
6. Remove the axle shaft and discard the gaskets.
7. With the axle shaft removed, remove the gasket from the axle shaft flange studs.

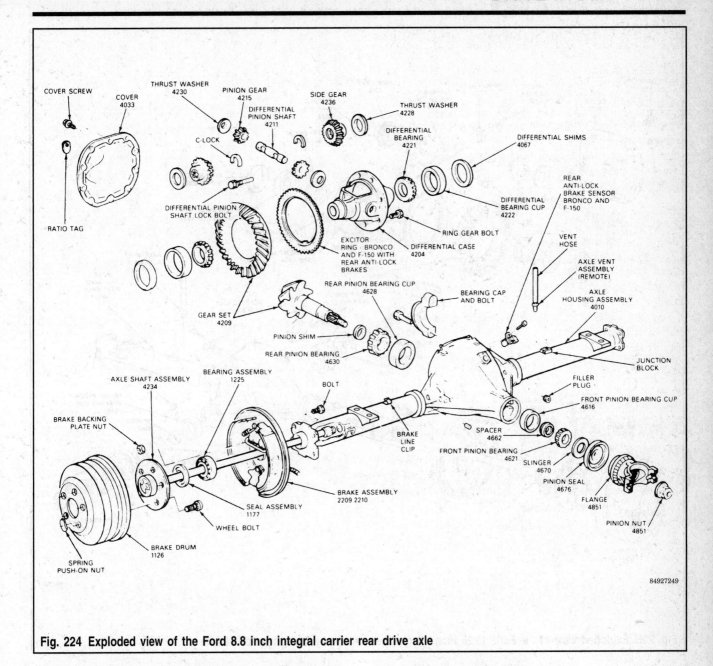

COVER SCREW
COVER 4033
RATIO TAG
THRUST WASHER 4230
PINION GEAR 4215
DIFFERENTIAL PINION SHAFT 4211
C-LOCK
SIDE GEAR 4236
THRUST WASHER 4228
DIFFERENTIAL BEARING 4221
DIFFERENTIAL SHIMS 4067
REAR ANTI-LOCK BRAKE SENSOR BRONCO AND F-150
DIFFERENTIAL PINION SHAFT LOCK BOLT
DIFFERENTIAL BEARING CUP 4222
RING GEAR BOLT
DIFFERENTIAL CASE 4204
VENT HOSE
AXLE VENT ASSEMBLY (REMOTE)
EXCITOR RING - BRONCO AND F-150 WITH REAR ANTI-LOCK BRAKES
REAR PINION BEARING CUP 4628
BEARING CAP AND BOLT
AXLE HOUSING ASSEMBLY 4010
GEAR SET 4209
PINION SHIM
REAR PINION BEARING 4630
JUNCTION BLOCK
AXLE SHAFT ASSEMBLY 4234
BEARING ASSEMBLY 1225
BOLT
FILLER PLUG
FRONT PINION BEARING CUP 4616
BRAKE BACKING PLATE NUT
BRAKE LINE CLIP
SPACER 4662
FRONT PINION BEARING 4621
SLINGER 4670
BRAKE ASSEMBLY 2209 2210
PINION SEAL 4676
SEAL ASSEMBLY 1177
WHEEL BOLT
FLANGE 4851
BRAKE DRUM 1126
SPRING PUSH-ON NUT
PINION NUT 4851

84927249

Fig. 224 Exploded view of the Ford 8.8 inch integral carrier rear drive axle

8. Install Hub Wrench T85T-4252-AH, or equivalent, so that the drive tangs on the tool engage the slots in the hub nut.

➡**The hub nuts are right hand thread on the right hub and left hand thread on the left hub. The hub nuts should be stamped RH and LH.   Never use power or impact tools on these nuts!   The nuts will ratchet during removal.**

9. Remove the hub nut.
10. Install step plate adapter tool D80L-630-7, or equivalent, in the hub.
11. Install puller D80L-1002-L, or equivalent and loosen the hub to the point of removal. Remove the puller and step plate.
12. Remove the hub, taking care to catch the outer bearing as the hub comes off.
13. Install the hub in a soft-jawed vise and pry out the hub seal.

14. Lift out the inner bearing.
15. Drive out the inner and outer bearing races with a drift.
16. Wash all the old grease or axle lubricant out of the wheel hub, using a suitable solvent.
17. Wash the bearing races and rollers and inspect them for pitting, galling, and uneven wear patterns. Inspect the roller for end wear. Replace any bearing and race that appears in any way damaged. Always replace the bearings and races as a set.
18. Coat the race bores with a light coat of clean, water-proof wheel bearing grease and drive the races squarely into the bores until they are fully seated. A good indication that the race is seated is when you notice the grease from the bore squashing out under the race when it contact the shoulder. Another indication is a definite change in the metallic tone when you seat the race. Just be very careful to avoid damaging the bearing surface of the race!

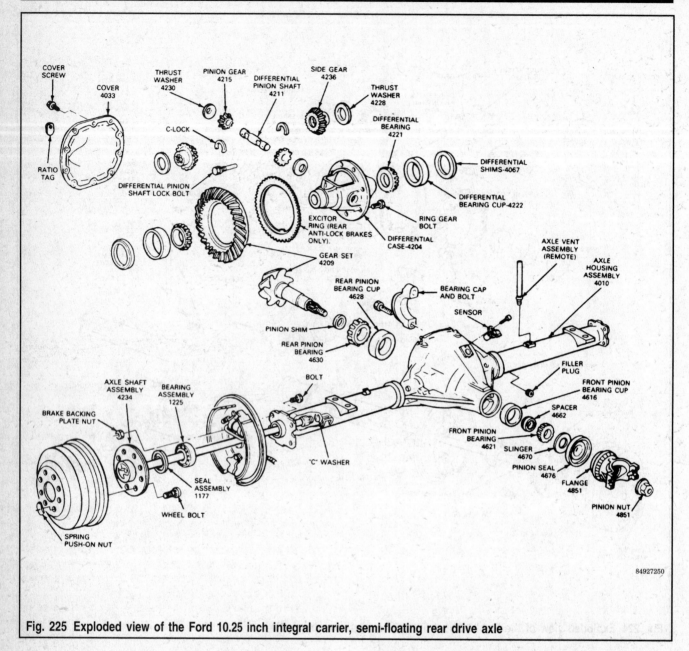

Fig. 225 Exploded view of the Ford 10.25 inch integral carrier, semi-floating rear drive axle

19. Pack each bearing cone and roller with a bearing packer or in the manner outlined in Section 1 for the front wheel bearings on 2-Wheel Drive trucks.

To install:

20. Place the inner bearing cone and roller assembly in the wheel hub.

➡**When installing the new seal, the words OIL SIDE must go inwards towards the bearing!**

21. Place the seal squarely in the hub and drive it into place. The best tool for the job is a seal driver such as T85T-1175-AH, which will stop when the seal is at the proper depth.

➡**If the seal is misaligned or damaged during installation, a new seal must be installed.**

22. Clean the spindle thoroughly. If the spindle is excessively pitted, damaged or has a predominately bluish tint (from overheating), it must be replaced.

23. Coat the spindle with 80W/90 oil.

24. Pack the hub with clean, waterproof wheel bearing grease.

25. Pack the outer bearing with clean, waterproof wheel bearing grease in the same manner as you packed the inner bearing.

26. Place the outer bearing in the hub and install the hub and bearing together on the spindle.

27. Install the hub nut on the spindle. Make sure that the nut tab is located in the keyway prior to thread engagement. Turn the hub nut onto the threads as far as you can by hand, noting the thread direction.

28. Install the hub wrench tool and tighten the nut to 55-65 ft. lbs. Rotate the hub occasionally during nut tightening.

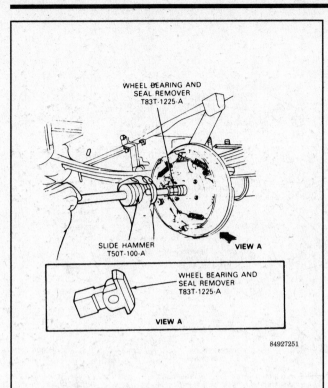

Fig. 226 Rear axle bearing and seal removal for the Ford 8.8 inch axle

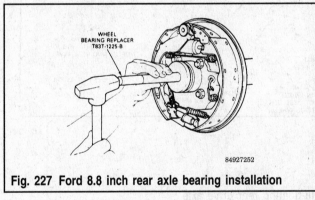

Fig. 227 Ford 8.8 inch rear axle bearing installation

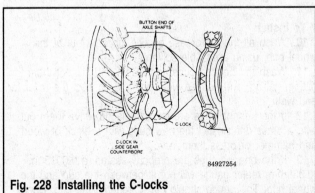

Fig. 228 Installing the C-locks

29. Ratchet the nut back 5 teeth. **Make sure that you hear 5 clicks!**

30. Inspect the axle shaft O-ring seal and replace it if it looks at all bad.

31. Install the axle shaft.

32. Coat the axle shaft bolt threads with waterproof seal and install them by hand until they seat. **Do not tighten them with a wrench at this time!**

33. Check the diameter across the center of the brake shoes. Check the diameter of the brake drum. Adjust the brake shoes so that their diameter is 0.030 in. (0.76mm) less than the drum diameter.

34. Install the brake drum

35. Install the wheel.

36. Loosen the differential filler plug. If lubricant starts to run out, retighten the plug. If not, remove the plug and fill the housing with 80W/90 gear oil.

37. Lower the truck to the floor.

38. Tighten the wheel lugs to 140 ft. lbs.

39. Now tighten the axle shaft bolts. Torque them to 60-80 ft. lbs.

Dana Model 80

▶ **See Figures 239, 240, 241, 242, 243 and 244**

❋❋CAUTION

New Dual Rear Wheel models have flat-faced lug nut replacing the old cone-shaped lug nuts. NEVER replace these new nuts with the older design! Never replace the newer designed wheels with older design wheels! The newer wheels have lug holes with special shoulders to accommodate the newly designed lug nuts.

1988-89 F-SUPER DUTY, STRIPPED CHASSIS AND MOTOR HOME CHASSIS

The wheel bearings on full floating rear axles are packed with wheel bearing grease. Axle lubricant can also flow into the wheel hubs and bearings, however, wheel bearing grease is the primary lubricant. The wheel bearing grease provides lubrication until the axle lubricant reaches the bearings during normal operation.

1. Set the parking brake and loosen — do not remove — the axle shaft bolts.

2. Raise the rear wheels off the floor and place jackstands under the rear axle housing so that the axle is parallel with the floor. Release the parking brake.

3. Remove the axle shaft bolts and lockwashers. They should not be re-used.

4. Place a heavy duty wheel dolly under the wheels and raise them so that all weight is off the wheel bearings.

5. Remove the axle shaft and gasket(s).

6. Remove the caliper. See Section 9.

7. Using a special hub nut wrench, remove the hub nut.

➡The hub nut on the right spindle is right hand thread; the one on the left spindle is left hand thread. They are marked RH and LH. NEVER use an impact wrench on the hub nut!

8. Remove the outer bearing cone and pull the wheel straight off the axle.

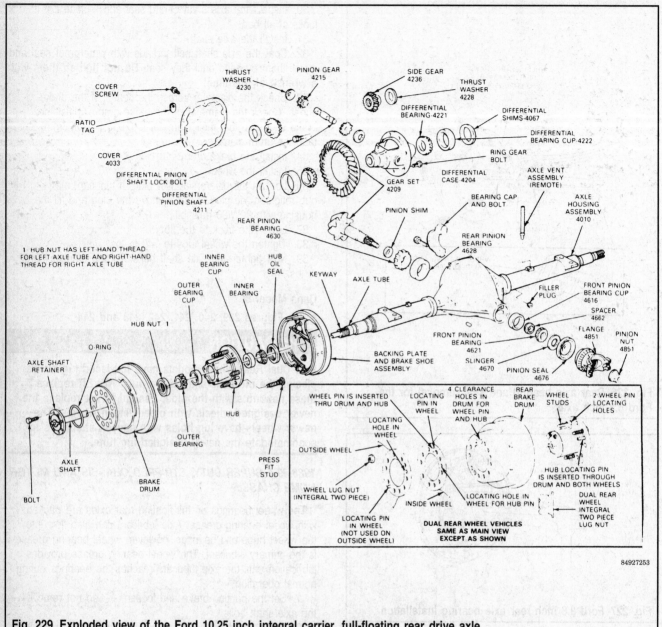

Fig. 229 Exploded view of the Ford 10.25 inch integral carrier, full-floating rear drive axle

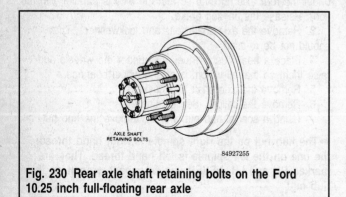

Fig. 230 Rear axle shaft retaining bolts on the Ford 10.25 inch full-floating rear axle

9. With a piece of hardwood or a brass drift which will just clear the outer bearing cup, drive the inner bearing cone and inner seal out of the wheel hub.

To install:

10. Wash all the old grease or axle lubricant out of the wheel hub, using a suitable solvent.

11. Wash the bearing cups and rollers and inspect them for pitting, galling, and uneven wear patterns. Inspect the roller for end wear.

12. If the bearing cups are to be replaced, drive them out with a brass drift. Install the new cups with a block of wood and hammer or press them in.

13. If the bearing cups are properly seated, a 0.0015 in. (0.038mm) feeler gauge will not fit between the cup and the wheel hub. The gauge should not fit beneath the cup. Check several places to make sure the cups are squarely seated.

14. Pack each bearing cone and roller with a bearing packer or in the manner outlined for the front wheel bearings on 2WD trucks in Section 1. Use a multi-purpose wheel bearing grease.

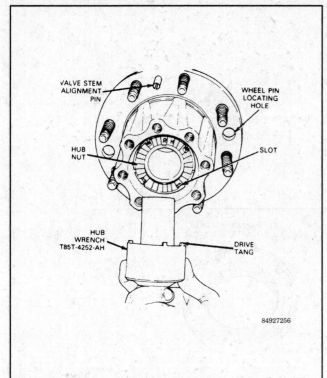

Fig. 231 Using a hub wrench to remove the hub nuts on the 10.25 inch full-floating axle

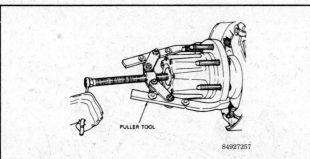

Fig. 232 Loosening the hub on the 10.25 inch full-floating axle

15. Place the inner bearing cone and roller assembly in the wheel hub. Install a new inner seal in the hub with a seal installation tool.

16. Wrap the threads of the spindle with tape and carefully slide the hub straight on the spindle. Take care to avoid damaging the seal! Remove the tape.

17. Install the outer bearing. Start the hub nut, making sure that the hub tab is engaged with the keyway prior to threading.

18. Tighten the nut to 65-75 ft.lbs. while rotating the wheel.

➡**The hub will ratchet at torque is applied. This ratcheting can be avoided by using Ford tool No. T88T-4252-A. Avoiding ratcheting will give more even bearing preloads.**

19. Back off (loosen) the adjusting nut 90° (¼ turn). Then, tighten it to 15-20 ft. lbs.

20. Using a dial indicator, check endplay of the hub. No endplay is permitted.

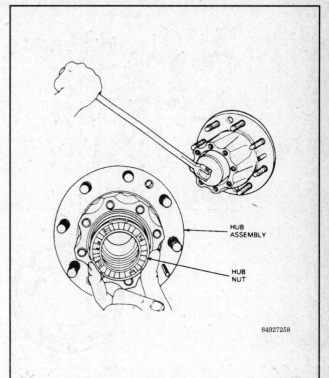

Fig. 233 Hub nut removal on the 10.25 inch full-floating axle

21. Clean the hub bolt holes thoroughly. Replace the hub if any cracks are found around the holes or if the threads in the holes are in any way damaged.

22. Install the axle shaft, new flange gasket, lock washers and **new** shaft retaining bolts. Coat the bolt threads with thread adhesive. Tighten them snugly, but not completely.

23. Install the calipe4r.

24. Install the wheels.

25. Lower the truck to the groups.

26. Tighten the wheel lug nuts.

27. Tighten the axle shaft bolts to 70-85 ft. lbs.

1990-93 F-SUPER DUTY, STRIPPED CHASSIS AND MOTOR HOME CHASSIS

The wheel bearings on full floating rear axles are packed with wheel bearing grease. Axle lubricant can also flow into the wheel hubs and bearings, however, wheel bearing grease is the primary lubricant. The wheel bearing grease provides lubrication until the axle lubricant reaches the bearings during normal operation.

1. Set the parking brake and loosen — do not remove — the axle shaft bolts.

2. Raise the rear wheels off the floor and place jackstands under the rear axle housing so that the axle is parallel with the floor. The axle shafts must turn freely, so release the parking brake.

3. Remove the axle shaft bolts and lockwashers. They should not be re-used.

4. Place a heavy duty wheel dolly under the wheels and raise them so that all weight is off the wheel bearings.

5. Remove the axle shaft and gasket(s).

6. Remove the brake caliper. See Section 9.

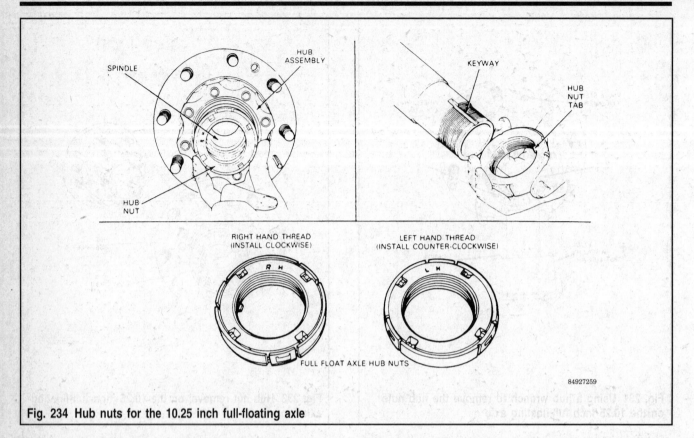

Fig. 234 Hub nuts for the 10.25 inch full-floating axle

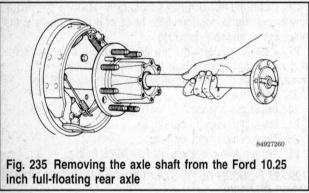

Fig. 235 Removing the axle shaft from the Ford 10.25 inch full-floating rear axle

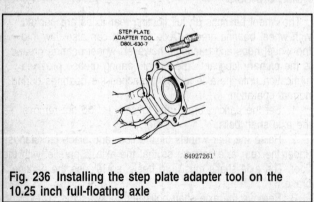

Fig. 236 Installing the step plate adapter tool on the 10.25 inch full-floating axle

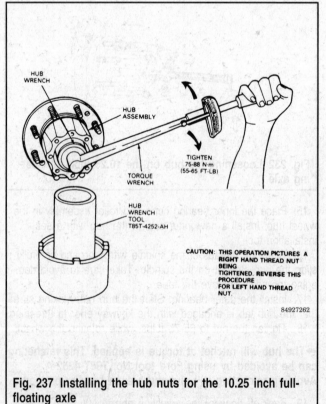

Fig. 237 Installing the hub nuts for the 10.25 inch full-floating axle

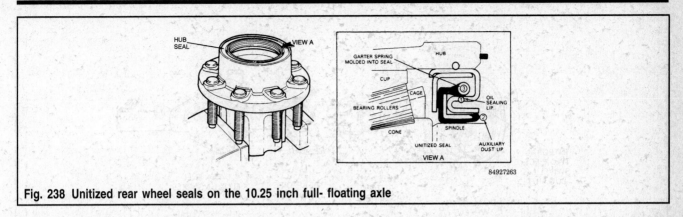

Fig. 238 Unitized rear wheel seals on the 10.25 inch full- floating axle

84927263

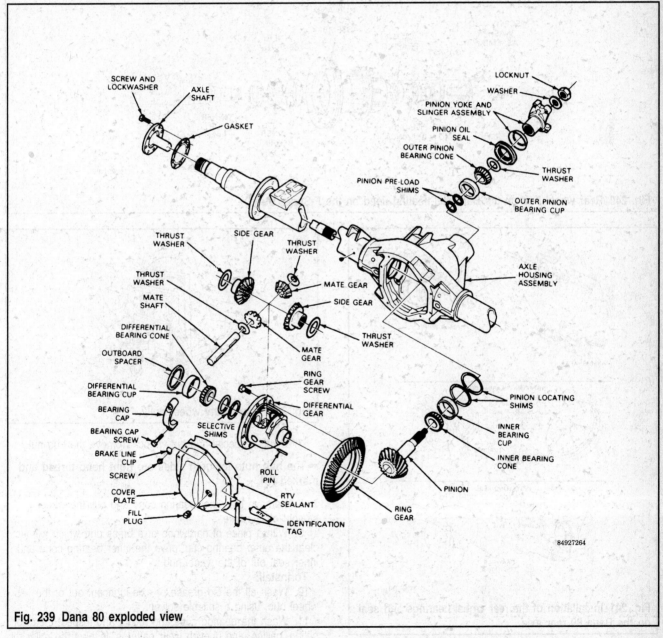

Fig. 239 Dana 80 exploded view

84927264

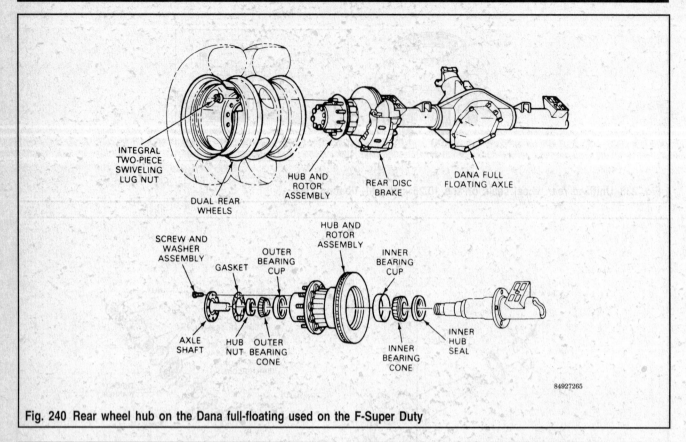

Fig. 240 Rear wheel hub on the Dana full-floating used on the F-Super Duty

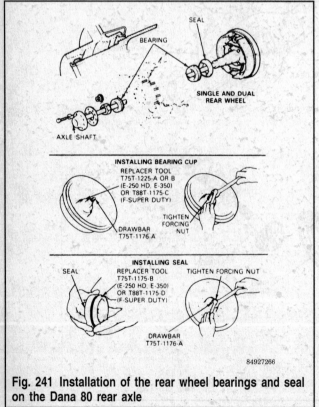

Fig. 241 Installation of the rear wheel bearings and seal on the Dana 80 rear axle

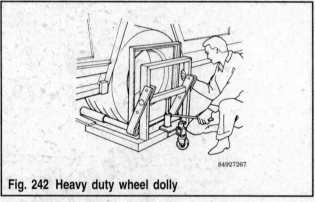

Fig. 242 Heavy duty wheel dolly

7. Using a special hub nut wrench, remove the hub nut.

➡ **The hub nuts for both sides are right hand thread and marked RH.**

8. Remove the outer bearing cone and pull the wheel straight off the axle.

9. With a piece of hardwood or a brass drift which will just clear the outer bearing cup, drive the inner bearing cone and inner seal out of the wheel hub.

To install:

10. Wash all the old grease or axle lubricant out of the wheel hub, using a suitable solvent.

11. Wash the bearing cups and rollers and inspect them for pitting, galling, and uneven wear patterns. Inspect the roller for end wear.

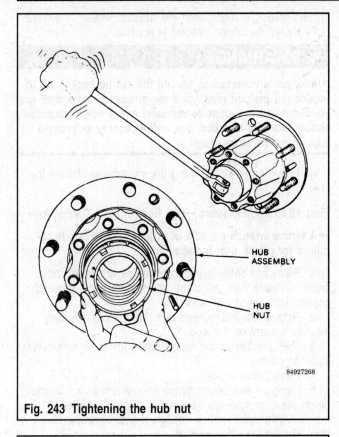

Fig. 243 Tightening the hub nut

HUB
ASSEMBLY

HUB
NUT

84927268

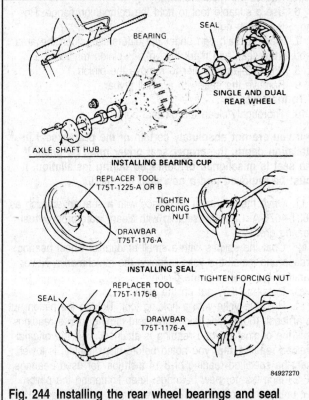

BEARING

SEAL

SINGLE AND DUAL
REAR WHEEL

AXLE SHAFT HUB

INSTALLING BEARING CUP

REPLACER TOOL
T75T-1225-A OR B

TIGHTEN
FORCING
NUT

DRAWBAR
T75T-1176-A

INSTALLING SEAL

REPLACER TOOL
T75T-1175-B

TIGHTEN FORCING NUT

SEAL

DRAWBAR
T75T-1176-A

84927270

Fig. 244 Installing the rear wheel bearings and seal

12. If the bearing cups are to be replaced, drive them out with a brass drift. Install the new cups with a block of wood and hammer or press them in.

13. If the bearing cups are properly seated, a 0.0015 in. (0.038mm) feeler gauge will not fit between the cup and the wheel hub. The gauge should not fit beneath the cup. Check several places to make sure the cups are squarely seated.

14. Pack each bearing cone and roller with a bearing packer or in the manner outlined for the front wheel bearings on 2WD trucks in Section 1. Use a multi-purpose wheel bearing grease.

15. Place the inner bearing cone and roller assembly in the wheel hub. Install a new inner seal in the hub with a seal installation tool.

16. Wrap the threads of the spindle with tape and carefully slide the hub straight on the spindle. Take care to avoid damaging the seal! Remove the tape.

17. Install the outer bearing. Start the hub nut, making sure that the hub tab is engaged with the keyway prior to threading.

18. Tighten the nut to 65-75 ft.lbs. while rotating the wheel.

➡**The hub will ratchet at torque is applied. This ratcheting can be avoided by using Ford tool No. T88T-4252-A. Avoiding ratcheting will give more even bearing preloads.**

19. Back off (loosen) the adjusting nut 90° (¼ turn). Then, tighten it to 15-20 ft. lbs.

20. Using a dial indicator, check endplay of the hub. No endplay is permitted.

21. Clean the hub bolt holes thoroughly. Replace the hub if any cracks are found around the holes or if the threads in the holes are in any way damaged.

22. Install the axle shaft, new flange gasket, lock washers and **new** shaft retaining bolts. Coat the bolt threads with thread adhesive. Tighten them snugly, but not completely.

23. Install the caliper.

24. Install the wheels.

25. Lower the truck to the groups.

26. Tighten the wheel lug nuts.

27. Tighten the axle shaft bolts to 40-55 ft. lbs.

Pinion Seal

REMOVAL & INSTALLATION

Ford 8.8 in. (223.5mm) Ring Gear Integral Carrier Axle

▶ **See Figures 245 and 246**

➡**A torque wrench capable of at least 225 ft. lbs. is required for pinion seal installation.**

1. Raise and safely support the vehicle with jackstands under the frame rails. Allow the axle to drop to rebound position for working clearance.

2. Remove the rear wheels and brake drums. No drag must be present on the axle.

3. Mark the companion flanges and U-joints for correct reinstallation position.

4. Remove the driveshaft.

5. Using an inch pound torque wrench and socket on the pinion yoke nut measure the amount of torque needed to maintain differential rotation through several clockwise revolutions. Record the measurement.

6. Use a suitable tool to hold the companion flange. Remove the pinion nut.

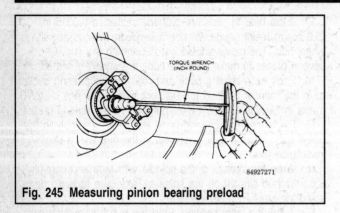

84927271

Fig. 245 Measuring pinion bearing preload

7. Place a drain pan under the differential, clean the area around the seal, and mark the yoke-to-pinion relation.

8. Use a 2-jawed puller to remove the pinion.

9. Remove the seal with a small prybar.

To install:

10. Thoroughly clean the oil seal bore.

➡**If you are not absolutely certain of the proper seal installation depth, the proper seal driver must be used. If the seal is misaligned or damaged during installation, it must be removed and a new seal installed.**

11. Drive the new seal into place with a seal driver such as T83T-4676-A. Coat the seal lip with clean, waterproof wheel bearing grease.

12. Coat the splines with a small amount of wheel bearing grease and install the yoke, aligning the matchmarks. Never hammer the yoke onto the pinion!

13. Install a NEW nut on the pinion.

14. Hold the yoke with a holding tool. Tighten the pinion nut to at least 160 ft. lbs., taking frequent turning torque readings until the original preload reading is attained.   If the original preload reading, that you noted before disassembly, is lower than the specified reading of 8-14 inch lbs. for used bearings; 16-29 inch lbs. for new bearings, keep tightening the pinion nut until the specified reading is reached.   If the original

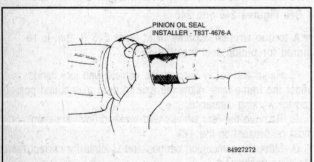

PINION OIL SEAL
INSTALLER - T83T-4676-A

84927272

Fig. 246 Pinion seal installation for the Ford 8.8 inch rear axle

preload reading is higher than the specified values, torque the nut just until the original reading is reached.

✳✳WARNING

Under no circumstances should the nut be backed off to reduce the preload reading! If the preload is exceeded, the yoke and bearing must be removed and a new collapsible spacer must be installed. The entire process of preload adjustment must be repeated.

15. Install the driveshaft using the matchmarks. Torque the nuts to 15 ft. lbs.

Ford 10.25 in. (260.35mm) Ring Gear Integral Carrier Axle

➡**A torque wrench capable of at least 225 ft. lbs. is required for pinion seal installation.**

1. Raise and safely support the vehicle with jackstands under the frame rails. Allow the axle to drop to the rebound position for working clearance.

2. Remove the rear wheels and brake drums. No drag must be present on the axle.

3. Mark the companion flanges and U-joints for correct reinstallation position.

4. Remove the driveshaft.

5. Using an inch pound torque wrench and socket on the pinion yoke nut measure the amount of torque needed to maintain differential rotation through several clockwise revolutions. Record the measurement.

6. Use a suitable tool to hold the companion flange. Remove the pinion nut.

7. Place a drain pan under the differential, clean the area around the seal, and mark the yoke-to-pinion relation.

8. Use a 2-jawed puller to remove the pinion.

9. Remove the seal with a small prybar.

To install:

10. Thoroughly clean the oil seal bore.

➡**If you are not absolutely certain of the proper seal installation depth, the proper seal driver must be used. If the seal is misaligned or damaged during installation, it must be removed and a new seal installed.**

11. Drive the new seal into place with a seal driver such as T83T-4676-A. Coat the seal lip with clean, waterproof wheel bearing grease.

12. Coat the splines with a small amount of wheel bearing grease and install the yoke, aligning the matchmarks. Never hammer the yoke onto the pinion!

13. Install a NEW nut on the pinion.

14. Hold the yoke with a holding tool. Tighten the pinion nut to at least 160 ft. lbs., taking frequent turning torque readings until the original preload reading is attained.   If the original preload reading, that you noted before disassembly, is lower than the specified reading of 8-14 inch lbs. for used bearings; 16-29 inch lbs. for new bearings, keep tightening the pinion nut until the specified reading is reached.   If the original

preload reading is higher than the specified values, torque the nut just until the original reading is reached.

✳✳WARNING

Under no circumstances should the nut be backed off to reduce the preload reading! If the preload is exceeded, the yoke and bearing must be removed and a new collapsible spacer must be installed. The entire process of preload adjustment must be repeated.

15. Install the driveshaft using the matchmarks. Torque the nuts to 15 ft. lbs.

Dana 80

➡**A torque wrench capable of at least 500 ft. lbs. is required for pinion seal installation.**

1. Raise and safely support the vehicle with jackstands under the frame rails. Allow the axle to drop to the rebound position for working clearance.
2. Remove the rear wheels and brake drums. No drag must be present on the axle.
3. Mark the companion flanges and U-joints for correct reinstallation position.
4. Remove the driveshaft.
5. Use a suitable tool to hold the companion flange. Remove the pinion nut.
6. Place a drain pan under the differential, clean the area around the seal, and mark the yoke-to-pinion relation.
7. Use a 2-jawed puller to remove the pinion.
8. Remove the seal with a small prybar.
To install:
9. Thoroughly clean the oil seal bore.

➡**If you are not absolutely certain of the proper seal installation depth, the proper seal driver must be used. If the seal is misaligned or damaged during installation, it must be removed and a new seal installed.**

10. Coat the new oil seal with wheel bearing grease. Install the seal using oil seal driver T56T-4676-B. After the seal is installed, make sure that the seal garter spring has not become dislodged. If it has, remove and replace the seal.
11. Install the yoke, using flange replacer tool D81T-4858-A if necessary to draw the yoke into place.
12. Install a new pinion nut and washer. Torque the nut to 440-500 ft. lbs.
13. Connect the driveshaft. Torque the fasteners to 15-20 ft. lbs.

Axle Damper

REMOVAL & INSTALLATION

▶ **See Figure 247**

This device is a large, heavy weight attached to a mounting flange on the differential carrier. Its purpose is to suppress driveline vibrations.

To remove/install the damper, simply support it and remove/install the bolts. Bolt torque is 40-60 ft. lbs.

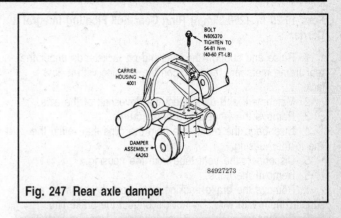

Fig. 247 Rear axle damper

Axle Housing

REMOVAL & INSTALLATION

Ford 8.8 in. (223.5mm) Ring Gear Integral Carrier Ford 10.25 in. (260.35mm) Ring Gear Semi-Floating Integral Carrier

1. Raise and support the rear end on jackstands under the rear frame members, and support the housing with a floor jack.
2. Matchmark and disconnect the driveshaft at the axle.
3. Remove the wheels and brake drums.
4. Disengage the brake line from the clips that retain the line to the housing.
5. Disconnect the vent tube from the housing.
6. Remove the axle shafts.
7. Remove the brake backing plate from the housing, and support them with wire. Do not disconnect the brake line.
8. Disconnect each rear shock absorber from the mounting bracket stud on the housing.
9. Lower the axle slightly to reduce some of the spring tension. At each rear spring, remove the spring clip (U-bolt) nuts, spring clips, and spring seat caps.
10. Remove the housing from under the vehicle.
To Install:
11. Position the axle housing under the rear springs. Install the spring clips (U-bolts), spring seat clamps and nuts. Tighten the spring clamps evenly to 115 ft. lbs.
12. If a new axle housing is being installed, remove the bolts that attach the brake backing plate and bearing retainer from the old housing flanges. Position the bolts in the new housing flanges to hold the brake backing plates in position. Torque the bolts to 40 ft. lbs.
13. Install the axle shafts.
14. Connect the vent tube to the housing.
15. Position the brake line to the housing, and secure it with the retaining clips.
16. Raise the axle housing and springs enough to allow connecting the rear shock absorbers to the mounting bracket studs on the housing. Torque the nuts to 60 ft. lbs.
17. Connect the driveshaft to the axle. Torque the nuts to 8-15 ft. lbs.
18. Install the brake drums and wheels.

Ford 10.25 in. (260.35mm) Ring Gear Full Floating Integral Carrier

1. Raise and support the rear end on jackstands under the rear frame members, and support the housing with a floor jack.

2. Matchmark and disconnect the driveshaft at the axle.

3. Remove the wheels and brake drums.

4. Disengage the brake line from the clips that retain the line to the housing.

5. Disconnect the vent tube from the housing.

6. Remove the hubs.

7. Remove the brake backing plate from the housing, and support them with wire. Do not disconnect the brake line.

8. Disconnect each rear shock absorber from the mounting bracket stud on the housing.

9. Lower the axle slightly to reduce some of the spring tension. At each rear spring, remove the spring clip (U-bolt) nuts, spring clips, and spring seat caps.

10. Remove the housing from under the vehicle.

To Install:

11. Position the axle housing under the rear springs. Install the spring clips (U-bolts), spring seat clamps and nuts. Tighten the spring clamps evenly to 200 ft. lbs.

12. If a new axle housing is being installed, remove the bolts that attach the brake backing plate and bearing retainer from the old housing flanges. Position the bolts in the new housing flanges to hold the brake backing plates in position. Torque the bolts to 40 ft. lbs.

13. Connect the vent tube to the housing.

14. Position the brake line to the housing, and secure it with the retaining clips.

15. Raise the axle housing and springs enough to allow connecting the rear shock absorbers to the mounting bracket studs on the housing. Torque the nuts to 60 ft. lbs.

16. Connect the driveshaft to the axle. Torque the nuts to 20 ft. lbs.

17. Install the brake drums and wheels.

Dana Axles

1. Disconnect the shock absorbers from the rear axle.

2. Loosen the rear axle shaft nuts.

3. Raise and support the rear end on jackstands placed under the frame.

4. Remove the rear wheels.

5. Disconnect the rear stabilizer bar.

6. Disconnect the brake hose at the frame.

7. Disconnect the parking brake cable at the equalizer and remove the cables from the support brackets.

8. Matchmark the driveshaft-to-axle flange position.

9. Disconnect the driveshaft from the rear axle and move it out of the way.

10. Take up the weight of the axle with a floor jack.

11. Remove the nuts from the spring U-bolts and remove the spring seat caps.

12. Lower the axle and roll it from under the van.

13. Installation is the reverse of removal. Torque the spring U-bolt nuts to 160 ft. lbs. Bleed the brake system.

Conventional Differential Overhaul Ford 8.8 in. Ring Gear

DISASSEMBLY

▶ **See Figures 248, 249, 250, 251, 252, 253, 254, 255, 256, 257, 258, 259 and 260**

Differential Carrier

1. Remove the cover and clean the lubricant from the internal parts.

2. Using a dial indicator, measure and record the ring gear backlash and the runout; the backlash should be 0.008-0.015 in. and the runout should be less than 0.004 in.

➡**On trucks with anti-lock brakes, there is room provided between the exciter ring and the ring gear for measuring backface runout.**

3. Mark 1 differential bearing cap to ensure it is installed its original position.

4. Loosen the differential bearing cap bolts.

5. Using a prybar, pry the differential carrier until the bearing cups and shims are loose in the bearing caps.

6. Remove the bearing caps and the differential assembly.

7. If necessary, remove ring gear-to-differential case bolts. Using a hammer and a punch, strike the alternate bolt holes around the ring gear to dislodge it from the differential.

8. If necessary, remove the exciter ring by striking it with a soft hammer.

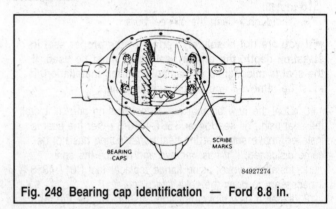

Fig. 248 Bearing cap identification — Ford 8.8 in.

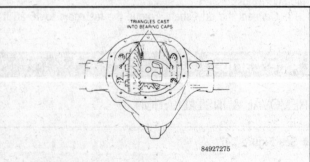

Fig. 249 Bearing cap identification marks cast into caps — Ford 8.8 in.

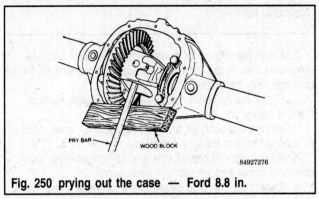

Fig. 250 prying out the case — Ford 8.8 in.

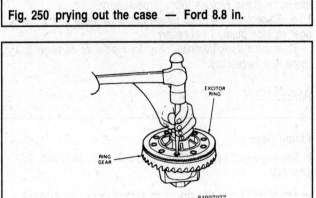

Fig. 251 Ring gear removal — Ford 8.8 in.

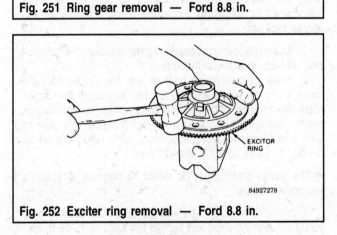

Fig. 252 Exciter ring removal — Ford 8.8 in.

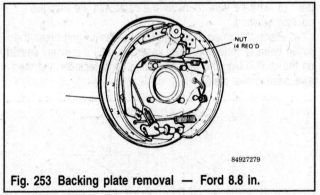

Fig. 253 Backing plate removal — Ford 8.8 in.

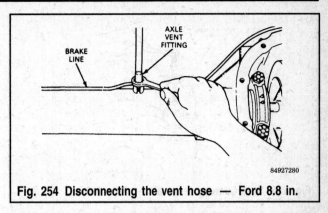

Fig. 254 Disconnecting the vent hose — Ford 8.8 in.

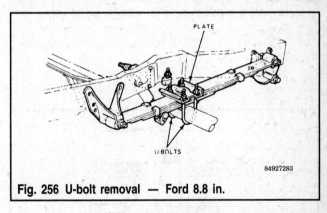

Fig. 255 Brake line clip — Ford 8.8 in.

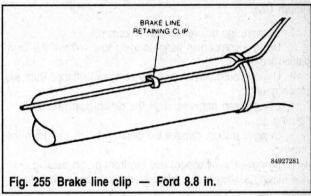

Fig. 256 U-bolt removal — Ford 8.8 in.

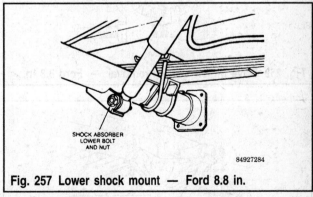

Fig. 257 Lower shock mount — Ford 8.8 in.

9. Remove the pinion shaft lock bolt from the differential case. Remove the differential pinion shaft, the pinion gears and the thrust washers.

10. Remove the side gears and thrust washers.

11. Using a bearing puller tool, press the bearings from the differential carrier.

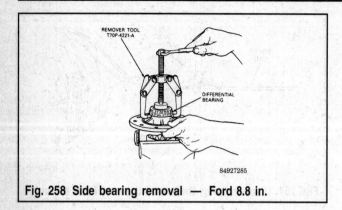

Fig. 258 Side bearing removal — Ford 8.8 in.

Pinion Gear

1. Remove the differential carrier assembly.
2. Using a companion flange holding tool, remove the companion flange nut.
3. Using a puller tool, press the companion flange from the pinion gear.
4. Using a soft hammer, drive the pinion gear from the housing.
5. Using a prybar, remove the pinion gear oil seal from the housing.
6. Remove the oil slinger and the front pinion bearing.
7. Using a shop press, press the bearing cone from the pinion gear.
8. Remove and record the shim from the pinion gear.

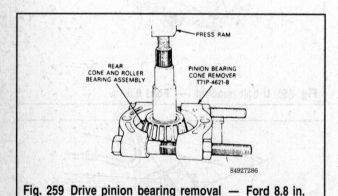

Fig. 259 Drive pinion bearing removal — Ford 8.8 in.

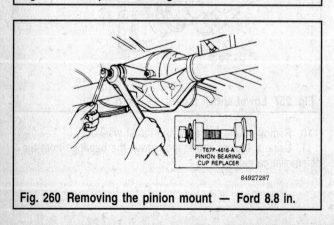

Fig. 260 Removing the pinion mount — Ford 8.8 in.

INSPECTION

1. Clean the differential components in solvent and use compressed air to dry them; do not use compressed air on the bearings, only shop towels.
2. Check the components for wear or damage; replace them, if necessary.
3. Inspect the bearings and bearing cups for wear, cracks or scoring; replace them, if necessary.
4. Inspect the differential side and pinion gears for wear, cracks or chips; replace them, if necessary.
5. Inspect the ring and pinion gears for wear and/or damage; replace them, if necessary.
6. Inspect the differential case for cracks or damage; replace it, if necessary.

ASSEMBLY

Pinion Gear

▶ See Figures 261, 262, 263, 264, 265, 266, 267, 268, 269 and 270

➡When replacing the ring and pinion gear, the correct shim thickness for the new gear set to be installed is determined by following procedure using a pinion depth gauge tool set.

1. Assemble the appropriate aligning adapter, the gauge disc and gauge block to the screw.
2. Place the rear pinion bearing over the aligning tool and insert it into the rear portion of the bearing cup of the carrier. Place the front bearing into the front bearing cup and assemble the tool handle into the screw. Roll the assembly back and forth a few times to seat the bearings while tightening the tool handle, by hand, to 20 ft. lbs. (27 Nm).

➡The gauge block must be offset 45 degrees to obtain an accurate reading.

3. Center the gauge tube into the differential bearing bore. Install the bearing caps and tighten the bolts to 70-85 ft. lbs. (96-115 Nm); be sure to install the caps with the triangles pointing outward.
4. Place the selected shim(s) on the pinion and press the pinion bearing cone and roller assembly until it is firmly seated on the shaft, using the pinion bearing cone replacer and the axle bearing/seal plate.

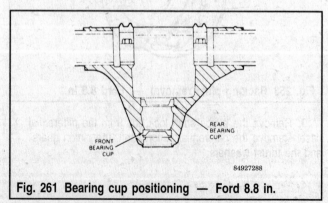

Fig. 261 Bearing cup positioning — Ford 8.8 in.

5. Place the collapsible spacer on the pinion stem against the pinion stem shoulder.

6. Install the front pinion bearing and oil slinger in the housing bore and install the pinion seal on the pinion seal replacer. Using a hammer, install the seal until it seats.

7. From the rear of the axle housing, install the drive pinion assembly into the housing pinion shaft bore.

8. Lubricate the pinion shaft splines and install the companion flange.

9. Using a companion flange holder tool, torque the pinion nut to 160 ft. lbs. (217 Nm); rotate the pinion gear, occasionally, to ensure proper bearing seating.

10. Using an inch pound torque wrench, frequently, measure the pinion bearing preload; it should be 8-14 inch lbs. for used bearings or 16-29 inch lbs. for new bearings.

➡**If the preload is higher than the specification, tighten to the original reading as recorded; never back off the pinion nut.**

Differential Carrier

▶ **See Figures 271, 272, 273, 274, 275, 276, 277, 278, 279, 280, 281, 282, 283, 284, 285, 286, 287, 288, 289, 290, 291, 292, 293, 294 and 295**

1. If the bearings were removed, use a shop press to press them onto the differential case.

2. Install the side gears and thrust washers. Install the pinion gears, the thrust washer, the pinion shaft and the pinion shaft lock bolt.

3. Using a shop press, align the exciter ring tab with the differential case slot and press the ring gear and exciter ring onto the differential case. Install the ring gear-to-differential case bolts and torque them to 100-120 ft. lbs. (135-162 Nm).

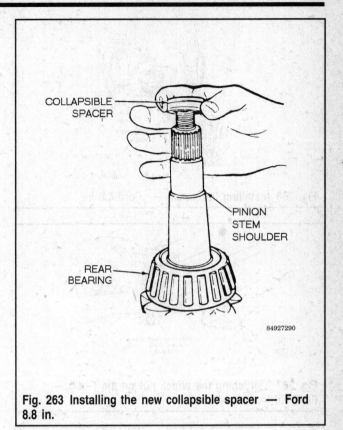

Fig. 263 Installing the new collapsible spacer — Ford 8.8 in.

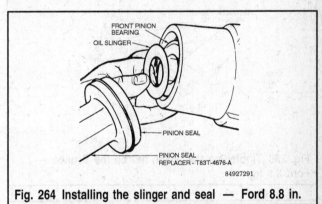

Fig. 264 Installing the slinger and seal — Ford 8.8 in.

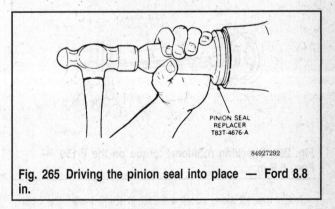

Fig. 265 Driving the pinion seal into place — Ford 8.8 in.

4. Place the differential case with the bearing cups into the housing.

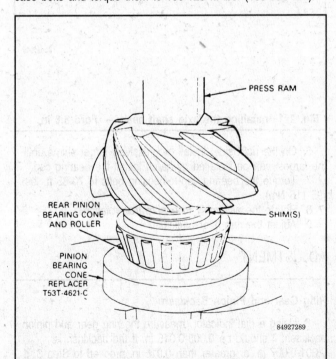

Fig. 262 Pinion bearing shim installation — Ford 8.8 in.

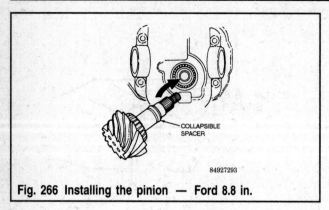

Fig. 266 Installing the pinion — Ford 8.8 in.

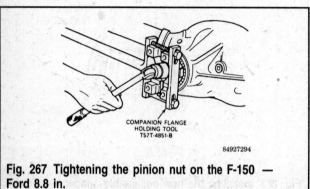

Fig. 267 Tightening the pinion nut on the F-150 — Ford 8.8 in.

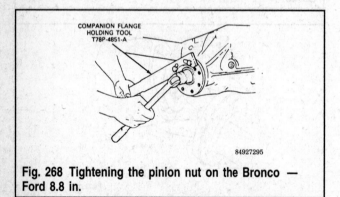

Fig. 268 Tightening the pinion nut on the Bronco — Ford 8.8 in.

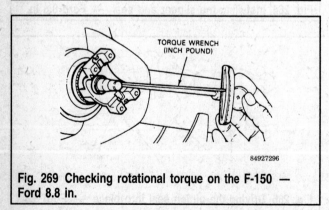

Fig. 269 Checking rotational torque on the F-150 — Ford 8.8 in.

5. On the left side, install a 0.265 in shim. Install the bearing cap and tighten the bolts finger tight.

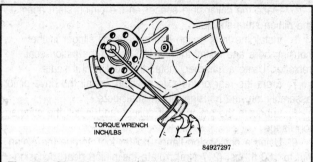

Fig. 270 Checking rotational torque on the Bronco — Ford 8.8 in.

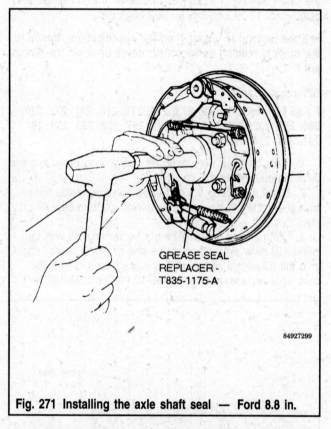

Fig. 271 Installing the axle shaft seal — Ford 8.8 in.

6. On the right side, install progressively larger shims until the largest can be installed by hand. Install the bearing cap.

7. Torque the bearing cap-to-housing bolts to 70-85 ft. lbs. (95-115 Nm).

8. Rotate the assembly to ensure free rotation.

9. Adjust the ring gear backlash.

ADJUSTMENT

Ring Gear and Pinion Backlash

1. Using a dial indicator, measure the ring gear and pinion backlash; it should be 0.008-0.015 in. If the backlash is 0.001-0.007 in. or greater than 0.015 in. proceed to Step 3. If the backlash is zero, proceed to Step 2.

2. If the backlash is zero, add 0.020 in. shim(s) to the right side and subtract a 0.020 in. shim(s) from the left side.

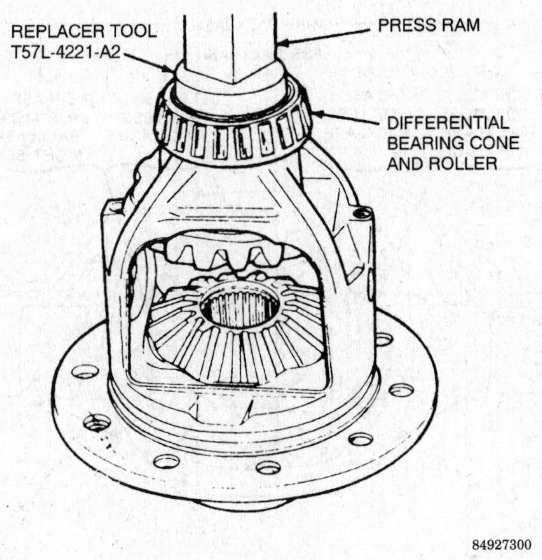

Fig. 272 Installing the side baring — Ford 8.8 in.

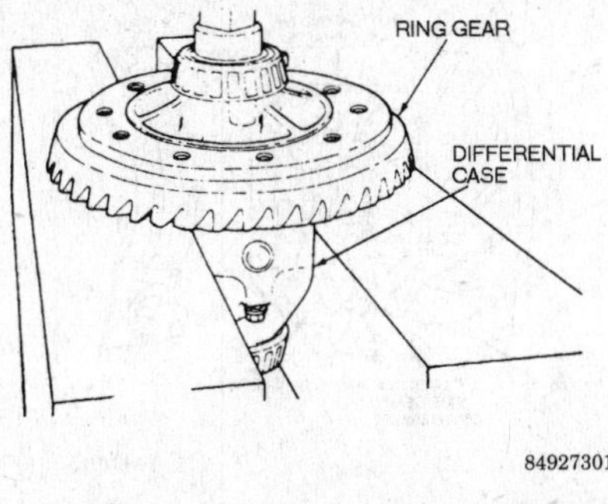

Fig. 273 Installing the exciter ring — Ford 8.8 in.

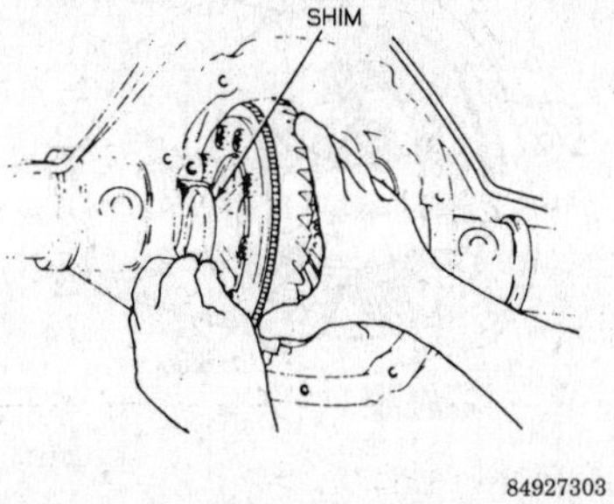

Fig. 274 Installing the left side shim — Ford 8.8 in.

3. If the backlash is within specification, go to step 7. If the backlash is 0.001-0.007 in. or greater than 0.015 in., increase the thickness of a shim on 1 side and decrease the same thickness of another shim on the other side, until the backlash comes within range.

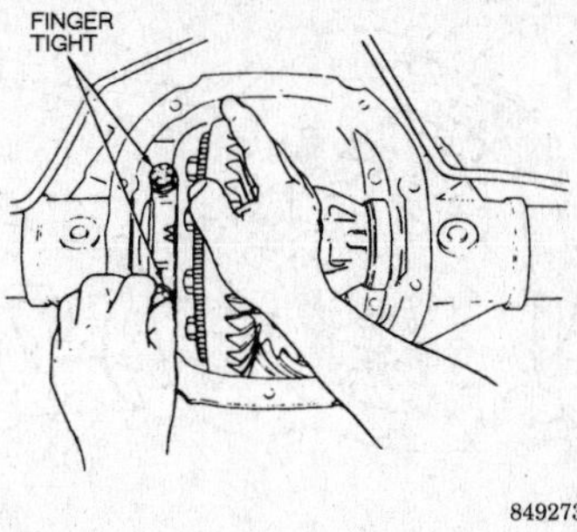

Fig. 275 Installing the left bearing cap — Ford 8.8 in.

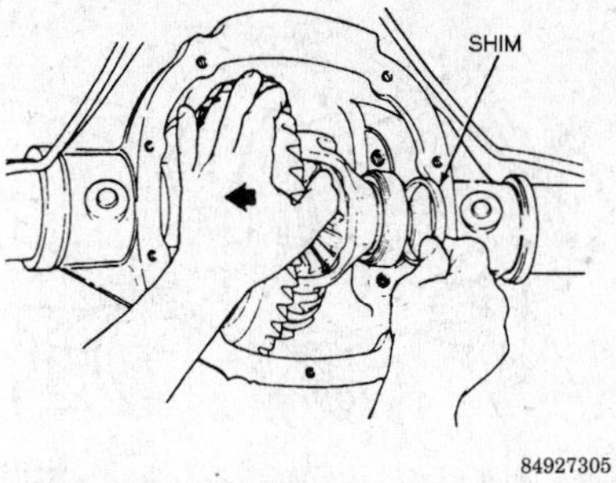

Fig. 276 Installing the right side shim — Ford 8.8 in.

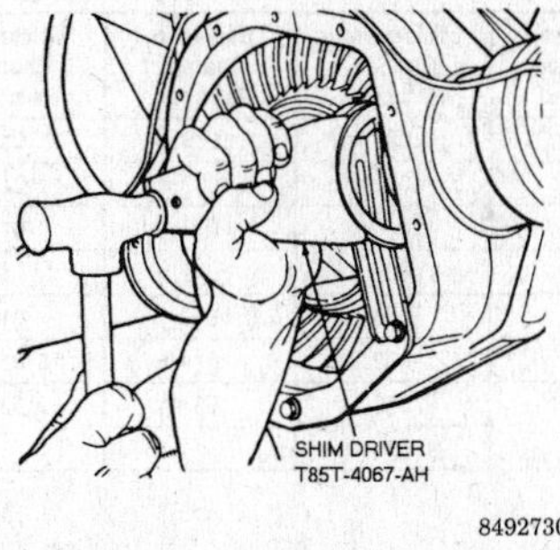

Fig. 277 Final shim installation — Ford 8.8 in.

4. Install and torque the bearing cap bolts to 80-95 ft. lbs. (109-128 Nm).

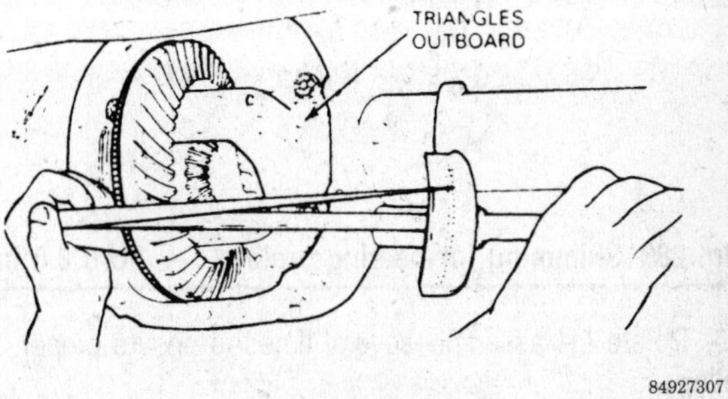

Fig. 278 Tightening the right side cap — Ford 8.8 in.

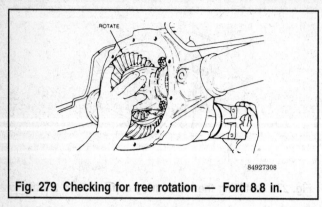

Fig. 279 Checking for free rotation — Ford 8.8 in.

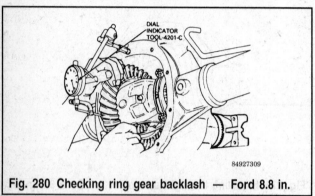

Fig. 280 Checking ring gear backlash — Ford 8.8 in.

Backlash Change Required	Thickness Change Required	Backlash Change Required	Thickness Change Required
.001	.002	.009	.012
.002	.002	.010	.014
.003	.004	.011	.014
.004	.006	.012	.016
.005	.006	.013	.018
.006	.008	.014	.018
.007	.010	.015	.020
.008	.010		

Fig. 281 Shim chart — Ford 8.8 in.

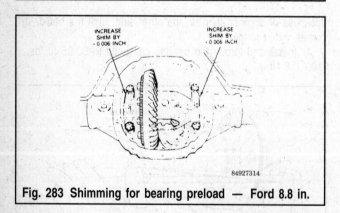

Fig. 283 Shimming for bearing preload — Ford 8.8 in.

5. Rotate the assembly several times to ensure proper seating.

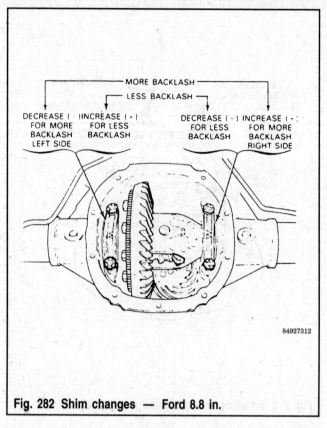

Fig. 282 Shim changes — Ford 8.8 in.

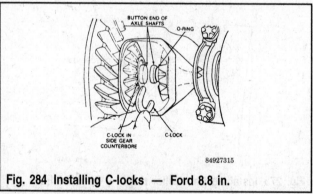

Fig. 284 Installing C-locks — Ford 8.8 in.

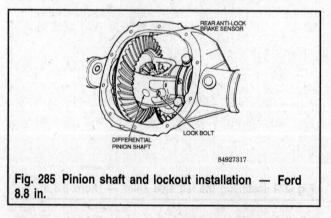

Fig. 285 Pinion shaft and lockout installation — Ford 8.8 in.

6. Recheck the backlash, if it is not within specification, go to step 7.

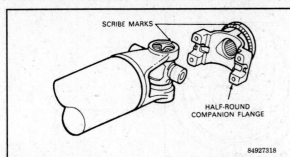

Fig. 286 Connecting the driveshaft on the F-150 — Ford 8.8 in.

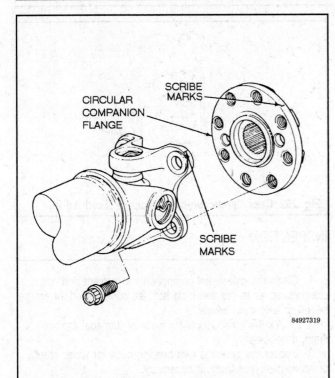

Fig. 287 Connecting the driveshaft on the Bronco — Ford 8.8 in

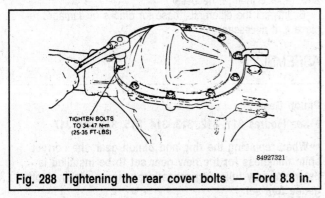

Fig. 288 Tightening the rear cover bolts — Ford 8.8 in.

7. Remove the bearing caps. Increase the shim sizes, on both sides by 0.006 in.; make sure the shims are fully seated

and the assembly turns freely. Use a shim driver to install the shims.

8. Install the bearing caps and torque the bearing caps to 80-95 ft. lbs. (109-128 Nm). Recheck the backlash; if not to specification, repeat this entire procedure.

Conventional Differential Overhaul Ford 10¼ in. Ring Gear

DISASSEMBLY

Differential Carrier

◆ **See Figures 296, 297, 298, 299, 300, 301, 302, 303 and 304**

1. Remove the cover and clean the lubricant from the internal parts.

2. Using a dial indicator, measure and record the ring gear backlash and the runout; the backlash should be 0.008-0.015 in. and the runout should be less than 0.004 in.

➡ **On trucks with anti-lock brakes, there is room provided between the exciter ring and the ring gear for measuring backface runout.**

3. Mark 1 differential bearing cap to ensure it is installed its original position.

4. Loosen the differential bearing cap bolts.

5. Using a prybar, pry the differential carrier until the bearing cups and shims are loose in the bearing caps.

6. Remove the bearing caps and the differential assembly.

7. If necessary, remove ring gear-to-differential case bolts. Using a hammer and a punch, strike the alternate bolt holes around the ring gear to dislodge it from the differential.

8. If necessary, remove the exciter ring by striking it with a soft hammer.

9. Remove the pinion shaft lock bolt from the differential case. Remove the differential pinion shaft, the pinion gears and the thrust washers.

10. Remove the side gears and thrust washers.

11. Using a bearing puller tool, press the bearings from the differential carrier.

Pinion Gear

◆ **See Figures 305, 306, 307, 308, 309 and 310**

1. Remove the differential carrier assembly.

2. Using a companion flange holding tool, remove the companion flange nut.

3. Using a puller tool, press the companion flange from the pinion gear.

4. Using a soft hammer, drive the pinion gear from the housing.

5. Using a prybar, remove the pinion gear oil seal from the housing.

6. Remove the oil slinger and the front pinion bearing.

7. Using a shop press, press the bearing cone from from the pinion gear.

8. Remove and record the shim from the pinion gear.

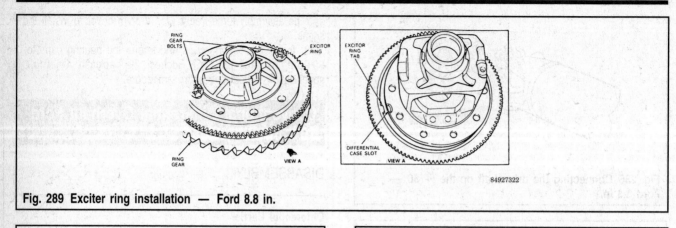

Fig. 289 Exciter ring installation — Ford 8.8 in.

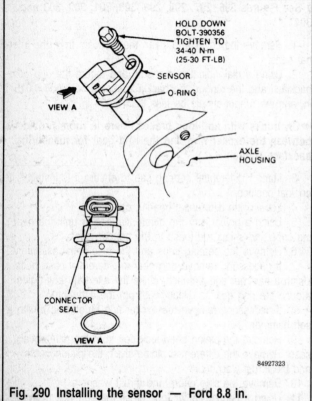

Fig. 290 Installing the sensor — Ford 8.8 in.

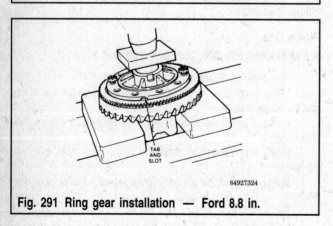

Fig. 291 Ring gear installation — Ford 8.8 in.

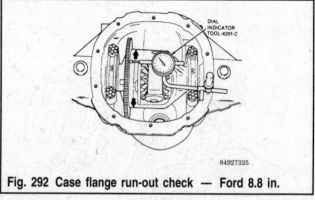

Fig. 292 Case flange run-out check — Ford 8.8 in.

INSPECTION

1. Clean the differential components in solvent and use compressed air to dry them; do not use compressed air on the bearings, only shop towels.
2. Check the components for wear or damage; replace them, if necessary.
3. Inspect the bearings and bearing cups for wear, cracks or scoring; replace them, if necessary.
4. Inspect the differential side and pinion gears for wear, cracks or chips; replace them, if necessary.
5. Inspect the ring and pinion gears for wear and/or damage; replace them, if necessary.
6. Inspect the differential case for cracks or damage; replace it, if necessary.

ASSEMBLY

Pinion Gear

▶ See Figures 311, 312, 313, 314, 315, 316 and 317

➡When replacing the ring and pinion gear, the correct shim thickness for the new gear set to be installed is determined by following procedure using a pinion depth gauge tool set.

1. Assemble the appropriate aligning adapter, the gauge disc and gauge block to the screw.
2. Place the rear pinion bearing over the aligning tool and insert it into the rear portion of the bearing cup of the carrier.

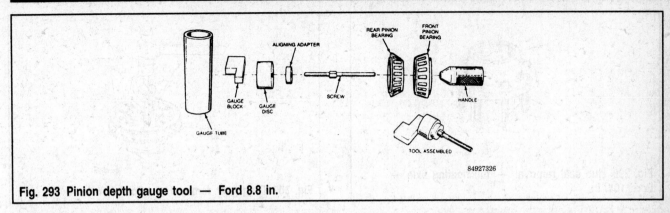

Fig. 293 Pinion depth gauge tool — Ford 8.8 in.

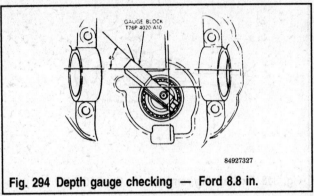

Fig. 294 Depth gauge checking — Ford 8.8 in.

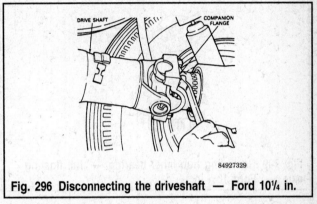

Fig. 296 Disconnecting the driveshaft — Ford 10¼ in.

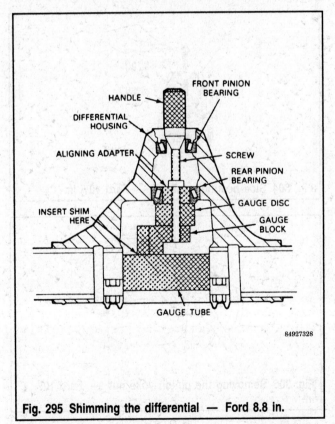

Fig. 295 Shimming the differential — Ford 8.8 in.

Place the front bearing into the front bearing cup and assemble the tool handle into the screw. Roll the assembly back and

forth a few times to seat the bearings while tightening the tool handle, by hand, to 20 ft. lbs. (27 Nm).

➡The gauge block must be offset 45 degrees to obtain an accurate reading.

3. Center the gauge tube into the differential bearing bore. Install the bearing caps and tighten the bolts to 70-85 ft. lbs. (96-115 Nm); be sure to install the caps with the triangles pointing outward.

4. Place the selected shim(s) on the pinion and press the pinion bearing cone and roller assembly until it is firmly seated on the shaft, using the pinion bearing cone replacer and the axle bearing/seal plate.

5. Place the collapsible spacer on the pinion stem against the pinion stem shoulder.

6. Install the front pinion bearing and oil slinger in the housing bore and install the pinion seal on the pinion seal replacer. Using a hammer, install the seal until it seats.

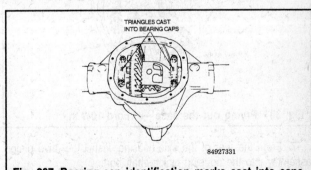

Fig. 297 Bearing cap identification marks cast into caps — Ford 10¼ in.

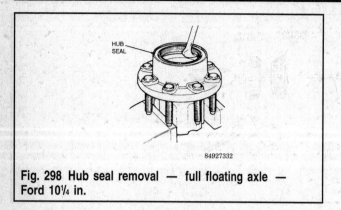

Fig. 298 Hub seal removal — full floating axle — Ford 10¼ in.

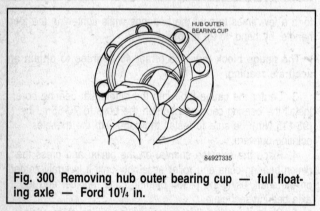

Fig. 299 Removing hub inner bearing — full floating axle — Ford 10¼ in.

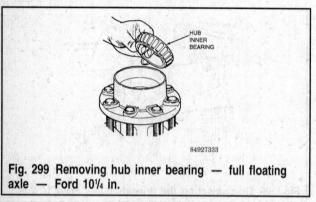

Fig. 300 Removing hub outer bearing cup — full floating axle — Ford 10¼ in.

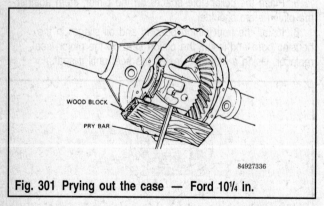

Fig. 301 Prying out the case — Ford 10¼ in.

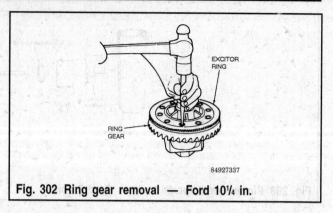

Fig. 302 Ring gear removal — Ford 10¼ in.

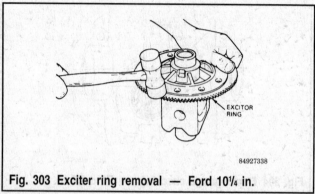

Fig. 303 Exciter ring removal — Ford 10¼ in.

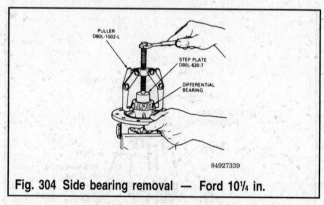

Fig. 304 Side bearing removal — Ford 10¼ in.

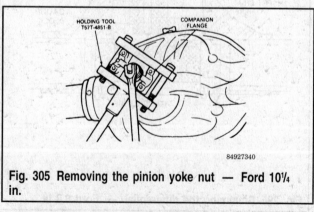

Fig. 305 Removing the pinion yoke nut — Ford 10¼ in.

7. From the rear of the axle housing, install the drive pinion assembly into the housing pinion shaft bore.

8. Lubricate the pinion shaft splines and install the companion flange.

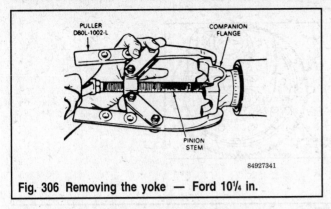

Fig. 306 Removing the yoke — Ford 10¼ in.

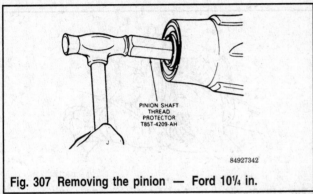

Fig. 307 Removing the pinion — Ford 10¼ in.

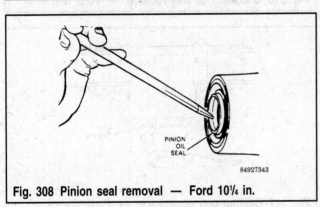

Fig. 308 Pinion seal removal — Ford 10¼ in.

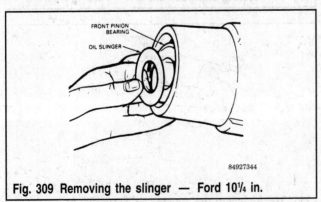

Fig. 309 Removing the slinger — Ford 10¼ in.

9. Using a companion flange holder tool, torque the pinion nut to 160 ft. lbs. (217 Nm); rotate the pinion gear, occasionally, to ensure proper bearing seating.

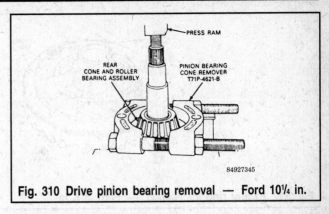

Fig. 310 Drive pinion bearing removal — Ford 10¼ in.

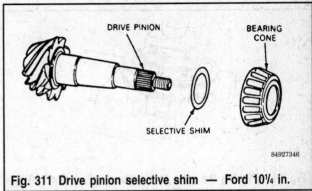

Fig. 311 Drive pinion selective shim — Ford 10¼ in.

10. Using an inch pound torque wrench, frequently, measure the pinion bearing preload; it should be 8-14 inch lbs. for used bearings or 16-29 inch lbs. for new bearings.

➡️ If the preload is higher than the specification, tighten to the original reading as recorded; never back off the pinion nut.

Differential Carrier

▶ See Figures 318, 319, 320, 321, 322, 323, 324, 325, 326, 327, 328, 329, 330, 331, 332, 333, 334 and 335

1. If the bearings were removed, use a shop press to press them onto the differential case.
2. Install the side gears and thrust washers. Install the pinion gears, the thrust washer, the pinion shaft and the pinion shaft lock bolt.
3. Using a shop press, align the exciter ring tab with the differential case slot and press the ring gear and exciter ring onto the differential case. Install the ring gear-to-differential case bolts and torque them to 100-120 ft. lbs. (135-162 Nm).
4. Place the differential case with the bearing cups into the housing.
5. On the left side, install a 0.265 in shim. Install the bearing cap and tighten the bolts finger tight.
6. On the right side, install progressively larger shims until the largest can be installed by hand. Install the bearing cap.
7. Torque the bearing cap-to-housing bolts to 70-85 ft. lbs. (95-115 Nm).
8. Rotate the assembly to ensure free rotation.
9. Adjust the ring gear backlash.

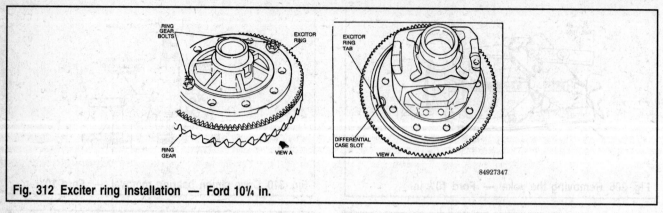

Fig. 312 Exciter ring installation — Ford 10¼ in.

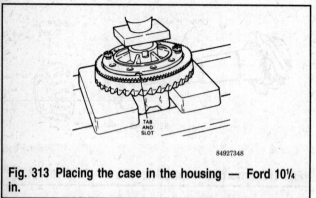

Fig. 313 Placing the case in the housing — Ford 10¼ in.

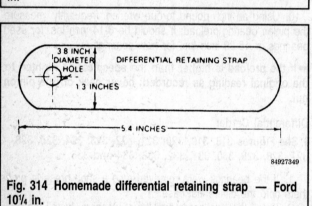

Fig. 314 Homemade differential retaining strap — Ford 10¼ in.

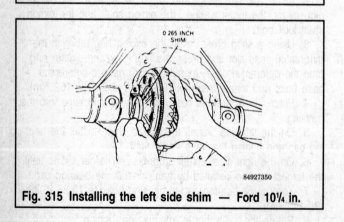

Fig. 315 Installing the left side shim — Ford 10¼ in.

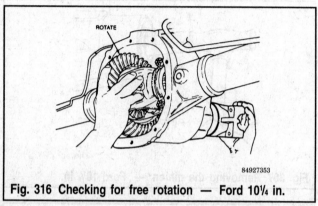

Fig. 316 Checking for free rotation — Ford 10¼ in.

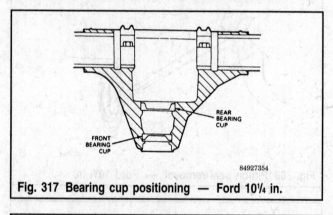

Fig. 317 Bearing cup positioning — Ford 10¼ in.

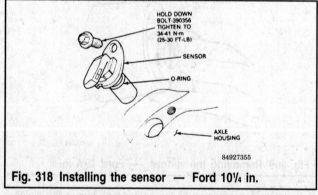

Fig. 318 Installing the sensor — Ford 10¼ in.

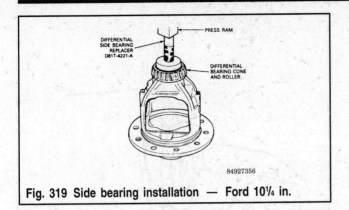

Fig. 319 Side bearing installation — Ford 10¼ in.

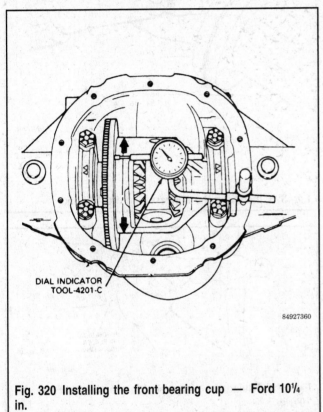

Fig. 320 Installing the front bearing cup — Ford 10¼ in.

ADJUSTMENT

Ring Gear and Pinion Backlash

1. Using a dial indicator, measure the ring gear and pinion backlash; it should be 0.008-0.015 in. If the backlash is 0.001-0.007 in. or greater than 0.015 in. proceed to step 3. If the backlash is zero, proceed to step 2.

2. If the backlash is zero, add 0.020 in. shim(s) to the right side and subtract a 0.020 in. shim(s) from the left side.

3. If the backlash is within specification, go to Step 7. If the backlash is 0.001-0.007 in. or greater than 0.015 in., increase the thickness of a shim on 1 side and decrease the same thickness of another shim on the other side, until the backlash comes within range.

4. Install and torque the bearing cap bolts to 80-95 ft. lbs. (109-128 Nm).

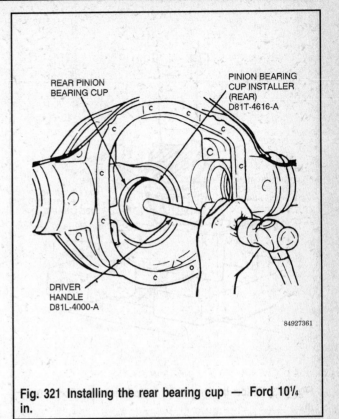

Fig. 321 Installing the rear bearing cup — Ford 10¼ in.

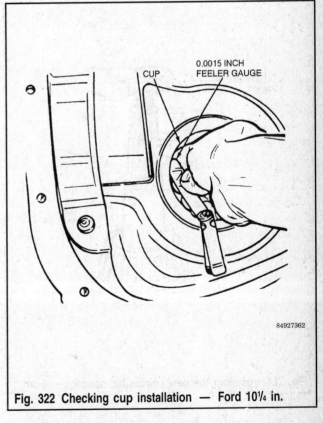

Fig. 322 Checking cup installation — Ford 10¼ in.

5. Rotate the assembly several times to ensure proper seating.

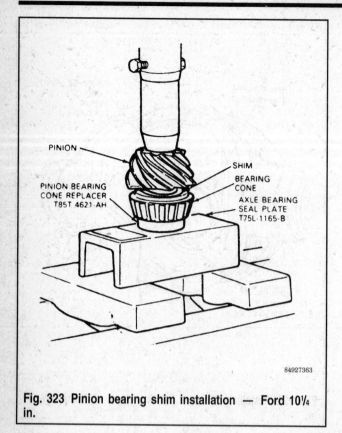

Fig. 323 Pinion bearing shim installation — Ford 10¼ in.

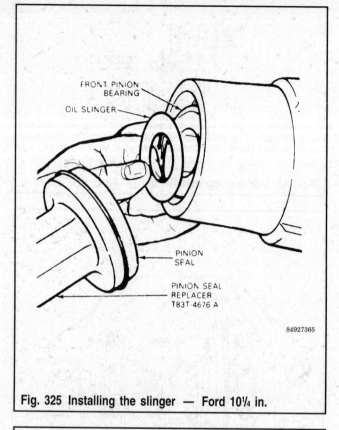

Fig. 325 Installing the slinger — Ford 10¼ in.

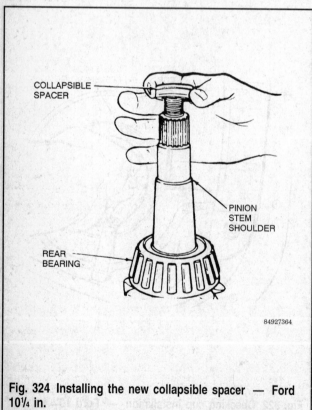

Fig. 324 Installing the new collapsible spacer — Ford 10¼ in.

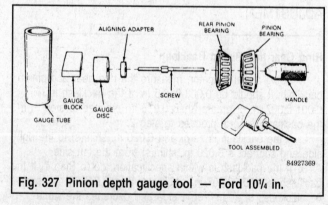

Fig. 326 Driving the pinion seal into place — Ford 10¼ in.

Fig. 327 Pinion depth gauge tool — Ford 10¼ in.

6. Recheck the backlash, if it is not within specification, go to Step 7.

7. Remove the bearing caps. Increase the shim sizes, on both sides by 0.006 in.; make sure the shims are fully seated

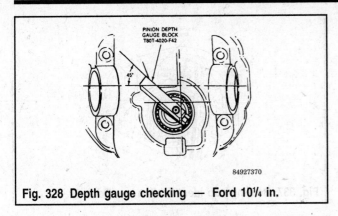

Fig. 328 Depth gauge checking — Ford 10¼ in.

Backlash Change Required	Thickness Change Required	Backlash Change Required	Thickness Change Required
.001	.002	.009	.012
.002	.002	.010	.014
.003	.004	.011	.014
.004	.006	.012	.016
.005	.006	.013	.018
.006	.008	.014	.018
.007	.010	.015	.020
.008	.010		

Fig. 332 Shim chart — Ford 10¼ in.

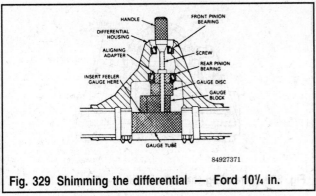

Fig. 329 Shimming the differential — Ford 10¼ in.

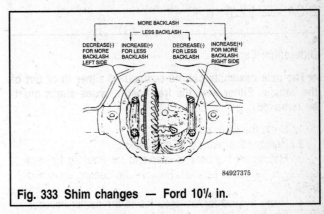

Fig. 333 Shim changes — Ford 10¼ in.

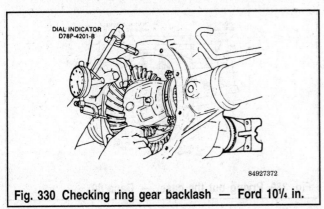

Fig. 330 Checking ring gear backlash — Ford 10¼ in.

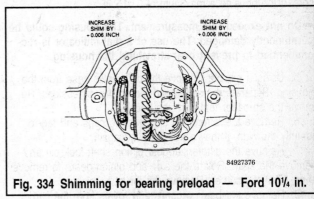

Fig. 334 Shimming for bearing preload — Ford 10¼ in.

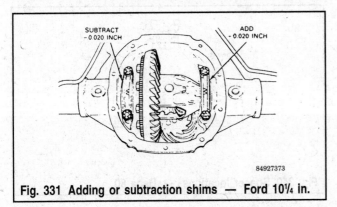

Fig. 331 Adding or subtraction shims — Ford 10¼ in.

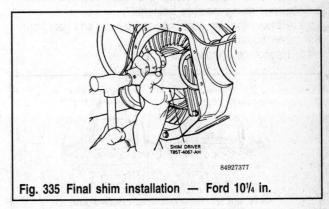

Fig. 335 Final shim installation — Ford 10¼ in.

and the assembly turns freely. Use a shim driver to install the shims.

8. Install the bearing caps and torque the bearing caps to 80-95 ft. lbs. (109-128 Nm). Recheck the backlash; if not to specification, repeat this entire procedure.

Conventional Differential Overhaul Dana Model 80

▶ See Figures 336, 337, 338, 339, 340, 341, 342, 343, 344, 345, 346, 347, 348, 349, 350, 351, 353, 354, 355, 356, 357, 358, 359, 360, 360, 361, 362, 363, 364, 365, 366, 367, 368, 369, 370, 371, 372, 373, 374, 375, 376, 377, 378, 379, 380 and 381

DISASSEMBLY

Differential Carrier

➡The axle assembly can be overhauled either in or out of the vehicle. Either way, the free-floating axles shafts must be removed.

1. Drain the lubricant.
2. Remove the rear cover and gasket.
3. Matchmark the bearing caps and the housing for reassembly in the same position. Remove the bearing caps and bolts.
4. Using a spreader tool mounted to the carrier housing, spread the housing a maximum of 0.015 in.

➡Do not exceed this measurement. The housing could be permanently damaged. The use of a dial indicator is recommended to prevent over-stretching the housing.

5. Using a pry bar, remove the differential case from the housing. Separate the shims and record the dimensions. Remove the spreader tool from the housing.
6. Remove the differential side bearing cups and tag to identify the side, if they are to be used again.
7. Remove the differential gear pinion shaft lock pin and remove the shaft. Rotate the side and pinion gears to remove them from the carrier. Remove the thrust bearings.
8. Remove the bearing cones and rollers from the carrier, marking and noting the shim locations.
9. Remove the ring gear bolts and tap the ring gear from the carrier housing.
10. Inspect the components.

NOTE: ANTILOCK EXCITOR RING PRESSED ON DIFFERENTIAL CASE FLANGE NOT SHOWN.

Fig. 336 Identifying the ring gears — Dana 80 axle

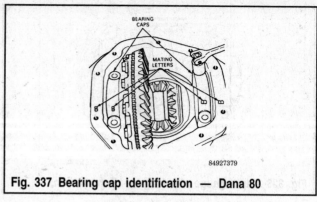

Fig. 337 Bearing cap identification — Dana 80

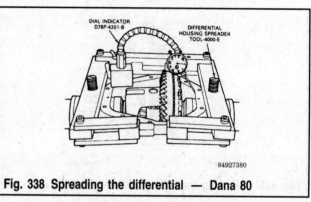

Fig. 338 Spreading the differential — Dana 80

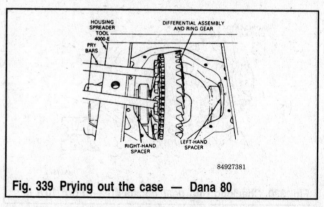

Fig. 339 Prying out the case — Dana 80

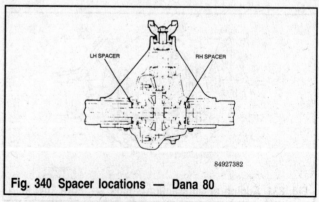

Fig. 340 Spacer locations — Dana 80

Drive Pinion

1. Remove the pinion nut and flange from the pinion gear.

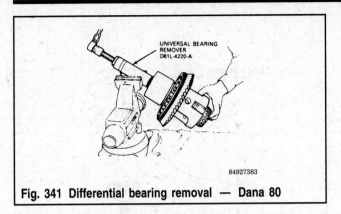

Fig. 341 Differential bearing removal — Dana 80

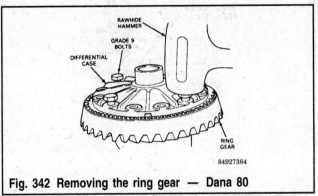

Fig. 342 Removing the ring gear — Dana 80

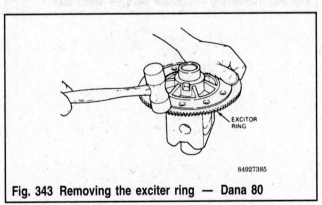

Fig. 343 Removing the exciter ring — Dana 80

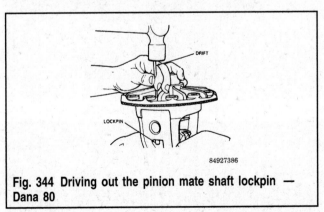

Fig. 344 Driving out the pinion mate shaft lockpin — Dana 80

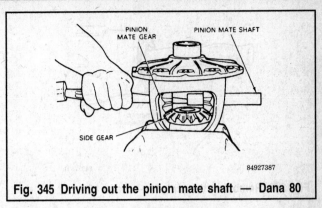

Fig. 345 Driving out the pinion mate shaft — Dana 80

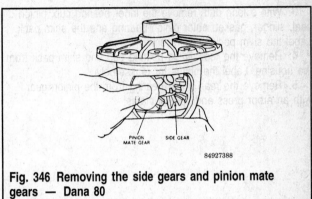

Fig. 346 Removing the side gears and pinion mate gears — Dana 80

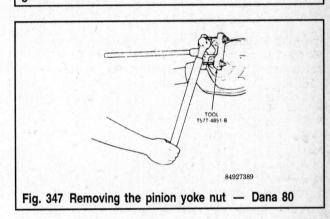

Fig. 347 Removing the pinion yoke nut — Dana 80

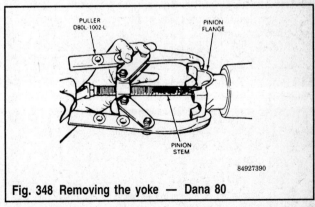

Fig. 348 Removing the yoke — Dana 80

2. Remove the pinion gear assembly from the housing. It may be necessary to tap the pinion from the housing with a soft faced hammer. Catch the pinion so as not to allow it to drop on the floor.

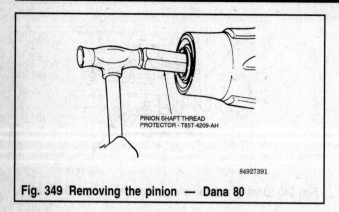

84927391

Fig. 349 Removing the pinion — Dana 80

3. With a long drift, remove the inner bearing cup, pinion seal, slinger, gasket, outer pinion bearing and the shim pack. Label the shim pack for reassembly.

4. Remove the rear pinion bearing cup and shim pack from the housing. Label the shims for reassembly.

5. Remove the rear pinion bearing from the pinion gear with an arbor press and special plates.

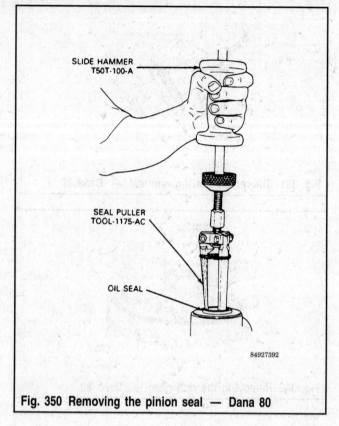

84927392

Fig. 350 Removing the pinion seal — Dana 80

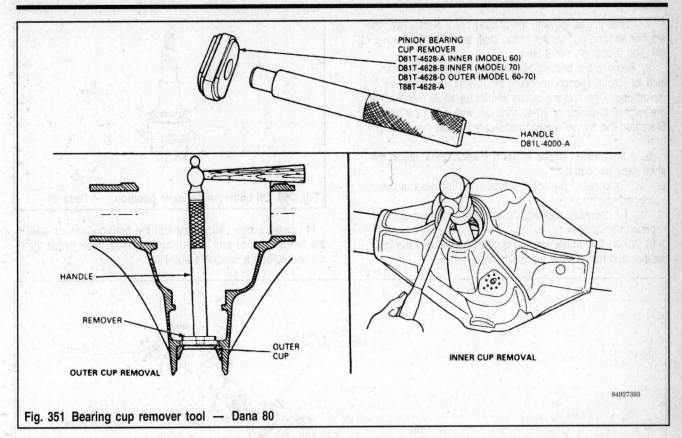

Fig. 351 Bearing cup remover tool — Dana 80

Fig. 352 Removing the pinion bearing — Dana 80

INSPECTION

1. Clean the gears, bearings and component parts with solvent and inspect for scoring, chipping or excessive wear.
2. Inspect the flanges and splines for excessive wear.
3. Replace the necessary parts as required.

PINION SHIM SELECTION

Ring gears and pinions are supplied in matched sets only. The matched numbers are etched on both gears for verification. On the rear face of the pinion, a plus (+) or a minus (-) number will be etched, indicating the best running position for each particular gear set. This dimension is controlled by the shimming behind the inner bearing cup. Whenever baffles or oil slingers are used, they become part of the adjusting shim pack. An example: If a pinion is etched +3, this pinion would require 0.003 in. less shims than a pinion etched 0. This means by removing shims, the mounting distance of the pinion is increased by 0.003 in., which is just what a plus (+) etching indicates. If a pinion is etched -3, it would be necessary to add 0.003 in. more shims than would be required if the pinion was etched 0. By adding the 0.003 in. shims, the mounting distance of the pinion is decreased 0.003 in., which is just what the minus (-) etching indicates. Pinion adjusting shims are available in thicknesses of 0.003, 0.005 and 0.010 in. An example: If a new gear set is used and the old pinion reads +2 and the new pinion reads -2, add 0.004 in. shims to the original shim pack.

ASSEMBLY

Drive Pinion

1. Select the correct pinion depth shims and install in the rear pinion bearing cup bore.
2. Install the rear bearing cup in the axle housing.
3. Add or subtract an equal amount of shim thickness to or from the preload or outer shim pack, as was added or subtracted from the inner shim pack.
4. Install the front pinion bearing cup into its bore in the axle housing.
5. Press the rear pinion bearing onto the pinion gear shaft and install the pinion gear with bearing into the axle housing.
6. Install the preload shims and the front pinion bearing; do not install the oil seal at this time.

7. Install the flange with the holding bar tool attached, the washer and the nut on the pinion shaft end. Torque the nut to 440-500 ft. lbs. (271-298 Nm).

8. Remove the holding bar from the flange and with an inch lb. torque wrench, measure the rotating torque of the pinion gear. The rotating torque should be 10-20 inch lbs. with the original bearings or 20-40 inch lbs. with new bearings. Disregard the torque reading necessary to start the shaft to turn.

9. If the preload torque is not in specifications, adjust the shim pack as required.

   a. To increase preload, decrease the thickness of the preload shim pack.

   b. To decrease preload, increase the thickness of the preload shim pack.

10. When the proper preload is obtained, remove the nut, washer and flange from the pinion shaft.

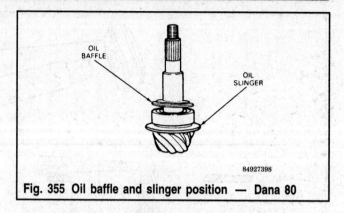

Fig. 355 Oil baffle and slinger position — Dana 80

11. Install a new pinion seal into the housing and reinstall the flange, washer and nut. Using the holder tool, torque the nut to 440-500 ft. lbs. (271-298 Nm).

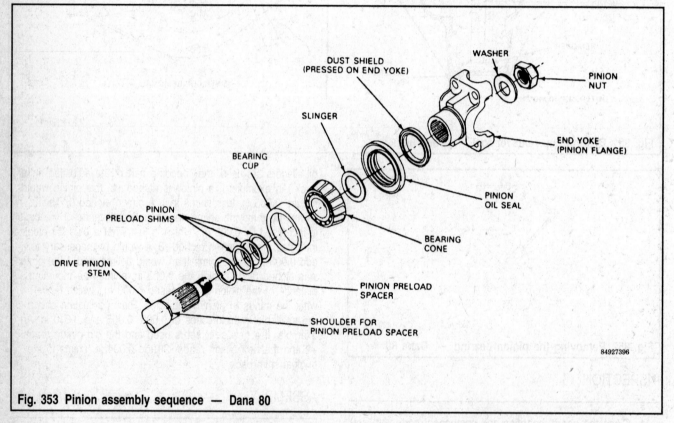

Fig. 353 Pinion assembly sequence — Dana 80

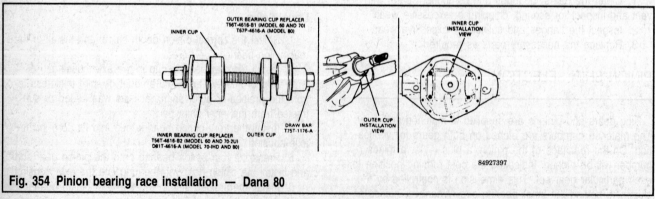

Fig. 354 Pinion bearing race installation — Dana 80

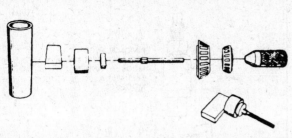

Description	Number	Model 60	Model 70-1HD	Model 70-2U	Model 80
Handle	T76P-4020-A11	X	X	X	T88T-4020-B
Screw	T80T-4020-F43	X	X	X	X
Gauge Block	T80T-4020-F42	X	X	X	X
Aligning Adapter	T76P-4020-A3	X			D80T-4020-R60
	T80T-4020-F48		X	X	
Gauge Disc	T78P-4020-A15	X			T88T-4020-A
	D80T-4020-F45		X	X	
Gauge Tube	D80T-4020-F48	X	X	X	D81T-4020-F51
Final Check (Not required with gear	D81T-4020-F54	X			
Gauge Block contact pattern method)	D81T-4020-F55		X	X	D81T-4020-F56

84927399

Fig. 356 Depth gauge checking tools — Dana 80

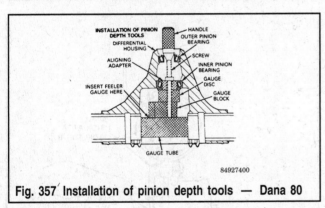

84927400

Fig. 357 Installation of pinion depth tools — Dana 80

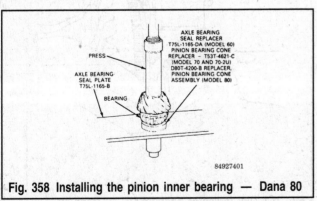

84927401

Fig. 358 Installing the pinion inner bearing — Dana 80

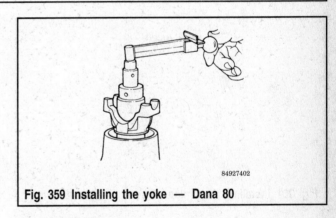

84927402

Fig. 359 Installing the yoke — Dana 80

Differential Carrier

1. Install the differential side gears, the differential pinion gears and new thrust washers into the differential carrier.

2. Align the pinion gear shaft holes and install the pinion shaft into the carrier. Align the lock pin hole in the shaft and carrier. Install the lock pin and peen the hole to avoid having the pin drop from the carrier.

3. Install the differential case side bearings with the proper installation tools. Do not install the shims at this time.

4. Place the carrier assembly into the axle housing with the bearing cups on the bearing cones. Install the bearing caps in their original position and tighten the bearing cap bolts enough to keep the bearing caps in place.

5. Install a dial indicator on the housing so the indicator button contacts the carrier flange. Press the differential carrier to prevent side-play and center the dial indicator. Rotate the carrier and check the flange for run-out. If the run-out is

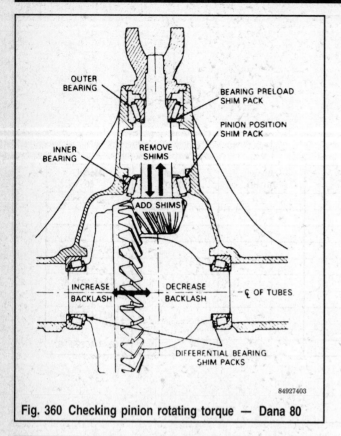

Fig. 360 Checking pinion rotating torque — Dana 80

Fig. 361 Installing the pinion oil seal — Dana 80

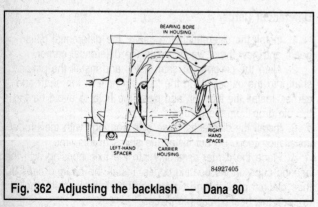

Fig. 362 Adjusting the backlash — Dana 80

greater than 0.002 in., the defect is probably due to the bearings or to the carrier and should be corrected.

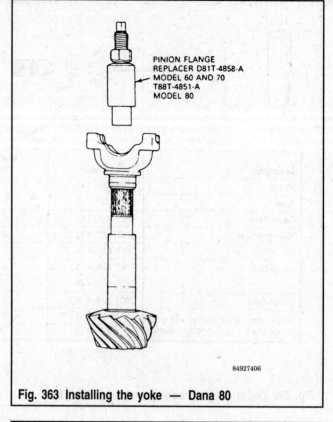

Fig. 363 Installing the yoke — Dana 80

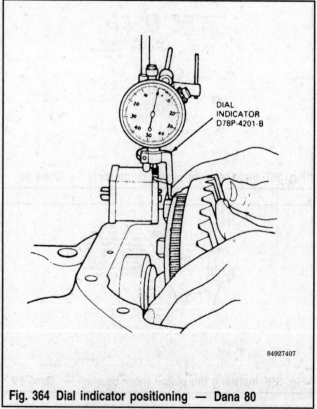

Fig. 364 Dial indicator positioning — Dana 80

6. Remove the assembly and install the ring gear. Torque the retaining bolts and reinstall the assembly into the housing.

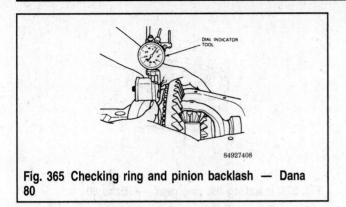

Fig. 365 Checking ring and pinion backlash — Dana 80

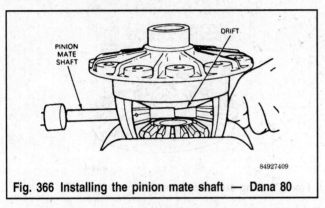

Fig. 366 Installing the pinion mate shaft — Dana 80

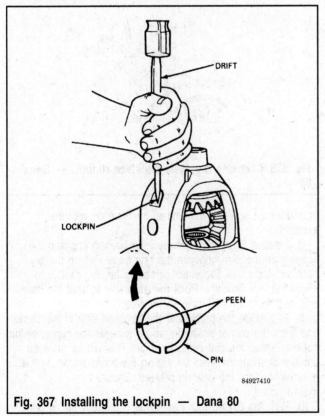

Fig. 367 Installing the lockpin — Dana 80

Install the bearing caps in their original position and tighten the cap bolts to keep the bearings caps in place.

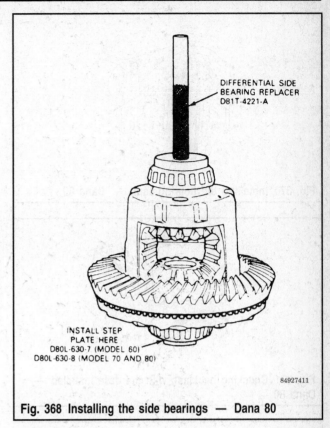

Fig. 368 Installing the side bearings — Dana 80

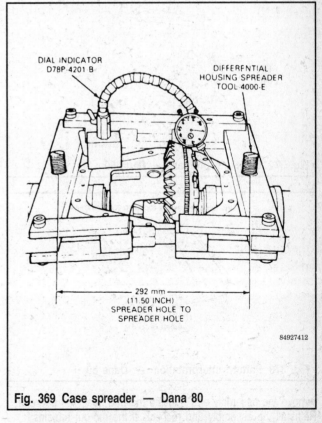

Fig. 369 Case spreader — Dana 80

7. Install the dial indicator and position the indicator button to contact the ring gear back surface. Rotate the assembly and the run-out should be less than 0.002 in. If over 0.002 in.,

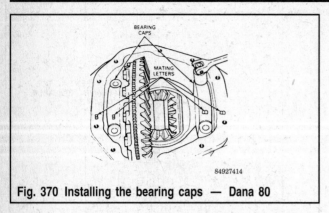

Fig. 370 Installing the bearing caps — Dana 80

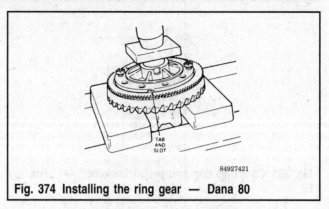

Fig. 374 Installing the ring gear — Dana 80

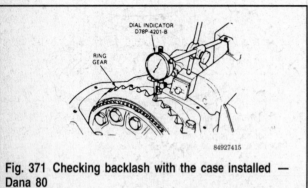

Fig. 371 Checking backlash with the case installed — Dana 80

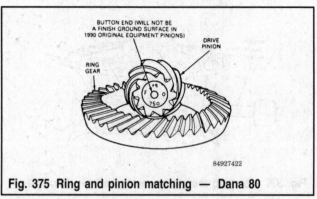

Fig. 375 Ring and pinion matching — Dana 80

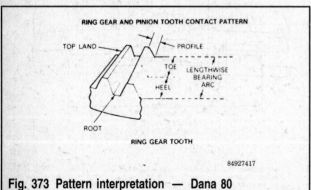

Fig. 372 Checking preload — Dana 80

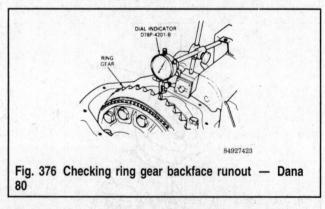

Fig. 376 Checking ring gear backface runout — Dana 80

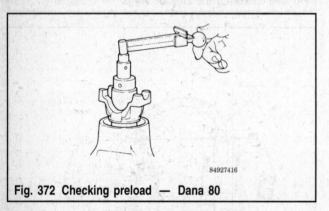

Fig. 373 Pattern interpretation — Dana 80

remove the assembly and relocate the ring gear 180 degrees. Reinstall the assembly and recheck. If the run-out remains over the 0.002 in. tolerance, the ring gear is defective. If the measurement is within tolerances, continue on with the assembly.

8. Position 2 pry bars between the bearing cap and the housing on the side opposite the ring gear. Pull on the pry bars and force the differential carrier as far as possible towards the dial indicator. Rock the assembly to seat the bearings and reset the dial indicator to zero.

9. Reposition the prybars to the opposite side of the carrier and force the carrier assembly as far towards the center of the housing. Read the dial indicator scale. This will be the total amount of shims required for setting the backlash during the reassembly, less the bearing preload. Record the measurement.

10. With the pinion gear installed and properly set, position the differential carrier assembly into the axle housing and install the bearing caps in their proper positions. Tighten the cap bolts just to hold the bearing cups in place.

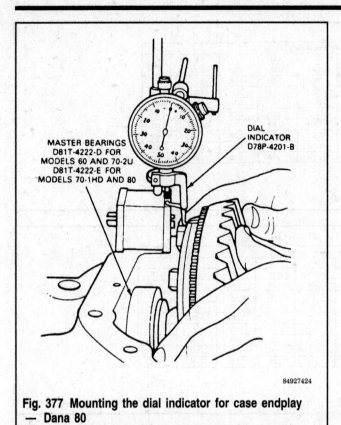

Fig. 377 Mounting the dial indicator for case endplay — Dana 80

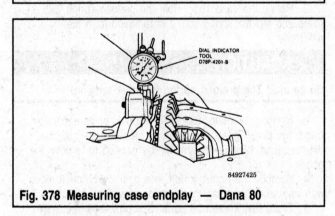

Fig. 378 Measuring case endplay — Dana 80

11. Install a dial indicator on the axle housing with the indicator button contacting the back of the ring gear.

12. Position 2 prybars between the bearing cup and the axle housing on the ring gear side of the case and pry the ring gear into mesh with the pinion gear teeth, as far as possible. Rock the ring gear to allow the teeth to mesh and the bearings to seat. With the pressure still applied by the prybars, set the dial indicator to zero.

13. Reposition the prybars on the opposite side of ring gear and pry the gear as far as it will go. Take the dial indicator reading. Repeat this procedure until the same reading is obtained each time. This reading represents the necessary amount of shims between the differential carrier and the bearing on the ring gear side.

14. Remove the bearing from the differential carrier on the ring gear side and install the proper amount of shims. Reinstall the bearing.

15. Remove the differential carrier bearing from the opposite side of the ring gear. To determine the amount of shims needed, use the following method.

   a. Subtract the size of the shim pack just installed on the ring gear side of the carrier from the reading obtained and recorded when measurement was taken without the pinion gear in place.

   b. To this figure, add an additional 0.015 in. to compensate for preload and backlash. An example: If the first reading was 0.085 in. and the shims installed on the ring gear side of the carrier were 0.055 in., the correct amount of shims would be 0.085 in. - 0.055 in. + 0.015 in. = 0.045 in.

16. Install the required shims as determined under step 15 and install the differential side bearing. The installation of the shims should give the proper preload to the bearings and the proper backlash to the ring and pinion gears.

17. Spread the axle housing with the spreader tool no more than 0.015 in. Install the differential bearing outer cups in their correct locations and install the cups in their respective locations.

18. Install the bolts and tighten finger-tight. Rotate the differential carrier and ring gear and tap with a soft-faced hammer to insure proper seating of the assembly in the axle housing.

19. Remove the spreader tool and torque the cap bolts to specifications.

20. Install a dial indicator and check the ring gear backlash at 4 equally spaced points of the ring gear circle. The backlash must be within a range of 0.005-0.008 in. and must not vary more than 0.002 in. between the points checked.

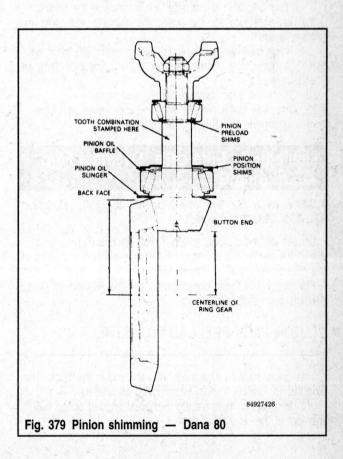

Fig. 379 Pinion shimming — Dana 80

SHIM SELECTION CHART — INCHES

Old Pinion Marking	New Pinion Marking								
	−4	−3	−2	−1	0	+1	+2	+3	+4
+4	+0.008	+0.007	+0.006	+0.005	+0.004	+0.003	+0.002	+0.001	0
+3	+0.007	+0.006	+0.005	+0.004	+0.003	+0.002	+0.001	0	−0.001
+2	+0.006	+0.005	+0.004	+0.003	+0.002	+0.001	0	−0.001	−0.002
+1	+0.005	+0.004	+0.003	+0.002	+0.001	0	−0.001	−0.002	−0.003
0	+0.004	+0.003	+0.002	+0.001	0	−0.001	−0.002	−0.003	−0.004
−1	+0.003	+0.002	+0.001	0	−0.001	−0.002	−0.003	−0.004	−0.005
−2	+0.002	+0.001	0	−0.001	−0.002	−0.003	−0.004	−0.005	−0.006
−3	+0.001	0	−0.001	−0.002	−0.003	−0.004	−0.005	−0.006	−0.007
−4	0	−0.001	−0.002	−0.003	−0.004	−0.005	−0.006	−0.007	−0.008

84927427

Fig. 380 Pinion setting chart — English measure — Dana 80

SHIM SELECTION CHART — METRIC

Old Pinion Marking	New Pinion Marking								
	−10	−8	−5	−3	0	+3	+5	+8	+10
+10	+.20	+.18	+.15	+.13	+.10	+.08	+.05	+.03	0
+8	+.18	+.15	+.13	+.10	+.08	+.05	+.03	0	−.03
+5	+.15	+.13	+.10	+.08	+.05	+.03	0	−.03	−.05
+3	+.13	+.10	+.08	+.05	+.03	0	−.03	−.05	−.08
0	+.10	+.08	+.05	+.03	0	−.03	−.05	−.08	−.10
−3	+.08	+.05	+.03	0	−.03	−.05	−.08	−.10	−.13
−5	+.05	+.03	0	−.03	−.05	−.08	−.10	−.13	−.15
−8	+.03	0	−.03	−.05	−.08	−.10	−.13	−.15	−.18
−10	0	−.03	−.05	−.08	−.10	−.13	−.15	−.18	−.20

84927428

Fig. 381 Pinion setting chart — Metric measure — Dana 80

21. If the backlash is not within specifications, the shim packs must be corrected to bring the backlash within limits.

  a. Low backlash is corrected by decreasing the shim on the ring gear side and increasing the opposite side shim an equal amount.

  b. High backlash is corrected by increasing the shim on the ring gear side and decreasing the opposite side shim an equal amount.

22. Check the tooth contact pattern and verify.

23. Complete the assembly, refill to proper level with lubricant and operate to verify proper assembly.

Limited Slip Differential Overhaul Ford. 8.8 in. Ring Gear

▶ **See Figures 382, 383, 384, 385, 386, 387, 388, 389, 390, 391, 392, 393, 394 and 395**

Other than the preload spring, pinion shaft and gears and the clutch packs, the overhaul of this unit is identical to that of the conventional 8.8 in. differential.

For removal of these components, see the Adjustment procedures immediately following.

CLUTCH PACK PRELOAD ADJUSTMENT

This adjustment can be made with the unit in the truck. The axle shafts, however, must be removed completely.

1. Using a punch, drive the S-shaped preload spring half way out of the differential case.

2. Rotate the case 180°. Hold the preload spring with a pliers and tap the spring until it is removed from the differential.

✳✳CAUTION

Be careful! The preload spring is under tension!

3. Using gear rotator tool T80P-4205-A, or its equivalent, rotate the pinion gears until the can be removed from the differential. A 12 in. extension will be needed to remove the gears.

4. Remove the right and left side gear clutch pack along with any shims, and tag them for identification.

5. Clean and inspect all parts. Use only acid-free, non-flammable cleaning agents. Use a lint-free cloth to wipe the parts dry. Replace any damaged parts.

6. Assemble the clutch packs — without the shims — on their side gears. Coat all friction plates with limited slip lubricant, such as Ford Additive Friction Modifier, or equivalent meeting EST-M2C118-A specifications.

7. Place the base portion of the Traction-Lok Clutch Gauge T87T-4946-A, or equivalent, in a vise. Install the clutch pack and side gear — without the shims — over the base.

8. Install the tool's disc over the base and on top of the clutch pack.

9. Install the top portion of the tool over the disc and base stud.

10. Install the tool's nut and torque it to 60 inch lbs.

11. Using feeler gauges, determine the distance between the tool and the clutch pack. This will be the thickness of the necessary shim.

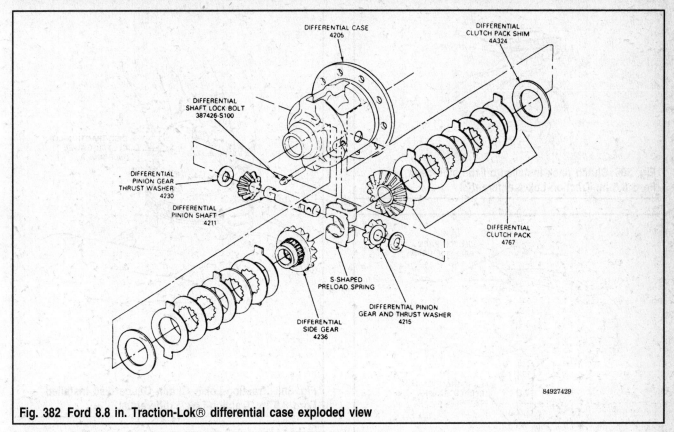

DIFFERENTIAL CASE
4205

DIFFERENTIAL
CLUTCH PACK SHIM
4A324

DIFFERENTIAL
SHAFT LOCK BOLT
387426-S100

DIFFERENTIAL
PINION GEAR
THRUST WASHER
4230

DIFFERENTIAL
PINION SHAFT
4211

DIFFERENTIAL
CLUTCH PACK
4767

S-SHAPED
PRELOAD SPRING

DIFFERENTIAL
SIDE GEAR
4236

DIFFERENTIAL PINION
GEAR AND THRUST WASHER
4215

84927429

Fig. 382 Ford 8.8 in. Traction-Lok® differential case exploded view

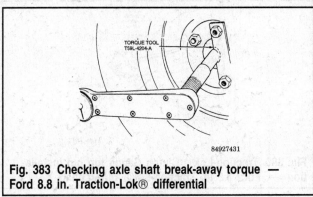

TORQUE TOOL
T59L-4204-A

84927431

**Fig. 383 Checking axle shaft break-away torque —
Ford 8.8 in. Traction-Lok® differential**

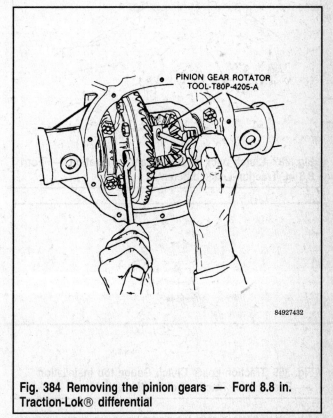

PINION GEAR ROTATOR
TOOL-T80P-4205-A

84927432

**Fig. 384 Removing the pinion gears — Ford 8.8 in.
Traction-Lok® differential**

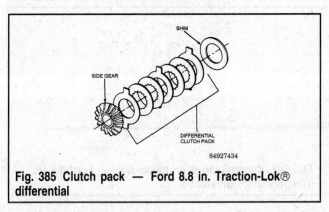

SHIM

SIDE GEAR

DIFFERENTIAL
CLUTCH PACK

84927434

**Fig. 385 Clutch pack — Ford 8.8 in. Traction-Lok®
differential**

12. Install the right side gear, clutch pack and new shim into the differential case. Repeat this for the left side.

13. Place the pinion gears and thrust washers 180° apart on the side gears. Install tool T80P-4205-A, or equivalent. A 12 in. extension should be used to install the gears.

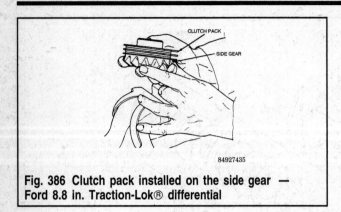

**Fig. 386 Clutch pack installed on the side gear —
Ford 8.8 in. Traction-Lok® differential**

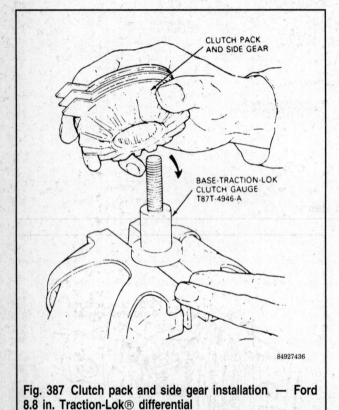

**Fig. 387 Clutch pack and side gear installation — Ford
8.8 in. Traction-Lok® differential**

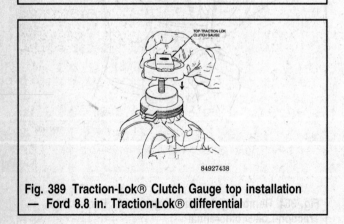

**Fig. 389 Traction-Lok® Clutch Gauge top installation
— Ford 8.8 in. Traction-Lok® differential**

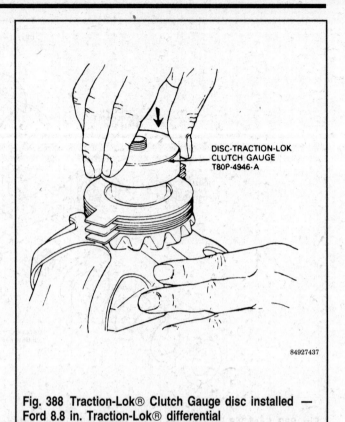

**Fig. 388 Traction-Lok® Clutch Gauge disc installed —
Ford 8.8 in. Traction-Lok® differential**

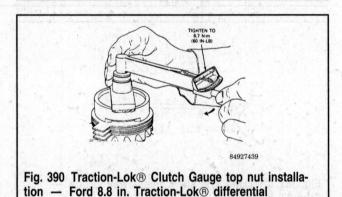

**Fig. 390 Traction-Lok® Clutch Gauge top nut installa-
tion — Ford 8.8 in. Traction-Lok® differential**

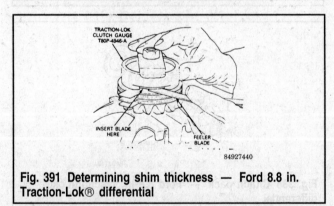

**Fig. 391 Determining shim thickness — Ford 8.8 in.
Traction-Lok® differential**

14. Rotate the tool until the pinion gears are aligned with the
pinion shaft hole. Remove the tool.

15. Hold the S-shaped preload spring at the differential case
window, and, with a plastic mallet, drive the spring into position. Check the spring for damage.

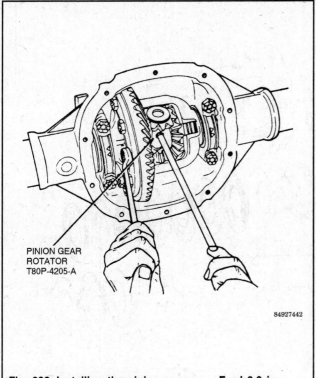

Fig. 392 Installing the pinion gears — Ford 8.8 in. Traction-Lok® differential

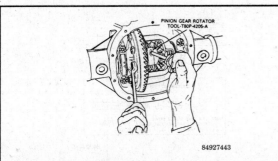

Fig. 393 Aligning the pinion gears — Ford 8.8 in. Traction-Lok® differential

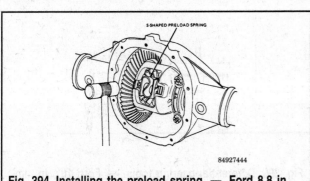

Fig. 394 Installing the preload spring — Ford 8.8 in. Traction-Lok® differential

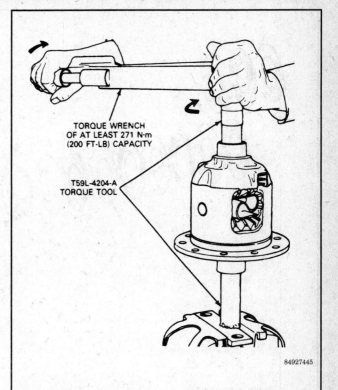

Fig. 395 Bench torque test — Ford 8.8 in. Traction-Lok® differential

BENCH TORQUE TEST

This test must be made any time the differential has been removed, or adjustments have been made.

Using the locker tools in set T59L-4204-A, or equivalent, check the torque required to rotate one side gear while the other is held stationary.

The initial breakaway torque, if original clutch plates are used, should be at least 20 ft. lbs.

The rotating torque needed to keep the side gear turning, with new plates, will fluctuate.

Limited Slip Differential Overhaul Ford 10½ in. Ring Gear

▶ **See Figures 396, 397, 398, 399, 400, 401, 402, 403, 404, 405, 406, 407, 408, 409, 410, 411, 412, 413, 414, 415, 416, 417, 418 and 419**

Overhaul of this differential, except for the differential case, is identical to the 10½ in. conventional axle.

For case removal and installation, see the conventional axle procedure.

DIFFERENTIAL CASE DISASSEMBLY

➡**The differential bearings need not be removed to overhaul the differential. If bearing removal is desired, refer to the conventional axle procedures.**

1. Remove the differential pinion lockshaft bolt.

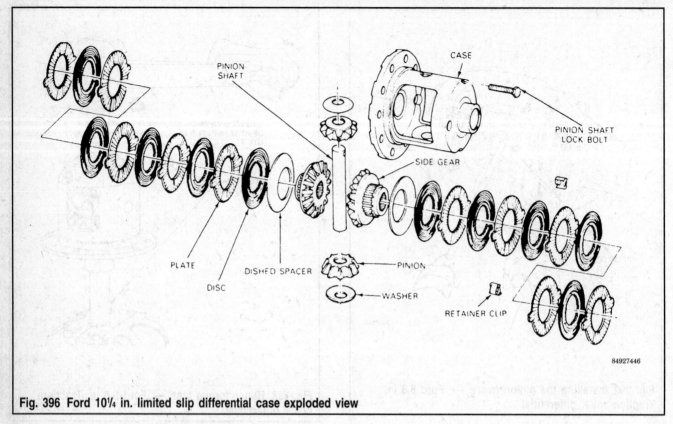

Fig. 396 Ford 10¼ in. limited slip differential case exploded view

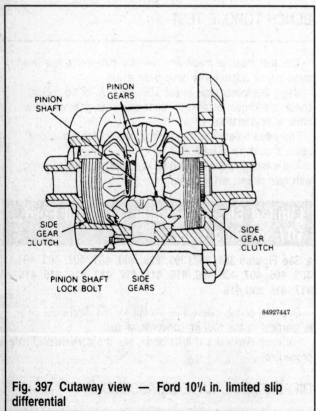

Fig. 397 Cutaway view — Ford 10¼ in. limited slip differential

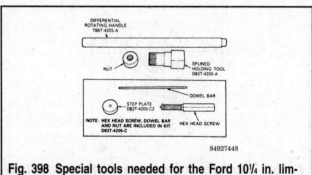

Fig. 398 Special tools needed for the Ford 10¼ in. limited slip differential

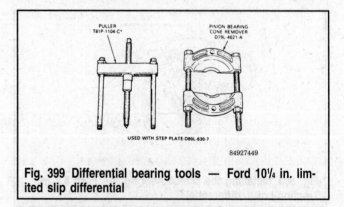

Fig. 399 Differential bearing tools — Ford 10¼ in. limited slip differential

2. Install a differential holding tool in a vise and install the differential on the tool, ring gear side up.

3. Using a punch, drive the pinion shaft from the case.

4. Install Step Plate D83T-4205-C2, or equivalent, in the bottom side gear bore. Apply a small amount of grease to the centering hole of the step plate.

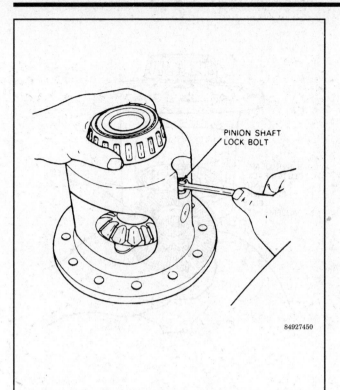

Fig. 400 Removing the pinion shaft lockbolt — Ford 10¼ in. limited slip differential

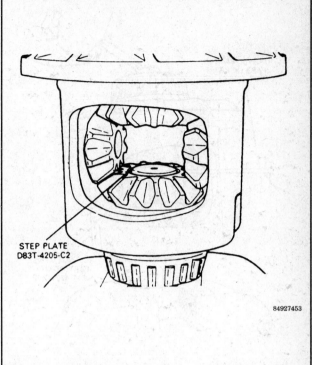

Fig. 402 Installing the step plate — Ford 10¼ in. limited slip differential

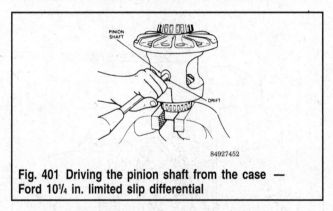

Fig. 401 Driving the pinion shaft from the case — Ford 10¼ in. limited slip differential

5. Install a nut on the upper side gear. Hold the nut in position while installing the hex screw tool, which is part of the step plate tool.

6. Install the dowel bar part of the tool in the hole in the nut. Tighten the forcing screw to force the side gears away from the pinion mating gears. The dowel bar is used to keep the nut from turning.

7. Using an appropriate sized feeler gauge, push the pinion gear thrust washers out from between the pinion gears and the case. Remove the thrust washers, then, back off the forcing screw until it is loose — about 1 full turn.

8. Insert rotating tool T86T-4205-A in the pinion shaft bore and turn the case to force the gears out of the case windows.

9. Remove the forcing screw and step plate. Remove the side gears, retainer clips and clutch packs.

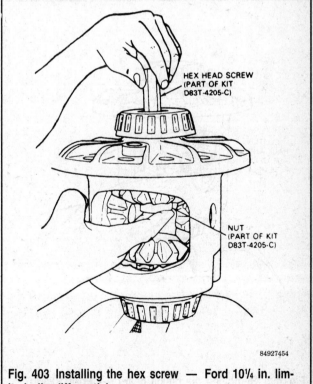

Fig. 403 Installing the hex screw — Ford 10¼ in. limited slip differential

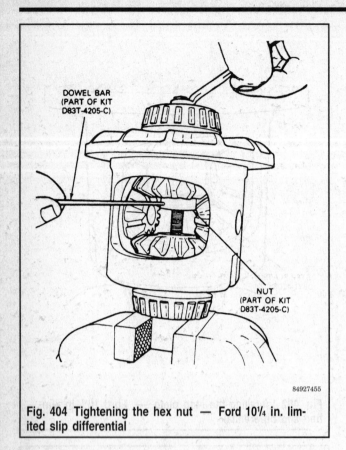

Fig. 404 Tightening the hex nut — Ford 10¼ in. limited slip differential

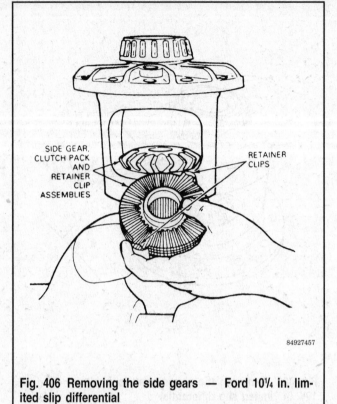

Fig. 406 Removing the side gears — Ford 10¼ in. limited slip differential

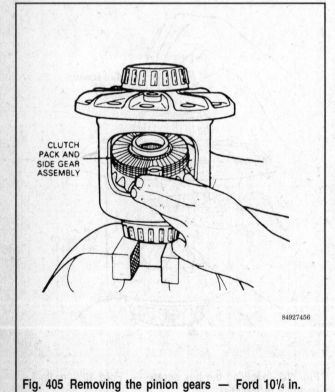

Fig. 405 Removing the pinion gears — Ford 10¼ in. limited slip differential

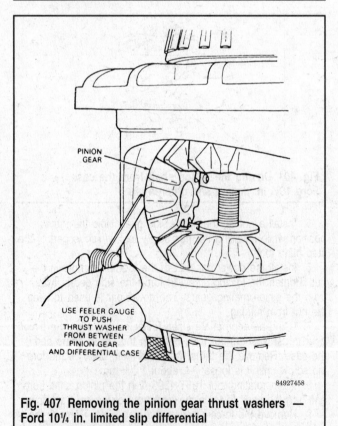

Fig. 407 Removing the pinion gear thrust washers — Ford 10¼ in. limited slip differential

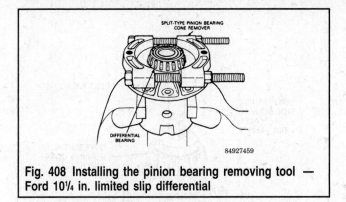

Fig. 408 Installing the pinion bearing removing tool — Ford 10¼ in. limited slip differential

10. Remove the retainer clips from both clutch packs so that you can separate the discs and plates for cleaning and inspection.

✳✳WARNING

Keep all parts in sequence and identified for re-assembly!

11. Coat all parts with the above-mentioned limited slip additive.

12. Assemble the plates and gears on the side gear splines. Make sure they are in the original sequence. Install the clips and make sure they are fully seated.

13. Install differential holding tool D83T-4205-A in a vise. Place the case on the tool with the ring gear side up. Install the clutch pack and side gear assemblies in the case. Make sure that the clutch packs stay assembled on the splines and that the clips stay seated.

14. Position the step plate in the bottom side gear bore. Apply a small amount of grease in the bore. Position the nut in the top side gear bore and hold it in place. Install the hex screw tool and tighten it 2 turns *after* it contacts the bottom step plate. Insert the dowel bar in the nut bolt.

15. Position the pinion gears in the case windows so that they mesh with the side gear teeth. Hold the pinion gears in place. Make sure that the pinion gears are 180° apart so that they will correctly align with the pinion shaft bore.

16. Insert the rotating tool into the pinion shaft bore and turn the case. This will cause the pinion gears to engage the side gears and 'walk' into the case. Rotate the case until the pinion

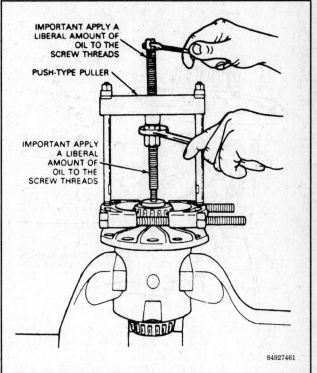

Fig. 410 Removing the pinion inner bearing — Ford 10¼ in. limited slip differential

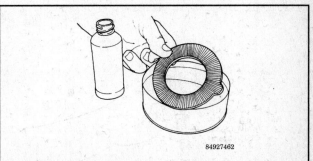

Fig. 411 Lubricating the disc — Ford 10¼ in. limited slip differential

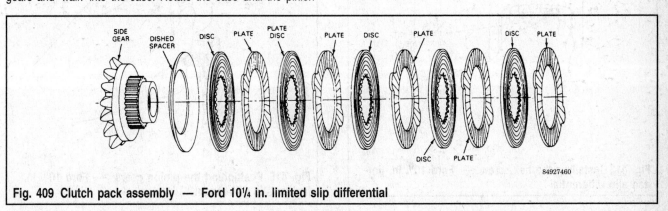

Fig. 409 Clutch pack assembly — Ford 10¼ in. limited slip differential

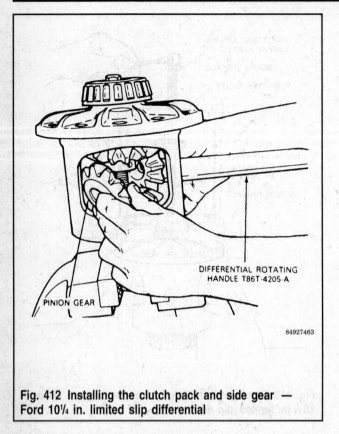

Fig. 412 Installing the clutch pack and side gear — Ford 10¼ in. limited slip differential

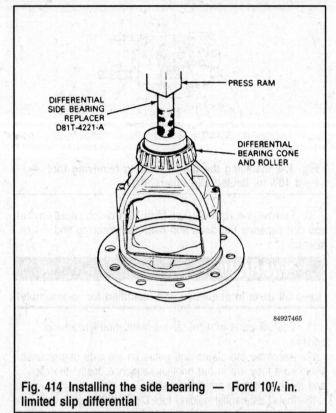

Fig. 414 Installing the side bearing — Ford 10¼ in. limited slip differential

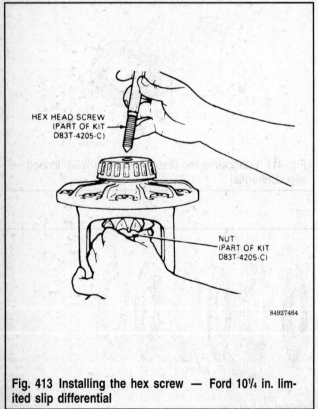

Fig. 413 Installing the hex screw — Ford 10¼ in. limited slip differential

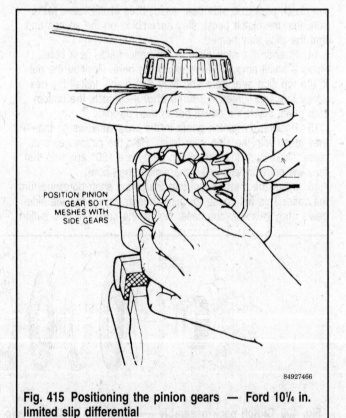

Fig. 415 Positioning the pinion gears — Ford 10¼ in. limited slip differential

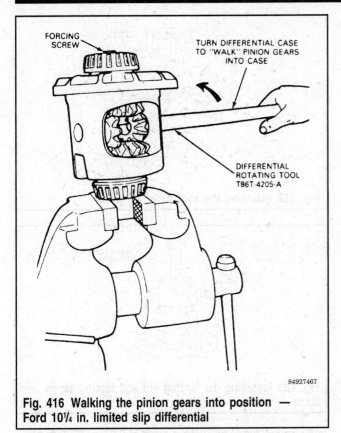

**Fig. 416 Walking the pinion gears into position —
Ford 10¼ in. limited slip differential**

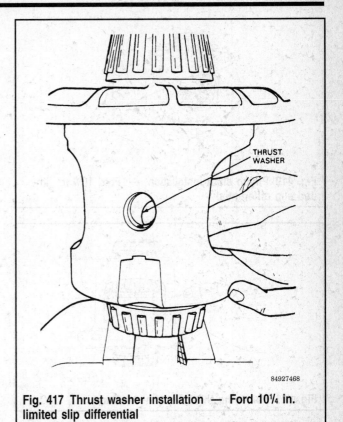

**Fig. 417 Thrust washer installation — Ford 10¼ in.
limited slip differential**

mating shaft holes are aligned exactly with the holes in the
pinion gears.

➡**It will probably be necessary to loosen or tighten the
forcing screw to allow the pinions and side gears to
rotate.**

17. Apply torque to the forcing screw to allow enough clearance to insert the thrust washers. Insert the pinion gear thrust
washers between the pinion gears and the differential case
with the concave side facing inwards.

18. Align the thrust washer holes with the bore in the differential case. Loosen the forcing screw and remove the step
plate and nut from the side gear bores. Install the pinion shaft
in the case. Install the shaft lockbolt and tighten it to 15-30 ft.
lbs.

19. If the ring gear was removed, install it now.

Limited Slip Differential Overhaul Dana Axles

▶ **See Figures 420, 421, 422, 423, 424, 425, 426, 427, 428,
429**

Overhaul of this differential, except for the differential case,
is identical to that of the conventional differential.

1. Remove the ring gear.
2. Place the case on a holding fixture mounted in a vise.
3. For full floating axles, use a small punch to drive out the
roll pin retaining the cross-shaft and drive out the cross-
shaft.   On semi-floating axles, remove the lock screw retaining the cross-shaft. The cross-shaft is a slip fit.

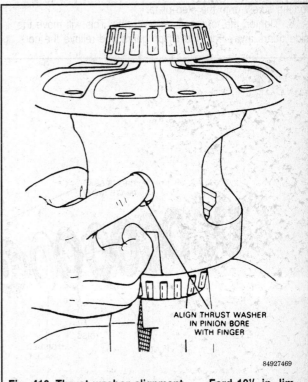

**Fig. 418 Thrust washer alignment — Ford 10¼ in. lim-
ited slip differential**

4. Position the Step Plate T83T-4205-A4, or equivalent, into
the bottom side gear. Apply a small amount of grease in the
centering hole.

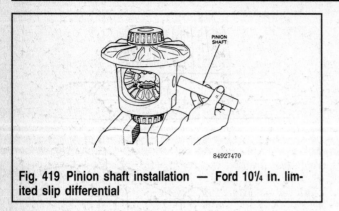

Fig. 419 Pinion shaft installation — Ford 10¼ in. limited slip differential

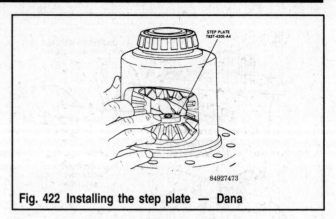

Fig. 422 Installing the step plate — Dana

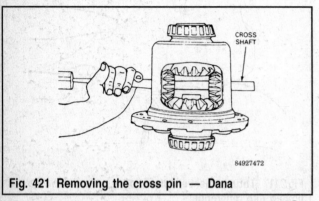

Fig. 421 Removing the cross pin — Dana

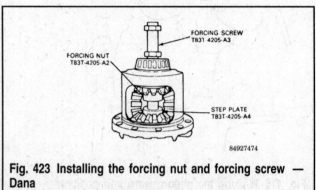

Fig. 423 Installing the forcing nut and forcing screw — Dana

5. Insert the forcing nut and screw into the case. Guide the forcing screw onto the step plate.

6. Tighten the forcing screw securely. This will move the side gears away from the pinion gears and relieve the nor-

mally loaded condition. Using a piece of 0.03 in. (0.762mm) shim stock, push out the differential spherical washers.

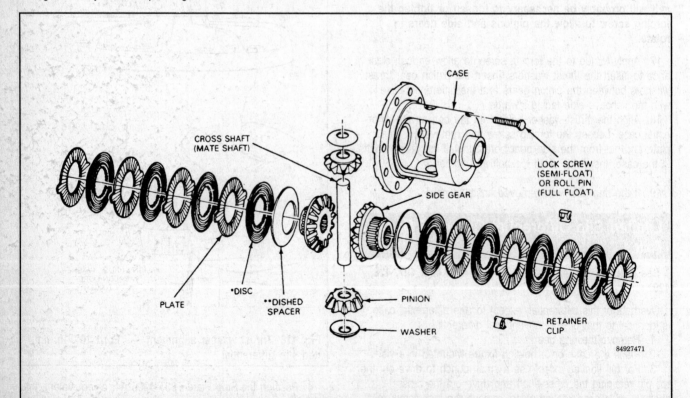

Fig. 420 2-pinion Trac-Lok® differential case exploded view — Dana

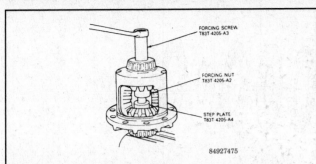

Fig. 424 Guiding the forcing screw into the step plate — Dana

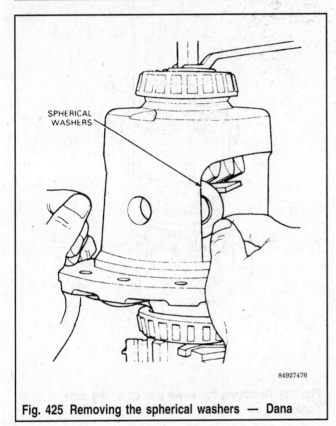

Fig. 425 Removing the spherical washers — Dana

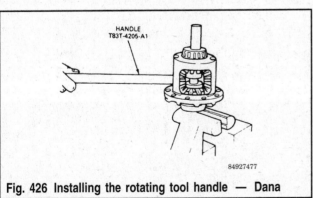

Fig. 426 Installing the rotating tool handle — Dana

7. Momentarily loosen the forcing screw to relieve the pressure on the clutch pack, then, tighten the screw until a slight movement of the pinion gears is seen.

8. Insert the tool handle into the pinion mating shaft bore and rotate the case until the pinion gears can be removed through the large openings in the case. Some tightening and loosening of the forcing screw will be required to permit gear movement.

9. Hold the top side gear and clutch pack in the case and remove the forcing screw and rotating tool. Then, remove the top side gear and clutch pack. Keep the stack of plates and discs in their exact order.

10. Turn the case so that the flange is up. Remove the step plate, side gear and clutch pack out of the case.

11. Remove the retainer clips from the clutch packs to allow separation of the discs and plates. Be sure to keep them in order!

To assemble:

12. Install the clutch packs, side gears and thrust washers. Assemble them is exactly the same order as the originals. Never replace just some of these parts. If any are damaged, replace the whole set.

13. Coat all parts with limited slip lubricant.

14. Assemble the plates and discs on the side gear splines.

➡ **Discs for the model 60 axle that are of the newer, coated design — without concentric grooves — must be soaked for 20 minutes in limited slip friction additive before assembly.**

15. Assemble the retainer clips on the plate ears. Make sure they are completely seated.

16. Assemble the clutch pack and side gear into the case. Make sure everything stays together and the clips stay in place.

17. Position the step plate in the case on the side gear. Apply a small glob of grease in the hole.

18. Assemble the other clutch pack and side gear. Install the step plate.

19. Hold the side gear in place and install the forcing screw down through the top of the case. Thread the forcing nut on the screw. The tip of the forcing screw must contact the step plate.

20. Position the case on the holding fixture.

21. Position the pinion gears in the case, opposite each other. Be sure the holes in the gears are aligned.

22. Turn the forcing screw so that the side gears move away from the differential pinion gears and relieve the loaded condition.

23. Insert the tool handle into the pinion shaft mating hole and turn the case to allow the pinion gears to rotate themselves into the case.

24. Rotate the case until the holes of the pinion gears align with those of the case.

25. Apply force to the forcing screw to allow clearance for the spherical washers. DO NOT OVERTIGHTEN THE SCREW!

26. Assemble the washers in the case. Be sure the holes in the washers and gears are aligned.

27. Remove all special tools.

28. Install the pinion shaft.

29. Install the cross-shaft locking pin.

30. Install the ring gear.

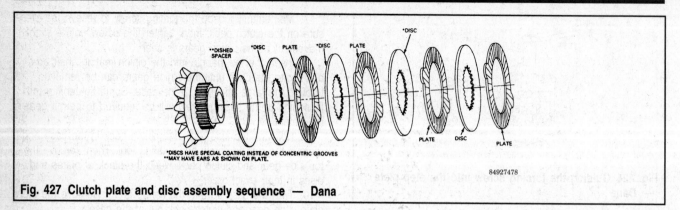

*DISCS HAVE SPECIAL COATING INSTEAD OF CONCENTRIC GROOVES
**MAY HAVE EARS AS SHOWN ON PLATE.

84927478

Fig. 427 Clutch plate and disc assembly sequence — Dana

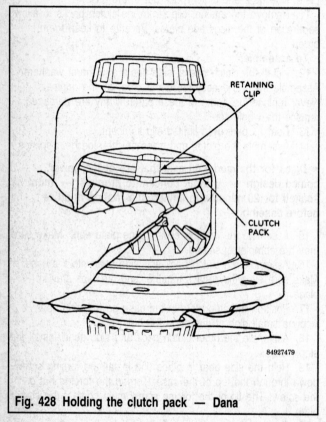

84927479

Fig. 428 Holding the clutch pack — Dana

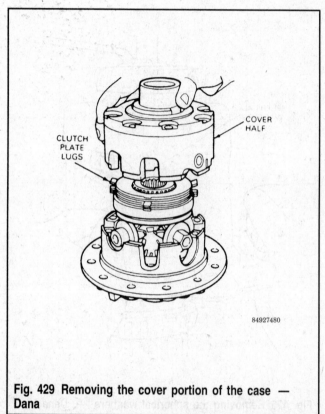

84927480

Fig. 429 Removing the cover portion of the case — Dana

8

STEERING AND SUSPENSION

WHEELS

✳✳CAUTION

Some aftermarket wheels may not be compatible with these vehicles. The use of incompatible wheels may result in equipment failure and possible personal injury! Use only approved wheels!

Front or Rear Wheels

REMOVAL & INSTALLATION

Bronco F-150 F-250 and F-350 with Single Rear Wheels
▶ **See Figures 1 and 2**

1. Set the parking brake and block the opposite wheel.
2. On trucks with an automatic transmission, place the selector lever in **P**. On trucks with a manual transmission, place the transmission in reverse.
3. If equipped, remove the wheel cover.
4. Break loose the lug nuts.
5. Raise the truck until the tire is clear of the ground.
6. Remove the lug nuts and remove the wheel.
To install:
7. Clean the wheel lugs and brake drum or hub of all foreign material.

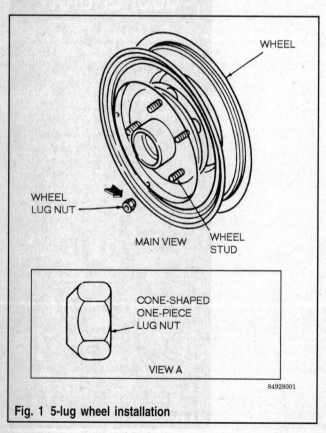

Fig. 1 5-lug wheel installation

8. Position the wheel on the hub or drum and hand-tighten the lug nuts. Make sure that the coned ends face inward.
9. Using the lug wrench, tighten all the lugs, in a criss-cross fashion until they are snug.
10. Lower the truck. Tighten the nuts, in the sequence shown, to 100 ft. lbs. for 5-lug wheels; 140 ft. lbs. for 8-lug wheels.

Front Wheels

REMOVAL & INSTALLATION

F-350 with Dual Rear Wheels F-Super Duty
▶ **See Figure 3**

✳✳CAUTION

Use only integral 2-piece, swiveling lug nuts. Do not attempt to use cone-shaped, one-piece lugs. The use of cone-shaped nuts will cause the nuts to come loose during vehicle operation! Do not attempt to use older-style wheels that use cone-shaped lug nuts. This practice will also cause the wheels to come loose!

1. Set the parking brake and block the opposite wheel.
2. On trucks with an automatic transmission, place the selector lever in **P**. On trucks with a manual transmission, place the transmission in reverse.
3. If equipped, remove the wheel cover.
4. Break loose the lug nuts.
5. Raise the truck until the tire is clear of the ground.
6. Remove the lug nuts and remove the wheel.
To install:
7. Clean the wheel lugs and brake drum or hub of all foreign material.
8. Position the wheel on the hub or drum and hand-tighten the lug nuts.
9. Using the lug wrench, tighten all the lugs, in a criss-cross fashion until they are snug.
10. Lower the truck. Tighten the nuts, in the sequence shown, to 140 ft. lbs.

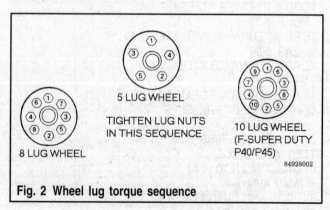

Fig. 2 Wheel lug torque sequence

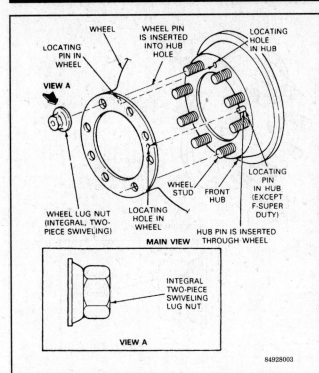

Fig. 3 Front wheel installation for F-350 w/dual rear wheels and F-Super Duty. The 10-lug wheel is identical except for the number of wheel lugs

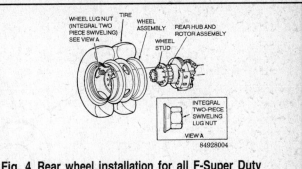

Fig. 4 Rear wheel installation for all F-Super Duty models

alignment pin on the hub. Make sure that the wheel is flush against the hub.

9. Install the outer wheel so that the protruding (convex) side is flush against the inner wheel. Make sure that the alignment pin is protruding through the wheel index hole.

10. Hand-tighten the lug nuts.

11. Using the lug wrench, tighten all the lugs, in a criss-cross fashion until they are snug.

12. Lower the truck. Tighten the nuts, in the sequence shown, to 140 ft. lbs.

❋❋CAUTION

The lug nuts on dual rear wheels should be retightened after the first 100 miles of new-vehicle operation. The lug nuts on dual rear wheels should be retightened at an interval of 500 miles after anytime a wheel has been removed and installed for any reason! Failure to observe this procedure may result in the wheel coming loose during vehicle operation!

Dual Rear Wheels

REMOVAL & INSTALLATION

◗ See Figures 4 and 5

❋❋CAUTION

Use only integral 2-piece, swiveling lug nuts. Do not attempt to use cone-shaped, one-piece lugs. The use of cone-shaped nuts will cause the nuts to come loose during vehicle operation! Do not attempt to use older-style wheels that use cone-shaped lug nuts. This practice will also cause the wheels to come loose!

➡F-Super Duty models require the use of center-pilot type wheels.

1. Set the parking brake and block the opposite wheel.

2. On trucks with an automatic transmission, place the selector lever in **P**. On trucks with a manual transmission, place the transmission in reverse.

3. If equipped, remove the wheel cover.

4. Break loose the lug nuts.

5. Raise the truck until the tire is clear of the ground.

6. Remove the lug nuts and remove the wheel(s).

To install:

7. Clean the wheel lugs and brake drum or hub of all foreign material.

8. Mount the inner wheel on the hub with the dished (concave) side inward. Align the wheel with the small indexing hole — located in the wheel between the stud holes — with the

Wheel Lug Nut Stud

REPLACEMENT

◗ See Figures 6, 7, 8, 9, 10 and 11

Front Wheels

USING A PRESS

1. Remove the wheel.

2. Place the hub/rotor assembly in a press, supported by the hub surface. NEVER rest the assembly on the rotor!

3. Press the stud from the hub.

4. Position the new stud in the hub and align the serrations. Make sure it is square and press it into place.

USING A HAMMER AND DRIVER

1. Remove the wheel.

2. Support the hub/rotor assembly on a flat, hard surface, resting the assembly on the hub. NEVER rest the assembly on the rotor!

3. Position a driver, such as a drift or broad punch, on the outer end of the stud and drive it from the hub.

4. Turn the assembly over, coat the serrations of the new stud with liquid soap, position the stud in the hole, aligning the

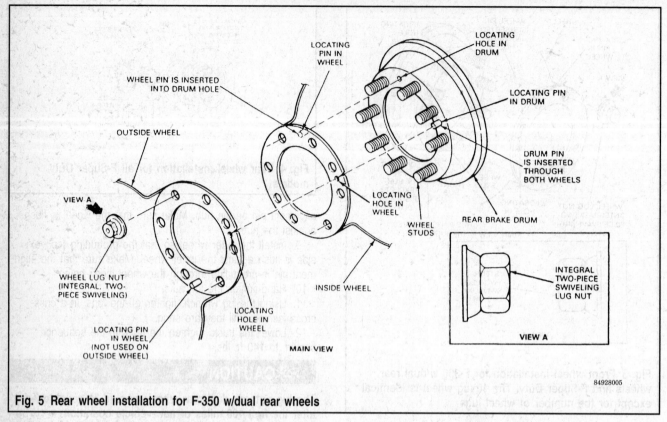

Fig. 5 Rear wheel installation for F-350 w/dual rear wheels

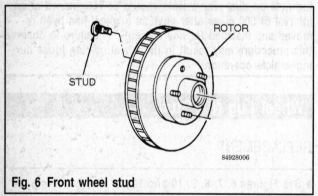

Fig. 6 Front wheel stud

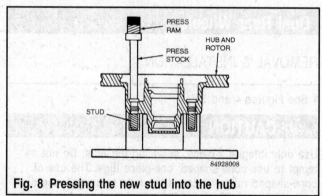

Fig. 8 Pressing the new stud into the hub

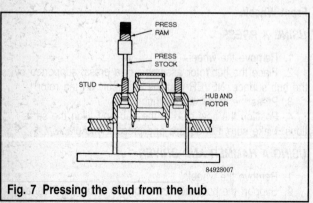

Fig. 7 Pressing the stud from the hub

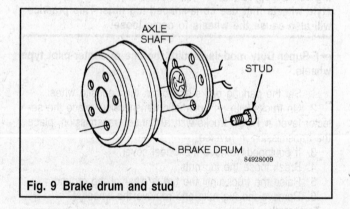

Fig. 9 Brake drum and stud

serrations, and, using the drift and hammer, drive it into place until fully seated.

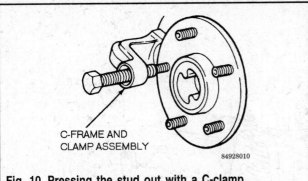

Fig. 10 Pressing the stud out with a C-clamp

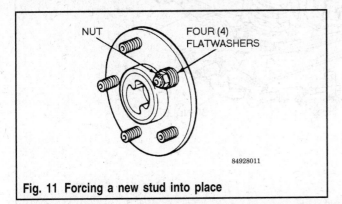

Fig. 11 Forcing a new stud into place

Rear Wheels

1. Remove the wheel.
2. Remove the drum or rotor from the axle shaft or hub studs.
3. Using a large C-clamp and socket, press the stud from the drum or rotor.
4. Coat the serrated part of the stud with liquid soap and place it in the hole. Align the serrations.
5. Place 3 or 4 flat washers on the outer end of the stud and thread a lug nut on the stud with the flat side against the washers. Tighten the lug nut until the stud is drawn all the way in.

✳✳WARNING

Do not use an impact wrench!

2-WHEEL DRIVE COIL SPRING FRONT SUSPENSION

▶ See Figure 12

Trucks with 2-Wheel Drive and coil springs use two I-beam type front axles; one for each wheel. One end of each axle is attached to the spindle and a radius arm, and the other end is attached to a frame pivot bracket on the opposite side of the truck.

Springs

REMOVAL & INSTALLATION

▶ See Figure 13

1. Raise the front of the vehicle and place jackstands under the frame and a jack under the axle.
2. Remove the wheels.
3. Disconnect the shock absorber from the lower bracket.
4. Remove one bolt and nut and remove the rebound bracket.
5. Remove the two spring upper retainer attaching bolts from the top of the spring upper seat and remove the retainer.
6. Remove the nut attaching the spring lower retainer to the lower seat and axle and remove the retainer.
7. Place a safety chain through the spring to prevent it from suddenly coming loose. Slowly lower the axle and remove the spring.

To install:

8. Place the spring in position and raise the front axle.
9. Position the spring lower retainer over the stud and lower seat, and install the two attaching bolts.
10. Position the upper retainer over the spring coil and against the spring upper seat, and install the two attaching bolts.
11. Tighten the upper retaining bolts to 13-18 ft. lbs.; the lower retainer attaching nuts to 70-100 ft. lbs.
12. Connect the shock absorber to the lower bracket. Torque the bolt and nut to 40-60 ft. lbs. Install the rebound bracket.
13. Remove the jack and safety stands.

Shock Absorbers

Most of these trucks are equipped with hydraulic shock absorbers as standard equipment. Some, however, are equipped with low pressure gas shock absorbers as standard equipment and all are available with gas shocks as optional equipment.

✳✳CAUTION

Low pressure gas shocks are charged with nitrogen gas to 135 psi. Do not puncture, attempt to open, or apply heat to the shock absorbers.

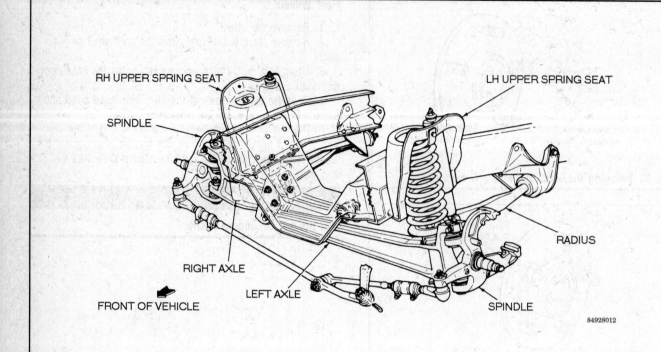

RH UPPER SPRING SEAT

LH UPPER SPRING SEAT

SPINDLE

RADIUS

RIGHT AXLE

LEFT AXLE

FRONT OF VEHICLE

SPINDLE

84928012

Fig. 12 2-wheel drive Twin I-Beam front suspension, w/ball joints

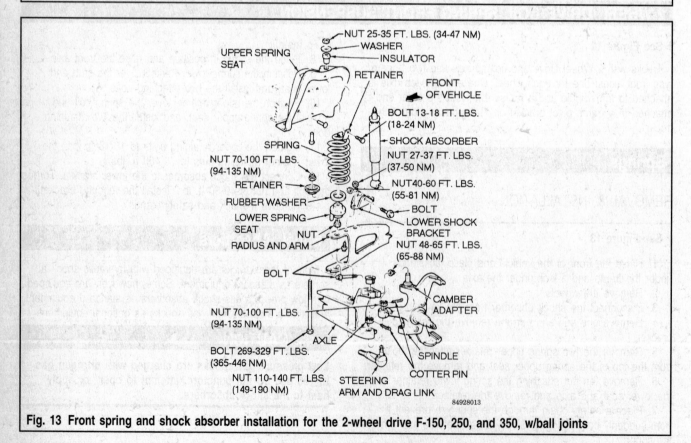

UPPER SPRING SEAT

NUT 25-35 FT. LBS. (34-47 NM)
WASHER
INSULATOR
RETAINER

FRONT OF VEHICLE

BOLT 13-18 FT. LBS. (18-24 NM)

SPRING

SHOCK ABSORBER

NUT 70-100 FT. LBS. (94-135 NM)

NUT 27-37 FT. LBS. (37-50 NM)

RETAINER

NUT 40-60 FT. LBS. (55-81 NM)

RUBBER WASHER

BOLT

LOWER SPRING SEAT

LOWER SHOCK BRACKET

NUT

RADIUS AND ARM

NUT 48-65 FT. LBS. (65-88 NM)

BOLT

CAMBER ADAPTER

NUT 70-100 FT. LBS. (94-135 NM)

AXLE

SPINDLE

BOLT 269-329 FT. LBS. (365-446 NM)

COTTER PIN

NUT 110-140 FT. LBS. (149-190 NM)

STEERING ARM AND DRAG LINK

84928013

Fig. 13 Front spring and shock absorber installation for the 2-wheel drive F-150, 250, and 350, w/ball joints

TESTING

Bounce Test

Each shock absorber can be tested by bouncing the corner of the truck until maximum up and down movement is obtained. Let go of the truck. It should stop bouncing in 1-2 bounces. If not, the shock should be inspected for damage and possibly replaced.

Inspect the Shock Mounts

Check the shock mountings for worn or defective grommets, loose mounting nuts, interference or missing bump stops. If no apparent defects are noted, continue testing.

Inspecting Hydraulic Shocks for Leaks

Disconnect each shock lower mount and pull down on the shock until it is fully extended. inspect for leaks in the seal area. Shock absorber fluid is very thin and has a characteristic odor and dark brown color. Don't confuse the glossy paint on some shocks with leaking fluid. A slight trace of fluid is a normal condition; they are designed to seep a certain amount of fluid past the seals for lubrication. If you are in doubt as to whether the fluid on the shock is coming from the shock itself or from some other source, wipe the seal area clean and manually operate the shock (see the following procedure). Fluid will appear if the unit is leaking.

Manually Operating the Shocks

It may be necessary to fabricate a holding fixture for certain types of shock absorbers. If a suspected problem is in the front shocks, disconnect both front shock lower mountings.

➡**When manually operating air shocks, the air line must be disconnected at the shock.**

Grip the lower end of the shock and pull down (rebound stroke) and then push up (compression stroke). The control arms will limit the movement of front shocks during the compression stroke. Compare the rebound resistance of both shocks and compare the compression resistance. Usually any shock showing a noticeable difference will be the one at fault.

If the shock has internal noises, extend the shock fully then exert an extra pull. If a small additional movement is felt, this usually means a loose piston and the shock should be replaced. Other noises that are cause for replacing shocks are a squeal after a full stroke in both directions, a clicking noise on fast reverse and a lag at reversal near mid-stroke.

REMOVAL & INSTALLATION

To replace the front shock absorber, remove the self-locking nut, steel washer, and rubber bushings at the upper end of the shock absorber. Remove the bolt and nut at the lower end and remove the shock absorber.

When installing a new shock absorber, use new rubber bushings. Position the shock absorber on the mounting brackets with the stud end at the top.

Install the rubber bushing, steel washer and self-locking nut at the upper end, and the bolt and nut at the lower end. Tighten the upper end to 25-35 ft. lbs. and the lower end to 40-60 ft. lbs.

Front Wheel Spindle

REMOVAL & INSTALLATION

▶ **See Figures 14 and 15**

➡**All 2-Wheel Drive pick-ups utilize upper and lower ball joints.**

1. Jack up the front of the truck and safely support it with jackstands.
2. Remove the wheels.
3. Remove the front brake caliper assembly and hold it out of the way with a piece of wire. Do not disconnect the brake line.
4. Remove the brake rotor from the spindle.
5. Remove the inner bearing cone and seal. Discard the seal, as you'll be fitting a new one during installation.
6. Remove the brake dust shield.
7. Disconnect the steering linkage from the spindle arm using a tie rod removal tool.
8. Remove the cotter from the upper and lower ball joint stud nuts. Discard the cotter pins, as new ones should be installed during reassembly.
9. Remove the upper ball joint nut and loosen the lower ball joint nut to the end of the threads.

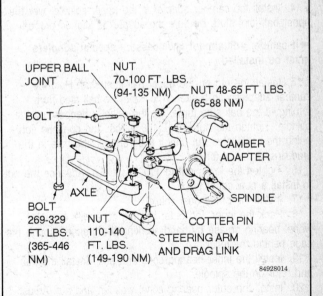

Fig. 14 Front wheel spindle installation for the 2-wheel drive F-150, 250 and 350 with ball joints

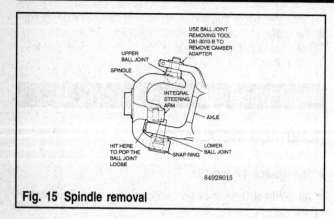

Fig. 15 Spindle removal

10. Strike the inside area or the spindle as shown in the illustration to pop the ball joints loose from the spindle.

✳✳WARNING

Do not use a forked ball joint removal tool to separate the ball joints as this will damage the seal and ball joint socket.

11. Remove the nut. Remove the spindle.

To install:

➡ **Before reassembly, be advised that new cotter pins should be used on the ball joints, and that new bearing seal(s) should also be used. Also, make sure the upper and lower ball joint seals are in place.**

12. Place the spindle over the ball joints.
13. Install the nuts on the lower ball joint stud and partially tighten to 35 ft. lbs. Turn the castellated nut until you are able to install the cotter pin.
14. Install the camber adapter in the upper spindle over the upper ball joint stud. Be sure the adapter is aligned properly.

➡ **If camber adjustment is necessary special adapters must be installed.**

15. Install the nut on the upper ball joint stud. Hold the camber adapter with a wrench to keep the ball stud from turning. If the ball stud turns, tap the adapter deeper into the spindle. Tighten the nut to 110-140 ft. lbs. and continue tightening the castellated nut until it lines up with the hole in the stud. Install the cotter pin.
16. Tighten the lower nut to 110-140 ft. lbs. Advance the nut to install a new cotter pin.
17. Install the brake dust shield.
18. Pack the inner and outer bearing cone with a quality wheel bearing grease by hand, working the grease through the cage behind the roller.
19. Install the inner bearing cone and seal. Install the hub and rotor on the spindle.
20. Install the outer bearing cone, washer, and nut. Adjust the bearing end-play and install the nut retainer, cotter pin and dust cap.
21. Install the brake caliper. connect the steering linkage to the spindle. Tighten the nut to 70-100 ft. lbs. and advance the nut as far necessary to install the cotter pin.
22. Install the wheels. Lower the truck and adjust toe-in if necessary.

Upper and Lower Ball Joints

INSPECTION

1. Before an inspection of the ball joints, make sure the front wheel bearings are properly packed and adjusted.
2. Jack up the front of the truck and safely support it with jackstands, placing the stands under the I-beam axle beneath the spring as shown in the accompanying illustration.
3. Have a helper grab the lower edge of the tire and move the wheel assembly in and out.
4. While the wheel is being moved, observe the lower spindle arm and the lower part of the axle jaw (the end of the axle to which the spindle assembly attaches). If there is 1/32 in. (0.8mm) or greater movement between the lower part of the axle jaw and the lower spindle arm, the lower ball must be replaced.
5. To check upper ball joints, grab the upper edge of the tire and move the wheel in and out. If there is 1/32 in. (0.8mm) or greater movement between the upper spindle arm and the upper part of the jaw, the upper ball joint must be replaced.

REMOVAL

◆ **See Figures 16, 17 and 18**

1. Remove the spindle as previously described.
2. Remove the snapring from the ball joints. Assemble the C-frame assembly T74P-4635-C and receiver cup D81T-3010-A, or equivalents, on the upper ball joint. Turn the

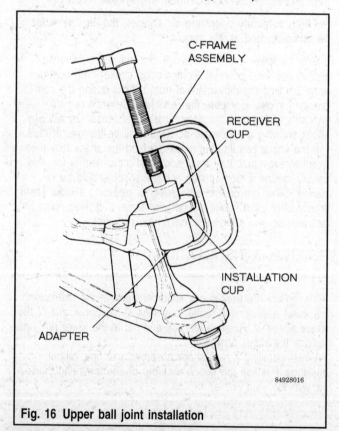

Fig. 16 Upper ball joint installation

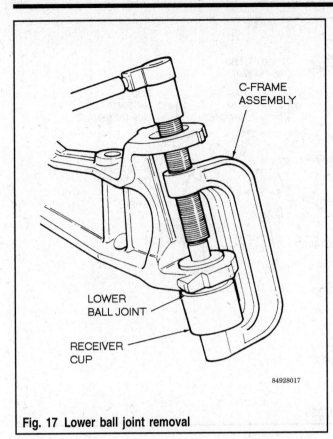

Fig. 17 Lower ball joint removal

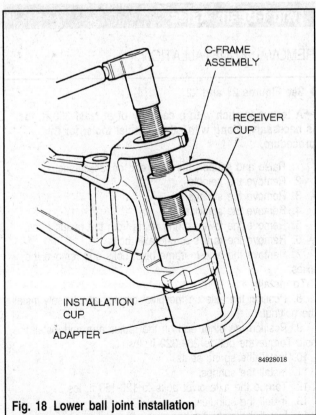

Fig. 18 Lower ball joint installation

forcing screw clockwise until the ball joint is removed from the axle.

3. Repeat Step 2 on the lower ball joint.

➡The upper ball joint must always be removed first. DO NOT heat the ball joint or spindle!

INSTALLATION

➡The lower ball joint must be installed first.

1. To install the lower ball joint, assemble the C-frame with ball joint receiver cup D81T-3010-A5 and installation cup D81T-3010-A1, and turn the forcing screw clockwise until the ball joint is seated. DO NOT heat the ball joint to aid in installation!
2. Install the snapring onto the ball joint.
3. Install the upper ball joint in the same manner as the lower ball joint.
4. Install the spindle assembly.

Radius Arm

REMOVAL & INSTALLATION

▶ See Figure 19

➡A torque wrench with a capacity of at least 350 ft. lbs. is necessary, along with other special tools, for this procedure.

1. Raise the front of the vehicle and place safety stands under the frame and a jack under the wheel or axle. Remove the wheels.
2. Disconnect the shock absorber from the radius arm bracket.
3. Remove the two spring upper retainer attaching bolts from the top of the spring upper seat and remove the retainer.
4. Remove the nut which attached the spring lower retainer to the lower seat and axle and remove the retainer.
5. Lower the axle and remove the spring.
6. Remove the spring lower seat and shim from the radius arm. The, remove the bolt and nut which attach the radius arm to the axle.
7. Remove the cotter pin, nut and washer from the radius arm rear attachment.
8. Remove the bushing from the radius arm and remove the radius arm from the vehicle.
9. Remove the inner bushing from the radius arm.
10. Position the radius arm to the axle and install the bolt and nut finger-tight.
11. Install the inner bushing on the radius arm and position the arm to the frame bracket.
12. Install the bushing, washer, and attaching nut. Tighten the nut to 120 ft. lbs. and install the cotter pin.
13. Tighten the radius arm-to-axle bolt to 269-329 ft. lbs.
14. Install the spring seat and insulator on the radius arm so that the hole in the seat fits over the arm-to-axle nut.
15. Install the spring.
16. Connect the shock absorber. Torque the nut and bolt to 40-60 ft. lbs.
17. Install the wheels.

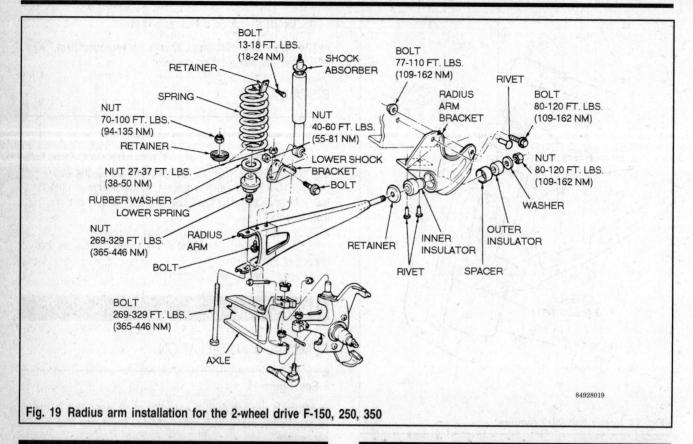

BOLT
13-18 FT. LBS.
(18-24 NM)

SHOCK
ABSORBER

BOLT
77-110 FT. LBS.
(109-162 NM)

RIVET

RETAINER

SPRING

RADIUS
ARM
BRACKET

BOLT
80-120 FT. LBS.
(109-162 NM)

NUT
70-100 FT. LBS.
(94-135 NM)

RETAINER

NUT
40-60 FT. LBS.
(55-81 NM)

NUT
80-120 FT. LBS.
(109-162 NM)

NUT 27-37 FT. LBS.
(38-50 NM)

LOWER SHOCK
BRACKET

BOLT

WASHER

RUBBER WASHER
LOWER SPRING

NUT
269-329 FT. LBS.
(365-446 NM)

RADIUS
ARM

RETAINER

INNER
INSULATOR

OUTER
INSULATOR

BOLT

RIVET

SPACER

BOLT
269-329 FT. LBS.
(365-446 NM)

AXLE

84928019

Fig. 19 Radius arm installation for the 2-wheel drive F-150, 250, 350

Stabilizer Bar

REMOVAL & INSTALLATION

▶ **See Figure 20**

1. Raise and support the front end on jackstands.
2. Disconnect the right and left stabilizer bar ends from the link assembly.
3. Disconnect the retainer bolts and remove the stabilizer bar.
4. Disconnect the stabilizer link assemblies by loosening the right and left locknuts from their respective brackets on the I-beams.

To install:

5. Loosely install the entire assembly. The links are marked with an **R** and **L** for identification.
6. Tighten the link-to-stabilizer bar and axle bracket fasteners to 70 ft. lbs.
7. Check to make sure that the insulators are properly seated and the stabilizer bar is centered.
8. On the F-150, torque the 6 stabilizer bar to cross-member attaching bolts to 35 ft. lbs.   On the F-250 and F-350, torque the stabilizer bar-to-frame retainer bolts to 35 ft. lbs.   Torque the frame mounting bracket nuts/bolts to 65 ft. lbs.

Twin I-Beam Axles

REMOVAL & INSTALLATION

▶ **See Figures 21 and 22**

➡ **A torque wrench with a capacity of at least 350 ft. lbs. is necessary, along with other special tools, for this procedure.**

1. Raise and support the front end on jackstands.
2. Remove the spindles.
3. Remove the springs.
4. Remove the stabilizer bar.
5. Remove the lower spring seats from the radius arms.
6. Remove the radius arm-to-axle bolts.
7. Remove the axle-to-frame pivot bolts and remove the axles.

To install:

8. Position the axle on the pivot bracket and loosely install the bolt/nut.
9. Position the other end on the radius arm and install the bolt. Torque the bolt to 269-329 ft. lbs.
10. Install the spring seats.
11. Install the springs.
12. Torque the axle pivot bolts to 120-150 ft. lbs.
13. Install the spindles.
14. Install the stabilizer bar.

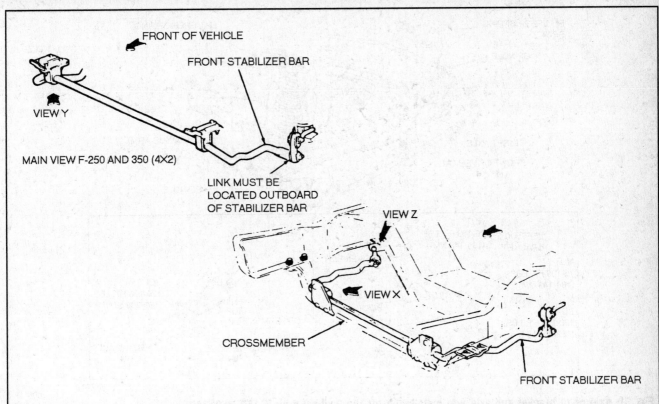

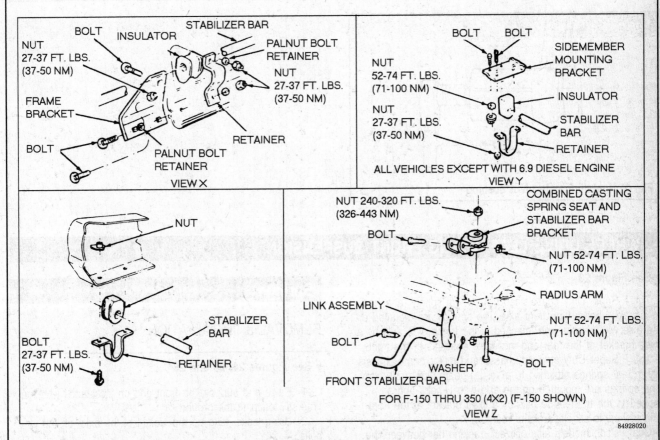

Fig. 20 Front stabilizer bar installation for the 2-wheel drive F-150, 250, 350

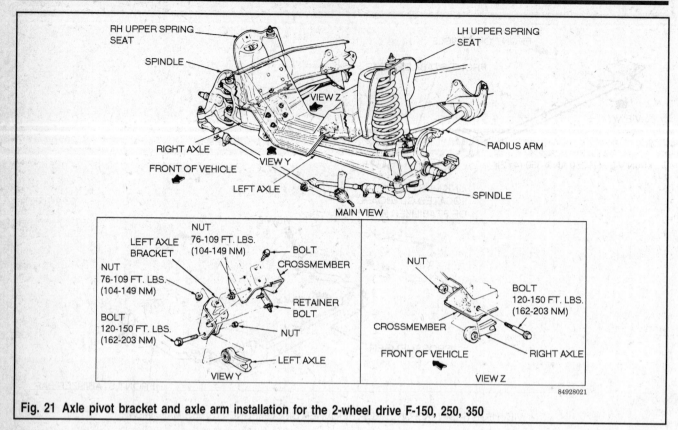

Fig. 21 Axle pivot bracket and axle arm installation for the 2-wheel drive F-150, 250, 350

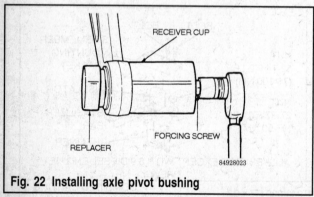

Fig. 22 Installing axle pivot bushing

2-WHEEL DRIVE LEAF SPRING FRONT SUSPENSION

◆ See Figure 23

The F-Super Duty chassis/cab utilizes leaf springs attached to a solid, I-beam type front axle. The springs are mounted on the axle with U-bolts and attached to the frame side rails by a fixed bracket at the rear and moveable shackles at the front.

The F-Super Duty stripped chassis and motor home chassis utilize leaf springs attached to a solid, I-beam type front axle. The springs are mounted on the axle with U-bolts and attached to the frame side rails by a fixed bracket at the front and moveable shackles at the rear.

Chassis/cab models also utilize a tracking bar between the left side of the No.1 crossmember and the right side of the axle beam, inboard of the right spring pad.

Springs

REMOVAL & INSTALLATION

◆ See Figures 24, 25 and 26

1. Raise and support the front end on jackstands with the tires still touching the ground.
2. Using jacks, take up the weight of the axle, off the U-bolts.
3. Disconnect the lower end of each shock absorber.
4. Disconnect the spring from the front bracket or shackle.

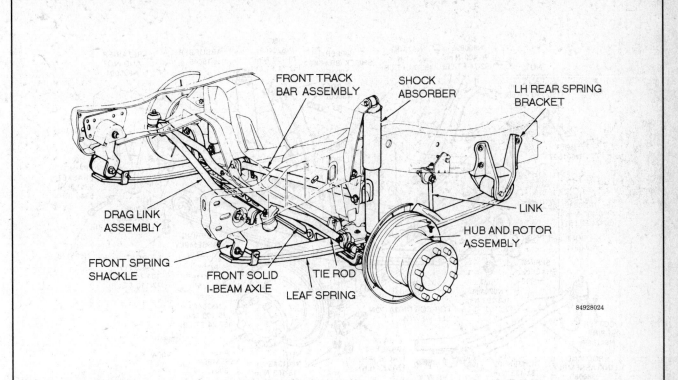

Fig. 23 F-Super Duty chassis/cab front suspension

5. Disconnect the spring from the rear bracket or shackle.

6. Remove the U-bolt nuts.

7. Remove the U-bolts.

8. Disconnect the jack bracket or stabilizer bar as necessary.

9. Lower the axle slightly and remove the spring. Take note of the position of the spring spacer.

To install

10. Position the spring on its seat on the axle and raise it to align the front of the spring with the bracket or shackle.

11. Coat the bushing with silicone grease.

12. Carefully guide the attaching bolt through the bracket or shackle, and the bushing.

13. Install the nut and, depending on model or which bolts you removed, torque it to:
- chassis/cab spring-to-shackle: 120-150 ft. lbs.
- chassis/cab shackle-to-frame: 150-210 ft. lbs.
- stripped chassis or motor home chassis spring-to-bracket: 148-207 ft. lbs.

14. In a similar fashion, attach the rear of the spring. The torques are:
- chassis/cab spring-to-bracket: 150-210 ft. lbs.
- stripped chassis or motor home chassis spring-to-shackle or shackle-to-bracket: 74-110 ft. lbs.

15. Position the spacer on the spring.

16. Install the U-bolts. Install the jack bracket or stabilizer bar bracket on the forward U-bolt. Install the U-bolt nuts. Torque the nuts, evenly and in gradual increments, in a criss-cross fashion, to:
- chassis/cab: 150-210 ft. lbs.
- stripped chassis and motor home chassis: 220-300 ft. lbs.

17. Connect the shock absorbers. Torque them to:
- chassis/cab models, shock absorber-to-bracket nuts to 52-74 ft. lbs.
- stripped chassis or motor home chassis models, lower attaching bolt to 220-300 ft. lbs.

Shock Absorbers

▶ **See Figures 23, 24 and 25**

These trucks are equipped with either hydraulic shock absorbers or with low pressure gas shock absorbers depending on equipment ordered.

✳✳CAUTION

Low pressure gas shocks are charged with nitrogen gas to 135 psi. Do not puncture, attempt to open, or apply heat to the shock absorbers.

TESTING

Bounce Test

Each shock absorber can be tested by bouncing the corner of the truck until maximum up and down movement is obtained. Let go of the truck. It should stop bouncing in 1-2 bounces. If not, the shock should be inspected for damage and possibly replaced.

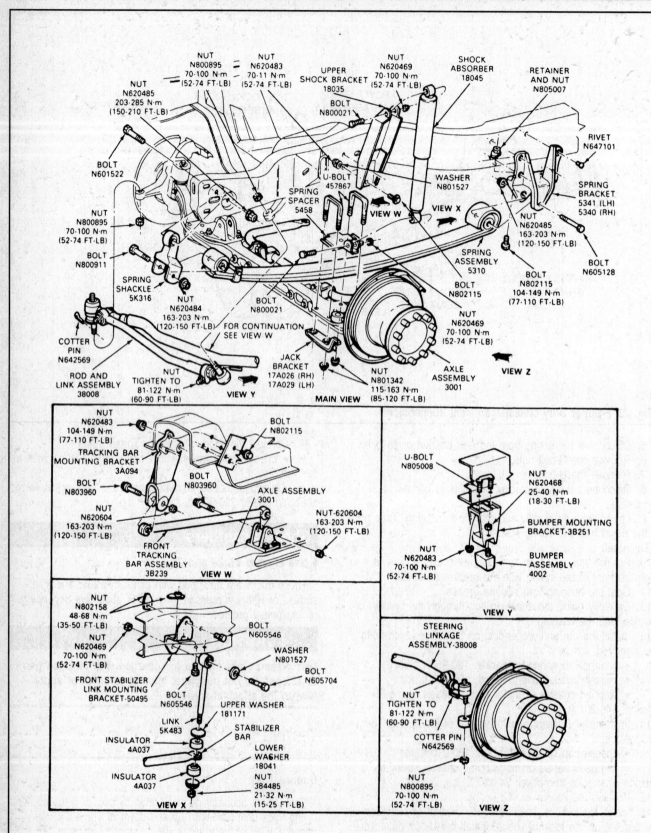

Fig. 24 Front spring and shock absorber installation for F-Super Duty chassis/cab

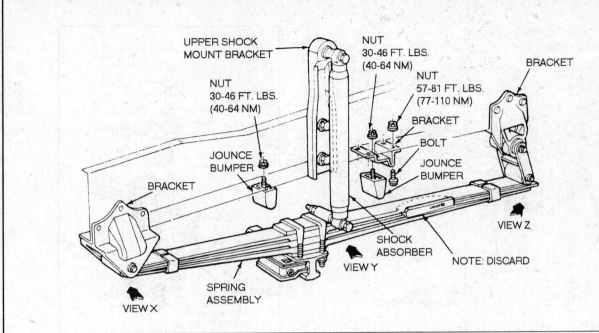

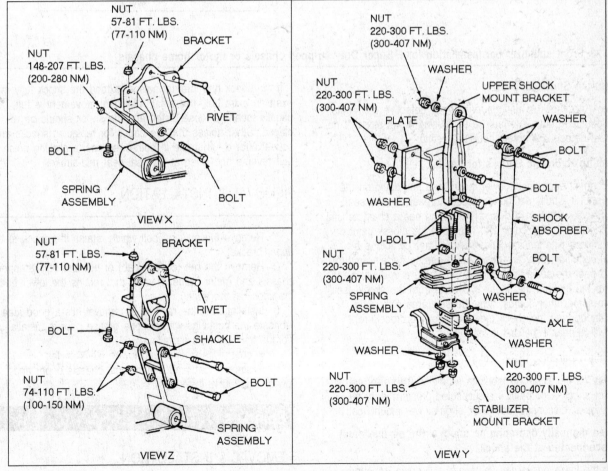

Fig. 25 Front spring and shock absorber installation for F-Super Duty stripped chassis or motor home chassis models

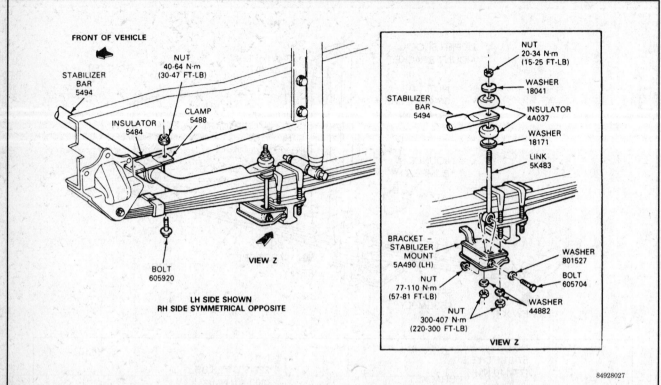

Fig. 26 Front stabilizer bar installation for F-Super Duty stripped chassis or motor home chassis

Inspect the Shock Mounts

Check the shock mountings for worn or defective grommets, loose mounting nuts, interference or missing bump stops. If no apparent defects are noted, continue testing.

Inspecting Hydraulic Shocks for Leaks

Disconnect each shock lower mount and pull down on the shock until it is fully extended. Inspect for leaks in the seal area. Shock absorber fluid is very thin and has a characteristic odor and dark brown color. Don't confuse the glossy paint on some shocks with leaking fluid. A slight trace of fluid is a normal condition; they are designed to seep a certain amount of fluid past the seals for lubrication. If you are in doubt as to whether the fluid on the shock is coming from the shock itself or from some other source, wipe the seal area clean and manually operate the shock (see the following procedure). Fluid will appear if the unit is leaking.

Manually Operating the Shocks

It may be necessary to fabricate a holding fixture for certain types of shock absorbers. If a suspected problem is in the front shocks, disconnect both front shock lower mountings.

➡**When manually operating air shocks, the air line must be disconnected at the shock.**

Grip the lower end of the shock and pull down (rebound stroke) and then push up (compression stroke). The control arms will limit the movement of front shocks during the compression stroke. Compare the rebound resistance of both shocks and compare the compression resistance. Usually any shock showing a noticeable difference will be the one at fault.

If the shock has internal noises, extend the shock fully then exert an extra pull. If a small additional movement is felt, this usually means a loose piston and the shock should be replaced. Other noises that are cause for replacing shocks are a squeal after a full stroke in both directions, a clicking noise on fast reverse and a lag at reversal near mid-stroke.

REMOVAL & INSTALLATION

1. Remove the nut and bolt which retains the shock to the upper bracket.
2. Remove the nut (chassis/cab) or nut and bolt (stripped chassis and motor home chassis) that retains the lower end of the shock at the spring.
3. Installation is the reverse of removal. It's a good idea to lubricate the bushings with silicone grease prior to installation. Torque the fasteners as follows:
   - chassis/cab upper and lower: 52-74 ft. lbs.
   - stripped cab and motor home chassis upper and lower: 220-300 ft. lbs.

Spindles

REMOVAL & INSTALLATION

▶ **See Figures 27, 28 and 29**

1. Raise and support the front end on jackstands.
2. Remove the wheels.

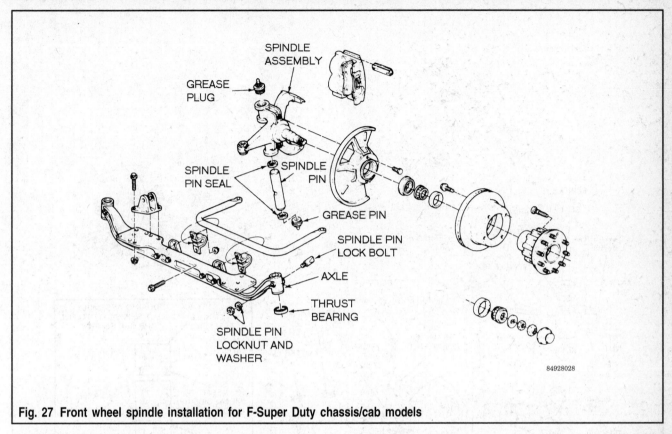

SPINDLE
ASSEMBLY

GREASE
PLUG

SPINDLE
PIN SEAL

SPINDLE
PIN

GREASE PIN

SPINDLE PIN
LOCK BOLT

AXLE

THRUST
BEARING

SPINDLE PIN
LOCKNUT AND
WASHER

84928028

Fig. 27 Front wheel spindle installation for F-Super Duty chassis/cab models

3. Remove the caliper and suspend it out of the way. See Section 9.

4. Remove the hub and rotor assembly. See Section 9.

5. Remove the inner bearing and seal. Discard the seal.

6. Remove the dust shield.

7. Remove the cotter pin and nut, and, using a ball joint separator — the forcing screw type, not the fork type — disconnect the tie rod end from the spindle arm.

8. On stripped chassis and motor home models, disconnect the drag link from the steering arm using a forcing type ball joint separator.

9. Remove the nut and washer from the spindle bolt lock pin and remove the lock pin.

10. Remove the upper and lower spindle pin plugs.

11. Using a brass drift, drive out the spindle pin from the top and remove the spindle and thrust bearing.

12. Remove the thrust bearing and seal.

To install:

13. Clean the spindle pin bore and make sure it is free of corrosion, nicks or burrs. Light corrosion and other irregularities can be removed.

14. Lightly coat the bore with lithium based grease meeting ESA-M1C75-B rating.

15. Install a new spindle pin seal with the metal side facing up into the spindle. Gently press the seal into position being careful to avoid distorting it.

16. Install a new thrust bearing with the lip flange facing downward. Press the bearing in until firmly seated against the surface of the spindle.

17. Lightly coat the bushing surface with lithium based grease and place the spindle on the axle.

18. Hold the spindle, with the thrust bearing in place, tightly against the axle, and measure the space between the axle and spindle at the top of the axle. Determine what thickness of shims is necessary to eliminate all play. Install the shims, available from the dealer.

19. One end of the spindle pin is stamped with a **T**. Install the spindle pin, from the top, with the **T** at the top and the notch aligned with the lock pin hole.

20. Install the lock pin with the threads forward and the wedge groove facing the spindle pin notch. Drive the lock pin in all the way and install the nut. Torque the nut to 40-50 ft. lbs.

21. Install the spindle pin plugs. Torque them to 35-50 ft. lbs.

22. Lubricate the spindle pin through the fittings until grease seeps past the upper seal and the thrust bearing slip joint at the bottom. If grease can't be forced past these points, the installation was probably done incorrectly and will have to be disassembled and re-assembled.

23. Install the dust shield.

24. Clean, pack and install the bearings. Install a new seal. See Section 1.

25. Install the hub and rotor assembly. See Section 9.

26. Install the caliper. See Section 9.

27. Connect the tie rod end and, if necessary, the drag link. Tighten the nuts to 50-70 ft. lbs. Always advance the nut to align the cotter pin holes. NEVER back them off! Always use new cotter pins!

28. Install the wheels.

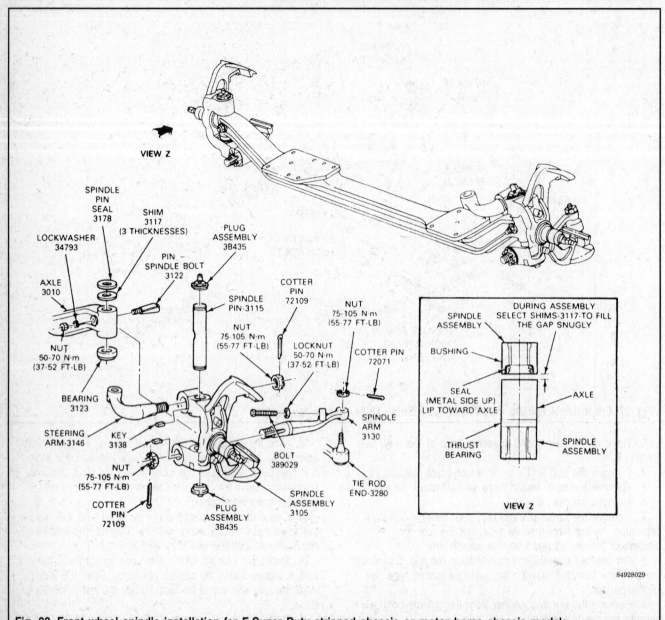

Fig. 28 Front wheel spindle installation for F-Super Duty stripped chassis or motor home chassis models

BRONZE SPINDLE BUSHING REPLACEMENT

▶ See Figures 29, 30, 31, 32, 33 and 34

1. Remove the spindle and secure it in a bench vise.
2. The bushings have an inside diameter of 1.301-1.302 in. (33.05-33.07mm). Use the following tools or their equivalents:
   - Reamer T88T-3110-BH
   - Bushing Remover/Installer T88T-3110-AH
   - Driver Handle T80T-4000-W   One side of the Remover/Installer is marked with a **T**; the other side with a **B**. The **T** side is used on the top bushing; the **B** side is for the bottom bushing.
3. Remove and discard the seal from the upper bushing bore.
4. Working on the upper bushing first, install the driver handle through the bottom bore. Position a new bushing on the **T** side of the tool. The bushing must be positioned so that the open end grooves will face outward when installed. Position the bushing and tool over the old bushing, insert the handle and drive out the old bushing while driving in the new bushing. Continue driving until the tool is fully seated. The new bushing should then be seated at the proper depth of 0.08 in. (2.03mm) minimum from the bottom of the upper spindle boss.

5. Working on the bottom bushing, position the driver handle through the top bushing bore. Position a new bushing on the **B** side of the tool. The bushing must be positioned so that the open end grooves will face outward when installed. Position the bushing and tool over the old bushing, insert the handle and drive out the old bushing while driving in the new bushing. Continue driving until the tool is fully seated. The new bushing should then be seated at the proper depth of 0.13 in. (3.3mm) minimum from the top of the lower spindle boss.

6. Ream the new bushings to 0.001-0.003 in. (0.025-0.076mm) larger than the diameter of the new spindle pin. Ream the top bushing first. Install the smaller diameter of

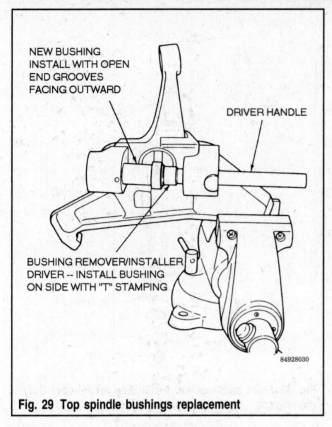

NEW BUSHING
INSTALL WITH OPEN
END GROOVES
FACING OUTWARD

DRIVER HANDLE

BUSHING REMOVER/INSTALLER
DRIVER -- INSTALL BUSHING
ON SIDE WITH "T" STAMPING

84928030

Fig. 29 Top spindle bushings replacement

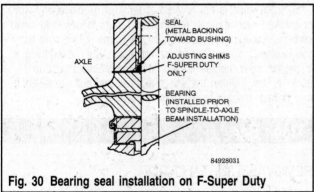

SEAL
(METAL BACKING
TOWARD BUSHING)

ADJUSTING SHIMS
F-SUPER DUTY
ONLY

AXLE

BEARING
(INSTALLED PRIOR
TO SPINDLE-TO-AXLE
BEAM INSTALLATION)

84928031

Fig. 30 Bearing seal installation on F-Super Duty

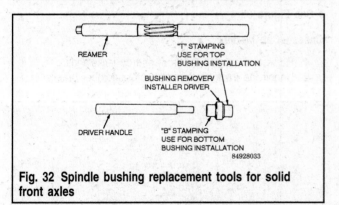

REAMER

"T" STAMPING
USE FOR TOP
BUSHING INSTALLATION

BUSHING REMOVER/
INSTALLER DRIVER

DRIVER HANDLE

"B" STAMPING
USE FOR BOTTOM
BUSHING INSTALLATION

84928033

Fig. 32 Spindle bushing replacement tools for solid front axles

the reamer through the top bore and into the bottom bore until the threads are in position is the top bushing. Ream the bushing until the threads exit the top bushing.   Ream the bot-

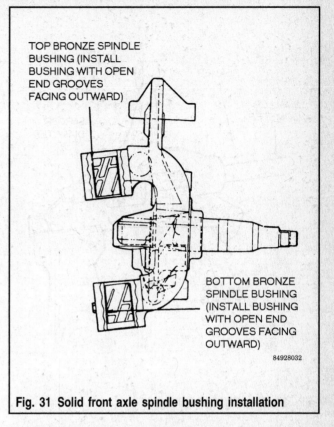

TOP BRONZE SPINDLE
BUSHING (INSTALL
BUSHING WITH OPEN
END GROOVES
FACING OUTWARD)

BOTTOM BRONZE
SPINDLE BUSHING
(INSTALL BUSHING
WITH OPEN END
GROOVES FACING
OUTWARD)

84928032

Fig. 31 Solid front axle spindle bushing installation

tom bushing. The larger diameter portion of the tool will act as a pilot in the top bushing to properly ream the bottom bushing.

7. Remove the tool and thoroughly clean all metal shavings from the bushings and surrounding parts. Coat the bushings

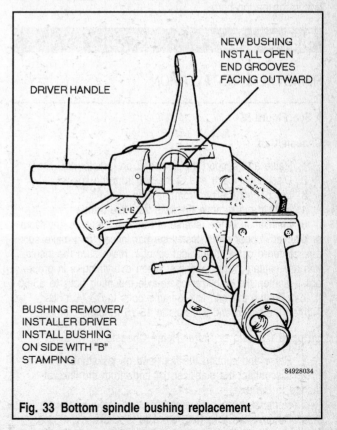

NEW BUSHING
INSTALL OPEN
END GROOVES
FACING OUTWARD

DRIVER HANDLE

BUSHING REMOVER/
INSTALLER DRIVER
INSTALL BUSHING
ON SIDE WITH "B"
STAMPING

84928034

Fig. 33 Bottom spindle bushing replacement

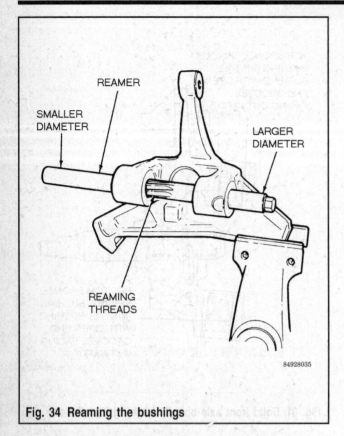

Fig. 34 Reaming the bushings

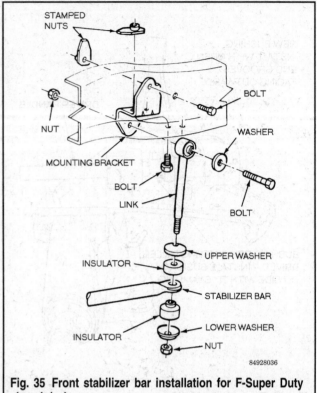

Fig. 35 Front stabilizer bar installation for F-Super Duty chassis/cab

and spindle pins with grease meeting specification ESA-M1C75-B.

8. Install a new seal on the Remover/Installer on the **T** side. Using the handle, push the seal into position in the bottom of the top bore.

Stabilizer Bar

REMOVAL & INSTALLATION

▶ See Figure 35

Chassis/Cab

1. Raise and support the front end on jackstands.
2. Disconnect each end of the bar from the links.
3. Disconnect the bar from the axle.
4. Unbolt and remove the links from the frame.
5. Installation is the reverse of removal. Replace any worn or cracked rubber parts. Install the bar loosely and make sure it is centered between the leaf springs. Make sure the insulators are seated in the retainers. When everything is in proper order, tighten the stabilizer bar-to-axle mounting bolts to 35-50 ft. lbs. Tighten the end link-to-frame bolts to 52-74 ft. lbs. Tighten the bar-to-end link nuts to 15-25 ft. lbs.

Stripped Chassis or Motor Home Chassis

1. Raise and support the front end on jackstands.
2. Disconnect the stabilizer bar ends from the links attached to the axle.
3. Remove the bar-to-frame bolts and remove the bar.
4. Remove the links from the axle brackets.

5. Installation is the reverse of removal. Replace any worn or cracked rubber parts. Assemble all parts loosely and make sure the assembly is centered on the frame. make sure that the insulators are seated in the retainers. When everything is in proper order, tighten the bar-to-frame brackets bolts to 30-47 ft. lbs. Tighten the link-to-axle bracket bolts to 57-81 ft. lbs. Tighten the bar-to-link nuts to 15-25 ft. lbs.

Track Bar

REMOVAL & INSTALLATION

▶ See Figure 36

Chassis/Cab Models

1. Raise and support the front end on jackstands.
2. Unbolt the track bar from the crossmember bracket.

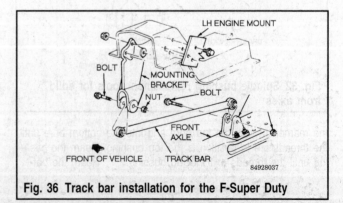

Fig. 36 Track bar installation for the F-Super Duty

3. Unbolt the track bar from the axle bracket.

4. Installation is the reverse of removal. Torque the bolts at each end to 120-150 ft. lbs.

Axle

REMOVAL & INSTALLATION

1. Raise and support the front end on jackstands positioned under the frame.

2. Remove the wheels.

3. Remove the brake calipers and suspend them out of the way. See Section 9.

4. Install the wheels with a few lug nuts finger-tight.

5. Adjust the height of the truck on the stands so that the weight is off the front springs, but the tires still touch the ground.

6. Disconnect the stabilizer bar from the axle.

7. Disconnect the tie rod end and, if applicable, the drag link, from the spindle.

8. On chassis/cab models, disconnect the track bar from the axle.

9. Remove the spring U-bolt nuts and remove the stabilizer bar brackets or jack brackets.

10. Remove the U-bolts.

11. Raise the truck and roll the axle from underneath.

To install:

12. Roll the axle into position under the truck and align it so that the spring seats align with the locating boss on each spring.

13. Install the U-bolts and jack brackets or stabilizer bar brackets. Install the U-bolt nuts and tighten them evenly, gradually and in a criss-cross fashion, to 150-210 ft. lbs. for chassis/cab models, or, 220-300 ft. lbs. for stripped chassis or motor home models.

14. Connect the tie rod ends and drag link.

15. Install the track bar on chassis/cab models.

16. Connect the stabilizer bar.

17. Install the calipers.

18. Install and tighten all the lug nuts.

4-WHEEL DRIVE FRONT SUSPENSION

▶ **See Figures 37, 38 and 39**

The suspension of an F-150 and Bronco 4-Wheel Drive consists of a Dana 44-IFS independent driving axle attached to the frame with two coil springs, two radius arms, and a stabilizer bar.

The front suspension on an F-250 4-Wheel Drive consists of a Dana 44- or 50-IFS independent driving axle attached to the frame with two semi-elliptic leaf springs. Each spring is clamped to the axle with two U-bolts. The front of the spring rests in a front shackle bracket and the rear is attached to a frame bracket.

The front suspension on an F-350 4-Wheel Drive consists of a Dana 60 Monobeam one piece driving axle attached to the frame with two semi-elliptic leaf springs. Each spring is clamped to the axle with two U-bolts. The front of the spring rests in a front shackle bracket and the rear is attached to a frame bracket. On the right spring cap a track bar is attached with the other end mounted on the crossmember.

Springs

REMOVAL & INSTALLATION

▶ **See Figures 37, 38 and 39**

F-150 and Bronco

1. Raise and support the front end on jackstands.

2. Remove the shock absorber lower attaching bolt and nut.

3. Remove the spring lower retainer nuts from inside of the spring coil.

4. Remove the upper spring retainer by removing the attaching screw.

5. Position safety stands under the frame side rails and lower the axle on a floor jack just enough to relieve tension from the spring.

➡**The axle must be supported on the jack throughout spring removal, and must not be permitted to hang from the brake hose. If the length of the brake hose does not provide sufficient clearance it may be necessary to remove and support the brake caliper.**

6. Remove the spring lower retainer and lower the spring from the vehicle.

To install:

7. Place the spring in position and slowly raise the front axle. Make sure the springs are positioned correctly in the upper spring seats.

8. Install the lower spring retainer and torque the nut to 100 ft. lbs.

9. Position the upper retainer over the spring coil and tighten the attaching screws to 13-18 ft. lbs.

10. Position the shock absorber to the lower bracket and torque the attaching bolt and nut to 65 ft. lbs.

11. Remove the safety stands and lower the vehicle.

F-250, F-350

1. Raise the vehicle frame until the weight is off the front spring with the wheels still touching the floor. Support the axle to prevent rotation.

2. Disconnect the lower end of the shock absorber from the U-bolt spacer. Remove the U-bolts, U-bolt cap and spacer.   On F-350 models, remove the 2 bolts retaining the track bar to the spring cap and the track bar bracket.

3. Remove the nut from the hanger bolt retaining the spring at the rear and drive out the hanger bolt.

4. Remove the nut connecting the front shackle and spring eye and drive out the shackle bolt and remove the spring.

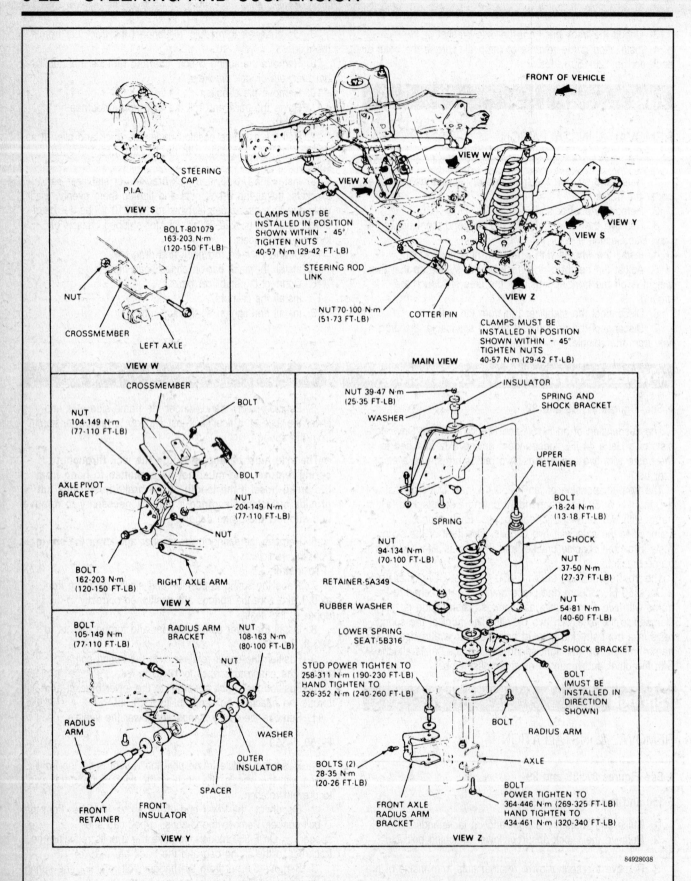

Fig. 37 Bronco and 4-wheel drive F-150 front suspension

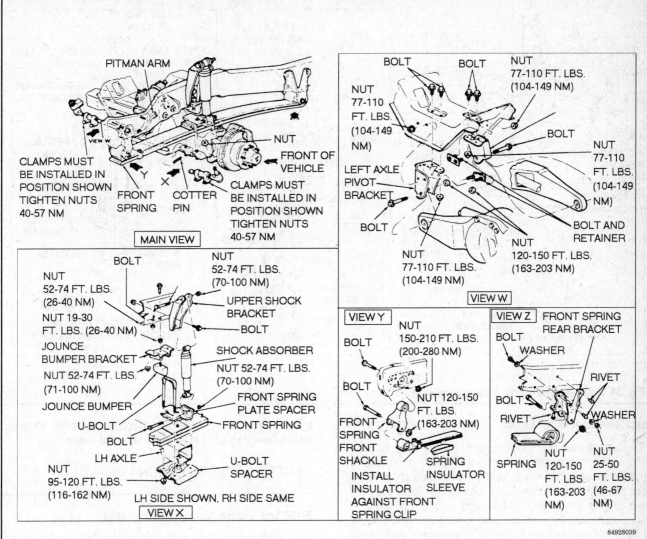

Fig. 38 F-250 4-wheel drive front suspension w/Dana 44-IFS-HD or Dana IFS

To install:

5. Position the spring on the spring seat. Install the shackle bolt through the shackle and spring. Torque the nuts to 150 ft. lbs.

6. Position the rear of the spring and install the hanger bolt. Torque the nut to 150 ft. lbs.

7. Position the U-bolt spacer and place the U-bolts in position through the holes in the spring seat cap. Install but do not tighten the U-bolt nut.   On the F-350, install the track bar. Torque the track bar-to-bracket bolts to 200 ft. lbs.

8. Connect the lower end of the shock absorber to the U-bolt spacer. Torque the fasteners to 60 ft. lbs. on the F-250; 70 ft. lbs. on the F-350.

9. Lower the vehicle and tighten the U-bolt nuts to 120 ft. lbs.

Shock Absorbers

TESTING

Bounce Test

Each shock absorber can be tested by bouncing the corner of the truck until maximum up and down movement is obtained. Let go of the truck. It should stop bouncing in 1-2 bounces. If not, the shock should be inspected for damage and possibly replaced.

Inspect the Shock Mounts

Check the shock mountings for worn or defective grommets, loose mounting nuts, interference or missing bump stops. If no apparent defects are noted, continue testing.

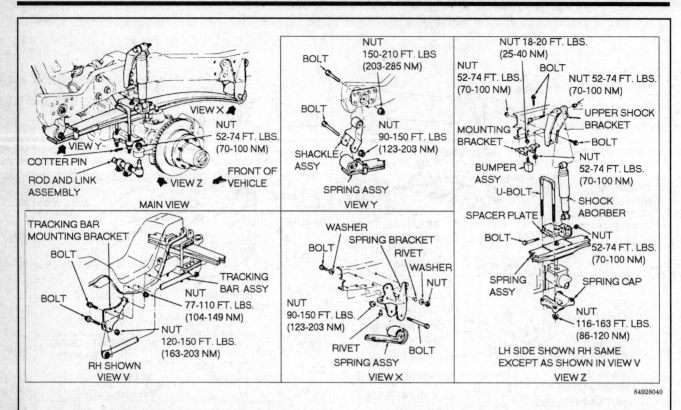

Fig. 39 F-350 4-wheel drive front suspension

Inspecting Shocks for Leaks

Disconnect each shock lower mount and pull down on the shock until it is fully extended. inspect for leaks in the seal area. Shock absorber fluid is very thin and has a characteristic odor and dark brown color. Don't confuse the glossy paint on some shocks with leaking fluid. A slight trace of fluid is a normal condition; they are designed to seep a certain amount of fluid past the seals for lubrication. If you are in doubt as to whether the fluid on the shock is coming from the shock itself or from some other source, wipe the seal area clean and manually operate the shock (see the following procedure). Fluid will appear if the unit is leaking.

Manually Operating the Shocks

It may be necessary to fabricate a holding fixture for certain types of shock absorbers. If a suspected problem is in the front shocks, disconnect both front shock lower mountings.

➡**When manually operating air shocks, the air line must be disconnected at the shock.**

Grip the lower end of the shock and pull down (rebound stroke) and then push up (compression stroke). The control arms will limit the movement of front shocks during the compression stroke. Compare the rebound resistance of both shocks and compare the compression resistance. Usually any shock showing a noticeable difference will be the one at fault.

If the shock has internal noises, extend the shock fully then exert an extra pull. If a small additional movement is felt, this usually means a loose piston and the shock should be replaced. Other noises that are cause for replacing shocks are a

squeal after a full stroke in both directions, a clicking noise on fast reverse and a lag at reversal near mid-stroke.

REMOVAL & INSTALLATION

F-150 and Bronco, except Quad Shocks

1. Remove the upper nut while holding the shock absorber stem.
2. Remove the lower mounting bolt/nut from the bracket.
3. Compress the shock and remove it.
4. Installation is the reverse of removal. Hold the stud while tightening the upper nut to 30 ft. lbs. Torque the lower bolt/nut to 60 ft. lbs.

F-150 and Bronco w/Quad Shocks

▶ **See Figure 40**

1. Remove the upper nut while holding the shock absorber stem on both forward and rearward shocks.
2. Remove the lower mounting bolt/nut from the rearward shock bracket; the nut and washer from the forward shock bracket.
3. Compress the shocks and remove them.
4. Cut the insulators from the upper spring seat.
5. Install new one piece insulators into the top surface of the upper spring seat. Coat them with a soap solution to aid in installation.
6. Installation of the shocks is the reverse of removal. Use a new steel washer under the upper nut. Hold the stud while tightening the upper nut to 30 ft. lbs. Torque the lower bolt/nut to 60 ft. lbs.

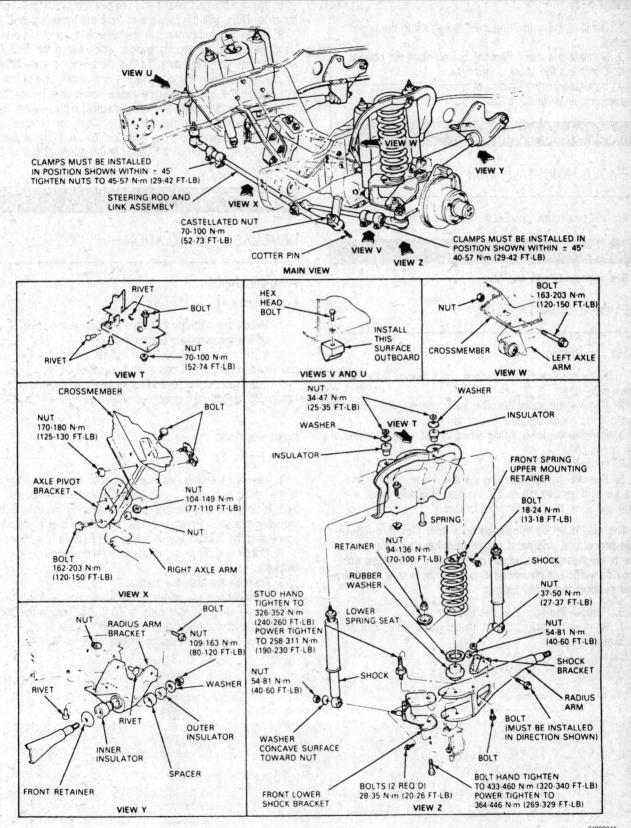

Fig. 40 Quad shock installation on the Bronco and 4-wheel drive F-150

F-250, F-350

1. Remove the nut/bolt retaining the shock to the upper bracket.
2. Remove the lower mounting bolt/nut from the bracket.
3. Compress the shock and remove it.
4. Installation is the reverse of removal. Tighten the upper and lower nut/bolt to 70 ft. lbs.

Front Wheel Spindle

REMOVAL & INSTALLATION

For this procedure, see Section 7 under Front Drive Axle.

Radius Arm

▶ **See Figures 37, 38 and 39**

REMOVAL & INSTALLATION

F-150 and Bronco

1. Raise the vehicle and position safety stands under the frame side rails.
2. Remove the shock absorber lower attaching bolt and nut and pull the shock absorber free of the radius arm.
3. Remove the lower spring retaining bolt from the inside of the spring coil.
4. Loosen the axle pivot bolt.
5. Remove the nut attaching the radius arm to the frame bracket and remove the radius arm rear insulator. Lower the axle and allow the axle to move forward.

➡**The axle must be supported on a floor jack throughout this procedure, and must not be permitted to hang from the brake hose. If the length of the brake hose does not provide sufficient clearance it may be necessary to remove and support the brake caliper.**

6. Remove the spring as described above.
7. Remove the bolt and stud attaching the radius arm and bracket to the axle.

8. Move the axle forward and remove the radius arm from the axle. Then, pull the radius arm from the frame bracket.
9. Install the components in the reverse order of removal. Install new bolts and stud type bolts which attach the radius arm and bracket to the axle. Torque the bracket-to-axle bolts to 25 ft. lbs. Torque the lower radius arm-to-axle bolt to 330 ft. lbs. Tighten the upper stud-type radius arm-to-axle bolt to 250 ft. lbs. Torque the radius arm rear attaching nut to 120 ft. lbs. Torque the lower spring retainer nut to 100 ft. lbs. Torque the upper spring retainer bolts to 15 ft. lbs. Torque the axle pivot bolt to 150 ft. lbs. Torque the lower shock absorber bolt to 60 ft. lbs.

Stabilizer Bar

REMOVAL & INSTALLATION

F-150 and Bronco

▶ **See Figure 41**

1. Unbolt the stabilizer bar from the connecting links.
2. Unbolt the stabilizer bar retainers.
3. If you have to remove the stabilizer bar mounting bracket, remove the coil springs as described above.
4. Installation is the reverse of removal. Torque the retainer nuts to 35 ft. lbs., then torque all other nuts at the links to 70 ft. lbs.

F-250 and F-350

▶ **See Figure 42**

1. Remove the bolts, washers and nuts securing the links to the spring seat caps.   On models with the Monobeam axle, remove the nut, washer and bolt securing the links to the mounting brackets. Remove the nuts, washers and insulators connecting the links to the stabilizer bar. Remove the links.
2. Unbolt and remove the retainers from the mounting brackets.
3. Remove the stabilizer bar.
4. Installation is the reverse of removal. Torque the connecting links-to-spring seat caps to 70 ft. lbs. Torque the nuts securing the connecting links to the stabilizer bar to 25 ft. lbs. Torque the retainer-to-mounting bracket nuts to 35 ft. lbs.

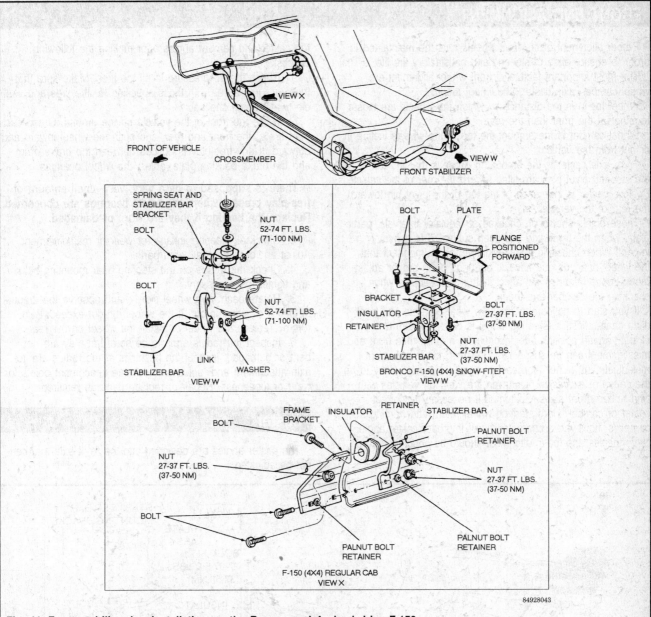

FRONT OF VEHICLE

CROSSMEMBER

VIEW X

VIEW W

FRONT STABILIZER

SPRING SEAT AND
STABILIZER BAR
BRACKET

BOLT

NUT
52-74 FT. LBS.
(71-100 NM)

BOLT

NUT
52-74 FT. LBS.
(71-100 NM)

STABILIZER BAR

LINK

WASHER

VIEW W

BOLT

PLATE

FLANGE
POSITIONED
FORWARD

BRACKET

INSULATOR

RETAINER

BOLT
27-37 FT. LBS.
(37-50 NM)

NUT
27-37 FT. LBS.
(37-50 NM)

STABILIZER BAR

BRONCO F-150 (4X4) SNOW-FITER
VIEW W

FRAME
BRACKET

INSULATOR

RETAINER

STABILIZER BAR

BOLT

PALNUT BOLT
RETAINER

NUT
27-37 FT. LBS.
(37-50 NM)

NUT
27-37 FT. LBS.
(37-50 NM)

BOLT

PALNUT BOLT
RETAINER

PALNUT BOLT
RETAINER

F-150 (4X4) REGULAR CAB
VIEW X

84928043

Fig. 41 Front stabilizer bar installation on the Bronco and 4-wheel drive F-150

FRONT END ALIGNMENT

Proper alignment of the front wheels must be maintained in order to ensure ease of steering and satisfactory tire life.

The most important factors of front wheel alignment are wheel camber, axle caster, and wheel toe-in.

Wheel toe-in is the distance by which the wheels are closer together at the front than the rear.

Wheel camber is the amount the top of the wheels incline in or out from the vertical.

From axle caster is the amount in degrees that the top of the steering pivot pins are tilted toward the rear of the vehicle. Positive caster is inclination of the top of the pivot pin toward the rear of the vehicle.

These points should be checked at regulator intervals, particularly when the front axle has been subjected to a heavy impact. When checking wheel alignment, it is important that the wheel bearings and knuckle bearings be in proper adjustment. Loose bearings will affect instrument readings when checking the camber and toe-in.

If you start to notice abnormal tire wear patterns and handling characteristics (steering wheel is hard to return to the straight ahead position after negotiating a turn), then front end misalignment can be suspected. However, toe-in alignment maladjustment, rather than cast or camber, is more likely to be the cause of excessive or uneven tire wear on vehicles with twin I-beam front axles. Seldom is it necessary to correct caster or camber. Hard steering wheel return after turning a corner is, however, a characteristic of improper caster angle. Nevertheless, the toe-in alignment should be checked before the caster and camber angles after making the following checks:

1. Check the air pressure in all the tires. Make sure that the pressures agree with those specified for the tires and vehicle model being checked.

2. Raise the front of the vehicle off the ground. Grasp each front tire at the front and rear, and push the wheel inward and outward. If any free-play is noticed between the brake drum and the brake backing plate, adjust the wheel bearings.

➡**There is supposed to be a very, very small amount of free-play present where the wheel bearings are concerned. Replace the bearing if they are worn or damaged.**

3. Check all steering linkage for wear or maladjustment. Adjust and/or replace all worn parts.

4. Check the torque on the steering gear mounting bolts and tighten as necessary.

5. Rotate each front wheel slowly, and observe the amount of lateral or side run-out. If the wheel run-out exceeds ⅛in. (3mm), replace the wheel or install the wheel on the rear.

6. Inspect the radius arms to be sure that they are not bent or damaged. Inspect the bushings at the radius arm-to-axle attachment and radius arm-to-frame attachment points for wear or looseness. Repair or replace parts as required.

Caster

The caster angles are designed into the front axle and cannot be adjusted.

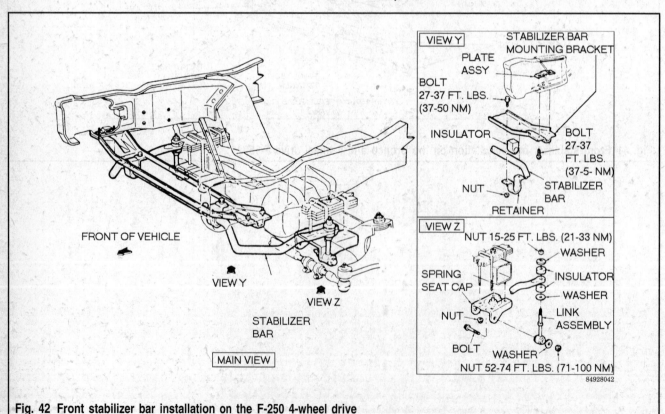

Fig. 42 Front stabilizer bar installation on the F-250 4-wheel drive

Camber

The camber angles are designed into the front axle and cannot be adjusted.

Toe-in Adjustment

ALL MODELS

Toe-in can be measured by using either a front end alignment machine or as follows. With the front wheels in the straight ahead position, measure the distance between the extreme front and the extreme rear of the front wheels. In other words, measure the distance across the undercarriage of the vehicle between the two front edges and the two rear edges of the two front wheels. Both of these measurements (front and rear of the two wheels) must be taken at an equal distance from the floor and at the approximate centerline of the spindle. The difference between these two distances is the amount that the wheels toe-in or toe-out. The wheels should be always adjusted to toe-in according to specifications.

1. Loosen the clamp bolts at each end of the left tie rod, seen from the front of the vehicle. Rotate the connecting rod tube until the correct toe-in is obtained, then tighten the clamp bolts.

2. Recheck the toe-in to make sure that no changes occurred when the bolts were tightened.

➡ **The clamps should be positioned 3/16 in. (5mm) from the end of the rod with the clamp bolts in a vertical position in front of the tube, with the nut down.**

WHEEL ALIGNMENT SPECIFICATIONS
1987–88 F-150 4x2

Ride Height (mm)	Caster (deg.) Range	Pref.	Camber (deg.) Range	Pref.	Toe-in (in.)	Front Wheel Angle (deg.)
80–90	5½P to 7½P	6¼P	1⅛N to 1¼P	0	1/32	12.5
90–100	4¼P to 7¼P	5¾P	½N to 2P	¾P	1/32	12.5
100–110	3¼P to 6¼P	4¾P	½P to 3P	1¾P	1/32	12.5
110–120	2⅜P to 5⅜P	3⅞P	1½P to 3½P	2¾P	1/32	12.5
120–130	1½P to 4½P	3P	2⅜P to 4⅜P	3⅜P	1/32	12.5
130–140	⅜P to 3⅜P	1⅞P	3⅜P to 5½P	4 7/16 P	1/32	12.5

Caster and Camber are determined based on ride height.
For all 2-wheel drive models, ride height is the measured distance between the bottom of the front spring tower and the top of the front axle beam, measured at the rebound bumper.

84928186

WHEEL ALIGNMENT SPECIFICATIONS
1987–88 F-150 4x4 and Bronco

Ride Height (mm)	Caster (deg.)		Camber (deg.)		Toe-in (in.)	Front Wheel Angle (deg.)
	Range	Pref.	Range	Pref.		
80–90	5P to 8P	6$\frac{1}{2}$P	1$\frac{1}{2}$N to $\frac{1}{2}$P	$\frac{1}{2}$N	$\frac{1}{32}$	13.0
90–100	4P to 7P	5$\frac{1}{2}$P	$\frac{3}{4}$N to 1$\frac{3}{4}$P	$\frac{1}{2}$P	$\frac{1}{32}$	13.0
100–110	3P to 6P	4$\frac{1}{2}$P	$\frac{1}{4}$P to 2$\frac{1}{2}$P	1$\frac{1}{2}$P	$\frac{1}{32}$	13.0
110–120	2P to 5P	3$\frac{1}{2}$P	1$\frac{1}{4}$P to 3$\frac{1}{2}$P	2$\frac{3}{8}$P	$\frac{1}{32}$	13.0

Caster and Camber are determined based on ride height.
For the F-150 4x4, ride height is the measured distance between the bottom of the front spring tower and the top of the front axle tube, measured at the rebound bumper.

84928187

WHEEL ALIGNMENT SPECIFICATIONS
1987–88 F-250 and F350 4x2

Ride Height (mm)	Caster (deg.)		Camber (deg.)		Toe-in (in.)	Front Wheel Angle (deg.)
	Range	Pref.	Range	Pref.		
70–80	—	—	2$\frac{7}{10}$N to $\frac{1}{2}$N	$\frac{3}{4}$N	$\frac{1}{32}$	12.5
80–90	7$\frac{1}{2}$P to 10$\frac{1}{2}$P	9P	1$\frac{1}{2}$N to $\frac{1}{2}$P	$\frac{1}{2}$N	$\frac{1}{32}$	12.5
90–100	6$\frac{1}{2}$P to 10P	8$\frac{1}{4}$P	2N to $\frac{1}{2}$P	1$\frac{1}{2}$N	$\frac{1}{32}$	12.5
100–110	5$\frac{3}{4}$P to 8$\frac{3}{4}$P	7$\frac{1}{4}$P	$\frac{1}{4}$P to 2$\frac{1}{2}$P	1$\frac{3}{8}$P	$\frac{1}{32}$	12.5
110–120	4$\frac{3}{4}$P to 7$\frac{3}{4}$P	6$\frac{1}{4}$P	1P to 4P	2$\frac{1}{2}$P	$\frac{1}{32}$	12.5
120–130	3$\frac{1}{2}$P to 6$\frac{3}{4}$P	4$\frac{7}{8}$P	2$\frac{1}{2}$P to 5P	3$\frac{3}{4}$P	$\frac{1}{32}$	12.5
130–140	2$\frac{3}{4}$P to 5$\frac{1}{2}$P	4$\frac{1}{8}$P	—	—	$\frac{1}{32}$	12.5

Caster and Camber are determined based on ride height.
For all 2-wheel drive models, ride height is the measured distance between the bottom of the front spring tower and the top of the front axle beam, measured at the rebound bumper.

84928188

WHEEL ALIGNMENT SPECIFICATIONS
1987–88 F-250 4x4

Ride Height (mm)	Caster (deg.)		Camber (deg.)		Toe-in (in.)	Front Wheel Angle (deg.)
	Range	Pref.	Range	Pref.		
125–140	3¹/₁₆P to 5¹/₈P	4¹/₈P	1³/₄N to ⁵/₈P	⁹/₁₆P	¹/₃₂	13.0
140–150	3¹/₄P to 5¹/₄P	4¹/₄P	³/₄N to 1³/₄P	¹/₂P	¹/₃₂	13.0
150–160	3³/₈P to 5³/₈P	4³/₈P	³/₈P to 3P	1¹¹/₁₆P	¹/₃₂	13.0
160–175	3⁷/₁₆P to 5¹/₂P	4¹⁹/₂₃P	1¹/₂P to 4¹/₄P	2³/₄P	¹/₃₂	13.0

Caster and Camber are determined based on ride height.

For the F-250 4x4, ride height is the measured distance between the bottom of the frame and the top of the front axle tube, measured at the rebound bumper.

84928189

WHEEL ALIGNMENT SPECIFICATIONS
1987–88 F-350 4x4

Ride Height (mm)	Caster (deg.)		Camber (deg.)		Toe-in (in.)	Front Wheel Angle (deg.)
	Range	Pref.	Range	Pref.		
95.25–111.75	6¹/₄P to 10P	8¹/₈P	³/₄N to 1¹/₂P	³/₄P	¹/₃₂	8
111.75–124.5	5P to 8¹/₄P	6⁵/₈P	¹/₄P to 2¹/₂P	1³/₈P	¹/₃₂	8
124.5–137.2	3³/₄P to 7P	5¹/₄P	1¹/₄P to 3¹/₂P	2³/₈P	¹/₃₂	8
137.2–146.0	3¹/₄P to 5³/₄P	4¹/₂P	2³/₈P to 4¹/₈P	3¹/₄P	¹/₃₂	8

Caster and Camber are determined based on ride height.

For the F-350 4x4, ride height is the measured distance between the bottom of the metal rebound stop to the top of the front spring plate spacer.

84928190

WHEEL ALIGNMENT SPECIFICATIONS
1987–88 F-Super Duty
(Caster and camber angles are not adjustable)

Ride Height (mm)	Caster (deg.)		Camber (deg.)		Toe-in (in.)	Front Wheel Angle (deg.)
	Range	Pref.	Range	Pref.		
108.0	—	5¹/₄P	—	³/₅P	¹/₃₂	9.6

For the F-Super Duty, ride height is the measured distance between the bottom of the metal rebound stop to the top fo the front spring plate spacer.

84928191

WHEEL ALIGNMENT SPECIFICATIONS
1989-93 ①

Models	Years	Caster (deg.) Range	Pref.	Camber (deg.) Range	Pref.	Toe (in.)
F-150 4x2	1989	1½P-4½P	—	0-1½P	—	0.2 out to 0.3 in
	1990	1P-4½P	—	½N-1½P	—	0.2 out to 0.3 in
	1991	2P-6P	—	—	¼P	0.03
	1992	2P-6P	—	—	¼P	0.09 out to 0.16 in
	1993	2P-6P	—	—	¼P	0.09 out to 0.16 in
F-250 4x2	1989	1½P-4½P	—	0-1½P	—	0.2 out to 0.3 in
	1990	1P-4½P	—	½N-1½P	—	0.2 out to 0.3 in
	1991	2P-6P	—	—	¼P	0.03
	1992	2P-6P	—	—	¼P	0.09 out to 0.16 in
	1993	2P-6P	—	—	¼P	0.09 out to 0.16 in
F-350 4x2	1989	1½P-4½P	—	0-1½P	—	0.2 out to 0.3 in
	1990	1P-4½P	—	½N-1½P	—	0.2 out to 0.3 in
	1991	②	—	—	½P	0.03
	1992	②	—	—	½P	0.09 out to 0.16 in
	1993	②	—	—	½P	0.09 out to 0.16 in
F-150 4x4/Bronco	1989	1P-4P	—	0-2P	—	0.16 in to 0.09 out
	1990	1P-4P	—	0-2P	—	0.3 in to 0.2 out
	1991	2P-6P	—	—	¼P	0.06
	1992	2P-6P	—	—	¼P	0.09 out to 0.16 in
	1993	2P-6P	—	—	¼P	0.09 out to 0.16 in
F-250 4x4	1989	1½P-4½P	—	0-2P	—	0.16 in to 0.09 out
	1990	1½P-4½P	—	0-2P	—	0.3 in to 0.2 out
	1991	2P-5P	—	—	¼P	0.5 out
	1992	2P-5P	—	—	¼P	0.09 out to 0.16 in
	1993	2P-5P	—	—	¼P	0.09 out to 0.16 in
F-350 4x4	1989	1½P-4½P	—	0-2P	—	0.16 in to 0.09 out
	1990	1½P-4½P	—	0-2P	—	0.3 in to 0.2 out
	1991	2P-4¾P	—	—	0	0.5 out
	1992	2P-4¾P	—	—	0	0.09 out to 0.16 in
	1993	2P-4¾P	—	—	0	0.09 out to 0.16 in
F-Super Duty	1989	1½P-4½P	—	0-2P	—	0.16 in to 0.09 out
	1990	1½P-4½P	—	0-2P	—	0.3 in to 0.2 out
	1991	2P-5P	—	—	0	0.3 in
	1992	2P-5P	—	—	0	0.09 out to 0.16 in
	1993	2P-5P	—	—	0	0.09 out to 0.16 in
F-Super Duty Stripped Chassis	All	2P-5½P	—	—	⅗P	0.03 in

① Vehicles without permanent aftermarket
   modifications
② Single rear wheels: 2P-6P
   Dual rear wheels: 2P-4½P

84928192

REAR SUSPENSION

Semi-elliptic, leaf type springs are used at the rear axle. The front end of the spring is attached to a spring bracket on the frame side member. The rear end of the spring is attached to the bracket on the frame side member with a shackle. Each spring is attached to the axle with two U-bolts. A spacer is located between the spring and the axle on some applications to obtain a level ride position.

Springs

REMOVAL & INSTALLATION

▶ **See Figures 43, 44, 45 and 46**

1. Raise the vehicle by the frame until the weight is off the rear spring with the tires still on the floor.
2. Remove the nuts from the spring U-bolts and drive the U-bolts from the U-bolt plate. Remove the auxiliary spring and spacer, if so equipped.
3. Remove the spring-to-bracket nut and bolt at the front of the spring.
4. Remove the upper and lower shackle nuts and bolts at the rear of the spring and remove the spring and shackle assembly from the rear shackle bracket.
5. Remove the bushings in the spring or shackle, if they are worn or damaged, and install new ones.

➡**When installing the components, snug down the fasteners. Don't apply final torque to the fasteners until the truck is back on the ground.**

6. Position the spring in the shackle and install the upper shackle-to-spring nut and bolt with the bolt head facing outward.
7. Position the front end of the spring in the bracket and install the nut and bolt.
8. Position the shackle in the rear bracket and install the nut and bolt.
9. Position the spring on top of the axle with the spring center bolts centered in the hole provided in the seat. Install the auxiliary spring and spacer, if so equipped.
10. Install the spring U-bolts, plate and nuts.
11. Lower the vehicle to the floor and tighten the attaching hardware as follows:**U-bolts nuts:**
  • Bronco, F-150 and F-250 under 8,500 lb. GVW: 75-115 ft. lbs.
  • F-250 HD and F-350: 150-210 ft. lbs.
  • F-Super Duty chassis/cab: 200-270 ft. lbs.
  • F-Super Duty stripped chassis and motor home chassis: 220-300 ft. lbs. **Spring to front spring hanger:**
  • F-150 2-wd: 75-115 ft. lbs.
  • F-250 2-wd, F-350 2-wd and Bronco: 150-210 ft. lbs.
  • F-150, 250, 350 4-wd: 150-175 ft. lbs.
  • F-Super Duty: 255-345 ft. lbs. **Spring to rear spring hanger:**
  • All except F-250 and F-350 2-wd Chassis Cab: 75-115 ft. lbs.
  • F-250 and F-350 2-wd Chassis Cab; F-Super Duty: 150-210 ft. lbs.

ADJUSTMENTS

Side-to-side lean can be adjusted by about ⅜ in. (10mm) by installing a shim between the spring and axle on the low side. A truck that is low in the rear on both sides can be similarly raised by the insertion of 1 shim on each side.

If the side-to-side lean is greater than ½ in., try switch the springs from one side to the other.

Shock Absorbers

TESTING

Check, inspect and test the rear shock absorbers in the same manner as outlined for the front shock absorbers.

REMOVAL & INSTALLATION

▶ **See Figures 47, 48 and 49**

1. Raise and support the rear end on jackstands.
2. Remove the self-locking nut, steel washer and bolt from the lower end of the shock absorber. Swing the lower end away from the bracket.
3. Remove the upper mounting nut and washer.
To install:
4. Attach the upper end first, then the lower end; don't tighten the nuts yet. If you are installing new gas shocks, attach the upper end loosely, aim the lower end at its bracket and cut the strap holding the shock compressed. Once extended, these shocks are very difficult to compress by hand!
5. Once the upper and lower ends are attached, tighten the nuts, for all models, as follows:
  • Lower end, except Super Duty stripped chassis and motor home chassis: 52-74 ft. lbs.
  • Upper end, except Super Duty stripped chassis and motor home chassis: 40-60 ft. lbs.
  • Super Duty stripped chassis and motor home chassis upper and lower ends: 220-300 ft. lbs.

Stabilizer Bar

REMOVAL & INSTALLATION

▶ **See Figures 50, 51, 52 and 53**

1. Remove the nuts from the lower ends of the stabilizer bar link.
2. Remove the outer washers and insulators.
3. Disconnect the bar from the links.
4. Remove the inner insulators and washers.
5. Unbolt the link from the frame.
6. Remove the U-bolts, brackets and retainers.

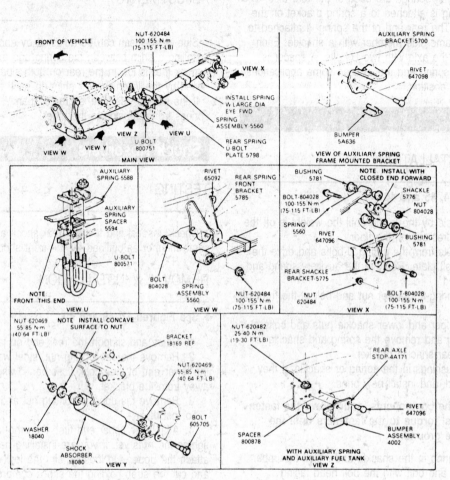

Fig. 43 2-wheel drive F-150 rear spring installation

7. Installation is the reverse of removal. Replace all worn or cracked rubber parts. Coat all new rubber parts with silicone grease. Assemble all parts loosely and make sure the bar assembly is centered before tightening the fasteners. Observe the following torque figures:

- Stabilizer bar-to-axle nut, except Super Duty: 30-42 ft. lbs.
- Stabilizer bar-to-axle bolt, Super Duty chassis/cab: 27-37 ft. lbs.

- Stabilizer bar-to-axle bolt, Super Duty stripped chassis and motor home chassis: 30-47 ft. lbs.
- Link bracket-to-frame nut, 4-wd: 30-42 ft. lbs.
- Link-to-bracket nut, 4-wd: 60 ft. lbs.
- Link-to-frame nut, 2-wd: 60 ft. lbs.
- Stabilizer bar-to-link: 15-25 ft. lbs.

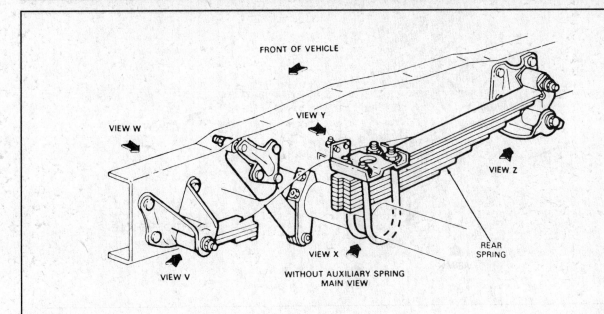

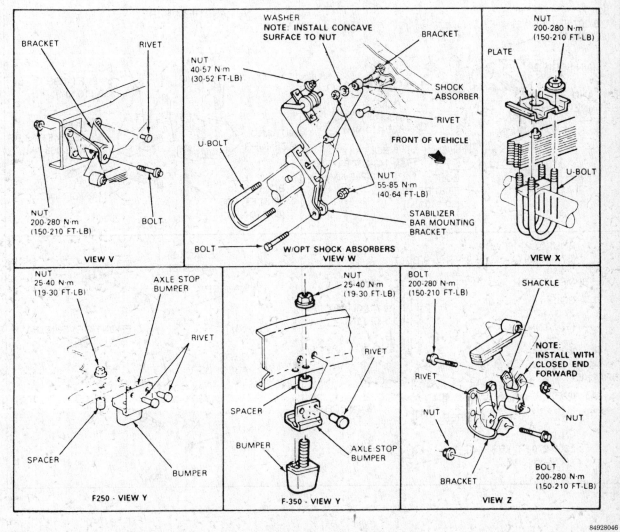

Fig. 44 Rear spring installation for F-250, 350 2-wheel Chassis Cab w/Dana axles

84928046

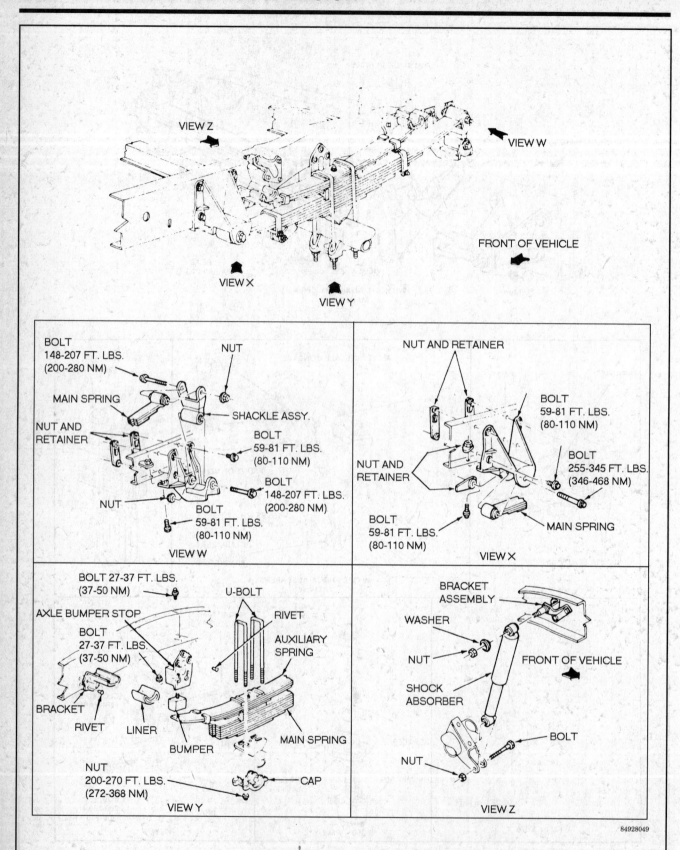

Fig. 45 Rear spring installation for F-Super Duty chassis/cab

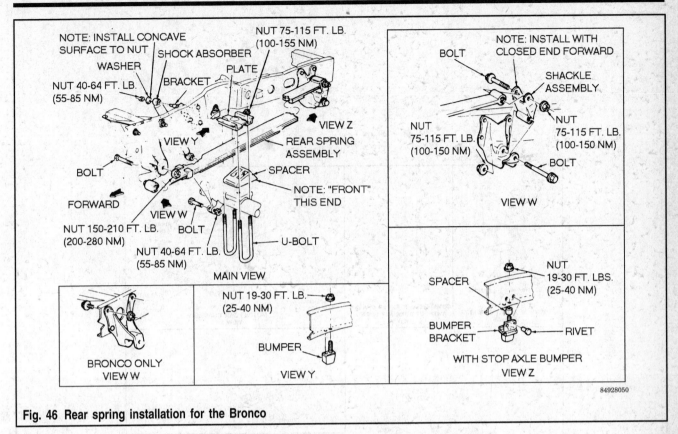

Fig. 46 Rear spring installation for the Bronco

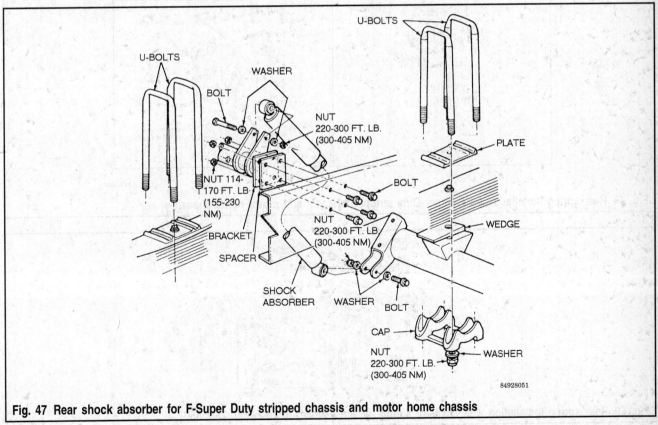

Fig. 47 Rear shock absorber for F-Super Duty stripped chassis and motor home chassis

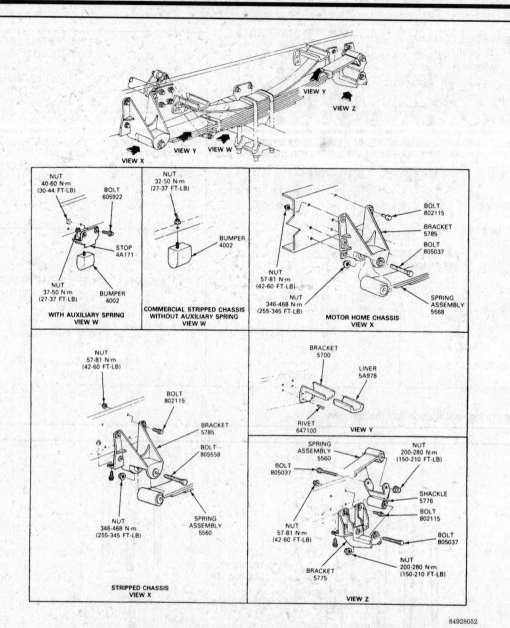

Fig. 48 Rear spring installation for F-Super Duty stripped chassis and motor home chassis

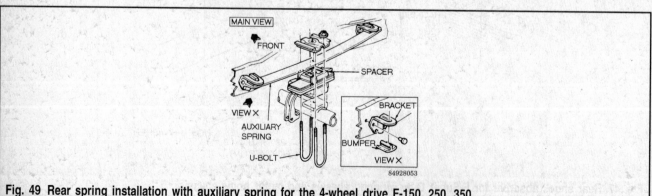

Fig. 49 Rear spring installation with auxiliary spring for the 4-wheel drive F-150, 250, 350

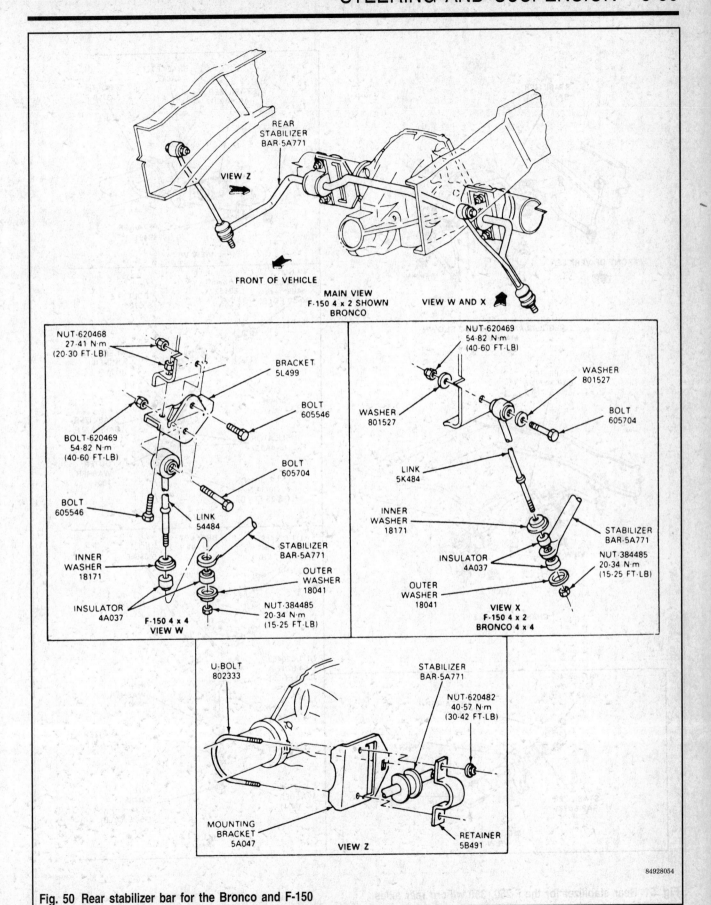

REAR STABILIZER BAR·5A771

VIEW Z

FRONT OF VEHICLE

MAIN VIEW
F-150 4 x 2 SHOWN
BRONCO

VIEW W AND X

NUT·620468
27·41 N·m
(20·30 FT·LB)

BRACKET
5L499

BOLT
605546

BOLT·620469
54·82 N·m
(40·60 FT·LB)

BOLT
605704

BOLT
605546

LINK
54484

STABILIZER
BAR·5A771

INNER
WASHER
18171

OUTER
WASHER
18041

INSULATOR
4A037

NUT·384485
20·34 N·m
(15·25 FT·LB)

F-150 4 x 4
VIEW W

NUT·620469
54·82 N·m
(40·60 FT·LB)

WASHER
801527

WASHER
801527

BOLT
605704

LINK
5K484

INNER
WASHER
18171

STABILIZER
BAR·5A771

INSULATOR
4A037

NUT·384485
20·34 N·m
(15·25 FT·LB)

OUTER
WASHER
18041

VIEW X
F-150 4 x 2
BRONCO 4 x 4

U-BOLT
802333

STABILIZER
BAR·5A771

NUT·620482
40·57 N·m
(30·42 FT·LB)

MOUNTING
BRACKET
5A047

RETAINER
5B491

VIEW Z

84928054

Fig. 50 Rear stabilizer bar for the Bronco and F-150

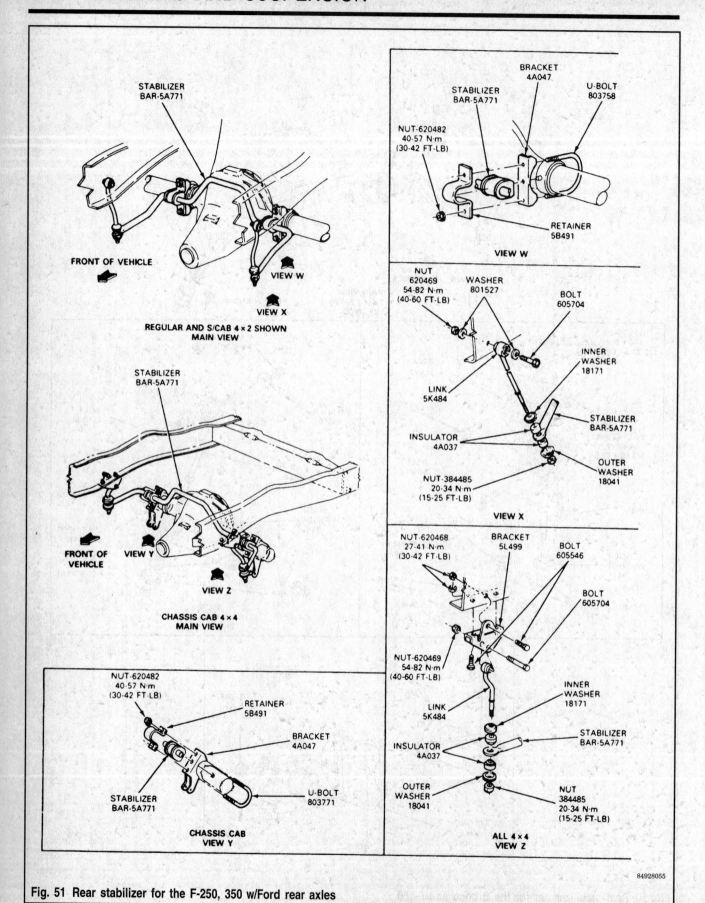

Fig. 51 Rear stabilizer for the F-250, 350 w/Ford rear axles

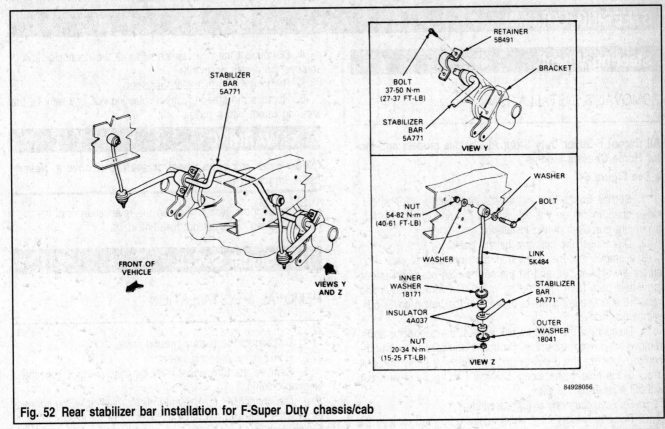

Fig. 52 Rear stabilizer bar installation for F-Super Duty chassis/cab

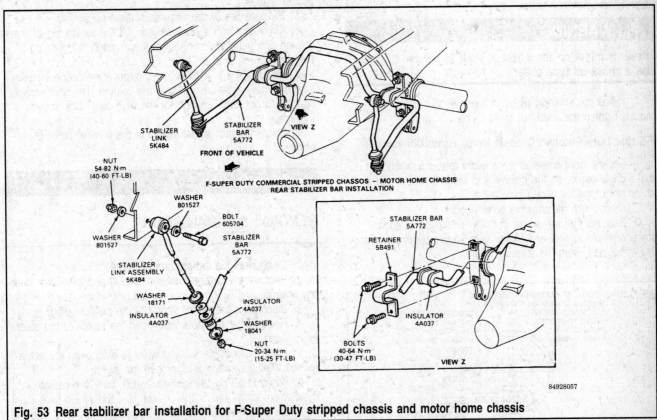

Fig. 53 Rear stabilizer bar installation for F-Super Duty stripped chassis and motor home chassis

STEERING COLUMN

Steering Wheel

REMOVAL & INSTALLATION

All Except F-Super Duty Stripped Chassis models and Motor Home Chassis Models

▶ **See Figure 54**

1. Set the front wheel in the straight ahead position and make chalk marks on the column and steering wheel hub for alignment purposes during installation.
2. Disconnect the negative battery cable.
3. Remove the one screw from the underside of each steering wheel spoke, and lift the horn switch assembly (steering wheel pad) from the steering wheel. On vehicles equipped with the sport steering wheel option, pry the button cover off with a screwdriver.
4. Disconnect the horn switch wires at the connector and remove the switch assembly. On trucks equipped with speed control, squeeze the J-clip ground wire terminal firmly and pull it out of the hole in the steering wheel. Don't pull the wire out without squeezing the clip.
5. Remove the horn switch assembly.
6. Remove the steering wheel retaining nut and remove the steering wheel with a puller.

✳✳WARNING

Never hammer on the wheel or shaft to remove it! Never use a knock-off type puller.

7. Install the steering wheel in the reverse order of removal. Tighten the shaft nut to 40 ft. lbs.

F-Super Duty Stripped Chassis Motor Home Chassis

1. Set the front wheel in the straight ahead position and make chalk marks on the column and steering wheel hub for alignment purposes during installation.
2. Disconnect the negative battery cable.
3. Remove the one screw from the underside of each steering wheel spoke, and lift the horn switch assembly (steering wheel pad) from the steering wheel.

4. Disconnect the horn switch wires at the connector and remove the switch assembly.
5. Remove the horn switch assembly.
6. Remove the steering wheel retaining nut and remove the steering wheel with a puller.

✳✳WARNING

Never hammer on the wheel or shaft to remove it! Never use a knock-off type puller.

7. Install the steering wheel in the reverse order of removal. Tighten the shaft nut to 30-42 ft. lbs.

Turn Signal Switch

REMOVAL & INSTALLATION

1. Disconnect the battery ground cable.
2. Remove the steering wheel.
3. Remove the turn signal lever by unscrewing it from the steering column.
4. Disconnect the turn signal indicator switch wiring connector plug by lifting up the tabs on the side of the plug and pulling it apart.
5. Remove the switch assembly attaching screws.
6. On trucks with a fixed column, lift the switch out of the column and guide the connector plug through the opening in the shift socket.
7. On trucks with a tilt column, remove the connector plug before removing the switch from the column. The shift socket opening is not large enough for the plug connector to pass through.
8. Install the turn signal switch in the reverse order of removal.

Ignition Switch

REMOVAL & INSTALLATION

1. Disconnect the battery ground cable.
2. Remove the steering column shroud and lower the steering column.
3. Disconnect the switch wiring at the multiple plug.
4. Remove the two nuts that retain the switch to the steering column.
5. Lift the switch vertically upward to disengage the actuator rod from the switch and remove the switch.
6. When installing the ignition switch, both the locking mechanism at the top of the column and the switch itself must be in the LOCK position for correct adjustment. To hold the mechanical parts of the column in the LOCK position, move the shift lever into PARK (with automatic transmissions) or REVERSE (with manual transmissions), turn the key to the LOCK position, and remove the key. New replacement

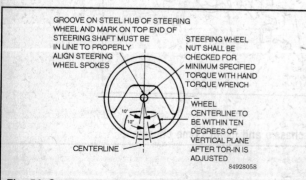

Fig. 54 Correct steering wheel installation

GROOVE ON STEEL HUB OF STEERING WHEEL AND MARK ON TOP END OF STEERING SHAFT MUST BE IN LINE TO PROPERLY ALIGN STEERING WHEEL SPOKES

STEERING WHEEL NUT SHALL BE CHECKED FOR MINIMUM SPECIFIED TORQUE WITH HAND TORQUE WRENCH

WHEEL CENTERLINE TO BE WITHIN TEN DEGREES OF VERTICAL PLANE AFTER TOR-IN IS ADJUSTED

CENTERLINE

84928058

switches, when received, are already pinned in the LOCK position by a metal shipping pin inserted in a locking hole on the side of the switch.

7. Engage the actuator rod in the switch.

8. Position the switch on the column and install the retaining nuts, but do not tighten them.

9. Move the switch up and down along the column to locate the mid-position of rod lash, and then tighten the retaining nuts.

10. Remove the locking pin, connect the battery cable, and check for proper start in PARK or NEUTRAL.   Also check to make certain that the start circuit cannot be actuated in the DRIVE and REVERSE position.

11. Raise the steering column into position at instrument panel. Install steering column shroud.

Ignition Lock Cylinder

REMOVAL & INSTALLATION

With Key

1. Disconnect the battery ground.

2. On tilt columns, remove the upper extension shroud by unsnapping the shroud from the retaining clip at the 9 o'clock position.

3. Remove the trim shroud halves.

4. Unplug the wire connector at the key warning switch.

5. Place the shift lever in PARK and turn the key to ON.

6. Place a 1/8in. (3mm) wire pin in the hole in the casting surrounding the lock cylinder and depress the retaining pin while pulling out on the cylinder.

7. When installing the cylinder, turn the lock cylinder to the RUN position and depress the retaining pin, then insert the lock cylinder into its housing in the flange casting. Assure that the cylinder is fully seated and aligned in the interlocking washer before turning the key to the OFF position. This will allow the cylinder retaining pin to extend into the cylinder cast housing hole.

8. The remainder of installation is the reverse of removal.

Non-Functioning Cylinder or No Key Available

FIXED COLUMNS

1. Disconnect the battery ground.

2. Remove the steering wheel.

3. Remove the turn signal lever.

4. Remove the column trim shrouds.

5. Unbolt the steering column and lower it carefully.

6. Remove the ignition switch and warning buzzer and pin the switch in the LOCK position.

7. Remove the turn signal switch.

8. Remove the snaping and T-bolt nuts that retain the flange casting to the column outer tube.

9. Remove the flange casting, upper shaft bearing, lock cylinder, ignition switch actuator and the actuator rod by pulling the entire assembly over the end of the steering column shaft.

10. Remove the lock actuator insert, the T-bolts and the automatic transmission indicator insert, or, with manual transmissions, the key release lever.

11. Upon reassembly, the following parts must be replaced with new parts:
- Flange
- Lock cylinder assembly
- Steering column lock gear
- Steering column lock bearing
- Steering column upper bearing retainer
- Lock actuator assembly

12. Assembly is a reversal of the disassembly procedure. It is best to install a new upper bearing. Check that the truck starts only in PARK and NEUTRAL.

TILT COLUMNS

▶ **See Figures 55, 56, 57, 58 and 59**

1. Disconnect the battery ground.

2. Remove the steering column shrouds.

3. Using masking tape, tape the gap between the steering wheel hub and the cover casting. Cover the entire circumference of the casting. Cover the seat and floor area with a dropcloth.

4. Pull out the hazard switch and tape it in a downward position.

5. The lock cylinder retaining pin is located on the outside of the steering column cover casting adjacent to the hazard flasher button.

6. Tilt the steering column to the full up position and prepunch the lock cylinder retaining pin with a sharp punch.

7. Using a 1/8in. (3mm) drill bit, mounted in a right angle drive drill adapter, drill out the retaining pin, going no deeper than 1/2 in. (13mm).

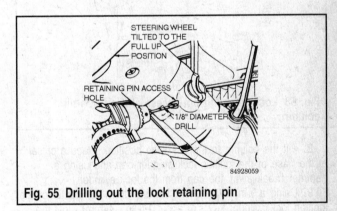

Fig. 55 Drilling out the lock retaining pin

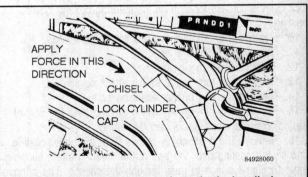

Fig. 56 Breaking the cap away from the lock cylinder

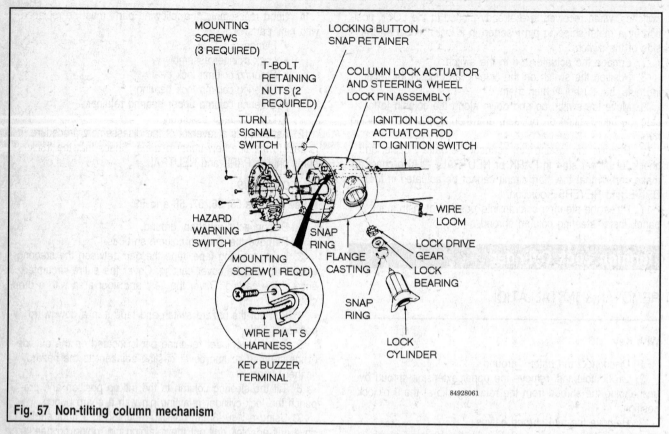

MOUNTING SCREWS (3 REQUIRED)

T-BOLT RETAINING NUTS (2 REQUIRED)

TURN SIGNAL SWITCH

LOCKING BUTTON SNAP RETAINER

COLUMN LOCK ACTUATOR AND STEERING WHEEL LOCK PIN ASSEMBLY

IGNITION LOCK ACTUATOR ROD TO IGNITION SWITCH

HAZARD WARNING SWITCH

MOUNTING SCREW(1 REQ'D)

WIRE PIA T S HARNESS

KEY BUZZER TERMINAL

SNAP RING

FLANGE CASTING

SNAP RING

WIRE LOOM

LOCK DRIVE GEAR

LOCK BEARING

LOCK CYLINDER

84928061

Fig. 57 Non-tilting column mechanism

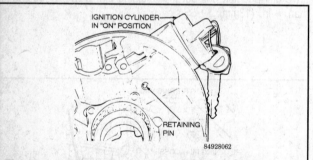

IGNITION CYLINDER IN "ON" POSITION

RETAINING PIN

84928062

Fig. 58 Lock retaining pin access slot on non-tilt column

8. Tilt the column to the full down position. Place a chisel at the base of the ignition lock cylinder cap and using a hammer break away the cap from the lock cylinder.

9. Using a ³⁄₈in. (10mm) drill bit, drill down the center of the ignition lock cylinder key slot about 1³⁄₄ in. (44mm), until the lock cylinder breaks loose from the steering column cover casting.

10. Remove the lock cylinder and the drill shavings.

11. Remove the steering wheel.

12. Remove the turn signal lever.

13. Remove the turn signal switch attaching screws.

14. Remove the key buzzer attaching screw.

15. Remove the turn signal switch up and over the end of the column, but don't disconnect the wiring.

16. Remove the 4 attaching screws from the cover casting and lift the casting over the end of the steering shaft, allowing the turn signal switch to pass through the casting. The removal

of the casting cover will expose the upper actuator. Remove the upper actuator.

17. Remove the drive gear, snapring and washer from the cover casting along with the upper actuator.

18. Clean all components and replace any that appear damaged or worn.

19. Installation is the reverse of removal.

Steering Column

REMOVAL & INSTALLATION

All Models Except F-Super Duty Stripped Chassis and Motor Home Chassis

▶ **See Figures 60 and 61**

1. Set the parking brake.
2. Disconnect the battery ground cable.
3. Unbolt the intermediate shaft from the steering column.
4. Disconnect the shift linkage rod(s) from the column.
5. Remove the steering wheel.

➡**If you have a tilt column, the steering wheel MUST be in the full UP position when it is removed.**

6. Remove the floor cover screws at the base of the column.

7. Remove the steering column shroud by place the bottom screw in the No.1 position and pulling the shroud up and away from the column.

8. On automatics, remove the shift indicator cable.

9. Remove the instrument panel column opening cover.

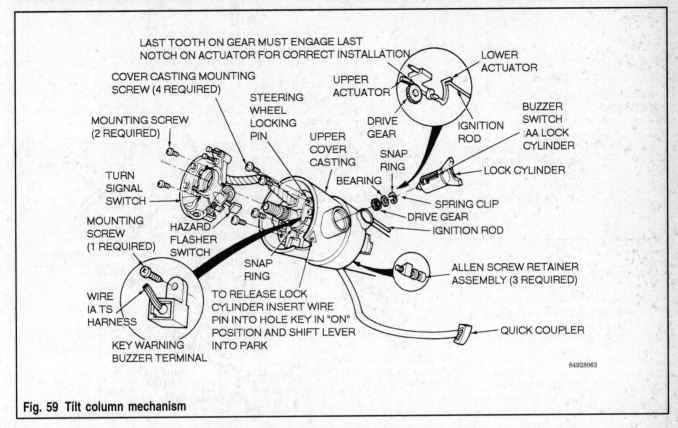

Fig. 59 Tilt column mechanism

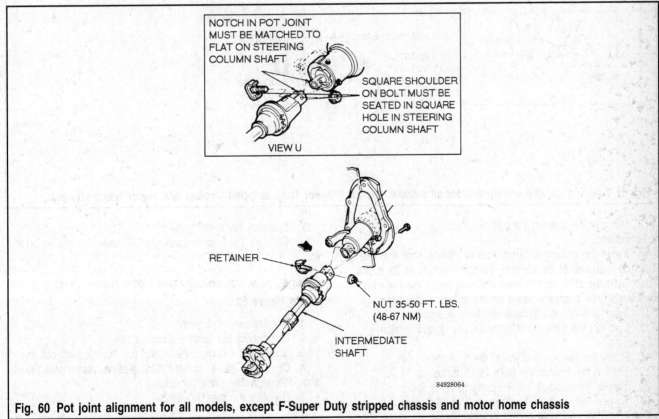

Fig. 60 Pot joint alignment for all models, except F-Super Duty stripped chassis and motor home chassis

10. Remove the bolts securing the column support bracket to the pedal support bracket.

11. Disconnect the turn signal/hazard warning harness and the ignition switch harness.

12. Lift the column from the truck.

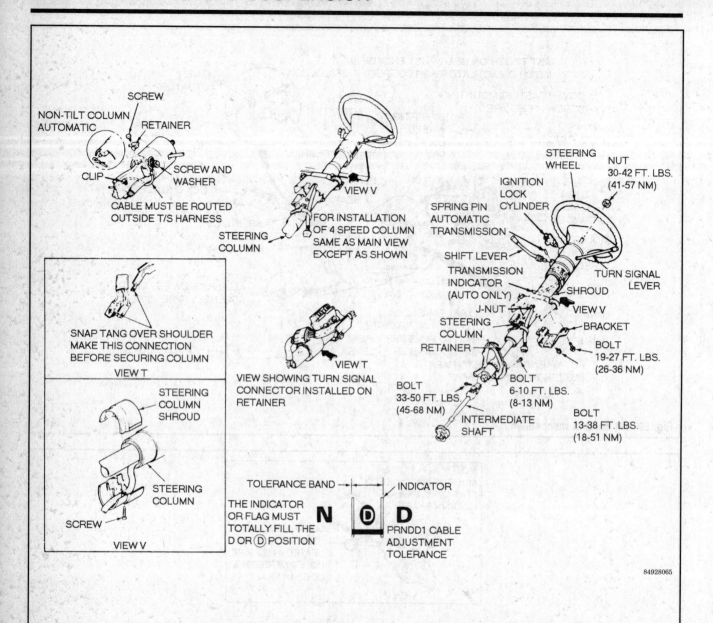

Fig. 61 Steering column installation for all models, except F-Super Duty stripped chassis and motor home chassis

13. Remove the column support bracket

To install:

14. Install the column support bracket making sure that the wiring is outboard of the column. Torque the nuts to 35 ft. lbs.

15. Start the floor cover clamp bolt and press the plate until the clamp flats touch the stops on the column outer tube.

16. Install the column through the floor opening.

17. Connect the turn signal/hazard warning and ignition harnesses.

18. Raise the column and install the 2 support bolts.

19. Tighten the floor cover bolts to 10 ft. lbs.

20. Torque the support bracket bolts to 25 ft. lbs.

21. Torque the cover plate clamp bolt to 18 ft. lbs.

22. Install and adjust the shift indicator cable, on automatics.

23. Install the instrument panel column opening cover.

24. Install the column shroud.

25. Torque the shroud bottom screw to 15 inch lbs.

26. Connect the shifter rod(s).

27. Connect the intermediate shaft. Torque the bolt to 50 ft. lbs.

F-Super Duty Stripped Chassis Motor Home Chassis

▶ See Figure 62

1. Set the parking brake.

2. Disconnect the battery ground cable.

3. Unbolt the intermediate shaft from the steering column.

4. On trucks with automatic transmission, disconnect the shift linkage rod(s) from the column.

5. Remove the steering wheel.

➡**If you have a tilt column, the steering wheel MUST be in the full UP position when it is removed.**

6. Disconnect the turn signal/hazard warning harness and the ignition switch and horn harnesses.

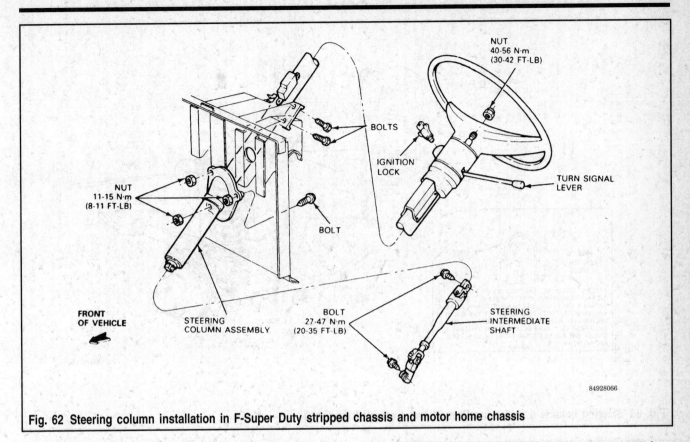

Fig. 62 Steering column installation in F-Super Duty stripped chassis and motor home chassis

7. Remove the floor cover screws at the base of the column.

8. Remove the column-to-support bracket bolts and lift the column from the truck.

To install:

9. Install the column through the floor opening.

10. Connect the wiring harnesses.

11. Raise the column and install the 2 support bolts.

12. Torque the column-to-support bracket bolts to 19-27 ft. lbs.

13. Connect the intermediate shaft. Torque the bolt to 20-35 ft. lbs.

14. Tighten the floor cover bolts to 10 ft. lbs.

15. Connect the shifter rod(s).

16. Install the steering wheel.

STEERING LINKAGE

▶ See Figures 63, 64, 65 and 66

Pitman Arm

REMOVAL & INSTALLATION

All Models Except F-Super Duty Stripped Chassis and Motor Home Chassis.

1. Place the wheels in a straight-ahead position.

2. Disconnect the drag link at the pitman arm. You'll need a puller such as a tie rod end remover.

3. Remove the pitman arm-to-gear nut and washer.

4. Matchmark the pitman arm and gear housing for installation purposes.

5. Using a 2-jawed puller, remove the pitman arm from the gear.

6. Installation is the reverse of removal. Align the matchmarks when installing the pitman arm. Torque the pitman arm nut to 170-230 ft. lbs.; torque the drag link ball stud nut to 50-75 ft. lbs., advancing the nut to align the cotter pin hole. Never back off the nut to align the hole.

F-Super Duty Stripped Chassis Motor Home Chassis

1. Matchmark the pitman arm and sector shaft.

2. Disconnect the drag link from the pitman arm.

3. Remove the bolt and nut securing the pitman arm to the sector shaft.

4. Using a 2-jawed gear puller, remove the pitman arm from the sector shaft.

To install:

5. Aligning the matchmarks, slide the pitman arm onto the sector shaft. If the arm won't slide on easily, use a cold chisel to spread the separation. NEVER HAMMER THE ARM ONTO THE SHAFT! Hammering on the arm will damage the steering gear!

6. Install the nut and bolt. Torque the nut to 220-300 ft. lbs.

7. Connect the drag link.

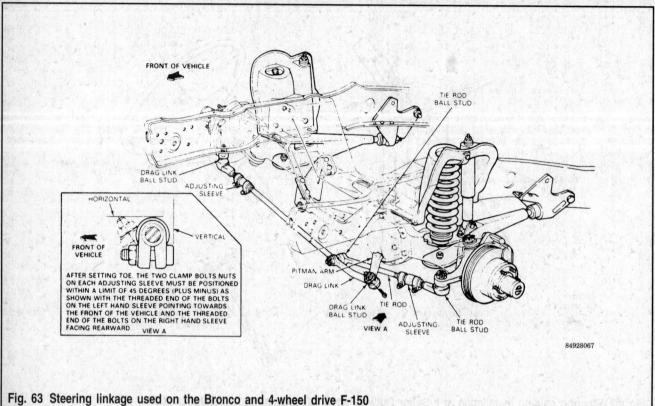

FRONT OF VEHICLE

TIE ROD
BALL STUD

DRAG LINK
BALL STUD

ADJUSTING
SLEEVE

HORIZONTAL

VERTICAL

FRONT OF
VEHICLE

AFTER SETTING TOE, THE TWO CLAMP BOLTS NUTS
ON EACH ADJUSTING SLEEVE MUST BE POSITIONED
WITHIN A LIMIT OF 45 DEGREES (PLUS MINUS) AS
SHOWN WITH THE THREADED END OF THE BOLTS
ON THE LEFT HAND SLEEVE POINTING TOWARDS
THE FRONT OF THE VEHICLE AND THE THREADED
END OF THE BOLTS ON THE RIGHT HAND SLEEVE
FACING REARWARD   VIEW A

PITMAN ARM

DRAG LINK

DRAG LINK
BALL STUD

TIE ROD

VIEW A

ADJUSTING
SLEEVE

TIE ROD
BALL STUD

84928067

Fig. 63 Steering linkage used on the Bronco and 4-wheel drive F-150

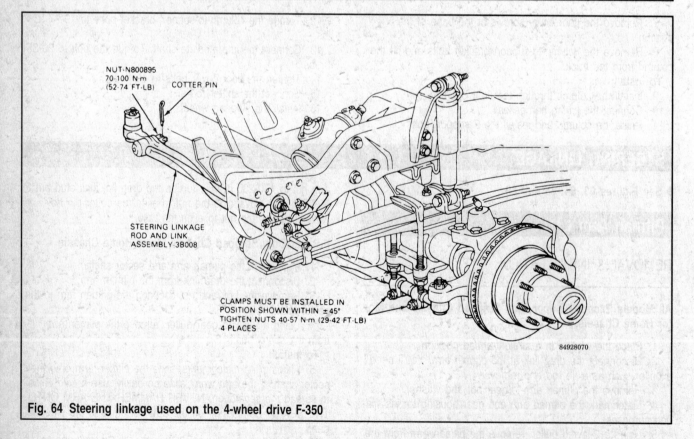

NUT-N800895
70-100 N·m
(52-74 FT-LB)

COTTER PIN

STEERING LINKAGE
ROD AND LINK
ASSEMBLY-3B008

CLAMPS MUST BE INSTALLED IN
POSITION SHOWN WITHIN ±45°
TIGHTEN NUTS 40-57 N·m (29-42 FT-LB)
4 PLACES

84928070

Fig. 64 Steering linkage used on the 4-wheel drive F-350

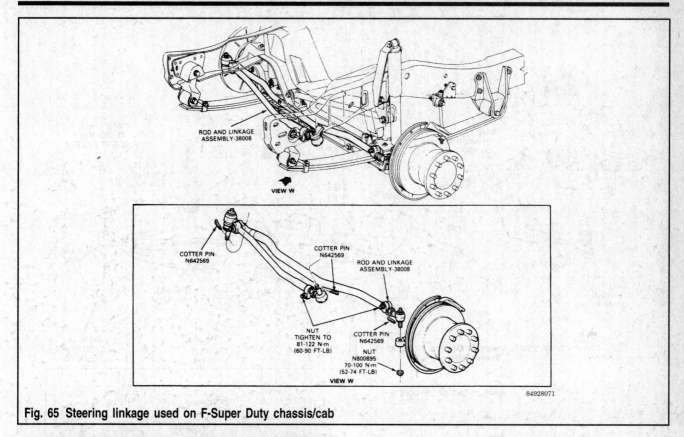

ROD AND LINKAGE
ASSEMBLY-38008

VIEW W

COTTER PIN
N642569

COTTER PIN
N642569

ROD AND LINKAGE
ASSEMBLY-38008

NUT
TIGHTEN TO
81-122 N·m
(60-90 FT-LB)

COTTER PIN
N642569

NUT
N800895
70-100 N·m
(52-74 FT-LB)

VIEW W

84928071

Fig. 65 Steering linkage used on F-Super Duty chassis/cab

Tie Rod and Drag Link

REMOVAL & INSTALLATION

Except Rubberized Ball Socket Linkage

1. Place the wheels in a straight-ahead position.
2. Remove the cotter pins and rust from the drag link and tie rod ball studs.
3. Remove the drag link ball studs from the right hand spindle and pitman arm.
4. Remove the tie rod ball studs from the left hand spindle and drag link.
5. Installation is the reverse of removal. Seat the studs in the tapered hole before tightening the nuts. This will avoid wrap-up of the rubber grommets during tightening of the nuts. Torque the nuts to 70 ft. lbs. Always use new cotter pins.
6. Have the front end alignment checked.

Rubberized Ball Socket Linkage

1. Raise and support the front end on jackstands.
2. Place the wheels in the straight-ahead position.
3. Remove the nuts connecting the drag link ball studs to the connecting rod and pitman arm.
4. Disconnect the drag link using a tie rod end remover.
5. Loosen the bolts on the adjuster clamp. Count the number of turns it take to remove the drag link from the adjuster.
To install:
6. Installation is the reverse of the removal procedure. Install the drag link with the same number of turns it took to

remove it. Make certain that the wheels remain in the straight-ahead position during installation. Seat the studs in the tapered hole before tightening the nuts. This will avoid wrap-up of the rubber grommets during tightening of the nuts. Torque the adjuster clamp nuts to 40 ft. lbs. Torque the ball stud nuts to 75 ft. lbs.
7. Have the front end alignment checked.

Connecting Rod

REMOVAL & INSTALLATION

Rubberized Ball Socket Linkage

1. Raise and support the front end on jackstands.
2. Place the wheels in the straight-ahead position.
3. Disconnect the connecting rod from the drag link by removing the nut and separating the two with a tie rod end remover.
4. Loosen the bolts on the adjusting sleeve clamps. Count the number of turns it takes to remove the connecting rod from the connecting rod from the adjuster sleeve and remove the rod.
5. Installation is the reverse of removal. Install the connecting rod the exact number of turns noted during removal. Torque the tie rod nuts to 40 ft. lbs.; the ball stud nut to 75 ft. lbs.
6. Have the front end alignment checked.

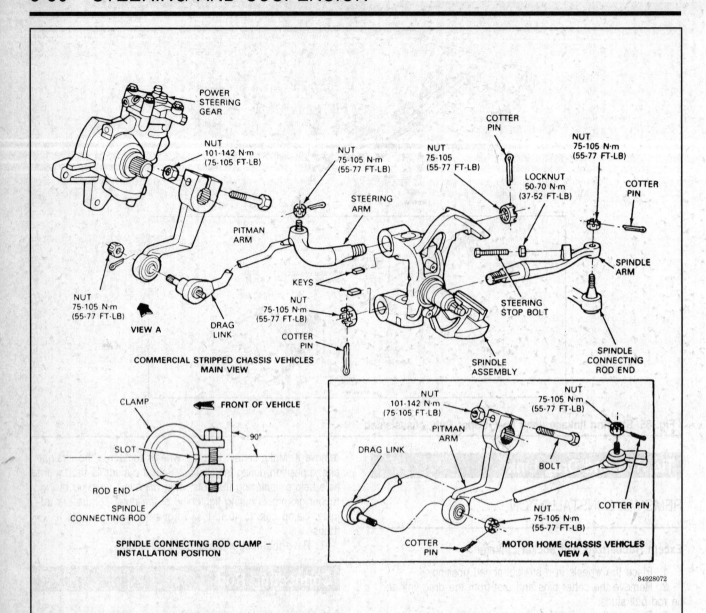

Fig. 66 Steering linkage for F-Super Duty stripped chassis and motor home chassis

Tie Rod Ends

REMOVAL & INSTALLATION

Rubberized Ball Socket Linkage

1. Raise and support the front end on jackstands.
2. Place the wheels in a straight-ahead position.
3. Remove the ball stud from the pitman arm using a tie rod end remover.

4. Loosen the nuts on the adjusting sleeve clamp. Remove the ball stud from the adjuster, or the adjuster from the tie rod. Count the number of turns it takes to remove the sleeve from the tie rod or ball stud from the sleeve.
   To install:
5. Install the sleeve on the tie rod, or the ball in the sleeve the same number of turns noted during removal. Make sure that the adjuster clamps are in the correct position, illustrated, and torque the clamp bolts to 40 ft. lbs.
6. Keep the wheels straight ahead and install the ball studs. Torque the nuts to 75 ft. lbs. Use new cotter pins.
7. Install the drag link and connecting rod.
8. Have the front end alignment checked.

STEERING GEAR

Manual Steering Gear

➡The Koyo recirculating ball manual steering gear is found only on 1987 2-wheel drive models.

ADJUSTMENTS

▸ **See Figures 67 and 68**

Preload and Meshload Check

1. Raise and support the front end on jackstands.
2. Disconnect the drag link from the pitman arm.

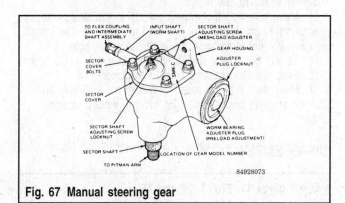

Fig. 67 Manual steering gear

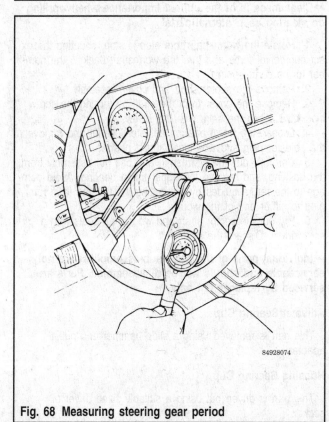

Fig. 68 Measuring steering gear period

3. Lubricate the wormshaft seal with a drop of automatic transmission fluid.
4. Remove the horn pad from the steering wheel.
5. Turn the steering wheel slowly to one stop.
6. Using an inch-pound torque wrench on the steering wheel nut, check the amount of torque needed to rotate the steering wheel through a 1½ turn cycle. The preload should be 5-9 inch lbs. If not, proceed with the rest of the steps.
7. Rotate the steering wheel from stop-to-stop, counting the total number of turns. Using that figure, center the steering wheel (½ the total turns).
8. Using the inch-pound torque wrench, rotate the steering wheel 90° to either side of center, noting the highest torque reading over center. The meshload should be 9-14 inch lbs., or at least 2 inch lbs. more than the preload figure.

Preload and Meshload Adjustment

1. Remove the steering gear.
2. Torque the sector cover bolts on the gear to 40 ft. lbs.
3. Loosen the preload adjuster nut and tighten the worm bearing adjuster nut until all end-play has been removed. Lubricate the wormshaft seal with a few drops of automatic transmission fluid.
4. Using an 11/16 in., 12-point socket and an inch-pound torque wrench, carefully turn the wormshaft all the way to the right.
5. Turn the shaft back to the left and measure the torque over a 1½ turn cycle. This is the preload reading.
6. Tighten or loosen the adjuster nut to bring the preload into range (7-9 inch lbs.).
7. Hold the adjuster nut while torquing the locknut to 187 ft. lbs.
8. Rotate the wormshaft stop-to-stop counting the total number of turns and center the shaft (½ the total turns).
9. Using the torque wrench and socket, measure the torque required to turn the shaft 90° to either side of center.
10. Turn the sector shaft adjusting screw as needed to bring the meshload torque within the 12-14 inch lbs. range, or at least 4 inch lbs. higher than the preload torque.
11. Hold the adjusting screw while tightening the locknut to 25 ft. lbs.
12. Install the gear.

REMOVAL & INSTALLATION

▸ **See Figures 69 and 70**

1. Raise and support the front end on jackstands.
2. Place the wheels in a straight-ahead position. Disengage the flex coupling shield from the steering gear input shaft shield and slide it up the intermediate shaft.
3. Disconnect the flexible coupling from the steering shaft flange by removing the 2 nuts.
4. Disconnect the drag link from the pitman arm.
5. Matchmark and remove the pitman arm.
6. Support the steering gear and remove the attaching bolts.

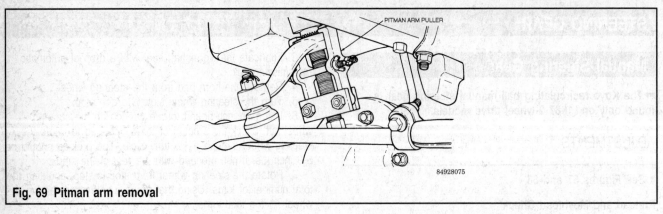

Fig. 69 Pitman arm removal

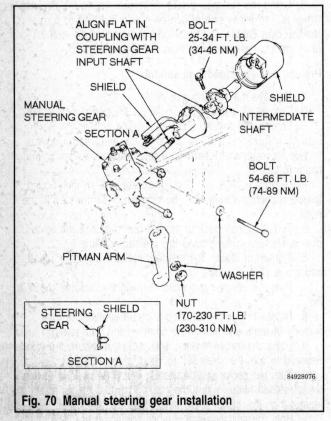

ALIGN FLAT IN COUPLING WITH STEERING GEAR INPUT SHAFT

BOLT 25-34 FT. LB. (34-46 NM)

SHIELD

SHIELD

MANUAL STEERING GEAR

INTERMEDIATE SHAFT

SECTION A

BOLT 54-66 FT. LB. (74-89 NM)

PITMAN ARM

WASHER

STEERING GEAR

SHIELD

NUT 170-230 FT. LB. (230-310 NM)

SECTION A

Fig. 70 Manual steering gear installation

7. Remove the coupling-to-gear attaching bolt and remove the coupling from the gear.

To install:

8. Install the flex coupling on the input shaft. Make sure that the flat on the gear is facing upward and aligns with the flat on the coupling. Install a new coupling-to-gear bolt and torque it to 30 ft. lbs.

9. Center the input shaft.

10. Place the steering gear into position. Make sure that all bolts and holes align.

11. Install the gear mounting bolts and torque them to 65 ft. lbs.

✳✳CAUTION

If you are using new mounting bolts, they MUST be grade 9!

12. Connect the drag link to the pitman arm and hand-tighten the nut.

13. Install the pitman arm on the sector shaft. Torque the sector shaft nut to 230 ft. lbs.

14. Make sure that the wheels are still in the straight-ahead position and tighten the drag link stud nut to 70 ft. lbs. Install a new cotter pin, advancing the nut to align the hole.

15. Torque the sector shaft-to-flex coupling nuts to 20 ft. lbs.

16. Snap the flex coupling shield into place.

17. Make sure that the steering system moves freely and that the steering wheel is straight with the wheels straight-ahead.

DISASSEMBLY

▶ **See Figures 71, 72, 73, 74 and 75**

➡**Cleanliness is of the utmost importance when working on steering gear internal parts!**

1. Rotate the wormshaft from stop-to-stop, counting the exact number of turns and turn the wormshaft back ½ the number to the center point.

2. Remove the sector shaft and cover assembly.

3. Remove the cover from the shaft by turning the screw clockwise. Keep the shim with the screw.

4. Loosen the worm bearing adjuster locknut and remove the adjuster plug and wormshaft thrust bearing.

5. Carefully pull the wormshaft and ball nut assembly from the housing, and remove the upper thrust bearing. Avoid damage to the return guides by preventing the ball nut from running to either end of the worm.

6. Pry out the sector shaft and wormshaft seals with a screwdriver. Discard the seals.

➡**Individual parts of the gear (sub-assemblies) are not serviceable and should not be disassembled. Parts are serviced by replacement only.**

Adjuster/Bearing Cup

This part is removed using a slide hammer and puller adapter.

Housing Bearing Cup

This part is driven out using a suitably sized driver or socket.

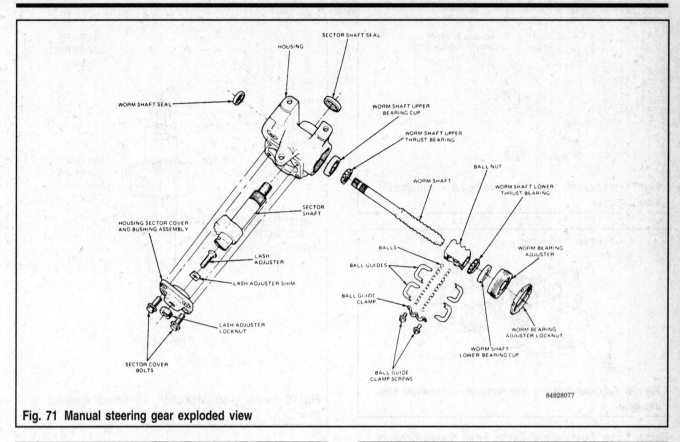

Fig. 71 Manual steering gear exploded view

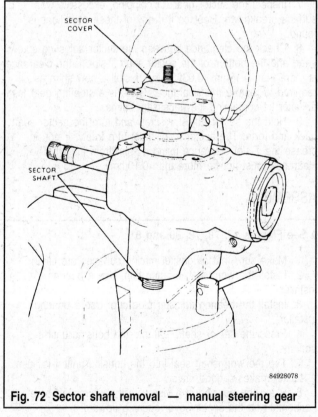

Fig. 72 Sector shaft removal — manual steering gear

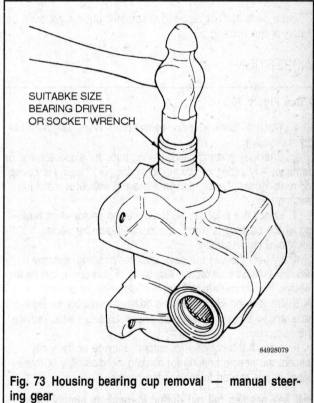

Fig. 73 Housing bearing cup removal — manual steering gear

Fig. 74 Wormshaft and ball nut removal — manual steering gear

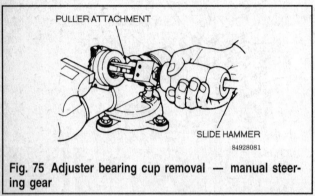

Fig. 75 Adjuster bearing cup removal — manual steering gear

Sector Cover Bushing and Sector Shaft Needle Bearing

These parts are not replaced separately, but are replaced as a part of the housing.

INSPECTION

▶ **See Figure 76**

1. Wash all parts in a non-flammable solvent. Let them air-dry thoroughly.
2. Check all bearings and bearing cups for signs of wear or damage. Any pitting or scoring, or bluing, or chipping is cause for replacement. Never replace a bearing without a matching bearing cup.
3. Check the fit of the sector shaft and sector shaft bushing. If the bushing is worn, you must replace the sector cover/bushing assembly.
4. Inspect the ball nut gear teeth for chipping, excessive wear or surface breakdown. Any wear or damage is cause to replace the wormshaft and ball nut assembly as a unit.
5. Inspect the wormshaft and ball nut assembly for tightness and/or binding. If tightness and/or binding exists, replace the assembly.
6. Inspect the housing for cracks, damage or deformity. Inspect the needle bearing for missing needles. Any of these conditions is reason to replace the housing.

➡**If any needles fall out during inspection, simply clean them and use steering gear lube to hold them in place.**

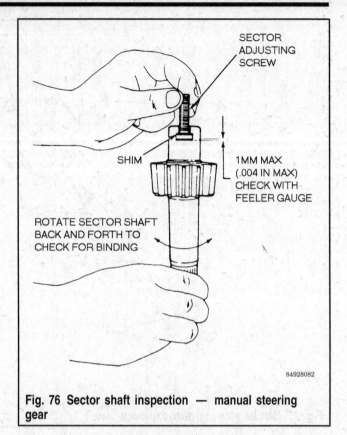

Fig. 76 Sector shaft inspection — manual steering gear

7. Inspect the sector gear for chipping, excessive wear and surface breakdown. Replace it if any of these conditions is found.
8. Check the clearance between the sector adjusting screw head and the bottom of the sector shaft T-slot. If the clearance is more than 0.10mm (0.03937 in.), install a new shim as required to restore the clearance. There is a steering gear lash adjuster kit containing the necessary shims.
9. Hold the sector adjuster screw and turn the sector shaft back and forth. The sector shaft must turn freely. If not, increase the T-slot clearance using a shim from the kit. The clearance must not be more than 0.10mm.

ASSEMBLY

▶ **See Figures 77, 78, 79, 80 and 81**

1. Make sure that all gasket mating surfaces are clean.
2. Install the wormshaft bearing cup. Use a bearing installer.
3. Install the bearing adjuster plug cup. Use a bearing installer.
4. Press the sector shaft seal into the housing until it bottoms.
5. Tap the wormshaft seal into the housing until it is flush. A socket makes a good driver.
6. Place the housing in a vise with the wormshaft bore horizontal and the sector cover opening upward.
7. Apply steering gear grease, meeting specification ESW-M1C87-A, to the wormshaft bearings, sector shaft needle bearings and the sector cover bushing.

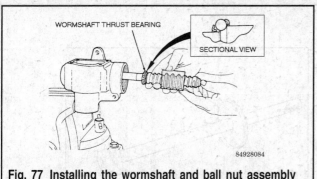

Fig. 77 Installing the wormshaft and ball nut assembly in the gear housing — manual steering gear

Fig. 78 Wormshaft seal installation — manual steering gear

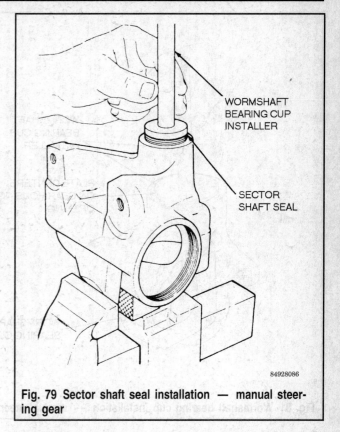

Fig. 79 Sector shaft seal installation — manual steering gear

without its squeezing out the sector shaft opening. Rotate the wormshaft to move the ball nut near the other end of its travel and pack more grease into the housing.

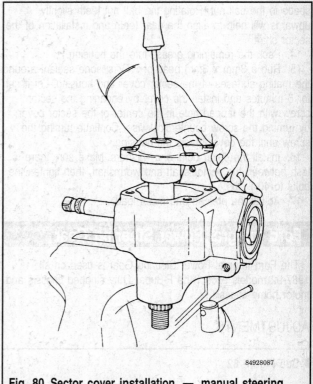

Fig. 80 Sector cover installation — manual steering gear

8. Slip one end of the wormshaft bearings over the wormshaft splined end. Be sure that the bearing cage is positioned correctly. Insert the wormshaft and ball nut into the housing. Feed the splined end of the wormshaft through the bearing cup and seal. Place the remaining wormshaft thrust bearing into the adjuster plug bearing cup.

9. Install the adjuster plug and locknut in the housing opening, being careful to guide the wormshaft end into the bearing until nearly all end-play is removed from the wormshaft.

10. Position the sector adjusting screw and shim in the sector shaft slot. Check the clearance between the screw head and the bottom of the sector shaft T-slot. The clearance must be less than 0.10mm. If the clearance exceeds 0.10mm, install a new shim as required.

11. Lubricate the steering gear with 420 grams (14.8 oz.) of steering gear grease. Rotate the wormshaft until the ball nut is near the end of its travel. Pack as much grease as possible

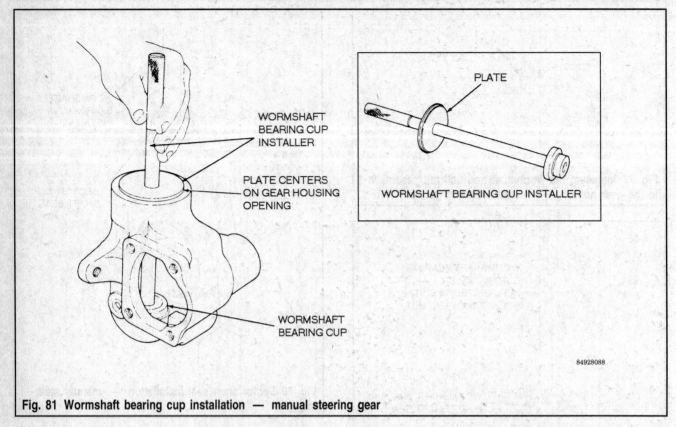

Fig. 81 Wormshaft bearing cup installation — manual steering gear

12. Rotate the wormshaft until the ball nut is in the center of its travel.

13. Install the sector shaft assembly into the housing so that the center tooth of the sector gear enters the center rack tooth space in the ball nut. Rotating the ball nut teeth slightly upwards will help to align the gear teeth and installation of the sector shaft.

14. Pack the remaining grease into the housing.

15. Run a 3mm **x** 3mm bead of RTV silicone sealant around the mating surfaces of the sector cover and housing. Let it set for 5 minutes and install the cover by engaging the sector screw with the tapped hole in the center of the sector cover, by turning the screw counterclockwise. Continue turning the screw until the cover meets the housing.

16. Install the cover bolts and washers. Make sure there is lash between the sector shaft and wormshaft, then tighten the bolts to 40 ft. lbs.

17. Adjust the preload and mesh load.

Ford Integral Power Steering Gear

The Ford Integral Power Steering Gear is used on all 1987-92 models except the F-Super Duty stripped chassis and motor home chassis

ADJUSTMENTS

▶ **See Figure 82**

Meshload

1. Raise and support the front end on jackstands.

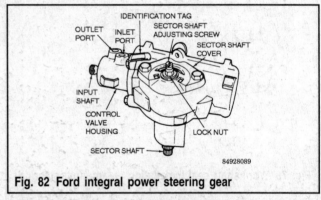

Fig. 82 Ford integral power steering gear

2. Matchmark the pitman arm and gear housing.

3. Set the wheels in a straight-ahead position.

4. Disconnect the pitman arm from the sector shaft.

5. Disconnect the fluid RETURN line at the pump reservoir and cap the reservoir nipple.

6. Place the end of the return line in a clean container and turn the steering wheel lock-to-lock a few times to expel the fluid from the gear.

7. Turn the steering wheel all the way to the right stop. Place a small piece of masking tape on the steering wheel rim as a reference and rotate the steering wheel 45° from the right stop.

8. Disconnect the battery ground.

9. Remove the horn pad.

10. Using an inch-pound torque wrench on the steering wheel nut, record the amount of torque needed to turn the steering wheel ⅛turn counterclockwise. The preload reading should be 4-9 inch lbs.

11. Center the steering wheel (½ the total lock-to-lock turns) and record the torque needed to turn the steering wheel 90° to either side of center. On a truck with fewer than 5,000 miles, the meshload should be 15-25 inch lbs. On a truck with 5,000 or more miles, the meshload should be 7 inch lbs. more than the preload torque.   On trucks with fewer than 5,000 miles, if the meshload is not within specifications, it should be reset to a figure 14-18 inch lbs. greater than the recorded preload torque.   On trucks with 5,000 or more miles, if the meshload is not within specifications, it should be reset to a figure 10-14 inch lbs. greater than the recorded preload torque.

12. If an adjustment is required, loosen the adjuster locknut and turn the sector shaft adjuster screw until the necessary torque is achieved.

13. Once adjustment is completed. hold the adjuster screw and tighten the locknut to 45 ft. lbs.

14. Recheck the adjustment readings and reset if necessary.

15. Connect the return line and refill the reservoir.

16. Install the pitman arm.

17. Install the horn pad.

REMOVAL & INSTALLATION

▶ **See Figure 83**

1. Raise and support the front end on jackstands.
2. Place the wheels in the straight-ahead position.
3. Place a drain pan under the gear and disconnect the pressure and return lines. Cap the openings.
4. Remove the splash shield from the flex coupling.
5. Disconnect the flex coupling at the gear.

6. Matchmark and remove the pitman arm from the sector shaft.

7. Support the steering gear and remove the mounting bolts.

8. Remove the steering gear. It may be necessary to work it free of the flex coupling.

To install:

9. Place the splash shield on the steering gear lugs.

10. Slide the flex coupling into place on the steering shaft. Make sure the steering wheel spokes are still horizontal.

11. Center the steering gear input shaft with the indexing flat facing downward.

12. Slide the steering gear input shaft into the flex coupling and into place on the frame side rail. Install the flex coupling bolt and torque it to 30 ft. lbs.

13. Install the gear mounting bolts and torque them to 65 ft. lbs.

14. Make sure that the wheels are still straight ahead and install the pitman arm. Torque the nut to 230 ft. lbs.

15. Connect the pressure, then, the return lines. Torque the pressure line to 25 ft. lbs.

16. Snap the flex coupling shield into place.

17. Fill the steering reservoir.

18. Run the engine and turn the steering wheel lock-to-lock several times to expel air. Check for leaks.

DISASSEMBLY

▶ **See Figures 84, 85, 86, 87, 88 and 89**

➡**It is essential that work on the internal parts of a power steering gear be done in a clean environment with reasonably clean hands!**

1. Hold the gear over a drain pan and rotate the input shaft several times to ensure that all fluid is expelled.

2. Clamp the gear, right side up, in a soft-jawed vise.

3. Remove the locknut from the sector shaft adjusting screw.

4. Turn the input shaft to either stop, then, back 2 full turns to center it. The flat on the splines should be facing downwards.

5. Remove the sector shaft cover bolts.

6. Using a plastic mallet, tap on the lower end of the sector shaft to loosen the cover, then, remove the cover and shaft assembly. Discard the O-ring.

7. Separate the cover and shaft by turning the cover counterclockwise.

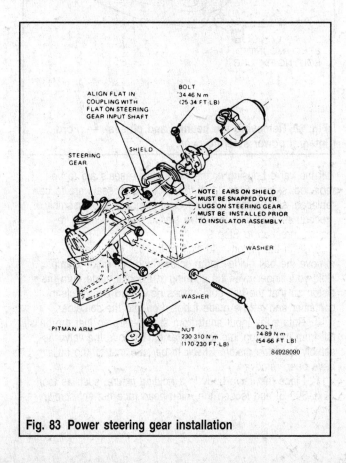

Fig. 83 Power steering gear installation

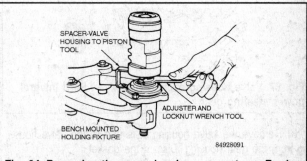

Fig. 84 Removing the worm bearing race nut — Ford integral power steering gear

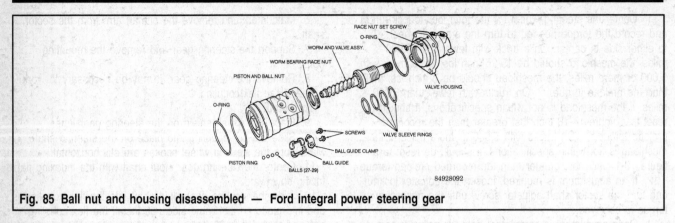

Fig. 85 Ball nut and housing disassembled — Ford integral power steering gear

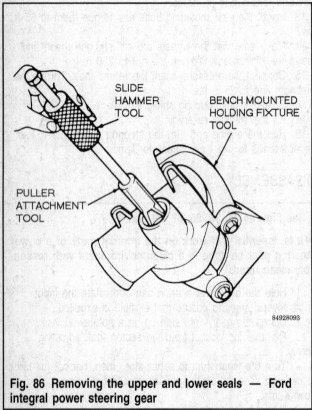

Fig. 86 Removing the upper and lower seals — Ford integral power steering gear

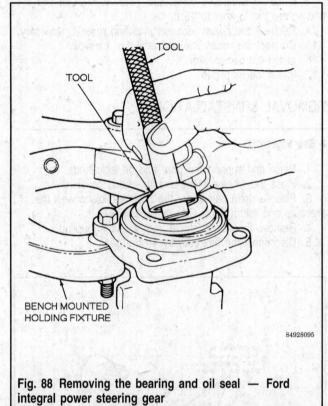

Fig. 88 Removing the bearing and oil seal — Ford integral power steering gear

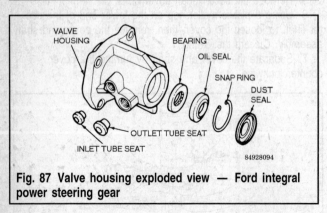

Fig. 87 Valve housing exploded view — Ford integral power steering gear

8. Remove the valve housing bolts and lift the valve housing from the gear housing. Discard the gasket.

If the valve housing or the valve sleeve seals are to be replaced, skip to Step 11. If the sector shaft seals are to be replaced, skip to the 'Steering Gear Housing' sub-assembly procedures, below. If the valve sleeve rings are being replaced, proceed to Step 9.

9. With the piston held so that the ball guide faces up, remove the ball guide clamp screws and ball guide clamp. Hold your finger over the opening in the ball guide, turn the piston so that the ball guide faces downward over a clean container and let the guide tubes drop into the container.

10. Rotate the input shaft from stop-to-stop so that the balls fall from the piston into the container. Remove the valve assembly from the piston. Check to be sure that all the balls have been removed.

11. Place the valve body in a holding fixture, such as tool T57L-500-B, and loosen the Allen head race nut set screw.

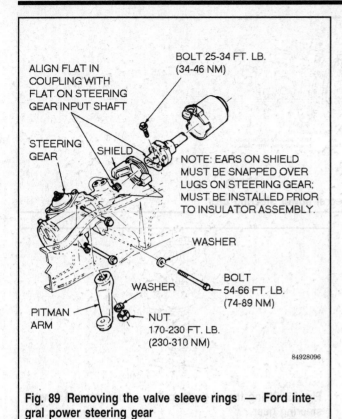

Fig. 89 Removing the valve sleeve rings — Ford integral power steering gear

Remove the worm bearing race nut using tools T66P-3553-B and T66P-3553-C, or their equivalents.

12. Carefully slide the input shaft, worm and valve assembly from the valve housing.

SUB-ASSEMBLY OVERHAUL

See Figures 90, 91 and 92

Steering Gear Housing

1. Remove the snapring from the lower end of the housing.
2. Using a slide hammer, remove the dust seal.
3. Using a slide hammer, remove the pressure seal.
4. Coat a new pressure seal and new dust seal with multi-purpose grease. Coat the seal bores with grease.
5. Install the seals with a seal driver. For the dust seal, the raised lip should face the seal driver. For the pressure seal,

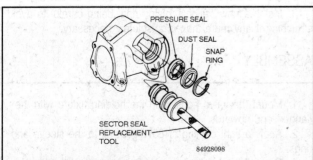

Fig. 90 Installing the sector shaft seals — Ford integral power steering gear

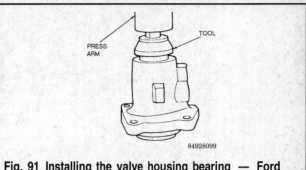

Fig. 91 Installing the valve housing bearing — Ford integral power steering gear

the lip should face away from the driver. The flat backs of the seals should be against each other when installed. DO NOT BOTTOM THE SEALS AGAINST THE BEARING! They will not function properly if bottomed.

6. Install the snapring.
7. Apply a generous amount of grease to the areas between the seal lips.

Valve Housing

1. Using a slide hammer, remove the dust seal from the rear of the housing.
2. Remove the snapring from the housing.
3. Invert the housing on the holding fixture.
4. Using tools T65P-3524-A2 and T65P-3524-A3, gently tap the bearing and seal from the housing, driving from the end opposite the seal. Take care to avoid damage to the housing when inserting and removing the tool.
5. If the tube seats are damaged, remove them with tool T74P-3504-L.
6. Coat the new tube seats with petroleum jelly and install them with tool T74P-3504-M.
7. Coat the bearing a seal surface of the housing with petroleum jelly.
8. Install the bearing with the metal side, covering the rollers, facing outward. Seat the bearing using tool T65P-3524-A1, or equivalent. Make sure the bearing rotates freely.
9. Dip the new oil seal in 80W gear oil and place it in the housing with the metal side outwards. Drive it into place until the outer edge does not quite clear the snapring groove.
10. Place the snapring in the housing and drive it into place until it seats in the groove.
11. Place the dust seal in the housing and drive it into place with the rubber side outwards. When fully seated, the seal should be behind the undercut in the input shaft.
12. Pack the area between the 2 seals with clean multi-purpose grease.

Worm and Valve Sleeve

See Figures 93, 94, 95 and 96

➡**This job is impossible without the proper sleeve ring installation tools found in tool set T75L-3517-A, or their equivalents!**

1. Remove the valve sleeve rings by slipping a sharp knife under them and cutting them away from the valve sleeve.
2. Grip the worm end of the worm and sleeve assembly in a soft-jawed vise.

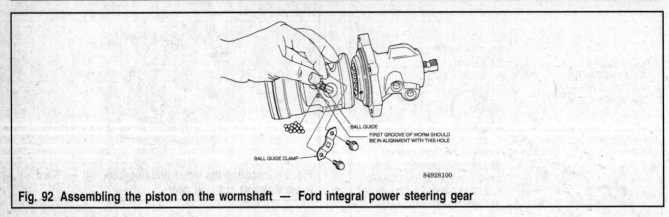

Fig. 92 Assembling the piston on the wormshaft — Ford integral power steering gear

3. Place tool T75L-3517-A1 over the sleeve and slide one new ring over the tool.

4. Slide pusher tool T75L-3517-A2 over the first tool and rapidly push down on the pusher tool, forcing the ring down the ramp and into the 4th groove in the sleeve. Repeat this procedure for each of the remaining rings, adding an additional spacer under the first tool to align the ring and groove.

5. After installing all 4 rings, apply a light coating of 80W gear oil to the sleeve and rings.

6. Install a spacer, T75L-3517-A3, over the input shaft. Slowly install sizing tube tool T75L-3517-A4 over the sleeve valve end of the wormshaft and onto the rings, using the spacer as a pilot. MAKE SURE THAT THE RINGS ARE NOT DISTORTED AS THE TOOL SLIDES OVER THEM!

7. Remove the sizing tube tool and check the rings. Make sure the rings turn freely in their grooves.

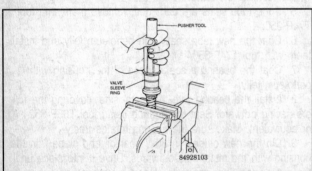

Fig. 93 Installing a ring — Ford integral power steering gear

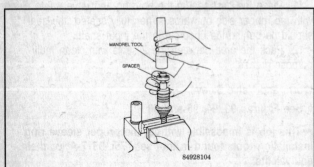

Fig. 94 Adding a spacer to install the next ring — Ford integral power steering gear

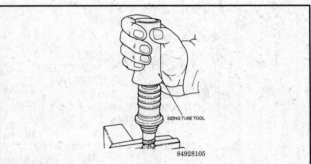

Fig. 95 Sizing the rings, step 1 — Ford integral power steering gear

Fig. 96 Seal installation tool kit — Ford integral power steering gear

Piston

1. Remove the Teflon® piston ring and the O-ring. Discard them.

2. Dip a new O-ring in 80W gear oil and install it on the piston.

3. Install a new Teflon® piston ring, being careful to avoid stretching it any more than is absolutely necessary.

ASSEMBLY

1. Mount the valve housing in the holding fixture with the flanged end upwards.

2. Apply a light coating of 80W gear oil to the sleeve and rings.

3. Carefully install the wormshaft and valve in the housing.

4. Install the race nut and torque it to 55-90 ft. lbs.

5. Install the set screw and torque it to 15-25 ft. lbs.

6. With the ball guide holes facing upwards, insert the wormshaft into the piston so that the first groove is aligned with the hole nearest the center of the piston.

7. Place the ball guides in the piston. Place the balls in the ball guide, turning the wormshaft as they are inserted. There should be at least 27 balls. All the balls removed MUST be installed! If there are still balls left over when the wormshaft reaches its stop, rotate it the other way, making room for all the balls.

8. Install the guide clamps and tighten the screws to 42-70 inch lbs.

9. Coat the Teflon® piston ring with petroleum jelly.

10. Install a new control valve O-ring on the housing.

11. Slide the piston and valve into the gear housing, taking care to avoid damage to the piston ring.

12. Align the oil passage in the valve housing with the passage in the gear housing. Place a new O-ring on the oil passage hole of the gear housing.

13. Place the ID tag on the housing. Install, but don't tighten, the housing bolts. The ID tag should be under the upper right bolt.

14. Rotate the ball nut so that the teeth are on the same plane as the sector teeth. Tighten the bolts to 55-70 ft. lbs.

15. Adjust the meshload.

Ford XR-50 Power Steering Gear

The XR-50 Power Steering Gear is used on all 1993 models except the F-Super Duty stripped chassis and motor home chassis.

ADJUSTMENTS

▶ **See Figure 97**

Meshload

1. Raise and support the front end on jackstands.

2. Matchmark the pitman arm and gear housing.

3. Set the wheels in a straight-ahead position.

4. Disconnect the pitman arm from the sector shaft.

5. Disconnect the fluid RETURN line at the pump reservoir and cap the reservoir nipple.

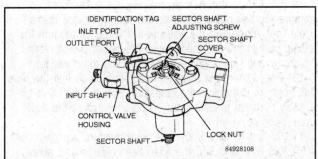

Fig. 97 Adjustment points — Ford XR-50 power steering gear

6. Place the end of the return line in a clean container and turn the steering wheel lock-to-lock a few times to expel the fluid from the gear.

7. Turn the steering wheel all the way to the right stop. Place a small piece of masking tape on the steering wheel rim as a reference and rotate the steering wheel 45° from the right stop.

8. Disconnect the battery ground.

9. Remove the horn pad.

10. Using an inch-pound torque wrench on the steering wheel nut, record the amount of torque needed to turn the steering wheel ⅛ turn counterclockwise. The preload reading should be 4-9 inch lbs.

11. Center the steering wheel (½ the total lock-to-lock turns) and record the torque needed to turn the steering wheel 90° to either side of center. On a truck with fewer than 5,000 miles, the meshload should be 15-25 inch lbs. On a truck with 5,000 or more miles, the meshload should be 7 inch lbs. more than the preload torque.   On trucks with fewer than 5,000 miles, if the meshload is not within specifications, it should be reset to a figure 14-18 inch lbs. greater than the recorded preload torque.   On trucks with 5,000 or more miles, if the meshload is not within specifications, it should be reset to a figure 10-14 inch lbs. greater than the recorded preload torque

12. If an adjustment is required, loosen the adjuster locknut and turn the sector shaft adjuster screw until the necessary torque is achieved.

13. Once adjustment is completed. hold the adjuster screw and tighten the locknut to 45 ft. lbs.

14. Recheck the adjustment readings and reset if necessary

15. Connect the return line and refill the reservoir.

16. Install the pitman arm.

17. Install the horn pad.

REMOVAL & INSTALLATION

▶ **See Figure 98**

1. Raise and support the front end on jackstands.

2. Place the wheels in the straight-ahead position.

3. Place a drain pan under the gear and disconnect the pressure and return lines. Cap the openings.

4. Remove the splash shield from the flex coupling.

5. Disconnect the flex coupling at the gear.

6. Matchmark and remove the pitman arm from the sector shaft.

7. Support the steering gear and remove the mounting bolts.

8. Remove the steering gear. It may be necessary to work it free of the flex coupling.

To install:

9. Place the splash shield on the steering gear lugs.

10. Slide the flex coupling into place on the steering shaft. Make sure the steering wheel spokes are still horizontal.

11. Center the steering gear input shaft with the indexing flat facing downward.

12. Slide the steering gear input shaft into the flex coupling and into place on the frame side rail. Install the flex coupling bolt and torque it to 30-42 ft. lbs.

13. Install the gear mounting bolts and torque them to 65 ft. lbs.

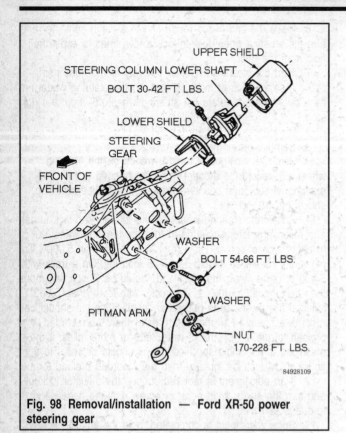

Fig. 98 Removal/installation — Ford XR-50 power steering gear

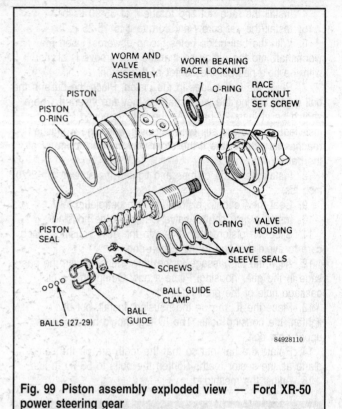

Fig. 99 Piston assembly exploded view — Ford XR-50 power steering gear

14. Make sure that the wheels are still straight ahead and install the pitman arm. Torque the nut to 170-288 ft. lbs.

15. Connect the pressure, then, the return lines. Torque the pressure line to 25 ft. lbs.

16. Snap the flex coupling shield into place.

17. Fill the steering reservoir.

18. Run the engine and turn the steering wheel lock-to-lock several times to expel air. Check for leaks.

DISASSEMBLY

▶ See Figures 99 and 100

➡It is essential that work on the internal parts of a power steering gear be done in a clean environment with reasonably clean hands!

1. Hold the gear over a drain pan and rotate the input shaft several times to ensure that all fluid is expelled.

2. Clamp the gear, right side up, in a soft-jawed vise.

3. Turn the input shaft to either stop, then, back 2 full turns to center it. The flat on the splines should be facing downwards.

4. Remove the locknut from the sector shaft adjusting screw.

5. Remove the sector shaft cover bolts.

6. Using a plastic mallet, tap on the lower end of the sector shaft to loosen the cover, then, remove the cover and shaft as an assembly. Discard the O-ring.

7. Separate the cover and shaft by turning the cover counterclockwise.

8. Remove the valve housing bolts and lift the valve housing from the gear housing. Discard the gasket.

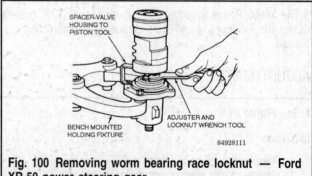

Fig. 100 Removing worm bearing race locknut — Ford XR-50 power steering gear

If the valve housing or the valve sleeve seals are to be replaced, skip to Step 11. If the sector shaft seals are to be replaced, skip to the 'Steering Gear Housing' sub-assembly procedures, below. If the valve sleeve rings are being replaced, proceed to Step 9.

9. With the piston held so that the ball guide faces up, remove the ball guide clamp screws and ball guide clamp. Hold your finger over the opening in the ball guide, turn the piston so that the ball guide faces downward over a clean container and let the guide tubes drop into the container.

10. Rotate the input shaft from stop-to-stop so that the balls fall from the piston into the container. Remove the valve assembly from the piston. Check to be sure that all the balls have been removed.

11. Place the valve body in a holding fixture, such as tool T57L-500-B, and loosen the Allen head race nut set screw. Remove the worm bearing race nut using tools T66P-3553-B and T66P-3553-C, or their equivalents.

12. Carefully slide the input shaft, worm and valve assembly from the valve housing.

SUB-ASSEMBLY OVERHAUL

Steering Gear Housing

▶ See Figures 101 and 102

1. Remove the snapring from the lower end of the housing.
2. Using a slide hammer, remove the dust seal.
3. Using a slide hammer, remove the pressure seal.
4. Coat a new pressure seal and new dust seal with multi-purpose grease. Coat the seal bores with grease.
5. Install the seals with a seal driver. For the dust seal, the raised lip should face the seal driver. For the pressure seal, the lip should face away from the driver. The flat backs of the seals should be against each other when installed. DO NOT BOTTOM THE SEALS AGAINST THE BEARING! They will not function properly if bottomed.
6. Install the snapring.
7. Apply a generous amount of grease to the areas between the seal lips.

Valve Housing

▶ See Figures 103, 104 and 105

1. Using a slide hammer, remove the dust seal from the rear of the housing.
2. Remove the snapring from the housing.
3. Invert the housing on the holding fixture.
4. Using tools T65P-3524-A2 and T65P-3524-A3, gently tap the bearing and seal from the housing, driving from the end

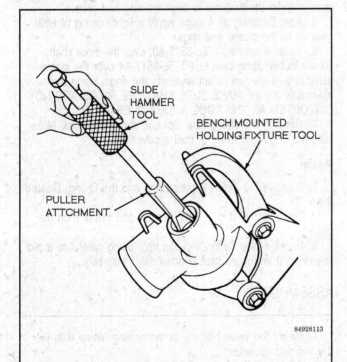

Fig. 101 Removing upper and lower seals — Ford XR-50 power steering gear

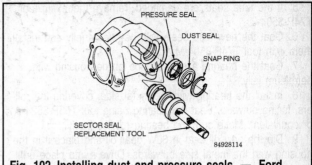

Fig. 102 Installing dust and pressure seals — Ford XR-50 power steering gear

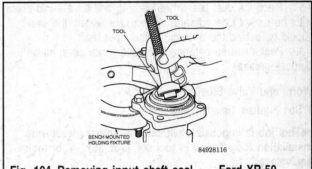

Fig. 104 Removing input shaft seal — Ford XR-50 power steering gear

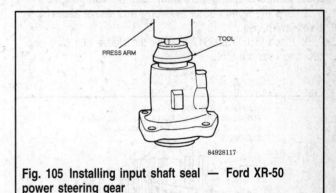

Fig. 105 Installing input shaft seal — Ford XR-50 power steering gear

opposite the seal. Take care to avoid damage to the housing when inserting and removing the tool.

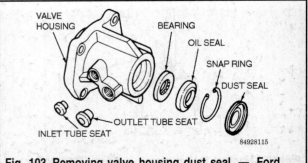

Fig. 103 Removing valve housing dust seal — Ford XR-50 power steering gear

5. If the tube seats are damaged, remove them with tool T74P-3504-L.

6. Coat the new tube seats with petroleum jelly and install them with tool T74P-3504-M.

7. Coat the bearing a seal surface of the housing with petroleum jelly.

8. Install the bearing with the metal side, covering the rollers, facing outward. Seat the bearing using tool T65P-3524-A1, or equivalent. Make sure the bearing rotates freely.

9. Dip the new oil seal in 80W gear oil and place it in the housing with the metal side outwards. Drive it into place until the outer edge does not quite clear the snapring groove.

10. Place the snapring in the housing and drive it into place until it seats in the groove.

11. Place the dust seal in the housing and drive it into place with the rubber side outwards. When fully seated, the seal should be behind the undercut in the input shaft.

12. Pack the area between the 2 seals with clean multipurpose grease.

Worm and Valve Sleeve

▶ See Figures 106, 107 and 108

➡This job is impossible without the proper sleeve ring installation tools found in tool set T75L-3517-A, or their equivalents!

1. Remove the valve sleeve rings by slipping a sharp knife under them and cutting them away from the valve sleeve.

2. Grip the worm end of the worm and sleeve assembly in a soft-jawed vise.

3. Place tool T75L-3517-A1 over the sleeve and slide one new ring over the tool.

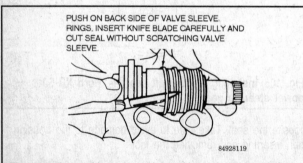

Fig. 106 Removing valve sleeve seals — Ford XR-50 power steering gear

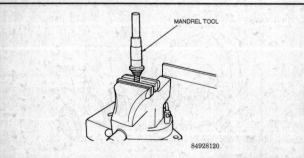

Fig. 107 Mandrel tool in place — Ford XR-50 steering gear

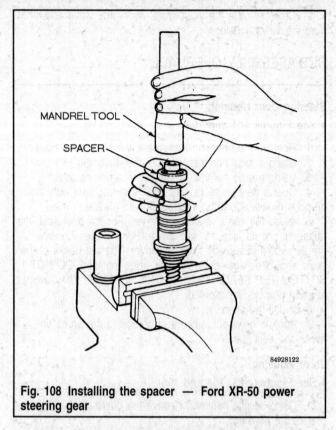

Fig. 108 Installing the spacer — Ford XR-50 power steering gear

4. Slide pusher tool T75L-3517-A2 over the first tool and rapidly push down on the pusher tool, forcing the ring down the ramp and into the 4th groove in the sleeve. Repeat this procedure for each of the remaining rings, adding an additional spacer under the first tool to align the ring and groove.

5. After installing all 4 rings, apply a light coating of 80W gear oil to the sleeve and rings.

6. Install a spacer, T75L-3517-A3, over the input shaft. Slowly install sizing tube tool T75L-3517-A4 over the sleeve valve end of the wormshaft and onto the rings, using the spacer as a pilot. MAKE SURE THAT THE RINGS ARE NOT DISTORTED AS THE TOOL SLIDES OVER THEM!

7. Remove the sizing tube tool and check the rings. Make sure the rings turn freely in their grooves.

Piston

1. Remove the Teflon® piston ring and the O-ring. Discard them.

2. Dip a new O-ring in 80W gear oil and install it on the piston.

3. Install a new Teflon® piston ring, being careful to avoid stretching it any more than is absolutely necessary.

ASSEMBLY

1. Mount the valve housing in the holding fixture with the flanged end upwards.

2. Apply a light coating of 80W gear oil to the sleeve and rings.

3. Carefully install the wormshaft and valve in the housing.

4. Install the race nut and torque it to 55-90 ft. lbs.

5. Install the set screw and torque it to 15-25 ft. lbs.

6. With the ball guide holes facing upwards, insert the wormshaft into the piston so that the first groove is aligned with the hole nearest the center of the piston.

7. Place the ball guides in the piston. Place the balls in the ball guide, turning the wormshaft as they are inserted. There should be at least 27 balls. All the balls removed MUST be installed! If there are still balls left over when the wormshaft reaches its stop, rotate it the other way, making room for all the balls.

8. Install the guide clamps and tighten the screws to 42-70 inch lbs.

9. Coat the Teflon® piston ring with petroleum jelly.

10. Install a new control valve O-ring on the housing.

11. Slide the piston and valve into the gear housing, taking care to avoid damage to the piston ring.

12. Align the oil passage in the valve housing with the passage in the gear housing. Place a new O-ring on the oil passage hole of the gear housing.

13. Place the ID tag on the housing. Install, but don't tighten, the housing bolts. The ID tag should be under the upper right bolt.

14. Rotate the ball nut so that the teeth are on the same plane as the sector teeth. Tighten the bolts to 55-70 ft. lbs.

15. Adjust the meshload.

Bendix C-300N Power Steering Gear

The Bendix gear is used on F-Super Duty stripped chassis models and motor home chassis models.

ADJUSTMENTS

Adjustments must be made with the steering gear removed and mounted in a vise.

Piston-to-Output Shaft Gear Backlash Adjustment
▶ **See Figure 109**

➡**Backlash is correct when a 4-18 inch lb. increase in rotational torque is noted at the input shaft as it is rotated and the piston passes the mid-point of its total travel in the housing. The torque increase should occur only at mid-point and should disappear after mid-point.**

1. Loosen the locknut and turn the adjusting screw counter-clockwise as far as it will go.

2. Using an inch-pound torque wrench, rotate the input shaft as far as it will go in one direction, then, counting the number of full turns and noting the rotational torque, rotate it to the opposite stop.

3. Turn the shaft back ½ the total number of turns to the mid-point.

4. Rotate the shaft 180° to both sides of the mid-point, noting the change in rotational torque. Turn the adjusting screw ⅛-¼ turn at a time until the proper reading of 4-18 inch lb. increase in torque is noted over the mid-point. This increase in torque must be plus the total rotational torque.

5. When the adjustment is correct, hold the adjusting screw and, using a crow's foot adapter, torque the locknut to 74-88 ft. lbs.

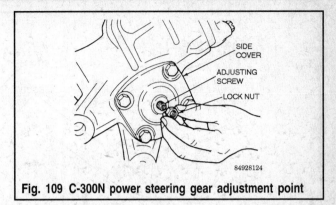

Fig. 109 C-300N power steering gear adjustment point

6. Check the adjustment to make sure it hasn't changed. Rotate the shaft through its entire travel. It must rotate smoothly.

REMOVAL & INSTALLATION

▶ **See Figures 110 and 111**

1. Raise and support the front end on jackstands.

2. Thoroughly clean all connections.

3. Place a drain pan under the area.

4. Disconnect the hydraulic lines at the gear. Cap all openings at once.

5. Remove the retaining bolt and nut and disconnect the pitman arm from the sector shaft.

6. Remove the bolt and nut securing the input shaft and U-joint.

7. Support the gear and remove the gear-to-frame bolts and nuts.

   To install:

8. Position the gear on the frame and install the bolts and nuts. Torque the nuts to 150-200 ft. lbs.

9. Install the U-joint bolt and nut. Torque the nut to 50-70 ft. lbs.

10. Install the pitman arm.

✳✳CAUTION

Never hammer the pitman shaft onto the sector shaft! Hammering will damage the gear. Use a cold chisel to separate the pitman arm opening.

11. Install the bolt and nut. Torque the nut to 220-300 ft. lbs.

12. Connect the hydraulic lines, fill the reservoir, run the engine and check for leaks.

DISASSEMBLY

✳✳WARNING

It is essential that work on the internal parts of a power steering gear be done in a clean environment with reasonably clean hands!

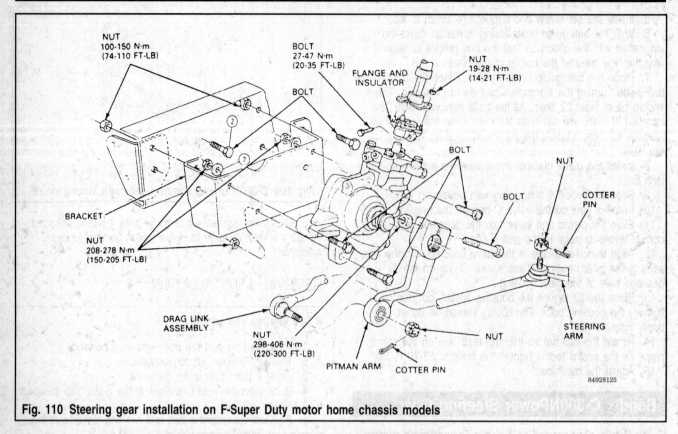

NUT
100-150 N·m
(74-110 FT-LB)

BOLT
27-47 N·m
(20-35 FT-LB)

BOLT

**FLANGE AND
INSULATOR**

NUT
19-28 N·m
(14-21 FT-LB)

BRACKET

NUT
208-278 N·m
(150-205 FT-LB)

BOLT

BOLT

NUT

**COTTER
PIN**

**DRAG LINK
ASSEMBLY**

NUT
298-406 N·m
(220-300 FT-LB)

**STEERING
ARM**

PITMAN ARM

COTTER PIN

NUT

84928125

Fig. 110 Steering gear installation on F-Super Duty motor home chassis models

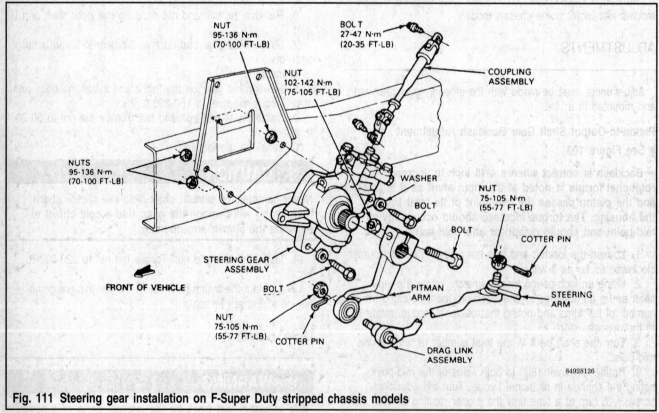

NUT
95-136 N·m
(70-100 FT-LB)

BOLT
27-47 N·m
(20-35 FT-LB)

**COUPLING
ASSEMBLY**

NUT
102-142 N·m
(75-105 FT-LB)

NUTS
95-136 N·m
(70-100 FT-LB)

WASHER

NUT
75-105 N·m
(55-77 FT-LB)

BOLT

BOLT

**COTTER
PIN**

**STEERING GEAR
ASSEMBLY**

FRONT OF VEHICLE

BOLT

**PITMAN
ARM**

**STEERING
ARM**

NUT
75-105 N·m
(55-77 FT-LB)

COTTER PIN

**DRAG LINK
ASSEMBLY**

84928126

Fig. 111 Steering gear installation on F-Super Duty stripped chassis models

Input/Output Shaft

▶ **See Figures 112, 113, 114, 115, 116, 117, 118, 119, 120, 121, 122 and 123**

➡ **This gear is built to metric standards with metric fasteners.**

1. Remove the dust boot from the input shaft splines.
2. Matchmark the valve body and housing. Remove the 4 valve body-to-housing bolts.
3. Rotate the output shaft to separate the valve boy from the housing. Continue rotating the shaft until both valve body O-rings are visible. Pull the valve body from the housing.
4. If not already done, matchmark and remove the pitman arm.
5. Remove the output shaft dust boot.
6. Thoroughly clean the exposed portion of the output shaft.

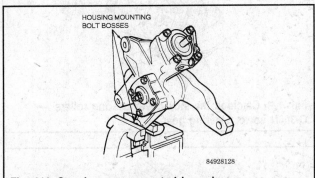

Fig. 113 Steering gear mounted in a vise

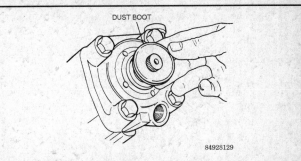

Fig. 114 Removing the dust boot from the input shaft — C-300N power steering gear

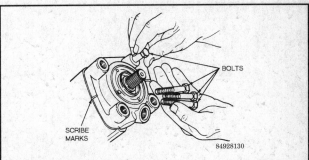

Fig. 115 Removing the valve body bolts — C-300N power steering gear

7. Remove the locknut from the adjusting screw on the side cover.

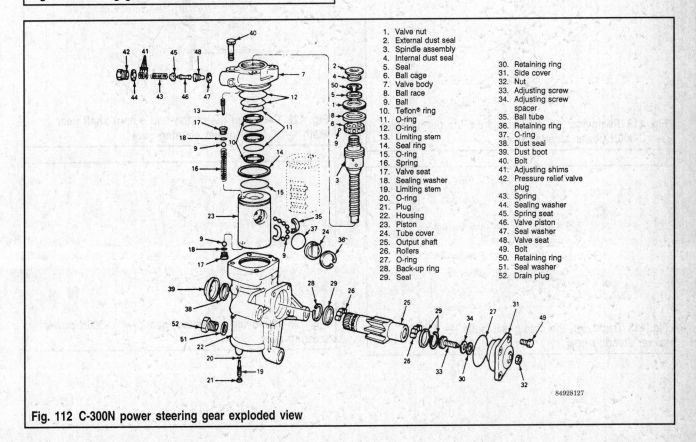

1. Valve nut	30. Retaining ring
2. External dust seal	31. Side cover
3. Spindle assembly	32. Nut
4. Internal dust seal	33. Adjusting screw
5. Seal	34. Adjusting screw
6. Ball cage	spacer
7. Valve body	35. Ball tube
8. Ball race	36. Retaining ring
9. Ball	37. O-ring
10. Teflon® ring	38. Dust seal
11. O-ring	39. Dust boot
12. O-ring	40. Bolt
13. Limiting stem	41. Adjusting shims
14. Seal ring	42. Pressure relief valve
15. O-ring	plug
16. Spring	43. Spring
17. Valve seat	44. Sealing washer
18. Sealing washer	45. Spring seat
19. Limiting stem	46. Valve piston
20. O-ring	47. Seal washer
21. Plug	48. Valve seat
22. Housing	49. Bolt
23. Piston	50. Retaining ring
24. Tube cover	51. Seal washer
25. Output shaft	52. Drain plug
26. Rollers	
27. O-ring	
28. Back-up ring	
29. Seal	

Fig. 112 C-300N power steering gear exploded view

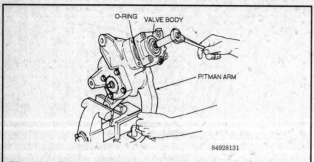

Fig. 116 Separating the valve body from the housing — C-300N power steering gear

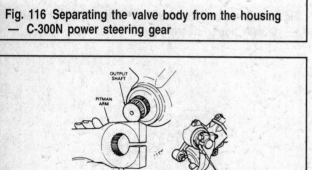

Fig. 117 Pitman arm removal — C-300N power steering gear

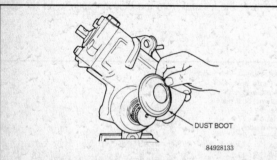

Fig. 118 Removing the dust boot from the output shaft — C-300N power steering gear

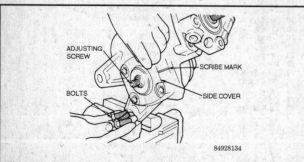

Fig. 119 Removing the side cover bolts — C-300N power steering gear

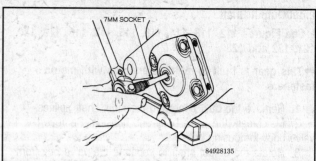

Fig. 120 Separating the side cover from the housing — C-300N power steering gear

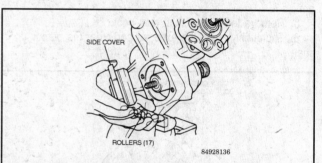

Fig. 121 Catching the side cover bearing rollers — C-300N power steering gear

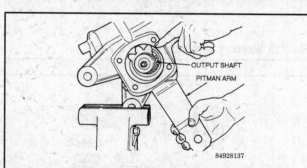

Fig. 122 Centering the piston and output shaft gear teeth — C-300N power steering gear

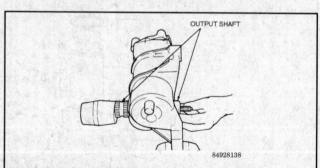

Fig. 123 Removing the output shaft — C-300N power steering gear

8. Matchmark the side cover and housing. Remove the 4 side cover bolts.

➡In the next step, you will be removing the side cover. When the cover is removed, the 17 rollers in the cover bearing will fall out. Don't lose any. And don't confuse them with the rollers in the housing bearing. They are not interchangeable.

9. Turn the adjusting screw clockwise to separate the side cover from the housing. Continue turning until the cover is free and remove it.

10. Slide the pitman arm onto the shaft and use it to center the piston and output shaft gear teeth.

➡In the next step, you will be removing the output shaft. When the shaft is removed, the 17 rollers in the housing bearing will fall out. Don't lose any. And don't confuse them with the rollers in the cover bearing. They are not interchangeable.

11. Remove the pitman arm and, tapping with a plastic mallet at the splined end, remove the output shaft.

Piston

▶ **See Figures 124, 125, 126, 127, 128, 129 and 130**

1. Hold the input end of the spindle and pull the valve body and piston from the housing.
2. Remove the retaining ring, ball tube cover, ball tube and 7 of the 26 balls from the piston.
3. Rotate the input shaft in whichever direction threads the spindle out of the piston and remove the remaining balls.
4. Separate the valve body and spindle from the piston. Check the inside of the piston for any remaining balls. There

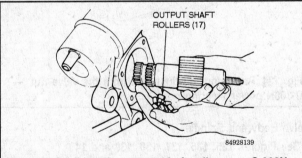

Fig. 124 Catching the output shaft rollers — C-300N power steering gear

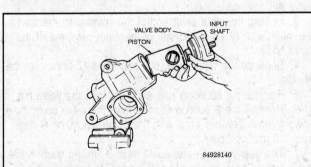

Fig. 125 Removing the valve body and piston — C-300N power steering gear

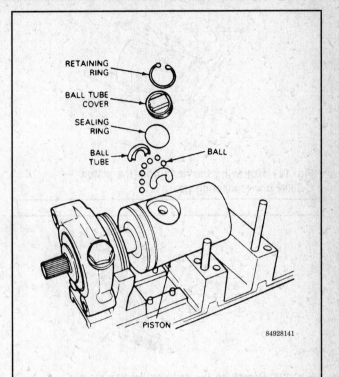

Fig. 126 Removing the ball tube and balls — C-300N power steering gear

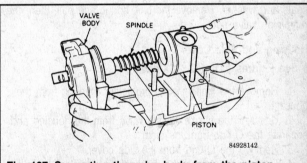

Fig. 127 Separating the valve body from the piston — C-300N power steering gear

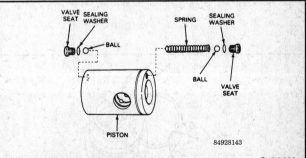

Fig. 128 Steering limiting valve components — C-300N power steering gear

should be a total of 26 balls removed from the tube and piston.

5. Remove the sealing ring and O-ring from the piston.

Fig. 129 Removing the rings from the piston —
C-300N power steering gear

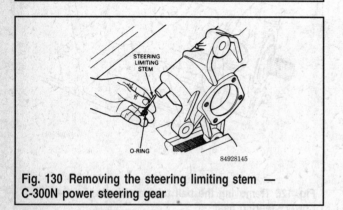

Fig. 130 Removing the steering limiting stem —
C-300N power steering gear

6. Using a screwdriver, remove one of the limiting valve seats and washer. Remove the ball, spring and ball, then, the remaining valve seat.

Housing and Side Cover

▶ **See Figures 131, 132, 133 and 134**

1. Remove the limiting stem protective covering from the housing.
2. Unscrew the stroke limiting valve from the housing and separate the O-ring from the stem.
3. Remove the O-ring from the side cover.
4. Remove the seal and nylon back-up ring from the side cover bore.
5. Remove the dust seal.
6. Remove the output shaft seal and nylon back-up ring.

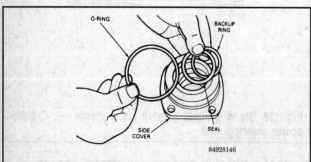

Fig. 131 Removing the side cover O-ring — C-300N
power steering gear

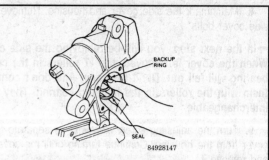

Fig. 132 Removing the housing dust seal — C-300N
power steering gear

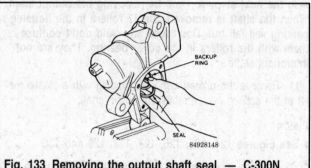

Fig. 133 Removing the output shaft seal — C-300N
power steering gear

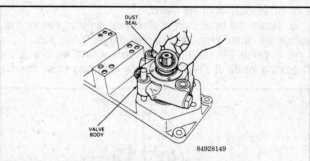

Fig. 134 Removing the dust seal from the valve nut —
C-300N power steering gear

Valve Body and Spindle

▶ **See Figures 135, 136, 137, 138, 139 and 140**

1. Remove the dust seal from the valve nut.
2. Using a punch, unlock the safety point between the valve nut and valve body.
3. Holding the input shaft end of the spindle, lift the spindle, ball cage, 17 balls and half of the outer race, out of the valve body.
4. Separate the outer race, ball cage and 17 balls from the spindle.
5. Remove the retaining ring and seal from the valve nut.
6. Remove the 2 outside O-rings from the valve body, then, remove the 3 Teflon® rings and the 3 corresponding O-rings from the spindle bore.
7. The gear in some trucks will have a limiting stem in the valve body. Check its condition. If it appears not to be damaged or compressed, leave it alone. If it needs to be replaced,

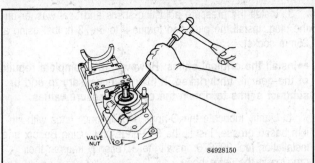

**Fig. 135 Unstaking the valve nut and valve body —
C-300N power steering gear**

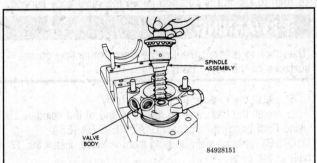

**Fig. 136 Removing the spindle assembly from the valve
body — C-300N power steering gear**

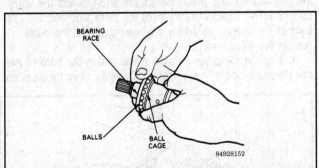

**Fig. 137 Removing the bearing assembly from the spin-
dle — C-300N power steering gear**

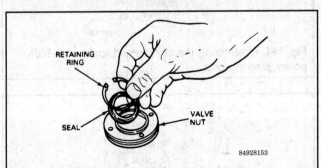

**Fig. 138 Removing the seal from the valve nut —
C-300N power steering gear**

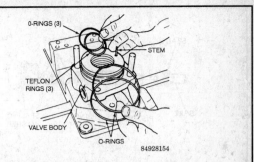

**Fig. 139 Removing the rings from the valve body —
C-300N power steering gear**

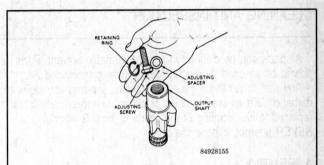

**Fig. 140 Removing the adjusting screw from the output
shaft — C-300N power steering gear**

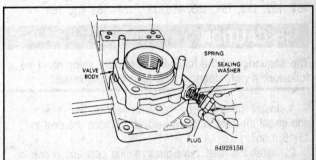

**Fig. 141 Removing the spring seat and shims from the
valve body — C-300N power steering gear**

remove it by heating the poppet stem to release the thread
locking compound and turning it counterclockwise.

Output Shaft

Remove the retaining ring, adjusting screw spacer and adjusting screw from the output shaft.

Pressure Relief Valve

▶ **See Figures 141 and 142**

1. Remove the plug and washer.
2. Remove the spring, seat and shims.
3. Using a wide-bladed screwdriver, remove the valve seat
and washer

Spindle

No attempt may be made to disassemble the spindle. It can
be serviced by replacement only. Moreover, if the spindle is
replaced, a matching piston must be installed as well.

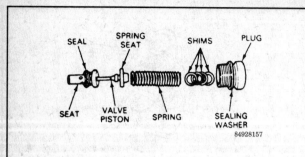

Fig. 142 Valve spring and seat components — C-300N power steering gear

CLEANING AND INSPECTION

All parts can be cleaned in a non-flammable solvent. Parts should be air-dried thoroughly. Do not use compressed air.

Any part found to be excessively worn, showing any signs of damage such as cracks, chips or pitting, or scored, should be replaced. Minor scuffing of the piston or bore is normal. NEVER attempt to hone the bore!

ASSEMBLY

▶ **See Figures 142, 143, 144, 145, 146, 147, 148, 149, 150, 151, 152, 153, 154, 155, 156, 157, 158, 159 and 160**

❄❄CAUTION

The sequence of the following assembly steps must be followed. If not, steering gear failure could result!

1. Install the pressure relief valve seal on the valve seat and install the seat in the valve body. Torque the seat to 15-18 ft. lbs.
2. Install the relief valve piston spring seat and spring in the valve body.

❄❄CAUTION

The spring must be installed as shown in the accompanying illustration. Incorrect installation will result in malfunction of the relief valve!

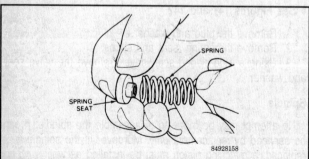

Fig. 143 Assembling the valve spring and seat — C-300N power steering gear

3. Install the pressure adjusting shims and seal washer on the plug. Install the plug and torque it to 66-73 ft. lbs. using a 26mm socket.

➡**Install the original shims. However, if a complete rebuild of the gear is undertaken, it may be necessary to add or subtract shims to obtain the correct pressure values.**

4. Lightly lubricate the O-rings and Teflon® rings with lithium based grease. Install the 3 O-rings and, using Bendix ring installation tool 297676, install the 3 Teflon® rings in their grooves in the valve body.
5. If the limiting valve was removed, install it now using Loctite®222 on the threads. Install it until a stem height of 18.7mm (0.736 in.) is obtained above the valve body surface.

❄❄WARNING

Use care to prevent the Loctite from contacting other surfaces of the valve body!

6. Install the O-rings on the valve body.
7. Install the ball cage on the input end of the spindle. Using Ford Long-Life lubricant C1AZ-19590-BA (ESA-M1C75-B), or equivalent, to hold them in place, install the 17 balls in the cage.
8. Install the outer bearing race half over the input end of the spindle assembly and insert the spindle assembly through the ring seating tool. Insert the spindle and tool into the valve body until the tool completely exits the other side and the 17 balls of the bearing assembly are resting against the outer race in the valve body.
9. Position the pressure side of the seal in the bore of the non-pressure side of the valve nut. Carefully drive the seal into

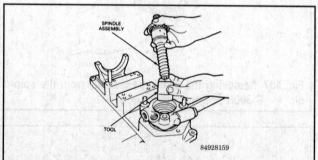

Fig. 144 Assembling the spindle and tool — C-300N power steering gear

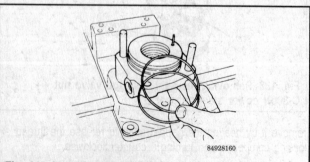

Fig. 145 Installing the O-rings on the valve body — C-300N power steering gear

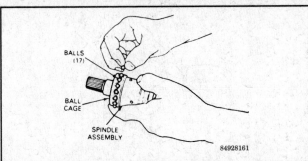

Fig. 146 Placing the 17 balls in the cage — C-300N power steering gear

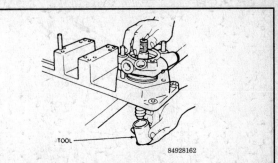

Fig. 147 Installing the spindle and tool in the valve body — C-300N power steering gear

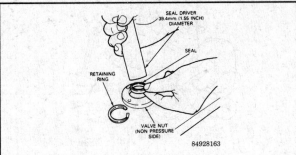

Fig. 148 Installing the seal in the valve nut — C-300N power steering gear

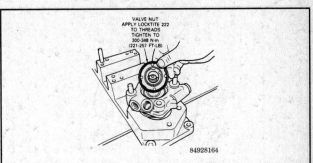

Fig. 149 Installing the valve nut — C-300N power steering gear

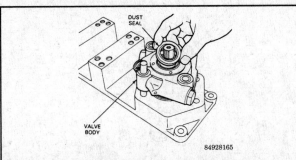

Fig. 150 Installing the dust seal on the valve nut — C-300N power steering gear

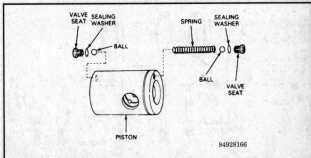

Fig. 151 Assembling the valve spring and seat in the piston — C-300N power steering gear

the bore until the snapring groove within the bore is visible. Install the retaining ring, making certain it is completely seated in the groove.

10. Gently tap the seal from the opposite side, until it rests squarely against the snapring. A driver can be made from round brass stock with a diameter of 39.4mm (1½ in.).

11. Apply Loctite®932 or 567 to the threads of the valve nut. Due to the proximity of the spindle bearing, use extreme care to avoid getting the Loctite on any other parts!

12. Carefully, install the valve nut over the input shaft end of the spindle and into the valve body. Tighten the valve nut to 221-257 ft. lbs. using Bendix tool 106243, or equivalent.

13. Stake the valve nut and body with a punch.

14. Install the dust seal in the valve nut.

15. Install one steering limiting valve seat and washer in the piston. Insert 1 of the balls, the spring and the other ball.

Install the remaining washer and seat. Torque each seat to 9-11 ft. lbs.

16. Install the O-ring on the piston.

17. Using a heat lamp or oven, heat the glide ring to 285-320°F (140-160°C) and immediately install it over the O-ring in the piston groove.

✳✳WARNING

Take great care to distort the glide ring as little as possible during installation.

18. Using a screw-type hose clamp, reshape the glide ring in the groove and allow it to cool at least 10 minutes before removing the hose clamp.

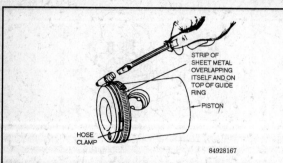

**Fig. 152 Using a hose clamp to size the glide ring —
C-300N power steering gear**

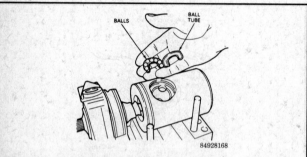

**Fig. 153 Installing the ball tube and 7 balls — C-300N
power steering gear**

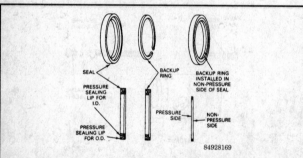

**Fig. 154 Proper installation alignment for seal and ny-
lon back-up rings — C-300N power steering gear**

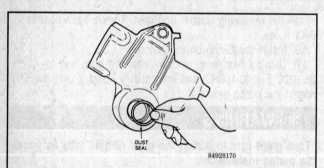

**Fig. 155 Installing the housing dust seal — C-300N
power steering gear**

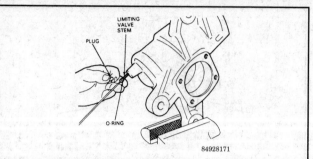

**Fig. 156 Installing the limiting stem — C-300N power
steering gear**

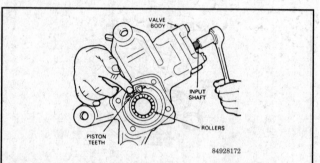

**Fig. 157 Installing the valve body — C-300N power
steering gear**

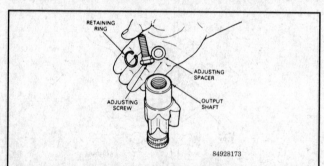

**Fig. 158 Installing the shim washer and adjusting screw
— C-300N power steering gear**

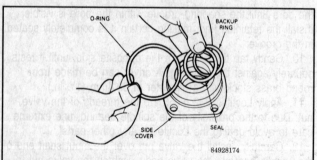

**Fig. 159 Installing the side cover O-ring — C-300N
power steering gear**

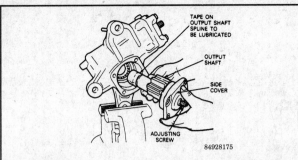

Fig. 160 Installing the output shaft — C-300N power steering gear

19. Install the O-ring in its groove in the ball return opening of the piston.

20. Insert the valve body and spindle assembly all the way into the piston, making certain that the stoke limiting stem is not damaged and that it mates with the valve seat in the piston.

21. Insert 19 of the balls, one at a time, into one of the ball tube holes in the ball return opening in the piston. Rotate the input shaft end of the spindle slightly after each ball is inserted. Rotate the spindle in one direction only, and do not alternate from clockwise to counterclockwise.

➡**If the procedure is performed correctly, the spindle and valve body should screw out of the piston and the balls should appear at the tube opposite the one used for installation. Make sure that the balls are at an equal depth in both holes.**

✳✳CAUTION

The assembly of this group of parts must be done with the utmost care. If the balls are dislodged during assembly, steering gear failure will result!

22. Install the remaining 7 balls in the tube halves, using lithium grease to hold them in place. Seat the tube halves containing the balls in the tube holes in the piston.

23. Lightly grease the sealing surface of the tube cover and install it in the piston, making certain that the slot in the underside of the cover mates with the tube in the piston. Install the retaining ring in the piston to secure the tube cover, making certain that it is completely seated in its groove. After assembly, check for smooth rotation of the spindle in both directions.

24. Working through the side cover opening, install the seal with its pressure side towards the interior of the housing.

25. Install the nylon back-up ring in the groove formed by the backside of the seal and housing. make sure the split surfaces of the ring mate properly.

26. Install the dust seal in the housing with its sealing lip towards the outside of the housing.

27. Install the O-ring in the groove around the limiting stem and screw the stem into the housing 5-6 full turns.

28. Install the 17 rollers of the housing bearing, holding them in place with Ford Long-Life lubricant, or equivalent.

29. Align the steering limiting stem in the valve body with the limiting valve seat in the piston. Insert the piston in the housing so that the rack teeth of the piston are visible through the side cover opening. Make sure the valve body is aligned so that the matchmarks are aligned.

30. Slide the piston and valve body completely into the housing, taking care not to damage the glide ring and O-rings. Secure the valve body using the 4 bolts. Torque the bolts to 80-88 ft. lbs. Rotate the input shaft end of the spindle until the rack teeth of the piston are centered in the side cover opening.

31. Install the shim and washer over the adjusting screw and secure them in the output shaft with the retaining ring. Check the end-play. Maximum end-play for these parts is 0.05mm (0.002 in.). If end-play is excessive, change the shim.

32. Install the seal in the side cover with the pressure side towards the outer race of the side cover roller bearing.

33. Install the nylon back-up ring by winding it into the groove formed by the side cover and seal. Install the O-ring.

34. Install the 17 rollers of the side cover bearing. Use lithium grease to hold them in place.

35. Coat the housing and side cover seals, and the sealing surface of the output shaft at the adjusting screw end, with lithium grease. Using a 77mm socket, install the side cover assembly on the output shaft adjuster screw and screw it on as far as it will go, then, back it off ⅛turn.

36. Wrap a single layer of masking tape around the output shaft splines. Coat the tape with lithium grease and slide the shaft and side cover assembly into the housing with a twisting motion. Remove the masking tape.

37. Install the side cover bolts. make certain the matchmarks are aligned. Torque the bolts to 80-88 ft. lbs.

38. Pack the cavities with lithium grease and install the dust boot on the output shaft and the dust seal on the input shaft.

39. Adjust the gear.

Ford C-II Power Steering Pump

This pump is used by all models except the F-Super Duty stripped chassis and motor home models.

REMOVAL & INSTALLATION

◗ **See Figures 161, 162, 163, 164, 165 and 166**

1. Disconnect the return line at the pump and drain the fluid into a container.

2. Disconnect the pressure line from the pump.

3. Loosen the pump bracket nuts and remove the drive belt. On the 6-4.9L and 8-5.0L with a serpentine drive belt, remove belt tension by lifting the tensioner out of position.

4. Remove the nuts and lift out the pump/bracket assembly.

5. If a new pump or bracket is being installed, you'll have to remove the pulley from the present pump. This is best done with a press and adapters.

6. Installation is the reverse of removal. Note the following torques:
- Pivot bolt (6-4.9L and 8-5.0L): 45 ft. lbs.
- Pump-to-adjustment bracket: 45 ft. lbs.
- Support bracket-to-engine (8-5.8L):65 ft. lbs.
- Support bracket-to-water pump housing (6-4.9L): 17 ft. lbs.
- Support bracket-to-water pump housing (8-5.0L, 5.8L): 45 ft. lbs.
- Pressure line-to-fitting: 29 ft. lbs.

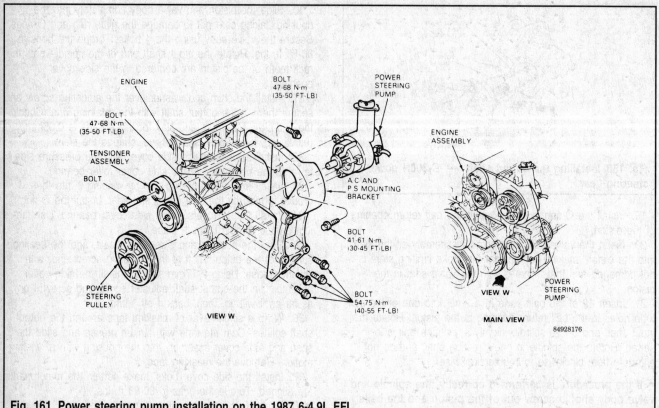

Fig. 161 Power steering pump installation on the 1987 6-4.9L EFI

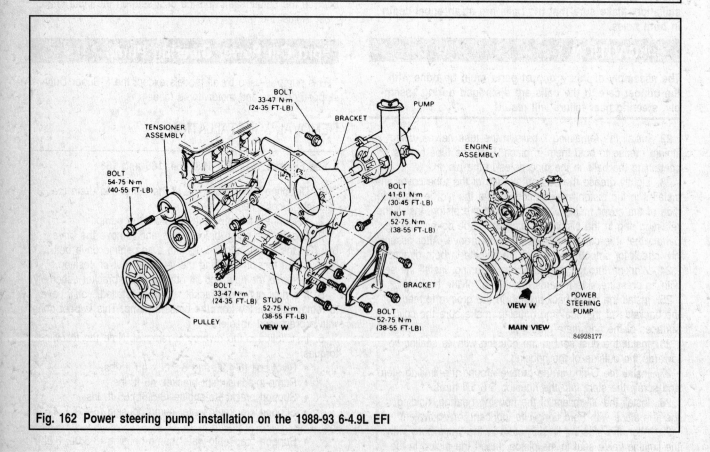

Fig. 162 Power steering pump installation on the 1988-93 6-4.9L EFI

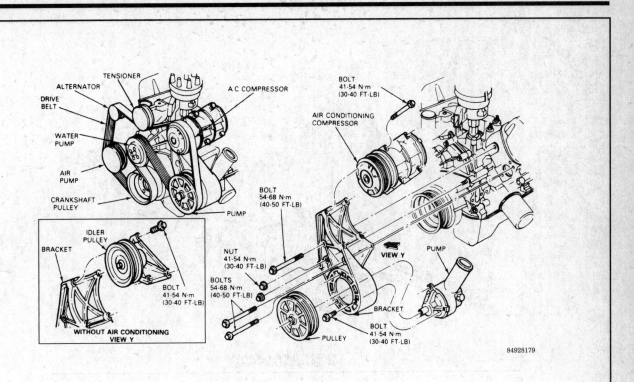

Fig. 163 Power steering pump installation on the 1988-93 8 — 5.0l EFI and 8-5.8L EFI

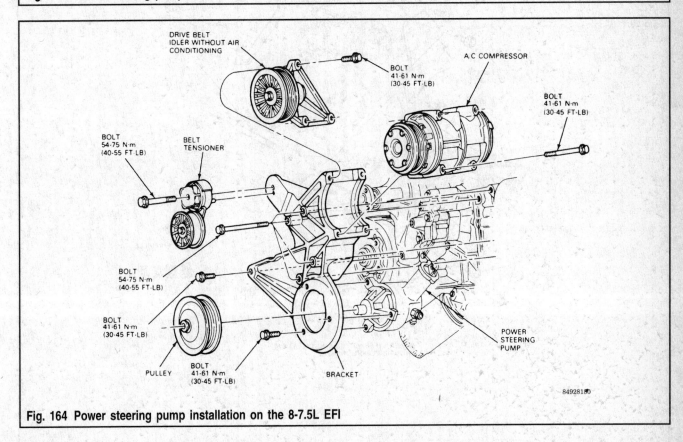

Fig. 164 Power steering pump installation on the 8-7.5L EFI

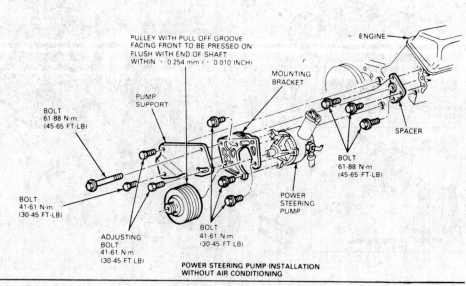

PULLEY WITH PULL OFF GROOVE
FACING FRONT TO BE PRESSED ON
FLUSH WITH END OF SHAFT
WITHIN · 0.254 mm (· 0.010 INCH)

ENGINE

MOUNTING
BRACKET

PUMP
SUPPORT

SPACER

BOLT
61-88 N·m
(45-65 FT-LB)

BOLT
61-88 N·m
(45-65 FT-LB)

BOLT
41-61 N·m
(30-45 FT-LB)

POWER
STEERING
PUMP

BOLT
41-61 N·m
(30-45 FT-LB)

ADJUSTING
BOLT
41-61 N·m
(30-45 FT-LB)

POWER STEERING PUMP INSTALLATION
WITHOUT AIR CONDITIONING

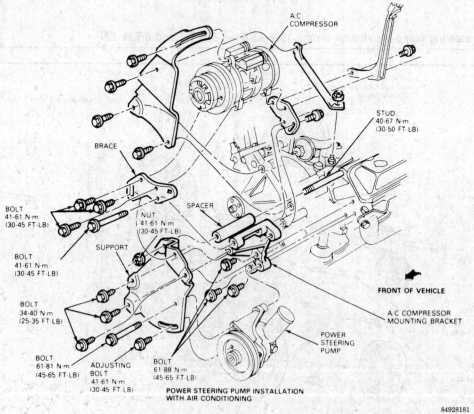

A C
COMPRESSOR

STUD
40-67 N·m
(30-50 FT-LB)

BRACE

BOLT
41-61 N·m
(30-45 FT-LB)

NUT
41-61 N·m
(30-45 FT-LB)

SPACER

BOLT
41-61 N·m
(30-45 FT-LB)

SUPPORT

FRONT OF VEHICLE

BOLT
34-40 N·m
(25-35 FT-LB)

A C COMPRESSOR
MOUNTING BRACKET

POWER
STEERING
PUMP

BOLT
61-81 N·m
(45-65 FT-LB)

ADJUSTING
BOLT
41-61 N·m
(30-45 FT-LB)

BOLT
61-88 N·m
(45-65 FT-LB)

POWER STEERING PUMP INSTALLATION
WITH AIR CONDITIONING

84928181

Fig. 165 Power steering pump installation on the 8-7.5L 4-bbl

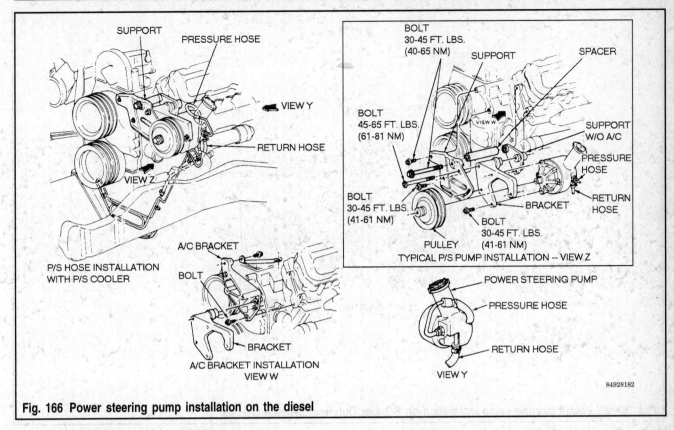

Fig. 166 Power steering pump installation on the diesel

- Adjustment bracket-to-support bracket:
- 6-4.9L, 8-5.0L, 8-5.8L: 45 ft. lbs.
- 8-7.5L and Diesel: Long bolt — 65 ft. lbs.
- Short bolt — 45 ft. lbs.

ZF Power Steering Pump

This pump is used on the F-Super Duty stripped chassis and motor home models.

REMOVAL & INSTALLATION

▶ **See Figures 167 and 168**

1. Place a drain pan under the pump, remove the return hose and drain the reservoir.
2. Disconnect the pressure line from the pump and tie up the ends of both hoses in a raised position. Cap the openings.

3. Loosen the pump pivot and adjusting bolts and remove the drive belt.
4. Remove the bolts and lift out the pump.
5. Installation is the reverse of removal. Adjust the belt tension. Tighten the bolts to 30-45 ft. lbs. Connect the hoses. Refill the reservoir. Run the engine and check for leaks.

Quick-Connect Pressure Line

▶ **See Figure 169**

Some pumps will have a quick-connect fitting for the pressure line. This fitting may, under certain circumstances, leak and/or be improperly engaged resulting in unplanned disconnection.

The leak is usually caused by a cut O-ring, imperfections in the outlet fitting inside diameter, or an improperly machined O-ring groove.

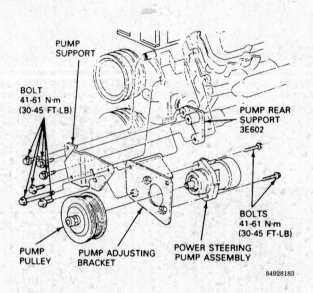

Fig. 167 ZF Power steering pump installation on F-Super Duty motor home chassis

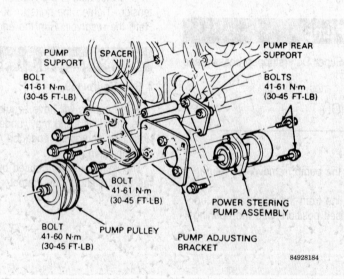

Fig. 168 ZF Power steering pump installation on F-Super Duty stripped chassis

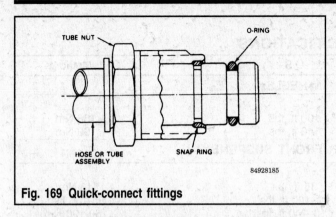

TUBE NUT

O-RING

HOSE OR TUBE ASSEMBLY

SNAP RING

84928185

Fig. 169 Quick-connect fittings

Improper engagement can be caused by an improperly machined tube end, tube nut, snapring, outlet fitting or gear port.

If a leak occurs, the O-ring should be replaced with new O-rings. Special O-rings are made for quick-disconnect fittings. Standard O-rings should never be used in their place. If the new O-rings do not solve the leak problem, replace the outlet fitting. If that doesn't work, replace the pressure line.

Improper engagement due to a missing or bent snapring, or improperly machined tube nut, may be corrected with a Ford snapring kit made for the purpose. If that doesn't work, replace the pressure hose.

When tightening a quick-connect tube nut, always use a tube nut wrench; never use an open-end wrench! Use of an open-end wrench will result in deformation of the nut! Tighten quick-connect tube nuts to 15 ft. lbs. maximum.

Swivel and/or end-play of quick-connect fittings is normal.

TORQUE SPECIFICATIONS

Component	U.S.	Metric
WHEELS		
Front or rear wheels		
5-lug	100 ft. lbs.	136 Nm
All others	140 ft. lbs.	190 Nm
2-WHEEL DRIVE COIL SPRING FRONT SUSPENSION		
Front Wheel Spindle		
Lower ball joint stud	35 ft. lbs.	48 Nm
Steering linkage to spindle nut	70–100 ft. lbs.	95-136 Nm
Upper ball joint stud	110–140 ft. lbs.	150-190 Nm
I-beam axle pivot bolts	120–150 ft. lbs.	163-204 Nm
Radius Arm		
Bushing nut	120 ft. lbs.	163 Nm
Radius arm-to-axle bolt	269–329 ft. lbs.	366-447 Nm
Shock Absorbers		
Lower end	40–60 ft. lbs.	54-82 Nm
Upper end	25–35 ft. lbs.	34-48 Nm
Springs		
Lower retainer attaching nuts	70–100 ft. lbs.	95-136 Nm
Upper retaining bolts	13–18 ft. lbs.	18-24 Nm
Stabilizer Bar		
Frame mounting bracket nuts/bolts		
F-250 and F-350	65 ft. lbs.	88 Nm
Link-to-stabilizer bar and axle bracket	70 ft. lbs.	95 Nm
Stabilizer bar-to-crossmember attaching bolts		
F-150	35 ft. lbs.	48 Nm
Stabilizer bar-to-frame retainer bolts		
F-250 and F-350	35 ft. lbs.	48 Nm
2-WHEEL DRIVE LEAF SPRING FRONT SUSPENSION		
Shock Absorbers		
Chassis/cab upper and lower	52–74 ft. lbs.	71-101 Nm
Stripped cab and motor home chassis upper and lower	220–300 ft. lbs.	299-408 Nm
Spindles		
Drag link nut	50–70 ft. lbs.	68-95 Nm
Lock pin nut	40–50 ft. lbs.	54-68 Nm
Spindle pin plugs	35–50 ft. lbs.	48-68 Nm
Tie rod end nut	50–70 ft. lbs.	68-95 Nm
Springs		
Front end of spring		
Chassis/cab spring-to-shackle	120–150 ft. lbs.	163-204 Nm
Chassis/cab shackle-to-frame	150–210 ft. lbs.	204-286 Nm
Stripped chassis or motor home chassis spring-to-bracket	148–207 ft. lbs.	201-282 Nm
Rear end of spring		
Chassis/cab spring-to-bracket	150–210 ft. lbs.	204-286 Nm
Stripped chassis or motor home chassis spring-to-shackle or shackle-to-bracket	74–110 ft. lbs.	101-150 Nm
U-bolts		
Chassis/cab	150–210 ft. lbs.	204-286 Nm
Stripped chassis and motor home chassis	220–300 ft. lbs.	299-408 Nm

TORQUE SPECIFICATIONS

Component	U.S.	Metric
2-WHEEL DRIVE LEAF SPRING FRONT SUSPENSION		
Stabilizer Bar		
Chassis/Cab		
End link-to-frame bolts	52–74 ft. lbs.	71-101 Nm
Stabilizer bar-to-axle mounting bolts	35–50 ft. lbs.	48-68 Nm
Stabilizer bar-to-end link nuts	15–25 ft. lbs.	20-34 Nm
Stripped Chassis or Motor Home Chassis		
Link-to-axle bracket bolts	57–81 ft. lbs.	78-110 Nm
Stabilizer bar-to-frame brackets bolts	30–47 ft. lbs.	41-64 Nm
Stabilizer bar-to-link nuts	15–25 ft. lbs.	20-34 Nm
Track Bar		
Chassis/Cab Models	120–150 ft. lbs.	163-204 Nm
4-WHEEL DRIVE FRONT SUSPENSION		
Axle pivot bolt	150 ft. lbs.	204 Nm
Radius Arm		
F-150 and Bronco		
Bracket-to-axle bolts	25 ft. lbs.	34 Nm
Radius arm-to-axle bolt	330 ft. lbs.	449 Nm
Radius arm rear attaching nut	120 ft. lbs.	163 Nm
Upper stud-type radius arm-to-axle bolt	250 ft. lbs.	340 Nm
Shock Absorbers		
F-150 and Bronco		
Upper nut	30 ft. lbs.	41 Nm
Lower bolt/nut	60 ft. lbs.	82 Nm
F-250, F-350, F-Super Duty		
Upper and lower nut/bolt	70 ft. lbs.	95 Nm
Springs		
U-bolt nuts 120 ft. lbs.	163 Nm	
F-150 and Bronco		
Lower spring retainer nut	100 ft. lbs.	136 Nm
Upper retainer bolts	13–18 ft. lbs.	18-24 Nm
F-250, F-350		
Shackle bolt nuts	150 ft. lbs.	204 Nm
Hanger bolt nut	150 ft. lbs.	204 Nm
Stabilizer Bar		
F-150 and Bronco		
Retainer nuts	35 ft. lbs.	48 Nm
All other nuts at the links	70 ft. lbs.	95 Nm
F-250 and F-350		
Connecting links-to-spring seat caps	70 ft. lbs.	95 Nm
Connecting links-to-stabilizer bar	25 ft. lbs.	34 Nm
Retainer-to-mounting bracket nuts	35 ft. lbs.	48 Nm
Track bar-to-bracket bolts		
F-350	200 ft. lbs.	272 Nm
REAR SUSPENSION		
Shock Absorbers		
Lower end		
exc. Super Duty stripped chassis & motor home	52–74 ft. lbs.	71-101 Nm
Upper end		
exc. Super Duty stripped chassis & motor home	40–60 ft. lbs.	54-82 Nm
Super Duty stripped chassis & motor home chassis		
Upper & lower ends	220–300 ft. lbs.	299-408 Nm

84928194

TORQUE SPECIFICATIONS

Component	U.S.	Metric
REAR SUSPENSION		
Springs		
Spring-to-front spring hanger		
F-150 2-wd	75–115 ft. lbs.	102-156 Nm
F-250 2-wd, F-350 2-wd and Bronco	150–210 ft. lbs.	204-286 Nm
F-150, 250, 350 4-wd	150–175 ft. lbs.	204-238 Nm
F-Super Duty	255–345 ft. lbs.	345-469 Nm
Spring-to-rear spring hanger		
All except F-250 and F-350 2-wd Chassis Cab	75–115 ft. lbs.	102-156 Nm
F-250 and F-350 2-wd Chassis Cab; F-Super Duty	150–210 ft. lbs.	204-286 Nm
U-bolts		
Bronco, F-150 and F-250 under 8,500 lb. GVW	75–115 ft. lbs.	102-156 Nm
F-250 HD and F-350	150–210 ft. lbs.	204-286 Nm
F-Super Duty chassis/cab	200–270 ft. lbs.	272-367 Nm
F-Super Duty stripped chassis and motor home chassis	220–300 ft. lbs.	299-408 Nm
Stabilizer Bar		
Link bracket-to-frame nut, 4-wd	30–42 ft. lbs.	41-57 Nm
Link-to-bracket nut, 4-wd	60 ft. lbs.	84 Nm
Link-to-frame nut, 2-wd	60 ft. lbs.	84 Nm
Stabilizer bar-to-axle bolt		
Super Duty stripped chassis and motor home chassis	30–47 ft. lbs.	41-64 Nm
Stabilizer bar-to-axle nut		
exc. Super Duty	30–42 ft. lbs.	41-57 Nm
Stabilizer bar-to-axle bolt		
Super Duty chassis/cab	27–37 ft. lbs.	37-50 Nm
Stabilizer bar-to-link	15–25 ft. lbs.	20-34 Nm
STEERING		
Bendix C-300N Power Steering Gear		
Adjusting screw locknut	74–88 ft. lbs.	101-120 Nm
Gear mounting bolts	150–200 ft. lbs.	204-272 Nm
Meshload	4–18 inch lb.*	0.5-2.0 Nm*
Piston and valve body bolts	80–88 ft. lbs.	109-120 Nm
Pressure relief plug	66–73 ft. lbs.	90-99 Nm
Pressure relief valve seat	15–18 ft. lbs.	20-24 Nm
Side cover bolts	80–88 ft. lbs.	109-120 Nm
Steering limiting valve seat	9–11 ft. lbs.	12-15 Nm
U-joint bolt and nut	50–70 ft. lbs.	68-95 Nm
Valve nut	221–257 ft. lbs.	301-350 Nm
*plus the total rotational torque		
Connecting rod ball stud nut	75 ft. lbs.	102 Nm
Drag link ball stud nut	50–75 ft. lbs.	68-102 Nm
Ford C-II Power Steering Pump		
Adjustment bracket-to-support bracket		
6-4.9L, 8-5.0L, 8-5.8L	45 ft. lbs.	61 Nm
8-7.5L and Diesel		
Long bolt	65 ft. lbs.	88 Nm
Short bolt	45 ft. lbs.	61 Nm
Pivot bolt		
6-4.9L and 8-5.0L	45 ft. lbs.	61 Nm
Pressure line-to-fitting	29 ft. lbs.	39 Nm
Pump-to-adjustment bracket	45 ft. lbs.	61 Nm
Support bracket-to-engine		
8-5.8L	65 ft. lbs.	88 Nm
Support bracket-to-water pump housing		
6-4.9L	17 ft. lbs.	23 Nm
8-5.0L, 5.8L	45 ft. lbs.	61 Nm

TORQUE SPECIFICATIONS

Component	U.S.	Metric
STEERING		
Ford Integral Power Steering Gear		
Adjuster screw locknut	45 ft. lbs.	61 Nm
Ball clamps	42–70 inch lbs.	4.7-7.8 Nm
Flex coupling bolt	30 ft. lbs.	41 Nm
Gear mounting bolts	65 ft. lbs.	88 Nm
Meshload		
Fewer than 5,000 miles	15–25 inch lbs.	1.7-2.8 Nm
5,000 or more miles	7 inch lbs.*	0.8 Nm*
Preload	4–9 inch lbs.	0.5-1.0
Pressure line	25 ft. lbs.	34 Nm
Race nut	55–90 ft. lbs.	75-122 Nm
Sector shaft bolts	55–70 ft. lbs.	75-95 Nm
*more than the preload		
Ford XR-50 Power Steering Gear		
Adjuster screw locknut	45 ft. lbs.	61 Nm
Ball clamps and tighten	42–70 inch lbs.	4.7-7.8 Nm
Flex coupling bolt	30-42 ft. lbs.	41-57 Nm
Gear mounting bolts	65 ft. lbs.	88 Nm
Meshload		
Fewer than 5,000 miles	15–25 inch lbs.	1.7-2.8 Nm
5,000 or more miles	7 inch lbs.*	0.8 Nm*
Preload	4-9 inch lbs.	0.5-1.0 Nm
Pressure line	25 ft. lbs.	34 Nm
Race nut	55–90 ft. lbs.	75-122 Nm
Sector bolts	55–70 ft. lbs.	75-95 Nm
* more than preload		
Manual Steering Gear		
Adjusting screw locknut	25 ft. lbs.	34 Nm
Flex coupling-to-gear bolt	30 ft. lbs.	41 Nm
Gear mounting bolts	65 ft. lbs.	88 Nm
Meshload	9–14 inch lbs.	1.0-1.5 Nm
Preload	5-9 inch lbs.	0.5-1.0 Nm
Sector cover bolts	40 ft. lbs.	54 Nm
Pitman arm nut		
All Except F-Super Duty Stripped Chassis & Motor Home	170–230 ft. lbs.	231-313 Nm
F-Super Duty Stripped Chassis & Motor Home	220–300 ft. lbs.	299-408 Nm
Quick-Connect Pressure Line		
Tube nuts	15 ft. lbs. max.	20 Nm max.
Steering Column		
All Models Except F-Super Duty Stripped Chassis and Motor Home		
Column support bracket nuts	35 ft. lbs.	48 Nm
Cover plate clamp bolt	18 ft. lbs.	24 Nm
Floor cover bolts	10 ft. lbs.	14 Nm
Intermediate shaft bolt	50 ft. lbs.	68 Nm
Shroud bottom screw	15 inch lbs.	1.7 Nm
Support bracket bolts	25 ft. lbs.	34 Nm
F-Super Duty Stripped Chassis & Motor Home		
Column-to-support bracket bolts	19–27 ft. lbs.	26-37 Nm
Floor cover bolts	10 ft. lbs.	14 Nm
Intermediate shaft bolt	20–35 ft. lbs.	27-48 Nm

84928196

TORQUE SPECIFICATIONS

	STEERING	
Component	U.S.	Metric
Steering wheel nut		
All Except F-Super Duty Stripped Chassis models & Motor Home	40 ft. lbs.	54 Nm
F-Super Duty Stripped Chassis & Motor Home	30–42 ft. lbs.	41-57 Nm
Tie Rod		
Adjuster clamp nuts	40 ft. lbs.	54 Nm
Except Rubberized Ball Socket Linkage	70 ft. lbs.	95 Nm
Rubberized Ball Socket Linkage	75 ft. lbs.	102 Nm
ZF Power Steering Pump		
Mounting bolts	30–45 ft. lbs.	41-61 Nm

84928197

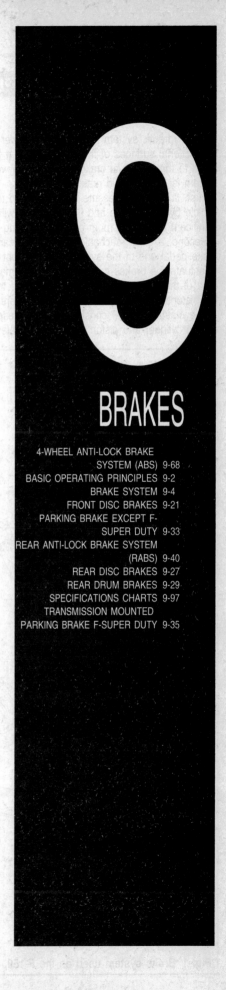

9

BRAKES

BASIC OPERATING PRINCIPLES

▶ See Figure 1

The hydraulic system transports the power required to force the frictional surfaces of the braking system together from the pedal to the individual brake units at each wheel. A hydraulic system is used for two reasons.

First, fluid under pressure can be carried to all parts of a vehicle by small pipes and flexible hoses without taking up a significant amount of room or posing routing problems.

Second, a great mechanical advantage can be given to the brake pedal end of the system, and the foot pressure required to actuate the brakes can be reduced by making the surface area of the master cylinder pistons smaller than that of any of the pistons in the wheel cylinders or calipers.

The master cylinder consists of a fluid reservoir and a double cylinder and piston assembly. Double type master cylin-ders are designed to separate the front and rear braking systems hydraulically in case of a leak.

Steel lines carry the brake fluid to a point on the vehicle's frame near each of the vehicle's wheels. The fluid is then carried to the calipers and wheel cylinders by flexible tubes and steel lines in order to allow for suspension and steering movements.

In drum brake systems, each wheel cylinder contains two pistons, one at either end, which push outward in opposite directions.

In disc brake systems, the cylinders are part of the calipers. The cylinders are used to force the brake pads against the disc.

All pistons employ some type of seal, usually made of rub-ber, to minimize fluid leakage. A rubber dust boot seals the

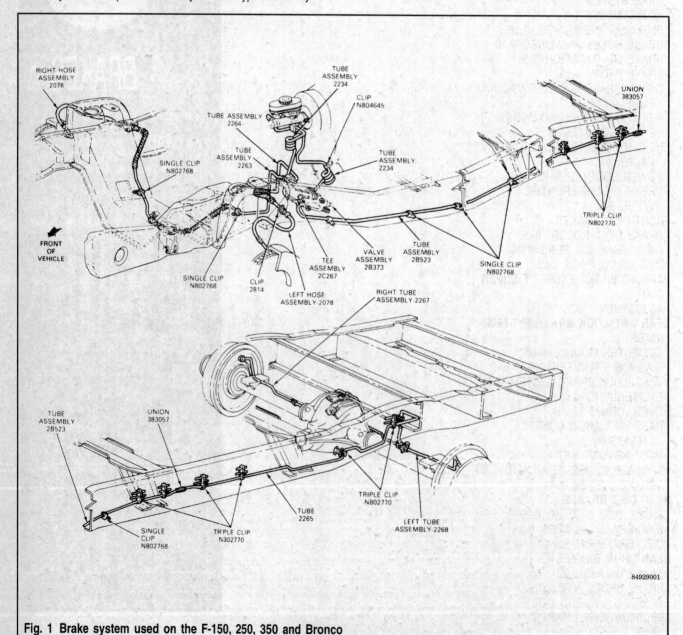

Fig. 1 Brake system used on the F-150, 250, 350 and Bronco

outer end of the cylinder against dust and dirt. The boot fits around the outer end of the piston on disc brake calipers, and around the brake actuating rod on wheel cylinders.

The hydraulic system operates as follows: When at rest, the entire system, from the piston(s) in the master cylinder to those in the wheel cylinders or calipers, is full of brake fluid. Upon application of the brake pedal, fluid trapped in front of the master cylinder piston(s) is forced through the lines to the wheel cylinders. Here, it forces the pistons outward, in the case of drum brakes, and inward toward the disc, in the case of disc brakes. The motion of the pistons is opposed by return springs mounted outside the cylinders in drum brakes, and by spring seals, in disc brakes.

Upon release of the brake pedal, a spring located inside the master cylinder immediately returns the master cylinder pistons to the normal position. The pistons contain check valves and the master cylinder has compensating ports drilled in it. These are uncovered as the pistons reach their normal position. The piston check valves allow fluid to flow toward the wheel cylinders or calipers as the pistons withdraw. Then, as the return springs force the brake pads or shoes into the released position, the excess fluid reservoir through the compensating ports. It is during the time the pedal is in the released position that any fluid that has leaked out of the system will be replaced through the compensating ports.

Dual circuit master cylinders employ two pistons, located one behind the other, in the same cylinder. The primary piston is actuated directly by mechanical linkage from the brake pedal through the power booster. The secondary piston is actuated by fluid trapped between the two pistons. If a leak develops in front of the secondary piston, it moves forward until it bottoms against the front of the master cylinder, and the fluid trapped between the pistons will operate the rear brakes. If the rear brakes develop a leak, the primary piston will move forward until direct contact with the secondary piston takes place, and it will force the secondary piston to actuate the front brakes. In either case, the brake pedal moves farther when the brakes are applied, and less braking power is available.

All dual circuit systems use a switch to warn the driver when only half of the brake system is operational. This switch is located in a valve body which is mounted on the firewall or the frame below the master cylinder. A hydraulic piston receives pressure from both circuits, each circuit's pressure being applied to one end of the piston. When the pressures are in balance, the piston remains stationary. When one circuit has a leak, however, the greater pressure in that circuit during application of the brakes will push the piston to one side, closing the switch and activating the brake warning light.

In disc brake systems, this valve body also contains a metering valve and, in some cases, a proportioning valve. The metering valve keeps pressure from traveling to the disc brakes on the front wheels until the brake shoes on the rear wheels have contacted the drums, ensuring that the front brakes will never be used alone. The proportioning valve controls the pressure to the rear brakes to lessen the chance of rear wheel lock-up during very hard braking.

Warning lights may be tested by depressing the brake pedal and holding it while opening one of the wheel cylinder bleeder screws. If this does not cause the light to go on, substitute a new lamp, make continuity checks, and, finally, replace the switch as necessary.

The hydraulic system may be checked for leaks by applying pressure to the pedal gradually and steadily. If the pedal sinks very slowly to the floor, the system has a leak. This is not to be confused with a springy or spongy feel due to the compression of air within the lines. If the system leaks, there will be a gradual change in the position of the pedal with a constant pressure.

Check for leaks along all lines and at wheel cylinders. If no external leaks are apparent, the problem is inside the master cylinder.

Disc Brakes

BASIC OPERATING PRINCIPLES

Instead of the traditional expanding brakes that press outward against a circular drum, disc brake systems utilize a disc (rotor) with brake pads positioned on either side of it. Braking effect is achieved in a manner similar to the way you would squeeze a spinning phonograph record between your fingers. The disc (rotor) is a casting with cooling fins between the two braking surfaces. This enables air to circulate between the braking surfaces making them less sensitive to heat buildup and more resistant to fade. Dirt and water do not affect braking action since contaminants are thrown off by the centrifugal action of the rotor or scraped off the by the pads. Also, the equal clamping action of the two brake pads tends to ensure uniform, straight line stops. Disc brakes are inherently self-adjusting. There are three general types of disc brake:

1. A fixed caliper.
2. A floating caliper.
3. A sliding caliper.

The fixed caliper design uses two pistons mounted on either side of the rotor (in each side of the caliper). The caliper is mounted rigidly and does not move.

The sliding and floating designs are quite similar. In fact, these two types are often lumped together. In both designs, the pad on the inside of the rotor is moved into contact with the rotor by hydraulic force. The caliper, which is not held in a fixed position, moves slightly, bringing the outside pad into contact with the rotor. There are various methods of attaching floating calipers. Some pivot at the bottom or top, and some slide on mounting bolts. In any event, the end result is the same.

Drum Brakes

BASIC OPERATING PRINCIPLES

Drum brakes employ two brake shoes mounted on a stationary backing plate. These shoes are positioned inside a circular drum which rotates with the wheel assembly. The shoes are held in place by springs. This allows them to slide toward the drums (when they are applied) while keeping the linings and drums in alignment. The shoes are actuated by a wheel cylinder which is mounted at the top of the backing plate. When the brakes are applied, hydraulic pressure forces the wheel cylinder's actuating links outward. Since these links bear directly against the top of the brake shoes, the tops of the shoes are then forced against the inner side of the drum. This action forces the bottoms of the two shoes to contact the brake drum by rotating the entire assembly slightly (known as servo action). When pressure within the wheel cylinder is relaxed, return springs pull the shoes back away from the drum.

Most modern drum brakes are designed to self-adjust themselves during application when the vehicle is moving in reverse. This motion causes both shoes to rotate very slightly with the drum, rocking an adjusting lever, thereby causing rotation of the adjusting screw.

Power Boosters

Power brakes operate just as non-power brake systems except in the actuation of the master cylinder pistons. A vacuum diaphragm is located on the front of the master cylinder and assists the driver in applying the brakes, reducing both the effort and travel he must put into moving the brake pedal.

The vacuum diaphragm housing is connected to the intake manifold by a vacuum hose. A check valve is placed at the point where the hose enters the diaphragm housing, so that during periods of low manifold vacuum brake assist vacuum will not be lost.

Depressing the brake pedal closes off the vacuum source and allows atmospheric pressure to enter on one side of the diaphragm. This causes the master cylinder pistons to move and apply the brakes. When the brake pedal is released, vac-

uum is applied to both sides of the diaphragm, and return springs return the diaphragm and master cylinder pistons to the released position. If the vacuum fails, the brake pedal rod will butt against the end of the master cylinder actuating rod, and direct mechanical application will occur as the pedal is depressed.

The hydraulic and mechanical problems that apply to conventional brake systems also apply to power brakes, and should be checked for if the tests below do not reveal the problem. **Test for a system vacuum leak as described below:**

1. Operate the engine at idle without touching the brake pedal for at least one minute.
2. Turn off the engine, and wait one minute.
3. Test for the presence of assist vacuum by depressing the brake pedal and releasing it several times. Light application will produce less and less pedal travel, if vacuum was present. If there is no vacuum, air is leaking into the system somewhere.

Test for system operation as follows:

4. Pump the brake pedal (with engine off) until the supply vacuum is entirely gone.
5. Put a light, steady pressure on the pedal.
6. Start the engine, and operate it at idle. If the system is operating, the brake pedal should fall toward the floor if constant pressure is maintained on the pedal.

Power brake systems may be tested for hydraulic leaks just as ordinary systems are tested.

BRAKE SYSTEM

✳✳WARNING

Clean, high quality brake fluid is essential to the safe and proper operation of the brake system. You should always buy the highest quality brake fluid that is available. If the brake fluid becomes contaminated, drain and flush the system and fill the master cylinder with new fluid.   Never reuse any brake fluid. Any brake fluid that is removed from the system should be discarded.

Adjustments

DRUM BRAKES

▶ See Figures 2, 3, 4, 5 and 6

The drum brakes are self-adjusting and require a manual adjustment only after the brake shoes have been replaced, or when the length of the adjusting screw has been changed while performing some other service operation, as i.e., taking off brake drums.

To adjust the brakes, follow the procedures given below:

Drum Installed

1. Raise and support the rear end on jackstands.
2. Remove the rubber plug from the adjusting slot on the backing plate.

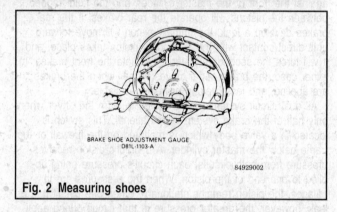

Fig. 2 Measuring shoes

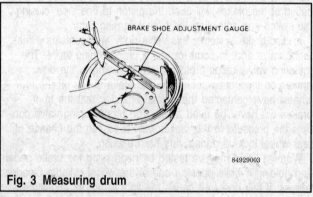

Fig. 3 Measuring drum

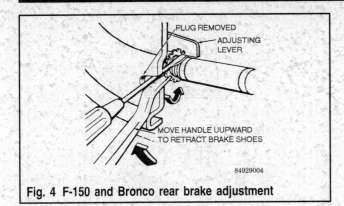

Fig. 4 F-150 and Bronco rear brake adjustment

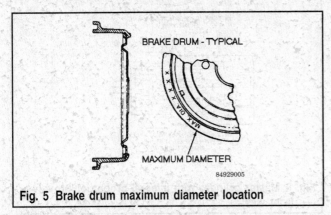

Fig. 5 Brake drum maximum diameter location

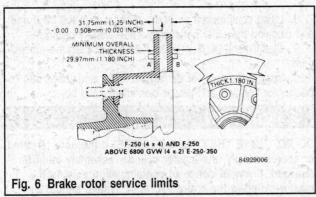

Fig. 6 Brake rotor service limits

3. Insert a brake adjusting spoon into the slot and engage the lowest possible tooth on the starwheel. Move the end of the brake spoon downward to move the starwheel upward and expand the adjusting screw. Repeat this operation until the brakes lock the wheels.

4. Insert a small screwdriver or piece of firm wire (coat hanger wire) into the adjusting slot and push the automatic adjusting lever out and free of the starwheel on the adjusting screw and hold it there.

5. Engage the topmost tooth possible on the starwheel with the brake adjusting spoon. Move the end of the adjusting spoon upward to move the adjusting screw starwheel downward and contract the adjusting screw. Back off the adjusting screw starwheel until the wheel spins freely with a minimum of drag. Keep track of the number of turns that the starwheel is backed off, or the number of strokes taken with the brake adjusting spoon.

6. Repeat this operation for the other side. When backing off the brakes on the other side, the starwheel adjuster must be backed off the same number of turns to prevent side-to-side brake pull.

7. When the brakes are adjusted make several stops while backing the vehicle, to equalize the brakes at both of the wheels.

8. Remove the safety stands and lower the vehicle. Road test the vehicle.

Drum Removed

❊❊CAUTION

Brake shoes contain asbestos, which has been determined to be a cancer causing agent. Never clean the brake surfaces with compressed air! Avoid inhaling any dust from any brake surface! When cleaning brake surfaces, use a commercially available brake cleaning fluid.

1. Make sure that the shoe-to-contact pad areas are clean and properly lubricated.

2. Using an inside caliper check the inside diameter of the drum. Measure across the diameter of the assembled brake shoes, at their widest point.

3. Turn the adjusting screw so that the diameter of the shoes is 0.030 in. (0.76mm) less than the brake drum inner diameter.

4. Install the drum.

Brake Light Switch

REMOVAL & INSTALLATION

▶ See Figure 7

1. Lift the locking tab on the switch connector and disconnect the wiring.

2. Remove the hairpin retainer, slide the stoplamp switch, pushrod and nylon washer off of the pedal. Remove the washer, then the switch by sliding it up or down.

➡**On trucks equipped with speed control, the spacer washer is replaced by the dump valve adapter washer.**

3. To install the switch, position it so that the U-shaped side is nearest the pedal and directly over/under the pin.

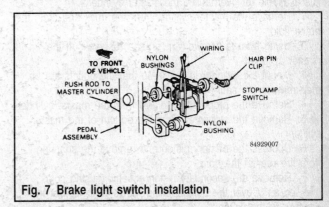

Fig. 7 Brake light switch installation

4. Slide the switch up or down, trapping the master cylinder pushrod and bushing between the switch side plates.

5. Push the switch and pushrod assembly firmly towards the brake pedal arm. Assemble the outside white plastic washer to the pin and install the hairpin retainer.

✳✳CAUTION

Don't substitute any other type of retainer. Use only the Ford specified hairpin retainer.

6. Assemble the connector on the switch.
7. Check stoplamp operation.

✳✳CAUTION

Make sure that the stoplamp switch wiring has sufficient travel during a full pedal stroke!

REMOVAL & INSTALLATION

▶ **See Figures 8, 9, 10, 11, 12, 13 and 14**

1. With the engine off, depress the brake pedal several times to expel any vacuum.
2. Disconnect the fluid level warning switch wire.
3. Disconnect the hydraulic system brake lines at the master cylinder.
4. Remove the master cylinder retaining nuts and remove the master cylinder.
To install the master cylinder:
5. Position the master cylinder assembly on the booster and install the retaining nuts. Torque the nuts to 18-25 ft. lbs.
6. Connect the hydraulic brake system lines to the master cylinder.
7. Connect the wiring.
8. Bleed the master cylinder as described below.

OVERHAUL

The most important thing to remember when rebuilding the master cylinder is cleanliness. Work in clean surroundings with clean tools and clean cloths or paper for drying purposes. Have plenty of clean alcohol and brake fluid on hand to clean and lubricate the internal components. There are service repair kits available for overhauling the master cylinder.

1. Remove the master cylinder from the truck and drain the brake fluid.
2. Using a large screwdriver, pry the reservoir off the master cylinder.
3. Mount the cylinder in a vise so that the outlets are up then remove the seal from the hub.
4. Remove the proportioning valve from the master cylinder.
5. Remove the stopscrew from the bottom of the master cylinder.
6. Depress the primary piston and remove the snapring from the rear of the bore.
7. Remove the secondary piston assembly using compressed air. Cover the bore opening with a cloth to prevent damage to the piston.

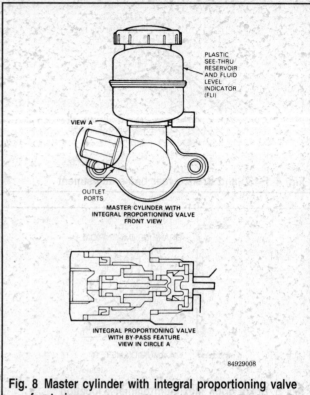

Fig. 8 Master cylinder with integral proportioning valve — front view

8. Using compressed air in the outlet port at the blind end and plugging the other port, remove the primary piston.
9. Clean metal parts in brake fluid and discard the rubber parts.
10. Inspect the bore for damage or wear, and check the pistons for damage and proper clearance in the bore.

✳✳CAUTION

DO NOT HONE THE CYLINDER BORE! If the bore is pitted or scored deeply, the master cylinder assembly must be replaced. If any evidence of contamination exist in the master cylinder, the entire hydraulic system should be flushed and refilled with clean brake fluid. Blow out the passages with compressed air.

11. If the master cylinder is not damaged, it may be serviced with a rebuilding kit. The rebuilding kit may contain secondary and primary piston assemblies instead of just rubber seals. In this case, seal installation is not required.
12. Clean all parts in isopropyl alcohol.
13. Install new secondary seals in the two grooves in the flat end of the front piston. The lips of the seals will be facing away from each other.
14. Install a new primary seal and the seal protector on the opposite end of the front piston with the lips of the seal facing outward.
15. Coat the seals with brake fluid. Install the spring on the front piston with the spring retainer in the primary seal.
16. Insert the piston assembly, spring end first, into the bore and use a wooden rod to seat it.

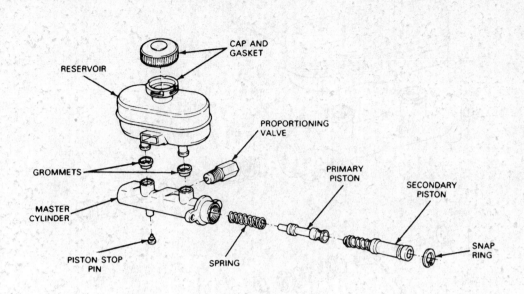

Fig. 9 1988-93 master cylinder

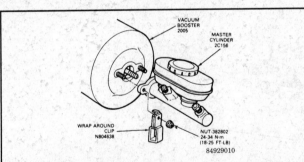

Fig. 10 Master cylinder installation on 1988-93 F-150, 250, 350 and Bronco

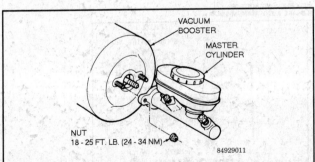

Fig. 11 Master cylinder installation on 1987 F-150, 250, 350 and Bronco

17. Coat the rear piston seals with brake fluid and install them into the piston grooves with the lips facing the spring end.

18. Assemble the spring onto the piston and install the assembly into the bore spring first. Install the snapring.

19. Hold the piston train at the bottom of the bore and install the stopscrew. Install a new seal on the hub.

➡**Whenever the reservoir or master cylinder is replaced, new reservoir grommets should be used.**

20. Coat the new grommet with clean brake fluid and insert them into the master cylinder. Bench-bleed the cylinder or install and bleed the cylinder on the car.

21. Press the reservoir into place. A snap should be felt, indicating that the reservoir is properly positioned.

Pressure Differential Valve

REMOVAL & INSTALLATION

1. Disconnect the electrical leads from the valve.
2. Unscrew the valve from the master cylinder.
3. Install the valve in the reverse order of removal.
4. Bleed the master cylinder.

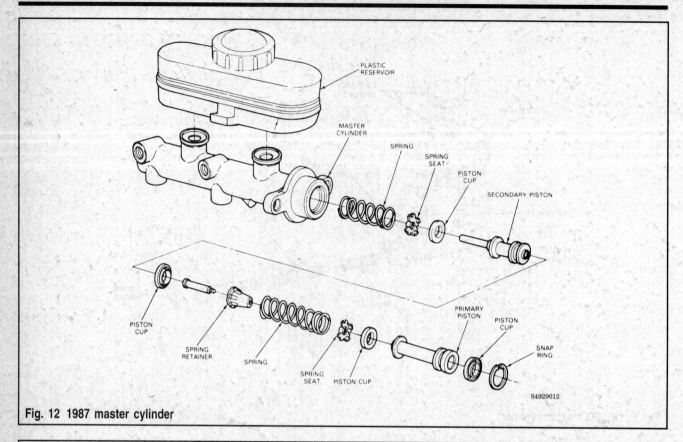

Fig. 12 1987 master cylinder

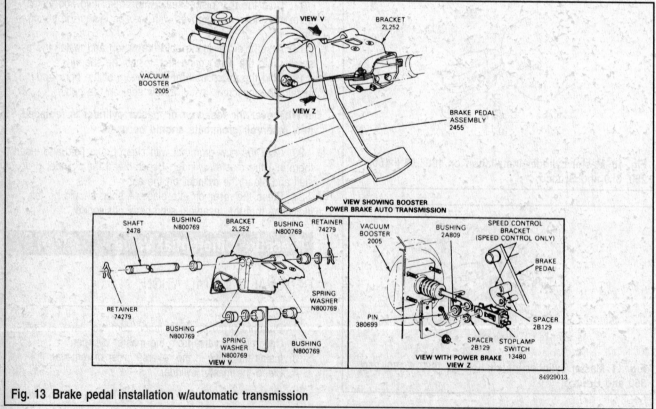

Fig. 13 Brake pedal installation w/automatic transmission

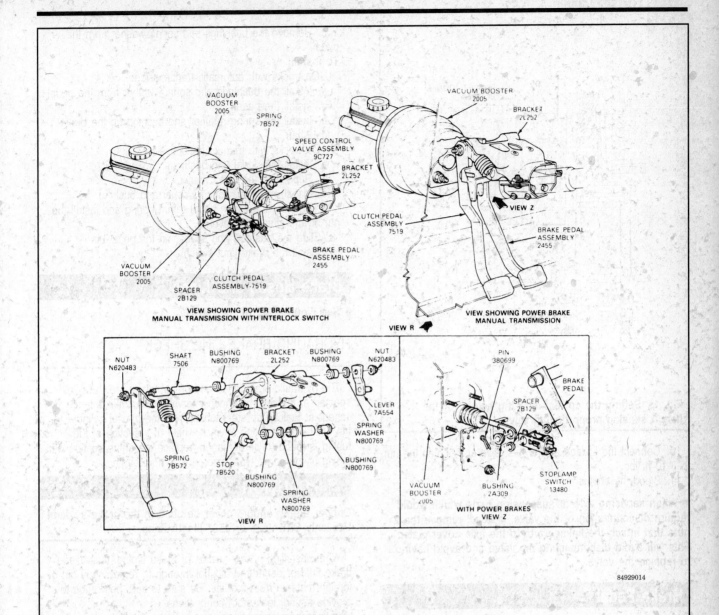

Fig. 14 Brake pedal installation w/manual transmission

Height Sensing Proportioning Valve

REMOVAL & INSTALLATION

▶ **See Figures 15 and 16**

F-Super Duty Only

➡If the linkage is disconnected from the valve, the proper setting of the valve will be lost and a new valve will have to be installed. The new valve will have the shaft preset and secured internally. If the shaft of the new valve turns freely, DO NOT USE IT! The valve cannot be repaired or disassembled. It is to be replaced as a unit. If the linkage is damaged or broken and requires replacement, a new sensing valve will also be required.

1. Raise and support the rear end on jackstands.
2. Raise the frame to obtain a clearance of 6⅝in. (168.3mm) between the bottom edge of the rubber jounce bumper and the top of the axle tube — on BOTH sides of the axle. The is the correct indexing height for the valve.
3. Remove the nut holding the linkage arm to the valve and disconnect the arm.
4. Remove the bolt holding the flexible brake hose to the valve.
5. Disconnect the brake line from the valve.
6. Remove the 2 mounting bolts and remove the valve from its bracket.
   To install:
7. Place the new valve on the bracket and tighten the mounting bolts to 12-18 ft. lbs.
8. Install the brake hose, using new copper gaskets and tighten the bolt to 28-34 ft. lbs.
9. Attach the brake line to the lower part of the valve.

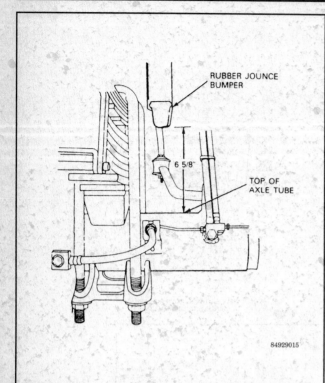

Fig. 15 Setting the correct indexing height for the height sensing proportioning valve

10. Connect the linkage arm to the valve and tighten the nut to 8-10 ft. lbs.
11. Bleed the brakes.

➡When servicing axle or suspension parts which would require disconnection of the valve, instead, remove the 2 nuts that attach the linkage arm to the axle cover plate. This will avoid disconnecting the valve and avoid having to replace the valve.

Brake Pedal

REMOVAL & INSTALLATION

1. Remove the brake light switch.
2. Slide the pushrod and spacer from the pedal pin.
3. If the truck is equipped with speed control, you can leave the speed control bracket in place.
4. On trucks with manual transmission:
   a. Disconnect the clutch pedal return spring and remove the nut on the clutch rod lever.
   b. Remove the lever, spring washer and bushing.
   c. Push the clutch pedal to the side far enough to allow the brake pedal to slide off the shaft.
   d. Remove the pedal and bushings.
5. On trucks with automatic transmission:
   a. Remove the spring retainer and bushing from the brake pedal shaft.
   b. From the other end, pull out the shaft and remove the pedal.

   c. Remove the bushings and spring washer from the pedal.
To install:
6. On trucks with automatic transmission:
   a. Install the bushings and spring washer from the pedal.
   b. Install the pedal.
   c. Install the spring retainer and bushing on the brake pedal shaft.
7. On trucks with manual transmission:
   a. Install the pedal and bushings.
   b. Reposition the clutch pedal.
   c. Install the lever, spring washer and bushing.
   d. Connect the clutch pedal return spring and install the nut on the clutch rod lever.
8. Slide the pushrod and spacer on the pedal pin.
9. Install the brake light switch.

Brake Hoses and Lines

▶ **See Figures 17, 18, 19 and 20**

HYDRAULIC BRAKE LINE CHECK

The hydraulic brake lines and brake linings are to be inspected at the recommended intervals in the maintenance schedule. Follow the steel tubing from the master cylinder to the flexible hose fitting at each wheel. If a section of the tubing is found to be damaged, replace the entire section with tubing of the same type, size, shape, and length.

❊❊CAUTION

Copper tubing should never be used in the brake system! Use only SAE J526 or J527 steel tubing.

When installing a new section of brake tubing, flush clean brake fluid or denatured alcohol through to remove any dirt or foreign material from the line. Be sure to flare both ends to provide sound, leak-proof connections.

❊❊CAUTION

Double-flare the lines! Never single-flare a brake line!

When bending the tubing to fit the underbody contours, be careful not to kink or crack the line. Torque all hydraulic connections to 10-15 ft. lbs.

Check the flexible brake hoses that connect the steel tubing to each wheel cylinder. Replace the hose if it shows any signs of softening, cracking, or other damage. When installing a new front brake hose, position the hose to avoid contact with other chassis parts. Place a new copper gasket over the hose fitting and thread the hose assembly into the front wheel cylinder. A new rear brake hose must be positioned clear of the exhaust pipe or shock absorber. Thread the hose into the rear brake tube connector. When installing either a new front or rear brake hose, engage the opposite end of the hose to the bracket on the frame. Install the horseshoe type retaining clip and connect the tube to the hose with the tube fitting nut.

Always bleed the system after hose or line replacement. Before bleeding, make sure that the master cylinder is topped

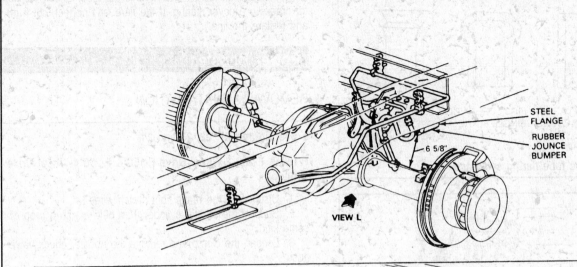

VIEW L

STEEL FLANGE

RUBBER JOUNCE BUMPER

6 5/8"

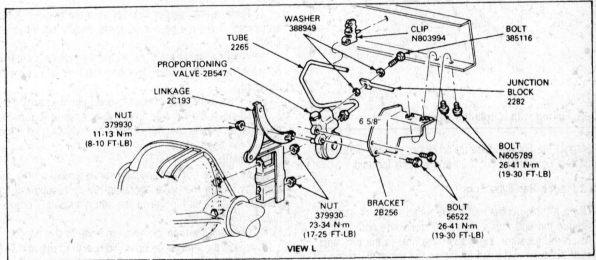

WASHER 388949

TUBE 2265

PROPORTIONING VALVE-2B547

LINKAGE 2C193

NUT 379930 11-13 N·m (8-10 FT-LB)

CLIP N803994

BOLT 385116

JUNCTION BLOCK 2282

6 5/8"

BOLT N605789 26-41 N·m (19-30 FT-LB)

NUT 379930 23-34 N·m (17-25 FT-LB)

BRACKET 2B256

BOLT 56522 26-41 N·m (19-30 FT-LB)

VIEW L

84929016

Fig. 16 Height sensing proportioning valve installation on F-Super Duty

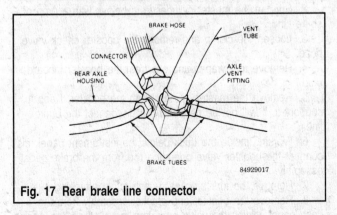

BRAKE HOSE

VENT TUBE

CONNECTOR

REAR AXLE HOUSING

AXLE VENT FITTING

BRAKE TUBES

84929017

Fig. 17 Rear brake line connector

up with high temperature, extra heavy duty fluid of at least SAE 70R3 (DOT 3) quality.

FLARING A BRAKE LINE

Using a Split-Die Type Flaring Tool

1. Using a tubing cutter, cut the required length of line.
2. Square the end with a file and chamfer the end.
3. Place the tube in the proper size die hole and position it so that it is flush with the die face. Lock the line with the wing nut.
4. The punches with most tools are marked to identify the sequence of flaring. Such marks are usually **Op.1** and **Op.2** or something similar.
5. Slide the **Op.1** punch into position and tighten the screw to form a single flare.
6. Remove the punch and position the **Op.2** punch. Tighten the screw to form the double flare.
7. Remove the punch and release the line from the die.

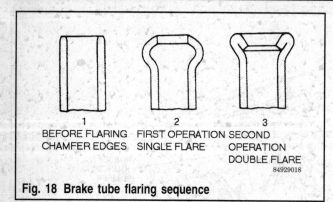

BEFORE FLARING
CHAMFER EDGES

FIRST OPERATION
SINGLE FLARE

SECOND
OPERATION
DOUBLE FLARE

84929018

Fig. 18 Brake tube flaring sequence

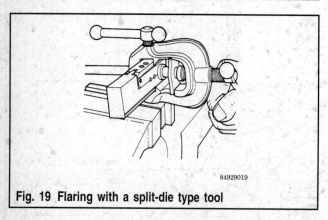

84929019

Fig. 19 Flaring with a split-die type tool

8. Inspect the finished flare for cracks or uneven flare form. If the flare is not perfect, cut it off and re-flare the end.

Using a Flaring Bar Type Tool

1. Using a tubing cutter, cut the required length of line.
2. Square the end with a file and chamfer the end.
3. Insert the tube into the proper size hole in the bar, until the end of the tube sticks out as far as the thickness of the adapter above the bar, or, depending on the tool, even with the bar face.
4. Fit the adapter onto the tube and slide the bar into the yoke. Lock the bar in position with the tube beneath the yoke screw.
5. Tighten the yoke screw and form the single flare.
6. Release the yoke screw and remove the adapter.
7. Install the second adapter and form the double flare.

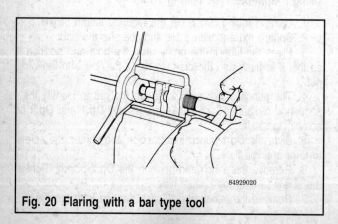

84929020

Fig. 20 Flaring with a bar type tool

8. Release the screw and remove the tube. Check the flare for cracks or uneven flaring. If the flare isn't perfect, cut it off and re-flare the line.

Power Booster

REMOVAL & INSTALLATION

▶ See Figures 21, 22, 23 and 24

F-150 & F-250 2-Wheel Drive F-150 & F-250 4-Wheel Drive Bronco

1. Disconnect the brake light switch wires.
2. Support the master cylinder from below, with a prop of some kind.
3. Loosen the clamp and remove the booster check valve hose.
4. Remove the master cylinder from the booster. Keep it supported. It will not be necessary to disconnect the brake lines.
5. Working inside the truck below the instrument panel, disconnect the booster valve operating rod from the brake pedal assembly.
6. Remove the four bracket-to-dash panel attaching nuts.
7. Remove the booster and bracket assembly from the dash panel, sliding the valve operating rod out from the engine side of the dash panel.

To install:

8. Mount the booster and bracket assembly on the dash panel by sliding the valve operating rod in through the hole in the dash panel, and installing the attaching nuts. Torque the nuts to 18-25 ft. lbs.
9. Connect the manifold vacuum hose to the booster.
10. Install the master cylinder. Torque the nuts to 18-25 ft. lbs.
11. Connect the stop light switch wires.
12. Working inside the truck below the instrument panel, connect the pushrod and stoplight switch.

F-250 HD 2- & 4-Wheel Drive F-350 2- & 4-Wheel Drive

1. Disconnect the brake light switch wires.
2. Support the master cylinder from below, with a prop of some kind.
3. Loosen the clamp and remove the booster check valve hose.
4. Remove the wraparound clip from the booster inboard stud.
5. Remove the master cylinder from the booster. Keep it supported. It will not be necessary to disconnect the brake lines.
6. Working inside the truck below the instrument panel, disconnect the booster valve operating rod from the brake pedal assembly.
7. Remove the four bracket-to-dash panel attaching nuts.
8. Remove the booster and bracket assembly from the dash panel, sliding the valve operating rod out from the engine side of the dash panel.

To install:

9. Mount the booster and bracket assembly on the dash panel by sliding the valve operating rod in through the hole in

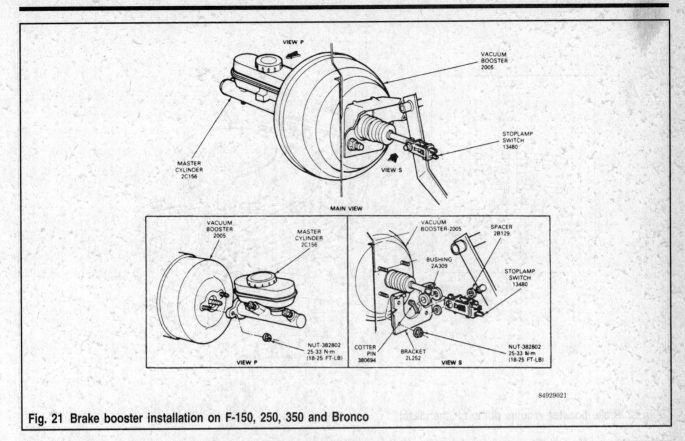

Fig. 21 Brake booster installation on F-150, 250, 350 and Bronco

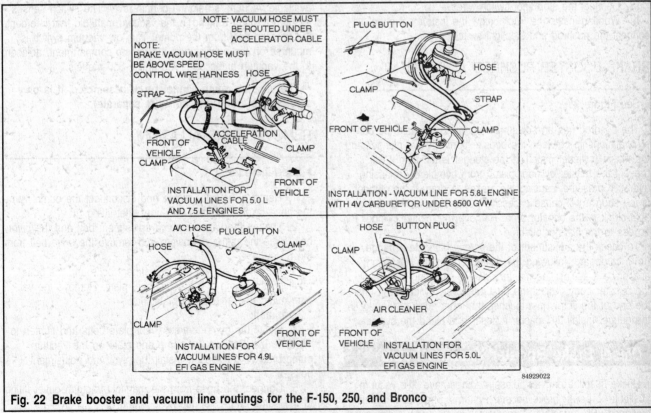

Fig. 22 Brake booster and vacuum line routings for the F-150, 250, and Bronco

the dash panel, and installing the attaching nuts. Torque the nuts to 18-25 ft. lbs.

10. Connect the manifold vacuum hose to the booster.

11. Install the master cylinder. Torque the nuts to 18-25 ft. lbs.

12. Install the wraparound clip.

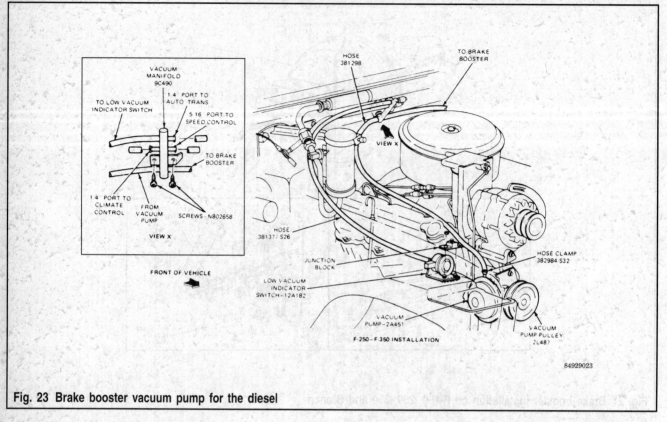

Fig. 23 Brake booster vacuum pump for the diesel

13. Connect the stop light switch wires.
14. Working inside the truck below the instrument panel, connect the pushrod and stoplight switch.

BRAKE BOOSTER PUSHROD ADJUSTMENT

▶ See Figure 25

The pushrod has an adjustment screw to maintain the correct relationship between the booster control valve plunger and the master cylinder piston. If the plunger is too long it will prevent the master cylinder piston from completely releasing hydraulic pressure, causing the brakes to drag. If the plunger is too short it will cause excessive pedal travel and an undesirable clunk in the booster area. Remove the master cylinder for access to the booster pushrod.

To check the adjustment of the screw, fabricate a gauge (from cardboard, following the dimensions in the illustration) and place it against the master cylinder mounting surface of the booster body. Adjust the pushrod screw by turning it until the end of the screw just touches the inner edge of the slot in the gauge. Install the master cylinder and bleed the system.

Diesel Brake Booster Vacuum Pump

Unlike gasoline engines, diesel engines have little vacuum available to power brake booster systems. The diesel is thus equipped with a vacuum pump, which is driven by a single belt off of the alternator. This pump is located on the top right side of the engine.

Diesel pickups are also equipped with a low vacuum indicator switch which actuates the BRAKE warning lamp when available vacuum is below a certain level. The switch senses vacuum through a fitting in the vacuum manifold that intercepts the vacuum flow from the pump. The low vacuum switch is mounted on the right side of the engine compartment, adjacent to the vacuum pump on F-250 and F-350 models.

➡The vacuum pump cannot be disassembled. It is only serviced as a unit (the pulley is separate).

REMOVAL & INSTALLATION

▶ See Figure 26

1. Remove the hose clamp and disconnect the pump from the hose on the manifold vacuum outlet fitting.
2. Loosen the vacuum pump adjustment bolt and the pivot bolt. Slide the pump downward and remove the drive belt from the pulley.
3. Remove the pivot and adjustment bolts and the bolts retaining the pump to the adjustment plate. Remove the vacuum pump and adjustment plate.
   To install:
4. Install the pump-to-adjustment plate bolts and tighten to 11-18 ft. lbs. Position the pump and plate on the vacuum pump bracket and loosely install the pivot and adjustment bolts.
5. Connect the hose from the manifold vacuum outlet fitting to the pump and install the hose clamp.
6. Install the drive belt on the pulley. Place a 3/8in. drive breaker bar or ratchet into the slot on the vacuum pump adjustment plate. Lift up on the assembly until the proper belt tension is obtained. Tighten the pivot and adjustment bolts to 11-18 ft. lbs.

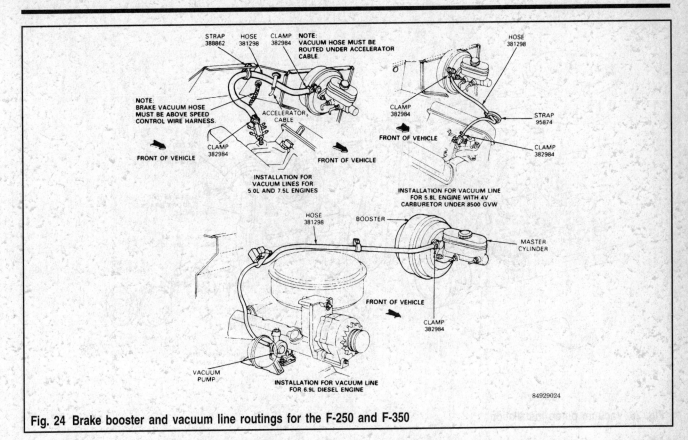

Fig. 24 Brake booster and vacuum line routings for the F-250 and F-350

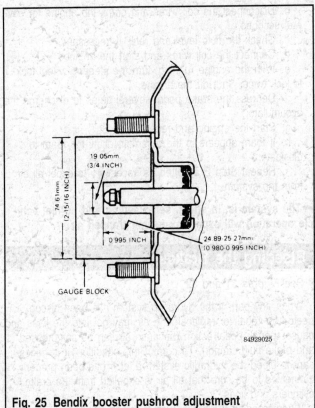

Fig. 25 Bendix booster pushrod adjustment

7. Start the engine and make sure the brake system functions properly.

➡ The **BRAKE** light will glow until brake vacuum builds up to the normal level.

F-Super Duty Hydro-Boost Brake Booster

▶ See Figures 27, 28, 29 and 30

A hydraulically powered brake booster is used on the F-Super Duty truck. The power steering pump provides the fluid pressure to operate both the brake booster and the power steering gear.

The Hydro-Boost assembly contains a valve which controls pump pressure while braking, a lever to control the position of the valve and a boost piston to provide the force to operate a conventional master cylinder attached to the front of the booster. The Hydro-Boost also has a reserve system, designed to store sufficient pressurized fluid to provide at least 2 brake applications in the event of insufficient fluid flow from the power steering pump. The brakes can also be applied unassisted if the reserve system is depleted.

✳✳WARNING

Before removing the Hydro-Boost, discharge the accumulator by making several brake applications until a hard pedal is felt.

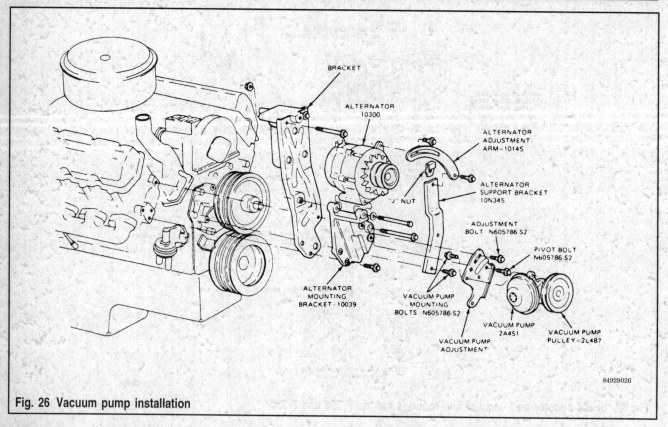

Fig. 26 Vacuum pump installation

REMOVAL & INSTALLATION

❋❋CAUTION

Do not depress the brake pedal with the master cylinder removed!

1. Remove the master cylinder from the Hydro-Boost unit. Do not disconnect the brake lines from the master cylinder! Position the master cylinder out of the way.
2. Disconnect the 3 hydraulic lines from the Hydro-Boost unit.
3. Disconnect the pushrod from the brake pedal.
4. Remove the booster mounting nuts and lift the booster from the firewall.

❋❋CAUTION

The booster should never be carried by the accumulator. The accumulator contains high pressure nitrogen and can be dangerous if mishandled! If the accumulator is to be disposed of, do not expose it to fire or other forms of incineration! Gas pressure can be relieved by drilling a 1/16 in. (1.5mm) hole in the end of the accumulator can. Always wear safety goggles during the drilling!

5. Installation is the reverse of removal. Torque the booster mounting nuts to 25 ft. lbs.; the master cylinder nuts to 25 ft. lbs.; connect the hydraulic lines, refill and bleed the booster as follows:
   a. Fill the pump reservoir with Dexron®II ATF.

b. Disconnect the coil wires and crank the engine for several seconds.
   c. Check the fluid level and refill, if necessary.
   d. Connect the coil wires and start the engine.
   e. With the engine running, turn the steering wheel lock-to-lock twice. Shut off the engine.
   f. Depress the brake pedal several times to discharge the accumulator.
   g. Start the engine and repeat Step E.
   h. If foam appears in the reservoir, allow the foam to dissipate.
   i. Repeat Step E as often as necessary to expel all air from the system.

➡**The system is, in effect, self-bleeding and normal vehicle operation will expel any further trapped air.**

Bleeding the Brakes

▶ **See Figures 31 and 32**

When any part of the hydraulic system has been disconnected for repair or replacement, air may get into the lines and cause spongy pedal action (because air can be compressed and brake fluid cannot). To correct this condition, it is necessary to bleed the hydraulic system after it has been properly connected to be sure that all air is expelled from the brake cylinders and lines.

When bleeding the brake system, bleed one brake cylinder at a time, beginning at the cylinder with the longest hydraulic line (farthest from the master cylinder) first. Keep the master cylinder reservoir filled with brake fluid during bleeding operation. Never use brake fluid that has been drained from the hydraulic system, no matter how clean it is.

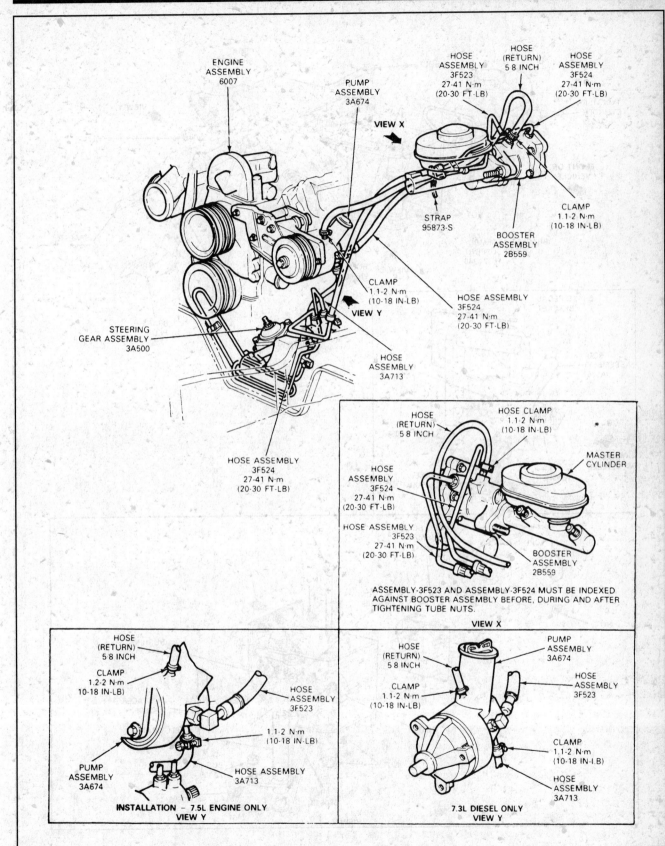

ENGINE
ASSEMBLY
6007

PUMP
ASSEMBLY
3A674

VIEW X

HOSE
ASSEMBLY
3F523
27-41 N·m
(20-30 FT-LB)

HOSE
(RETURN)
5 8 INCH

HOSE
ASSEMBLY
3F524
27-41 N·m
(20-30 FT-LB)

CLAMP
1.1-2 N·m
(10-18 IN-LB)

STRAP
95873-S

BOOSTER
ASSEMBLY
2B559

CLAMP
1.1-2 N·m
(10-18 IN-LB)

VIEW Y

HOSE ASSEMBLY
3F524
27-41 N·m
(20-30 FT-LB)

STEERING
GEAR ASSEMBLY
3A500

HOSE
ASSEMBLY
3A713

HOSE ASSEMBLY
3F524
27-41 N·m
(20-30 FT-LB)

HOSE
(RETURN)
5 8 INCH

HOSE CLAMP
1.1-2 N·m
(10-18 IN-LB)

MASTER
CYLINDER

HOSE
ASSEMBLY
3F524
27-41 N·m
(20-30 FT-LB)

HOSE ASSEMBLY
3F523
27-41 N·m
(20-30 FT-LB)

BOOSTER
ASSEMBLY
2B559

ASSEMBLY-3F523 AND ASSEMBLY-3F524 MUST BE INDEXED
AGAINST BOOSTER ASSEMBLY BEFORE, DURING AND AFTER
TIGHTENING TUBE NUTS.

VIEW X

HOSE
(RETURN)
5 8 INCH

CLAMP
1.2-2 N·m
10-18 IN-LB)

HOSE
ASSEMBLY
3F523

1.1-2 N·m
(10-18 IN-LB)

PUMP
ASSEMBLY
3A674

HOSE ASSEMBLY
3A713

INSTALLATION - 7.5L ENGINE ONLY
VIEW Y

HOSE
(RETURN)
5 8 INCH

PUMP
ASSEMBLY
3A674

HOSE
ASSEMBLY
3F523

CLAMP
1.1-2 N·m
(10-18 IN-LB)

CLAMP
1.1-2 N·m
(10-18 IN-LB)

HOSE
ASSEMBLY
3A713

7.3L DIESEL ONLY
VIEW Y

84929027

Fig. 27 Hydro-Boost system on the F-Super Duty chassis cab

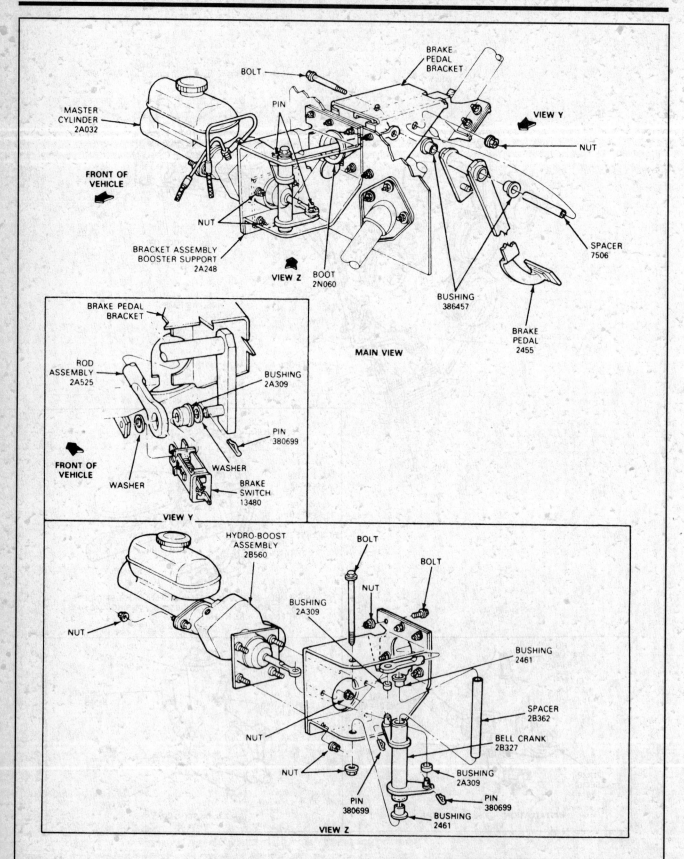

Fig. 28 Hydro-Boost system on the F-Super Duty commercial stripped chassis

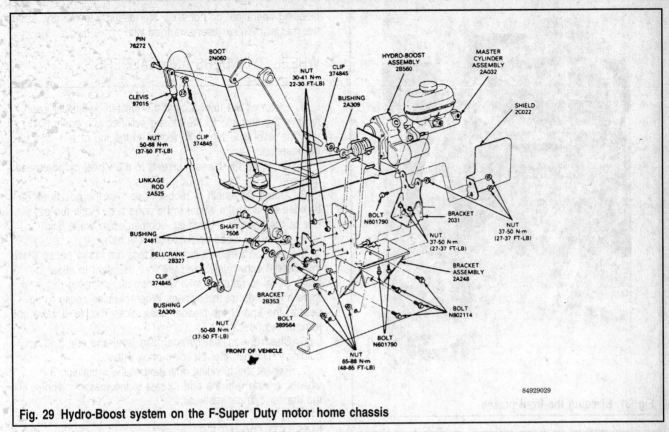

Fig. 29 Hydro-Boost system on the F-Super Duty motor home chassis

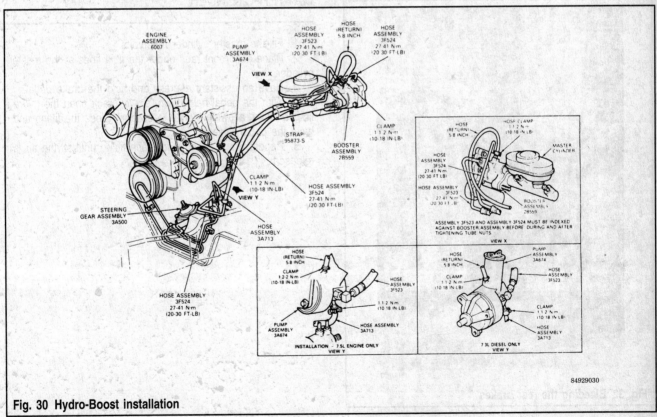

Fig. 30 Hydro-Boost installation

It will be necessary to centralize the pressure differential valve after a brake system failure has been corrected and the hydraulic system has been bled.

The primary and secondary hydraulic brake systems are individual systems and are bled separately. During the entire

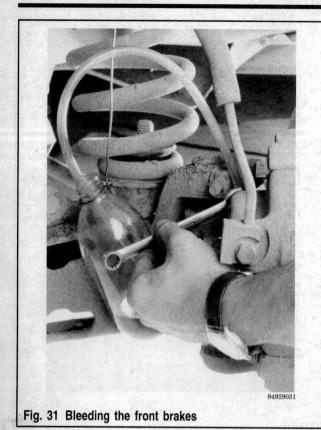

Fig. 31 Bleeding the front brakes

84929031

bleeding operation, do not allow the reservoir to run dry. Keep the master cylinder reservoirs filled with brake fluid.

WHEEL CYLINDERS AND CALIPERS

1. Clean all dirt from around the master cylinder fill cap, remove the cap and fill the master cylinder with brake fluid until the level is within 1/4 in. (6mm) of the top of the edge of the reservoir.
2. Clean off the bleeder screws at the wheel cylinders and calipers.
3. Attach the length of rubber hose over the nozzle of the bleeder screw at the wheel to be done first. Place the other end of the hose in a glass jar, submerged in brake fluid.
4. Open the bleed screw valve 1/2-3/4 turn.
5. Have an assistant slowly depress the brake pedal. Close the bleeder screw valve and tell your assistant to allow the brake pedal to return slowly. Continue this pumping action to force any air out of the system. When bubbles cease to appear at the end of the bleeder hose, close the bleed valve and remove the hose.
6. Check the master cylinder fluid level and add fluid accordingly. Do this after bleeding each wheel.
7. Repeat the bleeding operation at the remaining 3 wheels, ending with the one closest to the master cylinder. Fill the master cylinder reservoir.

MASTER CYLINDER

1. Fill the master cylinder reservoirs.
2. Place absorbent rags under the fluid lines at the master cylinder.
3. Have an assistant depress and hold the brake pedal.
4. With the pedal held down, slowly crack open the hydraulic line fitting, allowing the air to escape. Close the fitting and have the pedal released.
5. Repeat Steps 3 and 4 for each fitting until all the air is released.

Fig. 32 Bleeding the rear brakes

84929032

FRONT DISC BRAKES

There are two types of sliding calipers, the LD sliding caliper unit is operated by one piston per caliper. The caliper and steering arm are cast as one piece and combined with the spindle stem to form an integral spindle assembly.

The light duty system is used on all F-150 and Bronco models.

The HD slider caliper unit contains two pistons on the same side of the rotor. The caliper slides on the support assembly and is retained by a key and spring.

The heavy duty system is used on all F-250, F-350 and F-Super Duty models.

Disc Brake Pads

INSPECTION

Remove the brake pads as described below and measure the thickness of the lining. If the lining at any point on the pad assembly is less 1/16 in. (1.5mm) for LD brakes or 1/32 in. (0.8mm) for HD brakes, thick (above the backing plate or rivets), or there is evidence of the lining being contaminated by brake fluid or oil, replace the brake pad.

REMOVAL & INSTALLATION

➡Never replace the pads on one side only! Always replace pads on both wheels as a set!

LD Sliding Caliper (Single Piston)
▶ See Figures 33, 34, 35, 36, 37, 38, 39 and 40

1. To avoid overflowing of the master cylinder when the caliper pistons are pressed into the caliper cylinder bores, siphon or dip some brake fluid out of the larger reservoir.
2. Jack up the front of the truck, support it on jackstands, and remove the wheels.
3. Place an 8 in. (203mm) C-clamp on the caliper and tighten the clamp to bottom the caliper piston in the cylinder bore. Bear the clamp on the outer pad. NEVER PRESS DIRECTLY ON THE PISTON! Remove the C-clamp.
4. Clean the excess dirt from around the caliper pin tabs.
5. Drive the upper caliper pin inward until the tabs on the pin touch the spindle.
6. Insert a small prybar into the slot provided behind the pin tabs on the inboard side of the pin.
7. Using needlenose pliers, compress the outboard end of the pin while, at the same time, prying with the prybar until the tabs slip into the groove in the spindle.

8. Place the end of a 7/16 in. (11mm) punch against the end of the caliper pin and drive the pin out of the caliper slide groove.
9. Repeat this procedure for the lower pin.
10. Lift the caliper off of the rotor.
11. Remove the brake pads and anti-rattle spring.

➡Do not allow the caliper to hand by the brake hose.

To install:
12. Thoroughly clean the areas of the caliper and spindle assembly which contact each other during the sliding action of the caliper.
13. Place a new anti-rattle clip on the lower end of the inboard shoe. Make sure that the tabs on the clip are positioned correctly and the loop-type spring is away from the rotor.
14. Place the lower end of the inner brake pad in the spindle assembly pad abutment, against the anti-rattle clip, and slide the upper end of the pad into position. Be sure that the clip is still in position.
15. Check and make sure that the caliper piston is fully bottomed in the cylinder bore. Use a large C-clamp, bearing on a piece of wood, to bottom the piston, if necessary.
16. Position the outer brake pad on the caliper, and press the pad tabs into place with your fingers. If the pad cannot be pressed into place by hand, use a C-clamp. Be careful not to damage the lining with the clamp. Bend the tabs to prevent rattling.
17. Position the caliper on the spindle assembly. Lightly lubricate the caliper sliding grooves with caliper pin grease.
18. Position the a new upper pin with the retention tabs next to the spindle groove.

➡Don't use the bolt and nut with the new pin.

19. Carefully drive the pin, at the outboard end, inward until the tabs contact the spindle face.
20. Repeat the procedure for the lower pin.

21. Install the wheels.

HD Sliding Caliper (Two Piston)
▶ See Figures 41, 42, 43, 44 and 45

1. To avoid overflowing of the master cylinder when the caliper pistons are pressed into the caliper cylinder bores, siphon or dip some brake fluid out of the larger reservoir.
2. Raise and support the front end on jackstands.
3. Remove the wheels.
4. Place an 8 in. (203mm) C-clamp on the caliper and, with the clamp bearing on the outer pad, tighten the clamp to bottom the caliper pistons in the cylinder bores. Remove the C-clamp.
5. Clean the excess dirt from around the caliper pin tabs.

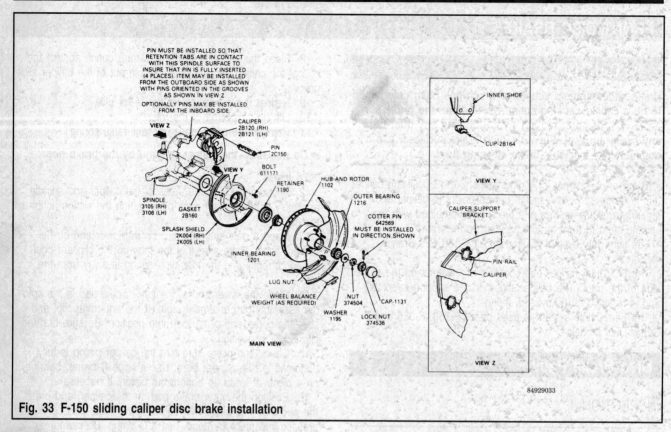

PIN MUST BE INSTALLED SO THAT
RETENTION TABS ARE IN CONTACT
WITH THIS SPINDLE SURFACE TO
INSURE THAT PIN IS FULLY INSERTED
(4 PLACES). ITEM MAY BE INSTALLED
FROM THE OUTBOARD SIDE AS SHOWN
WITH PINS ORIENTED IN THE GROOVES
AS SHOWN IN VIEW Z

OPTIONALLY PINS MAY BE INSTALLED
FROM THE INBOARD SIDE.

VIEW Z

CALIPER
2B120 (RH)
2B121 (LH)

PIN
2C150

VIEW Y

BOLT
611171

RETAINER
1190

HUB AND ROTOR
1102

OUTER BEARING
1216

COTTER PIN
642569
MUST BE INSTALLED
IN DIRECTION SHOWN

SPINDLE
3105 (RH)
3106 (LH)

GASKET
2B160

SPLASH SHIELD
2K004 (RH)
2K005 (LH)

INNER BEARING
1201

LUG NUT

WHEEL BALANCE
WEIGHT (AS REQUIRED)

NUT
374504

WASHER
1195

LOCK NUT
374536

CAP-1131

MAIN VIEW

INNER SHOE

CLIP-2B164

VIEW Y

CALIPER SUPPORT
BRACKET

PIN RAIL

CALIPER

VIEW Z

84929033

Fig. 33 F-150 sliding caliper disc brake installation

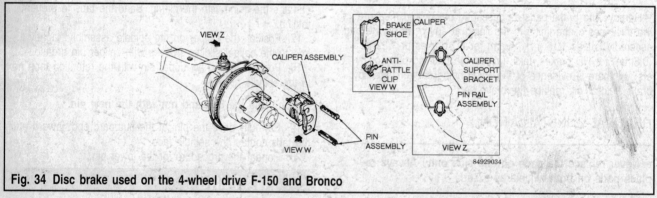

VIEW Z

CALIPER ASSEMBLY

BRAKE
SHOE

CALIPER

ANTI-
RATTLE
CLIP
VIEW W

CALIPER
SUPPORT
BRACKET

PIN RAIL
ASSEMBLY

VIEW Z

PIN
ASSEMBLY

VIEW W

84929034

Fig. 34 Disc brake used on the 4-wheel drive F-150 and Bronco

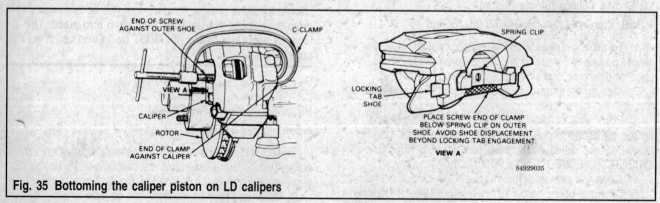

END OF SCREW
AGAINST OUTER SHOE

C-CLAMP

SPRING CLIP

VIEW A

CALIPER

ROTOR

END OF CLAMP
AGAINST CALIPER

LOCKING
TAB
SHOE

PLACE SCREW END OF CLAMP
BELOW SPRING CLIP ON OUTER
SHOE. AVOID SHOE DISPLACEMENT
BEYOND LOCKING TAB ENGAGEMENT.

VIEW A

84929035

Fig. 35 Bottoming the caliper piston on LD calipers

6. Drive the upper caliper pin inward until the tabs on the pin touch the spindle.

7. Insert a small prybar into the slot provided behind the pin tabs on the inboard side of the pin.

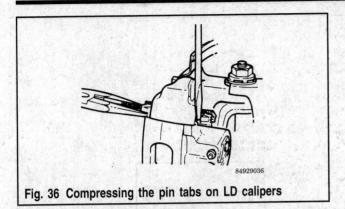

Fig. 36 Compressing the pin tabs on LD calipers

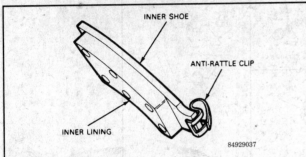

Fig. 37 Installing the inner shoe anti-rattle clip on LD calipers

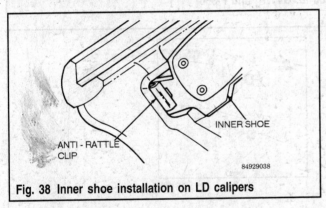

Fig. 38 Inner shoe installation on LD calipers

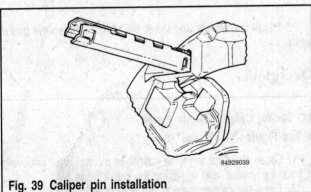

Fig. 39 Caliper pin installation

8. Using needlenose pliers, compress the outboard end of the pin while, at the same time, prying with the prybar until the tabs slip into the groove in the spindle.

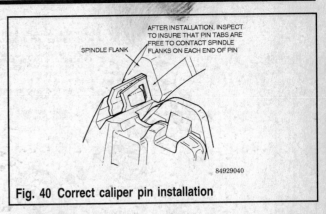

Fig. 40 Correct caliper pin installation

9. Place the end of a 7/16 in. (11mm) punch against the end of the caliper pin and drive the pin out of the caliper slide groove.
10. Repeat this procedure for the lower pin.
11. Lift the caliper off of the rotor.
12. Remove the brake pads and anti-rattle spring.

➡**Do not allow the caliper to hand by the brake hose.**

To install:
13. Thoroughly clean the areas of the caliper and spindle assembly which contact each other during the sliding action of the caliper.
14. Place a new anti-rattle clip on the lower end of the inboard shoe. Make sure that the tabs on the clip are positioned correctly and the loop-type spring is away from the rotor.
15. Place the lower end of the inner brake pad in the spindle assembly pad abutment, against the anti-rattle clip, and slide the upper end of the pad into position. Be sure that the clip is still in position.
16. Check and make sure that the caliper piston is fully bottomed in the cylinder bore. Use a large C-clamp to bottom the piston, if necessary.
17. Position the outer brake pad on the caliper, and press the pad tabs into place with your fingers. If the pad cannot be pressed into place by hand, use a C-clamp. Be careful not to damage the lining with the clamp. Bend the tabs to prevent rattling.
18. Position the caliper on the spindle assembly. Lightly lubricate the caliper sliding grooves with caliper pin grease.
19. Position the a new upper pin with the retention tabs next to the spindle groove.

➡**Don't use the bolt and nut with the new pin.**

20. Carefully drive the pin, at the outboard end, inward until the tabs contact the spindle face.
21. Repeat the procedure for the lower pin.

✳✳WARNING

Don't drive the pins in too far, or it will be necessary to drive them back out until the tabs snap into place. The tabs on each end of the pin MUST be free to catch on the spindle sides!

22. Install the wheels.

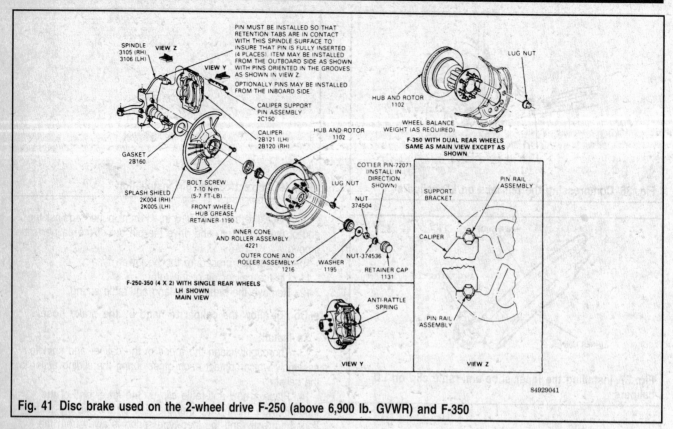

Fig. 41 Disc brake used on the 2-wheel drive F-250 (above 6,900 lb. GVWR) and F-350

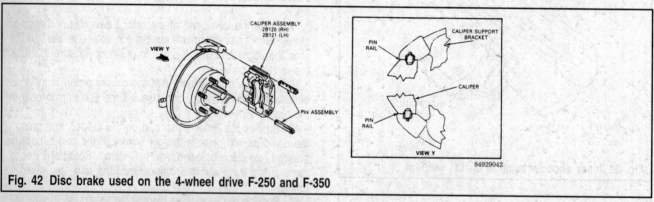

Fig. 42 Disc brake used on the 4-wheel drive F-250 and F-350

Disc Brake Calipers

REMOVAL & INSTALLATION

1. Raise and support the front end on jackstands.
2. Remove the wheels.
3. Remove the caliper and the brake pads as outlined under Disc Brake Pad Removal and Installation.
4. Disconnect the brake hose from the caliper.

To install:

5. Connect the brake hose to the caliper. When connecting the brake fluid hose to the caliper, it is recommended that a new copper washer be used at the connection of the brake hose and caliper.

6. Install the brake caliper and pads onto the vehicle as outlined in this Section.

7. Install the wheels and lower the vehicle. Bleed the brake system.

OVERHAUL

LD Sliding Caliper (Single Piston)

▶ **See Figures 46, 47 and 48**

1. Clean the outside of the caliper in alcohol after removing it from the vehicle and removing the brake pads.
2. Drain the caliper through the inlet port.
3. Roll some thick shop cloths or rags and place them between the piston and the outer legs of the caliper.
4. Apply compressed air to the caliper inlet port until the piston comes out of the caliper bore. Use low air pressure to avoid having the piston pop out too rapidly and possible causing injury.

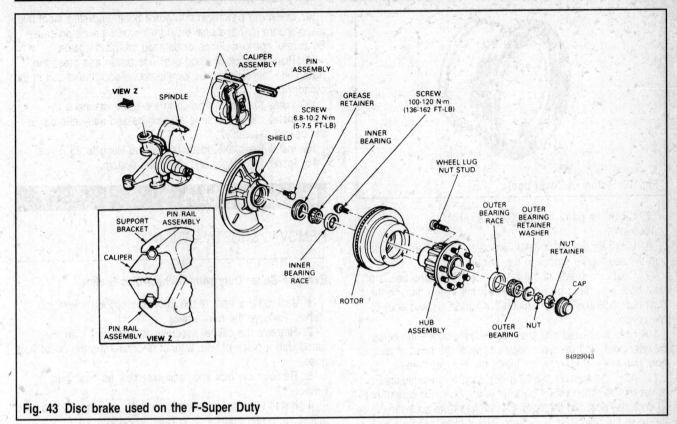

Fig. 43 Disc brake used on the F-Super Duty

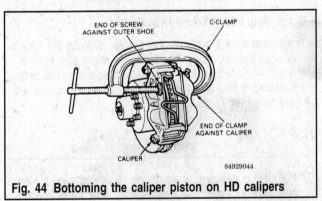

Fig. 44 Bottoming the caliper piston on HD calipers

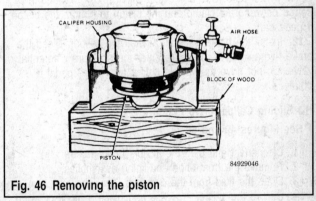

Fig. 46 Removing the piston

sharp tool or pry the piston out of the bore. Reapply the air pressure.

6. Remove the boot from the piston and seal from the caliper cylinder bore.

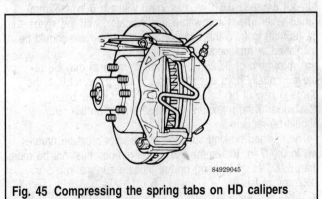

Fig. 45 Compressing the spring tabs on HD calipers

5. If the piston becomes cocked in the cylinder bore and will not come out, remove the air pressure and tap the piston with a soft hammer to try and straighten it. Do not use a

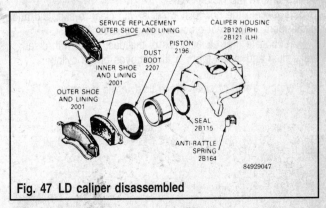

Fig. 47 LD caliper disassembled

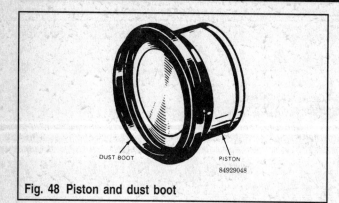

DUST BOOT   PISTON
84929048

Fig. 48 Piston and dust boot

7. Clean the piston and caliper in alcohol.

To install:

8. Lubricate the piston seal with clean brake fluid, and position the seal in the groove in the cylinder bore.

9. Coat the outside of the piston and both of the beads of dust boot with clean brake fluid. Insert the piston through the dust boot until the boot is around the bottom (closed end) of the piston.

10. Hold the piston and dust boot directly above the caliper cylinder bore, and use your fingers to work the bead of dust boot into the groove near the top of the cylinder bore.

11. After the bead is seated in the groove, press straight down on the piston until it bottoms in the bore. Be careful not to cock the piston in the bore. Be careful not to cock the piston in the bore. Use a C-clamp with a block of wood inserted between the clamp and the piston to bottom the piston, if necessary.

12. Install the brake pads and install the caliper. Bleed the brake hydraulic system and recenter the pressure differential valve. Do not drive the vehicle until a firm brake pedal is obtained.

HD Sliding Caliper (Two Piston)

▶ **See Figures 49 and 50**

1. Disconnect and plug the flexible brake hose.
2. Remove the front shoe and lining assemblies.
3. Drain the fluid from the cylinders.
4. Secure the caliper in a vise and place a block of wood between the caliper bridge and the cylinders.
5. Apply low pressure air to the brake hose inlet and the pistons will be forced out to the wood block.
6. Remove the block of wood and remove the pistons.
7. Remove the piston seals.
8. Lubricate the new piston seals with clean brake fluid and install them in the seal grooves in the cylinder bores.
9. Lubricate the retaining lips of the dust boots with clean brake fluid and install them in the grooves of the cylinder bores.
10. Apply a film of clean brake fluid to the pistons.

11. Insert the pistons into the dust boots and start them into the cylinders by hand until they are beyond the piston seals. Be careful not to dislodge or damage the piston seals.

12. Place a block of wood over one piston and press the piston into the cylinder. Be careful not to cock the piston in the cylinder bore.

13. Install the second piston in the same manner.

14. Install the brake shoe assemblies and anti-rattle clip in the caliper assembly.

15. Install the brake hose. Torque the fitting to 25 ft. lbs.

16. Install the caliper and bleed the system.

Brake Disc (Rotor)

REMOVAL & INSTALLATION

Except F-Super Duty with 4-Wheel Disc Brakes

1. Jack up the front of the truck and support it with jack-stands. Remove the front wheel.

2. Remove the caliper assembly and support it on the frame with a piece of wire without disconnecting the brake fluid hose.

3. Remove the hub and rotor assembly as described in Section 1.

4. Install the rotor in the reverse order of removal, and adjust the wheel bearing as outlined in Section 1.

F-Super Duty with 4-Wheel Disc Brakes

The hub and rotor are individual pieces, allowing the rotor to be replaced independently. The front and rear rotors are the same and are attached with 10 bolts and washers. The bolts are tightened a little at a time, in a criss-cross fashion, to an ultimate torque of 74-89 ft. lbs.

INSPECTION

If the rotor is deeply scarred or has shallow cracks, it may be refinished on a disc brake rotor lathe. Also, if the lateral run-out exceeds 0.010 in. (0.25mm) within a 6 in. (152mm) radius when measured with a dial indicator, with the stylus 1 in. (25mm) in from the edge of the rotor, the rotor should be refinished or replaced.

A maximum of 0.020 in. (0.5mm) of material may be removed equally from each friction surface of the rotor. If the damage cannot be corrected when the rotor has been machined to the minimum thickness shown on the rotor, it should be replaced.

The finished braking surfaces of the rotor must be parallel within 0.007 in. (0.18mm) and lateral run-out must not be more than 0.003 in. (0.076mm) on the inboard surface in a 5 in. (127mm) radius.

REAR DISC BRAKES

F-Super Duty models are equipped with the heavy duty, sliding 2-piston caliper similar to that used on the front axle.

Disc Brake Pads

INSPECTION

Remove the brake pads as described below and measure the thickness of the lining. If the lining at any point on the pad assembly is less than 1/16 in. (0.8mm) thick (above the backing plate or rivets), or there is evidence of the lining being contaminated by brake fluid or oil, replace the brake pad.

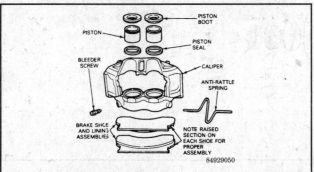

Fig. 50 HD caliper disassembled

REMOVAL & INSTALLATION

▶ **See Figure 51**

➡**Never replace the pads on one side only! Always replace pads on both wheels as a set!**

1. To avoid overflowing of the master cylinder when the caliper pistons are pressed into the caliper cylinder bores, siphon or dip some brake fluid out of the larger reservoir.
2. Raise and support the rear end on jackstands.
3. Remove the wheels.
4. Place an 8 in. (203mm) C-clamp on the caliper and tighten the clamp to bottom the caliper pistons in the cylinder bores. Remove the C-clamp.
5. Clean the excess dirt from around the caliper pin tabs.
6. Drive the upper caliper pin inward until the tabs on the pin touch the caliper support.
7. Insert a small prybar into the slot provided behind the pin tabs on the inboard side of the pin.
8. Using needlenose pliers, compress the outboard end of the pin while, at the same time, prying with the prybar until the tabs slip into the groove in the caliper support.
9. Place the end of a 7/16 in. (11mm) punch against the end of the caliper pin and drive the pin out of the caliper slide groove.
10. Repeat this procedure for the lower pin.
11. Lift the caliper off of the rotor.

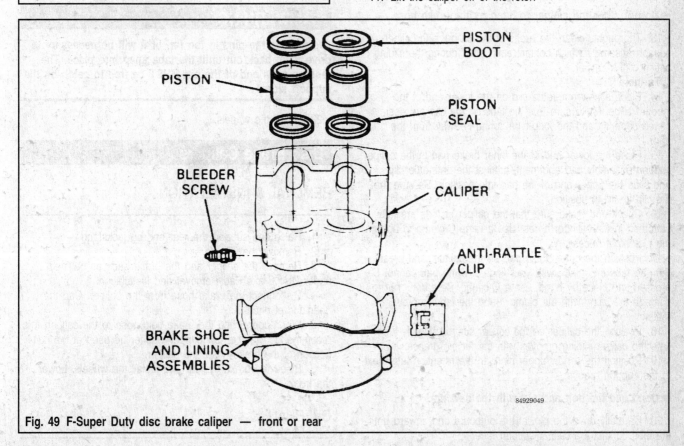

Fig. 49 F-Super Duty disc brake caliper — front or rear

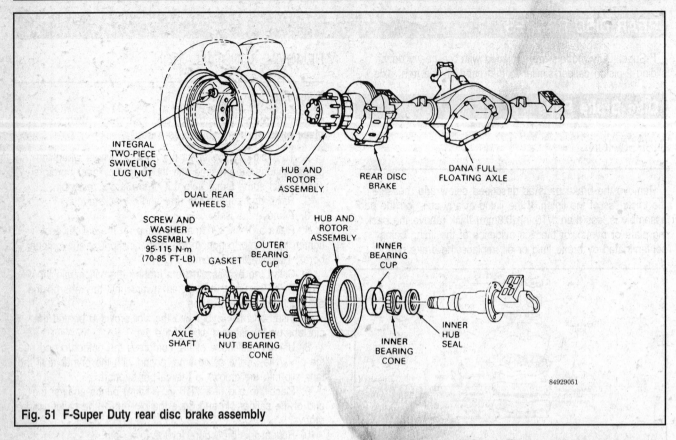

INTEGRAL
TWO-PIECE
SWIVELING
LUG NUT

DUAL REAR
WHEELS

HUB AND
ROTOR
ASSEMBLY

REAR DISC
BRAKE

DANA FULL
FLOATING AXLE

SCREW AND
WASHER
ASSEMBLY
95-115 N·m
(70-85 FT-LB)

GASKET

OUTER
BEARING
CUP

HUB AND
ROTOR
ASSEMBLY

INNER
BEARING
CUP

AXLE
SHAFT

HUB
NUT

OUTER
BEARING
CONE

INNER
BEARING
CONE

INNER
HUB
SEAL

84929051

Fig. 51 F-Super Duty rear disc brake assembly

12. Remove the brake pads and anti-rattle spring.

➡**Do not allow the caliper to hand by the brake hose.**

13. Thoroughly clean the areas of the caliper and caliper support assembly which contact each other during the sliding action of the caliper.

To install:

14. Place a new anti-rattle clip on the lower end of the inboard shoe. Make sure that the tabs on the clip are positioned correctly and the loop-type spring is away from the rotor.

15. Place the lower end of the inner brake pad in the caliper support assembly pad abutment, against the anti-rattle clip, and slide the upper end of the pad into position. Be sure that the clip is still in position.

16. Check and make sure that the caliper pistons are fully bottomed in the cylinder bores. Use a large C-clamp to bottom the pistons, if necessary.

17. Position the outer brake pad on the caliper, and press the pad tabs into place with your fingers. If the pad cannot be pressed into place by hand, use a C-clamp. Be careful not to damage the lining with the clamp. Bend the tabs to prevent rattling.

18. Position the caliper on the caliper support. Lightly lubricate the caliper sliding grooves with caliper pin grease.

19. Position the a new upper pin with the retention tabs next to the support groove.

➡**Don't use the bolt and nut with the new pin.**

20. Carefully drive the pin, at the outboard end, inward until the tabs contact the caliper support face.

21. Repeat the procedure for the lower pin.

✳✳WARNING

Don't drive the pins in too far, or it will be necessary to drive them back out until the tabs snap into place. The tabs on each end of the pin MUST be free to catch on the support sides!

22. Install the wheels.

Disc Brake Calipers

REMOVAL & INSTALLATION

1. Raise and support the rear end on jackstands.
2. Remove the wheels.
3. Remove the caliper and the brake pads as outlined under Disc Brake Pad Removal and Installation.
4. Disconnect the brake hose from the caliper. Cap the openings at once!
5. When connecting the brake fluid hose to the caliper, it is recommended that a new copper washer be used at the connection of the brake hose and caliper.
6. Bleed the brake system and install the wheels. Lower the truck.

OVERHAUL

1. Disconnect and plug the flexible brake hose.

2. Remove the caliper.

3. Drain the fluid from the cylinders.

4. Secure the caliper in a vise and place a block of wood between the caliper bridge and the cylinders.

5. Apply low pressure air to the brake hose inlet and the pistons will be forced out to the wood block.

6. Remove the block of wood and remove the pistons.

7. Remove the piston seals.

8. Lubricate the new piston seals with clean brake fluid and install them in the seal grooves in the cylinder bores.

9. Lubricate the retaining lips of the dust boots with clean brake fluid and install them in the grooves of the cylinder bores.

10. Apply a film of clean brake fluid to the pistons.

11. Insert the pistons into the dust boots and start them into the cylinders by hand until they are beyond the piston seals. Be careful not to dislodge or damage the piston seals.

12. Place a block of wood over one piston and press the piston into the cylinder. Be careful not to cock the piston in the cylinder bore.

13. Install the second piston in the same manner.

14. Install the brake shoe assemblies and anti-rattle clip in the caliper assembly.

15. Install the brake hose. Torque the fitting to 25 ft. lbs.

16. Install the caliper and bleed the system.

Brake Disc (Rotor)

REMOVAL & INSTALLATION

1. Jack up the rear of the truck and support it with jackstands. Remove the wheel.

2. Remove the caliper assembly and support it to the frame with a piece of wire without disconnecting the brake fluid hose.

3. Remove the axle hub and rotor assembly. See Section 7 under Dana 80 rear axle.

4. Install the rotor using the procedures found in Section 7.

INSPECTION

If the rotor is deeply scarred or has shallow cracks, it may be refinished on a disc brake rotor lathe. Also, if the lateral run-out exceeds 0.008 in. (0.20mm) within a 6 in. (152mm) radius when measured with a dial indicator, with the stylus 1 in. (25mm) in from the edge of the rotor, the rotor should be refinished or replaced.

A maximum of 0.020 in. (0.5mm) of material may be removed equally from each friction surface of the rotor. If the damage cannot be corrected when the rotor has been machined to the minimum thickness shown on the rotor, it should be replaced.

The finished braking surfaces of the rotor must be parallel within 0.0010 in. (0.025mm) and lateral run-out must not be more than 0.008 in. (0.20mm) on the inboard surface in a 5 in. (127mm) radius.

REAR DRUM BRAKES

✳✳CAUTION

Brake shoes contain asbestos, which has been determined to be a cancer causing agent. Never clean the brake surfaces with compressed air! Avoid inhaling any dust from any brake surface! When cleaning brake surfaces, use a commercially available brake cleaning fluid.

Brake Drums

INSPECTION

Check that there are no cracks or chips in the braking surface. Excessive bluing indicates overheating and a replacement drum is needed. The drum can be machined to remove minor damage and to establish a rounded braking surface on a warped drum. Never exceed the maximum oversize of the drum when machining the braking surface. The maximum inside diameter is stamped on the rim of the drum.

REMOVAL & INSTALLATION

Bronco, F-150, and F-250 Light Duty

1. Raise the vehicle so that the wheel to be worked on is clear of the floor and install jackstands under the vehicle.

2. Remove the wheel. Remove the three retaining nuts and remove the brake drum. It may be necessary to back off the brake shoe adjustment in order to remove the brake drum. This is because the drum might be grooved or worn from being in service for an extended period of time.

3. Before installing a new brake drum, be sure to remove any protective coating with carburetor degreaser.

4. Install the brake drum in the reverse order of removal and adjust the brakes.

F-250HD, F-350

1. Raise the vehicle and install jackstands.

2. Remove the wheel. Loosen the rear brake shoe adjustment.

3. Remove the rear axle retaining bolts and lockwashers, axle shaft, and gasket.

4. Remove the wheel bearing locknut, lockwasher, and adjusting nut.

5. Remove the hub and drum assembly from the axle.

6. Remove the brake drum-to-hub retaining screws, bolts or bolts and nut. Remove the brake drum from the hub.

To install:

7. Place the drum on the hub and attach it to the hub with the attaching nuts and bolts.

8. Place the hub and drum assembly on the axle and start the adjusting nut.

9. Adjust the wheel bearing nut and install the wheel bearing lockwasher and locknut.

10. Install the axle shaft with a new gasket and install the axle retaining bolts and lockwashers.

11. Install the wheel and adjust the brake shoes. Remove the jackstands and lower the vehicle.

Brake Shoes

REMOVAL & INSTALLATION

Bronco, F-150, F-250 Light Duty

▶ See Figures 52, 53 and 54

1. Raise and support the vehicle and remove the wheel and brake drum from the wheel to be worked on.

➡**If you have never replaced the brakes on a truck before and you are not too familiar with the procedures involved, only dissemble and assemble one side at a time, leaving the other side intact as a reference during reassembly.**

2. Install a clamp over the ends of the wheel cylinder to prevent the pistons of the wheel cylinder from coming out, causing loss of fluid and much grief.

3. Contract the brake shoes by pulling the self-adjusting lever away from the starwheel adjustment screw and turn the starwheel up and back until the pivot nut is drawn onto the starwheel as far as it will come.

4. Pull the adjusting lever, cable and automatic adjuster spring down and toward the rear to unhook the pivot hook from the large hole in the secondary shoe web. Do not attempt to pry the pivot hook from the hole.

5. Remove the automatic adjuster spring and the adjusting lever.

6. Remove the secondary shoe-to-anchor spring with a brake tool. (Brake tools are very common implements and are available to auto parts stores). Remove the primary shoe-to-anchor spring and unhook the cable anchor. Remove the anchor pin plate.

7. Remove the cable guide from the secondary shoe.

8. Remove the shoe holddown springs, shoes, adjusting screw, pivot nut, and socket. Note the color of each holddown spring for assembly. To remove the holddown springs, reach behind the brake backing plate and place one finger on the end of one of the brake holddown spring mounting pins. Using a pair of pliers, grasp the washer type retainer on top of the holddown spring that corresponds to the pin which you are holding. Push down on the pliers and turn them 90° to align the slot in the washer with the head on the spring mounting pin. Remove the spring and washer retainer and repeat this operation on the hold down spring on the other shoe.

9. Remove the parking brake link and spring. Disconnect the parking brake cable from the parking brake lever.

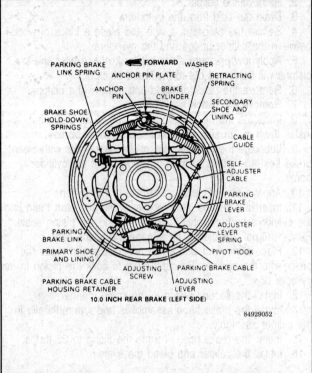

Fig. 52 Standard rear brakes used on the F-150 and Bronco

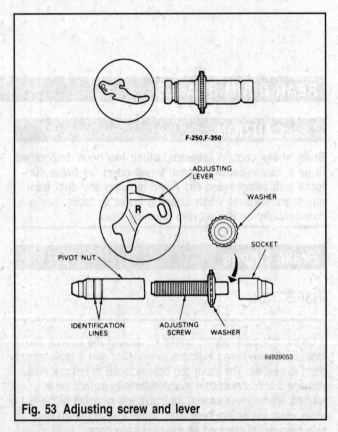

Fig. 53 Adjusting screw and lever

10. After removing the rear brake secondary shoe, disassemble the parking brake lever from the shoe by removing the retaining clip and spring washer.

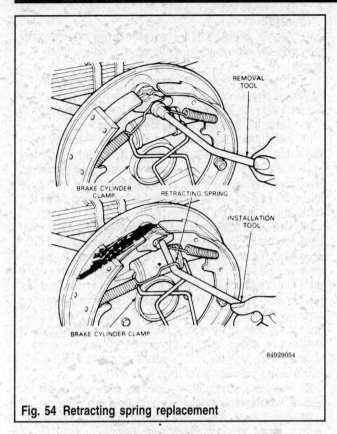

Fig. 54 Retracting spring replacement

11. Assemble the parking brake lever to the secondary shoe and secure it with the spring washer and retaining clip.

12. Apply a light coating of Lubriplate® at the points where the brake shoes contact the backing plate.

13. Position the brake shoes on the backing plate, and install the holddown spring pins, springs, and spring washer type retainers. On the rear brake, install the parking brake link, spring and washer. Connect the parking brake cable to the parking brake lever.

14. Install the anchor pin plate, and place the cable anchor over the anchor pin with the crimped side toward the backing plate.

15. Install the primary shoe-to-anchor spring with the brake tool.

16. Install the cable guide on the secondary shoe web with the flanged holes fitted into the hole in the secondary shoe web. Thread the cable around the cable guide groove.

17. Install the secondary shoe-to-anchor (long) spring. Be sure that the cable end is not cocked or binding on the anchor pin when installed. All of the parts should be flat on the anchor pin. Remove the wheel cylinder piston clamp.

18. Apply Lubriplate® to the threads and the socket end of the adjusting starwheel screw. Turn the adjusting screw into the adjusting pivot nut to the limit of the threads and then back off ½ turn.

➡Interchanging the brake shoe adjusting screw assemblies from one side of the vehicle to the other would cause the brake shoes to retract rather than expand each time the automatic adjusting mechanism is operated. To prevent this, the socket end of the adjusting screw is stamped with an 'R' or an 'L' for 'RIGHT' or 'LEFT'. The

adjusting pivot nuts can be distinguished by the number of lines machined around the body of the nut; one line indicates left hand nut and two lines indicate a right hand nut.

19. Place the adjusting socket on the screw and install this assembly between the shoe ends with the adjusting screw nearest to the secondary shoe.

20. Place the cable hook into the hole in the adjusting lever from the backing plate side. The adjusting levers are stamped with an **R** (right) or a **L** (left) to indicate their installation on the right or left hand brake assembly.

21. Position the hooked end of the adjuster spring in the primary shoe web and connect the loop end of the spring to the adjuster lever hole.

22. Pull the adjuster lever, cable and automatic adjuster spring down toward the rear to engage the pivot hook in the large hole in the secondary shoe web.

23. After installation, check the action of the adjuster by pulling the section of the cable guide and the adjusting lever toward the secondary shoe web far enough to lift the lever past a tooth on the adjusting screw starwheel. The lever should snap into position behind the next tooth, and release of the cable should cause the adjuster spring to return the lever to its original position. This return action of the lever will turn the adjusting screw starwheel one tooth. The lever should contact the adjusting screw starwheel one tooth above the centerline of the adjusting screw.

If the automatic adjusting mechanism does not perform properly, check the following:

24. Check the cable and fittings. The cable ends should fill or extend slightly beyond the crimped section of the fittings. If this is not the case, replace the cable.

25. Check the cable guide for damage. The cable groove should be parallel to the shoe web, and the body of the guide should lie flat against the web. Replace the cable guide if this is not so.

26. Check the pivot hook on the lever. The hook surfaces should be square with the body on the lever for proper pivoting. Repair or replace the hook as necessary.

27. Make sure that the adjusting screw starwheel is properly seated in the notch in the shoe web.

F-250 HD, F-350

▶ **See Figures 55, 56 and 57**

1. Raise and support the vehicle.
2. Remove the wheel and drum.
3. Remove the parking brake lever assembly retaining nut from behind the backing plate and remove the parking brake lever assembly.
4. Remove the adjusting cable assembly from the anchor pin, cable guide, and adjusting lever.
5. Remove the brake shoe retracting springs.
6. Remove the brake shoe holddown spring from each shoe.
7. Remove the brake shoes and adjusting screw assembly.
8. Disassemble the adjusting screw assembly.
9. Clean the ledge pads on the backing plate. Apply a light coat of Lubriplate® to the ledge pads (where the brake shoes rub the backing plate).

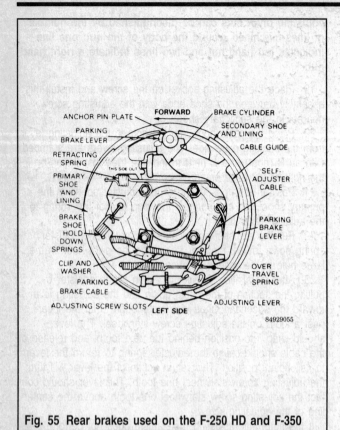

Fig. 55 Rear brakes used on the F-250 HD and F-350

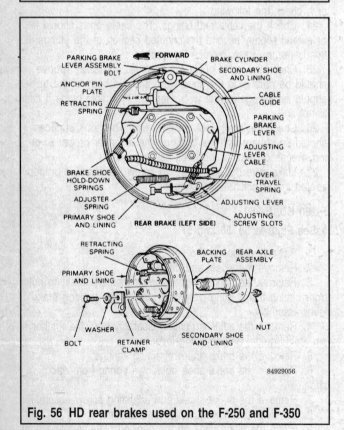

Fig. 56 HD rear brakes used on the F-250 and F-350

To install:

10. Apply Lubriplate® to the adjusting screw assembly and the holddown and retracting spring contacts on the brake shoes.

11. Install the upper retracting spring on the primary and secondary shoes and position the shoe assembly on the backing plate with the wheel cylinder pushrods in the shoe slots.

12. Install the brake shoe holddown springs.

13. Install the brake shoe adjustment screw assembly with the slot in the head of the adjusting screw toward the primary shoe, lower retracting spring, adjusting lever spring, adjusting lever assembly, and connect the adjusting cable to the adjusting lever. Position the cable in the cable guide and install the cable anchor fitting on the anchor pin.

14. Install the adjusting screw assemblies in the same locations from which they were removed. Interchanging the brake shoe adjusting screws from one side of the vehicle to the other will cause the brake shoes to retract rather than expand each time the automatic adjusting mechanism is operated. To prevent incorrect installation, the socket end of each adjusting screw is stamped with an **R** or an **L** to indicate their installation on the right or left side of the vehicle. The adjusting pivot nuts can be distinguished by the number of lines machined around the body of the nut. Two lines indicate a right hand nut; one line indicates a left hand nut.

15. Install the parking brake assembly in the anchor pin and secure with the retaining nut behind the backing plate.

16. Adjust the brakes before installing the brake drums and wheels. Install the brake drums and wheels.

17. Lower the vehicle and road test the brakes. New brakes may pull to one side or the other before they are seated. Continued pulling or erratic braking should not occur.

Wheel Cylinders

REMOVAL & INSTALLATION

▶ See Figure 58

1. Remove the brake drum.
2. Remove the brake shoes.
3. Loosen the brake line at the wheel cylinder.
4. Remove the wheel cylinder attaching bolt and unscrew the cylinder from the brake line.
5. Installation is the reverse of removal.

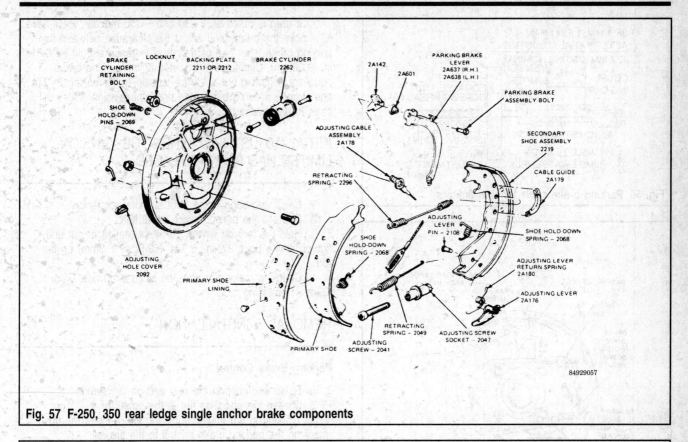

Fig. 57 F-250, 350 rear ledge single anchor brake components

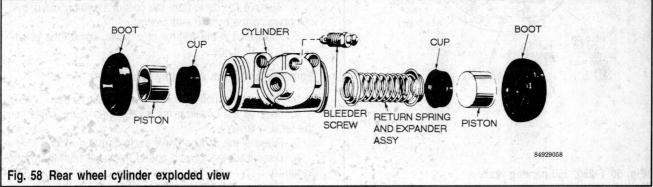

Fig. 58 Rear wheel cylinder exploded view

OVERHAUL

Purchase a brake cylinder repair kit. Remove and disassemble the wheel cylinder. Follow the instructions in the kit. Never repair only one cylinder. Repair both at the same time.

PARKING BRAKE EXCEPT F-SUPER DUTY

▶ See Figures 59, 60, 61 and 62

➡Before making any parking brake adjustment, make sure that the drum brakes are properly adjusted.

ADJUSTMENT

1. Raise and support the rear end on jackstands.

2. The brake drums should be cold.
3. Make sure that the parking brake pedal is fully released.
4. While holding the tension equalizer, tighten the equalizer nut 6 full turns past its original position.
5. Fully depress the parking brake pedal. Using a cable tension gauge, check rear cable tension. Cable tension should be 350 lbs. minimum.

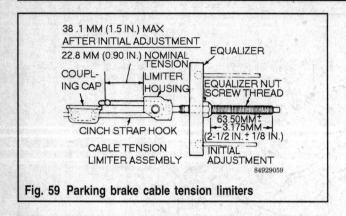

Fig. 59 Parking brake cable tension limiters

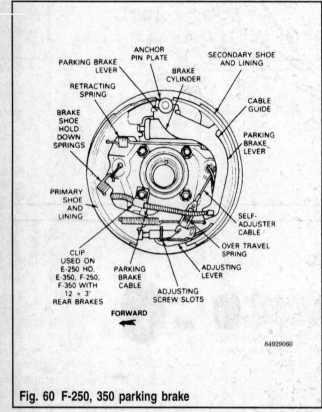

Fig. 60 F-250, 350 parking brake

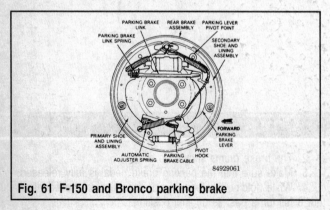

Fig. 61 F-150 and Bronco parking brake

6. Fully release the parking brake. No drag should be noted at the wheels.

7. If drag is noted on F-250 and F-350 models, you'll have to remove the drums and adjust the clearance between the parking brake lever and cam plate. Clearance should be 0.015 in. (0.38mm). Clearance is adjusted at the parking brake equalizer adjusting nut. If the tension limiter on the F-150 and Bronco doesn't release the drag, the tension limiter will have to be replaced.

INITIAL ADJUSTMENT WHEN THE TENSION LIMITER HAS BEEN REPLACED

1. Raise and support the front end on jackstands.
2. Depress the parking brake pedal fully.
3. Hold the tension limiter, install the equalizer nut and tighten it to a point $2\frac{1}{2}$ in. $\pm \frac{1}{8}$in. (63.5mm $\pm$ 3mm) up the rod.
4. Check to make sure that the cinch strap has $1\frac{3}{8}$in. (35mm) remaining.

REMOVAL & INSTALLATION

Parking Brake Control

1. Raise and support the rear end on jackstands.
2. Loosen the adjusting nut at the equalizer.
3. Working in the engine compartment, remove the nuts attaching the parking brake control to the firewall.
4. Remove the cable from the control assembly clevis by compressing the conduit end prongs.
5. Installation is the reverse of removal. Torque the attaching nuts to 15 ft. lbs.

Equalizer-to-Control Assembly Cable

1. Raise and support the rear end on jackstands.
2. Back off the equalizer nut and disconnect the cable from the tension limiter.
3. Remove the parking brake cable from the mount.
4. Disconnect the forward end of the cable from the control assembly.
5. Using a cord attached to the upper end of the cable, pull the cable from the truck.
6. Installation is the reverse of removal. Adjust the parking brake.

Equalizer-to-Rear Wheel Cable

1. Raise and support the rear end on jackstands.
2. Remove the wheels and brake drums.
3. Remove the tension limiter.
4. Remove the locknut from the threaded rod and disconnect the cable from the equalizer.
5. Disconnect the cable housing from the frame bracket and pull the cable and housing out of the bracket.
6. Disconnect the cables from the brake backing plates.
7. With the spring tension removed from the lever, lift the cable out of the slot in the lever and remove the cable through the backing plate hole.
8. Installation is the reverse of removal. On the F-250 and F-350, check the clearance between the parking brake operat-

ing lever and the cam plate. Clearance should be 0.015 in. (0.38mm) with the brakes fully released.

9. Adjust the brakes.

TRANSMISSION MOUNTED PARKING BRAKE F-SUPER DUTY

Parking Brake Unit

➡**To replace the brake shoes, or any other component, the unit must be disassembled.**

REMOVAL

➧ **See Figures 63, 64, 65, 66, 67, 68 and 69**

1. Place the transmission in gear.
2. Fully release the parking brake pedal.
3. Raise and support the truck on jackstands.
4. Disconnect the speedometer cable.
5. Spray penetrating oil on the adjusting clevis, jam nut and threaded end of the cable.
6. Loosen the jam nut and remove the locking pin from the clevis pin.
7. Remove the clevis pin, clevis and jam nut from the cable.
8. Remove the cable from the bracket on the case.
9. Matchmark the driveshaft and disconnect it from the flange.
10. Remove the 6 hex-head bolts securing the parking brake unit to the transmission extension housing and lift off the unit.

➡**The unit is filled with Ford Type H ATF.**

✻✻CAUTION

Brake shoes contain asbestos, which has been determined to be a cancer causing agent. Never clean the brake surfaces with compressed air! Avoid inhaling any dust from any brake surface! When cleaning brake surfaces, use a commercially available brake cleaning fluid.

DISASSEMBLY

➡**Several special tools and a hydraulic press are necessary.**

1. Remove the unit from the truck.
2. Remove the 4 bolts securing the yoke flange and drum, and remove the flange and drum.
3. Remove the 75mm hex nut from the mainshaft, using tool T88T-2598-G, or equivalent.
4. Press the mainshaft, drum and output flange from the case.
5. Remove the speedometer drive gear from the case.
6. Using tools D80L-1002-2, D79L-4621-A and D80L-630-6, remove the outer bearing cone from the mainshaft.
7. Place the threaded end of the output shaft in a soft-jawed vise.
8. Matchmark the drum, flange/yoke and mainshaft. Remove the 4 nuts securing the flange and drum to the output shaft and remove the flange and drum.
9. Using tool T77F-1102-A, remove the input shaft oil seal, spacer, O-ring, bearing cone and race from the input shaft end of the case.
10. Remove the 4 bolts securing the splash shield and brake assembly from the case. Remove the brake assembly and splash shield.
11. Remove the brake actuating lever and spring from the case.
12. Using tool T77F-1102-A, remove the outer bearing cup and oil seal.
13. Unscrew the vent from the case.
14. Hold the brake assembly securely and remove the 2 brake sure return springs.
15. Spread the free ends of the shoes and remove the shoes from the lower anchor pin. Remove the shoe-to-shoe spring.

ASSEMBLY

➧ **See Figures 70 and 71**

1. Clean the brake assembly thoroughly with a brake cleaning solvent.
2. Using a brake caliper grease, place a light coating on:
   - Camshaft lugs and ball on the actuating lever
   - Shoe guide lugs and support pads on the support plate
   - Upper and lower anchor pins
   - Brake shoe anchor pin contact points
3. Connect a NEW shoe-to-shoe spring between the brake shoes, spread the shoes and position them on the lower anchor pin.
4. Position the upper ends on the upper anchor pin, inserting the show webs between the shoe guide lugs and the pads on the support plate.
5. Install 2 NEW return springs.
6. Drive a new inner bearing race into place.
7. Drive a new outer bearing race into the case making sure it bottoms evenly.
8. Install a new outer bearing.
9. Coat the outer edge of a new outer oil seal with sealer and drive the seal into place with the lip facing inward. The seal must be flush with the bore surface.
10. Install the actuating lever spring.
11. Apply a light coating of brake grease on the actuating lever ball and install the lever through the coiled end of the spring.
12. Position the brake assembly into the case. Insert the lever into position in the brake assembly.
13. Torque the 4 brake assembly attaching bolts to 90 ft. lbs.
14. Attach the retracting spring to the actuating lever while bending the long end to snap over the lever.
15. Place the mainshaft in a soft-jawed vise with the flanged end upward.

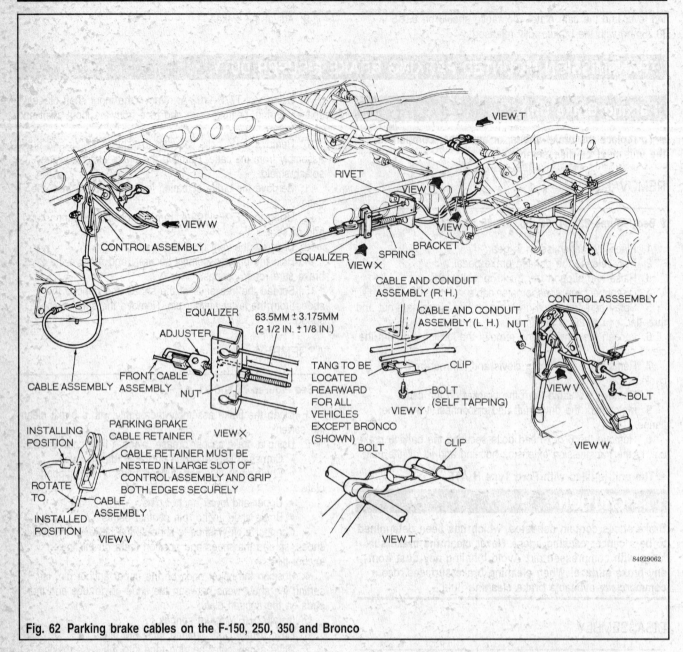

Fig. 62 Parking brake cables on the F-150, 250, 350 and Bronco

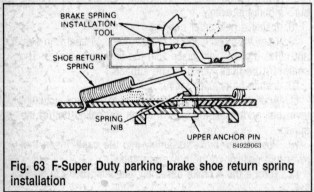

Fig. 63 F-Super Duty parking brake shoe return spring installation

18. Turn the mainshaft over and clamp it in the vise.

19. Install the case, with the outer bearing installed loosely on the mainshaft, guiding the mainshaft through the oil seal and bearing cone.

16. Install the brake drum and output flange onto the mainshaft, being aware of the matchmarks.

17. Install the 4 nuts and torque them to 85 ft. lbs.

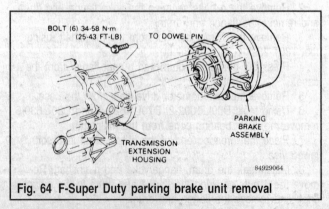

Fig. 64 F-Super Duty parking brake unit removal

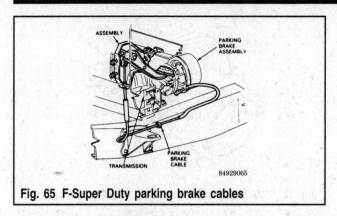

Fig. 65 F-Super Duty parking brake cables

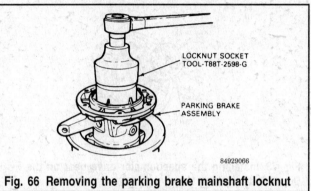

Fig. 66 Removing the parking brake mainshaft locknut

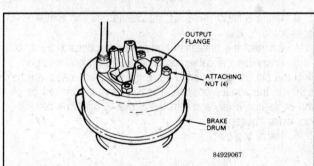

Fig. 67 Removing the F-Super Duty parking brake output flange

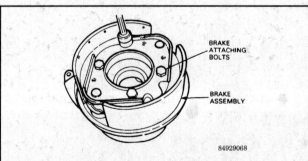

Fig. 68 Removing the F-Super Duty parking brake splash shield

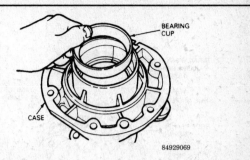

Fig. 69 Removing the F-Super Duty parking brake outer bearing cup

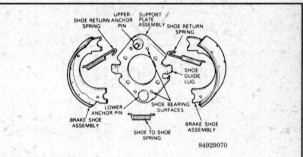

Fig. 70 Exploded view of the F-Super Duty parking brake shoes

20. Install the outer bearing cone on the mainshaft using tool T88T-2598-F to seat the bearing on the shaft.
21. Install the speedometer gear and snapring.
22. Install the shim on the mainshaft.

➡This shim determines end-play. It is available in several thicknesses with variations of 0.05mm (0.0019 in.).

23. Install the inner bearing cone and spacer on the mainshaft.

➡To check end-play, first install the inner bearing spacer without the O-ring.

24. Thread the 75mm nut onto the shaft and torque it to 215 ft. lbs.
25. Mount a dial indicator and bracket with the dial indicator between the mainshaft and case to check end-play. While rotating the case assembly on the mainshaft to center the bearings, apply pressure up and down. An end-play reading of 0.05-0.10mm (0.0019-0.0039 in.) is desired. Shim as necessary.
26. Remove the 75mm nut, spacer and bearing to install the shim(s).
27. Install the bearing.
28. Coat the outer edge of a new seal with sealer and seat it in the case bore with the lip facing inward.
29. Install a new O-ring in the spacer and install the spacer on the mainshaft until it butts against the shoulder of the shaft.
30. Install a NEW 75mm nut and torque it to 215 ft. lbs.
31. Install the vent.

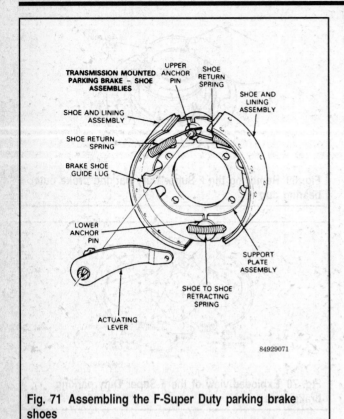

Fig. 71 Assembling the F-Super Duty parking brake shoes

INSTALLATION

▶ See Figures 72, 73, 74, 75 and 76

1. Refill the unit through the filler plug to the bottom of the plug hole. Install the plug and tighten it to 45 ft. lbs.

2. Position the unit on the extension housing using 2 guide pins.

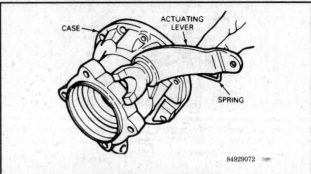

Fig. 72 Installing the F-Super Duty parking brake lever

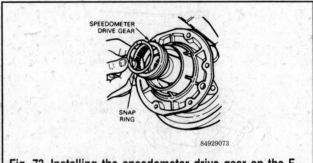

Fig. 73 Installing the speedometer drive gear on the F-Super Duty parking brake

3. Using 6 NEW hex-bolts, attach the unit and torque the bolts to 40 ft. lbs.

4. Connect the driveshaft and torque the bolts to 20 ft. lbs.

5. Assemble the cable components. Screw on the clevis until the pin can be inserted while the lever and cable are held tightly in the applied position. Then, remove the pin, let go of the cable and lever, and turn the clevis 10 full turns counter-clockwise (loosen).

6. Install the pin.

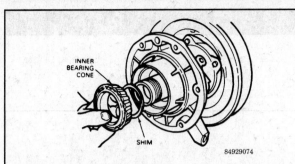

Fig. 74 Installing the inner bearing cone and shim on the F-Super Duty parking brake

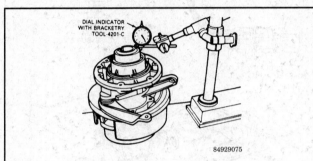

Fig. 75 Measuring endplay on the F-Super Duty parking brake

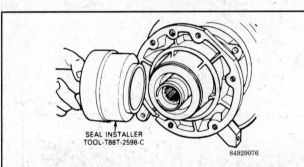

Fig. 76 Installing the inner seal on the F-Super Duty parking brake

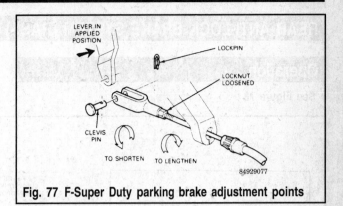

Fig. 77 F-Super Duty parking brake adjustment points

ADJUSTMENT

▶ See Figure 77

1. Fully release the brake pedal.
2. Spray penetrating oil on the adjusting clevis, jam nut and threaded end of the cable.
3. Loosen the jam nut and remove the locking pin from the clevis.
4. Back off on the clevis until there is slack in the cable.
5. Screw on the clevis until the pin can be inserted while the lever and cable are held tightly in the applied position. Then, remove the pin, let go of the cable and lever, and turn the clevis 10 full turns counterclockwise (loosen).
6. Install the pin.

REAR ANTI-LOCK BRAKE SYSTEM (RABS)

Operation

▶ See Figure 78

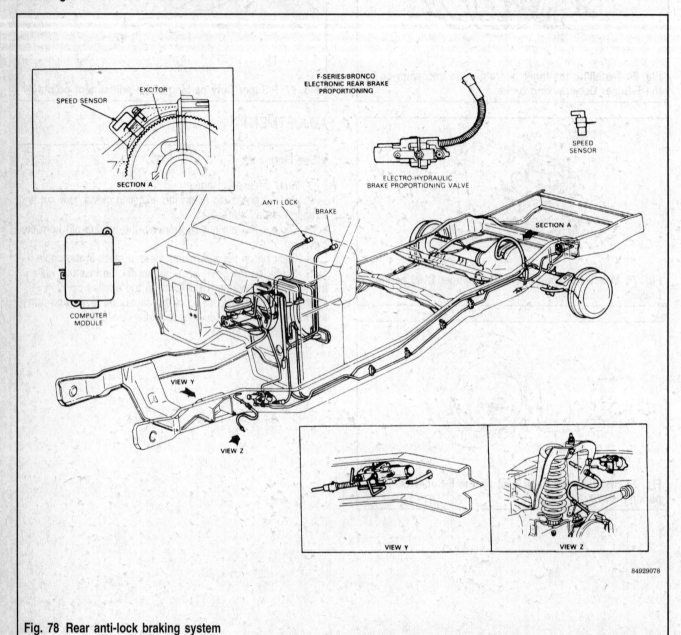

Fig. 78 Rear anti-lock braking system

The RABS system is found on all models except the F-Super Duty and the 1993 Bronco.

The system constantly monitors rear wheel speed and, in the event of impending rear wheel lock-up in a sudden stop, regulates the brake fluid hydraulic pressure at the rear brakes to prevent total wheel lock-up, thus reducing the possibility of skidding.

Trouble Codes- Rear Anti-lock Brake System

RABS FLASH CODES CHART — EXCEPT 1993 BRONCO

FLASHOUT CODES CHART

CONDITION	ACTION TO TAKE
No Flashout Code	See Flashout Code 0
Yellow REAR ABS Light Flashes 1 Time This Code Should Not Occur	See Flashout Code 1
Yellow REAR ABS Light Flashes 2 Times Open Isolate Circuit	See Flashout Code 2
Yellow REAR ABS Light Flashes 3 Times Open Dump Circuit	See Flashout Code 3
Yellow REAR ABS Light Flashes 4 Times Red Brake Warning Light Illuminated RABS Valve Switch Closed	See Flashout Code 4
Yellow REAR ABS Light Flashes 5 Times System Dumps Too Many Times in 2WD (2WD and 4WD vehicles). Condition Occurs While Making Normal or Hard Stops. Rear Brake May Lock	See Flashout Code 5
Yellow REAR ABS Light Flashes 6 Times (Sensor Signal Rapidly Cuts In and Out). Condition Only Occurs While Driving	See Flashout Code 6
Yellow REAR ABS Light Flashes 7 Times No Isolate Valve Self Test	See Flashout Code 7
Yellow REAR ABS Light Flashes 8 Times No Dump Valve Self Test	See Flashout Code 8
Yellow REAR ABS Light Flashes 9 Times High Sensor Resistance	See Flashout Code 9
Yellow REAR ABS Light Flashes 10 Times Low Sensor Resistance	See Flashout Code 10
Yellow REAR ABS Light Flashes 11 Times Stoplamp Switch Circuit Defective. Condition Indicated Only When Driving Above 35 mph	See Flashout Code 11
Yellow REAR ABS Light Flashes 12 Times Fluid Level Switch Grounded During a RABS Stop	See Flashout Code 12
Yellow REAR ABS Light Flashes 13 Times Speed Processor Check	See Flashout Code 13
Yellow REAR ABS Light Flashes 14 Times Program Check	See Flashout Code 14
Yellow REAR ABS Light Flashes 15 Times Memory Failure	See Flashout Code 15
Yellow REAR ABS Light Flashes 16 Times or More 16 or More Flashes Should Not Occur	See Flashout Code 16

NOTE: Refer to Obtaining the Flashout Code in this section for procedure to obtain flashout code.

CAUTION: WHEN CHECKING RESISTANCE IN THE RABS SYSTEM, ALWAYS DISCONNECT THE BATTERY. IMPROPER RESISTANCE READINGS MAY OCCUR WITH THE VEHICLE BATTERY CONNECTED.

84929400

Diagnosis and Testing- Rear Anti-lock Brake System

The following charts should be used for system diagnosis.

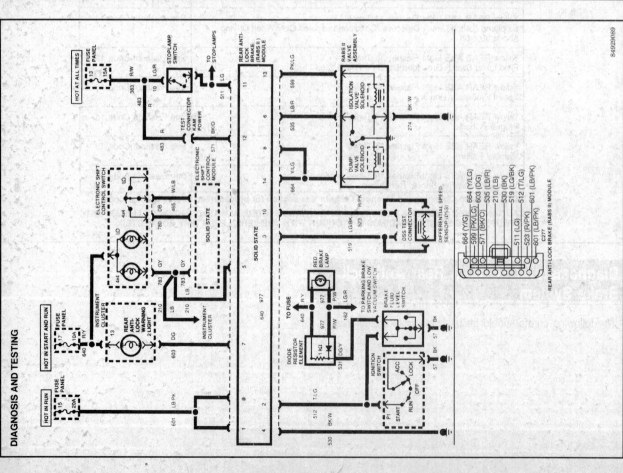

REAR ANTI-LOCK BRAKE SYSTEM TESTING — EXCEPT 1993 BRONCO

DIAGNOSIS AND TESTING (Continued)

Clearing the Keep Alive Memory (KAM)

The last step of the System Pre-Check always includes clearing the Keep Alive Memory (KAM). To do this, simply turn off the ignition while the diagnostic connector halves are separated as described in the procedures for obtaining the diagnostic trouble code above, after which the diagnostic connector should be re-assembled to provide KAM power to the RABS II module. If at this time a valid code has been obtained, go to the appropriate pinpoint test for that code.

BRAKE AND REAR ABS WARNING LAMP SYSTEM PRE-CHECK CHART

Condition	Action To Take
Yellow REAR ABS Light OFF and Does not Self Check	See System Pre-Check Test A
Red Brake Light OFF and Does Not Self-Check	See System Pre-Check Test B
Yellow REAR ABS Light Self-Check OK, but light automatically begins flashing	See System Pre-Check Test C
Yellow REAR ABS Light Self-Check OK, but no flashout code when diagnostics is started	See System Pre-Check Test D
Red Brake light ON when key in RUN position	See System Pre-Check Test E

System Pre-Check Test A

System Pre-Check Test A: Yellow REAR ABS Light OFF and Does Not Self-Check

Affected Circuit(s)/Electrical Component(s)

MODULE HARNESS CONNECTOR-PIN VIEW

ALL VIEWS LOOKING INTO CONNECTOR

Description

The RABS II module will turn on the REAR ABS light for 1-2 seconds after the key has been turned from the OFF to the RUN position. If REAR ABS light prove-out fails to occur, it may be caused by a burned-out bulb or an open fuse or Circuit 640(R/Y). An open in Circuit 603(DG) will also keep the light prove-out from occurring.

Possible Contributing Base Brake Component/Vehicle Wiring Concerns

- Open fuse Circuit 640(R/Y)
- Missing power to warning lamp (open circuit 640(R/Y))
- Open circuit 603(DG)
- Burned out REAR ABS warning bulb
- Terminal backout in the module harness connector at Pin 7

84929090

REAR ANTI-LOCK BRAKE SYSTEM TESTING — EXCEPT 1993 BRONCO

DIAGNOSIS AND TESTING

84929089

REAR ANTI-LOCK BRAKE SYSTEM TESTING — EXCEPT 1993 BRONCO

DIAGNOSIS AND TESTING (Continued)

System Pre-Check Test B

System Pre-Check Test B: Red BRAKE Light OFF and Does Not Self-Check

Affected Circuit(s)/Electrical Component(s)

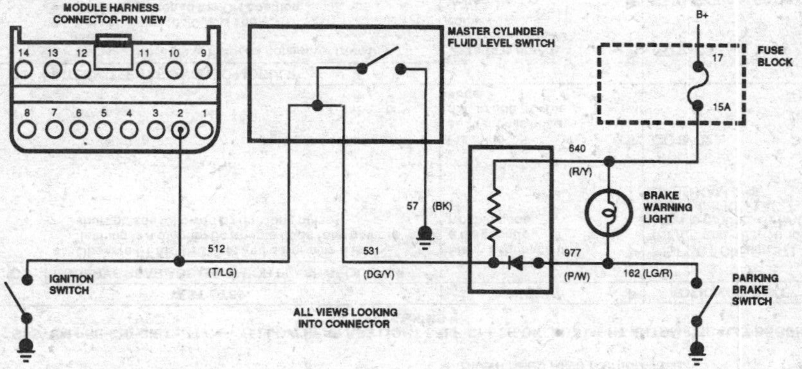

ALL VIEWS LOOKING INTO CONNECTOR

Description

If the red BRAKE light does not turn on when the key is in the START position, service the warning bulb system as required. The most likely cause of non-functioning red BRAKE lights is a burned out bulb or an open fuse.

Possible Contributing Base Brake Component/Vehicle Wiring Concerns

- Open brake warning light bulb (RED)
- Open power fuse

- Open circuit 640(R/Y), 977(P/W), 512(T/LG), 531(DG/Y), 162(LG/R)
- Open resistor/diode circuit
- Unseated master cylinder fluid level switch connector
- Defective ignition bulb prove-out switch.

SYSTEM PRE-CHECK TEST B — RED BRAKE LIGHT OFF AND DOES NOT SELF-CHECK

	TEST STEP	RESULT		ACTION TO TAKE
B1	**RED BRAKE WARNING LIGHT/FUSE**			
	• Turn ignition to RUN position.	Red BRAKE warning light turns on	▲	RELEASE parking brake GO to **B2**.
	• Apply parking brake			
	• Observe red BRAKE warning light.	Red BRAKE warning light does not turn on	▲	REPAIR brake warning circuit. CHECK for burned-out bulb or open fuse. CHECK for open Circuit 640 (R/Y), 162 (LG/R). REPEAT System Pre-Check.

REAR ANTI-LOCK BRAKE SYSTEM TESTING — EXCEPT 1993 BRONCO

DIAGNOSIS AND TESTING (Continued)

- Module connector not fully mated with RABS II module
- Defective RABS II module
- Open REAR ABS ground (Circuit 530(BK/W)

YELLOW REAR ABS LIGHT OFF AND DOES NOT SELF-CHECK

	TEST STEP	RESULT		ACTION TO TAKE
A1	**MODULE HARNESS CONNECTOR**			
	• Check to make sure module harness is fully plugged into RABS II module.	Harness is fully plugged in	▲	GO to **A2**.
		Harness is not fully plugged in	▲	CONNECT harness to module. REPEAT System Pre-Check.
A2	**RABS II MODULE GROUND**			
	• Check for good RABS II module ground:	Resistance less than 1 ohm	▲	RECONNECT battery. GO to **A3**.
	— Disconnect battery.			
	— Remove harness connector from module.	Resistance 1 ohm or greater	▲	CHECK for open in module ground wire.
	— Set ohmmeter on the 200 ohm scale.			CHECK for loose, dirty or broken connector pins. REPAIR as necessary. REPEAT System Pre-Check.
	— Check for resistance between harness connector Pin 4 and chassis ground.			
	NOTE: When checking resistance in the anti-lock system, always disconnect the battery. Improper resistance may occur with the vehicle battery connected.			
A3	**REAR ABS LIGHT POWER**			
	• Check for voltage to REAR ABS light:	Voltage greater than 9V	▲	REPLACE module. REPEAT System Pre-Check.
	— Remove harness connector from module.			
	— Set voltmeter on 20 VDC scale position.	Voltage less than 9V	▲	GO to **A4**.
	— Turn ignition to the ON position.			
	— Check voltage between harness connector Pin 7 and a known good chassis ground.			
A4	**REAR ABS LIGHT 15 AMP FUSE**			
	• Remove and inspect REAR ABS light 15 amp fuse.	Fuse is OK	▲	RE-INSTALL fuse and GO to **A5**.
		Fuse is blown	▲	CHECK for short to ground between fuse panel and warning lights. REPAIR short and replace 15 amp fuse. REPEAT System Pre-Check.
A5	**POWER TO REAR ABS LIGHT FUSE**			
	• Check for voltage to fuse.	Voltage greater than 9V	▲	GO to **A6**.
	— Set voltmeter on 20 VDC scale.			
	— Turn ignition to the ON position.	Voltage less than 9V	▲	REPAIR fuse panel or vehicle electrical system. REPEAT System Pre-Check.
	— Check voltage between panel fuse connector and known good chassis ground.			
A6	**RABS LIGHT BULB**			
	• Check REAR ABS light bulb.	Bulb is OK	▲	REPAIR open between RABS light fuse and Pin 7 of the module wiring harness connector. REPEAT System Pre-Check.
		Bulb is not OK	▲	REPLACE bulb. REPEAT System Pre-Check.

REAR ANTI-LOCK BRAKE SYSTEM TESTING — EXCEPT 1993 BRONCO

DIAGNOSIS AND TESTING (Continued)

SYSTEM PRE-CHECK TEST B — RED BRAKE LIGHT OFF AND DOES NOT SELF-CHECK (Continued)

	TEST STEP	RESULT	ACTION TO TAKE
B2	CHECK FOR CORRODED FLUID LEVEL CONNECTOR PINS • Remove fluid level switch connector located on master cylinder. • Inspect both halves of fluid level switch connector for corrosion or connector pin back-out.	Connector pins not corroded and pins seated properly	GO to **B3**.
		Corroded or bent connector pins	REPAIR/REPLACE connector as needed. REPEAT System Pre-Check.
B3	CHECK FOR UNSEATED CONNECTOR • Firmly reconnect fluid level switch connector located on master cylinder. • Turn key to START position. • Observe red BRAKE light.	Red BRAKE light is ON when key in START position	Condition is resolved. REPEAT System Pre-Check.
		Red BRAKE light remains OFF when key in START position	GO to **B4**.
B4	DIODE RESISTOR ELEMENT/CIRCUIT 531 • Disconnect fluid level switch. • Connect jumper wire from Circuit 531 (DG/Y) to known chassis ground. • Turn key to START position. • Observe red BRAKE light.	Red BRAKE light is OFF	REPAIR open Circuit 977 (P/W), 531 (DG/Y) or open diode/resistor element. REPEAT System Pre-Check.
		Red BRAKE light is ON	LEAVE fluid level switch disconnected. GO to **B5**.
B5	MASTER CYLINDER FLUID LEVEL SWITCH • Connect jumper wire from Circuit 531 (DG/Y) to Circuit 512 (T/LG). • Turn key to START position. • Observe red BRAKE light.	Red BRAKE light turns ON when key in START position	Master Cylinder fluid level switch is defective.
		Red BRAKE light remains OFF when key in START position	Open in Circuit 512 (T/LG) or defective ignition switch. REPAIR/REPLACE and REPEAT System Pre-Check.

84929093

REAR ANTI-LOCK BRAKE SYSTEM TESTING — EXCEPT 1993 BRONCO

DIAGNOSIS AND TESTING (Continued)

System Pre-Check Test C

System Pre-Check Test C: Yellow REAR ABS Light Self-Check OK, but light automatically begins flashing

Affected Circuit(s)/Electrical Component(s)

Possible Contributing Base Brake Component/Vehicle Wiring Concerns
- Intermittent RABS II module power circuit.
- Intermittent RABS II module ground circuit.
- Intermittent RABS II light circuit.
- Blown Keep Alive Memory fuse.

Description

The RABS II warning light will automatically begin a flash-out sequence if the diagnostic connector is shorted to ground. An open Keep Alive Memory (KAM) fuse is the most likely cause of a grounded diagnostic connector.

SYSTEM PRE-CHECK TEST C — YELLOW REAR ABS LIGHT SELF-CHECK OK, BUT LIGHT AUTOMATICALLY BEGINS FLASHING

	TEST STEP	RESULT	ACTION TO TAKE
C1	OBSERVE REAR ABS LIGHT FOR FLASH SEQUENCE • Observe REAR ABS light and determine if the flashing is a diagnostic trouble code (one or more short pulses followed by one long pulse).	Flash sequence is a diagnostic trouble code	INSPECT Circuits 571 (BK/O) and 483 (R) for short to ground. REPAIR circuit and REPLACE RABS KAM fuse.
		Flashing sequence is not a diagnostic trouble code	GO to **C2**.
C2	INTERMITTENT POWER TO MODULE • Remove the module harness connector from the module. • Set voltmeter to 20VDC scale. • Turn the ignition to the ON position. • Shake the instrument panel harness while measuring battery voltage between Pin 1, Pin 9 and chassis ground.	Voltage is steady and greater than 9 volts	GO to **C3**.
		Voltage is intermittent or less than 9 volts	REPAIR Circuit 601 (LB/PK). REPEAT System Pre-Check.

84929094

REAR ANTI-LOCK BRAKE SYSTEM TESTING — EXCEPT 1993 BRONCO

DIAGNOSIS AND TESTING (Continued)

SYSTEM PRE-CHECK TEST D — YELLOW REAR ABS LIGHT SELF-CHECK OK, BUT NO FLASHOUT CODE WHEN DIAGNOSTICS IS STARTED

TEST STEP	RESULT	ACTION TO TAKE
D1 DETERMINE IF SYSTEM IS RABS I OR RABS II • Determine if the ABS system is a RABS I or a RABS II system. (See TABLE 1 below for assistance.)	► Control module is a RABS II ► Control module is a RABS I	► GO to **D2**. ► This shop manual does not cover RABS I control module. See appropriate shop manual for vehicle which you are servicing.
D2 CHECK FOR SHORTED BRAKE SWITCH • Observe rear brake lights.	► Rear brake lights turned on continuously ► Rear brake lights not turned on continuously	► REPAIR shorted stoplamp switch. REPEAT System Pre-Check. ► GO to **D3**.
D3 CHECK FOR BURNED-OUT REAR BRAKE LIGHTS • Press on brake pedal while observing rear brake lights.	► Rear brake lights turn on when brake pedal is pushed ► Rear brake lights do not turn on when brake pedal is pushed	► GO to **D4**. ► REPAIR brake light system: Burned-out bulbs or open Circuit 511 (LG). REPEAT System Pre-Check.
D4 CHECK FOR LOSS OF BRAKE INPUT TO MODULE • Remove the module harness connector from the module. Check for terminal back-out. • Set voltmeter to 20 VDC range. • Press on brake pedal hard enough to turn on rear brake lights. • Measure voltage from RABS harness connector Pin 11 to chassis ground while brake pedal is pressed.	► Voltage is greater than 9 volts ► Voltage is less than 9 volts	► LEAVE module disconnected. GO to **D5**. ► REPAIR open in Circuit 511 (LG). RECONNECT module. REPEAT System Pre-Check.
D5 CHECK POWER TO THE MODULE • Turn the ignition to the ON position. • Measure the voltage between RABS harness connector Pin 1 (or Pin 9) and chassis ground.	► Voltage is less than 9 volts ► Voltage is greater than 9 volts	► REPAIR Circuit 601 (LB/PK) or associated fuse. RECONNECT module. REPEAT System Pre-Check. ► LEAVE module disconnected. GO to **D6**.
D6 CHECK FOR SHORTS IN MODULE HARNESS CONNECTOR • With same set up as in Step D5, observe yellow REAR ABS light.	► REAR ABS light is off ► REAR ABS light is on	► GO to **D7**. ► CHECK for short to ground in Circuit 603 (DG). RECONNECT the module. REPEAT System Pre-Check.
D7 CHECK CIRCUIT 571 (BK/O) CONTINUITY • Set the voltmeter to the 200 ohm scale. • Disconnect the RABS diagnostic connector from its mating half (Circuits 571 [BK/O] and 483 [R]). • Measure resistance of Circuit 571 (BK/O) from diagnostic connector to module harness connector Pin 12. • Is the resistance less than 20 ohms?	► Yes ► No	► REPLACE ECU. ► REPAIR Circuit 571 (BK/O). RECONNECT RABS II module. REPEAT System Pre-Check.

84929096

REAR ANTI-LOCK BRAKE SYSTEM TESTING — EXCEPT 1993 BRONCO

DIAGNOSIS AND TESTING (Continued)

SYSTEM PRE-CHECK TEST C — YELLOW REAR ABS LIGHT SELF-CHECK OK, BUT LIGHT AUTOMATICALLY BEGINS FLASHING (Continued)

TEST STEP	RESULT	ACTION TO TAKE
C3 DAMAGED MODULE GROUND • Disconnect the battery. • Set the voltmeter on the 200 ohm scale. • Shake the module harness while reading the resistance between Pin 4 and chassis ground.	► Resistance is less than 1 ohm and steady ► Resistance is greater than 1 ohm or fluctuates	► REPLACE module. RE-CONNECT the battery. REPEAT System Pre-Check. ► REPAIR poor ground in Circuit 530 (BK/W). RE-CONNECT the battery. REPEAT System Pre-Check.

System Pre-Check Test D

System Pre-Check Test D: Yellow REAR ABS Light Self-Check OK, but no diagnostic trouble code when diagnostics is started.

Affected Circuit(s)/Electrical Component(s)

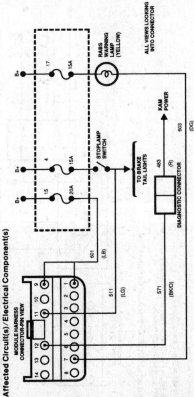

MODULE HARNESS CONNECTOR-PIN VIEW

601 (LB) 511 (LG) 571 (BK/O)

STOPLAMP SWITCH

RABS WARNING LAMP (YELLOW)

TO BRAKE TAIL LIGHTS — 483 (R)

DIAGNOSTIC CONNECTOR

KAM POWER — 603 (DG)

ALL VIEWS LOOKING INTO CONNECTOR

Description

The RABS II warning light should automatically begin a flash-out sequence if the diagnostic connector is shorted to ground for at least one second. This flashout sequence can be observed by watching the REAR ABS light. There are a few conditions which will prevent the flashout from occurring. These must be resolved before continuing the RABS II repair process.

Possible Contributing Base Brake Component/Vehicle Wiring Concerns

- Burned-out brake tail lights.
- Missing RABS II power (Circuit 601 [LB/PK] and associated fuse).
- Shorted RABS II light circuit (Circuit 603 [DG]).
- Incorrect module type (RABS I vs. RABS II).

84929095

REAR ANTI-LOCK BRAKE SYSTEM TESTING — EXCEPT 1993 BRONCO

DIAGNOSIS AND TESTING (Continued)

SYSTEM PRE-CHECK TEST E — RED BRAKE LIGHT ON

TEST STEP	RESULT	ACTION TO TAKE
E1 PULL CODE • Pull code. • Is code 4 obtained?	Yes	▲ RECONNECT data link connector and KAM connector. GO to Pinpoint Test — Code 4.
	No, no code is obtained	GO to System Pre-Check Test D.
	No, code is not code 4	GO to E2.
E2 CHECK BRAKE FLUID LEVEL IN MASTER CYLINDER • Check the brake fluid level at the master cylinder reservoir. • Is the fluid level within specification?	Yes	▲ GO to E3.
	No	▲ CHECK for leaks in the vehicle brake system and REPAIR as required. FILL the master cylinder reservoir to the required level. REPEAT E1.
E3 VERIFY FLOAT BOUYANCY • Remove the cap from the master cylinder reservoir. • Using a clean steel implement, attempt to push the float down. • Does the float move down?	Yes	▲ GO to E4.
	No, the float sits on the bottom	REPLACE the master cylinder reservoir. BLEED the brake system. REPEAT E1.
E4 CHECK RABS II MODULE • Key OFF. • Disconnect RABS II module harness connector. • Key ON. • Does the red BRAKE light turn on?	Yes	▲ RECONNECT RABS II module connector. GO to E5.
	No	▲ REPLACE RABS II module. RECONNECT RABS II module connector. REPEAT E1.
E5 LOCATE CAUSE OF RED BRAKE LIGHT ON • Key OFF. • Disconnect the fluid level switch harness connector from the master cylinder. • Key ON. • Does the red BRAKE light turn on?	Yes	▲ Diesel Only: GO to E6. All others: GO to E7.
	No	GO to E8.
E6 LOW VACUUM SWITCH CHECK (DIESEL ONLY) • Key OFF. • Disconnect low vacuum switch harness connector. • Key ON. • Does the red BRAKE light turn on?	Yes	GO to E7.
	No	RECONNECT all loose connections.
E7 PARKING BRAKE SWITCH • Key OFF. • Disconnect parking brake switch harness connector. • Key ON. • Does the red BRAKE light turn on?	Yes	▲ Key OFF. LOCATE and SERVICE short to ground in Circuit 977(P/W), 640(R/Y), 531(DG/Y), or 162(LG/R). RECONNECT all loose connections. REPEAT E1.
	No	Key OFF. REPLACE parking brake switch. RECONNECT all loose connections. REPEAT E1.

84929098

REAR ANTI-LOCK BRAKE SYSTEM TESTING — EXCEPT 1993 BRONCO

DIAGNOSIS AND TESTING (Continued)

TABLE I. ORIGINAL EQUIPMENT — RABS I VS. RABS II

Vehicle Type	Model Year	RABS System
F-Series	87-92	RABS I (see note)
F-Series	93	RABS II
Econoline	90-92	RABS I (see note)
Econoline	93	RABS II

NOTE: A RABS I system which has previously been serviced may have had its control module upgraded to a RABS II. In the event that you are uncertain whether you have a RABS I or RABS II control module, check the module part number to be certain of the type of system you have.
Part number F3TF-2C018- RABS II Module
Part number F3UF-2C018- RABS II Module
All other part numbers are RABS I Module

CAUTION: RABS I vehicles which have been upgraded with RABS II modules will NOT have Keep Alive Memory and therefore will not be able to store codes when the vehicle is turned off.

System Pre-Check Test E

System Pre-Check Test E: Red BRAKE Light ON When Key in RUN Position

Affected Circuit(s)/Electrical Component(s)

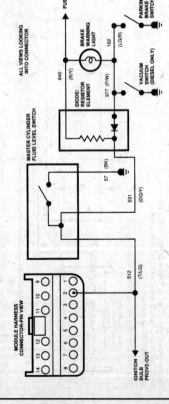

Description
- Red BRAKE light ON with ignition switch ON and parking brake released.

Possible Contributing Base Brake Component/Vehicle Wiring Concerns
- Brake fluid level low in master cylinder.
- Wiring between diode/resistor network and module is shorted to ground.
- RABS II module.
- Worn or damaged brake fluid level switch.

84929097

REAR ANTI-LOCK BRAKE SYSTEM TESTING — EXCEPT 1993 BRONCO

DIAGNOSIS AND TESTING (Continued)

SYSTEM PRE-CHECK TEST E — RED BRAKE LIGHT ON (Continued)

TEST STEP	RESULT	ACTION TO TAKE
E8 CHECK FLUID LEVEL SWITCH • Key OFF. • With the fluid level switch harness connector disconnected, jumper between Circuits 512(T/LG) and 531 (DG/Y). • Key ON. • Does the red BRAKE light turn on?	Yes ▲ No ▲	LOCATE and SERVICE short to ground in Circuit 512(T/LG). RECONNECT all loose connections. REPEAT E1. REPLACE master cylinder reservoir. BLEED brake system. RECONNECT all loose connections. REPEAT E1.

CIRCUIT 531 CIRCUIT 512

MASTER CYLINDER FLUID LEVEL SWITCH CONNECTOR

INTERMITTENT DIAGNOSIS PROCEDURE

TEST STEP	RESULT	ACTION TO TAKE
ID1 CLEAR CODES, RECONNECT COMPONENTS • Reinstall any components removed and reconnect all connections. • Clear all codes. • Key ON. • Does the REAR ABS warning light prove out?	Yes ▲ No, light stays on ▲	GO to ID3. GO to ID2.
ID2 SERVICE CONNECTOR/TERMINAL FAULT • Most likely problem is at one of the affected component connectors such that terminals unseat or back out upon installation. At each affected connection, look for: — Bent terminals. — Damaged connector terminal locks. — Damaged connector wedge. • Are any of the above conditions noted? NOTE: If one of the above conditions is found, check the length of the affected circuit once the connection is remade. If the wire is too tight (short), damage is likely to recur once vehicle is given back to the customer. Service the wire as necessary to correct tight wire conditions.	Yes ▲ No ▲	SERVICE connector and terminal as necessary. GO to ID7. GO to ID6.
ID3 WIGGLE TEST • Leave key on. • Wiggle an affected circuit in one location only. NOTE: Start at one component and wiggle connector by connector until the whole circuit has been tested. • Observe REAR ABS warning light. • Is the REAR ABS warning light on?	Yes ▲ No ▲	SERVICE the wire terminal or connector as identified in the wiggle test. GO to ID5. GO to ID4.
ID4 VERIFY ALL CIRCUITS HAVE BEEN TESTED • Have all affected circuits for the code being serviced been tested?	Yes ▲ No ▲	Key off. GO to ID6. GO to ID3 and check next circuit.

84929099

REAR ANTI-LOCK BRAKE SYSTEM TESTING — EXCEPT 1993 BRONCO

DIAGNOSIS AND TESTING (Continued)

INTERMITTENT DIAGNOSIS PROCEDURE (Continued)

TEST STEP	RESULT	ACTION TO TAKE
ID5 RETRIEVE CODE • Retrieve code. • Is this code different than the code being serviced?	Yes ▲ No ▲	GO to the appropriate pinpoint test. SERVICE the wire, terminal, or connector as necessary. GO to ID7.
ID6 VERIFY ALL APPROPRIATE DIAGNOSTIC PROCEDURES HAVE BEEN RUN • Has the System Pre-Check been run and a code been retrieved? • Have all steps of the pinpoint test for the code being serviced been performed? (If some tests were performed, then go the pinpoint step last completed and continue.)	Yes, all diagnostic procedures have been run ▲ No ▲	RETURN to the pinpoint test and proceed. RETURN to procedure(s) not yet performed and proceed.
ID7 VERIFY CONDITION RESOLVED • Clear all codes. • Key OFF. • Retrieve code. • Is Code 16 set?	Yes ▲ No, code being serviced still exists ▲ No, different code is set ▲	STOP. Concern has been corrected. GO to ID4. GO to appropriate pinpoint test.

PSOM Signal Verification Procedure

This procedure is intended to determine whether the cause for loss of or erratic Programmable Speedometer/Odometer Module (PSOM) function is due to the lack of a signal from the Rear Axle Sensor.

There are two basic reasons that PSOM would not receive a signal from the Rear Axle Sensor:

- The Rear Axle Sensor or the signal from the Rear Axle Sensor is faulty and either not being generated or is not reaching the RABS II module and/or PSOM. In cases where the concern is not intermittent and not reaching the RABS II module, the ABS warning light will be on upon vehicle startup and a rear axle diagnostic trouble code should be obtained upon RABS II diagnostic trouble code retrieval. Where the concern is intermittent and the ABS warning light does NOT come on during vehicle startup, a rear sensor diagnostic trouble code may still be stored in the RABS II module (see RABS II Diagnostic Codes).

- The wiring or interconnections in the vehicle harness between the RABS II and the PSOM module is faulty. This may lead to erratic PSOM function and is difficult to diagnose.

This procedure will only determine whether the Rear Axle Sensor is functioning based upon whether a signal is received at the PSOM module. If it is determined that the Rear Axle Sensor is sending out a proper signal, refer to Section 13-02A, PSOM System Diagnosis.

PROGRAMMABLE SPEEDOMETER/ODOMETER MODULE (PSOM) SIGNAL VERIFICATION PROCEDURE

TEST STEP	RESULT	ACTION TO TAKE
SV1 DETERMINE STATE OF ABS WARNING LIGHT • Observe ABS warning light. • Turn ignition to START. • Allow ignition to return to the RUN position. • Does the ABS warning light turn on?	Yes ▲ No ▲	GO to SV2. GO to System Pre-Check Test A. RETURN when ABS warning light fault is repaired.

84929100

REAR ANTI-LOCK BRAKE SYSTEM TESTING — EXCEPT 1993 BRONCO

DIAGNOSIS AND TESTING (Continued)

STATIC PINPOINT TEST (Cont'd)

CONDITION	ACTION TO TAKE
Yellow REAR ABS Light Flashes 12 Times Base Brake Hydraulic Loss or Worn or Damaged Master Cylinder Switch or Wiring	See Pinpoint Test — Code 12
Yellow REAR ABS Light Flashes 13 Times Module Failure	See Pinpoint Test — Code 13
Yellow REAR ABS Light Flashes 16 Times or More System OK	See Pinpoint Test — Code 16

NOTE: Refer to Obtaining the Diagnostic Trouble Code in this section for procedure to obtain flashout code.

Pinpoint Test Code 2

Code 2 — Open RABS II Valve Isolation Solenoid or Isolation Solenoid Wiring

Affected Circuit(s)/Electrical Component(s)

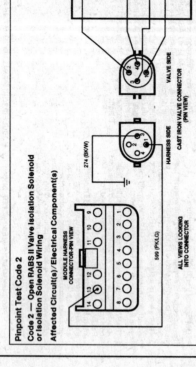

Description

Code 2 is generated by the module's detection of an open circuit in Circuit 599(PK/LG). The code may also be generated by a failed isolation solenoid (open coil) internal to the RABS II valve or a failed internal module circuit.

Possible Contributing Base Brake Component/Vehicle Wiring Concerns

- Terminal backout in the module harness connector at Pin 13.
- Terminal backout in the RABS II valve harness connector at Pin 1.
- Bulkhead connector (between engine compartment and instrument panel) terminal backout or loose connection.
- Module or RABS II valve connectors not fully mated with component.
- Intermittent open circuit in Circuit 599(PK/LG).

84929102

REAR ANTI-LOCK BRAKE SYSTEM TESTING — EXCEPT 1993 BRONCO

DIAGNOSIS AND TESTING (Continued)

PROGRAMMABLE SPEEDOMETER/ODOMETER MODULE (PSOM) SIGNAL VERIFICATION PROCEDURE (Continued)

	TEST STEP	RESULT	ACTION TO TAKE
SV2	OBTAIN ABS CODE • Obtain ABS code (refer System Pre-Check). • Are any of the following codes obtained: 6, 9, or 10? NOTE: Any other code obtained represents an ABS system concern and does NOT have an effect on the ability of the rear axle sensor to send the speed signal to PSOM. Resolve the ABS system concern indicated by the diagnostic trouble code first. When the ABS system concern is corrected, repeat this step to continue PSOM concern diagnosis.	Yes No, code 16 is obtained No, a code other than 6, 9, 10, 16 is obtained No, no code is obtained	▶ GO to the pinpoint test for the code obtained. ▶ GO to SV3. ▶ GO to appropriate pinpoint test (refer to Service Code Index). ▶ Go to System Pre-Check Test D.
SV3	VERIFY REAR AXLE SENSOR SPEED SIGNAL AT RABS II CONNECTOR • Key OFF. • Remove the RABS II module connector from the RABS II module. • Raise the vehicle so that all the wheels are clear of the ground. If the vehicle is a 4x4, verify the transfer case is in the 4x2 mode. • Connect a Hand-Held Automotive Meter, Rotunda 105-00053 or equivalent between RABS II harness connector pin 10 (circuit 523-R/PK) and pin 3 (circuit 519 — LG/BK). • Set the meter up to the frequency counter (Hz) setting. • Gradually spin up the rear wheels. • Does the frequency increase as the rear wheel speed increases?	Yes No	▶ RABS II module is receiving a proper signal. ▶ GO to Drive Test — Code 6, Step DT6.3.

CAUTION: When checking resistance in the RABS II system, always disconnect the battery. Improper resistance readings may occur with the vehicle battery connected.

STATIC PINPOINT TEST

CONDITION	ACTION TO TAKE
Yellow REAR ABS Light Flashes 2 Times Open Isolation Valve Circuit	See Pinpoint Test — Code 2
Yellow REAR ABS Light Flashes 3 Times Open Dump Valve Circuit	See Pinpoint Test — Code 3
Yellow REAR ABS Light Flashes 4 Times RABS Valve Switch Closed or Open Dump Valve	See Pinpoint Test — Code 4
Yellow REAR ABS Light Flashes 5 Times System Dumps Too Many Times in 2WD (2WD and 4WD Vehicles). Condition Occurs While Making Normal or Hard Stops. Rear Brake May Lock	See Pinpoint Test — Code 5
Yellow REAR ABS Light Flashes 6 Times (Sensor Signal Rapidly Cuts In and Out). Condition Only Occurs While Driving	See Pinpoint Test — Code 6
Yellow REAR ABS Light Flashes 7 Times No Isolate Valve Self-Test	See Pinpoint Test — Code 7
Yellow REAR ABS Light Flashes 8 Times No Dump Valve Self-Test	See Pinpoint Test — Code 8
Yellow REAR ABS Light Flashes 9 Times High Sensor Resistance	See Pinpoint Test — Code 9
Yellow REAR ABS Light Flashes 10 Times Low Sensor Resistance	See Pinpoint Test — Code 10
Yellow REAR ABS Light Flashes 11 Times Stoplamp Switch Circuit Defective. Condition Indicated Only When Driving Above 35 mph	See Pinpoint Test — Code 11

(Continued)

84929101

REAR ANTI-LOCK BRAKE SYSTEM TESTING — EXCEPT 1993 BRONCO

DIAGNOSIS AND TESTING (Continued)

PINPOINT TEST — CODE 2 (Continued)

	TEST STEP	RESULT	ACTION TO TAKE
2.5	**MAKE SURE ALL STEPS ARE COMPLETED** • This step requires that a valid diagnostic trouble code has been obtained, ALL prior diagnostic steps have been completed, and the affected wiring integrity has been verified. **CAUTION: If the above is not complete, chances are that replacement of this or any other system component without specific direction will not, in most circumstances, resolve the concern and will consequently result in customer dissatisfaction.** Have all prior diagnostic steps been completed as described above?	Yes	REPLACE ECU GO to Step **2.6**. If ECU has been replaced and no resolution has been reached, REPLACE RABS Valve GO to Step **2.6**.
		No	GO to diagnostic step last completed and continue.
2.6	**CLEAR CODE/PULL CODE** • Turn ignition OFF. • Reconnect battery ground cable. NOTE: On vehicles equipped with EEC, when the battery has been disconnected and reconnected, some abnormal drive symptoms may occur while the Powertrain Control Module (PCM) relearns its adaptive strategy. The vehicle may need to be driven 10 miles or more to relearn the strategy. • Verify all connectors are installed. • Locate and disconnect the diagnostic connector from its mating half (Circuits 571 [BK/O] and 483 [R]). • Turn ignition ON. • Begin diagnostic trouble code flashout by connecting Circuit 571 (BK/O) to a chassis ground for at least 1 second. • Observe and count code.	Diagnostic trouble code = 16	GO to Test Drive Code 16.
		Diagnostic trouble code = 2	GO to **2.7**.
		Diagnostic trouble code is different than before	GO to Pinpoint Test for corresponding code.
2.7	**PINPOINT TEST STATUS** • Has pinpoint test been completed?	Yes	GO to **2.8**.
		No	RETURN to last pinpoint test completed.
2.8	**VERIFY INTEGRITY OF VEHICLE WIRING** If the above steps have been completed, the MOST LIKELY cause of the concern is wiring related. • REFER to the Intermittent Wiring Diagnosis Porcedure and perform for ALL affected circuits as shown on this pinpoint test mini-schematic. • Is resolution achieved?	Yes	STOP. Repair is complete GO to Drive Test — Code 16.
		No	GO to **2.5**.

84929104

REAR ANTI-LOCK BRAKE SYSTEM TESTING — EXCEPT 1993 BRONCO

DIAGNOSIS AND TESTING (Continued)

PINPOINT TEST — CODE 2

	TEST STEP	RESULT	ACTION TO TAKE
2.1	**VERIFY INTEGRITY OF MODULE CONNECTION** • Turn the ignition OFF. • Disconnect battery ground cable. • Remove the module connector. • Pull gently on Pin 13 (PK/LG) just behind the harness connector.	Terminal is fully engaged	LEAVE module connector disconnected. GO to **2.2**.
		Terminal(s) in component connector are loose, bent, deformed, corroded, or missing	SERVICE terminal or connector as needed. If not, REPLACE RABS II module. GO to **2.6**.
		Terminal(s) are loose in harness connector or pull completely out of connector	SERVICE terminal or connector as needed. GO to **2.6**.
2.2	**VERIFY INTEGRITY OF VALVE CONNECTION** • Remove valve connector. • Inspect valve component connector for contamination or loose terminals. • Pull gently on Pin 1 (PK/LG) just behind the harness connector.	Terminals in component connector are clean and firmly in place. Terminal in harness connector is firmly engaged	LEAVE valve connector disconnected. GO to **2.3**.
		Terminal(s) in component connector are loose, bent, deformed, corroded, or missing	REPLACE RABS valve. GO to **2.6**.
		Terminal in harness connector moves back or comes free of connector	SERVICE terminal or connector as needed. GO to **2.6**.
2.3	**CHECK FOR CONTINUITY ALONG HARNESS CIRCUIT 599 (PK/LG)** • Verify ohmmeter is on 200 ohm scale. • Measure resistance between module harness connector Pin 13 and valve harness connector Pin 1.	Resistance is less than 10 ohms	Circuit is not open. GO to **2.4**.
		Resistance is greater than 10 ohms	FIND and REPAIR open circuit along Circuit 599 (PK/LG). GO to **2.6**.
2.4	**CHECK FOR OPEN RABS VALVE ISOLATION SOLENOID** • Verify ohmmeter is on 200 ohm scale. • Measure resistance between RABS valve Pins 1 and 3.	Resistance is less than 6 ohms	Circuit is not open. GO to **2.5**.
		Resistance is greater than 6 ohms	Open circuit in RABS valve is indicated. REPLACE RABS valve. GO to **2.6**.

84929103

REAR ANTI-LOCK BRAKE SYSTEM TESTING — EXCEPT 1993 BRONCO

DIAGNOSIS AND TESTING (Continued)

PINPOINT TEST — CODE 3 (Continued)

TEST STEP	RESULT	►	ACTION TO TAKE
3.2 VERIFY INTEGRITY OF VALVE CONNECTION			
● Remove valve connector. ● Inspect valve connector Pin 4. ● Gently pull on Pin 4 wire just behind harness connector.	Terminals in valve connector are clean and firmly in place. Terminals in harness connector are firmly engaged.	►	LEAVE valve connector disconnected. GO to **3.3**.
	Terminal(s) in valve connector are loose, bent, deformed, corroded, or missing	►	SERVICE terminal or connector as needed. If not serviceable, REPLACE RABS valve. GO to **3.6**.
	Terminal(s) in harness connector move back or come free of connector	►	SERVICE terminal or connector as needed. GO to **3.6**.
3.3 CHECK FOR CONTINUITY ALONG HARNESS CIRCUIT 664 (Y / LG) FROM MODULE CONNECTOR PINS 8 AND 14			
● Set ohmmeter on 200 ohm scale. ● Measure resistance between module harness connector Pin 8 and valve harness connector Pin 4. ● Measure resistance between module harness connector Pin 14 and valve harness connector Pin 4.	Resistance is less than 10 ohms between module harness Pin 8 and valve harness Pin 4 **AND** Resistance is less than 10 ohms between module harness Pin 14 and valve harness Pin 4	►	Circuit is not open. GO to **3.4**.
	Resistance is greater than 10 ohms between module harness Pin 8 and valve harness Pin 4	►	FIND and REPAIR open circuit along 664 (Y / LG). GO to **3.6**.
	Resistance is greater than 10 ohms between module harness Pin 14 and valve harness Pin 4	►	FIND and REPAIR open circuit along 664 (Y / LG). GO to **3.6**.
3.4 CHECK FOR OPEN RABS DUMP VALVE SOLENOID			
● Verify ohmmeter is on 200 ohm scale. ● Measure resistance between RABS valve Pins 4 and 3.	Resistance is less than 3 ohms	►	Circuit is not open. GO to **3.5**.
	Resistance is greater than 3 ohms	►	Open circuit in RABS valve is indicated. REPLACE RABS valve. GO to **3.6**.

84929106

REAR ANTI-LOCK BRAKE SYSTEM TESTING — EXCEPT 1993 BRONCO

DIAGNOSIS AND TESTING (Continued)

Pinpoint Test Code 3

Code: 3 — Open RABS II Valve Dump Solenoid or Dump Solenoid Wiring

Affected Circuit(s)/Electrical Component(s)

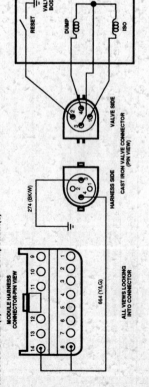

MODULE HARNESS
CONNECTOR-PIN VIEW

274 (BK/W)

664 (Y/LG)

ALL VIEWS LOOKING
INTO CONNECTOR

RESET
VALVE BODY
DUMP
ISO

HARNESS SIDE

VALVE SIDE

CAST IRON VALVE CONNECTOR
(PIN VIEW)

Description

Code 3 is generated by the module's detection of an open circuit in line 664(Y / LG) or 274(BK / W). The code may also be generated by a failed dump solenoid (open coil) internal to the RABS II valve or a failed internal module circuit.

Possible Contributing Base Brake Component/Vehicle Wiring Concerns

● Terminal backout in the module harness connector at Pin 8 or 14.

● Terminal backout in the RABS II valve harness connector at Pin 4.

● Bulkhead connector (between engine compartment and instrument panel) terminal backout or loose connection.

● Module or RABS II valve connectors not fully mated with component.

● Intermittent open circuit in line 664(Y / LG).

PINPOINT TEST — CODE 3

TEST STEP	RESULT	►	ACTION TO TAKE
3.1 VERIFY INTEGRITY OF MODULE CONNECTION			
● Turn ignition to the OFF position. ● Disconnect battery ground cable. ● Remove the module connector. ● Inspect module Pins 8 and 14. ● Pull gently on each wire just behind Pins 8 and 14 on harness connector.	Terminals in module connector are clean and firmly in place. Terminals 8 and 14 in harness connector are firmly engaged	►	LEAVE module connector disconnected. GO to **3.2**.
	Terminal(s) in module connector are loose, bent, deformed, corroded, or missing	►	SERVICE terminal or connector as needed. If not serviceable, REPLACE module. GO to **3.6**.
	Terminals 8 or 14 in harness connector move back or come free of connector	►	SERVICE terminal or connector as needed. GO to **3.6**.

84929105

REAR ANTI-LOCK BRAKE SYSTEM TESTING — EXCEPT 1993 BRONCO

DIAGNOSIS AND TESTING (Continued)

PINPOINT TEST — CODE 3 (Continued)

TEST STEP	RESULT	ACTION TO TAKE
3.5 MAKE SURE ALL STEPS ARE COMPLETED • This step requires that a valid diagnostic trouble code has been obtained, ALL prior diagnostic steps have been completed, and the affected wiring integrity has been verified. **CAUTION: If the above is not complete, chances are that replacement of this or any other system component without specific direction will not, in most circumstances, resolve the concern and will consequently result in customer dissatisfaction.** Have all prior diagnostic steps been completed as described above?	Yes	REPLACE ECU GO GO to Step 3.6. If ECU has been replaced and no resolution has been reached, REPLACE RABS Valve GO to Step 3.6.
	No	GO to diagnostic step last completed and continue.
3.6 CLEAR CODE/PULL CODE • Turn ignition OFF. • Reconnect battery ground cable. NOTE: On vehicles equipped with EEC, when the battery has been disconnected and reconnected, some abnormal drive symptoms may occur while the Powertrain Control Module (PCM) relearns its adaptive strategy. The vehicle may need to be driven 10 miles or more to relearn the strategy. • Verify all connectors are installed. • Locate and disconnect the diagnostic connector from its mating half (Circuits 571 [BK/O] and 483 [R]). • Turn ignition ON. • Begin diagnostic trouble code flashout by connecting Circuit 571 (BK/O) to a chassis ground for at least 1 second. • Observe and count code.	Diagnostic trouble code = 16	GO to Test Drive Code 16.
	Diagnostic trouble code = 3	GO to 3.7.
	Diagnostic trouble code is different than before	GO to Pinpoint Test for corresponding code.
3.7 PINPOINT TEST STATUS • Has pinpoint test been completed?	Yes	GO to 3.8.
	No	RETURN to last pinpoint test completed.
3.8 VERIFY INTEGRITY OF VEHICLE WIRING If the above steps have been completed, the MOST LIKELY cause of the concern is wiring related. • REFER to the Intermittent Wiring Diagnosis Procedure and perform for ALL affected circuits as shown on this pinpoint test mini-schematic. • Is resolution achieved?	Yes	STOP. Repair is complete GO to Drive Test — Code 16.
	No	GO to 3.5.

84929107

REAR ANTI-LOCK BRAKE SYSTEM TESTING — EXCEPT 1993 BRONCO

DIAGNOSIS AND TESTING (Continued)

Pinpoint Test Code 4

Code: 4 — Open / Grounded RABS Valve Reset Switch Circuit

Affected Circuit(s) / Electrical Component(s)

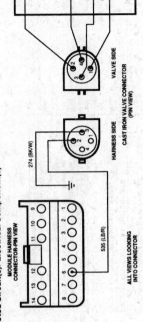

MODULE HARNESS CONNECTOR-PIN VIEW

535 (LB/R)   274 (BK/W)

HARNESS SIDE   VALVE SIDE

CAST IRON VALVE CONNECTOR (PIN VIEW)

ALL VIEWS LOOKING INTO CONNECTOR

RESET   VALVE BODY   DUMP   ISO

Description

Code 4 is generated by the module's detection of a resistance falling below 18k ohms (short) or above 26k ohms (open) in circuit 535(LB/R). This can indicate an open or short in the reset switch circuit, or a hydraulic leak into dump section of the valve.

Possible Contributing Base Brake Component / Vehicle Wiring Concerns

- Terminal backout in the module harness connector at Pin 6.
- Terminal backout in the RABS valve harness connector at Pins 2 or 3.
- Bulkhead connector (between engine compartment and instrument panel) terminal backout or loose connection.
- Module or RABS valve connectors not fully matted with component.
- Intermittent open or open circuit in Circuits 535 (LB/R), or 274 (BK/W).
- Intermittent short or short circuit in Circuit 535 (LB/R).
- Defective RABS valve (hydraulic or electrical).

PINPOINT TEST CODE 4

TEST STEP	RESULT	ACTION TO TAKE
4.1 VERIFY INTEGRITY OF MODULE CONNECTION • Turn the ignition OFF. • Disconnect battery ground cable. • Inspect module component connector Pin 6. • Inspect module harness connector Pin 6. • Pull gently on Pin 6 wire just behind the harness connector.	Terminals in module connector are clean and firmly in place. Terminal 6 in harness connector is firmly engaged	Leave module connector disconnected. GO to 4.2.
	Terminal(s) in module connector are loose, bent, deformed, corroded, or missing	SERVICE terminal or connector as needed. If not serviceable, REPLACE module. GO to 4.10.
	Terminal 6 in harness connector moves back or comes free of connector	SERVICE terminal or connector as needed. GO to 4.10.

84929108

REAR ANTI-LOCK BRAKE SYSTEM TESTING — EXCEPT 1993 BRONCO

DIAGNOSIS AND TESTING (Continued)

PINPOINT TEST CODE 4 (Continued)

TEST STEP	RESULT	ACTION TO TAKE
4.2 VERIFY INTEGRITY OF VALVE CONNECTION • Remove valve connector. • Inspect valve component connector Pins 2 and 3. • Inspect valve harness connector Pins 2 and 3. • Pull gently on Pin 2 wire just behind the harness connector. • Pull gently on Pin 3 just behind the harness connector.	▲ Terminals in valve connector are clean and firmly in place. Terminals 3 and 2 in harness connector are firmly engaged. ▲ Terminals in valve connector are loose, bent, deformed, corroded, or missing. ▲ Terminal(s) in harness connector move back or come free of connector	▲ Leave valve connector disconnected. GO to **4.3**. ▲ SERVICE terminal or connector as needed. If not serviceable, REPLACE valve. GO to **4.10**. ▲ SERVICE terminal or connector as needed. GO to **4.10**.
4.3 CHECK FOR CONTINUITY ALONG HARNESS CIRCUIT 535 (LB/R) • Set ohmmeter on 200 ohm scale. • Measure resistance between module harness connector Pin 6 and valve harness connector Pin 2.	▲ Resistance is less than 10 ohms ▲ Resistance is greater than 10 ohms	▲ Circuit is not open. GO to **4.4**. ▲ FIND and REPAIR open circuit along Circuit 535(LB/R). GO to **4.10**.
4.4 CHECK FOR CONTINUITY ALONG GROUND CIRCUIT 274(BK/W) • Set ohmmeter on 200 ohm scale. • Measure resistance between valve harness connector Pin 3 and negative battery post.	▲ Resistance is less than 12 ohms ▲ Resistance is greater than 12 ohms	▲ Circuit is not open. GO to **4.5**. ▲ FIND and REPAIR open circuit along Circuit 535(LB/R). GO to **4.10**.
4.5 CHECK FOR SHORT ALONG HARNESS CIRCUIT 535(LB/R) • Set ohmmeter on 200 ohm scale. • Measure resistance between module harness connector Pin 6 and chassis ground.	▲ Resistance is greater than 12 ohms ▲ Resistance is less than 12 ohms	▲ Circuit is not shorted. GO to **4.6**. ▲ FIND and REPAIR short circuit along Circuit 535(LB/R). GO to **4.10**.
4.6 CHECK FOR CLOSED RABS VALVE RESET SWITCH • Verify ohmmeter is on 200k ohm scale. • Measure resistance between RABS valve connector Pin 2 and RABS valve body.	▲ Resistance is greater than 10k ohms ▲ Resistance is less than 10k ohms	▲ Reset switch is not closed. GO to **4.7**. ▲ Shorted circuit in RABS valve is indicated. REPLACE RABS valve. GO to **4.10**.
4.7 CHECK RESISTANCE BETWEEN VALVE SWITCH AND VALVE COMMON • Verify ohmmeter is on 200k ohm scale. • Measure resistance between RABS valve Pins 2 and 3.	▲ Resistance greater than 10k ohms for cast iron valve ▲ Resistance less than 10k ohms for cast iron valve	▲ RABS valve internal circuit is OK. GO to **4.8**. ▲ Shorted or open circuit in RABS valve is indicated. REPLACE RABS valve. GO to **4.10**.

849293109

REAR ANTI-LOCK BRAKE SYSTEM TESTING — EXCEPT 1993 BRONCO

DIAGNOSIS AND TESTING (Continued)

PINPOINT TEST CODE 4 (Continued)

TEST STEP	RESULT	ACTION TO TAKE
4.8 CONSIDER PROBLEM TO BE INTERMITTENT OPEN CIRCUIT ALONG CIRCUIT 535(LB/R) • Consult generic intermittent wiring diagnostic procedure to find open circuit. • Reconnect battery negative cable. NOTE: On vehicles equipped with EEC, when the battery has been disconnected and reconnected, some abnormal drive symptoms may occur while the Powertrain Control Module (PCM) relearns its adaptive strategy. The vehicle may need to be driven 10 miles or more to relearn the strategy.	Intermittent open found Intermittent open not found	▲ REPAIR as needed. GO to **4.10**. ▲ GO to **4.10**.
4.9 MAKE SURE ALL STEPS ARE COMPLETED • This step requires that a valid diagnostic trouble code has been obtained, ALL prior diagnostic steps have been completed, and the affected wiring integrity has been verified. CAUTION: If the above is not complete, chances are that replacement of this or any other system component without specific direction will not, in most circumstances, resolve the concern and will consequently result in customer dissatisfaction. Have all prior diagnostic steps been completed as described above?	Yes No	▲ REPLACE ECU GO to Step **4.10**. If ECU has been replaced and no resolution have been reached, REPLACE RABS Valve. GO to Step **4.10**. ▲ GO to diagnostic step last completed and continue.
4.10 CLEAR CODE / PULL CODE • Turn ignition OFF. • Reconnect battery ground cable. NOTE: On vehicles equipped with EEC, when the battery has been disconnected and reconnected, some abnormal drive symptoms may occur while the Powertrain Control Module (PCM) relearns its adaptive strategy. The vehicle may need to be driven 10 miles or more to relearn the strategy. • Verify all connectors are installed. • Locate and disconnect the diagnostic connector from its mating half (Circuits 57-1 (BK/O and 481 (R)). • Turn ignition ON. Begin diagnostic trouble code flashout by connector circuit 571 (BK/O) to a chassis ground for at least 1 second. • Observe and count code.	Diagnostic Trouble Code = 16. Diagnostic Trouble Code = 4. Diagnostic Trouble Code is different than before.	▲ GO to Drive Test — Code 16. ▲ GO to **4.11**. ▲ GO to the pinpoint test for the corresponding code.
4.11 VERIFY PINPOINT TEST IS COMPLETE Has the pinpoint test been completed?	Yes No	▲ GO to **4.12**. ▲ RETURN to last pinpoint test step completed.
4.12 VERIFY INTEGRITY OF VEHICLE WIRING If the above steps have been completed, the MOST LIKELY cause of the concern is wiring related. • REFER to the Intermittent Wiring Diagnosis Procedure and perform for ALL affected circuits as shown on this pinpoint test mini-schematic. • Is resolution achieved?	Yes No	▲ STOP. Repair is complete GO to Drive Test — Code 16. ▲ GO to **4.9**.

849293110

REAR ANTI-LOCK BRAKE SYSTEM TESTING — EXCEPT 1993 BRONCO

DIAGNOSIS AND TESTING (Continued)

Pinpoint Test Code 5

Code: 5 Excessive dump solenoid activity. System dumps too many times in 2WD mode (2WD and 4WD vehicles).

Affected Circuit(s)/Electrical Component(s)

Description

Code 5 is generated when the maximum number of allowable dump pulses has been exceeded. The system will only recognize this condition during an anti-lock stop in 2WD mode. The code may be caused by a blocked RABS dump valve orifice, a stuck dump valve, an open circuit in Circuit 210 (LB), a worn or damaged 4x4 transfer case that causes the vehicle to remain in 4x4 after 4x2 has been selected, or mechanical problems in the rear brake system. (Rear brakes may lock.)

Possible Contributing Base Brake Component/Vehicle Wiring Concerns

- Parking brake drag.
- Worn or damaged 4x4 switch.
- Rear brake assembly grabby or hanging up.
- Connector corrosion or contamination.
- Intermittent open circuit in Circuit 210 (LB).
- Pierced wire insulation to battery power (4x4 only).

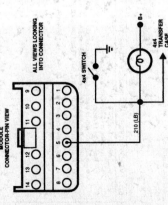

MODULE CONNECTOR-PIN VIEW — ALL VIEWS LOOKING INTO CONNECTOR

4x4 SWITCH — 210 (LB) — B+ — 4x4 TRANSFER CASE

PINPOINT TEST — CODE 5

TEST STEP	RESULT	ACTION TO TAKE
5.1 DRIVE STATUS • Determine if vehicle is in 2-or 4-wheel drive when code occurred (except all wheel drive Aerostar).	4-wheel drive 2-wheel drive	▲ GO to **5.2.** ▲ GO to **5.3.**
5.2 CHECK FOR INCORRECT 4WD SWITCH SIGNAL, OR SHORT TO POWER TO RABS II MODULE • Disconnect RABS II module harness connector from module to deactivate RABS. • Key ON. • Shift into 4x4 mode. • Set voltmeter to 20VDC scale. • Measure voltage between Pin 5 of the module harness and chassis ground. • Is the measured voltage less than 1V?	Yes No, greater than 1V	▲ GO to **5.3.** ▲ REPAIR 4x4 indicator switch or REPAIR short in Circuit 210 (LB). REFER to the appropriate section . . . GO to **5.4.**
5.3 CHECK FOR LOW OR ERRATIC SENSOR SIGNAL • Disconnect module harness connector. • Position vehicle on hoist and raise both front and rear wheels just enough to clear the floor. • Start the engine and turn the wheels at 5 mph. • Place voltmeter on 2000mV AC scale. • Measure the voltage across module harness connector Pins 3 and 10. • Is the voltage less than 650mV RMS or is sensor signal erratic?	Yes No, voltage is greater than 650mV RMS	▲ COMPLETE pinpoint test for Code 5, steps 6.2 through 6.8, then RETURN. GO to 5.4 to verify. ▲ REINSTALL module connector. GO to drive test for Code 5.

84929111

REAR ANTI-LOCK BRAKE SYSTEM TESTING — EXCEPT 1993 BRONCO

DIAGNOSIS AND TESTING (Continued)

PINPOINT TEST — CODE 5 (Continued)

TEST STEP	RESULT	ACTION TO TAKE
5.4 MAKE SURE ALL STEPS ARE COMPLETED • This step requires that a valid diagnostic troulbe code has been obtained, ALL prior diagnostic steps have been completed, and the affected wiring integrity has been verified. CAUTION: If the above is not complete, chances are that replacement of this or any other system component without specific direction will not, in most circumstances, resolve the concern and will consequently result in customer dissatisfaction. Have all prior diagnostic steps been completed as described above?	Yes No	▲ REPLACE ECU GO to Step **5.5.** If ECU has been replaced and no resolution has been reached, REPLACE RABS Valve GO to Step **5.5.** ▲ GO to diagnostic step last completed and continue.
5.5 CLEAR CODE / PULL CODE • Turn ignition OFF. • Reconnect battery ground cable. NOTE: On vehicles equipped with EEC, when the battery has been disconnected and reconnected, some abnormal drive symptoms may occur while the Powertrain Control Module (PCM) relearns its adaptive strategy. The vehicle may need to be driven 10 miles or more to relearn the strategy. • Verify all connectors are installed. • Locate and disconnect the diagnostic connector from its mating half (Circuits 571 [BK/O] and 481 [R]). • Turn ignition ON. • Begin diagnostic trouble code flashout by connecting Circuit 571 (BK/O) to a chassis ground for at least 1 second. • Observe and count code.	Diagnostic trouble code = 16 Diagnostic trouble code = 5 Diagnostic trouble code is different than before	▲ GO to Test Drive Code 16. ▲ GO to **5.6.** ▲ GO to Pinpoint Test for corresponding code.
5.6 PINPOINT TEST STATUS • Has pinpoint test been completed?	Yes No	▲ GO to **5.7.** ▲ RETURN to last pinpoint test completed.
5.7 VERIFY INTEGRITY OF VEHICLE WIRING • If the above steps have been completed, the MOST LIKELY cause of the concern is wiring related. • REFER to the Intermittent Wiring Diagnosis Porcedure and perform for ALL affected circuits as shown on this pinpoint test mini-schematic. • Is resolution achieved?	Yes No	▲ STOP. Repair is complete GO to Drive Test — Code 16. ▲ GO to **5.4.**

84929112

REAR ANTI-LOCK BRAKE SYSTEM TESTING — EXCEPT 1993 BRONCO

DIAGNOSIS AND TESTING (Continued)

PINPOINT TEST — CODE 6 (Continued)

TEST STEP	RESULT	ACTION TO TAKE
6.2 VERIFY INTEGRITY OF SENSOR CONNECTION • Verify ignition is OFF. • Remove sensor connector. • Inspect sensor component connector for contamination and bent or loose terminals. • Gently pull on Circuit 519 (LG/BK) behind Pin B of harness connector. • Gently pull on Circuit 523 (R/PK) behind Pin A of harness connector.	Terminals in component connector are clean and firmly in place. Terminal in harness connector is firmly engaged.	▲ REINSTALL RABS sensor connector. GO to **6.3**.
	Terminal(s) in component connector are corroded, bent, or loose.	▲ REPLACE RABS sensor. GO to **6.7**.
	Terminal(s) in harness connector are corroded, bent, or move back or come free of connector.	▲ SERVICE terminal or connector as needed. GO to **6.7**.
6.3 VERIFY PROPER SENSOR WIRE ROUTING • Inspect wire routing.	Wires are properly secured and show no sign of wear or being pinched.	▲ GO to **6.4**.
	Wire(s) are worn, insulation is pinched, or almost completely severed.	▲ FIND and REPAIR as necessary. GO to **6.7**.
6.4 CHECK FOR ERRATIC SENSOR SIGNAL AND LOOSE WIRE CONNECTORS • Set ohmmeter on the 20 K ohm scale. • Check resistance between Pin 10 and Pin 3 of the harness connector while shaking the harness from sensor to module.	Constant reading of 900 to 2500 ohms	▲ Signal is not erratic. GO to **6.5**.
	Reading is erratic or out of range	▲ FIND and REPAIR open/short circuit along Circuits 519 (LG/BK) and 523 (R/PK). GO to **6.7**.
6.5 VERIFY SENSOR INTEGRITY • Set ohmmeter on the 20 K ohm scale. • Check resistance between Pins A and B of the sensor connector.	Resistance between 900-2500 ohms	▲ GO to **6.6**.
	Resistance out of 900-2500 ohm range	▲ REPLACE RABS speed sensor. GO to **6.7**.
6.6 CHECK FOR METAL CHIPS ON SENSOR MAGNET POLE PIECE • Verify ignition is OFF. • Remove the sensor from the differential and inspect for a build up of metal chips on sensor magnetic pole.	No metal chips are present	▲ Leave speed sensor out. GO to **6.7**.
	Metal chips are present	▲ DRAIN and CLEAN differential. GO to **6.7**.

84929114

REAR ANTI-LOCK BRAKE SYSTEM TESTING — EXCEPT 1993 BRONCO

DIAGNOSIS AND TESTING (Continued)

Pinpoint Test Code 6

Code: 6 — Erratic speed sensor while rolling or bad speed sensor wiring.

Affected Circuit(s)/Electrical Component(s)

MODULE HARNESS CONNECTOR-PIN VIEW

RABS SENSOR CONNECTORS (PIN VIEW)

HARNESS SIDE — SENSOR SIDE

A   B

ALL VIEWS LOOKING INTO CONNECTOR

523 (R/PK)   519 (LG/BK)   (TWISTED)

Description

Code 6 is generated by the module's detection of an interruption in the continuous signal from the speed sensor while rolling, caused by an intermittent open internal to the speed sensor, Circuit 519 (LG/BK) or Circuit 523 (R/PK), or a damaged speed sensor ring. This condition can be detected anytime the brake pedal is not applied and 20 seconds has elapsed since the ignition self-test.

Possible Contributing Base Brake Component/Vehicle Wiring Concerns

• Terminal backout in the module harness connector at Pins 3 and 10.
• Terminal backout in the RABS speed sensor harness connector at Pins A and B.
• Bulkhead connector (between engine compartment and instrument panel) terminal backout or loose connection.
• Module or RABS speed sensor connectors are not fully mated with component.
• Intermittent open/short circuit in Circuits 519 (LG/BK) or 523 (R/PK).
• Damaged speed sensor (possibly metal shavings on pole piece).
• Damaged speed sensor ring (possibly teeth missing).

PINPOINT TEST — CODE 6

TEST STEP	RESULT	ACTION TO TAKE
6.1 VERIFY INTEGRITY OF MODULE CONNECTION • Turn ignition OFF. • Disconnect battery negative cable. • Remove the module connector. • Inspect module component connector for contamination and loose or bent terminals. • Pull gently on Circuit 519 (LG/BK) just behind Pin 3 on the harness connector. • Pull gently on Circuit 523 (R/PK) just behind Pin 10 on the harness connector.	Terminals in component connector are clean and firmly in place. Terminals in harness connector are firmly engaged.	▲ Leave module connector disconnected. GO to **6.2**.
	Terminal(s) in component connector are corroded, bent, or loose.	▲ SERVICE terminals or connector as needed. GO to **6.7**.
	Terminal(s) in harness connector are corroded, bent, or come free back or come free of connector.	▲ SERVICE terminals or connector as needed. GO to **6.7**.

84929113

REAR ANTI-LOCK BRAKE SYSTEM TESTING — EXCEPT 1993 BRONCO

DIAGNOSIS AND TESTING (Continued)

Pinpoint Test Code 7

Code: 7 — No Isolation Solenoid During Self-Check

Affected Circuit(s)/Electrical Component(s)

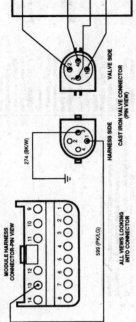

MODULE HARNESS CONNECTOR-PIN VIEW

14 13 12 11 10 9
8 7 6 5 4 3 2 1

599 (PK/LG)

ALL VIEWS LOOKING INTO CONNECTOR

274 (BK/W)

HARNESS SIDE — CAST IRON VALVE CONNECTOR (PIN VIEW)

VALVE SIDE

RESET — VALVE BODY — DUMP — ISO

Possible Contributing Base Brake Component/Vehicle Wiring Concerns

- Module internal fuse blown or internal open circuit.
- Shorted isolation solenoid internal to the RABS valve.
- Intermittent short or shorted circuit in Circuit 599 (PK/LG).
- Contamination or bent Pins 1 and 3 of valve connector shorting together.

Description

Code 7 is generated when the module detects a missing Isolation solenoid output. This can only be detected during an ignition self-check or during RABS stop.

PINPOINT TEST — CODE 7

	TEST STEP	RESULT	ACTION TO TAKE
7.1	CHECK FOR RABS VALVE ISOLATION SOLENOID OR WIRING SHORTED TO GROUND • Turn the ignition OFF. • Disconnect battery negative cable. • Remove the module connector. • Set the ohmmeter on the 200 ohm scale. • Measure the resistance between module harness connector Pin 13 and chassis ground.	Resistance greater than 10 ohms Resistance less than 10 ohms	Circuit is not shorted. Leave module connector disconnected. GO to 7.5. Circuit is shorted. Leave module connector disconnected. GO to 7.2.
7.2	CHECK INTEGRITY OF VALVE CONNECTION • Remove valve connector. • Inspect valve component connector and Pins 1 and 3.	Terminals in valve connector are clean and firmly in place. Terminal(s) in valve connector are loose, bent, deformed, or corroded.	Circuit is not shorted. Leave valve connector disconnected. GO to 7.3. SERVICE terminals or connector as needed. If not serviceable, REPLACE RABS valve. GO to 7.6.

REAR ANTI-LOCK BRAKE SYSTEM TESTING — EXCEPT 1993 BRONCO

DIAGNOSIS AND TESTING (Continued)

PINPOINT TEST — CODE 6 (Continued)

	TEST STEP	RESULT	ACTION TO TAKE
6.7	MAKE SURE ALL STEPS ARE COMPLETED • This step requires that a valid diagnostic trouble code has been obtained, ALL prior diagnostic steps have been completed, and the affected wiring integrity has been verified. CAUTION: If the above is not complete, chances are that replacement of this or any other system component without specific direction will not, in most circumstances, resolve the concern and will consequently result in customer dissatisfaction. Have all prior diagnostic steps been completed as described above?	Yes No	REPLACE ECU. GO to Step 5.8. If ECU has been replaced and no resolution has been reached, REPLACE rear axle sensor. GO to Step 6.8. GO to diagnostic step last completed and continue.
6.8	CLEAR CODE/PULL CODE • Turn ignition OFF. • Reconnect battery ground cable. NOTE: On vehicles equipped with EEC, when the battery has been disconnected and reconnected, some abnormal drive symptoms may occur while the Powertrain Control Module (PCM) relearns its adaptive strategy. The vehicle may need to be driven 10 miles or more to relearn the strategy. • Verify all connectors are installed. • Locate and disconnect the diagnostic connector from its mating half (Circuits 571 [BK/O] and 481 [R]). • Turn ignition ON. • Begin diagnostic trouble code flashout by connecting Circuit 571 (BK/O) to a chassis ground for at least 1 second. • Observe and count code.	Diagnostic trouble code = 16 Diagnostic trouble code = 6 Diagnostic trouble code is different than before	GO to Test Drive Code 16. GO to 6.9. GO to Pinpoint Test for corresponding code.
6.9	PINPOINT TEST STATUS • Has pinpoint test been completed?	Yes No	GO to 6.10. RETURN to last pinpoint test completed.
6.10	VERIFY INTEGRITY OF VEHICLE WIRING If the above steps have been completed, the MOST LIKELY cause of the concern is wiring related. • REFER to the Intermittent Wiring Diagnosis Porcedure and perform for ALL affected circuits as shown on this pinpoint test mini-schematic. • Is resolution achieved?	Yes No	STOP. Repair is complete. GO to Drive Test — Code 16. GO to 6.7.

REAR ANTI-LOCK BRAKE SYSTEM TESTING — EXCEPT 1993 BRONCO

DIAGNOSIS AND TESTING (Continued)

Pinpoint Test Code 8

Code: 8 — No Dump Solenoid During Self-Check

Affected Circuit(s)/Electrical Component(s)

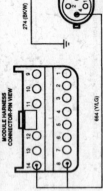

MODULE HARNESS CONNECTOR-PIN VIEW

274 (BK/W)

664 (Y/LG)

ALL VIEWS LOOKING INTO CONNECTOR

CAST IRON VALVE CONNECTOR (PIN VIEW)

VALVE BODY — RESET — DUMP — ISO — VALVE SIDE — HARNESS SIDE

Description

Code 8 is generated when the module detects a missing Dump solenoid output. This concern can only be detected during an ignition self-test or during a REAR ABS stop.

Possible Contributing Base Brake Component/Vehicle Wiring Concerns

- Module internal fuse blown or internal open circuit.
- Shorted Dump solenoid internal to RABS valve.
- Intermittent short or shorted circuit in Circuit 664 (Y/LG).
- Bulkhead connector between engine compartment and instrument panel terminals shorted.

PINPOINT TEST — CODE 8

TEST STEP	RESULT	ACTION TO TAKE
8.1 CHECK FOR RABS VALVE DUMP SOLENOID OR WIRING SHORTED TO GROUND • Turn the ignition OFF. • Disconnect battery negative cable. • Remove the module connector. • Set the ohmmeter on the 200 ohm scale. • Measure the resistance between module harness connector Pin 8 and chassis ground. • Measure the resistance between module harness connector Pin 14 and chassis ground.	▶ Resistance greater than 10 ohms between module harness Pin 8 and ground AND Resistance greater than 10 ohms between module harness Pin 14 and ground	▶ Leave module connector disconnected. GO to **8.4.**
	▶ Resistance less than 10 ohms between module harness Pin 8 ground	▶ Leave module connector disconnected. GO to **8.2.**
	▶ Resistance less than 10 ohms between module harness Pin 14 and ground	▶ Leave module connector disconnected. GO to **8.2.**

84929118

REAR ANTI-LOCK BRAKE SYSTEM TESTING — EXCEPT 1993 BRONCO

DIAGNOSIS AND TESTING (Continued)

PINPOINT TEST — CODE 7 (Continued)

TEST STEP	RESULT	ACTION TO TAKE
7.3 CHECK FOR SHORTED RABS ISOLATION SOLENOID • Verify valve connector removed. • Set the ohmmeter on the 200 ohm scale. • Measure the resistance between Pins 1 and 3 of valve connector.	▶ Resistance greater than 3 ohms	▶ LEAVE valve connector disconnected. GO to **7.4.**
	▶ Resistance less than 3 ohms	▶ REPLACE RABS valve. GO to **7.6.**
7.4 CHECK FOR SHORT TO GROUND ALONG HARNESS CIRCUIT 599 (PK/LG) • Set ohmmeter on 20K ohm scale. • Measure resistance between module harness connector Pin 13 (PK/LG) and chassis ground.	▶ Resistance less than 20 K ohms	▶ REPAIR short in Circuit 599 (PK/LG) between module and RABS valve. GO to **7.6.**
	▶ Resistance greater than 20 K ohms	▶ Conflict of information. REPEAT **7.2.**
7.5 MAKE SURE ALL STEPS ARE COMPLETED • This step requires that a valid diagnostic trouble code has been obtained, ALL prior diagnostic steps have been completed, and the affected wiring integrity has been verified. **CAUTION: If the above is not complete, chances are that replacement of this or any other system component without specific direction will not, in most circumstances, resolve the concern and will consequently result in customer dissatisfaction.** Have all prior diagnostic steps been completed as described above?	▶ Yes	▶ REPLACE ECU GO to Step **7.6.** If ECU has been replaced and no resolution has been reached, REPLACE RABS Valve GO to Step **7.6.**
	▶ No	▶ GO to diagnostic step last completed and continue.
7.6 CLEAR CODE/PULL CODE • Turn ignition OFF. • Reconnect battery ground cable. NOTE: On vehicles equipped with EEC, when the battery has been disconnected and reconnected, some abnormal drive symptoms may occur while the Powertrain Control Module (PCM) relearns its adaptive strategy. The vehicle may need to be driven 10 miles or more to relearn the strategy. • Verify all connectors are installed. • Locate and disconnect the diagnostic connector from its mating half (Circuits 571 [BK/O] and 481 [R]). • Turn ignition ON. • Begin diagnostic trouble code flashout by connecting Circuit 571 (BK/O) to a chassis ground for at least 1 second. • Observe and count code.	▶ Diagnostic trouble code = 16	▶ GO to Test Drive Code 16.
	▶ Diagnostic trouble code = 7	▶ GO to **7.7.**
	▶ Diagnostic trouble code is different than before	▶ GO to Pinpoint Test for corresponding code.
7.7 PINPOINT TEST STATUS • Has pinpoint test been completed?	▶ Yes	▶ GO to **7.8.**
	▶ No	▶ RETURN to last pinpoint test completed.
7.8 VERIFY INTEGRITY OF VEHICLE WIRING • After the above steps have been completed, the MOST LIKELY cause of the concern is wiring related. • REFER to the Intermittent Wiring Diagnosis Procedure and perform for ALL affected circuits as shown on this pinpoint test mini-schematic. • Is resolution achieved?	▶ Yes	▶ STOP. Repair is complete GO to Drive Test — Code 16.
	▶ No	▶ GO to **7.5.**

84929117

REAR ANTI-LOCK BRAKE SYSTEM TESTING — EXCEPT 1993 BRONCO

DIAGNOSIS AND TESTING (Continued)

PINPOINT TEST — CODE 8 (Continued)

TEST STEP	RESULT	ACTION TO TAKE
8.2 CHECK FOR SHORTED RABS DUMP SOLENOID • Remove valve connector. • Set the ohmmeter on the 200 ohm scale. • Measure the resistance between Pins 3 and 4 of valve connector.	Resistance greater than 1 ohm Resistance less than 1 ohm	Leave valve connector disconnected. GO to **8.3.** REPLACE RABS II valve. GO to **8.5.**
8.3 CHECK FOR SHORT TO GROUND ALONG HARNESS CIRCUIT 664 (Y/LG) • Set ohmmeter on 20 ohm scale. • Measure resistance between module harness connector Pin 8 and valve harness connector Pin 4. • Measure resistance between module harness connector Pin 14 and valve harness connector Pin 4.	Resistance less than 10 ohms between module Pin 8 and valve Pin 4 Resistance less than 10 ohms between module Pin 14 and valve Pin 4 Resistance greater than 10 ohms between module Pin 8 and valve Pin 4 AND Resistance greater than 10 ohms between module Pin 14 and valve Pin 4	REPAIR short in Circuit 664 (Y/LG) between module and RABS valve. GO to **8.5.** REPAIR short in Circuit 664 (Y/LG) between module and RABS valve. GO to **8.5.** Conflict of information. REPEAT **8.1.**
8.4 MAKE SURE ALL STEPS ARE COMPLETED • This step requires that a valid diagnostic trouble code has been obtained, ALL prior diagnostic steps have been completed, and the affected wiring integrity has been verified. **CAUTION: If the above is not complete, chances are that replacement of this or any other system component without specific direction will not, in most circumstances, resolve the concern and will consequently result in customer dissatisfaction.** Have all prior diagnostic steps been completed as described above?	Yes No	REPLACE ECU GO to Step **8.5.** If ECU has been replaced and no resolution has been reached, REPLACE RABS Valve GO to Step **8.5.** GO to diagnostic step last completed and continue.
8.5 CLEAR CODE / PULL CODE • Turn ignition OFF. • Reconnect battery ground cable. • NOTE: On vehicles equipped with EEC, when the battery has been disconnected and reconnected, some abnormal drive symptoms may occur while the Powertrain Control Module (PCM) relearns its adaptive strategy. The vehicle may need to be driven 10 miles or more to relearn the strategy. • Verify all connectors are installed. • Locate and disconnect the diagnostic connector from its mating half (Circuits 571 [BK/O] and 481 [R]). • Turn ignition ON. • Begin diagnostic trouble code flashout by connecting Circuit 571 (BK/O) to a chassis ground for at least 1 second. • Observe and count code.	Diagnostic trouble code = 16 Diagnostic trouble code = 8 Diagnostic trouble code is different than before	GO to Test Drive Code 16. GO to **8.6.** GO to Pinpoint Test for corresponding code.

REAR ANTI-LOCK BRAKE SYSTEM TESTING — EXCEPT 1993 BRONCO

DIAGNOSIS AND TESTING (Continued)

PINPOINT TEST — CODE 8 (Continued)

TEST STEP	RESULT	ACTION TO TAKE
8.6 PINPOINT TEST STATUS • Has pinpoint test been completed?	Yes No	GO to **8.7.** RETURN to last pinpoint test completed.
8.7 VERIFY INTEGRITY OF VEHICLE WIRING If the above steps have been completed, the MOST LIKELY cause of the concern is wiring related. • REFER to the Intermittent Wiring Diagnosis Procedure and perform for ALL affected circuits as shown on this pinpoint test mini-schematic. • Is resolution achieved?	Yes No	STOP. Repair is complete. GO to Drive Test — Code 16. GO to **8.4.**

Pinpoint Test Code 9

Code: 9 — High Speed Sensor Resistance or Open Speed Sensor Wiring

Affected Circuit(s)/Electrical Component(s)

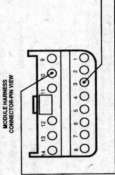

MODULE HARNESS CONNECTOR-PIN VIEW

RABS SENSOR CONNECTORS (PIN VIEW)
SENSOR SIDE
HARNESS SIDE

ALL VIEWS LOOKING INTO CONNECTOR

523 (R/PK)
519 (LG/BK)
(TWISTED)

Description

Code 9 is generated by the module's detection of high speed sensor resistance. The module will consider the speed sensor circuit to have a high resistance when it exceeds approximately 3 K ohms. The code may also be generated by a failed internal module circuit. The module can only detect this condition when the vehicle is at rest.

Possible Contributing Base Brake Component/Vehicle Wiring Concerns

- Terminal backout in the module harness connector at Pin 3 or Pin 10.
- Terminal backout in the RABS speed sensor harness connector at Pins A or B.
- Module or RABS speed sensor connectors not fully mated with component.
- Open or intermittent open circuit in Circuits 519 (LG/BK) or 523 (R/PK).

84929119

84929120

REAR ANTI-LOCK BRAKE SYSTEM TESTING — EXCEPT 1993 BRONCO

DIAGNOSIS AND TESTING (Continued)

PINPOINT TEST — CODE 9 (Continued)

TEST STEP	RESULT	ACTION TO TAKE
9.6 CLEAR CODE / PULL CODE • Turn ignition OFF. • Reconnect battery ground cable. NOTE: On vehicles equipped with EEC, when the battery has been disconnected and reconnected, some abnormal drive symptoms may occur while the Powertrain Control Module (PCM) relearns its adaptive strategy. The vehicle may need to be driven 10 miles or more to relearn the strategy. • Verify all connectors are installed. • Locate and disconnect the diagnostic connector from its mating half (Circuits 571 [BK/O] and 481 [R]). • Turn ignition ON. • Begin diagnostic trouble code flashout by connecting Circuit 571 (BK/O) to a chassis ground for at least 1 second. • Observe and count code.	Diagnostic trouble code = 16 Diagnostic trouble code = 9 Diagnostic trouble code is different than before	▲ GO to Test Drive Code 16. ▲ GO to 9.7. ▲ GO to Pinpoint Test for corresponding code.
9.7 PINPOINT TEST STATUS • Has pinpoint test been completed?	Yes No	▲ GO to 9.8. ▲ RETURN to last pinpoint test completed.
9.8 VERIFY INTEGRITY OF VEHICLE WIRING If the above steps have been completed, the MOST LIKELY cause of the concern is wiring related. • REFER to the Intermittent Wiring Diagnosis Porcedure and perform for ALL affected circuits as shown on this pinpoint test mini-schematic. • Is resolution achieved?	Yes No	▲ STOP. Repair is complete GO to Drive Test — Code 16. ▲ GO to 9.5.

Pinpoint Test Code 10

Code: 10 — Low Speed Sensor Resistance or Shorted Speed Sensor Wiring

Affected Circuit(s)/Electrical Component(s)

MODULE HARNESS CONNECTOR-PIN VIEW

RABS SENSOR CONNECTORS (PIN VIEW)
HARNESS SIDE   SENSOR SIDE

ALL VIEWS LOOKING INTO CONNECTOR

523 (R/PK)
519 (LG/BK)
(TWISTED)

84929122

REAR ANTI-LOCK BRAKE SYSTEM TESTING — EXCEPT 1993 BRONCO

DIAGNOSIS AND TESTING (Continued)

PINPOINT TEST — CODE 9

TEST STEP	RESULT	ACTION TO TAKE
9.1 VERIFY INTEGRITY OF MODULE CONNECTION • Turn ignition OFF. • Disconnect battery negative cable. • Remove the module connector. • Pull gently on Circuit 519 (LG/BK) just behind Pin 3 on the harness connector. • Pull gently on Circuit 523 (R/PK) just behind Pin 10 on the harness connector.	Terminal is fully engaged Terminal moves back or comes free of connector	▲ Leave module connector disconnected. GO to 9.2. ▲ SERVICE terminal or connector as needed. GO to 9.6.
9.2 VERIFY INTEGRITY OF SENSOR CONNECTION • Remove sensor connector. • Inspect sensor component connector for contamination or loose terminals. • Gently pull on Circuit 519 (LG/BK) behind Pin B of harness connector. • Gently pull on Circuit 523 (R/PK) behind Pin A of harness connector.	Terminals in component connector are clean and firmly in place. Terminal in harness connector is firmly engaged. Terminals in component connector are loose. Terminal in harness connector moves back or comes free of connector.	▲ Leave sensor connector disconnected. GO to 9.3. ▲ REPLACE RABS sensor. GO to 9.6. ▲ SERVICE terminal or connector as needed. GO to 9.6.
9.3 CHECK FOR CONTINUITY ALONG HARNESS CIRCUITS 519 (LG/BK) and 523 (R/PK) • Set ohmmeter on 200 ohm scale. • Measure resistance between module harness connector Pin 3 and sensor harness connector Pin B. • Measure resistance between module harness connector Pin 10 and sensor harness connector Pin A.	Resistance is less than 10 ohms Resistance is greater than 10 ohms	▲ Circuit is not open. GO to 9.4. ▲ FIND and REPAIR open circuit along Circuit 519 (LG/BK) and 523 (R/PK). GO to 9.6.
9.4 CHECK FOR OPEN SENSOR • Verify ohmmeter is on 20 K ohm scale. • Measure resistance between RABS sensor Pins A and B.	Resistance is less than 2500 ohms Resistance is greater than 2500 ohms	▲ GO to 9.5. ▲ REPLACE RABS sensor. GO to 9.6.
9.5 MAKE SURE ALL STEPS ARE COMPLETED • This step requires that a valid diagnostic trouble code has been obtained, ALL prior diagnostic steps have been completed, and the affected wiring integrity has been verified. CAUTION: If the above is not complete, chances are that replacement of this or any other system component without specific direction will not, in most circumstances, resolve the concern and will consequently result in customer dissatisfaction. • Have all prior diagnostic steps been completed as described above?	Yes No	▲ REPLACE ECU GO to Step 9.6. If ECU has been replaced and no resolution has been reached, REPLACE rear axle sensor. GO to Step 9.6. ▲ GO to diagnostic step last completed and continue.

84929121

REAR ANTI-LOCK BRAKE SYSTEM TESTING — EXCEPT 1993 BRONCO

DIAGNOSIS AND TESTING (Continued)

PINPOINT TEST — CODE 10 (Continued)

	TEST STEP	RESULT	ACTION TO TAKE
10.5	**CHECK FOR SHORTED SENSOR** • Verify ohmmeter is on 20 K ohm scale. • Measure resistance between RABS sensor Pins A and B.	▲ Resistance is greater than 900 ohms ▲ Resistance is less than 900 ohms	▲ GO to **10.6.** ▲ REPLACE rear axle speed sensor. GO to **10.7.**
10.6	**MAKE SURE ALL STEPS ARE COMPLETED** • This step requires that a valid diagnostic troulbe code has been obtained, ALL prior diagnostic steps have been completed, and the affected wiring integrity has been verified. **CAUTION: If the above is not complete, chances are that replacement of this or any other system component without specific direction will not, in most circumstances, resolve the concern and will consequently result in customer dissatisfaction.** • Have all prior diagnostic steps been completed as described above?	▲ Yes ▲ No	▲ REPLACE ECU GO to Step **10.7.** If ECU has been replaced and no resolution has been reached, REPLACE rear axle sensor. GO to Step **10.7.** ▲ GO to diagnostic step last completed and continue.
10.7	**CLEAR CODE / PULL CODE** • Turn ignition OFF. • Reconnect battery ground cable. **NOTE: On vehicles equipped with EEC, when the battery has been disconnected and reconnected, some abnormal drive symptoms may occur while the Powertrain Control Module (PCM) relearns its adaptive strategy. The vehicle may need to be driven 10 miles or more to relearn the strategy.** • Verify all connectors are installed. • Locate and disconnect the diagnostic connector from its mating half (Circuits 571 [BK/O] and 483 [R]). • Turn ignition ON. • Begin diagnostic trouble code flashout by connecting Circuit 571 (BK/O) to a chassis ground for at least 1 second. • Observe and count code.	▲ Diagnostic trouble code = 16 ▲ Diagnostic trouble code = 10 ▲ Diagnostic trouble code is different than before	▲ GO to Test Drive Code 16. ▲ GO to **10.8.** ▲ GO to Pinpoint Test for corresponding code.
10.8	**PINPOINT TEST STATUS** • Has pinpoint test been completed?	▲ Yes ▲ No	▲ GO to **10.9.** ▲ RETURN to last pinpoint test completed.
10.9	**VERIFY INTEGRITY OF VEHICLE WIRING** If the above steps have been completed, the MOST LIKELY cause of the concern is wiring related. • REFER to the Intermittent Wiring Diagnosis Porcedure and perform for ALL affected circuits as shown on this pinpoint test mini-schematic. • Is resolution achieved?	▲ Yes ▲ No	▲ STOP. Repair is complete GO to Drive Test — Code 16. ▲ GO to **10.6.**

84929124

REAR ANTI-LOCK BRAKE SYSTEM TESTING — EXCEPT 1993 BRONCO

DIAGNOSIS AND TESTING (Continued)

Description

Code 10 is generated by the module's detection of low sensor resistance. The code may also be generated by a short circuit in the Circuits 519 (LG/BK) or 523 (R/PK), or a failed internal module circuit. Module can only detect when vehicle is at rest.

Possible Contributing Base Brake Component/Vehicle Wiring Concerns

- Short between module harness connector Pin 3 and Pin 10.
- Short between RABS speed sensor connector Pins A and B.
- Bulkhead connector (between engine compartment and instrument panel) sensor terminals shorted together.
- Intermittent short circuit in Circuits 519 (LG/BK) or 523 (R/PK).

PINPOINT TEST — CODE 10

	TEST STEP	RESULT	ACTION TO TAKE
10.1	**VERIFY INTEGRITY OF MODULE CONNECTION** • Turn ignition OFF. • Disconnect battery negative cable. • Remove the module connector. • Pull gently on wire just behind Pin 3 on the harness connector. • Pull gently on wire just behind Pin 10 on the harness connector.	▲ Terminal is fully engaged ▲ Terminal moves back and comes free of connector	▲ Leave module connector disconnected. GO to **10.2.** ▲ SERVICE terminal or connector as needed. GO to **10.7.**
10.2	**VERIFY INTEGRITY OF SENSOR CONNECTION** • Remove sensor connector. • Inspect sensor component connector. • Gently pull on wire behind Pin B of harness connector. • Gently pull on wire behind Pin A of harness connector.	▲ Terminals in component connector are clean and firmly in place. Terminals in harness connector are firmly engaged ▲ Terminal(s) in component connector are loose, bent, deformed, or corroded ▲ Terminal(s) in harness connector move back or come free of connector	▲ Leave sensor connector disconnected. GO to **10.3.** ▲ REPLACE RABS II sensor. GO to **10.7.** ▲ SERVICE terminal or connector as needed. GO to **10.7.**
10.3	**CHECK FOR SHORT ALONG HARNESS CIRCUIT 519 (LG/BK) WITH CIRCUIT 523 (R/PK)** • Set ohmmeter on 20 K ohm scale. • Verify sensor connector is disconnected. • Measure resistance between module harness connector Pin 3 and Pin 10.	▲ Resistance is greater than 20 K ohms ▲ Resistance is less than 20 K ohms	▲ Circuits are not shorted. GO to **10.4.** ▲ FIND and REPAIR short along Circuits 519 (LG/BK) and 523 (R/PK). GO to **10.7.**
10.4	**CHECK FOR SHORT TO CHASSIS GROUND ALONG CIRCUIT 523 (R/PK)** • Verify ohmmeter is on 20 K ohm scale. • Measure resistance between module harness connector Pin 10 and chassis ground.	▲ Resistance is greater than 20 K ohms ▲ Resistance is less than 20 K ohms	▲ Circuit is not shorted. GO to **10.5.** ▲ FIND and REPAIR short circuit along Circuit 523 (R/PK). GO to **10.7.**

84929123

REAR ANTI-LOCK BRAKE SYSTEM TESTING — EXCEPT 1993 BRONCO

DIAGNOSIS AND TESTING (Continued)

PINPOINT TEST — CODE 11 (Continued)

TEST STEP	RESULT	ACTION TO TAKE
11.2 CHECK VEHICLE STOPLAMPS • Check vehicle stoplamp bulbs. NOTE: Both bulbs need to be burned out to cause a Code 11).	▲ Bulbs are not burned out ▲ Bulbs are burned out	▲ GO to 11.3. ▲ REPLACE stoplamp bulbs and GO to 11.6.
11.3 CHECK FOR BLOWN STOPLAMP FUSE • Remove and visually inspect stoplamp fuse located in the fuse panel.	▲ Fuse is blown ▲ Fuse is not blown	▲ REPLACE fuse and investigate reason for blown fuse. GO to 11.6. ▲ CHECK Circuit 511 (LG) for open condition. If none found, then REPAIR or REPLACE vehicle stoplamp switch. GO to 11.6.
11.4 CHECK FOR CONTINUITY BETWEEN MODULE CONNECTOR PIN 11 AND THE STOPLAMP SWITCH • Set ohmmeter on 20 volt scale. • Step on brake pedal. • Measure voltage between module connector Pin 11 and chassis ground.	▲ Voltage greater than 9 volts ▲ Voltage is less than 2 volts	▲ REINSTALL all connectors. GO to 11.5. ▲ FIND and REPAIR open circuit between RABS II module connector (Pin 11), and stoplamp switch. REINSTALL all connectors. GO to 11.6.
11.5 MAKE SURE ALL STEPS ARE COMPLETED • This step requires that a valid diagnostic trouble code has been obtained, ALL prior diagnostic steps have been completed, and the affected wiring integrity has been verified. **CAUTION: If the above is not complete, chances are that replacement of this or any other system component without specific direction will not, in most circumstances, resolve the concern and will consequently result in customer dissatisfaction.** Have all prior diagnostic steps been completed as described above?	▲ Yes ▲ No	▲ REPLACE ECU GO to Step 11.6. If ECU has been replaced and no resolution has been reached, REPLACE stoplamp switch. GO to Step 11.6. ▲ GO to diagnostic step last completed and continue.
11.6 CLEAR CODE / PULL CODE • Turn ignition OFF. • Reconnect battery ground cable. NOTE: On vehicles equipped with EEC, when the battery has been disconnected and reconnected, some abnormal drive symptoms may occur while the Powertrain Control Module (PCM) relearns its adaptive strategy. The vehicle may need to be driven 10 miles or more to relearn the strategy. • Verify all connectors are installed. • Locate and disconnect the diagnostic connector from its mating half (Circuits 571 [BK/O] and 481 [R]). • Turn ignition ON. • Begin diagnostic trouble code flashout by connecting Circuit 571 (BK/O) to a chassis ground for at least 1 second. • Observe and count code.	▲ Diagnostic trouble code = 16 ▲ Diagnostic trouble code = 11 ▲ Diagnostic trouble code is different than before	▲ GO to Test Drive Code 16. ▲ GO to 11.7. ▲ GO to Pinpoint Test for corresponding code.

84929126

REAR ANTI-LOCK BRAKE SYSTEM TESTING — EXCEPT 1993 BRONCO

DIAGNOSIS AND TESTING (Continued)

Pinpoint Test Code 11

Code: 11 — Stoplamp switch always closed or stoplamp switch circuit worn or damaged.

Affected Circuit(s) / Electrical Component(s)

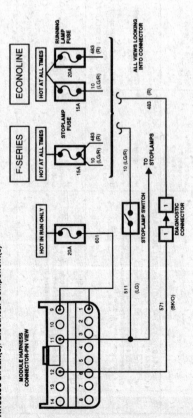

Description

Code 11 is caused by the stoplamp switch always being closed prior to the vehicle moving. If the stoplamp switch remains closed when the vehicle begins to move, the REAR ABS warning light will turn on at approximately 16 mph. Code 11 will not be latched in the control modules memory until the speed of the vehicle exceeds 37 mph for at least 10 seconds. If the vehicle does not exceed 37 mph for at least 10 seconds, then the REAR ABS warning light will turn on but the module will not latch a code. Code 11 can be caused by a driver who is resting their foot on the brake with just enough pressure to close the stoplamp switch, while driving at least 37 mph for a minimum of ten seconds. When this occurs, a Code 11 will be latched by the control unit.

Possible Contributing Base Brake Component/Vehicle Wiring Concerns

• Terminal backout in the module harness connector at Pin 11.

• Missing (burned-out) stoplamps. All stoplamps must be missing or burned out to cause a Code 11.

• An intermittent/continuous open in Circuit 511 (LG). This open would be between module connector Pin 11 and the stoplamp switch.

• Worn or damaged stoplamp switch.

PINPOINT TEST — CODE 11

TEST STEP	RESULT	ACTION TO TAKE
11.1 CHECK VEHICLE STOPLAMP OPERATION • Turn ignition to the OFF position. • Apply pressure to the brake pedal and then release pressure while observing the stoplamps.	▲ Lamps illuminate when pressure is applied to pedal, and turn off when pressure is released ▲ Lamps do not illuminate ▲ Lamps always illuminated	▲ GO to 11.4. ▲ GO to 11.2. ▲ REPAIR or REPLACE vehicle stoplamp switch GO to 11.6.

84929125

REAR ANTI-LOCK BRAKE SYSTEM TESTING — EXCEPT 1993 BRONCO

DIAGNOSIS AND TESTING (Continued)

PINPOINT TEST — CODE 11 (Continued)

TEST STEP	RESULT	ACTION TO TAKE
11.7 PINPOINT TEST STATUS		
• Has pinpoint test been completed?	Yes	GO to 11.5.
	No	RETURN to last pinpoint test completed.

Pinpoint Test Code 12

Code: 12 — Loss of hydraulic brake fluid for one second or more during an anti-lock stop.

Affected Circuit(s)/Electrical Component(s)

Description

Code 12 is generated when the module detects that the brake fluid level in the master cylinder reservoir is low for one or more seconds during an anti-lock stop. It can also be generated by a short in the stoplamp circuit.

Possible Contributing Base Brake Component/Vehicle Wiring Concerns

• Low master cylinder fill level.
• Fluid leaks in vehicle brake system.
• Worn or damaged master cylinder fluid level switch, or fluid level circuit shorted to ground.
• Master cylinder float that sticks in the bottom of reservoir or does not float.
• Failed diode-resistor element in stoplamp circuit.

REAR ANTI-LOCK BRAKE SYSTEM TESTING — EXCEPT 1993 BRONCO

DIAGNOSIS AND TESTING (Continued)

PINPOINT TEST — CODE 12

TEST STEP	RESULT	ACTION TO TAKE
12.1 DIODE RESISTOR ELEMENT NOTE: This pinpoint test should not be attempted until after the base brake system has been verified to be operating correctly. This means that the red BRAKE light should not be ON. See System Pre-Check section for assistance in correcting the condition of red BRAKE light is ON when key is in the RUN position. • Turn ignition to the OFF position. • Release the parking brake. • DIESEL VEHICLES ONLY: remove diesel low vacuum switch. • Turn ignition from the OFF position to the ON position. • Observe REAR ABS light (after 2 second bulb prove-out).	REAR ABS light is OFF, red BRAKE light is OFF	LEAVE key in the ON position. GO to 12.2.
	REAR ABS light is ON, red BRAKE light is OFF	GO to 12.5.
	REAR ABS light is OFF or ON, red BRAKE light is ON	GO to System Pre-Check Test E.
12.2 DIODE RESISTOR ELEMENT (Continued) • Set parking brake ON. • Observe REAR ABS warning light.	REAR ABS light turns ON	CHECK for open Circuit 640 (R/Y). If circuit is OK, REPLACE diode/resistor element.
	REAR ABS light remains OFF	GO to 12.3.
12.3 CHECK TERMINALS • Inspect and clean master cylinder fluid level switch as necessary. • Are terminals clean?	Yes	RECONNECT connectors. GO to 12.5.
	No	CLEAN terminals. RECONNECT connectors. GO to 12.5.
12.4 MAKE SURE ALL STEPS ARE COMPLETED • This step requires that a valid diagnostic troulbe code has been obtained, and ALL prior diagnostic steps have been completed, and the affected wiring integrity has been verified. CAUTION: If the above is not complete, chances are that replacement of this or any other system component without specific direction will not, in most circumstances, resolve the concern and will consequently result in customer dissatisfaction. • Have all prior diagnostic steps been completed as described above?	Yes	REPLACE ECU GO to Step 12.5. If ECU has been replaced and no resolution has been reached, REPLACE RABS Valve GO to Step 12.5.
	No	GO to diagnostic step last completed and continue.
12.5 CLEAR CODE / PULL CODE • Turn ignition OFF. • Reconnect battery ground cable. NOTE: On vehicles equipped with EEC, when the battery has been disconnected and reconnected, some abnormal drive symptoms may occur while the Powertrain Control Module (PCM) relearns its adaptive strategy. The vehicle may need to be driven 10 miles or more to relearn the strategy. • Verify all connectors are installed. • Turn ignition ON. • Locate and disconnect the diagnostic connector from its mating half (Circuits 571 [BK/O] and 481 [R]). • Turn ignition ON. • Begin diagnostic trouble code flashout by connecting Circuit 571 (BK/O) to a chassis ground for at least 1 second. • Observe and count code.	Diagnostic trouble code = 16	GO to Test Drive Code 16.
	Diagnostic trouble code = 18	GO to 12.6.
	Diagnostic trouble code is different than before	GO to Pinpoint Test for corresponding code.

REAR ANTI-LOCK BRAKE SYSTEM TESTING — EXCEPT 1993 BRONCO

DIAGNOSIS AND TESTING (Continued)

PINPOINT TEST — CODE 12 (Continued)

TEST STEP	RESULT	ACTION TO TAKE
12.6 PINPOINT TEST STATUS • Has pinpoint test been completed?	Yes	GO to 12.7.
	No	RETURN to last pinpoint test completed.
12.7 VERIFY INTEGRITY OF VEHICLE WIRING If the above steps have been completed, the MOST LIKELY cause of the concern is wiring related. • REFER to the Intermittent Wiring Diagnosis Porcedure and perform for ALL affected circuits as shown on this pinpoint test mini-schematic. • Is resolution achieved?	Yes	STOP. Repair is complete GO to Drive Test — Code 16.
	No	GO to 12.4.

Pinpoint Test Code 13

RABS II Module Failure

Description

Code 13 is generated when a fault is found with the RABS II module. Module must be replaced and Test Drive Code 16 must be performed.

Pinpoint Test Code 16

Affected Circuit(s) / Electrical Component(s)

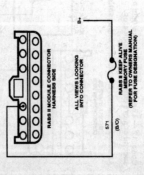

Description

Code 16 is always present, unless a system concern has been detected and a diagnostic trouble code has been stored. This code should be used by the technician to verify that the RABS II system is OK.

Code 16 will be output by the module when one of two conditions exist:

1. The technician ground Circuit 571 (BK/O).

2. The RABS II Keep Alive Memory (KAM) fuse has blown.

If the KAM fuse has blown, the REAR ABS warning light will begin flashing Code 16 (or a diagnostic trouble code if a concern has been detected) if the stoplamp switch is depressed (F-Series), or the running lamps are turned on (Econoline).

Therefore, check the KAM fuse when diagnosing complaints of REAR ABS light flashing.

Drive Test — Code 16

Purpose

This drive test will be used when either of the two conditions listed below exists.

1. **Required Repair Verification**

This drive procedure will be used after all vehicle repairs. Once a vehicle has been repaired, it is necessary to verify the repair by driving the vehicle. This is because the RABS II module is unable to detect some system concerns until the vehicle is being driven a certain way. Therefore the drive verification test is a very important step.

2. **Symptom Evaluation Drive**

When a vehicle is brought to the dealer, the customer may only have a general concern about the way their vehicle is braking. In these situations there may not be a clear system concern to troubleshoot. In this type of situation, this drive test is designed to produce common system concern symptoms. Use this drive test to determine a symptom. Once a symptom is found, a symptom troubleshooting procedure can be followed to repair the vehicle.

Drive Description

This drive test is designed to be a generic drive test that is used for three purposes listed below.

1. To verify a repair of the RABS II system on a vehicle.

REAR ANTI-LOCK BRAKE SYSTEM TESTING — EXCEPT 1993 BRONCO

DIAGNOSIS AND TESTING (Continued)

2. To attempt to recreate an intermittent concern.

3. To attempt to detect a symptom when a diagnostic trouble code or a concern symptom is not known.

DRIVE TEST — CODE 16

TEST STEP	RESULT	ACTION TO TAKE
DT1.1 KEEP ALIVE MEMORY (KAM) FUSE CHECK • Key ON. Observe REAR ABS light prove-out. • Turn on headlamps and press on the brake pedal. With the headlamps ON and while pushing on the brake pedal, monitor the yellow REAR ABS light in the dash for 10 seconds. • Does the REAR ABS light prove out normally?	Yes	GO to DT1.2.
	No, the REAR ABS light flashes	REPLACE KAM fuse
DT1.2 LOW SPEED REAR ABS STOP NOTE: Wetting down the area where stop is to be performed will aid this test. • Drive vehicle at approximately 10 mph. • Press on brake pedal hard enough to lock all four wheels, and observe the left rear wheel in the driver's mirror. • Repeat the second step, except observe right rear wheel in passenger mirror. • Do both rear wheels lock or does one wheel lock consistently? (Momentary lock up is permissible.) NOTE: An assistant to observe rear wheels would be helpful.	Yes, and REAR ABS light is not on	GO to Symptom B. One or both rear wheels lock up.
	No, but other symptoms are detected	GO to DT1.6.
	No, and REAR ABS light is not on	GO to DT1.3.
	REAR ABS light comes on and stays on	GO to DT1.7.
DT1.3 CHECK FOR UNWARRANTED RABS II ACTIVITY NOTE: Stop should be performed on dry pavement. • Drive vehicle at approximately 20 mph. • Perform a light to medium (normal traffic) stop. • Turn off the windshield wipers if they are on. (Wipers can cause a pulsation in the brake pedal that can be mistaken for RABS II activity.) Feel for pulsation in the brake pedal within 10 seconds after the vehicle has come to a stop. • Is there any pulsation in the pedal any time during the stop or within 10 seconds after the vehicle has stopped?	Yes, and REAR ABS light is not on	GO to Symptom A, Unwarranted RABS II Activity.
	No, but other symptoms are detected	GO to DT1.6.
	No, and REAR ABS light is not on	GO to DT1.4.
	REAR ABS light comes on and stays on	GO to DT1.7.
DT1.4 BRAKE STOP LAMP / SWITCH CHECK • Turn key ON. • Press on the brake pedal. • Release brake pedal. • Do the stoplamps come on and then turn off properly?	Yes	GO to DT1.5.
	No	GO to pinpoint test Code 11.
DT1.5 DETERMINE DRIVE TEST IS COMPLETE • Has customer concern been addressed and corrected by previous actions?	Yes	STOP. Vehicle RABS II function has been verified.
	No	REFER to Symptom Chart.
DT1.6 DETERMINE NEXT DIAGNOSTIC STEP BASED ON BRAKE SYMPTOM • Are any of the following symptoms present? — Hard or soft brake pedal — Lack of sufficient vehicle deceleration upon brake application	Yes	GO to Symptom Chart.
	No	Concern is not in the RABS II system.

REAR ANTI-LOCK BRAKE SYSTEM TESTING — EXCEPT 1993 BRONCO

DIAGNOSIS AND TESTING (Continued)

DRIVE TEST — CODE 16 (Continued)

TEST STEP	RESULT	ACTION TO TAKE
DT1.7 OBTAIN DIAGNOSTIC TROUBLE CODE • Obtain diagnostic trouble code. • Is the diagnostic trouble code the same as before and has the entire pinpoint test for the code been completed?	Yes	▶ REDO steps once more.
	No, pinpoint test is not complete	▶ RETURN to the last step completed in the pinpoint test.
	No, code obtained is different	▶ GO to the pinpoint test for the code obtained.
	No, no code or Code 16 is obtained	▶ GO to System Pre-Check, Test D.

Drive Test — Code 4 Only

Purpose

If Pinpoint Test Code 4 is not successful in resolving the system concern, this drive test can be used to conduct additional, more in depth, diagnostics.

CAUTION: Only perform this test when directed to do so. This drive test is only designed to resolve a Code 4 condition. Performing this test for any other reason will often lead to incorrect diagnosis of system problem and incorrect replacement of components.

This drive test assumes that pinpoint test Code 4 has been completed. If this is not the case, complete the test before proceeding.

Drive Description

This drive test is designed to induce a Code 4 if there is a system concern that can create a Code 4 on a repeatable basis. Carefully record the data when performing the drive test. It is important to know what part of the drive test you are in when a diagnostic trouble Code 4 is detected.

TEST STEP	RESULT	ACTION TO TAKE
DT4.1 VERIFY PROPER WARNING LIGHT PROVE-OUT • Start the vehicle and observe the REAR ABS warning light for proper warning light prove-out. • Does the REAR ABS warning light prove-out properly?	Yes No	▶ GO to DT4.2. ▶ GO to System Pre-Check, Test A.
DT4.2 VALVE RESET SWITCH CHECK • Drive the vehicle at approximately 10 mph on dry pavement. **CAUTION: Do not exceed 10 mph to prevent flat-spotting of tires.** • Press on brake pedal hard enough to lock all four wheels. • After the vehicle has stopped, place the vehicle in PARK and take foot off the brake pedal. • Wait 30 seconds. • Does the RABS warning light come on?	Yes No	▶ Key OFF. Go to DT4.4. ▶ Key OFF. GO to DT4.3.
DT4.3 RABS HYDRAULIC VALVE LEAK TEST • Press hard on the brake pedal and keep pressure on the brake pedal for 30 seconds. • While keeping pressure on the brake, monitor the height of the brake pedal. • Does the brake pedal drop slowly toward the floor? NOTE: The condition is similar to the Master Cylinder Bypass condition. It is important that the pedal be quickly and forcefully applied to rule out Master Cylinder Bypass as the cause if a hydraulic leak is detected. Typically, Master Cylinder Bypass only occurs at low line pressures.	Yes No	▶ REPLACE RABS Valve. GO to Drive Test — Code 16 to verify concern is resolved. ▶ RETURN to the pinpoint test for code 4, Step 4.11.

84929131

REAR ANTI-LOCK BRAKE SYSTEM TESTING — EXCEPT 1993 BRONCO

DIAGNOSIS AND TESTING (Continued)

TEST STEP	RESULT	ACTION TO TAKE
DT4.4 OBTAIN DIAGNOSTIC TROUBLE CODE • Obtain Diagnostic Trouble Code. • Is Code 4 Obtained?	Yes	▶ REPLACE RABS Valve. GO to Drive Test — Code 16 to verify concern is resolved.
	No, code obtained is Code 16	▶ INCONSISTENT result If RABS Warning light did come on in Step DT4.2, then a Diagnostic Trouble Code other than Code 16 should be stored. REPEAT DT4.4 and verify Code 16 is obtained.
	No, code obtained is NOT code 4	▶ GO to the pinpoint test for the code obtained.
	No, no code is obtained	▶ GO to System Pre-Check, Test D.
DT4.5 BLOCKED ISOLATION ORIFICE • Disconnect RABS II module. • Raise the vehicle on a hoist far enough to allow all wheels to spin freely. • Verify that the vehicle is in 4x2 mode and the hubs are unlocked (4x4 only). • Start the vehicle, place in DRIVE and allow rear wheels to spin at idle for at least 30 seconds. • Apply the brake pedal with the force of a normal traffic stop. • Do the rear wheels react uncharacteristically slowly or continue to spin?	Yes No, rear wheels stop normally	▶ RECONNECT RABS II module. REPLACE RABS II valve. GO to Drive Test — Code 16 to verify concern is resolved. ▶ RABS II valve is OK. RECONNECT RABS II module. RETURN to Pinpoint Test for Code 4 (Step 4.11).

Drive Test — Code 5 Only

Purpose

If pinpoint test Code 5 is not successful in resolving the system concern, this drive test can be used to conduct additional, more in depth, diagnostics.

CAUTION: Only perform this test when directed to do so. This drive test is only designed to resolve a Code 5 condition. Performing this test for any other reason will often lead to incorrect diagnosis of system problem and incorrect replacement of components.

This drive test assumes that pinpoint test Code 5 has been completed. If this is not the case, complete the test before proceeding.

Drive Description

This drive test is designed to induce a Code 5 if there is a system that can create a Code 5 on a repeatable basis. Carefully record the data when performing the drive test. It is important to know what part of the drive test you are in when diagnostic trouble Code 5 is detected.

NOTE: Four Wheel Drive Issue

Discuss with the customer to determine if the vehicle was in four wheel drive when the light came on. During normal 4x2 anti-lock operation, the module energizes the dump solenoid a maximum of 16 times without interruption. Conditions experienced in 4x2 operation will not require more than 16 dump pulses. If the module notices that conditions call for a 17th dump pulse, it assumes there is a problem with RABS II, deactivates the system (turning the REAR ABS warning light on), and sets a Code 5. During normal 4x4 operation, the module only allows 16 dump pulses but does not deactivate the RABS II or light the yellow REAR ABS warning light if more than 16 dump pulses are requested. If, for reasons described below, the module receives incorrect information from the 4x4 switch, and therefore improperly assumes the vehicle is in 4x2, a Code 5 will often be improperly set. The most common reasons for incorrect information being sent to the RABS II module are:

- 4x4 indicator switch worn or damaged.
- Vehicle wiring concern in Circuit 210 (LB) between the 4x4 indicator switch and the RABS II module.
- Customer has switched from 4x4 to 4x2 but the transfer case has not yet disengaged.

NOTE: The customer must also enter an anti-lock stop, at the same time, for this event to occur.

84929132

REAR ANTI-LOCK BRAKE SYSTEM TESTING — EXCEPT 1993 BRONCO

DIAGNOSIS AND TESTING (Continued)

DRIVE TEST — CODE 5

TEST STEP	RESULT	ACTION TO TAKE
DT5.1 VERIFY PROPER WARNING LIGHT PROVE-OUT		
• Start the vehicle and observe the REAR ABS warning light for proper warning light prove-out. • Does the REAR ABS warning light prove-out properly?	Yes	▲ GO to **DT5.2.**
	No	▲ GO to System Pre-Check Test A.
DT5.2 BASE BRAKE STOPPING TEST		
• Remove the harness connector from the RABS II module. • Drive the vehicle at approximately 20 mph. • Perform a light to medium (normal traffic) stop. • Do the rear wheels lock up?	Yes	▲ RECONNECT RABS II module.
	No	▲ RECONNECT RABS II module. GO to **DT5.3.**
DT5.3 DRY ROAD STOP TEST		
• Drive the vehicle at approximately 10 mph on dry pavement. **CAUTION: Do not exceed 10 mph to prevent flat-spotting of tires.**	Yes	▲ REPLACE RABS valve. GO to Drive Test — Code 16 to verify concern is resolved.
• Press on brake pedal hard enough to lock all four wheels and observe the left rear wheel in the driver's mirror. • Do the rear wheels lock up? (Momentary lock up followed by spinup is permissible.)	No	▲ GO to **DT5.4.**
DT5.4 VERIFY PROPER RABS II OPERATION IN 4X2		
WARNING: PERFORM THIS TEST ON AN AXLE HOIST ONLY.	Yes	▲ LEAVE key ON. GO to **DT5.5.**
• Place vehicle on the hoist and raise high enough to clear all wheels off the ground. • Verify vehicle is in 4x2 mode. (4x4 vehicles only.) • Place vehicle transmission in Drive Low (automatic) or First gear (manual). • Accelerate vehicle drive wheels to 10 mph. • Press hard on the brake pedal until wheels stop. • Do the rear wheels first lock up and then spin?	No, wheels lock up and remain locked up	▲ REPLACE RABS valve. GO to Drive Test — Code 16 to verify concern is resolved.
NOTE: Because vehicle is not on the ground, wheels will spin for a significant time. This is not indicative of vehicle braking performance.		
DT5.5 OBTAIN DIAGNOSTIC TROUBLE CODE		
• Obtain diagnostic trouble code. • Is Code 5 obtained?	Yes	▲ INCONSISTENT result DT5.4 indicates RABS Valve is functioning correctly. CLEAR code REPEAT DT5.4. If result repeats, RETURN to pinpoint test for Code 5, Step 5.6.
	No, code obtained is Code 16	▲ RETURN to pinpoint test for Code 5, Step 5.6.
	No, code obtained is NOT code 5	▲ GO to the pinpoint test for the code obtained.
	No, no code is obtained	▲ Go to System Pre-Check, Test D.

84929133

REAR ANTI-LOCK BRAKE SYSTEM TESTING — EXCEPT 1993 BRONCO

DIAGNOSIS AND TESTING (Continued)

Drive Test — Code 6

Purpose

If pinpoint test Code 6 is not successful in resolving the system concern, this drive test can be used to conduct additional, more in depth, diagnostics.

CAUTION: Only perform this test when directed to do so. This drive test is only designed to resolve a Code 6 condition. Performing this test for any other reason will often lead to incorrect diagnosis of system problem and incorrect replacement of components.

This drive test assumes that pinpoint test Code 6 has been completed. If this is not the case, complete the test before proceeding.

Drive Description

This drive test is designed to induce a Code 6 if there is a system concern that can create a Code 6 on a repeatable basis. Carefully record the data when performing the drive test. It is important to know what part of the drive test you are in when a Code 6 diagnostic trouble code is detected.

DRIVE TEST — CODE 6

TEST STEP	RESULT	ACTION TO TAKE
DT6.1 VERIFY PROPER WARNING LIGHT PROVE-OUT		
• Key ON and observe the REAR ABS warning light for proper bulb prove-out. • Does the REAR ABS warning light prove-out properly?	Yes	▲ Key OFF. GO to **DT6.2.**
	No	▲ GO to System Pre-Check, Test A.
DT6.2 MEASURE SENSOR OUTPUT		
• Put vehicle on hoist and raise so that the rear wheels can rotate freely. • Verify the vehicle is in 4x2 mode and hubs are unlocked. • Set an AC voltmeter on the 2000mV scale. • Remove the cap from the sensor test connector and connect the AC voltmeter across the connector leads. • Start the engine and turn the rear wheels at 5 mph. • Measure the voltage output of the sensor.	Voltage is 650mV (RMS) or greater	▲ REINSTALL the sensor test connector cap. GO to **DT6.3.**
	Voltage is less than 650mV (RMS)	▲ REINSTALL the sensor test connector cap. REPLACE sensor. GO to Drive Test — Code 16 to verify concern is resolved.
DT6.3 MEASURE SENSOR AIR GAP		
• Remove Rear Axle Differential Cover. • Measure the shortest distance from the sensor pole piece to the teeth on the speed sensor ring. • Rotate the axle 60°-90°. • Repeat the second and third steps for a total of five measurements. • Are all measurements between 0.005 inch and 0.050 inch and within 0.010 inch of each other?	Yes	▲ GO to **DT6.5.**
	No, measurements are not between 0.005 inch and 0.050 inch	▲ CHECK for foreign material under sensor mounting flange and on carrier housing. REPLACE sensor GO to **DT6.4.**
	No, not all measurements are within 0.010 inch of each other	▲ REINSTALL sensor. GO to Drive Test — Code 16 to verify concern is resolved.
DT6.4 IMPROPER SENSOR GAP RESOLUTION		
• Verify that the installed sensor is seated fully in the bore and the hold-down bolt is tightened to specification. • Repeat measurements from Step DT6.3. • Are all measurements between 0.005 inch and 0.050 inch and within 0.010 inch of each other?	Yes	▲ GO to Drive Test — Code 16 to verify concern is resolved.
	No	▲ REPLACE rear axle. GO to Drive Test — Code 16 to verify concern is resolved.
DT6.5 CHECK CONDITION OF SPEED SENSOR RING TEETH		
• Carefully inspect each tooth on the speed sensor ring. (Rear Axle Differential cover should still be off.) • Are any teeth missing, malformed, or damaged?	Yes	▲ REPLACE rear axle. GO to Drive Test — Code 16 to verify concern is resolved.
	No	▲ RETURN to pinpoint test for Code 6, Step 6.9.

84929134

REAR ANTI-LOCK BRAKE SYSTEM TESTING — EXCEPT 1993 BRONCO

DIAGNOSIS AND TESTING (Continued)

SYMPTOM B: ONE OR BOTH REAR WHEELS LOCK UP (Continued)

CONDITION	POSSIBLE SOURCE	ACTION
Base brake mechanical concern.	• Brake related concern: — Damp or contaminated rear brake shoe linings — Stuck/leaking wheel cylinder. — Overadjusted rear brakes. • Hung-up parking brake. • Leaking rear axle seal.	
4x4 system mechanical electrical concern.	• Hubs engaged although shift lever is in 4x2 position. • Faulty 4x4 indicator switch or short to 12V in 4x4 circuit 210 (LB).	• Refer to pinpoint test for Code 5, steps 5.3 and 5.5 only.
Vehicle electrical concern.	• Stoplamp input to RABS II module not present. • Stoplamps inoperative.	• Refer to pinpoint test for Code 11, steps 11.1-11.4 only. — Refer to Section 17-01.

SYMPTOM C: HARD OR SOFT BRAKE PEDAL

CONDITION	POSSIBLE SOURCE	ACTION
RABS valve inoperative (hard/soft).	• Stuck shut isolation valve (hard). • Leaky dump valve (soft). • Leaky isolation valve during RABS stop (soft).	• Refer to drive test — DT4.5 only. • Refer to drive test — Code 4, step DT4.3 only. • Refer to drive test — Code 5, step DT5.4 only.
Vehicle electrical concern.	• Stoplamp switch always on while driving.	• Refer to pinpoint test for Code 11, steps 11.1-11.4 only.
Base brake hydraulic concern (soft).	• Hydraulic leak in brake line or hose, fitting, master cylinder, wheel cylinder, or caliper. • Air in brake system.	
Base brake mechanical concern (hard).	Brake related concern: — Little or no vacuum boost. — Stuck or inoperative wheel cylinder or caliper. — Pinched or crimped brake line or hose.	

84929138

REAR ANTI-LOCK BRAKE SYSTEM TESTING — EXCEPT 1993 BRONCO

DIAGNOSIS AND TESTING (Continued)

SYMPTOM DIAGNOSTIC CHART

WARNING: PERFORM INDICATED PINPOINT TEST OR DRIVE TEST STEPS ONLY. DO NOT PERFORM OTHER STEPS, ALTHOUGH WITHIN THE TEST BOX YOU MAY APPEAR TO BE DIRECTED TO DO SO. ALWAYS RETURN TO THE SYMPTOM CONDITION CHART IF NO RESOLUTION IS REACHED BY PERFORMING A PARTICULAR TEST.

Symptom Description	Refer to
Unwarranted RABS II Activity	Symptom A
Rear Wheels Lockup	Symptom B
Hard/Soft Brake Pedal	Symptom C
Lack of Decel (Med/Hard Braking)	Symptom D

SYMPTOM A: UNWARRANTED RABS II ACTIVITY

CONDITION	POSSIBLE SOURCE	ACTION
Premature loss of rear axle sensor signal during decel.	• Metal chips on sensor pole piece. • Gap between sensor and speed sensor ring is too large (greater than 0.050 inches). • Missing or damaged speed sensor ring teeth. • Sensor/speed sensor ring interference (gap is too small [less than 0.005 inches]).	• Refer to pinpoint test, Code 6, step 6 only. • Refer to drive test — Code 6, step DT6.3-DT6.4 only. • Refer to drive test — Code 6, step DT6.5 only. • Refer to drive test — Code 6, step DT6.5 only.
Intermittent sensor signal to RABS II module during decel.	• Intermittent open or shorted sensor circuit. • Intermittent open sensor circuit at intermediate connections especially bulkhead. • Chafed wire insulation or pinched wire due to improper routing causing intermittent short. • Underhood sensor test connector shorted.	• Perform intermittent diagnosis for Circuits 519(LG/BK) and 523(R/PK) between RABS II module and sensor. • Perform intermittent diagnosis for Circuit 519(LG/BK) and 523(R/PK) at intermediate connectors. • Inspect wiring harness from rear axle to frame for chafing or rub marks. • Inspect underhood sensor test connector for presence of cap, corrosion, and excessive dirt in the terminal cavities.
Maladjusted rear brakes or "grabby" brake shoe linings.	• Rear brake adjustment too tight. • Linings are "grabby".	

SYMPTOM B: ONE OR BOTH REAR WHEELS LOCK UP

CONDITION	POSSIBLE SOURCE	ACTION
RABS valve failure.	• Damaged RABS valve reset switch. • Leaky dump valve. • Hydraulically inoperative RABS valve.	• Refer to drive test — Code 4, steps DT4.2 and DT4.4 only. • Refer to drive test — Code 4, step DT4.3 only. • Refer to drive test — Code 4, step DT4.5 only.
RABS sensor output low or lost at lower vehicle speeds.	• Sensor air gap too large. • Sensor/speed sensor ring assembly does not produce sufficient output.	• Refer to drive test — Code 6, step DT6.3 only. • Refer to drive test — Code 6, step DT6.2 only. • Perform intermittent diagnosis for Circuit 519 (LG/BK) and 523 (R/PK) between RABS II module and sensor. • Perform intermittent diagnosis for Circuit 519 (LG/BK) and 523 (R/PK) at intermediate connectors.

84929137

REAR ANTI-LOCK BRAKE SYSTEM TESTING — EXCEPT 1993 BRONCO

DIAGNOSIS AND TESTING (Continued)

SYMPTOM D: LACK OF DECELERATION DURING MEDIUM/HARD BRAKE APPLICATIONS

CONDITION	POSSIBLE SOURCE	ACTION
RABS valve inoperative.	• Leaky dump valve. • Stuck shut isolation valve.	• Refer to drive test — Code 4, step DT4.3. • Refer to Drive Test — Code 4, step DT4.5 ONLY.
RABS sensor input to RABS II module intermittent or improper.	• Short/open in frame or instrument panel harness (Circuits 519 and/or 523) — At RABS II module connector (Pins 3 and 10) — At RABS sensor connector — At bulkhead or other interconnection — Pinched wire or worn insulation due to improper routing — Test connector (in engine compartment) • Metal chips on sensor. • Borderline high sensor to speed sensor ring air gap, excessive speed sensor ring radial runout, damaged or missing speed sensor ring teeth.	• Refer to pinpoint test Code 6, steps 6.1-6.5 only. • Refer to pinpoint test Code 6, step 6.6 only. • Refer to drive test — Code 6 steps DT6.3-DT6.4 only.
Vehicle electrical concern.	• Low vacuum switch inoperative (diesel only).	
Base brake hydraulic concern.	• Hydraulic leak in brake line or hose, fitting, master cylinder, wheel cylinder, or caliper. • Air in brake system.	
Base brake mechanical concern.	• Brake related concern: — Little or no vacuum boost. — Stuck or inoperative wheel cylinder or caliper. — Pinched or crimped brake line or hose. — Ineffective brake shoe or pad linings.	

84929139

RABS Hydraulic Control Valve

REMOVAL & INSTALLATION

▶ **See Figure 81**

The valve is located in the brake lines, below the master cylinder.

1. Disconnect the brake lines from the valve and plug the lines.
2. Disconnect the wiring harness at the valve.
3. Remove the 3 nuts retaining the valve to the frame rail and lift out the valve.

4. Installation is the reverse of removal. Don't overtighten the brake lines. Bleed the brakes.

Computer Module

REMOVAL & INSTALLATION

▶ **See Figure 82**

The module is located on the firewall just inboard of the master cylinder.

1. Disconnect the wiring harness.
2. Remove the 2 attaching screws and lift out the module.
3. Installation is the reverse of removal.

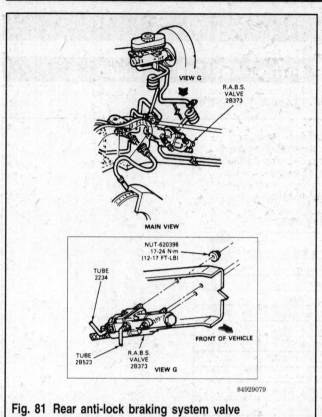

Fig. 81 Rear anti-lock braking system valve

RABS Sensor

REMOVAL & INSTALLATION

The sensor is located on the rear axle housing.
1. Remove the sensor holddown bolt.
2. Remove the sensor.
3. Carefully clean the axle surface to keep dirt from entering the housing.
4. If a new sensor is being installed, lubricate the O-ring with clean engine oil. Carefully push the sensor into the housing aligning the mounting flange hole with the threaded hole in the housing. Torque the holddown bolt to 30 ft. lbs.   If the old sensor is being installed, clean it thoroughly and install a new O-ring coated with clean engine oil.

Exciter Ring

The ring is located on the differential case inside the axle housing. Once it is pressed of the case it cannot be reused. See Section 7 for the procedure.

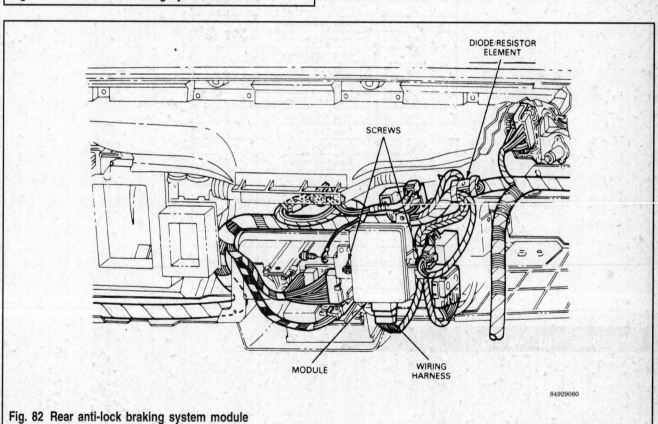

Fig. 82 Rear anti-lock braking system module

4-WHEEL ANTI-LOCK BRAKE SYSTEM (ABS)

This system is used on 1993 Bronco.

4-Wheel ABS Trouble Codes

4-WHEEL ABS TROUBLE CODE INDEX — 1993 BRONCO

NOTE: Check for continuity between Pin 60 and chassis ground or invalid results may be obtained. Results not matching specification indicate either a wiring or component concern. Further analysis is needed before any component replacement. Refer to pinpoint tests for proper diagnostic procedures.

SERVICE CODE INDEX

Service Code	Component	Pinpoint Test Step
11	ECU Failure	Replace ECU
16	System OK	—
17	Reference Voltage	A
22	Front Left Inlet Valve	B
23	Front Left Outlet Valve	C
24	Front Right Inlet Valve	D
25	Front Right Outlet Valve	E
26	Rear Axle Inlet Valve	F
27	Rear Axle Outlet Valve	G
31	Front Left Sensor	H
32	Front Right Sensor	J
33	Rear Axle Sensor	K
35	Front Left Sensor	H
36	Front Right Sensor	J
37	Rear Axle Sensor	K
41	Front Left Sensor	H
42	Front Right Sensor	J
43	Rear Axle Sensor	K
55	Front Left Sensor	H
56	Front Right Sensor	J
57	Rear Axle Sensor	K
51	Front Left Outlet Valve	L
52	Front Right Outlet Valve	M
53	Rear Axle Outlet Valve	N
63	Pump Motor	P
65	G Switch	Q
67	Pump Motor	R
No Code Obtained	No ECU Initialization	S

84929401

Diagnosis and Testing

4-WHEEL ABS TESTING — 1993 BRONCO

DIAGNOSIS AND TESTING (Continued)

PRE-CHECK

TEST STEP	RESULT	ACTION TO TAKE
PC1 PERFORM UNDERHOOD SYSTEM PRE-CHECK • Verify that all of the following connectors are connected and the terminals are secure and free of contaminants or corrosion. — 40-pin ECU connector — 8-pin HCU connector — 4-pin pump motor connector — 2-pin front sensor connectors (2) • Open power distribution box and verify that both the system relay and pump motor relay and diode are fully seated. • Gently pull on relay and diode terminals beneath power distribution box to make sure all are secure. • Verify that both the system fuse and pump motor fuse are present and intact. • Verify that the system ground eyelet at the left hand radiator support is firmly attached to the weld stud and is free of corrosion and excessive dirt. • Are all connectors, terminals and grounds secure?	All connections, terminals and grounds are secure. Fuses are intact Any of the above are missing, not connected or loose	▲ GO to PC2. ▲ Correct condition. GO to PC2.
PC2 PERFORM UNDER-VEHICLE SYSTEM PRE-CHECK • Verify that the 3-pin acceleration connector and the 2-pin rear axle sensor connector are connected and the terminals are secure and free of contaminants or corrosion. • Are all connectors, terminals and grounds secure?	Yes No	▲ GO to PC3. ▲ SERVICE as required. GO to PC3.
PC3 CHECK ABS WARNING LIGHT SEQUENCE (KEY ON / ENGINE OFF) • Observe ABS warning light on dash. • Turn ignition to ON. • Does ABS warning light come on?	Yes, and stays on for 3 seconds and goes out (normal bulb proveout) Yes, comes on and stays on (hard light) No	▲ GO to PC6. ▲ Go to PC4. ▲ GO to PC7.

84929140

4-WHEEL ABS TESTING — 1993 BRONCO

DIAGNOSIS AND TESTING (Continued)

PRE-CHECK (Continued)

TEST STEP	RESULT	ACTION TO TAKE
PC4 CODE RETRIEVAL EQUIPMENT HOOKUP • Verify that an ABS concern has been detected (ABS warning light ON). • Key OFF. • Using SUPER STAR II Tester: — Connect tester to red ABS data link connector located near ECU. — Turn test power ON and put HOLD / TEST button in TEST position. • Using 12V test light or ABS warning light: — Locate red ABS data link connector near ECU and install 12V test light between Pins C (Circuit 603 [DG]) and E (Circuit 57 [BK]). — If no test light is available, ABS warning light will flash. • Jumper ABS data link connector pins B (Circuit 606 [BK/LB]) and E (Circuit 57 [BK]). • Is equipment hooked up properly?	Yes No	▲ GO to PC5. ▲ RE-ATTEMPT PC4. SERVICE as required.

PC5 RETRIEVE ABS DIAGNOSTIC TROUBLE CODES
• Using SUPER STAR II Tester:
— Key in RUN.
— Read out and record all diagnostic trouble codes.
  CAUTION: Be sure to read out and record all codes. Failure to do so may result in improper diagnosis and unnecessary repairs.
  NOTE: After first code, the remaining codes will follow in 15-second intervals. Leave STAR Tester HOLD / TEST button in the TEST position.
• Using 12V test light or ABS warning light:
— Key in RUN.
— Count flashes.
  NOTE: Digits will be separated by 3-6 seconds. Diagnostic trouble codes will be separated by 15 seconds.
— Record all codes. When flashing stops there are no codes remaining.
— Remove jumper in ABS TEST connector.
• Are there any codes present?
	Yes (other than Code 16)
	
	Yes (Code 16)
	
	No, no code is obtained
		▲ Starting with the first code recorded, GO to the pinpoint test for that code.
		
		▲ If previous action has been taken, concern most likely has been corrected and ABS system is OK. Otherwise, GO to Symptom Chart.
		▲ GO to Pinpoint Test S.

84929141

4-WHEEL ABS TESTING — 1993 BRONCO

DIAGNOSIS AND TESTING

PRE-CHECK (Continued)

TEST STEP	RESULT	ACTION TO TAKE
PC11 CHECK GROUND BETWEEN ABS SYSTEM RELAY AND CHASSIS GROUNDS • Inspect chassis ground stud at left-hand radiator support for loose or corroded eyelets. • Clean and tighten any loose or dirty ground eyelets. • Check for continuity between ABS system relay Circuit 57 (BK) and left-hand radiator support chassis ground stud. • Is there continuity?	Yes	REINSERT ABS system relay. REPLACE ABS warning bulb. REPEAT Steps **PC8-PC11** looking for intermittent condition (see Intermittent Diagnosis).
	No	SERVICE open circuit between ABS system relay and chassis ground. REINSERT ABS system relay. GO to **PC3**.

INTERMITTENT DIAGNOSIS PROCEDURE

TEST STEP	RESULT	ACTION TO TAKE
ID1 CLEAR CODES, RECONNECT COMPONENTS • Remove the pinout box. • Reinstall any components removed and remake all connections. • Clear all codes. • Key ON. • Does the ABS warning light prove out?	Yes	GO to **ID3**.
	No, light stays on.	GO to **ID2**.
ID2 SERVICE CONNECTOR/TERMINAL CONCERN • Most likely concern is at one of the affected component connectors such that terminals unseat or back out upon installation. At EACH affected connection, including intermediate connections, look for: — Bent terminals. — Damaged connector terminal locks. — Damaged connector wedge. • Are any of the above conditions noted? NOTE: If one of the above conditions is found, check the tightness of the affected circuit once the connection is remade. If the wire is too tight (short), damage is likely to recur once vehicle is given back to the customer. Service the wire as necessary to correct tight wire conditions.	Yes	SERVICE connector and terminal as necessary. GO to **ID7**.
	No	GO to **ID6**.
ID3 WIGGLE TEST • Leave key ON. • Wiggle an affected circuit in one location only. NOTE: Start at one component and wiggle connector by connector until the whole circuit has been tested. • Observe ABS warning light. • Is the ABS warning light on?	Yes	Key off. GO to **ID5**.
	No	GO to **ID4**.
ID4 VERIFY ALL CIRCUITS HAVE BEEN TESTED • Have all affected circuits for the code being serviced been tested?	Yes	Key off. GO to **ID6**.
	No	GO to **ID3** and check next circuit.
ID5 RETRIEVE CODE • Retrieve code. • Is this code different than the code being serviced?	Yes	GO to the appropriate pinpoint test.
	No	SERVICE the wire, terminal, or connector as necessary. GO to **ID7**.

84929143

4-WHEEL ABS TESTING — 1993 BRONCO

DIAGNOSIS AND TESTING

PRE-CHECK (Continued)

TEST STEP	RESULT	ACTION TO TAKE
PC6 ROAD TEST VEHICLE NOTE: Step PC6 is optional, for additional information only. • Drive vehicle and observe ABS warning light. • Does ABS warning light come on during any of the following? — When vehicle moves initially (light comes on at or near 6 mph). — While driving under 25 mph. — While driving at or over 25 mph. — While in an anti-lock stop.	Yes, at or near 6 mph, concern most likely found during pump check	GO to **PC4**. VERIFY pump diagnostic trouble code has been set.
	Yes, while driving under 25 mph, most likely cause is missing wheel speed sensor output	GO to **PC4**. VERIFY sensor diagnostic trouble code has been set.
	Yes, while driving over 25 mph, most likely cause is an erratic wheel speed sensor output	GO to **PC4**. VERIFY sensor diagnostic trouble code has been set.
	No, but vehicle has abnormal ABS or brake system operation	GO to symptom chart.
	No, and no abnormal operation or symptoms detected	GO to **PC4**. VERIFY Code 16 (System OK) is present.
PC7 ABS WARNING LIGHT DOES NOT PROVE-OUT/CHECK BULB • Inspect ABS warning light bulb in dash. • Is the bulb blown?	Yes	REPLACE bulb. GO to **PC3**.
	No	LEAVE bulb out. GO to **PC8**.
PC8 VERIFY ABS WARNING LAMP FEED IS INTACT • Insert 12V test light between ABS bulb socket (+) and a known good chassis ground. • Does test light illuminate?	Yes	GO to **PC9**.
	No	SERVICE open circuit or short to ground in warning light feed. REINSERT bulb back into socket. GO to **PC3**.
PC9 VERIFY ABS WARNING LAMP GROUND BETWEEN BULB AND ABS DIODE • Open power network box and remove ABS diode. • Verify diode terminals are clean and firmly in place. • Check for continuity between ABS bulb socket ground and diode terminal in power network box for Circuit 603 (DG). • Is there continuity?	Yes	GO to **PC10**.
	No	SERVICE open circuit in warning light ground or loose terminal. REINSERT ABS diode. GO to **PC3**.
PC10 VERIFY INTACT ABS WARNING LAMP GROUND BETWEEN ABS DIODE AND ABS SYSTEM RELAY • Remove ABS system relay. • Verify relay terminals are clean and firmly in place. • Check for continuity between ABS diode Circuit 532 (O/Y) and ABS System Relay Circuit 532 (O/Y). • Is there continuity?	Yes	GO to **PC11**.
	No	SERVICE open circuit in Circuit 532 (O/Y) between ABS diode and ABS system relay or loose terminals. REINSERT ABS diode and system relay. GO to **PC3**.

84929142

4-WHEEL ABS TESTING — 1993 BRONCO

DIAGNOSIS AND TESTING (Continued)

INTERMITTENT DIAGNOSIS PROCEDURE (Continued)

	TEST STEP	RESULT	ACTION TO TAKE
ID6	VERIFY ALL APPROPRIATE DIAGNOSTIC PROCEDURES HAVE BEEN RUN • Has the System Pre-Check been run and a code been retrieved? • Have all steps of the pinpoint test for the code being serviced been performed. If only some tests were performed, then go to the pinpoint step last completed and continue. • Have ALL steps of the symptom pinpoint test (if applicable) been performed. If only some tests were performed, go to the pinpoint step last completed and continue.	Yes, all diagnostic procedures have been run. No	▲ RETURN to the pinpoint test and proceed. ▲ RETURN to procedure(s) not yet performed and proceed.
ID7	VERIFY CONDITION RESOLVED • Clear all codes. • Key OFF. • Retrieve code. • Is Code 16 set?	Yes No, code being serviced still exists. No, different code is set.	▲ STOP. Concern has been corrected. ▲ GO to ID4. ▲ GO to appropriate pinpoint test.

• The wiring or interconnections in the vehicle harness between the ECU and the PSOM module is damaged. This, in most cases, will lead to erratic PSOM function, and is the most difficult to diagnose.

NOTE: The ECU will continue to send a signal to PSOM in all other cases, including when the ABS system is disabled, with the exception of the first two ABS system concerns.

This procedure will only determine if the ECU is not sending out a signal. If it is determined that the ECU is sending out a proper signal, Section 13-02A should be consulted with the knowledge that a proper signal is available from the ABS system.

PSOM Signal from ABS Verification Procedure

This procedure is intended to determine whether the cause for loss of or erratic Programmable Speedometer/Odometer Module (PSOM) function is due to the lack of a signal from the ECU.

There are three basic reasons that PSOM would not receive a signal from the ABS ECU:

• The ECU has no ignition power and therefore cannot initialize or function. In this case, the ABS warning light will come on and stay on upon vehicle start-up.

• The Rear Axle Sensor or the signal from the Rear Axle Sensor is either damaged, not being generated or is not reaching the ECU. The ECU, in turn, is unable to provide the speed signal to PSOM. In cases where the concern is not intermittent, the ABS warning light will be on upon vehicle start-up. Where the concern is intermittent, and the ABS warning light does NOT come on during vehicle start-up, a rear sensor diagnostic trouble code will often be stored in the ECU (see ABS Diagnostic Trouble Codes).

PROGRAMMABLE SPEEDOMETER/ODOMETER MODULE (PSOM) SIGNAL VERIFICATION PROCEDURE

	TEST STEP	RESULT	ACTION TO TAKE
SV1	DETERMINE STATE OF ABS WARNING LIGHT • Observe ABS warning light. • Turn ignition to START. • Allow ignition to return to the RUN position. • Does the ABS warning light turn on?	Yes No	▲ GO to SV2. ▲ GO to PC7. RETURN when ABS warning light concern is repaired.

4-WHEEL ABS TESTING — 1993 BRONCO

DIAGNOSIS AND TESTING (Continued)

PROGRAMMABLE SPEEDOMETER/ODOMETER MODULE (PSOM) SIGNAL VERIFICATION PROCEDURE (Continued)

	TEST STEP	RESULT	ACTION TO TAKE
SV2	OBTAIN ABS DIAGNOSTIC TROUBLE CODE • Obtain ABS diagnostic trouble code (refer to PC4 and PC5). • Are any of the following codes obtained: 33, 37, 43, or 57? NOTE: Any other code obtained represents an ABS system concern and does NOT have an effect on the ability of the ECU to send the speed signal to PSOM. Resolve the ABS system concern indicated by the diagnostic service code first. When the ABS system concern is corrected, repeat this step to continue PSOM diagnosis.	Yes No, Code 16 is obtained No, a code other than 16/33/37/43/57 is obtained No code is obtained	▲ GO to K1 to address rear axle sensor concern. ▲ GO to SV3. ▲ GO to appropriate pinpoint test (refer to Service Code Index). ▲ GO to PC12 to resolve lack of power to ECU concern. REPEAT SV2 If PSOM still does not function.
SV3	VERIFY ECU SPEED SIGNAL AT PSOM CONNECTOR • Key OFF. • Remove the PSOM harness connector from the PSOM module. • Raise the vehicle so that the rear wheels are clear of the ground. If the vehicle is a 4x4, verify the transfer case is in the 4x2 mode. • Connect Rotunda Hand-Held Automotive Meter 105-00053, or equivalent between PSOM harness connector Pin 7 (Circuit 491 [O/LB]) and Pin 2 (Circuit 530 [LG/Y]). • Set the meter to the frequency counter (Hz) setting. • Gradually spin up the rear wheels. • Does the frequency increase as the rear wheel speed increases? CAUTION: The terminals in the PSOM harness connector spread very easily and upon reconnection will often result in erratic PSOM operation. Use an assistant to aid in the measurement of the speed signal. Make sure that no more pressure than absolutely necessary to obtain a reading is applied between the meter probes and the connector terminals.	Yes No	▲ ECU is providing a proper signal. ▲ GO to K1.

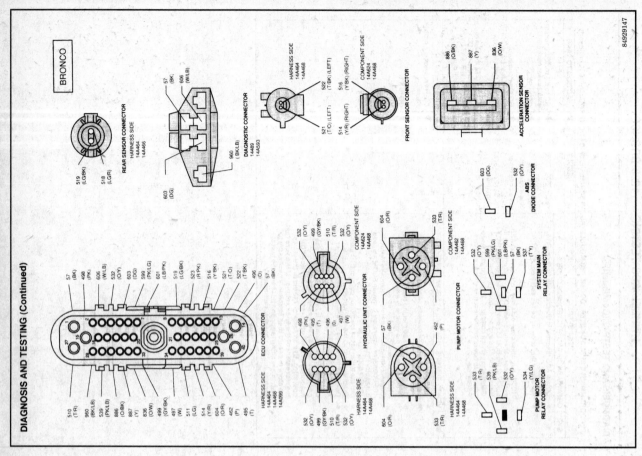

4-WHEEL ABS TESTING — 1993 BRONCO

DIAGNOSIS AND TESTING (Continued)

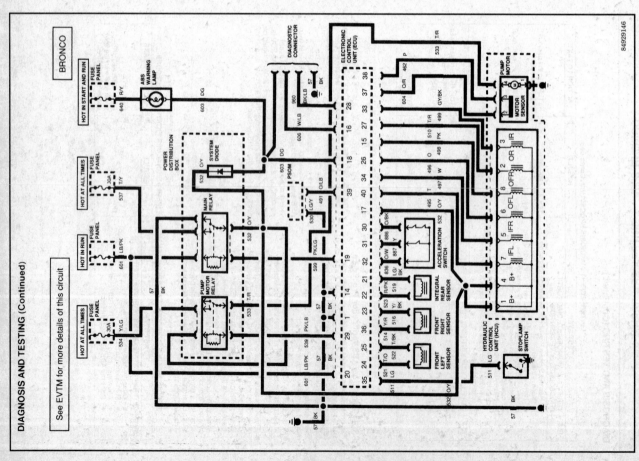

4-WHEEL ABS TESTING — 1993 BRONCO

DIAGNOSIS AND TESTING (Continued)

4-WHEEL ABS TESTING — 1993 BRONCO

DIAGNOSIS AND TESTING (Continued)

NOTE: Perform the following measurements with Rotunda 105-00053 Hand-Held Automotive Meter, or equivalent.

ANTI-LOCK QUICK CHECK SHEET

Item To Be Tested	Measure Between Pin Number(s)	Ignition Mode	Scale/Range	Specification
ECU Ground Check	60 + Chassis Gnd	Off	Ohms	Continuity
	14 + Chassis Gnd	Off	Ohms	Continuity
	17 + Chassis Gnd	Off	Ohms	Continuity
Battery Power to ECU Check	20 + 60	On	Volts	8V minimum
Jumper Pins 80 + 19 (Energizing System Relay) Power from System Relay	17 + 60	On	Volts	• 8V Minimum • Verify ABS warning lamp is OFF
System Relay Coil	19 + 20	Off	Ohms	54-68 Ohms
Pump Motor Relay Coil	17 + 29	Off	Ohms	54-68 Ohms
ABS Warning Light Ground through System Relay	17 + 60	Off	Ohms	Continuity
IFR Isolation (Inlet) Valve Resistance	17 + 34	Off	Ohms	5-8 Ohms
IFL Isolation (Inlet) Valve Resistance	17 + 40	Off	Ohms	5-8 Ohms
IRA Isolation (Inlet) Valve Resistance	17 + 33	Off	Ohms	5-8 Ohms
OFR Dump (Outlet) Valve Resistance	17 + 15	Off	Ohms	3-6 Ohms
OFL Dump (Outlet) Valve Resistance	17 + 28	Off	Ohms	3-6 Ohms
ORA Dump (Outlet) Valve Resistance	17 + 27	Off	Ohms	3-6 Ohms
FR Wheel Speed Sensor Resistance	23 + 38	Off	kOhms	1.0-1.2 kOhms
FL Wheel Speed Sensor Resistance	24 + 25	Off	kOhms	1.0-1.2 kOhms
RA Speed Sensor Resistance	21 + 22	Off	kOhms	0.8-1.4 kOhms
Motor Speed Sensor Resistance	37 + 38	Off	Hz	Greater than 150 Hz, pump motor ON / Less than 70 Hz, pump motor OFF
Sensor Output: Rotate Front Wheels and Rear Axle 60 rpm FR	24 + 25	Off	Hz and mV	3.4 mV/Hz, or greater
FL	21 + 22	Off	Hz and mV	6 mV/Hz, or greater
RA	37 + 38	Off	Hz and mV	6 mV/Hz, or greater
Diode	18 (Meter Polarity +) or 17 (Meter Polarity -)	Off	Diode Check	0.5 Volts
Remove System Relay	18 (Meter Polarity +) or 17 (Meter Polarity -)	Off	Diode Check	Infinity mOhms

NOTE: Check for continuity between Pin 60 and chassis ground or invalid results may be obtained. Results not matching specification indicate either a wiring or component concern. Further analysis is needed before any component replacement. Refer to pinpoint tests for proper diagnostic procedures.

SERVICE CODE INDEX

Service Code	Component	Pinpoint Test Step
11	ECU Failure	Replace ECU
16	System OK	—
17	Reference Voltage	A
22	Front Left Inlet Valve	B
23	Front Left Outlet Valve	C
24	Front Right Inlet Valve	D
26	Front Right Outlet Valve	E

(Continued)

SERVICE CODE INDEX (Cont'd)

Service Code	Component	Pinpoint Test Step
26	Rear Axle Inlet Valve	F
27	Rear Axle Outlet Valve	G
31	Front Left Sensor	H
32	Front Right Sensor	J
33	Rear Axle Sensor	K
35	Front Left Sensor	H
36	Front Right Sensor	J

(Continued)

84929148

4-WHEEL ABS TESTING — 1993 BRONCO

DIAGNOSIS AND TESTING (Continued)

SERVICE CODE INDEX (Cont'd)

Service Code	Component	Pinpoint Test Step
37	Rear Axle Sensor	K
41	Front Left Sensor	H
42	Front Right Sensor	J
43	Rear Axle Sensor	K
55	Front Left Sensor	H
56	Front Right Sensor	J
57	Rear Axle Sensor	K

(Continued)

SERVICE CODE INDEX (Cont'd)

Service Code	Component	Pinpoint Test Step
51	Front Left Outlet Valve	L
52	Front Right Outlet Valve	M
53	Rear Axle Outlet Valve	N
63	Pump Motor	P
65	G Switch	Q
67	Pump Motor	R
No Code Obtained	No ECU Initialization	S

ECU CONNECTOR HARNESS SIDE — HYDRAULIC UNIT CONNECTOR HARNESS SIDE — SYSTEM RELAY HARNESS SIDE — SYSTEM RELAY COMPONENT SIDE — ALL VIEWS LOOKING INTO CONNECTOR — IGNITION 12V — BATTERY — FUSE 30A

84929149

Pinpoint Test A — Code 17

Possible Code(s)

17 — Open circuit from battery, main relay open or 30 amp fuse open.

Affected Circuit(s)/Electrical Component(s)

Description

Code 17 is generated by the ECU indicating a loss of system reference voltage.

Possible Contributing Component/Vehicle Wiring Concerns

- 30 amp fuse open
- Intermittent connections to battery, main relay or ground
- Main relay coil or contacts open

4-WHEEL ABS TESTING — 1993 BRONCO

DIAGNOSIS AND TESTING (Continued)

- Open or short to ground in Circuit 532 (O/Y)
- Open or short to ground in Circuit 599 (PK/LG)
- Open or short to ground in Circuit 601 (LB/PK)

CODE 17 REFERENCE VOLTAGE — TEST A

	TEST STEP	RESULT	ACTION TO TAKE
A1	INSTALL PINOUT BOX AND CHECK CONNECTIONS • Install pinout box. • Check connections to battery, power network box battery feed lugs, and grounds. • Are all connections clean and secure?	Yes No	▲ GO to A2. ▲ SECURE all connections. GO to A2.
A2	INSPECT 30A FUSE IN POWER NETWORK BOX • Open power network box and locate 30A fuse for Circuit 537 (T/Y). • Check fuse for continuity. • Verify fuse terminals are clean and secure in the power network box. • Is the fuse blown?	Yes No	▲ REPLACE fuse. GO to A12. ▲ REINSTALL fuse. GO to A3.
A3	CHECK GROUND CONNECTIONS TO ECU • Key OFF. • Verify ground eyelets at left hand radiator support are free of excessive dirt and corrosion and are securely fastened. • Check for continuity between Pin 60 and Pin 14 on pinout box. • If OK, check for continuity between Pin 60 on pinout box and chassis ground at left-hand radiator support ground stud. • Is there continuity?	Yes No, continuity between Pins 60 and 14 does not exist No, continuity between Pin 60 and chassis ground does not exist	▲ GO to A4. ▲ SERVICE open circuit immediately behind ECU connector. REPEAT A3. ▲ SERVICE open circuit in ground between ECU connector and left-hand radiator support ground stud. REPEAT A3.
A4	CHECK FOR PROPER VOLTAGE AT ECU CONNECTOR • Connect a jumper wire between Pins 19 and 60 on the pinout box. • Check for terminal backout on 40-way connector. • Key ON. • Measure voltage between Pins 17 and 14 on the pinout box. • Is there at least 8V?	Yes No	▲ Key OFF. REMOVE jumper. REPLACE ECU. GO to A12. ▲ Key OFF; REMOVE jumper. GO to A5.
A5	VERIFY WIRING TO ECU CONNECTOR IS INTACT • Disconnect battery negative cable. • Remove ABS system relay from power network box. • Connect a jumper wire between pins for Circuits 537 (T/Y) and 532 (O/Y) in the power network box. • Reconnect battery negative cable. NOTE: On vehicles equipped with EEC, when the battery has been disconnected and reconnected, some abnormal drive symptoms may occur while the Powertrain Control Module (PCM) relearns its adaptive strategy. The vehicle may need to be driven 10 miles or more to relearn the strategy. • Key ON. • Measure voltage between Pins 17 and 60 on the pinout box. • Is there at least 8V?	Yes No	▲ Key OFF. GO to A9. ▲ DISCONNECT battery negative cable. REMOVE jumper. RECONNECT battery negative cable. Key OFF. GO to A6.

84929150

4-WHEEL ABS TESTING — 1993 BRONCO

DIAGNOSIS AND TESTING (Continued)

CODE 17 REFERENCE VOLTAGE — TEST A (Continued)

	TEST STEP	RESULT	ACTION TO TAKE
A6	VERIFY VOLTAGE PRESENT AT RELAY CONTACTS • Key ON. • Measure voltage between pins for Circuits 537 (T/Y) and 57 (BK) in the power network box. • Is there at least 8V?	Yes No, no voltage is present No, voltage is less than 8V but greater than 0V	▲ Key OFF. GO to A8. ▲ Key OFF. GO to A7. ▲ Key OFF. ECU does not have enough reference voltage to function. ABS system is working as intended. RE-INSTALL ABS system relay. Refer to the appropriate section.
A7	CHECK FOR OPEN CIRCUIT BETWEEN BATTERY POSITIVE VOLTAGE (B+) AND RELAY • Check for continuity between Battery Positive Voltage (B+) terminal and pin for Circuit 537 (T/Y) in power network box. • Is there continuity?	Yes No	▲ REPEAT A6, looking for loose or intermittent connections/circuits (see Intermittent Diagnosis). ▲ SERVICE open circuit in battery feed to power network box or relay. RE-INSTALL ABS system relay. GO to A12.
A8	CHECK FOR PROPER VOLTAGE AT 8-WAY VALVE BLOCK CONNECTOR • Disconnect 8-way connector from valve block. • Connect a jumper wire between pins for Circuits 537 (T/Y) and 532 (O/Y) in the power network box. • Key ON. • Measure voltage between 8-way harness connector Pin 1 or Pin 4 and Pin 60 on pinout box. • Is there at least 8V?	Yes No	▲ Key OFF. SERVICE open circuit or short to ground in circuit 532 (O/Y) between valve block and ECU. REMOVE jumper. GO to A12. ▲ Key OFF. SERVICE open circuit or short to ground in Circuit 532 (O/Y) between relay and valve block connector. REMOVE jumper. GO to A12.
A9	VERIFY CIRCUITS TO SYSTEM RELAY COIL ARE INTACT • Check continuity between pin for Circuit 599 (PK/LG) in the power network box and Pin 19 on the pinout box. • Check continuity between pin for Circuit 601 (LB/PK) in the power network box and Pin 20 on the pinout box. • Is there continuity?	Yes No	▲ GO to A10. ▲ SERVICE open Circuits in 599 (LB/PK) or 601 (LB/PK). RE-INSTALL ABS system relay. GO to A12.
A10	CHECK CIRCUITS TO SYSTEM RELAY COIL FOR SHORTS TO GROUND • Check continuity between pin for Circuit 599 (PK/LG) in the power network box and Pin 60 in the pinout box. • Check continuity between pin for Circuit 601 (LB/PK) in the power network box and Pin 60 in the pinout box. • Is there continuity?	Yes No	▲ SERVICE short to ground in Circuits 599 (PK/LG) or 601 (LB/PK). RE-INSTALL ABS system relay. GO to A12. ▲ REPLACE ABS system relay. GO to A12.

84929151

4-WHEEL ABS TESTING — 1993 BRONCO

DIAGNOSIS AND TESTING (Continued)

CODE 17 REFERENCE VOLTAGE — TEST A (Continued)

	TEST STEP	RESULT	▲	ACTION TO TAKE
A11	CHECK IF ALL STEPS HAVE BEEN COMPLETED			
	• This step requires that a valid diagnostic trouble code has been obtained. ALL prior diagnostic steps have been completed, and the affected wiring integrity has been verified.	Yes	▲	REPLACE ECU. GO to A12.
		No	▲	GO to last diagnostic step completed and continue.
	CAUTION: If the above is not complete, changes are that replacement of this or any other system component without specific direction will not, in most circumstances, resolve the concern and will consequently result in customer dissatisfaction.			
	• Have all prior diagnostic steps been completed as described above?			
A12	VERIFY CONDITION RESOLVED	Yes	▲	STOP. Concern has been corrected.
	• Clear all codes.	No, Code 17 still exists	▲	GO to next pinpoint step.
	• Key OFF.	No, different code is set	▲	GO to appropriate pinpoint test.
	• Retrieve code.	No, Code 17 still exists and Step A10 is completed	▲	GO to A13.
	• Is Code 16 set?			
A13	VERIFY INTEGRITY OF VEHICLE WIRING	Yes	▲	STOP. Repair is complete.
	NOTE: If the above steps have been completed, the MOST LIKELY cause of the concern is wiring related.	No	▲	GO to A11.
	• Refer to the Intermittent Diagnosis Procedure and perform for ALL affected circuits as shown on the pinpoint test mini-schematic.			
	• Does wiring check OK?			

Pinpoint Test B — Code 22

Possible Code(s)

22 — Open circuit to valve block or ECU, open or shorted valve coil or internal ECU defect.

84929152

4-WHEEL ABS TESTING — 1993 BRONCO

DIAGNOSIS AND TESTING (Continued)

Affected Circuit(s)/Electrical Component(s)

IFL ISOLATION (INLET) VALVE (5-8 Ω)

HYDRAULIC UNIT CONNECTOR

COMPONENT SIDE

HARNESS SIDE

ALL VIEWS LOOKING INTO CONNECTOR

ECU CONNECTOR
HARNESS SIDE

Possible Contributing Component/Vehicle Wiring Concerns

- Intermittent open Circuit 495 (T)
- Terminal backout in ECU connector Pins 17 and 40
- Terminal backout in valve block connector Pins 1, 4 and 7
- Open or shorted inlet front left (IFL) valve coil
- Open or shorted driver in ECU

Description

Code 22 is generated by the ECU's detection of an open or shorted Circuit 495 (T) and by an open or shorted inlet front left (IFL) valve coil or an open or shorted driver in the ECU.

FRONT LEFT INLET SOLENOID VALVE CONCERN DIAGNOSIS — TEST B

	TEST STEP	RESULT	▲	ACTION TO TAKE
B1	SERVICE CODE 22: CHECK VALVE COIL, CIRCUIT 495 (T) AND THE ECU			
	• Ignition OFF.	Yes	▲	GO to B4.
	• Install pinout box.	No	▲▲	GO to B2.
	• Verify terminals at Pins 17 and 40 are clean and secure in the ECU connector.			
	• Measure resistance between Pins 17 and 40.			
	• Is reading between 5 and 8 ohms?			

84929153

4-WHEEL ABS TESTING — 1993 BRONCO

DIAGNOSIS AND TESTING (Continued)

FRONT LEFT INLET SOLENOID VALVE CONCERN DIAGNOSIS — TEST B (Continued)

TEST STEP	RESULT	▶ ACTION TO TAKE
B2 CHECK VALVE COIL • Disconnect 8-pin valve block connector. • Verify terminals on both halves of the 8-way connector are clean and secure. • Measure resistance between Pins 1 and 7 and Pins 1 and 4 on the valve block. • Are both readings between 5 and 8 ohms?	Yes No	▲ SERVICE open or short to ground in Circuits 496 (T) or 532 (O/Y) between valve block harness connector and ECU connector. GO to **B4**. ▲ REPLACE valve block. GO to **B4**.
B3 CHECK IF ALL STEPS HAVE BEEN COMPLETED • This step requires that a valid diagnostic trouble code has been obtained, ALL prior diagnostic steps have been completed, and the affected wiring integrity has been verified. **CAUTION: If the above is not complete, changes are that replacement of this or any other system component without specific direction will not, in most circumstances, resolve the concern and will consequently result in customer dissatisfaction.** • Have all prior diagnostic steps been completed as described above?	Yes No	▲ REPLACE ECU. GO to **B4**. ▲ GO to last diagnostic step completed and continue.
B4 VERIFY CONDITION RESOLVED • Clear all codes. • Key OFF. • Retrieve code. • Is Code 16 set?	Yes No, Code 22 still exists No, different code is set No, Code 22 still exists and Step B2 is completed	▲ STOP. Concern has been corrected. ▲ GO to next pinpoint step. ▲ GO to appropriate pinpoint test. ▲ GO to **B5**.
B5 VERIFY INTEGRITY OF VEHICLE WIRING NOTE: If the above steps have been completed, the MOST LIKELY cause of the concern is wiring related. • Refer to the Intermittent Diagnosis Procedure and perform for ALL affected circuits as shown on the pinpoint test mini-schematic. • Does wiring check OK?	Yes No	▲ STOP. Repair is complete. ▲ GO to **B3**.

Pinpoint Test C — Code 23

Possible Code(s)

23 — Open circuit to valve block or ECU, open or shorted valve coil or internal ECU damage.

84929154

4-WHEEL ABS TESTING — 1993 BRONCO

DIAGNOSIS AND TESTING (Continued)

Affected Circuit(s)/Electrical Component(s)

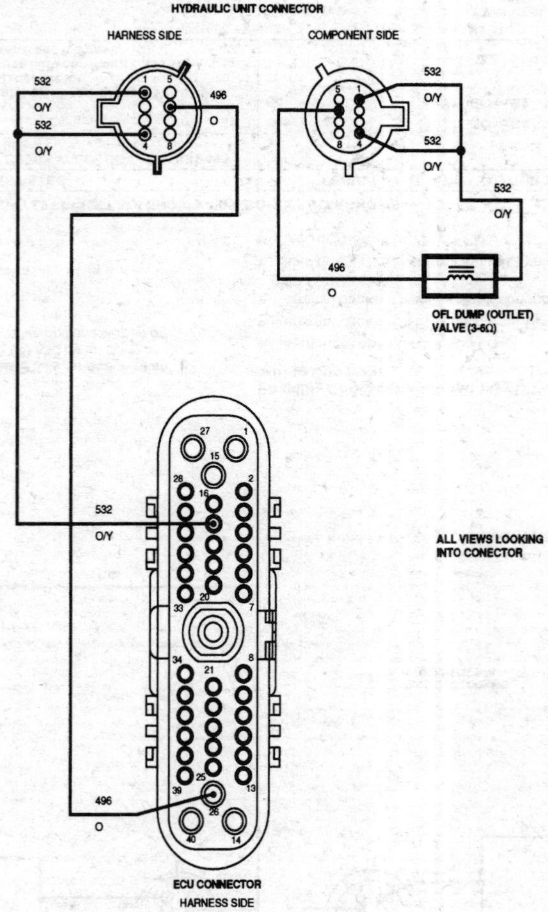

HYDRAULIC UNIT CONNECTOR

COMPONENT SIDE

HARNESS SIDE

532 O/Y 496 O

OFL DUMP (OUTLET) VALVE (3-6Ω)

ALL VIEWS LOOKING INTO CONECTOR

ECU CONNECTOR

HARNESS SIDE

532 O/Y 496 O

84929155

4-WHEEL ABS TESTING — 1993 BRONCO

DIAGNOSIS AND TESTING (Continued)

Description
Code 23 is generated by the ECU's detection of an open or shorted Circuit 496 (O) and by an open or shorted outlet front left (OFL) valve coil or an open or shorted driver in the ECU.

Possible Contributing Component/Vehicle Wiring Concerns
- Intermittent open Circuit 496 (O)
- Terminal backout in ECU connector Pins 17 and 26
- Terminal backout in valve block connector Pins 1 and 6
- Open or shorted outlet front left (OFL) valve coil
- Open or shorted driver in ECU

FRONT LEFT OUTLET SOLENOID CONCERN DIAGNOSIS — TEST C

	TEST STEP	RESULT	ACTION TO TAKE
C1	SERVICE CODE 23: CHECK VALVE COIL, CIRCUIT 496 AND THE ECU • Ignition OFF. • Install pinout box. • Verify terminals at Pins 17 and 26 are clean and secure in the ECU connector. • Measure resistance between Pins 17 and 26. • Is reading between 5 and 8 ohms?	Yes No	GO to C4. GO to C2.
C2	CHECK VALVE COIL • Disconnect 8-pin valve block connector. • Verify terminals on both halves of the valve block 8-way connector are clean and secure. • Measure resistance between Pins 1 and 6 on the valve block. • Is reading between 3 and 6 ohms?	Yes No	SERVICE open or short to ground in Circuits 496 (O) or 532 (O/Y) between valve block harness connector and ECU connector. GO to C4. REPLACE valve block. GO to C4.
C3	CHECK IF ALL STEPS HAVE BEEN COMPLETED • This step requires that a valid diagnostic trouble code has been obtained, ALL prior diagnostic steps have been completed, and the affected wiring integrity has been verified. CAUTION: If the above is not complete, changes that are that replacement of this or any other system component without specific direction will not, in most circumstances, resolve the concern and will consequently result in customer dissatisfaction. • Have all prior diagnostic steps been completed as described above?	Yes No	REPLACE ECU. GO to C4. GO to last diagnostic step completed and continue.
C4	VERIFY CONDITION RESOLVED • Clear all codes. • Key OFF. • Retrieve code. • Is Code 16 set?	Yes No, Code 23 still exists No, different code is set No, Code 23 still exists and Step C2 is completed	STOP. Concern has been corrected. GO to next pinpoint step. GO to appropriate pinpoint test. GO to C5.
C5	VERIFY INTEGRITY OF VEHICLE WIRING NOTE: If the above steps have been completed, the MOST LIKELY cause of the concern is wiring related. • Refer to the Intermittent Diagnosis Procedure and perform for ALL affected circuits as shown on the pinpoint test mini-schematic. • Does wiring check OK?	Yes No	STOP. Repair is complete. GO to C3.

84929156

4-WHEEL ABS TESTING — 1993 BRONCO

DIAGNOSIS AND TESTING (Continued)

Pinpoint Test D — Code 24

Possible Code(s)
24 — Open circuit to valve block or ECU, open or shorted valve coil or internal ECU damage.

Affected Circuit(s)/Electrical Component(s)

Description
Code 24 is generated by the ECU's detection of an open or shorted Circuit 497 (W) and by an open or shorted inlet front right (IFR) valve coil or an open or shorted driver in the ECU.

Possible Contributing Component/Vehicle Wiring Concerns
- Intermittent open Circuit 497 (W)
- Terminal backout in ECU connector Pins 17 and 34
- Terminal backout in valve block connector Pins 1 and 5
- Open or shorted inlet front right (IFR) valve coil
- Open or shorted driver in ECU

84929157

4-WHEEL ABS TESTING — 1993 BRONCO

DIAGNOSIS AND TESTING (Continued)

Description

Code 25 is generated by the ECU's detection of an open or shorted Circuit 498 (PK) and by an open or shorted outlet front right (OFR) valve coil or an open or shorted driver in the ECU.

Possible Contributing Component/Vehicle Wiring Concerns

- Intermittent open Circuit 498 (PK)
- Terminal backout in ECU connector Pins 17 and 15
- Terminal backout in valve block connector Pins 1 and 8
- Open or shorted outlet front right (OFR) valve coil
- Open or shorted driver in ECU

Affected Circuit(s)/Electrical Component(s)

HYDRAULIC UNIT CONNECTOR — HARNESS SIDE / COMPONENT SIDE — 532 O/Y 498 PK — OFR DUMP (OUTLET) VALVE (3-4Ω) — ECU CONNECTOR — HARNESS SIDE — ALL VIEWS LOOKING INTO CONECTOR

FRONT RIGHT OUTLET SOLENOID VALVE CONCERN DIAGNOSIS — TEST E

	TEST STEP	RESULT	ACTION TO TAKE
E1	**SERVICE CODE 25: CHECK VALVE COIL, CIRCUIT 498 AND THE ECU** • Ignition OFF. • Install pinout box. • Verify terminals at Pins 17 and 15 are clean and secure in the ECU connector. • Measure resistance between Pins 17 and 15. • Is reading between 5 and 8 ohms?	Yes No	▲ GO to **E4**. ▲ GO to **E2**.
E2	**CHECK VALVE COIL** • Disconnect 8-pin valve block connector. • Verify terminals on both halves of the valve block 8-way connector are clean and secure. • Measure resistance between Pins 1 and 8 on the valve block. • Is reading between 5 and 8 ohms?	Yes No	▲ SERVICE open or short to ground in Circuits 498 (PK) or 532 (O/Y) between valve block harness connector and ECU connector. GO to **E4**. ▲ REPLACE valve block. GO to **E4**.

84929159

4-WHEEL ABS TESTING — 1993 BRONCO

DIAGNOSIS AND TESTING (Continued)

FRONT RIGHT INLET SOLENOID VALVE CONCERN DIAGNOSIS — TEST D

	TEST STEP	RESULT	ACTION TO TAKE
D1	**SERVICE CODE 24: CHECK VALVE COIL CIRCUIT 497 AND THE ECU** • Ignition OFF. • Install pinout box. • Verify terminals at Pins 17 and 34 are clean and secure in the ECU connector. • Measure resistance between Pins 17 and 34. • Is reading between 5 and 8 ohms?	Yes No	▲ GO to **D4**. ▲ GO to **D2**.
D2	**CHECK VALVE COIL** • Disconnect 8-pin valve block connector. • Verify terminals on both halves of the valve block 8-way connector are clean and secure. • Measure resistance between Pins 1 and 5 on the valve block. • Is reading between 5 and 8 ohms?	Yes No	▲ SERVICE open or short to ground in Circuits 497 (W) or 532 (O/Y) between valve block harness connector and ECU connector. GO to **D4**. ▲ REPLACE valve block. GO to **D4**.
D3	**CHECK IF ALL STEPS HAVE BEEN COMPLETED** • This step requires that a valid diagnostic trouble code has been obtained, ALL prior diagnostic steps have been completed, and the affected wiring integrity has been verified. **CAUTION: If the above is not complete, changes are that replacement of this or any other system component without specific direction will not, in most circumstances, resolve the concern and will consequently result in customer dissatisfaction.** • Have all prior diagnostic steps been completed as described above?	Yes No	▲ REPLACE ECU. GO to **D4**. ▲ GO to last diagnostic step completed and continue.
D4	**VERIFY CONDITION RESOLVED** • Clear all codes. • Key OFF. • Retrieve code. • Is Code 16 set?	Yes No, Code 24 still exists No, different code is set No, Code 24 still exists and Step D2 is completed	▲ STOP. Concern has been corrected. ▲ GO to next pinpoint step. ▲ GO to appropriate pinpoint test. ▲ GO to **D5**.
D5	**VERIFY INTEGRITY OF VEHICLE WIRING** NOTE: If the above steps have been completed, the MOST LIKELY cause of the concern is wiring related. • Refer to the Intermittent Diagnosis Procedure and perform for ALL affected circuits as shown on the pinpoint test mini-schematic. • Does wiring check OK?	Yes No	▲ STOP. Repair is complete. ▲ GO to **D3**.

Pinpoint Test E — Code 25

Possible Code(s)

25 — Open circuit to valve block or ECU, open or shorted valve coil or internal ECU damage.

84929158

4-WHEEL ABS TESTING — 1993 BRONCO

DIAGNOSIS AND TESTING (Continued)

FRONT RIGHT OUTLET SOLENOID VALVE CONCERN DIAGNOSIS — TEST E (Continued)

	TEST STEP	RESULT		ACTION TO TAKE
E3	CHECK IF ALL STEPS HAVE BEEN COMPLETED			
	• This step requires that a valid diagnostic trouble code has been obtained, ALL prior diagnostic steps have been completed, and the affected wiring integrity has been verified.	Yes	▲	REPLACE ECU. GO to **E4**.
		No	▲	GO to last diagnostic step completed and continue.
	CAUTION: If the above is not complete, changes are that replacement of this or any other system component without specific direction will not, in most circumstances, resolve the concern and will consequently result in customer dissatisfaction.			
	• Have all prior diagnostic steps been completed as described above?			
E4	VERIFY CONDITION RESOLVED			
	• Clear all codes.	Yes	▲	STOP. Concern has been corrected.
	• Key OFF.	No, Code 25 still exists	▲	GO to next pinpoint step.
	• Retrieve code.	No, different code is set	▲	GO to appropriate pinpoint test.
	• Is Code 16 set?	No, Code 25 still exists and Step E2 is complete	▲	GO to E5.
E5	VERIFY INTEGRITY OF VEHICLE WIRING			
	NOTE: If the above steps have been completed, the MOST LIKELY cause of the concern is wiring related.	Yes	▲	STOP. Repair is complete.
	• Refer to the Intermittent Diagnosis Procedure and perform for ALL affected circuits as shown on the pinpoint test mini-schematic.	No	▲	GO to E3.
	• Does wiring check OK?			

Pinpoint Test F — Code 26

Possible Code(s)

26 — Open circuit to valve block or ECU, open or shorted valve coil or internal ECU damage.

84929160

4-WHEEL ABS TESTING — 1993 BRONCO

DIAGNOSIS AND TESTING (Continued)

Affected Circuit(s) / Electrical Component(s)

IRA ISOLATION (INLET) VALVE (5-6-12)

499 GY/BK
532 O/Y
532 O/Y

ALL VIEWS LOOKING INTO CONNECTOR

HARNESS SIDE — COMPONENT SIDE
HYDRAULIC UNIT CONNECTOR

ECU CONNECTOR HARNESS SIDE

532 O/Y
499 GY/BK
532 O/Y

Description

Code 26 is generated by the ECU's detection of an open or shorted Circuit 499 (GY / BK) and by an open or shorted inlet rear axle (IRA) valve coil or an open or shorted driver in the ECU.

Possible Contributing Component / Vehicle Wiring Concerns

- Intermittent open Circuit 499 (GY / BK)
- Terminal backout in ECU connector Pins 17 and 33
- Terminal backout in valve block connector Pins 1 and 3
- Open or shorted inlet rear axle (IRA) valve coil
- Open or shorted driver in ECU

REAR AXLE INLET SOLENOID VALVE CONCERN DIAGNOSIS — TEST F

	TEST STEP	RESULT		ACTION TO TAKE
F1	SERVICE CODE 26: CHECK VALVE COIL, CIRCUIT 499 AND THE ECU			
	• Ignition OFF.	Yes	▲	GO to **F4**.
	• Install pinout box.	No	▲	GO to **F2**.
	• Verify terminals at Pins 17 and 33 are clean and secure in the ECU connector.			
	• Measure resistance between Pins 17 and 33.			
	• Is reading between 5 and 8 ohms?			

84929161

4-WHEEL ABS TESTING — 1993 BRONCO

DIAGNOSIS AND TESTING (Continued)

REAR AXLE INLET SOLENOID VALVE CONCERN DIAGNOSIS — TEST F (Continued)

TEST STEP	RESULT	ACTION TO TAKE
F2 CHECK VALVE COIL • Disconnect 8-pin valve block connector. • Verify terminals in both halves of the valve block 8-way connector are clean and secure. • Measure resistance between Pins 1 and 3 on the valve block. • Is reading between 5 and 8 ohms?	Yes ▸	SERVICE open or short to ground in Circuits 499 (GY/BK) or 532 (O/Y) between the valve block harness connector and the ECU connector. GO to F4.
	No ▸	REPLACE valve block. GO to F4.
F3 CHECK IF ALL STEPS HAVE BEEN COMPLETED • This step requires that a valid diagnostic trouble code has been obtained, ALL prior diagnostic steps have been completed, and the affected wiring integrity has been verified. **CAUTION: If the above is not complete, changes are that replacement of this or any other system component without specific direction will not, in most circumstances, resolve the concern and will consequently result in customer dissatisfaction.** • Have all prior diagnostic steps been completed as described above?	Yes ▸ No ▸	REPLACE ECU. GO to F4. GO to last diagnostic step completed and continue.
F4 VERIFY CONDITION RESOLVED • Clear all codes. • Key OFF. • Retrieve code. • Is Code 16 set?	Yes ▸ No, Code 26 still exists ▸ No, different code is set ▸ No, Code 26 still exists and Step F2 is complete	STOP. Concern has been corrected. GO to next pinpoint step. GO to appropriate pinpoint test. GO to F5.
F5 VERIFY INTEGRITY OF VEHICLE WIRING NOTE: If the above steps have been completed, the MOST LIKELY cause of the concern is wiring related. • Refer to the Intermittent Diagnosis Procedure and perform for ALL affected circuits as shown on the pinpoint test mini-schematic. • Does wiring check OK?	Yes ▸ No ▸	STOP. Repair is complete. GO to F3.

Pinpoint Test G — Code 27

Possible Code(s)

27 — Open circuit to valve block or ECU, open or shorted valve coil or internal ECU damage.

4-WHEEL ABS TESTING — 1993 BRONCO

DIAGNOSIS AND TESTING (Continued)

Affected Circuit(s)/Electrical Component(s)

ORA DUMP (OUTLET) VALVE (5-6 Ω)
510 T/R 532 O/Y

HYDRAULIC UNIT CONNECTOR
COMPONENT SIDE HARNESS SIDE

ECU CONNECTOR HARNESS SIDE

ALL VIEWS LOOKING INTO CONNECTOR

Description

Code 27 is generated by the ECU's detection of an open or shorted Circuit 510 (T/R) and by an open or shorted outlet rear axle (ORA) valve coil or an open or shorted driver in the ECU.

Possible Contributing Component/Vehicle Wiring Concerns

- Intermittent open Circuit 510 (T/R)
- Terminal backout in ECU connector Pins 17 and 27
- Terminal backout in valve block connector Pins 1 and 2
- Open or shorted outlet rear axle (ORA) valve coil
- Open or shorted driver in ECU

REAR AXLE OUTLET SOLENOID CONCERN DIAGNOSIS — TEST G

TEST STEP	RESULT	ACTION TO TAKE
G1 SERVICE CODE 27: CHECK VALVE COIL, CIRCUIT 510 AND THE ECU • Ignition OFF. • Install pinout box. • Verify terminals at Pins 17 and 27 are clean and secure in the ECU connector. • Measure resistance between Pins 17 and 27. • Is reading between 5 and 8 ohms?	Yes ▸ No ▸	GO to G4. GO to G2.
G2 CHECK VALVE COIL • Disconnect 8-pin valve block connector. • Verify terminals on both halves of the valve block 8-way connector are clean and secure. • Measure resistance between Pins 1 and 2 on the valve block. • Is reading between 3 and 6 ohms?	Yes ▸ No ▸	SERVICE open or short to ground in Circuits 510 (T/R) or 532 (O/Y) between valve block harness connector and ECU connector. REPLACE valve block.

84929163

84929162

4-WHEEL ABS TESTING — 1993 BRONCO

DIAGNOSIS AND TESTING (Continued)

Affected Circuit(s)/Electrical Component(s)

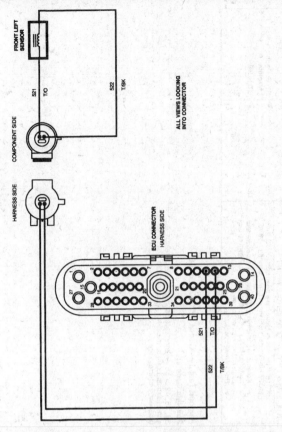

FRONT LEFT
SENSOR CONNECTOR

HARNESS SIDE   COMPONENT SIDE

FRONT LEFT
SENSOR

521   T/O

522   T/BK

ALL VIEWS LOOKING
INTO CONNECTOR

ECU CONNECTOR

HARNESS SIDE

521   T/O

522   T/BK

- Open or shorted front left sensor coil
- Open or shorted Circuit 521 (T/O) or 522 (T/BK)
- Damaged or missing tone rings
- Air gap too small or too large
- Excessive axle vibration
- Disturbances caused by ignition or RFI
- Defective trigger circuit in ECU

Description

Codes 31, 35, 41 or 55 are generated by the ECU's detection of an open or intermittent Circuit 521 (T/O) or 522 (T/BK); by misadjusted, loose or improperly installed sensor components; and by external interference or internal ECU concerns.

Possible Contributing Component/Vehicle Wiring Concerns

- Poor connection at front left wheel sensor
- Terminal backout on ECU connector pins

FRONT LEFT WHEEL SPEED SENSOR DIAGNOSIS — TEST H

TEST STEP	RESULT		ACTION TO TAKE
H1 SERVICE CODES: 31, 35, 41 OR 55 CHECK FRONT LEFT SENSOR • Ignition OFF. • Install pinout box. • Measure resistance between Pins 24 and 25. • Is reading between 800 and 1400 ohms?	Yes	▲	GO to H7.
	No	▲	GO to H2.

84929165

4-WHEEL ABS TESTING — 1993 BRONCO

DIAGNOSIS AND TESTING (Continued)

REAR AXLE OUTLET SOLENOID CONCERN DIAGNOSIS — TEST G (Continued)

TEST STEP	RESULT		ACTION TO TAKE
G3 CHECK IF ALL STEPS HAVE BEEN COMPLETED • This step requires that a valid diagnostic, trouble code has been obtained, ALL prior diagnostic steps have been completed, and the affected wiring integrity has been verified. **CAUTION: If the above is not complete, changes are that replacement of this or any other system component without specific direction will not, in most circumstances, resolve the concern and will consequently result in customer dissatisfaction.** • Have all prior diagnostic steps been completed as described above?	Yes	▲	REPLACE ECU. GO to G4.
	No	▲	GO to last diagnostic step completed and continue.
G4 VERIFY CONDITION RESOLVED • Clear all codes. • Key OFF. • Retrieve code. • Is Code 16 set?	Yes	▲	STOP. Concern has been corrected.
	No, Code 27 still exists	▲	GO to next pinpoint step.
	No, different code is set	▲	GO to appropriate pinpoint test.
	No, Code 27 still exists and Step G2 is complete	▲	GO to G5.
G5 VERIFY INTEGRITY OF VEHICLE WIRING NOTE: If the above steps have been completed, the MOST LIKELY cause of the concern is wiring related: • Refer to the Intermittent Diagnosis Procedure and perform for ALL affected circuits as shown on the pinpoint test mini-schematic. • Does wiring check OK?	Yes	▲	STOP. Repair is complete.
	No	▲	GO to G3.

Pinpoint Test H — Codes 31, 35, 41 or 55

Possible Code(s)

31, 35, 41 or 55 — Interrupted sensor signal, missing short term and long term sensor signal or radio frequency interference.

84929164

4-WHEEL ABS TESTING — 1993 BRONCO

DIAGNOSIS AND TESTING (Continued)

FRONT LEFT WHEEL SPEED SENSOR DIAGNOSIS — TEST H (Continued)

TEST STEP	RESULT	ACTION TO TAKE
H2 CHECK RESISTANCE AT FRONT LEFT WHEEL SENSOR • Disconnect left front sensor connector. • Measure resistance between the two pins on the sensor. • Is reading between 800 and 1400 ohms?	Yes ▶ No ▶	GO to **H3**. REPLACE sensor. GO to **H10**.
H3 CHECK CIRCUIT 521 (T/O) CONTINUITY • Measure resistance between pinout box Pin 24 and wheel sensor harness connector Pin 2. • Is there continuity (zero or near zero ohms)?	Yes ▶ No ▶	GO to **H4**. REPAIR open or high resistance on Circuit 521 (T/O). GO to **H10**.
H4 CHECK CIRCUIT 522 (T/BK) CONTINUITY • Measure resistance between pinout box Pin 25 and wheel sensor harness connector Pin 1. • Is there continuity (zero or near zero ohms)?	Yes ▶ No ▶	GO to **H5**. REPAIR open or high resistance on Circuit 522 (T/BK). GO to **H10**.
H5 CHECK CIRCUIT 521 (T/O) SHORT TO GROUND • Disconnect left front wheel sensor connector. • Measure resistance between Pins 60 and 24 on pinout box. • Is there continuity?	Yes ▶ No ▶	REPAIR short to ground on Circuit 521 (T/O). GO to **H10**. GO to **H6**.
H6 CHECK CIRCUIT 522 (T/BK) SHORT TO GROUND • Measure resistance between Pins 60 and 25 on pinout box. • Is there continuity?	Yes ▶ No ▶	REPAIR short to ground on Circuit 522 (T/BK). GO to **H10**. GO to **H7**.
H7 CHECK FL SENSOR OUTPUT AT ECU • Key OFF. • Install pinout box. • Raise vehicle so that left front wheel is off the ground. • Remove left front wheel. Knock back the caliper so that the wheel can move as freely as possible. Remount the wheel. • Place transfer case in 4x4 LOW. Key ON and allow wheel to spin at engine idle speed. • Set the Hand-Held Automotive Meter, Rotunda 105-00053 or equivalent to the frequency counter (Hz) setting. Measure and record the frequency between pinout box Pins 24 and 25. • Change the meter to the A/C mV setting. Measure and record the voltage output between pinout box Pins 24 and 25. • Determine the sensor output in mV/Hz: • Output = Voltage/Frequency • Is the sensor output greater than 3.4 mV/Hz?	Yes ▶ No ▶	GO to **H10**. GO to **H8**.
H8 CHECK FL SENSOR OUTPUT AT SENSOR • Key OFF. • Place the transfer case in 4x4 LOW. Key ON and allow wheel to spin at engine idle speed. • Set the Hand-Held Automotive Meter, Rotunda 105-00053 or equivalent to the frequency counter (Hz) setting. Measure and record the frequency across the two pins of the sensor component connector. • Change the meter to the A/C mV setting. Measure and record the voltage output across the two pins of the sensor component connector. • Determine the sensor output in mV/Hz: • Output = Voltage/Frequency • Is the sensor output greater than 3.4 mV/Hz?	Yes ▶ No ▶	Sensor is OK. REPAIR sensor open or short to ground on Circuits 521 (T/O) or 522 (T/BK). GO to **H10**. REPLACE sensor. GO to **H10**.

84929166

4-WHEEL ABS TESTING — 1993 BRONCO

DIAGNOSIS AND TESTING (Continued)

FRONT LEFT WHEEL SPEED SENSOR DIAGNOSIS — TEST H (Continued)

TEST STEP	RESULT	ACTION TO TAKE
H9 CHECK IF ALL STEPS HAVE BEEN COMPLETED • This step requires that a valid diagnostic trouble code has been obtained, ALL prior diagnostic steps have been completed, and the affected wiring integrity has been verified. **CAUTION:** If the above is not complete, changes are that replacement of this or any other system component without specific direction will not, in most circumstances, resolve the concern and will consequently result in customer dissatisfaction. • Have all prior diagnostic steps been completed as described above?	Yes ▶ No ▶	REPLACE sensor. GO to **H10**. If no resolution, REPLACE ECU. GO to **H10**. GO to last diagnostic step completed and continue.
H10 VERIFY CONDITION RESOLVED • Clear all codes. • Key OFF. • Retrieve code. • Is Code 16 set?	Yes ▶ No, code being serviced still exists ▶ No, different code is set ▶ No, code being serviced still exists and Step H8 is completed ▶	STOP. Concern has been corrected. GO to next pinpoint step. GO to appropriate pinpoint test. GO to **H11**.
H11 VERIFY INTEGRITY OF VEHICLE WIRING NOTE: If the above steps have been completed, the MOST LIKELY cause of the concern is wiring related. • Refer to the Intermittent Diagnosis Procedure and perform for ALL affected circuits as shown on the pinpoint test mini-schematic. • Does wiring check OK?	Yes ▶ No ▶	STOP. Repair is complete. GO to **H9**.

Pinpoint Test J — Codes 32, 36, 42 or 56 — Interrupted sensor signal missing short term and long term sensor signal or radio frequency interference.

Possible Code(s)

32, 36, 42 or 56

84929167

4-WHEEL ABS TESTING — 1993 BRONCO

DIAGNOSIS AND TESTING (Continued)

Affected Circuit(s)/Electrical Component(s)

- Open or shorted front right sensor coil
- Open or shorted Circuit 516 (Y/BK) or 514 (Y/R)
- Damaged or missing tone rings
- Air gap too small or too large
- Excessive axle vibration
- Disturbances caused by ignition or RFI
- Defective trigger circuit in ECU

Description

Codes 32, 36, 42 or 56 are generated by the ECU's detection of an open or intermittent Circuit 516 (Y/BK) or 514 (Y/R); by misadjusted, loose or improperly installed sensor components; and by external interference or internal ECU concerns.

Possible Contributing Component/Vehicle Wiring Concerns

- Poor connection at front right wheel sensor
- Terminal backout in ECU connector pins

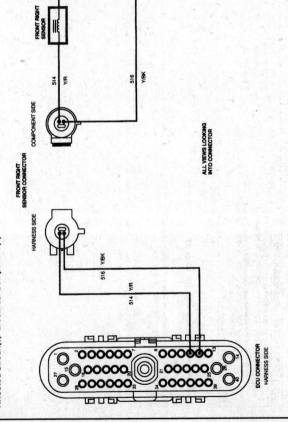

FRONT RIGHT SENSOR — COMPONENT SIDE — FRONT RIGHT SENSOR CONNECTOR — HARNESS SIDE — 514 Y/R — 516 Y/BK — ECU CONNECTOR HARNESS SIDE — ALL VIEWS LOOKING INTO CONNECTOR

84929168

FRONT RIGHT WHEEL SPEED SENSOR DIAGNOSIS — TEST J

	TEST STEP	RESULT	ACTION TO TAKE
J1	SERVICE CODES: 32, 36, 42 OR 56 CHECK FRONT RIGHT SENSOR • Ignition OFF. • Install pinout box. • Measure resistance between Pins 23 and 36. • Is reading between 800 and 1400 ohms?	Yes No	► GO to J7. ► GO to J2.

4-WHEEL ABS TESTING — 1993 BRONCO

DIAGNOSIS AND TESTING (Continued)

FRONT RIGHT WHEEL SPEED SENSOR DIAGNOSIS — TEST J (Continued)

	TEST STEP	RESULT	ACTION TO TAKE
J2	CHECK RESISTANCE AT FRONT RIGHT WHEEL SENSOR • Disconnect right front sensor connector. • Measure resistance between the two pins on the sensor. • Is reading between 800 and 1400 ohms?	Yes No	► GO to J3. ► REPLACE sensor. GO to J10.
J3	CHECK CIRCUIT 516 (Y/BK) CONTINUITY • Measure resistance between pinout box Pin 23 and wheel sensor harness connector Pin 2. • Is there continuity (Zero or near zero ohms)?	Yes No	► GO to J4. ► REPAIR open or high resistance on Circuit 516 (Y/BK). GO to J10.
J4	CHECK CIRCUIT 514 (Y/R) CONTINUITY • Measure resistance between pinout box Pin 36 and wheel sensor harness connector Pin 1. • Is there continuity (Zero or near zero ohms)?	Yes No	► REVERIFY symptoms. ► REPAIR open or high resistance on Circuit 514 (Y/R). GO to J10.
J5	CHECK CIRCUIT 516 (Y/BK) SHORT TO GROUND • Disconnect right front wheel sensor connector. • Measure resistance between Pins 60 and 23 on pinout box. • Is there continuity?	Yes No	► REPAIR short to ground on Circuit 516 (Y/BK). GO to J10. ► GO to J6.
J6	CHECK CIRCUIT 514 (Y/R) SHORT TO GROUND • Measure resistance between Pins 60 and 36 on pinout box. • Is there continuity?	Yes No	► REPAIR short to ground on Circuit 514 (Y/R). GO to J10. ► GO to J7.
J7	CHECK FR SENSOR OUTPUT AT ECU • Key OFF. • Install pinout box. • Raise vehicle so that right front wheel is off the ground. • Remove left front wheel. Knock back the caliper so that the wheel can move as freely as possible. Remount the wheel. • Place transfer case in 4x4 LOW. Key ON and allow wheel to spin at engine idle speed. • Set the Hand-Held Automotive Meter, Rotunda 105-00053 or equivalent to the frequency counter (Hz) setting. Measure and record the frequency between pinout box Pins 23 and 36. • Change the meter to the A/C mV setting. Measure and record the voltage output between pinout box Pins 23 and 36. • Determine the sensor output in mV/Hz: Output = Voltage/Frequency • Is the sensor output greater than 3.4 mV/Hz?	Yes No	► GO to J10. ► GO to J8.
J8	CHECK FR SENSOR OUTPUT AT SENSOR • Key OFF. • Place transfer case in 4x4 LOW. Key ON and allow wheel to spin at engine idle speed. • Set the Hand-Held Automotive Meter, Rotunda 105-00053 or equivalent to the frequency counter (Hz) setting. Measure and record the frequency across the two pins of the sensor component connector. • Change the meter to the A/C mV setting. Measure and record the voltage output across the two pins of the sensor component connector. • Determine the sensor output in mV/Hz: Output = Voltage/Frequency • Is the sensor output greater than 3.4 mV/Hz?	Yes No	► Sensor is OK. REPAIR open or short to ground on Circuits 514 (Y/R) or 516 (Y/BK). GO to J10. ► REPLACE sensor. GO to J10.

84929169

4-WHEEL ABS TESTING — 1993 BRONCO

DIAGNOSIS AND TESTING (Continued)

FRONT RIGHT WHEEL SPEED SENSOR DIAGNOSIS — TEST J (Continued)

TEST STEP	RESULT	ACTION TO TAKE
J9 CHECK IF ALL STEPS HAVE BEEN COMPLETED • This step requires that a valid diagnostic trouble code has been obtained, ALL prior diagnostic steps have been completed, and the affected wiring integrity has been verified. **CAUTION:** If the above is not complete, changes are that replacement of this or any other system component without specific direction will not, in most circumstances, resolve the concern and will consequently result in customer dissatisfaction. • Have all prior diagnostic steps been completed as described above?	Yes No	▲ REPLACE sensor. GO to J10. If no resolution, REPLACE ECU. GO to J10. ▲ GO to last diagnostic step completed and continue.
J10 VERIFY CONDITION RESOLVED • Clear all codes. • Key OFF. • Retrieve code. • Is Code 16 set?	Yes No, code being serviced still exists No, different code is set No, code being serviced still exists and Step J8 is complete	▲ STOP. Concern has been corrected. ▲ GO to next pinpoint step. ▲ GO to appropriate pinpoint test. ▲ GO to J11.
J11 VERIFY INTEGRITY OF VEHICLE WIRING NOTE: If the above steps have been completed, the MOST LIKELY cause of the concern is wiring related. • Refer to the Intermittent Diagnosis Procedure and perform for ALL affected circuits as shown on the pinpoint test mini-schematic. • Does wiring check OK?	Yes No	▲ STOP. Repair is complete. ▲ GO to **J9**.

Pinpoint Test K — Codes 33, 37, 43 or 57

Possible Code(s)

33, 37, 43 or 57 — Interrupted sensor signal, missing short term and long term sensor signal or radio frequency interference.

4-WHEEL ABS TESTING — 1993 BRONCO

DIAGNOSIS AND TESTING (Continued)

Affected Circuit(s)/Electrical Component(s)

REAR SENSOR CONNECTOR — HARNESS SIDE / COMPONENT SIDE
REAR SENSOR — 519 LG/BK, 518 LG/R
ECU CONNECTOR — HARNESS SIDE
ALL VIEWS LOOKING INTO CONNECTOR

Description

Codes 33, 37, 43 or 57 are generated by the ECU's detection of an open or intermittent Circuit 518 (LG/R) or 519 (LG/BK); by misadjusted, loose or improperly installed sensor components; and by external interference or internal ECU concerns.

Possible Contributing Component/Vehicle Wiring Concerns

- Poor connection at rear axle wheel sensor
- Terminal backout in ECU connector pins
- Open or shorted front left sensor coil
- Open or shorted Circuit 519 (LG/BK) or 518 (LG/R)
- Damaged or missing tone rings
- Air gap too small or too large
- Excessive axle vibration
- Disturbances caused by ignition or RFI
- Defective trigger circuit in ECU

REAR AXLE WHEEL SPEED SENSOR DIAGNOSIS — TEST K

TEST STEP	RESULT	ACTION TO TAKE
K1 SERVICE CODES 33, 37, 43 OR 57: CHECK REAR AXLE SENSOR • Ignition OFF. • Install pinout box. • Measure resistance between Pins 21 and 22. • Is reading between 1300 and 1550 ohms? NOTE: Rear differential reading can be between 1300-2100 ohms.	Yes No	▲ GO to K7. ▲ GO to K2.

4-WHEEL ABS TESTING — 1993 BRONCO

DIAGNOSIS AND TESTING (Continued)

REAR AXLE WHEEL SPEED SENSOR DIAGNOSIS — TEST K (Continued)

	TEST STEP	RESULT	ACTION TO TAKE
K2	**CHECK RESISTANCE AT REAR AXLE SENSOR** • Disconnect rear axle sensor connector. • Measure resistance between the two pins on the sensor. • Is reading between 800 and 1400 ohms?	Yes No	GO to **K3**. REPLACE sensor. GO to **K10**.
K3	**CHECK CIRCUIT 519 (LG/BK) CONTINUITY** • Measure resistance between pinout box Pin 21 and wheel speed sensor harness connector Pin 2. • Is there continuity (zero or near zero ohms)?	Yes No	GO to **K4**. REPAIR open or high resistance on Circuit 519 (LG/BK). GO to **K10**.
K4	**CHECK CIRCUIT 518 (LG/R) CONTINUITY** • Measure resistance between pinout box Pin 22 and wheel speed sensor harness connector Pin 1. • Is there continuity (zero or near zero ohms)?	Yes No	REVERIFY symptoms. REPAIR open or high resistance on Circuit 518 (LG/R). GO to **K10**.
K5	**CHECK CIRCUIT 519 (LG/BK) SHORT TO GROUND** • Disconnect rear axle sensor connector. • Measure resistance between Pins 60 and 21 on pinout box. • Is there continuity?	Yes No	REPAIR short to ground on Circuit 519 (LG/BK). GO to **K10**. GO to **K6**.
K6	**CHECK CIRCUIT 518 (LG/R) SHORT TO GROUND** • Measure resistance between Pins 60 and 22 on pinout box. • Is there continuity?	Yes No	REPAIR short to ground on Circuit 518 (LG/R). GO to **K10**. GO to **K7**.
K7	**CHECK REAR AXLE SENSOR OUTPUT AT ECU** • Key OFF. • Install pinout box. • Raise vehicle so that the rear wheels are off the ground. • Place transfer case in 4x4 LOW. • Key ON and allow wheels to spin at engine idle speed. • Set the Hand-Held Automotive Meter, Rotunda 105-00053 or equivalent to the frequency counter (Hz) setting. Measure and record the frequency between pinout box Pins 23 and 36. • Change the meter to the A/C mV setting. Measure and record the voltage output between pinout box Pins 23 and 36. • Determine the sensor output in mV/Hz: Output = Voltage/Frequency • Is the sensor output greater than 6 mV/Hz?	Yes No	GO to **K10**. GO to **K8**.
K8	**CHECK REAR AXLE SENSOR OUTPUT AT SENSOR** • Key OFF. • Place transfer case in 4x4 LOW. • Key ON and allow wheels to spin at engine idle speed. • Set the Hand-Held Automotive Meter, Rotunda 105-00053 or equivalent to the frequency counter (Hz) setting. Measure and record the frequency across the two pins of the sensor component connector. • Change the meter to the A/C mV setting. Measure and record the voltage output across the two pins of the sensor component connector. • Determine the sensor output in mV/Hz: Output = Voltage/Frequency • Is the sensor output greater than 6 mV/Hz?	Yes No	Sensor is OK. REPAIR open or short to ground on Circuits 519 (LG/BK) or 523 (R/PK). GO to **K10**. REPLACE sensor. GO to **K10**.

DIAGNOSIS AND TESTING (Continued)

REAR AXLE WHEEL SPEED SENSOR DIAGNOSIS — TEST K (Continued)

	TEST STEP	RESULT	ACTION TO TAKE
K9	**CHECK IF ALL STEPS HAVE BEEN COMPLETED** • This step requires that a valid diagnostic trouble code has been obtained, ALL prior diagnostic steps have been completed, and the affected wiring integrity has been verified. **CAUTION: If the above is not complete, changes are that replacement of this or any other system component without specific direction will not, in most circumstances, resolve the concern and will consequently result in customer dissatisfaction.** • Have all prior diagnostic steps been completed as described above?	Yes No	REPLACE sensor. GO to **K10**. If no resolution, REPLACE ECU. GO to **K10**. GO to last diagnostic step completed and continue.
K10	**VERIFY CONDITION RESOLVED** • Clear all codes. • Key OFF. • Retrieve code. • Is Code 16 set?	Yes No, code being serviced still exists No, different code is set No, code being serviced still exists and Step K8 is complete	STOP. Concern has been corrected. GO to next pinpoint step. GO to appropriate pinpoint test. GO to **K11**.
K11	**VERIFY INTEGRITY OF VEHICLE WIRING** NOTE: If the above steps have been completed, the MOST LIKELY cause of the concern is wiring related. • Refer to the Intermittent Diagnosis Procedure and perform for ALL affected circuits as shown on the pinpoint test mini-schematic. • Does wiring check OK?	Yes No	STOP. Repair is complete. GO to **K9**.

Pinpoint Test L — Code 51

Possible Code(s)

51 — Hydraulically inoperative front left outlet valve, pinched or closed brake line or hose, worn or clogged valve.

4-WHEEL ABS TESTING — 1993 BRONCO

DIAGNOSIS AND TESTING (Continued)

Affected Circuit(s)/Electrical Component(s)

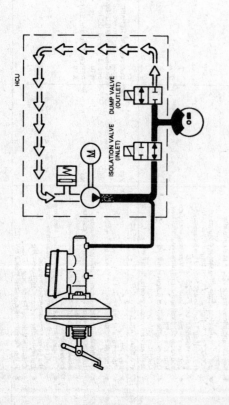

Description

Code 51 is generated by the ECU's detection of a sensor disturbance or hydraulically inoperative left front outlet valve.

Possible Contributing Component/Vehicle Wiring Concerns

- Pinched or closed brake line or hose
- Worn or clogged front left outlet valve

HYDRAULICALLY INOPERATIVE FRONT LEFT OUTLET VALVE OR SENSOR DISTURBANCE DETECTED DIAGNOSIS — TEST L

	TEST STEP	RESULT	ACTION TO TAKE
L1	CHECK BRAKE LINES/HOSES • Visually inspect brake lines from valve block to front left wheel. • Are they damaged?	Yes No	REPLACE/REPAIR brake lines. GO to L2.
L2	SERVICE CODE 51: CHECK FRONT LEFT OUTLET VALVE • Key OFF. • Install pinout box. • Jumper pinout box Pins 19, 26, 40, and 60 together. • Raise vehicle so front left wheel is just off the ground. • Press hard on the brake pedal and have an assistant try to turn the wheel. • Does the wheel turn or the pedal drop slowly? NOTE: This condition is similar to the master cylinder bypass condition. It is important that the pedal be quickly and forcefully applied to rule out master cylinder bypass as the cause if a hydraulic leak is detected. Typically, master cylinder bypass only occurs at low line pressures.	Yes No	REPLACE HCU. BLEED Brake System. GO to L4. GO to L3.

84929174

4-WHEEL ABS TESTING — 1993 BRONCO

DIAGNOSIS AND TESTING (Continued)

HYDRAULICALLY INOPERATIVE FRONT LEFT OUTLET VALVE OR SENSOR DISTURBANCE DETECTED DIAGNOSIS — TEST L (Continued)

	TEST STEP	RESULT	ACTION TO TAKE
L3	CHECK FRONT LEFT OUTLET VALVE OPERATION • Apply brake pedal force, turn ignition on and have assistant try to turn wheel. CAUTION: Do not leave ignition on for more than 30 seconds with the jumper installed. • Does wheel turn now?	Yes No	VALVE is OK. GO to Drive Test — Code 16 Step DT1.1. REPLACE valve block.
L4	VERIFY CONDITION RESOLVED • Clear all codes. • Key OFF. • Retrieve code. • Is Code 16 set?	Yes No, code being serviced still exists No, different code is set	STOP. Concern has been corrected. GO to next pinpoint step. GO to appropriate pinpoint test.

Pinpoint Test M — Code 52

Possible Code(s)

52 — Hydraulically inoperative front right outlet valve, pinched or closed brake line or hose, worn or clogged valve.

Affected Circuit(s)/Electrical Component(s)

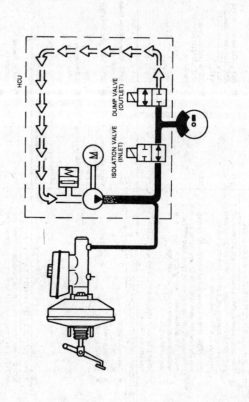

84929175

4-WHEEL ABS TESTING — 1993 BRONCO

DIAGNOSIS AND TESTING (Continued)

Affected Circuit(s)/Electrical Component(s)

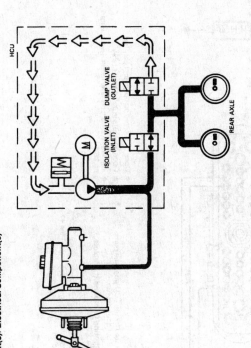

Description

Code 53 is generated by the ECU's detection of a hydraulically inoperative rear axle outlet valve.

Possible Contributing Component/Vehicle Wiring Concerns
- Pinched or closed brake line or hose
- Worn or clogged rear axle outlet valve

HYDRAULICALLY INOPERATIVE REAR AXLE OUTLET VALVE OR SENSOR DISTURBANCE DETECTED DIAGNOSIS — TEST N

	TEST STEP	RESULT	ACTION TO TAKE
N1	CHECK BRAKE LINES • Visually inspect brake lines from valve block to rear wheel. • Are lines damaged?	Yes	REPAIR/REPLACE lines.
		No	GO to **N2**.
N2	SERVICE CODE 53: CHECK REAR AXLE OUTLET VALVE • Key OFF. • Install pinout box. • Jumper pinout box Pins 19, 27, 33, and 60 together. • Raise vehicle so rear wheels are just off the ground. • Press hard on the brake pedal and have an assistant try to turn a rear wheel. • Does the wheel turn or the pedal drop slowly? NOTE: This condition is similar to the master cylinder bypass condition. It is important that the pedal be quickly and forcefully applied to rule out master cylinder bypass as the cause if a hydraulic leak is detected. Typically, master cylinder bypass only occurs at low line pressures.	Yes	REPLACE HCU. BLEED Brake System. GO to **N4**.
		No	GO to **N3**.

84929177

4-WHEEL ABS TESTING — 1993 BRONCO

DIAGNOSIS AND TESTING (Continued)

Description

Code 52 is generated by the ECU's detection of a hydraulically inoperative right front outlet valve.

Possible Contributing Component/Vehicle Wiring Concerns
- Pinched or closed brake line or hose
- Worn or clogged front right outlet valve

HYDRAULICALLY INOPERATIVE RIGHT FRONT OUTLET VALVE OR SENSOR DISTURBANCE DETECTED DIAGNOSIS — TEST M

	TEST STEP	RESULT	ACTION TO TAKE
M1	CHECK BRAKE LINES/HOSES • Visually inspect brake lines from valve block to right front wheel. • Are lines damaged?	Yes	REPAIR/REPLACE lines.
		No	GO to **M2**.
M2	SERVICE CODE 52: CHECK FRONT RIGHT OUTLET VALVE • Key OFF. • Install pinout box. • Jumper pinout box Pins 15, 19, 34, and 60 together. • Raise vehicle so front right wheel is just off the ground. • Press hard on the brake pedal and have an assistant try to turn the wheel. • Does the wheel turn or the pedal drop slowly? NOTE: This condition is similar to the master cylinder bypass condition. It is important that the pedal be quickly and forcefully applied to rule out master cylinder bypass as the cause if a hydraulic leak is detected. Typically, master cylinder bypass only occurs at low line pressures.	Yes	REPLACE HCU. BLEED Brake System. GO to **M4**.
		No	GO to **M3**.
M3	CHECK FRONT RIGHT OUTLET VALVE OPERATION • Apply brake pedal force, turn ignition ON and have assistant try to turn wheel. CAUTION: Do not leave ignition on for more than 30 seconds with the jumper installed. • Does wheel turn now?	Yes	VALVE is OK. GO to Drive Test — Code 16, Step DT1.1.
		No	REPLACE valve block.
M4	VERIFY CONDITION RESOLVED • Clear all codes. • Key OFF. • Retrieve code. • Is Code 16 set?	Yes	STOP. Concern has been corrected.
		No, code being serviced still exists	GO to next pinpoint step.
		No, different code is set	GO to appropriate pinpoint test.

Pinpoint Test N — Code 53

Possible Code(s)

53 — Hydraulically inoperative rear axle outlet valve, pinched or closed brake line or hose, worn or clogged valve.

84929176

4-WHEEL ABS TESTING — 1993 BRONCO

DIAGNOSIS AND TESTING (Continued)

HYDRAULICALLY INOPERATIVE REAR AXLE OUTLET VALVE OR SENSOR DISTURBANCE DETECTED DIAGNOSIS — TEST N (Continued)

	TEST STEP		RESULT	▲	ACTION TO TAKE
N3	CHECK REAR AXLE OUTLET VALVE OPERATION				
	● Apply brake pedal force, turn ignition on and have assistant try to turn wheel.		Yes	▲	Valve is OK. GO to Drive Test — Code 16, Step DT 1.1.
	CAUTION: Do not leave ignition on for more than 30 seconds with the jumper installed.		No	▲	REPLACE valve block.
	● Does wheel turn now?				
N4	VERIFY CONDITION RESOLVED		Yes	▲	STOP. Concern has been corrected.
	● Clear all codes.		No, code being serviced still exists	▲	GO to next pinpoint step.
	● Key OFF.				
	● Retrieve code.		No, different code is set	▲	GO to appropriate pinpoint test.
	● Is Code 16 set?				

Pinpoint Test P — Code 63

Possible Code(s)

63 — Open or intermittent connection to relay pump motor, damaged relay coil or contacts, damaged pump motor.

84929178

DIAGNOSIS AND TESTING (Continued)

Affected Circuit(s)/Electrical Component(s)

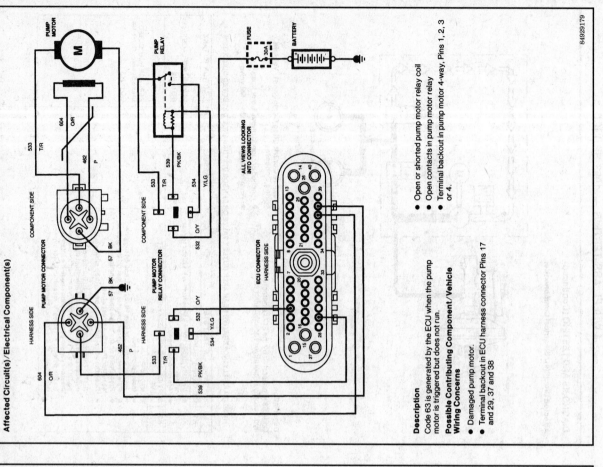

ALL VIEWS LOOKING INTO CONNECTOR

Description

Code 63 is generated by the ECU when the pump motor is triggered but does not run.

Possible Contributing Component/Vehicle Wiring Concerns

● Damaged pump motor.
● Terminal backout in ECU harness connector Pins 17 and 29, 37 and 38

● Open or shorted pump motor relay coil
● Open contacts in pump motor relay
● Terminal backout in pump motor 4-way, Pins 1, 2, 3 or 4.

84929179

4-WHEEL ABS TESTING — 1993 BRONCO

DIAGNOSIS AND TESTING (Continued)

MOTOR TRIGGERED BUT DID NOT RUN (CODE 63) — TEST P

	TEST STEP	RESULT	ACTION TO TAKE
P1	VISUAL INSPECTION AND EQUIPMENT HOOK-UP • Make sure the battery is OK. Refer to Section 14-01. • Inspect ECU pins, 30 amp fuse, battery and ground connections, relay connections and pump motor connections. • Remove ECU, install breakout box and verify ground. • Jumper Pins 60 and 19 together. • Key ON (energize system relay). • Jumper Pins 60 and 29 together (energize pump motor relay). • Is pump motor running?	Yes No	GO to P8. GO to P2.
P2	VOLTAGE CHECK, PINS 1 AND 4 • Disconnect 4-pin pump motor connector. • Measure voltage between Pins 1 and 4. • Is there at least 8 volts?	Yes No	REPLACE HCU. GO to P11. GO to P3.
P3	CHECK PIN 1 GROUND • Check for continuity between Pin 1 and a known good chassis ground. • Is there continuity?	Yes No	GO to P4. REPAIR open in Circuit 57 (BK). GO to P11.
P4	CONTINUITY CHECK, CIRCUIT 533 (T/R) • Key OFF. • Disconnect pump motor relay. • Check continuity on Circuit 533 (T/R). • Is there continuity?	Yes No	GO to P5. REPAIR open in Circuit 532 (O/Y). GO to P11.
P5	CONTINUITY CHECK, PUMP MOTOR RELAY TO SYSTEM RELAY • Remove system relay. • Check continuity between pump motor relay Circuit 532 (O/Y) and system relay Circuit 533 (T/R). • Is there continuity?	Yes No	GO to P6. REPAIR Circuit 532 (O/Y). GO to P11.
P6	CONTINUITY CHECK, PUMP MOTOR RELAY CIRCUIT 534 (Y/LG) • Check continuity from pump motor relay Circuit 534 (Y/LG) to battery connection point. • Is there continuity?	Yes No	GO to P7. REPAIR open in Circuit 534 (Y/LG) or REPLACE 30A fuse. GO to P11.
P7	CONTINUITY CHECK, PUMP MOTOR RELAY CIRCUIT 539 (PK/BK) • Check continuity from pump motor relay Circuit 539 (PK/BK) to breakout box Pin 29. • Is there continuity?	Yes No	REPLACE pump motor relay. GO to P11. REPAIR open in Circuit 539 (PK/BK). GO to P11.
P8	CHECK MOTOR SPEED SENSOR RESISTANCE • Key OFF. • Connect digital volt-ohmmeter to pinout box Pins 37 and 38 and measure resistance. • Is resistance between 5-40 ohms?	Yes No	GO to P9. REPLACE HCU. BLEED brake system. GO to P11.
P9	CHECK MOTOR SPEED SENSOR OUTPUT • Switch Rotunda Hand-Held Automotive Meter 105-00063, or equivalent, to frequency (Hz). • Key ON. • Measure motor speed sensor output. • Is output between 70-150 Hz?	Yes No	GO to P11. REPLACE HCU. BLEED brake system. GO to P11.

84929180

4-WHEEL ABS TESTING — 1993 BRONCO

DIAGNOSIS AND TESTING (Continued)

MOTOR TRIGGERED BUT DID NOT RUN (CODE 63) — TEST P (Continued)

	TEST STEP	RESULT	ACTION TO TAKE
P10	CHECK IF ALL STEPS HAVE BEEN COMPLETED • This step requires that a valid diagnostic trouble code has been obtained, ALL prior diagnostic steps have been completed, and the affected wiring integrity has been verified. CAUTION: If the above is not complete, changes are that replacement of this or any other system component without specific direction will not, in most circumstances, resolve the concern and will consequently result in customer dissatisfaction. • Have all prior diagnostic steps been completed as described above?	Yes No	REPLACE ECU. GO to P11. GO to last diagnostic step completed and continue.
P11	VERIFY CONDITION RESOLVED • Clear all codes. • Key OFF. • Retrieve code. • Is Code 16 set?	Yes No, Code 63 still exists No, different code is set No, Code 63 still exists and Step P9 is complete	STOP. Concern has been corrected. GO to next pinpoint step. GO to appropriate pinpoint test. GO to P12.
P12	VERIFY INTEGRITY OF VEHICLE WIRING NOTE: If the above steps have been completed, the MOST LIKELY cause of the concern is wiring related. • Refer to the Intermittent Diagnosis Procedure and perform for ALL affected circuits as shown on the pinpoint test mini-schematic. • Does wiring check OK?	Yes No	STOP. Repair is complete. GO to P10.

Pinpoint Test Q — Code 65

Possible Code(s)

65 — Intermittent or open connection between ECU and acceleration switch, damaged acceleration switch or circuit in ECU.

84929181

4-WHEEL ABS TESTING — 1993 BRONCO

DIAGNOSIS AND TESTING (Continued)

ACCELERATION SENSOR (CODE 65) — TEST Q

	TEST STEP	RESULT	ACTION TO TAKE
Q1	**RESISTANCE CHECK, SENSOR RAISED 38MM (1.5 IN)** • Disconnect acceleration sensor harness connector. • Remove the acceleration sensor from vehicle. • Check for water or terminal corrosion. Service as necessary. • Place acceleration sensor on a level surface and raise the front of the sensor 38mm (1.5 in). • Measure the resistance between Circuits 836 (O/W) and 886 (O/BK). • Is the resistance greater than 5 ohms (open circuit)?	Yes No	▲ GO to **Q2**. ▲ REPLACE the sensor. GO to **Q12**.
Q2	**RESISTANCE CHECK, SENSOR RAISED 25.4MM (1.0 IN)** • Place acceleration sensor on a level surface and raise the front of the sensor 25.4mm (1.0 in). • Measure the resistance between Circuits 836 (O/W) and 887 (Y). • Is the resistance greater than 5 ohms (open circuit)?	Yes No	▲ Acceleration switch OK. GO to **Q3**. ▲ REPLACE the sensor. GO to **Q12**.
Q3	**RESISTANCE CHECK ECU PIN 32 AND ACCELERATION SENSOR PIN 1** • Disconnect ECU. • Disconnect acceleration sensor. • Measure resistance between ECU Pin 32 and acceleration sensor Pin 1. • Is resistance less than 5 ohms?	Yes No	▲ GO to **Q4**. ▲ REPAIR Circuit 836 (O/W) between ECU and acceleration sensor. GO to **Q12**.
Q4	**RESISTANCE CHECK ECU PIN 31 AND ACCELERATION SENSOR PIN 2** • Measure resistance between ECU Pin 31 and acceleration sensor Pin 2. • Is resistance less than 5 ohms?	Yes No	▲ GO to **Q5**. ▲ REPAIR Circuit 887 (Y) between ECU and acceleration sensor. GO to **Q12**.
Q5	**RESISTANCE CHECK ECU PIN 30 AND ACCELERATION SENSOR PIN 3** • Measure resistance between ECU Pin 30 and acceleration sensor Pin 3. • Is resistance less than 5 ohms?	Yes No	▲ RECONNECT acceleration switch. GO to **Q6**. ▲ REPAIR Circuit 886 (O/BK) between ECU and acceleration sensor. GO to **Q12**.
Q6	**RESISTANCE CHECK, ECU PIN 32 TO GROUND** • Measure resistance between ECU Pin 32 and ground. • Is resistance greater than 5 ohms?	Yes No	▲ GO to **Q7**. ▲ REPAIR Circuit 836 (O/W) between ECU and acceleration sensor. GO to **Q12**.
Q7	**RESISTANCE CHECK, ECU PIN 31 TO GROUND** • Measure resistance between ECU Pin 31 and ground. • Is resistance greater than 5 ohms?	Yes No	▲ GO to **Q8**. ▲ REPAIR Circuit 887 (Y) between ECU and acceleration sensor. GO to **Q12**.
Q8	**RESISTANCE CHECK, ECU PIN 30 TO GROUND** • Measure resistance between ECU Pin 30 and ground. • Is resistance greater than 5 ohms?	Yes No	▲ GO to **Q9**. ▲ REPAIR Circuit 886 (O/BK) between ECU and acceleration sensor. GO to **Q12**.

84929183

4-WHEEL ABS TESTING — 1993 BRONCO

DIAGNOSIS AND TESTING (Continued)

Affected Circuit(s)/Electrical Component(s)

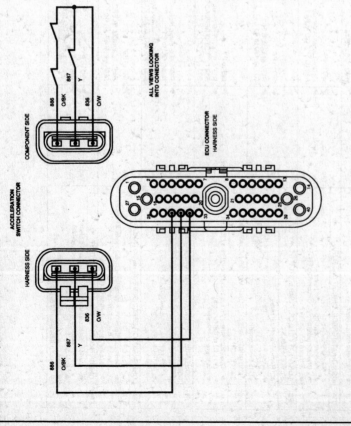

Description

Code 65 is generated by the ECU's detection of an open circuit between the ECU and the acceleration switch and by a failed acceleration switch or internal ECU damage.

Possible Contributing Component/Vehicle Wiring Concerns

- Terminal backout in ECU wiring harness connector Pins 30, 31 and 32.
- Worn or damaged acceleration switch.
- Worn or damaged ECU.
- Acceleration switch terminal backout, Pins 1, 2 and 3.
- Short to ground in Circuits 836 (O/W), 886 (O/BK) and 887 (Y).

84929182

4-WHEEL ABS TESTING — 1993 BRONCO

DIAGNOSIS AND TESTING (Continued)

ACCELERATION SENSOR (CODE 65) — TEST Q (Continued)

	TEST STEP	RESULT	ACTION TO TAKE
Q9	LEVEL SURFACE RESISTANCE CHECK, CIRCUITS 836 (O/W) AND 886 (O/BK) • Remove acceleration sensor from vehicle. • Place sensor on a level surface. • Measure the resistance between Circuits 836 (O/W) and 886 (O/BK). • Is the resistance less than 5 ohms?	Yes No	GO to Q10. REPLACE acceleration sensor, GO to Q12.
Q10	LEVEL SURFACE RESISTANCE CHECK, CIRCUITS 836 (O/W) AND 887 (Y) • Measure the resistance between Circuits 836 (O/W) and 887 (Y). • Is the resistance less than 5 ohms?	Yes No	REPLACE the acceleration sensor. GO to Q12. GO to Q12.
Q11	CHECK IF ALL STEPS HAVE BEEN COMPLETED • This step requires that a valid diagnostic trouble code has been obtained, ALL prior diagnostic steps have been completed, and the affected wiring integrity has been verified. CAUTION: If the above is not complete, changes are that replacement of this or any other system component without specific direction will not, in most circumstances, resolve the concern and will consequently result in customer dissatisfaction. • Have all prior diagnostic steps been completed as described above?	Yes No	REPLACE acceleration sensor. GO to Q12. If no resolution, REPLACE ECU. GO to Q12. GO to last diagnostic step completed and continue.
Q12	VERIFY CONDITION RESOLVED • Clear all codes. • Key OFF. • Retrieve code. • Is Code 16 set?	Yes No, Code 65 still exists No, different code is set No, Code 65 still exists and Step Q10 is complete	STOP. Concern has been corrected. GO to next pinpoint step. GO to appropriate pinpoint test. GO to Q13.
Q13	VERIFY INTEGRITY OF VEHICLE WIRING NOTE: If the above steps have been completed, the MOST LIKELY cause of the concern is wiring related. • Refer to the Intermittent Diagnosis Procedure and perform for ALL affected circuits as shown on the pinpoint test mini-schematic. • Does wiring check OK?	Yes No	STOP. Repair is complete. GO to Q11.

Pinpoint Test R — Code 67

Possible Code(s)

67 — Intermittent or open connection on ECU connector and/or motor speed sensor, damaged motor speed sensor or trigger circuit in ECU.

84929184

4-WHEEL ABS TESTING — 1993 BRONCO

DIAGNOSIS AND TESTING (Continued)

Affected Circuit(s)/Electrical Component(s)

ALL VIEWS LOOKING INTO CONNECTOR

Possible Contributing Component/Vehicle Wiring Concerns

- Damaged motor speed sensor.
- Damaged trigger circuit in ECU.
- Terminal backout in ECU harness connector Pins 2 and 3.

Description

Code 67 is generated by the ECU when the pump motor is running but is not triggered.

MOTOR RUNNING BUT NOT TRIGGERED (CODE 67) — TEST R

	TEST STEP	RESULT	ACTION TO TAKE
R1	MOTOR CHECK, KEY OFF • Make sure the battery is OK. Refer to Section 14-01. • Key OFF. • Is the motor running?	Yes No	REPLACE motor relay. GO to R4. GO to R2.

84929185

4-WHEEL ABS TESTING — 1993 BRONCO

DIAGNOSIS AND TESTING (Continued)

MOTOR RUNNING BUT NOT TRIGGERED (CODE 67) — TEST R (Continued)

	TEST STEP	RESULT		ACTION TO TAKE
R2	CHECK CIRCUIT 539 (PK/LB) • Remove ECU, install breakout box and verify Pin 60 is ground. • Key ON. • Jumper Pins 60 and 19 to energize main relay. • Is motor running?	Yes No	▲ ▲	REPAIR short to ground in Circuit 539 (PK/LB). GO to **R4**. GO to **R4**.
R3	CHECK IF ALL STEPS HAVE BEEN COMPLETED • This step requires that a valid diagnostic trouble code has been obtained, ALL prior diagnostic steps have been completed, and the affected wiring integrity has been verified. • Have all prior diagnostic steps been completed as described above? **CAUTION: If the above is not complete, changes are that replacement of this or any other system component without specific direction will not, in most circumstances, resolve the concern and will consequently result in customer dissatisfaction.**	Yes No	▲ ▲	REPLACE ECU. GO to **R4**. GO to last diagnostic step completed and continue.
R4	VERIFY CONDITION RESOLVED • Clear all codes. • Key OFF. • Retrieve code. • Is code 16 set?	Yes No, Code 67 still exists No, different code is set	▲ ▲ ▲	STOP. Concern has been corrected. GO to next pinpoint step. Go to appropriate pinpoint test. GO to **R5**.
		No, Code 67 still exists and Step R2 is complete		
R5	VERIFY INTEGRITY OF VEHICLE WIRING NOTE: If the above steps have been completed, the MOST LIKELY cause of the concern is wiring related. • Refer to the Intermittent Diagnosis Procedure and perform for ALL affected circuits as shown on the pinpoint test mini-schematic. • Does wiring check OK?	Yes No	▲ ▲	STOP. Repair is complete. GO to **R3**.

Pinpoint Test S — No Code

Hard Light — No Code

Affected Circuit(s)/Electrical Components

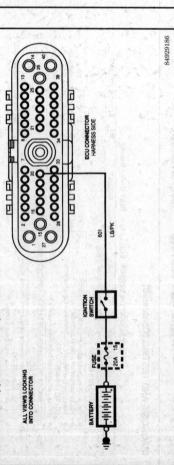

ALL VIEWS LOOKING INTO CONNECTOR

BATTERY — FUSE 20A 15 — IGNITION SWITCH — 601 LB/PK — ECU CONNECTOR HARNESS SIDE

84929186

4-WHEEL ABS TESTING — 1993 BRONCO

DIAGNOSIS AND TESTING (Continued)

Description

If no vehicle battery voltage is available to the ECU, or the voltage available is less than 8 volts, the ECU cannot initialize. As a result, the system relay cannot be energized and the ABS warning light remains on. No diagnostics are possible; no codes can be read.

Possible Contributing Base Brake Component/Vehicle Wiring Concerns

- Worn or damaged ignition switch
- Open ignition feed circuit to ECU
- Low battery voltage (less than 8V)
- Blown ignition fuse
- Open system ground

NO CODE — TEST S

	TEST STEP	RESULT		ACTION TO TAKE
S1	INSTALL PINOUT BOX • Install pinout box. • Open power network box and locate ignition fuse 15 (20A). • Check fuse for continuity. • Verify both fuse terminals in the power network box are clean and secure. • Is there continuity and are terminals clean and secure?	Yes No	▲ ▲	REINSTALL fuse. GO to **S2**. REPLACE fuse or SERVICE terminal as appropriate. GO to **PC3**.
S2	VERIFY ECU GROUND • Key OFF. • Inspect ground eyelet at left radiator support for excessive dirt, corrosion, or looseness. Clean and tighten as necessary. • Check for continuity between Pin 60 and the ground stud at left radiator support. • Check for continuity between Pin 14 and the ground stud at left radiator support. • Is there continuity at both pins?	Yes No	▲ ▲	GO to **S3**. SERVICE open circuit in ground between ECU harness connector and ground stud. GO to **PC3**.
S3	VERIFY PROPER IGNITION VOLTAGE AT ECU HARNESS CONNECTOR • Key ON. • Measure voltage between Pins 20 and 60. • Is there at least 8 volts?	Yes No, there is voltage greater than 0 volts but less than 8 volts No, there is 0 volts	▲ ▲ ▲	REPLACE ECU. GO to **PC3**. ECU cannot initialize due to insufficient ignition voltage. Problem is NOT in ABS system. SERVICE open circuit between ignition and ECU harness connector in 601 (LB/PK). GO to **PC3**.

Drive Test

Purpose

This drive test will be used when either of two conditions exists.

1. Required Repair Verification — This drive procedure will be used after all vehicle repairs. Once a vehicle has been repaired it is necessary to verify the repair by driving the vehicle. This is because the ABS module is unable to detect some system concerns until the vehicle is being driven a certain way. Therefore the drive verification test is a very important step.

2. Symptom Evaluation Drive — When a vehicle is brought to the dealer, the customer may only have a general concern about the way the vehicle is braking. In these situations there may not be a clear system concern to troubleshoot. This drive test is designed to produce common system concern symptoms. Use this drive test to determine a symptom. Once a symptom is found, a symptom troubleshooting procedure can be followed to repair the vehicle.

Drive Description

This is designed to be a generic drive test that used for three purposes listed below.

1. To verify a repair of the ABS system on a vehicle.

84929187

4-WHEEL ABS TESTING — 1993 BRONCO

DIAGNOSIS AND TESTING (Continued)

2. To attempt to recreate an intermittent concern.
3. To attempt to detect a symptom when a diagnostic trouble code or a concern symptom is not known.

DRIVE TEST — CODE 16

TEST STEP	RESULT	ACTION TO TAKE
DT1.1 LOW SPEED ABS STOP NOTE: Wetting down the area where stop is to be performed will aid this test. • Drive vehicle at approximately 10 mph. • Press on brake pedal hard enough to lock all four wheels. • Does one wheel lock consistently? NOTE: Momentary lock up is permissible. NOTE: An assistant should be used to monitor the wheels during the ABS stop.	Yes, and ABS light is not on	▲ GO to Symptom B, Wheel Lock-Up.
	Yes, and ABS light comes on and stays on	▲ GO to DT1.7.
	No, but other symptoms are detected	▲ GO to DT1.6.
	No, and ABS light is not on	▲ GO to DT1.2.
DT1.2 CHECK FOR UNWARRANTED ABS ACTIVITY • Drive vehicle at approximately 20 mph. • Perform a light to medium (normal traffic) stop. • Turn off the windshield wipers if they are on. Feel for pulsation in the brake pedal. • Does the pump motor turn on and are brake pedal pulsations felt any time during the stop? NOTE: In this event, the vehicle may pull as soon as the pump motor begins to run. If the vehicle does pull when the pump motor turns on, the front sensor opposite the pull should be checked using the UNWARRANTED ABS ACTIVITY Symptom, Sensor. If the pump motor turns on and no pull is felt, the rear sensor should be checked using the UNWARRANTED ABS ACTIVITY Symptom, Sensor. If a vehicle pulls immediately upon braking and the pump motor does not run, use the VEHICLE PULLS WHILE BRAKING Symptom to diagnose the concern.	Yes, and ABS light is not on	▲ GO to Symptom A, Unwarranted ABS Activity.
	Yes, and ABS light comes on and stays on	▲ GO to DT1.7.
	No, but other symptoms are detected	▲ GO to DT1.6.
	No, and ABS light is not on	▲ GO to DT1.3.
DT1.3 CHECK FOR MARGINALLY HIGH SENSOR GAP • Clear all codes. • Key OFF. • Start vehicle and select Drive Low (Automatic) or 1st forward gear (Manual). • Allow vehicle to creep forward at idle for at least 45 seconds. • Does the ABS warning light come on?	Yes	▲ GO to DT1.8.
	No	▲ GO to DT1.4.
DT1.4 CHECK FOR MARGINALLY HIGH SENSOR GAP • Clear all codes. • Key OFF. • Start vehicle and accelerate slowly to 25 mph. Let at least 45 seconds elapse before reaching 25 mph. • Does the ABS warning light come on?	Yes	▲ GO to DT1.8.
	No	▲ GO to DT1.5.
DT1.5 DETERMINE DRIVE TEST IS COMPLETE • Has customer concern been addressed and corrected by previous actions?	Yes	▲ STOP. Vehicle RABS function has been verified.
	No	▲ REFER to Symptom Chart.

84929188

4-WHEEL ABS TESTING — 1993 BRONCO

DIAGNOSIS AND TESTING (Continued)

DRIVE TEST — CODE 16 (Continued)

TEST STEP	RESULT	ACTION TO TAKE
DT1.6 DETERMINE NEXT DIAGNOSTIC STEP BASED ON BRAKE SYMPTOM • Are any of the following symptoms present? — Hard or soft brake pedal. — Lack of sufficient vehicle deceleration upon brake application. — Vehicle pulls during braking and pump motor does NOT run.	Yes	▲ GO to Symptom Chart. Concern is NOT in the ABS system.
	No	
DT1.7 OBTAIN DIAGNOSTIC TROUBLE CODE • Obtain ABS diagnostic trouble code. • Is the diagnostic trouble code the same as before and the ENTIRE pinpoint test for the code completed?	Yes	▲ PERFORM intermittent diagnosis.
	No, pinpoint test is NOT complete	▲ RETURN to the last step completed in the pinpoint test.
	No, code obtained is NOT the same	▲ GO to the pinpoint test for the code obtained.
	No, no code or Code 16 is obtained	▲ GO to System Pre-Check.
DT1.8 DETERMINE WHICH SENSOR SIGNAL IS INCORRECT • Obtain diagnostic trouble code. • Is code obtained 31-33/ 35-37/ 41-43/ 55-57?	Yes	▲ GO to DT1.9.
	No, and Code 16 is not obtained	▲ GO to the pinpoint test for the code obtained.
	No, no code or Code 16 is obtained	▲ GO to System Pre-Check.
DT1.9 RESOLVE SENSOR SIGNAL CONCERN • For the code received, perform the following checks on the appropriate wheel end and or rear axle (refer to Service Code Index). • Check for metal chips or ferrous debris on the sensor pole piece or can. • Verify that the gap between the sensor can or pole piece and speed sensor ring is less than 0.070 inch for the front sensors and less than 0.050 inch for the rear axle sensor. • Inspect the speed sensor ring for damaged or missing teeth. • FRONT SENSORS ONLY — Inspect the speed sensor ring for ferrous material built up between the teeth. • Are any of the above conditions present?	Yes, chips or ferrous debris on the sensor	▲ REMOVE debris from sensor. If rear axle sensor, DRAIN and CLEAN rear carrier. GO to DT1.3.
	No, the gap is greater than specified	▲ GO to DT1.10.
	Yes, speed sensor ring teeth are missing or damaged	▲ REPLACE speed sensor ring. GO to DT1.3.
	Yes, material is built up between the sensor ring teeth	▲ CLEAN speed sensor ring. GO to DT1.3.
	No, none of the above conditions are present	▲ PERFORM intermittent diagnosis.
DT1.10 DETERMINE FRONT OR REAR SENSOR • Is the affected sensor a front wheel sensor or the rear axle sensor?	Front Wheel	▲ REPLACE sensor. Make sure mounting area is clean.
	Rear Axle	▲ GO to DT1.11.

84929189

DIAGNOSIS AND TESTING (Continued)

DRIVE TEST — CODE 16 (Continued)

TEST STEP	RESULT	▶	ACTION TO TAKE
DT1.11 IMPROPER SENSOR GAP RESOLUTION			
REAR AXLE SENSOR ONLY • Remove speed sensor from the rear axle carrier bore. • Clean axle housing and remove all debris from mounting area. • Inspect the sensor mounting flange and clean as required. • Install a new speed sensor O-ring onto the sensor. • Reinstall the speed sensor. Make sure the sensor is fully seated in the bore and the hold-down bolt is torqued to specification. • Measure the gap between the sensor and ring. • Is the gap less than 0.050 inch?	Yes No	▶ ▶	GO to **DT1.3**. REPLACE rear axle.

SYMPTOM DIAGNOSTIC CHART

Symptom Description	Refer To
Unwarranted ABS Activity	Symptom A
Wheels Lockup	Symptom B
Hard / Soft Brake Pedal	Symptom C
Lack of Decel (Med / Hard Braking)	Symptom D
Vehicle Pulls During Braking	Symptom E

WARNING: PERFORM INDICATED PINPOINT TEST OR DRIVE TEST STEPS ONLY — DO NOT PERFORM OTHER STEPS (ALTHOUGH WITHIN THE TEST BOX, YOU MAY APPEAR TO BE DIRECTED TO DO SO). ALWAYS RETURN TO THE SYMPTOM CONDITION CHART IF NO RESOLUTION IS REACHED BY PERFORMING A PARTICULAR TEST.

NOTE: Ignore directions to CALL Hotline within pinpoint and drive tests until all Symptom options are exhausted.

SYMPTOM A: UNWARRANTED ABS ACTIVITY

CONDITION	POSSIBLE SOURCE	ACTION
Premature loss of sensor signal during vehicle deceleration.	• Sensor signal is weak or erratic.	• Refer to Drive Test — Code 16, Step DT1.3.
Intermittent sensor signal to ECU during decel.	• Intermittent open or shorted sensor circuit. • Intermittent open sensor circuit at intermediate connections especially bulkhead. • Chafed wire insulation or pinched wire due to improper routing causing intermittent short.	• Perform Intermittent Diagnosis for Circuits 514 (Y/R), 516 (Y/BK), 521 (T/O), 522 (T/BK), 519 (LG/BK), and 523 (R/PK). • Perform Intermittent Diagnosis for Circuit 514 (Y/R), 516 (Y/BK), 521 (T/O), 522 (T/BK), 519 (LG/BK), and 523 (R/PK) at intermediate connectors. • Inspect wiring harness from front sensor on knuckle to the frame and from the rear axle to the frame for worn or chafed wire insulation.
Maladjusted rear brakes or "grabby" brake shoe or pad linings	• Rear brake adjustment too tight. • Linings are "grabby".	

84929190

Hydraulic Control Unit

REMOVAL & INSTALLATION

▶ **See Figure 85**

1. Disconnect the battery ground cable.
2. Unplug the 8-pin connector from the unit, and the 4-pin connector from the pump motor.
3. Disconnect the 5 inlet and outlet tubes from the unit. Immediately plug the ports.
4. Remove the 3 unit attaching nuts and lift out the unit.
5. Installation is the reverse of removal. Torque the mounting nuts to 12-18 ft. lbs. and the tube fittings to 10-18 ft. lbs.

➡**After reconnecting the battery, it may take 10 miles or more of driving for the Powertrain Control Module to relearn its driveability codes.**

6. Bleed the brakes.

Electronic Control Unit

REMOVAL & INSTALLATION

▶ **See Figure 85**

1. Disconnect the battery ground cable.
2. Unplug the wiring from the ECU.

3. Remove the mounting bolts, slide the ECU off its bracket.
4. Installation is the reverse of removal. Torque the mounting screw to 5-6 ft. lbs. and the connector bolt to 4-5 ft. lbs.

➡**After reconnecting the battery, it may take 10 miles or more of driving for the Powertrain Control Module to relearn its driveability codes.**

Front Wheel Speed Sensor

REMOVAL & INSTALLATION

1. Inside the engine compartment, disconnect the sensor from the harness.
2. Unclip the sensor cable from the brake hose clips.
3. Remove the retaining bolt from the spindle and slide the sensor from its hole.
4. Installation is the reverse of removal. Torque the retaining bolt to 40-60 inch lbs.

Rear Speed Sensor

REMOVAL & INSTALLATION

▶ **See Figure 86**

1. Disconnect the wiring from the harness.
2. Remove the sensor holddown bolt and remove the sensor from the axle.

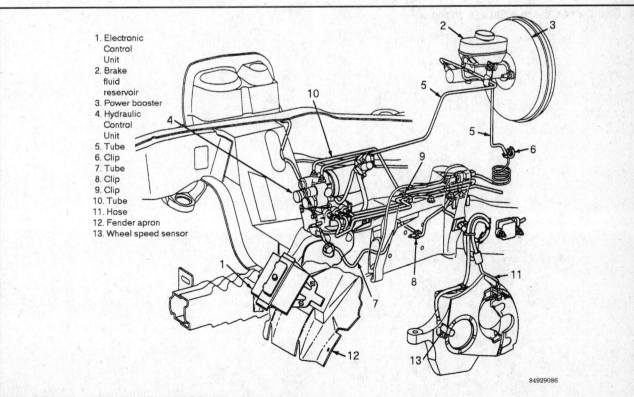

1. Electronic Control Unit
2. Brake fluid reservoir
3. Power booster
4. Hydraulic Control Unit
5. Tube
6. Clip
7. Tube
8. Clip
9. Clip
10. Tube
11. Hose
12. Fender apron
13. Wheel speed sensor

84929086

Fig. 85 Front end of the 4-wheel ABS system

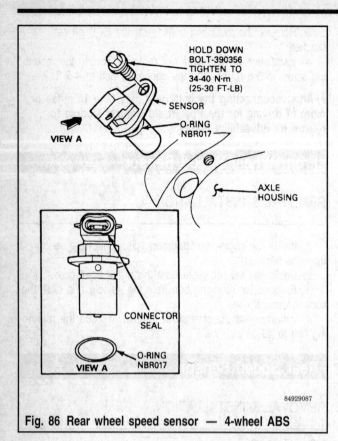

Fig. 86 Rear wheel speed sensor — 4-wheel ABS

To install:

3. Thoroughly clean the mounting surfaces. Make sure no dirt falls into the axle. Clean the magnetized sensor pole piece. Metal particles can cause sensor problems. Replace the O-ring.

4. Coat the new O-ring with clean engine oil.

5. Position the new sensor on the axle. It should slide into place easily. Correct installation will allow a gap of 0.005-0.045 in.

6. Torque the holddown bolt to 25-30 ft. lbs.

7. Connect the wiring.

Front Speed Sensor Ring

REMOVAL & INSTALLATION

▶ **See Figure 87**

1. Raise and support the front end on jackstands.
2. Remove the wheels.
3. Remove the caliper, rotor and hub.
4. Using a 3-jawed puller, remove the ring from the hub. The ring cannot be reused; it must be replaced.

To install:

5. Support the hub in a press so that the lug studs do not rest on the work surface.

6. Position the **new** sensor ring on the hub. Using a cylindrical adapter 98mm ID · 106mm OD, press the ring into place. The ring **must** be fully seated!

7. The remainder of installation is the reverse of removal.

Rear Speed Sensor Ring

REMOVAL & INSTALLATION

This procedure requires the removal of the differential. See Section 7.

BRAKE SPECIFICATIONS

All measurements in inches unless noted.

Year	Model	Master Cylinder Bore	Brake Disc Original Thickness	Brake Disc Minimum Thickness	Brake Disc Maximum Runout	Brake Drum Diameter Original Inside Diameter	Brake Drum Diameter Max. Wear Limit	Brake Drum Diameter Maximum Machine Diameter	Minimum Lining Thickness Front	Minimum Lining Thickness Rear
1987	F-150	1.000	NA	1.120	0.003	11.03	11.09	11.09	①	①
	Bronco	1.000	NA	1.120	0.003	11.03	11.09	11.09	①	①
	F-250	1.062	NA	1.180	0.003	12.00	12.06	12.06	①	①
	F-250HD	1.125	NA	1.180	0.003	12.00	12.06	12.06	①	①
	F-350	1.125	NA	1.180	0.003	12.00	12.06	12.06	①	①
1988	F-150	1.000	NA	1.120	0.003	11.03	11.09	11.09	①	①
	Bronco	1.000	NA	1.120	0.003	11.03	11.09	11.09	①	①
	F-250	1.062	NA	1.180	0.003	12.00	12.06	12.06	①	①
	F-250HD	1.125	NA	1.180	0.005	12.00	12.06	12.06	①	①
	F-350	1.125	NA	1.180	0.005	12.00	12.06	12.06	①	①
	F-Super Duty	1.125	NA	1.430	0.008	12.00	12.06	12.06	①	①
1989	F-150	1.000	NA	1.120	0.003	11.03	11.09	11.09	①	①
	Bronco	1.000	NA	1.120	0.003	11.03	11.09	11.09	①	①
	F-250	1.062	NA	1.180	0.003	12.00	12.06	12.06	①	①
	F-250HD	1.125	NA	1.180	0.005	12.00	12.06	12.06	①	①
	F-350	1.125	NA	1.180	0.005	12.00	12.06	12.06	①	①
	F-Super Duty	1.125	NA	1.430	0.008	12.00	12.06	12.06	①	①
1990	F-150	1.000	NA	1.120	0.003	11.03	11.09	11.09	①	①
	Bronco	1.000	NA	1.120	0.003	11.03	11.09	11.09	①	①
	F-250	1.062	NA	1.180	0.003	12.00	12.06	12.06	①	①
	F-250HD	1.125	NA	1.180	0.005	12.00	12.06	12.06	①	①
	F-350	1.125	NA	1.180	0.005	12.00	12.06	12.06	①	①
	F-Super Duty	1.125	NA	1.430	0.008	12.00	12.06	12.06	①	①
1991	F-150	1.000	NA	1.120	0.003	11.03	11.09	11.09	①	①
	Bronco	1.000	NA	1.120	0.003	11.03	11.09	11.09	①	①
	F-250	1.062	NA	1.180	0.003	12.00	12.06	12.06	①	①
	F-250HD	1.125	NA	1.180	0.005	12.00	12.06	12.06	①	①
	F-350	1.125	NA	1.180	0.005	12.00	12.06	12.06	①	①
	F-Super Duty	1.125	NA	1.430	0.008	12.00	12.06	12.06	①	①
1992	F-150	1.000	NA	1.120	0.003	11.03	11.09	11.09	①	①
	Bronco	1.000	NA	1.120	0.003	11.03	11.09	11.09	①	①
	F-250	1.062	NA	1.180	0.003	12.00	12.06	12.06	①	①
	F-250HD	1.125	NA	1.180	0.005	12.00	12.06	12.06	①	①
	F-350	1.125	NA	1.180	0.005	12.00	12.06	12.06	①	①
	F-Super Duty	1.125	NA	1.430	0.008	12.00	12.06	12.06	①	①
1993	F-150	1.000	NA	1.120	0.003	11.03	11.09	11.09	①	①
	Bronco	1.000	NA	1.120	0.003	11.03	11.09	11.09	①	①
	F-250	1.062	NA	1.180	0.003	12.00	12.06	12.06	①	①
	F-250HD	1.125	NA	1.180	0.005	12.00	12.06	12.06	①	①
	F-350	1.125	NA	1.180	0.005	12.00	12.06	12.06	①	①
	F-Super Duty	1.125	NA	1.430	0.008	12.00	12.06	12.06	①	①

NA—Information not available
① 1/16 inch above the backing plate or 1/32 inch above the rivet heads

84929191

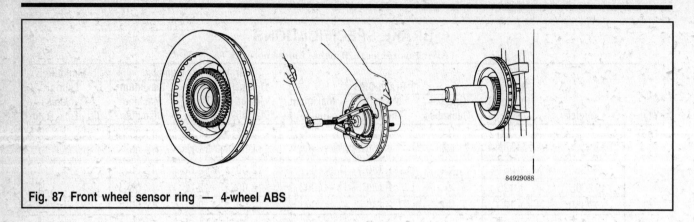

Fig. 87 Front wheel sensor ring — 4-wheel ABS

TORQUE SPECIFICATIONS

Component	U.S.	Metric
ABS Hydraulic Control Unit		
Mounting nuts	12-18 ft. lbs.	16-24 Nm
Tube fittings	10-18 ft. lbs.	14--24 Nm
ABS Electronic Control Unit		
Connector bolt	4-5 ft. lbs.	5-7 Nm
Mounting screw	5-6 ft. lbs.	7-8 Nm
ABS Front Wheel Speed Sensor bolt	40-60 inch lbs.	4-7 Nm
ABS Rear Speed Sensor bolt	25-30 ft. lbs.	34-41 Nm
Brake tubing hydraulic connections	10–15 ft. lbs.	14-20 Nm
Booster bracket-to-dash panel nuts	18–25 ft. lbs.	24-34 Nm
Diesel Brake Booster Vacuum Pump		
Pivot adjustment bolts	11–18 ft. lbs.	15-25 Nm
Pump-to-adjustment plate bolts	11–18 ft. lbs.	15-24 Nm
Height Sensing Proportioning Valve		
F-Super Duty Only		
Brake hose bolt	28–34 ft. lbs.	38-46 Nm
Linkage arm-to-valve nut	8–10 ft. lbs.	11-14 Nm
Valve-to-bracket bolts	12–18 ft. lbs.	16-24 Nm
Hydro-Boost Brake Booster		
Booster mounting nuts	25 ft. lbs.	34 Nm
Master cylinder-to-booster	18–25 ft. lbs.	24-34 Nm
Parking brake control-to-firewall	15 ft. lbs.	20 Nm
RABS sensor holddown bolt	30 ft. lbs.	41 Nm
Rotor attaching bolts		
F-Super Duty		
Front or rear	74–89 ft. lbs.	101-121 Nm
Transmission Mounted Parking Brake		
F-Super Duty		
Brake assembly-to-case	90 ft. lbs.	122 Nm
Brake drum and output flange nuts	85 ft. lbs.	116 Nm
Brake unit-to-extension housing	40 ft. lbs.	54 Nm
Driveshaft bolts	20 ft. lbs.	27 Nm
Filler plug	45 ft. lbs.	61 Nm
Mainshaft 75mm nut	215 ft. lbs.	292 Nm

84929192

10

BODY AND TRIM

EXTERIOR

Doors

ADJUSTMENT

▶ **See Figures 1 and 2**

➡**Loosen the hinge-to-door bolts for lateral adjustment only. Loosen the hinge-to-body bolts for both lateral and vertical adjustment.**

1. Determine which hinge bolts are to be loosened and back them out just enough to allow movement.

2. To move the door safely, use a padded pry bar. When the door is in the proper position, tighten the bolts to 24 ft. lbs. and check the door operation. There should be no binding or interference when the door is closed and opened.

3. Door closing adjustment can also be affected by the position of the lock striker plate. Loosen the striker plate bolts and move the striker plate just enough to permit proper closing and locking of the door.

REMOVAL & INSTALLATION

1. Matchmark the hinge-to-body and hinge-to-door locations. Support the door either on jackstands or have somebody hold it for you.

2. Remove the lower hinge-to-door bolts.

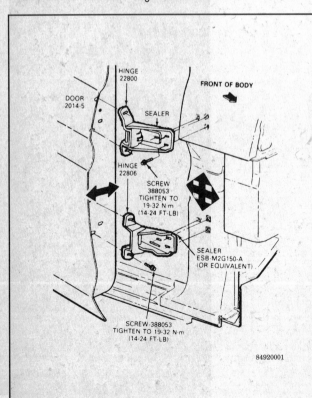

Fig. 1 Door hinge adjustment

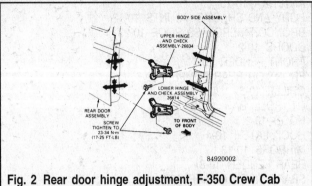

Fig. 2 Rear door hinge adjustment, F-350 Crew Cab

3. Remove the upper hinge-to-door bolts and lift the door off the hinges.

4. If the hinges are being replaced, remove them from the door pillar.

To install:

5. Install the door and hinges with the bolts finger tight.

6. Adjust the door and torque the hinge bolts to 24 ft. lbs.

Hood

REMOVAL & INSTALLATION

▶ **See Figures 3 and 4**

➡**You'll need an assistant for this job.**

1. Open the hood.

2. Remove the 2 link assembly bolts.

3. Matchmark the hood-to-hinge position.

4. Remove the hood-to-hinge bolts and lift off the hood.

5. Installation is the reverse of removal. Loosely install the hood and align the matchmarks. Torque all bolts to 20 ft. lbs.

ADJUSTMENT

1. Open the hood and matchmark the hinge and latch positions.

2. Loosen the hinge-to-fender bolts just enough to allow movement of the hood.

3. Move the hood as required to obtain the proper fit and alignment between the hood and the top of the cowl panel. Tighten the bolts to 34 ft. lbs.

4. Loosen the 2 latch attaching bolts.

5. Loosen the hinge-to-hood bolts just enough to allow movement of the hood.

6. Move the hood forward/backward and/or side-to-side to obtain a proper hood fit.

7. Tighten the hood-to-hinge bolts to 20 ft. lbs.

8. Move the latch from side-to-side to align the latch with the striker. Torque the latch bolts.

9. Lubricate the latch and hinges and check the hood fit several times.

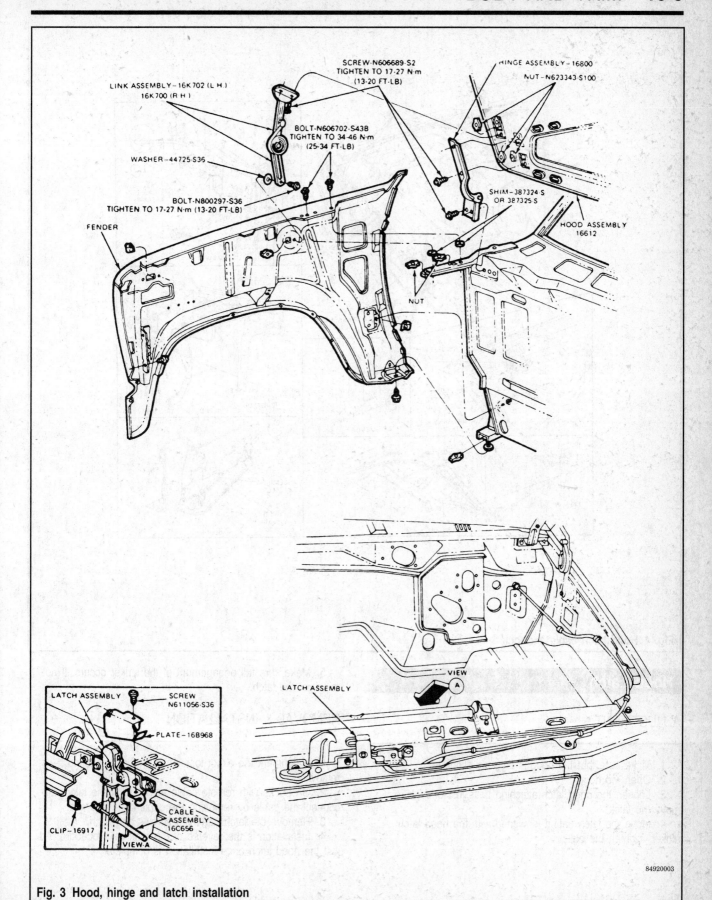

LINK ASSEMBLY-16K702 (L.H.)
16K700 (R.H.)

WASHER-44725-S36

BOLT-N800297-S36
TIGHTEN TO 17-27 N·m (13-20 FT·LB)

FENDER

SCREW-N606689-S2
TIGHTEN TO 17-27 N·m
(13-20 FT·LB)

BOLT-N606702-S43B
TIGHTEN TO 34-46 N·m
(25-34 FT·LB)

HINGE ASSEMBLY-16800

NUT-N623343-S100

SHIM-387324-S
OR 387325-S

HOOD ASSEMBLY
16612

NUT

LATCH ASSEMBLY

SCREW
N611056-S36

PLATE-16B968

CLIP-16917

CABLE
ASSEMBLY
16C656

VIEW-A

LATCH ASSEMBLY

VIEW
A

84920003

Fig. 3 Hood, hinge and latch installation

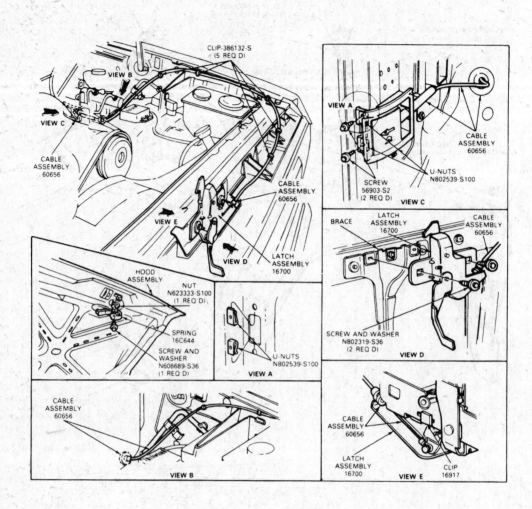

Fig. 4 Hood latch cable and lock

Hood Latch

ADJUSTMENT

1. Make sure that the hood is properly aligned.
2. Open the hood.
3. Loosen the hood latch attaching bolts just enough to move the latch.
4. Move the latch until it is aligned with the hood latch striker. Tighten the bolts.

5. Make sure full engagement of the striker occurs. If not, re-adjust the latch.

REMOVAL & INSTALLATION

1. Matchmark the exact location of the latch prior to removal.
2. On trucks with remote cable actuation of the latch, disconnect the cable by removing the cable plate and clip.
3. Remove the latch attaching screws and latch.
4. Installation is the reverse of the removal procedure. Adjust the hood latch once installation is complete.

Tailgate

REMOVAL & INSTALLATION

Bronco
▶ See Figure 5

1. Lower the tailgate.
2. Disconnect the cable at each end.
3. Disconnect the tailgate wiring at the connector.
4. Pull the wiring from the tailgate body rail.
5. Have someone support the tailgate and remove the torsion bar retainer from the body.
6. Matchmark the hinge-to-body positions and unbolt the hinges from the body.
7. Installation is the reverse of removal. Torque the hinge bolts to 11 ft. lbs.; the cable bolts to 30 ft. lbs.

Styleside Pickup
▶ See Figures 6 and 7

1. Remove the tailgate support strap at the pillar T-head pivot.
2. Lift off the tailgate at the right hinge.
3. Pull off the left hinge.
4. Installation is the reverse of removal.

Flareside Pickup

1. Unhook the chain.
2. Remove the movable pivot-to-body bolts and remove the pivot.

3. Slide the tailgate off the stationary pivot.
4. Installation is the reverse of removal.

Tailgate Latch Release Handle and Lock Release Control Assemblies

REMOVAL & INSTALLATION

Bronco

1. Lower the tailgate and remove the inner access cover.
2. Remove the 2 screws securing the handle to the tailgate.
3. Remove the rod from the clip that holds the handle rod to the lock control.
4. Remove the handle and rod assembly.
5. Disconnect the latch release links and latch control rod.
6. Disconnect the wiring from the interlock switch.
7. Remove the 3 lock control-to-tailgate retaining screws.
8. Remove the lock control from the tailgate.

To install:

9. Install the lock control and tighten the screws to 11 ft. lbs.
10. Connect the wires.
11. Place the latch control rod in position and install the clip.
12. Place the latch release links in position and install the clips.
13. Place the handle and rod assembly in the tailgate. Connect the rod to the lock control and install the clip.
14. Install and tighten the handle attaching screws.
15. Install the access cover.

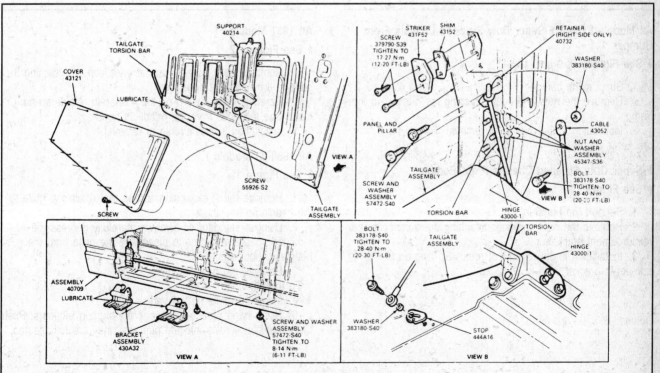

Fig. 5 Bronco tailgate installation

84920005

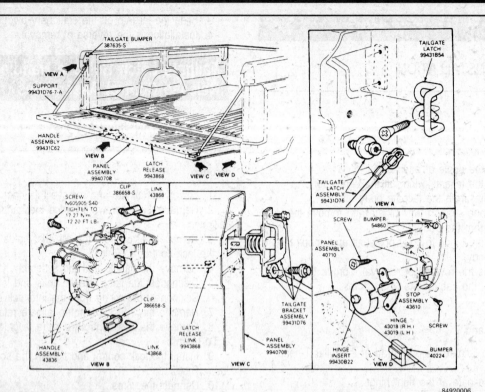

Fig. 6 1987 Styleside pickup tailgate

Front or Rear Bumper

REMOVAL & INSTALLATION

All Models Except F-Super Duty Stripped Chassis Front Bumper

▶ See Figures 8, 9 and 10

1. Support the bumper.
2. Remove the nuts and bolts attaching the bumper to the frame.
3. Installation is the reverse of removal. Torque the bracket-to-frame bolts to 100 ft. lbs.

F-Super Duty Stripped Chassis Front Bumper

▶ See Figure 11

1. Support the bumper.
2. Remove the nuts and bolts attaching the bumper to the reinforcement brackets.
3. Installation is the reverse of removal. Torque the bumper-to-bracket bolts to 88 ft. lbs.

Grille

REMOVAL & INSTALLATION

All 1987 Models

▶ See Figure 12

1. Remove the 4 screws, one at each corner, attaching the grille to the headlight housings.
2. Carefully push inward on the 4 snap-in retainers and disengage the grille from the headlight housings.
3. Installation is the reverse of removal.

All 1988-93 Models

▶ See Figure 13

1. Remove the 2 expansion screws that retain the grille to the headlamp housings.
2. Using a standard screwdriver, carefully depress the 4 moulded snap-in retainers to disengage the grille from the headlamp housings.
3. Remove the grille.
   To install:
4. Install the grille on the vehicle.
5. Using hand pressure, engage the snap-in retainers. Push the expansion screws into the nuts until they are fully seated.

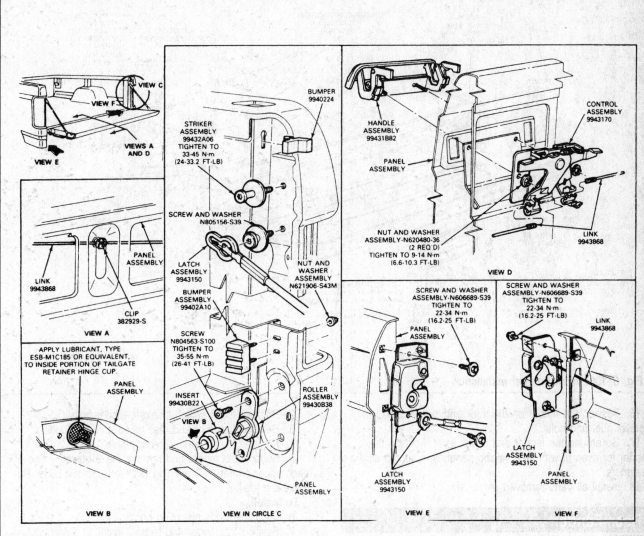

Fig. 7 1988-93 Styleside pickup tailgate

84920007

Front Fender

REMOVAL & INSTALLATION

All Models

▶ See Figures 14, 15 and 16

1. Clean all fender fasteners and liberally apply penetrating oil, such as Liquid Wrench®, WD-40®, or equivalent.
2. Remove the headlamp assemblies.
3. Remove the fender-to-radiator support screws.
4. Remove the screw attaching the fender to the lower corner of the cab.
5. Remove the screw — inside the cab — attaching the lower end of the fender to the cowl.
6. Remove the screws attaching the top edge of the fender to the cowl extension.
7. Remove the screws that attach the fender to the apron, around the wheel opening.
8. Remove the top fender-to-apron bolts.
9. On the right side, remove the battery and the battery tray.
10. On the left side, remove the auxiliary battery and/or tool box — both options.
11. On the right side, detach the main wiring harness from the fender.
12. On the left side, detach the hood latch cable from the fender.
13. Remove the hood prop spring from the fender.
14. Remove the fender.
To install:
15. Apply sealer to the upper edge of the apron.

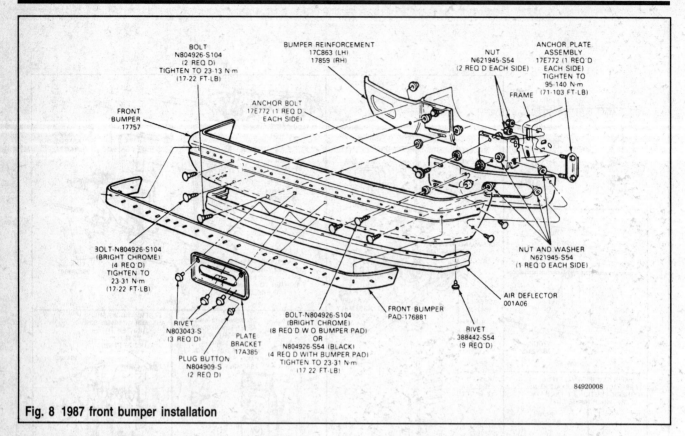

Fig. 8 1987 front bumper installation

16. Position the fender on the truck and loosely install all screws nuts and bolts.

17. Go around the fender and check its fit. Position the fender for even fit with all adjoining panels and tighten all the fasteners.

18. Install all parts removed previously.

Rear Fender

REMOVAL & INSTALLATION

F-150, 250, 350 Flare Side

1. Clean all fender fasteners and liberally apply penetrating oil, such as Liquid Wrench®, WD-40®, or equivalent.
2. Remove the fender brace-to-fender nut and bolt.
3. Remove the 12 fender-to-body nuts.
4. Remove the 3 fender-to-running board nuts and bolts.
5. Remove the fender.
   To install:
6. Clean the body mounting points.
7. Position the fender and loosely install all fasteners.
8. Go around the fender and check for proper clearance. Position the fender for even fit with all adjoining panels and tighten all the fasteners.

F-350 with Dual Rear Wheels

1. Clean all fender fasteners and liberally apply penetrating oil, such as Liquid Wrench®, WD-40®, or equivalent.

2. Remove the 3 splash shield-to-fender bolts.
3. Remove the front and rear fender-to-brace bolts.
4. Remove the 11 fender-to-body bolts.
5. Support the fender and remove the 2 nuts — one at each upper corner — retaining the fender to the body. Remove the fender.
   To install:
6. Clean the body mounting points.
7. Position the fender and loosely install all fasteners.
8. Go around the fender and check its fit. Position the fender for even fit with all adjoining panels and tighten all the fasteners.

Spare Tire Carrier

REMOVAL & INSTALLATION

All Except Bronco
▶ See Figures 17 and 18

✷✷CAUTION

A slow leak in the tire can cause the tire to become loose in its carrier. It's a good idea to check the tire pressure every 2 weeks. If the valve is not accessible, check the tire with hand or foot pressure.

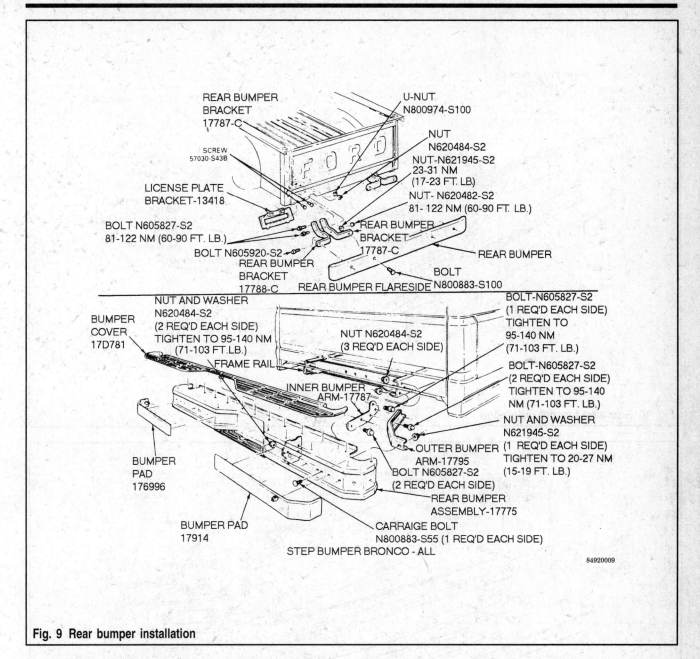

REAR BUMPER
BRACKET
17787-C

SCREW
57030-S43B

LICENSE PLATE
BRACKET-13418

BOLT N605827-S2
81-122 NM (60-90 FT. LB.)

BOLT N605920-S2
REAR BUMPER
BRACKET
17788-C

U-NUT
N800974-S100

NUT
N620484-S2
NUT-N621945-S2
23-31 NM
(17-23 FT. LB.)
NUT- N620482-S2
81- 122 NM (60-90 FT. LB.)

REAR BUMPER
BRACKET
17787-C

REAR BUMPER

BOLT
N800883-S100
REAR BUMPER FLARESIDE

NUT AND WASHER
N620484-S2
(2 REQ'D EACH SIDE)
TIGHTEN TO 95-140 NM
(71-103 FT.LB.)

FRAME RAIL

BUMPER
COVER
17D781

BUMPER
PAD
176996

BUMPER PAD
17914

NUT N620484-S2
(3 REQ'D EACH SIDE)

INNER BUMPER
ARM-17787

OUTER BUMPER
ARM-17795
BOLT N605827-S2
(2 REQ'D EACH SIDE)
REAR BUMPER
ASSEMBLY-17775

CARRAIGE BOLT
N800883-S55 (1 REQ'D EACH SIDE)
STEP BUMPER BRONCO - ALL

BOLT-N605827-S2
(1 REQ'D EACH SIDE)
TIGHTEN TO
95-140 NM
(71-103 FT. LB.)

BOLT-N605827-S2
(2 REQ'D EACH SIDE)
TIGHTEN TO 95-140
NM (71-103 FT. LB.)

NUT AND WASHER
N621945-S2
(1 REQ'D EACH SIDE)
TIGHTEN TO 20-27 NM
(15-19 FT. LB.)

84920009

Fig. 9 Rear bumper installation

1. Insert the tang of the lug wrench through the tire retaining eyebolt, and turn the bolt until the tire is loose from the upper retaining support.

✳✳CAUTION

Never position any part of your body under the tire or carrier during removal! To avoid a sudden drop of the tire, don't turn the end of the eyebolt out of the retaining nut.

2. Align the eye of the eyebolt with the channel slot.
3. While holding the nut end of the wrench parallel with the ground, insert the tang of the wrench into the channel assembly tube.

4. Lift up on the wrench and, at the same time, pull the eyebolt towards the tube and push on the wrench to pass the eyebolt shoulder through the keyhole in the channel.
5. Lower the tire. Swing the channel to the rear and remove the wrench.
6. Remove the wheel retainer from the center bolt.
7. Remove the wheel from the channel.
To install:
8. Balance the wheel on the channel. Install and tighten the center bolt.
9. Using the lug wrench, swing the channel under the eyebolt.
10. Lift the channel and insert the eyebolt through the keyhole. Shift the channel and eyebolt until the shoulder of the eyebolt is pushed all the way into the slot.

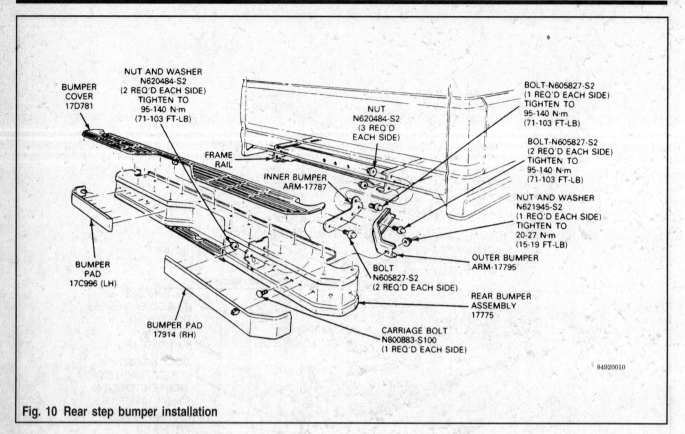

BUMPER
COVER
17D781

NUT AND WASHER
N620484-S2
(2 REQ'D EACH SIDE)
TIGHTEN TO
95-140 N·m
(71-103 FT-LB)

NUT
N620484-S2
(3 REQ'D
EACH SIDE)

FRAME
RAIL

INNER BUMPER
ARM-17787

BUMPER
PAD
17C996 (LH)

BUMPER PAD
17914 (RH)

BOLT
N605827-S2
(2 REQ'D EACH SIDE)

CARRIAGE BOLT
N800883-S100
(1 REQ'D EACH SIDE)

BOLT-N605827-S2
(1 REQ'D EACH SIDE)
TIGHTEN TO
95-140 N·m
(71-103 FT-LB)

BOLT-N605827-S2
(2 REQ'D EACH SIDE)
TIGHTEN TO
95-140 N·m
(71-103 FT-LB)

NUT AND WASHER
N621945-S2
(1 REQ'D EACH SIDE)
TIGHTEN TO
20-27 N·m
(15-19 FT-LB)

OUTER BUMPER
ARM-17795

REAR BUMPER
ASSEMBLY
17775

84920010

Fig. 10 Rear step bumper installation

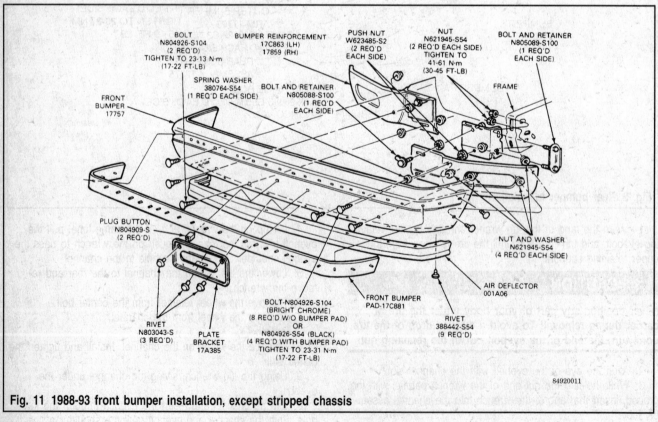

BOLT
N804926-S104
(2 REQ'D)
TIGHTEN TO 23-13 N·m
(17-22 FT-LB)

BUMPER REINFORCEMENT
17C863 (LH)
17859 (RH)

PUSH NUT
W623485-S2
(2 REQ'D
EACH SIDE)

NUT
N621945-S54
(2 REQ'D EACH SIDE)
TIGHTEN TO
41-61 N·m
(30-45 FT-LB)

BOLT AND RETAINER
N805089-S100
(1 REQ'D
EACH SIDE)

SPRING WASHER
380764-S54
(1 REQ'D EACH SIDE)

BOLT AND RETAINER
N805088-S100
(1 REQ'D
EACH SIDE)

FRAME

FRONT
BUMPER
17757

PLUG BUTTON
N804909-S
(2 REQ'D)

NUT AND WASHER
N621945-S54
(4 REQ'D EACH SIDE)

RIVET
N803043-S
(3 REQ'D)

PLATE
BRACKET
17A385

BOLT-N804926-S104
(BRIGHT CHROME)
(8 REQ'D W/O BUMPER PAD)
OR
N804926-S54 (BLACK)
(4 REQ'D WITH BUMPER PAD)
TIGHTEN TO 23-31 N·m
(17-22 FT-LB)

FRONT BUMPER
PAD-17C881

RIVET
388442-S54
(9 REQ'D)

AIR DEFLECTOR
001A06

84920011

Fig. 11 1988-93 front bumper installation, except stripped chassis

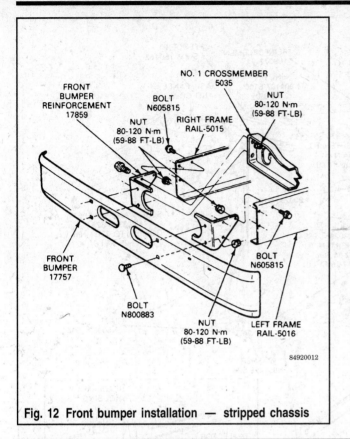

FRONT
BUMPER
REINFORCEMENT
17859

NUT
80-120 N·m
(59-88 FT-LB)

BOLT
N605815

RIGHT FRAME
RAIL-5015

NO. 1 CROSSMEMBER
5035

NUT
80-120 N·m
(59-88 FT-LB)

FRONT
BUMPER
17757

BOLT
N800883

NUT
80-120 N·m
(59-88 FT-LB)

BOLT
N605815

LEFT FRAME
RAIL-5016

84920012

Fig. 12 Front bumper installation — stripped chassis

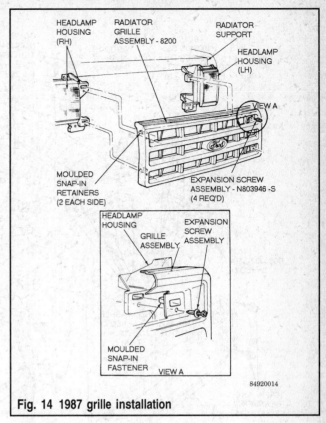

HEADLAMP
HOUSING
(RH)

RADIATOR GRILLE
ASSEMBLY - 8200

RADIATOR
SUPPORT

HEADLAMP
HOUSING
(LH)

VIEW A

MOULDED
SNAP-IN
RETAINERS
(2 EACH SIDE)

EXPANSION SCREW
ASSEMBLY - N803946 -S
(4 REQ'D)

HEADLAMP
HOUSING

GRILLE
ASSEMBLY

EXPANSION
SCREW
ASSEMBLY

MOULDED
SNAP-IN
FASTENER   VIEW A

84920014

Fig. 14 1987 grille installation

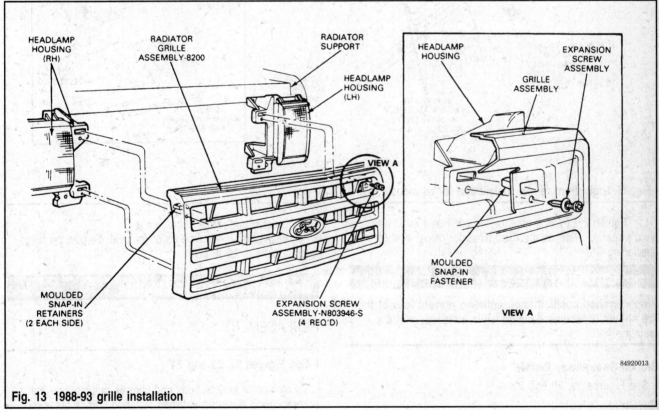

HEADLAMP
HOUSING
(RH)

RADIATOR
GRILLE
ASSEMBLY-8200

RADIATOR
SUPPORT

HEADLAMP
HOUSING
(LH)

VIEW A

MOULDED
SNAP-IN
RETAINERS
(2 EACH SIDE)

EXPANSION SCREW
ASSEMBLY-N803946-S
(4 REQ'D)

HEADLAMP
HOUSING

GRILLE
ASSEMBLY

EXPANSION
SCREW
ASSEMBLY

MOULDED
SNAP-IN
FASTENER

VIEW A

84920013

Fig. 13 1988-93 grille installation

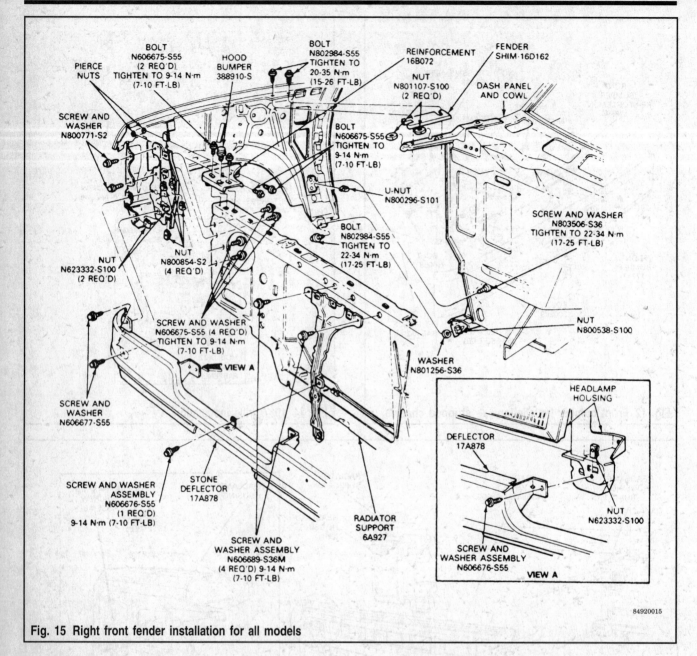

Fig. 15 Right front fender installation for all models

11. Tighten the eyebolt until the tire can't be moved with hand pressure. Refer to the illustrations for proper eyebolt positioning.

✳✳CAUTION

Proper eyebolt position is essential to prevent loss of the tire should it become deflated while installed, or if it's installed flat!

Bronco Swing-Away Carrier

▶ **See Figures 19, 20 and 21**

1. Remove the tire.
2. With the carrier latched in place, remove the carrier hinge-to-body bolts.

3. Unlatch and remove the carrier.
4. Installation is the reverse of removal. Torque the hinge-to-body bolts to 20 ft. lbs.

Body and Chassis Mounts

REPLACEMENT

▶ **See Figures 22, 23 and 24**

To replace or service body and chassis mounts, use the accompanying illustrations. When installing body mounts, do not use **any** lubricants on the mounts!

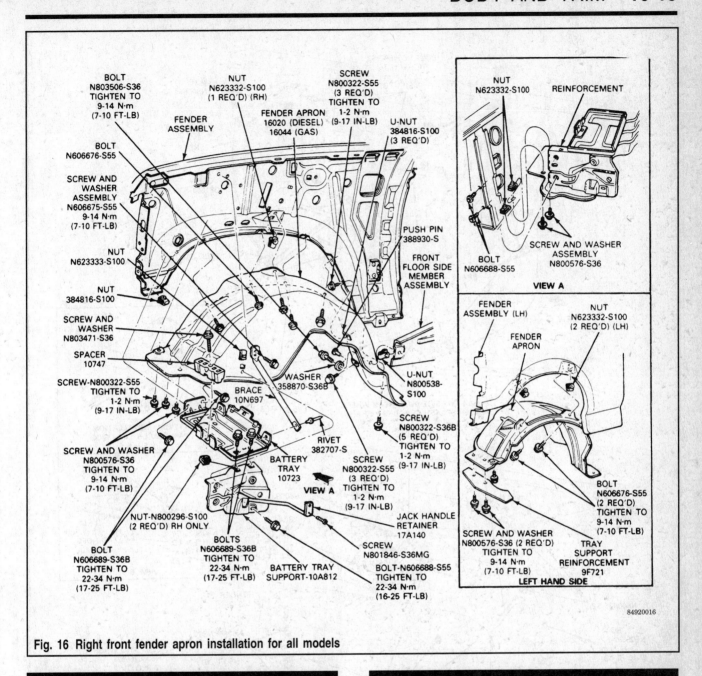

Fig. 16 Right front fender apron installation for all models

GT (Roll) Bar

REMOVAL & INSTALLATION

▶ See Figure 25

To service the roll bar, see the accompanying illustration. Make sure you replace any damaged sealer.

Mirrors

REMOVAL & INSTALLATION

All mirrors are remove by removing the mounting screws and lifting off the mirror and gasket.

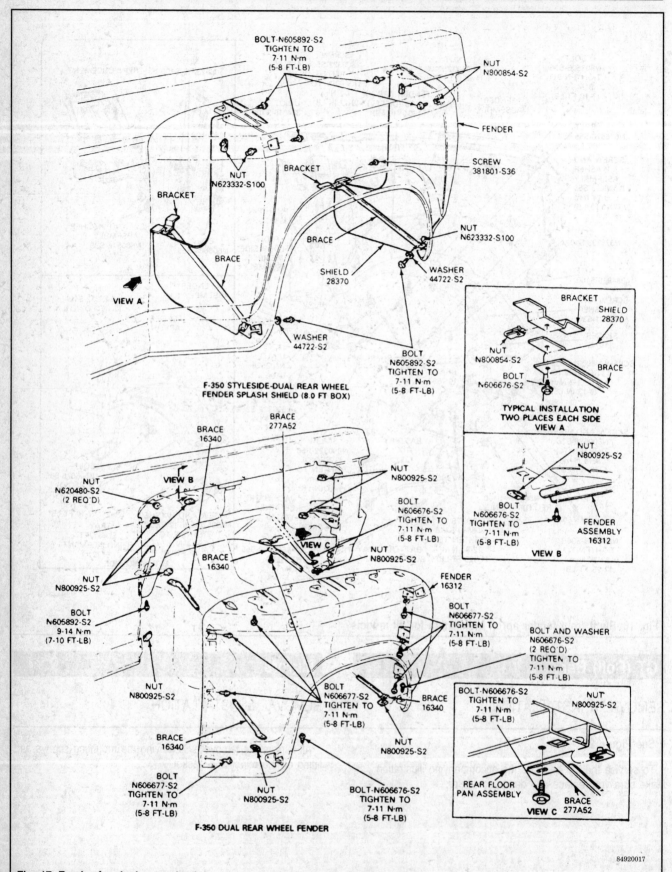

BOLT-N605892-S2
TIGHTEN TO
7-11 N·m
(5-8 FT-LB)

NUT
N800854-S2

FENDER

SCREW
381801-S36

NUT
N623332-S100

BRACKET

NUT
N623332-S100

BRACE

WASHER
44722-S2

BRACKET

BRACE

SHIELD
28370

VIEW A

WASHER
44722-S2

BOLT
N605892-S2
TIGHTEN TO
7-11 N·m
(5-8 FT-LB)

**F-350 STYLESIDE-DUAL REAR WHEEL
FENDER SPLASH SHIELD (8.0 FT BOX)**

BRACKET

SHIELD
28370

NUT
N800854-S2

BOLT
N606676-S2

BRACE

**TYPICAL INSTALLATION
TWO PLACES EACH SIDE
VIEW A**

NUT
N800925-S2

BOLT
N606676-S2
TIGHTEN TO
7-11 N·m
(5-8 FT-LB)

FENDER
ASSEMBLY
16312

VIEW B

BRACE
277A52

BRACE
16340

VIEW B

NUT
N800925-S2

NUT
N620480-S2
(2 REQ'D)

BOLT
N606676-S2
TIGHTEN TO
7-11 N·m
(5-8 FT-LB)

BRACE
16340

VIEW C

NUT
N800925-S2

NUT
N800925-S2

BOLT
N605892-S2
9-14 N·m
(7-10 FT-LB)

FENDER
16312

BOLT
N606677-S2
TIGHTEN TO
7-11 N·m
(5-8 FT-LB)

BOLT AND WASHER
N606676-S2
(2 REQ'D)
TIGHTEN TO
7-11 N·m
(5-8 FT-LB)

NUT
N800925-S2

BOLT
N606677-S2
TIGHTEN TO
7-11 N·m
(5-8 FT-LB)

BRACE
16340

BRACE
16340

BOLT-N606676-S2
TIGHTEN TO
7-11 N·m
(5-8 FT-LB)

NUT
N800925-S2

NUT
N800925-S2

BOLT
N606677-S2
TIGHTEN TO
7-11 N·m
(5-8 FT-LB)

NUT
N800925-S2

BOLT-N606676-S2
TIGHTEN TO
7-11 N·m
(5-8 FT-LB)

REAR FLOOR
PAN ASSEMBLY

VIEW C

BRACE
277A52

F-350 DUAL REAR WHEEL FENDER

84920017

Fig. 17 Fender for dual rear wheels

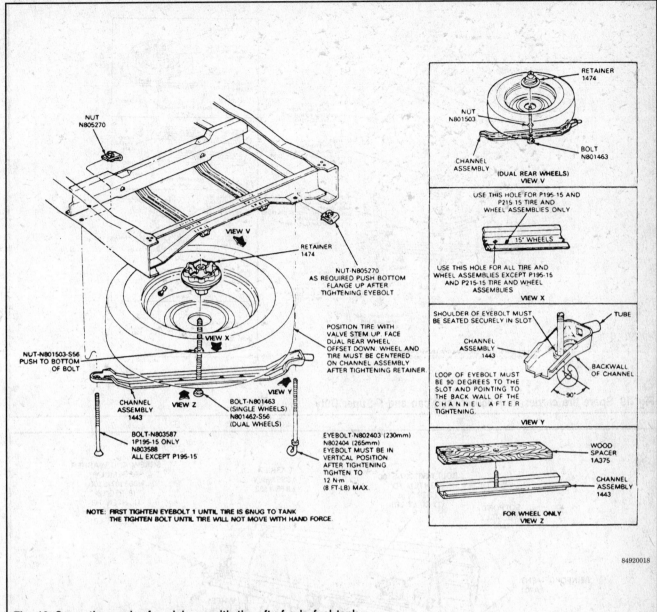

RETAINER
1474

NUT
N801503

CHANNEL
ASSEMBLY

BOLT
N801463

(DUAL REAR WHEELS)
VIEW V

USE THIS HOLE FOR P195-15 AND
P215-15 TIRE AND
WHEEL ASSEMBLIES ONLY

15" WHEELS

USE THIS HOLE FOR ALL TIRE AND
WHEEL ASSEMBLIES EXCEPT P195-15
AND P215-15 TIRE AND WHEEL
ASSEMBLIES

VIEW X

SHOULDER OF EYEBOLT MUST
BE SEATED SECURELY IN SLOT

TUBE

CHANNEL
ASSEMBLY
1443

BACKWALL
OF CHANNEL

LOOP OF EYEBOLT MUST
BE 90 DEGREES TO THE
SLOT AND POINTING TO
THE BACK WALL OF THE
CHANNEL AFTER
TIGHTENING.

VIEW Y

WOOD
SPACER
1A375

CHANNEL
ASSEMBLY
1443

FOR WHEEL ONLY
VIEW Z

NUT
N805270

VIEW V

RETAINER
1474

NUT-N805270
AS REQUIRED PUSH BOTTOM
FLANGE UP AFTER
TIGHTENING EYEBOLT

NUT-N801503-S56
PUSH TO BOTTOM
OF BOLT

VIEW X

POSITION TIRE WITH
VALVE STEM UP. FACE
DUAL REAR WHEEL
OFFSET DOWN. WHEEL AND
TIRE MUST BE CENTERED
ON CHANNEL ASSEMBLY
AFTER TIGHTENING RETAINER.

VIEW Y

CHANNEL
ASSEMBLY
1443

VIEW Z

BOLT-N801463
(SINGLE WHEELS)
N801462-S56
(DUAL WHEELS)

BOLT-N803587
1P195-15 ONLY
N803588
ALL EXCEPT P195-15

EYEBOLT-N802403 (230mm)
N802404 (265mm)
EYEBOLT MUST BE IN
VERTICAL POSITION
AFTER TIGHTENING
TIGHTEN TO
12 N·m
(8 FT-LB) MAX.

NOTE: FIRST TIGHTEN EYEBOLT 1 UNTIL TIRE IS SNUG TO TANK
THE TIGHTEN BOLT UNTIL TIRE WILL NOT MOVE WITH HAND FORCE.

84920018

Fig. 18 Spare tire carrier for pickups with the aft-of-axle fuel tank

Antenna

REMOVAL & INSTALLATION

▸ **See Figures 26 and 27**

1. Disconnect the antenna cable at the radio by pulling it straight out of the set.

2. Working under the instrument panel, disengage the cable from its retainers.

➡**On some models, it may be necessary to remove the instrument panel pad to get at the cable. See Section 6.**

3. Outside, unsnap the cap from the antenna base.

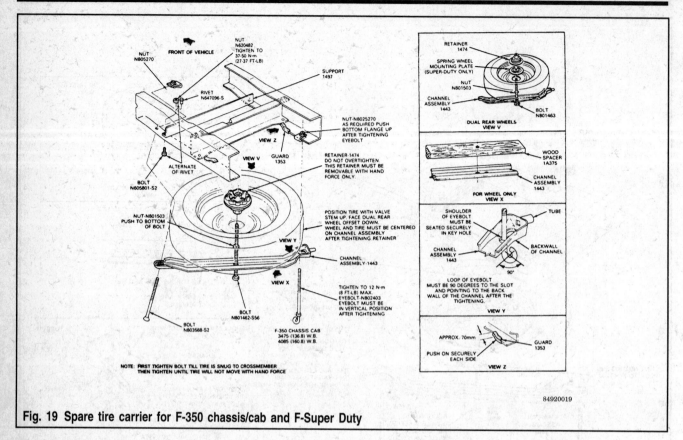

Fig. 19 Spare tire carrier for F-350 chassis/cab and F-Super Duty

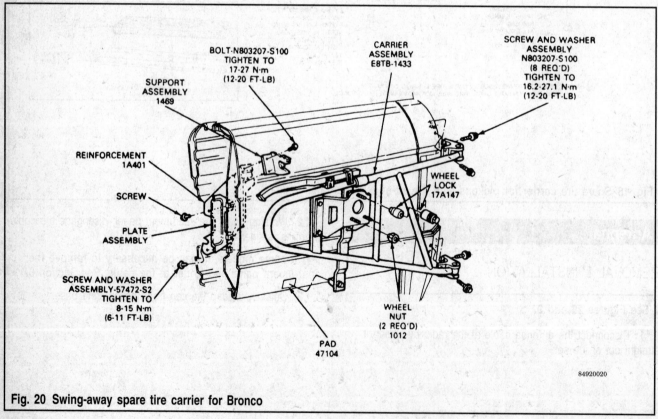

Fig. 20 Swing-away spare tire carrier for Bronco

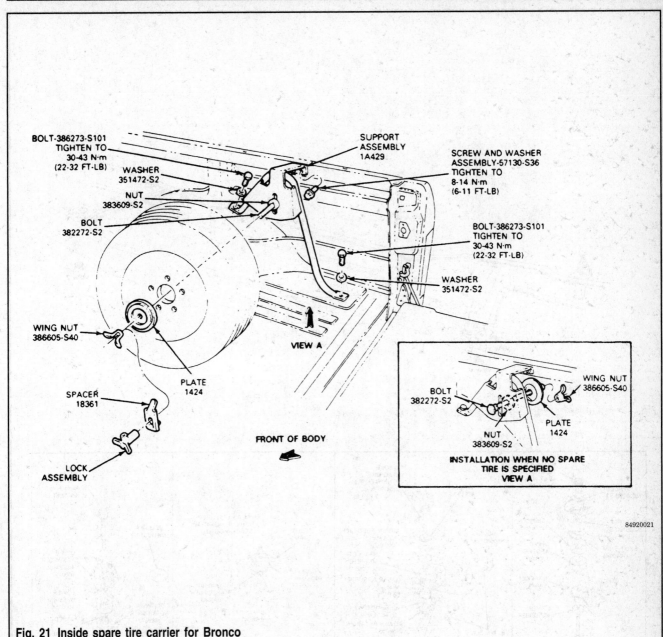

BOLT-386273-S101
TIGHTEN TO
30-43 N·m
(22-32 FT-LB)

WASHER
351472-S2

NUT
383609-S2

BOLT
382272-S2

WING NUT
386605-S40

SPACER
18361

LOCK
ASSEMBLY

PLATE
1424

SUPPORT
ASSEMBLY
1A429

SCREW AND WASHER
ASSEMBLY-57130-S36
TIGHTEN TO
8-14 N·m
(6-11 FT-LB)

BOLT-386273-S101
TIGHTEN TO
30-43 N·m
(22-32 FT-LB)

WASHER
351472-S2

VIEW A

FRONT OF BODY

BOLT
382272-S2

WING NUT
386605-S40

NUT
383609-S2

PLATE
1424

INSTALLATION WHEN NO SPARE
TIRE IS SPECIFIED
VIEW A

84920021

Fig. 21 Inside spare tire carrier for Bronco

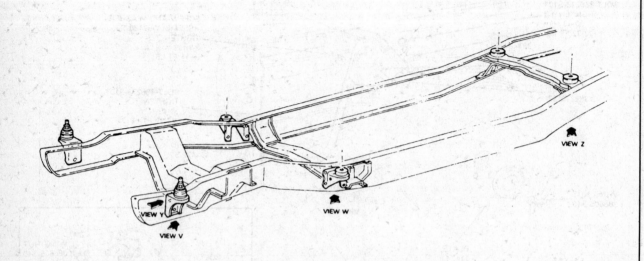

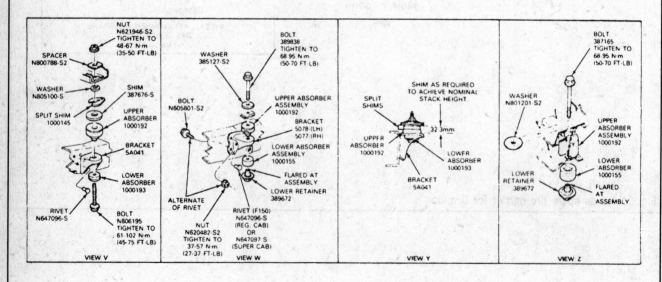

84920022

Fig. 22 Body mounts for the F-150, 250, 350 and F-Super Duty chassis/cab

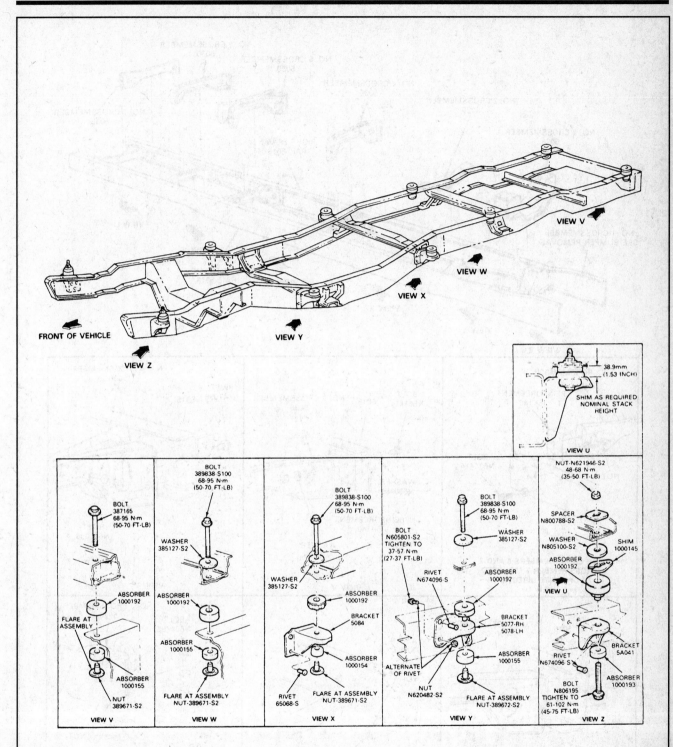

Fig. 23 Body mounts for the Bronco

84920023

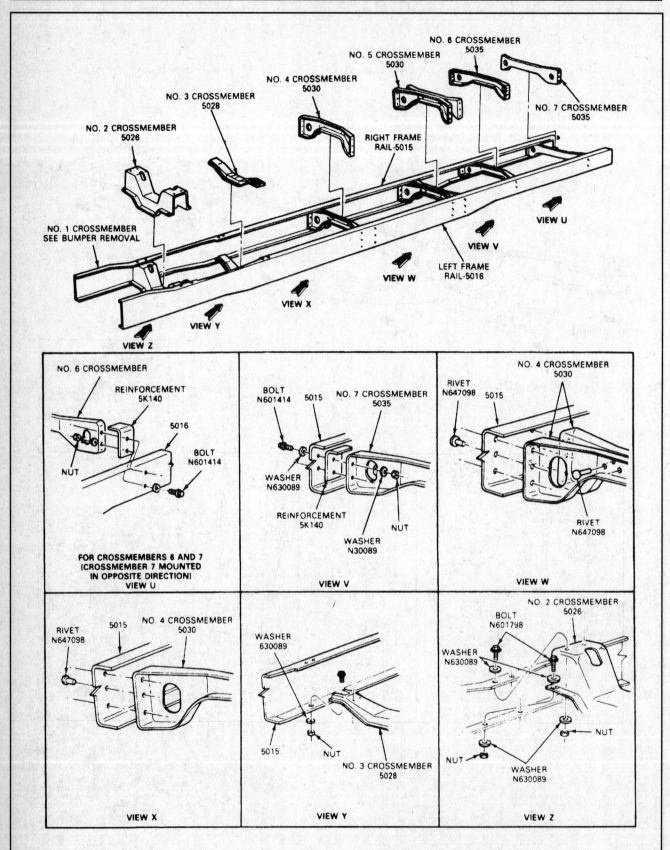

Fig. 24 Frame and crossmember installation for the F-Super Duty stripped chassis — 158 in.

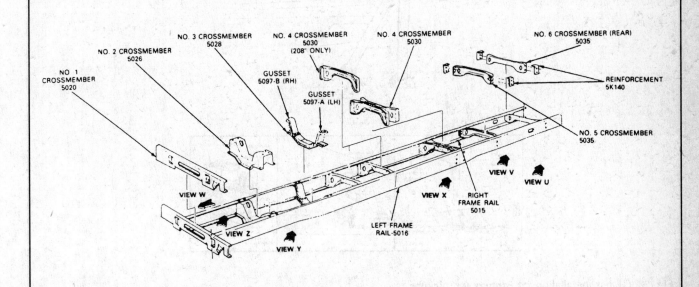

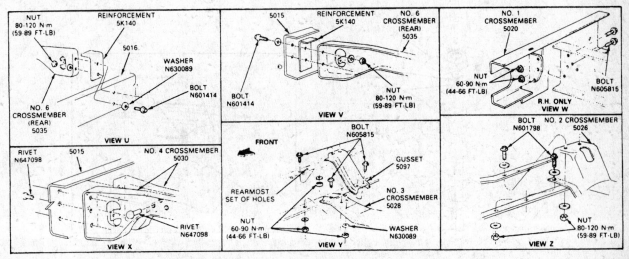

Fig. 25 Frame and crossmember installation for the F-Super Duty motor home chassis — 178 in. and 208 in.

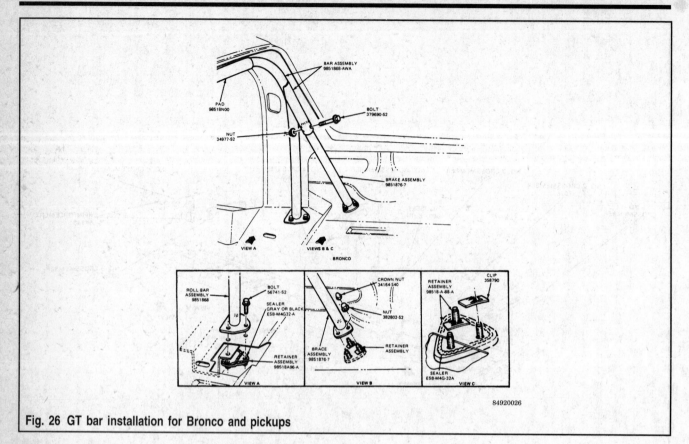

Fig. 26 GT bar installation for Bronco and pickups

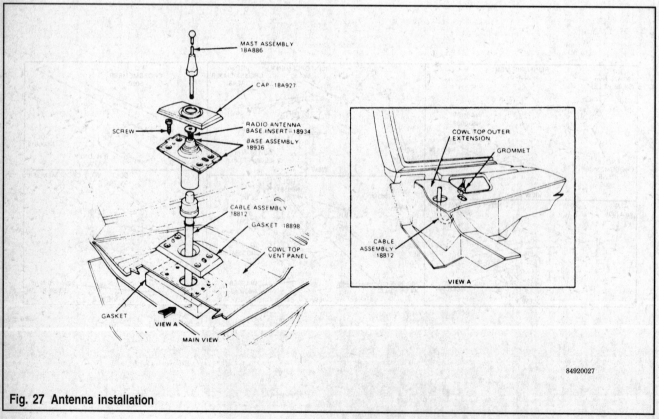

Fig. 27 Antenna installation

4. Remove the 4 screws and lift off the antenna, pulling the cable with it, carefully.

5. Installation is the reverse of removal.

Bronco Fiberglass Roof

REMOVAL & INSTALLATION

Roof

▶ **See Figure 28**

1. Lower the tailgate.

2. Remove the lower trim mouldings from the roof panels.

3. Scribe the locations of each trim moulding bracket and number each bracket as it is removed.

4. Remove all the roof attaching bolts and trim bolts.

5. With at least one other person, carefully lift the roof off of the body. Be careful to avoid tearing the weather-stripping. Be careful to avoid over-flexing the roof. The roof weighs about 120 lbs.

6. Installation is the reverse of removal. Torque the roof retaining bolts to 72-84 inch lbs.

Stationary Window

▶ **See Figures 29 and 30**

➡ **You'll need an assistant for this job.**

1. Have your assistant stand outside and support the glass.

2. Working from the inside truck, start at one upper corner and work the weather-stripping across the top of the glass, pulling the weather-stripping down and pushing outward on the glass until your assistant can grab the glass and lift it out.

3. Remove the mouldings.

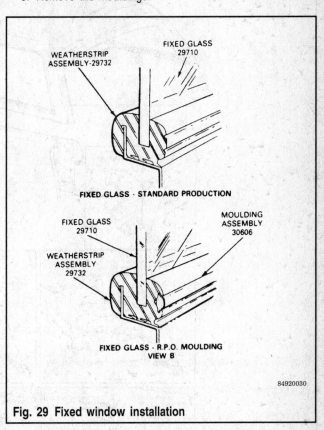

Fig. 29 Fixed window installation

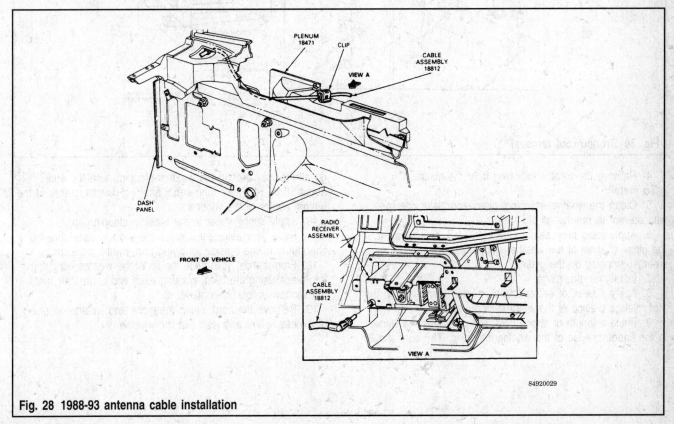

Fig. 28 1988-93 antenna cable installation

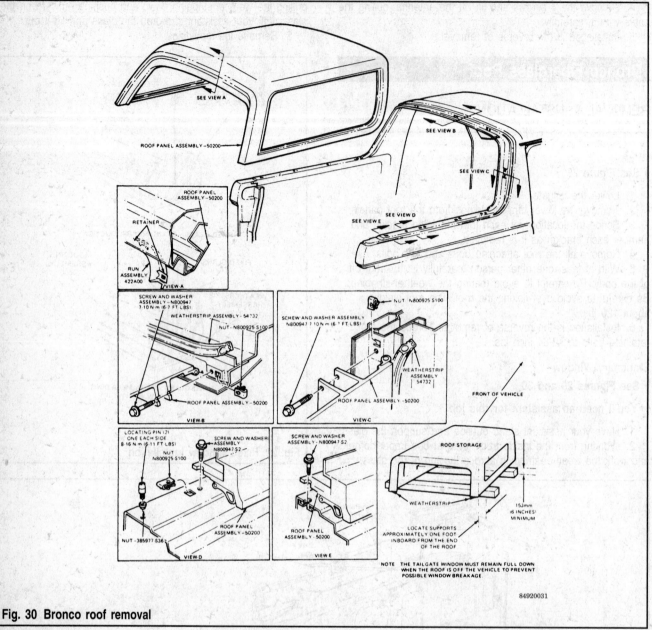

Fig. 30 Bronco roof removal

4. Remove the weather-stripping from the glass.

To install:

5. Clean the weather-stripping, glass and glass opening with solvent to remove all old sealer.

6. Apply liquid butyl sealer C9AZ-19554-B, or equivalent, in the glass channel of the weather-stripping and install the weather-stripping on the glass.

7. Install the mouldings.

8. Apply a bead of sealer to the opening flange and in the inner flange crevice of the weather-stripping lip.

9. Place a length of strong cord, such as butcher's twine, in the flange crevice of the weather-stripping. The cord should go all the way around the weather-stripping with the ends, about 18 in. (457mm) long each, hanging down together at the bottom center of the window.

10. Apply soapy water to the weather-stripping lip.

11. Have your assistant position the window assembly in the channel from the outside, applying firm inward pressure.

12. From inside, you guide the lip of the weather-stripping into place using the cord, working each end alternately, until the window is locked in place.

13. Remove the cord, clean the glass and weather-stripping of excess sealer and leak test the window.

INTERIOR

Door Trim Panels

REMOVAL & INSTALLATION

▶ **See Figure 31**

1. Remove the armrest.
2. Remove the door handle screw and pull off the handle.
3. If equipped with manual windows, remove the window regulator handle screw and pull off the handle. On vehicles with power windows, remove the power window switch housing.
4. If equipped with manual door locks, remove the door lock control. On vehicles with power door locks, remove the power door lock switch housing.
5. On models with electric outside rear view mirrors, remove the power mirror switch housing.

6. Using a flat wood spatula, insert it carefully behind the panel and slide it along to find the push-pins. When you encounter a pin, pry the pin outward. Do this until all the pins are out. NEVER PULL ON THE PANEL TO REMOVE THE PINS!
7. Installation is the reverse of removal.

Interior Trim Panels

REMOVAL & INSTALLATION

▶ **See Figures 32 and 33**

All interior trim panels are retained by either screws or push pins. Illustrations show the panels and their positioning. In the case of push pins, use a flat bladed tool such as a spatula and pry out on the panel next to each pin.

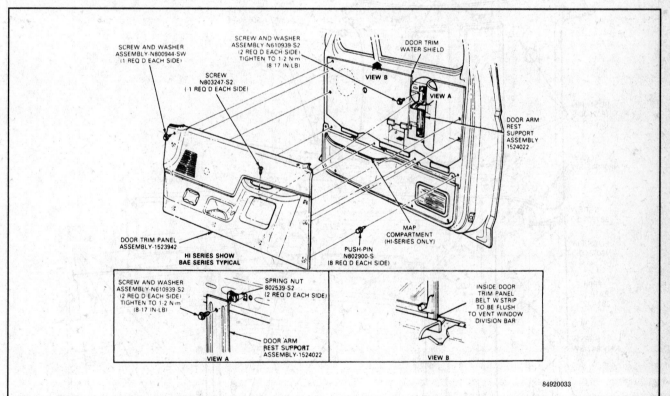

Fig. 31 Door trim panel installation

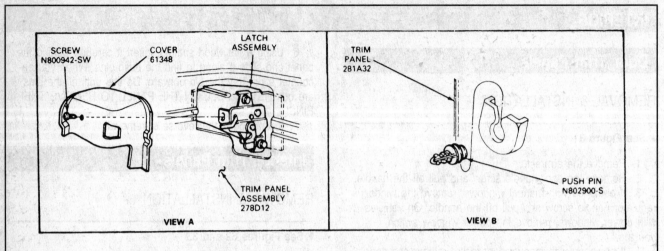

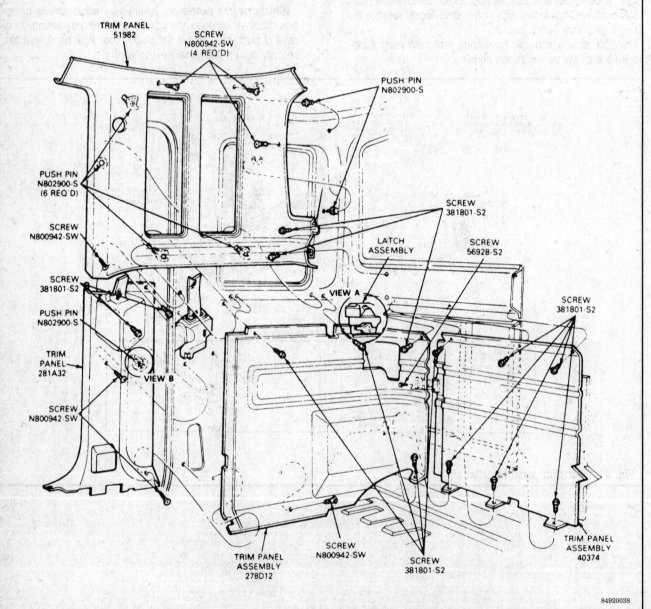

Fig. 32 F-150, 250, 350 super cab body trim panels

84920038

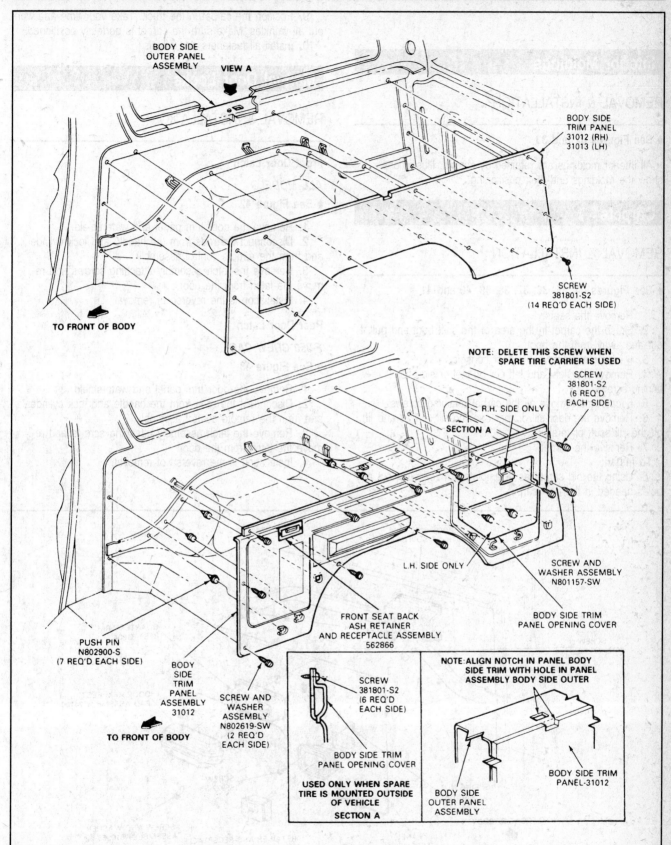

BODY SIDE OUTER PANEL ASSEMBLY

VIEW A

BODY SIDE TRIM PANEL
31012 (RH)
31013 (LH)

SCREW
381801-S2
(14 REQ'D EACH SIDE)

TO FRONT OF BODY

NOTE: DELETE THIS SCREW WHEN SPARE TIRE CARRIER IS USED

SCREW
381801-S2
(6 REQ'D EACH SIDE)

R.H. SIDE ONLY

SECTION A

L.H. SIDE ONLY

FRONT SEAT BACK ASH RETAINER AND RECEPTACLE ASSEMBLY
562866

SCREW AND WASHER ASSEMBLY
N801157-SW

BODY SIDE TRIM PANEL OPENING COVER

PUSH PIN
N802900-S
(7 REQ'D EACH SIDE)

BODY SIDE TRIM PANEL ASSEMBLY
31012

SCREW AND WASHER ASSEMBLY
N802619-SW
(2 REQ'D EACH SIDE)

TO FRONT OF BODY

SCREW
381801-S2
(6 REQ'D EACH SIDE)

BODY SIDE TRIM PANEL OPENING COVER

USED ONLY WHEN SPARE TIRE IS MOUNTED OUTSIDE OF VEHICLE

SECTION A

NOTE: ALIGN NOTCH IN PANEL BODY SIDE TRIM WITH HOLE IN PANEL ASSEMBLY BODY SIDE OUTER

BODY SIDE TRIM PANEL-31012

BODY SIDE OUTER PANEL ASSEMBLY

84920041

Fig. 33 Bronco standard side trim panels

Interior Moldings

REMOVAL & INSTALLATION

▶ **See Figures 32 and 33**

All interior moldings are retained by screws. Illustrations show the moldings and their positioning.

Carpets

REMOVAL & INSTALLATION

▶ **See Figures 34, 35, 36, 37, 38, 39, 40 and 41**

1. Remove the seats.
2. Grasp the carpet in the area of the shift boot and pull it out and away from the boot.
3. If equipped, remove the floor console.
4. Remove the right and left cowl panel or side panel retaining screws.
5. Locate and remove all the carpet retaining screws.
6. Remove the door sill or rear opening sill screws and lift off the sill scuff plate(s).
7. Remove the carpet.

To install:

8. Using the old carpet as a template, if necessary, cut any holes needed in the new carpet.

9. Position the carpet in the truck. Take your time and work out all wrinkles. Make sure the carpet is perfectly positioned.
10. Install all fasteners and panels.

Manual Door Locks

REMOVAL & INSTALLATION

Front Door Latch

ALL MODELS

▶ **See Figure 42**

1. Remove the door trim panel and watershield.
2. Disconnect the rods from the handle and lock cylinder, and from the remote control assembly.
3. Remove the latch assembly attaching screws and remove the latch from the door.
4. Installation is the reverse of removal.

Rear Door Latch

F-350 CREW CAB

▶ **See Figure 43**

1. Remove the door trim panel and watershield.
2. Disconnect the rods from the handle and lock cylinder, and from the remote control assembly.
3. Remove the latch assembly attaching screws and remove the latch from the door.
4. Installation is the reverse of removal.

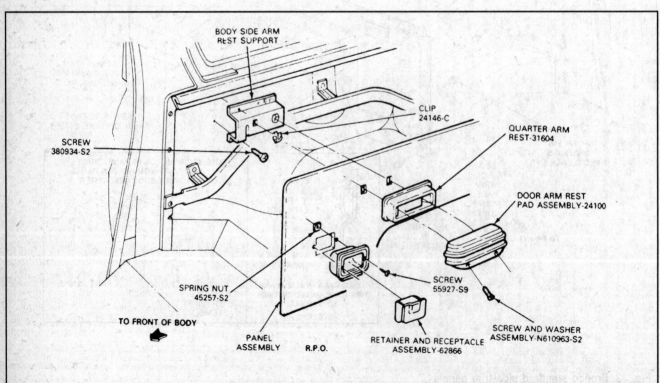

Fig. 34 Bronco optional side trim armrest and ashtray

84920042

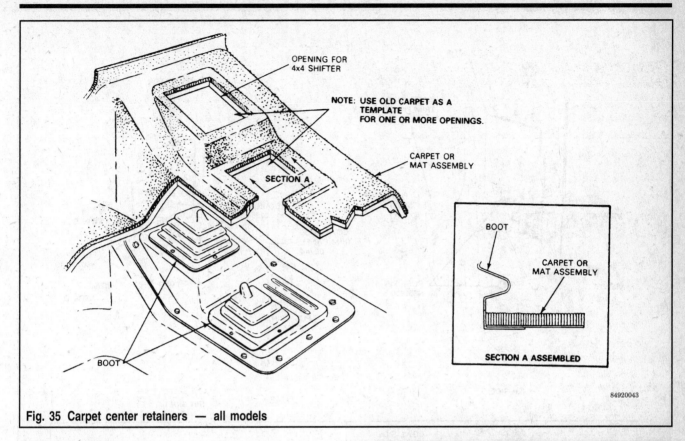

OPENING FOR
4x4 SHIFTER

NOTE: USE OLD CARPET AS A
TEMPLATE
FOR ONE OR MORE OPENINGS.

CARPET OR
MAT ASSEMBLY

SECTION A

BOOT

BOOT

CARPET OR
MAT ASSEMBLY

SECTION A ASSEMBLED

84920043

Fig. 35 Carpet center retainers — all models

Door Lock Linkage

1. Remove the door trim panels.
2. Remove the door lock control attaching screws and remove the control from the door.
3. Disconnect the linkage rod from the control.
4. Installation is the reverse of removal. Transfer the clip to the new linkage.

Door Lock Cylinder

1. Place the window in the UP position.
2. Remove the trim panel and watershield.
3. Disconnect the actuating rod from the lock control link clip.
4. Slide the retainer away from the lock cylinder.
5. Pull the cylinder from the door.
6. Installation is the reverse of removal.

Tailgate Lock Cylinder

1. Remove the tailgate access cover.
2. Raise the glass. If the glass can't be raised, remove it as described below.
3. Remove the lock cylinder retainer.
4. Disengage the lock cylinder from the switch and remove it from the tailgate.
5. Installation is the reverse of removal.

Power Door Locks

REMOVAL & INSTALLATION

Actuator Motor

▶ See Figures 44 and 45

1. Remove the door trim panel.
2. Disconnect the motor from the door latch.
3. Remove the motor and swivel bracket from the door by drilling out the pop rivet.
4. Disconnect the wiring harness.
5. Installation is the reverse of removal. Make sure that the pop rivet is tight.

Control Switch

1. Insert a small, thin-bladed screwdriver into the spring tab slots at the front and rear of the switch housing, and pop the housing out.
2. Remove the 3 connector attaching screws from the switch housing.
3. The switch is held in place by the electrical contact pins. Carefully pry the switch away from the connector to remove it.
4. Installation is the reverse of removal. The switch can be install only one way.

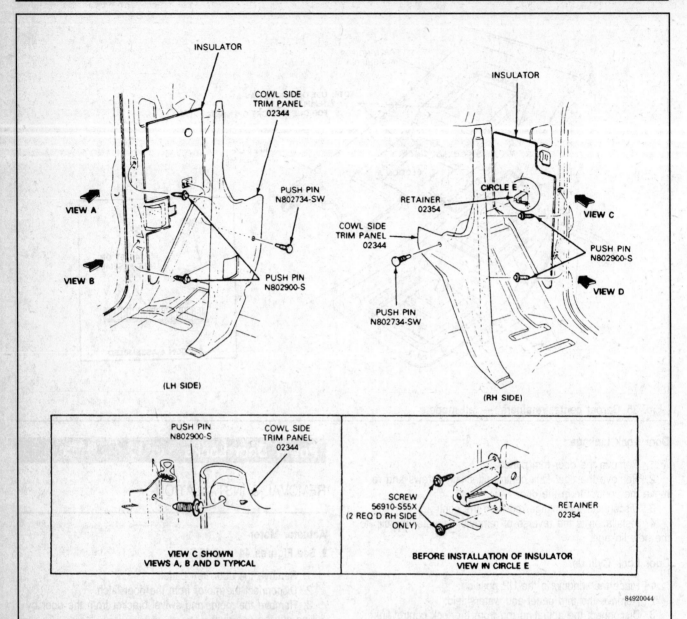

Fig. 36 Cowl side trim panels — all models

Vent Window

REMOVAL & INSTALLATION

1. Remove the door trim panel.
2. Remove the division bar-to-door panel screw.
3. Remove the 2 screws retaining the vent window to the door leading edge.
4. Lower the door window all the way.
5. Pull the glass run part of the way out of the door run retainer in the area of the division bar.
6. Tilt the vent window and division bar rearwards and pull the vent window assembly from the door.

7. Remove the 2 pivot-to-frame screws.
8. Remove the nut and spring from the lower pivot.
9. Separate the glass retainer and the pivot stops from the frame and weather-stripping.

To install:

10. Re-assemble the parts of the window and install the 2 pivot-to-frame screws.
11. Install the spring and nut. The spring tension should be adjusted so that the window will stay open at highway speeds.
12. Place the run assembly in the vent assembly.
13. Place the window and division bar in the door. Make sure the spacer is in position.
14. Install the window-to-door edge screws.
15. Install the division bar screw. Adjust the run for proper window operation.
16. Install the door trim.

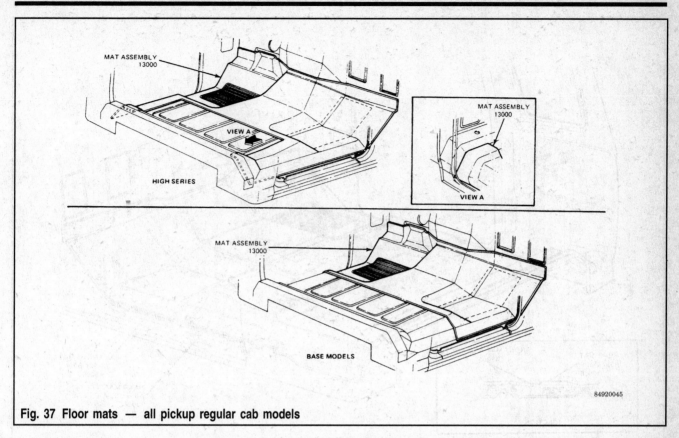

Fig. 37 Floor mats — all pickup regular cab models

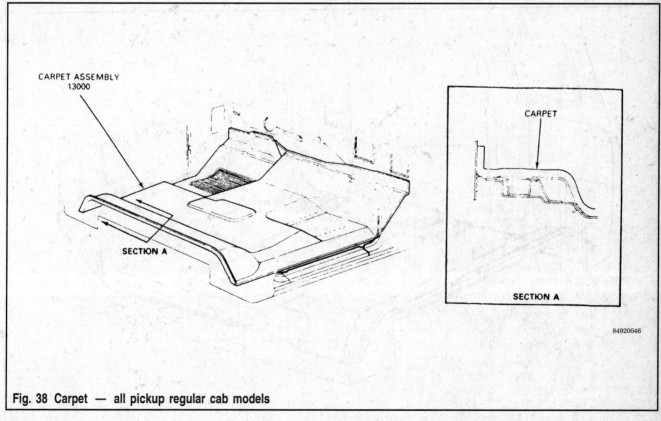

Fig. 38 Carpet — all pickup regular cab models

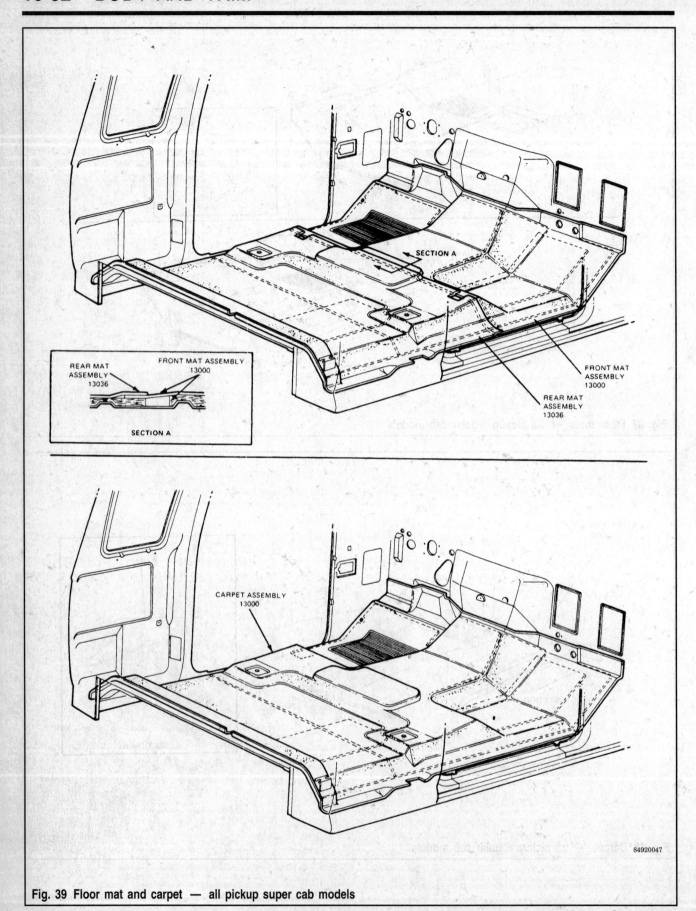

Fig. 39 Floor mat and carpet — all pickup super cab models

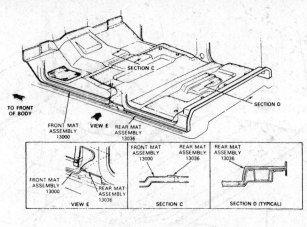

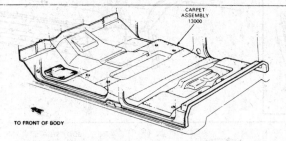

Fig. 40 Floor mat and carpet — F-350 crew cab models

Stationary Window Glass

REMOVAL & INSTALLATION

F-150, 250, 350, Super Duty Back Window

▶ See Figure 46

➡ You'll need an assistant for this job.

1. Have your assistant stand outside and support the glass.
2. Working from the inside truck, start at one upper corner and work the weather-stripping across the top of the glass, pulling the weather-stripping down and pushing outward on the glass until your assistant can grab the glass and lift it out.
3. Remove the mouldings.
4. Remove the weather-stripping from the glass.

To install:

5. Clean the weather-stripping, glass and glass opening with solvent to remove all old sealer.
6. Apply liquid butyl sealer C9AZ-19554-B, or equivalent, in the glass channel of the weather-stripping and install the weather-stripping on the glass.
7. Install the mouldings.
8. Apply a bead of sealer to the opening flange and in the inner flange crevice of the weather-stripping lip.
9. Place a length of strong cord, such as butcher's twine, in the flange crevice of the weather-stripping. The cord should go all the way around the weather-stripping with the ends, about 18 in. (457mm) long each, hanging down together at the bottom center of the window.
10. Apply soapy water to the weather-stripping lip.

11. Have your assistant position the window assembly in the channel from the outside, applying firm inward pressure.
12. From inside, you guide the lip of the weather-stripping into place using the cord, working each end alternately, until the window is locked in place.
13. Remove the cord, clean the glass and weather-stripping of excess sealer and leak test the window.

Super Cab Quarter Window

▶ See Figures 47 and 48

1. Remove the quarter trim panel.
2. Remove the nuts retaining the molding.
3. Remove the window and seal.
4. Installation is the reverse of removal.

F-150, 250, 350, Super Duty Movable Back Window

▶ See Figure 49

➡ You'll need a helper to catch the glass.

1. Working inside, pull down the weather-stripping lip and push the window frame and weather-stripping out.
2. Remove the weather-stripping from the frame and place the window in the open position.
3. Remove the division bar-to-frame screws.
4. Remove the 2 anchor plate-to-window track screws and remove the plate.
5. Spread the frame and work the glass out of its track.
6. If new glass is being installed, remove the division bar.

To install:

7. Apply silicone grease to the weather-stripping and track. Spread the frame slightly and slide the glass into place. Don't bunch the weather-stripping.

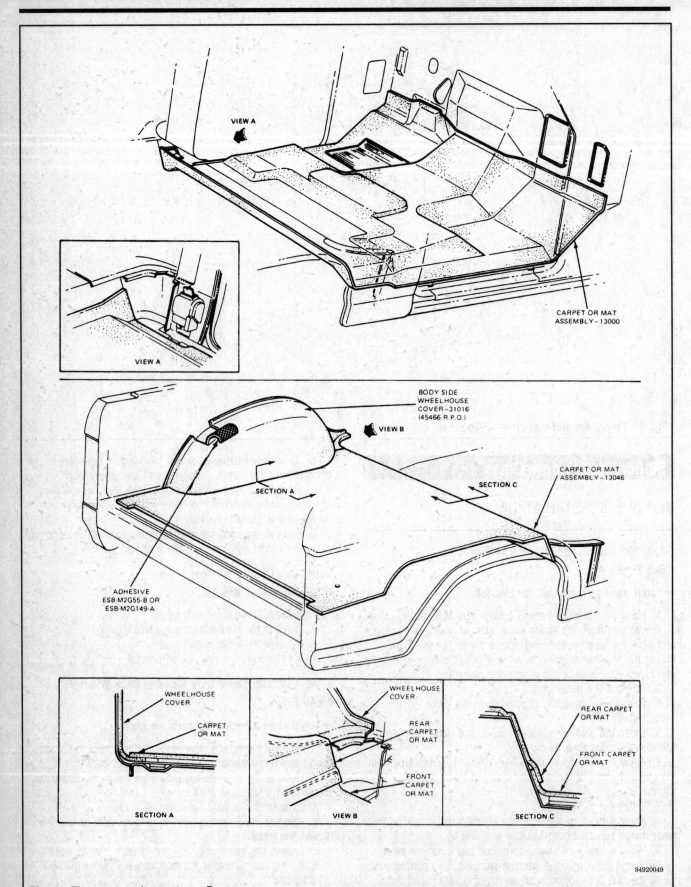

Fig. 41 Floor mat and carpet — Bronco

VIEW A

VIEW A

CARPET OR MAT
ASSEMBLY—13000

BODY SIDE
WHEELHOUSE
COVER—31016
(45466 R.P.O.)

VIEW B

CARPET OR MAT
ASSEMBLY—13046

SECTION A

SECTION C

ADHESIVE
ESB-M2G55-B OR
ESB-M2G149-A

WHEELHOUSE
COVER

CARPET
OR MAT

SECTION A

WHEELHOUSE
COVER

REAR
CARPET
OR MAT

FRONT
CARPET
OR MAT

VIEW B

REAR CARPET
OR MAT

FRONT CARPET
OR MAT

SECTION C

84920049

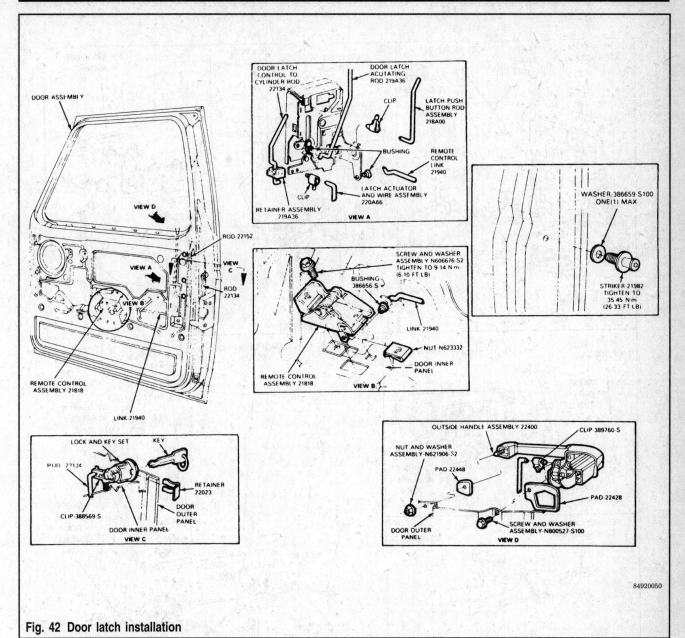

Fig. 42 Door latch installation

8. Install the division bar.
9. Spread the frame slightly and install the sliding glass.
10. Install the anchor plate.
11. Install the anchor plate.
12. Clean the weather-stripping, glass and glass opening with solvent to remove all old sealer.
13. Position the weather-stripping on the frame.
14. Apply a 203mm (8 in.) bead of liquid butyl sealer C9AZ-19554-B, or equivalent, between the two secondary sealing fins centered in each upper corner.
15. Place a length of strong cord, such as butcher's twine, in the flange crevice of the weather-stripping. The cord should go all the way around the weather-stripping with the ends, about 18 in. (457mm) long each, hanging down together at the bottom center of the window.
16. Have your assistant position the window assembly in the channel from the outside, applying firm inward pressure.

17. From inside, you guide the lip of the weather-stripping into place using the cord, working each end alternately, until the window is locked in place.
18. Remove the cord, clean the glass and weather-stripping of excess sealer and leak test the window.

Windshield

REMOVAL & INSTALLATION

▶ **See Figures 50 and 51**

➡**You'll need Windshield Installation Kit E0AZ-19562-A, or equivalent urethane installation kit, and a helper.**

1. Remove the windshield wiper arms.
2. Remove all windshield moldings and retainers.

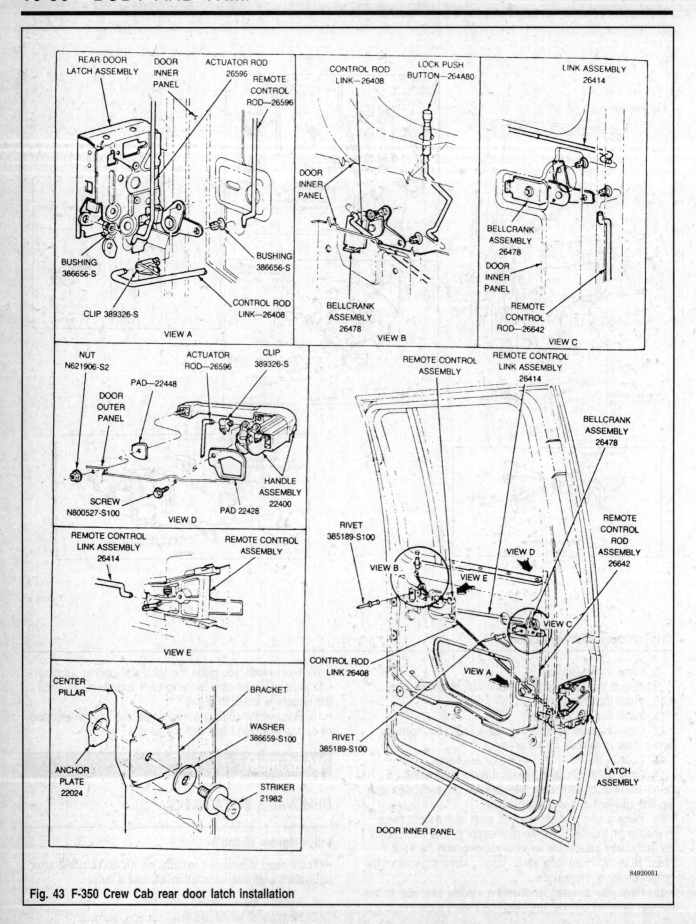

Fig. 43 F-350 Crew Cab rear door latch installation

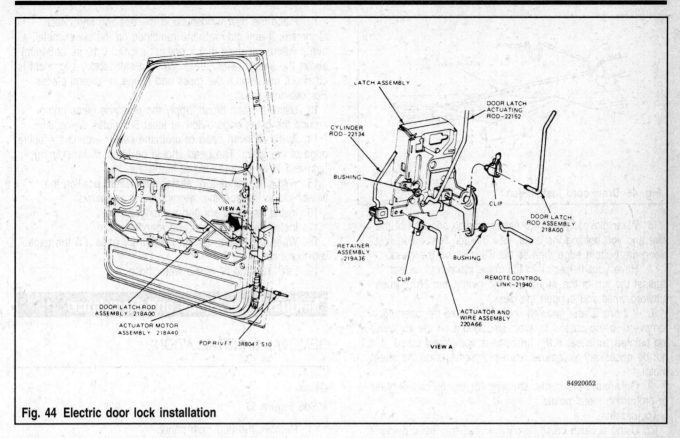

Fig. 44 Electric door lock installation

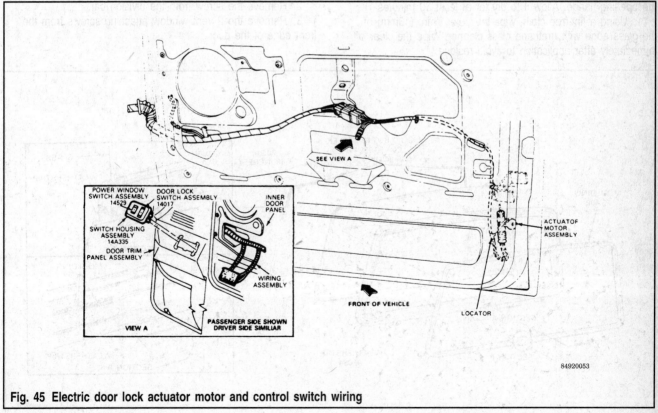

Fig. 45 Electric door lock actuator motor and control switch wiring

3. Remove the rearview mirror.

4. Obtain a 914mm (36 in.) length of steel piano wire. The wire should be the smallest diameter available.

5. Using an aluminum rod, 3/16 in. in diameter with a notch in one end, force the wire through the urethane seal at the bottom of the windshield at one corner.

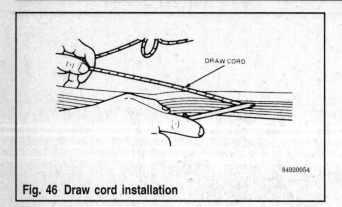

Fig. 46 Draw cord installation

6. Wear gloves. With your helper holding one end of the wire and you holding the other, saw through the sealer, first along the bottom edge then all the way around the glass.

7. Have your helper sit in the truck, place his/her feet against the top of the windshield and gently, but firmly push outward while you support the glass.

8. If there is any uncured urethane around the opening, remove it, being careful to avoid smearing it on the surrounding painted surfaces. If the urethane is completely cured, it will not be necessary to remove any which remains on the sheet metal.

9. Go around the frame, checking for broken bits of glass or protruding metal points.

To install:

10. Using a clean brush, apply the urethane metal primer to the opening flange. Allow it to dry for at least 30 minutes.

11. Using a lint-free cloth, wipe the outer ½ in. (13mm) of the glass edge with urethane glass cleaner. Wipe the clear off immediately after application to avoid residue.

12. Place the new windshield in the opening and check alignment. If any old urethane remained on the sheet metal, trim it with a razor so that it doesn't exceed 0.10 in. (2.54mm) above the sheet metal flange. When a satisfactory alignment is obtained, matchmark the glass and flange in several places. Remove the glass.

13. Using a clean brush, apply the urethane glass primer around the glass edge. Allow at least 5 minutes drying time.

14. Apply an even bead of urethane sealer around the entire edge of the glass. The bead should be about ½ in. (13mm) high and ¼ in. (6mm) wide at its base.

15. Within 15 minutes of sealer application, position the windshield in the opening, aligning the matchmarks.

16. Install the retainers and moldings.

17. Install the wiper arms and rearview mirror.

18. When the sealer is dry, check it for gaps. Fill the gaps with butyl sealer.

19. Leak test the fit with a water hose.

Manual Door Glass and Regulator

REMOVAL & INSTALLATION

Glass

▶ See Figure 52

1. Remove the door trim panel.

2. Remove the screw from the division bar.

3. Remove the 2 vent window attaching screws from the front edge of the door.

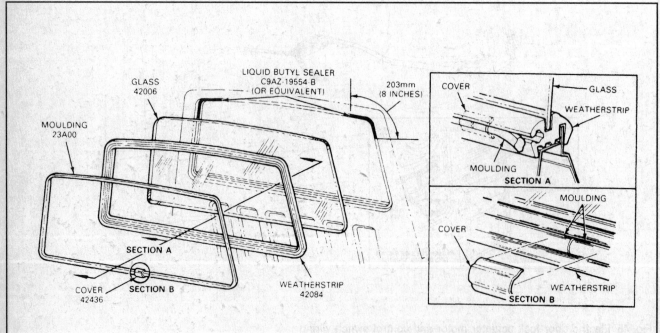

Fig. 47 Stationary back window — pickups and Super Duty

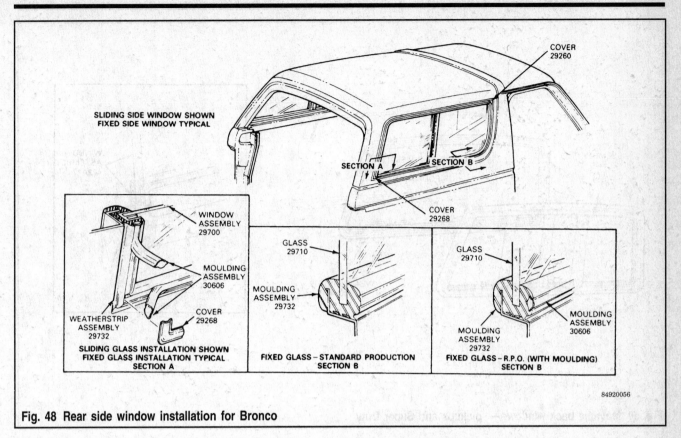

Fig. 48 Rear side window installation for Bronco

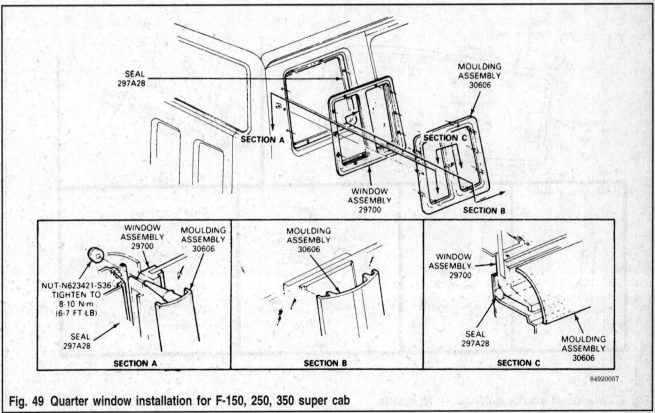

Fig. 49 Quarter window installation for F-150, 250, 350 super cab

4. Lower the glass and pull the glass out of the run retainer near the vent window division bar, just enough to allow the removal of the vent window.

5. Push the front edge of the glass downward and remove it from the door.

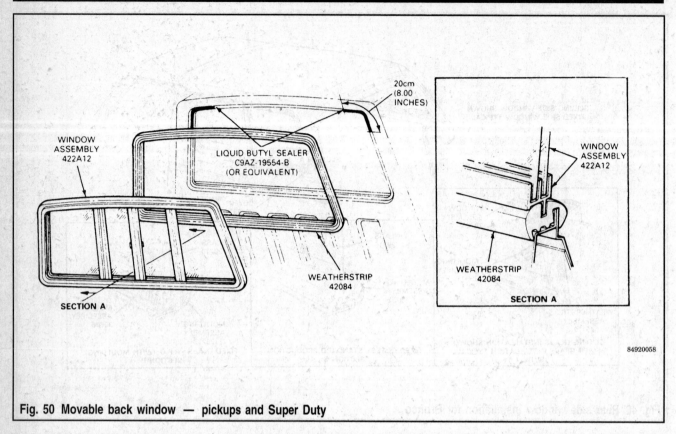

Fig. 50 Movable back window — pickups and Super Duty

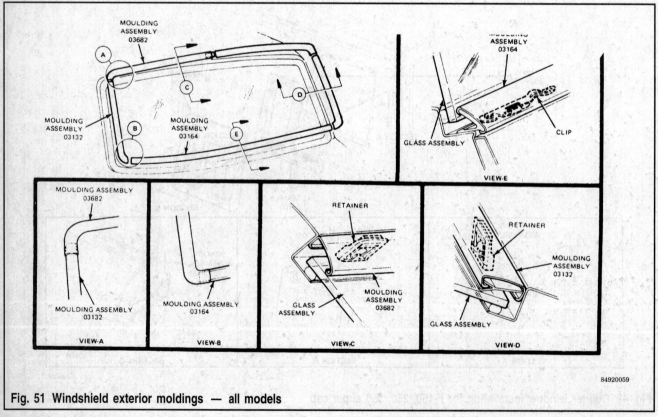

Fig. 51 Windshield exterior moldings — all models

6. Remove the glass from the channel using Glass and Channel Removal Tool 2900, made by the Sommer and Mala Glass Machine Co. of Chicago, ILL., or its equivalent.

7. Glass installation is the reverse of removal. Check the operation of the window before installing the trim panel.

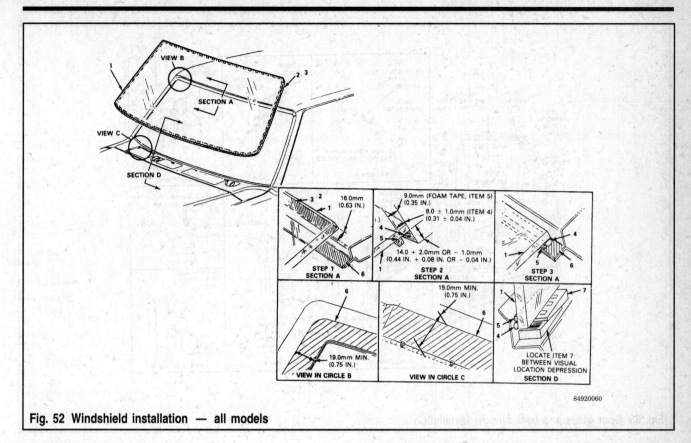

Fig. 52 Windshield installation — all models

Regulator

▶ **See Figure 53**

1. Remove the door trim panel.
2. Support the glass in the full UP position.
3. Drill out the regulator attaching rivets using a ¼ in. (6mm) drill bit.
4. Disengage the regulator arm from the glass bracket and remove the regulator.
5. Installation is the reverse of removal. ¼ in.-20 · ½ in. bolts and nuts may be used in place of the rivets to attach the regulator.

Power Door Glass and Regulator Motor

REMOVAL & INSTALLATION

Glass

▶ **See Figure 54**

1. Remove the door trim panel.
2. Remove the screw from the division bar.
3. Remove the 2 vent window attaching screws from the front edge of the door.
4. Lower the glass and pull the glass out of the run retainer near the vent window division bar, just enough to allow the removal of the vent window.

5. Push the front edge of the glass downward and remove it from the door.
6. Remove the glass from the channel using Glass and Channel Removal Tool 2900, made by the Sommer and Mala Glass Machine Co. of Chicago, ILL., or its equivalent.
7. Glass installation is the reverse of removal. Check the operation of the window before installing the trim panel.

Regulator

1. Disconnect the battery ground.
2. Remove the door trim panel.
3. Disconnect the window motor wiring harness.
4. There are 2 dimples in the door panel, opposite the 2 concealed motor retaining bolts. Using a ½ in. (13mm) drill bit, drill out these dimples to gain access to the motor bolts. Be careful to avoid damage to the wires.
5. Remove the 3 motor mounting bolts.
6. Push the motor towards the outside of the door to disengage it from the gears. You'll have to support the window glass once the motor is disengaged.
7. Remove the motor from the door.
8. Installation is the reverse of removal. To avoid rusting in the drilled areas, prime and paint the exposed metal, or, cover the holes with waterproof body tape. Torque the motor mounting bolts to 50-85 inch lbs. Make sure that the motor works properly before installing the trim panel.

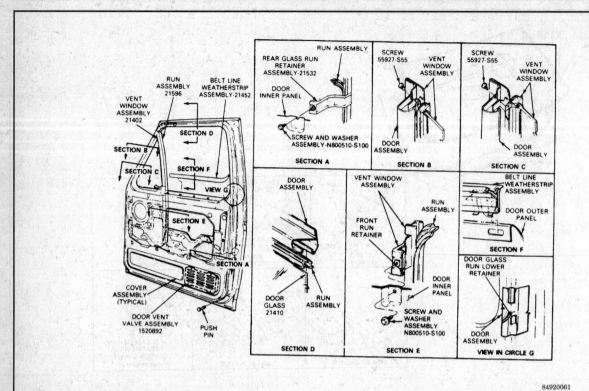

Fig. 53 Door glass and vent window installation

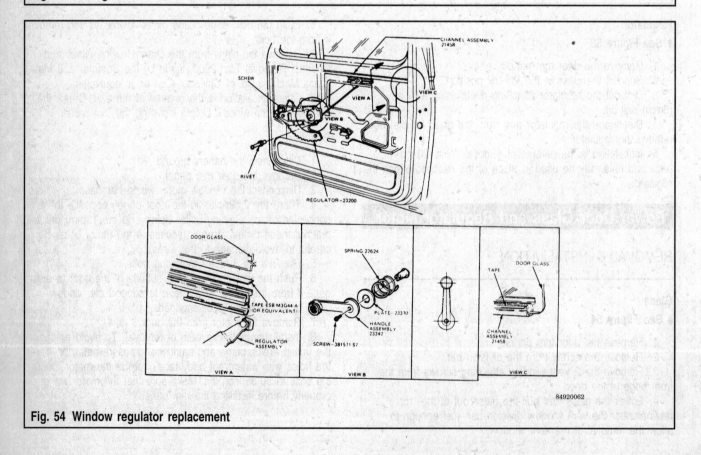

Fig. 54 Window regulator replacement

Bronco Tailgate Window Glass

ADJUSTMENT

1. Fore-aft adjustment is made by loosening the glass run attaching screws and positioning the glass as required. Tighten the screws to 10 ft. lbs.

2. Side-to-side adjustment is made by loosening the glass-to-window bracket nuts and positioning the glass as required. Torque the nuts to 10 ft. lbs.

REMOVAL & INSTALLATION

▶ **See Figures 55, 56, 57 and 58**

1. Open the tailgate.
2. Remove the access cover.
3. Remove the watershield.
4. Remove the cover panel support.
5. Using the template illustrated, centerpunch the holes noted on the inner panel.

➡**The template shown is not actual size. The actual template can be purchased at a Ford dealer.**

6. Using a ⅝ in. (16mm) holesaw, cut 4 holes at the template hole location.

❄❄WARNING

Cover the glass with protective padding prior to cutting the holes.

7. Working through the holes, remove the 4 glass bracket retaining nuts.
8. Using a ⁵⁄₁₆ in. (8mm) drift punch, remove the glass bracket C-channel from the glass and bracket.
9. Remove the padding and drillings.
10. Grasp the glass at the 2 bottom cutouts and slide it to the half-open position. Disconnect the rear window grid wire, if so equipped, and remove the glass from the tailgate.
11. Make sure that you remove all the drillings from the tailgate. Vacuuming them out is a good idea. These drillings, if left in the tailgate will lead to rusting of the surrounding metal. Prime and paint the drilled out holes to prevent rusting.

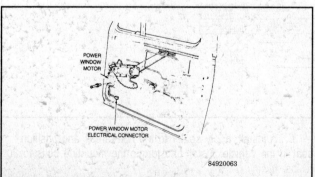

POWER
WINDOW
MOTOR

POWER WINDOW MOTOR
ELECTRICAL CONNECTOR

84920063

Fig. 55 Power window installation

12. Installation is the reve... retaining nuts to 10 ft. lbs.

Bronco Tailgate W... Motor

REMOVAL & INSTALL...

▶ **See Figures 59 and 60**

1. Lower the tailgate and remove the access panel. If the glass cannot be lowered, remove the access panel and depress the lockout rod located in the bottom center of the tailgate.
2. Using a jumper to the tailgate motor, raise the glass to the full up position. If the glass cannot be raised it will have to be removed as outlined above.
3. Remove the regulator mounting bolts and nuts and lift out the regulator.
4. Disconnect the motor harness.

❄❄CAUTION

The counterbalance spring is under considerable tension. To prevent injury from sudden movement of the regulator components, clamp or lock the gear sectors prior to removing the components!

5. Detach the motor from the tailgate and remove it.
6. Installation is the reverse of removal. Torque the regulator mounting bolts to 10 ft. lbs.

Inside Rear View Mirror

The mirror is held in place with a single setscrew. Loosen the screw and lift the mirror off. Repair kit for damaged mirrors are available and most auto parts stores.

Front Bench Seat

REMOVAL & INSTALLATION

▶ **See Figure 61**

1. Remove the 4 seat track-to-floor pan bolts.
2. Carefully lift the seat and remove from the vehicle.
To install:
3. Apply sealer to the mounting hole areas.
4. Install the seat in the vehicle and adjust position.
5. Install the mounting bolts and torque to 30 ft. lbs.

Driver's Bucket Seat

REMOVAL & INSTALLATION

▶ **See Figures 62 and 63**

1. Remove the 4 seat track-to-floor pan bolts.

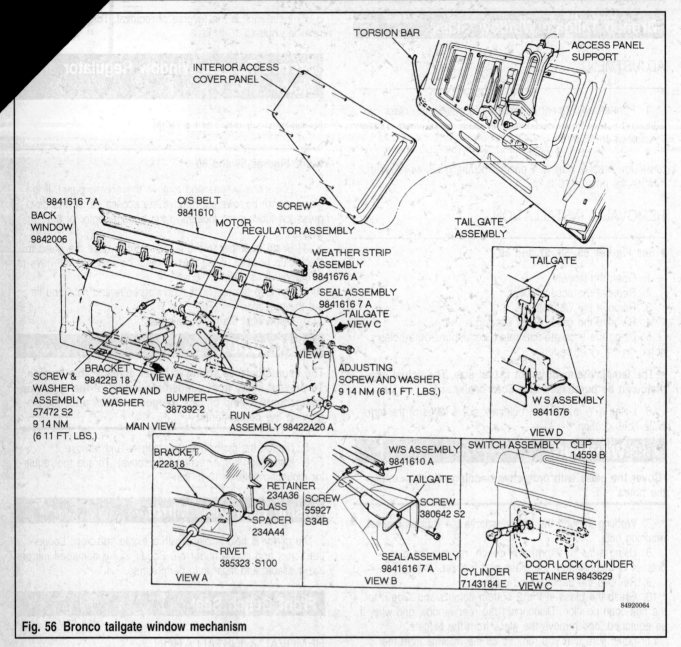

Fig. 56 Bronco tailgate window mechanism

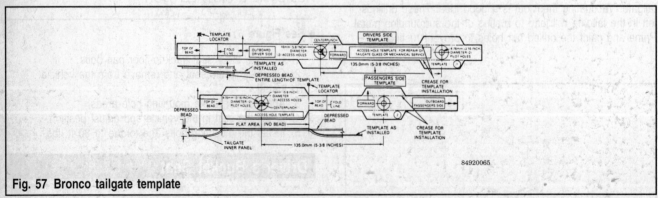

Fig. 57 Bronco tailgate template

2. Lift the seat and remove from the vehicle.

3. To install, apply sealer to the hole areas and position seat in the vehicle. Install and torque the mounting bolts to 30 ft. lbs.

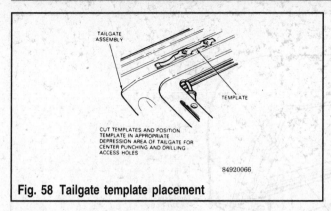

Fig. 58 Tailgate template placement

Fig. 59 Bronco tailgate glass bracket installation

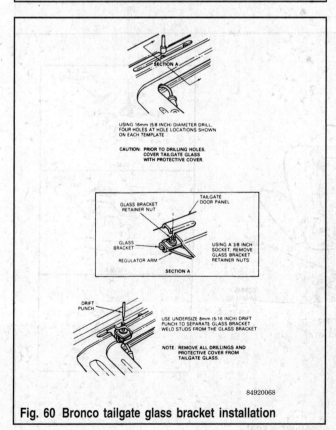

Fig. 60 Bronco tailgate glass bracket installation

Driver's Captain's Chair

REMOVAL & INSTALLATION

▶ **See Figure 64**

1. Remove the 4 seat track-to-floor pan bolts and lift out the seat.
2. Apply sealer to the hole areas and install the seat. Torque the bolts to 30 ft. lbs.

Passenger's Bucket Seat or Captain's Chair

REMOVAL & INSTALLATION

1. Remove the 2 front bolts retaining the passenger's seat and support assembly to the floor pan.
2. Move the seat release lever rearward allowing the seat to pop-up and fold forward.
3. Remove the 2 rear seat assembly-to-floor pan bolts.
4. Disengage one end of the passenger's seat support stop cable.
5. Move the seat and support assembly rearward until the seat back clears the instrument panel when folded forward.
6. Fold the seat fully forward and disengage the ends of the 3 assist springs from their retainers. NEVER TRY TO REMOVE THE SEAT WITH THE SPRINGS ATTACHED!
7. Return the seat to the upright position and push the seat back down firmly until the seat is latched.
8. Remove the seat from the truck.
   To install:
9. Position the seat in the truck far enough rearward to enable the seat to clear the instrument panel when folded forward.
10. Fold the seat forward.
11. Attach the assist springs to their retainers.
12. Place the seat in the upright position. Push the seat down firmly to latch it.
13. Position the seat and install the 2 front holddown bolt. Hand-tighten them only at this time.
14. Connect the end of the passenger's seat support stop cable.
15. Pop the seat up and fold it forward.
16. Install the 2 rear seat bolts and tighten all 4 bolts to 30 ft. lbs.
17. Position the seat upright again and latch it into place.

✳✳WARNING

To insure that the seat support assembly is in an unlatched position, a measured distance of 102mm, or more, is required between the bumper and the lower support.

18. For captain's chairs:
   a. Push the seat support release lever rearward.

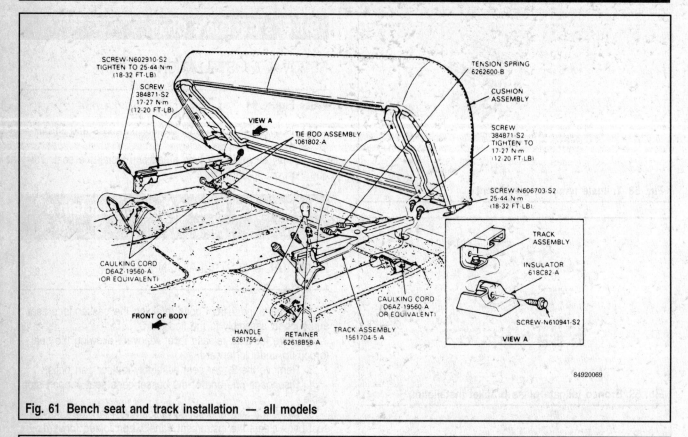

Fig. 61 Bench seat and track installation — all models

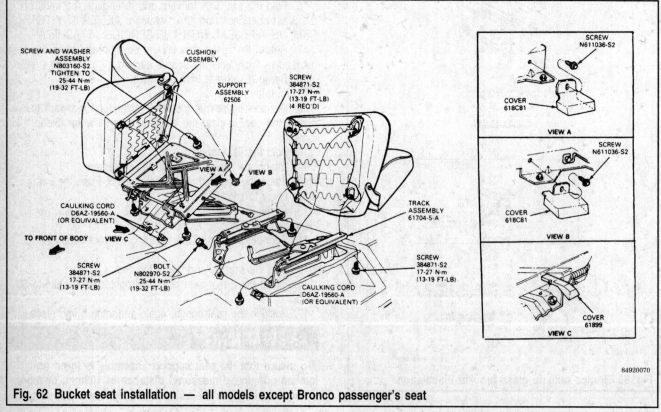

Fig. 62 Bucket seat installation — all models except Bronco passenger's seat

b. Make sure that the seat back adjuster is actuated allowing the seat back to fold forward at approximately the same time that the seat support assembly pops up.

c. If the seat assembly and/or the seat back does not release properly, it will be necessary to adjust the release

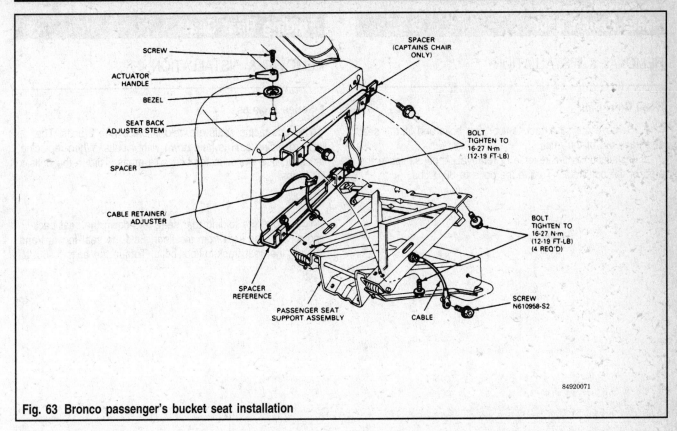

Fig. 63 Bronco passenger's bucket seat installation

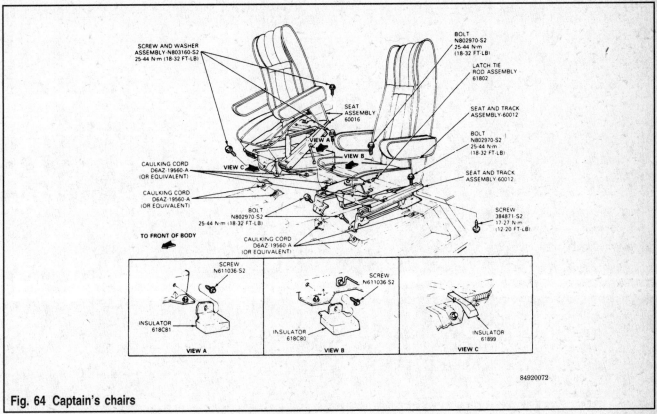

Fig. 64 Captain's chairs

cable by moving the slotted cable retainer fore or aft as needed.

Rear Bench Seat

REMOVAL & INSTALLATION

F-350 Crew Cab

1. Remove the seat track-to-floor pan bolts and lift the seat and track out of the truck.

2. Installation is the reverse of removal. Apply sealer to the area of the bolt holes. Torque the bolts to 30 ft. lbs.

Folding Rear Seat

REMOVAL & INSTALLATION

F-Series Pickups

The side-facing seats are held in place with 2 bolts. The forward facing seat is held down with 4 bolts. When replacing the seat, use sealer in the bolt hole areas. Torque the bolts to 30 ft. lbs.

Bronco

To remove the folding rear seat, fold down the seat back and unlatch the seat from the floor. Fold the seat forward and remove the seat track-to-floor bolts. Torque the bolts to 60 ft. lbs.

TORQUE SPECIFICATIONS

Component	U.S.	Metric
Bumpers		
Front or Rear		
Bracket-to-frame bolts		
All Except F-Super Duty Stripped		
Chassis Front Bumper	100 ft. lbs.	136 Nm
F-Super Duty Stripped Chassis		
Front Bumper	88 ft. lbs.	120 Nm
Doors		
Hinge bolts	24 ft. lbs.	33 Nm
Fiberglass Roof		
Bronco		
Roof retaining bolts	72–84 inch lbs.	8-9 Nm
Hood		
Hood-to-hinge bolts	20 ft. lbs.	27 Nm
Hood hinge-to-cowl panel bolts	34 ft. lbs.	46 Nm
Power door glass regulator motor mounting bolts	50–85 inch lbs.	6-10 Nm
Seats		
Front Bench Seat bolts	30 ft. lbs.	41 Nm
Bucket Seat bolts	30 ft. lbs.	41 Nm
Captain's Chair bolts	30 ft. lbs.	41 Nm
Rear Bench Seat bolts	30 ft. lbs.	41 Nm
Folding Rear Seat		
F-Series Pickups	30 ft. lbs.	41 Nm
Bronco	60 ft. lbs.	81 Nm
Swing-Away Spare Tire Carrier		
Bronco		
Hinge-to-body bolts	20 ft. lbs.	27 Nm
Tailgate		
Bronco		
Hinge bolts	11 ft. lbs.	15 Nm
Cable bolts	30 ft. lbs.	41 Nm
Lock control screws	11 ft. lbs.	15 Nm
Tailgate Window Glass		
Bronco		
Glass run attaching screws	10 ft. lbs.	14 Nm
Glass-to-window bracket nuts	10 ft. lbs.	14 Nm
Regulator mounting bolts	10 ft. lbs.	14 Nm

84920074

GLOSSARY

AIR/FUEL RATIO: The ratio of air to gasoline by weight in the fuel mixture drawn into the engine.

AIR INJECTION: One method of reducing harmful exhaust emissions by injecting air into each of the exhaust ports of an engine. The fresh air entering the hot exhaust manifold causes any remaining fuel to be burned before it can exit the tailpipe.

ALTERNATOR: A device used for converting mechanical energy into electrical energy.

AMMETER: An instrument, calibrated in amperes, used to measure the flow of an electrical current in a circuit. Ammeters are always connected in series with the circuit being tested.

AMPERE: The rate of flow of electrical current present when one volt of electrical pressure is applied against one ohm of electrical resistance.

ANALOG COMPUTER: Any microprocessor that uses similar (analogous) electrical signals to make its calculations.

ARMATURE: A laminated, soft iron core wrapped by a wire that converts electrical energy to mechanical energy as in a motor or relay. When rotated in a magnetic field, it changes mechanical energy into electrical energy as in a generator.

ATMOSPHERIC PRESSURE: The pressure on the Earth's surface caused by the weight of the air in the atmosphere. At sea level, this pressure is 14.7 psi at 32{248}F (101 kPa at 0{248}C).

ATOMIZATION: The breaking down of a liquid into a fine mist that can be suspended in air.

AXIAL PLAY: Movement parallel to a shaft or bearing bore.

BACKFIRE: The sudden combustion of gases in the intake or exhaust system that results in a loud explosion.

BACKLASH: The clearance or play between two parts, such as meshed gears.

BACKPRESSURE: Restrictions in the exhaust system that slow the exit of exhaust gases from the combustion chamber.

BAKELITE: A heat resistant, plastic insulator material commonly used in printed circuit boards and transistorized components.

BALL BEARING: A bearing made up of hardened inner and outer races between which hardened steel balls roll.

BALLAST RESISTOR: A resistor in the primary ignition circuit that lowers voltage after the engine is started to reduce wear on ignition components.

BEARING: A friction reducing, supportive device usually located between a stationary part and a moving part.

BIMETAL TEMPERATURE SENSOR: Any sensor or switch made of two dissimilar types of metal that bend when heated or cooled due to the different expansion rates of the alloys. These types of sensors usually function as an on/off switch.

BLOWBY: Combustion gases, composed of water vapor and unburned fuel, that leak past the piston rings into the crankcase during normal engine operation. These gases are removed by the PCV system to prevent the buildup of harmful acids in the crankcase.

BRAKE PAD: A brake shoe and lining assembly used with disc brakes.

BRAKE SHOE: The backing for the brake lining. The term is, however, usually applied to the assembly of the brake backing and lining.

BUSHING: A liner, usually removable, for a bearing; an anti-friction liner used in place of a bearing.

CALIPER: A hydraulically activated device in a disc brake system, which is mounted straddling the brake rotor (disc). The caliper contains at least one piston and two brake pads. Hydraulic pressure on the piston(s) forces the pads against the rotor.

CAMSHAFT: A shaft in the engine on which are the lobes (cams) which operate the valves. The camshaft is driven by the crankshaft, via a belt, chain or gears, at one half the crankshaft speed.

CAPACITOR: A device which stores an electrical charge.

CARBON MONOXIDE (CO): A colorless, odorless gas given off as a normal byproduct of combustion. It is poisonous and extremely dangerous in confined areas, building up slowly to toxic levels without warning if adequate ventilation is not available.

CARBURETOR: A device, usually mounted on the intake manifold of an engine, which mixes the air and fuel in the proper proportion to allow even combustion.

CATALYTIC CONVERTER: A device installed in the exhaust system, like a muffler, that converts harmful byproducts of combustion into carbon dioxide and water vapor by means of a heat-producing chemical reaction.

CENTRIFUGAL ADVANCE: A mechanical method of advancing the spark timing by using flyweights in the distributor that react to centrifugal force generated by the distributor shaft rotation.

CHECK VALVE: Any one-way valve installed to permit the flow of air, fuel or vacuum in one direction only.

CHOKE: A device, usually a moveable valve, placed in the intake path of a carburetor to restrict the flow of air.

CIRCUIT: Any unbroken path through which an electrical current can flow. Also used to describe fuel flow in some instances.

CIRCUIT BREAKER: A switch which protects an electrical circuit from overload by opening the circuit when the current flow exceeds a predetermined level. Some circuit breakers must be reset manually, while most reset automatically

COIL (IGNITION): A transformer in the ignition circuit which steps up the voltage provided to the spark plugs.

COMBINATION MANIFOLD: An assembly which includes both the intake and exhaust manifolds in one casting.

COMBINATION VALVE: A device used in some fuel systems that routes fuel vapors to a charcoal storage canister instead of venting them into the atmosphere. The valve relieves fuel tank pressure and allows fresh air into the tank as the fuel level drops to prevent a vapor lock situation.

COMPRESSION RATIO: The comparison of the total volume of the cylinder and combustion chamber with the piston at BDC and the piston at TDC.

CONDENSER: 1. An electrical device which acts to store an electrical charge, preventing voltage surges.
2. A radiator-like device in the air conditioning system in which refrigerant gas condenses into a liquid, giving off heat.

CONDUCTOR: Any material through which an electrical current can be transmitted easily.

CONTINUITY: Continuous or complete circuit. Can be checked with an ohmmeter.

COUNTERSHAFT: An intermediate shaft which is rotated by a mainshaft and transmits, in turn, that rotation to a working part.

CRANKCASE: The lower part of an engine in which the crankshaft and related parts operate.

CRANKSHAFT: The main driving shaft of an engine which receives reciprocating motion from the pistons and converts it to rotary motion.

CYLINDER: In an engine, the round hole in the engine block in which the piston(s) ride.

CYLINDER BLOCK: The main structural member of an engine in which is found the cylinders, crankshaft and other principal parts.

CYLINDER HEAD: The detachable portion of the engine, fastened, usually, to the top of the cylinder block, containing all or most of the combustion chambers. On overhead valve engines, it contains the valves and their operating parts. On overhead cam engines, it contains the camshaft as well.

DEAD CENTER: The extreme top or bottom of the piston stroke.

DETONATION: An unwanted explosion of the air/fuel mixture in the combustion chamber caused by excess heat and compression, advanced timing, or an overly lean mixture. Also referred to as "ping".

DIAPHRAGM: A thin, flexible wall separating two cavities, such as in a vacuum advance unit.

DIESELING: A condition in which hot spots in the combustion chamber cause the engine to run on after the key is turned off.

DIFFERENTIAL: A geared assembly which allows the transmission of motion between drive axles, giving one axle the ability to turn faster than the other.

DIODE: An electrical device that will allow current to flow in one direction only.

DISC BRAKE: A hydraulic braking assembly consisting of a brake disc, or rotor, mounted on an axle, and a caliper assembly containing, usually two brake pads which are activated by hydraulic pressure. The pads are forced against the sides of the disc, creating friction which slows the vehicle.

DISTRIBUTOR: A mechanically driven device on an engine which is responsible for electrically firing the spark plug at a predetermined point of the piston stroke.

DOWEL PIN: A pin, inserted in mating holes in two different parts allowing those parts to maintain a fixed relationship.

DRUM BRAKE: A braking system which consists of two brake shoes and one or two wheel cylinders, mounted on a fixed backing plate, and a brake drum, mounted on an axle, which revolves around the assembly.

DWELL: The rate, measured in degrees of shaft rotation, at which an electrical circuit cycles on and off.

ELECTRONIC CONTROL UNIT (ECU): Ignition module, module, amplifier or igniter. See Module for definition.

ELECTRONIC IGNITION: A system in which the timing and firing of the spark plugs is controlled by an electronic control unit, usually called a module. These systems have no points or condenser.

ENDPLAY: The measured amount of axial movement in a shaft.

ENGINE: A device that converts heat into mechanical energy.

EXHAUST MANIFOLD: A set of cast passages or pipes which conduct exhaust gases from the engine.

FEELER GAUGE: A blade, usually metal, of precisely predetermined thickness, used to measure the clearance between two parts.

FIRING ORDER: The order in which combustion occurs in the cylinders of an engine. Also the order in which spark is distributed to the plugs by the distributor.

FLOODING: The presence of too much fuel in the intake manifold and combustion chamber which prevents the air/fuel mixture from firing, thereby causing a no-start situation.

FLYWHEEL: A disc shaped part bolted to the rear end of the crankshaft. Around the outer perimeter is affixed the ring gear. The starter drive engages the ring gear, turning the flywheel, which rotates the crankshaft, imparting the initial starting motion to the engine.

FOOT POUND (ft.lb. or sometimes, ft. lbs.): The amount of energy or work needed to raise an item weighing one pound, a distance of one foot.

FUSE: A protective device in a circuit which prevents circuit overload by breaking the circuit when a specific amperage is present. The device is constructed around a strip or wire of a lower amperage rating than the circuit it is designed to protect. When an amperage higher than that stamped on the fuse is present in the circuit, the strip or wire melts, opening the circuit.

GEAR RATIO: The ratio between the number of teeth on meshing gears.

GENERATOR: A device which converts mechanical energy into electrical energy.

HEAT RANGE: The measure of a spark plug's ability to dissipate heat from its firing end. The higher the heat range, the hotter the plug fires.

HUB: The center part of a wheel or gear.

HYDROCARBON (HC): Any chemical compound made up of hydrogen and carbon. A major pollutant formed by the engine as a byproduct of combustion.

HYDROMETER: An instrument used to measure the specific gravity of a solution.

INCH POUND (in.lb. or sometimes, in. lbs.): One twelfth of a foot pound.

INDUCTION: A means of transferring electrical energy in the form of a magnetic field. Principle used in the ignition coil to increase voltage.

INJECTOR: A device which receives metered fuel under relatively low pressure and is activated to inject the fuel into the engine under relatively high pressure at a predetermined time.

INPUT SHAFT: The shaft to which torque is applied, usually carrying the driving gear or gears.

INTAKE MANIFOLD: A casting of passages or pipes used to conduct air or a fuel/air mixture to the cylinders.

JOURNAL: The bearing surface within which a shaft operates.

KEY: A small block usually fitted in a notch between a shaft and a hub to prevent slippage of the two parts.

MANIFOLD: A casting of passages or set of pipes which connect the cylinders to an inlet or outlet source.

MANIFOLD VACUUM: Low pressure in an engine intake manifold formed just below the throttle plates. Manifold vacuum is highest at idle and drops under acceleration.

MASTER CYLINDER: The primary fluid pressurizing device in a hydraulic system. In automotive use, it is found in brake and hydraulic clutch systems and is pedal activated, either directly or, in a power brake system, through the power booster.

MODULE: Electronic control unit, amplifier or igniter of solid state or integrated design which controls the current flow in the ignition primary circuit based on input from the pick-up coil. When the module opens the primary circuit, the high secondary voltage is induced in the coil.

NEEDLE BEARING: A bearing which consists of a number (usually a large number) of long, thin rollers.

OHM:(Ω) The unit used to measure the resistance of conductor to electrical flow. One ohm is the amount of resistance that limits current flow to one ampere in a circuit with one volt of pressure.

OHMMETER: An instrument used for measuring the resistance, in ohms, in an electrical circuit.

OUTPUT SHAFT: The shaft which transmits torque from a device, such as a transmission.

OVERDRIVE: A gear assembly which produces more shaft revolutions than that transmitted to it.

OVERHEAD CAMSHAFT (OHC): An engine configuration in which the camshaft is mounted on top of the cylinder head and operates the valve either directly or by means of rocker arms.

OVERHEAD VALVE (OHV): An engine configuration in which all of the valves are located in the cylinder head and the camshaft is located in the cylinder block. The camshaft operates the valves via lifters and pushrods.

OXIDES OF NITROGEN (NOx): Chemical compounds of nitrogen produced as a byproduct of combustion. They combine with hydrocarbons to produce smog.

OXYGEN SENSOR: Used with the feedback system to sense the presence of oxygen in the exhaust gas and signal the computer which can reference the voltage signal to an air/fuel ratio.

PINION: The smaller of two meshing gears.

PISTON RING: An open ended ring which fits into a groove on the outer diameter of the piston. Its chief function is to form a seal between the piston and cylinder wall. Most automotive pistons have three rings: two for compression sealing; one for oil sealing.

PRELOAD: A predetermined load placed on a bearing during assembly or by adjustment.

PRIMARY CIRCUIT: Is the low voltage side of the ignition system which consists of the ignition switch, ballast resistor or resistance wire, bypass, coil, electronic control unit and pick-up coil as well as the connecting wires and harnesses.

PRESS FIT: The mating of two parts under pressure, due to the inner diameter of one being smaller than the outer diameter of the other, or vice versa; an interference fit.

RACE: The surface on the inner or outer ring of a bearing on which the balls, needles or rollers move.

REGULATOR: A device which maintains the amperage and/or voltage levels of a circuit at predetermined values.

RELAY: A switch which automatically opens and/or closes a circuit.

RESISTANCE: The opposition to the flow of current through a circuit or electrical device, and is measured in ohms. Resistance is equal to the voltage divided by the amperage.

RESISTOR: A device, usually made of wire, which offers a preset amount of resistance in an electrical circuit.

RING GEAR: The name given to a ring-shaped gear attached to a differential case, or affixed to a flywheel or as part a planetary gear set.

ROLLER BEARING: A bearing made up of hardened inner and outer races between which hardened steel rollers move.

ROTOR: 1. The disc-shaped part of a disc brake assembly, upon which the brake pads bear; also called, brake disc.
2. The device mounted atop the distributor shaft, which passes current to the distributor cap tower contacts.

SECONDARY CIRCUIT: The high voltage side of the ignition system, usually above 20,000 volts. The secondary includes the ignition coil, coil wire, distributor cap and rotor, spark plug wires and spark plugs.

SENDING UNIT: A mechanical, electrical, hydraulic or electromagnetic device which transmits information to a gauge.

SENSOR: Any device designed to measure engine operating conditions or ambient pressures and temperatures. Usually electronic in nature and designed to send a voltage signal to an on-board computer, some sensors may operate as a simple on/off switch or they may provide a variable voltage signal (like a potentiometer) as conditions or measured parameters change.

SHIM: Spacers of precise, predetermined thickness used between parts to establish a proper working relationship.

SLAVE CYLINDER: In automotive use, a device in the hydraulic clutch system which is activated by hydraulic force, disengaging the clutch.

SOLENOID: A coil used to produce a magnetic field, the effect of which is produce work.

SPARK PLUG: A device screwed into the combustion chamber of a spark ignition engine. The basic construction is a conductive core inside of a ceramic insulator, mounted in an outer conductive base. An electrical charge from the spark plug wire travels along the conductive core and jumps a preset air gap to a grounding point or points at the end of the conductive base. The resultant spark ignites the fuel/air mixture in the combustion chamber.

SPLINES: Ridges machined or cast onto the outer diameter of a shaft or inner diameter of a bore to enable parts to mate without rotation.

TACHOMETER: A device used to measure the rotary speed of an engine, shaft, gear, etc., usually in rotations per minute.

THERMOSTAT: A valve, located in the cooling system of an engine, which is closed when cold and opens gradually in response to engine heating, controlling the temperature of the coolant and rate of coolant flow.

TOP DEAD CENTER (TDC): The point at which the piston reaches the top of its travel on the compression stroke.

TORQUE: The twisting force applied to an object.

TORQUE CONVERTER: A turbine used to transmit power from a driving member to a driven member via hydraulic action, providing changes in drive ratio and torque. In automotive use, it links the driveplate at the rear of the engine to the automatic transmission.

TRANSDUCER: A device used to change a force into an electrical signal.

TRANSISTOR: A semi-conductor component which can be actuated by a small voltage to perform an electrical switching function.

TUNE-UP: A regular maintenance function, usually associated with the replacement and adjustment of parts and components in the electrical and fuel systems of a vehicle for the purpose of attaining optimum performance.

TURBOCHARGER: An exhaust driven pump which compresses intake air and forces it into the combustion chambers at higher than atmospheric pressures. The increased air pressure allows more fuel to be burned and results in increased horsepower being produced.

VACUUM ADVANCE: A device which advances the ignition timing in response to increased engine vacuum.

VACUUM GAUGE: An instrument used to measure the presence of vacuum in a chamber.

VALVE: A device which control the pressure, direction of flow or rate of flow of a liquid or gas.

VALVE CLEARANCE: The measured gap between the end of the valve stem and the rocker arm, cam lobe or follower that activates the valve.

VISCOSITY: The rating of a liquid's internal resistance to flow.

VOLTMETER: An instrument used for measuring electrical force in units called volts. Voltmeters are always connected parallel with the circuit being tested.

WHEEL CYLINDER: Found in the automotive drum brake assembly, it is a device, actuated by hydraulic pressure, which, through internal pistons, pushes the brake shoes outward against the drums.

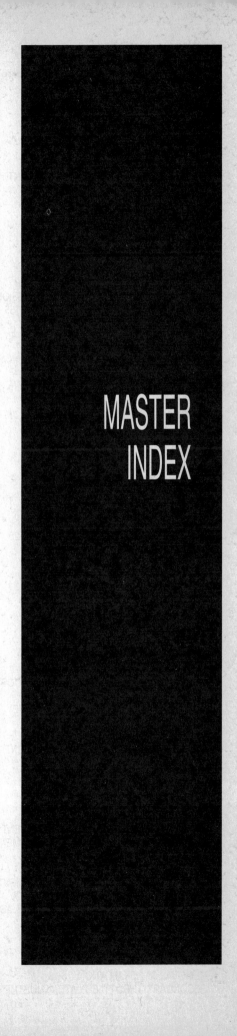

MASTER
INDEX